NATIONAL UND

a division of ALM Media, LLC

2021 TAX FACTS ON INSURANCE & EMPLOYEE BENEFITS
Robert Bloink, J.D., LL.M., William H. Byrnes, Esq., LL.M, CWM®

2021 Tax Facts on Insurance & Employee Benefits is your complete source for tax information as it relates to these two critical business and financial planning areas. With thousands of easy-to-use questions & answers that cover the most critical topics, Tax Facts helps advisers of all kinds understand the tax implications of the recommendations that they make for their clients.

Insurance and employee benefits are complicated tools that each carry their own set of tax issues, and advisers cannot possibly make the thorough and complete assessments that clients depend on without understanding this ever-changing area. These two volumes provide guidance on:

- *Annuities and life insurance products*

- *ERISA regulations for employee benefit plans*

- *Health and long-term care insurance*

- *Disclosure and recordkeeping requirements*

- *Qualified and nonqualified compensation plans*

- *Defined contribution and defined benefit deferred compensation plans*

- *Funded and unfunded plans*

- *PBGC requirements*

- *Estate and gift tax planning and consequences*

- *And more!*

The 2021 edition has been completely updated, featuring:

- *Extensive coverage of the effect of the SECURE Act on qualified plans, including new RMD rules, new rules on inherited IRAs, and contributions beyond age 72*

- *Complete updates on the legal and regulatory changes related to the CARES Act*

- *Updated paid leave requirements under the Families First Coronavirus Response Act*

- *Updated withholding and employment tax requirements*

- *Complete set of updated inflation number adjustments*

Tax Facts on Insurance & Employee Benefits provides practical advice for any professional, including in-house HR professionals, insurance producers and third-party advisers on how to handle real-world issues. Having the right tax information helps to avoid problems before they become costly mistakes, as well as correct problems when they do occur.

Related titles also available:

- *Tax Facts on Investments*

- *Tax Facts on Individuals & Small Business*

- *ERISA Facts*

- *Field Guide: Estate & Retirement Planning, Business Planning & Employee Benefits*

- *Social Security & Medicare Facts*

- *Healthcare Reform Facts*

- *The Tools & Techniques of Employee Benefit and Retirement Planning*

For customer service questions or to place additional orders, please call 1-800-543-0874 or email CustomerService@nuco.com.

Dear *Tax Facts* Readers,

As the editor of *Tax Facts*, this is a time that is always spent reflecting on what we have seen in the past year as we prepare for the release of the next year's editions. And what a year it has been! We started with the enactment of the SECURE Act, which by itself would have made for a busy year for tax-planning professionals. The arrival of the COVID-19 pandemic, and the tax changes that came along with it, have made this one of the most significant years for tax changes since 1986.

Through all of these changes we have kept the *Tax Facts Online* content current to bring you the latest information that you'll need and to best serve your clients. As always, the most up-to-date information will form the core of the 2021 print edition of *Tax Facts*. However, because of the unusual nature of this year, and the last minute passage of the SECURE Act in 2019, we're doing a few things differently for the 2021 edition.

Here's what you need to know:

- We've all had too many surprises this year, so there will be **no price increases** for any of the *Tax Facts* print and online products in 2021.

- Customers who have purchased any volume of the 2021 print editions of *Tax Facts* will receive a complimentary print supplement in February that will cover **new tax updates** no matter how late in 2020 they were enacted.

- The *Tax Facts Intelligence Weekly* newsletter with the latest updates will continue to be provided to all *Tax Facts* online subscribers.

- The *Tax Facts Intelligence Weekly* newsletter now will also provide all of the week's content from our authors, Robert Bloink and William Byrnes, including their in-depth feature articles and the always timely Thumbs Up/Thumbs Down commentary pieces.

- We are also introducing the *Tax Facts News Flash*, a new component to our electronic services. With the *News Flash* we will be able to update our subscribers to major tax-related news events regardless of when they happen. Don't worry, we'll still have the same weekly in-depth updates that you have come to rely on in *Tax Facts Intelligence* weekly.

We thank you for your loyalty to *Tax Facts*. We hope you stay safe, we hope you stay healthy, and we hope *Tax Facts* helps you stay smart.

Sincerely,

Jason R. Gilbert, J.D., M.A.

Editor, *Tax Facts*

2021
TAX FACTS

ON INSURANCE &
EMPLOYEE BENEFITS

- Annuities • Cafeteria Plans • Compensation
- Disclosure Requirements • CARES Act • MEPs
- Estate and Gift Taxation • Health Insurance
- Healthcare Reform • International Tax
- Life Insurance • Long-Term Care Insurance
- Pensions and Profit Sharing • Structured Settlements
- Taxation of Individuals

Robert Bloink, Esq., LL.M.
William H. Byrnes, Esq., LL.M., CWM®

2021 Edition

Tax Facts on Insurance and Employee Benefits (formerly *Tax Facts 1*) is published annually by the Professional Publishing Division of The National Underwriter Company. This edition reflects selected pertinent legislation, regulations, rulings and court decisions as of October 15, 2020.

This publication is designed to provide accurate and authoritative information in regard to the subject matter covered. It is sold with the understanding that the publisher is not engaged in rendering legal, accounting or other professional service. If legal advice or other expert assistance is required, the services of a competent professional person should be sought. —From a Declaration of Principles jointly adopted by a Committee of the American Bar Association and a Committee of Publishers and Associations.

Circular 230 Notice – The content in this publication is not intended or written to be used, and it cannot be used, for the purposes of avoiding U.S. tax penalties.

ISBN 978-1-949506-87-7
ISSN 0496-9685

The National Underwriter Company
4157 Olympic Blvd., Suite 225
Erlanger, KY 41018

Printed in U.S.A.

TABLE OF CONTENTS

TAX FACTS ON INSURANCE & EMPLOYEE BENEFITS – VOLUME 1

TAX FACTS ON INSURANCE & EMPLOYEE BENEFITS – VOLUME 2

APPENDICES AND TABLES

TAX FACTS ON INVESTMENTS

APPENDICES AND TABLES

TAX FACTS ON INDIVIDUALS & SMALL BUSINESS

APPENDICES AND TABLES

ABOUT THE NATIONAL UNDERWRITER COMPANY

a division of ALM Media, LLC

For over 120 years, The National Underwriter Company, *a division of ALM Media, LLC* has been the first in line with the targeted tax, insurance, and financial planning information you need to make critical business decisions. Boasting nearly a century of expert experience, our reputable editors are dedicated to putting accurate and relevant information right at your fingertips. With *Tax Facts, FC&S® Expert Coverage Interpretation, Tools & Techniques, Field Guide, Insurance Coverage Law Center, Property & Casualty Coverage Guides* and other resources available in print, eBook, or online, you can be assured that as the industry evolves National Underwriter will be at the forefront with the thorough and easy-to-use resources you rely on for success.

Update Service Notification

This National Underwriter Company publication is regularly updated to include coverage of developments and changes that affect the content. If you did not purchase this publication directly from The National Underwriter Company, *a division of ALM Media, LLC* and you want to receive these important updates sent on a 30-day review basis and billed separately, please contact us at (800) 543-0874. Or you can mail your request with your name, company, address, and the title of the book to:

The National Underwriter Company
a division of ALM Media, LLC
4157 Olympic Boulevard
Suite 225
Erlanger, KY 41018

If you purchased this publication from The National Underwriter Company, *a division of ALM Media, LLC,* directly, you have already been registered for the update service.

Contact Information

To order any National Underwriter Company title, please

- call 1-800-543-0874, 8-6 ET Monday – Thursday and 8 to 5 ET Friday

- online bookstore at www.nationalunderwriter.com, or

- mail to Orders Department, The National Underwriter Company, *a division of ALM Media, LLC*, 4157 Olympic Blvd., Ste. 225, Erlanger, KY 41018

INTRODUCTION TO 2021 TAX FACTS ON INSURANCE & EMPLOYEE BENEFITS

Welcome to the 2021 edition of *Tax Facts on Insurance & Employee Benefits*. This year's *Tax Facts* features both new and enhanced content designed to help you provide clients with the most relevant tax planning advice possible. Clearly the most significant updates for this year's edition involve the changes made by the SECURE Act, passed at the very end of 2019, and the legislative and regulatory changes that were made during 2020 in response to the COVID-19 pandemic.

The SECURE Act was a legislative change, but over the past year we have also seen a number of administrative updates that have filled in the gaps where further interpretation was needed. The SECURE Act changes are long-term in nature. We are likely to see more administrative updates in 2021, and the new regime for inherited IRAs and the potential for qualified plan contributions to be made later in life will shift long-term retirement and legacy planning strategies for many advisors and their clients.

The COVID-19 related changes a more short-term in nature, but they have potential tax consequences for a very broad range of areas that affect individuals and businesses. There are significant issues to consider for employee benefits through the CARES Act's new paid leave requirements, potential payroll tax changes for all businesses, and retirement plan changes with new COVID-19 hardship distributions. While the window of applicability may be short for many of these changes, they all have potential long-term planning consequences.

We have also continued our comprehensive coverage of the 2017 tax reform legislation in this year's edition, explaining how the newly revamped tax code, regulations and administrative guidance diverge from previously existing law. As the IRS continues to release guidance implementing the changes, we continue to keep you up-to-date on how those developments might impact your clients.

Throughout this year's edition of *Tax Facts*, we have provided more than a bare bones discussion of the tax code changes. This year's materials also discuss the planning implications brought about by the new rules that might impact your clients.

Throughout *Tax Facts*, we have continued the expansion of our "planning points," each offering a piece of practical advice written by a practitioner who is an expert in the field, which will assist you in providing your clients with the most knowledgeable guidance possible. Many of these planning points in our 2021 edition continue to focus on tax reform, both with respect to planning opportunities that have been created and questions that remain. We have also continued to reorganize many of our more complicated questions, splitting questions into discrete subparts that make these questions simpler and easier to understand. When combined with our updated IRS code-based index, we believe this will streamline your research process and save you time and effort.

Additional changes throughout the year—including revenue rulings, case law decisions, and legislative and regulatory activity—are available through subscription to our online tax service, *Tax Facts Online*. We continue to produce *Tax Facts Intelligence Weekly*, a weekly electronic newsletter that delivers updates every week to your email on recent rulings, regulations and cases affecting *Tax Facts* content—including analysis of tax reform issues that could most strongly impact your clients and business. This publication is automatically sent to you as part of your Tax Facts subscription.

This edition of *Tax Facts* was developed with the assistance of authors Professor William H. Byrnes and Professor Robert Bloink. Prof. Byrnes serves as an Associate Dean and Professor of Law at the Texas A&M School of Law and has been the author of numerous books, treatises and scholarly articles. Prof. Bloink is an insurance industry expert whose practice incorporates sophisticated wealth transfer techniques, as well as counseling institutions in the context of their insurance portfolios. He is also a professor of tax at Texas A&M Law School.

ABOUT THE EDITORS

ABOUT THE AUTHORS

Robert Bloink, Esq., LL.M.

Robert Bloink worked to put in force in excess of $2B of longevity pegged portfolios for the insurance industry's producers in the past five years. His insurance practice incorporates sophisticated wealth transfer techniques, as well as counseling institutions in the context of their insurance portfolios and other mortality based exposures. Professor Bloink is working with William Byrnes, Associate Dean of Special Projects of Texas A&M School of Law, on development of executive programs for insurance underwriters, wealth managers and financial planners.

Previously, Mr. Bloink served as Senior Attorney in the IRS Office of Chief Counsel, Large and Mid-Sized Business Division, where he litigated many cases in the U.S. Tax Court, served as Liaison Counsel for the Offshore Compliance Technical Assistance Program, coordinated examination programs audit teams on the development of issues for large corporate taxpayers, and taught continuing education seminars to Senior Revenue Agents involved in Large Case Exams. In his governmental capacity, Mr. Bloink became recognized as an expert in the taxation of financial structured products and was responsible for the IRS' first FSA addressing variable forward contracts. Mr. Bloink's core competencies led to his involvement in prosecuting some of the biggest corporate tax shelters in the history of our country

William H. Byrnes, Esq., LL.M.

William Byrnes is the leader of National Underwriter's Financial Advisory Publications, having been appointed in 2010. He is a professor and an associate dean of Texas A&M University School of Law. He is one of the leading authors and best-selling authors in the professional markets with 30 books that have sold in excess of 100,000 copies in print and online, with thousands of online database subscribers. His National Underwriter publications include Tax Facts, Advanced Markets, and Sales Essentials.

Mr. Byrnes held senior positions of international tax for Coopers & Lybrand and has been commissioned and consulted by a number of governments on their tax and fiscal policy. He has served as an operational board member for companies in several industries including fashion, durable medical equipment, office furniture and technology.

He pioneered online legal education in 1994. In 1998 he developed the first online program to achieve American Bar Association acquiescence. His Master, LL.M. and doctoral programs are leveraged by wealth managers, financial planners and life insurance underwriters.

LEAD CONTRIBUTING EDITOR

<u>Alexis Long, J.D.</u>

Alexis Long formerly practiced corporate law as an associate with the business transactions group at Schulte Roth & Zabel in New York City. She was a corporate, securities and finance editor for the Practical Law Company before moving to Thomas Jefferson School of Law as publications director. Alexis is currently publications director at the Texas A&M School of Law. She holds a J.D. from the University of Michigan Law School.

THE TAX FACTS EDITORIAL ADVISORY BOARD

<u>Kevin W. Blanton, J.D.</u>

Kevin W. Blanton, J.D., is Assistant Vice President and Associate Counsel, Advanced Markets, for the U.S. Individual Life operations of John Hancock Financial, a Manulife company. In his current position Mr. Blanton provides advanced marketing support to John Hancock's home office employees, field personnel, and producers. In addition, he is responsible for the development of innovative advanced marketing materials, programs, and strategies. Mr. Blanton is also a recurring host on John Hancock's weekly JHAM Radio program and a regular speaker at industry meetings around the country.

Prior to joining Manulife Financial in 1999, Mr. Blanton practiced law in the private sector for many years in the Boston area, concentrating on estate planning, probate, business succession planning, corporate benefits, and charitable planning for high net worth individuals and companies. Mr. Blanton also provided tax compliance advice for several large national mutual fund companies as part of the

Tax Department of Coopers & Lybrand in Boston and served as bond counsel for more than 100 New England municipalities and state agencies.

Mr. Blanton received his Bachelor of Arts degree in economics from The University of Michigan, Ann Arbor, Michigan, and his Juris Doctor degree *cum laude* from Boston University School of Law. Mr. Blanton is licensed to practice law in the Commonwealth of Massachusetts, the State of New York, and the State of Texas, and is a member of the American Bar Association, the Massachusetts Bar Association, the New York State Bar Association, the Texas State Bar Association, and the Boston Bar Association.

Caroline Brooks, J.D., CFP®

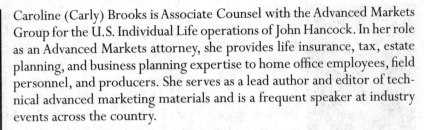

Caroline (Carly) Brooks is Associate Counsel with the Advanced Markets Group for the U.S. Individual Life operations of John Hancock. In her role as an Advanced Markets attorney, she provides life insurance, tax, estate planning, and business planning expertise to home office employees, field personnel, and producers. She serves as a lead author and editor of technical advanced marketing materials and is a frequent speaker at industry events across the country.

Carly received her Bachelor of Arts degree, *magna cum laude*, in Criminal Justice and Political Science from the University at Albany, SUNY, in Albany, New York. Carly received her Juris Doctor with a concentration in Estate Planning and her Master of Business Administration from Western New England University School of Law, Springfield, Massachusetts. Carly is licensed to practice law in the Commonwealth of Massachusetts and holds the Certified Financial Planner (CFP®) designation. She currently serves on the Editorial Advisory Board for Tax Facts, a publication of The National Underwriter Company, is a co-author of the 19th Edition of the Tools and Techniques of Estate Planning, a Leimberg Library publication, and has been published in Broker World.

Carly lives in Boston, Massachusetts, where she is very active in the greater Boston trusts and estates and legal community. She is the current President of the Boston Trusts and Estates Consortium, serves on the Member Involvement Committee for the Boston Estate Planning Council, and is active in the Massachusetts Women's Bar Association.

Martin J. Burke, III, Esq.

Martin Burke is a principal owner of the Matthews Benefit Group, Inc., a third party administration firm in St. Petersburg Florida. In addition to ensuring the firm's continued compliance with all applicable regulations, he is involved in the development of custom-tailored retirement plans designed to meet specific goals for business owners.

Mr. Burke is a graduate of Lycoming College, Pennsylvania, and the University of Maryland School of Law. Mr. Burke is licensed to practice law in Maryland and Florida.

He is coauthor of the *403(b) Answer Book Forms & Worksheets for Aspen Publishers* as well as a regular contributing editor for the *401(k) Advisor*.

Anne Berre Downing, J.D.

Anne Berre Downing, J.D. has a Bachelors of Arts in English and Political Science from Agnes Scott College, and received her Doctor of Law degree from Emory University School of Law. She has practiced labor, employment, and commercial law, and served as adjunct faculty for 24 years before transitioning to academe full time. She speaks and writes internationally on issues involving law, leadership, conflict resolution and academic employment. She has served as a Professor of Business Law and Dispute Resolution at Western Carolina University and has directed other universities' pre-law, dispute resolution, and Moot Court programs. She is an accomplished mediator, author and editor and is currently a Fellow at the Israeli Center for Peace.

Jonathan H. Ellis, J.D., LL.M. (Taxation)

Mr. Ellis is currently a Shareholder in the law firm of Plotnick & Ellis, P.C., where his practice focuses primarily on estate planning, estate administration, elder law, and the representation of closely held businesses.

He has a B.S. in Accounting from Pennsylvania State University, J.D. from Widener University, and LL.M. (Taxation) from Temple University. In addition, Mr. Ellis is Executive Editor and Co-author, and along with Stephen Leimberg, et.al., of *Tools and Techniques of Estate Planning*, 16th Edition, The National Underwriter Company, as well as a Co-Author of the 15th Edition. Also, Mr. Ellis is the author of the book "Drafting Wills and Trusts in Pennsylvania", 2010 Edition for PBI Press. Mr. Ellis is also a member of the Editorial Advisory Board for Tax Facts 2012 through 2015, The National Underwriter Company. In addition, he is the author of 30 articles for Pennsylvania Tax Service Insights (LexisNexis Matthew Bender). Finally, he is a former member of the Adjunct Faculty at Villanova Law School where he taught Family Wealth Planning.

Mr. Ellis frequently speaks to a variety of groups, including attorneys, accountants and financial planners throughout Pennsylvania, New Jersey, Delaware and Maryland. Mr. Ellis is also the Course Planner for the PBI Courses "Drafting Wills and Trusts in Pennsylvania", "Wills v. Trusts: A Primer on the Right Tool for Your Clients", "Use of Trusts", and "Post-Mortem Estate Planning", and a participant in a variety of additional courses for PBI. He is also an annual participant in the Villanova University's annual tax conference, cosponsored with the Internal Revenue Service.

He is a member of the Pennsylvania, New Jersey and Florida Bars; the Montgomery County Bar Association; and the Philadelphia Estate Planning Council. Mr. Ellis is also a Fellow of the American College of Trust and Estate Counsel.

Stephen D. Forman, CLTC

Stephen Forman is senior vice president and co-founder of Long Term Care Associates, Inc. (LTCA), a national marketing firm focused exclusively on long-term care solutions. LTCA helped pioneer this field, with roots stretching back to 1972, pre-dating the LTC entry of many of today's carriers.

Mr. Forman has authored more than 50 articles on the topics of long-term care insurance, sales, marketing and regulation, and was chosen by National Underwriter to revise the latest edition of its popular franchise, "The Advisor's Guide to Long-Term Care." He has advised several major carriers in the design phase of their products, helped re-design Washington State's LTC Training requirement, and speaks frequently with the media, including Kiplinger's and Consumer Reports. His columns have been honored as as one of "7 Health Insurance Blogs You Should Know About," and he was recently named one of the "Top 20 Most Creative People in the Insurance Industry."

Mr. Forman graduated magna cum laude from UCLA and has been an active member of American MENSA since 2012.

Randy Gardner J.D., LL.M., MBA, CPA, CFP®

Randy Gardner is a Professor of Tax and Financial Planning and former Director of the Certificate in Financial Planning Program at the University of Missouri – Kansas City. He is an estate planning attorney with over 30 years of experience and one of the founders of onlineestateplanning.com. He is coauthor of *101 Tax Saving Ideas* and *Tools and Techniques of Income Tax Planning* and is a highly rated discussion leader who has been recognized as an Outstanding Educator by the Missouri Society of CPAs. Mr. Gardner brings his teaching experience and tax planning expertise to Garrett Members as the Network Tax, Estate & Financial Planning Coach.

In addition to teaching, Mr. Gardner is a member of WealthCounsel, LLC, serves on the Editorial Board of The Journal of Financial Planning, and is former member of the Council on Examinations of the Certified Financial Planner Board of Standards. He is a member of the AICPA, the Missouri Society of CPAs, and the Kansas Bar Association. He has also written many articles for publications such as the Journal of Financial Planning, Taxation for Accountants, Practical Tax Strategies, and Tax Adviser.

Johni Hays, J.D.

Johni Hays is Vice-President of Thompson and Associates. With almost 20 years' experience as a practicing attorney in charitable and estate planning, Johni Hays is a recognized expert on the subject of charitable gift planning. Johni is the author of the book, *Essentials of Annuities* and co-author of the book, *The Tools and Techniques of Charitable Planning*. Johni serves on the Editorial Advisory Board for the books *Tax Facts on Investments* and *Tax Facts on Insurance and Employee Benefits*. She serves as a charitable planning author of Steve Leimberg's electronic newsletter service, LISI, found at www.leimbergservices.com. Johni has been quoted in the Wall Street Journal and has published charitable planning articles in Estate Planning Magazine, Planned Giving Today, Fundraising Success, Life Insurance Selling and the National Underwriter magazines.

Johni is in demand as a national lecturer on estate and charitable planning, probate, living wills, annuities, life insurance, retirement planning and IRAs, as well as income, estate and gift taxation. Johni has been engaged in the practice of law with an emphasis in charitable and estate planning since 1993.

Prior to joining Thompson & Associates, Johni served as the Senior Gift Planning Consultant for The Stelter Company. Prior to that Johni was the Executive Director of the Greater Des Moines Community Foundation Planned Giving Institute. In addition, Johni practiced estate planning with Myers Krause and Stevens, Chartered law firm in Naples Florida, where she specialized in estate planning.

Johni graduated cum laude with a Juris Doctor degree from Drake University in Des Moines, Iowa, in 1993. She also holds a Bachelor of Science degree in Business Administration from Drake University and graduated magna cum laude in 1988.

Johni is the president of the Charitable Estate Planning Institute and she also serves on the national board of the Partnership for Philanthropic Planning (PPP) formerly the National Committee on Planned Giving. Johni serves on the Technical Advisory Board for the Stelter Company and is a charter member of PPP's Leadership Institute. She is also a member of the Mid-Iowa Planned Giving Council and the Mid-Iowa Estate and Financial Planners Council (president 2007-2008). Johni has been a member of both the Iowa Bar and the Florida Bar since 1993. She resides in Johnston, Iowa, with her husband, Dave Schlindwein.

Chuck Hodges, J.D., LL.M.

Chuck Hodges is the Chair of the Domestic & International Tax Team of the law firm of Kilpatrick Townsend & Stockton. Mr. Hodges focuses his practice on civil and criminal federal tax controversies and complex tax planning. He has been involved in more than 100 cases against the IRS and state revenue agencies, involving all areas of tax law. Mr. Hodges handles approximately 15 cases against the IRS per year, recovering more than

$1 million for his clients from the IRS in reimbursement of attorneys' fees at the conclusion of their trial victory. As a tax litigator, he has handled all stages of tax controversies, including all administrative and judicial levels from examination through court proceedings.

Mr. Hodges has represented a broad range of taxpayers, including individuals, estates, closely held businesses, tax-exempt organizations, and publicly traded corporations. A substantial number of these engagements have involved the defense of TEFRA partnerships and limited liability companies. He has represented taxpayers in many different federal courts, including the U.S. Tax Court, the U.S. District Court for the Northern District of Georgia, the U.S. District Courts for the Middle District and Southern District of Florida, the U.S. District Court for the Southern District of Mississippi, the U.S. District Court for the District of Arizona, the U.S. District Court for the District of South Carolina, the U.S. Court of Federal Claims, and the U.S. Court of Appeals for the Fifth, Ninth and Eleventh Circuits.

Mr. Hodges has been a key litigator in various cases earning him honors and recognition. He has been listed as a "Leader in the Field" for Taxation by Chambers USA: *America's Leading Lawyers for Business* each year since 2005. He was recognized by his peers in the 2015 edition of *The Best Lawyers in America*®, and each of the five years immediately preceding, for the area of Tax Law. In 2014 and each of the five years immediately preceding, Mr. Hodges was named a Georgia "Super Lawyer" and previously a Georgia "Rising Star" by *SuperLawyers* magazine. Throughout his career, Mr. Hodges has provided insight as an industry leader for some of the nation's top news outlets including the *Wall Street Journal, Bloomberg, BusinessWeek, Forbes and Law360*. He is AV® rated by Martindale-Hubbell.*

Paul Hood, Jr., J.D., LL.M.

L. Paul Hood L, Jr. received his J.D. from Louisiana State University Law Center in 1986 and Master of Laws in Taxation from Georgetown University Law Center in 1988. Paul is a frequent speaker, is widely quoted and his articles have appeared in a number of publications, including BNA Tax Management Memorandum, BNA Estates, Gifts & Trusts Journal, CCH Journal of Practical Estate Planning, Estate Planning, Valuation Strategies, Digest of Federal Tax Articles, Loyola Law Review, Louisiana Bar Journal, Tax Ideas, The Value Examiner and Charitable Gift Planning News. He has spoken at programs sponsored by a number of law schools, including Duke University, Georgetown University, New York University, Tulane University, Loyola (N.O.) University, and Louisiana State University, as well as many other professional organizations, including AICPA and NACVA. From 1996-2004, Paul served on the Louisiana Board of Tax Appeals, a three member board that has jurisdiction over all State of Louisiana tax matters.

A self-described "recovering tax lawyer," Paul is the author or co-author of four other books, and is the proud father of two boys who are the apples of his eye, Paul III and Evan. Happily married to Carol A. Sobczak, Paul lives with Carol in Toledo OH, where he serves as the Director of Planned Giving for The University of Toledo Foundation.

Erik M. Jensen

Erik Jensen is the Burke Professor of Law at Case Western Reserve University in Cleveland, Ohio, where he has been on the faculty for over 30 years. Professor Jensen has also taught at the Cornell Law School, from which he earned his law degree in 1979. His work has been recognized through election as a fellow of the American College of Tax Counsel and as a member of the American Law Institute.

Professor Jensen's professional activities have been extensive. Before entering teaching, Professor Jensen was a tax associate with the New York City law firm of Sullivan & Cromwell.

He has spoken widely on tax matters and is author of *The Taxing Power* (Praeger 2005) and of several dozen articles on taxation and other subjects. He is also Editor of the *Journal of Taxation of Investments*. He serves as Vice-Chair for Law Development of the Sales, Exchanges, and Basis Committee of the American Bar Association Section of Taxation.

Jay Katz, J.D., LL.M.

Jay Katz is a tax attorney in Delaware with more than a decade of experience in private practice litigating tax cases and handling audits, collection matters, and offers in compromise for corporate and individual clients. He has earned LLMs in taxation from both the NYU and University of Florida graduate tax programs. During 12 years as a professor at Widener University Law School and Beasley School of Law at Temple University, Jay has taught virtually every tax and estate planning course on the curriculum and was the director of the Widener tax clinic.

In addition to being a coauthor of the 4th Edition of *The Tools & Techniques of Income Tax Planning*, Jay has penned seven published tax articles, including "An Offer in Compromise You Can't Confuse: It is not the Opening Bid of a Delinquent Taxpayer to Play Let's Make a Tax Deal with the Internal Revenue Service," 81 *Miss. L. J.* 1673 (2012) (lead article); "The William O. Douglas Tax Factor: Where Did the Spin Stop and Who Was He Looking Out For?" 3 *Charlotte Law Review* 133 (2012) (lead article); and "The Untold Story of Crane v. Commissioner Reveals an Inconvenient Tax Truth: Useless Depreciation Deductions Cause Global Basis Erosion to Bait A Hazardous Tax Trap For Unwitting Taxpayers," 30 *Va. Tax Rev.* 559 (2011).

Robert S. Keebler, CPA, MST, AEP (Distinguished)

Robert Keebler is a partner with Keebler & Associates, LLP. He is a 2007 recipient of the prestigious Distinguished Estate Planners award from the National Association of Estate Planning Counsels. Mr. Keebler has several times been named by *CPA Magazine* as one of the top 100 most influential practitioners in the United States. His practice includes family wealth transfer and preservation planning, charitable giving, retirement distribution planning, and estate administration.

Mr. Keebler frequently represents clients before the IRS National Office in the private letter ruling process and in estate, gift, and income tax examinations and appeals, and he has received more than 150 favorable private letter rulings including several key rulings of first impression. He is the author of over 100 articles and columns and is the editor, author, or coauthor of many books and treatises on wealth transfer and taxation.

Sonya King, J.D., LL.M.

Sonya King has been involved with tax issues affecting estate, retirement, business, and charitable planning for 15 years. Prior to joining New York Life's Advanced Planning Group in 2010, Ms. King worked at the National Underwriter Company where she was an editor of *Tax Facts* and the *Tools & Techniques* series. She authored numerous articles on life insurance, annuities, retirement, income tax, health and welfare plans, and charitable and estate planning. Sonya is a coauthor of the *Tools & Techniques of Income Tax Planning*.

Before that, Ms. King served as a judicial law clerk to the Honorable Donald R. Ford at the Eleventh District Court of Appeals in Warren, Ohio, and also as a trust officer with Key Bank. Prior to attending law school, she was a registered principal (Series 24) and licensed insurance agent for a major life insurance company.

Ms. King graduated from Duke University where she received her Bachelor of Arts degree. She earned her law degree (J.D.) from the University of Akron and her tax law degree (LL.M.) from Case Western Reserve University. She is a member in good standing of the Ohio State Bar Association.

Alson R. Martin, J.D., LL.M.

Alson R. Martin is a Partner of Lathrop & Gage LLP in Overland Park, Kansas. The firm also has offices in Los Angeles, California; Denver & Boulder, Colorado; Washington, D.C.; Chicago, Illinois; Kansas City, St. Louis, Jefferson City, Springfield & Columbia, Missouri; Boston, Massachusetts; and New York, New York.

Al is a Fellow of the American College of Tax Counsel and American College of Employee Benefits Counsel, as well as a charter Life Member of the American Tax Policy Institute. Mr. Martin is listed in the book The Best Lawyers in America (from inception in three categories), Outstanding Lawyers of America, Missouri-Kansas Super Lawyers, Ingram's Best Lawyers in Kansas City (three categories), American Lawyer Media & Martindale-Hubbell™ Top Rated Lawyers in Health Care, and Guide to Leading U.S. Tax Lawyers. He was selected by Best Lawyers as the 2010 Kansas City, KS Corporate Lawyer of the Year and 2013 Tax Lawyer of the Year.

Al is the author of *Healthcare Reform Facts* (2015), *Limited Liability Companies and Partnerships* (3rd edition, 2011) and coauthor of *Kansas Corporation Law & Practice (Including Tax Aspects)* (5th edition,

2011), and has written many articles in various publications. He was also Technical Editor of Panel Publication's monthly newsletter *The 401k Advisor* from 1990- 2012. He has published numerous articles and made hundreds of speeches. Mr. Martin was for many years Co-Chair and speaker at the Annual Advanced Course of Study Professional Service Organizations, a faculty member for the ALI-ABA Courses Estate Planning for the Family Business Owner and Sophisticated Estate Planning Techniques, as well as speaker at many national meetings of the American Bar Association Tax Section, the ESOP Association Annual Convention, Mountain States Pension Conference, Southern Federal Tax Conference, Notre Dame Estate Planning Symposium and the Ohio Pension Conference, as well as the Alabama, Georgia Federal, Kansas, Missouri, and Tennessee Tax conferences.

He is President and Director of the Small Business Council of America, and he was a delegate to the 1995 White House Conference on Small Business and the 2006 Savers' Summit, Washington, D.C. Mr. Martin has testified in Congress.

Al graduated with Highest Distinction from Kansas University and was a Phi Beta Kappa, Summerfield Scholar, Student Body President. He received his J.D., *cum laude*, and LL.M. in taxation from New York University School of Law, where he was a Root-Tilden Scholar and Note & Comment Editor, *New York University Law Review*.

Gregory E. Matthews, CPA

Gregory Matthews is a principal and CEO and senior benefit and compliance consultant with Matthews Benefit Group, Inc., in St. Petersburg, Florida. He is the creator and author of the monthly employee benefits newsletter *401(k) Advisor*, author of the *Payroll Answer Book*, and coauthor of the *403(b) Answer Book Forms & Worksheets* for Aspen Publishers. He is a frequent speaker at regional and national benefit programs. Mr. Matthews also authored and taught Course 6 of the American Institute of CPAs' "Compensation and Benefits" in the Tax Certificate Program.

Mr. Matthews is the past chair of the IRS Gulf Coast EP/EO Liaison Council and has participated as a speaker in national AICPA, ASPPA, ABA, and ALI-ABA tax/ benefits programs.

Gregory is a graduate of the University of Tampa (mathematics) and completed his accounting and mathematical studies at Strayer University and American University, Washington, D.C.

Mr. Matthews is a member of the Florida Institute of Certified Public Accountants, the American Institute of Certified Public Accountants, the ESOP Association, the Profit Sharing Council of America, and the American Society of Pension Professionals & Actuaries.

Caroline B. McKay, J.D.

Caroline B. McKay is an Associate Counsel of the Advanced Markets department for John Hancock Insurance (USA). In her current position, Caroline provides estate and business planning support to home office employees, field personnel, and producers. Caroline is also a recurring host on John Hancock's weekly JHAM Radio program and a regular speaker at industry meetings around the country.

Caroline is a contributing author of the 16th edition of *The Tools & Techniques of Estate Planning* by Stephan Leimberg and previously has been published on Wealth Management.com.

Prior to joining John Hancock, Caroline was in private practice in the Boston area where she concentrated her practice on estate planning, probate, business succession planning, and charitable planning for moderate and high net worth individuals and companies.

Caroline received her Bachelor of Arts degree, *magna cum laude*, in History from Colby College in Waterville, Maine, and her Juris Doctor degree *cum laude* from Suffolk University Law School, Boston, Massachusetts. While at Suffolk Law, she was a member of the Law Review and was published in the Suffolk University Law Review. Upon receiving her J.D., Caroline spent one year clerking for the Honorable Chief Justice Paul Suttell of the Rhode Island Supreme Court.

Jonathan Neal

Jonathan Neal has more than 30 years of experience in the retirement planning industry dealing directly with seniors. He writes both public and industry related articles on retirement planning issues and products that are primarily focused on the senior marketplace. In April 2009 his book "Reverse Mortgages – What Every Financial Advisor Should Know" was released. This book tackles the complexities of reverse mortgages and the various perceptions that seniors, financial and insurance advisors, and mortgage brokers are presently dealing with.

Over the years his articles have introduced some unique ideas and tools designed to help seniors better understand different insurance and investing concepts, such as The LTC Calculator, which is a tool that helps LTCi representatives and seniors work together to find a realistic daily LTCi coverage needs. Another example is the premium versus cost formula he developed in order to provide advisors with an functional mathematical formula to provide seniors with realistic quantified numbers based on their individual situation to help them understand not only what it would take to fund a LTCi policy, but also identify where those funds can be found in their present portfolio.

In addition to his articles, he has written 25 continuing education courses that have been approved by various state insurance departments, which include but are not limited to the following: Basic Long-Term Care, Long-Term Care, The History of Long-Term Care in the United States, Service Providers for Long-Term Care Patients, The Stats, Facts & Myths of Long-Term Care Planning, Funding Long-Term Care Annuities, Long-Term Care Annuities, Life Long-Term

Care, Fixed Annuities, Immediate Annuities, Basic Variable Annuities, The Fundamentals of Long-Term Care Polices, Professional Ethics, Retirement Planning, IRA Fundamentals, Stretch IRA Concepts, Retirement Plans, and Reverse Mortgages.

John L. Olsen, CLU, ChFC, AEP

John Olsen is a financial and estate planner practicing in St. Louis County, Missouri. He has been active in the financial services industry for more than 40 years. John is a past President of the St. Louis chapter of the National Association of Insurance and Financial Advisors, a current Board member of the St. Louis chapter of the Society of Financial Service Professionals, and the current Vice President of the St. Louis Estate Planning Council.

Mr. Olsen is coauthor, with Michael Kitces, CLU, ChFC, CFP, MSFS, of *The Advisor's Guide to Annuities* (National Underwriter Co. 4th ed., 2014), with Jack Marrion, D.M, of *Index Annuities: A Suitable Approach* (www.indexannuitybook.com) and author of *Taxation and Suitability of Annuities for the Professional Advisor"* (2nd expanded Kindle edition to be released in Fall, 2014) and numerous articles on annuities, insurance, and financial planning. He offers consulting services on annuities to other advisors and expert witness services in litigation involving annuities or life insurance.

David Pratt

David Pratt was born in England and received a law degree from Oxford University. He worked for law firms in London and Cleveland before moving to Albany, New York. In Albany, he practiced with a law firm and two accounting firms before joining the faculty of Albany Law School in 1994. He continues to advise clients and serves as an expert witness on employee benefits issues.

He has written numerous articles on employee compensation and benefits topics, and is a Senior Editor of the *Journal of Pension Benefits* and a fellow of the American College of Employee Benefits Counsel. He is the author of *The Social Security and Medicare Answer Book* and the coauthor of *Pension and Employee Benefit Law, 5th edition* (with John Langbein and Susan Stabile), *Taxation of Distributions from Qualified Plans* (with Dianne Bennett and others) and *ERISA and Employee Benefit Law: the Essentials* (with Sharon Reese, ABA Publications).

Louis R. Richey, J.D.

Lou Richey is recognized as an experienced executive and employee benefits & business insurance attorney and consultant, with special expertise on "top hat" 409A nonqualified deferred compensation and welfare benefit plans, as well as other employee retirement plans. He has over 40 years of experience in executive and employee benefits compensation consulting, planning, and insurance for Fortune 1000 public companies, as well as closely-held and tax-exempt organizations.

Currently, Mr. Richey is an independent executive and employee benefits, business insurance & benefits, and business insurance marketing consultant located in Blairsville, Georgia, located just north of Atlanta. He retired in 2020 as legacy Senior Vice- President with Infosys McCamish Systems, LLC. Infosys McCamish Systems is one of the nation's leading providers of outsourced administrative and other back-office support services for life insurance carriers and other major financial services organizations. Mr. Richey helped lead the McCamish *Retirement Services Group* and was the legal and *content expert* for all of Infosys McCamish's executive, employee, and qualified and nonqualified pension benefit web-based marketing, design, and plan administration platforms.

At earlier points in his career, Mr. Richey served as a senior marketing officer, as well as a compensation and senior consultant with employers like American Express Company, the General American Life Insurance Company, William M. Mercer, Magner Network, and several offices of the Management Compensation Group (MCG) and M Group.

Lou is a graduate of Wabash College in Indiana, a cum laude graduate of the IU McKinney Law School, and a member of the Georgia Bar. He is currently a member of the BNA and the ALM/NUCO Editorial Advisory Boards and has served on the editorial advisory boards of several other major industry publications. He is also a retired Chairman of the Board of Visitors of the IU McKinney Law School, Indianapolis. He has been named a Kentucky Colonel and an Arkansas Traveler in recognition of his professional contributions to the legal profession.

Mr. Richey lectures widely on the impact and implications of 409A, executive and employee benefit topics, retirement planning, business insurance, financial services marketing, insurance, and financial planning, at major conferences and institutes such as the New York University Federal Tax Institute , the Southwest Federal Tax Conference, the Notre Dame Estate Planning Institute , the American Society of Actuaries Annual Conference, the LIMRA Advance Marketing Conference, the LIMRA/LOMA Conference, the NACD Conference and a host of other professional services conferences and local meetings.

Mr. Richey's comments have appeared in <u>Business Week</u>, <u>The Wall Street Journal</u>, <u>Forbe's Magazine</u>, and <u>Investor's Daily</u>, and he has appeared on the <u>Financial News Network</u> for National Public Radio. He has authored or co-authored a number of books, and portfolios with organizations like the American Bar Association and Bloomberg BNA, plus more than 500 articles, audios and videos on compensation, business insurance and tax topics. One article was used by the IRS in its own training materials for its audit agents, and another publication he coauthored was cited in a recent Tax Court opinion.

Mr. Richey can be reached at LouRichey@aol.com.

Jeff Sadler

Jeff Sadler began his career as an underwriter in the disability income brokerage division of the Paul Revere Life Insurance Company following his graduation from the University of Vermont in 1975. Disability income and long-term care insurance have been the primary focus of his career, leading to the founding of Sadler Disability Services, Inc. with his father, Raymond Sadler, in 1989.

Over the last several years, Mr. Sadler has authored a number of insurance books, including *The Long Term Care Handbook* (1996, 1998 and 2003), *How To Sell Long Term Care Insurance* (2001 and 2006), *Disability Income: The Sale, The Product, The Market* (1991 and 1995), *How To Sell Disability Income* (2005), and *The Managed Care and Group Health Handbook* (1997), all published by the National Underwriter Company. Other books by Mr. Sadler include *Business Disability Income* (1993) and *Understanding LTC Insurance* (1992).

He has been very active in the industry, currently serving as the Chair of the National Association of Health Underwriters' Long-Term Care Advisory Group. He is a past president of the Central Florida Association of Health Underwriters, the Gulf Coast Health Underwriters, the Florida Association of Health Underwriters, and the Central Florida General Agents and Managers Association. He is a past winner of the Stanley Greenspun Health Insurance Person of the Year Award and the NAHU Distinguished Service Award.

Jamie Scott, J.D.

Jamie Scott serves as Chair of Cincinnati law firm Graydon Head's Employee Benefits and Executive Compensation Practice Group. He has worked with clients of all sizes to design and implement qualified retirement plans (including ESOPs), nonqualified deferred compensation plans, incentive compensation plans, and welfare benefit plans.

He also has significant experience in working with the Internal Revenue Service and Department of Labor on compliance issues. Mr. Scott has extensive estate planning experience, which enables him to advise clients on estate planning issues that arise when a large part of a client's estate consists of retirement plan assets. In 2010, he was named an "Ohio Super Lawyer" by Super Lawyers Magazine for his work in Employee Benefits/ERISA. Based on the grading and comments of his peers, Jamie is recognized with an AV Rating, the highest rating given to lawyers by Martindale-Hubbell.

Mr. Scott received his J.D. from Brigham Young University in 1983 and a B.B.A in Accounting from the University of Cincinnati in 1978. He is admitted to practice law in Ohio and Texas. He is member and former chair of the Cincinnati Bar Association, Employee Benefits Committee; Warren County Bar Association; ASPPA Benefits Council of Greater Cincinnati; Warren County MRDD Board Member; and member of the Lebanon City Schools Citizens Audit Advisory Committee.

Lou Shuntich, J.D., LL.M.

Lou Shuntich has a wealth of knowledge and expert advice to offer in the Advanced Planning arena. He earned his B.S. Cum Laude from Rider University, his J.D. from The College of William and Mary, and his LL.M. (in Taxation) from New York University. He is a Certified Retirement Counselor and is licensed for life, health, variable annuities, and Series 6 and 63.

He is the Associate Editor of the *Journal of Financial Service Professionals*. He previously served in the Law Department of Prudential-Financial as

Vice President and Corporate Counsel specializing in business insurance, estate planning, and compensation planning. He also served as Senior Vice President, Advanced Planning for Lincoln Benefit Life Company.

He is a member of the Association for Advanced Life Underwriting Business Insurance and Estate Planning and Nonqualified Plans Broad Committees. He is past chairman of the American Council of Life Insurance Split Dollar Task Force and has served on the Life Underwriter Training Council's Content and Techniques Committee.

In addition, he is a member of the Speakers Bureau of the Society of Financial Service Professionals and the Speakers Bureau of the National Association of Estate Planners and Councils. He has appeared on the CNBC Power Lunch and Health and Lifestyles programs answering questions about retirement and estate planning. He has five published books on advanced marketing subjects, including *The Estate Planning Today Handbook, The Complete Guide to Compensation Planning With Life Insurance*, and *The Life Insurance Handbook*, all published by Marketplace, as well as *Key Life Insurance Model Agreements* and *The Next Step, Successfully Graduating To Life Insurance Advanced Markets*, both published by the National Underwriter Company.

He has also published multiple articles including those in the *Journal of Financial Service Professionals, AALU Quarterly Magazine, Brokers World Magazine* and *Life Insurance Selling*.

Joseph F. Stenken, J.D., CLU, ChFC

 Joseph F. Stenken, J.D., CLU, ChFC, has over 20 years of experience in insurance and financial services and worked in advanced markets for over 10 years. After graduating from the University of Cincinnati College of Law, he worked at the National Underwriter Company as an Associate Editor for over 12 years. While at National Underwriter he worked on numerous publications, including *Tax Facts on Insurance & Employee Benefits, Field Guide to Estate, Employee, & Business Planning, The Social Security Source Book*, and books in the *Tools and Techniques* series.

While working in advanced markets he assisted agents with case design in areas such as Estate Planning and Business Continuation planning. He has given numerous educational webinars for agents throughout the country and has given CE lectures for various NAIFA chapters.

He is the co-author of *Tools and Techniques of Employee Benefits and Retirement Planning*. He has written articles for *Think About It* as well as Retirement Daily, and has been quoted in USA Today and theStreet.com.

Joseph served as President of the Cincinnati Chapter of the Society of FSP for the 2009-2010 year and as President of the Cincinnati NAIFA chapter in 2020. He earned his Bachelor of Science from Miami University and served in the U.S. Navy aboard USS Haddock (SSN-621).

Bruce A. Tannahill, J.D., CPA/PFS, CLU, ChFC, AEP

Bruce Tannahill is an experienced tax, estate and business planning attorney and CPA with expertise in estate and business planning, qualified plans, IRAs, life insurance, and annuities. In his role as Director, Estate and Business Planning for Massachusetts Mutual Life Insurance Company, he assists MassMutual agents in serving their clients on estate planning, business planning, Social Security, and personal planning matters.

Bruce is a nationally recognized author on the topics of retirement planning and trust and estate issues. He is a co-author of three books. His articles have been published in various industry and professional publications, including *Trusts & Estates, Estate Planning, Probate & Property*, and the *Journal of Financial Service Professionals*. He was the Qualified Plans & Retirement Counseling columnist for the *Journal of Financial Service Professionals* from 2012 through May 2015.

He serves as CLE Committee vice Chair for the ABA Real Property, Trust & Estate Law Section and is a former Director of the Society of Financial Service Professionals. He also served as Chair of the Synergy Summit, an organization of leading financial service professional organizations.

He received his Juris Doctor, with distinction, from the University of Missouri at Kansas City, Kansas City, MO and his BSBA in Accounting, Summa Cum Laude, from University of Dayton. He is admitted to practice before the U.S. Tax Court and the Supreme Courts of Kansas, Missouri, and Ohio.

In his spare time, he enjoys volunteering for the FIRST Robotics Competition, reading, and watching baseball.

Robert Toth, J.D., ACEBC

Bob Toth is the Principal of the Law Office of Robert J. Toth, Jr., LLC, and has been practicing employee benefits law since 1983. His practice focuses on the design, administration, and distribution of financial products and services for retirement plans, particularly on complex fiduciary and prohibited transaction issues, annuities in deferred compensation plans, and 403(b) plans. Mr. Toth is a Fellow of American College of Employee Benefits Counsel and is on the faculty of ALI-ABA Advance Law of Pensions. In addition, he managed the legal affairs of Lincoln Financial Group's retirement plan business. Mr. Toth is also an Adjunct Professor at John Marshall Law School where he teaches 403(b) and 457 plan courses.

Mr. Toth coauthored Thompson Publishing's *403(b) and 457 Technical Requirements Handbook* and is a contributing author to Aspen Publishing's *403(b) Answer Book*. He is also Chair of ASPPA's IRS Governmental Affairs Sub-Committee and writes on current employee benefits issues at the *businessofbenefits.com*, where more on his background, publications, and presentations can be found.

William J. Wagner, J.D., LL.M., CLU

William J. Wagner is a Senior Editor with Forefield, Inc., a provider of Web-based applications that facilitate the communication of financial planning knowledge and advice between financial institutions, their advisors, and their customers.

Mr. Wagner is the author of the *Ultimate IRA Resource* (including the IRA Calculator) and the *Ultimate Trust Resource* (including the Trust Calculator). Previously, he was a Senior Associate Editor of *Tax Facts on Insurance & Employee Benefits*, *Tax Facts on Investments*, and *Tax Facts News*, all published by The National Underwriter Company.

Jayne Elizabeth Zanglein

Jayne Elizabeth Zanglein is a prolific writer on employee benefits. She contributes regularly to journals such as the *ABA Supreme Court Preview*, the *Journal of Taxation of Employee Benefits*, and the *NYU Review of Employee Benefits and Executive Compensation*. Her treatise, *ERISA Litigation*, was published in 2003 and is now in its fourth edition. She serves as an employee benefits expert and neutral in class action cases.

She is the cochair of the Fiduciary Duties Committee of the ABA Section on Labor and Employment Law's subcommittee on Employee Benefits. She has served on various task forces including Governor Cuomo's Task Force on Pension Fund Investments. She has worked on pension fund reform in Ontario and South Africa. She currently teaches law and dispute resolution at Western Carolina University.

Randy L. Zipse, J.D., AEP (Distinguished)

Randy Zipse serves as Vice President, Advanced Markets, at Prudential. In this position, Mr. Zipse provides advanced sales support across the company, assisting distribution channels and working with sales vice presidents, independent producers, and financial institutions to develop business opportunities and enhanced advanced marketing solutions for clients.

Mr. Zipse has written numerous articles on trust taxation, estate planning, and business succession planning, which have appeared in the Journal of *Financial Service Professionals, BrokerWorld, Estate Planning, Life Insurance Selling, LAN*, and the National Underwriter news magazines. He is coauthor with Stephan R. Leimberg of *Tools and Techniques of Charitable Planning*. He has also been a frequent lecturer at industry meetings, including AALU, International Forum, Million Dollar Round Table, New York University Tax Institute, University of Miami Heckerling Tax Institute, and the Hawaii Tax Institute.

Mr. Zipse also serves as author of National Underwriter's popular *Field Guide on Estate Planning, Business Planning, & Employee Benefits* publication.

Prior to joining Prudential, Mr. Zipse was Senior Vice President at Highland Capital where he was responsible for the Advanced Markets group, which provided estate and business planning support to home office employees, field personnel, and producers.

Mr. Zipse was Senior Counsel and VP of the Manulife Financial Advanced Markets team. Before that he worked as an attorney in private practice. An honors graduate of the University of Northern Iowa, Mr. Zipse subsequently received his J.D. from Drake University College of Law (Order of the Coif, class rank number one), and is a member of the Iowa, Texas, and Missouri Bars.

OTHER CONTRIBUTORS

William H. Alley, CLU, ChFC, RHU, LUTCF, MSFS, AEP, CLTC, is Principal and CEO of Alley Financial Group, LLC in Lexington, Kentucky. Bill entered the life insurance business in 1960, having graduated from Columbia Military Academy and attended the University of Kentucky. Bill has developed a successful practice in the areas of retirement and succession planning, estate analysis, financial planning, and business insurance. Bill is a past president of the Lexington and Kentucky Life Underwriters Association, past president of the Lexington Chapter of the Society of Financial Service Professionals, a past trustee of the National Association of Insurance and Financial Advisors and a 25 year member of the Million Dollar Round Table. He is also a past National Director for the Society of Financial Service Professionals. Bill is a frequent speaker on insurance and financial planning as well as the author of numerous articles on insurance and financial matters.

Ward B. Anderson, CLU, ChFC, is president of Compensation Planning & Administration Systems, Inc., an employee benefit consulting firm involved in the design, installation and funding of tax qualified retirement plans, selective executive benefit plans and group life, health and disability plans. Ward is immediate past president of the Society of Financial Service Professionals. He has been a frequent speaker to legal, accounting and financial planning groups on the topics of estate planning, uses of life insurance, employee benefit planning, taxation of employee benefit plans and planning for retirement plan distributions. Ward attended the University of Kansas and the University of Kansas School of Law.

Marcela S. Aroca is a litigator based in Windsor, Ontario practicing exclusively in tax and civil litigation. During her 18 year career, Marcela has developed into an expert in the field and has appeared at all trial and appellate Courts in Ontario, the Federal Court, the Federal Court of Appeal and has appeared in writing to the Supreme Court of Canada. When Marcela is not working at her practice, she teaches Income Tax Law, Advanced Tax Law, Civil Procedure, and Contract Law at the University of Windsor, Faculty of Law.

Gregory W. Baker, J.D., CFP®, CAP, is Senior Vice President of Legal Services for Renaissance, the nation's leading third-party administrator of charitable gifts. For the past 18 years, he has provided trust, tax and philanthropic financial planning advice to over 4,000 attorneys and 7,000 financial planners in all 50 states regarding more than 14,000 charitable remainder trusts, more than 800 charitable lead trusts, and numerous foundations, charitable gift annuities and donor-advised funds. Baker's advice has helped advisors close cases for their high net worth clients in the areas of charitable, investment, retirement, gift, estate and tax planning.

Baker is currently an Advisory Board Member of the Chartered Advisor in Philanthropy designation at the American College, member of the Financial Planning Association, National Committee on Planned Giving and the Indiana Bar. Baker was previously VP, Charitable Fiduciary Risk Manager for the Merrill Lynch Center for Philanthropy & Nonprofit Management in Princeton, NJ. Baker speaks at national and local conferences for professional advisors, high net worth clients and charities regarding charitable gift planning, asset-allocation, investment modeling and tax issues.

Ted R. Batson, Jr., MBA, CPA, is Senior Vice President of Professional Services for Renaissance, the nation's leading third-party administrator of charitable gifts. Since his employment in 1993, Batson has developed a wealth of practical, hands-on experience in dealing with complex issues related to the creative use of unmarketable and unusual assets to fund charitable gifts. He routinely consults with the more than 2,000 attorneys, CPAs and financial service professionals who look to Renaissance for case assistance. Batson has spoken to numerous groups regarding charitable planning and has been published in several professional publications. Batson is a member of the American Institute of Certified Public Accountants (AICPA) and the Indiana CPA Society. He is a graduate of Asbury College (BA in computer science) and Indiana University (MBA in accounting).

Lawrence Brody, J.D., LL.M, is a partner in Bryan Cave LLP, a national and international law firm, and a member of the firm's Private Client Group. He is an adjunct professor at Washington University School of Law and a visiting adjunct professor at the University of Miami School of Law. Mr. Brody focuses his practice on estate planning for high net worth individuals and the use of life insurance in estate and nonqualified deferred compensation planning, He is the author of two BNA Tax Management Portfolios and two books for the National Underwriter Company, and is a frequent lecturer at national conferences on estate and insurance planning. Mr. Brody received the designation of Accredited Estate Planner by the National Association of Estate Planners and Councils, and was awarded its Distinguished Accredited Estate Planner designation in 2004.

Fred Burkey, CLU, APA, is a retired Advanced Sales Consultant with Ameritas Life Insurance Corporation (previously Union Central Life Insurance Corporation). He joined Union Central in 1981 after nine years of insurance sales in the greater Cincinnati area. He served in agent support departments including pension sales, agency development, and individual annuity sales. Fred is a member of the National Association for Variable Annuities, the Society of Financial Service Professionals, and the National Institute of Pension Administrators.

Donald F. Cady, J.D., LL.M., CLU, is the author of *Field Guide to Estate, Employee, & Business Planning* and *Field Guide to Financial Planning*. He is a graduate of St. Lawrence University with a B.A. in Economics, where he received the Wall Street Journal Award for excellence in that subject. He received his J.D. degree from Columbia University School of Law, holds the degree of LL.M. (Taxation) from Emory University School of Law, and is a member of the New York Bar. For 20 years, Don was with the Aetna Life Insurance & Annuity Company in various advanced underwriting positions. Don is a frequent speaker on the subjects of estate planning, business planning and employee benefits for business and professional organizations.

Natalie B. Choate, Esq., is an estate planning attorney with the firm of Nutter, McClennen, and Fish, LLP. A Regent of the American College of Trust & Estate Counsel, she is the author of two books, *Life and Death Planning for Retirement Benefits* and *The QPRT Manual*, and is a frequent lecturer on estate planning topics. She is listed in *The Best Lawyers in America*.

Stephan R. Leimberg is CEO of LISI, Leimberg Information Services, Inc., a provider of email/internet news and commentary for professionals on recent cases, rulings, and legislation. He is also CEO of Leimberg & LeClair, Inc., an estate and financial planning software company, and President of Leimberg Associates, Inc., a publishing and software company in Bryn Mawr, Pennsylvania. Leimberg is the author of the acclaimed *Tools and Techniques* series, with titles on estate planning, employee benefits, financial planning, charitable planning, life insurance planning, income tax planning, investment planning, and practice management. Mr. Leimberg is a nationally known speaker and an award-winning author.

Martin A. Silfen, Esq., is an attorney and author with 25 years of practice in the areas of retirement planning and estate planning. Mr. Silfen was senior partner in the law firm of Silfen, Segal, Fryer & Shuster, P.C. in Atlanta. He is currently Senior Vice President of Brown Brothers Harriman Trust Company, New York, New York. Mr. Silfen is a nationally recognized expert in retirement tax planning, having authored *The Retirement Plan Distribution Advisor* and served as Retirement Planning columnist for *Personal Financial Planning*. He has also authored several articles for *Estate Planning*.

Editor

Jason Gilbert, J.D., M.A., is a senior editor with the Practical Insights Division of The National Underwriter Company, a division of ALM Media, LLC. He edits and develops publications related to tax and insurance products, including titles in the *Advisor's Guide* and the *Tools & Techniques* series of investment and planning products. He also develops content for National Underwriter's other financial services publications and online products. He has worked on insurance and tax publications for more than nine years.

Jason has been a practicing attorney for more than a dozen years in the areas of criminal defense, products liability, and regulatory enforcement actions. Prior to joining National Underwriter, his experience in the insurance and tax fields has included work as a Westlaw contributor for Thomson Reuters and a tax advisor and social media contributor for Intuit. He is an honors graduate from Wright State University and holds a J.D. from the University of Cincinnati College of Law as well as a master's degree in Economics from Miami University in Ohio.

Editorial Services

Connie L. Jump, Sr. Manager, Editorial Operations

Patti O'Leary, Sr. Editorial Assistant

Emily Brunner, Editorial Assistant

ABBREVIATIONS

ACA	Affordable Care Act
Acq. (Nonacq.)	Commissioner's acquiescence (nonacquiescence) in decision
AFTR	American Federal Tax Reports (Research Institute of America, early decisions)
AFTR2d	American Federal Tax Reports (Research Institute of America, second series)
AJCA 2004	American Jobs Creation Act of 2004
ARRA 2009	American Recovery and Reinvestment Act of 2009
ATRA 2012	American Taxpayer Relief Act of 2012
BTA	Board of Tax Appeals decisions (now Tax Court)
BTA Memo	Board of Tax Appeals memorandum decisions
CA or -- Cir.	United States Court of Appeals
CARES	Coronavirus Aid, Relief, and Economic Security Act
CB	Cumulative Bulletin of Internal Revenue Service
CCA	Chief Counsel Advice
Cl. Ct.	U.S. Claims Court (designated U.S. Court of Federal Claims in 1992)
CLASS Act	Community Living Assistance Services and Support Act
COBRA	Consolidated Omnibus Budget Reconciliation Act of 1985
CRTRA 2000	Community Renewal Tax Relief Act of 2000
Ct. Cl.	Court of Claims (designated U.S. Claims Court in 1982)
DOL Adv. Op.	Department of Labor Advisory Opinion
EGTRRA 2001	Economic Growth and Tax Relief Reconciliation Act of 2001
EIEA 2008	Energy Improvement and Extension Act of 2008
ERISA	Employee Retirement Income Security Act of 1974
ERTA	Economic Recovery Tax Act of 1981
Fed.	Federal Reporter (early decisions)
Fed. Cl.	U.S. Court of Federal Claims
Fed. Reg.	Federal Register
F.2d	Federal Reporter, second series (later decisions of U.S. Court of Appeals to Mid-1993)
F.3rd	Federal Reporter, third series (decisions of U.S. Court of Appeals since Mid-1993)
F. Supp.	Federal Supplement (decisions of U.S. District Courts)
FFCRA	Families First Coronavirus Response Act
FMLA	Family Medical Leave Act
FSA	Field Service Advice
FSA	Flexible spending account
FTE	Full-time equivalent employee
GCM	General Counsel Memorandum (IRS)
HCE	Highly compensated employee
HIPAA '96	Health Insurance Portability and Accountability Act
HHS	The Department of Health and Human Services
HRA	Health Reimbursement Account
HSA	Health Savings Account
IR	Internal Revenue News Release
HIREA (2010)	Hiring Incentives to Restore Employment Act
IRB	Internal Revenue Bulletin of Internal Revenue Service
IRC	Internal Revenue Code
IRS	Internal Revenue Service
IRSRRA '98	IRS Restructuring and Reform Act of 1998
IT	Income Tax Ruling Series (IRS)
ITCA	Installment Tax Correction Act of 2000
JCWAA	Job Creation and Worker Assistance Act of 2002
JGTRRA 2003	Jobs and Growth Tax Relief Reconciliation Act of 2003

KETRA 2005	Katrina Emergency Tax Relief Act of 2005
Let. Rul.	Letter Ruling (issued by IRS)
MERP	Medical Expense Reimbursement Plan
MFDRA 2007	Mortgage Forgiveness Debt Relief Act of 2007
MHPAEA	Mental Health Parity and Addiction Equity Act
MSA	Archer medical savings account
NHCE	Non highly compensated employee
NMHPA	Newborns' and Mothers' Health Protection Act
OBRA	Omnibus Budget Reconciliation Act of (year of enactment)
P.L.	Public Law
PLR	Private Letter Ruling
P&PS Rept.	Pension and Profit Sharing Report (Prentice-Hall)
PBGC	Pension Benefit Guaranty Corporation
PFEA 2004	Pension Funding Equity Act of 2004
PHSA	Public Health Service Act
PPA 2006	Pension Protection Act of 2006
PPACA	Patient Protection and Affordable Care Act
PPPFA	Paycheck Protection Program Flexibility Act
Prop. Reg.	Proposed Regulation
PTE	Prohibited Transaction Exemption
REA '84	Retirement Equity Act of 1984
Rev. Proc.	Revenue Procedure (issued by IRS)
Rev. Rul.	Revenue Ruling (issued by IRS)
SBJPA '96	Small Business Job Protection Act of 1996
SBWOTA 2007	Small Business and Work Opportunity Tax Act of 2007
SCA	IRS Service Center Advice
SECURE	Setting Up Every Community for Retirement Act
TAM	Technical Advice Memorandum (IRS)
TAMRA '88	Technical and Miscellaneous Revenue Act of 1988
TC	Tax Court (official reports)
TC Memo	Tax Court memorandum decisions (official reports)
TC Summary Opinion	Tax Court Summary Opinion
TD	Treasury Decision
TEAMTRA 2008	Tax Extenders and Alternative Minimum Tax Relief Act of 2008
TEFRA	Tax Equity and Fiscal Responsibility Act of 1982
Temp. Reg.	Temporary Regulation
TIPA 2007	Tax Increase Prevention Act of 2007
TIPRA 2005	Tax Increase Prevention and Reconciliation Act of 2005
TIR	Technical Information Release (from the IRS)
TRA	Tax Reform Act of (year of enactment)
TRA '97	Taxpayer Relief Act of 1997
TRA 2010	Tax Relief Act of 2010
TRHCA 2006	Tax Relief and Health Care Act of 2006
TTCA 2007	Tax Technical Corrections Act of 2007
URAA '94	Uruguay Round Agreements Act of 1994
US	United States Supreme Court decisions
USERRA '94	Uniformed Services Employment and Reemployment Rights Act of 1994
USTC	United States Tax Cases (Commerce Clearing House)
VTTRA 2001	Victims of Terrorism Tax Relief Act of 2001
WFTRA 2004	Working Families Tax Relief Act of 2004
WHBAA 2009	Worker, Homeownership, and Business Assistance Act of 2009
WHCRA	Women's Health and Cancer Rights Act
WRERA 2008	Worker, Retiree, and Employer Recovery Act of 2008

COMPLETE LIST OF QUESTIONS

2021 TAX FACTS ON INSURANCE & EMPLOYEE BENEFITS, VOLUME 2

PART X: CAFETERIA PLANS

Overview

3501. What is a cafeteria plan?

3502. What benefits may be offered under a cafeteria plan?

3503. What are the income tax benefits of a cafeteria plan?

3504. What nondiscrimination requirements apply to cafeteria plans?

3505. What are the rules that apply to simple cafeteria plans for small businesses?

3506. When can benefit elections under a cafeteria plan be changed?

3507. When can benefit elections under a cafeteria plan be changed due to a change in an employee's status?

3508. Can an employee change benefit elections under a cafeteria plan because of significant cost or coverage changes?

3509. How are health-related benefits offered under a cafeteria plan affected by the Family and Medical Leave Act?

3510. How are non-health-related benefits offered under a cafeteria plan affected by the Family and Medical Leave Act?

3511. What are the payment options that must be made available to employees on FMLA leave?

3512. What is the new tax credit for employers that provide paid family and medical leave to employees?

3513. Are amounts received under a cafeteria plan subject to Social Security and federal unemployment taxes?

3514. Must an employer sponsoring a cafeteria plan file an information return with the IRS?

Flexible Spending Arrangements

3515. What is a flexible spending arrangement?

3516. What is a health flexible spending arrangement?

PART XIII: UNFUNDED DEFERRED COMPENSATION

Overview

Section 409A

Informal Funding Arrangements

3567. What is a "rabbi" trust?

3568. What is the impact of Section 409A(b) on a "rabbi" trust?

3569. What pre-409A issues were raised by the IRS model rabbi trust?

3570. Pre-409A, if a taxpayer wanted to adopt the model trust and wished to obtain an advance ruling from the IRS on the underlying deferred compensation plan, what additional guidelines was it required to follow?

Account and Nonaccount Balance Plans

3571. Can a private IRC Section 451 unfunded nonqualified deferred compensation employee account balance plan be used in connection with a qualified 401(k) elective deferral plan to maximize the annual deferrals into the qualified 401(k) and also to receive employee contributions that cannot go into the qualified plan because of nondiscrimination testing issues?

3572. What approved wrap plan structure exists to allow employees to maximize 401(k) plan deferrals using a nonqualified deferred compensation account balance plan to temporarily hold elective deferrals?

3573. When are deferred amounts under an unfunded nonqualified account and nonaccount balance plan deductible by the employer?

3574. How are deferred compensation account balances and nonaccount balance payments taxed when received by the employee or the beneficiary?

3575. How are deferred compensation account balances and nonaccount balance payments taxed when they are received by an ex-spouse pursuant to divorce?

FICA and FUTA Taxes

3576. Are contributions to, and postretirement payments from, a deferred compensation account balance or nonaccount balance plan subject to FICA and FUTA taxes?

3577. When is a nonqualified deferred compensation plan excluded for purposes of determining FICA and FUTA taxes?

3578. How is the amount deferred for employment tax purposes impacted by whether the account is an account balance plan or a nonaccount balance plan?

3579. Are self-employed individuals and corporate directors subject to FICA and FUTA taxes for deferred compensation arrangements?

3580. What is the wage base subject to FICA and FUTA taxes for deferred compensation arrangements?

Section 457 Plans

Overview

Section 457(b) "Eligible" Plans

Excess Benefit Pension Plans

Stock Options

PART XIV: NON-TRADITIONAL EMPLOYMENT BENEFITS

Dependent Care Assistance Programs

Social Security Planning

Distributions

Required Minimum Distributions

3728. How are Section 415 limits applied to defined contribution plans?

3729. What is counted as compensation for purposes of applying the Section 415 limits to defined contribution plans?

3730. What are savings and thrift plans, and "side car" accounts?

3731. What special rules apply to the sale of employer securities to a defined contribution plan?

3732. What is the diversification requirement for defined contribution plans?

Pensions

3733. What is a pension plan?

3734. What is a target benefit plan?

3735. What is the maximum amount that an employer may deduct annually for contributions on behalf of employees to a qualified defined benefit pension plan?

3736. What special qualification requirements regarding the payment of definitely determinable benefits apply to pension plans but not to profit sharing plans?

3737. What special qualification requirements regarding retirement age apply to pension plans but not to profit sharing plans?

3738. Can a pension plan allow participants to retire in phases and still remain qualified?

3739. Under the Multiemployer Pension Reform Act of 2014, can a plan reduce a participant's benefit levels?

3740. Are there any limitations on a pension plan's ability to reduce participant benefit levels under the Multiemployer Pension Reform Act of 2014?

3741. What procedures and notices are required in order for a pension plan to reduce participant benefit levels under the Multiemployer Pension Reform Act of 2014?

3742. What is the minimum funding standard that applied in plan years before 2008?

3743. What is the funding requirement for defined benefit plans beginning after PPA 2006, MAP-21 and HATFA 2014?

3744. What requirements apply to defined benefit plans that are "at risk" beginning after 2007?

3745. When are pension plan contributions credited for funding standard account purposes?

3746. What other special requirements applied in plan years prior to 2008 when a qualified plan was subject to the minimum funding standard?

Nondiscrimination

Minimum Participation and Coverage

3840. What are the age and service requirements that can be used for qualified plans?

3841. What is the minimum coverage requirement for qualified plans?

3842. What is the ratio percentage test that can be used to determine whether a qualified plan satisfies the minimum coverage requirement?

3843. What is the average benefit test that can be used to determine whether a qualified plan satisfies the minimum coverage requirement?

3844. What are the miscellaneous rules associated with the minimum coverage requirement for qualified plans?

3845. What effect does noncompliance with the minimum coverage requirements have upon a qualified plan?

3846. Can a qualified plan be established for the sole shareholder of a corporation?

Nondiscrimination

3847. When is a plan nondiscriminatory?

3848. What safe harbor designs allow a defined contribution plan to satisfy the nondiscrimination requirements?

3849. How can a defined contribution plan that does not satisfy one of the safe harbor designs show that it does not discriminate in favor of highly compensated employees?

3850. What safe harbors exist that allow a defined benefit plan to satisfy the nondiscrimination requirements?

3851. How can a defined benefit plan that does not satisfy one of the safe harbors show that it does not discriminate in favor of highly compensated employees?

3852. Can a plan satisfy the nondiscrimination requirements by limiting participation to highly compensated employees and nonhighly compensated employees with very short periods of service?

3853. What safe harbor designs allow a target benefit plan to satisfy the nondiscrimination requirements?

3854. How do 401(k) plans satisfy the IRC nondiscrimination requirements?

3855. Can a plan satisfy the IRC nondiscrimination requirements through aggregating multiple plans or restructuring the plan?

3856. Will a plan be considered discriminatory if it is integrated with Social Security?

I

Vesting

Anti-Cutback Rule

3897. How are defined benefit plan annuity payments to children treated for purposes of the minimum distribution requirements?

3898. Are there any situations in which a defined benefit plan participant's benefit must, or may, be increased?

3899. How are the minimum distribution requirements met after the death of an employee?

3900. How are the minimum distribution requirements met if an employee died before the required beginning date?

3901. How are the minimum distribution requirements met if an employee died on or after the required beginning date?

3902. What is an eligible designated beneficiary? How does this designation impact the rules governing retirement plan distributions after an account owner's death?

3903. How is the designated beneficiary determined for purposes of the minimum distribution requirements?

3904. How does the presence of multiple, contingent or successor beneficiaries impact the minimum distribution requirements?

3905. What are the separate account rules for purposes of the minimum distribution requirements?

3906. When may a trust be a designated beneficiary for purposes of the minimum distribution requirements?

3907. Who is the employee's spouse or surviving spouse for purposes of the minimum distribution requirements? What is the effect of a QDRO?

3908. What is the incidental benefit rule for qualified plans?

3909. How is an individual taxed when a qualified plan distribution fails to meet the minimum distribution requirements?

3910. How is an individual taxed when a qualified plan distribution made under an annuity contract or defined benefit plan annuity option fails to meet the minimum distribution requirements?

3911. What restrictions apply to the assignment or alienation of a participant's qualified plan benefit?

3912. Do anti-alienation rules prevent collections of federal taxes or judgments from qualified plan assets?

3913. Do anti-alienation rules prevent collections of payments from qualified plan assets if the payment is required because the participant committed a crime or violated his or her fiduciary duties?

3914. What is a qualified domestic relations order?

Top-Heavy Plan Requirements

3915. What do the top-heavy rules require with respect to a qualified plan?

3916. When is a single plan top-heavy?

3917. When are multiple plans top-heavy?

3918. How do the top-heavy rules apply to simplified employee pension plans?

3919. Are rollover plans subject to the top-heavy rules?

3920. Are there simplified calculation methods for a top-heavy plan?

3921. What special qualification requirements apply to top-heavy plans?

3922. What vesting requirements apply to top-heavy plans?

3923. What requirements with respect to minimum benefits and contributions apply to top-heavy defined benefit plans?

3924. What requirements with respect to minimum benefits and contributions apply to top-heavy defined contribution plans?

3925. What requirements with respect to minimum benefits and contributions apply to top-heavy plans if the employer has both a top-heavy defined contribution plan and a top-heavy defined benefit plan?

3926. What miscellaneous qualification requirements must be met in order for a plan to be qualified?

3927. Who is an employee for purposes of meeting the requirements applicable to qualified plans?

3928. What special rules apply to leased employees for purposes of the requirements that apply to qualified plans?

3929. Who are highly compensated employees for purposes of the requirements that apply to qualified plans?

3930. Who is a key employee for purposes of the top-heavy rules for qualified plans?

3931. Who is an owner-employee for purposes of the requirements that apply to qualified plans?

3932. What is a controlled group of corporations?

3933. When are trades or businesses under common control?

3934. What is an affiliated service group?

3935. Can the IRS retroactively apply a finding that a plan does not meet qualification requirements?

Employer Deduction

Taxation of Distributions

3976. What general rules apply to withholding of income tax from qualified retirement plan benefits?

3977. When are the earnings of a qualified pension or profit sharing trust taxable to the trust or to participants? When does trust income constitute unrelated business income?

3978. What is the tax treatment of trust assets that revert to a plan sponsor?

Prohibited Transactions

3979. What are prohibited transactions?

3980. What is a "disqualified person" for purposes of the prohibited transaction rules?

3981. Who is a fiduciary for purposes of the prohibited transaction rules?

3982. What exemptions to the prohibited transaction rules are provided by the Internal Revenue Code?

3983. When is a plan loan exempted from the prohibited transaction rules?

3984. What is the prohibited transaction exemption that allows life insurance agents, brokers, or pension consultants (including fiduciaries) who are disqualified persons to receive commission or effect transactions related to certain life insurance and annuities?

3985. What requirements must be satisfied for an investment advice fiduciary to qualify under the fiduciary PTE proposed by the DOL in 2020?

3986. When does the 2020 DOL investment advice fiduciary PTE apply to rollover transactions?

3987. What is the PTE that permits certain insurance agents or brokers who are employers (or related) maintaining a plan to sell insurance or annuity contracts to the plan and receive commission?

3988. What is the PTE that permits disqualified persons other than a plan to make unsecured interest-free loans to a plan to pay ordinary operating expenses?

3989. What are the PTEs that establish conditions for the transfer of life insurance and annuity contracts to and from plans?

3990. What is the PTE that allows banks and brokers to offer no or low cost services based on account balances in IRAs and Keogh plans?

3991. What are the penalties for engaging in a prohibited transaction?

Qualified Plans and Estate Taxes

3992. Is the value of a death benefit payable from a qualified plan includable in the employee's gross estate?

4013. May a surviving spouse make a rollover contribution?

4014. May a surviving non-spouse beneficiary make a rollover contribution?

4015. How is the 60-day time limit on rollovers applied?

4016. What is the self-certification process that can potentially allow individuals to obtain a waiver of the 60-day time limit on rollovers?

4017. May an individual who has attained age 70½ make a rollover?

4018. May a recipient of a distribution roll over the amount into another person's individual retirement plan?

4019. May a taxpayer roll over amounts from a defined contribution plan into a defined benefit plan? What special rules apply to the rolled over funds?

4020. How does the Department of Labor fiduciary standard impact advisors who provide advice with respect to IRA rollovers?

PART XVIII: SPLIT DOLLAR PLAN

4021. What is a split dollar plan?

4022. What are the income tax results of a split dollar plan entered into, or materially modified, after September 17, 2003?

4023. When is a split dollar plan that was entered into or materially modified after September 17, 2003 governed by the economic benefit theory and what are the tax consequences?

4024. When is a split dollar plan that was entered into or materially modified after September 17, 2003 treated as a loan and what are the tax consequences?

4025. When will a split dollar plan that is entered into before September 17, 2003 found to be "materially modified" so that it is governed by the 2003 regulations?

4026. What are the income tax results of a split dollar plan entered into before September 18, 2003?

4027. What are the income tax consequences of the transfer or rollout of a policy subject to a split dollar arrangement entered into after September 17, 2003?

4028. What are the income tax consequences of the transfer or rollout of a policy subject to a split dollar arrangement entered into before September 18, 2003?

4029. What is reverse split dollar and how is it taxed?

4030. What is private split dollar and how is it taxed?

PART XIX: TAX SHELTERED ANNUITIES FOR EMPLOYEES OF SECTION 501(C)(3) ORGANIZATIONS AND PUBLIC SCHOOLS

Overview

Contract Requirements

Contributions

4047. What is the special increase to the limit on amounts contributed to a tax sheltered annuity plan under a salary reduction agreement for employees who have completed 15 years of service?

4048. What are the consequences of exceeding the limit on elective deferrals to a tax sheltered annuity plan?

4049. Can participants in a tax sheltered annuity plan who are age 50 and over contribute a "catch-up" contribution each year?

4050. Are the elective deferral limits for tax sheltered annuity plans coordinated with the limits applicable to IRC Section 457 plans?

4051. What special rules apply to tax sheltered annuities for church employees?

4052. What is an excess contribution and an excess aggregate contribution to a tax sheltered annuity? What excise taxes apply to them?

4053. What are the requirements for an automatic enrollment provision in a 403(b) plan?

4054. Can an employer make post-retirement contributions to a tax sheltered annuity on behalf of a retired employee?

4055. What is a Roth 403(b) contribution program?

4056. May an employee exchange his or her tax sheltered annuity contract for another contract within the same plan?

4057. May an employee exchange his or her tax sheltered annuity contract for another contract in another 403(b) plan?

Amounts Received Under the Plan

4058. May an employee, the employee's surviving spouse, or a non-spouse beneficiary rollover a distribution from a tax sheltered annuity?

4059. May an employee transfer funds from a 403(b) account to purchase past service credit?

4060. Is an employee taxed on incidental life insurance protection and waiver of premium benefits under a tax sheltered annuity contract?

4061. How are dividends under a tax sheltered annuity treated for income tax purposes?

4062. Are amounts borrowed under a tax sheltered annuity taxable income?

4063. How long can a loan under a tax sheltered annuity remain outstanding and still avoid treatment as a deemed distribution and inclusion in the participant's taxable income?

4064. What is the substantially level amortization requirement applicable to a loan taken under a tax sheltered annuity that seeks to avoid taxation as a deemed distribution?

4065. Does a loan taken under a tax sheltered annuity plan have to be evidenced by an enforceable agreement in order to avoid taxation as a deemed distribution?

4066. Is there a dollar limit on the amount that a participant can borrow under a tax sheltered annuity and avoid the loan being treated as a taxable distribution?

4067. When is a loan taken under a tax sheltered annuity considered to be a deemed distribution? How does subsequent repayment of the loan, or subsequent failure to repay the loan, impact the participant's ability to receive additional loans?

4068. What is the process for determining whether loans taken under a tax sheltered annuity are taxable income when the participant receives multiple loans?

4069. Can loans taken under a tax sheltered annuity be refinanced? What is the effect of a refinancing on determining whether the outstanding loans constitute deemed distributions?

4070. When are amounts borrowed under a tax sheltered annuity taxable income as actual distributions?

4071. What is the tax treatment when amounts borrowed under a tax sheltered annuity are found to constitute deemed distributions?

4072. Is interest on a loan under a tax sheltered annuity deductible?

4073. What distributions from a tax sheltered annuity are subject to a penalty for early or premature distributions?

Distributions

4074. When must distributions begin from a tax sheltered annuity?

4075. How are distribution requirements from a tax sheltered annuity satisfied if an individual has more than one tax sheltered annuity?

4076. What is the effect of failure to make timely distributions from a tax sheltered annuity?

4077. What minimum distributions must be made under Section 401(a)(9) from a tax sheltered annuity during the life of the participant?

4078. What minimum distributions requirements apply under Section 401(a)(9) during the life of a tax sheltered annuity participant if distributions are not made as annuity payments?

4079. What minimum distributions requirements apply under Section 401(a)(9) during the life of a tax sheltered annuity participant if distributions are made as annuity payments?

4080. How is the designated beneficiary under a tax sheltered annuity determined?

4081. What is the minimum distribution incidental benefit requirement with respect to tax sheltered annuities?

4118. What requirements apply to a 501(c)(9) trust ("VEBA") that provides severance pay arrangements?

4119. Are an employer's contributions to a 501(c)(9) trust ("VEBA") deductible?

4120. How are contributions to 501(c)(9) trusts ("VEBAs") taxed to participants?

4121. How are benefits payable under 501(c)(9) trusts ("VEBAs") taxed to participants?

4122. How are rebates and termination distributions taxed to participants in 501(c)(9) trusts ("VEBAs")?

PART XXI: DISCLOSURE REQUIREMENTS

Disclosure Regulations for Retirement Plan Service Providers

4123. What are the fee disclosure requirements imposed by the Department of Labor ("DOL")?

4124. What is the purpose of the Department of Labor ("DOL") 408(b)(2) covered service provider disclosure regulations?

4125. What disclosures are required under the 408(b)(2) regulations?

4126. When does a service provider arrangement result in a prohibited transaction?

4127. Does a plan fiduciary still have to evaluate the reasonableness of compensation paid under a service provider's arrangement?

4128. How can a covered service provider correct a prohibited transaction arising from a failure to timely disclose required information?

4129. What penalties typically apply if there has been a prohibited transaction?

4130. What does a responsible plan fiduciary need to do to avoid the penalties of a prohibited transaction from a disclosure failure?

4131. Are new fiduciary responsibilities imposed upon plan fiduciaries under the DOL 408(b)(2) regulations?

4132. What is a responsible plan fiduciary?

4133. How can a qualified plan loan impact the analysis of the plan sponsor's fiduciary status? What new considerations did tax reform create?

4134. What is a reasonable service provider agreement?

4135. What are covered service providers?

PART X: CAFETERIA PLANS

Overview

3501. What is a cafeteria plan?

A cafeteria plan (or "flexible benefit plan") is a written plan in which all participants are employees who may choose among two or more benefits consisting of cash and "qualified benefits." With certain limited exceptions, a cafeteria plan cannot provide for deferred compensation. See Q 3502.[1]

Some cafeteria plans provide for salary reduction contributions by the employee and others provide benefits in addition to salary. In either case, the effect is to permit participants to purchase certain benefits with pre-tax dollars.

A plan may provide for automatic enrollment whereby an employee's salary is reduced to pay for "qualified benefits" unless the employee affirmatively elects cash.[2]

Under the 2007 proposed regulations (effective for plan years beginning on or after January 1, 2009), the written plan document must contain the following: (1) a specific description of the benefits, including periods of coverage; (2) the rules regarding eligibility for participation; (3) the procedures governing elections; (4) the manner in which employer contributions are to be made, such as by salary reduction or nonelective employer contributions; (5) the plan year; (6) the maximum amount of employer contributions available to any employee stated as (a) a maximum dollar amount or maximum percentage of compensation or (b) the method for determining the maximum amount or percentage; (7) a description of whether the plan offers paid time off, and the required ordering rules for use of nonelective and elective paid time off; (8) the plan's provisions related to any flexible spending arrangements (FSAs) included in the plan; (9) the plan's provisions related to any grace period offered under the plan; and (10) the rules governing distributions from a health FSA to employee health savings accounts (HSAs), if the plan permits such distributions.[3] The plan document need not be self-contained, but may incorporate by reference separate written plans.[4]

Note that under the ACA[5], the cost of an over-the-counter medicine or drug could not be reimbursed from FSAs or health reimbursement arrangements (HRAs) unless a prescription is obtained prior to 2020 (the CAREs Act permanently eliminated the prescription rule). The ACA rule did not affect insulin or other health care expenses such as medical devices, eyeglasses, contact lenses, co-pays and deductibles.

The IRS advises employers and employees to take these changes into account as they make health benefit decisions.[6] FSA and HRA participants may continue using debit cards to buy

---

1.   IRC Sec. 125(d).
2.   Rev. Rul. 2002-27, 2002-1 CB 925.
3.   Prop. Treas. Reg. §1.125-1(c).
4.   Prop. Treas. Reg. §1.125-1(c)(4).
5.   P.L. 111-148.
6.   See IRS News Release IR-2010-95 (Sept. 3, 2010).

prescribed over-the-counter medicines, if requirements are met.[1] In addition, starting in 2013, there were new rules about the amount that can be contributed to an FSA. For instance, a cafeteria plan may not allow an employee to request salary reduction contributions for a health FSA in excess of $2,750 (as indexed for 2020 and 2021, the amount was $2,700 in 2019). A cafeteria plan offering a health FSA must be amended to specify the contribution limit (or any lower limit set by the employer). While cafeteria plans generally must be amended on a prospective basis, an amendment that was adopted on or before December 31, 2014, could be made effective retroactively, if in operation the cafeteria plan met the limit for plan years beginning after December 31, 2012. A cafeteria plan that does not limit health FSA contributions to the annual limit is not a cafeteria plan and all benefits offered under the plan are includible in the employee's gross income.

IRS Notice 2012-40 provided information about these rules (see Q 3503) and flexibility for employers applying the new rules.

On June 28, 2012, the Supreme Court, in *National Federation of Independent Business v. Sebelius*, upheld the constitutionality of the *Affordable Care Act,* with only minor changes to certain Medicaid provisions. While most attempts to repeal or seriously modify the ACA have failed in Congress so implementation of the ACA and its requirements continues for the time-being, the individual mandate was repealed for tax years beginning after 2018.[2]

Former employees may be participants (although the plan may not be established predominantly for their benefit), but self-employed individuals may not.[3] A full-time life insurance salesperson who is treated as an employee for Social Security purposes will also be considered an employee for cafeteria plan purposes.[4]

3502. What benefits may be offered under a cafeteria plan?

Participants in a cafeteria plan may choose among two or more benefits consisting of cash and qualified benefits.[5] A cash benefit includes not only cash, but a benefit that may be purchased with after-tax dollars or the value of which is generally treated as taxable compensation to the employee (provided the benefit does not defer receipt of compensation).[6]

A qualified benefit is a benefit that is not includable in the gross income of the employee because of an express statutory exclusion and that does not defer receipt of compensation. Contributions to Archer Medical Savings Accounts (Q 420), qualified scholarships, educational assistance programs, or excludable fringe benefits are not qualified benefits. No product that is advertised, marketed, or offered as long-term care insurance is a qualified benefit.[7]

---

1.   IRS News Release IR-2010-128 (Dec. 23, 2010).
2.   See e.g., Miller, "The ACA Remains, but Targeted reforms Will be Sought'" SHRM, Jul. 24, 2017 at www.shrm.org.
3.   Prop. Treas. Reg. §1.125-1(g).
4.   IRC Sec. 7701(a)(20); Prop. Treas. Reg. §1.125-1(g)(1)(iii).
5.   IRC Sec. 125(d)(1)(B).
6.   Prop. Treas. Reg. §1.125-1(a)(2).
7.   IRC Sec. 125(f); Prop. Treas. Reg. §1.125-1(q).

With respect to insurance benefits, such as those provided under accident and health plans and group term life insurance plans, the benefit is the coverage under the plan. Accident and health benefits are qualified benefits to the extent that coverage is excludable under IRC Section 106.[1] Accidental death coverage offered in a cafeteria plan under an individual accident insurance policy is excludable from the employee's income under IRC Section 106.[2] A cafeteria plan can offer group term life insurance coverage on employees participating in the plan. Coverage that is includable in income only because it exceeds the $50,000 excludable limit under IRC Section 79 also may be offered in a cafeteria plan.[3] The application of IRC Section 79 to group term life insurance and IRC Section 106 to accident or health benefits is explained in Q 240 to Q 249 and Q 332.

Accident and health coverage, group term life insurance coverage, and benefits under a dependent care assistance program remain "qualified" even if they must be included in income because a nondiscrimination requirement has been violated.[4] (See Q 3625.) Health coverage and dependent care assistance under flexible spending arrangements (FSAs) are qualified benefits if they meet the requirements explained in Q 3515.

For taxable years beginning after December 31, 2012, a health FSA offered through a cafeteria plan will not be treated as a qualified benefit unless the plan provides that an employee may not elect for any taxable year to have salary reduction contributions in excess of $ 2,750 in 2020 and 2021 ($2,700 in 2019) made to such arrangement.[5] See Q 3501.

A cafeteria plan generally cannot provide for deferred compensation, permit participants to carry over unused benefits or contributions from one plan year to another, or permit participants to purchase a benefit that will be provided in a subsequent plan year. A cafeteria plan, however, may permit a participant in a profit sharing, stock bonus, or rural cooperative plan that has a qualified cash or deferred arrangement to elect to have the employer contribute on the employee's behalf to the plan (Q 3753).[6] After-tax employee contributions to a qualified plan subject to IRC Section 401(m) (Q 3803) are permissible under a cafeteria plan, even if matching contributions are made by the employer.[7]

A FSA may allow a grace period of no more than 2½ months following the end of the plan year for participants to incur and submit expenses for reimbursement (Q 3515).[8] FSAs may now be amended so that $500 of unused amounts remaining at the end of the plan year may be carried forward to the next plan year. However, plans that incorporate the carry forward provision may not also offer the two and one-half month grace period.[9]

---

1.   Prop. Treas. Reg. §1.125-1(h)(2).
2.   Let. Ruls. 8801015, 8922048.
3.   Prop. Treas. Reg. §1.125-1(k).
4.   IRC Sec. 129(d); Prop. Treas. Reg. §1.125-1(b)(2).
5.   IRC Sec. 125(i); Rev. Proc. 2018-57, Rev. Proc. 2019-44, Rev Proc. 2020-45.
6.   IRC Sec. 125(d)(2).
7.   Prop. Treas. Reg. §1.125-1(o)(3)(ii).
8.   Prop. Treas. Reg. §1.125-1(e); Notice 2005-42, 2005-1 CB 1204.
9.   Notice 2013-71, 2013-47 IRB 532.

A cafeteria plan also may permit a participant to elect to have the employer contribute to a health savings account (HSA) on the participant's behalf (Q 388).[1] Unused balances in HSAs funded through a cafeteria plan may be carried over from one plan year to another.

Under the general rule, life, health, disability, or long-term care insurance with an investment feature, such as whole life insurance, or an arrangement that reimburses premium payments for other accident or health coverage extending beyond the end of the plan year cannot be purchased.[2] Supplemental health insurance policies that provide coverage for cancer and other specific diseases do not result in the deferral of compensation and are properly considered accident and health benefits under IRC Section 106.[3]

A cafeteria plan maintained by an educational organization described in IRC Section 170(b)(1)(A)(ii) (i.e., one with a regular curriculum and an on-site faculty and student body) can allow participants to elect postretirement term life insurance coverage. The postretirement life insurance coverage must be fully paid up on retirement and must not have a cash surrender value at any time. Postretirement life insurance coverage meeting these conditions will be treated as group term life insurance under IRC Section 79.[4]

To provide tax favored benefits to highly compensated employees and "key employees," a cafeteria plan must meet certain nondiscrimination requirements and avoid concentration of benefits in key employees (Q 3504).

The Affordable Care Act requires plans and issuers that offer dependent coverage to make the coverage available until a child reaches the age of 26.[5] To implement the expanded coverage, the ACA allows employers with cafeteria plans to permit employees to immediately make pre-tax salary reduction contributions to provide coverage for children under age 27, even if the cafeteria plan has not yet been amended to cover these individuals.

Both married and unmarried children qualify for this coverage. This rule applies to all plans in the individual market and to new employer plans. It also applies to existing employer plans unless the adult child has another offer of employer-based coverage. Beginning in 2014, children up to age 26 can stay on their parent's employer plan even if they have another offer of coverage through an employer.

Employees are eligible for the new tax benefit from March 30, 2010 forward if the children are already covered under the employer's plan or are added to the employer's plan at any time. For this purpose, a child includes a son, daughter, stepchild, adopted child, or eligible foster child. This "up to age 26" standard replaces the lower age limits that applied under prior tax law, as well as the requirement that a child generally qualify as a dependent for tax purposes.

---

1.   IRC Sec. 125(d)(2)(D).
2.   Prop. Treas. Reg. §1.125-1(p)(1)(ii).
3.   TAM 199936046.
4.   IRC Sec. 125(d)(2)(C).
5.   See IRC Sec. 105(b); Notice 2010-38.

3503. What are the income tax benefits of a cafeteria plan?

As a general rule, a participant in a cafeteria plan (as defined in Q 3501), is not treated as being in constructive receipt of taxable income solely because he has the opportunity – before a cash benefit becomes available – to elect among cash and "qualified" benefits (generally, nontaxable benefits, but as defined in Q 3502).[1]

In order to avoid taxation, a participant must elect the qualified benefits before the cash benefit becomes currently available. That is, the election must be made before the specified period for which the benefit will be provided begins—generally, the plan year.[2]

A cafeteria plan may, but is not required to, provide default elections for one or more qualified benefits for new employees or for current employees who fail to timely elect between permitted taxable and qualified benefits.[3]

Note that a benefit provided under a cafeteria plan through employer contributions to a health flexible spending arrangement (FSA) is not treated as a qualified benefit unless the plan provides that an employee may not elect for any taxable year to have salary reduction contributions in excess of the annual contribution cap ($2,750 in 2020 and 2021, as adjusted annually for inflation) made to the FSA.[4]

Under IRS Notice 2012-40:

(1)   the contribution limit does not apply for plan years that begin before 2013;

(2)   the term "taxable year" in IRC Section 125(i) refers to the plan year of the cafeteria plan, as this is the period for which salary reduction elections are made;

(3)   plans were permitted to adopt the required amendments to reflect the contribution limit at any time through the end of calendar year 2014;

(4)   in the case of a plan providing a grace period (which may be up to two months and fifteen days), unused salary reduction contributions to the health FSA for plan years beginning in 2012 or later that are carried over into the grace period for that plan year will not count against the contribution limit for the subsequent plan year; and

(5)   unless a plan's benefits are under examination by the IRS, relief is provided for certain salary reduction contributions exceeding the contribution limit that are due to a reasonable mistake and not willful neglect, and that are corrected by the employer.

For the income tax effect of a discriminatory plan on highly compensated individuals, see Q 3504.

---

1.   IRC Sec. 125; Prop. Treas. Reg. §1.125-1.
2.   Prop. Treas. Reg. §1.125-2.
3.   Prop. Treas. Reg. §1.125-2(b).
4.   IRC Sec. 125(i), Rev. Proc. 2018-57, Rev. Proc. 2019-44, Rev. Proc. 2020-45.

3504. What nondiscrimination requirements apply to cafeteria plans?

If a cafeteria plan discriminates in favor of highly compensated individuals as to eligibility to participate or discriminates in favor of highly compensated participants as to contributions or benefits, highly compensated participants will be considered in constructive receipt of the available cash benefit.[1] "Highly compensated" individuals are officers, shareholders owning more than 5 percent of the voting power or value of all classes of stock, those who are "highly compensated," and any of their spouses or dependents. For this purpose, "highly compensated" means any individual or participant who, for the preceding plan year (or the current plan year in the case of the first year of employment), had compensation from the employer in excess of the compensation amount specified in IRC Section 414(q)(1)(B) ($130,000 in 2020 and 2021 and $125,000 in 2019), and, if elected by the employer, also was in the top-paid group of employees (determined by reference to Section 414(q)(3)) for such preceding plan year (or for the current plan year in the case of the first year of employment).[2]

Participation will be nondiscriminatory if (1) it benefits a classification of employees found by the Secretary of Treasury not to discriminate in favor of employees who are officers, shareholders, or highly compensated, (2) no more than three years of employment are required for participation and the employment requirement for each employee is the same, and (3) eligible employees begin participation by the first day of the first plan year after the employment requirement is satisfied.[3]

According to proposed regulations, a cafeteria plan does not discriminate in favor of highly compensated individuals if the plan benefits a group of employees who qualify under a reasonable classification established by the employer and the group of employees included in the classification satisfies the safe harbor percentage test or the unsafe harbor percentage test. These are the same nondiscriminatory classification tests used for qualified plans (Q 3841).[4]

If a cafeteria plan offers health benefits, the plan is not discriminatory as to contributions and benefits if (1) contributions for each participant include an amount that either (x) equals 100 percent of the cost of the health benefit coverage under the plan of the majority of the highly compensated participants who are similarly situated (e.g., same family size); or (y) equals or exceeds 75 percent of the cost of the most expensive health benefit coverage elected by any similarly-situated participant; and (2) contributions or benefits in excess of (1) above bear a uniform relationship to compensation.[5]

A plan is considered to satisfy all nondiscrimination tests if it is maintained under a collective bargaining agreement between employee representatives and one or more employers.[6]

---

1.   IRC Sec. 125(b) (1); Prop. Treas. Reg. §1.125-7(m) (2).
2.   IRC Sec. 125 (e); Prop. Treas. Reg. §1.125-7(a)(3); IR-2014-99 (Oct. 23, 2014), IR-2015-118 (Oct. 21, 2015), Notice 2016-62, Notice 2017-64, Notice 2018-83, Notice 2019-59 Notice 2020-79.
3.   IRC Sec. 125 (g) (3); Prop. Treas. Reg. §1.125-7.
4.   Prop. Treas. Reg. §1.125-7(b) (1).
5.   IRC Sec. 125 (g) (2); Prop. Treas. Reg. §1.125-7(e).
6.   IRC Sec. 125 (g) (1).

In addition, a "key employee," as defined for purposes of the top-heavy rules (Q 3930), will be considered in constructive receipt of the available cash benefit option in any plan year in which nontaxable benefits provided under the plan to key employees exceed 25 percent of the aggregate of such benefits provided to all employees under the plan. For this purpose, excess group term life insurance coverage that is includable in income is not considered a nontaxable benefit.[1]

Employees of a controlled group of corporations, employers under common control, or members of an "affiliated service group" (Q 3934) are treated as employed by a single employer.[2]

Amounts that the employer contributes to a cafeteria plan pursuant to a salary reduction agreement will be treated as employer contributions to the extent that the agreement relates to compensation that has not been actually or constructively received by the employee as of the date of the agreement and subsequently does not become currently available to the employee.[3]

3505. What are the rules that apply to simple cafeteria plans for small businesses?

A "simple cafeteria plan" means a cafeteria plan that is established and maintained by an eligible employer and with respect to which contribution, eligibility, and participation requirements are met.[4]

The Affordable Care Act of 2010 (ACA) provides a safe harbor "simple cafeteria plan" under which an "eligible employer" (generally an employer with fewer than 100 employees) is treated as meeting any applicable nondiscrimination requirements for the year.[5]

The employer is required to make contributions on behalf of each "qualified employee" in an amount equal to the following: (1) a uniform percentage (not less than 2 percent) of the employee's compensation; or (2) an amount not less than the lesser of (x) 6 percent of the employee's compensation for the plan year, or (y) twice the amount of salary deduction contributions of each qualified employee.[6] Contribution requirement option (2) is not met if the rate of contributions with respect to the salary contributions of any highly compensated or key employee at any rate of contribution is greater than that with respect to an employee who is not a highly compensated or key employee.[7]

All employees with at least 1,000 hours of service during the preceding plan year must be eligible to participate. Each employee who is eligible to participate must be able to select any benefit available under the plan.[8] An employee can be excluded if the employee:

(1)   is under age 21;

(2)   has less than one year of service;

---

1.   IRC Sec. 125 (b) (2).
2.   IRC Sec. 125 (g) (4).
3.   Prop. Treas. Reg. §1.125-1(r).
4.   IRC Sec. 125(j)(2); IRS Publication 15-B (2019).
5.   IRC Sec. 125(j)(1).
6.   IRC Sec. 125(j)(3)(A).
7.   IRC Sec. 125(j)(3)(B).
8.   IRC Sec. 125(j)(4)(A).

(3)   is covered by a collective bargaining agreement and the benefits of a cafeteria plan were the subject of good faith bargaining; or

(4)   is a nonresident alien working outside of the United States.[1]

"Eligible employer" means, with respect to any year, any employer that employed an average of 100 or fewer employees on business days during either of the two preceding years.[2] An employer that initially qualifies for a simple cafeteria plan ceases to qualify in the year after the number of employees reaches 200.[3]

Planning Point: If the employer's business was not in existence throughout the preceding year, it is eligible to establish a simple cafeteria plan if the employer reasonably expects to employ an average of 100 or fewer employees in the current year. If the employer establishes a simple cafeteria plan in a year it employs an average of 100 or fewer employees, it is considered an eligible employer for any subsequent year as long as the employer does not employ an average of 200 or more employees in a subsequent year.

A qualified employee is any employee who is eligible to participate in the cafeteria plan and who is not a highly compensated or key employee.[4]

3506. When can benefit elections under a cafeteria plan be changed?

Editor's Note: The IRS provided relief to permit certain mid-year election changes in the wake of the COVID-19 pandemic. For mid-year elections made during calendar year 2020, a Section 125 cafeteria plan may permit employees who are eligible to make salary reduction contributions under the plan to:

(1)   with respect to employer-sponsored health coverage, (a) make a new election on a prospective basis, if the employee initially declined to elect employer-sponsored health coverage; (b) revoke an existing election and make a new election to enroll in different health coverage sponsored by the same employer on a prospective basis; and (c) revoke an existing election on a prospective basis, provided that the employee confirms in writing that the employee is enrolled, or immediately will enroll, in other health coverage not sponsored by the employer; and

(2)   revoke an election, make a new election, or decrease or increase an existing election applicable to a health FSA or dependent care assistance program on a prospective basis.

If an employee has unused amounts remaining in a health FSA or a dependent care assistance program under the cafeteria plan at the end of a grace period or plan year ending in 2020, the cafeteria plan may permit employees to apply those unused amounts to pay or reimburse medical care expenses or dependent care expenses incurred through December 31, 2020.[5]

---

1.   IRC Sec. 125(j)(4)(B).
2.   IRC Sec. 125(j)(5)(A).
3.   IRC Sec. 125(j)(5)(C).
4.   IRC Sec. 125(j)(3)(D).
5.   Notice 2020-29.

There are only certain instances when a cafeteria plan may permit an employee to revoke an election during a period of coverage and to make a new election relating to a qualified benefits plan.[1]

A cafeteria plan may permit an employee to revoke an election for coverage under a group health plan during a period of coverage and make a new election that corresponds with the special enrollment rights of IRC Section 9801(f). (This section deals generally with special enrollment periods for persons losing other group health plan coverage and dependent beneficiaries.)[2] An election change with respect to the Section 9801(f) enrollment rights can be funded through salary reduction under a cafeteria plan only on a prospective basis, except for the retroactive enrollment right under Section 9801(f) that applies in the case of elections made within 30 days of a birth, adoption, or placement for adoption.[3]

Certain changes are permitted with respect to a judgment, decree, or order resulting from a divorce, legal separation, annulment, or change in legal custody (including a qualified medical child support order) that requires accident or health coverage for an employee's child or for a foster child who is a dependent of the employee. A cafeteria plan may change the employee's election to provide coverage for the child if an order requires coverage for the child under the employer's plan. Also, the plan may permit the employee to make an election change to cancel coverage for the child if an order requires the spouse, former spouse, or other individual to provide coverage for the child and that coverage actually is provided.[4]

Additionally, if an employee, spouse, or dependent who is enrolled in the employer's accident or health plan becomes entitled to coverage (i.e., becomes enrolled) under Medicaid or Part A or Part B of Medicare, the plan may permit the employee to make a prospective election change to reduce or cancel coverage of that employee, spouse, or dependent under the accident or health plan. Note that this does not apply to coverage consisting solely of benefits under the Social Security Act Section 1928 program for distribution of pediatric vaccines.

If an employee, spouse, or dependent that has been entitled to Medicaid or Medicare Part A or Part B coverage loses eligibility for the coverage, the plan may allow the employee to make a prospective election to commence or increase coverage of that employee, spouse, or dependent under the accident or health plan.[5]

An employee taking a leave under the Family and Medical Leave Act (FMLA) may revoke an existing election of accident or health plan coverage and make such election as provided for under the FMLA for the remaining portion of the period of coverage (Q 3509).[6]

Regarding contributions under a qualified cash or deferred arrangement, the regulations state that these provisions do not apply to elective contributions under such

---

1.   Treas. Reg. §1.125-4(a).
2.   Treas. Reg. §1.125-4(b).
3.   Treas. Reg. §1.125-4(b)(2).
4.   Treas. Reg. §1.125-4(d).
5.   Treas. Reg. §1.125-4(e).
6.   Treas. Reg. §1.125-4(g).

an arrangement, within the meaning of IRC Section 401(k), or employee contributions subject to IRC Section 401(m). Therefore, a cafeteria plan may allow an employee to modify or revoke elections as provided by these sections and applicable regulations.[1]

If a cafeteria plan offers salary reduction contributions to health savings accounts (HSAs), the plan must allow participants to prospectively change or revoke salary reduction elections for HSA contributions on a monthly, or more frequent, basis.[2]

3507. When can benefit elections under a cafeteria plan be changed due to a change in an employee's status?

A plan may permit an employee to revoke an election during a period of coverage with respect to a qualified benefits plan and make a new election for the remaining portion of the period if a change in status (as defined below) occurs and the election change meets the consistency rule (as explained below).[3] For this purpose, changes in status events include:

(1)   events that change an employee's legal marital status, including marriage, death of a spouse, divorce, legal separation, and annulment;

(2)   events that change an employee's number of dependents such as birth, death, adoption, and placement for adoption;

(3)   events that change the employment status of an employee, an employee's spouse, or an employee's dependent, such as a termination or commencement of employment, a strike or lockout, a commencement of or return from an unpaid leave of absence, or a change in work site, if the employee, spouse, or dependent becomes or ceases to be eligible under the plan;

(4)   events that cause an employee's dependent to satisfy or cease to satisfy eligibility requirements for coverage due to reaching a certain age, student status, or any other similar provision;

(5)   a change in the place of residence of the employee, spouse, or dependent; and

(6)   for purposes of adoption assistance provided through a cafeteria plan, the commencement or termination of an adoption proceeding.[4]

Consistency Rule

The consistency rule states that an election change is not properly made with respect to accident or health coverage or group term life insurance unless it is on account of or corresponds with a change in status that affects eligibility for coverage under an employer's plan.

1.   Treas. Reg. §1.125-4(h).
2.   Prop. Treas. Reg. §1.125-2(c).
3.   Treas. Reg. §1.125-4(c)(1); Prop. Treas. Reg. §1.125-2(a)(4).
4.   Treas. Reg. §1.125-4(c)(2).

With respect to accident or health coverage, the consistency rule requires that any employee who wishes to decrease or cancel coverage because they become eligible for coverage under a spouse's or dependent's plan due to a marital or employment change in status can do so only if they actually obtain coverage under that other plan. Employers may generally rely on an employee's certification that the employee has or will obtain coverage under the other plan (assuming that the employer has no reason to believe that the employee certification is incorrect).[1]

A change in status that affects eligibility under an employer's plan includes a change in status that results in an increase or decrease in the number of an employee's family members or dependents who may benefit from coverage under the plan.[2]

If a dependent dies or otherwise ceases to satisfy the eligibility requirements for coverage, the employee's election to cancel health insurance coverage for any other dependent, for the employee, or the employee's spouse does not correspond to the change in status.

Planning Point: The application of the consistency rule is illustrated as follows: If the change in status is the employee's divorce, annulment or legal separation from a spouse, the death of a spouse or dependent, or a dependent ceasing to satisfy the eligibility requirements for coverage, an employee's election under the cafeteria plan to cancel accident or health insurance coverage for any individual other than the spouse involved in the divorce, annulment or legal separation, the deceased spouse or dependent, or the dependent that ceased to satisfy the eligibility requirements for coverage, respectively, fails to correspond with that change in status. Thus, if a dependent dies or ceases to satisfy the eligibility requirements for coverage, the employee's election to cancel accident or health coverage for any other dependent, for the employee, or for the employee's spouse fails to correspond with that change in status.[3]

There is an exception to the consistency rule for COBRA coverage. If the employee, spouse, or dependent becomes eligible for COBRA continuation coverage (Q 356) under the employer's group health plan, a cafeteria plan may allow the employee to elect to increase payments under the cafeteria plan to pay for the COBRA coverage.

With respect to group term life insurance and disability coverage, as well as coverage to which IRC Section 105(c) (coverage for permanent loss or loss of use of a member or function of the body) applies, an election under a cafeteria plan to increase or decrease coverage in response to any of the above listed changes in status is deemed to correspond to that change in status.[4]

An election change satisfies the consistency rule with respect to other qualified benefits if it is on account of and corresponds with a change in status that affects eligibility for coverage under an employer's plan. An election change also satisfies the consistency rule if it is on account of and corresponds with a change in status that affects dependent care expenses, as set forth in IRC Section 129 (Q 3625), or adoption assistance expenses, as described in IRC Section 137. Regulations provide examples of the application of the consistency rule.[5]

---

1.   Treas. Reg. §1.125-4(c)(4).
2.   Treas. Reg. §1.125-4(c)(3)(i).
3.   Treas. Reg. §1.125-4(c)(3)(iii).
4.   Treas. Reg. §1.125-4(c)(3).
5.   Treas. Reg. §1.125-4(c)(3).

3508. Can an employee change benefit elections under a cafeteria plan because of significant cost or coverage changes?

The rules regarding election changes due to a significant cost or coverage changes apply to all types of qualified benefits offered under a cafeteria plan, but <u>not</u> to health flexible spending arrangements (FSAs).[1]

A plan may automatically make a prospective change in an employee's salary reduction amount if the cost of a qualified benefits plan increases or decreases during a period of coverage. If the cost of a benefit package option significantly increases during a period of coverage, the cafeteria plan may allow employees to either increase their salary reduction amounts or revoke their elections for this benefit and elect another benefit package option that offers similar coverage on a prospective basis. If the cost of a qualified benefits plan significantly decreases during the year, the cafeteria plan may allow all employees, even those who have previously not participated in the plan, to elect to participate in the plan for the option with such decrease in cost. A cost change applies in the case of dependent care assistance only if the cost change is imposed by a dependent care provider who is not a relative of the employee, as defined in IRC Section 152.[2]

If an employee has a significant curtailment of coverage under a plan during a period of coverage that is a "loss of coverage," the cafeteria plan may permit the employee to revoke his or her election under the plan and elect to receive, on a prospective basis, coverage under another option providing similar coverage. The employee may drop the coverage if no similar option is available. A "loss of coverage" means a complete loss of coverage under the benefit package option or other coverage option (e.g., the elimination of an option, an HMO ceasing to be available in the area, or losing all coverage under the option by reason of an overall lifetime or annual limitation).[3]

Other events constituting a loss of coverage include:

(1) a substantial decrease in medical care providers (such as a major hospital ceasing to be a member of a preferred provider network or a substantial decrease in the physicians participating in a preferred provider network or an HMO),

(2) a reduction in the benefits for a specific type of medical condition or treatment with respect to which the employee or the employee's spouse or dependent is currently in a course of treatment, or

(3) any other similar fundamental loss of coverage.[4]

If an employee has a significant curtailment of coverage under a plan during a period of coverage that is not a "loss of coverage" (e.g., a significant increase in the deductible, the co-pay, or the out-of-pocket expense), the cafeteria plan may permit the employee to revoke his or

---

1. Treas. Reg. §1.125-4(f)(1).
2. Treas. Reg. §1.125-4(f)(2).
3. Treas. Reg. §1.125-4(f)(3)(ii).
4. Treas. Reg. §1.125-4(f)(3)(ii).

her election under the plan and elect to receive, on a prospective basis, coverage under another option providing similar coverage.[1]

If a plan adds a new benefit package option or improves an existing benefit package option or other coverage option during a period of coverage, the cafeteria plan may allow eligible employees (whether or not they have previously made an election under the cafeteria plan) to revoke their election and to make an election on a prospective basis for coverage under the new or improved option.[2]

A cafeteria plan may allow an employee to make a prospective election change that corresponds to a change made under another employer plan (including a plan of the same employer or of another employer) or to add coverage under a cafeteria plan for the employee, spouse, or dependent if the employee, spouse, or dependent loses coverage under any group health plan sponsored by a governmental or educational institution.[3]

3509. How are health-related benefits offered under a cafeteria plan affected by the Family and Medical Leave Act?

The interaction between IRC Section 125 and the Family and Medical Leave Act ("FMLA") of 1993 was first addressed in proposed regulations published in 1995. Final regulations were published in October 2001, and are applicable for plan years beginning on or after January 1, 2002.

Under the 1995 proposed regulations, employers had to permit employees on FMLA leave to revoke an existing election of group health plan coverage (including a flexible spending arrangement, see Q 3515) under a cafeteria plan for the remainder of the coverage period.[4] Under the 2001 final regulations, employers may require employees to continue coverage if the employer pays the employee's portion of the coverage cost.[5]

Employees on FMLA leave are generally entitled to revoke or change elections in the same manner as the employees not on FMLA leave. Upon returning from the FMLA leave, the employee is entitled to be reinstated in the plan if the employee's coverage terminated during the leave, either by revocation or nonpayment of premiums.[6]

Health FSAs

A health flexible spending arrangement (health FSA, see Q 3515) is subject to the same general rules as a traditional cafeteria plan, as discussed above.

The employee must be permitted to reinstate his coverage under the plan following the FMLA leave, as if he had not taken the leave. The employer may require that employees be

---

1. Treas. Reg. §1.125-4(f)(3)(i).
2. Treas. Reg. §1.125-4(f)(3)(iii).
3. See Treas. Reg. §§1.125-4(f)(4), 1.125-4(f)(5).
4. Prop. Treas. Reg. §1.125-3, A-1.
5. Treas. Reg. §1.125-3, A-1.
6. Treas. Reg. §1.125-3, A-1.

reinstated following an FMLA leave if it also requires reinstatement for employees returning from non-FMLA leave.[1]

For so long as the employee's coverage under the health FSA is continued (whether voluntarily or involuntarily), the entire amount of his health FSA, less any previous reimbursements, must be available for reimbursement of his health expenses. If the employee's coverage is terminated at any time during FMLA leave, he may not be reimbursed for expenses incurred while coverage was terminated.[2]

3510. How are non-health-related benefits offered under a cafeteria plan affected by the Family and Medical Leave Act?

Under both the proposed and final regulations, employers are not required to continue an employees' non-health benefits provided under a cafeteria plan (e.g., life insurance) during an FMLA leave. Rather, whether an employee is entitled to the continuation of non-health benefits must be decided under the employer's policy applicable to employees on non-FMLA leave.[3]

3511. What are the payment options that must be made available to employees on FMLA leave?

Editor's Note: The 2017 Tax Act created a new tax credit for employers that provide paid family and medical leave to employees. See Q 3512 for details.

Whatever payment options are available to employees on non-FMLA leave must also be made available to employees on FMLA leave.[4] *Employers* must continue to contribute the same share of the premium cost that they were paying prior to the FMLA leave. *Employees* who choose to continue health coverage during an FMLA leave must pay the same portion of the cost of such coverage that they paid while actively at work.[5] Employers may choose to waive this requirement, provided that they do so on a nondiscriminatory basis.

A cafeteria plan may generally offer employees on *unpaid* FMLA leave up to three options for paying for their health coverage under a cafeteria plan or health FSA.[6] These rules do not apply where paid leave is substituted for unpaid FMLA leave, in which case the employer must offer the payment method normally available during other types of paid leave.[7]

Any of the three payment options discussed below may generally be made on a pre-tax salary reduction basis to the extent that the employee on FMLA leave has any taxable compensation (including the cash value of unused sick days or vacation days). A restriction applies when an employee's FMLA leave spans two plan years. In such a case, the plan may not operate in a

---

1.   Treas. Reg. §1.125-3, A-6(a)(2).
2.   Treas. Reg. §1.125-3, A-6(b).
3.   Treas. Reg. §1.125-3, A-7.
4.   Treas. Reg. §1.125-3, A-3(b).
5.   Treas. Reg. §1.125-3, A-2.
6.   Treas. Reg. §1.125-3, A-3(a).
7.   Treas. Reg. §1.125-3, A-4.

manner that would allow employees on FMLA leave to defer compensation from one plan year to a subsequent plan year.[1] Any of the three payment options may also be made on an after-tax basis.

A cafeteria plan may offer one or more of the following payment options, or a combination of these options, to an employee who continues group health plan coverage (including a health FSA) while on unpaid FMLA leave; provided that the payment options for employees on FMLA leave are offered on terms at least as favorable as those offered to employees not on FMLA leave.

"Pre-pay" Option. Under this option, the employer allows the employee to pay the amounts due for the FMLA leave period prior to the commencement of FMLA leave.[2] Under no circumstances may the pre-pay option be the only option offered to employees on FMLA leave. The employer may offer the pre-pay option to employees on FMLA leave even if such option is not offered to employees on other types of unpaid leave.[3]

"Pay-as-you-go" Option. Under this option, employees pay their portion of the health care costs according to a payment schedule. This schedule may be (1) the same as the schedule that would be in effect if they were not on FMLA leave; (2) the same schedule upon which COBRA payments would be made (see Q 368); (3) the same schedule as applies to other employees on other, unpaid non-FMLA leave; or (4) any other schedule that (a) the employee and the employer voluntarily agree upon and (b) is not inconsistent with the regulations. The employer may not offer employees on FMLA leave only the pre-pay option and the catch-up option if the pay-as-you-go option is offered to employees on unpaid non-FMLA leave.[4]

"Catch-up" Option. Under this option, an employer continues providing coverage during FMLA leave. The catch-up option may be the sole option offered by the employer only if it is the sole option offered to employees on unpaid non-FMLA leave.[5]

In general, the employer and the employee must agree in advance that (1) coverage will continue during the FMLA leave, (2) the employer assumes responsibility for the payment of employee's portion of the health care costs during the FMLA leave, and (3) the employee will repay such amounts when he returns from FMLA leave.

Employer's Right of Recoupment. An employer is not required to continue the coverage of an employee on FMLA leave who fails to make the required premium payments when due. But if the employer *does* continue coverage, the employer is entitled to recoup the missed payments under the "catch-up" option, without the employee's prior agreement.[6]

Health FSAs. Health FSAs are generally subject to the same payment rules as traditional cafeteria plans.[7] The regulations do not make clear whether the employer's right of recoupment,

1.   Treas. Reg. §1.125-3, A-5.
2.   Treas. Reg. §1.125-3(a)(1)(i).
3.   Treas. Reg. §1.125-3, A-3(b)(1).
4.   Treas. Reg. §1.125-3, A-3.
5.   Treas. Reg. §1.125-3, A-3.
6.   Treas. Reg. §1.125-3, A-3(a).
7.   Treas. Reg. §1.125-3, A-6(a)(1).

discussed above, applies to health FSAs. If so, it would appear to represent a significant departure from the general risk-shifting rule applicable to health FSAs. See Q 3515.

3512. What is the new tax credit for employers that provide paid family and medical leave to employees?

The 2017 Tax Act created a new temporary tax credit for employers that provide paid family and medical leave to employees.[1] The credit is an amount equal to 12.5 percent of the wages that are paid to qualifying employees during a period where the employee was on family and medical leave if the employee is paid 50 percent of the normal wages that he or she would receive from the employer. The credit increases by 0.25 percentage points (but can never exceed 25 percent) for each percentage point by which the rate of payment exceeds 50 percent of wages.

For purposes of the 50 percent of wages requirement, overtime and discretionary bonuses are excluded from the wages that are normally paid. Wages paid by a third-party payor, such as an insurance company or professional employer organization, are taken into account if based on services provided by the employee to the eligible employer. Similarly, amounts paid under the employer's short-term disability program are taken into account. The rate of pay does not have to be uniform.

> *Example:* The employer provides six weeks paid leave for a qualifying employee for the birth or adoption of a child, at a rate of 100 percent of wages. The same employer provides two weeks of annual leave paid at a rate of 75 percent of wages for all other FMLA purposes. The policy satisfies the paid leave requirements. Note that the rate of pay cannot vary based on the employee's classification (i.e., the employee cannot be paid leave only to employees not covered by a collective bargaining agreement).[2]

Only twelve weeks of family and medical leave can be taken into account for any one employee. Further, all part-time employees must be allowed a pro-rated amount of paid family and medical leave.[3] Any leave paid for by the state or local government is not taken into account.[4]

In order to qualify, employers must have a written policy in place to allow all qualifying full-time employees no less than two weeks of paid family and medical leave each year. The written policy may be set forth in a single document, or in multiple documents that cover different classes of employee or different types of leave. The policy must be in place before the leave for which the employer claims the credit is taken, except as otherwise provided in a transition rule. A policy is considered to be "in place" at the later of its adoption date or effective date. Under the transition rule, the policy is considered "in place" as of its effective date, rather than a later adoption date, for the first tax year beginning after December 31, 2017 if the policy (a) is adopted before December 31, 2018 and (b) the employer complies with the terms of the policy for the entire retroactive period.[5]

---

1. IRC Sec. 45S (added by the Tax Cuts and Jobs Act).
2. Notice 2018-71.
3. IRC Sec. 45S(c)(1).
4. IRC Sec. 45S(c)(4).
5. Notice 2018-71.

The employer need not be subject to title 1 of the Family and Medical Leave Act of 1993 (FMLA) to be a qualifying employer. However, employers who employee at least one employee who is not subject to title 1 of the FMLA must include and comply with "noninterference" language in the required written policy. This language must generally state that the employer will not attempt to interfere with the employee's exercise of his or her rights under the written policy, and will not discharge or discriminate against an employee who opposes any practice prohibited by the written policy.[1]

"Qualifying employees" are those who have been employed by the employer for one year or more and who had compensation that did not exceed 60 percent of the compensation threshold for highly compensated employees[2] in the previous year.[3] The employer can use any reasonable method to determine how long the employee has been employed. Further, there is no minimum hours requirement in determining how long the employee has been employed, and requiring the employee to work a minimum number of hours would **not** be treated as a reasonable method for determining whether an employee has been employed for one year (the requirement that an employee work at least 1,250 hours to be an FMLA-eligible employee does not apply to the Section 45S credit).

If the employee is otherwise a qualifying employee, the employer's written policy cannot exclude any class of employees (although the amount of paid leave provided may be pro-rated for part-time employees who customarily work fewer than 30 hours per week). For part-time employees, the paid leave ratio must be at least equal to the ratio of the expected weekly hours worked by a qualifying employee who is a part-time employee to the expected weekly hours worked by an equivalent qualifying employee who is not a part-time employee.[4]

Planning Point: The employee must be a qualifying employee at the date the paid leave is taken for the credit to apply.

"Family and medical leave" means leave as defined under Section 102(a)(1)(a)-(e) or Section 102(a)(3) of the FMLA. It includes leave taken as a result of: (1) the birth of a child, (2) adoption or fostering of a child, (3) the need to care for the employee's spouse, child or parent who has a serious health condition, (4) a serious health condition that makes the employee unable to perform his or her job, (5) issues arising due to the employee's spouse, child or parent being on covered active duty (or being notified of an impending order to covered duty), or (6) the need to care for a service member who is the employee's spouse, child, parent or next of kin. Paid leave that is vacation leave, personal leave or other medical or sick leave does not qualify for the new tax credit.[5]

The employer's policy must strictly apply to only leave that qualifies as an FMLA purpose—meaning that the employer cannot give the employee a choice between an FMLA purpose and vacation leave, for example. This is the case even if the employee actually does use the leave for

---

1.   Notice 2018-71.
2.   Under IRC Sec. 414(g)(1)(B).
3.   IRC Sec. 45S(d).
4.   Notice 2018-71.
5.   IRC Sec. 45S(e).

a qualifying purpose. The IRS has carved out an exception for situations where the employer provides leave to care for a group of individuals, and one or more of those individuals is not a qualified individual for FMLA purposes. In this case, the policy will continue to qualify, except that if an employee takes the leave to care for a non-qualified individual, the employer will not be entitled to the credit with respect to that employee.[1]

This credit is only available for tax years beginning after December 31, 2017 and before December 31, 2020 (as extended), and is a part of the general business tax credit.[2] The credit is allowed against the alternative minimum tax (AMT).

3513. Are amounts received under a cafeteria plan subject to Social Security and federal unemployment taxes?

Amounts received by participants, or their beneficiaries, under a cafeteria plan are not treated as wages. Thus, these amounts are not subject to tax under the Federal Insurance Contributions Act (FICA) or under the Federal Unemployment Tax Act (FUTA) if such payments would not be treated as wages without regard to the plan, and if it is reasonable to believe that IRC Section 125 would not treat any wages as constructively received.[3]

3514. Must an employer sponsoring a cafeteria plan file an information return with the IRS?

Under IRC Section 6039D, an employer sponsoring a cafeteria plan was required to file an information return with the IRS. This return indicated the number of the employer's employees, the number of employees eligible to participate in the plan, the number of employees actually participating in the plan, the cost of the plan, the identity of the employer, the type of business in which it is engaged, and the number of its highly compensated employees in the above categories.

Under prior law, all employers that maintained cafeteria plans were required to file an information return (Form 5500 series with Schedule F) for each year.[4]

However, the IRS has currently suspended the operation of these reporting requirements with respect to cafeteria plans.[5] This suspension is in effect for plan years beginning prior to the issuance of further guidance from the IRS. Proposed Form 5500 regulations released in July 2016 would require plans that provide group health benefits to provide information on whether health plan funding and benefit arrangements are through a health insurance issuer and whether benefits are paid through a trust or from the employer's general assets. Further, Schedule J to Form 5500 would require these plans to disclose whether there were participant and/or employer contributions. "Participant contributions" include all elective contributions made under a cafeteria plan.[6]

---

1.   Notice 2018-71.
2.   IRC Sec. 45S(a)(1).
3.   IRC Secs. 3121(a)(5)(G), 3306(b)(5)(G).
4.   IRS Office of Chief Counsel Training Manual No. 4213-018 (Rev. 5/98).
5.   Notice 2002-24, 2002-1 CB 785.
6.   Proposed Revision of Annual Information Return/Reports, RIN 1210-AB63, p96.

The proposed regulations would not require welfare benefit plans (including cafeteria plans) to file Form 5500 if the plan (1) does not provide health benefits, (2) covers fewer than 100 participants and (3) is unfunded, fully insured or a combination of insured and unfunded (unfunded plans have benefits paid directly from the general assets of the employer or sponsoring employee organization). If the plan receives participant contributions, it is funded.[1] Despite this, a cafeteria plan may be treated as though it is unfunded if it meets the requirements of DOL Technical Release 92-01, 57 FR 23272 (June 2, 1992) and 58 FR 45359 (Aug. 27, 1993).

The IRS action does not affect annual reporting requirements under Title I of ERISA, or relieve administrators of employee benefit plans from any obligation to file a Form 5500 and any required schedules (other than the Schedule F) under that title. However, many practitioners believe that, under ERISA and the new proposed Form 5500 regulations, cafeteria plans containing Health FSAs with more than 100 participants are required to file Forms 5500 because the FSA is a welfare benefit that provides health benefits. And because the IRS Section 6039D suspension does not affect ERISA filing requirements, such cafeteria plans are therefore required to file.

Flexible Spending Arrangements

3515. What is a flexible spending arrangement?

A flexible spending arrangement (FSA) is a program under IRC Section 125 under which incurred expenses may be reimbursed. This benefit may be provided as a stand-alone plan or as part of a traditional cafeteria plan. The most common types are health FSAs (Q 3516) and dependent care assistance FSAs (Q 3517).

In order for the coverage provided through an FSA to qualify for the exclusion from income under IRC Sections 105 and 106 (for health FSAs, see Q 332, Q 334) or IRC Section 129 (for dependent care FSAs, see Q 3625), the FSA must meet the requirements set forth in Q 3516 and Q 3517.

3516. What is a health flexible spending arrangement?

Although health coverage under an FSA need not be provided under commercial insurance, it must demonstrate the risk shifting and risk distribution characteristics of insurance. Reimbursements under a health FSA must be paid specifically to reimburse medical expenses that have been incurred previously. A health FSA cannot operate so as to provide coverage only for periods during which the participants expect to incur medical expenses, if such period is shorter than a plan year. In addition, the maximum amount of reimbursement must be available at all times throughout the period of coverage (properly reduced for prior reimbursements for the same period of coverage), without regard to the extent to which the participant has paid the required premiums for the coverage period, and without a premium payment schedule based on the rate or amount of covered claims incurred in the coverage period.[2] Before 2013, there was no statutory limit on contributions to a health FSA, but most employers imposed a limit to protect themselves against large claims that had not yet been funded by salary reductions.

---

1. Appendix B to Instructions for Form 5500 Annual Return/Report of Employee Benefit Plan, p. 314.
2. Prop. Treas. Reg. §1.125-5(d).

The period of coverage must be twelve months, or in the case of a short first plan year, the entire first year (or the short plan year where the plan year is changed). Election changes may not be permitted to increase or decrease coverage during a coverage year, but prospective changes may be allowed if they are consistent with certain changes in family status. See Q 3506. The plan may permit the period of coverage to be terminated if the employee fails to pay premiums, provided that the terms of the plan prohibit the employee from making a new election during the remaining period of coverage. The plan may permit revocation of existing elections by an employee who terminated service.[1]

A plan may provide a grace period of no more than 2½ months following the end of the plan year for participants to incur and submit expenses for reimbursement. The grace period must apply to all participants in the plan. Plans may adopt a grace period for the current plan year by amending the plan document before the end of the current plan year.[2] Further, beginning in 2014, health FSAs may be amended so that $500 of each participant's unused amounts remaining at the end of the plan year may be carried forward to the next plan year. However, plans that incorporate the carryover provision may not also offer the 2½ month grace period.[3]

In 2020, the IRS clarified that the amount that may be carried forward will be inflation-adjusted, so that the amount that can be carried over to the following year from a health FSA will equal 20 percent of the maximum inflation-indexed salary reduction amount under Section 125 (increasing the carryover amount to $550 for 2020).[4] This change, while enacted in the wake of the COVID-19 pandemic, is permanent.

Planning Point: The IRS has released guidance clarifying application of the carryover provision. The IRS guidance has made clear that, unlike health savings accounts (HSAs) or health reimbursement arrangements (HRAs), the FSA cannot allow the participant to accumulate funds from year to year. The carryover applies only to the single year that immediately follows the year of contribution.[5]

The plan may reimburse medical expenses of the kind described under IRC Section 213(d), but may not reimburse for premiums paid for other health plan coverage.[6]

Editor's Note: Under current law, the plan can reimburse for nonprescription over-the-counter drugs.[7] However, for taxable years beginning after December 31, 2010 and before March 2020, reimbursements for medicine were limited to doctor-prescribed drugs and insulin. That requirement was repealed by the 2020 CARES Act in the wake of the COVID-19 pandemic.[8]

---

1.   Prop. Treas. Reg. §1.125-5(e).
2.   Prop. Treas. Reg. §1.125-1(e); Notice 2005-42, 2005-1 CB 1204.
3.   Notice 2013-71, 2013-47 IRB 532.
4.   Notice 2020-33.
5.   IRS INFO 2018-0012.
6.   Prop. Treas. Reg. §1.125-5(k).
7.   Rev. Rul. 2003-102, 2003-2 CB 559.
8.   IRC Sec. 106(f), as added by ACA 2010.

The medical expenses must be for medical care provided during the period of coverage with substantiation that the expense claimed has been incurred and is not reimbursable under other health coverage.[1]

Planning Point: Employees should remember that health expenses are deemed to be "incurred" when the service is actually provided--not when the employee is billed.

The IRS has approved the use of employer-issued debit and credit cards to pay for medical expenses as incurred, provided that the employer requires subsequent substantiation of the expenses or has in place sufficient procedures to substantiate the payments at the time of purchase.[2] On a one-time basis, a plan may allow a qualified HSA distribution. See Q 411.

Employer-provided coverage for qualified long-term care services provided through an FSA is included in the employee's gross income.[3]

Informal IRS Guidance on FSAs. In August of 2001, the IRS provided informal, *nonbinding* guidance regarding FSAs. In a departure from previous informal guidance, the IRS indicated that orthodontia expenses should be treated differently from other medical expenses. Under this reasoning, if orthodontia expenses are paid in a lump sum when treatment commences, rather than over the course of treatment, they could be reimbursed under an FSA when paid. Finally, the IRS informally clarified that there is no *de minimis* claim amount that need not be substantiated; employers and plan administrators may not disregard the substantiation requirements for small claims.

3517. What is a dependent care flexible spending arrangement?

Substantially the same rules apply to dependent care FSAs as health FSAs, except that the maximum amount of reimbursement need not be available throughout the period of coverage. A plan may limit a participant's reimbursement to amounts actually contributed to the plan and still available in the participant's account.[4] Contributions to a dependent care FSA may not exceed $5,000 during a taxable year.[5]

Planning Point: With so many employees working from home in 2020, many employees are rethinking contributions to dependent care FSAs. The rules governing changes to dependent care FSA contributions are more flexible than health FSAs. Employees are permitted to make mid-year changes in pre-tax contributions if their circumstances relating to the need for dependent care changes. Employees can reduce their contributions if they are working from home and do not need childcare, or they can increase the contributions when they return to work and need to provide for increased childcare costs.

Further, employees who have been furloughed and laid off might want to ask whether their plan contains a spend-down feature. These features are optional but allow former employees to seek reimbursement for dependent care expenses incurred through the end of the tax year (even if

1.   Prop. Treas. Reg. §1.125-6(b); Rev. Proc. 2003-43, 2003-1 CB 935. See *Grande v. Allison Engine Co.*, 2000 U.S Dist. LEXIS 12220 (S.D. Ind. 2000).
2.   Notice 2006-69, 2006-2 CB 107. See also Notice 2007-2, 2007-1 CB 254.
3.   IRC Sec. 106(c)(1).
4.   Prop. Treas. Reg. §1.125-5.
5.   IRC Sec. 129(a)(2)(A). This limit is not currently adjusted for inflation.

their employment has been terminated). Employers have the option of adding a spend-down feature at any time.

Like a health FSA, a dependent care FSA may permit a grace period of no more than 2½ months following the end of the plan year for participants to incur and submit expenses for reimbursement.[1] The $500 carryover rule applicable for health FSAs after 2013, however, is not available for participants in a dependent care FSA.

The IRS has also approved the use of employer-issued debit and credit cards to reimburse for recurring dependent care expenses. Because expenses may not be reimbursed until the dependent care services are provided, reimbursements through debit cards must flow in arrears of expenses incurred.[2]

3518. How are gains or income from a flexible spending arrangement treated?

Any gain or income from an FSA may be (1) used to reduce premiums for the following year; or (2) returned to the premium payors as dividends or premium refunds on a reasonable basis, but in no case based on their individual claims experience.[3]

The maximum amount of reimbursement for a period of coverage under an FSA may not be substantially in excess of the total "premium" for the coverage. The maximum amount of reimbursement is not considered to be substantially in excess of the total premium if the maximum amount is less than 500 percent of the premium. This definition is applicable to plan years beginning after December 31, 1989.[4]

Since 2013, there are two possible plan options for a participant with *unspent funds* in a health FSA. The plan may (1) allow for a carryover of up to $500 to the next year, but forfeit amounts in excess of $500 ($550 in 2020, see Q 3516) at year end; or (2) allow for a grace period giving participants up to an additional 2½ months (through March 15) to spend the unused funds, but forfeit any remaining at the end of the grace period. The employer can offer either option, but not both. Or it can offer neither option resulting in forfeiture of all unspent funds at end of year.

---

1.   Notice 2005-42, 2005-1 CB 1204.
2.   Notice 2006-69, 2006-2 CB 107.
3.   Prop. Treas. Reg. §1.125-5(o).
4.   Prop. Treas. Reg. §1.125-5(a).

PART XI: EXECUTIVE COMPENSATION

Overview

3519. What are the limits on an employer's ability to deduct compensation paid to an employee?

Editor's Note: The Tax Cuts & Jobs Act of 2017 (2017 Tax Act) changed the rules governing the deductibility of compensation, including nonqualified deferred compensation, under Code Section 162(m) for certain companies as to "performance-based compensation" and the $1 million cap, except as to amounts under narrowly crafted grandfathering provisions. See Q 3520 for details.

An employer may deduct all ordinary and necessary business expenses including "a reasonable allowance for salaries or other compensation for personal services actually rendered."[1] "Reasonable" compensation is "such amount as would ordinarily be paid for like services by like enterprises under like circumstances."[2] A salary that exceeds what is customarily paid for such services is considered unreasonable or excessive. Items other than wages may be considered in determining whether compensation is excessive. For example, the amount of loans forgiven on key person insurance policies for two top executives when the policies were transferred to them was used in determining whether their compensation was unreasonable.[3] Compensation generally is the total amount of compensation paid to an employee, rather than that paid to all employees as a group.[4]

The issue of reasonable compensation has been almost exclusively a problem in connection with employee-shareholders of closely-held companies. If the IRS finds compensation to be unreasonable, it may reclassify it as a dividend if it had been paid to an employee-shareholder.[5] The fact that the corporation had never declared a dividend was a factor in determining whether amounts paid to an individual who was president, director, and sole shareholder were actually disguised dividends.[6] Bonuses that are disproportionately high in relation to salaries actually may be dividends in disguise, especially if the employee receiving the "bonus" is the company's sole or majority shareholder.[7] This even includes the value of qualified and nonqualified pension-like benefits, although valuing them for this purpose is not entirely clear.[8]

---

1.   IRC Sec. 162(a)(1) as amended by PL 115-97
2.   Treas. Reg. §1.162-7(b)(3).
3.   *Avis Indus. Corp. v. Comm.*, TC Memo 1995-434.
4.   *L. Schepp Co.*, 25 BTA 419 (1932).
5.   See Treas. Reg. §1.162-7(b)(1).
6.   *Eberl's Claim Serv., Inc. v. Comm.*, 249 F.3d 994 (10th Cir. 2001).
7.   *Rapco, Inc. v. Comm.*, 85 F 3d 950 (2nd Cir. 1996),96-1 USTC ¶50,297 (2nd Cir. 1996); *Labelgraphics, Inc. v. Comm.*, TC Memo 1998-343, aff'd 2000-2 USTC ¶50,648 (9th Cir. 2000). But see *Exacto Spring Corp. v. Comm.*, 196 F. 3d 833, 99-2 USTC ¶50,964 (7th Cir. 1999).
8.   See e.g., *The Thousand Oaks Residential Care Home v. Comm.*, TC Memo 2013-10.

3520. Is there an upper limit on the amount of executive compensation that a publicly-traded corporation may deduct? How did the 2017 Tax Act impact this limit?

IRC Section 162(m) mandates an upper limit on the amount that a publicly-traded corporation may deduct for compensation paid to certain executives, even though it may well otherwise be reasonable.[1] No deduction is permitted for "applicable employee remuneration" in excess of $1 million paid to any "covered employee" by any "publicly-held corporation."[2]

Prior to 2018, a "covered employee" was defined as the corporation's principal executive officer or any other employee who is one of the corporation's three highest compensated officers (other than the corporation's principal financial officer).[3] This determination is made under the executive compensation disclosure rules of the Securities Exchange Act of 1934.[4] The 2017 Tax Act expanded the definition of "covered employee" to include the chief financial officer and the chief executive officer (if the individual holds one of these positions at any time during the tax year). A covered employee now includes the three (rather than four) most highly compensated officers (other than the CEO and CFO) for the tax year who must be reported on the company's proxy statement for the tax year (or who would be required to be reported if the company is not required to provide a proxy statement).[5]

Planning Point: The IRS proposed regulations provide that the employee need not have served as an executive officer as of the end of the company's tax year in order to be treated as a covered employee (adopting the rule set forth in Notice 2018-68). Further, executive officers can be covered employees even if their compensation need not be disclosed. In determining the three most highly compensated employees, employers are entitled to rely on a reasonable, good faith interpretation of the statute until further guidance is released. The guidance also clarified that covered employees identified during a tax year that began in 2017 in accordance with pre-tax reform rules will continue to be covered employees for 2018 and beyond.

For tax years beginning after 2017, once the employee becomes a covered employee, he or she will stay a covered employee (even if the compensation is eventually paid to a beneficiary after the individual has died, to a beneficiary of a qualified domestic relations order or if the employee is no longer employed by the employer).[6]

The term "covered employee" also means any employee who was a covered employee of any predecessor of a publicly held corporation of the taxpayer for any preceding taxable year beginning after December 31, 2016. The proposed regulations use the term "predecessor of a publicly held corporation" for clarity. An individual who is a covered employee for one taxable year (including a taxable year of a predecessor of a publicly held corporation) remains a covered employee for subsequent taxable years. Specifically, a predecessor of a publicly held corporation includes a publicly held corporation that, after becoming privately held, again becomes a publicly

---

1.   IRC Sec. 162(m).
2.   IRC Sec. 162(m)(1).
3.   IRC Sec. 162(m)(3); Notice 2007-49, 2007-25 IRB 1429.
4.   Treas. Reg. §1.162-27(c)(2)(ii).
5.   IRC Sec. 162(m)(3).
6.   IRC Sec. 162(m)(4)(F).

held corporation for a taxable year ending before the 36-month anniversary of the due date for the corporation's federal income tax return (excluding any extensions) for the last taxable year for which the corporation was previously publicly held.

The proposed regulations also provide that the term "predecessor of a publicly held corporation" includes a publicly held corporation that is acquired (as a target corporation), or the assets of which are acquired, by another publicly held corporation (the acquiror corporation) in certain transactions. The covered employees of the target corporation in those transactions are also covered employees of the acquiror corporation. With respect to asset acquisitions, if an acquiror corporation or one or more members of an affiliated group (acquiror group) acquires at least 80 percent of the operating assets (determined by fair market value on the date of acquisition) of a publicly held target corporation, then the target corporation is a predecessor of the acquiror corporation or group. For acquisitions of assets that occur over time, only acquisitions that occur within a twelve-month period are taken into account to determine whether at least 80 percent of the target corporation's operating assets were acquired.

The 2017 Tax Act also expanded the category of publicly held companies that are subject to the limit to include any company that is required to file reports with the SEC under Section 15(d) of the Securities Exchange Act of 1934, as well as any company with securities registered under Section 12 of the Act.[1] The proposed regulations clarify that this determination is made as of the last day of the company's tax year. However, a corporation will not be considered publicly held if its obligation to file reports under section 15(d) of the Exchange Act is suspended. A publicly held subsidiary is separately subject to section 162(m) and, therefore, has its own set of covered employees (in other words, a subsidiary is treated separately from its parent company) under the proposed rules.

Planning Point: Late in 2019, the SEC proposed amendments to the definition that would add new categories of individuals and expand the types of entitles that will qualify as accredited investors. The definition of "accredited investor" is generally important because satisfying those criteria allows taxpayers to participate in certain private investments. Relevant criteria include things like the taxpayer's net worth, but the new definition would also consider professional knowledge, experience or certifications (for example, a Series 7 license). Entities that meet an "investments test" would also qualify. Importantly, a company may be exempt from SEC registration requirements under Section 12(g) if fewer than 2,000 persons hold their securities, if fewer than 500 of those people are **not** accredited investors. Exemption from registration can exempt a company from the Section 162(m) requirements.

If a disregarded entity that is owned by a privately held corporation is an issuer of securities that are required to be registered under section 12(b) of the Exchange Act or is required to file reports under section 15(d) of the Exchange Act, these proposed regulations treat the privately held corporation as a publicly held corporation for purposes of section 162(m). Similarly, a Qualified Subchapter S Subsidiary (QSub)'s S corporation parent will be treated as a publicly held corporation for purposes of section 162(m) if the QSub is an issuer of securities that are

---

1.   IRC Sec. 162(m)(2).

required to be registered under section 12(b) of the Exchange Act, or is required to file reports under section 15(d) of the Exchange Act.[1]

See Q 3522 for a discussion of the transition relief that applies with respect to certain executive compensation agreements entered into before the enactment of the 2017 tax reform legislation.

"Applicable employee remuneration" is the aggregate amount of remuneration paid to an employee for services performed (whether or not during the taxable year) that would be deductible if not for this limitation.[2] Amounts not considered to be wages for FICA purposes under IRC Sections 3121(a)(5)(A) through 3121(a)(5)(D), including payments to or from any qualified plan, SEP, or Section 403(b) tax sheltered annuity, are not included.[3] Pension plan payments received by a chief executive officer who retired and then returned to work within the same tax year were not considered applicable employee remuneration.[4] Also excluded are any benefits provided to an employee that are reasonably believed to be excludable from his or her gross income and salary reduction contributions described in IRC Section 3121(v)(1) (Q 3940).[5]

Questions also arose as to how a company should identify its most highly compensated employees if their tax year was not also a fiscal year. The proposed regulations provide that the amount of compensation used to identify the three most highly compensated executive officers is determined pursuant to the executive compensation disclosure rules under the Exchange Act using the taxable year as the fiscal year for purposes of making the determination. For example, if a publicly held corporation uses a calendar year fiscal year for SEC reporting purposes, but has a taxable year beginning July 1, 2019, and ending June 30, 2020, then the three most highly compensated executive officers are determined for the taxable year ending June 30, 2020, by applying the executive compensation disclosure rules under the Exchange Act as if the fiscal year ran from July 1, 2019 to June 30, 2020. The same rule applies to short taxable years.

The 2017 Tax Act provided for only limited grandfathering of existing remuneration payable under a written binding contract that was in effect on November 2, 2017 (not the date of enactment or later date) and not thereafter modified in any material respect on or after that date.[6] Notice 2018-68 narrowed the grandfathering even further by requiring the contract to be binding under applicable law (i.e., primarily applicable state contract law) if the employee performs services or satisfies any vesting requirements. The Notice also ends grandfathering as soon as the written contract is unilaterally terminable or cancelable by the employer, or is renewable. However, amounts under the contract remain grandfathered if: (a) the written binding contract is terminated or cancelable only by terminating the employee's employment relationship; (b) employee consent is require; or (c) the amount is required to be paid under an arrangement in place as of November 2, 2017, even though the employee was not eligible on that date to participate, as long as that employee had the right to participate in the arrangement

---

1. Prop. Treas. Reg. §1.162-33(c)(1)(iv).
2. IRC Sec. 162(m)(4).
3. Treas. Reg. §1.162-27(c)(3)(ii)(A).
4. Let. Rul. 9745002.
5. Treas. Reg. §1.162-27(c)(3)(ii)(B).
6. 162(m) as amended by PL 115-97.

under a written binding contract on November 2, 2017.[1] Grandfathering is complicated since it not only requires that the administrator identify the covered and noncovered employees in a plan but maintain the grandfathered and nongrandfathered amounts separately for each group, based upon the transition rule (using the November 2, 2017 or other date as determined appropriate). See Q. 3522 for more detail.

3521. What was the pre-2018 exception for performance-based compensation to the rules for deduction executive compensation?

Prior to 2018, specifically excluded from the definition of applicable employee remuneration were commission payments, which generally were defined as any remuneration paid on a commission basis solely due to income generated directly by the employee's performance.[2] The 2017 Tax Act repealed the exception that allows a corporation to deduct compensation in excess of $1 million to the top executive employees of a public company if that compensation is performance based. As a result, public companies are now only entitled to deduct $1 million in compensation.[3]

Planning Point: Companies that offer a deferred compensation program should be advised that the Section 409A performance-based compensation definition has not changed. However, deferred compensation is subject to the new rules, except to the extent accrued accounts/amounts and nonforfeitable benefits are grandfathered under the transition rules. See below.

Planning Point: State law implications should also be examined by companies in light of the now firm $1 million cap on the deductibility of compensation. Most states calculate state taxable income based upon the company's federal taxable income at some point (either before or after NOL and other special federal-level deductions). The impact will vary based on how closely a state conforms its tax rules to the IRC. Some states may conform to the IRC on a rolling basis (i.e., the new changes will immediately flow through to the state level), while others may conform at a fixed date. If the state uses the IRC as in effect at a fixed date (before the passage of tax reform), corporations in these states may have to separately track their starting point (for measurement of the amount of compensation paid during the one-year period) for state tax purposes.

Certain other performance-based compensation (e.g., stock options and stock appreciation rights) payable solely on the attainment of at least one performance goal also was excluded, but only if (1) the goals were set by a compensation committee of the corporation's board of directors, made up solely of at least two outside directors, (2) the terms under which the compensation would be paid were disclosed to the corporation's shareholders and approved by a majority vote prior to the time of payment, and (3) the compensation committee certified that the performance goals had been attained before payment was made.[4]

A plan would not be considered performance-based compensation, however, if payment would be made when the employee was terminated or retired regardless of whether or not the goal was met.[5]

---

1.   Notice 2018-68
2.   IRC Sec. 162(m)(4)(B).
3.   IRC Sec. 162(m).
4.   IRC Sec. 162(m)(4)(C).
5.   Rev. Rul. 2008-13, 2008-10 IRB 518.

Amounts paid under a binding contract in effect on February 17, 1993, and not modified before the remuneration is paid, also are excluded.[1] If a contract entered into on or before February 17, 1993 is renewed after this date, it becomes subject to the deduction limitation.[2]

The IRS has concluded that a proposed supplemental executive retirement plan ("SERP") (Q 3540) affecting employees subject to pre-1993 employment contracts did not provide for increased compensation or the payment of additional compensation under substantially the same elements and conditions covered under the employment agreements and thus was not considered a material modification of those agreements pursuant to Treasury Regulation Section 1.162-27(h)(1)(iii)(C).[3]

The IRS has released guidance clarifying that the CFO of a smaller reporting company will be treated as a covered employee for purposes of Section 162(m) if the CFO is one of the business' two most highly compensated employees. In a notice released in 2007, the IRS had stated that a covered employee does not include an employee for whom disclosure is required because the employee is the company's CFO. A 2015 CCA, however, clarified this rule in the case of smaller reporting companies. The new guidance provides that, in the case of a smaller reporting company, the principal financial officer is a covered employee if he or she is also one of the two most highly compensated employees (other than the CEO) at the end of the tax year. Disclosure is not required only because of the individual's status as CFO, however.[4] Under the 2017 Tax Act, however, the CFO of a company is now generally treated as a covered employee.

Revenue Ruling 2008-13

In Revenue Ruling 2008-13, the IRS took the new position that agreements providing for vesting acceleration on performance-based equity or cash awards following an executive's termination without cause, without good reason, or due to retirement, or if the plan or agreement does not pay remuneration solely on account of the attainment of one or more performance goals and regardless of actual performance, will cause the plan to fail the requirements of Section 162(m), even if the accelerated vesting and payout is never triggered under the plan.

In effect, the IRS said that provisions in a plan for vesting and payment accelerations upon terminations without cause, for good reason, or due to involuntary retirement are not permissible payment events under Section 162(m) regulations. The provisions alone thereby cause loss of the compensation deduction, even if the acceleration of vesting and payment never occurs. Under the ruling, the IRS gave employers until January 1, 2009, to modify performance-based plans and agreements with "covered employees" to comply for years after 2009.

---

1.   IRC Sec. 162(m)(4)(D); Treas. Reg. §1.162-27(h)(1)(iii).
2.   Treas. Reg. §1.162-27(h)(1)(i).
3.   Let. Rul. 9619046.
4.   IRS CCA 201543003.

3522. What is the grandfathering rule that provides transition relief with respect to executive compensation agreements entered into before the 2017 Tax Act was enacted?

A transition rule applies to exempt compensation paid pursuant to a written binding contract in effect on November 2, 2017 and which was not materially modified on or after that date. If the contract is renewed after November 2, 2017, it does not qualify for the transition relief (i.e., it is treated as a new contract). The IRS has provided guidance with respect to this transition relief, and has clarified that the grandfathering provision applies only with respect to amounts that the employer is obligated to pay under applicable law (i.e., state contract law) if the employee provides the relevant services or satisfies applicable vesting conditions. If the employer pays more than this amount, those excess amounts are subject to the 2017 Tax Act amendments to Section 162(m).

Contracts that can be terminated unconditionally by either party without the other party's consent, or by both parties, are treated as new contracts entered into on the date the termination would be effective if it was made (contracts that can only be terminated by terminating the employment relationship are not treated as new contracts under this provision).[1] For example, if the terms of a contract provide that the contract will be automatically renewed unless one party provides notice of termination at least 30 days prior to the renewal date, the contract is treated as though it was renewed as of the date the termination would have been effective if the notice was given.

If the employer remains legally obligated to perform under the contract beyond a certain date at the sole discretion of the employee, the contract will **not** be treated as renewed as of that date if the employee exercises the discretion to keep the corporation bound to the contract. A contract will **not** be treated as though it was renewed if, upon termination or cancellation of the contract, the employment relationship continues but is no longer covered by the contract. If the employment relationship continues, payments with respect to the employment are not made pursuant to the contract, so they are no longer grandfathered.[2]

If a compensation arrangement is binding, amounts required to be paid as of November 2, 2017 pursuant to the plan are not subject to the Section 162(m) amendments even if the employee was not eligible to participate in the plan as of that date. The amendments **do** apply if the employee was not employed by the employer as of November 2, 2017, or if the employee had the right to participate in the plan under a binding written contract.

---

1.   Pub. Law. No. 115-97, Sec. 13601.
2.   Notice 2018-68.

The Section 162(m) amendments apply to plans that are materially modified after November 2, 2017. Amounts received pursuant to the agreement before the material modification occurs are not subject to the Section 162(m) amendments, but amounts received after the material modification occurs are subject to the Section 162(m) amendments. The IRS has provided examples of when a material modification will occur:

- The contract is amended to increase the amount of compensation payable to the employee,

- The contract is amended to accelerate payment of compensation, unless the amount paid is discounted to reasonably reflect the time value of money,

- A supplemental contract or agreement that provides for increased compensation, or the payment of additional compensation, if the facts and circumstances demonstrate that the additional compensation is paid on the basis of substantially the same elements or conditions of the compensation that is otherwise paid pursuant to the written binding agreement (although supplemental plans that provide for reasonable cost of living increases do not result in material modification).

Failure to exercise negative discretion under a contract does not result in material modification. Additionally, if the contract is modified to defer the payment of compensation, any compensation paid (or to be paid) in excess of the original amount payable to the employee under the contract is not a material modification if the additional amount is based on either a reasonable rate of interest or a predetermined actual investment (whether or not assets associated with the amount originally owed are actually invested as such) so that the amount payable by the employer at the later date will be based on the actual rate of return on the predetermined actual investment (including any decrease, as well as any increase, in the value of the investment).[1]

Planning Point: Pre-reform, companies could deduct certain compensation in excess of the $1 million limit so long as the compensation was based on performance goals certified by the company's compensation committee. Tax reform eliminated that exception so that companies cannot deduct this excess compensation even if it is performance based--therefore, many companies may decide there is no tangible tax benefit to having a compensation committee certify that those goals were met. Despite this, in order to qualify under the grandfathering provisions, performance-based compensation must continue to satisfy all of the standards that existed prior to the reform, so it is important to continue the certification practice if the compensation otherwise qualifies for grandfathering treatment.

3523. Did the TARP program place any limitations on the deductibility of executive compensation of program recipients?

The Emergency Economic Stabilization Act of 2008 added new rules to limit the deductibility of compensation paid to certain executives of companies participating in the federal

---

1.   Notice 2018-68.

government's Troubled Assets Relief Program ("TARP").[1] These companies generally may not deduct more than $500,000 in compensation, including deferred compensation.[2]

In effect, the compensation in excess of the limit is taxed twice. It is taxed once when the employee pays tax on the compensation, and it is taxed again to the extent the employer cannot deduct the compensation in excess of the limitation. Most large recipients under the program have sought to make their reimbursement of advances under the program to remove these special deduction limitations.

3524. Do the health care reform laws place any limitations on the deductibility of executive compensation?

Yes. The Affordable Care Act (ACA) has added rules to limit the deductibility of compensation paid to certain executives of certain "health care insurers" as defined under the law (and applying the controlled group rules). The definition of "health care insurers" includes insurance companies, health maintenance organizations, and any other entity that receives premiums for providing "health insurance coverage." The ACA places a $500,000 limit on the deduction of compensation that otherwise would be deductible to each employee during an applicable tax year. This limit includes any deferred compensation amounts earned in that tax year, even if it will not be paid until a later year. The deduction then would not be available when the deferred compensation is later paid if it is used up.

In effect, the compensation in excess of the limit is taxed twice. It is taxed once when the employee pays tax on the compensation, and it is taxed again to the extent the employer cannot deduct the compensation in excess of the limit.

This limit is effective for compensation earned in 2013 and later tax years, but includes compensation earned in 2010 or later tax years and deferred until later than 2012.

3525. Did the Dodd-Frank Act place any limitations on the deductibility of executive compensation?

The Dodd-Frank Wall Street Reform and Consumer Protection Act of 2010 (DFA) added new law to prohibit any covered financial institution (those not already covered by TARP restrictions) from offering any type of incentive-based compensation arrangement that encourages inappropriate risk by providing "excessive compensation, fees or benefits," or would lead to "material loss" to the covered financial institution.

A "covered financial institution" is one that has assets greater than $1 billion and is:

(1)   a depository institution or depository holding institution;

(2)   a broker-dealer;

---

1.   As of 2020, there were 984 recipient organizations under the TARP program originally, See "Bailout Recipients" on ProPublica website at https://projects.propublica.org/bailout/list/index for a list and current status of the recipients under the program.
2.   IRC Sec. 162(m)(5), as added by EESA 2008.

(3)   a credit union;

(4)   an investment advisor;

(5)   the Federal National Mortgage Association;

(6)   the Federal Loan Mortgage Corporation; or

(7)   any other financial institution that federal regulators determine should be treated as a covered financial institution.

Many of these new prohibition rules could look very much like those already in place for TARP-covered financial institutions. It is important to see the final regulations for the details of the operation of this broad and vague compensation limiting prohibition. However, in 2017, the President ordered a review of all of Dodd Frank with regard to regulations, existing or yet to be issued.[1] As of the date of this publication, most of the focus has been on current regulations already issued, like the CEO pay ratio regulations.

3526. Did the Temporary Pension Contribution Relief Act place any limitations on the deductibility of executive compensation?

Editor's Note: The 2017 Tax Act changed the rules governing the deductibility of compensation, including deferred compensation, for certain companies, except to the extent amounts are grandfathered. See Q 3520 for details.

Although not a deduction limitation, the Preservation of Access to Care for Medicare Beneficiaries and Pension Relief Act of 2010 ("BPRA") indirectly affects an employer's compensation deductions (and it affects the employer's cash and accounting in other ways).

The law added new rules to permit employers to amortize any qualified pension contribution shortfalls – from the required amount – over a longer time period. A public or private company must give up portions of its annual pension contribution relief permitted under the BPRA, based on "excess compensation" paid to employees (not just executives) of companies. Under the BPRA, there is a formula for calculating the permitted relief reduction in the annual pension contribution; the formula requires the employer to offset certain amounts (i.e., to make an add-back adjustment), primarily stock redemptions, dividends, and so-called "excess compensation." Under the BPRA, "excess compensation" is defined as all taxable compensation of an employee from the employer during a year exceeding $1 million, including all nonqualified deferred compensation as defined by Section 409A, which includes a broad segment of an employee's compensation under current law.

The definition of "excess compensation" also includes certain amounts that are not currently taxable to an employee. The BPRA requires an employer to include in "excess compensation" employer contributions made to any trust (or similar arrangement) to fund any nonqualified deferred compensation plan, even though these employer contribution amounts are not currently taxable. Although it is not yet clear, this requirement could

---

1.   Executive Order 13772 (Feb. 3, 2017).

include premium payments made to EOLI/COLI or annuities acquired in connection with an employer's nonqualified deferred compensation plan. Although excess compensation cannot ever exceed the permitted temporary reduction, it could cancel the benefit of the reduction for a year. Moreover, there is some concern that, subject to getting the IRS interpretation from further guidance on the statutory language, the formula and its operation with regard to excess compensation actually could cost the employer a $2 increase in pension contribution for each $1 of excess compensation.

In summary, a public or private employer seeking to take advantage of the temporary qualified pension contribution relief law will need to evaluate both the alternative schedules of pension contribution relief offered by the BPRA, and also then consider the potential impact of various scenarios of excess compensation, taking account of both taxable compensation and non-taxable employer contributions to nonqualified plans on that schedule.

3527. Did the 2017 Tax Act place any limitations on the deductibility of executive compensation in the tax-exempt entity context?

For tax years beginning after 2017, the 2017 Tax Act imposed a 21 percent excise penalty tax on remuneration that exceeds $1 million or an excess parachute payment (see below) that is paid by an applicable tax-exempt organization (ATEO, or related organization) to a covered employee.[1] This excise tax is imposed on the ATEO and not the employee. Covered employees include any of the ATEO's five most highly compensated employees. This penalty also applies to remuneration paid to an employee who was a covered employee for any tax year beginning after December 31, 2016.[2]

"Compensation" for purposes of the tax is determined based on a calendar year, not on the taxable year of the tax-exempt employer. Further, compensation is counted when there is no substantial risk of forfeiture (i.e., when it is vested), rather than when it is paid. If compensation vested before 2018, it is not counted toward the $1 million threshold.[3] In determining the five most highly paid employees for the year (and when calculating the tax itself), all compensation paid by the ATEO and related organizations is counted.[4]

Planning Point: Once an employee is a covered employee, the employee remains a covered employee indefinitely, even as compensation and services change in future years. Because of this, tax-exempt employers must maintain a record of all covered employees indefinitely.

The 21 percent penalty also applies to excess parachute payments made by tax-exempt employers to any of its five most highly compensated employees even if their compensation does not exceed $1 million. Excess parachute payments are those contingent on the employee's leaving employment with the employer and that exceed three times the employee's five-year average annual compensation.[5] Parachute payments do not include payments under a qualified

---

1. IRC Sec. 4960(a)(1). "Employee" generally means common law employee, although a facts and circumstances analysis may apply. See. Prop. Treas. Reg. §53.4960-1(e).
2. P.L. 115-97, IRC Sec. 4960(c)(2).
3. Notice 2019-09.
4. Prop. Treas. Reg. §53.4960-1(d)(2)(i).
5. IRC Secs. 4960(a)(2), 4960(c)(5).

retirement plan, a simplified employee pension plan, a simple retirement account, a tax-deferred annuity, or an eligible deferred compensation plan of a state or local government employer. The excess parachute payment need not exceed $1 million in order to trigger the excise tax.

Under the IRS guidance, a parachute payment must be conditioned upon an involuntary separation from employment, and generally means any payment that the employer would not make absent an involuntary separation from employment. If the amount is vested before separation from employment, it should not be treated as a parachute payment. Further, payment that vests early because of a separation from employment, but would have vested at a later date absent that separation, also will not be treated as a parachute payment because it would have been paid to the employee eventually. However, the value of receiving the payment early can be treated as a parachute payment if the accelerated payment is due to an involuntary separation from employment. Under the proposed regulations, the value of parachute payment is the present value calculated using reasonable actuarial assumptions and using the applicable discount rate for the present value calculation. In other words, even deferred payments are counted in determining whether an excess parachute payment has been made.[1]

Planning Point: Under the proposed regulations, excess parachute payments paid by the employer, a predecessor or a related organization are counted. Payments made by related organizations to the employee are also counted in determining the employee's base compensation amount. However, only excess parachute payments made by the ATEO (not the related entity) are subject to the tax.

However, the regulations contain an anti-abuse rule that allows reallocation of payments if the excess parachute payment was only made by the non-employer to avoid application of the excise tax.

An employee "separates from employment" if the level of services provided by that employee is reduced to no more than 20 percent of the level of services provided in the prior 36-month period. If the employee is willing and able to continue providing services, and does not request the separation, the separation will be considered involuntary.[2]

Planning Point: The 21 percent tax is imposed on the tax-exempt organization (the employer), not the employee receiving the compensation. Therefore, the tax is a plan design and/or budgeting problem for the ATEO.

Planning Point: Whether or not an employee is a covered employee must be determined separately for each tax-exempt employer within a group of tax-exempt employers. This means that larger groups of tax-exempt entities could have many employees that trigger the new tax. In some cases, payment of the tax must be allocated among multiple tax-exempt employers within a group of entities.[3]

"Remuneration" is defined to include wages for income tax withholding purposes. Designated Roth contributions are excluded. Remuneration also includes amounts included in income as compensation for services as an employee pursuant to a below-market loan.[4] Remuneration

---

1.   See Prop. Treas. Reg. §53.4960-3(h).
2.   Notice 2019-09.
3.   Notice 2019-09.
4.   Prop. Treas. Reg. §53.4960-2(a)(1).

paid (or a grant of a legally binding right to non-vested remuneration) by a third-party payor for services performed as an employee of an employer is deemed paid (or payable) by the employer. Third-party payors may include related organizations, payroll agents or other entities.[1]

Planning Point: Remuneration that is regular wages for employment is counted when it is actually or constructively paid.[2] Hence, historically popular nonqualified 457(f) supplemental executive benefit plans (SERPs) that become taxable on the entire discounted present value of the future benefit payments upon the lapse or termination of the necessary 457(f) substantial risk of forfeiture present a special problem for ATEOs under this law. Moreover, if the pay period spans two calendar years, the same rules for determining "counting" wages for Form W-2 purposes apply (i.e., the wages are counted in the year they are paid).

Any payments made with respect to the employment of the covered employee by a person or governmental entity that is related to the ATEO are included in the definition of remuneration. A person or governmental entity is treated as related to the tax-exempt organization if the person or governmental entity (1) controls, or is controlled by, the organization, (2) is controlled by one or more persons that control the organization, (3) is a supported organization during the taxable year with respect to the organization, (4) is a supporting organization during the taxable year with respect to the organization, or (5) in the case of a voluntary employees' beneficiary association ("VEBA"), establishes, maintains, or makes contributions to the VEBA.[3]

Under proposed regulations that generally follow Notice 2019-09, remuneration includes compensation paid by the ATEO, and also remuneration paid for services rendered as an employee of a related organization. Related organizations are any entity (regardless of tax-exempt status), using a 50 percent control test. An individual can be an employee of more than ATEO.[4]

Compensation paid to employees who are not highly compensated employees (under IRC Section 414(q)) is exempt from the definition of parachute payment.

Further, compensation attributable to medical services of certain qualified medical professionals is exempt from the definitions of remuneration and parachute payment.[5] To qualify, the payment must be directly related to the performance of medical or veterinary services by the professional, while payments to the professional in any other capacity is not exempt. A medical professional for this purpose means a doctor, nurse, or veterinarian.[6]

Remuneration is treated as paid when there is no substantial risk of forfeiture (the IRC Section 457(f)(3)(B) definition applies in determining when there is a substantial risk of forfeiture).[7]

---

1. Prop. Treas. Reg. §53.4960-2(b)(1).
2. See Prop. Treas. Reg. §53.4960-2(d)(1).
3. IRC Sec. 4960(c)(3).
4. Notice 2019-09.
5. Prop. Treas. Reg. §53.4960-2(a)(2).
6. IRC Sec. 4960(c)(5)(C). See also Prop. Treas. Reg. § 53.4960-1(g), which contains several examples designed to illustrate application of this rule.
7. IRC Sec. 4960(a) (flush language).

3528. Are there any exceptions to the application of the 21 percent excise tax on certain individuals who provide services for tax-exempt organizations?

In order to be covered by the new regulations, the individual receiving remuneration from the ATEO must be an employee, not an independent contractor. The typical facts-and-circumstances analysis is used to determine whether independent contractor status is appropriate.

The proposed regulations also contain exceptions designed to exempt certain individuals who provide minimal services for the ATEO. This new rule is meant to exclude "employees" who donate services to tax-exempt organizations.

Under the exceptions, (1) a director is not an employee in the capacity as a director and (2) an officer performing minor or no services and not receiving any remuneration for those services is not an employee. Employees of a related non-ATEO are not considered for purposes of determining the five highest-compensated employees if they are never employees of the ATEO. In addition, individuals who receive no remuneration (or a legally binding right to remuneration) from the ATEO or a related organization cannot be among the ATEO's five highest-compensated employees.[1]

Under the limited hours exception, an ATEO's five highest-compensated employees also exclude an employee of the ATEO who receives no remuneration from the ATEO and performs only limited services for the ATEO, which means that no more than 10 percent of total annual hours worked for the ATEO and related organizations are for services performed for the ATEO.[2] An employee who performs fewer than 100 hours of services as an employee of an ATEO and its related ATEOs is treated as having worked less than 10 percent of total hours for the ATEO and related ATEOs.[3]

Under the non-exempt funds exception, an employee who is not compensated by an ATEO, related ATEO, or any taxable related organization controlled by the ATEO and who primarily (more than 50 percent of total hours worked) provides services to a related non-ATEO is also disregarded.

Similarly, an employee is disregarded if an ATEO paid less than 10 percent of the employee's total remuneration for services performed for the ATEO and all related organizations. However, in the case of related ATEOs, if neither the ATEO nor any related ATEO paid more than 10 percent of the employee's total remuneration, then the ATEO that paid the highest percent of remuneration does not meet this exception. Basically, this exception only applies in the case of multiple ATEOs paying compensation to the same employee.

An employee is disregarded for purposes of determining an ATEO's five highest-compensated employees for a taxable year even though the ATEO paid remuneration to the employee if, for the applicable year, all of the following requirements are met:

1.   Prop. Treas. Reg. §53.4960-1(d)(2)(i).
2.   Prop. Treas. Reg. §53.4960-1(d)(2)(ii)(A)(2).
3.   Prop. Treas. Reg. §53.4960-1(d)(2)(ii)(C).

    (1)   Remuneration requirement. The ATEO did not pay 10 percent or more of the employee's total remuneration for services performed as an employee of the ATEO and all related organizations; and

    (2)   Related organization requirement. The ATEO had at least one related ATEO and one of the following conditions apply:

        a.   Ten percent remuneration condition. A related ATEO paid at least 10 percent of the remuneration paid by the ATEO and all related organizations; or

        b.   Less remuneration condition. No related ATEO paid at least 10 percent of the total remuneration paid by the ATEO and all related organizations and the ATEO paid less remuneration to the employee than at least one related ATEO.[1]

3529. Did the 2017 Tax Act make any changes to the rules for calculating unrelated business taxable income (UBTI) in the tax-exempt entity context?

Editor's Note: The Taxpayer Certainty and Disaster Relief Act of 2019[2] *repealed* the expansion of the UBTI definition. The repeal was made retroactive to the date of enactment, *so it is essentially as though the new provision never existed.* However, organizations can file an amended Form 990-T to claim a refund for taxes paid under the repealed provision. The rules discussed below reflect the rule as it would have stood had the repeal not happened.

The 2017 Tax Act created a new IRC Section 512(a)(6) requirement that tax-exempt entities now separately compute unrelated business taxable income (UBTI) for each trade or business, so that losses from one business can no longer be used to offset gains in another business. In interpreting this new rule, several questions arose that the IRS began to address in Notice 2018-67.

Notice 2018-67 makes clear that the IRS will not penalize entities for using any reasonable good faith interpretation of the statute in calculating UBTI, and requests comments on implementation of the new rules. The Notice proposes that entities distinguish between their trades and businesses by using the codes provided by the North American Industry Classification System (NAICS) in order to aggregate certain business lines.

The notice also requests comments on the IRS' proposal to create a separate category of "business" for gains and losses generated from partnership investments. Notice 2018-67 contains a safe harbor for organizations to rely upon in the meantime. Under the safe harbor rule, organizations can aggregate income from a single partnership that conducts multiple trades or businesses if the holdings are qualified partnership interests. Gains and losses from all qualifying partnership interests can also be aggregated under the safe harbor. A "qualifying partnership interest" for this purpose is an investment that satisfies one of the following tests:

---

1.   Prop. Treas. Reg. §53.4960-1(d)(iv).

2.   Part of PL 116-94,

- De minimis test where the organization has no more than a 2 percent interest in the profits and capital of the partnership, or

- Control test, where the organization has no more than a 20 percent interest in the partnership and does not exert any control or influence over the partnership.

A transition rule allows aggregation of all income from a single partnership as one trade or business if the interest was acquired before August 21, 2018 (although aggregation across partnerships is not addressed).

Planning Point: After enactment of the 2020 law, UBTI now will **not** include amounts paid for (1) qualified transportation fringe benefits, (2) parking facilities used in connection with qualified parking or (3) on-premise athletic facilities, if the amounts are not paid in direct connection with an unrelated trade or business regularly conducted by the organization.

With respect to other fringe benefits, an IRS official has commented on the link between the IRC Section 274 expensing rules and the Section 512 UBTI. The official noted that tax-exempts should look to the Section 274 allowances to determine whether they are offering a fringe benefit that would become subject to the UBTI.

3530. What are "excess parachute payments" and how are they taxed?

Editor's Note: The 2017 Tax Act changed the rules governing the taxability of certain compensation amounts paid by the employer (not the employee), including certain "excess parachute payments", for certain tax-exempt entities. See Q 3527 for details of coverage for purposes of the 21 percent excise tax penalty.

Agreements providing a generous package of severance and benefits to top executives and key personnel in the event of a takeover or merger are commonly referred to as "golden parachutes." "Excess parachute payments," as defined in IRC Section 280G, are subject to the following two tax sanctions: (1) no employer deduction is allowed; and (2) the recipient is subject to a 20 percent penalty tax.[1] Note that this tax penalty is not the same 20 percent penalty imposed by plans covered by and failing IRC Section 409A requirements (Q 3540).

A "parachute payment" is defined in the IRC as any payment in the nature of compensation to a disqualified individual that is (1) contingent on a change in the ownership or effective control of the corporation or a substantial portion of its assets and the present value of the payments contingent on such change equals or exceeds three times the individual's average annual compensation from the corporation in the five taxable years ending before the date of the change, or (2) pursuant to an agreement that violates any generally enforced securities laws or regulations.[2] The present value of the payments contingent on the change in ownership or control is to be determined as of the date of the change, using a discount rate equal to 120 percent of the applicable federal rate.[3] A transfer of property will be treated as a payment and taken into account at its fair market value.[4]

---

1. IRC Secs. 280G, 4999.
2. IRC Sec. 280G(b)(2).
3. IRC Sec. 280G(d)(4).
4. IRC Sec. 280G(d)(3).

A "disqualified individual" is any employee, independent contractor, or other person specified in the regulations who performs personal services for a corporation and who is an officer, shareholder, or highly compensated individual of the corporation. For this purpose, "highly compensated individual" only includes an individual who is a member of the group consisting of the highest paid 1 percent of the employees of the corporation or, if less, the highest paid 250 employees of the corporation.

A payment generally will not be considered contingent if it is substantially certain at the time of the change that the payment would have been made whether or not the change occurred. If a payment is made under a contract entered into or amended within one year of a change in ownership or control, it is presumed to be a parachute payment, unless it can be shown "by clear and convincing evidence" that the payment was not contingent on the change in ownership or control.[1]

The term "parachute payment" does not include:

(1)   any payment to a disqualified individual with respect to a "small business corporation" as defined in IRC Section 1361(b) (which does not have more than one class of stock and not more than 100 stockholders, all of whom are generally individuals but none of whom are nonresident aliens),

(2)   any payment to a disqualified individual with respect to a corporation if, immediately before the change, no stock was readily tradable on an established securities market or otherwise and shareholder approval of the payment was obtained after adequate and informed disclosure by a vote of persons, who, immediately before the change, owned more than 75 percent of the voting power of all outstanding stock of the corporation, or

(3)   any payment to or from a qualified pension, profit sharing or stock bonus plan, a tax sheltered annuity plan, or a simplified employee pension plan.[2]

IRC Section 280G applies to agreements entered into or amended after June 14, 1984.[3]

See Q 3531 for a discussion of how to calculate the nondeductible portion of a parachute payment.

Section 409A Impact

Because Section 280G and Section 409A both can cover a plan providing severance/separation benefits in the case of a change in control, and Section 280G and Section 409A have separate definitions of what constitutes a change in control (Section 409A imposing a narrower

---

1.   IRC Sec. 280G(b)(2)(C).
2.   IRC Secs. 280G(b)(5) and (6). Based upon the Conference Report to the Tax Reform Act of 1984 that enacted the 280G tax, true nonqualified deferral plans are probably excluded since they are compensation earned prior to the change of control. Nonqualified supplemental plans would generally be included, except for one case, supplemental plans installed to replace an executive's qualified plan benefits lost under a prior employer's qualified plan since they were also deemed as earned prior to change of control in the report.
3.   Treas. Reg. §1.280G-1, Q&A 47.

definition), it is necessary to carefully coordinate the plan provisions when both IRC sections might apply (Q 535).

3531. How is the nondeductible amount of a parachute payment calculated?

Editor's Note: The 2017 Tax Act changed the rules governing taxability to the employer (not the employee) of certain compensation, including certain "excess parachute payments", for certain tax-exempt entities. See Q 3527 for details.

The amount of a parachute payment that is nondeductible and subject to the excise tax (i.e., the "excess parachute payment," see Q 3530) is the amount of the payment in excess of the portion of the base amount allocable to that payment.

The "base amount" is the average of the individual's annual compensation paid by the corporation undergoing the change in ownership and includable in the gross income of the individual in the most recent five taxable years ending before the date on which the change in ownership or control occurs. If the individual has been employed by the corporation for fewer than five years, then the base amount is figured using the annual compensation for the years actually employed. Compensation of individuals employed for a portion of a taxable year should be annualized (i.e., $30,000 in compensation for four months of employment with the corporation would be $90,000 on an annual basis).

To determine the "excess parachute payment," the base amount is multiplied by the ratio of the present value of the parachute payment to the present value of all parachute payments expected; the result is then subtracted from the amount of the parachute payment.

$$
\begin{array}{c}
\text{excess} \\
\text{parachute} \\
\text{payment}
\end{array}
=
\begin{array}{c}
\text{parachute} \\
\text{payment}
\end{array}
-
\frac{
\begin{array}{c}
\text{present value} \\
\text{of the} \\
\text{parachute payment}
\end{array}
}{
\begin{array}{c}
\text{present value of} \\
\text{all parachute} \\
\text{payments expected}
\end{array}
}
\times \text{base amount}
$$

The present value is to be determined at the time the contingency occurs, using a discount rate of 120 percent of the applicable federal rate.

Any amount the taxpayer can prove is "reasonable compensation" will not be treated as a parachute payment.[1] See Q 3519 for a general discussion on standards for "reasonable compensation."

Planning Point: The original documentation should allow the sponsor the option to pay the maximum amount payable (2.99 × average annual compensation) without equaling or exceeding the total amount that would make some portion "excess compensation," which would cause loss of a portion of the deduction. This option often may result in the participant ultimately receiving a larger dollar amount than if the participant had received "excessive compensation," after consideration for income taxes in both cases. In addition, the sponsor will have retained its compensation deduction for the payment.

---

1.   IRC Sec. 280G(b)(4); Treas. Reg. §1.280G-1, Q&A 40-44.

PART XII: FUNDED DEFERRED COMPENSATION

Overview

3532. What are the tax consequences for the employee of a Section 83 funded deferred compensation agreement?

Under IRC Section 83, as a general rule, an employee is currently taxed on a contribution to a trust or a premium paid for an annuity contract (paid after August 1, 1969), or other "transfer of property" to the extent that the interest is substantially vested when the contribution or transfer is made.

An interest is substantially vested if it is transferable or not subject to a Section 83 substantial risk of forfeiture. Under Section 83, an interest is transferable if it can be transferred free of a substantial risk of forfeiture (Q 3538).[1] On May 29, 2012, the IRS released proposed regulations clarifying the definition of "substantial risk of forfeiture" under Section 83,[2] and incorporating its ruling in Revenue Ruling 2005-48 as to Section 83 equity plans (for details on the changes see Q 3538). On February 25, 2014, the IRS issued final regulations that are substantially similar to the proposed regulations. These regulations will apply to all transfers of property on or after January 1, 2013, and the proposed regulations may be relied on as to transfers after May 30, 2012.[3]

A partner is immediately taxable on the partner's distributive share of contributions made to a trust in which the partnership has a substantially vested interest even if the partner's right is not substantially vested.[4]

If an employee's rights change from substantially nonvested to substantially vested, the value of the employee's interest in the trust or the value of the annuity contract on the date of change (to the extent such value is attributable to contributions made after August 1, 1969) must be included in the employee's gross income for the taxable year in which the change occurs. The value on the date of change also probably constitutes "wages" for the purposes of withholding[5] and for purposes of FICA and FUTA (Q 3576). The value of an annuity contract is its cash surrender value.[6]

If only part of an employee's interest in a trust or an annuity contract changes from substantially nonvested to substantially vested during any taxable year, only that corresponding part is includable in gross income for the year.[7]

---

1.   IRC Secs. 402(b)(1), 403(c), 83(a); Treas. Reg. §§1.402(b)-1(a)(1), 1.403(c)-1(a), 1.83-1(a)(1), 1.83-3(b), 1.83-3(d).
2.   It is important to note that there multiple definitions of "substantial risk of forfeiture" under different Internal Revenue Code Sections (there are seven definitions now since the release of the new proposed 457/409A integration regulations), and *they are not exactly the same* so it is important to follow the definition required for the section applicable to the tax question. For example, compare Q 3538, Q 3550 and Q 3601.
3.   Proposed Treas. Reg. §1.83-3, 5-29-2012., made final in TD 9659, 2014-12 IRB (Mar. 17, 2014) with minor modification on Example 4.
4.   *U.S. v. Basye*, 410 U.S. 441 (1973).
5.   Temp. Treas. Reg. §35.3405-1T, A-18; Let. Rul. 9417013.
6.   IRC Secs. 402(b)(1), 403(c), 83(a); Treas. Reg. §§1.402(b)-1(b), 1.403(c)-1(b).
7.   Treas. Reg. §§1.402(b)-1(b)(4), 1.403(c)-1(b)(3).

An employee is not taxed on the value of a vested interest in a trust attributable to contributions made while the trust was exempt under IRC Section 501(a).[1]

Special rules apply to trusts that lose their tax qualification because of a failure to satisfy the applicable minimum participation or minimum coverage tests.[2] The IRS has taken the controversial position that these special rules apply to nonexempt trusts that were never intended to be tax qualified. As a result, the IRS would tax highly compensated employees ("HCEs") (Q 3927) participating in trust-funded nonqualified plans that fail the minimum participation or minimum coverage tests applicable to qualified plans (Q 3847 through Q 3860), which most nonqualified plans will fail (Q 3534).

There is no tax liability when an employee's rights in the value of a trust or annuity (attributable to contributions or premiums paid on or before August 1, 1969) change from forfeitable to nonforfeitable. Prior to August 1, 1969, an employee was not taxed when payments were made to a nonqualified trust or as premiums to a nonqualified annuity plan if the employee's rights at the time were forfeitable.[3] Thus, the employee did not incur tax liability when the employee's forfeitable rights later became nonforfeitable. This old law still applies to trust and annuity values attributable to payments made on or before August 1, 1969.[4]

Where an employer amended its Section 451 "unfunded" nonqualified deferred compensation plan (one subject to the claims of the employer's general creditors in bankruptcy) to provide those participants with a choice between a lump sum payment of the present value of their future benefits or an annuity contract securing their rights to the remaining payments under the plan (with a corresponding tax gross-up payment from the employer), any participant who chose the annuity contract would be required to include the purchase price for such participant's benefits under the contract in gross income (as well as the tax gross-up payment) in the year paid or made available, if earlier.[5]

In July 2015, the IRS proposed new regulations that would eliminate the requirement to file a Section 83(b) election with the IRS by attaching a copy to a federal income tax return (since this requirement generally prohibits an electronic filing.)[6] These regulations were finalized in 2016. Individuals are still required to keep records sufficient to show basis of the property and the original cost (if any).

For taxation of annuity payments to an employee, see Q 3539.

---

1.   Treas. Reg. §1.402(b)-1(b)(1).
2.   IRC Sec. 402(b)(4).
3.   IRC Secs. 402(b) and 403(b), prior to amendment by P.L. 91-172 (TRA '69).
4.   Treas. Reg. §§1.402(b)-1(d), 1.403(c)-1(d).
5.   Let. Rul. 9713006. This transaction would now likely be subject to Section 409A, and the change to the plan would constitute a violation as a prohibited "substitution" by way of an alternative benefit.
6.   Prop. Treas. Reg. §1.83-2(c).

3533. What are the tax consequences of a Section 83 funded deferred compensation agreement for the employer?

Editor's Note: The 2017 Tax Act created a new Section 83(i), which permits tax deferral with respect to certain broad-based employee stock options and restricted stock units of private companies, especially start-ups, on an attractive basis. See Q 3613 for details.

Whether a cash or accrual basis taxpayer, an employer can take a deduction for a contribution or premium paid in the year in which an amount attributable thereto is includable in an employee's gross income.[1] This deduction cannot be more than the amount of the contribution and it cannot include any earnings on the contribution before they are included in the employee's income.[2] If more than one employee participates in a funded deferred compensation plan, the deduction will be allowed only if separate accounts are maintained for each employee.[3] The employer is not allowed a deduction at any time for contributions made or premiums paid on or before August 1, 1969, if the employee's rights were forfeitable at the time.[4] Contributions or premiums paid or accrued on behalf of an independent contractor may be deducted only in the year in which amounts attributable thereto are includable in the independent contractor's gross income.[5]

With respect to contributions made after February 28, 1986 to annuity contracts held by a corporation, partnership, or trust (i.e., a nonnatural person), the "income on the contract" for the tax year of the policyholder generally is treated as ordinary income received or accrued by the contract owner during such taxable year (Q 511).[6]

Prior to the 2017 Tax Act, corporate ownership of life insurance could result in exposure to the corporate alternative minimum tax (Q 316), although the corporate AMT was permanently repealed beginning in 2018.

The IRS has taken the position that a nonexempt employee's Section 83 funded trust deferred compensation agreement cannot be considered an employer-grantor trust. As a result, the employer will not be taxed on the trust's income, but it also cannot claim the trust's deductions and credits.[7] Proposed regulations have affirmed the position of the IRS (Q 3534).[8]

Funded deferred compensation may take the form of either an employer-paid supplemental or voluntary deferred compensation plan (Q 3540), although supplemental plans using equity or SARs are most common.

---

1. IRC Sec. 404(a)(5); Treas. Reg. §1.404(a)-1(c).
2. Treas. Reg. §1.404(a)-12(b)(1).
3. Treas. Reg. §1.404(a)-12(b)(3).
4. Treas. Reg. §1.404(a)-12(c).
5. IRC Sec. 404(d); Temp. Treas. Reg. §1.404(d)-1T.
6. IRC Sec. 72(u). See also H.R. Rep. 99-426 (TRA '86), *reprinted in* 1986-3 CB (vol. 2) 703, 704; the General Explanation of TRA '86, at 658.
7. Let. Rul. 9302017.
8. Prop. Treas. Reg. §1.671-1(g).

The fact that the addition of a trust to fund a previously unfunded deferred compensation agreement was established as part of a nontaxable[1] corporate liquidation did not alter its treatment as an employee trust.[2]

A nonqualified deferred compensation plan funded by a trust or annuity other than an "excess benefit plan" (Q 3608) must provide for minimum vesting generally comparable to that required in qualified retirement plans (Q 3868).[3] Government plans and many church plans, however, are exempt from ERISA.

The above rules do not apply to nonqualified annuities purchased by tax-exempt organizations and public schools (Q 4031 to Q 4092) or to individual retirement accounts and annuities (Q 3641 to Q 3699).

IRC Section 404(a)(11)

If vacation pay is paid to an employee within 2½ months after the end of the applicable tax year, it generally is deductible for the tax year in which it is earned (vested) and is not treated as deferred compensation.[4] Employers may not deduct accrued vacation or severance pay unless it actually is received by employees.[5]

Actual receipt is not:

(1)   a note or letter evidencing the employer's indebtedness (whether or not guaranteed by an instrument or third party);

(2)   a promise to provide future service or property (whether or not evidenced by written agreement);

(3)   an amount transferred by a loan, refundable deposit, or contingent payment; or

(4)   amounts set aside in a trust for an employee.[6]

The IRS provided settlement options for taxpayers who had accelerated the deduction of accrued employee benefits (primarily vacation pay, disability pay, and sick pay) secured by a letter of credit, bond, or similar financial instrument, in reliance on *Schmidt Baking Co., Inc. v. Comm.*,[7] which Section 404(a)(11) expressly overturned for years ending after July 22, 1998.[8] The IRS also has published guidance explaining the automatic accounting method change necessary to comply with IRC Section 404(a)(11).[9]

---

1.   IRC Sec. 337.
2.   *Teget v. U.S.*, 552 F.2d 236, 77-1 USTC ¶9315 (8th Cir. 1977).
3.   ERISA Sec. 201.
4.   Temp. Treas. Reg. §1.404(b)-1T, A-2.
5.   IRC Sec. 404(a)(11).
6.   IRSRRA '98, Sec. 7001, H.R. Conf. Rep. No. 105-599.
7.   107 TC 271 (1996) (employer allowed to deduct accrued vacation liabilities because it had obtained an irrevocable letter of credit guaranteeing such obligation within 2½ months of the year of deduction).
8.   Rev. Proc. 99-26, 1999-1 CB 1244.
9.   Notice 99-16, 1999-1 CB 501.

IRC Section 409A

Section 409A covers "inclusion in gross income of deferred compensation under nonqualified deferred compensation plans."[1] This definition of "nonqualified deferred compensation plans" is so expansive that it generally applies to most arrangements of deferred fringe benefits, including funded arrangements covered by Section 83, and is not limited to cash payments, unless the arrangement is outside certain statutory exemptions or regulatory exceptions to Section 409A. Plan sponsors should routinely seek to design their fringe benefit and incentive compensation arrangements covered by Section 83 to fall within these Section 409A exemptions and exceptions whenever possible, especially those involving equity that impose strict Section 409A requirements to claim an exception.

3534. What is a "secular trust" and how is it taxed?

A secular trust is an irrevocable trust established to formally fund and secure nonqualified deferred compensation benefits and is referred to as a secular trust to distinguish it from a grantor rabbi trust (Q 3567). Funds placed in a secular trust are not subject to the claims of the employer's creditors. Thus, unlike a rabbi trust, a secular trust can protect its participants against both the employer's future unwillingness to pay promised benefits and the employer's future inability to pay promised benefits, including sponsor insolvency or bankruptcy situations.

Secular trusts have not been as popular as rabbi trusts, in part because of questions surrounding their taxation (see Q 3535 to Q 3537), but they have historically received more consideration during severe economic downturns when companies are more at risk to fail, or the future for success of an industry appears unclear or highly volatile (such as the airline industry during the first decade of the 21st century).

ERISA Implications

Use of a secular trust (at least other than an employee-grantor trust) probably will cause a deferred compensation plan subject to ERISA to be funded for ERISA purposes.[2] Funded plans generally are required to meet ERISA's Title I requirements.

Section 409A Inapplicable

Section 409A generally is inapplicable to a secular trust arrangement because the contributions and earnings are made subject to current annual income taxation to a plan participant and thus the plan is eligible to claim the Section 409A short term deferral exception for current compensation (Q 3541). In effect, the plan is an after-tax plan that involves current compensation, not Section 409A nonqualified deferred compensation. Whether this is entirely true as to a plan participant when a nontaxable investment vehicle is used inside the trust to shelter any

---

1.   See generally Treas. Reg. §§1.409A-1(b)(9)(v) and 1.409A-3(i)(1)(iv); see also Notice 2007-34, 2007-17 IRB 996 (governing split dollar life insurance as to the limited types of split dollar arrangements excepted from Section 409A).
2.   See, e.g., *Dependahl v. Falstaff Brewing Corp.*, 653 F.2d 1208 (8th Cir. 1981) (plan is funded when employee can look to property separate from employer's ordinary assets for satisfaction of benefit obligations), *aff'g in part* 491 F. Supp. 1188 (E.D. Mo. 1980), *cert. denied*, 454 U.S. 968 (1981) and 454 U.S. 1084 (1981).

earnings growth from taxation as to the plan sponsor is not entirely clear as of the date of this publication.

Planning Point: Although essentially an "after-tax" technique, the secular trust technique is usually used when an employer wants to provide a supplemental retirement benefit that is protected against the claims of the employer's creditors. In private companies, the Section 162 bonus life insurance or annuity technique is often used as an inexpensive substitute for a secular trust.

3535. What are the tax consequences to an employee when a secular trust is used to provide deferred compensation?

The IRS takes the position that IRC Section 402(b)(1) through IRC Section 402(b)(4) govern the taxation of employee-participants in an employer-funded secular trust.[1] Under the general timing rule of IRC Section 402(b)(1), contributions to a secular trust are immediately included in the income of the employee to the extent that they are substantially vested.[2] Further, in any tax year in which any part of an employee's interest in the trust changes from substantially nonvested to substantially vested, the employee will be required to include that portion in income as of the date of the change.[3]

An interest is substantially vested if it is transferable or not subject to a substantial risk of forfeiture (Q 3538).[4]

With respect to the taxation of distributions from an employer-funded secular trust, the IRS previously has indicated that the rules of IRC Section 72 (except IRC Section 72(e)(5)) apply (Q 3539). Under this approach, distributions would be taxable except to the extent that they represent amounts previously taxed. Consequently, it would seem that a highly compensated employee who has been taxed on his or her entire "vested accrued benefit" would not be taxed again on receipt of a lump sum distribution.

The IRS has questioned the applicability of IRC Section 72 to distributions from employer-funded secular trusts to highly compensated employees ("HCEs," as defined in IRC Section 414(q) (Q 3929)) participating in plans that fail the minimum participation or the minimum coverage tests applicable to qualified retirement plans (which most nonqualified plans will fail). The IRS has adopted the controversial position that a special rule under IRC Section 402(b)(4) should be applied to tax HCEs each year on their "vested accrued benefit" in the trust (minus amounts previously taxed). Thus, HCEs will be taxed on vested contributions and on vested earnings on those contributions. Apparently, the IRS would tax HCEs on their vested earnings even where they consist of unrealized appreciation of capital assets or nominally tax-free or tax deferred income (e.g., from municipal bonds or life insurance). Further, the IRS has ruled that any right to receive trust payments in compensation for these taxes also will be taxable as part of the vested accrued benefit.[5]

---

1. Let. Ruls. 9502030, 9302017, 9212024, 9212019, 9207010, 9206009.
2. Treas. Reg. §1.402(b)-1(a)(1).
3. IRC Sec. 402(b)(1); Treas. Reg. §§1.402(b)-1(b)(1), 1.402(b)-1(b)(4).
4. Treas. Reg. §§1.402(b)-1(a)(1), 1.83-3(b).
5. Let. Ruls. 9502030, 9417013, 9302017, 9212024, 9212019, 9207010.

According to the IRS, as long as a failure to satisfy the minimum participation test or the minimum coverage test is not the only feature of the plan that keeps the secular trust from being treated as a tax-qualified trust (and it generally will not be so treated), then any participants who are not highly compensated will be taxed under the general rules of IRC Section 402(b)(1), described above.

The 10 percent penalty for certain early (premature) annuity distributions under IRC Section 72(q) may apply to distributions from employer-funded secular trusts if the deferred compensation plan behind the trust is considered to be an annuity (i.e., if it provides for the payment of benefits in a series of periodic payments over a fixed period of time, or over a lifetime).[1]

Employee-funded secular trusts (where the employee establishes the trust, but the employer administers it and contributes to it) are analyzed differently. The employee generally has a choice between currently receiving cash or its equivalent, e.g., an annuity that can be surrendered immediately or life insurance policy, or a cash contribution to the trust. Sometimes the employee has the choice between withdrawing contributions from the trust or leaving them in. In these situations, the IRS generally has ruled that the employee constructively received the employer-contributed cash and then assigned it to the trust. Thus, the IRS generally has held the employee to be currently taxable on employer contributions to the trust.[2]

An employee who establishes and is considered to be the owner of an employee-funded secular trust under the grantor-trust rules should not have to include the income on annuity contracts held by the trust in income each year (Q 511).[3]

3536. What are the tax consequences to an employer that uses a secular trust to fund a deferred compensation plan for employees?

It is the position of the IRS that an employer can take a deduction for a contribution to an employer-funded secular trust in the year in which it is includable in employee income.[4] The rules of IRC Section 404(a)(5) limit the employer's deduction to the amount of the contribution; it never can include "earnings" on that amount between contribution and inclusion in the employee's income.[5] Moreover, these deductions potentially may be subject to certain limitations based on aggregations of defined "nonqualified deferred compensation," depending on the type of sponsor (Q 3519).

An employer cannot increase its "contributions" and thus its deductions by drafting the trust agreement to require that the trust distribute its earnings to the employer and that the trustee retain those earnings as "recontributions" to the trust. The IRS has indicated that it will not recognize such deemed distributions and recontributions.[6]

---

1. Let. Ruls. 9502030, 9212024, 9212019.
2. See Let. Ruls. 9548015, 9548014. See also Let. Rul. 9450004 (employee who could keep or contribute cash to trust was currently taxable on amounts contributed, although keeping cash would jeopardize future contributions and benefits).
3. Let. Ruls. 9322011, 9316018.
4. Let. Ruls. 9502030, 9417013, 9302017, 9212024, 9212019.
5. Treas. Reg. §1.404(a)-12(b)(1); Let. Ruls. 9502030, 9417013, 9302017, 9212024, 9212019.
6. Let. Rul. 9302017.

If a secular trust covers more than one employee, the employer will be able to take a deduction for contributions only if the trust maintains separate accounts for the various employees. According to the IRS, the separate account rule is satisfied only if the trust document requires that the income earned on participants' accounts be allocated to the accounts.[1]

The IRS also has granted employers immediate deductions for trust contributions where participants could choose between receiving current compensation outright or having it contributed to a trust, and where trust participants could choose between withdrawing contributions from the trust or leaving them in the trust. The IRS regarded these situations as employee-funded trusts and gave the employers deductions for the payment of compensation.[2] Moreover, these deductions potentially may be subject to certain limitations based on aggregations of defined "nonqualified deferred compensation" depending on the type of sponsor (Q 3519).

3537. If a secular trust is used to fund employer-provided deferred compensation, is the trust itself subject to taxation?

The IRS has ruled that a secular trust can never be an employer-grantor trust. Thus, an employer-funded secular trust is a separate, taxable entity. Unless secular trust earnings are distributable or are distributed annually, the trust will be taxed on those earnings.[3]

Proposed regulations have affirmed this position.[4]

Because the IRS generally would tax highly compensated employees each year on vested trust earnings (and generally would tax other employees on at least some trust earnings when a substantially nonvested interest becomes substantially vested), double taxation of trust earnings is a very real possibility. Funding secular trusts with life insurance may eliminate this by eliminating taxation of the trust. The IRS has not considered the use of life insurance in secular trusts, but under generally applicable tax rules, the inside build-up (or "earnings") on life insurance should not be taxed to the trust while it holds the policies. The use of life insurance probably will not save employees from taxation on trust earnings, however.

It also is possible to avoid trust (and therefore double) taxation by using employee-funded secular trusts. Employee-funded trusts generally are treated as employee-grantor trusts, because the trust income generally is held solely for the employee's benefit. As a result, the trust income generally is taxed to the employee only.[5]

---

1. Treas. Reg. §1.404(a)-12(b)(3); Let. Ruls. 9502030, 9302017, 9212024.
2. Let. Ruls. 9548015, 9548014. See also Let. Rul. 9450004 (employer allowed immediate deduction where employee could keep or contribute cash to employee-funded trust). See also Treas. Reg. §1.404(a)-12(b)(1); Let. Ruls. 9502030, 9417013, 9302017, 9212024, 9212019.
3. Let. Ruls. 9502030, 9417013, 9302017, 9212024.
4. Prop. Treas. Reg. §1.671-1(g) (employer not treated as an owner of any portion of a domestic, nonexempt employees' trust under IRC Section 402(b) if part of a deferred compensation plan, regardless of whether the employer has power of interest described in IRC Section 673 through IRC Section 677).
5. See Let. Ruls. 9548015, 9548014, 9450004. Compare Let. Rul. 9620005 (group of secular trusts, each with a separate employee grantor, pooled investment resources together to form a master trust, will be taxed as a partnership, thereby avoiding double taxation applicable to corporations).

3538. What is "a substantial risk of forfeiture" under IRC Section 83?

A person's rights in a Section 83 funded plan, where there has been a "transfer of property," are subject to a substantial risk of forfeiture[1] requirement under the IRC Section 83 definition. Full enjoyment of the property must be conditioned on the future performance (or the refraining from performance) of substantial services by any individual.[2]

On February 25, 2014, the IRS issued final regulations[3] clarifying the Section 83 definition of "substantial risk of forfeiture" (which are substantially similar to the proposed regulations released on May 29, 2012) as follows:

A risk of forfeiture may be established only through a service condition or a condition related to the purpose of the transfer.

Both the likelihood of a forfeiture event and the likelihood the forfeiture will be enforced must be considered in evaluating whether a service condition is related to a purpose of the transfer in establishing whether there is a Section 83 substantial risk of forfeiture.

Property is *not* transferred subject to a Section 83 substantial risk of forfeiture to the extent that an employer is required to pay the fair market value of a portion of such property to the employee if the employee returns the property. In other words, the risk that the value of the property will decline during a period of time is not a Section 83 substantial risk of forfeiture.

A nonlapse restriction, by itself, will not result in a Section 83 substantial risk of forfeiture.

In the case of equity compensation primarily, transfer restrictions mandated under the securities laws, including lock-up agreement restrictions, and restrictions related to insider trading under Rule 10b-5 under the Securities Exchange Act of 1934 [except as specifically outlined in Treasury Regulation Sections 1.83-3(j) and (k)] do NOT create a substantial risk of forfeiture.

These final regulations apply to property transferred on or after January 1, 2013. The proposed regulations can be relied upon for property transferred after May 30, 2012.

Planning Point: Planners should review the final regulations for the final guidelines that must be followed in order to create a valid Section 83 "substantial risk of forfeiture" for a Section 83 plan after January 1, 2013. For transfers made prior to this date, they may rely on the proposed regulations. It should be noted that the regulations appear to be an attempt by the IRS to better integrate the definitions of "substantial risk of forfeiture" under Sections 83 and 409A. In doing so, the clarifications do potentially have special implications for plans involving majority or sole shareholders of closely-held companies as noted herein. In addition, planners must now consider the proposed regulations, released in 2016, integrating Section 457 with Section 409A that address top hat 457(f) "ineligible" plans specifically covered by Section 409A (and other plans,

---

1. Note that there are currently seven definitions of "substantial risk of forfeiture" and "substantial limitation" (which is usually referred to a substantial risk of forfeiture) contained in the Internal Revenue Code and that they are not all the same. This can be very confusing to planners and attorneys alike. They are in IRC Sections: a.) 409A, b.) 83, c.) 457(f), d.) 457A, e.) 312, f.) 451 and g.) 61. "Substantial limitation," is commonly referred to as a "substantial risk of forfeiture," applicable to unfunded unsecured plans and is the least burdensome standard of the seven. However, to the extent an unfunded plan is also covered by 409A, its more restrictive form and operational requirements must be considered.
2. IRC Sec. 83(c)(1); Treas. Reg. §1.83-3(c)(1).
3. Treas. Reg. §1.83-3.

like severance plans) (Q 3602). 457(f) plans formerly looked to Section 83 regulations for their definition of a "substantial risk of forfeiture" and now, unexpectedly,[1] have their own separate and unique definition. This unique new 457 definition is generally a positive for the creation of most types of 457(f) plans, especially those involving deferral of vested compensation (for example, salary) as well as severance plans covered by 457.

Even with this clarification, however, whether there is a risk of forfeiture and whether it is substantial still largely depends on the facts and circumstances at the time the plan is created.[2]

Because the inquiry remains so fact-based, little definitive guidance as to the sorts of services considered substantial existed prior to the release of the proposed Section 83 regulations, and even this guidance may now need to be considered in light of the new final Section 83 regulations. The regularity of performance and the time spent in performing the required services tend to indicate whether they are substantial.[3] Furthermore, it is not clear how far into the future an arrangement must require substantial services to require adequate "future performance." Nonetheless, the regulations' examples describe arrangements requiring employees to work for periods as short as one or two years as imposing substantial risks of forfeiture, although two full tax years is probably the safe choice.[4]

Some things are clear. Requiring that property be returned if the employee is discharged for cause or for committing a crime will not create a substantial risk of forfeiture.[5] The IRS has indicated that benefits would be taxable once a participant has met age and service requirements under an IRC Section 457 governmental plan (Q 3584). Although the benefits remained forfeitable if participants were fired for cause, the IRS noted that forfeiture on termination for cause was not sufficient to constitute a substantial risk of forfeiture.[6]

A covenant not to compete will not ordinarily result in a substantial risk of forfeiture unless the particular facts and circumstances indicate otherwise.[7]

Similarly, the requirement that a retiring employee render consulting services on the request of a former employer does not result in a substantial risk of forfeiture, unless the employee is, in fact, expected to perform substantial consulting services.[8]

Special scrutiny will be applied in determining whether the risk of forfeiture is substantial if the case involves a property transfer from a corporation to a controlling shareholder-employee.

---

1. It was thought that the final 457/409A integration regulations would follow the IRS's preliminary position on this important definition stated in IRS Notice 2007-62, which downloaded the 409A definition rather than the Section 83 definition of "substantial risk of forfeiture," for use with 457(f) plans. However, the IRS proposed regulations covering 457 plans unexpectedly have an additional and unique definition of "substantial risk of forfeiture" for use with 457(f) plans, even though the proposed regulations note that a 457(f) plan must generally comply with both 457(f) as well as 409A form and operational requirements to achieve and maintain income tax deferral for plan participants.
2. Treas. Reg. §1.83-3(c)(1).
3. Treas. Reg. §1.83-3(c)(2).
4. See Treas. Reg. §1.83-3(c)(4), Ex. 1 and Ex. 3. For examples of service requirements that have constituted a substantial risk of forfeiture in the context of Section 457(f) plans prior to the current proposed 457 regulations (Q 3602), see generally Letter Rulings 9642046, 9642038, 9628020, 9627007, 9623027. However, these older rulings must now be considered in light of the new proposed 457 regulations.
5. Treas. Reg. §1.83-3(c)(2).
6. TAM 199902032.
7. Treas. Reg. §1.83-3(c)(2); see also Let. Ruls. 9548015, 9548014.
8. Treas. Reg. §1.83-3(c)(2).

In such situations, a restriction that would otherwise be considered to impose a substantial risk of forfeiture will be considered to impose such a risk only if the chance that the corporation will enforce the restriction is substantial.[1]

Planning Point: To the extent these new regulations are drawing down Section 409A concepts into the Section 83 definition of substantial risk of forfeiture with regard to the likelihood forfeiture conditions will be enforced, sole or majority shareholders (and perhaps even the relatives of such persons) in closely-held companies may have a difficult time creating plans for themselves under Section 83. This is because the control they exercise over such a plan raises the issue of whether any forfeiture provision is likely to be enforced, as in the *Ludden* case.

In addition, under Section 409A, a noncompete and a consulting agreement can never constitute a substantial risk of forfeiture under Section 83 as compared with Section 457(f) under the new proposed 457/409A regulations. However, the more stringent definition of "substantial risk of forfeiture" in Section 409A is used only to define the scope of the short term deferral exception under Section 409A to define the scope of the application of Section 409A coverage (and not the incidence of taxation) under the current regulations. In contrast, the phrase is now used to determine incidence of deferral or taxation under Section 83. This could mean a substantive transfer of the narrower 409A definition down into Section 83 more broadly.

Lack of a substantial risk of forfeiture under Section 409A means only that a plan cannot escape 409A coverage (as under the "short-term deferral" exception) and must comply fully with 409A to achieve deferral and avoid taxation, which then largely controls the incidence of taxation for constructive receipt purposes. Under Section 83 as to funded plans, it actually governs the incidence of deferral of taxation in the first place. This situation may cause great confusion for planners and attorneys.

Imposing a sufficient condition on the full enjoyment of the property is not in itself enough to create a substantial risk of forfeiture; the possibility of forfeiture if the condition is not satisfied must be substantial. This possibility may be substantial even if there are circumstances under which the failure to satisfy the condition will not result in forfeiture of the property. For example, the possibility of forfeiture is substantial where an employee would generally lose his or her deferred compensation on termination of employment before completing the required services, but would not forfeit those benefits if his or her early termination were due to death or permanent disability.[2] The possibility that a forfeiture might not be enforced in the event of normal or early retirement before the satisfaction of the condition might not undermine the substantial risk of forfeiture.

The risk that property will decline in value over time does not create a substantial risk of forfeiture. The example below, taken from the final regulations, illustrates.

> *Example:* Employer, ABC Corp., gives its employee, in connection with his performance of services for ABC Corp., a bonus of 100 shares of ABC Corp. stock. Under the terms of the agreement, employee is required to return the stock to ABC Corp. if he terminates his employment for any reason. However, for each year occurring after January 1, 2010, during which employee remains employed with ABC Corp.,

---

1. See Treas. Reg. §1.83-3(c)(3). Compare *Ludden v. Comm.*, 68 TC 826 (1977) (possibility of forfeiture did not amount to a substantial risk of forfeiture because there was too little chance that the shareholder-employees would cause themselves to be fired), aff'd on other grounds, 620 F.2d 700, 45 AFTR 2d 80-1068 (9th Cir. 1980).
2. Rev. Rul. 75-448, 1975-2 CB 55.

employee ceases to be obligated to return 10 shares of stock. Employee's rights in 10 shares each year for 10 years cease to be subject to a substantial risk of forfeiture in each year he remains employed.

Example 2: Same facts as above, except for each year that employee remains employed after January 1, 2010, ABC Corp. agrees to pay, in redemption of the bonus shares given to the employee if he terminates employment for any reason, 10 percent of the fair market value of each share of stock on the date of termination. Since ABC Corp. will pay employee 10 percent of the value of his bonus stock for each year (up to 10 years when the stock becomes 100 percent vested) he remains employed with ABC Corp., and the risk of decline in value is not a substantial risk of forfeiture, employee's interest in 10 percent of the bonus stock becomes substantially vested in each of those years.[1]

It is not clear whether one can effectively extend a substantial risk of forfeiture. One letter ruling has concluded that as long as the future services required of the employee were and would continue to be substantial, an agreement between the employer and the employee postponing the vesting date of restricted stock would not in itself trigger taxation of the stock.[2] The ruling generated controversy, particularly with respect to efforts to extend this reasoning to ineligible Section 457(f) plans prior to the release of the proposed 457/409A integration regulations. To the extent that the narrower Section 409A definition of substantial risk of forfeiture was substituted for the one in 457(f) by Notice 2007-62, it could not necessarily be used, because Section 409A prohibits extensions of the risk of forfeiture. The proposed 457/409A integration regulations (which did not follow Notice 2007-62) now allow for a continuation of a substantial risk of forfeiture, but under a narrow and restricted set of requirements that would not generally support this specific extension interpretation. See Q 3602.

3539. How is an employee taxed on the payment received from a nonqualified annuity or nonexempt trust?

Annuity payments are taxable to employees under the general rules in IRC Section 72 relating to the taxation of annuities (see Q 525 as to payments in annuitization phase, Q 513 as to payments in accumulation phase).[3] An employee's investment in the contract, for purposes of figuring the exclusion ratio, consists of all amounts attributable to employer contributions that were taxed to the employee and premiums paid by the employee, if any. Investment in the contract includes the value of the annuity taxed to the employee when the employee's interest changed from nonvested to vested.[4]

Payments under a nonexempt trust are also generally taxed under the same rules relating to annuities, except that distributions of trust income before the annuity starting date are subject to inclusion in income under the generally applicable "interest first" rule without regard to the "cost recovery" rule retained (for certain cases) by IRC Section 72(e)(5) (Q 525, Q 513).[5] Furthermore, a distribution from the trust before the "annuity starting date" for the periodic payments will be treated as distributed in the following order:

(1)   Income earned on employee contributions made after August 1, 1969

---

1.   Treas. Reg. §1.83-3(c)(4), Ex. 3 and 4.
2.   Let. Rul. 9431021.
3.   IRC Sec. 403(c).
4.   Let. Rul. 7728042.
5.   IRC Sec. 402(b)(2).

(2)   Other amounts attributable to employee contributions

(3)   Amounts attributable to employer contributions (made after August 1, 1969 and not previously includable in employee's gross income)

(4)   Amounts attributable to employer contributions made on or before August 1, 1969

(5)   The remaining interest in the trust attributable to employer contributions[1]

The IRS has privately questioned whether the annuity rules of IRC Section 72 are applicable to distributions to highly compensated employees from an employer-funded nonexempt trust under a plan that fails the minimum participation or the minimum coverage tests applicable to qualified plans (Q 3840, Q 3841); the taxation of such distributions is unclear (Q 3534).[2] In fact, according to the IRS website, the tax treatment of an employee who has participated in a failed qualified plan is as follows:

General Rule – Employees Include Contributions in Gross Income

Generally, an employee would include in income any employer contributions made to the trust for his or her benefit in the calendar years the plan is disqualified to the extent the employee is vested in those contributions.

Exceptions: There are exceptions to the general rule (see IRC Section 402(b)(4)):

- **If one of the reasons** the plan is disqualified is for failure to meet either the additional participation or minimum coverage requirements (see IRC Sections 401(a)(26) and 410(b)) and Pat is a highly compensated employee (see IRC Section 414(q)), then Pat would include all of her vested account balance (any amount that wasn't already taxed) in her income. A non-highly compensated employee would only include employer contributions made to his or her account in the years that the plan is not qualified to the extent the employee is vested in those contributions.

- **If the sole reason** the plan is disqualified is that it fails either the additional participation or minimum coverage requirements, and Pat is a highly compensated employee, then Pat still would include any previously untaxed amount of her entire vested account balance in her income. Nonhighly compensated employees, however, do not include in income any employer contributions made to their accounts in the disqualified years in that case until the amounts are paid to them.

Note: Any failure to satisfy the nondiscrimination requirements (see IRC Section 401(a)(4)) is considered a failure to meet the minimum coverage requirements.[3]

---

1.   Treas. Reg. §1.402(b)-1(c)(2).
2.   Let. Ruls. 9502030, 9417013.
3.   See IRS website at https://www.irs.gov/retirement-plans/tax-consequences-of-plan-disqualification, last reviewed by the IRS December 20, 2019.

If a distribution consists of an annuity contract, the entire value of the annuity, less the investment in the contract, is included in gross income.[1]

For applications of FICA and FUTA to deferred compensation payments, see Q 3576.

---

1.   Treas. Reg. §1.402(b)-1(c)(1).

PART XIII: UNFUNDED DEFERRED COMPENSATION

Overview

3540. What are the tax benefits for a participant of an unfunded deferred compensation agreement with an employer?

A properly constructed unfunded[1] nonqualified deferred compensation agreement can postpone payment of compensation for currently rendered services until a future date, with the intended objective of postponing the taxation of such compensation until it is actually received. Since the enactment of IRC Section 409A (generally effective as to contributions/deferrals to plans as of January 1, 2005), such an agreement, at least with respect to vested compensation, likely will create a plan that is covered by the additional tax law requirements of Section 409A, unless the plan is either specifically exempted by the statute or can claim an exception under the regulations. The IRS released proposed regulations in June 2016 that made amendments to clarify the final regulations under Section 409A (TD 9321, 72 FR 19234). This document also withdraws a specific provision of the notice of proposed rulemaking (REG-148326-05) published in the Federal Register on December 8, 2008 (73 FR 74380) regarding the calculation of amounts includible in income under Section 409A(a)(1). The provision is replaced by revised proposed regulations. These proposed regulations affect participants, beneficiaries, sponsors, and administrators of nonqualified deferred compensation plans.[2]

Section 409A also creates an entirely new and greatly expanded group of compensation plan types that may be covered by Section 409A under the law's broad definition of a "nonqualified deferred compensation plan" (see the nine plan types that follow). This definition constitutes an expansion beyond what historically was considered a deferred compensation plan and now pulls in almost all executive compensation plans and some employee benefit plans.

Under Section 409A, a nonqualified deferred compensation plan is one involving a deferral of compensation that is legally binding in the present tax year and not payable until a future tax year (beyond the current tax year plus 2½ months), and is not specifically statutorily exempted or excepted by regulation.

As noted, under the current Section 409A regulations, there are nine types or categories of nonqualified deferred compensation plans, per the so-called "aggregation rule," as follows:

(1)   Employee account balance plans (voluntary salary, bonus, commission deferral plans)

(2)   Employer account balance plans (defined contribution, "phantom stock" plans)

(3)   Employer nonaccount balance plans (defined benefit plans)

---

1.   "Unfunded" does not mean that assets may not be set aside in a sponsor's general asset reserve for a plan; just that they may not be escrowed from sponsor's general creditors or constitute "plan assets" under ERISA. It also means that the plan is an unsecured promise-to-pay subject to Sections 61 and 451, and not a "transfer of property" plan under Section 83.

2.   Reg. 123854-12, 81 FR 40569 (Jun. 22, 2016).

(4)   Split dollar life insurance plans (except for the two limited formats detailed in Revenue Ruling 2008-36)

(5)   Stock equity plans

(6)   Severance/separation plans

(7)   Reimbursement or fringe benefit plans

(8)   Foreign plans

(9)   Other miscellaneous plans

This list is duplicated for directors participating in covered plans.

Under a typical "pension" type deferred compensation agreement (primarily employee and employer account balance plans and employer nonaccount balance plans using 409A language), an employer promises to pay an employee fixed or variable amounts for life or for a guaranteed number of years or to pay out an account containing pre-tax contributions plus credited gains and losses. The employer can make this promise to an employee without creating current taxation, subject to compliance with IRC Section 409A, when applicable.

When the deferred amount is received, the employee may be in a lower income tax bracket, but at least has another future income source (Q 3574). Additionally, many employers use the employer-paid types (account or nonaccount balance) of plans to provide benefits in excess of the limitations placed on qualified plan benefits. For example, a Supplemental Executive Retirement Plan ("SERP"), in either an account balance or nonaccount balance design, for a selected group of executives generally provides extra retirement benefits. An "excess benefit plan" is a special kind of supplemental plan that addresses only the benefits lost under qualified plan limits and caps (Q 3608).

Nonqualified deferred compensation plans have been divided into two broad categories: (1) voluntary employee deferred compensation plans and (2) employer-paid supplemental plans. Both unfunded deferred compensation plans (governed by IRC Sections 61 and 451) and funded deferred compensation plans (governed by IRC Section 83) may be divided into these categories (Q 3532). Under prior law, taxation of these two plan categories was the same based on whether the plan was an unfunded plan (one that was merely an "unsecured promise-to-pay") or a funded plan (one that involved the "transfer of property").

The enactment of Section 409A, however, has added a new additional categorization: whether the plan (unfunded or unfunded) is covered or excepted from coverage from the additional Section 409A requirements. That is because Section 409A is additive tax law and only changes prior income tax law applicable to nonqualified deferred compensation to the extent specifically indicated. The term "nonqualified deferred compensation plans" should be understood to refer to both voluntary employee deferred compensation plans and employer-paid supplemental plans that are covered by Section 409A requirements, as well as all the other plan types now covered by Section 409A, unless exempted or excepted.

A "voluntary employee deferred compensation plan" involves an agreement between the employer and employee, whereby the employee defers receipt of some portion of present compensation (or a raise or bonus, or a portion thereof) in exchange for the employer's promise to pay a deferred benefit in the future. This has been referred to as an "in lieu of" plan. As noted, under Section 409A, these plans are employee account balance plans.

An "employer-paid supplemental plan" is a compensation benefit provided by the employer to an employee in the future in addition to all other forms of compensation; the employer promises to pay a deferred benefit, but there is no corresponding reduction in the employee's present compensation, raise, or bonus. Under Section 409A, these plans are employer account balance or nonaccount balance plans. If they are designed with a Section 409A substantial risk of forfeiture, and are paid in lump sum in the year the risk of forfeiture lapses or within 2½ months afterwards, a supplemental plan might be designed to be excepted under the Section 409A "short-term deferral exception".

3541. What requirements must be met by a private nonqualified deferred compensation plan?

An unfunded private nonqualified deferred compensation plan is a plan entered into with any employer <u>other than</u>:

(1)   a state;

(2)   a political subdivision of a state (e.g., a local government);

(3)   an agency or instrumentality of (1) or (2);[1] or

(4)   an organization exempt from tax under IRC Section 501.

Although private nonqualified deferred compensation agreements most frequently are entered into with employees of corporations, they also may be entered into with employees of other business organizations and with independent contractors.[2] For example, a director's fees can be deferred through an unfunded deferred compensation agreement with the corporation.[3] This remains true for plans covered by IRC Section 409A. If an employer or service recipient transfers its payment obligation to a third party, efforts to defer payments from the third party may not be effective.[4]

For rules concerning nonqualified deferred compensation plans sponsored by governmental or private tax-exempt not-for-profit employers, see Q 3581 through Q 3602.

---

1.   Federal credit unions, in additions to state chartered credit unions, per the IRS, are considered tax-exempt organizations for purposes of 457.

2.   Rev. Rul. 60-31, 1960-1 CB 174, as modified by Rev. Rul. 70-435, 1970-2 CB 100.

3.   Rev. Rul. 71-419, 1971-2 CB 220.

4.   Rev. Rul. 69-50, 1969-1 CB 140, as amplified in Rev. Rul. 77-420, 1977-2 CB 172 (deferral of physicians' payments from Blue Shield type organization ineffective); TAM 9336001 (deferral of plaintiffs' attorney's fees under structured settlement with defendants' liability insurers ineffective); *contra Childs v. Comm.*, 103 TC 634 (1994), *aff'd*, 89 F.3d 856 (11th Cir. 1996) (deferral of plaintiffs' attorneys' fees under structured settlement with defendant's liability insurers effective).

General Taxation Rules for Unfunded Plans

IRC Section 409A is *additive law* that further defines the income tax doctrine of constructive receipt. Therefore, prior income tax law and theories (for example, the economic benefit theory) continue to apply, unless specifically replaced by Section 409A. This means that a plan subject to Section 409A must comply with both prior income tax law (except as specifically changed) as well as Section 409A requirements. Plans that are statutorily exempted or excepted by regulations from the Section 409A requirements (such as amounts grandfathered from 409A coverage) must continue to comply with prior income tax law only.

Pre-409A Income Tax Law Requirements

1. An employer may contractually agree to pay deferred amounts as additional compensation, or employees may voluntarily agree pursuant to contract to reduce current salary.[1]

2. The plan must provide that participants only have the status of general unsecured creditors of the employer in bankruptcy and that the plan constitutes a mere unsecured promise-to-pay benefits by the employer in the future.

3. The plan also should state that it is the intention of the parties that it is unfunded for tax (and ERISA) purposes; that is without ERISA "plan assets."

4. The plan should prohibit and void the anticipatory assignment of the benefits by a participating employee.

5. The plan should define the time and form for paying deferred compensation for each event (e.g., retirement) that would entitle a participant to a distribution of benefits.

6. The plan should include any provisions necessary to designate and comply with controlling state law requirements.

These requirements continue after the enactment of Section 409A, and are the primary requirements for portions of plans that are grandfathered from 409A coverage or excepted from 409A coverage, such as plans that can claim the "short term deferral exception."

If the plan refers to a trust or other informal funding mechanism, additional rules must be satisfied (Q 3564, Q 3567).

3542. What is the doctrine of constructive receipt and how does it apply to nonqualified deferred compensation plans?

Under pre-409A income tax law, tax deferment is not achieved if, prior to the actual receipt of payments, the employee is in constructive receipt of the income under the agreement. Income is constructively received if the employee can draw upon it at any time. Income is not constructively received if the employee's control of its receipt is subject to substantial limitations or restrictions. Some agreements contain contingencies that may cause the employee to forfeit

---

1.   Rev. Rul. 69-650, 1969-2 CB 106.

future payments. So long as the employee's rights are forfeitable, there can be no constructive receipt.[1] The IRS has ruled, however, that the employee will not be in constructive receipt of income even though rights are nonforfeitable if the agreement is entered into before the compensation is earned and the employer's promise to pay is not secured in any way.[2]

IRC Section 409A created new requirements for elections to defer compensation for covered nonqualified deferred compensation plans.[3] Under pre-IRC Section 409A income tax law (which is still applicable to amounts grandfathered and plans excepted from Section 409A coverage), there was some conflict between the IRS and the courts with respect to the consequences of an election to defer compensation after the earning period commences. The IRS always has seemed to believe that a deferral election made after the earning period commences will result in constructive receipt of the deferred amounts, even if made before the deferred amounts are payable.[4]

For example, in TAM 8632003, the IRS found constructive receipt where a participant in a shadow stock plan elected, just prior to surrendering his shares, to take the value of his shares in 10 installment payments rather than in one lump sum. The IRS refused to permit further deferral of amounts already earned and determinable, believing that the fact that the benefits were not yet payable at the time of the election was an insufficient restriction on the availability of the money.[5] A plan allowing elections to defer bonus payments on or before May 31 of the year for which the deferral was effective did not cause constructive receipt. There was no express consideration of the effect of the election provision, however.[6]

In another ruling, contributions to a rabbi trust did not result in income to participants or beneficiaries until benefits would be paid or made available in the context of the plan allowing an election to further defer compensation through choice of the payout method after termination of services; there was no express consideration of the effect of the election provision.[7]

Pre-Section 409A, courts looked more favorably on elections to defer compensation after the earning period commenced but before the compensation was payable. For example, the Tax Court considered the same plan addressed in TAM 8632003, above, and reaffirmed its position that an election to further defer compensation not yet due under the original deferred compensation agreement does not necessarily result in constructive receipt.[8] Although the IRS did acquiesce in *Oates* and in the first *Veit* case, it tried to distinguish those cases and the second *Veit* case in TAM 8632003.

---

1. Treas. Reg. §1.451-1, 1.451-2.
2. Rev. Rul. 60-31, 1960-1 CB 174, as modified by Rev. Rul. 70-435, 1970-2 CB 100.
3. IRC Sec. 409A(a)(4).
4. The IRS made elections to defer prior to the tax year in which compensation is earned a requirement for a letter ruling on plans prior to enactment of Section 409A. Such IRS rulings are not available currently as to the income tax consequences of nonqualified deferred compensation plans.
5. See also Let. Rul. 9336001 (election to defer must be made before earning compensation to avoid constructive receipt); Rev. Proc. 71-19, 1971-1 CB 698, as amplified by Rev. Proc. 92-65, 1992-2 CB 428.
6. See Let. Rul. 9506008.
7. See also Let. Rul. 9525031.
8. See *Martin v. Comm.*, 96 TC 814 (1991). See also *Childs v. Comm.*, 103 TC 634 (1994), *aff'd*, 89 F.3d 856 (11th Cir. 1996); *Oates v. Comm.*, 18 TC 570 (1952), *aff'd*, 207 F.2d 711 (7th Cir. 1953), *acq.*, 1960-1 CB 5; *Veit v. Comm.*, 8 TCM 919 (1949); *Veit v. Comm.*, 8 TC 809 (1947), *acq.*, 1947-2 CB 4.

The 409A general rule requires an election prior to the tax year in which the compensation is to be earned, which is the historic position of the IRS. Because the IRS was charged by Congress in the Congressional Commentary to Section 409A to pursue plans not conforming to Section 409A, it could be expected that the IRS likely will challenge plans excepted from Section 409A, and perhaps even grandfathered plans, that generally do not follow the income tax guidelines established by Section 409A, especially this one governing fundamental tax deferral.

Planning Point: To date, the IRS has only continued to do some audits for general 409A compliance.[1] Staffing problems at the IRS have forced it to forgo any broader enforcement beyond covered plans, and the focus is currently on FICA tax compliance.

Whether Section 409A is applicable or not, special concerns are present if compensation is deferred for a controlling shareholder-employee, typically in the closely-held corporate situation. If a controlling shareholder-employee can (through control of the corporation) effectively remove any restrictions on immediate receipt of the money, the IRS can argue that he or she is in constructive receipt because nothing really stands between the shareholder-employee and the money.[2] It is hard to eliminate these concerns in advance, because the IRS continues to refuse to issue advance rulings on the tax consequences of a controlling shareholder-employee's participation in a nonqualified deferred compensation plan.[3] Courts seemed to be less willing to impose constructive receipt in such situations prior to Section 409A.[4]

Under Section 409A, the definition of "substantial risk of forfeiture" in the regulations embedded this IRS argument into law. The regulations to Section 409A prevent such a shareholder-employee from using the short term deferral exception to escape the coverage of Section 409A, even on a "vest and pay lump sum" Supplemental Executive Retirement Plan ("SERP"). However, they do not seem to prohibit such a nonqualified deferred compensation plan for such a shareholder-employee if the plan thereby fully complies with the documentary and operational requirements of the law. Such a plan could not claim the short term deferral exception to escape Section 409A coverage, even as to a SERP. Under the Section 409A regulations the shareholder's control causes a loss of the substantial risk of forfeiture needed to claim the short term deferral exception. Even then, the IRS still might attempt to attack a plan for such a shareholder-employee, even if the plan is otherwise fully complying with the form and operational requirements of Section 409A. Therefore, special consideration and review must be applied to such a situation before implementing any plan, whether a voluntary deferral or employer-paid supplemental design.

Finally, a nonqualified deferred compensation plan that is subject to registration as a security with the SEC, but that fails to register, may suffer adverse tax consequences. In such a case,

---

1.   The IRS indicated in the spring of 2015 that it was going to do an audit of only a small number of large companies due to undergo audit for FICA tax compliance, and that the results would be used to help create guidance for its audit staff. However, if these special 409A audits occurred, none of the results seem to have shown up in the IRS's release of its updated *Nonqualified Deferred Compensation Audit Technique Guide* in June, 2015. In fact, the portion covering 409A is such a small part of the new guide that there is little helpful information for practitioners as to structuring plans to avoid audit issues and the primary focus was on the FICA rules which seems to parallel the IRS's current audit focus.

2.   See, e.g., TAM 8828004.

3.   See Rev. Proc. 2008-3, Sec. 3.01(43), 2008-1 IRB 110, Rev. Proc. 2009-3, 2009-1 IRB 107.

4.   See, e.g., *Carnahan v. Comm.*, TC Memo 1994-163 (controlling shareholder's power to withdraw corporate funds is not sufficient to cause constructive receipt), *aff'd without opinion*, 95-2 USTC ¶50,592 (D.C. Cir. 1995).

a participant may be able to rescind the deferral of compensation under SEC rules. A right to rescind could cause the participant to be in constructive receipt of the deferred amounts. Currently, the IRS has not resolved either the nature or extent of any tax implications arising from a failure to register a plan with the SEC, and this is further complicated by the enactment of Section 409A. Further complicating matters, the SEC has not formally clarified in detail the nonqualified deferred compensation plans that are subject to the "security" registration requirements and has provided little useable informal guidance in this area, except to suggest that contemporary voluntary multi-account deferral designs might require registration.[1]

Section 409A

3543. What requirements are there for a private nonqualified deferred compensation plan under IRC Section 409A?

Congress imposed additional documentary and operational requirements in IRC Section 409A to avoid a current constructive receipt on a "nonqualified deferred compensation plan" at inception and during the life of a covered plan. Many of these new requirements actually are those that the IRS formerly required to receive a favorable private letter ruling on income tax deferral under a plan and so are not new.

Section 409A imposes requirements on plans in four primary areas:

1. Minimum plan documentation

2. Permissible Distributions

3. Elections to defer

4. Prohibited Accelerations

See Q 3544 to Q 3547 for a detailed discussion of each of these requirements.

Planning Point: Planners should assume that any compensation plan is covered by Section 409A and plan to comply with the form and operational requirements until and unless they have satisfied themselves that the plan (which may be for only a single person) is either 1.) specifically statutorily exempted – such as a 457(b) plan – or 2.) meets (or can be designed to claim) a regulatory exception – such as the short term deferral exception.

3544. What are the minimum plan documentation requirements for a private nonqualified deferred compensation plan under IRC Section 409A?

Under Section 409A, a covered plan must be compliant both in *form* (documentation) and *operation* (administration). Therefore, there are certain minimum requirements for plan documentation to comply with Section 409A at the outset. In general, any plan subject to Section 409A must meet the following minimum requirements.

---

1.   For a more detailed discussion of this thorny issue, see Part V., Insurance-Related Compensation, Tax Management Portfolio, 386-4th T.M., Brody, Richey, Baier, Bloomberg, BNA (2017); and "Securities Registration Requirements and Issues," pgs. 255-257, in Chapter 5, "SEC Considerations," The Advisor's Guide to Nonqualified Deferred Compensation, 2014 Edition, Richey, Baier, Phelan, National Underwriter Company."

As to Section 409A:

1. The plan must be in writing, but there are no IRS prototype plans available as is the case for qualified plans. In effect, a plan is in violation of Section 409A if it is a covered arrangement but not in writing. However, the plan may be in more than one document, such as a plan and joinder agreement. The IRS will currently not issue letter rulings in regard to 409A.[1]

    This also suggests that plans claiming exception from 409A ought to be in writing to make the exception from coverage clear if audited. There are indications that the IRS auditors are asking for an identification of those plans that are covered and those claiming a 409A coverage exception to include the relevant exception and justification in pre-audit requests.[2]

2. The plan must state either the amount of the deferred compensation or the method for calculating the amount and the plan also must state the time and form of payment distribution, which would include:

    a. all of the Section 409A rules for elections (and appropriate timing) to defer on salary, commissions, performance-based compensation bonuses, and non-performance-based compensation bonuses, and newly eligible participants as applicable (see Q 3545 and Q 3546); and

    b. all of the Section 409A permissible distributions, "earlier of" sequencing, and a prohibition against all other non-Section 409A distributions and accelerations (see Q 3547).

3. The plan must contain all the unique definitions (e.g., "separation from service") and key terminology (e.g., "leave of absence") from Section 409A that apply to the plan, including the special plan termination rules.

4. The plan should contain a "Section 409A interpretation clause" defining undefined, ambiguous, or missing plan definitions and other language consistent with Section 409A.

5. The plan should include the Section 409A compliant timing for distribution following a permissible distribution event.

6. The plan should state the inclusion or prohibition of permitted Section 409A acceleration events (e.g., domestic relations orders).

7. The plan should state the requirements for a voluntary plan termination by the employer.

---

1. Rev. Proc. 2019-3.
2. During early audits, several counsel shared pre-audit IRS written requests online at various tax blogs in the past several years, and generally suggested the wisdom of a written plans, even if claiming an exception to 409A coverage. This remains good advice to document the claimed exception for the sponsor and for the IRS in case of an audit of all its various plans.

8. The plan should include an indemnification provision that either accepts or refuses the responsibility of the employer for any Section 409A violations and the adverse tax consequences that may result.

9. The plan should state whether it will allow subsequent elections and whether a series of installment payments shall be treated as a single distribution or a series of individual distributions for purposes of the plan, and subsequent elections to extend deferral.

10. The plan should include a provision for a delay of the payment start date for six calendar months when there is a separation from service of "specified employees," including the desired optional "catch-up" treatment (the provision is required if the plan is sponsored by a publicly-traded company; the provision is conditional (or unnecessary) if the sponsor is a closely-held company or tax-exempt organization).

11. The plan should include a prohibition provision against crediting interest on any participant accounts during any period that the plan sponsor is not in compliance with the minimum funding requirements for any qualified defined benefit pension plan.

12. The plan optionally may include a provision for:

   a. the very limited Section 409A right of the employer to offset participant liabilities to the employer against a participant's account, unless extended in the normal course of business as outlined in Section 409A, which should be clearly documented if this very narrow exception to the rule will be relied upon;

   b. accelerated cash-outs for certain allowed small amounts (those amounts less than the annual $402(g)(1)(b)$ amount) upon a separation from service; and

   c. automatic cancellation of a participant's deferral election for the balance of the plan year upon a request for an "unforeseeable emergency" request.

As to continuing prior law:

1. The plan should contain a provision in which the employer contractually agrees to pay deferred amounts at a future date as additional compensation, or employees contractually voluntarily agree with the employer to reduce current salary.[1]

2. The plan must provide that participants only have the status of general unsecured creditors of the employer in bankruptcy and that the plan constitutes mere promise-to-pay benefits by the employer in the future.

---

1. Rev. Rul. 69-650, 1969-2 CB 106.

3. The plan also should state that it is the intention of the parties that it be unfunded for tax (and ERISA) purposes.

4. The plan should prohibit and void the anticipatory assignment of the benefits by a participating employee.

5. The plan should include any provisions necessary to designate and comply with controlling state law requirements.

3545. When can a participant in a private nonqualified deferred compensation plan receive a distribution of previously deferred compensation under IRC Section 409A?

Under Section 409A, a participant may only receive a distribution of previously deferred compensation upon the occurrence of one of six primary events.

- Separation from service (which has a detailed definition with only limited flexibility to modify)

- Date the participant becomes disabled (requires the Social Security definition of a disability)

- Death

- A fixed date or time (or pursuant to a fixed scheduled) specified in the plan at the date of the deferral

- A change in the ownership or effective control of the corporation or assets of the corporation, to the extent provided in regulations (but an equity investment by the federal government under the Troubled Asset Relief Program (TARP) is not considered a change in ownership or control)[1]

- The occurrence of an unforeseeable emergency[2]

Most of these events have definitions unique to Section 409A and *must* be used in covered plans. Generally speaking, the definitions are narrower than one might suppose, and have special rules. There are also a limited number of other regulatory permissible accelerated distribution events covering plan termination; domestic relations orders (DRO); payment to avoid conflict of interest statutes; payment of applicable employment (FICA) taxes and distribution withholdings; payment of amounts because of 409A violations; payment of "small amounts" under Section 402(g)(i)(B); payment of applicable local, state and foreign taxes; payment to avoid a "nonallocation year" under Section 409A(p) with respect to an ESOP sponsored by an S corporation; and payment of applicable employment and income tax withholding because of taxable vesting under Section 457(f) plan of a tax exempt entity (see Q 3547).[3]

---

1. Notice 2009-49, 2009-25 IRB 1093.
2. IRC Sec. 409A(a)(2)(A); Treas. Reg. § 1.409A-3.
3. See specific subsections, Treas. Reg. §§ 1.409A-1 and 409A-3 for permissible regulatory accelerations.

Under 409A, "specified employees" ("key employees" as defined under IRC Section 416(i)) of publicly-traded corporations may not take distributions until six calendar months after a 409A separation from service (or the date of death of the employee, if earlier).[1] In general, plan distribution in other situations and at earlier times, except as permitted under "combination elections", and is prohibited under Section 409A (see below).

Under final regulations, a change in ownership occurs when an individual or persons acting as a group acquires more than 50 percent of the total fair market value or total voting power of the corporation. Ownership under these rules is subject to attribution under IRC Section 318(a). A change in effective control occurs when (1) an individual or persons acting as a group acquires 35 percent or more of the total voting power of the stock of the corporation within a twelve month period or (2) where there is an adversarial change in a majority of the membership of the board of directors within a twelve month period. A change in the ownership of a substantial portion of the assets of the corporation occurs when an individual or persons acting as a group acquire assets equal to or greater than 40 percent of the total gross fair market value of the corporation.[2]

An "unforeseeable emergency" under Section 409A means "a severe financial hardship to the participant resulting from an illness or accident" of the participant, the participant's spouse, or a dependent (as defined in IRC Section 152(a)) of the participant, loss of the participant's property due to casualty, or other similar "extraordinary and unforeseeable circumstances" arising as a result of events beyond the control of the participant.[3] A nonqualified deferred compensation plan financial hardship withdrawal under this provision may be taken without taking a financial hardship distribution from any qualified 401(k) plan balance of the employee, and the plan may require that the balance of remaining voluntary employee deferral elections for the plan year be cancelled if a financial hardship distribution is taken from an employee's 401(k) plan balance (to comply with 401(k) plan financial hardship requirements).[4]

Planning Point: The IRS confirmed that a coronavirus-related distribution is a distribution that can be treated as a hardship distribution for nonqualified deferred compensation plan purposes. This allows nonqualified deferred compensation plans to amend their terms to allow either (1) automatic suspension of the individual's deferral elections throughout 2020 or (2) the right for qualified individuals to elect to suspend their deferral elections during 2020.[5]

Under the technical 409A Proposed Amendments in June 2016, the IRS clarified the definition of a "payment", which is important for meeting distribution and subsequent election requirements. A "payment" is made under Section 409A when any taxable benefit is actually or constructively received.[6]

---

1. IRC Sec. 409A(a)(2)(B)(i).
2. Treas. Reg. § 1.409A-3(i)(5).
3. Treas. Reg. § 1.409A-3(i)(3).
4. Treas. Reg. §1.409A-3(j)(4)(viii); Preamble Section VII.D., Section 409A Proposed Treasury Regulations, 9-23-2005.
5. Notice 2020-50.
6. *See generally*, Prop. Treas. Reg. § 1.409A-2 and 3, as amended by REG. 123854-12, 81 FR 40569, Para. 4 and 5 (June 22, 2016). *See also*, Preamble Section IV. To the REG.

3546. When must a participant in a private nonqualified deferred compensation plan elect to defer compensation under IRC Section 409A?

IRC Section 409A imposes timing requirements for participants electing to defer compensation. The general rule is that participants now generally must make deferral elections prior to the end of the preceding taxable year (December 31 in most cases) in which the income is earned.[1] There are two major exceptions to the general rule, as follows:

1. In the first year of a plan, a participant can make a pro rata election on compensation, based upon the number of days remaining in the year.

2. In the case of any "performance-based compensation," (PBC) as defined in the regulations to Section 409A, a participant must make an election to defer not later than six months before the end of the covered period (June 30 for a calendar year performance period) and performance period in the case of a fiscal year. The compensation must meet this unique Section 409A definition, which includes (among other important requirements) a twelve month performance period.[2] This rule also allows an election on fiscal year performance-based compensation to be made six months prior to the end of the fiscal year if that is the end of the performance period.[3] This rule changes the common practice on bonus compensation under prior law, especially as to new plans, to make elections late in the performance period. Now it is essential to start and enroll a deferral plan prior to the six month deadline to maximize the deferral opportunity.

    In the case of existing plans, participants need not make a final election on PBC until the six-month prior deadline, even if they make a preliminary election on it in the prior tax year.

Newly eligible participants must make an election within 30 days after the date of eligibility, but only with respect to services to be performed subsequent to the election. In addition, elections to defer on plans of the same Section 409A plan type (for example, all employee account balance plans) under the "aggregation rule," if there is more than one, must occur at the same time.

Planning Point: Employers with more than one plan of the same Section 409A type (e.g., employee account balance plans) only should allow enrollment in plans, including for newly eligible employees, during perhaps a mid-year and end-of calendar year enrollment window to comply with the requirement of a common enrollment period for similar Section 409A plans.

Section 409A also requires a plan to specify whether any elected series of installment payments shall be treated as a single distribution or a series of individual distributions.

---

1. IRC Sec. 409A(a)(4)(B)(i).
2. IRC Sec. 409A(a)(4)(B); Treas. Reg. §1.409A-2.
3. However, this rule only covers fiscal year performance-based compensation and not salary or other types of compensation. The IRS requires the election on these types of compensation to be made before the end of the taxable calendar year in advance of the beginning of the specific fiscal year. In effect, these other types of compensation cannot be deferred based upon a fiscal year.

Subsequent Elections: Using this rule, Section 409A allows participants to elect to make a "subsequent election" to delay the timing of an existing elected distribution or change the form of that distribution from a plan so long as the plan provides for such subsequent election right. To make such a subsequent election, the plan document and the administration must require the subsequent election to be made at least twelve months in advance of the original distribution date, and the subsequent election must delay the timing of the distribution at least five years from the date of the original distribution (unless made on account of disability, death, or an unforeseeable emergency).

In addition, there is a twelve month waiting period requirement after the subsequent election during which the old election must be applied for an event-based separation from service. An election related to a scheduled series of installment payments made pursuant to a fixed schedule and treated as a single distribution must be made at least twelve months in advance of the first such scheduled installment payment.[1] In general, it is usually preferable to create more flexibility for a participant in a plan by designating that a series of installment payments be treated as a series of individual distributions. However, it is necessary to have a plan administrator who can manage this complex flexibility and thereby comply with Section 409A to include it in a plan.

Current regulations generally also provide that a separately identified amount of an installment (either by percentage or fixed dollar amounts) that an employee is entitled to receive on a determinable date may be deferred subject to the subsequent election rules.[2] In effect, a portion of an installment, if a series of installment payments are treated as a series of individual distributions, may be subsequently deferred.

3547. When do prohibited (and permissible) acceleration of payment requirements apply to private nonqualified deferred compensation plans under IRC Section 409A?

Accelerations of plan distributions outside the six primary permissible listed distributions are prohibited. Final regulations, however, define specified circumstances under which a plan may permit the acceleration of plan payments and, in effect, widen permissible plan distributions, as follows:

(1)   To comply with a domestic relations order (a DRO, not a QDRO since there are no "plan assets" in a promise-to-pay nonqualified deferred compensation plan to levy against).

(2)   To comply with a conflict-of-interest divestiture requirement, including foreign conflict of interest per 2016 409A clarifications.[3]

(3)   To pay income taxes due on a vesting event under a plan subject to IRC Section 457(f).

---

1.   IRC Sec. 409A(a)(4)(C); Treas. Reg. §1.409A-2(b).

2.   Treas. Reg. §1.409A-2(b)(2).

3.   IRC Sec. 1043.

(4)   To pay FICA or other employment taxes imposed on compensation deferred under the plan.

(5)   To pay any amount included in income under IRC Section 409A.

(6)   To pay only the proper amount due, based on a valid unforeseeable emergency request.

(7)   To terminate a participant's entire interest in a plan:

    a.   after a separation from service where the payment is not greater than the IRC Section 402(g)(1)(B) amount- so-called "small amounts" ($19,500 in 2020 and 2021, $19,000 in 2019, $18,500 in 2018); or

    b.   in the calendar month prior to, or twelve months following, a Section 409A change in control event date.

(8)   To terminate the plan entirely at the employer's discretion (and distribute) so long as:

    a.   all the plans of the same Section 409A type are terminated;

    b.   all plan termination distributions will be made no earlier than twelve months, but not later than 24 months, following the date of termination; and

    c.   no new plan of the same Section 409A type is established for at least three years following the termination (or a retroactive violation occurs).

(9)   To terminate a plan pursuant to an IRC Section 331 corporate dissolution with the approval of a bankruptcy court judge.[1]

The IRS has informally advised[2] that a "salary advance" plan that allows an employer to offset any unpaid compensation advances against an employee's balance under a Section 409A non-qualified deferred compensation plan violates the Section 409A prohibition against acceleration of payments, and requires the amendment of the salary advance plan to prevent a violation of Section 409A for the deferred compensation plan (the terms of the two plans would be combined to determine a Section 409A violation).

Offsets and substitutions of plans to achieve an earlier distribution of compensation deferred under Section 409A generally are prohibited, except for a narrow exception that allows "debt incurred in the normal course of the service relationship" to be offset in the year debt is due up to $5,000."[3]

---

1.   Treas. Reg. §1.409A-3(j); Prop. Treas. Reg. REG 123854-12, June 22, 2016.
2.   CCA 200935029, Released 8-28-2009.
3.   Treas. Reg. §1.409A-3(j)(4)(D)(xiii).

3548. What is a "short term deferral exception" under Section 409A?

The "short term deferral exception" in the regulations to Section 409A is perhaps the most important exception to coverage by Section 409A for many compensation plans.

Its name is a misnomer because this regulatory exception actually can be claimed for plan benefit distributions far in the future so long as (1) the benefit is subject to a Section 409A "substantial risk of forfeiture," which is the most stringent definition of the seven definitions of "substantial risk of forfeiture" currently in the IRC, and (2) the plan distribution essentially is made in a lump sum on the lapse of the 409A substantial risk of forfeiture. Both of these requirements must be met to claim the Section 409A short term deferral exception.

For example, an employer-paid supplemental executive retirement plan (SERP) for a 45 year-old key employee might provide for payment upon vesting at age 62, but it might also provide for a forfeiture of the entire benefit if the executive terminates employment prior to age 62. If that promised benefit is also payable in a lump sum in that year of vesting (resulting in lapse of the substantial risk of forfeiture) or within 2½ months following that year, the plan might qualify as a so-called "vest-and-pay lump sum" plan to claim an exception from Section 409A coverage, even though the plan defers payment for 17 years. Under the short term deferral exception, no Section 409A "deferral of compensation" occurs if amounts are paid within 2½ months after the end of the tax year in which the employee obtains a legally-binding right to the amounts or any Section 409A substantial risk of forfeiture lapses. Under this rule, many multiyear bonus arrangements, including bonus life insurance or bonus annuity arrangements and "vest-and-pay lump sum" SERPs that require payments in lump sum promptly after the amounts "vest" (under Section 409A substantial risk of forfeiture requirements), as in the example, will not be subject to coverage under Section 409A.[1] Of course, in contrast, the employee loses the potential tax advantage of spreading the income across several tax years that installment payments might offer, so there are considerations other than the application (or nonapplication) of the Section 409A rules.

Planning Point: The 2007 regulations always permitted certain delays beyond the 2½ month distribution deadline that would not cause a loss of the short term deferral exception. The exception included delays for reason of administrative impracticality so long as the delayed payments were then made as soon as administratively practical. In June 2016, the IRS released proposed 409A clarification regulations that expand these permissible delays to include payments delayed in order to comply with federal securities or other applicable laws so long as the payment is made on the first date the employer believes the payment will not violate the applicable law.[2] These proposed regulations, which may be relied upon now, also allow for delay of payment of covered plan death benefits until the end of the calendar year following the year of a participant's death.

3549. What penalties can be imposed under Section 409A?

IRC Section 409A imposes substantial penalties for failing to meet either the Section 409A *form* (documentation) or *operational* (administration) requirements at inception and during the life of a covered plan. One of the peculiarities of Section 409A is that the tax falls on the

---

1.   Treas. Reg. §1.409A-1(b)(4).
2.   Prop Treas. Regulation, REG 123854-12, June 22, 2016.

participant and not the employer.[1] In the worst-case situation, any violation of the Section 409A documentary or operational requirements results in retroactive constructive receipt, with the vested portion of the deferred compensation being taxable to the participant back to the date of the violation, which might be the date of the intended deferral.[2]

However, in June 2016, the IRS released technical proposed amendments[3] to the inclusion regulations that limit the ability of plan sponsors to use the existing exclusion of nonvested amounts from taxation to make changes in the time and form of payment in a plan document without engaging the subsequent election five-year setback. Under the proposed amendment, the nonvested amounts of a benefit cannot be excluded from the calculation of the tax in the event of a violation unless the following conditions are met: 1) the plan provisions must be non-compliant prior to the correction of the document, meaning the amendments to the document must not create the noncompliance); 2) there must be no prior history of the employer making and correcting such intentional failures; 3) there must be a consistency in how the employer makes corrections in such cases; and, 4) there must be full conformity and compliance with the IRS guidance on such plan corrections (i.e., Notice 2010-6).[4] IRS treatment of prior instances of using the pre-June 22 exclusion of nonvested amounts in such intentional violation of 409A instances is uncertain. No specific grandfathering of such instances was provided in the June 2016 proposed amendments.

This proposed amendment apparently ends a practice of some sponsors intentionally mak-ing changes in time and form of payment (probably at the request of a senior plan participant) on individualized supplemental plans in which the benefits were substantially nonvested until a late distribution date, like retirement. By not applying the subsequent election five-year set-back rule, a sponsor violates Section 409A, but avoids reporting because of the prior exclusion for nonvested benefits. In such cases now, all amounts, whether non-vested or vested, must be included in the calculation of the penalty taxes.

In addition, IRS Counsel has taken the position that the correction of a form error prior to the date of vesting, *but in the tax year of the vesting date,* did not cure the plan sponsor's failure to correct the error in time. Therefore, the entire amount of the plan benefits must be included in taxable income under Section 409A. The Chief Counsel's memorandum indicated that 409A and the proposed regulations governing income inclusion require that the form correction should have been made before the end of the tax year prior to the tax year in which vesting occurred for it to have avoided application of the 409A inclusion rules for the error in form.[5]

---

1.   Based upon the logic in *Davidson v. Henkel*, No. 12-cv-14103, 2015 WL 74257 (E.D. Mich. Jan. 6, 2015), a plan sponsor can be held liable for extra FICA taxes imposed on plan participants because of an employer's failure to withhold and pay them during their working career, and there might also be exposure to a sponsor for the extra penalty taxes imposed on plan participants because of its failure to document and operate a plan according to the requirements of 409A. There might be a risk even if the sponsor disclaims such liability in the plan documentation.

2.   IRC Sec. 409A(a)(1)(A)(i); Prop. Treas. Reg. §1.409A-4 as to valuation when worst-case taxation is required.

3.   Per the release, the IRS provided that the proposed regulations can be immediately relied upon by taxpayers.

4.   *See generally,* Prop. Treas. Reg. § 1.409A-4, as amended by REG 148362-05, 73 FR 74380, Para. 6 (June 22, 2016); *See also,* Preamble Section VII to the REG.

5.   CCM 201518013 (May 1, 2015).

In addition to the normal income tax on the compensation, the participant must pay an additional 20 percent tax, as well as interest at a "premium" penalty rate 1 percent higher than the normal AFR underpayment rate.[1] Fortunately, there are now methods under Notices 2008-113 (in the case of operational errors), Notice 2010-6 (in the case of documentation error), and Notice 2010-80 (updating both prior Notices) for correcting many common documentary and operational errors that may avoid the full impact of taxation under Section 409A.

Planning Point: With regard to penalties for violations of Section 409A, at least one state – California – currently adds its own 5[2] percent excise state income tax penalty when the federal penalty is imposed for a Section 409A error. Planners should therefore check the relevant applicable state rules at the time any voluntary deferral plan is created, to determine the additional state income tax exposure for likely eligible participants. If the sponsor and its participants are substantially all located (and likely to remain) in a state(s) that also imposes its own penalty excise tax, a discussion of other potential approaches to a 409A nonqualified deferred compensation plan may be in order if the total potential federal and state income tax for an error appears excessive. If the plan desired is an employer-paid SERP, the 409A penalty state income tax possibility may be less of an issue, but still ought to be discussed.

3550. What is a "substantial risk of forfeiture" for Section 409A purposes?

The definition of "substantial risk of forfeiture" under Section 409A (409A SROF) further defines the constructive receipt doctrine and is more stringent than any of the other definitions under the IRC (Q 3538, footnote 1), especially as to closely-held companies and tax-exempt organizations. The 409A definition starts with the language from the Section 83 definition that there is substantial risk of forfeiture only if compensation is conditioned on the performance of substantial future services, the occurrence of a condition related to the purpose of the compensation, and the possibility of forfeiture is substantial. Whether there is a 409A SROF is based on the likelihood of enforcement, given all the facts and circumstances according to the IRS. This regulatory position presents the most problems as to participants who are majority or controlling shareholder and family members of such participants.

On May 29, 2012, the IRS released proposed Section 83 regulations clarifying "substantial risk of forfeiture" as to *funded* Section 83 "transfer of property plans" and it has drawn some language from Section 409A in doing so (Q 3538). On February 25, 2014, the IRS released final Section 83 regulations that are substantially similar to the proposed regulations. It appears that the IRS may be trying to better integrate Section 83 with 409A by dropping 409A concepts into these Section 83 regulations. However, in doing so, it may be making substantive changes to "substantial risk of forfeiture" requirements for Section 83 plans by adopting the more stringent 409A requirements, although the IRS has always claimed that its interpretation of regulations under Section 83 have never changed. Of course these changes to Section 83 impact only funded "transfer of property" plans and not unfunded promise-to-pay plans that are specifically exempt from Section 83 coverage.

---

1.   IRC Sec. 409A(a)(1)(B); Prop. Treas. Reg. §1.409A-4 as to valuation when worst-case taxation is required.
2.   This penalty excise tax in California was initially 20 percent but reduced to 5 percent on October 4, 2013. On that date, California signed into law an amendment to the California Revenue and Taxation Code reducing its state excise income tax rate effective for taxable years beginning *on or after January 1, 2013.*

For example, the final Section 409A regulations note the following as to certain specific circumstances that do not constitute a 409A SROF:

- Voluntary salary deferrals (because the deferrals are fully vested and so such a plan is covered and *therefore must comply with Section 409A requirements as to form and operation*);

- A covenant not to compete, even if the compensation is forfeitable in the event of on a breach;

- Compensation following an extension or modification of an existing 409A SROF (hence rolling vesting dates do not create a 409A SROF and, unless there is new consideration for the extension or modification, the amount will be treated as vested and subject to 409A compliance requirements);

- Compensation beyond the time at which the employee could have otherwise received it, unless the present value of the amount subject to the 409A SROF is materially greater than the present value of the amount the employee could have elected to receive in the absence of the 409A SROF;

Planning Point: These 2007 rules primarily created a problem for "ineligible" 457(f) voluntary deferral plans operating under the then-applicable guidance of IRS Notice 2007-62. This was because in the Notice the IRS proposed to substitute the 409A SROF definition for the definition found in 457(f). In addition, the IRS indicated that it did not believe any risks of forfeiture are real in a Section 457(f) voluntary deferral design unless there is a significant employer match that would provide a materially greater benefit on a present value basis to the employee for deferring and placing otherwise vested compensation back at risk. However, the IRS failed to provide guidance on a minimum safe harbor employer amount.

Then, in June 2016 the IRS released the long-delayed proposed 457/409A integration regulations. In these proposed regulations, the IRS created a unique definition of substantial risk of forfeiture for Section 457, and did not adopt the current 409A definition directly into Section 457. These proposed regulations still seem to drive planners toward Section 457(b) "eligible" plans as the preferred alternative for voluntary deferral plans under Section 457, especially if the employer does not and cannot make the substantial employer match as proposed.

However, if a match can be contemplated, the minimum safe harbor for a "materially greater" safe harbor match has been defined as more than 125 percent on a present value basis as required for a 457(f) "ineligible" voluntary deferral plan covering vested compensation (for example, salary, bonus deferral) to establish a substantial risk of forfeiture for purposes of a plan covered by Section 457. However, there is no guidance in the 2016 proposed regulations as to treatment or correction for a 457(f) plan that may have used a lesser employer matching percentage during the long interim in which there was no substantive guidance defining a "materially greater" match. Practitioners should check for guidance when the propped regulations are finalized.

- Payments based on attainment of a prescribed level of earnings, unless there is a substantial risk that this level may not be achieved;

- Payments based on an initial IPO unless the risk there will be no initial IPO is substantial from the beginning; and

- Stock options immediately exercisable in exchange for substantially vested stock, even if the ability to exercise the option would terminate on a separation from service.

In the first reported Section 409A case (where the facts occurred during the transition period in 2005 when there were no regulations and only the bare statute and IRS Notice 2005-1 to review), the Tax Court held in a summary opinion (meaning it is not legal precedent) that a surrender charge on an annuity was not a substantial risk of forfeiture. The case is confusing at best because the taxpayer was arguing that the situation was covered by Section 409A and a deferral existed, while the IRS argued only that there was a constructive receipt of income under Section 61 and made no 409A violation arguments at all.[1]

In 2016, IRS Chief Counsel advised an audit team in a memo that the use of a 25 percent matching formula on a continuation of a voluntary deferral of current salary until a future fixed date, but forfeitable (along with the match) was sufficient to create a materially greater present value amount to qualify as a 409A SROF.[2]

3551. What factors determine whether a Section 409A substantial risk of forfeiture exists if the individual has significant voting power in the entity paying the nonqualified deferred compensation?

Where individuals have significant voting power in the entity paying the nonqualified deferred compensation, the following relevant factors must be considered to determine if there is a 409A SROF:

- The employee-shareholders' relationship to the other shareholders and the extent of their control and potential control over the decision, and possible loss of control of the employee;

- The position of the employee at the employer and the extent to which the employee-shareholder is subordinate to the other employees, especially other employee shareholders;

- The relationship of the employee to the employer's officers and directors (i.e., whether they are family);

- The person or persons who would approve the employee's discharge; and

- The past actions of the employer in enforcing any restrictions on employees, especially employee-shareholders.[3]

---

1. *Slater v. Comm.*, T.C. Summary Opinion 2010-1, 1-11-2010.
2. CCM 201645012, Nov. 27, 2016. This CCM predated and anticipated the 125 percent PV increase (25 percent employer DC match) safe harbor incorporated into the June 2016 proposed 457/409A integration regulations.
3. *See generally*, Treas. Reg. §1.409A-1(d).

Of course, this means that majority or controlling shareholders in for-profit entities may find it difficult, if not impossible, to establish that there is a 409A SROF.[1] The failure to establish a 409A SROF in such situations apparently does not mean that a nonqualified deferred compensation plan cannot be created for such an employee-shareholder, or so it has been thought to date. This is because the 409A SROF definition is used for a special purpose under Section 409A, rather than to establish whether there is current taxation. Except in the case of 457(f) plans, based on its separate definition of substantial risk of forfeiture under the proposed regulations, the 409A definition is used to determine access to the short term deferral exception that allows the plan to entirely avoid compliance with the so-called 409A "detail" requirements. If a plan has no 409A SROF and cannot claim the short term deferral exception under the final 409A regulations, it must comply with all the form and operational requirements of Section 409A. Because Section 409A is additive income tax law, the plan would then also have to comply with the other applicable pre-409A IRC income tax sections (for example, Section 61/451 substantial limitation or risk of forfeiture requirements in the case of an unfunded deferred compensation plan) in order to achieve income tax deferral for the plan.

3552. What are the reporting and withholding requirements under Section 409A?

Section 409A requires both informational annual tax reporting and tax reporting of amounts in violation of Section 409A (to determine the special taxes). Under IRC Section 409A, employers are required to make an informational tax report on all employee deferrals for a year on a Form W-2 or a Form 1099-MISC, regardless of whether such deferred compensation currently is includable in gross income. These amounts are reportable for informational purposes, whether or not they are treated as wages under IRC Section 3401(a).[2] The IRS temporarily waived the informational reporting obligations of employers for 2005-2010.[3] The IRS has since indicated that no informational reporting will be required until the proposed regulations on income taxation under Section 409A are made final.[4] Employers should annually check with their administrator to determine if informational reporting will be required for the coming tax year.

Employers also must annually report amounts includable in gross taxable income under IRC Section 409A on a Form W-2 or a Form 1099-MISC for any documentary or operational violations of Section 409A. This includes violations that require "worst case" tax reporting for a violation, or amounts includible under the documentary and operational correction procedures allowed under current IRS Notices 2008-113, 2010-6, and 2010-80.

Amounts reportable for violations of Section 409A should be reported as wages on line 2 in Form 941 and then in Box 12 of Form W-2 using a "Z" code. *No code is added on Box 12 if the compensation is taxable but not subject to the penalties of Section 409A.* The amounts for an independent contractor should be reported as nonemployee compensation in Box 7 and Box 15b of Form 1099-MISC. This includible income is treated as supplemental wages

---

1.　It is less clear how these factors would be applied to 457(f) plans for employees in tax-exempt organizations that have no shareholders.
2.　IRC Secs. 6041, 6051.
3.　Notices 2005-1; 2005-94; 2006-100; 2007-89, 2008-115 and 2010-80.
4.　Prop. Treas. Reg. §1.409A-4. As of September 2020 these proposed income inclusion regulations have not yet been made final and annual reporting has not yet been made mandatory.

subject to withholding, but there is no requirement for an employer to withhold on the 20 percent excise penalty and late interest tax penalty amounts.[1]

3553. What are the correction procedures under Section 409A?

With respect to nonqualified deferred compensation plans, it is important to note that the IRS EPCS and the SCP correction procedures applying to qualified plans[2] *do not* apply to non-qualified deferred compensation plans, whether subject to Section 409A or not.

Fortunately, it is not always necessary to suffer worst case taxation under Section 409A for an unintentional error in either plan documentation or operation. The IRS has released three notices, one that addresses Section 409A documentation errors, Notice 2010-6,[3] one that addresses Section 409A operational administrative errors, Notice 2008-113,[4] and Notice 2010-80 that updates both on certain select issues.[5] All notices require that certain preconditions be met to take advantage of the special correction processes made available. In general, the notice correction procedures allow for corrections based on the timing of the correction of the error, the party involved (whether an "insider" or another employee), and in some cases the magnitude of the error.

The general remedy under the notices is to include in an employee's income only the amount in error, in the case of operational errors, or some specified portion of the amount, such as 50 percent or 25 percent in the case of documentation errors. The 20 percent excise tax and premium penalty tax is often avoided, unless the affected participant is an "insider" (applying SEC Section 16(b) named officer standards, including by analogy those in closely-held companies). Both the employer and the employee have to report the correction of the error on tax returns to the IRS to claim the benefit of these correction procedures, unless the error is caught and corrected in the year of error. In that case, reporting is not required.

Some commentators think that it also may be possible to correct some documentary and operational errors in covered plans outside the parameters of these three notices under correction concepts applicable prior to the enactment of Section 409A. However, it should be recognized that the IRS takes a strict constructionist view of errors and error correction under Section 409A, and is unlikely to agree with these alternative procedures, even though 409A is additive law and arguably historic contract and tax bookkeeping correction procedures should remain available. However, plans excepted from 409A coverage and grandfathered portions of plans would remain covered by these pre-409A correction procedures and not the formal correction procedures provided in the notices.[6]

---

1.   Notice 2008-115.
2.   See generally, Rev. Proc. 2008-50 effective for qualified plan errors after 1-1-2009, as modified and superseded in part by Rev. Proc. 2013-12, Rev. Proc. 2016-51 and Rev. Proc. 2018-52.
3.   Notice 2010-6, 2010-3 IRB, 1-6-2010.
4.   2008-51, 12-23-2008.
5.   Notice 2010-80, 2010-51 IRB 853.
6.   See for example, Olshan, Regina & Schohn, Erica, Expert Q&A on Correcting Section 409A Documentary Violations, Practicallaw.com, October, 2010; Baker, Rosina, 409A Failures: Correcting Outside of the IRS's Formal Correction Programs, Presentation at DC Bar Luncheon Program, February 25, 2010, available at ipbtax.com; and Barker, Rosina & O'Brien, Kevin, Document Failures in the Section 409A Plan: Correcting With and Without Notice 2010-6, Pension & Benefits Daily, BNA, April 12, 2010.

Notices 2009-113 and 2010-6 were expanded in late 2010 under Notice 2010-80. Notice 2010-80 modified Notice 2008-113, governing operational errors, to eliminate employer and employee reporting when an operational error correction is made within the same year as the error. It also modified Notice 2010-6, governing documentation errors, to allow correction of severance/separation plans with incorrect release of claims provisions if completed by December 31, 2012, and to allow nonqualified plans "linked" to other nonqualified plans (e.g., excessive benefit plans) and stock plans to use Notice 2010-6 to make corrections for document failures prior to that date. However, this last opportunity to correct the form errors outlined in Notice 2010-80 expired on December 31, 2012.

Documentary Error Correction

In the case of documentation errors, there are some errors that may be corrected without an amendment or paying any tax or penalties at all. Notice 2010-6 provides an extensive digest of various (but not all possible) documentation errors and the remedies that permit the employee to report less than the amount that would be required in the worst case Section 409A taxation situation and avoid the full Section 409A 20 percent excise and premium interest penalty taxes in many cases. Notice 2010-6 highlights specific documentation errors, with corrective procedures and costs.

Because it is focused on language and structures that create errors under Section 409A, it also provides a useful checklist for plan drafting to avoid common Section 409A drafting errors for various types of Section 409A-covered plans. Notice 2010-6 also gives new plans a grace period of twelve months from the effective date to correct errors found in the plan documentation.

Operational Error Correction

In the case of operational errors, Notice 2008-113 defines operational errors based on Section 409A requirements. It organizes them into useful categories of Section 409A operational violations, such as distributions made before the six month delay period for highly compensated employees. It outlines the Notice 2008-113 special corrective procedure required to correct that category of error without having to incur the worst case tax event. In general, full relief is available when operational errors involving any employee are discovered and corrected in the same tax year, and by the second tax year in the case of employees that are not "insiders," as defined under Section 16(b) of the federal securities laws notwithstanding whether the employer is a public or private corporation. In other words, the "insider" rule for 409A correction purposes applies to public companies and also to private, closely-held for-profit and tax-exempt organizations by analogy.

Planning Point: Notice 2010-6 allowed a final opportunity to correct documentation errors in plans not later than December 31, 2010, and to have these corrections apply retroactively back to the January 1, 2009, effective date for actual document compliance. As of January 1, 2011, this opportunity passed, and sponsors now must use Notice 2010-6, as modified by Notice 2010-80 to make formal corrections. In addition, all errors in plans, whether of a documentary or operational nature, usually can be corrected in order to minimize the negative tax impact on an employee if the error is identified and corrected sooner rather than later, especially if caught and corrected in the same tax year. Therefore, plan sponsors should routinely audit their plans in the late fall to discover and correct any operational or documentation errors before the end of the current tax year. They should also build in a review audit in the first year of a plan in order to catch initial plan drafting errors and then correct them during the correction grace period provided for new plans that do not generally constitute an error or require formal correction under Notice 2010-6.

Planning Point: On May 9, 2014, in a subcommittee meeting at the American Bar Association annual conference, the IRS announced that it was launching a new, limited CIP 409A audit. Although the audit was to impact only 50 public companies also targeted for an audit on employment taxes, the audit was used to sharpen IRS future audit practice on 409A plans for even broader audits that will surely follow.[1]

This and prior IRS 409A audit initiatives suggest the wisdom of periodic "self-audits" of both the required **documentary** and **operational** compliance. A periodic self-audit makes sense anyway, since the special correction programs, which provide a less than worse-case results under the penalty provisions of 409A, are NOT available for companies once they are in an IRS audit. Moreover, the IRS currently applies a strict application of 409A penalties when they are discovered in audit. Therefore, it is recommended that companies routinely self-audit their 409A plans annually for **operational** compliance. Documents can be reviewed less frequently, but certainly should be reviewed any time they are amended or restated. However, compliant plan documentation and operation should always be in sync at all times.

3554. How is the penalty tax under Section 409A calculated?

If it is necessary to compute the worst case scenario, the directions for completing the calculations, including the calculation of the late premium penalty interest, as applicable, can be found in Proposed Treasury Regulation Section 1.409A-4. This proposed regulation for calculation of the tax under Section 409A was issued in December 2008, and was subject to a proposed amendment in 2016 as to the inclusion or exclusion of nonvested amounts under the anti-abuse rule. Both the 2008 and 2016 proposed amendments are still not yet final as of the date of this publication.

One of the positive elements in the calculations under the 2008 proposed regulations was that the calculation applied only to vested benefit amounts unless there was an indication that vesting was being used as a subterfuge to avoid the application of Section 409A. In general, this anti-abuse rule provided that amounts would not be treated as unvested (hence would require inclusion) to the extent there is an indication of a pattern or practice of permitting changes of the time and form of payment on unvested amounts contrary to the rules providing for such changes (primarily the so-called "subsequent election" rule).

The anit-abuse rule has since been made more stringent)by proposed 409A technical clarifications regulations released in June, 2016 to address the apparent issue of abusive changes in timing or form of payment being made to plans, especially with long vesting periods. The anti-abuse rule now provides that any unvested amounts will be treated as vested for purposes of income inclusion if there is a change in a plan provision otherwise not permitted by 409A as to time and form of payment and has otherwise to comply with the applicable 409A change rules.

---

1. However, there has been little evidence of any results from any such CIP audit. Even the IRS's revised *"Nonqualified deferred Compensation Audit Techniques Guide,"* released on June 9, 2015 has little additional detail on what the Service will look for when it audits plans that might be covered by 409A as versus the information gained from its first set of 409A audits back soon after the final regulations were issued.

To remain unvested, there must be a reasonable good faith basis to conclude: 1) the original provision did not meet 409A requirements, and 2) the change is necessary to bring the plan into compliance with the form requirements. The proposed technical regulations actually provide examples of patterns of permitting impermissible change in time and form of payment, and dictate the appropriate, 409A correction procedure to be applied.[1]

Planning Point: Under this revised anti-abuse portion of the unvested amounts noninclusion exception rule, corrections cannot now made on a SERP design with vesting delayed until nearly retirement (as many SERPs for key employees in closely-held companies are structured), and still be able to make corrections to the plan for errors during nearly the entire period of the plan, if the form correction were made in a tax year prior to the tax year in which separation from service occurred,[2] without worrying about imposition of a tax under Section 409A. This is because the benefits will be treated as vested, and therefore includible in any calculations for an error, unless the error is discovered at that late date and the change made is necessary to assure compliance. Even then, if the time and form of payment would be changed, the 409A rules for changes in the timing and form of payment would need to be followed, and the appropriate correction procedure must be followed as part of the error correction.

Of course, such plans might be better designed as a plan excepted from 409A coverage entirely, so as to avoid IRS questions on whether the exclusion of unvested amounts will be recognized. Presumably, the IRS would ignore this rule if the plan is drafted outside the requirements of Section 409A, or if there appears to be a pattern of ignoring Section 409A with regard to the plan, or making periodic changes to plan provisions that are not necessary to bring a plan into compliance, or change a provision that is already compliant.

3555. What rules apply to correction of errors in nonqualified deferred compensation plans excepted from Section 409A?

The IRS procedures for the voluntary correction of errors in qualified pension plans (e.g., VCP) do not apply to the correction of errors in nonqualified deferred compensation plans. Moreover, the correction of errors in connection with nonqualified deferred compensation plans was not the subject of much discussion prior to the enactment of Section 409A. However, there were legal theories for the correction of both documentation and operational administrative errors in connection with nonqualified deferred compensation plans that existed prior to Section 409A (Q 3553).

Most documentary errors, in general, were corrected under various legal theories for the reformation of contracts (such as correction of "scrivener errors") because nonqualified deferred compensation plans are contracts. Likewise, longstanding tax bookkeeping theories and principles were applied to correct operation plan administration errors, such as the correction of incorrectly calculated participant phantom account balances (Q 3553).

Where plans can claim a regulatory exception from Section 409A coverage or are grandfathered from Section 409A coverage, these pre-409A legal theories remain the appropriate methods for correcting both documentary and operational plan administration errors. Some

---

1.   Prop Treas. Regulation, REG 123854-12, June 22, 2016.
2.   *See,* CCA 201518013 (April 14, 2015) in which the IRS Chief Counsel's Office took the position that a correction of a plan error prior to the vesting date, *but not prior to the tax year in which the vesting date occurred,* was made too late to prevent an inclusion of all the plan benefit amounts to participants for the failure of form compliance under Section 409A.

commentators believe these pre-409A legal theories still can be used to correct errors as to 409A-covered plans not covered by Notices 2008-113 and 2010-6 (as modified by Notice 2010-80), and even as to errors specifically covered by these notices. The fact that Section 409A is additive law would seem to support this position. However, the IRS takes a strict view as to the correction of errors in 409A covered plans and is unlikely to agree with corrections made outside the notices at this stage, except as to grandfathered and 409A-excepted plans, and plans that fall under the short term deferral exception (Q 3548).

3556. Does Section 409A apply to independent contractors?

IRC Section 409A generally does not apply to amounts deferred under an arrangement between an employer and either an accrual-based independent contractor or an unrelated independent contractor. If both the employer and the independent contractor are accrual-based taxpayers, the agreement is not a nonqualified deferred compensation plan covered by Section 409A. However, the IRS has clarified that a "service recipient" may be an entity and not just a natural person.[1]

In addition, if, during a contractor's taxable year in which an amount is deferred, the contractor provides significant services to each of two or more service recipients that are unrelated, both to each other and to the independent contractor, the arrangement does not involve a deferral of compensation under Section 409A; the plan is not covered by Section 409A. For this exception, a safe harbor rule provides that an independent contractor will be treated as providing significant services to more than one service recipient where not more than 70 percent of the total revenue of the trade or business is derived from any particular service recipient or group of related service recipients. Unfortunately, there is no three-of-five or similar multiyear feature in this safe harbor rule.[2]

Practice Point: The IRS has clarified that when an employee changes status to an independent contractor the former employee will be treated as having separated from service for purposes of 409A if at the time of separation the level of services to be reasonably expected would result in a separation of services under the employee rules (generally less than 20-50 percent of the prior level of services).[3]

3557. What are Section 409A's effective dates, compliance deadlines and grandfathering rules?

The requirements of Section 409A generally apply to amounts deferred (or prior unvested amounts) after December 31, 2004. The requirements also apply to amounts deferred prior to January 1, 2005, if the plan under which the deferral is made is "materially modified" after October 3, 2004. There is an exception for material modifications made pursuant to IRS guidance. The IRS deferred the date to comply in both form and operation with the final regulations under Section 409A until December 31, 2008, and actual compliance began as of January 1,

---

1.   Prop Treas. Regulation, REG 123854-12, June 22, 2016.
2.   Treas. Reg. §1.409A-1(f)(2)(C)(iii).
3.   Op. Cite., F. 1.

2009.[1] Prior to January 1, 2009, plans were required to operate in "good faith" compliance with Section 409A documentary and operational requirements.[2]

The proposed 409A technical clarification regulations that change the final 409A regulations can be relied upon until the clarifications are made final.[3] The 457/409A integration regulations apply to compensation deferred under a plan for calendar years after the date the rules are published as final. However, they may be relied on immediately.[4] Unfortunately, there is no grandfathering or transition language for plans impacted by any the changes, especially as to ineligible 457(f) plans, for the long period between the final regulations and the 2016 release date of proposed regulations for such plans.

It should be noted that, under IRS Notice 2010-6, addressing documentation errors, sponsors were given until not later than December 31, 2010, to make corrections to documents not made compliant by December 31, 2008, and to have these corrections deemed retroactively in compliance as of the January 1, 2009 actual compliance deadline under Section 409A (see prior discussion on correction of documentation and operational plan errors in Q 3553). This deadline has passed and generally has not been extended except for certain specific corrections outlined in Notice 2010-80 that expired after December 31, 2012.

Finally, plans with certain assets in offshore rabbi trusts were given only until December 31, 2007 to disconnect or terminate the trust so as to comply with the 409A(b) funding requirements. Notice 2008-33 provided temporary guidance on complying with these requirements. Currently, no regulations on Section 409A(b) have been released, so further guidance as to the structuring of assets in such rabbi trusts is not yet available. A plan is "materially modified" if a new benefit or right is added or if a benefit or right existing as of October 3, 2004 is materially enhanced and such addition or enhancement affects amounts earned and vested before January 1, 2005. The reduction of an existing benefit is not a material modification.[5] Adding a participant right to a grandfathered plan that it did not possess, even though it was technically permissible under Section 409A, will be considered to be a material modification (for example, an "unforeseeable emergency" distribution right).

Planning Point: Employers should use great care in making any modifications to existing pre-409A deferred compensation arrangements until they are paid out to avoid the application of IRC Section 409A. According to the final regulations, a "material modification" that causes loss of grandfathering may be considered to be a formal plan amendment and may occur simply by virtue of an employer's exercise of administrative discretion in the plan participant's favor. Any amendment effected by form or practice that adds a beneficial right to a plan, even if it was allowed prior to the enactment of Section 409A and remained permissible after enactment (for example, a financial hardship provision), can cause loss of grandfather protection.

---

1.   Notice 2007-86, 2007- 46 IRB 990; Notice 2006-79, 2006-43 IRB 763.
2.   Notice 2005-1.
3.   Prop. Treas. Regulations, REG 123854-12, June 22, 2016.
4.   Prop. Treas. Regulations, REG 147196-07, June 21, 2016.
5.   Treas. Reg. §1.409A-6(a)(4).

3558. What elements of an unfunded arrangement met regulatory requirements before the enactment of Section 409A?

Prior to the enactment of Section 409A, the IRS generally would issue advance determination rulings concerning the tax consequences of an unfunded arrangement if the arrangement met the requirements outlined below. Some of the requirements parallel those now required in IRC Section 409A.[1] Currently, the IRS generally will not issue a letter ruling to a plan sponsor on the income tax consequences of a plan under Section 409A and does not plan to issue any prototype documents under Section 409A (there were no prototype documents prior to the enactment of Section 409A either).[2]

Any initial election to defer compensation generally had to be made before the beginning of the period of service for which the compensation was payable, regardless of the existence of forfeiture provisions. If any election other than the initial election to defer compensation could be made after the beginning of the period of service, the plan had to set forth substantial forfeiture provisions that had to remain in effect throughout the entire period of the deferral. The plan had to define the time and method for paying deferred compensation for each event (such as retirement) entitling a participant to benefits. The plan could specify the date of payment or provide that payments would begin within 30 days after a triggering event.

If the plan provided for the early payment of benefits in the case of an "unforeseeable emergency," that term was defined as an unanticipated emergency caused by an event beyond the control of the participant or beneficiary that would cause severe financial hardship if early withdrawal were not permitted. The plan also had to provide that any early withdrawal would be limited to the amount necessary to meet the emergency. Language similar to that in Treasury Regulations Sections 1.457-2(h)(4) and 1.457-2(h)(5) could be used. The plan had to provide that participants had the status of general unsecured creditors of the employer and that the plan constituted a mere promise by the employer to pay benefits in the future. The plan also had to state that it was the intention of the parties that it be unfunded both for tax and ERISA purposes. The plan had to provide that a participant's rights to benefits could not be anticipated, alienated, sold, transferred, assigned, pledged, encumbered, attached, or garnished by the participant's or the participant's beneficiary's creditors.[3]

3559. What are the deferred compensation rules applicable to foreign nonqualified entities under Section 457A?

In the Emergency Economic Stabilization Act of 2008, Congress created new IRC Section 457A to impose immediate taxation on deferred compensation where the employer is a foreign "nonqualified entity" (as defined in the law) that is not subject to U.S. taxation. This section is comparable to Section 409A, which potentially applies to nonqualified deferred

---

1. Rev. Proc. 2009-3, 2009-1 IRB 107, 2008-1 IRB 110. It should be noted that many plans operated without a letter ruling pre-409A anyway because of the IRS's rigid positions on some features and provisions as versus favorable court decisions.

2. Rev. Proc. 2008-61, 2008-30 IRB 180 (superseded by Rev. Proc. 2018-3), amplifying Rev. Proc. 2008-3, 2008-1 IRB 110. Also see Section 3.01(67), Rev. Proc. 2020-3.

3. Rev. Proc. 2009-3, Sec. 3.01(42), 2009-1 IRB 107; Rev. Proc. 71-19, 1971-1 CB 698, as amplified by Rev. Proc. 92-65, 1992-2 CB 428.

compensation paid by any entity, U.S. domestic or foreign. In addition, 457A applies to both cash and accrual method taxpayers while Section 409A applies to just cash method taxpayers.

Under IRC Section 457A, all compensation deferred under a nonqualified deferred compensation plan of a nonqualified entity is includable in gross income of a plan participant when there is no longer any Section 457A substantial risk of forfeiture of the rights to such compensation. IRC Section 457A has its own definition of substantial risk of forfeiture that defines a substantial risk of forfeiture as applicable "only if" a person's rights are conditioned on the future performance of substantial services.[1] This definition is therefore not exactly the same as that in Section 409A but is generally consistent. For instance, Section 409A includes attainment of performance goals in addition to performance of substantial services. However, the 2016 409A technical amendments make it clear that these types of plans may also be covered by both Sections 409A and 457. The 2016 proposed regulations for 457(f) and those for nonelective deferred compensation plans[2] under Section 457(e)(12) do not substitute for or supersede 409A compliance requirements. In such cases, the plan must comply with Section 409A and 457 in addition to Section 457A, if and as necessary, which makes for complex compliance coordination indeed.[3]

IRC Section 457A defines a nonqualified entity as (1) any foreign corporation, unless substantially all of its income is "effectively connected with the conduct of a trade or business in the United States" or is "subject to a comprehensive foreign income tax," or (2) any partnership, unless substantially all of its income is allocated to persons other than "foreign persons with respect to whom such income is not subject to a comprehensive foreign income tax" and "organizations which are exempt from tax under this title."[4] (IRC Section 457A provides a limited exception for deferred compensation payable by foreign corporations that have "effectively connected income" under IRC Section 882.)

A "comprehensive foreign income tax" is the income tax of a foreign country if there is an applicable comprehensive income tax treaty between that country and the United States or the Secretary of the Treasury is otherwise satisfied that it is a comprehensive foreign income tax.[5]

IRC Section 457A generally applies to nonqualified deferred compensation within the same broad scope as IRC Section 409A. IRC Section 457A explicitly applies to all stock options and stock appreciation rights, even those issued with the option price or measurement price at fair market value.[6] IRC Section 457A also extends the 2½ month short term deferral exemption in IRC Section 409A to twelve months, meaning that IRC Section 457A does not apply to compensation received during the taxable year following that year in which the compensation is no longer subject to a substantial risk of forfeiture.[7]

---

1.   IRC Sec. 457A(d)(1)(A).
2.   Only a Section 457(e)(11)(A)(ii) length of service award program (LOSAP) is not considered a "nonqualified deferred compensation plan" for purposes of Section 409A.
3.   Prop Treas. Reg., REG 123854-12 June 22, 2016.
4.   IRC Sec. 457A(b).
5.   IRC Sec. 457A(d)(2).
6.   IRC Sec. 457A(d)(3)(A).
7.   IRC Sec. 457A(d)(3)(B).

If the amount of any deferred compensation taxable under IRC Section 457A is not determinable at the time it is otherwise includable under that section, it is subject to a penalty and interest when so determinable. In addition to the normal tax, the amount includable is subject to a 20 percent penalty tax and interest on the underpayment of taxes at the normal underpayment rate plus 1 percent.[1]

IRC Section 457A applies to deferred amounts attributable to services performed after December 31, 2008. Congress also directed the IRS to provide guidance within 120 days on amending plans to conform to IRC Section 457A and providing a limited period of time to do so without violating IRC Section 409A.

In 2017, the Treasury Department and the IRS indicated they would issue regulations applicable as of December 8, 2017 providing the relief for plan distributions made for taxes on pre-2009 457A foreign deferred compensation. The agencies also indicated taxpayers can rely on the relief until the regulations are finalized. The coming regulations will permit the acceleration of payments under a nonqualified deferred compensation plan to pay federal, state, local, and foreign income taxes due on pre-2009 section 457A deferrals that are includible in gross income.

Specifically, the Notice indicates Treasury Department and the IRS intend to issue regulations providing that a change in the time and form of payment under a nonqualified deferred compensation plan to pay federal, state, local, and foreign income taxes on pre-2009 section 457A deferrals will not be treated as an impermissible acceleration under sections 409A(a)(3) and 1.409A-3(j)(1). These regulations will also provide that, to the extent a deferred amount attributable to services performed before January 1, 2009, was earned and vested before December 31, 2004, and is not otherwise subject to the requirements of section 409A due to the effective date rules under section 1.409A-6, a change in the time and form of payment of the deferred amount to pay federal, state, local, and foreign income taxes on pre-2009 section 457A deferrals will not be treated as a material modification of such arrangement under section 1.409A-6(a)(4). The relief provided in these regulations will apply only to the extent that that the amount of any distribution to pay federal, state, local, and foreign income taxes on pre-2009 section 457A deferrals is not more than an amount equal to the federal, state, local, and foreign income tax withholding that would have been remitted by an employer if there had been a payment of wages equal to the income includible by the service provider under section 801(d)(2) of TEAMTRA.[2]

3560. What are the tax consequences of a transfer of interests in a nonqualified deferred compensation plan to a qualified plan?

Under Section 409A, "substitutions" of another benefit involving a nonqualified deferred compensation plan results in a prohibited acceleration of the nonqualified benefit that is immediately taxable.[3] In a pre-409A private letter ruling, the IRS determined that employees electing to cancel their interests in an unfunded nonqualified deferred compensation plan in exchange

---

1.   IRC Sec. 457A(c).
2.   IRS Notice 2017-75, 12-8-2017.
3.   Treas. Reg. § 1.409A-3(f).

for substitute interests in a qualified plan would be taxable on the present value of their accrued benefits in the qualified plan upon the funding of those new interests. They would have to include the value of future benefits attributable to future compensation when the cash, which otherwise would have been received under the nonqualified plan, would have been includable.[1] Under Section 409A, such a transaction should also constitute a violation of 409A that attracts immediate inclusion and penalties.

Planning Point: This IRS letter ruling was released prior to, but is largely consistent with, Section 409A, which broadly prohibits "substitutions" of benefits, and deems them a prohibited acceleration that results in immediate taxation and the application of penalty taxes. Therefore, such a substitution should be taxable under Section 409A. However, this prohibition does not apply to an annual transfer from a nonqualified plan to a qualified 401(k) plan that occurs within the framework of a "wrap-around" nonqualified plan, which remains potentially possible under Section 409A, so long as the IRS guidance on the technique is followed.[2] Nor does Section 409A apply to the process of using alternative qualified nondiscrimination testing rules to determine and then allocate the largest possible benefit into the qualified plan as between an excess benefit nonqualified plan and the qualified plan.

3561. What ERISA requirements are imposed on deferred compensation employee benefit pension plans?

Deferred compensation employee pension benefit plans may be required to meet various requirements under ERISA, including reporting, funding, vesting and fiduciary requirements, unless they can find an exemption from coverage and meet those ERISA exemption requirements.[3]

Certain pension type plans, including "top hat" plans for an unfunded "select group," of management or "excess benefit plans" (Q 3608), and plans that provide payments to a retired partner or a deceased partner's successor in interest under IRC Section 736, are exempt from some or all of these more onerous ERISA requirements.[4] For exempt plans, there is currently only a one-time short-form filing report at the inception of an ERISA-exempt plan, no funding or vesting requirements, and only a written plan document (which is necessary for purposes of Section 409A anyway) and a claims procedure (recently revised as to disability claims) as nominal partial fiduciary responsibility. As of January 1, 2017, the one-time filing must now be made online at the DOL website (See Q 3562). For comparison, "employee welfare benefit plans", like split dollar insurance plans, also have certain available ERISA exemptions that parallel those for ERISA pension benefit plans, but they are not the same. Section 162 bonus life insurance programs, when properly designed and operated, are not ERISA "employee benefit plans," pension or welfare, at all and would be expected to escape all ERISA requirements.[5]

---

1. Let. Rul. 9436051.
2. The approved wrap plan format is contained in IRS Let. Rul. 9436051, as modified by Section 409A. However, note that the ERISA rules that require a very limited amount of sponsor delay to deposit qualified plan contributions may apply to further limit the use of the nonqualified wrap-around 401(k) mirror plan technique.
3. See, generally, ERISA, Titles I and IV. ERISA covers "employee pension benefit" plans and "employee welfare benefit" plans. The exemptions are different for pension type plans (ex. SERP) versus welfare benefit (e.g., split dollar) plans.
4. ERISA Secs. 4(b), 201, 301, 401, 4021.
5. See *Mozingo v. Trend Personnel*, No. 15-11263 (5th Cir. App. Ct. Aug. 13, 2016).

In a 2017 case involving a nonqualified deferred compensation plan, a U.S. Appellate Court has affirmed a lower district court holding that a company can change its phantom crediting rates on employee deferrals into the plan prospectively without violating its fiduciary duties under ERISA. The court said in a de novo review that the changes appeared proper on the facts and were an expected normal exercise of the plan's authority and judgment of discretion concerning crediting exercises crediting indices, and were uniformly applied to all plan participant. In effect, the court said that participants have no contractual right to a specific expectation of specific crediting indices over the life of a plan.[1]

In a 2018 case involving a nonqualified deferred compensation plan, another U.S. Appellate Court held a plan participant had no standing to make a claim against the plan sponsor for violating its fiduciary duty or engaging in a prohibited transaction in order to recover benefits or obtain a declaratory judgment against the plan sponsor as to the participant's qualified as well as nonqualified plans. In this case, the Siemen's Corporation transferred the employee participant's specific nonqualified deferred compensation plan benefit liabilities as a part of a sale of a division of the sponsor's business Sivantos, Inc., the buying company. The buying company agreed to assume all the plan liabilities, including those of the participant, as part of the purchase. The participant was upset because the buying company was much smaller and financially less significant than Siemens. The Appellate Court affirmed the district court dismissal of the case for slightly different reasons saying the plaintiff's claim did not shown an "injury in fact' of an invasion of a legally protected interest" that is "concrete and particularized" and there is a casual relationship between the injury and the conduct complained of" and a "likelihood" that the injury will be redressed by a favorable decision. The Appellate court said the claims were too speculative in the absence of a real showing of actual loss, or failure to pay or some similar injury, even though the participant alleged that the informal COLI funding behind the plan in a Rabbi Trust was eliminated thereby reducing the security of the participant's benefits.[2]

In considering this decision, it should be noted that nonqualified deferred compensation plans are not mandated and cannot escrow or trustee assets for a plan without causing current income taxation to plan participants. Moreover, plan sponsors are not even required to informally create a general asset reserve (as in this case of COLI in Rabbi Trust) to help support a plans liabilities, unless the plan requires it, which it apparently did not. Hence there was fiduciary duty violated in the plan sponsor's actions under the facts.

3562. What rules govern "top hat" employee pension benefit plans?

Under ERISA, a "top hat" pension benefit plan is an unfunded plan maintained "primarily" to provide deferred compensation for a "select group of management or highly compensated employees".[3] The determination of whether a plan is offered to a "select group" is a facts and circumstance determination.[4] The factors that are to be applied and the weight to be given each to determine whether any specific group qualifies as an ERISA select group remains in

---

1. *Plotnick v. Computer Sciences Corporation*, No. 1q6-1606 (4th Cir Ct App. Dec. 8, 2017, aff'g 182 F. Supp.3d 573 (2016)).
2. *Krauter v. Siemens Corporation*, No. 2-16-CV-02015 (3rd Cir. Ct, App. Feb. 16, 2018).
3. ERISA Sec. 201(2), 301(a)(3), 4021(b)(6); also see DOL Reg. Section 2520.104-23 providing an alternative, one-time short-form of reporting.
4. See, e.g., *Demery v. Extebank*, 216 F.3d 283 (2d Cir. 2000) ("select group" requirement was met where plan was offered to 15.34 percent of employees, since they were all either management or highly compensated employees).

much dispute.[1] The DOL inserted itself into the ongoing debate among the federal circuits by filing an amicus brief in the *Bond* case in 2015 to support its interpretations of the exemption, including its own so-called "qualitative" requirement.[2] However, one federal district court has expressly rejected this as a requirement to claim the exemption.[3] In one strange case, where all management employees were eligible for a plan, the plan did not meet the select group requirement because the group was apparently not select enough.[4] The maximum amount a court has approved is 15.4 percent of the workforce,[5] but less is desirable. The inclusion of even one nonhighly compensated employee might cause loss of the exemption under the DOL's position as described in its amicus brief.

The second requirement to claim the select group exemption is that the plan be "unfunded" for ERISA purposes. Generally speaking, this requirement means that there should not be any ERISA "plan assets" in connection with the plan, but only general assets supporting the plan's liabilities. In a 2015 case, a court reaffirmed that the question to ask is whether an employer has set aside funds, separate from its general assets, for payment of plan benefits and whether plan beneficiaries have a legal right greater than that of a general, unsecured creditor to the corporation's assets. Applying this question, the court held that the use of employer-owned COLI contracts did not cause a plan to be funded for ERISA purposes.[6]

Top hat plans are subject to a different standard of review from other ERISA plans, because they are exempt from most of ERISA's substantive rules. They are subject to a de novo review unless the plan documents expressly grant deference to the plan administrator, rather than to the "arbitrary and capricious"[7] standard of *Firestone v. Bruch*.[8]

There is another ERISA exemption available for "excess benefit plans" that make up the difference between what the qualified plan pays and what it would have paid but for the caps on qualified plan benefits to the highly compensated. This type of plan is also commonly referred to as a "top hat" plan since by its definitional terms it applies only to highly compensated employees.[9]

Planning Point: Plans claiming either the "top hat" or "excess benefit" ERISA exemption must file a one-time letter statement with the DOL for a new pension benefit plan. This statement relieves the sponsor from having to file the more complex and detailed Form 5500 annually on the plan and all other pension reporting and disclosure requirements. This one-time statement must be filed within 120 days of the inception of a plan.[10] Historically, the filing involved a letter statement

1.   Consider, *Tolbert v. RBC Capital Markets Corporation*, 758 F.3d 619 (5th Cir. App. Ct. 2014), *Bond v. Marriott International, Inc.*, 971 F.Supp.2d 480 (Dist. Ct. Md. Dist. 2013).

2.   DOL amicus brief filed July, 2015, *Bond v. Marriott International, Inc.*, 971 F.Supp.2d 480 (Dist. Ct., Md. Dist. 2013). *Also see specifically*, DOL Adv. Opin. 90-14A. The US Chamber of Commerce, ERIC and ABC also filed its own amicus brief in opposition to the DOL position brief on July 2, 2015. SIFMA filed an amicus brief in *Tolbert* Case. The three amicus briefs make for comprehensive reading of the issues and positions.

3.   *Sikora v. UPMC*, 153 F.Supp. 3d 820 (2015).

4.   *Carrabba v. Randalls Food Mkts, Inc.*, 252 F.3d 721 (5th Cir. 2001), *cert. denied*, 26 EBC 2920 (US Sup. Ct. 2001).

5.   *See*, Footnote 2, the *Demery* Case.

6.   *Huber v. Lightforce USA*, 367 P.2d 228 (2015).

7.   *Goldstein v. Johnson & Johnson*, 251 F.3d 433 (3d Cir. 2001).

8.   489 U.S. 101 (1989).

9.   ERISA Sections 4(b)(5), 201(7), 301(a)(9), 4021(b)(6).

10. *See* DOL. Reg. Section 2520.104-23(b).

mailed to the DOL. However, as of January 1, 2017, this filing must be made electronically on the DOL's website.[1]

As to income taxation, top hat plans will generally be Section 409A "nonqualified deferred compensation plans" and thereby be covered by 409A additive requirements sections (as well as prior income tax law), unless an exception to Section 409A coverage can be claimed (example, short term deferral exception for SERPs).

3563. What is the "economic benefit" theory and how does it apply to nonqualified deferred compensation plans?

Under the economic benefit income tax theory, an employee is taxed when the employee receives something other than cash that has a determinable, present economic value. The danger, in the nonqualified deferred compensation context, is that an arrangement for providing future benefits will be considered to provide the employee with a current economic benefit capable of valuation. Current taxation arises when assets are unconditionally and irrevocably paid into a fund or trust to be used for the employee's sole benefit.[2]

An employer can establish a reserve for satisfying its future deferred compensation obligations while preserving the "unfunded and unsecured" nature of its promise, provided that the reserve is wholly owned by the employer and remains subject to the claims of its general creditors. A mere promise to pay, not represented by notes or secured in any way, is not regarded as a receipt of income.[3] Unfunded plans do not confer a present, taxable economic benefit.[4] An unfunded and unsecured promise of future payment is specifically excluded from coverage under IRC Section 83, which codifies the economic benefit theory.[5]

It generally has been accepted that deferred compensation benefits can be backed by life insurance or annuities (or any other assets) in a general asset reserve of the employer without creating a currently taxable economic benefit to a participant.[6]

In the old *Goldsmith* case,[7] the court found that the promises of preretirement death and disability benefits provided the employee with a current economic benefit – current life insurance and disability insurance protection – even though the corporation was the owner and beneficiary of the policy, which was subject to the claims of its general creditors. The court did not find constructive receipt of the promised future deferred compensation payments, but ruled that the portion of the premium attributable to life, accidental death, and disability benefits was taxable as a current economic benefit to the employee. The *Goldsmith* case appears to be anomalous. Since it was decided, the IRS has not treated pre-retirement death or disability benefits paid

1.   To access the DOL's electronic statement filing site go to www.dol.gov/efiletophatfilinginstructions.html. The site provides instructions as well as the electronic form to file. Of interest, the new statement is slightly different than the prior letter filing format (e.g., requires name and address, including email, of plan administrator). However, the DOL has indicated in the Preamble to the Proposed Regulations changing the filing procedures that no substantive change in content is contemplated by the new statement.

2.   *Sproull v. Comm.*, 16 TC 244 (1951), *aff'd per curiam*, 194 F.2d 541 (6th Cir. 1952); Rev. Rul. 60-31, sit. 4, 1960-1 CB 174.

3.   Rev. Rul. 60-31, 1960-1 CB 174, 177; Rev. Rul. 70-435, 1970-2 CB 100.

4.   *Minor v. U.S.*, 772 F.2d 1472, 85-2 USTC ¶9717 (9th Cir. 1985).

5.   Cf. Treas. Reg. §1.83-3(e).

6.   See, e.g., *Casale v. Comm.*, 247 F.2d 440 (2d Cir. 1957) (the IRS has said it will follow this decision, Rev. Rul. 59-184, 1959-1 CB 65); Rev. Rul. 72-25, 1972-1 CB 127; Rev. Rul. 68-99, 1968-1 CB 193; TAM 8828004; Rev. Rul. 60-31, 1960-1 CB 174.

7.   *Goldsmith v. U.S.*, 586 F.2d 810, 78-2 USTC ¶9804 (Ct. Cl. 1978).

out as ordinary income under a nonqualified deferred compensation plan as creating a currently taxable economic benefit.[1] This income tax treatment can be compared with that intended by Congress for deferred compensation plans under IRC Section 457 (Q 3600).

It should be noted that the economic benefit tax theory has not been eliminated by the enactment of Section 409A, because Section 409A is *additive* law and actually further defines constructive receipt. Therefore, the IRS still can apply this theory and all other pre-409A income taxation theories (e.g., assignment of benefit) to impose taxation on deferred compensation when supported by the facts of any nonqualified deferred compensation arrangement situation, regardless of whether it is covered by, grandfathered, or excepted from Section 409A coverage. Therefore, the nonassignability and unfunded plan provisions commonly placed in nonqualified deferred compensation, whether covered by or excepted from 409A coverage, remain a necessity to reduce the chance of the IRS applying the economic benefit as well as assignment of benefit tax theories to impose premature income taxation on plan participants.

Informal Funding Arrangements

3564. How does an informal funding affect a private IRC Section 451 unfunded nonqualified deferred compensation account balance or non-account balance plan?

An IRC Section 451 unfunded deferred compensation account balance or nonaccount balance arrangement cannot be formally funded. That is, the employee cannot be given any secured interest in any trust or escrowed fund or in any asset, such as an annuity or life insurance contract, without adverse tax consequences to a participant. If a secured interest is given, the arrangement is treated as a funded arrangement under IRC Section 83 and must be handled according to its specific tax deferral requirements (Q 3532 to Q 3539).

A nonqualified deferred compensation account balance or nonaccount balance arrangement can be informally funded without jeopardizing tax deferral, even after enactment of Section 409A. Under 409A(b), an employer can specifically set aside assets as a general reserve in a rabbi trust (Q 3567) to provide funds for payment of deferred compensation obligations, as long as the following requirements are met:

(1)   the plan participants have no interest in those assets and they remain the employer's property, subject to the claims of the employer's general creditors in bankruptcy;

(2)   the trust or assets supporting the plan are not placed offshore (in light of IRC Section 409A(d));

(3)   the trust does not receive assets or pay out deferred compensation to participants during the period of an employer's declining economic circumstances [as detailed in IRC Section 409A(b)(2)]; and

---

1.   *See*, e.g., Let. Ruls. 9517019, 9510009, 9505012, 9504006, 9427018, 9403016, 9347012, 9323025, 9309017, 9142020.

(4)   there is no transfer of assets to a trust during a period the sponsor's qualified defined benefit pension plan, if any, is "at risk" or underfunded.[1]

Rabbi trusts remain very popular devices for reserving assets acquired to support the liabilities of a nonqualified deferred compensation account balance or nonaccount balance arrangement. Currently, however, there are no proposed regulations for the so-called "funding" rules under Section 409A; there is only the bare language of the law under 409A(b). Practitioners should watch for these regulations, which are likely to further clarify these "funding" prohibition requirements in connection with the use of such a trust.

Even before Section 409A(b), the IRS historically did not consider a plan that sets aside assets in an escrow account to be "formally funded" if the assets are subject to the claims of the employer's general creditors.[2] Of course, the Section 409A prohibition on the use of offshore trusts to hold assets intended to hold general company assets adds a new requirement as do the others listed above to the use of such a trust.

It has been accepted for some time that an employer may informally fund its obligation by setting aside an employer-owned fund composed of life insurance contracts, annuities, mutual funds, securities, etc., without adverse tax consequences to the employee so long as the fund remains the unrestricted asset of the employer and the employee has no interest in it.[3] Thus, a deferred compensation plan should not be regarded as "funded" for income tax purposes (although there is another issue of funding for ERISA purposes) merely because the employer purchases a life insurance policy or an annuity contract to ensure that funds will be available when needed. The Tax Court stretched these rules a bit in ruling that payment obligations to attorneys under a structured settlement were unfunded even though the attorneys were annuitants under the annuities financing the obligations; it is not clear if this decision can be extended to more traditional nonqualified deferred account balance and nonaccount balance plans.[4] In general, the sponsoring company must be the owner and recipient of all benefits from any insurance contracts in the general reserve for the arrangement to be treated as unsecured and thereby unfunded for income tax purposes, although the use of a split dollar endorsement of portions of the death benefit proceeds to a participant on an EOLI/COLI supporting a plan does not seem to be a problem for the IRS.

Since the enactment of Section 409A, securing or distributing deferred compensation on the employer's falling net worth or other financial events unacceptably secures the payment of the promised benefits.[5] This now includes hybrid rabbi/secular trust arrangements that distribute assets from nominal rabbi trusts to secular trusts on the occurrence of triggering events based on the employer's financial difficulty. Under any such arrangement, compensation otherwise successfully deferred is immediately taxable as a violation of Section 409A, and is subject to its

1.   *Minor v. U.S.*, 772 F.2d 1472, 85-2 USTC ¶9717 (9th Cir. 1985); see also *McAllister v. Resolution Trust Corp.*, 201 F.3d 570 (5th Cir. 2000); *Goodman v. Resolution Trust Corp.*, 7 F.3d 1123 (4th Cir. 1993).

2.   Let. Ruls. 8901041, 8509023.

3.   Rev. Rul. 72-25, 1972-1 CB 127 (annuity contract); Rev. Rul. 68-99, 1968-1 CB 193 (life insurance).

4.   *Childs v. Comm.*, 103 TC 634 (1994), *aff'd*, 89 F.3d 856 (11th Cir. 1996).

5.   IRC Sec. 409A(b)(2); Notice 2006-33, 2006-15 IRB 754.

20 percent excise tax, plus premium penalty interest on the underpayment of taxes (the normal underpayment AFR rate plus 1 percent).[1]

As noted, setting aside assets in an offshore trust to directly or indirectly fund deferred compensation now also unacceptably secures the payment of the promised benefits under the funding provisions of Section 409A.[2] Under any such arrangement, the compensation otherwise successfully deferred is immediately taxable and subject to a 20 percent excise tax, and premium penalty interest is due at the normal underpayment AFR rate plus 1 percent.[3]

Both the Section 409A prohibition on financial triggers and on offshore trusts apply even to deferrals of compensation earned and vested on or before December 31, 2004 (and thus not generally subject to the requirements of Section 409A). The IRS provided transition relief through December 31, 2007, for amounts otherwise subject to Section 409A(b), if those assets relate to compensation deferred on or before December 31, 2004, and if those assets were set aside, transferred, or restricted on or before March 21, 2006.[4] This relief was not extended to coincide with the extension of compliance relief under Section 409A to December 31, 2008. Compliance with the Section 409A funding requirements needed to be completed by December 31, 2007.

In addition, the Section 409A funding requirements also prohibit top executives – individuals described in IRC Section 162(m)(3) or subject to Section 16(a) of the Securities Exchange Act of 1934 – from setting aside assets in a rabbi trust or other informal funding device during a "restricted period." The restricted period is any period during which the employer is in bankruptcy, during which a company's qualified defined benefit plan is in "at-risk" status (underfunded per the statutory requirements), or during the six months before or after an insufficient plan termination. The restrictions apply to any transfers or reservations after August 17, 2006. If any Section 409A prohibited transfer occurs, compensation otherwise successfully deferred is immediately taxable and subject to a 20 percent excise tax and premium penalty interest on the underpayment of taxes is due at the normal underpayment AFR rate plus 1 percent.[5]

Pre-409A, one court had ruled that a "death benefit only" plan backed by corporate-owned life insurance was "funded" for ERISA purposes.[6] The decision has been criticized and largely limited to its unusual facts by other courts. However, the result, if ever accepted by other courts, could have far reaching tax implications.

If a plan is "funded" for ERISA purposes (meaning that assets are ERISA "plan assets"), it generally is required to satisfy ERISA's exclusive purpose rule and to meet certain minimum vesting and funding standards. Once these requirements are met, the plan may no longer be considered "informally funded" for tax purposes as well, and adverse income tax consequences may follow. In 1987, the same court that decided *Dependahl* distinguished it from a second case,

---

1.   IRC Sec. 409A(b)(5).
2.   IRC Sec. 409A(b)(1); Notice 2006-33, 2006-15 IRB 754.
3.   IRC Sec. 409A(b)(5).
4.   Notice 2006-33, 2006-15 IRB 754.
5.   IRC Secs. 409A(b)(3), 409A(b)(5).
6.   See *Dependahl v. Falstaff Brewing Corp.*, 491 F. Supp. 1188 (E.D. Mo. 1980), *aff'd in part*, 653 F.2d 1208 (8th Cir. 1981), *cert. denied*, 454 U.S. 968 (1981) and 454 U.S. 1084 (1981).

concluding that a nonqualified deferred compensation plan informally funded with life insurance contracts was not funded for ERISA purposes and thus was not subject to minimum vesting and funding standards.[1] The court distinguished this case from *Dependahl*, in part, by noting that the *Belsky* agreement stated specifically that the employee's only right against the employer was that of an unsecured creditor.[2]

Over the years, the Department of Labor ("DOL") has issued various advisory opinions permitting the use of an employer-owned asset to finance different types of plans while the plans maintained their "unfunded" status under ERISA.[3] The DOL has stated that plan assets include any property, tangible or intangible, in which the plan has a beneficial ownership interest.[4] According to footnote three in Advisory Opinion 94-31A, the "beneficial ownership interest" analysis is not relevant in the context of excess benefit and top hat plans.[5] The DOL reasoned that its position was supported by the special nature of these plans, the participating employees' ability to affect or substantially influence the design and operation of the plan, and the rulings of the IRS surrounding the tax consequences of using rabbi trusts with these plans. The kind of plan asset analysis relevant in that context is not clear, although the DOL does have a working premise that rabbi trusts meeting with IRS approval will not cause excess benefit or top hat plans to be funded for ERISA purposes.[6] The impact on the ERISA treatment of assets after application of the Section 409A funding rules is yet to be determined. The basic concept of the prior DOL position that a plan is "unfunded" for ERISA purposes if it is "unfunded" for income tax purposes still would seem to work.

Pre-409A, a key associate insurance policy used to informally fund a plan should be held by the employer (as owner) and not distributed to the employee at any time; otherwise, the employee would be taxed on the value of the contract when received.[7] This result would not change under Section 409A since a key associate policy, as an informal funding device, generally would not be subject to Section 409A when set up correctly (Q 297). The employer cannot deduct its premium payments, but the employer receives the death proceeds tax-free.[8] Prior to the repeal of the corporate AMT, proceeds paid to a corporation may have been includable, at least in part, in the corporation's income for alternative minimum tax purposes (Q 316).[9] For tax results on the surrender of a policy, see Q 51, Q 52. For a discussion of accumulated earnings tax, see Q 308.

1. *Belsky v. First Nat'l Life Ins. Co.*, 818 F.2d 661 (8th Cir. 1987).
2. For courts finding plans backed by life insurance or annuities to be unfunded, see *Reliable Home Health Care Inc. v. Union Central Ins. Co.*, 295 F.3d 505 (5th Cir. 2002); *Miller v. Heller*, 915 F. Supp. 651 (S.D.N.Y. 1996); *The Northwestern Mut. Ins. Co. v. Resolution Trust Corp.*, 848 F. Supp. 1515 (N.D. Ala. 1994); *Darden v. Nationwide Mut. Life Ins. Co.*, 717 F. Supp. 388 (E.D.N.C. 1989), *aff'd*, 922 F.2d 203 (4th Cir.), *cert. denied*, 502 U.S. 906 (1991); *Belka v. Rowe Furniture Corp.*, 571 F. Supp. 1249 (D. Md. 1983).
3. *See* DOL Adv. 92-22A (cash value element of split dollar life insurance policy under death benefit plan is not a plan asset); DOL Adv. Op. 92-02A (stop-loss insurance policy backing medical expense plan obligations is not plan asset of death benefit plan); DOL Adv. Op. 81-11A (corporate-owned life insurance is not plan asset of death benefit plan).
4. DOL Adv. Op. 94-31A.
5. But see *Miller v. Heller*, 915 F. Supp. 651 (S.D.N.Y. 1996) (in holding that a deferred compensation plan is an unfunded top hat plan, the court interpreted footnote three in Advisory Opinion 94-31A to mean that the DOL's *entire* analysis for determining whether assets are plan assets is not relevant to the issue of whether the plan is funded).
6. *See*, e.g., DOL Adv. Op. 92-13A. See also DOL Adv. Op. 90-14A (great deference is given to the position of the IRS regarding deferred compensation plans when determining, for ERISA purposes, whether a top hat plan is funded).
7. *Centre v. Comm.*, 55 TC 16 (1970); *Morse v. Comm.*, 17 TC 1244 (1952), *aff'd*, 202 F.2d 69 (2nd Cir. 1953). See Treas. Reg. §1.83-3(e).
8. IRC Sec. 264(a)(1).
9. IRC Secs. 56-59.

Even after Section 409A, an employee generally is not taxable on the premiums paid by the employer or on any portion of the value of the policy or annuity, provided that the employer applies for, owns, is beneficiary of, and pays for the policy or annuity contract and uses it merely as a general reserve asset for the employer's obligations under the deferred compensation agreement.[1] Properly structured funding arrangements should not be treated as nonqualified deferred compensation subject to Section 409A.

With respect to contributions made after February 28, 1986 to annuity contracts held by a corporation, partnership, or trust (i.e., a non-natural person), "the income on the contract" for the tax year of the policyholder generally is treated as ordinary income received or accrued by the contract owner during such taxable year (Q 511).[2] Prior to 2018, corporate ownership of life insurance could result in exposure to the corporate alternative minimum tax (Q 316). However, the corporate AMT was repealed for tax years beginning after 2017.

3565. Can a split dollar arrangement be subject to the Section 409A rules?

Where an employee receives a basic vested right in cash values of a policy, or basic life insurance protection and a vested right in the cash surrender values of a policy, the policy becomes a split dollar life insurance arrangement. A split dollar arrangement is also subject to Section 409A, unless it is structured as one of the two excepted variations under IRS Notice 2007-34.[3]

Premiums for a split dollar policy should be taxable to the employee under both split dollar and Section 409A rules (making it subject to the Section 409A penalty taxes and interest if the arrangement does not comply with Section 409A requirements in both form and operation). The Tax Court has held that employer-paid life insurance premiums on an employee's life, where the annual increase in the cash surrender value benefits the employee and the employee also receives annual insurance protection for both the employee and family, will be includable in the employee's gross income.[4] Only an endorsement split dollar (where the participant receives only an interest in a portion of the policy death benefits and pays only an economic benefit tax cost) seems to escape additional taxation under both split dollar and Section 409A tax rules.

3566. How does a surety bond, indemnification insurance or a third party guarantee affect a private IRC Section 451 unfunded nonqualified deferred compensation account balance or nonaccount balance plan?

The IRS has privately ruled that an employee's purchase of a surety bond (with no reimbursement from the employer) as protection against nonpayment of unfunded deferred compensation benefits would not, by itself, cause deferred amounts to be includable in income prior to receipt.[5] The IRS also warned, however, that an employer-paid surety bond would cause current

1.   *Casale v. Comm.*, 247 F.2d 440 (2nd Cir. 1957) (the IRS has said it will follow this decision, Rev. Rul. 59-184, 1959-1 CB 65); Rev. Rul. 72-25, 1972-1 CB 127; Rev. Rul. 68-99, 1968-1 CB 193; Let. Ruls. 8607032, 8607031; TAM 8828004. See also Let. Rul. 9122019. But see *Goldsmith v. U.S.*, 586 F.2d 810, 78-2 USTC ¶9804 (Ct. Cl. 1978) discussed in Q 3561..

2   IRC Sec. 72(u).

3.   IRS Notice 2007-34 was issued as the same time as the final Section 409A regulations in April of 2007 and were intended to specifically discuss the application of Section 409A to split dollar life insurance plans in more detail.

4.   *Frost v. Comm.*, 52 TC 89 (1969).

5.   Let. Rul. 8406012.

taxation. A later letter ruling has blurred the line between employee-provided and employer-provided surety bonds; the IRS hinted, without clearly distinguishing between employee-paid and employer-paid surety bonds, that the use of a surety bond to protect deferred compensation could cause the promise to be secured, resulting in taxation under IRC Section 83 when the deferred compensation is substantially vested (that is, either not subject to a substantial risk of forfeiture or transferable to a third party free of such a risk).[1] Whether the IRS meant to question both employer-provided and employee-provided surety bonds is not clear.

The IRS has also ruled privately that an employee can buy indemnification insurance to protect deferred benefits without causing immediate taxation. This result holds even if the employer reimburses the employee for the premium payments as long as the employer has no other involvement in the arrangement (the employee's premium payments must be treated as nondeductible personal expenses, and any premium reimbursements must be included in the employee's income).[2] The ERISA consequences of such an arrangement are not clear.

On occasion, third party guarantees of benefit promises have received favorable treatment. For example, a parent corporation's guarantee of its subsidiary's deferred compensation obligations did not accelerate the taxation of the benefits.[3] The conclusion that the plaintiffs' promise to pay their attorney was funded and secured (and subject to IRC Section 83) where they irrevocably ordered the defendants' insurers to pay the plaintiffs' attorney his fees out of the plaintiffs' recovery and the defendants' insurers paid the attorney by purchasing annuities for him was "strengthened" by the fact that a defendant and the defendants' insurers guaranteed to make the annuity payments should the annuity issuer default.[4]

The current value of protection provided by an employer-paid surety bond or other guarantee arrangement constitutes a taxable economic benefit;[5] protecting deferred compensation benefits by giving employees certificates of participation secured by irrevocable standby letters of credit secured the promise and triggered application of IRC Section 83.[6] Further, an employer's purchase of irrevocable standby letters of credit that were beyond the reach of its general creditors to back its promise to pay accrued vacation benefits secured the promise and triggered taxation under IRC Section 83.[7]

There is some controversy between the IRS and the Tax Court over whether a promise to pay will be "funded" for tax purposes if the benefit obligation is transferred to a third party. The IRS is likely to think that the employer's promise is funded, even if the third party pays the transferred obligations out of general revenues or sets aside a fund that remains its general asset

---

1.   Let. Rul. 9241006.
2.   Let. Rul. 9344038. The age (1993) and the nonprecedental nature of this private letter ruling makes reliance uncertain, especially in light of the passage of Section 409A that expands the constructive receipt doctrine. Unfortunately, letter rulings are not currently available on the income tax issues of deferred compensation plans under Section 409A. Presumably this means letter rulings would also not be available on the economic benefit doctrine that can still be applied to transactions by the IRS, since 409A is additive income tax law.
3.   Let. Ruls. 8906022, 8741078. See also *Berry v. U.S.*, 593 F. Supp. 80 (M.D.N.C. 1984), *aff'd per curiam*, 760 F.2d 85 (4th Cir. 1985) (a guarantee does not make a promise secured, because the guarantee is itself a mere promise to pay); *Childs v. Comm.*, 103 TC 634 (1994) (same), *aff'd*, 89 F.3d 856 (11th Cir. 1996).
4.   TAM 9336001
5.   Let. Rul. 8406012.
6.   Let. Rul. 9331006.
7.   Let. Rul. 9443006.

and to which the employee has no special claim.[1] The Tax Court does not seem to think that the transfer will automatically result in funding; rather, the Tax Court is more likely to examine whether any property is specially set aside (secured) by the new obligor for the employee.[2]

A US firm has recently released a proprietary technique to protect nonqualified plan benefits that pools small groups of executives from publicly-traded companies with similar debt credit ratings (e.g.; AAA) in trusts that pay a participant's benefits up to the limits of a participant's agreed benefit coverage in the event that his or her employer plan sponsor should go bankrupt during a fixed time frame (apparently either 5 or 10 year periods). Based upon this editor's most current information, this technique relies on the 1993 IRS letter ruling on indemnity insurance purchased by the employee for the lack of any tax impact to the employee as their plan benefits. This technique is not indemnity insurance (or a surety bond), although there are surface parallels to indemnity insurance. Time will tell if this technique can pass IRS scrutiny, especially in light of enactment of Section 409A and the expansion of the constructive receipt doctrine.[3]

3567. What is a "rabbi" trust?

A rabbi trust is a trust vehicle for accumulating assets to support an employer's unfunded deferred compensation plan obligations. Under the IRC, this trust is considered an IRC Section 671 "grantor" trust. Established by the employer with an independent trustee, a rabbi trust is designed to provide employees with some assurance that their promised benefits will be paid while preserving the tax deferral that is at the heart of unfunded deferred compensation plans. To accomplish these ends, a rabbi trust is generally irrevocable.

The use of such trusts with nonqualified deferred compensation plans has been affirmed under Section 409A(b). However, plans must meet the funding rules contained in 409A(b) that include prohibitions against funding or distribution while in declining financial circumstances, placing them offshore,[4] and placing assets into one during the "restricted period" when a sponsor is underfunded on any qualified defined benefit plan.[5] There are currently no regulations covering these 409A(b) funding rules but they are expected to be released at some point in the future.

Planning Point: Planners need to watch for the proposed regulations covering these funding rules under Section 409A(b). Although Section 409A(b) now statutorily confirms use of rabbi trusts in connection with nonqualified plans, these regulations are likely to make substantive changes in the requirements for a 409A(b) compliant rabbi trust. They will likely revoke or replace the current rabbi trust model trust in Revenue Procedure 92-64[6] (Q 3569).

In addition to the new funding requirements of Section 409A(b), the key characteristic of a rabbi trust is that it must provide that its assets remain subject to the claims of the employer's

---

1.   Rev. Rul. 69-50, 1969-1 CB 140, as amplified in Rev. Rul. 77-420, 1977-2 CB 172; TAM 9336001.
2.   *Childs v. Comm.*, 103 TC 634 (1994), *aff'd*, 89 F.3d 856 (11th Cir. 1996).
3.   The editor continues to watch for developments and to evaluate updates on this proposed benefit security technique, which continues to be presented to the marketplace as of the date of this publication.
4.   26 USC Section 409A(b)(2) as amended by the Gulf Opportunity Zone Act of 2005 ("GOZA").
5.   27 USC Section 409A(b)(3) in the Pension Protection Act of 2006.
6.   1992-2 C.B. 422.

general creditors in the event of the employer's insolvency or bankruptcy.[1] This result has been affirmed even when there was a delay in making a distribution of account, based on a legitimate participant request under the plan, until a bankruptcy filing prevented any distribution.[2]

These trusts are called "rabbi" trusts because the first such trust approved by the IRS was set up by a synagogue for a rabbi.[3] Historically, the combination of security (albeit imperfect; a rabbi trust can protect an employee against the employer's future unwillingness to pay promised benefits, but it cannot protect an employee against the employer's future inability to pay) and the tax deferral offered to participants in a nonqualified deferred compensation plan supported by a rabbi trust has made such trusts very popular, even though the new Section 409A(b) funding rules have reduced the ability to use the trust device to provide security for the payment of benefits (for example, placing it offshore).

3568. What is the impact of Section 409A(b) on a "rabbi" trust?

IRC Section 409A has statutorily codified the use of rabbi trusts subject to certain limitations on their use. Since enactment of the Section 409A(b) funding rules, there have been three funding prohibitions on the use of a rabbi trust.

(1)   The securing or distribution of deferred compensation during a period when the employer's net worth is falling or during other financial events that unacceptably secure the payment of the promised benefits is treated as a violation of Section 409A.[4] This includes hybrid rabbi/secular trust arrangements that distribute assets from nominal rabbi trusts to secular trusts on the occurrence of triggering events indicating the employer's financial difficulty. Under any such arrangement, otherwise deferred compensation is immediately taxable and subject to the 20 percent additional tax, plus premium interest on the underpayment of taxes (at the normal underpayment AFR rate plus 1 percent).[5]

(2)   Also, under the Section 409A(b) funding rules, setting aside assets in an offshore trust (one outside the United States) to directly or indirectly fund deferred compensation also unacceptably secures the payment of the promised benefits.[6] Under any such arrangement, the otherwise deferred compensation is immediately taxable and subject to the 20 percent additional tax, plus premium interest on the underpayment of taxes (at the normal underpayment AFR rate plus 1 percent).[7]

The Section 409A funding rules on both (a) prohibition on financial triggers and (b) offshore trusts apply even to deferrals of compensation earned and vested on

---

1.   See *McAllister v. Resolution Trust Corp.* 201 F.3d 570 (5th Cir. 2000); *Goodman v. Resolution Trust Corp.* 7 F.3d 1123 (4th Cir. 1993) (both underscoring that beneficiaries of rabbi trusts take the risk of trust assets being subject to the claims of the employer's general creditors for the benefit of favorable tax treatment).

2.   *In re Washington Mutual Inc.*, 450 B.R. 490 (June 1, 2011) (denying motion for "constructive trust" for payments).

3.   Let. Rul. 8113017.

4.   IRC Sec. 409A(b)(2); Notice 2006-33, 2006-15 IRB 754. As of the date of this publication, there are still no regulations covering the funding rules of Section 409A.

5.   IRC Sec. 409A(b)(4).

6.   IRC Sec. 409A(b)(1); Notice 2006-33, 2006-15 IRB 754.

7.   IRC Sec. 409A(b)(4).

or before December 31, 2004 (and thus not generally subject to the requirements of IRC Section 409A). The IRS provided transition relief through December 31, 2007, for amounts otherwise subject to IRC Section 409A(b), if those assets relate to compensation deferred on or before December 31, 2004, and if those assets were set aside, transferred, or restricted on or before March 21, 2006.[1] *Note: the IRS did not further extend the deadline for compliance on the funding rules to December 31, 2008, as it did for other documentary and operational compliance with Section 409A. December 31, 2007, was the deadline for compliance with the Section 409A(b) funding requirements.* All existing trusts out of compliance with the Section 409A funding requirements should have been terminated and assets distributed or the trust amended as of December 31, 2007. A trust that has not done so is in violation of Section 409A.

(3)   Finally, a trust is in violation of the funding requirements of Section 409A if it makes contributions or transfers assets to a trust during the period that any qualified defined benefit pension plan is "at risk" (below the required percentage statutory funding levels) under the qualified pension funding rules enacted in the Pension Reform Act of 2006, or during the period of any reorganizational bankruptcy.

Planning Point: IRC Section 409A has called into question many prior decisions and rulings in the deferred compensation arena, and there are no detailed regulations on the new funding rules of Section 409A(b), even though the law has been in effect for more than a decade. Moreover, during this time, there has been no IRS update on the model trust in light of the enactment of Section 409A. Employers and employees therefore should rely on their own legal counsel in structuring deferred compensation when using rabbi trusts and any other informal funding mechanisms. There currently are not even proposed regulations for Section 409A(b) requirements, so much detail for guidance in trust construction, especially in the absence of a revised model trust, is lacking. Using the model trust document modified to add the current three funding prohibitions of Section 409A(b) should be acceptable. The planner needs to continue watch for the release of Section 409A proposed regulations, even though there seems to be no IRS priority for it. These regulations will likely make substantive changes in the requirements under these new rules governing rabbi trusts that will impact documentation and operation. The fate of Revenue Procedure 92-64 governing the model rabbi trust document should also be part of this proposed regulation release. Ideally, a new prototype rabbi trust document will be part of the release. However, as of the date of this publication, no such revised revenue procedure or prototype grantor rabbi trust document exists.

3569. What pre-409A issues were raised by the IRS model rabbi trust?

The rabbi trust has been so popular historically that the IRS released a model rabbi trust instrument in 1992 to aid taxpayers and to relieve the processing of requests on the IRS for advance rulings on these arrangements.[2] The IRS model trust was intended to serve as a safe harbor document for employers. Used properly, pre-409A, the model trust assured employers that plan participants either were not in constructive receipt of income or that they incurred no economic benefit because of the trust. Of course, whether an unfunded deferred compensation

---

1.   Notice 2006-33, 2006-15 IRB 754.
2.   1992-2 C.B. 422.

plan using the model rabbi trust effectively deferred taxation depended on whether the underlying plan effectively deferred compensation.

Pre-Section 409A, the IRS would issue advance rulings on the tax treatment of unfunded deferred compensation plans that did not use a trust and unfunded deferred compensation plans that used the model trust in Revenue Procedure 92-64. The IRS announced at that time that it would not issue advance rulings on unfunded nonqualified deferred compensation arrangements *that use a trust* other than the model trust.[1] With the enactment of Section 409A, the IRS announced that it would not issue any advance letter rulings on the income tax consequences of nonqualified deferred compensation plans, but would continue to advise on peripheral tax issues, such as gift tax issues. It also declined to issue prototype plans, although it did not indicate that this pronouncement also includes a revision of its model rabbi trust under the existing revenue procedure. The status of the model trust as provided in the revenue procedure has remained in limbo pending Section 409A regulations, and the funding portion of the law that include rules on trusts.[2]

The current model trust language contains all the pre-409A provisions necessary for operation of a trust separate from the underlying plan except provisions describing the trustee's investment powers. The parties involved are still required to provide language describing the investment powers of the trustee, and those powers must include some investment discretion. Proper use of the model trust requires that its language be adopted verbatim, except where substitute language is expressly permitted. Although it is somewhat puzzling in light of the claim by the IRS that it will not rule on plans that do not use the model trust, the employer may add additional text to the model trust language, as long as such text is "not inconsistent with" the model trust language.[3] The enactment of Section 409A, and specifically the new funding rules (see Q 3568) that impact trusts used in connection with such plans, places the use of the model rabbi trust requirements at issue, even if the grantor adds language incorporating the essential language contained in Section 409A(b), including all the amendments since the enactment of Section 409A.

Under the pre-409A model trust, the rights of plan participants to trust assets had to be merely the rights of unsecured creditors. Participants' rights could not be alienable or assignable. The assets of the trust were required to remain subject to the claims of the employer's general creditors in the event of insolvency or bankruptcy.[4]

In at least one older pre-409A letter ruling, the IRS held that the use of a third party guarantee as an additional security measure did not undermine the tax-effectiveness of a rabbi trust.[5]

---

1. See Rev. Proc. 92-64, 1992-2 CB 422, 423.
2. See Rev. Proc. 2008-61, 2008-42 IRB, 934 and Rev. Proc. 2009-3, 2009-1 IRB 107, Section 3.01(42).
3. Rev. Proc. 92-64, 1992-2 CB 422, 423, Secs. 4.01 and 5.01.
4. Sections 1(d) and 13(b) of the model trust, at 1992-2 CB 424 and 427; but see *Goodman v. Resolution Trust Corp.*, 7 F.3d 1123 (4th Cir. 1993) (assets in a rabbi trust must be subject to the claims of creditors at all times).
5. See Let. Rul. 8906022 (employer established a rabbi trust and its corporate parent also guaranteed the obligations).

Under the pre-409A process, the board of directors and the highest ranking officer of the employer were required to notify the trustee of the employer's insolvency or bankruptcy, and the trustee must be required to cease benefit payments on the company's insolvency or bankruptcy.[1]

Under pre-409A process, if the model trust was used properly, it should not cause a plan to lose its status as "unfunded." In other words, contributions to a rabbi trust should not cause immediate taxation to employees; employees should not have income until the deferred benefits are received or otherwise made available.[2] Contributions to a rabbi trust for the benefit of a corporation's directors have been treated similarly.[3] Likewise, contributions to a rabbi trust should not be considered "wages" subject to income tax withholding until benefits are actually or constructively received.[4]

Pre-409A, a proper rabbi trust would not be considered an IRC Section 402(b) nonexempt employees' trust. Contributions to a proper rabbi trust would not be subject to IRC Section 83.[5]

Pre-409A, the employer would receive no deduction for amounts contributed to the trust, but would receive a deduction when benefit payments were includable in the employee's income (Q 3573). In pre-409A and premodel trust days, the employer generally was considered the owner of the trust under IRC Section 677 and was required to include the income, deductions, and credits generated by the trust in computing the employer's taxable income.[6] This is normal grantor trust tax treatment.

Pre-409A, the IRS generally would issue advance rulings on the grantor trust status of trusts following the model trust.[7] Those pre-409A model trust rulings seem entirely consistent with earlier rulings.[8] In pre-409A and premodel trust rulings, the IRS generally conditioned favorable tax treatment upon the satisfaction of two additional requirements: that creation of the trust did not cause the plan to be other than unfunded for ERISA purposes, and that trust provisions requiring that the trust's assets be available to satisfy the claims of general creditors in the event of insolvency or bankruptcy were enforceable under state and federal law.[9] The same conditions were imposed in earlier model trust rulings.[10]

Pre-409A, the concern of the IRS with respect to ERISA seems to have been that if the DOL took the position that the use of a rabbi trust causes the underlying plan to be other than unfunded for ERISA purposes, then this would cause the plan to be funded for tax purposes and require the accelerated taxation of contributions to the rabbi trust. The DOL's position has been that rabbi trusts maintained in connection with excess benefit or top hat plans will not cause

---

1.   See section 3(b)(1) of the model trust, at 1992-2 CB 425.
2.   Rev. Proc. 92-64, Sec. 3, 1992-2 CB 422, 423; Let. Ruls. 9732008, 9723013, 9601036.
3.   Let. Ruls. 9525031, 9505012, 9452035.
4.   Let. Rul. 9525031.
5.   Let. Ruls. 9732006, 9548015, 9542032, 9536027.
6.   Let. Ruls. 9314005, 9242007, 9214035.
7.   Rev. Proc. 92-64, Sec. 3, 1992-2 CB 422, 423.
8.   Let. Ruls. 9542032, 9536027, 9443016.
9.   Let. Ruls. 9314005, 9242007, 9214035, 8634031.
10.   See, e.g., Let. Ruls. 9548015, 9517019, 9504006; see also Rev. Proc. 92-64, Sec. 4.02, 1992-2 CB 422, 423; sections 1(d), 1(e) and 3(b) of the model trust, at 1992-2 CB 424, 425.

the underlying plans to be funded for ERISA purposes so long as the IRS maintains they are not taxable because they are unsecured (hence not funded for tax purposes).[1]

Also, at least one court prior to the enactment of Section 409A noted that the use of a rabbi trust will not cause a top hat plan to lose its ERISA exemption as long as the trust assets remain subject to the claims of the employer's creditors in the event of insolvency, and the participants' interests are inalienable and unassignable.[2] Nonetheless, pre-Section 409A rulings on plans using the model trust are supposed to state that the IRS expresses no opinion on the ERISA consequences of using a rabbi trust.[3]

In earlier pre-409A private letter rulings, the IRS had allowed the use of a rabbi trust in conjunction with a deferred compensation plan that permitted hardship withdrawals, ruling that the hardship withdrawal provision did not cause amounts deferred to be taxable before they are paid or made available. In these letter rulings, "hardship" generally was defined as an unforeseeable financial emergency caused by events beyond the participant's control. The amount that could be withdrawn generally was limited to the amount needed to satisfy the emergency need.[4]

Pre-409A IRS guidelines for giving advanced rulings on unfunded deferred compensation plans expressly permitted the use of certain hardship withdrawal provisions (Q 3541).[5] Therefore, pre-409A, it seemed that a rabbi trust conforming to the model trust could be used in conjunction with a deferred compensation plan permitting an acceptable hardship withdrawal.[6] Pre-409A, an appropriate hardship withdrawal provision was not expected to trigger taxation before deferred amounts are paid or made available. Such a provision might have triggered constructive receipt; however, at the time a qualifying emergency arose.[7]

Pre-409A, the trustee could be given the power to invest in the employer's securities. If the trustee was given that power, the trust had to be revocable or include a provision that the employer could substitute assets of equal value for any assets held by the trust.[8]

Where presumably model trusts separately serving a parent and affiliates could invest in the parent's stock, it was ruled that:

(1)   dividends paid on the parent's stock held by the parent's trusts would not be includable in the parent's income in the year paid;

(2)   no gain or loss would be recognized by the parent on transfer of its stock from its trusts to its participants or their beneficiaries; and

---

1.   See DOL Adv. Op. 94-31A, fn.3; DOL Adv. Op. 92-13A.
2.   See *Nagy v. Riblet Prod. Corp.*, 13 EBC 1743 (N.D. Ind. 1990), *amended on other grounds and reconsideration denied*, 1991 U.S. Dist. Lexis 11739 (N.D. Ind. 1991).
3.   See Rev. Proc. 92-64, Sec. 3, 1992-2 CB 422, 423.
4.   See Let. Ruls. 9242007, 9121069. Section 409A allows hardship distributions from covered plans but uses the 457 definition of "unforeseeable emergency" rather than the hardship definition under 401(k).
5.   Rev. Proc. 92-65, Sec. 3.01(c), 1992-2 CB 428.
6.   Let. Rul. 9505012.
7.   Let. Rul. 9501032.
8.   See IRS Model Trust, section 5(a), Rev. Proc. 92-64, 1992-2 CB 425.

(3)   no gain or loss would be recognized by the affiliates on the direct transfer of the parent's stock to the affiliates' participants or their beneficiaries if that stock was transferred directly by the parent to the participants or beneficiaries and neither the affiliates nor their trusts were the legal or beneficial owners of parent's stock.[1]

Regulations under IRC Section 1032 (Q 307) generally permit nonrecognition treatment for transfers of stock from an issuing corporation to an acquiring corporation if the acquiring corporation immediately disposes of such stock. A transfer of a parent corporation's stock to a rabbi trust for the benefit of a subsidiary's employee would not qualify for this nonrecognition treatment because the stock is not immediately distributed to the participant. The IRS has announced that nonrecognition treatment is available for such transfers, albeit under a different theory. The IRS treated the parent corporation, rather than the subsidiary corporation, as the grantor and owner of the rabbi trust, so long as the trust provided that stock not transferred to the subsidiary's employees reverts to the parent and the parent's creditors can reach the stock.[2] Pre-409A, the IRS had indicated that it would rule on model rabbi trusts that have been modified to comply with this notice.

Pre-409A, the trust had to provide that, if life insurance would be held by the trust, the trustee would have no power to name any entity other than the trust as beneficiary, assign the policy to any entity other than a successor trustee, or loan to any entity the proceeds of any borrowing against the policy (but an optional provision permits the loan of such borrowings to the employer).[3]

Pre-409A, the IRS issued several private letter rulings addressing the deductibility of interest paid on life insurance policy loans after the policies were transferred to a rabbi trust (Q 30).

Planning Point: Until proposed regulations under Section 409A(b) are released, the model trust will need to be amended to comply with all the new Section 409A(b) funding requirements if it is to be used with a Section 409A plan and remain 409A compliant under Section 409A(b). These forthcoming regulations under Section 409A(b) will be important in determining what will happen to Revenue Procedure 94-64 and the model trust contained in it, as well as the details that may be required to draft such trust provisions and guide trust operations. Planners and sponsors need to continue to watch for these proposed regulations or action on Rev. Proc. 92-64. In the meantime, they need to rely on legal counsel's expert guidance to integrate the 409A(b) requirements with those in the revenue procedure, especially in light of more than a decade of inaction by the IRS

3570. Pre-409A, if a taxpayer wanted to adopt the model trust and wished to obtain an advance ruling from the IRS on the underlying deferred compensation plan, what additional guidelines was it required to follow?

Pre-409A, taxpayers that wanted to adopt the model trust and wished to obtain an advance ruling on the underlying deferred compensation plan had to follow not only the standard guidelines for obtaining a ruling on an unfunded deferred compensation plan (Q 3541) but had to also follow other guidelines unique to plans using a trust.

1.   Let. Rul. 9505012.
2.   Notice 2000-56, 2000-43 IRB 393.
3.   See IRS Model Trust, sections 8(e) and 8(f), Rev. Proc. 92-64, 1992-2 CB 426.

First, the plan had to provide that the trust and any assets would be held to conform to the terms of the model trust.

Second, taxpayers had to generally include a representation that the plan was not inconsistent with the terms of the trust with the letter ruling request.

Third, the language of the trust had to conform generally with the model text, and tax-payers generally had to include a representation that the trust conformed to the model trust language (including the order in which the provisions appear) and that the trust did not contain any inconsistent language (in substituted portions or elsewhere) that conflicted with the model trust language. Provisions were permitted to be renumbered if appropriate, any bracketed model trust language could be omitted, and blanks could be filled in.

Fourth, the request for a letter ruling generally had to include a copy of the trust document on which all substituted or added language was clearly marked and on which the required investment authority text was indicated.

Fifth, the request for a ruling generally had to contain a representation that the trust was a valid trust under state law, and that all of the material terms and provisions of the trust, including the creditors' rights clause, were enforceable under the appropriate state laws.

Finally, the trustee generally had to be an independent third party that could be granted corporate trustee powers under state law, such as a bank trust department or a similar party.[1]

In summary, as of the date of this publication, a plan sponsor can neither obtain an advance ruling on the income taxation consequences for plan participants in a 409A covered unfunded nonqualified deferred compensation plan or an associated rabbi trust designed to follow the trust revenue procedure updated for 409A requirements.

Account and Nonaccount Balance Plans

3571. Can a private IRC Section 451 unfunded nonqualified deferred compensation employee account balance plan be used in connection with a qualified 401(k) elective deferral plan to maximize the annual deferrals into the qualified 401(k) and also to receive employee contributions that cannot go into the qualified plan because of nondiscrimination testing issues?

Yes. However, 409A income tax and ERISA developments governing participant deposits have raised questions about the so-called 401(k) "wrap-around" technique.

A 1995 private letter ruling approved a particular nonqualified/401(k) "wrap-around" "spill-over" or "pour-over" plan.[2] Since then, more rulings approving the use of wrap-around

---

1.   Rev. Proc. 2003-3, Secs. 3.01(35), 4.01(33), 2003-1 IRB 113; Rev. Proc. 92-64, Secs. 3 and 4, 1992-2 CB 422, 423.
2.   See Let. Rul. 9530038.

plans have been issued.[1] Wrap-around plans have been primarily used to maximize elective deferrals under both an IRC Section 401(k) plan and a nonqualified voluntary employee account balance plan, which generally is subject to IRS Section 409A. These plans are referred to as "linked" plans by the IRS for purposes of Section 409A, as are "excess benefit" plans. Such a nonqualified arrangement may be unnecessary due to the method by which the actual deferral percentage test for 401(k) plans now is administered (Q 3801).

For employers that continue to elect to use the current year testing method on their qualified plans, use of a wrap-around nonqualified employee account balance plan will continue to provide planning opportunities and any employer, regardless of method, may desire a nonqualified employee account balance plan to permit highly compensated employees to voluntarily defer more than that permitted under a qualified plan.

Section 409A Impact

Under final regulations to IRC Section 409A, the IRS advised that such a wrap-around nonqualified plan is still possible under IRC Section 409A if it meets certain requirements:

(1)   The plan must follow the structure provided in the favorable IRS letter rulings (contributions must all go first into the nonqualified employee account balance plan and then spill into the qualified 401(k) as it becomes clear the qualified plan may receive them, based on discrimination testing).

(2)   Such a linkage may not result in a decrease in deferrals in the nonqualified arrangement in excess of the deferral limits under IRC Section 402(g)(1)(b) ($19,500 in 2020 and 2021, $19,000 in 2019, $18,500 in 2018).[2] For existing nonqualified wrap-around arrangements, the IRS offered transition relief through December 31, 2008. For these plans, elections as to the timing and form of payment under the nonqualified plan that are controlled by the qualified plan were permitted through December 31, 2008. Elections had to be made in accordance with the terms of the nonqualified plan as of October 3, 2004.[3] In Notice 2010-80, the IRS modified Notice 2010-6 governing plan documentation correction to allow "linked" plan documentation under the notice's guidance so long as certain prerequisites are met.

DOL Guidance Potentially Impacting Wrap Plans

Although Section 409A does not seem to preclude a nonqualified wrap-around plan based upon income tax considerations after Section 409A, the DOL's released guidance and ongoing focus[4] on the timeliness of qualified plan deposits and the required deadlines raises ERISA issues for wrap-around plans that need to be discussed with legal counsel, if a wrap design is to be

---

1.   Let. Ruls. 200116046, 200012083, 199924067, 9752018, 9752017.
2.   Treas. Reg. §§1.409A-2(a)(9), 1.409A-3(j)(5); Notice 2017-64, Notice 2018-83, Notice 2019-59, Notice 2020-79.
3.   Notice 2006-79, 2006-43 IRB 763.
4.   The DOL continues to make timely deposit of employee contributions a priority focus of its audits. It is unclear if the DOL has addressed a situation where the employer has a wrap plan for HCEs and is not necessarily making deposits to the 401(k) plan on the timing normally expected. As of the date of this publication, there is no special guidance from the DOL on thus unique situation.

used. This discussion is necessary because the currently approved wrap plan structure does not conform to these more recent DOL timely deposit rules.

3572. What approved wrap plan structure exists to allow employees to maximize 401(k) plan deferrals using a nonqualified deferred compensation account balance plan to temporarily hold elective deferrals?

An employer seeking to maximize highly compensated employees' ("HCEs") elective deferrals to its 401(k) plan established in an unfunded, nonqualified salary reduction plan (employee account balance plan) to temporarily hold elective deferrals until the maximum amount of 401(k) elective deferrals could be determined for the tax year. Employees could defer compensation into the proposed nonqualified plan by entering into salary reduction agreements by December 31 of the prior year. These employees then would receive "matching" contributions under the nonqualified plan equal to their matching contributions under the 401(k) plan. The employer would determine the maximum amount of elective contributions that the HCEs could make to the 401(k) plan for the current year as soon as practicable each year, but no later than January 31 of the next year.

Then, the lesser of the maximum allowable amount or the amount actually deferred under the nonqualified plan would be distributed in cash to the HCEs by March 15 of the following year unless they irrevocably elected to have such amounts contributed as elective deferrals to the 401(k) plan at the same time they elected to defer compensation into the nonqualified plan. Where such election is made, the "elective deferrals" and the appropriate "matching" contributions under the nonqualified plan would be contributed directly to the 401(k) plan. Earnings under the nonqualified plan would not be contributed to the 401(k) plan. Presumably, any balance in the nonqualified plan would remain in the nonqualified plan.

In a pre-409A ruling, the IRS determined that amounts initially held in the nonqualified employee account balance plan would be treated as made to the 401(k) plan in the year of deferral under the nonqualified plan, and would be excluded from income under IRC Section 402(e)(3). Amounts distributed to an employee that the employee did not elect to contribute to the 401(k) plan would be taxable in the year the compensation was earned. This is the linked plan design structure for a nonqualified wrap-around plan approved under Section 409A.

Apparently, the key to the success of this wrap-around arrangement was the requirement that the election to transfer amounts to the 401(k) plan had to be made at the same time as the election to initially defer compensation into the nonqualified plan, before the beginning of the year in which the compensation was earned. The IRS earlier had approved, and then revoked in 1995, its approval of a similar arrangement where the election to transfer excess amounts flowed from a 401(k) plan into a nonqualified plan, even after the close of the year in which the amounts were earned.[1] Apparently, the IRS was concerned that this arrangement raised the specter of constructive receipt and violated qualified 401(k) plan law (Q 3541).

---

1.   See Let. Ruls. 9423034 and 9414051, revoking Let. Rul. 9317037.

Another pre-409A private letter ruling approved a similar arrangement utilizing a rabbi trust (Q 3567) in connection with the nonqualified plan.[1] One ruling (involving a top hat plan, Q 3541) specifically indicated that amounts must be transferred from the nonqualified plan to the 401(k) plan no later than March 15th.[2]

A 401(k) plan will be disqualified if any employer-provided benefit (other than matching contributions) is contingent on the employee's elective deferrals under the 401(k) plan (Q 3753). The 401(k) regulations provide that participation in a nonqualified deferred compensation plan is treated as contingent only to the extent that the employee may receive additional deferred compensation under the nonqualified deferred compensation plan based on whether he or she makes elective deferrals under the 401(k) plan. These regulations explicitly state that a provision under a nonqualified deferred compensation plan requiring an employee to have made the maximum permissible elective deferral under the 401(k) plan is not treated as contingent (deferrals under a nonqualified plan permitting deferral of up to 15 percent of compensation if participants have made maximum allowable 401(k) elective deferrals were not impermissibly conditioned on elective deferrals).[3]

In determining how this structure compares to the final regulations published by the DOL (as finalized on January 14, 2010), it should be noted that the written rule provides that employers have a fiduciary duty to remit employee contributions to the qualified plan as soon as they can be reasonably segregated from the employer's general assets, but not later than the 15th business day of the month following the month in which the participant contributions are withheld or received.[4] Unfortunately, the DOL has taken the position that the "reasonable segregation" language takes precedence over the "no later than the 15th day of the month following the month" language.

The 2010 regulations provided a safe harbor for retirement and health and welfare plans with fewer than 100 participants (often referred to as "small plans"). The DOL has said that "… employee contributions are deemed to be timely if the amounts are deposited with the plan no later than the 7th business day following the date the contributions (including loan repayments) are received by the employer."

The DOL has declined to extend the same or similar safe harbor to large plans. The rule for large plans is a facts-and-circumstances determination, which is no rule at all. But, in either case, the rule for timely deposits to the qualified plan, and many versions of the wrap-around design, especially those that need to wait until the following year to determine and move deposits to the qualified plan, do NOT meet these DOL timely deposit rule requirements. There are some qualified plan systems that may facilitate the approved wrap-around plan design by functionally being able to move the money virtually in real time from the nonqualified plan to the qualified plan almost instantly as it comes in on a timely deposit basis until the qualified plan caps out

---

1.   See Let. Rul. 9752018.
2.   Let. Rul. 200116046.
3.   See, e.g., Let. Rul. 199902002.
4.   DOL Reg. 2510.3-102(b).

and thereafter leaves the balance of the deposits in the nonqualified plan. If the qualified plan system cannot do this, then the timely deposit rules are an issue for use of a wrap-around design.

Planning Point: Of interest is the fact that the DOL timely deposit rules have always been an issue since the wrap design first appeared in the mid-1990s. What has changed is the DOL's heavy continuing focus on timely deposit compliance, and the emphasis on the shortest period possible for remission of employee contributions to the qualified plan. The IRS, for its part, has apparently given the wrap-around design basic approval, even under Section 409A, so long as certain nominal requirements discussed heretofore are met.

It is important, however, not to overlook the ERISA issue concerning the timeliness of contributions to the qualified 401(k) plan under such a wrap-around plan linked to the employer's qualified 401(k) plan, and to determine the measure of the risk. Obtaining clearance from the DOL for the design may be in order, based upon the ability of the qualified plan recordkeeping and nondiscrimination testing capabilities system to move deposits from the nonqualified plan to the qualified plan on a timely basis. If it cannot meet or approach the timely deposit requirements, counsel must help the sponsor understand the measure of the risk involved if this 401(k) wrap-around design is to be implemented.

3573. When are deferred amounts under an unfunded nonqualified account and nonaccount balance plan deductible by the employer?

An employer can take an income tax expense deduction for nonqualified deferred compensation only when it is includable in the employee's income, regardless of whether the employer is on a cash or accrual basis of accounting.[1] Likewise, deduction of amounts deferred for an independent contractor can be taken only when they are includable in the independent contractor's gross income.[2] Section 409A has not changed the income tax deduction timing for the employer; only the potential timing of income tax inclusion by a participant. Nor does the enactment of the 2017 Tax Reform Act seem to change the timing of this deferred tax deduction of nonqualified deferred compensation for the sponsoring business entity, although it may impact the amount of the deduction if the aggregate compensation, including nongrandfathered nonqualified deferred compensation, for a participant exceeds $1M.

The IRS has confirmed that payments made under an executive compensation plan within 2½ months of the end of the year in which employees vest do not constitute deferred compensation and thus may be deducted in the year in which employees vest, rather than the year in which the employees actually receive the payments.[3] Previously, there was some controversy over the proper timing of an accrual basis employer's deduction for amounts credited as "interest" to employee accounts under a nonqualified deferred compensation plan. The weight of authority currently holds that IRC Section 404(a)(5) governs the deduction for such amounts, which must be postponed until such amounts are includable in employee income. Amounts representing "interest" cannot be currently deducted by an accrual basis employer under IRC Section 163.[4]

---

1. IRC Sec. 404(a)(5); Treas. Reg. §§1.404(a)-1(c), 1.404(a)-12(b)(2). See also *Lundy Packing Co. v. U.S.*, 302 F. Supp. 182 (E.D.N.C. 1969), *aff'd per curiam*, 421 F.2d 850 (4th Cir. 1970); *Springfield Prod., Inc. v. Comm.*, TC Memo 1979-23.
2. IRC Sec. 404(d).
3. Let. Rul. 199923045.
4. *Albertson's, Inc. v. Comm.*, 42 F.3d 537 (9th Cir. 1994), *vacating in part* 12 F.3d 1529 (9th Cir. 1993), *aff'g in part* 95 TC 415 (1990) (divided court), *en banc reh'g denied*, (9th Cir. 1995), *cert. denied*, 516 U.S. 807 (1995); Notice 94-38, 1994-1 CB 350; Let. Rul. 9201019; TAM 8619006.

To be deductible, deferred compensation payments must represent reasonable compensation for the employee's services when added to current compensation. The question of what is reasonable is question of fact in each case. One factor considered in determining the reasonableness of compensation is whether amounts paid are intended to compensate for past, under-compensated services (Q 3519). Thus, deferred compensation for past services may be deductible, even if the total of such compensation and other compensation for the current year is in excess of reasonable compensation for services performed in the current year, as long as that total, plus all compensation paid to the employee in prior years, is reasonable for all of the services performed through the current year.[1]

Planning Point: Substantiating the rationale behind the deferred compensation can be particularly important in a plan that is implemented for the benefit of an owner-operator nearing retirement in a closely-held company, because this substantiation can make the difference between whether the post-retirement payments are considered tax deductible compensation, rather than a nondeductible dividend. This is especially true in light of the increases in dividend tax rates for clients in the highest income tax bracket, which took effect beginning January 1, 2013. Proposed reductions in income tax rates may change this.

Historically, best practice dictated documenting that the deferred compensation is partial compensation to make up for past "under compensation" in board resolutions and supporting materials, as well as the plan document itself (if written as a separate individual agreement) in order to support it as reasonable compensation. This also suggests the wisdom of creating such a plan for an owner-operator as far in advance of retirement as possible, so as to make the deferred compensation part of compensation for as many tax years as possible, thereby helping establish its long-term reasonableness, even if resources to initially fund it are not readily available.

However, if the desired plan design is 409A covered, under the current regulations the IRS may be expected to take the position that the deferral of taxation is not effective because of the unlikelihood that the 409A plan operational requirements will be followed by a majority or controlling shareholder with respect to his or her own benefit.

Reasonableness of compensation is usually not an issue as to non-shareholder or minority shareholder employees. A finding of unreasonableness in the case of a controlling shareholder is more likely. In one case, benefits paid to a surviving spouse of a controlling shareholder of a closely-held corporation were held not reasonable compensation where:

(1)   the controlling shareholder had not been under-compensated in previous years;

(2)   the controlling shareholder's compensation exceeded the amounts paid by comparable companies;

(3)   the payments were not part of a pattern of benefits provided to employees; and

(4)   there was an absence of dividends.[2]

In a second case, deferred compensation payments were held to be reasonable where the controlling shareholder was inadequately paid during the controlling shareholder's life and the

---

1.   Treas. Reg. §1.404(a)-1(b).
2.   See, e.g., *Nelson Bros., Inc. v. Comm.*, TC Memo 1992-726.

surviving spouse, to whom payments were made, did not inherit a controlling stock ownership.[1] Proper documentation (e.g., board of directors' minutes) is important to help substantiate the reasonableness of the compensation.

Publicly-traded corporations generally do not run into the reasonable compensation issue. This is because public companies are not permitted to deduct compensation in excess of $1 million per tax year to certain top-level employees (note that the exception for performance-based incentive compensation was eliminated for tax years beginning after 2017 (Q 3519)).[2]

Golden parachute rules may limit the amount of the deduction for deferred compensation payments that are contingent upon a change in ownership or control of a corporation or made under an agreement that violates a generally enforced securities law or regulation (Q 3530).[3]

3574. How are deferred compensation account balances and nonaccount balance payments taxed when received by the employee or the beneficiary?

Plans Subject to Section 409A

Section 409A is a refinement of the constructive receipt doctrine. Plans that are "nonqualified deferred compensation plans," as defined in Section 409A, have additional requirements added to the prior tax law, unless specifically replaced by Section 409A, that are now necessary to achieve and maintain income tax deferral as to plan participants until the date of distribution under the terms of the plan. Under Section 409A, its regulations, and guidance, a participant is taxed on deferred compensation immediately upon violation of Section 409A in either form (documentation) or operation (administration). These additional 409A plan requirements (for plans not involving a trust) are primarily:

(1)   minimum required plan documentation;

(2)   limited permissible distributions;

(3)   prohibited accelerations of these distributions; and

(4)   required timing of elections to defer.

Plans Excepted or Grandfathered from Section 409A Coverage (Residual Rules for 409A Plans)

When deferred compensation payments are actually or constructively received, they are taxed as ordinary income. Deferred compensation payments are "wages" subject to regular income tax withholding (and not the special withholding rules that apply to pensions, etc.) when actually or constructively received.[4] Section 409A greatly expands the existing definition

---

1.   *Andrews Distrib. Co., Inc. v. Comm.*, TC Memo 1972-146.
2.   IRC Sec. 162(m).
3.   IRC Sec. 280G.
4.   See IRC Sec. 3401(a); Rev. Rul. 82-176, 1982-2 CB 223; Rev. Rul. 77-25, 1977-1 CB 301; Temp. Treas. Reg. §35.3405-1T, A-18; cf. Let. Rul. 9525031 (contributions to rabbi trust were not subject to income tax withholding because they were not the actual or constructive payment of wages).

of constructive receipt so that violations of Section 409A requirements in either form documentation or administrative operation cause immediate taxation.

In the worst case taxation situation, deferred compensation that is subject to constructive receipt not only is immediately taxed under IRC Section 409A, but it is also subject to a 20 percent excise tax in addition to the normal tax on all vested amounts (Q 3541, Q 3564). Interest on the underpayment of taxes is also retroactively imposed to the date of error and is also due at the normal underpayment AFR rate plus 1 percent.[1] The IRS has provided for certain corrections of documentation and operational errors that may entirely or substantially avoid worst-case taxation under Section 409A. The tax outcome under these correction procedures depends largely on the nature of the error, when the error occurred and is corrected, and the specific participant involved (an "insider" or not, regardless whether the company is publicly traded or privately held).

Certain Foreign Plans of "Nonqualified Entities" under IRC Section 457A

A nonqualified deferred compensation plan of a uniquely defined "nonqualified entity" (offshore fund or partnership located in a tax indifferent situs) is subject to IRC Section 457A. This is a different IRC section than Section 409A, which covers the "nonqualified deferred compensation" plans of all entities, except to the extent they are exempted or excepted from coverage. Deferred compensation provided by such 457A nonqualified entities is taxable at the time any 457A "substantial risk of forfeiture" lapses (Q 3541). If the deferred compensation is deferred beyond the year in which the risk of forfeiture lapses, the participant is subject to a 20 percent excise tax and premium penalty interest on the underpayment of taxes at the normal underpayment AFR rate plus 1 percent on the amount.[2] However, in 2016 the IRS clarified that plans subject to 457A may be covered by Section 409A and when covered must comply with it in addition to complying with 457A requirements.[3] The 2016 proposed regulations indicate that 457A plans will have to separately and independently comply with Section 409A and 457 as well as 457A in order to postpone taxation.

Annuity Payout

Where an unfunded plan paid deferred compensation benefits in the form of a commercial single premium annuity at the termination of the participant's employment, the IRS privately ruled that the full value of the contract would be includable in the recipient's income at the time of distribution, in accordance with IRC Section 83.[4] Unless the payment was due in a lump sum rather than in installments under the plan, this technique would now also violate Section 409A as an impermissible acceleration of the benefits.

---

1.   IRC Sec. 409A(b)(4).
2.   IRC Sec. 457A(c).
3.   Prop. Treas. Regs., REG 123854-12, June 22, 2016.
4.   Let. Rul. 9521029.

Beneficiary Payments

Payments made to a beneficiary from an unfunded plan are "income in respect of a decedent" for income tax purposes and, as such, are taxed, as they would have been to the employee. It is not clear whether the same withholding rules apply. For treatment of death benefits under deferred compensation agreements, see Q 3638.

3575. How are deferred compensation account balances and nonaccount balance payments taxed when they are received by an ex-spouse pursuant to divorce?

Prior to Section 409A (but continuing for excepted and grandfathered plans), benefits assigned by an employee to an ex-spouse in a divorce agreement can be split and, if so, are income taxed to the employee and the ex-spouse according to their split. However, the employee retains the tax liability for FICA/FUTA purposes. Pre-409A, generally speaking, there was no specific framework for the assignment of nonqualified deferred compensation for any reason, other than for eligible Section 457 plans (Q 3584), which is similar to the framework for the assignment of qualified plan benefits through a qualified domestic relations order ("QDRO").[1] In fact, plans frequently prohibit such assignments (as well as all others) to avoid constructive receipt, economic benefit and assignment of income issues for plan participants since it was required under Rev. Proc. 1992-65[2] in order to get a positive letter ruling prior to the enactment of Section 409A. They sometimes did allow splitting of the vested nonqualified account, but prohibited accelerated distribution of the ex-spouse's portion granted in a divorce until it was due.

Section 409A final regulations now specifically permit the accelerated distribution of a nonqualified account balance or nonaccount balance benefit to an ex-spouse under a domestic relations order ("DRO"). Note that this is not a QDRO, and the DRO form, which generally should parallel a QDRO, cannot actually do so in all respects because a nonqualified plan has no "plan assets" (to which the standard QDRO attaches). Under Section 409A, this right is optional and a plan still does not have to provide for this divorce participant right if the employer does not want to include it in the plan. Moreover, it is not clear if the prior rulings (involving the responsible party for income tax and FICA purposes) continue to apply in the case of a 409A plan DRO divorce distribution to an ex-spouse.

Finally, even if the plan does not provide for a participant to split their account/benefit under a DRO, does a plan sponsor have the right, by virtue of the ERISA preemption of state law to ERISA plans, to refuse a properly presented DRO from a state family law court under ERISA even though Section 409A allows it "optionally"? In general, this area remains a mess for all parties involved, especially the employer who is caught in the middle and may not even have general account reserves set aside to address a requested payout of a spouse's vested portion of a nonqualified benefit or account, especially in the case of a supplemental plan.

---

1.   See Let. Rul. 9340032.
2.   1992 C.B 428.

FICA and FUTA Taxes

3576. Are contributions to, and postretirement payments from, a deferred compensation account balance or nonaccount balance plan subject to FICA and FUTA taxes?

Yes.

There are two timing rules for the treatment of deferred compensation amounts under the Federal Insurance Contributions Act ("FICA") and the Federal Unemployment Tax Act ("FUTA"): (1) the "general timing rule," and (2) the "special timing rule."

The general timing rule provides that amounts taxable as wages generally are taxed when paid or "constructively received" (Q 3541).

The special timing rule applies to amounts deferred by an employee under any deferred compensation plan of an employer covered by FICA. The special timing rule applies to voluntary salary, commission and bonus reduction plans, employer-paid supplemental plans, funded and unfunded plans, private plans, and eligible or ineligible Section 457 plans. It does not apply to excess (golden) parachute payments.

In a 2016 case, the 11th Circuit affirmed this application of FICA taxation to an employer-paid SERP in a case where the taxpayer sought to argue that the subject plan was not a supplementary deferred compensation plan that constituted FICA taxable "wages".[1]

Section 409A has not changed the application or calculation of employment taxes. Under these rules, vested nonqualified plan contributions (and the earnings on them) generally are taxable for employment tax purposes (compared with income tax purposes) when they are contributed (as in the case of most voluntary salary/bonus deferral plans) or when they are vested (as in the case of an employer-paid supplemental plan with risks of forfeiture on the benefits).

General Timing Rule

Under the general timing rule, an employee's "amount deferred" is considered to be "wages" for FICA purposes at the later of the date when the services are performed or the employee's rights to such amount are no longer subject to a Section 3121 "substantial risk of forfeiture" governing the timing of the imposition of FICA taxes on compensation.[2] This definition of substantial risk of forfeiture or limitation should not be confused with the seven others discussed in Q 3538 and Q 3541; it is similar but not the same as the others and should be reviewed separately for FICA inclusion questions.

1.　　*Peterson v. Comm.*, 827 F.3d 968 (11th Cir. 2016).

2.　　See IRC Secs. 3121(v)(2)(A), 3121(v)(2)(C); Treas. Reg. §31.3121(v)(2)-1(a)(2); *Buffalo Bills, Inc. v. U.S.*, 31 Fed. Cl. 794 (1994), *appeal dismissed without opinion*, 56 F.3d 84, 1995 U.S. App. Lexis 27184 (Fed. Cir. 1995); *Hoerl & Assoc., P.C. v. U.S.*, 996 F.2d 226 (10th Cir. 1993), *aff'g in part, rev'g in part, and remanding* 785 F. Supp. 1430 (D. Colo. 1992); Let. Ruls. 9443006 (fn. 1), 9442012, 9417013; 9347006, 9024069 *as revised by* Let. Rul. 9025067; TAMs 9051003, 9050006.

Similar rules apply for FUTA (federal unemployment tax) purposes, although the taxable wage base for FUTA purposes is substantially smaller ($7,000).[1]

Where an amount deferred cannot be readily calculated by the last day of the year, employers may choose between two alternative methods: the estimated method and the lag method.

Under the estimated method, the employer treats a reasonably estimated amount as wages paid on the last day of the calendar year. If the employer underestimates, it may treat the shortfall as wages in the first year (or in the first quarter of the second year). If the employer overestimates, it may claim a refund or credit.

Under the lag method, the employer may calculate the end-of-year amount deferred on any date in the first quarter of the next calendar year. The amount deferred will be treated as wages paid and received on that date, and the amount deferred that otherwise would have been taken into account on the last day of the year must be increased by income through the date on which the amount is taken into account.[2]

Special Timing (Nonduplication) Rule

The "special timing" (nonduplication) rule is designed to prevent double taxation once an amount is treated as wages. Under this rule, any amount (and any income attributable to it) will not again be treated as wages for FICA or FUTA purposes in any later year.[3] A deferred amount is treated as taken into account for FICA and FUTA purposes when it is included in computing the amount of wages, but only to the extent that any additional tax for the year resulting from the inclusion actually is paid before the expiration of the period of limitation for the year. A failure to take a deferred amount into account subjects it (and any income attributable thereto) to inclusion when actually or constructively paid.[4]

Planning Point: In an important case development, in 2016 a Federal District Court (affirmed on appeal by the 11th circuit) held that an employer was responsible under the plan provisions for some FICA taxes paid by its plan participants on plan benefits because of its failure to withhold FICA taxes in connection with a SERP during the active working life of those plan participants rather than at the time the benefits were paid.[5]

The participants argued that the employer was obligated to pay those taxes under the plan and by failing to withhold during the working period they incurred FICA taxes on their benefits that would not have been due otherwise. Because of annual caps on total FICA contributions, the FICA taxes were often muted or avoided entirely for deferred compensation plan participants, except for the Medicare portion. Under the application of the FICA rules to the plan, by failing to withhold on FICA during the working period, their benefits were thereby subjected to FICA taxation as paid contrary to the plan provisions.

---

1.   See IRC Secs. 3306(r)(2), 3306(b)(1).
2.   Treas. Reg. §§31.3121(v)(2)-1(f), 31.3306(r)(2)-1(a).
3.   IRC Secs. 3121(v)(2)(B), 3306(r)(2)(B).
4.   Treas. Reg. §§31.3121(v)(2)-1(a)(2)(iii), 31.3306(r)(2)-1(a).
5.   *Davidson v. Henkel Corp.*, 2015WL 74257 (E.D. Mich. 2015). It is understood that the employer eventually settled with the participants for a significant portion of the taxes including a tax gross up (as well as attorneys' fees).

3577. When is a nonqualified deferred compensation plan excluded for purposes of determining FICA and FUTA taxes?

The following plans and benefits are not considered deferred compensation "wages" for FICA and FUTA purposes (but may well be a "nonqualified deferred compensation plan" for 409A purposes and includible for income tax purposes for noncompliance):

(1)   Stock options, stock appreciation rights, and other stock value rights, but not phantom stock plans or other arrangements under which an employee is awarded the right to receive a fixed payment equal to the value of a specified number of shares of employer stock

(2)   Some restricted property received in connection with the performance of services

(3)   Compensatory time, disability pay, severance pay, and death benefits

(4)   Certain benefits provided in connection with impending termination, including window benefits

(5)   Excess (golden) parachute payments

(6)   Benefits established twelve months before an employee's termination, if there was an indication that benefits were provided in contemplation of termination

(7)   Benefits established after termination of employment

(8)   Compensation paid for current services[1]

3578. How is the amount deferred for employment tax purposes impacted by whether the account is an account balance plan or a nonaccount balance plan?

The manner of determining the amount deferred for employment tax purposes under Section 3121 for a given period depends on whether the deferred compensation plan is an account balance plan or a nonaccount balance plan.[2]

Account Balance Plan

A plan is an account balance plan only if, under its terms, a principal amount is credited to an employee's individual account, the income attributable to each principal amount is credited or debited to the individual account, and the benefits payable to the employee are based solely on the balance credited to the individual account.[3] This is the typical voluntary top hat salary/bonus deferral plan and the defined contribution version of an employer-paid supplemental plan.

---

1.   Treas. Reg. §§31.3121(v)(2)-1(b)(4), 31.3306(r)(2)-1(a).
2.   Treas. Reg. §§31.3121(v)(2)-1(c)(1), 31.3306(r)(2)-1(a).
3.   Treas. Reg. §§31.3121(v)(2)-1(c)(1), 31.3306(r)(2)-1(a).

If the plan is an account balance plan, the amount deferred for a period equals the principal amount credited to the employee's account for the period, increased or decreased by any income or loss attributable thereto through the date when the principal amount must be taken into account as wages for FICA and FUTA purposes. See Q 3576 for a discission of the application of the Section 3121 "nonduplication rule" to account balance plans.

The regulations explain that "income attributable to the amount taken into account" means any amount that, under the terms of the plan, is credited on behalf of an employee and attributable to an amount previously taken into account, but only if the income is based on a rate of return that does not exceed either the actual rate of return on a predetermined actual investment or a reasonable rate of interest, if no predetermined actual investment has been specified.

Nonaccount Balance Plan

If the plan is a nonaccount balance plan, the amount deferred for a given period equals the present value of the additional future payment or payments to which the employee has obtained a legally binding right under the plan during that period; that is, when they become vested and no longer subject to a substantial risk of forfeiture The present value must be determined as of the date when the amount deferred must be taken into account as FICA taxable "wages," using actuarial assumptions and methods that are reasonable as of that date.[1]

With respect to these defined-benefit-type plans, the IRS has ruled privately that when a deferred compensation plan promises to pay a fixed amount in the future, the "amount deferred" is the present value of the expected benefits at the time when the benefits are considered wages for FICA purposes. The discount (that is, the income attributable to the amount deferred) is not treated as wages in that or any later year.[2] Thus, if the deferred compensation payments under such a plan do not vest (i.e., become nonforfeitable) until retirement, then the present value of the expected payments will not be treated as wages for FICA purposes until the year of retirement.

An employer may treat a portion of a nonaccount balance plan as a separate account balance plan if that portion satisfies the definition of an account balance plan and the amount payable under that portion is determined independently of the amount payable under the other portion of the plan.[3]

The "income attributable to the amount taken into account" means the increase, due solely to the passage of time, in the present value of the future payments to which the employee has obtained a legally binding right, the present value of which constitutes the amount taken into account, but only if determined using reasonable actuarial methods.[4]

Final Section 3121 regulations provide that an amount deferred under a nonaccount balance plan need not be taken into account as wages under the special timing rule (see Q 3577) until the earliest date on which the amount deferred is reasonably ascertainable. An amount

---

1.   Treas. Reg. §§31.3121(v)(2)-1(c)(2), 31.3306(r)(2)-1(a).
2.   TAMs 9051003, 9050006.
3.   Treas. Reg. §§31.3121(v)(2)-1(c)(1)(iii)(B), 31.3306(r)(2)-1(a).
4.   Treas. Reg. §§31.3121(v)(2)-1(d)(2), 31.3306(r)(2)-1(a).

deferred is reasonably ascertainable when there are no actuarial (or other) assumptions needed to determine the amount deferred other than interest, mortality, or cost-of-living assumptions.[1] For example, the IRS ruled that a participant's benefits under an IRC Section 457 plan (Q 3584) would not be subject to FICA tax simply because the plan's age and service requirements had been met, because benefits were not "reasonably ascertainable" at that time. Similarly, the benefits would not be subject to income tax withholding at that time, because they are not treated as constructively received until actually received for income tax withholding.[2]

Planning Point: It usually is better not to vest an employee in employer amounts subject to forfeiture until immediately before payment is scheduled to start, because there is currently no refund or credit ability for FICA taxes paid if the employee should leave the employer and forfeit his or her benefit under the plan. It usually is desirable to vest the benefit in the final year the employee is actively at work when the participant is above the wage limit and effectively incurs no FICA/FUTA taxation on the amounts (except for the portion that has no cap) By employing this strategy, the benefit payments avoid FICA/FUTA taxation following retirement. This strategy also reduces the risk that the employer will be liable for these employment taxes on post retirement payments by failing to include them during the participants' active working period when there would be little actual FICA/FUTA tax on the amounts, whether incrementally vested on portions of the benefit or vested on the entire benefit just prior to retirement.[3]

No amount deferred under a deferred compensation plan may be taken into account as FICA or FUTA wages before the plan is established.[4]

3579. Are self-employed individuals and corporate directors subject to FICA and FUTA taxes for deferred compensation arrangements?

Self-employed individuals pay Social Security taxes through self-employment ("SECA") taxes rather than FICA taxes. Deferred compensation of self-employed individuals is usually counted for SECA tax purposes when it is includable in income for income tax purposes.[5] Deferred compensation of self-employed individuals generally is counted for SECA purposes when paid, or when it is constructively received, if earlier.[6]

Likewise, corporate directors who defer their fees generally count those fees for SECA purposes when paid or constructively received (Q 3541).[7] This pattern of SECA imposition makes deferral of board fees a less attractive deferral technique for corporate directors as compared to deferred compensation for executive employees.

For a discussion of the SECA taxation of deferred commission payments to self-employed life insurance agents, see Q 650.

---

1.   Treas. Reg. §§31.3121(v)(2)-1(e)(4)(i), 31.3306(r)(2)-1(a).
2.   TAM 199902032.
3.   *See, Davidson v. Henkel* (Q 3576) in the Planning Point for discussion of a case in which a group of participants sought recovery from the employer in such a failure to include such deferred compensation amounts during their active employment period.
4.   Treas. Reg. §§31.3121(v)(2)-1(e)(1), 31.3306(r)(2)-1(a).
5.   See IRC Sec. 1402(a); Treas. Reg. §1.1402(a)-1(c).
6.   See, e.g., Let. Ruls. 9609011, 9540003.
7.   IRC Secs. 1402(a), 5123(a); Treas. Reg. §1.1402(a)-1(c); Let. Rul. 8819012.

3580. What is the wage base subject to FICA and FUTA taxes for deferred compensation arrangements?

The wage base for the Old Age, Survivors, and Disability Insurance ("OASDI") portion of the FICA tax and the taxable earnings base for the OASDI portion of the SECA tax are both $137,700 (up from $132,900 in 2019, $128,400 in 2018, $127,200 in 2017 and $118,500 for 2015 and 2016).

Medicare Hospital Insurance Portion and Health Care Reform Changes

There is no taxable wage base cap for the Medicare hospital insurance ("HI") portion of the FICA tax, so all deferred compensation counted as wages for FICA purposes is subject to at least the hospital portion of the FICA tax without limit.[1] There also is no earnings base cap for the hospital insurance portion of the SECA tax.[2]

Currently, the Medicare payroll tax on all wages is 2.9 percent, with the employer and employee each paying 1.45 percent. The Medicare payroll tax rate for the employee was raised to 2.35 percent beginning January 1, 2013 for individuals making more than $200,000 and couples making more than $250,000 annually. Also, a new 3.8 percent Medicare tax on the lesser of "investment income" or the amount of adjusted gross income in excess of the income breakpoints became effective January 1, 2013 on individuals making more than $200,000 of specially defined adjusted gross income concerning investment and other income, and couples making $250,000 ($125,000 for married couples filing separately).[3]

Section 457 Plans

Overview

3581. Are the tax benefits of a nonqualified deferred compensation account balance or nonaccount balance plan available through an agreement with a state or local government or other tax-exempt employer?

Yes.

Such plans for employees of tax exempt organizations generally are available under and covered by IRC Section 457 (but see Q 3607). It should be noted that governmental plans have slightly different rules under Section 457 than those of private tax-exempt organizations, such as charities and private colleges.[4] For both types of tax-exempt organizations – governmental or private – there are two kinds of plans under IRC Section 457: 1) "eligible" plans under Section 457(b), and 2) "ineligible" plans under Section 457(f). Receipt and taxation of compensation for services performed for a state or local government may be deferred under a Section 457 plan. See Q 3583 for a discussion of the impact of Section 409A on Section 457 plans.

---

1.   IRC Sec. 3121(a)(1).
2.   IRC Sec. 1402(b)(1).
3.   Health Care Reform Act of 2010, PL 111-148.
4.   Also, governmental plans are usually not subject to ERISA requirements but may have certain state rules for trusteeing or escrowing assets acquired for a plan.

For this purpose, a state or local government includes a state, a political subdivision of a state, or any agency or instrumentality of either of them, and a federal credit union since 2012 (see discussion infra.). A plan of a tax-exempt rural electric cooperative and its tax-exempt affiliates is included under these same rules. Deferred compensation plans covering state judges may not be governed under these rules (Q 3607). Although the IRC does not appear to provide for tax-exempt employers and governmental entities to maintain SIMPLE IRA plans (Q 3706), the IRS has stated that they may do so.[1] (SIMPLE IRA plans of tax-exempt employers and governmental entities are not subject to the limits of IRC Section 457.) IRC Section 409A specifically exempts 457(b) eligible plans from coverage by Section 409A, but specifically applies Section 409A to so-called 457(f) ineligible top hat plans.

IRC Section 457 also generally applies to deferred compensation agreements entered into with private, nongovernmental organizations exempt from tax under IRC Section 501 (for the most part, nonprofit organizations serving some public or charitable purpose). Amounts deferred under agreements with such tax-exempt organizations (other than tax-exempt rural electric cooperatives) in taxable years prior to December 31, 1986, do not fall within the rules applicable to Section 457 plans (for a discussion of the "Grandfather Rule," see Q 3582).

Churches fit into their own unique category within tax-exempt organizations. Neither a church (as defined in IRC Section 3121(w)(3)(A)), nor a church-controlled organization (as defined in IRC Section 3121(w)(3)(B)) is an eligible employer for purposes of IRC Section 457.[2] The plan of such a church employer, however, is subject to Section 409A unless the plan can claim one of the exceptions to coverage, such as the "short term deferral exception" (Q 3548). Such a church plan generally is not subject to ERISA requirements as well, unless so elected.[3]

In Notice 2005-58,[4] the IRS initially determined that a federal credit union was not covered by Section 457 because of its federal chartering, reversing a decision from a 2004 private letter ruling.[5] The notice said that a federally chartered credit union was not an eligible employer under IRC Section 457 because it was a federal instrumentality under IRC Section 501(c)(1). Under this Notice, a federal credit union that consistently claimed the status of a nongovernmental tax-exempt organization for employee benefit plan purposes was permitted to maintain an "eligible" or "ineligible" plan under IRC Section 457 if implemented on or before the August 2005 cutoff date provided in the notice. The Notice did not offer an interim solution for the creation of non-qualified plans pending resolution of the federal instrumentality issue, which was incorporated into a bigger project primarily dealing with the status of Indian tribe agency units.

The guidance in this Notice was the only guidance on this issue until 2012, when the IRS issued proposed regulations defining a federal instrumentality, and determined that a federal

---

1.   Notice 97-6, 1997-1 CB 353. See also *General Explanation of Tax Legislation Enacted in the 104th Congress* (JCT-12-96), n. 130, p. 140 (the 1996 Blue Book).
2.   IRC Sec. 457(e)(13); Treas. Reg. §1.457-2(e).
3.   Note that the issue of the ERISA coverage of a qualified retirement plan is a different issue and there have been a number of cases contesting the ERISA coverage of "church plans". Whether the legal logic in these cases can be applied to nonqualified deferred compensation plans is unclear. See Vol. 2, Part VIII Pensions & Profit Sharing for more discussion on this issue and recent cases.
4.   2005-33 IRB 295.
5.   Let. Rul. 200430013.

credit union was, in fact, a federal instrumentality. However, the IRS still concluded that, for purposes of available retirement plan authority, federal credit unions will look to Section 457 for construction of nonqualified plans, just like their state chartered peers.[1] This means that federal credit unions are authorized to have 457(b) eligible and 457(f) ineligible nonqualified plans, thus ending the eight year mystery of their proper authority for nonqualified plans. As to plans created by federal credit unions during the intervening period without guidance, plans created pursuant to 457(b) and 457(f) would seem to be safe from attack. In addition, a plan created during that period that complied with both Sections 409A and Section 83 (which was used by reference in Section 457(f)) would seemingly satisfy the most stringent income tax hurdles and avoid taxation. However, sponsors of such plans would need to consider modifications necessary to fit their plan entirely within the bounds of 457(f) as the most likely target. Designs that used other Code sections for plans are less certain and will probably require special procedures with the IRS in light of the proposed regulations, including the 2016 regulations integrating Sections 457 and 409A that took unexpected directions.

An "eligible" Section 457(b) plan is one that meets the annual deferral limits and other requirements of IRC Section 457 (Q 3584).[2] 457(b) plans are specifically exempt from 409A coverage. Plans that do not meet these limits are referred to as 457(f) "ineligible" plans and generally are top hat plans because of the ability to impose vesting on the benefits (and generally can be provided only to a select group of management or highly compensated employees for ERISA purposes) (Q 3602).[3] 457(f) plans are specifically covered by 409A. In 2016, the IRS finally released long-delayed proposed regulations integrating Sections 457 and 409A, especially as to 409A-covered 457(f) "ineligible" plans (Q 3583).

Plans Not Subject to IRC Section 457

For amounts deferred under plans of nongovernmental tax-exempt organizations under written agreements prior to December 31, 1986, see Q 3582.

Bona fide vacation leave, sick leave, compensatory time, severance pay (including certain voluntary early retirement incentive plans), disability pay, and death benefit plans, as well as a plan providing for payment of recurring part-year compensation (i.e., educational salaries), generally are not considered to be plans providing for the deferral of compensation and, thus, are not subject to IRC Section 457. The IRS has issued interim guidance for certain broad-based, nonelective severance pay plans of a state or local government in existence before 1999 with respect to the timing of reporting payments.[4] The 2016 proposed 457/409A integration regulations also clarify those 457 severance plans that are not also covered by Section 409A.[5]

Length of service awards (so-called LOSAPs) that accrue to bona fide volunteers (or their beneficiaries) due to "qualified services" after December 31, 1996 are also excluded from

---

1.   2005-33 IRB 295.
2.   Treas. Reg. §1.457-2(f).
3.   Treas. Reg. §1.457-2(h).
4.   Ann. 2000-1, 2000-2 IRB 294.
5.   Prop. Reg., REG 147196-07, June 22, 2016. Per the IRS release, the regulations may be relied upon immediately.

coverage.[1] "Qualified services," for this purpose, means firefighting and prevention services, emergency medical services, and ambulance services.[2] This exclusion does not apply when the accrued aggregate amount of the award in any year of service exceeds $6,000 ($3,000 for tax years beginning prior to 2018).[3]

IRC Section 457 also does not apply to nonelective deferred compensation attributable to services not performed as an employee. Deferred compensation is treated as nonelective for this purpose if all individuals with the same relationship to the employer are covered under the same plan, with no individual variations or options under the plan.[4]

3582. When will amounts deferred under certain grandfathered plans of nongovernmental tax-exempt organizations be exempt from IRC Section 457 requirements?

Amounts deferred under plans of nongovernmental tax-exempt organizations for taxable years beginning after December 31, 1986 are not subject to IRC Section 457 if made pursuant to an agreement that was in writing on August 16, 1986, and provides for yearly deferrals of a fixed amount or an amount determined by a fixed formula.[5] This grandfather provision is available only to those individuals covered under such a plan on August 16, 1986.[6]

Any modification to a written plan that directly or indirectly alters the fixed amount or the fixed formula will subject the plan to the limitations of IRC Section 457.[7] Modifications that reduce benefits apparently will not.[8]

Where promised retirement benefits provided (as a matter of practice) solely through a grandfathered nonqualified plan were offset by benefits from a qualified plan without altering the fixed formula determining the total amount of promised benefits, the grandfathered status of the nonqualified plan was not affected.[9] Similarly, an amendment to allow for the diversification into different mutual funds for the deemed investment of a participant's account and not limiting such participant to his or her original mutual fund investment options was found not to modify the basic formula and not to affect the grandfather status of the plan.[10]

Where, in the context of a parent-subsidiary structure established before August 16, 1986, a participant in the subsidiary's plan became an employee of the parent and was paid by the parent but retained his positions and responsibilities with, but not his compensation from, the subsidiary, a proposal to amend the subsidiary's plan to cover the participant's employment with the parent did not modify the plan's fixed formula and did not affect the grandfathered status of the plan.[11]

---

1.   IRC Sec. 457(e)(11)(A)(ii).
2.   IRC Sec. 457(e)(11)(C).
3.   IRC Sec. 457(e)(11)(B).
4.   IRC Sec. 457(e)(12).
5.   TRA '86, Sec. 1107(c)(3)(B).
6.   TAMRA '88, Sec. 1011(e)(6).
7.   Notice 87-13, 1987-1 CB 432, Notice 98-49, 1998-2 CB 365.
8.   See TAMRA '88, Sec. 6064(d)(3); Let. Ruls. 9538021, 9334021, 9250008.
9.   Let. Rul. 9549003.
10. Let. Rul. 9721012.
11. Let. Rul. 9548006.

The IRS has indicated that amendments providing for selection of investment alternatives and an election to receive an annual cash payment did not adversely affect the plan's grandfathered status under the Tax Reform Act of 1986.[1] In addition, the IRS has ruled that amendments to make such a pre-August 16, 1986 plan compliant with Section 409A (these old plans were not included in the Section 409A exemptions or exceptions) does not cause loss of the plan's grandfathering against coverage by Section 457.[2]

3583. How does Code Section 409A impact Section 457(b) "eligible" and Section 457(f) "ineligible" plans?

Nonqualified deferred compensation plans subject to Section 457 may also be covered by Section 409A. In such cases, a plan must comply with Section 409A separately and in addition to compliance with Section 457.[3] Section 409A does not apply to Section 457(b) "eligible" plans at all. 457(b) plans are specifically exempted from coverage under Section 409A.[4] However, Section 409A does apply to Section 457(f) "ineligible" top hat plans, thereby requiring such plans to comply with both Code sections. Unfortunately, the requirements of these IRC provisions do not mesh easily because Section 457(f) requires taxation upon vesting of a benefit. Vesting does not cause taxation for unfunded nonqualified deferred compensation plans of for-profit entities under Section 409A.

In an initial attempt to reconcile the requirements of Section 457(f) with Section 409A, the IRS released Notice 2007-62 while promising the future release of comprehensive integration regulations.[5] In the Notice, the IRS redefined certain terms for Section 457(f) purposes. Of significance, the IRS made the Section 409A definition of a "substantial risk of forfeiture" (SROF) the 457(f) definition. The 409A definition of SROF was and remains the most stringent and is more of a timing rule (it governs the availability of the short-term deferral exception) than a taxation rule. Therefore, the Notice had a significant negative impact on the design of certain 457(f) plans.

The negative impact of the guidance in the Notice primarily applied to voluntary deferral plans of vested compensation. Under the Notice, such plans could not achieve a substantial risk of forfeiture for 457(f) purposes to avoid current taxation. This was the result of the 409A/457(f) definition that precluded the existence of a SROF unless there was a substantial employer contribution to create a "materially larger benefit" (which was ill defined in 409A). Under 409A, as transposed into 457(f) under the Notice, it was unclear how much of an employer match was required to satisfy the 409A/457(f) requirement.

Before the Notice, a plan might have independently satisfied the old 457(f) SROF requirements (as then understood) and the individual "detail" Section 409A requirements (i.e., minimum

---

1.   Let. Rul. 9822038.
2.   Let. Rul. 201117001.
3.   Treas. Reg. § 1.409A-1(a)(4).
4.   IRC Sec. 409A(d); Treas. Reg. §1.409A-1(a)-(b).
5.   *See generally,* Notice 2007-62, 2007-31 IRB 311. The IRS promised the regulations integrating 409A and 457, especially as to 457(f) "ineligible" plans, for nearly 10 years before finally being released in June 2016, leaving only the IRS Notice for 457(f) plan design guidance during the interim.

documentation, permissible distributions, prohibitions against accelerations, and the timing of elections). The Notice's use of the Section 409A definition in Section 457(f) also eliminated the possibility of installment payments being treated as taxable as received under all designs. Such taxation was based upon using noncompetiton provisions to parallel the installment period and thus extend the vesting period until each payment was made.[1] The Section 409A definition (made the 457(f) definition under the Notice) does not recognize noncompetition and consulting agreements as a SROF to further delay taxation.

The IRS in Notice 2007-62 also redefined the definition of "severance plans" as to a voluntary and involuntary separation from service for purposes of Section 457(f) to engraft the 409A definition.

However, in June 2016 the IRS release the long-overdue proposed 457(f) regulations. In these proposed 457/409A integration regulations, the IRS has taken a surprising favorable change of direction and does not follow Notice 2007-62. Importantly, the IRS has adopted a separate definition for "substantial risk of forfeiture" than the one used in Section 409A (or other Code sections). It does remain clear that 457(f) plans are covered by Section 409A as well as 457(f), and therefore must comply with both Sections 457(f) and 409A to achieve and maintain deferral of taxation. However, these 2016 proposed 457(f)/409A integration regulations provide significant revised guidance on how to design both voluntary deferral plans of vested compensation (i.e., salary and bonus) as well as employer-paid SERPs to comply with both 457(f) and 409A. Detail on these proposed regulations can be found in Q 3603.

However, the 2016 proposed 457 regulations do not provide grandfathering or any specific guidance for dealing with or amending plans designed under Notice 2007-62 during the long interim period.

Planning Point: Under Notice 2007-62, employer-paid supplemental plans (account balance or nonaccount balance), were largely left unhindered, but even here the payments had to be made in a lump sum (or risk Section 72 taxation). Unless a voluntary deferral plan involved a significant employer match, a voluntary deferred compensation account balance plan was unlikely to satisfy the revised standard for income deferral under Section 457(f).

In the June 2016 proposed integration regulations, the IRS surprised everyone and took a different and more helpful approach to its integration of Sections 457(f) and 409A. These proposed regulations not only provide clarity on how to achieve tax deferral on vested compensation (by providing a safe harbor "materially greater benefit" rule), but also allow use of a "rolling risk of forfeiture" and noncompetition provisions to extend vesting again (although within very narrowly prescribed and defined conditions). Moreover, these regulations may immediately be relied upon for designing compliant new plans. However, these proposed regulations do not provide any grandfathering for existing plans so it is not clear how to address the many plans created during the period when only the Notice was available. In general, many of those plans will require modification because of the substantial differences between the Notice and the proposed regulations. Planners will need to follow the IRS's handling of the final regulations where it is hoped some guidance on handling existing 457(f) plans will be provided.

---

1.   In the absence of such a plan construction using noncompetiton provisions paralleling the installment period, Section 72 taxation would be applied to a sequence of installment payments from a 457(f) plan.

Section 457(b) "Eligible" Plans

3584. What are the requirements for a Section 457(b) "eligible" nonqualified deferred compensation plan of a tax-exempt or governmental organization?

There are two types of retirement-oriented nonqualified deferred compensation plans under Section 457: (1) the 457(b) "eligible" plan, and (2) the 457(f) "ineligible" plan. A deferred compensation plan under IRC Section 457(b) must meet certain requirements as set forth in Q 3585 to Q 3602. These requirements do not contain a prohibition against discrimination among employees. A Section 457 plan that is not designed and administered in accordance with these requirements will be treated as "ineligible," and must meet certain extra requirements (Q 3602).[1] Plans paying benefit awards based solely on length of service to bona fide volunteers or their beneficiaries on account of such volunteers' qualified services are exempt from Section 457.[2]

It should be noted that the Economic Growth and Tax Relief Reconciliation Act of 2001 (EGTRRA 2001) made many changes in the rules applicable to Section 457 plans. In addition, final regulations were issued in 2003 and were generally effective for taxable years beginning after December 31, 2001.[3] In addition, IRC Section 409A, enacted in 2004, specifically excludes 457(b) "eligible" plans from Section 409A coverage, but specifically includes 457(f) "ineligible" plans. Finally, the proposed regulations issued by the IRS in June 2016 to integrate 457 and 409A, especially as to 457(f) plans, clarified the application/nonapplication of Section 409A to various 457 plan types [e.g., 457(e)(11) severance plans].[4]

Governmental Versus Private Tax-Exempt Organizations

In general, 457(b) "eligible" plans separate into two different categories: (1) plans for governmental plans (i.e., state and local, also federal credit unions), and (2) plans for private tax-exempt organizations (e.g., Section 501(c)(3) organizations). The tax and ERISA rules for an eligible plan will vary according to the category the plan. See Q 3585 to Q 3602 for details.

3585. What are the rules regarding permissible participants in a Section 457(b) "eligible" nonqualified deferred compensation plan?

Under "eligible" plans, only individuals may participate, but they may be either employees or independent contractors. Partnerships and corporations cannot be participants.[5] Where local government employees were hired by a for-profit water company as part of privatization, they could no longer continue to participate in the local government's Section 457 plan.[6]

It should be noted that plans for nongovernmental private tax-exempt employers are subject to ERISA (unlike a governmental plan), except for church plans. Therefore, private tax-exempts

---

1. IRC Sec. 457(b)(6). An "ineligible" plan under Section 457(f) is also required to specifically comply with Code Section 409A.
2. IRC Sec. 457(e)(11)(A)(ii).
3. Treas. Reg. §1.457-12.
4. Per the IRS release, these 2016 proposed regulations may be relied upon immediately as of the release date.
5. Sen. Rep. 95-1263 (Revenue Act of 1978), *reprinted in* 1978-3 CB (vol. 1) 364.)
6. IRS Information Letter 2000-0300.

must structure their 457 plans to take advantage of a top hat ERISA exemption (e.g., by allowing only a select group of management or highly compensated employees to participate). Otherwise, the plan would be subject to the exclusive purpose and funding requirements of Title I of ERISA, and a nongovernmental tax-exempt Section 457 plan cannot, by definition, meet those requirements.[1]

3586. What are the timing requirements for deferred compensation under a Section 457(b) "eligible" nonqualified deferred compensation plan?

Generally, unlike 457(f) plans subject to Section 409A election timing requirements, compensation may be deferred into 457(b) plan for any calendar month. However, the deferral agreement must be entered into *before* the beginning of that month.[2] Despite this, a Section 457 plan may permit a newly hired employee to enter into an agreement before his or her first day of employment, under which deferrals will be made for the first month of employment. Non-elective employer contributions are treated as being made under an agreement entered into before the first day of the calendar month.[3] As noted, this timing of elections to defer should be contrasted with that required for 457(f) "ineligible" plans, which are subject to Section 409A and its election timing and deferral rules, including those requirements to exclude certain educational compensation that spans more than two calendar years, so-called educator annualized "recurring part-year compensation"[4]

A Section 457 plan may permit deferrals pursuant to an automatic election, under which a fixed percentage of an employee's compensation is deferred unless he or she affirmatively elects to receive it in cash.[5]

3587. What are the rules regarding the availability of the amounts payable under a Section 457(b) "eligible" nonqualified deferred compensation plan?

A Section 457(b) plan generally cannot provide that amounts will be made available before (1) the calendar year in which the participant attains age 70½, unless the employer is a state, political subdivision of a state or an agency or instrumentality thereof, in which case the age is 59½, (2) the date when the participant has a severance from employment (see Q 3588), or (3) the date when the participant is faced with "an unforeseeable emergency" (see Q 3589).[6] Here again the difference in the rules for a permissible distribution for a 457(b) "eligible" plan and a 457(f) "ineligible" plan , and the timing of taxation, need to be contrasted.

A participant in an eligible nongovernmental private tax-exempt Section 457 plan may make a one-time election, *after* amounts are available and *before* commencement of distributions, to

---

1.   See Let. Rul. 8950056.
2.   IRC Sec. 457(b)(4).
3.   Treas. Reg. §1.457-4(b).
4.   Treas. Reg. §1.409A-2(a)(14); Notice 2008-62; IR 2007-142; Preamble to 2016 Proposed 409A Regulations, §II.F. Prop. Reg. § 1,409A-1(b) (13) (2016).
5.   Rev. Rul. 2000-33, 2000-2 CB 142.
6.   IRC Sec. 457(d)(1)(A).

defer commencement of distributions (Q 3602).[1] Further deferral of taxation under amounts under an "ineligible" 457(f) plan is subject to very restrictive preconditions/conditions.[2]

The early distribution penalty applicable to qualified retirement plans generally does not apply to distributions from a Section 457 plan, except to the extent that the distribution is attributable to rollovers from a qualified retirement plan or a Section 403(b) plan, for which Section 457 plans are required to separately account (see Q 3576).[3]

Planning Point: This treatment should be contrasted with accelerated distributions from an "ineligible" 457(f) plan that is also subject to Section 409A requirements and distribution penalties for impermissible accelerated distributions, and income taxation upon vesting even if distribution does not occur.

3588. When does a "severance from employment" occur under a Section 457(b) "eligible" nonqualified deferred compensation plan?

A severance from employment occurs when a participant ceases to be employed by the employer sponsoring the plan.[4] An employee will not experience a severance from employment merely because any portion of his benefit is transferred (other than by a rollover or elective transfer) from his former employer's plan to the plan of his new employer.[5] This should be contrasted with the definition of separation of service for a 457(f) "ineligible" plan that is subject to Section 409A restrictive termination of employment definition. It should also be noted that unlike 457(b) "eligible" plans, roll-overs are not allowed for 457(f) "ineligible" plans.

Under the regulations for 457(b) plans, an independent contractor is considered to have separated from service upon an expiration of all contracts under which services are performed, if such expiration is considered a good faith and complete termination of the contractual relationship. Good faith is lacking where a renewal of the contractual relationship or the independent contractor becoming an employee is anticipated.[6] Note the similarity of the definition used here in a 457(b) plan for independent contractors and for a 457(f) plan, which are subject to very similar rules covering a separation from service distribution for independent contractors under the Section 409A regulations.

3589. Is a Section 457(b) "eligible" nonqualified deferred compensation plan required to include provisions regarding unforeseeable emergency situations?

A financial hardship provision allowing distributions to participants with financial difficulties is optional at the employer's option. However, if included an "unforeseeable emergency" must be defined in the plan as a severe financial hardship of participants or beneficiaries resulting from illnesses or accidents of the participants or beneficiaries or of their spouses or dependents, the

---

1.   IRC Sec. 457(e)(9)(B).
2.   Prop. Treas. Reg. § 1.457-12(e)(2) (2016); Preamble to 2016 Proposed 457 Regulations, §IV.E.
3.   IRC Sec. 72(t)(9).
4.   IRC Sec. 457(d)(1)(A)(ii); Treas. Reg. §1.457-6(b).
5.   EGTRRA 2001 Conf. Rep., *reprinted in* the General Explanation of EGTRRA 2001, p. 161.
6.   Treas. Reg. §1.457-6(b)(2).

loss of the participants' or beneficiaries' property due to casualty, or other similar extraordinary and unforeseeable circumstances arising as a result of events beyond their control. It should be noted that Section 457 uses terminology that is different from that in 401(k) and 403(b) plans but very similar to that used in Section 409A, which is also an optional plan provision. Moreover, the IRS has made it clear that it intends to treat the definitions as having the same meaning in both Code sections, especially as to 457(f) "ineligible" plans.[1]

Examples of valid emergencies in the Section 457 regulations and in Revenue Ruling 2010-27 include the imminent foreclosure of, or eviction from, a primary residence; the need to pay for medical or funeral expenses, including funeral expenses for an adult child who is not a dependent; and significant water damage to a principal residence. However, the most recent ruling indicates that paying off high credit card debt is not unforeseeable and therefore does not qualify.

Whether an event is an unforeseeable emergency will depend upon the relevant facts and circumstances of each case. However, a distribution on account of an unforeseeable emergency may not be made where the emergency may be relieved through reimbursement or compensation from insurance or otherwise, by liquidation of a participant's assets if liquidation in itself would not cause severe financial hardship, or cessation of deferrals under the plan. In addition, the distribution must be limited to the amount reasonably necessary to satisfy the emergency need (including amounts necessary to pay taxes or penalties reasonably expected to result from the distribution).[2] In order to ensure that the distribution is limited to the amount reasonably necessary to satisfy the emergency need, the IRS requires documentation in the form of receipts so that the plan administrator can verify the necessity of the amounts requested.[3]

Distributions made at any time on or after August 25, 2005 and before January 1, 2007 by an individual whose principal place of abode on August 28, 2005 was located in the Hurricane Katrina disaster area and who sustained an economic loss by reason of Hurricane Katrina are treated as permissible distributions under IRC Section 457(d)(1)(A). Total distributions under this provision may not exceed $100,000.[4]

A court *did* find a severe financial hardship where the participant's spouse gave birth to a severely ill child and had to cease working in order to care for such child.[5]

3590. How are loans treated under a Section 457(b) "eligible" nonqualified deferred compensation plan?

There is a difference in treatment of loans between nongovernmental and governmental entities. Any amount received by a participant as a loan from an eligible nongovernmental private tax-exempt Section 457(b) plan is treated as a distribution in violation of the distribution

---

1.   Rev. Rul. 2010-27. Also *see*, www.irs.gov/retirement-plans/employee-plans-news-december-17-2010-unforeseeable emergency. In this website entry, the IRS says, "In addition to 457(b) plans, the examples and related rules cited in the ruling also apply to emergency distributions from a nonqualified deferred compensation plan subject to IRC Section 409A".
2.   Treas. Reg. §1.457-6(c)(2).
3.   See IRS INFO 2014-0041.
4.   KETRA 2005 Sec. 101; Notice 2005-92, 2005-51 IRB 1165.
5.   *Sanchez v. City of Hartford*, 89 F. Supp. 2d 210 (DC 2000).

requirements and is prohibited.[1] But a facts and circumstances standard is applied to amounts received as loans from a governmental Section 457 "eligible" plan to determine whether the loan is bona fide and for the exclusive purpose of benefitting participants and beneficiaries. Factors considered include whether the loan has a fixed repayment schedule, a reasonable rate of interest, and repayment safeguards.[2] Such loans are taxed under the rules of IRC Section 72(p) (Q 3952).[3]

Contrast this with the treatment of loans under 457(f) "ineligible" plans covered by Section 409A where loans are expressly prohibited and an attempted loan would generate immediate taxation and penalties (Q 3541). Loans were prohibited prior to the enactment of Section 409A on nonqualified deferred compensation plans to avoid current taxation on the deferral accounts or plan benefits, including 457(f) plans, so this prohibition is not new.

3591. How are domestic relations orders treated in conjunction with Section 457(b) "eligible" nonqualified deferred compensation plans?

The Qualified Domestic Relations Order (QDRO) rules applicable to qualified plans (Q 3914) also apply to eligible Section 457 plans, so that the IRC Section 457(d) distribution rules are not violated if an eligible Section 457 plan makes a distribution to an alternate payee pursuant to a valid QDRO.[4]

Contrast this with a 457(f) "ineligible" plan where a DRO outlined by Section 409A regulations applies (Q 3541). Although there are parallels, the DRO has significant differences from the QDRO that a QDRO is designed to act on escrowed "plan assets" of a qualified plan that do not and must not exist in the case of a 457(f) "ineligible" plan that is and must be unfunded and unsecured (even if placed in a Rabbi Trust).

3592. What required minimum distribution ("RMD") requirements are imposed with regard to Section 457(b) "eligible" nonqualified deferred compensation plans?

For distributions *after December 31, 2001*, an eligible Section 457(b) plan is generally subject only to the same required minimum distribution rules as apply to qualified retirement plans.[5] These rules generally require a plan to begin distribution of an employee's interest no later than his or her required beginning date.[6] For a detailed discussion of the rules that apply to qualified retirement plans, see Q 3891 through Q 3908. The Worker, Retiree, and Employer Recovery Act of 2008 (WRERA 2008) provided that RMDs from governmental Section 457(b) defined contribution plans for calendar year 2009 were waived. Also, the five-year rule was to be determined without regard to 2009. The CARES Act also waived RMDs for 2020.

---

1.   Treas. Reg. §1.457-6(f)(1).
2.   Treas. Reg. §1.457-6(f)(2).
3.   Treas. Reg. §1.457-7(b)(3).
4.   IRC Secs. 414(p)(10), 414(p)(11).
5.   IRC Sec. 457(d)(2).
6.   IRC Sec. 401(a)(9)(A).

In contrast, a 457(f) "ineligible" plan is not subject to the minimum distribution rules, but must follow the distribution rules, especially the prohibitions against accelerations, in 457(f) and 409A.

For purposes of 457(b) plans, "Required beginning date" generally means April 1 of the calendar year following the *later* of (1) the year in which the employee attains age 70½ (except for certain government employers, where the age is 59½ beginning in 2020 under the SECURE Act)[1] or (2) the year in which the employee retires.[2] A special rule applies to a "5 percent owner" (as defined in IRC Section 416 (Q 3930), for whom "required beginning date" means April 1 of the calendar year following the year in which he or she attains age 70½).[3] Although this rule technically applies to Section 457 (b) plans maintained by tax-exempt employers (and not to governmental or church plans), as a practical matter, tax-exempt employers are as unlikely as governments and churches to have 5 percent owners. A Section 457 (b) plan may provide that the required beginning date for *all employees* is April 1 of the calendar year following the calendar year in which the employee attains age 70½.[4]

Penalty. An excise tax of 50 percent of the amount by which the required minimum distribution for the year exceeds the amount actually distributed is imposed on the payee (Q 3909).[5]

3593. What requirements involving the treatment of plan assets are imposed upon Section 457(b) "eligible" nonqualified deferred compensation plans?

Governmental plans. An eligible Section 457 plan of a governmental employer must hold all plan assets and income thereon in a trust, custodial account, or annuity contract for the exclusive benefit of participants and their beneficiaries. This rule allows them to comply with common state laws specifying specific funding requirements for retirement plans of state and local retirement plans. This account is exempt from tax under IRC Section 501(a).[6] A 457(b) plan is exempt and not subject to Section 409A; hence not subject to the funding rules in 409A(b).

Nongovernmental tax-exempt plans. A Section 457 plan, whether a 457(b) "eligible" plan or 457(f) "ineligible" plan, of a nongovernmental private tax-exempt employer must provide that amounts deferred, all property purchased with those amounts, and the income thereon will remain the property of the employer sponsoring the plan, and subject to the claims of its general creditors, commonly referred to as an unfunded and unsecured plan.[7] The participants may not have a secured interest in property held under such a Section 457 plan. A rabbi trust (Q 3567) may be established without causing such a Section 457 plan to violate this requirement.[8] Moreover, Section 457(f) "ineligible" plans are subject to additional and more stringent requirements, including the funding limitations and prohibitions under Code Section 409A(b) (Q 3603).

---

1.   See IRC Sec. 457(d)(1)(A)(i).
2.   IRC Sec. 401(a)(9)(C).
3.   IRC Sec. 401(a)(9)(C)(ii)(I).
4.   Treas. Reg. §1.401(a)(9)-2, A-2(e).
5.   IRC Sec. 4974.
6.   IRC Sec. 457(g); Treas. Reg. §1.457-8(a).
7.   IRC Sec. 457(b)(6); Treas. Reg. §1.457-8(b).
8.   Let. Ruls. 9517026, 9436015.

3594. What limitations on the amount of deferrals apply to Section 457(b) "eligible" nonqualified deferred compensation plans?

A Section 457(b) plan must provide that the annual deferral amount may not exceed the lesser of (1) 100 percent of includable compensation or (2) the applicable dollar limit. The dollar limit is $19,500 in 2020 and 2021, $19,000 in 2019 and $18,500 in 2018.[1] In tax years beginning after 2006, annual cost-of-living adjustments are made in $500 increments.[2] "Annual deferral" includes not only elective salary deferral contributions, but also nonelective employer contributions.[3] The annual deferral amount does not include any rollover amounts received by the plan on behalf of the participant.[4]

Any amount deferred in excess of the Section 457(b) plan's deferral limits is considered an "excess deferral". Likewise, where an individual participates in more than one Section 457 plan, amounts deferred not in excess of the applicable plan's deferral limits, but that exceeds the individual participant's deferral limit, are also considered excess deferrals.[5] Amounts that exceed a governmental Section 457 plan's deferral limits must be distributed to the participant, along with allocable net income, as soon as administratively practicable after the plan determines that the amount constitutes an excess deferral.[6] If a nongovernmental tax-exempt Section 457(b) plan's deferral limits are exceeded, the plan will be treated as a Section 457(f) "ineligible" plan.[7]

For these purposes, all plans in which the individual participates as a result of his or her relationship with a single employer are treated as a single plan.[8] Where excess deferrals have arisen out of a failure to satisfy the individual deferral limitation, a Section 457(b) plan may provide that the excess deferral will be distributed as soon as administratively practicable after the plan determines that the amount constitutes an excess deferral. If the Section 457(b) plan does not distribute the excess deferral, it will not lose its status as an eligible plan, but the participant must include the excess amount in income for the later of (1) the taxable year in which it was deferred or (2) the first taxable year in which there is no longer a 457(f) substantial risk of forfeiture.[9]

The contribution limits under IRC Section 457(b) are _not_ coordinated with the IRC Section 402(g) limits on elective deferrals under IRC Section 401(k) plans and IRC Section 403(b) plans.[10] These limitations do not apply to qualified governmental excess benefit arrangements under IRC Section 415(m) (3).[11]

---

1.   Notice 2017-64, Notice 2018-83, Notice 2019-59, Notice 2020-79.
2.   IRC Sec. 457 (b) (2).
3.   Treas. Reg. §1.457-2(b).
4.   Treas. Reg. §1.457-4(c)(1)(iii).
5.   Treas. Reg. §§1.457-4(e)(1), 1.457-5.
6.   Treas. Reg. §1.457-4(e)(2).
7.   Treas. Reg. §1.457-4(e)(3).
8.   Treas. Reg. §§1.457-4(e)(2), 1.457-4(e)(3).
9.   Treas. Reg. §1.457-4(e) (4).
10.   IRC Sec. 457 (c).
11.   IRC Sec. 457 (e) (14).

Pre-409A, some employers avoided the deferral limitations by deliberately failing to satisfy the trust requirements under IRC Section 457(g) – so that the IRS would rule the plan to be an *ineligible* plan (Q 3602) – while maintaining a Section 457 (f) "substantial risk of forfeiture" (Q 3538) in order to avoid current taxation.[1] Under Section 409A and its guidance and the 2016 Proposed Regulations integrating 457 with 409A, the plan would also need to satisfy the requirements of both the unique 457(f) "substantial risk of forfeiture" definition and as well as the 409A "substantial risk of forfeiture" definition.. In most cases the unique and very stringent 457(f) definition requirements to achieve deferral, especially as to voluntary deferral 457(f) plans, will present the most difficult and perhaps impossible hurdle for potential plan sponsors. SERPs will find compliance with both definitions much less of a challenge.

Compensation. "Includable compensation" has the meaning given to "participant's compensation" by IRC Section 415(c) (3) (Q 3866). Includable compensation is determined without regard to community property laws. Compensation is taken into account at its present value in the plan year in which it is deferred (or, if the compensation deferred, is subject to a Section 457(f) substantial risk of forfeiture, at its present value in the plan year in which such risk is first eliminated).[2]

3595. Can participants in a Section 457(b) "eligible" nonqualified deferred compensation plan make catch-up contributions?

IRC Section 457(b) Catch-up Rules. An eligible Section 457(b) plan can provide for catch-up contributions in one or more of a participant's last three taxable years ending before the participant attains normal retirement age under the plan. For those years, in addition to the normal limits, a participant may defer a catch-up amount equal to the portions of normal deferral limits unused in prior taxable years for which the participant was eligible to participate in the plan.[3] During those years, the limit on deferrals is increased to the lesser of (1) twice the amount of the regularly applicable dollar limit (2 × $19,500 in 2020 and 2021); or (2) the underutilized limitation.[4] Note that the IRC Section 457(b) catch-up rules cannot be used for the year in which the participant attains normal retirement age.[5] The underutilized limitation is the sum of (1) the otherwise applicable limit for the year; plus (2) the amount by which the applicable limit in preceding years exceeded the participant's actual deferral for those years.[6]

For purposes of determining the underutilized limitation for pre-2002 years, participants remain subject to the rules in effect for those prior years (e.g., includable compensation is reduced by all pre-tax contributions and the previous coordination rules apply.).[7] A participant cannot elect to have the IRC Section 457(b) catch-up rules apply more than once, even if the participant failed to use it in all three years before reaching retirement age, and even if he or she rejoined the plan or participated in another plan after retirement.

---

1. See, e.g., Let. Rul. 9823014.
2. IRC Secs. 457(e)(5), 457(e)(6), 457(e)(7).
3. IRC Sec. 457(b)(3); Treas. Reg. §1.457-4(c)(3).
4. Treas. Reg. §1.457-4(c)(3)(i).
5. See, e.g., Treas. Reg. §1.457-4(c)(3)(D)(vi), Ex. 3.
6. Treas. Reg. §1.457-4(c)(3)(ii).
7. Treas. Reg. §§1.457-4(c)(3)(iii), 1.457-4(c)(iv).

For purposes of the IRC Section 457(b) catch-up rules, the Section 457(b) plan must generally specify the plan's normal retirement age. Under the regulations, a Section 457(b) plan may define normal retirement age as any age on or after the earlier of (1) age 65 or (2) the age when participants may retire and receive immediate retirement benefits (without actuarial or other reduction) under the basic defined benefit plan of the government or tax-exempt entity, but in any event, no later than age 70½ (even post-SECURE Act for these types of plans). A special rule provides that Section 457(b) plans may permit participants to designate a normal retirement age within these ages instead of designating a normal retirement age. A participant may not have more than one normal retirement age under different plans sponsored by the employer sponsoring the Section 457(b) plan for purposes of the IRC Section 457(b) catch-up rules. Plans that include among their participants qualified police or firefighters may designate an earlier normal retirement age for such qualified police and firefighters.[1]

Age 50 Catch-up Rules. An additional catch-up rule applies for eligible Section 457(b) plans of governmental employers.[2] Additional contributions are allowed for participants who have attained age 50 by the end of the taxable year.[3] (See also Q 3761.) All eligible IRC Section 457(b) governmental plans of an employer are treated as a single plan.[4] The additional amount is the lesser of (1) the applicable dollar amount; or (2) the participant's compensation, reduced by the amount of any other elective deferrals that the participant made for that year.[5]

The applicable dollar amount for eligible IRC Section 457(b) governmental plans is $6,500 in 200, up from $6,000 in 2015-2019.[6] The limit is indexed for inflation in $500 increments for years beginning after 2006.[7] An individual participating in more than one plan is subject to one annual dollar limit for all catch-up contributions during the taxable year.[8] Catch-up contributions by participants age 50 or over, made under the provisions of IRC Section 414(v), are not subject to any otherwise-applicable limitation of IRC Section 457(b)(2) (determined without regard to IRC Section 457(b)(3)).[9] See Q 3761 for additional details on the requirements for the new catch-up contributions.

During the last three years before a participant reaches normal retirement age, the age 50 catch-up rules do not apply if a higher catch-up amount would be permitted under the IRC Section 457(b) catch-up rules referenced above. Thus, an individual who is eligible for additional deferrals under both the age 50 catch-up and the IRC Section 457(b) catch-up rules is entitled to the greater of (1) the applicable dollar limit in effect for the plan year plus the age 50 catch-up contribution amount, disregarding the IRC Section 457(b) catch-up rules or (2) the applicable

---

1. Treas. Reg. §1.457-4(c)(3)(v).
2. IRC Sec. 414(v)(6)(A)(iii); Treas. Reg. §1.414(v)-1(a)(1).
3. IRC Sec. 414(v)(5).
4. IRC Sec. 414(v)(2)(D).
5. Treas. Reg. §1.457-4(c)(2)(i).
6. IR-2014-99 (Oct. 23, 2014), IR-2015-118 (Oct. 21, 2015), Notice 2016-62, Notice 2017-64, Notice 2018-83, Notice 2019-59.
7. IRC Sec. 457(e)(15); Treas. Reg. §1.457-4(c)(2)(i).
8. Treas. Reg. §1.414(v)-1(f)(1).
9. IRC Sec. 414(v)(3)(A).

dollar limit in effect for the plan year plus the contribution amount under the IRC Section 457(b) catch-up rules, disregarding the age 50 catch-up rules.[1]

The catch up rules do not apply to 457(f) plans, but do not generally present a problem since employee and employer deferrals are not limited any way for "ineligible" plans. In fact, the requirement of specific levels of employer contributions in order to achieve deferral of taxation when participant deferrals are involved is more the challenge.

For the taxation of amounts deferred under a Section 457(b) plan, see Q 3602.

3596. Do any special rules regarding small distributions and transfers apply to Section 457(b) "eligible" nonqualified deferred compensation plans?

Yes. If a participant's total distribution is $5,000 or less, the participant may elect to receive such amount (or the Section 457(b) plan may provide for an involuntary cashout of such amount) if (1) no amount has been deferred by the participant during the two-year period ending on the date of distribution; and (2) there has been no prior distribution under this provision.[2] Contrast this with the small amount distribution rules for 457(f) "ineligible" plans subject to 409A that permits distribution of the 402(g)(1)(b) amount ($19,500 in 2020 and 2021).

Participants are permitted to make tax-free transfers between eligible Section 457(b) plans as long as the amounts transferred are not actually or constructively received prior to the transfer.[3] But according to the regulations, plan-to-plan transfers must meet certain requirements and are permitted only from one governmental plan to another, or from one nongovernmental private tax-exempt plan to another, but *not* between a governmental plan and a nongovernmental private tax-exempt plan. In addition, no direct transfer may be made from a governmental plan to a qualified retirement plan except in the context of a service credit purchase, discussed in Q 3598. A tax-exempt plan may *not* directly transfer assets to a qualified retirement plan, and a qualified retirement plan may *not* directly transfer assets to either a governmental plan or a nongovernmental tax-exempt plan.[4]

Employees that deferred amounts to a Section 457(b) plan in which they were ineligible to participate cannot transfer such amounts, under IRC Section 457(e)(10), to a Section 457(b) plan in which they *are* eligible to participate.[5]

3597. Are rollover distributions permitted in the context of Section 457(b) "eligible" nonqualified deferred compensation plans?

Yes. Distributions may be rolled over to and from eligible Section 457(b) plans of governmental employers under rules similar to those for qualified retirement plans and tax-sheltered annuities.[6] If an eligible Section 457(b) plan of a governmental employer receives a rollover

---

1.   Treas. Reg. §1.457-4(c)(2)(ii).
2.   IRC Sec. 457(e)(9); Notice 98-8, 1998-4 IRB 6.
3.   See IRC Sec. 457(e)(10); Let. Ruls. 199923010, 8946019, 8906066.
4.   Treas. Reg. §1.457-10(b)(1).
5.   Let. Rul. 9540057.
6.   IRC Sec. 457(d)(1)(C); Treas. Reg. §1.457-7(b)(2).

from a qualified retirement plan or a TSA, it must separately account for such rollover amounts thereafter.[1]

The following rules applicable to rollovers from qualified retirement plans (Q 3997) are also applicable to rollovers to and from eligible Section 457(b) plans of governmental employers:

(1) Maximum amount of rollover

(2) 60-day limitation

(3) Definition of eligible rollover distribution

(4) Sales of distributed property

(5) Frozen deposits

(6) Surviving spouse rollovers

(7) For distributions after December 31, 2006, nonspouse beneficiary rollovers[2]

The direct rollover rules, automatic rollover option, and withholding rules applicable to qualified retirement plans (Q 4000) also apply.[3]

Transfers between eligible Section 457(b) plans remain the only option for eligible Section 457(b) plans of *nongovernmental private tax-exempt organizations*.[4]

Contrast this with a 457(f) "ineligible" plan benefit that may not be rolled over into another qualified retirement plan, 457(b), another 457(f) plan or an IRA at all, and is taxable upon vesting according to 457(f) and subject to the inclusion rules for violations of Section 409A.[5]

3598. What is a service credit purchase in the context of a governmental Section 457(b) "eligible" nonqualified deferred compensation plan?

In many states, participants may use "permissive service credits" to increase their retirement benefits under a state's governmental 457(b) "eligible" defined benefit retirement plan(s). For this purpose, permissive service credit means credit for a period of service that a plan recognizes only if the employee contributes an amount, determined by the plan, which does not exceed the amount necessary to fund the benefit attributable to such period of service. Such contributions must be voluntary and made in addition to regular employee contributions, and are generally subject to the limits of IRC Section 415.[6]

Participants may exclude from income amounts directly transferred (i.e., from trustee to trustee) from a Section 457(b) contributory plan of a governmental employer to a governmental

---

1.   IRC Secs. 402(c)(8)(B), 403(b)(8)(A)(ii).
2.   IRC Sec. 457(e)(16).
3.   IRC Secs. 457(d)(1)(C), 3401(a)(12)(E).
4.   IRC Sec. 457(d)(1)(C).
5.   See Prop Treas. Reg., REG 1238196-12, June 22, 2016.
6.   EGTRRA 2001 Conf. Rep., *reprinted in* the General Explanation of EGTRRA 2001, pp. 161, 162.

defined benefit plan in order to purchase permissive service credits. Likewise, a participant may use such directly transferred amounts to repay contributions or earnings that were previously refunded because of a forfeiture of service credit, under either the transferee plan or another Section 457(b) plan maintained by a governmental employer in the same state.[1]

There is no parallel concept for nongovernmental private tax-exempts, nor for 457(f) "ineligible" plans.

3599. Will the IRS issue advance rulings on the tax consequences of Section 457(b) "eligible" and Section 457(f) "ineligible" nonqualified deferred compensation plans?

Since the enactment of IRC Section 409A, the IRS has refused to issue advance rulings on the tax consequences of nonqualified deferred compensation plans of for-profit companies as it once did prior to Section 409A (Q 3541). The availability and requirements for favorable letter rulings for plans under Section 457(b) were not clear even before the enactment of Section 409A (and even before the IRS' release of guidance refusing to issue letter rulings on all plans in for-profit entities).

It was clear though, prior to the enactment of Section 409A, that the IRS would not issue an advance ruling on the tax consequences of a Section 457(b) plan covering independent contractors, unless all such independent contractors were identified.[2] Now that 457(b) "eligible" plans are specifically exempted from, and 457(f) "ineligible" plans are specifically covered by, Section 409A statutorily, perhaps the IRS will begin to provide letter rulings on 457(b) "eligible" plans. However, the IRS has indicated its direction will be to issue fewer letter rulings on qualified plans, so it is currently not likely that 457(b) plan can obtain a letter ruling either. As noted, the IRS specifically will not issue letter rulings on the income tax consequences of plans that are covered by Section 409A, which would include 457(f) "ineligible" plans (see Q 3541).

3600. Is the cost of current life insurance protection under a Section 457 plan taxable to participants?

If life insurance is purchased with amounts deferred under a Section 457 plan, whether a 457(b) "eligible" or 457(f) "ineligible" plan, the cost of current life insurance protection is not taxed to the participant, as long as the plan retains all the incidents of ownership in the policy, is the sole beneficiary under the policy, and is under no obligation to transfer the policy or to pass through the life insurance proceeds of the policy. To have an "eligible" plan, under a nongovernmental private tax-exempt entity, the plan must be unfunded and the plan assets cannot be set aside (escrowed) for any participants or their beneficiaries (Q 3581).[3] This plan ownership requirement does not allow for the combination of endorsement split dollar and informal

---

1.   IRC Sec. 457(e)(17).
2.   Rev. Proc. 2003-3, Sec. 3.01(36), 2003-1 CB 113, as modified by Rev. Proc. 2011-56.
3.   Treas. Reg. §1.457-8(b)(1).

deferred compensation funding on the same life insurance policy as is frequently done with nonqualified deferred compensation plans for-profit entities (Q 3959).

3601. Are death benefits under a Section 457 plan excludable from gross income?

If a death benefit is provided by a nongovernmental Section 457 plan, whether a 457(b) "eligible" or 457(f) "ineligible" plan, any such death benefit will not qualify for exclusion from gross income as the proceeds of life insurance under IRC Section 101(a). The life insurance proceeds must first be paid to the employer as sole beneficiary; hence, are "washed" through the employing entity and lose their tax-free character.[1] Prior to the enactment of Section 409A, both 457 "eligible" and "ineligible" plans would have to be treated under the deferred compensation rules of Section 457.[2]

Since the enactment of Section 409A, however, an "eligible" plan would be subject only to Section 457 treatment on the deferred compensation death benefit, while a Section 457(f) ineligible plan would have to comply with both Sections 457 and 409A. However, the outcome is still the same because a death benefit paid from the employer rather than directly from the life insurance carrier (e.g., as in the case of endorsement split dollar) will still be treated as deferred compensation and thereby as income-in-respect of a decedent, etc. rather than the proceeds of life insurance (Q 3602). The proposed 457/409A integration regulations have not changed this result.

Planning Point: As a practical matter, what this means is that tax-exempt organizations cannot create the combination of an endorsement split dollar life insurance arrangement on a single organization-owned policy acquired to help support a 457 supplemental deferred compensation plan. It will only be able to support a DBO plan and the payment will produce IRD.

3602. How are the participants in a Section 457(b) "eligible" plan taxed?

Amounts deferred under a governmental Section 457(b) "eligible" plan, and any income attributable to such amounts, are includable in the participant's gross income for the taxable year in which they are distributed/paid to the participant (or to the beneficiary).[3]

Unless a taxpayer elects otherwise, any amount of a qualified Hurricane Katrina distribution required to be included in gross income shall be so included ratably over the three-year taxable period beginning with such year. Qualified Hurricane Katrina distributions are distributions not exceeding $100,000 in the aggregate from qualified retirement plans, individual retirement plans, Section 403(b) tax-sheltered annuities, or eligible governmental Section 457 plans made at any time on or after August 25, 2005, and before January 1, 2007, by an individual whose principal place of abode on August 28, 2005, was located in the Hurricane Katrina disaster area and who sustained an economic loss by reason of Hurricane Katrina.[4]

---

1.   Treas. Reg. §1.457-10(d).
2.   Let. Rul. 9008043.
3.   IRC Sec. 457(a)(1)(A); Treas. Reg. §1.457-7(b)(1).
4.   Section 101(e), KETRA 2005; Notice 2005-92, 2005-51 IRB 1165.

Nongovernmental (Private) Tax-Exempt Section 457(b) Eligible Plan

Distributions of amounts deferred under Section 457 eligible plans sponsored by nongovernmental tax-exempt organizations (private charitable organizations and colleges, etc.) are includable in the participant's gross income for the taxable year in which they are made available to the participant (or to the beneficiary), without regard to whether they actually have been distributed.[1] These amounts are not considered to be available simply because the participant or beneficiary is permitted to direct the investment of amounts deferred under the plan.[2]

Amounts generally are considered made available and, hence, includable in income as of the earliest date on which the plan permits distributions to be made on or after the severance of employment, but not later than the date on which the required minimum distribution rules of IRC Section 401(a)(9) would require commencement of distributions.[3]

Section 457(b) plans of private nongovernmental tax exempts may provide a period during which participants are permitted to elect to defer the payment of all or a portion of amounts deferred until a fixed or determinable date in the future. This election period must expire before the first time when any amounts deferred are considered made available to the participant.[4] If the participant fails to make this election, the amounts deferred generally would be includable in income when made available as discussed above. Plans may provide, however, for a "default payment schedule" to be used if no election is made, in which case amounts deferred are includable in income for the year in which such amounts first are made available under the default payment schedule.[5] In addition, a plan may provide for a second, one-time election to further defer payment of amounts deferred beyond the initial distribution deferral.

Participants may not elect to accelerate commencement of such distributions, however. Amounts deferred are not treated as available merely because the participant may elect this second deferral. Participants may be permitted to make this second deferral election even if they:

(1) have previously received a distribution on account of an unforeseeable emergency;

(2) have previously received a cash-out distribution of an amount of $5,000 or less;

(3) have previously made (or revoked) other elections regarding deferral or mode of payment; or

(4) are subject to a default payment schedule deferring the commencement of benefit distribution.[6]

A plan may provide participants with an opportunity to elect among methods of payment, provided such election is made before the amounts deferred are to be distributed according

---

1.   IRC Sec. 457(a)(1)(B); Treas. Reg. §1.457-7(c)(1).
2.   Treas. Reg. §1.457-7(c)(1).
3.   Treas. Reg. §1.457-7(c)(2)(i).
4.   Treas. Reg. §1.457-7(c)(2)(ii)(A).
5.   Treas. Reg. §1.457-7(c)(2)(ii)(B).
6.   Treas. Reg. §1.457-7(c)(2)(iii).

to the participant's (or beneficiary's) initial or additional distribution deferral election. If the participant does not make an election regarding the mode of payment, the amounts deferred are included in the participant's gross income when they become available pursuant to either the participant's initial or additional election, unless such amounts are subject to, and includable in income according to, a default payment schedule.[1]

In addition, amounts are not considered made available to a participant or beneficiary solely because a participant or beneficiary may elect to receive a distribution on account of an unforeseeable emergency or a cash-out distribution of $5,000 or less.[2]

The use of a properly drafted and operated rabbi trust in connection with a nongovernmental private tax-exempt Section 457 eligible plan should not affect the tax treatment of participants or their beneficiaries.[3]

Contrast this treatment to the distribution/payment and detailed and complex subsequent election rules imposed on 457(f) "ineligible" plans under 457(f) rules and those governing Section 409A.

3603. How are the participants in a Section 457(f) "ineligible" plan taxed?

Prior to the enactment of Section 409A,[4] the general income tax rule was that compensation deferred under an ineligible and unfunded Section 457(f) plan was includable in gross income in the first taxable year during which it is not subject to a Section 457(f) "substantial risk of forfeiture" that pointed to Section 83, governing *funded* deferred compensation plans, for its definition of substantial risk of forfeiture (Q 3538).[5] Where no 457(f) substantial risk of forfeiture existed in the initial year of deferral, all compensation deferred under the plan had to be included in the participant's gross income for that year. This rule still applies to any 457(f) plan amounts in plans in existence prior to the enactment of Section 409A that may be eligible to be grandfathered. They would also apply to amounts in a plan if it can claim the short-term deferral exception to Section 409A coverage, since it has been made clear that 457(f) plans can claim the 409A short- term deferral exception.

Section 409A, which specifically included 457(f) ineligible plans under Section 409A coverage, requires such ineligible plans to comply with both the requirements under Section 457(f) and Section 409A. Unfortunately, the two IRC sections did not integrate smoothly. The IRS tried to reconcile them in IRS Notice 2007-62 shortly after the final regulations to Section 409A were issued in 2007. The IRS also promised to issue comprehensive 457/409A integration regulations (see Q 3603 for a discussion of these regulations). Commentators saw significant problems in the Notice's proposed solutions, at least as to the substantial risk of forfeiture requirement that proposed to substitute the 409A definition of substantial risk of forfeiture for the one in 457(f), which had been less onerous.

1.   Treas. Reg. §1.457-7(c)(2)(iv).
2.   Treas. Reg. §1.457-7(c)(2)(i).
3.   Let. Ruls. 9517026, 9436015.
4.   Section 409A generally became effective January 1, 2005.
5.   IRC Sec. 457(f)(1)(A); Treas. Reg. §1.457-11(a)(1). Section 409A generally became effective January 1, 2005.

Prior Guidance: Prior to the enactment of Section 409A, a participant's right to deferred compensation under an ineligible Section 457 plan was subject to a 457(f) substantial risk of forfeiture if it was conditioned on the future performance of substantial services by any individual.[1] Because this is the same language as used in IRC Section 83, governing transfers of property as compensation, it generally was believed that Section 83 concepts governed this definition for 457(f) purposes. Hence, distributions would become taxable when no longer subject to a Section 457(f) substantial risk of forfeiture, which might be as late as the date of each payment by the proper use of covenants not to compete, consulting agreements, and similar devices to continue the risk of forfeiture until payment actually was made.[2]

If the risk were to lapse before or at the time payments began, however, distributions from an ineligible plan would be taxable according to the Section 72 annuity rules.[3] Property (including an insurance contract or annuity) distributed from an ineligible plan is includable in gross income at its fair market value.[4] Once the annuity contract has been distributed, payments or withdrawals from that contract may be subject to the "interest first" rule (Q 10, Q 513).

Prior to the enactment of Section 409A and the Section 457 final regulations, it was not entirely clear when earnings on compensation deferred under an ineligible plan would be includable in gross income. The Section 457 final regulations currently provide that if amounts deferred are subject to a 457(f) substantial risk of forfeiture, then the amount includable in gross income for the first taxable year in which there is no Section 457(f) substantial risk of forfeiture includes earnings up to the date of the lapse. Earnings accruing after the date of the lapse are not includable in gross income until paid or otherwise made available, provided that the participant's (or the beneficiary's) interest in any assets of the employer is not senior to that of the employer's general creditors.[5] Based upon Notice 2007-62, the substantial risk of forfeiture applied for this purpose would become the more stringent 409A substantial risk of forfeiture definition, which for example, specifically excludes non-competes and consulting services as valid risks of forfeiture.

After enactment and release of IRS Notice 2007-62, the IRS proposed to use the Section 409A definition of substantial risk of forfeiture in place of that in Section 457(f) in an attempt to reconcile the sections. The impact of this proposed definition substitution was severely detrimental to 457(f) plans, especially 457(f) voluntary deferral plans.

Before the notice, it would have been possible for a 457(f) plan (whether a voluntary deferral or employer-paid supplemental plan) to have complied with the requirements under 457(f) as to substantial risk of forfeiture and then to have complied with the detailed coverage requirements of Section 409A separately, and avoided current income taxation under both sections.

---

1. IRC Sec. 457(f)(3)(B); Treas. Reg. §1.83-3(c).
2. Note that the IRS released proposed regulations, clarifying the Section 83 definition of "substantial risk of forfeiture" on May 29, 2012. Final regulations that are substantially similar to these proposed regulations were released February 25, 2014. The IRS claims that the final Section 83 regulations make no substantive change in its positions on the necessary risks of forfeiture and the factors that make them sufficiently substantial.
3. IRC Sec. 457(f)(1)(B); Treas. Reg. §1.457-11(a)(4).
4. H. Rep. 95-1445 (Revenue Act of 1978), reprinted in 1978-3 CB (vol. 1) 227; Sen. Rep. 95-1263 (Revenue Act of 1978), reprinted in 1978-3 CB (vol. 1) 364.
5. Treas. Reg. §1.457-11(a).

After Notice 2007-62, this became impossible. Moreover, the Section 409A definition is the most severe definition of substantial risk of forfeiture of all the definitions currently in the IRC because it is used primarily to limit the availability of the short term deferral exception (Q 3548) that would allow plans to escape Section 409A coverage. Hence, this most stringent Section 409A rule governed taxation under Section 457(f) plans, so that a 457(f) ineligible plan became taxable (for 457(f) purposes) when the 409A substantial risk of forfeiture lapsed. This meant that a plan could be fully compliant with the Section 409A detailed form and operation requirements and yet still fail the 457(f) substantial risk of forfeiture requirement because of the IRS's proposed move to use the Section 409A definition in Section 457(f).

Note that under the Section 409A definition, devices such as covenants not to compete do not constitute a valid substantial risk of forfeiture (however, see the discussion of the applicability of the new proposed 409A/457 regulations to noncompetition agreements, Q 3604). This means that 457(f) distributions could only be paid either as a lump sum, or under Section 72 annuity treatment if paid in installments, based on Notice 2007-62 guidance. Moreover, the IRS requires a voluntary employee or director deferral plan to have an employer contribution such that it creates an amount, on a present value basis, that would make the amount of the benefit "materially greater" than the benefit without it, before it considers that a 457(f) ineligible plan has the necessary substantial risk of forfeiture (for 457(f) purposes) to permit a deferral of income taxation. This situation existed since the release of Notice 2007-62 until the release of the 2016 proposed regulations integrating 457, especially 409A-covered plans, with Section 409A. The proposed regulations did not follow the Notice, and created a more favorable, but unique and complex, rules for tax deferral under 457(f) plans.

Additionally, these 2016 Section 457 (not 409A) rules (made immediately effective) that continue to apply to the tax treatment of ineligible Section 457 plans do not extend these rules to any of the following: (1) any plan qualified under IRC Section 401, IRC Section 403, or IRC Section 415(m), (2) that portion of any plan that consists of a nonexempt trust to which IRC Section 402(b) applies, and (3) any transfer of property to which IRC Section 83 applies.[1]

The Section 457 regulations also clarify that these provisions do not apply if a IRC Section 83 transfer occurs before the lapse of a 457(f) substantial risk of forfeiture applicable to amounts deferred under an ineligible plan. If, on the other hand, the IRC Section 83 transfer occurs after the lapse of a 457(f) substantial risk of forfeiture, the provisions do apply. If such property is includable in income under IRC Section 457(f) on the lapse of a substantial risk of forfeiture, when the property is later made available to the participant, the amount includable is the excess of the value of the property when made available over the amount previously included in income on the lapse.[2] This section does not apply to an equity option that has no readily ascertainable fair market value (as defined in IRC Section 83(e)(3)) and that was granted on or before May 8, 2002.[3]

If a plan starts but then ceases to be an 457(b) eligible governmental plan by operation, amounts subsequently deferred by participants will be includable in income when deferred, or,

---

1. IRC Sec. 457(f)(2); Treas. Reg. §1.457-11(b).
2. Treas. Reg. §1.457-11(d)(1).
3. Treas. Reg. §1.457-12.

if later, when the amounts deferred cease to be subject to a 457(f) substantial risk of forfeiture. Amounts deferred before the date on which the plan ceases to be an "eligible" governmental plan, and any earnings thereon, will be treated as if the plan continues to be an "eligible" governmental plan and, thus, will not be includable in income until paid to the participant or beneficiary.[1]

Rulings on "Ineligible" Plans

Prior to the enactment of Section 409A, the creation of a rabbi trust in connection with an "ineligible" Section 457 plan to hold employer assets in connection with the plan did not affect the tax treatment of amounts deferred thereunder.[2] Since the enactment of Section 409A, use of a rabbi trust is still possible so long as the requirements under the Section 409A(b) funding rules (e.g., the trust may not be placed offshore) are met (Q 3567).

The right to designate "deemed" investments in an ineligible Section 457 plan will not result in current taxation under the constructive receipt doctrine (Q 3542), the economic benefit doctrine (Q 3563), or on account of a transfer of property under IRC Section 83.[3] Section 409A has not changed this rule.

A Section 457 plan created prior to the enactment of Section 409A and established to provide additional benefits for an employee on an extended leave of absence was an "ineligible" plan rather than an "eligible" plan because it was unfunded and no trust was established (as would otherwise be required by IRC Section 457(g)), and because a settlement agreement called for deferrals in excess of the IRC Section 457(b) maximum amount. The IRS found, however, that a plan provision requiring service of the participant (then age 44) until age 50 was a 457(f) substantial risk of forfeiture.[4]

3604. What new rules regarding the tax treatment of participants in "ineligible" Section 457(f) plans were released in proposed Section 457/ Section 409A integration regulations?

As noted in Q 3603, nearly 10 years passed without the promised proposed integration regulations leaving only Notice 2007-62 for guidance. The Notice had a significant negative design impact on 457(f) case designs, especially voluntary deferral plans of vested compensation (i.e., salary and bonus). Finally, in June 2016,[5] the IRS released its long-awaited proposed comprehensive 457/409A integration regulations. These 2016 proposed regulations had been expected to follow the logic in IRS Notice 2007-62. However, the IRS surprised everyone by issuing proposed 457 regulations that took a distinctly different, but welcome, direction that would allow more flexibility in plan design, including a separate and unique definition for the definition of 'substantial risk of forfeiture' for purposes of 457(f) "ineligible" plans.[6]

---

1.   Treas. Reg. §1.457-9.
2.   See, e.g., Let. Ruls. 200009051, 9713014, 9701024, 9444028, 9430013, 9422038.
3.   Let. Ruls. 9815039, 9805030.
4.   Let. Rul. 9835017.
5.   June 22, 2016. See Prop. Treas. Reg., REG-123854-12.
6.   Although a positive step for 457(f) plan design, there are now *seven* different definitions of "substantial risk of forfeiture" or "substantial limitation" for different purposes under the IRC. This situation of similar but different definitions can (and does) cause confusion for planners. See Q 3532, Footnote 2.

Planning Point: The 2016 proposed 457/409A integration regulations may be relied upon immediately pending finalization. Therefore, planners may immediately use them for designing new 457 plans, especially 457(f) "ineligible" plans. However, there is no grandfathering currently in the proposed regulations for "ineligible" plans created in the interim. While the proposed regulations generally provide for more liberal plan designs and provide more clarity for compliant plan design, amendment of existing plans will be more complex. For instance, it is not clear how to address noncompliant design in existing plans, such as a voluntary deferral plan of vested compensation that does not provide more than 125 percent present value increase safe harbor match/benefit increase (25 percent employer match) under the "materially greater benefit" rule. Nor does it direct how to handle an existing severance plan that was thought to be exempt from coverage by Sections 457 and 409A that does not meet the new definition of an exempt 457 severance plan. It is hoped that the finalized regulations will provide guidance on these plans and similar questions caused by the unfortunate long delay in significant guidance.

Planning Point: Based on guidance available to date, there is a conflict between the proposed regulations and IRS chief counsel guidance on whether a "minimum" 125 percent present value increase or "more than" 125 percent present value increase is required. Perhaps this point will be clarified in the final regulations. Stanfield Hill, stanhill@richerassociates.com

Proposed Guidance: The general rule of taxation for 457(f) plans under the 2016 proposed regulations affirms that compliance requires both the Section 457(f) guidance and Section 409A guidance. This was not unexpected since Section 409A is *additive* tax law further defining the constructive receipt doctrine (Q 3542). The proposed regulations are most helpful in this regard, but do not eliminate all issues in regard to integration of the two Sections. For example, it remains unclear whether a 457(f) plan need only comply with the proposed rolling risk of forfeiture rules (that permits an extension of a substantial risk of forfeiture) or whether it must integrate both this rule and the subsequent election rules under Section 409A. Informally, the IRS has suggested the former,[1] but until this is clarified, planners may wish to take a more conservative approach, at least with regard to voluntary deferral plans of vested compensation. Continuation of deferral of compensation under a renewed employment contract presents a more difficult situation if integration is required.

Under the 2016 proposed regulations, there is also a deferral of compensation, and a covered 457(f)/409A plan will exist, if the plan 1) provides for compensation that is or may be payable in a future year, and 2) there is a legally binding right to such compensation in the tax year. In general, a participant does not have a legally binding right if the employer may unilaterally reduce or eliminate compensation. In addition, any plan that can qualify for the "short-term deferral" exception under 409A is also not subject to 457(f).

As noted, the 2016 proposed regulations did not adopt the Section 409A definition of a "substantial risk of forfeiture". Although similar to the 409A definition in some respects, a 457(f) plan will be subject to a 457(f) substantial risk of forfeiture and achieve deferral from current taxation if the amount is conditioned on the: 1) future performance of substantial service (which appears to be a minimum of two tax years, although the hours need to be

---

1.   Comment made by attorney speaker at Trucker Huss, APC in webinar, entitled, "Compensation Planning for Non-Profits and Governmental Entities-Newly Issued Code Section 457(f)," on July 27, 2016 following release of the proposed regulations.. Planners should look for more clarification in the final regulations on these types of difficult integration situations.

substantial in respect to the amount of the compensation provided); or 2) occurrence of a condition that is related to the compensation. An amount will not be subject to a 457(f) substantial risk of forfeiture if the facts and circumstances suggest that the forfeiture condition is unlikely to be enforced, based upon factors such as the participant's level of influence and control as to payment (majority shareholder), enforceability under applicable law (noncompetition agreements), and past practices of the employer, as well as other relevant applicable factors governing enforceability.

Under the 457(f) definition in the proposed regulations (and contrary to Notice 2007-64), a noncompetition agreement is allowed as a potential substantial risk of forfeiture. However, the requirements for a noncompetition agreement to be considered a substantial risk of forfeiture for purposes of a 457(f) plan are: 1) a written agreement that is enforceable under applicable law, which is state law (for instance, noncompetition agreements are not generally enforceable under California law); 2) the employer is consistently making reasonable efforts to enforce all of its noncompetition agreements; and 3) the facts and circumstances indicate that the employer has a bona fide interest in preventing competition and the employee has a reasonable bona fide interest to compete.

Planning Point: Prior to enactment of Section 409A and Notice 2007-62, noncompetition agreements were often added to 457(f) plans to justify installment (annuity-like) payment of benefits by continuing a substantial risk of forfeiture into the benefit distribution period so benefit payments would be taxed as paid rather than under the IRC Section 72 (annuity) rules. Noncompetition agreements may again constitute a substantial risk of forfeiture. This approach is available under the proposed regulations so long as the noncompetition agreement is valid under the proposed regulations, but the requirements present a high hurdle. The rules for the calculation of the present value (PV) for tax purposes under Section 457(f) specifies that the PV of deferred compensation (including earnings) is taxable when the risk lapses; but future earnings (if amounts are left in the plan) are includible when finally paid or made available.

There are circumstances in which the PV of future earnings must also be included at the time of the first income tax inclusion. This taxation structure as proposed suggests that installments taxable as received, even if there is a valid noncompetition agreement, may not avoid Section 72 taxation on the benefit stream in the tax year in which the primary (substantial service vesting date or occurrence of a condition tied to employment) substantial risk of forfeiture lapses. Here again, more clarification is necessary, since a noncompetition agreement would seem to be able to serve as the primary condition, and layering of conditions does not seem to be precluded. On the positive side, delaying distribution should not be a violation of Section 409A that attracts its penalties.

Extensions of the period of risks of forfeiture (referred to as "rolling risks of forfeitures" in the tax-exempt context) are permitted by the proposed regulations so long as certain conditions are met. The same conditions are required in order to achieve and maintain deferral of vested compensation (i.e., salary and bonus). These requirements are:

(1)   PV of amount to be paid upon the lapse of the risk of forfeiture (extended or otherwise) must be materially greater than the amount the employee would have otherwise been paid absent the risk of forfeiture. The safe harbor required by the proposed regulations is more than 125 percent on a PV basis. The proposed

regulations provide a specific example of a voluntary account balance deferral plan with a match of 30 percent as clearly more than meeting the safe harbor requirement.

(2)   Initial or renewed risk of forfeiture must be based only upon the performance of substantial services, or compliance with a noncompetition agreement (but not for the achievement of a performance goal or other condition related to a purpose of the compensation).

(3)   The period of future services *must* be for a minimum of two tax years, except in the case of death, disability, or involuntary severance from employment without cause.

(4)   A written agreement that meets the following requirements:

   A.   For an initial deferral of vested compensation, the agreement *must* be in writing in the calendar year prior to the year in which the compensation is being earned;

   B.   For an extension, the agreement *must* be in writing at least 90 days prior to the date on which the 457(f) substantial risk of forfeiture would have lapsed; and

   C.   For newly hired employees, the agreement must be writing within 30 days after the date of hire, but only as to amounts attributable to services rendered after the extension or deferral is agreed to in writing.

Planning Point: Subject to the need for an employer match or increased benefit that achieves more than 125 percent present value increase safe harbor to satisfy the "materially greater benefit" requirement for achieving and maintaining a 457(f) substantial risk of forfeiture, the revival of the ability to create plans that allow voluntary deferral of vested compensation, or to allow renewal and, therefore, a continuation of deferral under a 457(f) substantial risk of forfeiture (as in a sequence of employment contracts that are typically three to five years in length) is a very positive development for planners to design useful plans under 457(f) for tax-exempt employers. However, because of the differences between 457(f) and 409A definitions of substantial risk of forfeiture, the compensation might be tax-deferred for 457(f) purposes and yet still need to comply with 409A in its design.

A 457(f) plan under the regulations can also allow for: 1) an involuntary termination by an employer without cause; or 2) a voluntary termination by an employee with good reason if the possibility is substantial. This allows an early payment event that does not void an otherwise valid 457(f) substantial risk of forfeiture. The definition of "voluntary termination for good reason" is similar, but not identical to, the Section 409A definition. A termination is for "good reason" under 457(f) if it results from a unilateral action of the employer that creates a material adverse or negative change to the working relationship. It includes changes like reduction in duties or position, working conditions, or pay. These "good reason" changes should be established in a written agreement, which is required by 409A anyway.

Planning Point: These are very important provisions for 457(f) plans, notably voluntary deferral plans involving deferral of an employee's vested compensation. A 457(f) plan must provide for a real forfeiture event so an employee cannot have the right to voluntarily terminate employment (just walk away) prior to the vesting or lapse of the substantial risk of forfeiture and still receive the benefit without voiding the risk of forfeiture. These termination right provisions provide two cases in which termination of the employee may occur early and the employee may still receive the plan benefits.

3605. What are the reporting and withholding requirements for a Section 457(b) plan?

Deferrals under an eligible Section 457(b) plan (and earnings thereon) are not subject to withholding when deferred, but they must be reported annually on a participant's Form W-2 (according to the Form W-2 instructions).[1]

Payments from Section 457(b) plans are W-2 wages subject to regular income tax withholding, not under the withholding rules that apply to pensions.[2]

Employers generally are liable for withholding from Section 457(b) plan distributions. If a trustee (or custodian or insurance carrier treated as a trustee) of a governmental plan makes distributions from such plan's trust or custodial account to participants, then that person/entity is responsible for withholding income tax and reporting the distributions.[3]

Amounts deferred under both Section 457 nongovernmental "eligible" and "ineligible" plans generally are subject to Social Security taxes under the Federal Insurance Contributions Act ("FICA") and federal unemployment taxes under the Federal Unemployment Tax Act ("FUTA") at the later of the date when the services are performed or the date when the employee's right to such amounts is no longer subject to a Section 3121 substantial risk of forfeiture (Q 3538).[4] For more detail on the application of FICA and FUTA taxes to deferred compensation, see Q 3576.

Service performed in the employ of a state or political subdivision is exempt from FUTA, and also may be exempt from FICA.[5]

Length of service awards from an eligible employer accruing to bona fide volunteers[6] (or their beneficiaries) due to "qualified services" after December 31, 1996, which are exempted from the Section 457 plan requirements (Q 3581, Q 3584) and which are maintained by an eligible employer are not considered "wages" for FICA purposes.[7]

Deferrals under a Section 457(f) "ineligible" plan (and earnings thereon) are not subject to taxation or withholding when deferred, but they must be reported annually on the participant's

---

1.   Notice 2000-38, 2000-33 IRB 174, as superseded by Notice 2003-20, 2003-19 IRB 894.
2.   Rev. Rul. 82-46, 1982-1 CB 158; Temp. Treas. Reg. §35.3405-1T, A-23.
3.   Notice 2000-38, 2000-33 IRB 174, as superseded by Notice 2003-20, 2003-1 CB 894.
4.   See IRC Secs. 3121(a)(5), 3121(v)(2), 3306(b)(5), 3306(r)(2). See also Let. Rul. 9024069, as modified by Let. Rul. 9025067; compare SSA Inf. Rel. No. 112 (Dec. 1993).
5.   IRC Secs. 3306(c)(7), 3121(b)(7).
6.   This typically applies to plans for members of volunteer fire departments.
7.   IRC Sec. 3121(a)(5)(I).

Form W-2 (according to the Form W-2 instructions). As of the date of this publication, this annual informational reporting requirement has been waived until the proposed 409A compensation inclusion regulations are finalized. Plan sponsors should check with their administrators at the end of each year to determine if they must report and to obtain the necessary information for current tax year W-2s (Q 3541).

Income Tax Informational and 409A Violation Reporting

For employees, independent contractors and income tax withholding purposes, the rules are the same as for other plans covered by Section 409A (Q 3541).

FICA and FUTA: Section 409A has not changed the application of FICA to 457(f) plans. For more detail on the application of FICA and FUTA taxes to deferred compensation, see Q 3576.

3606. How did the 2017 Tax Reform Act impact Section 457(b) and Section 457(f) plans?

The 2017 Tax Act did not directly change the rules governing Section 457(b) or Section 457(f) plans. However, the final law did contain a provision that could indirectly subject a tax-exempt employer that offers these plans to a steep excise penalty tax.

For tax years beginning after 2017, the 2017 Tax Act imposes a 21 percent penalty tax (see Q 3527) on compensation that exceeds $1 million per year when paid by a tax-exempt employer to a "covered employee".[1] "Covered employee" includes any of the five most highly compensated employees. This penalty also applies to compensation paid to an employee who was a covered employee for any tax year beginning after December 31, 2016.[2] The 21 percent tax is imposed on the tax-exempt organization (the employer), not the employee receiving the compensation.

This tax can create problems for tax-exempt employers that provide 457(b) plans for nongovernmental employees or 457(f) plans.[3] Both types of plans essentially defer the recognition of compensation until a later year. When the employee withdraws all (or even a substantial portion) of the 457(b) funds in his or her last year of account, especially with reference to large SERPs,, the funds will be counted toward the $1 million limit and could trigger the excise tax depending upon the amount of his or her other regular compensation and the account value. Further, 457(f) plans are generally taxable in the year the funds become vested, which means the total account value could become vested in the employee's final year of employment (and, when added to regular compensation for the year, could trigger the excise tax).

---

1.   IRC Sec. 4960(a)(1).
2.   P.L. 115-97, IRC Sec. 4960(c)(2).
3.   Since this penalty tax is imposed on the tax-exempt entity and not the individual, it appears that this excise tax cannot be applied to the plans of certain state/local governmental entities that have governmental sovereign powers (like police power, eminent domain, issuance of financing bonds, and the like), since it is an understood fundamental principal of our federal constitutional structure that the federal government cannot tax states, which ought to include most state instrumentalities (e.g., public universities) A few entities do not have these characteristics. A brief review of the "governmental" entities charter should reveal if it is exempt or potentially subject to the new excise tax. This is likely to be an area of clarifying guidance and/or litigation.

Planning Point: In light of this new excise tax, tax-exempt employers may wish to encourage 457(b) plan participants to withdraw funds in a later year, when they have no other compensation, and in installments to the extent possible. In that regard, an employer could also encourage 457(f) plan participants, who are covered employees, to continue to provide services (i.e., in a consulting role) in some capacity to delay vesting in hopes of spreading income recognition over a period of years to avoid the new tax. The degree of services provided would have to be relatively substantial (when compared to the amount of 457(f) funds that will vest) in order to delay vesting. Because of the many questions raised by this new tax on private nongovernment tax exempt entities, it will be important to review proposed regulations on this penalty tax when they are made available. In light of the IRS's history of slow delivery of guidance in the case of tax-exempt entities, such guidance could be long time coming.

3607. What tax rules apply to nonqualified deferred compensation plans covering state judges?

The participants in a governmental nonqualified deferred compensation plan covering state judges are taxed under the rules applicable to funded or unfunded nonqualified deferred compensation plans [but a plan is not subject to the requirements of 457 as deferred compensation, especially 457(f)] if:

(1)   the plan has been continuously in existence since December 31, 1978;

(2)   the plan requires all eligible judges to participate and contribute the same fixed percentage of their basic or regular compensation;

(3)   the plan provides no judge with an option as to contributions or benefits, which, if exercised, would affect the amount of his or her includable compensation;

(4)   retirement benefits under the plan are a percentage of the compensation of judges holding similar positions in the state; and

(5)   benefits paid to any participant in any year do not exceed the limitation of IRC Section 415(b) (Q 3867).[1]

However, plans for judges that do not meet these conditions must comply with requirements of a Section 457(b) eligible or 457(f) ineligible plan, as applicable.

Excess Benefit Pension Plans

3608. What is an excess benefit pension plan? How is it taxed?

ERISA Section 3(36) defines an "excess benefit" plan as a nonqualified employee pension benefit plan maintained by an employer solely for the purpose of providing only those benefit amounts for certain "select employees" in excess of the limitations on contributions and benefits imposed by IRC Section 415 (Q 3867). Curiously, ERISA Section 3(36) has never been amended to include the limitations on covered compensation imposed by IRC

---

1.   Rev. Act of 1978 Sec. 131 (as amended by TEFRA 1982 Sec. 252); TRA 1986 Sec. 1107(c)(4); PL 97-514 (TEFRA), Section 252, and reaffirmed in Prop. Treas. Reg. Section 1.457-11(b)(1), REG 1147197, June 22, 2016. See also *Foil v. Comm.*, 91-1 USTC ¶50,016 (5th Cir. 1990); *Yegan v. Comm.*, TC Memo 1989-291.

Section 401(a)(17) ($290,000 in 2021, $285,000 in 2020, and $280,000 in 2019).[1] If an excess benefit plan cannot restore these benefits, its usefulness is limited.

One case seems to indicate that an excess benefit plan can replace benefits limited by IRC Section 401(a)(17), provided that the plan was never amended to take the 401(a)(17) limits into account.[2] On the other hand, in another case, a Supplemental Executive Retirement Plan (Q 3540) intended as an excess benefit plan was held to be a "top hat" plan for a "select group" (Q 3541), rather than an excess benefit plan, because it was not specifically limited to restoring benefits lost under IRC Section 415.[3] Until ERISA is amended to add the IRC Section 401(a)(17) limits to the excess benefit plan exemption, this area of ERISA law is likely to remain muddled and pose a risk to its use by a plan sponsor. For this reason, a sponsor should attempt to use the ERISA "select group" exemption to cover a plan that also has an objective of restoring lost qualified plan benefits. This will prove easier for defined contribution plans than defined benefit plans.

A pure excess benefit plan under the ERISA exemption can be funded or unfunded as compared to an employee benefit pension plan for "select group of management or highly compensated employees" ERISA-exempt top hat plan that *must* be unfunded. If the excess benefit plan is unfunded (as defined for ERISA purposes), it apparently need not comply with any of ERISA's requirements. Even if it is funded, an excess benefit plan is exempt from ERISA's minimum participation, vesting, funding, and plan termination insurance provisions.[4] However, the ERISA exemption does not drive income tax law, so a funded plan for ERISA purposes could be deemed a funded (secured) plan for income tax purposes and be currently taxable (Q 3609). Depending on how it is structured such a plan might be subject to Section 409A or designed as a plan exempt under the short-term deferral rule. It is often made an employer contribution under a basic 409A voluntary account balance plan and may or may not be subject to vesting rules in the plan.

As noted, the alternative ERISA exemption is the so-called ERISA "top hat" exemption of ERISA Section 201(2) for a "select group of management and highly compensated employees". However, as noted, the plan must be limited to only a select group of management, and also be unfunded to claim this exemption. The definition of the scope of this ERISA exemption has been a point of increasingly significant legal controversy for a number of years since most of the guidance comes from a sequence of federal cases.

See Q 3609 for detailed information as to how an excess benefit pension plan is taxed.

Qualified Governmental Excess Benefit Arrangements

"Qualified governmental excess benefit arrangements" are excess benefit plans maintained by state and local governmental employers. The requirements for such plans are set forth in

---

1.   IRC Sec. 401(a)(17); Notice 2018-83, Notice 2019-59, Notice 2020-79.
2.   *Gamble v. Group Hospitalization*, 38 F.3d 126 (4th Cir. 1994).
3.   *Garratt v. Knowles*, 245 F.3d 941 (7th Cir. 2001).
4.   ERISA Secs. 4(b)(5), 201(7), 301(a)(9), 4021(b)(8).

IRC Section 415(m).[1] For a discussion of the interaction between IRC Section 415(m) and IRC Section 457, see Q 3584.

3609. How is an excess benefit pension plan taxed?

In contrast to the special tax treatment afforded by ERISA, excess benefit plans remain subject to the tax rules applicable to nonqualified deferred compensation plans. This includes the full range of Section 409A form and operational requirements, unless the plan can claim an exception from Section 409A coverage, such as the "short term deferral exception" by structuring a "vest and pay lump sum" plan (Q 3548). The employer's deduction is likewise deferred until amounts are includable in the employee's gross income, and the employee generally is taxed on payments when they are received (Q 3532, Q 3573).

Planning Point: Funding the plan for ERISA "excess benefit" plan exemption purposes (as compared to the "select group" ERISA exemption) is permitted, and does not present ERISA "plan asset" problems. However, it would change the applicable income tax consequences if the amounts do not remain subject to the claims of the sponsor's general creditors in bankruptcy. Funding the plan would subject the amounts to the Section 83 tax rules applicable to "transfers of property" and vested amounts would be taxable. Therefore, an excess benefit plan should generally always be unfunded to assure the desired income tax consequences, in spite of the ERISA rules. Moreover, pre-409A, it was common for the qualified plan distribution events to control the distribution of the nonqualified excess benefit plan benefits. Under Section 409A, these "excess benefit" plans are now described as "linked" plans, and, if form and timing of distributions from the nonqualified plan are governed by the qualified plan (and deferral stop-and-start timing as well for DC plans), the nonqualified plan is in violation of Section 409A. In effect, distributions and deferral timing rules under any qualified plan cannot control the non-qualified excess benefit/linked plan distribution or deferral timing. This is because the qualified distribution rules are different from, and incompatible with, those under Section 409A. In general, qualified plan provisions may govern only the calculation of the benefit amount that may be due under the nonqualified plan.

As a consequence, post-409A, the nonqualified plan documentation must be written to calculate the benefit in an excess benefit/linked defined benefit plan using a single pre-established benefit form, frequently lump sum (even if a different form is selected by a participant under the DB qualified plan at separation of service, and even if that benefit form is not available under the qualified DB plan). As noted, this is because the distribution form and timing in the nonqualified plan must generally be selected in advance under Section 409A and not at the time of distribution as is the case with a qualified plan. Therefore, one form of distribution must be established in advance.

Of course, these 409A "linked" plan rules mean that existing linked qualified and nonqualified "excess benefit" nonqualified plans should already be delinked as to distribution timing and the timing of deferrals (stop and start) in the case of DC plans. Moreover, the IRS has applied similar logic to multiple nonqualified plans linked together. Movement of benefit amounts between one nonqualified plan linked to another can impermissibly delay or accelerate distribution of benefits under Section 409A. The IRS has thus required that they also be delinked so one nonqualified plan cannot control the distribution of benefits from another.

---

1.   See, e.g., Let. Rul. 199923056.

Stock Options

3610. What are employee stock options and how are they taxed?

An employee stock option gives an employee the right to buy a certain number of shares in the employer's corporation at a fixed price within a specified period of time. The price at which the option is offered is the "grant" price and generally must be issued at the stock's current market value since the enactment of Section 409A.[1] Failure to do so results in the option being outside the exemption from 409A coverage for most Section 83 funded plans. The exemption includes various forms of stock options. The result of issuance at less than FMV is a violation of Section of 409A causing inclusion of the full value of the option with imposition of the 20 percent penalty. However, assuming proper issuance at FMV, it is assumed that the stock will increase in value, allowing the employee to profit by the difference. Should the stock price decrease below the grant price, the option is "underwater" and the employee simply does not "exercise" the option to purchase the stock; the employee is not at risk for out-of-pocket losses.

There are two principal kinds of stock option programs, each with unique rules and tax consequences: (1) "qualified" or "incentive stock options" ("ISOs"), sometimes also referred to as "statutory stock options," (see Q 3611) and (2) non-qualified stock options ("NQSOs"), sometimes also referred to as "nonstatutory stock options" (see Q 3618).

Some executive plans use performance-based options, which provide that the option holder will not realize any value from the option unless specified conditions are met, such as the share price exceeding a certain value above the grant price or the company outperforming the industry. Performance-based plans can require special plan accounting.

3611. What are ISOs?

For a stock option to qualify as an ISO (and thus receive special tax treatment under IRC Section 421(a)), it must meet the requirements of IRC Section 422 when granted and at all times from the grant until its exercise. The key requirements are that an ISO have an exercise price not less than the fair market value of the stock at the time of the grant, expire within no more than 10 years, and be generally nontransferable and exercisable only by the grantee.[2]

Planning Point: Although technically ISOs are exempt from Section 409A, they are required to be issued at fair market value at the date of grant in order to qualify as an ISO. If they are not issued at fair market value at the date of grant, they become an NQSO that has not been issued at fair market value and thereby subject to Section 409A, because they fail to meet the requirements for the Section 409A exemption. Therefore, the planner must make certain that the ISO, like an NQSO, is issued at fair market value at the date of grant in order to avoid the application of Section 409A to the stock, which is not desirable, since it will loss the exemption and fail 409A with the imposition of 409A tax and penalties.

---

1.   Treas. Reg. §1.409A-1(b)(5). Note that an ISO must be issued at FMV to be an ISO so both NQSOs and ISOs must be issued at FMV to claim the exemption and avoid application of Section 409A.
2.   IRC Sec. 422; Treas. Reg. §1.422-2.

3612. What are the tax implications of ISOs for employees?

Editor's Note: The 2017 Tax Act created a new Section 83(i), which permits attractive tax deferral with respect to certain broad-based employee stock options and restricted stock units for closely held companies, especially start-ups. See Q 3613 and Q 3614 for details.

An employee receiving an ISO realizes no income upon its receipt or exercise.[1] Instead, the employee is taxed when he or she disposes of the ISO stock. The ISO should not normally be subject to Section 409A. However, the definition of an ISO requires that the stock be issued at FMV. Failure to do so turns the ISO into a nonqualified stock option (NQSO) and issuance at less than FMV causes it to become subject to Section 409A and fail it with the immediate imposition of income taxation along with the 20 percent penalty.

Disposition generally means any sale, exchange, gift, or transfer of legal title of stock. It does not include a transfer from a decedent to the estate, a transfer by a bequest or inheritance, or any transfer of ISO stock between spouses or incident to a divorce.[2]

The tax treatment of the disposition of ISO stock depends on whether it was disposed of within the statutory holding period for ISO stock. The ISO statutory holding period is the later of two years from the date of the grant or one year from the date when the shares were transferred to the employee upon exercise.[3]

If the employee disposes of the stock within the holding period, the employee first recognizes ordinary income, measured by the difference between the option price and the fair market value of the stock at the time of exercise, and second, capital gain measured by the difference between the fair market value of the stock at exercise and the proceeds of the sale.[4] When an employee disposes of ISO stock after the holding period, all of the gain is capital gain, measured by the difference between the option price and the sale proceeds.[5]

Although the exercise of an ISO does not result in an immediate taxable event, any deferred gain is includable as an adjustment in calculating the Alternative Minimum Tax ("AMT").

3613. Can gain on certain stock options and restricted stock units be deferred under the 2017 Tax Act?

The 2017 Tax Act created a new IRC Section 83(i) that changes the rules that govern certain stock options and restricted stock units (RSUs) that are granted to employees.[6] Under the 2017 Tax Act, qualifying employees are now permitted to defer gain on these benefits for up to five years.

---

1.   See IRC Sec. 422(a) (incorporating by reference the nonrecognition provisions of IRC Sec. 421(a)(1)).
2.   IRC Secs. 424(c)(1), 424(c)(4).
3.   IRC Sec. 422(a)(1).
4.   IRC Secs. 421(b), 422(c)(2).
5.   IRC Sec. 1001(a).
6.   IRC Sec. 83(i)(2).

Generally, IRC Section 83(a) requires that, when a taxpayer receives property in exchange for services, the value of the property is taxable when it becomes transferrable or when it is vested (basically, when it is no longer subject to a substantial risk of forfeiture). As a result, when an employee receives an equity grant, appreciation on the stock can be taxed at ordinary income tax rates during the time between granting and vesting. Section 83(b) allows taxpayers to make an irrevocable election to pay income taxes on the unvested stock at its fair market value on the date of transfer (so that subsequent appreciation is taxed at capital gains rates). However, many employees who receive equity grants do not have the funds to make this election and cover the tax liability, especially with respect to companies where the stock is not readily tradeable (i.e., the employee cannot sell the stock to help pay the taxes).

New IRC Section 83(i) allows employees who receive these specific types of equity grants to elect to defer taxation for five years after the stock vests. Essentially, this can be helpful to employees when the stock that will be transferred to them is not readily tradeable, making it potentially difficult to pay the associated taxes immediately.

The election must be made within 30 days after the date upon which the employee's rights in the stock are transferable or are no longer subject to a substantial risk of forfeiture (whichever is earlier). The election must be filed with the IRS and the employee must also provide a copy to the employer.[1] The employer is required to provide notice of the potential to defer income to the employee receiving the grant. If a deferral election is made with respect to an incentive stock option, that option is treated as a nonqualified stock option for FICA tax purposes.[2]

Planning Point: Only income taxes are deferred during the deferral period. Employment related taxes (Social Security and Medicare taxes) still must be paid.

At the end of the deferral period, the employee recognizes income based upon the value of the stock on the vesting date (regardless of whether the value has decreased during the deferral period).

Planning Point: While the eventual tax paid is based on the value of the stock at vesting, the holding period for long-term capital gains treatment will begin to run during the deferral period. Therefore, if the stock value increases during the deferral period, ordinary income tax rates will only apply to the stock value at the start of the deferral period. The remainder will be taxed at the lower long-term capital gains rates if the stock is not sold for at least one year.

Income must be recognized for the first taxable year that includes one of the following (1) the first date the qualified stock becomes transferable (including transferable to the employer), (2) the date the employee becomes an "excluded employee", (3) the date on which any of the stock becomes readily tradeable on an established securities market, (4) five years after the first date the employee's right to the stock becomes substantially vested or (5) the date upon which the employee revokes the deferral election.[3]

---

1.   IRC Sec. 83(i)(4). Making this election is similar to making the Section 83(b) election.
2.   IRC Sec. 83(i)(1)(B).
3.   IRC Sec. 83(i)(1)(B). Revocation of a deferral election will be as established by the Secretary.

Planning Point: Under the rules that have been provided thus far, it does not appear that termination of employment with the employer will cause the deferral period to end.

"Excluded employees" include any individual (1) who was a 1-percent owner of the corporation at any time during the 10 previous calendar years, (2) who is, or has ever been, CEO or CFO of the company (or has acted in that capacity), (3) who is a family member of an individual described in (1) or (2), or (4) who has been one of the four most highly compensated officers of the company for any of the 10 previous tax years.[1] Under guidance contained in Notice 2018-97, employees must also agree to an escrow provision in order to take advantage of the new deferral option. All deferral stock must be held in an escrow arrangement established by the employer to qualify.

Planning Point: Failure to establish an escrow account to hold the deferral stock provides employers with the option to compensate employees with stock, but preclude them from making the new Section 83(i) election. The terms of the stock option or RSU can also provide that no Section 83(i) election will be available.

The election is only available with respect to qualified stock, which means stock in an employee's employer that is (1) received in connection with the exercise of an option or in settlement of an RSU and (2) granted in connection with services that are being performed by the employee. The stock will no longer be qualified if the employee may sell the stock, or otherwise receive cash in lieu of the stock from, the corporation.[2]

To issue equity grants that qualify for the Section 83(i) deferral election, the employer must be a private company that has a written plan in place stating that at least 80 percent of the employer's full-time U.S. employees will be granted stock options or RSUs on substantially the same terms. The number of shares granted to each employee need not be equal, so long as each employee is entitled to a more than de minimis amount. Rights and privileges with respect to the exercise of a stock option are not treated for this purpose as the same as rights and privileges with respect to the settlement of an RSU.[3]

Planning Point: The IRS has released guidance clarifying that this 80 percent requirement is based only on stock options or RSUs granted in a particular calendar year. Further, the employer is required to take the total number of employees employed at any time during the year into account in calculating the 80 percent requirement, as well as all of the employees receiving grants, regardless of whether the person was employed at the beginning or the end of the year in question.[4]

All related entities are considered in determining whether the 80 percent requirement is satisfied. The definition of controlled group under IRC Section 414(b) applies for purposes of determining corporations that are members of a controlled group (and are thus treated as a single corporation).[5] Further, only corporations that make grants to employees are eligible under this provision (LLCs that elect partnership taxation are excluded).

---

1.   IRC Sec. 83(i)(3)(B).
2.   IRC Sec. 83(i)(2)(B).
3.   IRC Sec. 83(i)(2)(C).
4.   Notice 2018-97.
5.   IRC Sec. 83(i)(5).

The election is not available if the company has repurchased any of its stock in the past year, unless at least 25 percent of the stock repurchased is stock that has been deferred under Section 83(i) elections (and determination of which employees to repurchase the stock from is made on a reasonable basis).[1] If the company repurchases all Section 83(i) stock, the 25 percent requirement and reasonable basis requirement are deemed to have been satisfied.[2]

A transition rule provides that a corporation will be deemed to comply with this "80 percent" restriction if it complies with a reasonable good faith interpretation of the rules. Further, an employer will be treated as satisfying the notice requirements if it complies with a reasonable good faith interpretation of the rules. This transition relief will apply until the IRS releases regulations or other guidance on the 80 percent rule and notice requirements (employers are now required to comply with the rules for calculating the 80 percent rule found in Notice 2018-97).[3]

If the Section 83(i) election is made, RSUs are not eligible for the IRC Section 83(b) election. Further, qualified stock will not be treated as a nonqualified deferred compensation plan for Section 409A purposes, but only with respect to employees who may receive qualified stock.

See Q 3614 for a discussion of the notice and reporting requirements that apply with respect to the deferral election. See Q 3615 for a discussion of the new escrow requirement.

3614. What notice, reporting and withholding requirements apply to an employer that transfers to its employees' stock options or restricted stock units upon gain deferral is possible?

Corporations that transfer qualified stock options or restricted stock units (RSUs) to qualified employees are subject to certain notice requirements under the 2017 Tax Act. Pursuant to the new rules, the company must provide a notice at the time (or a reasonable period before) the employee's rights are substantially vested (and income would therefore be recognized if no deferral election was made.

The notice must:

(1)   certify that the stock is qualified stock,

(2)   notify the employee that he or she may elect to defer income recognition with respect to the stock,

(3)   notify the employee that at the end of the income deferral period, the value of the stock to be recognized will be based on the value of the stock when the employee's rights first become substantially vested, even if the value has subsequently declined, and

---

1.   IRC Sec. 83(i)(4)(B)(iii).
2.   IRC Sec. 83I(i)(4)(C)(iii).
3.   IRC Sec. 83(i)(7)(g).

(4)   notify the employee that the value as recognized will be subject to withholding at the end of the deferral period.[1]

Failure to satisfy the notice requirements will subject the company to a penalty of $100 per failure, with a $50,000 annual maximum.

On Form W-2, the employer must report the amount of income covered by the deferral election both in the year of deferral and in the year that the income is required to be included in income by the employee. Further, the employer must report the total amount of income deferred through income deferral elections for the calendar year on Form W-2 each year (as determined at year-end).

Initial IRS guidance provides that the IRS intends to release further guidance clarifying that the rate of withholding on deferral stock will be the maximum rate of withholding under IRC Section 1, and that deferral stock will essentially be treated as wages for withholding purposes. Withholding will be applied:

(1)   without reference to the payment of regular wages,

(2)   without allowance for the number of allowances or other dollar amounts claimed on the employee's Form W-4,

(3)   without regard to whether the employee requests additional withholding, and

(4)   without regard to the withholding method used by the employer.[2]

3615. What is the escrow requirement that employers must satisfy in order to give employees the option of deferring tax on certain stock options and RSUs under new Section 83(i)?

IRS guidance interpreting the new Section 83(i) tax deferral option requires employers to establish an escrow arrangement if they wish to provide employees with the opportunity to defer taxes under the new code section. This escrow arrangement is designed to solve potential income tax withholding issues associated with the new rules. If the employee and employer do not agree to the escrow arrangement, the employee is not a qualified employee for purposes of the Section 83(i) deferral option.

All deferral stock must be deposited in the escrow account before the end of the calendar year in which the Section 83(i) election is made, and must remain in the account until the employer recovers the income tax withholding obligation from the employer. At any time between the date of income inclusion under Section 83(i)(1)(B) and March 31 of the following year, the employer is permitted to remove from escrow and retain the number of shares of deferral stock with a fair market value equal to the income tax withholding obligation that has not been otherwise received from the employee.

---

1.   IRC Sec. 83(i)(6).
2.   Notice 2018-97.

Planning Point: Practically, this escrow arrangement could force corporations to repurchase their own stock in order to satisfy the employee's income tax withholding obligations, potentially making the Section 83(i) deferral option less attractive for employers who may not wish to use their own funds to satisfy these obligations.

Fair market value, for purposes of these rules, means the fair market value as determined under the Section 409A regulations, and is the fair market value of the shares at the time the corporations retains the shares held in escrow to satisfy the employee's income tax withholding obligations.

After the employee has satisfied his or her income tax withholding obligations, the shares held in escrow must be delivered to the employee as soon as reasonably practicable.[1]

3616. What are the tax implications of ISOs for employers?

An employer granting an ISO is not entitled to an income tax deduction with respect to the option on its grant or its exercise.[2] The amount received by the employer as the exercise price will be considered the amount received by the employer for the transfer of the ISO stock.[3] If the employee disposes of the stock prior to the end of the requisite holding period, the employer generally may take a deduction for the amount that the employee recognized as ordinary income in the same year in which the employee recognizes the income.[4]

3617. What are the reporting and withholding requirements that apply with respect to ISOs?

The employer has no obligation to pay FICA or FUTA taxes, or to withhold federal income taxes, when an option is granted. Pending further guidance from the IRS, employers also are not obligated to pay or withhold FICA and FUTA taxes on the exercise of ISOs.[5] However, the IRS has announced that any sponsor determination to impose FICA or FUTA on the exercise of ISOs will not take effect before January 1 following the second anniversary of the announcement.

IRC Section 6039 requires employers to provide a written statement to each employee regarding any exercise of an ISO and, beginning for transfers occurring in 2009 or later, to file a similar information return with the IRS by January 31 of the year following the transfer.[6] Under proposed regulations, the information return must identify the parties and provide the following information:

- The date the option was granted

- The exercise price per share

- The date the option was exercised

---

1.   Notice 2018-97.
2.   IRC Sec. 421(a)(2).
3.   IRC Sec. 421(a)(3).
4.   IRC Sec. 421(b).
5.   Notice 2002-47, 2002-28 IRB 97.
6.   Prop. Treas. Reg. §§1.6039-1, 1.6039-2.

- The fair market value of a share on the date of exercise

- The number of shares transferred pursuant to the exercise

3618. What are NQSOs and how are they taxed?

A Nonqualified Stock Option ("NQSO") is generally an option to purchase employer stock that does not satisfy the legal requirements of an ISO (Q 3611).

Tax Implications for Employees

The tax implications of an NQSO are governed by IRC Section 83, and potentially by Section 409A, because they give a participant a legally binding right to compensation that will be realized in a later taxable year. Final regulations to Section 409A allow an NQSO to be structured to claim the equity plan exception and avoid Section 409A coverage. The requirements to claim the regulatory exception from Section 409A coverage are:

- the option stock must be Section 409A "service recipient stock;"

- the exercise price must be at fair market value on the option grant date;

- the option share total must be fixed on the grant date;

- the option stock must be subject to taxation under Section 83 and Treasury Regulation Section 1.83-7; and

- the option cannot provide for any additional deferral of compensation features.

If an option does not meet these preconditions, and is issued below fair market value, it must comply with Section 409A, which usually destroys the intended objective and subjects the award to immediate 409A taxation with penalties. Fortunately, the IRS has provided for a correction method for such failures that allows the participants to avoid experiencing the 409A taxation scenario if the error is discovered early and corrected quickly (Q 3541).

Under Section 83, an employee generally is not taxed on an NQSO at grant unless it has a readily ascertainable fair market value and is not subject to a substantial risk of forfeiture.[1] Options generally do not have a readily ascertainable fair market value unless they are publicly traded.[2] If an NQSO does not have a readily ascertainable fair market value at grant, it is taxed at the time of exercise.[3] If an NQSO with a readily ascertainable fair market value is subject to a Section 83 substantial risk of forfeiture, it is taxed when the risk of forfeiture lapses. When taxed, the employee will recognize the excess of the market value of shares receivable over the grant price as ordinary income subject to FICA, FUTA, and federal income tax.[4]

---

1.   IRC Secs. 83(a), 83(e)(3).
2.   Treas. Reg. §1.83-7(b)(1).
3.   Treas. Reg. §1.83-7(a).
4.   IRC Sec. 83(a).

On May 29, 2012, the IRS released proposed regulations clarifying the key definition of "substantial risk of forfeiture" for purposes of Section 83. On February 25, 2014, the IRS released final regulations that are substantially similar to the proposed regulations. (For details, see Q 3538.)[1] These clarifications incorporate the IRS' position in Revenue Ruling 2005-48, in which it rejected the extension of the court's logic in the case of *Robinson v. Comm.* that implied that restrictions other than those related to the purpose of the transfer, such as lock-up agreement restrictions and Rule 10b-5 trading restrictions mandated by U.S. securities law, could result in the deferral of taxation. It also ruled that Section 16(b) of the Securities Exchange Act of 1934 is the ONLY securities law provision that will defer taxation under Section 83. The regulations apply to property transferred on or after January 1, 2013. The proposed regulations can be relied upon for transfers after May 30, 2012.

Planning Point: These regulations would seem to clarify that federally mandated clawback requirements as in Dodd-Frank, TARP, and Sarbanes-Oxley will NOT defer taxation on stock options post exercise, or restricted stock awards post vesting, even if the stock is potentially subject to forfeiture or disgorgement upon triggering of such a clawback. They might even limit use of noncompete agreements and consulting agreements to defer taxation, given that the IRS has drawn language from Section 409A, and Section 409A specifically provides that noncompete and consulting agreements will not constitute a substantial risk of forfeiture, although this is less clear at the date of publication (note that the proposed Section 409A/457 integration regulations may change this result, as well). Time will tell if these regulations are only "clarifications" or substantive changes, so planners must follow the progress of the IRS' administration of these regulations, now that they are finally effective.

Within 30 days of the grant of an NQSO subject to a Section 83 substantial risk of forfeiture, an employee may elect under IRC Section 83(b) to be taxed currently on the fair market value of the option. Any appreciation after the election is taxable as a capital gain. If the NQSO is ultimately forfeited, no deduction is allowed for that forfeiture.[2]

It is possible to escape state income taxation on certain nonqualified deferred compensation benefits by establishing new residence in a different state that does not impose income tax (e.g., Nevada) before distribution of the benefit begins However, the Supreme Court of Connecticut has held in a Connecticut case[3] involving NQSOs that a former taxpayer cannot escape Connecticut state income taxation on options that are already issued only for services performed while in Connecticut. The Connecticut Supreme Court reached this conclusion even though the nonqualified options were exercised at the time. The taxpayer was a resident of another state. The SCOTUS denied review on appeal so the Connecticut holding imposing taxation on the vested NQSOs was allowed to stand despite the taxpayer's argument that the Connecticut ruling was at variance with a number of the other federal appellate circuits.[4]

---

1. Prop. Treas. Reg, §1.83-3, Treas. Reg. §1.83-3.
2. IRC Sec. 83(b)(1).
3. *Allen v. Comm. of Rev. Services*, 152 A. 3d. 488 (Conn. Supreme Court (2016)).
4. Cert. den., 423 U.S. 845 (2017).

Tax Implications for Employers

An employer has a corresponding deduction (in the same amount and at the same time) as the ordinary income recognized by the employee.[1] Compensation paid in the form of stock options normally triggers the receipt of wages for the purpose of employment tax and withholding provisions in the amount of the income generated under IRC Section 83(a).[2]

3619. When will a nonqualified stock option constitute deferred compensation that is subject to the IRC Section 409A rules?

NQSOs that are exercisable at less than their fair market value at the date of grant,[3] or where there are additional deferral features in the NQSO, will be subject to the rules governing deferred compensation plans under IRC Section 409A (Q 3541). Where the exercise price can never be less than the fair market value of the underlying stock at the date of grant, and where there is no other feature for the deferral of compensation, a stock option will not constitute deferred compensation subject to IRC Section 409A, which is the desired design objective.[4] Plans generally could substitute non-discounted stock options and stock appreciation rights for discounted options and rights until December 31, 2007.[5] See Q 3541 for exceptions to this rule.

Under a pre-409A ruling, stock options could be "converted" to a deferred compensation plan free of tax under limited circumstances. Where employees could choose to retain or surrender both ISOs and NQSOs in exchange for an initial deferral amount under a nonqualified deferred compensation plan, the IRS indicated that neither the opportunity to surrender the options, nor their actual surrender, would create taxable income for participants under either the constructive receipt or economic benefit doctrines.[6] For a discussion of the theories of constructive receipt and economic benefit, see Q 3541 and Q 3563, respectively.

3620. What reporting and withholding requirements apply for employers who grant nonqualified stock options?

An employer has no obligation to pay employment taxes or to withhold federal income taxes upon the grant of NQSOs, unless the plan fails to place itself in the desired exception to Section 409A. In that case, Section 409A taxation, reporting, and withholding would be required. Under Section 83 (assuming exception from Section 409A coverage), on exercise, the employer must treat the excess of the market value of shares received over the grant price as wages subject to FICA, FUTA, and federal income tax withholding in the pay period in which the income arises. The employer has no obligation to withhold or pay federal income or employment taxes on the sale of shares purchased by option.

---

1. IRC Sec. 83(h).
2. See Rev. Rul. 79-305, 1979-2 CB 550; Rev. Rul. 78-185, 1978-1 CB 304.
3. *See Sutardja v. U.S.*, (U.S. Ct. of Claims Feb. 2-27-2013). To emphasize the IRS's hard position on the FMV requirement, *Sutardja* involved a transition case of a grant made before enactment of Section 409A but the IRS successfully applied IRS Notice 2005-1, which was the first guidance on new Section 409A.
4. Treas. Reg. §1.409A-1(b)(5). *Also see* CCM 132502-09 (Jun. 6, 2009), released July 17, 2009 for additional guidance on proper NQSOs release steps for both IRC Sections 162(m) and 409A.
5. Notice 2006-79, 2006-43 IRB 763.
6. Let. Rul. 199901006.

Employers are to use code "V" in Box 12 on Form W-2 to identify the amount of compensation to be included in an employee's wages in connection with the exercise of an employer-provided NQSO. Completion of code V is addressed in the instructions for Forms W-2 and W-3. Employers must report the excess of the fair market value of the stock received on exercise of the option over the amount paid for that stock on Form W-2 in boxes 1, 3 (up to the Social Security wage base), 5, and 12 (using code V) when an employee (or former employee) exercises his or her options.[1] If an employer were to fail to claim the exception to 409A and violate Section 409A, it would follow reporting and withholding required for Section 409A plans (Q 3541).

3621. Are ISOs subject to ERISA reporting requirements?

An ISO generally is not subject to ERISA's reporting requirements since it is usually not a covered ERISA "employee benefit plan." Therefore, a summary plan description need not be distributed to participants. An employer must furnish a statement to an employee on or before January 31 of the year following the year in which the employee exercises the ISO, stating details about the options granted.[2]

3622. What is restricted stock?

A restricted stock award, which is considered a funded Section 83 "transfer of property" for income tax purposes, is an outright grant of shares by a company to an individual, usually an employee, without any payment by the recipient (or for only a nominal payment). The shares of stock generally are subject to a contractual provision under which the granting company has the right (but not the obligation) to repurchase or reacquire the shares from the recipient on the occurrence of a specified event (e.g., termination of employment). This right of repurchase or reacquisition expires after a specified period of time, either all at once or in increments (for example, a grant of 1,000 shares with 200 shares vesting annually over a five year period). The expiration of this right is referred to as "vesting." During the period that the shares of stock may be repurchased or reacquired, the recipient is prohibited from selling (or otherwise transferring) the shares. This is why the shares are called "restricted stock." The passage of time typically serves as the primary restriction for such stock and is the normal substantial risk of forfeiture in the grant necessary to prevent current taxation under IRC Section 83 and also to claim the "short term deferral exception" to avoid Section 409A coverage. Restricted stock vesting may depend on restrictions other than time (e.g., satisfying corporate performance goals, such as reaching a specified level of profitability) that also might satisfy these requirements.

On May 29, 2012, the IRS released proposed regulations clarifying the definition of "substantial risk of forfeiture" under Section 83, and incorporating its ruling in Revenue Ruling 2005-48 (for details on the changes see Q 3610 and Q 3538). On February 25, 2014, the IRS released final regulations that are substantially similar to the proposed regulations. These regulations apply to all transfers of property on or after January 1, 2013, though the final regulations may be relied on as to transfers after May 30, 2012.[3] Hence, they apply to restricted stock plans that

---

1. Ann. 2000-97, 2000-48 IRB 557; Ann. 2001-7, 2001-3 IRB 357.
2. IRC Sec. 6039(a).
3. Prop. Treas. Reg. §1.83-3, Treas. Reg. §1.83-3.

usually achieve income deferral because they require substantial future service, which provides an adequate Section 83 "substantial risk of forfeiture".

For the tax treatment of restricted stock, including the taxability of dividends on restricted stock, see Q 3623.

3623. How is restricted stock taxed?

Taxation of restricted stock is governed by IRC Section 83, even after the enactment of Section 409A, if structured properly. This is because restricted stock must be structured and issued subject to a Section 409A substantial risk of forfeiture (in addition to a Section 83 substantial risk of forfeiture) that also makes it eligible to claim the Section 409A "short term deferral exception" to escape Section 409A coverage requirements. The distribution must be made during the 409A exception safe harbor time period to claim this exception to Section 409A (Q 3541).

Section 83 restricted stock generally does not constitute taxable income to the employee at the time it is granted (unless at the time of the grant it is "substantially vested," see below). An employee who receives restricted stock must include the fair market value of that stock in his or her income in the year the stock becomes "substantially vested." The amount the employee paid for the restricted stock, if any, must be subtracted from this amount. Restricted stock becomes substantially vested in the year in which the stock becomes transferable or the stock is no longer subject to a Section 83 substantial risk of forfeiture.[1]

Within 30 days of receiving the restricted stock, an employee may elect under IRC Section 83(b) to be taxed on the fair market value of the stock currently, rather than in the year the stock becomes substantially vested. Any appreciation after the election is thereafter taxable as a capital gain. If the restricted stock is ultimately forfeited, no deduction is allowed for that forfeiture.[2]

Where restricted stock that is substantially vested is subjected to new restrictions that cause it to become substantially nonvested, the stock is not subject to IRC Section 83(b) in the absence of an exchange of stock. Where substantially vested stock is exchanged for substantially nonvested stock, the new restricted stock is subject to IRC Section 83(b).[3]

An employer is entitled to a corresponding deduction in the same amount and at the same time as the ordinary income recognized by the employee.[4] Compensation paid in the form of restricted stock normally triggers the receipt of wages for the purpose of employment tax and withholding provisions in the amount of the income generated under IRC Section 83(a).[5]

1. IRC Sec. 83(a).
2. IRC Sec. 83(b).
3. Rev. Rul. 2007-49, 2007-31 IRB 237.
4. IRC Sec. 83(h).
5. See Rev. Rul. 79-305, 1979-2 CB 350.

On May 29, 2012, the IRS released proposed regulations clarifying the definition of "substantial risk of forfeiture"[1] under Section 83, integrating more closely with the Section 409A definition of "substantial risk of forfeiture" and incorporating its ruling in Revenue Ruling 2005-48 (for details on the changes see Q 3622, Q 3610, and especially Q 3538). On February 25, 2014, the IRS released final regulations that are substantially similar to the proposed regulations. These regulations will apply to all transfers of property on or after January 1, 2013, though the final regulations may be relied on as to transfers after May 30, 2012.[2]

3624. How are dividends on restricted stock taxed?

Dividends received on restricted stock are extra compensation to an employee that must be included on the employee's Form W-2. Dividends received on restricted stock that the employee chooses to include in his or her income in the year transferred are treated the same as any other dividends. The employee should receive a Form 1099-DIV showing these dividends. These dividends should not be included in the employee's wages on the income tax return; instead, the employee should report them as dividends.

---

1.   As noted several places in *Tax Facts*, there are currently seven definitions of "substantial risk of forfeiture" in the IRC (including the definition of "substantial limitation," which historically has been referred to by attorneys and judges as a "substantial risk of forfeiture"). These seven definitions are usually similar but also not exactly the same (e.g., the Section 457(f) definition for ineligible nonqualified deferred compensation plans versus the definition for purposes of Section 409A). They frequently are additive to each other, which is helpful if a planner is aware there are more than one that is applicable. These multiple definitions create considerable confusion for all parties concerned trying to properly construct and administer compensation plans of all types. See Q 3538 for a listing of the seven.
2.   Prop. Treas. Reg. §1.83-3.

PART XIV: NON-TRADITIONAL EMPLOYMENT BENEFITS

Dependent Care Assistance Programs

3625. What are the income tax consequences of an employer-sponsored dependent care assistance program?

A dependent care assistance program (DCAP) is a separate written plan of an employer for the exclusive benefit of providing employees with payment for or the provision of services that, if paid for by the employee, would be considered employment-related expenses under IRC Section 21(b)(2).[1] Employment-related expenses are amounts incurred to permit the taxpayer to be gainfully employed while he or she has one or more dependents under age 13 (for whom he or she is entitled to a personal exemption deduction under IRC Section 151(c) (note, however, that the exemption was suspended for 2018-2025)) or a dependent or spouse who cannot care for themselves. The expenses may be for household services or for the care of the dependents.[2] The plan is not required to be funded.[3]

Nonhighly compensated employees may exclude from income a limited amount for services paid or incurred by the employer under such a program provided during a taxable year.[4] For highly compensated employees to enjoy the same income tax exclusion, the program must meet the following additional requirements:

(1) Plan contributions or benefits must not discriminate in favor of highly compensated employees (as defined in IRC Section 414(q) (Q 3929)) or their dependents.

(2) The program must benefit employees in a classification that does not discriminate in favor of highly compensated employees or their dependents.

(3) No more than 25 percent of the amounts paid by the employer for dependent care assistance may be provided for the class of shareholders and owners each of whom owns more than 5 percent of the stock or of the capital or profits interest in the employer (certain attribution rules under IRC Section 1563 apply).

(4) Reasonable notification of the availability and terms of the program must be provided to eligible employees.

(5) The plan must provide each employee, on or before January 31, with a written statement of the expenses or amounts paid by the employer in providing such employee with dependent care assistance during the previous calendar year.

---

1. IRC Secs. 129(d)(1), 129(e)(1).
2. IRC Sec. 21(b)(2).
3. IRS Sec. 129(d)(5).
4. IRC Sec. 129(d)(1).

(6)   The average benefits provided to nonhighly compensated employees under all plans of the employer must equal at least 55 percent of the average benefits provided to the highly compensated employees under all plans of the employer.[1]

If benefits are provided through a salary reduction agreement, the plan may disregard any employee with compensation less than $25,000 for purposes of the 55 percent test.[2] For this purpose, compensation is defined in IRC Section 414(q)(4), but regulations may permit an employer to elect to determine compensation on any other nondiscriminatory basis.[3]

For purposes of the eligibility and benefits requirements (items (2) and (6) above), the employer may exclude from consideration (1) employees who have not attained age 21 and completed one year of service (provided all such employees are excluded), and (2) employees covered by a collective bargaining agreement (provided there is evidence of good faith bargaining regarding dependent care assistance).[4]

A program will not fail to meet the requirements above, other than the 25 percent test applicable to more than 5 percent shareholders, or the 55 percent test applicable to benefits, merely because of the utilization rates for different types of assistance available under the program. The 55 percent test may be applied on a separate line of business basis.[5]

Grace Period

An employer may, at the employer's option, amend its plan document to include a grace period, which must not extend beyond the 15th day of the third calendar month after the end of the immediately preceding plan year to which it relates (i.e., the "2½ month rule"). If a plan document is amended to include a grace period, a participant who has unused benefits or contributions relating to a particular qualified benefit from the immediately preceding plan year, and who incurs expenses for that same qualified benefit during the grace period, may be paid or reimbursed for those expenses from the unused benefits or contributions as if the expenses had been incurred in the immediately preceding plan year. The effect of the grace period is that the participant may have as long as 14 months and 15 days (i.e., the twelve months in the current plan year plus the grace period to March 15) to use the benefits or contributions for a plan year before those amounts are "forfeited" under the "use-it-or-lose-it" rule.[6] (For the clarified Form W-2 reporting requirements, which apply when an employer has amended a cafeteria plan document to provide a grace period for qualified dependent care assistance immediately following the end of a cafeteria plan year, see Notice 2005-61.)[7]

---

1.   IRC Sec. 129(d).
2.   IRC Sec. 129(d)(8)(B).
3.   IRC Sec. 129(d)(8)(B).
4.   IRC Sec. 129(d)(9).
5.   See IRC Sec. 414(r).
6.   Notice 2005-42, 2005-23 IRB 1204.
7.   2005-39 IRB 607, *amplifying*, Notice 89-11, 1989-2 CB 449.

Coordination with Dependent Care Credit

The amount of employment-related expenses available in calculating the dependent care credit of IRC Section 21 is reduced by the amount excludable from gross income under IRC Section 129.[1]

Employer's Deduction

The employer's expenses incurred in providing benefits under a dependent care assistance program generally are deductible by the employer as ordinary and necessary business expenses under IRC Section 162.

Sole Proprietors and Partners

An individual who owns the entire interest in an unincorporated trade or business is treated as his or her own employer. A partnership is treated as the employer of each partner who is an employee under the plan.[2] A self-employed individual (within the meaning of 401(c)(1)) is considered an employee.[3]

3626. What exclusion is available for employee participants in an employer-sponsored dependent care assistance program?

An employee may exclude up to $5,000 paid or incurred by the employer for dependent care assistance provided during a tax year.[4] For a married individual filing separately, the excludable amount is limited to $2,500. Furthermore, the amount excluded cannot exceed the earned income of an unmarried employee or the lesser of the earned income of a married employee or the earned income of the employee's spouse.[5]

An employee cannot exclude from gross income any amount paid to an individual with respect to whom the employee or the employee's spouse was entitled to take a personal exemption deduction under IRC Section 151(c) (prior to the suspension of the personal exemption from 2018-2025) or who is a child of the employee under 19 years of age at the close of the taxable year.[6]

With respect to on-site facilities, the amount of dependent care assistance excluded is based on utilization by a dependent and the value of the services provided with respect to that dependent.[7]

---

1. IRC Sec. 21(c).
2. IRC Sec. 129(e)(4).
3. IRC Sec. 129(e)(3).
4. IRC Sec. 129(a). The dependent care maximum limit is set by federal statute. It is not subject to inflation-related adjustments as many other benefits. The limits have not been raised in several years.
5. IRC Sec. 129(b).
6. IRC Sec. 129(c).
7. IRC Sec. 129(e)(8).

3627. What reporting requirements apply with respect to an employer-sponsored dependent care assistance program?

An employee cannot exclude from gross income any amount paid or incurred by the employer for dependent care assistance unless the name, address, and taxpayer identification number of the person (name and address in the case of a tax-exempt 501(c)(3) organization) providing the services are included on the return. If this information was not provided, but the taxpayer exercised due diligence in attempting to do so, the amount shall not be included in the employee's gross income.[1]

IRC Section 6039D generally requires an employer maintaining a dependent care assistance plan to file an information return with the IRS that indicates:

(1)   its number of employees;

(2)   the number of employees eligible to participate in the plan;

(3)   the number of employees participating in the plan;

(4)   the number of highly compensated employees ("HCEs") of the employer;

(5)   the number of HCEs eligible to participate in the plan;

(6)   the number of HCEs actually participating in the plan;

(7)   the cost of the plan;

(8)   the identity of the employer; and

(9)   the type of business in which it is engaged.

For plan years beginning prior to the issuance of further guidance from the IRS, these reporting requirements are suspended for dependent care assistance plans.[2]

Social Security Planning

3628. When should an individual claim Social Security benefits?

The earliest date that an individual can begin claiming Social Security is age 62, and the latest is when the individual reaches age 70. Full retirement age has historically been age 66 for people born between 1943 and 1954, but will gradually increase with time so that for individuals born after 1960, full retirement age is 67. For individuals born between 1954 and 1960, full retirement age is somewhere between 66 and 67 based on the actual date of birth.

Determining when to claim Social Security benefits requires a detailed personalized calculation that often results in different answers for different clients. The conventional rule is that

---

1.   IRC Sec. 129(e)(9).
2.   Notice 2002-24, 2002-16 IRB 785; Notice 90-24, 1990-1 CB 335.

the longer a client can wait to claim Social Security, the better. This is because a client's Social Security benefit level will increase by 8 percent for each year the client delays claiming benefits beyond full retirement age, and claiming benefits early will actually lead to a reduction in benefits. However, this rule will not work perfectly in all circumstances.

Clients must also consider past health issues and their impact on anticipated life expectancy in determining whether waiting until after age 70 to claim benefits is advantageous. The date at which the client intends to retire is also relevant. Clients who wish to keep working until age 70 may be best served by adhering to the traditional approach in delaying Social Security for as long as possible. For those clients who wish to retire early, however, claiming benefits early may actually enable them to make better use of their hard-earned retirement dollars by using Social Security to fund the bulk of their living expenses while retirement funds continue to grow on a tax-preferred basis.

3629. Is "file and suspend" a viable Social Security planning option?

The rules governing Social Security claiming have changed so that the file and suspend strategy is now generally unavailable for most individuals. Although the file and suspend strategy is generally now unavailable for most, for older clients (those who were at least 66 years of age by April 29, 2016) who have already filed and suspended, the strategy remains available. Under the new rules, individuals can still file and suspend, but the benefits received by others (a spouse or dependent) that are based on the individual's earnings record are also suspended.

Divorced spouses, however, may continue to receive benefits even if one spouse chooses to suspend his or her benefits. A spouse of a client who filed and suspended before the deadline is entitled to collect his or her full retirement benefit if he or she was 62 years of age on January 1, 2016.

For individuals who were born in 1954 or thereafter, the option of choosing between two spouses' benefits is no longer available—the individual will automatically receive the higher of the two benefits when he or she applies for Social Security (known as a "deemed filing" requirement). The individual will automatically be deemed to apply for both available benefits.

Surviving spouses (or divorced surviving spouses) are not subject to this rule, and are still permitted to apply for survivor benefits and subsequently switch to his or her own retirement benefits at a later date if the retirement benefit would produce a higher total benefit. Deemed filing also does not apply to a individual who is receiving a spouse's benefit and is also entitled to disability benefits.

In the past, the file and suspend strategy allowed one spouse to begin collecting spousal benefits without jeopardizing the amount of the second spouse's retirement benefit. The second spouse was permitted to file for his or her benefits and then make a subsequent filing to suspend those benefits.

During the time that the benefits were suspended, one spouse earned delayed retirement credits, which increased the eventual benefit level by 8 percent for each year in which benefits were suspended. The taxpayer was, however, required to begin collecting benefits by age 70, by which point the benefit level could be increased substantially.

A spouse who was still working was permitted to collect spousal benefits but could similarly suspend any work-related benefit, so that it too could continue to grow until the working spouse reached age 70. At that point, both spouses would be entitled to a larger benefit and would still have collected some Social Security income in the intervening years.

3630. When can an individual claim retroactive Social Security benefits?

In general, if an individual waits until full retirement age to claim Social Security benefits, he or she may be eligible for up to six months' worth of retroactive benefits. For example, if an individual claimed Social Security benefits at age 67 and his or her full retirement age was 66, he or she would be entitled to up to six months' worth of retroactive benefits. If the individual claimed Social Security benefits at age 66 and 3 months, and his or her full retirement age was 66, he or she would be entitled to up to three months' worth of retroactive benefits.

If the individual chooses to claim retroactive benefits, his or her permanent ongoing monthly benefit will be reduced based upon the number of months' worth of retroactive benefits that are claimed.

Planning Point: Delayed retirement credits allow an individual's eventual monthly benefit to grow by 0.66 percent per month, or 8.0 percent per year, in the time that elapses between full retirement age and claiming benefits. The latest that an individual can claim Social Security benefits is age 70.

Retroactive benefits are received in a lump sum payment.

Planning Point: Individuals considering claiming retroactive benefits should consider the potential tax consequences of the lump sum distribution, as well as any potential impact on income levels for purposes of the Medicare income-based surcharge.

Retroactive Social Security benefits can be valuable with respect to survivor and spousal benefits, which do not earn delayed retirement credits and reach 100 percent of their value when the surviving spouse or spouse reaches full retirement age. If a surviving spouse or spouse claims these benefits after reaching full retirement age, he or she should request up to six months' worth of retroactive benefits (depending upon the time period that has elapsed between reaching full retirement age and claiming spousal or survivor benefits). However, in order to do so, the deceased spouse must have begun collecting Social Security benefits before full retirement age.

The surviving spouse or spouse's own Social Security retirement benefits (i.e., based on the spouse's own earnings record) will not be impacted, and can continue to earn delayed retirement credits until he or she eventually claims Social Security benefits.

3631. What are spousal Social Security benefits and how can these benefits impact Social Security planning?

Spousal benefits are benefits that an individual may be entitled to receive based on his or her spouse's earnings record. This essentially means that married clients may be eligible for Social

Security benefits regardless of whether they have ever earned income. This spousal benefit can equal up to 50 percent of the working spouse's benefit if the nonworking spouse waits until his or her full retirement age to claim Social Security benefits. If the spouse claims benefits early, the percentage is reduced based on the number of months remaining until the nonworking spouse reaches full retirement age.

It is also possible that the nonworking spouse actually did have enough earned income to qualify for traditional Social Security benefits, but those benefits may equal less than the 50 percent spousal benefit. In this case, that spouse is eligible for the higher level benefit, but it will be made up of a combination of the nonworking spouse's own benefit and a portion of the spousal benefit—the full amount of both benefits cannot be claimed.

3632. What are Social Security survivor benefits? What planning considerations can arise when claiming survivor benefits?

After the death of a spouse, the surviving spouse can begin to claim Social Security survivor benefits as early as age 60, although the benefit will be reduced based on the number of months remaining until the survivor reaches full retirement age. Like a traditional spousal benefit that is received when both spouses are alive, the amount of the survivor benefit is based on the deceased spouse's traditional retirement benefit, meaning that the benefit increases in proportion to how much the spouse earned during working years.

If the surviving spouse reached full retirement age before his or her death, the survivor's benefit will equal 100 percent of the deceased spouse's benefit. If the deceased spouse was receiving a reduced benefit, the survivor is only entitled to receive that reduced amount. However, if the surviving spouse had reached full retirement age at the time of the claim, he or she will be entitled to the higher of the reduced benefit or 82.5 percent of the deceased spouse's full benefit.

If a surviving spouse is between ages 50 and 59½ and is disabled, he or she is entitled to receive a reduced benefit (71.5 percent of the deceased spouse's benefit).

However, additional complexities come into play when a surviving spouse is also entitled to claim his or her own retirement benefit. If both spouses are already claiming benefits, the higher benefit amount automatically will become the survivor's benefit. If the surviving spouse has not yet claimed his or her own benefit, he or she is entitled to receive the survivor's benefit *or* his or her own benefit. For many surviving spouses who have yet to reach full retirement age, it can be beneficial to take the survivor benefit and allow his or her own benefit to grow. When the surviving spouse reaches age 70, he or she can switch from the survivor benefit to his or her own benefit, and receive an increased benefit.

In determining which benefit to choose (and when), it is important that both the size of the benefits and the client's life expectancy are taken into account. A client who has a long remaining life expectancy may choose to take a lower survivor benefit for several years in order to eventually switch to an increased benefit at age 70 (survivor benefits do not increase if claimed later than full retirement age).

3633. Can a surviving spouse continue to receive survivor benefits if he or she remarries?

If the surviving spouse remarries before reaching age 60, he or she will no longer be entitled to Social Security survivor benefits based on the prior spouse's record unless the subsequent marriage ends. Remarriage that occurs at age 60 or later does not impact the survivor benefit rules.

Further, an ex-spouse who was married to the deceased spouse for at least 10 years is entitled to survivor benefits based on his or her former spouse's earnings record even if the deceased spouse had remarried.

3634. What should dual income households consider with respect to Social Security planning?

One complication that arises in applying the Social Security earnings test applies in cases where both spouses in a marriage have their own independent earnings records upon which Social Security benefits can be based. Further, it is entirely possible that only one spouse will continue to work during retirement, so that uncertainty can arise over whether and when the earnings test will apply to reduce benefits.

Generally, the reduction, or working retirement tax, on Social Security benefits will only apply if the spouse whose earnings record is used to determine the amount of the benefits is also the spouse who continues to work. However, added complications can arise when one spouse decides to file a restricted application (an option that remains even after the phase-out of "file and suspend", see Q 3629) in order to cease receiving his or her own benefits and collect half of the other spouse's available benefit. This strategy can prove useful in situations where it is beneficial to allow the "restricting" spouse's benefit to grow until he or she reaches age 70.

In this case, the spousal benefit that is received is based on the spouse's earnings record, so if that spouse continues to work, the earnings test and applicable taxes will apply even though the spouse who is actually collecting the benefits has reached full retirement age (so is no longer subject to the earnings test) and does not work. However, once the working spouse reaches full retirement age, the Social Security Administration recalculates his or her benefits to treat that spouse as though he or she had waited to claim benefits (i.e., if the earnings test results in three months' worth of lost benefits for three years, the client will be treated as though he or she had begun claiming benefits nine months after the actual claim was made).

With divorced spouses, the continued earnings of a former spouse does not impact the ability of the other ex-spouse to claim benefits based on that working ex-spouse's earnings record, however.

3635. What should taxpayers who continue to work during retirement consider with respect to Social Security planning? Are Social Security benefits taxed?

Generally, an individual can begin to collect Social Security benefits even while he or she continues to work and earn income. However, a portion of that benefit will be subject to tax rules that differ from the otherwise applicable tax rates. In 2021, if an individual is younger than full retirement age, collects Social Security early and earns more than $18,960, his or her Social Security benefit will be reduced by $1 for every $2 that he or she earns over that limit. This earnings limit is applied on a calendar year basis (January-December), rather than based on the individual client's birthday. The limit is also indexed annually for inflation (the amount for 2020 was $18,240).

During the year in which the individual reaches full retirement age, the lower $18,960 amount is increased to $50,520 in the months prior to the month in which the individual actually reaches full retirement age. Further, during those months, his or her Social Security benefits are only reduced by $1 for every $3 that is earned above the $50,520 limit. For example, if the individual reaches full retirement age in September, his or her benefit will be reduced during the months of January through August, assuming his or her earned income exceeds $50,520.

Once the individual reaches full retirement age, his or her benefit is no longer reduced regardless of earned income.

It should be noted that these reductions are made in addition to any otherwise applicable income taxes that apply to the individual's Social Security benefit—when an individual earns over $25,000 per year ($32,000 for a married individual), one-half of his or her Social Security benefit plus any earned income will be taxable.

Despite all of this, if an individual's Social Security benefit is reduced because he or she continues to work during retirement, the individual will actually receive a higher monthly benefit amount once he or she actually reaches full retirement age. Essentially, the system treats such an individual as though he or she did not choose to claim benefits as early as he or she actually did claim benefits (because a portion of those benefits was actually withheld).

Earnings restrictions apply to a surviving spouse that is receiving Social Security survivor benefits in the same manner as they apply to any other recipient. In 2021, if a client a client is younger than full retirement age, collects Social Security early and earns more than $18,960, his or her Social Security benefit will be reduced by $1 for every $2 that he or she earns over that limit. When the client reaches full retirement age, the earnings cap increases to $50,520 and the reduction is only $1 for every $3 earned above the limit.

3636. How are Social Security benefits impacted by divorce?

If two individuals divorce, but have been married for at least 10 years, a divorced spouse can continue to receive benefits based on his or her ex-spouse's earnings record, even if that ex-spouse has remarried, in the following situations:

- The individual is unmarried,

- The individual is age 62 or older,

- The ex-spouse is entitled to Social Security or disability benefits, and

- The benefit the individual is entitled to receive based on his or her own earnings record is less than the benefit the individual would receive based on the ex-spouse's working record.

The benefit received as a divorced spouse is generally equal to half of the ex-spouse's full retirement amount if the individual begins to receive benefits at full retirement age. The individual's benefit based on the ex-spouse's record does not include delayed retirement credits that the ex-spouse may receive.

Planning Point: Even if the ex-spouse has not yet claimed benefits, but would qualify to do so, a divorced spouse can claim benefits based on that ex-spouse's earnings record if they have been divorced for at least two years.

With divorced spouses, the continued earnings of a former spouse also does not impact the ability of the other ex-spouse to claim benefits based on that working ex-spouse's earnings record. Further, a divorced spouse's claim to Social Security benefits based upon the earnings record of his or her ex-spouse does not impact the Social Security benefits that the ex-spouse and his or her current spouse are entitled to receive.

Planning Point: The file and suspend strategy may still be available for divorced spouses who have reached full retirement age if they were born before January 2, 1954.

3637. How can a client use a qualified longevity annuity contract in conjunction with his or her Social Security planning?

As most clients know, waiting past the normal retirement age to begin collecting Social Security allows the client to earn delayed retirement credits, which increase the eventual benefit by 8 percent for each year in which benefits are delayed. Because of this special treatment, most advisors counsel clients to delay claiming benefits for as long as possible in order to ensure the maximum monthly benefit level. Clients who do not wish to follow this advice, and who choose to instead claim Social Security early, can potentially benefit from using a qualified longevity annuity contract (QLAC) in their Social Security planning.

A QLAC is an annuity contract that is purchased within a traditional retirement plan, under which the annuity payments are deferred until the client reaches old age (they must begin by the month following the month in which the client reaches age 85) in order to provide retirement income security late in life. The value of the QLAC is excluded from the retirement account value when calculating the client's required minimum distributions (RMDs) once the client reaches age 70½, though the client is limited to purchasing a QLAC with an annuity premium value equal to the lesser of 25 percent of the account value or $130,000.

The introduction of QLACs can now allow clients who have saved for retirement to avoid delaying Social Security benefits entirely-and, because of volatility in the Social Security system and the uncertainty of a client's lifespan generally, many clients are receptive to this idea because they are reluctant to delay in the first place. For most clients, delaying Social Security benefits past retirement age means that withdrawals from tax-preferred accounts must increase during the deferral period in order to ensure sufficient income while maximizing the benefit level for a later time. However, this means that tax-preferred accounts are depleted at a much more rapid rate early in the client's retirement-leaving a lower account value to grow over subsequent years.

By purchasing a QLAC within the retirement account, the client can reduce his or her account distributions and eliminate the associated income tax liability, yet still secure a higher level of guaranteed income to supplement Social Security later in retirement. If the client claims Social Security benefits early in retirement, the amount that must be withdrawn from tax-preferred accounts is reduced and a larger portion of his or her retirement savings can be left intact to grow-generating a higher account balance in the long run. With the QLAC, the client still has a guaranteed source of income late in life-regardless of poor market performance or unforeseen circumstances-to supplement the lower Social Security benefit level that reduced the need for high withdrawals early in retirement.

Employee Death Benefits

3638. If an employer is under contract to pay a death benefit to an employee's surviving spouse, is the benefit taxable income to the surviving spouse?

Yes. Death benefits payable under a contract, or pursuant to an established plan of the employer (usually referred to as a "death benefit only" plan), are taxable income, and for this reason are frequently paid in installments.[1] Employee death benefits that are payable by reason of the death of certain terrorist attack victims or astronauts are excludable from gross income.[2]

Frequently, death benefits are funded by insurance on the life of the employee, with the insurance owned by and payable to the employer (traditional key associate life insurance). The fact that the death payments originate from life insurance proceeds received tax-free by the employer does not cause them to be tax-exempt to the employee's surviving spouse. The surviving spouse receives them as compensation payments from the employer and not as life insurance proceeds.[3] (For tax effects of insurance funding, see Q 262, Q 263, and Q 276.) Employee death benefits rarely qualify as life insurance benefits wholly excludable under IRC Section 101(a) (Q 63, Q 65, and Q 260).[4] Death benefits payable to an employee's surviving spouse under a split dollar life insurance arrangement, however, may be received free of income tax obligations (Q 4021, Q 4022).

Contractual death benefits are "income in respect of a decedent."[5] Consequently, where an estate tax has been paid, the recipient of the death payments is entitled to an income tax deduction for that portion of the estate tax attributable to the value of the payments, which may not prove very valuable.

---

1.   *Simpson v. U.S.*, 261 F.2d 497 (7th Cir. 1958); *Robinson v. Comm.*, 42 TC 403 (1964).
2.   IRC Sec. 101(i).
3.   *Essenfeld v. Comm.*, 311 F.2d 208 (2nd Cir. 1962).
4.   See *Edgar v. Comm.*, TC Memo 1979-524.
5.   *Est. of Wright v. Comm.*, 336 F.2d 121 (2nd Cir. 1964).

Planning Point: For the reasons mentioned above -income taxation of the death benefit to the beneficiary and only a potential deduction to the estate – it is often more attractive to create an endorsement split dollar life insurance plan for an employee so that the death benefits will be treated as the proceeds of life insurance to the beneficiary. The trade-off is some annual current economic benefit to the employee.

3639. Is a contractual death benefit payable to a surviving spouse deductible by an employer?

The employer can deduct the death benefit payments provided they represent reasonable additional compensation for the employee's services (Q 3519).[1] Payments can be deducted only in the year they are includable in the employee's income, regardless of the accounting method used by the employer.[2] An employer may not deduct a death benefit paid to (or received by) a surviving spouse to the extent that the employee recognized the value of the arrangement for income tax purposes or purchased the contractual right to the death benefit (Q 4021, Q 4022).

Questions as to whether death payments constitute compensation for an employee's services and, if so, whether the compensation is reasonable typically arise only in connection with payments for stockholder-employees of a close corporation. In several cases it has been held that the payments, even though made under contract, were not compensation but were payments under a plan to provide financial security for the families of the stockholder-employees. Hence, the deductions were disallowed.[3] On the other hand, payments were held reasonable and for a substantial business purpose in *M. Buten and Sons, Inc. v. Comm.*[4]

An employer who prefunds welfare benefit fund benefits will be subject to limits discussed in Q 4096 and Q 4100. If the funded benefit is considered deferred compensation, the deduction is subject to the rules in Q 3532 or Q 3573.

3640. If an employer voluntarily pays a death benefit to an employee's surviving spouse, is the benefit taxable income to the surviving spouse, and is it deductible by the employer?

The IRS has taken the position that voluntary death benefits are not gifts, but are compensation and therefore taxable income.[5] The courts, following the rules developed by the United States Supreme Court in *Commissioner v. Duberstein*,[6] have divided on the question of whether these payments are tax-free gifts or taxable compensation. Each case has been decided on its facts.[7]

Payments made after December 31, 1986 by an employer "to, or for the benefit of" an employee are not excludable as gifts, however.[8] Thus, a death benefit paid by an employer after

---

1.   *Southern Fruit Distributors v. U.S.*, 32 AFTR 2d 5598 (M.D. Fla. 1973).
2.   IRC Sec. 404(a)(5); Rev. Rul. 55-212, 1955-1 CB 299.
3.   *Willmark Serv. Sys., Inc. v. Comm.*, 368 F.2d 359 (2d Cir. 1966); *Wallace v. Comm.*, TC Memo 1967-11; M.S.D. Inc. v. U.S., 611 F. 2d 373 (6th Cir. 1979).
4.   TC Memo 1972-44.
5.   Rev. Rul. 62-102, 1962-2 CB 37.
6.   363 U.S. 278 (1960).
7.   See *Sweeney v. Comm.*, TC Memo 1987-550.
8.   IRC Sec. 102(c).

December 31, 1986 would appear to be a payment for the benefit of an employee and, if so, would be taxable compensation not an excludable gift. Employee death benefits that are payable by reason of the death of certain terrorist attack victims or astronauts are excludable from gross income.[1]

To be deductible by the employer, a voluntary death benefit must qualify as an ordinary and necessary business expense.[2] Payments will be deductible, therefore, if the circumstances show that they are additional reasonable compensation for the employee's services, or otherwise qualify as an ordinary and necessary business expense.[3]

The deduction will be denied if the facts indicate that the payment was purely a gift or was made for the personal satisfaction of the directors.[4]

Where the surviving spouse is a controlling stockholder, the payments may very likely be treated as constructive dividends. In such a case, the entire death benefit would be taxable to the surviving spouse but not deductible by the corporation.[5] Even where the surviving spouse does not own a controlling interest, the payments may be treated as dividends, if the corporation is owned by a closely knit family group.[6] The payments will not be treated as dividends merely because the employee was a minority stockholder. They also will not be treated as dividends in all cases where the surviving spouse is a substantial, but not a controlling, stockholder.[7]

1.   IRC Sec. 101(i).
2.   IRC Sec. 404(a)(5); Treas. Reg. §1.404(a)-12.
3.   *Rubber Assoc., Inc. v. Comm.*, 335 F.2d 75 (6th Cir. 1964); *Associated Ark. Newspapers Inc. v. Johnson*, 18 AFTR 2d 5894 (E.D. Ark. 1966); *Fifth Ave. Coach Lines, Inc. v. Comm.*, 31 TC 1080 (1959).
4.   *Loewy Drug Co. v. Comm.*, 356 F.2d 928 (4th Cir. 1966); *Vesuvius Crucible Co. v. Comm.*, 356 F.2d 948 (3rd Cir. 1965); *Montgomery Eng'g Co. v. Comm.*, 344 F.2d 996 (3rd Cir. 1965); *Greentree's Inc. v. U.S.* 16 AFTR 2d 5368 (E.D. Va. 1965); *Fouke Fur Co. v. Comm.*, 261 F. Supp. 367 (E.D. Mo. 1966).
5.   *Schner-Block Co., Inc. v. Comm.*, 329 F.2d 875 (2nd Cir. 1964); *Nickerson Lumber Co. v. U.S.*, 214 F. Supp. 87 (D. Mass. 1963); *Bacon v. Comm.*, 12 AFTR 2d 6076 (E.D. Ky. 1963).
6.   *Jordanos, Inc. v. Comm.*, 396 F.2d 829 (9th Cir. 1968).
7.   *Plastic Binding Corp. v. Comm.*, TC Memo 1967-147; see also *John C. Nordt Co. v. Comm.*, 46 TC 431 (1966).

PART XV: INDIVIDUAL RETIREMENT PLANS

In General

3641. What is an individual retirement plan? What is an individual retirement account and a Roth individual retirement account?

Individual retirement plans are tax favored personal savings arrangements that allow an individual to set aside money for retirement.

A traditional individual retirement plan generally allows an individual to contribute both deductible (where eligible) and nondeductible payments to receive the benefit of tax-deferred buildup on income.

Alternatively, a Roth individual retirement plan allows eligible individuals to contribute only nondeductible payments with the benefit of tax-free buildup of income (Q 3673). A Roth individual retirement plan must clearly be designated as such at the time of establishment, and that designation cannot later be changed; the recharacterization of a Roth IRA will require the execution of new documents (Q 3662).[1] Note that tax reform eliminated the traditional ability to convert traditional IRA funds to a Roth account and later recharacterize the transaction for tax years beginning after 2017.

With respect to both traditional and Roth individual retirement plans, some individuals also may contribute to such plans for their spouses.

There are two kinds of traditional and Roth individual retirement plans: individual retirement accounts (discussed below) and individual retirement annuities (Q 3642).

An individual retirement account (IRA) is a written trust or custodial account created for the purpose of saving money for retirement that allows individuals to make yearly contributions, up to specific annual limits, that will grow tax-free.

A "traditional" IRA allows an individual to make both pre-tax (where eligible) and after-tax contributions to the account, which will grow free of income taxes, but are taxable when distributed to the participant (see Q 3649, Q 3671). Alternatively, a Roth IRA only allows after-tax contributions, but such contributions also grow tax-free and usually can be distributed tax-free to the extent they are considered "qualified distributions" (see Q 3673).

Contributions to such accounts must be in cash (except for rollovers) and may not exceed the maximum annual contribution limit for the tax year – $5,500 in 2018 and $6,000 (in 2019-2021) (Q 3656) – except for rollover contributions (Q 3991), for contributions to a SIMPLE IRA (Q 3706), and for employer contributions to simplified employee pensions (Q 3701).[2] A wire order from a broker to a custodian will constitute a "cash contribution" on the date payment and registration instructions are received by the broker, provided an agency

---

1.   IRC Sec. 408A(b); Treas. Reg. §1.408A-2, A-2.
2.   IRC Sec. 408(a)(1).

arrangement recognized by and binding under state law exists between the broker and the custodian.[1]

With respect to traditional individual retirement accounts, distribution of an individual's interest must begin by April 1 of the year after the year in which he or she reaches age 72 (70½ before 2020) and must be made over a limited period. In addition, distributions must comply with the incidental death benefit requirements of IRC Section 401(a)(9) (Q 3686).[2] With respect to both traditional and Roth accounts, required minimum distribution (RMD) requirements must be met upon death of the owner (Q 3687).[3]

The trustee or custodian of an individual retirement account must be a bank, a federally insured credit union, a building and loan association, or an entity that satisfies IRS requirements.[4] A trustee or custodian acceptable to the IRS cannot be an individual but can be a corporation or partnership that demonstrates that it has fiduciary ability (including continuity of life, established location, fiduciary experience, and fiduciary and financial responsibility), capacity to account for the interests of a large number of individuals, fitness to handle retirement funds, ability to administer fiduciary powers (including maintenance of a separate trust division), and adequate net worth (at least $250,000 initially).[5]

The interest of the individual in the balance of his or her individual retirement account must be nonforfeitable, and the assets must not be commingled with other property except in a common trust fund or common investment fund. In such a trust, they may be pooled with trust funds of regular qualified plans.[6] No part of the trust funds may be invested in life insurance.[7] An account generally may not invest in collectibles without adverse tax consequences (Q 3649). An account may invest in annuity contracts that, in the case of death prior to the time distributions commence, provide for a payment equal to the sum of the premiums paid or, if greater, the cash value of the contract.[8] An account may not use any part of its assets to purchase an endowment contract issued after November 6, 1978.[9]

Planning Point: Effective for tax years beginning after December 31, 2012, distributions from individual retirement arrangements (as well as from qualified plans, Section 403(b) tax-sheltered annuities, and eligible 457 governmental plans) are exempted from the unearned income Medicare contribution tax imposed under the Affordable Care Act.[10] The ACA imposes a tax of 3.8 percent on individuals, estates, and trusts on the lesser of net investment income, or the excess of modified adjusted gross income (AGI + foreign earned income) over a threshold of $200,000 (individual) or $250,000 (joint). Investors may therefore find it beneficial to direct wages and investments into IRAs to reduce income and remain below these thresholds.[11]

---

1.   Let. Ruls. 9034068, 8837034.
2.   IRC Secs. 408(a)(6), 408A(c)(4).
3.   IRC Secs. 408(a)(6), 408A(c)(4).
4.   IRC Secs. 408(a)(2), 408(n).
5.   Treas. Reg. §§1.408-2(b)(2), 1.408-2(e).
6.   IRC Secs. 408(a)(4), 408(a)(5), 408(e)(6); Rev. Rul. 81-100, 1981-1 CB 326; see also *Nichola v. Comm.*, TC Memo 1992-105.
7.   IRC Sec. 408(a)(3).
8.   Treas. Reg. §1.408-2(b)(3).
9.   Treas. Reg. §§1.408-4(f), 1.408-3(e)(1)(ix).
10.   P.L. 111-148.
11.   See IRC Sec. 1411.

3642. What is an individual retirement annuity?

An individual retirement annuity is an annuity or an endowment contract issued by an insurance company that is structured similarly to an individual retirement account, but must meet certain additional requirements to qualify as a retirement plan.[1] An endowment contract issued after November 6, 1978 will not qualify.[2]

To qualify as an individual retirement annuity, as provided by IRC Section 408(b):

(1)   The contract must be nontransferable.

(2)   Contracts issued after November 6, 1978 may not have fixed premiums.

(3)   The annual premium on behalf of any individual may not exceed the maximum annual contribution limit for the tax year except in the case of a SIMPLE IRA (Q 3706) or a simplified employee pension (SEP, see Q 3701).

(4)   Any refund of premium must be applied to the payment of future premiums or the purchase of additional benefits before the close of the calendar year of the refund.

(5)   With respect to non-Roth individual retirement annuities, distribution must begin by April 1 of the year after the year in which the owner reaches age 70½ and the period over which distribution may be made is limited.

(6)   With respect to both traditional and Roth annuities, required minimum distribution requirements must be met on the owner's death (Q 3687).[3]

(7)   Distributions must comply with the incidental death benefit requirements of IRC Section 401(a)(9) (Q 3686).[4]

(8)   The interest of the owner must be nonforfeitable.

A contract will be considered transferable if it can be used as security for any loan other than a loan from the issuer in an amount not greater than the cash value of the contract. Even so, a policy loan would cause the contract to cease to be an individual retirement annuity or endowment contract as of the first day of the owner's tax year in which the loan was made (Q 3649).[5]

The Eighth Circuit has held that a premium was not fixed when a lump sum was rolled from an IRA into an individual retirement annuity because funds taken from an IRA did not constitute a premium if used to pay for an individual retirement annuity.[6]

---

1.   IRC Secs. 408(b), 408A(a).
2.   Treas. Reg. §1.408-3(e)(1)(ix).
3.   IRC Secs. 408(a)(6), 408A(c)(6).
4.   IRC Secs. 408(b)(3), 408A(c)(6).
5.   IRC Sec. 408(e)(3); Treas. Reg. §1.408-3(c).
6.   *Running v. Miller*, 778 F.3d 711 (8th Cir. 2015).

Proposed regulations state that for a flexible premium annuity to qualify as an individual retirement annuity, the contract must provide that (1) at no time after the initial premium has been paid will a specified renewal premium be required, (2) the contract may be continued as a paid-up annuity under its nonforfeiture provision if premium payments cease altogether, and (3) if the contract is continued on a paid-up basis, it may be reinstated at any date prior to its maturity date by a payment of premium to the insurer.

Two exceptions allow the insurer to set a minimum premium, not in excess of $50, and to terminate certain contracts where premiums have not been paid for an extended period and the paid-up benefit would be less than $20 a month.

A flexible premium contract will not be considered to have fixed premiums merely because a maximum annual premium is set, an annual charge is placed against the policy value, or because the contract requires a level annual premium for supplementary benefits (such as a waiver of premium feature).[1]

The IRS has privately ruled that a contract that includes a substantial element of life insurance will not qualify as an individual retirement annuity.[2]

A participation certificate in a group annuity contract meeting the above requirements will be considered an individual retirement annuity if there is a separate accounting for the benefit allocable to each participant-owner and the group contract is for the exclusive benefit of the participant-owners and their beneficiaries.[3]

A "wraparound annuity" contract entered into on or before September 25, 1981 as an individual retirement annuity will continue to be treated for tax purposes as an individual retirement annuity provided no contributions are made on behalf of any individual who was not included under the contract on that date. "Wraparound annuity" refers to an insurance company contract containing typical deferred annuity provisions but that also promises to allocate net premiums to an account invested in shares of a specific mutual fund that is available to the general public without purchase of the annuity contract.[4]

Effective November 16, 1999, annuity contracts in which the premiums are invested at the direction of the IRA owners in "publicly available securities" (i.e., mutual funds that are available for public purchase) will be treated as an individual retirement annuity contract if no additional federal income tax liability would have been incurred if the owner had instead contributed such amount into an individual retirement account where the funds were commingled in a common investment fund.[5]

---

1.   Prop. Treas. Reg. §1.408-3(f).
2.   Let. Rul. 8439026.
3.   Treas. Reg. §1.408-3(a).
4.   Rev. Rul. 81-225, 1981-2 CB 12, as clarified by Rev. Rul. 82-55, 1982-1 CB 12.
5.   Rev. Proc. 99-44, 1999-2 CB 598, modifying Rev. Rul. 81-225, 1981-2 CB 12.

3643. What are some of the potential benefits and consequences of holding a fixed income annuity within an IRA?

The primary benefit of holding fixed income annuities within an IRA is the simplification of the required minimum distribution process. Fixed income annuities held inside a taxpayer's IRA usually comply with the RMD rules automatically because their payments are determined in the same way that the RMD itself is calculated—using a formula based on the life expectancy of the individual and the amount invested.

While a cash RMD is required each year after the taxpayer turns 72 (70½ before 2020) regardless of general market conditions, it is important to remember that IRA assets may be invested in a variety of holdings, including securities and funds that will fluctuate with the equity markets. Unfortunately, the RMD requirements may, depending on market performance, cause taxpayers to miss market upswings by requiring that the taxpayer liquidate securities held within the IRA in order to satisfy his or her RMDs. Using a fixed income annuity can help reduce this risk because the payments are fixed in advance. Note that RMD requirements were suspended for the 2020 tax year under the CARES Act.

In other words, there is no investment decision required each year because the taxpayer has already determined the value of the payout (whether it is made monthly, quarterly or annually). While the RMD for any non-annuitized portion of the IRA will still have to be calculated, the value of the annuity is excluded from this calculation, thereby reducing the risk that the taxpayer will be forced to make an unfavorable investment decision simply to comply with the RMD rules.

Further, the fixed income annuity actually allows the taxpayer to set an income level in advance—RMDs will fluctuate with the IRA value in any given year, but the annuity payments will remain constant regardless of the performance of the remaining underlying IRA assets. Taxpayers also have the option of adding a cost of living increase to the annuity payouts to ensure sufficient income during retirement.

As with any planning strategy, however, there are potential objections. Most commonly, advisors may feel that it makes little sense for some taxpayers (especially younger individuals) to hold an annuity within the IRA because both types of investments are tax-deferred, so the annuity could be held separately from IRA assets with similar consequences. As a result, some might feel that the strategy is simply redundant.

Additionally, amounts held in an annuity are more difficult to access than other IRA funds without incurring significant penalty charges—if the taxpayer has a financial emergency after age 72, he or she could access non-annuitized IRA funds without penalty. Taxpayers should, therefore, only consider purchasing the annuity with IRA funds if they have sufficient assets held outside of the annuity to cover any unforeseen expenses.

Further, while holding an annuity within an IRA can allow the taxpayer to avoid selling IRA assets during unfavorable market swings, it can also mean that the taxpayer has no reason to liquidate those holdings when their value is high, potentially avoiding a loss if the value eventually falls.

Planning Point: Advisors considering recommending that a client purchase an annuity inside of an IRA should carefully consider the costs and the benefits of the arrangement, and should carefully review and comply with any applicable fiduciary rules, although the Department of Labor fiduciary rule was vacated in 2018.

3644. What are U.S. Individual Retirement Bonds?

Prior to TRA '84, the IRC provided for the issuance of retirement bonds.[1] These bonds were issued by the U.S. government, with interest to be paid on redemption. Sales of these bonds were suspended as of April 30, 1982.[2] Subsequently, the Treasury Department announced that existing bonds could be redeemed by their holders at any time without being subject to an early distribution penalty (Q 3677).[3] Existing bonds also can be rolled over into other individual retirement plans under rules applicable to rollovers from individual retirement plans (Q 4003).[4]

3645. What is a "deemed IRA"?

A deemed IRA is an account or annuity created under an employer's qualified retirement plan. A deemed IRA is treated as a traditional IRA or Roth IRA and is subject to the same rules regarding contributions and distributions.

For plan years beginning after December 31, 2002, a qualified plan, Section 403(b) tax sheltered annuity plan, or eligible Section 457 governmental plan may allow employees to make voluntary employee contributions to a separate account or annuity established under the plan. If such account or annuity meets the rules for traditional IRAs under IRC Section 408 or for Roth IRAs under IRC Section 408A, then such account or annuity will be "deemed" an IRA and not a qualified employer plan.

A voluntary employee contribution is any nonmandatory contribution that the individual designates as such. Such "deemed IRAs" will not be subject to the IRC rules governing the employer plan, but they will be subject to the exclusive benefit and fiduciary rules of ERISA to the extent they otherwise apply to the employer plan.[5]

Under final regulations, a deemed IRA and the plan under which it is adopted generally are treated as separate entities, with each subject to the rules generally applicable to that type of entity.[6] The regulations further provide that the "availability of a deemed IRA is not a benefit, right, or feature of the qualified employer plan," meaning that eligibility for and contributions to deemed IRAs are not subject to the general nondiscrimination requirements applicable to qualified plans.[7]

---

1.   IRC Sec. 409, as in effect prior to repeal by TRA '84.
2.   Treasury Release (4-27-82).
3.   Treasury Announcement (7-26-84).
4.   IRC Sec. 409(b)(3)(C), prior to repeal.
5.   IRC Sec. 408(q). See Rev. Proc. 2003-13, 2003-1 CB 317.
6.   Treas. Reg. §1.408(q)-1.
7.   Treas. Reg. §1.408(q)-1(f)(6).

The regulations provide three exceptions to treating a qualified plan and deemed IRAs as separate entities:

(1)   The qualified plan documents must contain the deemed IRA provisions and be in effect at the time the deemed IRA contributions are accepted. (Plans offering deemed IRAs for the 2002 or 2003 plan years had until the plan year beginning in 2004 to have such provisions in writing).[1]

(2)   Deemed IRA and qualified plan assets may be commingled. The prohibition against commingling in IRC Section 408(a)(5) (Q 3641) does not apply to deemed IRA and qualified plan assets. Deemed IRA and qualified plan assets still may not be further commingled with nonplan assets.[2]

(3)   If deemed IRA and qualified plan assets are commingled in a single trust, the failure of any of the deemed IRAs maintained by a plan to meet the requirements of IRC Section 408 (traditional IRAs) or IRC Section 408A (Roth IRAs) can disqualify the qualified plan, requiring correction through the Employee Plans Compliance Resolution System or another administrative procedure (Q 3837). Likewise, the disqualification of a plan can cause the individual accounts to no longer be considered deemed IRAs.[3]

If deemed IRA and qualified plan assets are maintained in separate trusts, a qualified plan will not be disqualified solely because of the failure of any of the deemed IRAs to meet the requirements of IRC Section 408 (traditional IRAs) or IRC Section 408A (Roth IRAs). Likewise, if separate trusts are maintained, individual accounts will not fail to be deemed IRAs solely because of the disqualification of the plan.[4]

Planning Point: The advantages of a deemed IRA as part of the employer plan include the ability of the employee to consolidate retirement investment savings, perceived ease of making additional contributions to retirement savings, and more investment options may be available with a deemed IRA than with a stand-alone IRA.

However, a participant may prefer to create IRAs outside of a an employer's qualified plan or use separate trusts to avoid any possibility of either the IRA or the qualified plan causing disqualification of the other.

3646. What information must be provided to a buyer of an IRA?

The trustee or issuer (i.e. "the sponsor") of an IRA must furnish the plan participant with a "disclosure statement" and a copy of the governing instrument at least seven days before the plan is purchased or established, whichever is earlier. Alternatively, the sponsor can wait to provide the disclosure statement to the participant until the time it is purchased or established, whichever is earlier, provided that the individual is permitted to revoke the plan within at least seven days from that date.

---

1.   Treas. Reg. §1.408(q)-1(d)(1).
2.   Treas. Reg. §1.408(q)-1(d)(2).
3.   Treas. Reg. §1.408(q)-1(g).
4.   Treas. Reg. §1.408(q)-1(g).

The disclosure statement must include certain items in plain language such as provisions related to when and how the IRA can be revoked and the contact information for the person to receive the notice of cancellation. An individual revoking his or her plan is entitled to the return of the full amount he or she paid without adjustment for sales commission, administrative expenses, or fluctuation in market value. If the governing instrument is amended after the IRA is no longer subject to revocation, a copy of the amendment (and possibly a "disclosure statement") must be furnished to the individual not later than the 30th day after the later of the date the amendment is adopted or becomes effective.[1]

IRS regulations also provide that, if values under an individual retirement arrangement are guaranteed or can be projected, the trustee or issuer must in certain instances disclose to an IRA purchaser the amounts guaranteed or projected to be withdrawable. Basically, these regulations provide that the trustee must show the owner the amount the owner could receive if he or she closed the account and paid any surrender charges or penalties at the end of each of the first five years after the initial contribution and at ages 60, 65, and 70.[2] In making the disclosure, the trustee must show the amount guaranteed (or projected) to be withdrawable, after reduction for all charges or penalties that may be applied. The disclosures required for values at an owner's ages 60, 65, and 70 must be based on the actual age of the individual at the time of the disclosure. If a guaranteed rate is actually lower than the rate currently being paid on an account, the disclosure statement may use the higher rate, but must clearly indicate that the guaranteed rate is lower.[3]

For the reporting requirements imposed on IRA trustees with respect to required minimum distributions, see Q 3698.

3647. What is sequence of returns risk? How can sequence of returns risk affect a taxpayer's retirement income strategy?

Sequence of returns risk is a market volatility issue surrounding the order in which returns on a taxpayer's investments occur when the taxpayer is taking distributions or withdrawals from the portfolio.

Essentially, if a greater proportion of low or negative returns occur during the early years of retirement, when taxpayer is taking withdrawals, the taxpayer's overall returns are going to be lower than if those negative or low returns occurred at a later point in the taxpayer's (and the investment's) lifetime. Mathematically, this is because the withdrawal of a fixed dollar amount from a portfolio when the portfolio value is down requires the liquidation and distribution of a larger percentage of the portfolio than would be required when the portfolio value is high. These early low (or negative) returns and distributions have a larger impact on the compounded value of the portfolio if they occur in early years. Negative returns could even cause a portion of the principal investment to be lost.

---

1.   Treas. Reg. §1.408-6(d)(4).
2.   Treas. Reg. §1.408-6(d)(4)(v).
3.   Rev. Rul. 86-78, 1986-1 CB 208.

Even if the return is simply lower than average in the early years while distributions are being taken, the investment will generate an overall lower return because the investment will gain less value early on, meaning there will be a lower account value to generate growth even in later, higher return periods.

When the taxpayer is making withdrawals from his or her investment accounts, the risk of outliving the retirement assets is magnified when negative returns occur in early years.

Planning Point: Financial planners modeling sequence of returns risk for their clients can illustrate the potential impact of (1) reducing market volatility of the overall portfolio, (2) reducing withdrawal amounts in early years or delaying withdrawals from the portfolio in down markets, and (3) maintaining a balanced portfolio so that withdrawal amounts can be paid from assets with a stable asset value rather than from selling volatile assets in a depressed market – as strategies to mitigate the potential impact of sequence of returns risk.

3648. What is the saver's credit and who can claim it?

Editor's Note: The 2017 Tax Act modified the rules governing ABLE accounts to permit a contributing beneficiary to claim the saver's credit for tax years beginning after 2017 and before 2026. See Q 385 to Q 387.

The saver's credit (formally known as the retirement savings contributions credit) permits certain lower-income taxpayers to claim a nonrefundable credit for qualified retirement savings contributions.[1] Qualified retirement savings contributions include contributions to Roth or traditional IRAs, as well as elective deferrals to a 401(k) plan (Q 3752), an IRC Section 403(b) tax sheltered annuity (Q 4029), an eligible Section 457 governmental plan (Q 3584), a SIMPLE IRA (Q 3706), and a salary reduction SEP (Q 3705). Voluntary after-tax contributions to a qualified plan or Section 403(b) tax sheltered annuity are also eligible for the credit.[2] The fact that contributions are made pursuant to a negative election (i.e., automatic enrollment) will not preclude a participant from claiming the saver's credit.[3] Contributions made to an IRA that are withdrawn, together with the net income attributable to such contribution, on or before the due date (including extensions of time) for filing the federal income tax return of the contributing individual are not considered eligible contributions.[4]

To prevent churning (simply switching existing retirement funds from one account to another to qualify for the credit), the total of qualified retirement savings contributions is reduced by certain distributions received by the taxpayer during the prior two taxable years and the current taxable year for which the credit is claimed, including the period up to the due date (plus extensions) for filing the federal income tax return for the current taxable year. Distributions received by the taxpayer's spouse during the same time period are also counted if the taxpayer and spouse filed jointly both for the year during which a distribution was made and the year for which the credit is taken.[5]

---

1.   IRC Sec. 25B.
2.   IRC Sec. 25B(d)(1); Ann. 2001-106, 2001-44 IRB 416, A-5.
3.   See Ann. 2001-106, 2001-44 IRB 416.
4.   See Ann. 2001-106, 2001-44 IRB 416, A-5.
5.   See Ann. 2001-106 Q-4.

Corrective distributions of excess contributions and excess aggregate contributions (Q 3807), excess deferrals (Q 3760), dividends paid on employer securities under Section 404(k) (Q 3823), and loans treated as distributions (Q 3948) are not taken into account.[1]

To be eligible to claim the credit, the taxpayer must be at least 18 as of the end of the tax year, cannot be claimed as a dependent on someone else's tax return, and cannot be a full-time student. Full-time students include any individual who is enrolled in school during some part of each of five months during the year and is enrolled for the number of hours or courses the school considers to be full-time.[2]

The amount of the credit is limited to an applicable percentage of IRA contributions and elective deferrals up to $2,000.

The applicable percentages for 2021 are as follows:[3]

ADJUSTED GROSS INCOME

| Joint return | | Head of a household | | All other cases | | Applicable |
Over	Not over	Over	Not over	Over	Not over	Percentage
0	$39,500	0	$29,625	0	$19,750	50%
39,500	43,000	29,625	32,250	19,750	21,500	20%
43,000	66,000	32,250	49,500	21,500	33,000	10%
66,000		49,500		33,000		0%

The applicable percentages for 2020 are as follows:[4]

ADJUSTED GROSS INCOME

| Joint return | | Head of a household | | All other cases | | Applicable |
Over	Not over	Over	Not over	Over	Not over	Percentage
0	$39,000	0	$29,250	0	$19,500	50%
39,000	42,500	29,250	31,875	19,500	21,250	20%
42,500	65,000	31,875	48,750	21,250	32,500	10%
65,000		48,750		32,500		0%

The income limits are indexed for inflation.[5] For this purpose, adjusted gross income is calculated without regard to the exclusions for income derived from certain foreign sources or sources within United States possessions.[6]

Taxpayers have until their tax filing deadline to contribute to traditional and Roth IRAs and still claim the credit on the prior year's tax return.

---

1.   IRC Sec. 25B(d)(2); Ann. 2001-106, above, A-4.
2.   IRC Sec. 25B(c); Ann. 2001-106, 2001-44 IRB 416, A-2.
3.   Notice 2020-79.
4.   Notice 2019-59.
5.   IRC Sec. 25B(b)(3).
6.   IRC Sec. 25B(e).

The maximum credit that can be claimed is $1,000, or $2,000 for married taxpayers filing jointly. For married couples, contributions by or for either or both spouses may give rise to the credit.[1]

> *Example:* Susan, who is married, earned $39,500 in 2021. Her husband did not have any earnings. During 2020, Susan contributed $1,200 to her IRA, which she deducted on her tax return, which reduced her adjusted gross income to $38,300. Susan is eligible to claim a 50 percent saver's credit, or $600.

3649. When are funds in an IRA taxed?

Funds accumulated in a traditional IRA generally are not taxable until they are distributed (Q 3671). Funds accumulated in a Roth IRA may or may not be taxable on distribution (Q 3673). Special rules may treat funds accumulated in an IRA as a "deemed distribution" and, thus, includable in income under the rules discussed in Q 3671 for traditional IRAs and in Q 3673 for Roth IRAs.

A distribution of a nontransferable, nonforfeitable annuity contract that provides for payments to begin by age 72 (70½ prior to 2020) and not to extend beyond certain limits is not taxable, but payments made under such an annuity would be includable in income under the appropriate rules.

Contributions to an IRA may be returned to the participant in a tax-free manner if certain conditions are met as discussed in Q 3670 (provided, in the case of a traditional IRA that no deduction was allowed for the contribution). If net income allocable to the contribution is distributed before the due date for filing the tax return for the year in which the contribution was made, it must be included in income for the tax year for which the contribution was made even if the distribution actually was made after the end of that year.[2] With respect to distributions of excess contributions after this deadline, the net income amount is included in income in the year distributed. Any net income amount also may be subject to penalty tax as an early distribution.

Where a taxpayer transferred funds from a single IRA into two newly-created IRAs, the direct trustee-to-trustee transfers were not considered distributions under IRC Section 408(d)(1).[3] The division of a decedent's IRA into separate subaccounts does not result in current taxation of the IRA beneficiaries.[4]

A distribution of any amount may be received free of federal income tax to the extent the amount is then contributed within 60 days to another plan under qualified rollover rules (Q 4003).

For the penalty tax imposed on accumulated amounts not distributed in accordance with the required minimum distribution rules, see Q 3682.

---

1.   Ann. 2001-106, 2001-44 IRB 416, A-9.
2.   IRC Sec. 408(d)(4); Treas. Reg. §1.408-4(c).
3.   Let. Rul. 9438019. See also Rev. Rul. 78-406, 1978-2 CB 157; Let. Rul. 9433032.
4.   Let. Rul. 200008044.

If any assets of an individual retirement account are used to purchase collectibles (works of art, gems, antiques, metals, etc.), the amount so used will be treated as distributed from the account (and also may be subject to penalty as an early distribution). A plan may invest in certain gold or silver coins issued by the United States, any coins issued under the laws of a state, and certain platinum coins. A plan may buy gold, silver, platinum, and palladium bullion of a fineness sufficient for the commodities market if the bullion remains in the physical possession of the IRA trustee.[1] A plan may purchase shares in a grantor trust holding such bullion.[2]

If any part of an individual retirement account is used by the individual as security for a loan, that portion is deemed distributed on the first day of the tax year in which the loan was made.[3] Amounts rolled over into an IRA from a qualified plan by one of the 25 highest paid employees, however, may be pledged as security for repayments that may have to be made to the plan in the event of an early plan termination.[4] A less-than-60-day interest-free loan from IRA accumulations is possible under the rollover rules (Q 4011).[5]

If the owner of an individual retirement annuity borrows money under or by use of the contract in any tax year, including a policy loan, the annuity ceases to qualify as an individual retirement annuity as of the first day of the tax year and the fair market value of the contract would be deemed distributed on that day.[6]

If an individual engages in a prohibited transaction (Q 3975) with his or her IRA, such IRA ceases to qualify as such as of the first day of that tax year when the prohibited transaction occurred; the individual, however, is not liable for a prohibited transaction tax.[7] The fair market value of all the assets in the account is deemed distributed on that day.[8] If the account is maintained by an employer, only the separate account of the individual involved is disqualified and deemed distributed.[9]

The transfer to an individual retirement account of a personal note received in a terminating distribution from a qualified plan and the holding of that note is a prohibited transaction.[10]

The use of IRA funds to invest in a personal retirement residence of the taxpayer is considered a prohibited transaction under IRC Section 4975(c)(1)(D) and, thus, is treated as a distribution.[11]

Whether a purchase of life insurance in conjunction with an individual retirement plan but with non-plan funds constitutes a prohibited transaction apparently depends on the circumstances. The IRS has held that the purchase of insurance on the depositor's life by the

1.   IRC Sec. 408(m); Let. Rul. 200217059.
2.   Let. Ruls. 200732026, 200732027.
3.   IRC Sec. 408(e)(4); Treas. Reg. §1.408-4(d)(2); Let. Ruls. 8335117, 8019103, 8011116.
4.   See, e.g., Let. Ruls. 8845060, 8803087, 8751049. See also Treas. Reg. §1.401-4(c).
5.   See Let. Rul. 9010007.
6.   See IRC Sec. 408(e)(3). See also *Griswold v. Comm.*, 85 TC 869 (1985).
7.   IRC Sec. 4975(c)(3).
8.   See Treas. Reg. §1.408-1(c)(2).
9.   IRC Sec. 408(e)(2).
10.   TAM 8849001.
11.   *Harris v. Comm.*, TC Memo 1994-22.

trustee of the account with non-plan funds amounted to an indirect prohibited transaction by the depositor.[1] The IRS also has ruled that the solicitation by an association of individuals who maintain individual retirement plans with the association for enrollment in a group life plan did not result in a prohibited transaction where premiums would be paid by the individuals and not out of plan funds.[2]

Institutions may offer limited financial incentives to IRA and Keogh holders without running afoul of the prohibited transaction rules provided certain conditions are met. Generally speaking, the value of the incentive must not exceed $10 for deposits of less than $5,000 and $20 for deposits of $5,000 or more. These requirements also are applicable to SEPs that allow participants to transfer their SEP balances to IRAs sponsored by other financial institutions and to SIMPLE IRAs.[3]

3650. When are IRA funds transferred between spouses or incident to a divorce treated as taxable distributions?

An individual may transfer, without tax, the individual's IRA to his or her spouse or former spouse under a divorce or separate maintenance decree or a written instrument incident to the divorce. The IRA then is maintained for the benefit of the former spouse.[4] Any other assignment of an IRA is a deemed distribution of the amount assigned.[5]

Planning Point: It is especially important for clients to revisit IRA beneficiary designations upon divorce. The U.S. Supreme Court recently upheld a Minnesota law that operates to revoke a life insurance beneficiary designation in favor of an ex-spouse upon divorce. In that case, the policy owner's two children from a prior marriage claimed that they, not the owner's ex-spouse, were the rightful beneficiaries and the Supreme Court agreed. While this case involved life insurance policies, it is important to remember that it could also impact a client's IRA.[6]

Where an individual rolled over his interest in a tax sheltered annuity to an IRA, pursuant to a qualified domestic relations order ("QDRO") (Q 3908), the subsequent transfer of the IRA to the individual's spouse was considered a "transfer incident to a divorce" and, thus, nontaxable to either spouse.[7]

A taxpayer was liable for taxes on a distribution from his IRA that he subsequently turned over to his ex-wife in satisfaction of a family court order because it was not a "transfer incident to divorce" and the family court order was not a QDRO because it did not specifically require the transfer of assets to come from the IRA.[8] A transfer of funds between the IRAs of two spouses that does not come within the divorce exception is a deemed distribution despite IRC provisions that provide that no gain is recognized on transfers between spouses.[9]

---

1.   Let. Rul. 8245075.
2.   Let. Rul. 8338141.
3.   PTE 93-1, 58 Fed. Reg. 3567, 1-11-93; PTE 93-33, 58 Fed. Reg. 31053, 5-28-93, as amended at 64 Fed. Reg. 11044 (Mar. 8, 1999).
4.   IRC Sec. 408(d)(6).
5.   Treas. Reg. §1.408-4(a)(2).
6.   *Sveen v. Melin*, 138 S. Ct. 939 (2018).
7.   Let. Rul. 8916083.
8.   *Czepiel v. Comm.*, TC Memo 1999-289.
9.   See Let. Ruls. 9422060, 8820086.

The transfer of a portion of a husband's IRA to his wife to be placed in an IRA for her benefit that was the result of a private written agreement between the two that was not considered incident to a divorce was not eligible for nontaxable treatment under IRC Section 408(d)(6).[1]

Where a taxpayer received a full distribution from his IRA and endorsed the distribution check over to his soon-to-be-ex-wife, the husband was determined to have failed to satisfy the requirements for a nontaxable transfer incident to divorce and was liable for taxation on the entire proceeds of the IRA distribution.[2]

State community property laws, although generally disregarded under IRC Section 408(g) with respect to IRAs, are not always preempted by Section 408(g). Where two traditional IRAs were classified as community property, the distributions of the deceased spouse's community property interest in the IRAs to relatives other than her surviving husband were taxable only to those recipients and not to the husband.[3]

Conversely, in a case of first impression, the Tax Court ruled that the recognition of community property interests in IRAs would conflict with existing federal tax rules under Section 408(g) treating IRA accounts as separate property. In this case, the taxpayer transferred money from his IRA, which was considered community property under California law, to his former spouse pursuant to his divorce decree. By reason of IRC Section 408(g), the Court held that the taxpayer, not the former spouse, was liable for the income taxes associated with the distribution because, despite the former spouse's community property interest in the IRA, taxable IRA distributions are separate property.[4]

Where taxpayers requested that an IRA be reclassified under state marital property law from individual property to marital property, no distribution under IRC Section 408(d)(1) was deemed to have occurred.[5]

The involuntary garnishment of a husband's IRA and resulting transfer of such funds to the former spouse to satisfy arrearages in child support payments was a deemed distribution to the husband because it discharged a legal obligation owed by the husband.[6]

Planning Point: An IRA being transferred to an ex-spouse pursuant to a divorce or separation agreement should made through a direct trustee-to-trustee transfer to avoid possible tax consequences.

3651. Are IRA distributions subject to the 3.8 percent net investment income tax?

Distributions from traditional and Roth IRAs are not subject to the 3.8 percent net investment income tax (also known as the Medicare contribution tax) imposed under the Affordable

---

1.   Let. Rul. 9344027.
2.   *Jones v. Comm.*, TC Memo 2000-219.
3.   Let. Rul. 8040101.
4.   *Bunney v. Comm.*, 114 TC 259 (2000). See also *Morris v. Comm.*, TC Memo 2002-17.
5.   Let. Ruls. 199937055, 9419036.
6.   *Vorwald v. Comm.*, TC Memo 1997-15.

Care Act. The tax equals 3.8 percent of the lesser of a taxpayer's net investment income for the taxable year, or the excess (if any) of the taxpayer's modified adjusted gross income for the year, over a threshold amount ($200,000 for a taxpayer filing an individual return and $250,000 for a taxpayer filing jointly).[1]

IRC Section 1411 specifically excludes distributions from both traditional and Roth IRAs and other qualified plans from the definition of "net investment income."

Planning Point: While taxable distributions from traditional IRAs are not subject to the net investment income tax, they do increase a taxpayer's modified adjusted gross income (MAGI) for the year. A higher MAGI may expose taxpayer's other investment income (or increase taxpayer's exposure) to this 3.8 percent tax. Planners should consider the effect of an IRA distribution on a client's MAGI and exposure to the net investment income tax.

3652. How are earnings on an IRA taxed?

An IRA offers tax-free build up on contributions. The earnings on a traditional IRA are tax deferred to the owner; that is, they are not taxed until the owner begins receiving distributions (Q 3671). The earnings on a Roth IRA may or may not be taxed upon distribution (Q 3673). Like a trust that is part of a qualified plan, an individual retirement account is subject to taxes for its unrelated business income (Q 3973, Q 4097).

Tax deferral is lost if an individual engages in a prohibited transaction (Q 3979) or borrows under an individual retirement annuity. The loss occurs as of the first day of the tax year in which the prohibited transaction or borrowing occurred.[2] For an account established by an employer or association of employees, only the separate account of the individual loses its deferred status.

Planning Point: Prohibited transactions include: borrowing money from the IRA, selling property to it and using IRA assets for personal use or as security for a personal loan. Additionally an IRA is prohibited from investing in collectibles (e.g. artwork, antiques, stamps) and life insurance.

3653. Are IRAs subject to attachment?

ERISA provides that benefits under "pension plans" must not be assigned or alienated.[3] This provision has been construed as protecting pension benefits from claims of creditors. ERISA defines a "pension plan" as a plan established or maintained by an employer to provide retirement income to employees. An individual retirement plan generally is not maintained by an employer and, thus, is not protected under federal law by ERISA's anti-alienation clause.[4]

Although qualified retirement plans, SEP IRAs, SIMPLE IRAs, and elective deferral Roths are *excluded* from bankruptcy (i.e. not part of the bankruptcy estate), the same is not true for traditional IRAs and Roth IRAs.[5] Traditional IRAs and Roth IRAs, however, may be *exempted* (i.e. protected) from bankruptcy depending on the size of these accounts (see below).

---

1. IRS Publication 550 (2018).
2. IRC Sec. 408(e); Treas. Reg. §1.408-1.
3. ERISA Sec. 206(d)(1).
4. *Patterson v. Shumate*, 504 U.S. 753 (1992).
5. 11 U.S.C. §§541(b)(7), 541(c)(2).

A debtor can choose to exempt property from the bankruptcy estate using federal exemptions or state exemptions, but not both.[1] Federal bankruptcy exemptions generally protect a debtor's right to receive payments under a stock bonus, pension, profit-sharing, annuity or similar plan on account of illness, disability, age, or length of service under Section 522(d)(10)(E) of the federal Bankruptcy Code. The U.S. Supreme Court has ruled that assets in a traditional IRA are eligible for this exemption.[2]

Although bankruptcy is governed by federal law, Congress has given states the power to create their own exemptions and to opt out of the federal exemption system. Each state now has its own set of exemptions and many, but not all, have opted out of the federal system entirely. For a debtor living in a state that has opted out, only applicable state law exemptions may be used in a bankruptcy proceeding to exempt assets. It should be noted, however, that many states also extend protections to IRAs and Roth IRAs and exempt (fully or partially) these accounts from attachment by creditors – even in non-bankruptcy cases.

Editor's Note: Note that inherited IRAs that are inherited by non-spouse beneficiaries are often not given the same bankruptcy protection.

Planning Point: When available, a debtor choosing between the available federal and state exemptions should examine all of his or her assets, not just the IRA provisions, to determine which method is more beneficial in bankruptcy.

The bankruptcy exemption for contributory (nonrollover) traditional and Roth IRAs is limited in the aggregate to $1 million (the amount is indexed every three years and the current limit (as adjusted April 1, 2019) is $1,362,800 per person, for 2016 through April 1, 2019, the amount was $1,283,025), unless the bankruptcy court determines that "the interests of justice" require otherwise.[3] The exemption for IRA balances rolled over from other retirement accounts with an unlimited exemption is unlimited.

The exemption limit applies to the aggregate of all retirement accounts, without regard to rollover contributions, and does not apply separately to each account. Amounts in excess of the limit are subject to the claims of creditors.[4]

The Eighth Circuit has upheld a bankruptcy appellate panel decision, finding that an annuity purchased with funds rolled over from a taxpayer's traditional IRA was exempt from the bankruptcy estate because the annuity complied with the IRC Section 408 requirements for qualified individual retirement annuities. This was held to be the case despite the fact that the taxpayer paid an initial lump sum for the annuity that exceeded the annual contribution limits under IRC Section 219(b). The court agreed with the taxpayer's argument that the amounts rolled over from the IRA into the annuity did not constitute premium payments, so that the IRC Section 408(b) prohibitions against fixed premium amounts or premiums that exceed the Section 219 annual limits were not violated. As a result, under the Eighth Circuit's logic, funds

---

1.   11 U.S.C. §§522(b)(1).
2.   *Rousey v. Jacoway*, 544 U.S. 320 (2005).
3.   11 U.S.C. §§104 and 522(n).
4.   11 U.S.C. §522(n).

from a traditional IRA can be rolled over into a qualified individual retirement annuity without losing the bankruptcy exemption granted to IRA funds.[1]

With respect to self-directed IRAs, the 11th Circuit recently confirmed that a taxpayer was not entitled to creditor protection in bankruptcy with respect to a self-directed IRA that he used for impermissible purposes. In this case, the taxpayer withdrew IRA funds to purchase cars, real estate and other assets not specifically permitted by the IRA, which prohibited using the retirement funds for pre-retirement personal benefit. The issue in this case was not whether IRA funds were used for prohibited personal use, however, but whether the assets left within the IRA could be protected from creditors in bankruptcy. The court ruled that the creditors could access amounts left in the IRA, regardless of whether that IRA continued to be tax-exempt, because the taxpayer failed to properly maintain the IRA by withdrawing funds for prohibited reasons.[2]

Planning Point: Although assets rolled over from non-Roth IRA retirement accounts, and future earnings on those assets, do not lose their unlimited exemption by virtue of a rollover, taxpayers with significant IRA balances are advised to keep their contributory and rollover IRA accounts segregated. Otherwise, to the extent that rollover IRA assets are commingled with contributory IRA assets, it may be difficult to calculate the value of the assets attributable to the rollover.

Outside the bankruptcy context, the U.S. Court of Appeals for the Seventh Circuit has ruled that because ERISA's anti-alienation provisions do not apply to assets contained in IRAs, such assets may be seized under criminal forfeiture proceedings brought by the federal government.[3] The 10th Circuit Court of Appeals has held that an IRA trustee was not in breach of its fiduciary duty to an IRA account holder when the trustee responded to an IRS service of notice of levy for delinquent taxes owed by the account holder by turning over to the IRS assets held in the account.[4]

3654. Who may establish an IRA?

Virtually any individual who wishes to do so may establish a traditional individual retirement plan. To deduct contributions to such a plan once it is established and avoid tax penalties for excess contributions, an individual must have compensation (either earned income of an employee or self-employed person, or alimony prior to 2019), and before 2020, must not have attained age 70½ during the taxable year for which the contribution is made.[5]

Note that the SECURE Act eliminated the age cap on IRA contributions. Further, the 2017 Tax Act eliminated the deduction for alimony payments and provides that alimony is no longer includable in the recipient's income for tax years beginning after 2018. Because only "taxable" alimony constitutes "compensation", alimony is no longer included after 2018.

---

1. *Running v. Miller,* 778 F.3d 711 (8th Cir. 2015).
2. *Yerian v. Webber,* 2019 WL 2610751 (11th Cir. 2019).
3. *Infelise v. U.S.,* 159 F.3d 300 (7th Cir. 1998).
4. *Kane v. Capital Guardian Trust Co.,* 145 F.3d 1218 (10th Cir. 1998).
5. IRC Sec. 219.

If an individual is an "active participant" (Q 3666), the deduction may be limited (Q 3656). Any individual who can make a rollover contribution (Q 3991) may establish an individual retirement plan (or more than one plan) to receive it (Q 3995 to Q 4011).[1]

To establish and contribute directly to a Roth individual retirement plan, an individual (1) must have compensation (either earned income of an employee or self-employed person, or alimony (but see above)), and (2) must not have adjusted gross income (in 2021) (a) of $208,000 or above in the case of a taxpayer filing a joint return, (b) of $140,000 or above in the case of a taxpayer filing a single or head-of-household return,[2] or (c) of $10,000 or above in the case of a married individual filing separately (Appendix E).[3] An individual who satisfies these requirements may establish and contribute to a Roth IRA (Q 3659).[4]

Planning Point: For taxpayers who exceed the income limits and are thus prohibited from contributing directly to a Roth IRA, a Roth IRA may still be established to receive rollover distributions from other IRAs or qualified plans (this strategy is commonly referred to as the backdoor Roth IRA).

As to what constitutes "compensation," see Q 3665.

An estate may not make a contribution on behalf of the decedent.[5]

3655. When must contributions to IRAs be made?

Contributions to both a traditional IRA and Roth IRA must be made by the tax filing deadline for the tax year in question, not including extensions. For example, a taxpayer who wishes to contribute to an IRA must do so prior to April 15 (July 15 in 2020) of the following year. This rule applies whether the IRA is an existing or new plan.

With respect to traditional IRAs, contributions may be deducted for that tax year if the contribution is made on account of that year. This applies both to contributions to individual plans and contributions to spousal plans.[6] A postmark is evidence of the timeliness of the contribution.[7]

3656. How much may an individual contribute to a traditional IRA? How much may be deducted?

Contributions to traditional IRAs are limited at two levels. First, there is a limit on the amount of contributions that may be deducted for income tax purposes. Second, there is a limit with respect to the amount of total contributions that can be made, including both deductible and nondeductible contributions.

Contributions to an individual retirement plan are not subject to the general limits on contributions and benefits of IRC Section 415 (Q 3867). (See Q 3701 for the effect of IRC

---

1.   Special Ruling 9-28-76.
2.   Notice 2020-79.
3.   IRS Pub. 590.
4.   IRC Secs. 219, 408A; IR-2011-103.
5.   Let. Rul. 8439066.
6.   IRC Secs. 219(f)(3), 408A(c)(6).
7.   Let. Ruls. 8633080, 8611090, 8536085.

Section 415 on simplified employee pensions.) The source of the funds contributed to an IRA is not determinative as to eligibility or deductibility so long as the contributing individual has includable compensation at least equal to the amount of the contribution.[1]

The IRA contribution limit does not apply to qualified rollovers into an IRA.[2]

Deductible Contributions

If an eligible individual contributes on his own behalf to a traditional IRA, he generally may deduct amounts contributed in cash up to the lesser of the "deductible amount" for the taxable year or 100 percent of *compensation* includable in his gross income for such year.[3]

The "deductible amount" is $6,000 for 2019-2021. It was $5,500 in 2014-2018 (Appendix E).[4] This amount is indexed for inflation.

> *Example 1:* Danny, an unmarried college student working part-time, earns $4,500 in 2021. Danny can contribute up to $4,500, the amount of his compensation (rather than the deductible amount), to his IRA in 2021.

> *Example 2:* George, who is 34 years old and single, earns $24,000 in 2021. His IRA contributions for 2021 are limited to $6,000 (the deductible amount).

The "deductible amount" is increased by a $1,000 catch-up contribution for individuals who have attained age 50 before the close of the tax year.[5]

> *Example: Samantha*, who is single, turned 50 in October of 2021. She earns $30,000 in 2021. Her IRA contributions for 2021 are limited to $7,000 - $6,000 plus a $1,000 catch-up.

Employer contributions to a simplified employee pension and any amounts contributed to a SIMPLE IRA are subject to different limitations.

Planning Point: Before 2020, contributions could not be made to a traditional IRA for the year in which the IRA participant reaches age 70½ or for any later year. The age cap was removed beginning in 2020 by the SECURE Act.

The overall maximum contribution limit is also equal to the "deductible amount."[6] Contributions made to Roth IRAs for the taxable year reduce both deductible and overall contribution limits (Q 3659). As to what constitutes "compensation," see Q 3665.

In taxable years beginning in 2007 through 2009, the "deductible amount" was increased by $3,000 for former employees of bankrupt companies with indicted executives (e.g., Enron), if the employer matched 50 percent or more of employee 401(k) contributions in the form of

---

1.   See Let. Rul. 8326163.
2.   IRC. Sec 408(a)(1).
3.   IRC Sec. 219(b)(1).
4.   IRC Sec. 219(b)(5)(A)); Notice 2013-73, IR-2014-99, Notice 2016-62, Notice 2017-64, Notice 2018-83, Notice 2019-59, Notice 2020-79.
5.   IRC Sec. 219(b)(5)(B).
6.   IRC Sec. 408(a)(1).

employer stock. For taxpayers age 50 or older, the enhanced catch-up contribution was available instead of the usual $1,000 catch-up provision.[1]

If a married couple files a joint return, both spouses may contribute to an IRA even if only one spouse has taxable compensation. The maximum deduction allowed to an individual for a cash contribution to a traditional IRA *for a nonworking spouse* for a taxable year is the lesser of (1) the "deductible amount" or (2) 100 percent of the nonworking spouse's includable compensation, plus 100 percent of the working spouse's includable compensation minus (a) the amount of any IRA deduction taken by the working spouse for the year, and (b) the amount of any contribution made to a Roth IRA by the working spouse.[2]

> *Example:* Sarah, age 52, is married with no taxable compensation for 2021. She and her spouse reported taxable compensation of $60,000 on their 2021 joint return. Sarah may contribute $7,000 to her IRA for 2021 ($6,000 plus an additional $1,000 contribution for age 50 and over).

While two spouses who file jointly are permitted a maximum deduction of up to $12,000 in 2021 (this amount is increased to $14,000 to include catch up contributions if they are both over 50), the deduction for each spouse is computed separately.[3]

The deduction is taken from gross income so that an individual who does not itemize his deductions may take advantage of the retirement savings deduction.[4] Prior to 2020, no deduction could be taken for a contribution *on behalf of* an individual who had attained age 70½ before the end of the tax year.[5] An individual over age 70½ could also take a deduction for a contribution made on behalf of a spouse who was under age 70½. An excess contribution made in one year can be deducted in a subsequent year to the extent the excess is absorbed in the later year (Q 3669).

The cost of a disability waiver of premium feature in an individual retirement annuity is deductible under IRC Section 219, but where an individual contributes to an annuity for the benefit of himself and his non-employed spouse, the waiver of premium feature may only be allocated to the working spouse's interest.[6]

No deduction is allowed for contributions to an IRA if the individual for whose benefit the IRA is maintained acquired that IRA by reason of the death of another individual after 1983. But this does not apply where the acquiring individual is the surviving spouse of the deceased individual.[7]

For the limits on contributions to Roth IRAs, see Q 3659. For limits on contributions to simplified employee pensions, see Q 3701. For limits on contributions to a SIMPLE IRA, see Q 3706. For a discussion of the nondeductible contributions that may be made to an IRA, see Q 3658.

---

1. IRC Sec. 219(b)(5)(C).
2. IRC Sec. 219(c)(1).
3. Notice 2020-79.
4. IRC Sec. 62(a)(7).
5. IRC Sec. 219(d)(1), prior to repeal by the SECURE Act.
6. Let. Rul. 7851087.
7. IRC Secs. 219(d)(4), 408(d)(3)(C)(ii).

3657. What are the active participant rules that can impact an individual's IRA contribution limit?

The deduction for contributions made to individual and spousal plans may be reduced or eliminated if the individual or his spouse is an "active participant" (Q 3666). The amount of the reduction is the amount that bears the same ratio to the overall limit as the taxpayer's *adjusted gross income* (AGI) in excess of an "applicable dollar amount" bears to $10,000 ($20,000 in the case of a joint return for taxable years beginning after 2006).[1] Applicable dollar amounts are indexed for inflation. Thus, the amount of the reduction is calculated as follows:

$$\text{"deductible amount"} \times \frac{\text{AGI} - \text{"applicable dollar amount"}}{\$10,000 \text{ (or } \$20,000 \text{ for joint return)}}$$

In the case of a taxpayer who is an active participant and files a single or head-of-household return, the "applicable dollar amount" is $66,000 in 2021 ($65,000 in 2020, $64,000 in 2019, $63,000 in 2018 (Appendix E)).[2]

In the case of married taxpayers who file a joint return, where one or both spouses are active participants, the "applicable dollar amount" for a spouse who is an active participant is $105,000 in 2021 ($104,000 in 2020, $103,000 in 2019, $101,000 in 2018 (Appendix E)).[3]

In the case of married taxpayers who file a joint return, where only one is an active participant, the "applicable dollar amount" for the nonactive participant spouse is $198,000 in 2021 ($196,000 in 2020, $193,000 in 2019, $189,000 in 2018 (Appendix E)).[4] The denominator in the fraction remains at $10,000 (it does not increase to $20,000).[5]

In the case of a married individual filing a separate return where either spouse is an active participant, the "applicable dollar amount" is $0.[6]

> *Example:* Jack and Jill are married and file a joint tax return for 2021. Jack is an active participant, but Jill is not. Their modified adjusted gross income is $111,000. Jack is under age 50 and is therefore able to contribute $6,000 to a traditional IRA.
>
> Using the formula above, Jack calculates his maximum deductible amount:
>
> = $6,000 × (111,000 – $105,000)/ $20,000
>
> = $1,800, which represents the amount of the reduction
>
> = $6,000 (the maximum contribution amount) minus $1,800 (the reduction amount)
>
> **Answer** = $4,200

---

1.   IRC Sec. 219(g)(2).
2.   IRC Sec. 219(g)(3)(B)(ii); IR-2015-118, Notice 2017-64, Notice 2018-83, Notice 2019-59, Notice 2020-79.
3.   IRC Sec. 219(g)(3)(B)(i); IR-2015-118, Notice 2017-64, Notice 2018-83, Notice 2019-59, Notice 2020-79.
4.   IR-2015-118, Notice 2017-64, Notice 2018-83, Notice 2019-59, Notice 2020-79.
5.   IRC Sec. 219(g)(7)(B); Notice 2013-73, IR-2014-99.
6.   IRC Sec. 219(g)(3)(B)(iii).

Because Jill is the nonactive participant with an active participant spouse, the "applicable dollar amount" for Jill is $198,000 (for 2021), well above Jack and Jill's AGI. Accordingly, a $6,000 contribution to Jill's IRA is fully deductible.

Due to these "active participant" limitations, a deduction for contributions made to an IRA in 2021 will be eliminated for:

(1) individuals who are active participants and file a single or head-of-household return with AGI of $76,000 and above;

(2) married individuals who are active participants and file a joint return with AGI of $125,000 and above;

(3) married individuals where only one spouse is an active participant and file a joint return with AGI of $208,000 and above; and

(4) married individuals who are active participants *or* their spouses are active participants and file separately with AGI of $10,000 and above (Appendix E).[1]

The amount of the reduction is rounded to the next lowest multiple of $10.[2] Unless the individual's deduction limit is reduced to zero, the IRC permits a minimum deduction of $200.[3]

For this purpose, AGI is calculated without regard to the exclusions for foreign earned income, qualified adoption expenses paid by the employer and interest on qualified United States savings bonds used to pay higher education expenses. Social Security benefits includable in gross income under IRC Section 86 and losses or gains on passive investments under IRC Section 469 are taken into account. Also for this purpose, contributions to a traditional IRA are not deducted in determining AGI.[4]

3658. What nondeductible contributions may be made to a traditional IRA?

Nondeductible contributions can also be made to a traditional IRA. The limit on nondeductible contributions is equal to the *excess of* the "deductible amount," discussed in Q 3656, over the actual maximum deduction allowed.[5] Contributions made to Roth IRAs for the taxable year reduce this limit (Q 3659). This limit is not reduced because an individual's AGI exceeds certain limits (in contrast, see Q 3659 with respect to contributions to Roth IRAs). A taxpayer may elect to treat contributions that would otherwise be deductible as nondeductible.[6] Nondeductible contributions must be reported on the individual's tax return and penalties apply if the required form is not filed or the amount of such contributions is overstated (Q 3699).

Planning Point: It is generally better to make nondeductible contributions to a Roth IRA (Q 3659) rather than nondeductible contributions to a traditional IRA because of the way the earnings are taxed.

---

1.   IR-2015-118, Notice 2020-79 2019-59.
2.   IRC Sec. 219(g)(2)(C).
3.   IRC Sec. 219(g)(2)(B).
4.   IRC Sec. 219(g)(3)(A); See Treas. Reg. §1.408A-3, A-5.
5.   IRC Sec. 408(o)(2)(B)(i).
6.   IRC Sec. 408(o)(2)(B)(ii).

Endowment Contracts

Endowment contracts issued after November 6, 1978 do not qualify as individual retirement annuities; therefore, contributions to such contracts are not deductible.[1] Furthermore, in the case of contributions to an endowment contract individual retirement annuity issued before November 7, 1978, no deduction is allowed for contributions that are allocable to the purchase of life insurance protection. The amount allocable to life insurance protection is determined by multiplying the death benefit payable during the tax year less the cash value at the end of the year by the net premium cost. (See Q 616 for purposes of valuing the economic benefit of current life insurance protection.) The nondeductible amount may be contributed to another funding medium and a deduction taken so that the maximum deduction may be used, but it may not be used to pay the premium for an annuity if the total premium on behalf of any one individual would then exceed the maximum annual contribution limit.

3659. How much may an individual contribute to a Roth IRA?

An eligible individual may contribute cash to a Roth IRA on his own behalf up to the *lesser of* the maximum annual contribution limit (equal to the "deductible amount" under IRC Section 219(b)(5)(A)) or 100 percent of *compensation* includable in his gross income for the taxable year. The amount that can be contributed, however, is *reduced by* any contributions made to traditional IRAs for the taxable year on his own behalf.[2]

The maximum annual contribution limit is $6,000 in 2021[3] (Appendix E). This amount is indexed for inflation. The maximum annual contribution limit is increased by $1,000 for individuals who have attained age 50 before the close of the tax year (i.e. $7,000 in 2020 and 2021) (Appendix E).[4]

SEPs and SIMPLE IRAs may not be designated as Roth IRAs, and contributions to a SEP or SIMPLE IRA will not affect the amount that an individual can contribute to a Roth IRA.[5] Qualified rollover contributions (Q 3662) do not count towards this limit.[6] As to what constitutes "compensation," see Q 3665. Roth IRA contributions are not deductible and can be made at any age.[7]

In taxable years beginning in 2007 through 2009, the maximum annual contribution limit was increased by $3,000 for former employees of bankrupt companies with indicted executives (e.g., Enron), if the employer matched 50 percent or more of employee 401(k) contributions in the form of employer stock. For taxpayers age 50 or older, the enhanced catch-up contribution was available instead of the usual $1,000 catch-up provision.[8]

---

1.   See Treas. Reg. §§1.408-4(f), 1.408-3(e)(1)(ix).
2.   IRC Sec. 408A(c)(2).
3.   Notice 2019-59, Notice 2020-79.
4.   IRC Sec. 219(b)(5); Notice 2019-59, Notice 2020-79.
5.   IRC Sec. 408A(f).
6.   IRC Sec. 408A(c)(5).
7.   IRC Secs. 408A(c)(1).
8.   IRC Sec. 219(b)(5)(C).

An individual may contribute cash to a Roth IRA *for a non-working spouse* for a taxable year up to the maximum deductible limit (disregarding active participant restrictions) permitted with respect to traditional IRAs for such non-working spouse (Q 3656), reduced by any such contributions made to traditional IRAs for the taxable year on behalf of the non-working spouse.[1] Thus, a married couple (both spouses under age 50) may be permitted a maximum contribution of up to $12,000 for 2020 and 2021 ($6,000 for each spouse).

The maximum contribution permitted to an individual Roth IRA or a spousal Roth IRA is reduced or eliminated for certain high-income taxpayers. The amount of the reduction is the amount that bears the same ratio to the overall limit as the taxpayer's *adjusted gross income* (AGI) in excess of an "applicable dollar amount" bears to $15,000 ($10,000 in the case of a joint return).[2] Thus, the amount of the reduction is calculated as follows:

$$\text{maximum contribution} \times \frac{\text{AGI} - \text{``applicable dollar amount''}}{\$15,000 \ (\$10,000 \text{ if a joint return})}$$

The "applicable dollar amount" in 2021 is (1) $125,000 in the case of an individual ($124,000 for 2020, $122,000 for 2019), (2) $198,000 ($196,000 for 2020, $193,000 in 2019) in the case of a married couple filing a joint return, and (3) $0 in the case of a married person filing separately.[3] (Appendix E.)

Thus in 2021, the Roth IRA contribution limit is $0 for (1) individuals with AGI of $140,000 and above ($139,000 in 2020, $137,000 in 2019), (2) married couples filing a joint return with AGI of $208,000 and above ($206,000 in 2020, $203,000 in 2019), and (3) a married individual filing separately with AGI of $10,000 and above (Appendix E).[4] Except for married individuals filing separately, the "applicable dollar amount" is indexed for inflation. The amount of the reduction is rounded to the next lowest multiple of $10. Unless the individual's contribution limit is reduced to zero, the IRC permits a minimum contribution of $200.[5]

For this purpose, AGI is calculated without regard to the exclusions for foreign earned income, qualified adoption expenses paid by the employer, and interest on qualified United States savings bonds used to pay higher education expenses. Social Security benefits includable in gross income under IRC Section 86 and losses or gains on passive investments under IRC Section 469 are taken into account. Also for this purpose, deductible contributions to a traditional IRA plan are not taken into account in determining AGI; amounts included in gross income as a result of a rollover or conversion from a traditional IRA to a Roth IRA are not taken into account for purposes of determining the maximum contribution limit for a Roth IRA.

---

1. See IRC Secs. 408A(c)(2), 219(b)(1), 219(c).
2. IRC Sec. 408A(c)(3).
3. Notice 2018-83, Notice 2019-59, Notice 2020-79.
4. IR-2015-118, Notice 2018-83, Notice 2019-59, Notice 2020-79.
5. IRC Sec. 408A(c)(3)(A).

3660. What is the difference between a Roth IRA and a traditional IRA?

The primary difference between a Roth IRA and a traditional IRA is the tax treatment of contributions to, and withdrawals from, the account. "Qualified distributions" (see Q 3673) from a Roth IRA are not includable in gross income. Thus, earnings are tax-free, not tax deferred, as is the case with traditional IRAs. Any nonqualified distribution from a Roth IRA will be includable in income, but only to the extent that the distribution, along with all previous distributions from the Roth IRA, exceeds the aggregate amount of contributions to the Roth IRA.

Contributions from a traditional IRA are contributed on a pre-tax basis (i.e., they are deductible up to the annual contribution limit), while Roth IRA contributions are not deductible. Before 2020, contributions to a traditional IRA had to cease when the account owner reached age 70½. The age limitation was eliminated by the SECURE Act.[1] An individual may make both pre-tax and after-tax (Q 3658) contributions to a traditional IRA, but may only make after-tax contributions to a Roth IRA.

Planning Point: Note that while the SECURE Act eliminated the age restriction for traditional IRA contributions, financial institutions are not required to accept post-age 70½ contributions. In other words, it is up to the specific institution to determine whether to accept these contributions beginning in 2020.[2]

Further, amounts accumulated in a traditional IRA or annuity must be distributed in compliance with the minimum distribution requirements (see Q 3682).[3] Roth IRAs are not subject to the lifetime minimum distribution requirements, but are subject to certain after-death distribution requirements (Q 3687). The chart below summarizes the primary differences between a traditional IRA and a Roth IRA.

	Traditional IRA	Roth IRA
Contribution Limit[4]	$6,000 + $1,000 catch-up if 50 or older.	$6,000 + $1,000 catch-up if 50 or older.
Taxation of Contributions	Made with pre-tax dollars	Made with after-tax dollars.
Age Limit for Contributions	None.	None.
Taxation of Distributions	Taxed at ordinary income tax rates.	Tax-free if certain conditions are met.
Required Distributions	Distributions must begin April 1 of the year after the owner turns 72.	No lifetime distribution requirements for original account owner.

For more information on the contribution limit that applies to both traditional IRAs and Roth IRAs, see Q 3656 and Q 3659. Also, Q 3659 and Q 3661 discuss the income limits that apply to Roth IRAs, and Q 3662 discusses the rules governing converting traditional IRA funds to Roth accounts.

1.　IRC Secs. 408A(c)(1), 408A(c)(4), prior to repeal by the SECURE Act.
2.　Notice 2020-68.
3.　IRC Secs. 408(a)(6), 408(b)(3), 401(a)(9).
4.　Notice 2019-59.

3661. Can a taxpayer whose income level exceeds the limitations for Roth IRA contributions maintain a Roth IRA?

Yes. Despite the fact that a taxpayer whose income level exceeds the Roth IRA contribution limits cannot contribute directly to a Roth IRA, he or she is permitted to maintain a Roth account. In 2021 the ability to make contributions to a Roth IRA begins to phase out for married taxpayers with income over $198,000 ($125,000 for single taxpayers). Roth contributions are completely disallowed for married taxpayers who earn over $208,000 and single taxpayers who earn over $140,000.[1]

While contributions cannot be made directly to the Roth IRA if the taxpayer's income exceeds the annual income threshold, for tax years beginning in 2010 and after, the income limits that applied to prevent high-income taxpayers from making rollovers from traditional IRAs were eliminated.[2]

Therefore, many high-income taxpayers may make contributions indirectly to a Roth account, via a series of rollovers from traditional IRAs. The taxpayer must first open a traditional IRA if he or she does not already maintain such an account (in 2021, each taxpayer can contribute up to $6,000 to an IRA ($7,000 if the taxpayer is 50 or older)).[3] Using the so-called "backdoor" Roth IRA technique, the taxpayer can then roll a portion of the traditional IRA into a Roth IRA account each year, though taxes must be paid on the amounts that are rolled over. See Q 3662 for rules regarding rollovers from an IRA to a Roth IRA.

3662. Can an individual roll over or convert a traditional IRA or other eligible retirement plan into a Roth IRA?

Editor's Note: The 2017 Tax Act eliminated the ability of taxpayers to recharacterize Roth IRA conversions for tax years beginning after 2017. Taxpayers were entitled to recharacterize 2017 conversions through October 15, 2018.

Yes.

A "qualified rollover contribution" can be made from a traditional IRA or any eligible retirement plan (Q 3995) to a Roth IRA.[4]

Amounts that are held in a SEP or a SIMPLE IRA that have been held in the account for two or more years also may be converted to a Roth IRA.[5]

The taxpayer must include in income the amount of the distribution from the traditional IRA or other eligible retirement plan that would be includable if the distribution were not rolled over.[6] (See Q 3671 for taxation of amounts distributed from such IRAs.) Thus, if only deductible

---

1.   Notice 2020-79.
2.   IRC Secs. 408A(c)(3)(B), 408A(e).
3.   Notice 2020-79.
4.   IRC Sec. 408A(e).
5.   Treas. Reg. §1.408A-4, A-4.
6.   IRC Secs. 408A(d)(3)(A)(i), 408A(d)(3)(C).

contributions were made to an eligible retirement plan, the entire amount of the distribution would be includable in income in the year rolled over or converted. (Special rules apply for conversions made in 2010.) While the 10 percent early distribution penalty (Q 3677) does not apply at the time of the conversion to a Roth IRA, it does apply to any converted amounts distributed during the five-year period beginning with the year of the conversion.[1]

When an individual retirement annuity is converted to a Roth IRA, or when an individual retirement account that holds an annuity contract as an asset is converted to a Roth IRA, the amount that is deemed distributed is the fair market value of the annuity contract on the date of the (deemed) distribution. If, in converting to a Roth IRA, an IRA annuity contract is completely surrendered for its cash value, regulations provide that the cash received will be the conversion amount.[2]

Non-rollover contributions made to a traditional IRA for a taxable year (and any earnings allocable thereto) may be transferred to a Roth IRA on or before the due date (excluding extensions of time) for filing the federal income tax return of the contributing individual and no such amount will be includable in income, provided no deduction was allowed with respect to such contributions.[3] Such contributions would be subject to the maximum annual contribution limits (Q 3659).

A "qualified rollover contribution" is any rollover contribution to a Roth IRA from a traditional IRA or other eligible retirement plan that meets the requirements of IRC Section 408(d)(3) (Q 4003). A rollover or conversion of a traditional IRA to a Roth IRA does not count in applying the one IRA-to-IRA rollover in any twelve month period limit (Q 4003).[4]

For years prior to 2010, the taxpayer's AGI was calculated without regard to the exclusions for foreign earned income, qualified adoption expenses paid by the employer, and interest on qualified United States savings bonds used to pay higher education expenses. Deductible contributions to a traditional IRA also were not taken into account in determining AGI. Amounts included in gross income as a result of a rollover or conversion from a traditional IRA or other eligible retirement plan to a Roth IRA were not taken into account.[5] Social Security benefits includable in gross income under IRC Section 86 and losses or gains on passive investments under IRC Section 469 were taken into account. The definition of AGI excludes minimum required distributions to IRA owners, solely for purposes of determining eligibility to convert a regular IRA to a Roth IRA.[6]

An eligible retirement plan, for this purpose, includes a qualified retirement plan, a IRC Section 403(b) tax sheltered annuity, or an eligible IRC Section 457 governmental plan. Taxpayers, including plan beneficiaries, can directly transfer (and thereby convert) money from these plans into a Roth IRA without the need for a conduit traditional IRA (as was required prior to

---

1. IRC Sec. 408A(d)(3)(F).
2. Treas. Reg. § 1.408A-4.
3. IRC Secs. 408(o)(3), 408A(c)(6).
4. IRC Sec. 408A(e).
5. IRC Sec. 408A(c)(3)(B)(i).
6. IRC Sec. 408A(c)(3)(B)(i).

2008).[1] (Other than by direct conversion from an eligible non-IRA retirement plan, a beneficiary may not convert to a Roth IRA.)[2]

Unless a taxpayer elects otherwise, income from conversions to Roth IRAs occurring in 2010 were to be reported ratably in 2011 and 2012.[3]

Qualified rollover contributions do not count toward the annual maximum contribution limit applicable to Roth IRAs (Q 3659).[4]

A rollover from a Roth IRA or a designated Roth account to a Roth IRA is not subject to the adjusted gross income limitation and is not subject to tax.[5]

Planning Point: Major reasons for converting to a Roth IRA often include obtaining tax-free quali-fied distributions from the Roth IRA and greater stretch from the Roth IRA because distributions from a Roth IRA are not required until after the death of the owner (or the death of the IRA owner's spouse if the spouse is the sole designated beneficiary and elects to treat the IRA as the spouse's own), rather than starting at age 72. A conversion also may make sense if it is expected that tax rates will increase (from the time of conversion to the time of distribution), but not if tax rates will decrease. Consider whether any special tax benefits, such as net unrealized appreciation, would be lost if a qualified plan is converted to a Roth IRA. Also, a qualified plan may offer better asset protection than a Roth IRA. State laws vary on this issue. If a taxpayer cannot qualify under the Roth AGI limitations, perhaps he or she can establish a traditional IRA, and then convert that into a Roth IRA. While this has not yet been addressed by the IRS, the strategy was blessed by Congress in its commentary to the 2017 tax reform legislation.

3663. What should an individual consider when choosing whether to convert retirement funds to a Roth IRA or to a Roth 401(k)?

Editor's Note: The 2017 Tax Act eliminated the ability of taxpayers to recharacterize Roth IRA conversions for tax years beginning after 2017. Taxpayers were entitled to recharacterize 2017 conversions through October 15, 2018.

Prior to 2018, one important characteristic of a Roth IRA conversion was the taxpayer's ability to undo the transaction through a recharacterization transaction that moves the funds back into the traditional account, eliminating the tax liability that the initial conversion created.[6] This option was unavailable if the individual chooses to convert to a Roth 401(k).

If the taxpayer's account performed poorly in the months after the conversion took place, or if the taxpayer otherwise found that he or she was unable to pay the tax bill that results from a Roth conversion, the taxpayer had until October 15 of the year following the conversion to recharacterize the funds. The tax reform changes to the recharacterization rules placed Roth IRAs on par with Roth 401(k)s, where once the conversion takes place, the taxpayer is required to pay the associated taxes regardless of any events that occur post-conversion.

---

1.   IRC Sec. 408A(d)(3); Notice 2008-30, 2008-1 CB 638, A-7.
2.   IRC 402(c)(11).
3.   IRC Sec. 408A(d)(3)(A)(iii).
4.   IRC Sec. 408A(c)(5)(B).
5.   IRC Secs. 408A(c)(3)(B); 408A(d)(3)(B).
6.   IRC Sec. 408A(d)(6).

A taxpayer who converts to a Roth IRA is able to escape the IRS's required minimum distribution (RMD) rules so that the funds in the account are permitted to grow tax-free over a longer period of time. Taxpayers who use Roth 401(k)s are often required to comply with the RMD rules when they turn 72 (70½ before 2020), possibly reducing the account's growth potential if the taxpayer does not need to access the funds.[1] A taxpayer who plans to use a Roth account as a wealth transfer vehicle may also prefer the Roth IRA because the entire account value can be passed to heirs upon his or her death.

Taxpayers who anticipate that they will need access to the funds before retirement should also consider how the application of the "five year rule" could impact the tax-free availability of these funds. To access the funds, a qualifying event must have occurred *and* the Roth must be at least five years old before a qualified distribution is permitted. However, if the taxpayer has multiple Roth IRAs, only *one* of the taxpayer's IRAs must be five years old before a tax-free withdrawal is permitted.[2] With a Roth 401(k), the particular account must be five years old or a penalty tax will apply.[3]

Importantly, for high-income taxpayers, post-conversion contributions may be limited or blocked entirely because of the income limits that apply to Roth IRA contributions (but not to Roth 401(k) contributions). In 2021, the ability to make contributions to a Roth IRA begins to phase out for married taxpayers with income over $198,000 ($125,000 for single filers). Roth IRA contributions are completely blocked for married taxpayers who earn over $208,000 and single filers who earn over $140,000.[4]

Stronger creditor protection rules also apply to Roth 401(k) accounts. While Roth IRAs are protected under state law, the rules that apply in some states offer much less in the way of creditor protection than can be found in others. Roth 401(k)s are always protected by ERISA-mandated federal creditor protection rules regardless of where the taxpayer lives.

3664. Can an individual correct a Roth conversion? What is a recharacterization?

Editor's Note: The 2017 Tax Act eliminated the ability of taxpayers to recharacterize Roth IRA conversions for tax years beginning after 2017. The IRS released a FAQ confirming that taxpayers were entitled to recharacterize 2017 conversions through October 15, 2018.

Prior to 2018, if a taxpayer rolled over funds from a traditional IRA or other eligible retirement plan to a Roth IRA during the taxable year, and later discovered that for any reason he or she wanted the transaction undone, the taxpayer generally had until the due date for filing his or her return (including extensions) to correct the conversion without penalty, to the extent all earnings and income allocable to the conversion were also transferred back to the original IRA, and no deduction had been allowed with respect to the original conversion.[5]

---

1.   Treas. Reg. §1.401(k)-1(f)(3).
2.   IRC Secs. 408A(d).
3.   Treas. Reg. §1.402A-1, A-4.
4.   IRC Sec. 408A(c)(3); IR-2014-99 (Oct. 23, 2014), Notice 2020-79.
5.   IRC Sec. 408A(d)(6); Notice 2008-30, 2008-1 CB 638, A-5.

This "recharacterization" in the form of a trustee-to-trustee transfer resulted in the recharacterized contribution being treated as a contribution made to the transferee IRA, instead of to the transferor IRA.[1] A taxpayer was able to apply to the IRS for relief from the time limit for making a recharacterization.[2]

Planning Point: After tax reform, if a taxpayer makes a Roth contribution, he or she is permitted to recharacterize the transaction as a contribution to a traditional IRA before the due date for his or her income tax return for the year.[3]

For purposes of a recharacterized contribution, the net income attributable to a contribution made to an IRA was determined by allocating to the contribution a pro-rata portion of the earnings or losses accrued by the IRA during the period the IRA held the contribution. This allowed the taxpayer to claim any net income that is a negative amount.[4]

A time restriction was placed on reconversions (i.e., converting to a Roth IRA a second time after recharacterizing a first conversion). A person could reconvert back to a Roth IRA but only after the later of the beginning of the next year or 30 days after the recharacterization.[5]

Planning Point: Prior to 2018, where the value of converted property dropped after a conversion to a Roth IRA, it was often useful to recharacterize the contribution back to a traditional IRA and then reconvert to a Roth IRA to reduce the amount taxable on converting to a Roth IRA. The time restriction on reconversions reduced, but did not eliminate, the potential value of this technique.

Reconversions and recharacterizations had to be reported to the IRS on Form 1099-R and Form 5498. Prior year recharacterizations had to be reported under separate codes. All recharacterized contributions received by an IRA in the same year were permitted to be totaled and reported on a single Form 5498.[6]

3665. What is "compensation" for purposes of IRA eligibility rules and deduction limits?

Editor's Note: The SECURE Act also modified the definition of compensation so that certain stipends provided to graduate students can be counted as compensation for IRA contribution purposes after December 31, 2019. Similarly, qualified foster care payments (excluded from income) can be treated as compensation for plan years effective after December 31, 2015 (retroactively) for defined contribution plans and after 2019 for IRAs.[7]

For purposes of the eligibility rules and deduction limits applicable to traditional and Roth IRAs, "compensation" means wages, salary, professional fees, or other amounts derived from, or received for, personal services actually rendered. "Compensation" also typically included alimony paid under a divorce or separation agreement that is includable in the income of the

---

1. See Treas. Reg. §1.408A-5.
2. See Let. Ruls. 200234073, 200213030.
3. IRC Sec. 408A(d)(6)(B)(iii).
4. Treas. Reg. §1.408A-5; Notice 2000-39, 2000-2 CB 132.
5. Treas. Reg. §1.408A-5, A-9.
6. Notice 2000-30, 2000-1 CB 1266.
7. SECURE Act, Sec. 106, Sec. 116.

recipient under IRC Section 71.[1] Because of the changes to the tax treatment of alimony payments following enactment of the 2017 tax reform legislation, non-taxable alimony payments are no longer "compensation" for these purposes.

In the case of a self-employed individual, "compensation" includes earned income from personal services, but in computing the maximum IRA or SEP contribution, such income must be reduced by (1) any qualified retirement plan contributions made by such individual on his or her own behalf and (2) the 50 percent of self-employment taxes deductible by the individual.

Earned income not subject to self-employment tax because of an individual's religious beliefs is "compensation."[2]

An individual whose income for the tax year consists solely of interest, dividend, and pension income has no "compensation" and cannot deduct any portion of a traditional IRA contribution.[3] In addition, such a person may not make a Roth IRA contribution.[4]

Compensation does not include earnings and profits from property, such as rental income, interest, and dividend income, or any amount received as pension or annuity income, or as deferred compensation (see IRS Tax Topics No. 451).

Further, "compensation" does not include any Social Security or railroad retirement benefits required to be included in gross income.[5] Payments made to employees terminated because of a restructuring of the company are deferred compensation and may not be used as a basis for IRA contributions.[6] Amounts received from an employer as deferred incentive awards, whether in the form of cash, stock options, or stock appreciation rights, also are not "compensation."[7] However, incentive pay awarded in one year for services performed in that year but paid in the following year is considered "compensation" in that second year.[8]

The IRS has ruled that disability income payments, whether made under public or private plans, do not constitute "compensation."[9] Also, unemployment benefits do not constitute "compensation" because they are paid due to an inability to earn wages and not for personal services actually rendered.[10]

Additionally, the IRS has issued a compensation "safe harbor." The amount properly shown in the box for "wages, tips, other compensation," less any amount properly shown in the box for "nonqualified plans," on Form W-2 is considered compensation for purposes of calculating an individual's IRA contribution.[11]

---

1.   IRC Secs. 219(f)(1), 408A(a); Treas. Reg. §1.408A-3, A-4.
2.   IRC Sec. 219(f)(1).
3.   *King v. Comm.*, TC Memo 1996-231.
4.   IRC Sec. 408A(c)(2).
5.   IRC Secs. 86(f)(3), 219(f)(1); Treas. Reg. §1.219-1(c)(1).
6.   Let. Ruls. 8534106, 8519051.
7.   Let. Rul. 8304088.
8.   Let. Rul. 8707051.
9.   See Let. Ruls. 8331069, 8325080, 8014110.
10.   *Russell v. Comm.*, TC Memo 1996-278.
11.   See Rev. Proc. 91-18, 1991-1 CB 522.

Amounts paid by one spouse to another spouse to manage their jointly-owned investment property may not be treated by the spouse, on a joint return, as compensation for purposes of an IRA contribution.[1] Similarly, wages paid to one spouse by another spouse and deposited in their joint account are not considered compensation because deposit in a joint account does not constitute actual payment of wages.[2]

Payment in hogs rather than cash by a husband to his wife for her services in running their farm, however, was considered to be compensation for purposes of making an IRA contribution.[3]

A self-employed individual who shows a net loss for the tax year cannot take any IRA deduction.[4] A salaried employee who also is self-employed should disregard net losses from self-employment when computing his or her maximum deduction.[5]

3666. Who is an "active participant" for purposes of IRA eligibility rules and deduction limits?

Suppose an individual is an "active participant" in:

(1)   a qualified corporate or Keogh pension, profit sharing, stock bonus, or annuity plan;

(2)   a simplified employee pension or SIMPLE IRA;

(3)   a Section 403(b) tax sheltered annuity; or

(4)   a government plan.

In those instances, the individual's deduction limit for contributions to a traditional IRA may be reduced or eliminated (Q 3657). The limitation applies if the individual or the individual's spouse was an active participant for any part of the plan year that ended with or within the taxable year.[6]

Participation in Social Security, Railroad Retirement (tier I or II), or in an eligible Code section 457 deferred compensation plan (Q 3581) is not taken into consideration.[7] Federal judges are treated as active participants.[8] Active participants include any individual who is an active participant in a plan established for employees by the United States, a state or political subdivision thereof, or an agency or instrumentality of any of the foregoing.[9]

---

1.   Let. Rul. 8535001.
2.   Let Rul. 8707004.
3.   TAM 9202003.
4.   *Est. of Hall v. Comm.*, TC Memo 1979-342.
5.   Rev. Rul. 79-286, 1979-2 CB 121.
6.   IRC Sec. 219(g)(1); see *Wartes v. Comm.*, TC Memo 1993-84.
7.   IRC Sec. 219(g)(5); Notice 87-16, 1987-1 CB 446, A-7; Notice 89-25, 1989-1 CB 662; Notice 98-49, 1998-2 CB 365.
8.   OBRA '87, Sec. 10103.
9.   IRC Sec. 219(g)(5)(A)(iii).

A district court judge in the state of Nebraska who participated in the Nebraska Retirement Fund for Judges was found to be an employee of the state (not an officer of the state) and, thus, was an active participant.[1]

Full-time active duty officers in the U.S. Air Force were found to be active participants.[2] Certain members of the armed forces reserves and certain volunteer firemen covered under government plans are not considered active participants.[3]

A teacher employed by a municipal school district in Michigan was found to be an active participant in the employment-based, qualified retirement plan provided by the state based upon his being an employee of a state or political subdivision through his employment in the school district.[4]

Active participant status for a tax year must be reported by the employer on the employee's Form W-2.

Active participant status is determined without regard to whether such individual's rights under the plan, trust, or contract are nonforfeitable.[5] Active participant status is further determined under the rules provided in Notice 87-16[6] and Treasury Regulation Section 1.219-2 (active participant rules in effect prior to the Economic Recovery Tax Act of 1981).

In the case of a defined benefit plan, an individual who is not excluded under the eligibility provisions of the plan for the plan year ending with or within the individual's taxable year is an active participant in the plan, regardless of whether such individual has elected to decline participation in the plan, has failed to make a mandatory contribution specified under the plan, or has failed to perform the minimum service required to accrue a benefit under the plan.[7] An individual in a plan under which accruals all have ceased is not an active participant. Where benefits may vary with future compensation, all accruals are not considered to have ceased.[8]

In the case of a profit sharing or stock bonus plan, an individual is an active participant if any employer contribution is deemed added or any forfeiture is allocated to the individual's account during the individual's taxable year.[9] A contribution is treated as made to an individual's account on the later of the date the contribution is made or allocated.[10]

If the right to an allocation is conditioned on the performance of a specified number of hours (or on the employment of the participant on a specified day) and the individual does not

---

1. *Fuhrman v. Comm.*, TC Memo 1997-34.
2. *Morales-Caban v. Comm.*, TC Memo 1993-466.
3. IRC Sec. 219(g)(6).
4. *Neumeister v. Comm.*, TC Memo 2000-41.
5. IRC Sec. 219(g)(5), flush language; see *Nicolai v. Comm.*, TC Memo 1997-108; *Wartes v. Comm.*, TC Memo 1993-84.
6. 1987-1 CB 446.
7. Notice 87-16, 1987-1 CB 446, A-15; Treas. Reg. §1.219-2(b)(1); see *Nicolai v. Comm.*, TC Memo 1997-108.
8. Notice 87-16, 1987-1 CB 446, A-16; Treas. Reg. §1.219-2(b)(3); Let. Rul. 8948008.
9. Treas. Reg. §1.219-2(d)(1); see *Tolley v. Comm.*, TC Memo 1997-244.
10. Treas. Reg. §1.219-2(d)(1).

meet the condition for a particular year, the individual is not an active participant with respect to the taxable year within which such plan year ends.[1]

Where contributions to a plan are purely discretionary and no amount attributable to forfeitures or contributions has been allocated to an individual's account by the last day of the plan year, the individual is not an active participant for the taxable year in which the plan year ends. If the employer contributes an amount after the end of the plan year for that prior plan year, however, the individual generally is an active participant for the taxable year in which the contribution is made.[2]

An individual is an active participant in a money purchase pension plan if any contribution or forfeiture is required to be allocated to his or her account for the plan year ending with or within his or her taxable year, even if the individual was not employed at any time during the taxable year.[3]

An individual is an active participant for any taxable year in which the individual makes a voluntary or a mandatory contribution.[4] The individual is not treated as an active participant if only earnings (rather than contributions or forfeitures) are allocated to his or her account.[5]

An individual is not considered an active participant in a plan integrated with Social Security if his or her compensation is less than the minimum needed to accrue a benefit or to be eligible for an allocation in the plan.[6]

There is no de minimis rule for active participant status. An individual may be an active participant even if no money is allocated to his or her account.[7] Active participant status is determined without regard to whether the individual is vested in any portion of his or her benefit.

3667. Are fees or commissions paid in connection with an IRA deductible?

The IRS has ruled that the payment of administrative or trustee fees incurred in connection with an individual retirement account may be claimed as a miscellaneous itemized deduction (i.e., for the production or collection of income) if such fees are separately billed and paid.[8] However, the 2017 tax reform legislation suspended all miscellaneous itemized deductions subject to the 2 percent floor for 2018-2025. Furthermore, if separately billed and paid, the payment of such fees does not constitute a contribution to the individual retirement account and thus will not be an excess contribution or reduce the amount that may be contributed to the account or, in the case of a traditional IRA, deducted (Q 3656).[9] Deduction of administrative fees is subject to the 2 percent floor on miscellaneous itemized deductions (prior to 2018).

1. Notice 87-16, 1987-1 CB 446, A-20; Let. Rul. 8919064.
2. Notice 87-16, 1987-1 CB 446; Let. Rul. 9008056.
3. Treas. Reg. §1.219-2(c).
4. Treas. Reg. §1.219-2(e); see *Felber v. Comm.*, TC Memo 1992-418; *Wade v. Comm.*, TC Memo 2001-114.
5. Notice 87-16, 1987-1 CB 446, A-16, A-19.
6. Notice 87-16, 1987-1 CB 446, A-9.
7. *Colombell v. Comm.*, TC Summ. Op. 2006-184.
8. Rev. Rul. 84-146, 1984-2 CB 61; Let. Ruls. 9005010, 8951010.
9. See Let. Ruls. 8432109, 8329058, 8329055, 8329049.

Sales commissions on individual retirement annuities that are billed directly by an insurance agent to the client and paid separately by the client are not separately deductible, but are subject to the overall limits on contributions and deductions.[1]

Similarly, broker's commissions incurred in connection with the purchase of securities on behalf of an IRA are not separately deductible, but are subject to the overall limits.[2]

An annual maintenance fee charged for self-directed brokerage accounts that did not vary with the number of transactions, the number of securities involved, or the dollar amount and that was paid to the trustee, not the broker, was not treated as a commission but was separately deductible as an administrative fee.[3]

In addition, brokerage account "wrap fees" that were based on a percentage of assets under management, but that did not vary based on the number of trades in the account, were not treated as a commission and were separately deductible as an administrative fee.[4]

The IRS has held that the payment of fees associated with flexible premium variable annuity contracts that are paid directly from subaccounts within the contract would not be considered a distribution from the contract.

The IRS ruled that assessing expenses against the contract is unrelated to whether or not the participant is currently entitled to benefits under the contract. Therefore, such payments are an expense of the contract and not a distribution.[5]

3668. Is interest paid on amounts borrowed to fund an IRA deductible?

The IRS has ruled that interest paid on amounts borrowed to fund an IRA is not allocable to tax-exempt income (Q 3652). Therefore, the deduction of such interest is not subject to the general prohibition against deducting interest incurred or carried to purchase tax-exempt assets.[6] Because such interest is "on amounts borrowed to buy or carry property held for investment," it would seem that it should be classified as "investment interest expense" and the deduction limited.

Interest paid on money borrowed to buy property held for investment is investment interest. Such interest is deductible but generally limited to the taxpayer's net investment income for the year.[7] Generally, interest incurred to produce tax-exempt income is not deductible.

Property held for investment includes property that produces interest, dividends, annuities, or royalties not derived in the ordinary course of a trade or business. It also includes property that produces gain or loss (not derived in the ordinary course of a trade or business) from the sale or trade of property producing these types of income or held for investment (other than an

---

1.   Let. Rul. 8747072.
2.   Rev. Rul. 86-142, 1986-2 CB 60; Let. Rul. 8711095.
3.   Let. Rul. 8835062.
4.   Let. Rul. 200507021.
5.   Let. Rul. 9845003.
6.   Let. Rul. 8527082. See IRC Secs. 163(a), 265.
7.   IRC Sec. 163(d).

interest in a passive activity). Investment property also includes an interest in a trade or business activity in which the taxpayer did not materially participate (other than a passive activity).[1]

3669. What is the penalty for making excess contributions to an IRA?

If contributions are made in excess of the maximum contribution limit for traditional IRAs (Q 3656) or for Roth IRAs (Q 3659), the contributing individual is liable for a nondeductible excise tax of six percent of the amount of the excess for every year the excess contribution remains in the IRA (not to exceed six percent of the value of the account or annuity, determined as of the close of the tax year).[2] A contribution by a person ineligible to make the contribution is an excess contribution even if it is made through inadvertence.[3]

In the case of an endowment contract described in IRC Section 408(b), the tax does not apply to amounts allocable to life, health, accident, or other insurance.[4] It also does not apply to premiums waived under a disability waiver of premium feature in an individual retirement annuity.[5]

The penalty tax does not apply to "rollover" contributions to a traditional IRA or "qualified rollover contributions" to a Roth IRA.[6] It does apply, however, if the "rollover" contribution does not qualify for rollover. The Tax Court did not accept the argument that an IRA created in a failed rollover attempt is not a valid IRA and, thus, the six percent penalty should not apply.[7] Likewise, a failed Roth IRA conversion that is not recharacterized is subject to the 6-percent penalty (the right to recharacterize IRA-to-Roth IRA conversions has generally been eliminated for tax years beginning after 2017, although recharacterizations to correct an excess contribution should remain permissible absent further guidance to the contrary).[8]

The IRS has ruled that earnings credited to an IRA that are attributable to a non-IRA companion account maintained at the same financial institution (a "super IRA") are treated as contributions to the IRA; when coupled with a cash contribution, these amounts may represent excess contributions subject to the penalty tax.[9] An interest bonus credited to an individual retirement account, however, is not included in the calculation of an excess contribution.[10]

3670. When can IRA contributions be withdrawn or reduced?

A taxpayer who wants to withdraw or reduce a contribution – whether to correct a problem, such as an excess or impermissible contribution, or merely because the taxpayer has changed his or her mind – generally may do so without recognizing income tax or penalties.

---

1.   IRS Publication 550 (2018).
2.   IRC Sec. 4973(a).
3.   *Orzechowski v. Comm.*, 69 TC 750 (1978), *aff'd* 79-1 USTC ¶9220 (2nd Cir. 1979); *Tallon v. Comm.*, TC Memo 1979-423; *Johnson v. Comm.*, 74 TC 1057 (1980).
4.   IRC Sec. 4973(a).
5.   See Let. Rul. 7851087.
6.   IRC Secs. 4973(b)(1)(A), 4973(f)(1)(A).
7.   *Martin v. Comm.*, TC Memo 1993-399; *Michel v. Comm.*, TC Memo 1989-670.
8.   SCA 200148051.
9.   Rev. Rul. 85-62, 1985-1 CB 153.
10.   Let. Rul. 8722068.

If the contribution is withdrawn, together with the net income attributable to such contribution, on or before the due date (including extensions of time) for filing the federal income tax return of the contributing individual, the amount distributed will be treated as if never contributed, regardless of the size of the contribution.[1] Thus, such a distribution is not included in gross income and is not subject to the 10 percent early distribution excise tax. A distribution of an excess contribution also is not subject to the 6 percent excess contribution excise tax. Moreover, no income tax deduction may be taken for such contribution (Q 3669).[2]

If there is net income included with the accompanying distribution, such income is includable in income and may be subject to penalty as an early distribution (Q 3671, Q 3677).[3] Net income attributable to a contribution is determined by allocating to the contribution a pro-rata portion of the earnings or losses accrued by the IRA during the period the IRA held the contribution. Net income may be a negative amount.[4]

Relief may be granted for failure to meet the above deadline if the taxpayer has taken all necessary and reasonable steps, such as properly notifying the financial institution, to comply with the law.[5] Excess amounts that are not withdrawn by this method are subject to the 6 percent excise tax (Q 3669) in the year of contribution and are carried over and taxed each year until the year the excess is eliminated.[6]

By contributing less than the maximum limit in a year, an excess contribution in a previous year may be absorbed up to the unused maximum limit for the year.[7] With respect to traditional IRAs, both the amount contributed and the amount of excess absorbed may be deductible subject to the active participant rules (Q 3656) and no taxable income or early distribution tax is involved. The deduction must be reduced if the excess was improperly deducted in a year closed to IRS challenge.[8]

Where all or a portion of the excess is attributable to an excess "rollover" contribution that resulted from the individual's reliance on erroneous information supplied by the plan, trust, or institution making the distribution, distribution of the portion of the excess attributable to the erroneous information is not included in income and is not subject to the 10 percent early distribution tax.[9] It is not necessary to withdraw earnings on the excess, but any earnings withdrawn would be taxable income and subject to the 10 percent tax if early.

The excess also may be reduced by a distribution includable in income. Such a distribution is subject to the 10 percent excise tax if it is an early distribution, as well as income tax.

---

1.   IRC Secs. 4973(b), 408(d)(4).
2.   IRC Sec. 408(d)(4)(B).
3.   IRC Sec. 408(d)(4).
4.   Treas. Reg. §1.408-11; Notice 2000-39, 2000-2 CB 132.
5.   *Childs v. Comm.*, TC Memo 1996-267; *Thompson v. Comm.*, TC Memo 1996-266.
6.   IRC Sec. 4973(a)
7.   IRC Secs. 4973(b)(2), 4973(f)(2).
8.   IRC Sec. 219(f)(6); Prop. Treas. Reg. §1.219-1(e).
9.   IRC Sec. 408(d)(5)(B).

Where a taxpayer amended his tax return to include an excess contribution in income in the year contributed, the Tax Court ruled that the distribution of the excess in a later year was not includable under the rules of IRC Section 72, that the excess contribution included in income in the prior year constituted an "investment in the contract," and that as a result it was not taxable a second time on the actual distribution of such excess.[1] The phrase "aggregate amount of * * * consideration paid for the contract" found in IRC Section 72(e)(6) encompassed the excess contribution made by the taxpayer. The contribution was therefore considered to be an amount paid in consideration for an IRA and, thus, an "investment in the contract." As a consequence, section 72 would provide a basis for the excess contribution and, upon distribution, such amount would be distributed tax-free.[2]

For purposes of the excess contribution rules, if an excess contribution is invested in a time deposit (such as a CD) that is subject to an early withdrawal penalty, the amount reportable as an excess contribution on distribution of the excess is the total amount actually distributed from the plan after the imposition of the early withdrawal penalty.[3]

A decline in asset value does not remove an excess contribution.[4]

Distributions

3671. How are amounts distributed from a traditional IRA taxed?

Distributions from a traditional IRA generally are taxed under IRC section 72 (relating to the taxation of annuities).[5] Under these rules, a portion of the distribution may be excludable from income. The amount excludable from the taxpayer's income in a given year is that portion of the distribution that bears the same ratio to the amount received as the taxpayer's investment in the contract (i.e., nondeductible contributions) bears to the expected return under the contract. In no case will the total amount excluded exceed the unrecovered investment in the contract.[6]

All traditional IRAs are treated as one contract, all distributions during the year are treated as one distribution, and the value of the contract, income on the contract, and investment in the contract are computed as of the close of the calendar year with or within which the taxable year begins.[7] Thus, the nontaxable portion of a distribution (whether from a traditional individual retirement annuity or account) is equal to the following:

$$\frac{\text{Unrecovered Nondeductible Contributions}}{\text{Total IRA Account Balance} + \text{Distribution amount} + \text{Outstanding Rollovers}} \times \text{Distribution Amount}$$

1.   *Campbell v. Comm.*, 108 TC 54 (1997).
2.   Id.
3.   Let. Ruls. 8643070, 8642061.
4.   H. R. Conf. Rep. 93-1280 (ERISA '74) *reprinted in* 1974-3 CB 501-502.
5.   IRC Sec. 408(d)(1).
6.   IRC Sec. 72(b).
7.   IRC Sec. 408(d)(2).

The total IRA account balance is the balance in all traditional IRAs owned by the taxpayer, as of December 31 of the year of the distribution. The amount of any distributions made (i.e., the amounts for which the nontaxable portion is being computed) and any outstanding rollover amounts (i.e., any amount distributed by a traditional IRA within 60 days of the end of the year, which has not yet been rolled over into another plan, but which is rolled over in the following year) are added to the total IRA account balance. If it is not rolled over, the amount is not treated as an outstanding rollover.[1]

> *Example:* Bill King has made nondeductible contributions to a traditional IRA totaling $2,000, giving him a basis at the end of 2021 of $2,000. By the end of 2022, his IRA earns $400 in interest income. In that year, Bill receives a distribution of $600. Of the $600 received by Bill, the nontaxable portion of the distribution is equal to $500, calculated as follows:

$$\frac{\$2,000 \text{ [total unrecovered nondeductible contributions]}}{\$2,400 \text{ [total IRA account balance + distribution]}} \times \$600 \text{ [distribution amount]}$$

> Thus, Bill will be taxed on only $100 of the $600 distribution and remaining IRA account balance will be $1,800 ($2,000+$400 − $600).

Nondeductible contributions will not be excluded from gross income as investment in the contract where the taxpayer is unable to document the nontaxable basis through the filing of Form 8606, Nondeductible IRAs (Contributions, Distributions and Basis) for the year in which such nondeductible contributions were made and the year in which they were distributed (Q 3699).[2]

An individual may recognize a loss on a traditional IRA, but only when all amounts have been distributed from all traditional IRAs and the total distributed is less than the individual's unrecovered basis.[3] The deduction for the loss was typically a miscellaneous itemized deduction (all of which were suspended for 2018-2025 by the 2017 tax reform legislation—the IRS has yet to issue guidance that would otherwise allow this loss deduction during this time period).[4]

Despite the pro-rata rule generally applicable to distributions from a traditional IRA, distributions after 2001 that are rolled over to a qualified plan, an IRC Section 403(b) tax sheltered annuity, or an eligible IRC Section 457 governmental plan are treated as coming first from all non-after-tax contributions and earnings in all of the IRAs of the owner.[5] Because after-tax contributions cannot be rolled over to eligible retirement plans other than another IRA (Q 3995, Q 4003), this ordering rule effectively allows the owner to rollover the maximum amount permitted. Appropriate adjustments must be made in applying IRC Section 72 to other IRA distributions in the same taxable year and subsequent years.[6]

---

1. Notice 87-16, 1987-1 CB 446.
2. *Alpern v. Comm.*, TC Memo 2000-246.
3. Notice 87-16, 1987-1 CB 446.
4. See IRS Pub 590-B (2017), p. 19.
5. IRC Sec. 408(d)(3)(H).
6. IRC Sec. 408(d)(3)(H)(ii)(III).

The fact that IRA funds were distributed by the financial institution's receiver following insolvency proceedings did not change the nature of the distribution. The taxpayers were taxed on the distribution since a timely rollover was not made.[1]

Likewise, the transfer of IRA funds by a financial institution into a "trust account" was a taxable distribution to the taxpayer even though the taxpayer had intended to transfer the IRA funds to another IRA and had named the account a "trust IRA" because the money was transferred into the trust account.[2]

In addition, a failed Roth IRA conversion that is not recharacterized is treated as a distribution from a traditional IRA and taxed accordingly (note that the typical Roth IRA recharacterization rules were eliminated for tax years beginning after 2017).[3]

Taxpayers who were defrauded of their account balances by their investment advisor, who convinced them to make IRA rollover investments that the advisor subsequently embezzled, were liable for taxes on the amount of assets stolen because the account holders failed to take the necessary steps required to properly set up IRA rollover accounts.[4]

Prior to 2018, special rules applied for qualified hurricane distributions, as follows: Unless a taxpayer elects otherwise, any amount of a qualified hurricane distribution required to be included in gross income shall be so included ratably over the three year taxable period beginning with such year.[5] If a qualified hurricane distribution is an eligible rollover distribution (Q 4003), it may be recontributed to an eligible rollover plan no later than three years from the day after such distribution was received (Q 4011).[6]

Certain early distributions are subject to additional tax (Q 3677). As to what constitutes a "deemed distribution" from a traditional IRA, see Q 3649. For the estate tax marital deduction implications of distributions from a traditional IRA, see Q 3713.

3672. Why is IRA basis important in determining the tax treatment of IRA distributions?

If an individual's IRA contains basis, a portion of each distribution will represent basis and those amounts can be withdrawn from the account tax-free. If a taxpayer maintains multiple IRAs, the cumulative amount of nondeductible IRA contributions is used in determining the portion of a withdrawal from any particular account that is nontaxable.

When clients think of IRA contribution limits, they generally think of the amount that the client may contribute and deduct from income (i.e., $6,000 in 2019-2021, $5,500 in 2018, with a $1,000 catch-up provision for clients age 50 and older). However, deductions are limited for those individuals whose income exceeds the annual inflation-adjusted thresholds.

1. *Aronson v. Comm.*, 98 TC 283 (1992).
2. Let. Rul. 199901029.
3. SCA 200148051.
4. FSA 199933038.
5. IRC Sec. 1400Q; Notice 2005-92, 2005-2 CB 1165.
6. IRC Sec. 1400Q; Notice 2005-92, 2005-2 CB 1165.

As a result, a taxpayer may make nondeductible contributions to an IRA even when his or her income is too high to qualify for a tax deduction. These nondeductible contributions represent the "basis" in the IRA, and are withdrawn tax-free (unlike traditional, deductible contributions, which are taxed under the general rules upon distribution). After-tax funds that are rolled over from another retirement account will also be added to the account's basis.

The Tax Court recently found that the bulk of a lump sum distribution received by a taxpayer was taxable even though the taxpayer was a high income taxpayer who would have been unable to deduct his IRA contributions. This is because the taxpayer was unable to produce documents that would prove the value of his basis in the account. Instead, the court relied upon Forms 5498 (Individual Retirement Arrangement Contribution Information) with respect to the taxpayer to limit his non-taxable distribution to the amount of nondeductible contributions that could be proven.[1]

Individuals keep track of IRA basis on Form 8606, which must be filed with the IRS if the individual made any nondeductible contributions to an IRA for the year, or if he or she received a distribution from an account that has a basis that is greater than zero. Further, the form is required if the individual made a Roth IRA conversion (unless the entire amount was later recharacterized). Form 8606 must also be filed if the taxpayer receives a distribution or transfers funds from an inherited IRA that has basis.

A $50 penalty applies for failure to file an annual Form 8606 when one is required, and a $100 penalty applies to individuals who overstate IRA basis.

3673. How are amounts distributed from a Roth IRA taxed?

"Qualified distributions" from a Roth IRA are not includable in gross income. Thus, earnings are tax-free, not tax deferred as with traditional IRAs. A "qualified distribution" is any distribution made after the five-taxable year period beginning with the first taxable year for which the individual made a contribution to a Roth IRA (or such individual's spouse made a contribution to a Roth IRA) established for such individual and such distribution meets one of the following requirements.[2]

(1)   It is made on or after the date on which the individual attains age 59½.

(2)   It is made to a beneficiary (or to the estate of the individual) on or after the death of the individual.

(3)   It is attributable to the individual's being disabled (within the meaning of IRC Section 72(m)(7)).

(4)   It is a "qualified first-time homebuyer distribution" (see below).

---

1.   *Shank v. Comm.*, No. 1752-17 (2018).
2.   IRC Sec. 408A(d).

A "qualified first-time homebuyer distribution" is any payment or distribution that is used within 120 days after the day it was received by the individual to pay the qualified acquisition costs of a principal residence for a first-time homebuyer.[1] The aggregate amount of payments or distributions received by an individual from all Roth and traditional IRAs that may be treated as qualified first-time homebuyer distributions is limited to a lifetime maximum of $10,000.[2] The first-time homebuyer may be the individual, his or her spouse, or any child, grandchild, parent, or other ancestor of the individual or his or her spouse. A first-time homebuyer is further defined as an individual (and, if married, such individual's spouse) who has had no present ownership interest in a principal residence during the two year period ending on the date of acquisition of the residence for which the distribution is being made.[3] The date of acquisition is the date on which a binding contract to acquire the residence is entered into or the date construction or reconstruction of the residence begins.[4] Qualified acquisition costs are defined as the costs of acquiring, constructing, or reconstructing a residence, including reasonable settlement, financing, or other closing costs.[5]

Planning Point: Although the first-time homebuyer exception allows a taxpayer to avoid paying taxes on earnings, an individual should consider the non-tax consequences of such a distribution. There is an "opportunity cost" associated with taking early distributions. By taking a distribution from a Roth IRA, the Roth funds are depleted and the individual could lose out on significant account growth over time.

In calculating the five-taxable-year period, it is important to remember that contributions to Roth IRAs, as with traditional IRAs, may be made as late as the due date for filing the individual's tax return for the year (without extensions) (Q 3655). For example, if a contribution is made to a Roth IRA between January 1, 2022 and April 15, 2022 for the 2021 taxable year, the five-taxable-year holding period begins to run in 2021.

For purposes of determining whether a distribution from a Roth IRA that is allocable to a "qualified rollover contribution" (Q 3662) from a traditional IRA is a "qualified distribution," the five-taxable-year period begins with the taxable year for which the conversion applies. A subsequent conversion will not start the running of a new five-taxable-year period.[6]

The five-taxable-year period for determining a "qualified distribution" is not recalculated on the death of the Roth IRA owner; the five-taxable-year period of the beneficiary includes the period the Roth IRA was held by the decedent.[7]

Any nonqualified distribution will be includable in income, but only to the extent that the distribution, along with all previous distributions from the Roth IRA, exceeds the aggregate amount of contributions to the Roth IRA. For this purpose, all Roth IRAs are aggregated. To the extent such distributions are taxable, the 10 percent early distribution penalty may apply

---

1.   IRC Sec. 72(t)(8)(A).
2.   IRC Sec. 72(t)(8)(B).
3.   IRC Sec. 72(t)(8)(D)(i).
4.   IRC Sec. 72(t)(8)(d)(iii).
5.   IRC Sec. 72(t)(8)(C).
6.   IRC Sec. 408A(d)(2)(B).
7.   Treas. Reg. §1.408A-6, A-7.

(Q 3677). Distributions allocable to "qualified rollover contributions" (Q 3662) will be subject to the early distribution penalty regardless of whether the distribution is taxable if the distribution is made within the five-year period beginning with the tax year in which the contribution was made.[1] Distributions of excess contributions and earnings on these contributions are not qualified distributions.[2]

When a Roth IRA contains both contributions and conversion amounts, there are ordering rules that apply in determining which amounts are withdrawn. In applying the ordering rules, traditional IRAs are not aggregated with Roth IRAs. All Roth IRAs are aggregated with each other. Regular Roth IRA contributions are deemed to be withdrawn first, then converted amounts second (in order if there has been more than one conversion). Withdrawals of converted amounts are treated first as coming from converted amounts that were includable in income. The ordering rules treat earnings as being withdrawn last after contributions and converted amounts.[3]

An individual may recognize a loss on a Roth IRA, but only when all amounts have been distributed from all Roth IRAs and the total distributed is less than the individual's unrecovered Roth IRA contributions.[4] The deduction for the loss was typically a miscellaneous itemized deduction, but all miscellaneous itemized deductions subject to the 2 percent floor were suspended for 2018-2025.[5]

A transfer of a Roth IRA by gift would constitute an assignment of the Roth IRA, with the effect that the assets of the Roth IRA would be deemed to be distributed to the Roth IRA owner and, accordingly, treated as no longer held in a Roth IRA.[6]

Prior to 2018, special rules applied for qualified hurricane distributions, as follows: Unless a taxpayer elects otherwise, any amount of a qualified hurricane distribution required to be included in gross income shall be so included ratably over the three year taxable period beginning with the year of distribution.[7] If a qualified hurricane distribution is an eligible rollover distribution (Q 4003), it may be recontributed to an eligible rollover plan no later than three years from the day after such distribution was received (Q 4011).[8]

For the estate tax marital deduction implications of distributions from a Roth IRA, see Q 3713.

3674. Are the death proceeds of an individual retirement endowment contract taxable?

An endowment contract is a policy under which a person is paid a specified amount of money on a certain date unless he or she dies before that date, in which case, the money is paid

---

1. Treas. Reg. §1.408A-6, A-5.
2. See IRC Sec. 408A(d).
3. IRC Sec. 408A(d)(4); Treas. Reg. §1.408A-6, A-8.
4. Notice 87-16, 1987-1 CB 446.
5. See IRS Pub 590-B (2015), p. 19.
6. Treas. Reg. §1.408A-6, A-19.
7. IRC Sec. 1400Q; Notice 2005-92, 2005-2 CB 1165.
8. IRC Sec. 1400Q; Notice 2005-92, 2005-2 CB 1165.

to a designated beneficiary. Endowment proceeds paid in a lump sum at maturity are taxable only if the proceeds are more than the cost of the policy. To determine the cost, subtract any amount previously received under the contract, and exclude from income the total premiums (or other consideration) paid for the contract. Include the part of the lump sum payment that is more than the cost in income.[1]

If no nondeductible contributions (Q 3656) have been made by the taxpayer to any traditional individual retirement plan, the portion of the death benefit of an endowment contract equal to the cash value immediately before death is included in gross income as a federal income taxable distribution. The balance is federal income tax-free as proceeds of life insurance under IRC Section 101(a). If the death benefit is paid in installments, the amount representing life insurance proceeds is prorated and recovered tax-free under IRC Section 101(d).[2]

If nondeductible contributions to any such individual retirement plan have been made, it would seem that a portion of the cash value of the contract should be treated as a recovery of basis and, as such, nontaxable (Q 3671).

3675. Are amounts received from IRAs subject to withholding?

Yes.

Taxable distributions from traditional IRAs are subject to income tax withholding. If the distribution is in the form of an annuity or similar payments, amounts are withheld as though each distribution were a payment of wages pursuant to the recipient's Form W-4. In the case of any other kind of distribution, a flat 10 percent must be withheld by the plan custodian unless a different withholding choice is elected by the owner.[3] A recipient generally can elect not to have the tax withheld; this election will continue until the recipient revokes the election.[4] Even though distributions from a traditional IRA may be partly nontaxable because of nondeductible contributions, the payor must report all withdrawn amounts to the IRS.[5] For states that impose income tax on IRA distributions, state income tax withholding may also be required.

Planning Point: A recipient of a taxable IRA distribution should project his or her income tax liability for the year and pay in an appropriate amount of estimated tax payments to avoid penalties for under-withholding. Withholding of 10 percent or even 20 percent may be insufficient to cover federal income tax liability. Taxpayers should project their state and local tax liabilities as well. *Martin Silfen, J.D., Brown Brothers, Harriman Trust Co., LLC.*

Distributions from Roth IRAs are subject to income tax withholding, but only to the extent that it is reasonable to believe the amount withdrawn would be includable in income.[6]

---

1.   IRS Pub. 17 (2019).
2.   Treas. Reg. §1.408-3(e)(2).
3.   IRC Sec. 3405(e) (1)(A); Treas. Reg. §35.3405-1.
4.   IRC Secs. 3405(a) (2), 3405(b)(2).
5.   IRC Sec. 3405(e) (1)(B).
6.   IRC Sec. 3405(e) (1)(B).

Planning Point: IRS withholding guidance, released in Notice 2018-14, could impact individuals who receive retirement benefits in the form of periodic payments (generally those that are annuitized). Individuals receiving periodic payments can use Form W-4P to waive or increase withholding, depending upon their expected income tax liability. With respect to periodic payments, the default method of withholding is based on whether the individual is single or married and the number of withholding allowances the individual could claim were the payments traditional wages. Under Notice 2018-14, the IRS has set the default withholding for periodic payments to equal the wage withholding of a married taxpayer who claims three withholding allowances in order to take the 2017 tax reform law into consideration. Individuals who receive periodic retirement payments may wish to examine their anticipated tax situation and use Form W-4P to modify this default treatment if appropriate. [1]

Planning Point: The IRS redesigned Form W-4, which previously mirrored Form W-4P, for 2020, to account for tax reform (so the 2020 forms will no longer match because the 2020 Form W-4P will continue to mirror the old version). The IRS has clarified that in 2020, the default rules for withholding from periodic payments under Section 3405(a) when no withholding certificate has been furnished will continue as in prior years (i.e., married with three allowances). The IRS guidance does note that it is studying whether changes for years after 2020 may be appropriate. The IRS also notes that 2020 Form W-4P will work with certain withholding tables and computational procedures in the 2020 Publication 15-T that are applicable to a 2019 or earlier Form W-4. [2]

IRS regulations clarify tax withholding rules for periodic retirement and annuity payments. Pre-tax reform, the default withholding rate was based on a married taxpayer with three withholding exemptions. Post-reform, the personal exemption has been suspended and Congress directed the Treasury to provide updated withholding rules. The regulations add several Q&A to explain that amounts withheld will be treated as though the payment were part of wages paid by an employer. If the payee has not provided a withholding certificate, the withholding amount is determined based on a married taxpayer with three withholding allowances. [3]

Generally, withholding for these types of payments should be determined based on the rules in applicable IRS forms, instructions, publications and other guidance. Rules similar to the wage withholding rules will apply, but the IRS has indicated that further forms, instructions, publications and other guidance will be issued when the rules are finalized. The regulations apply to payments made after December 31, 2020.

3676. What should taxpayers consider when determining their withholding for an IRA? Are taxpayers required to make estimated payments with respect to IRA distributions?

Taxpayers with IRA investments will face mandatory distributions (RMDs) from IRAs beginning April 1 of the year after the year the individual reaches age 72 (70½ before 2020). For those who have focused on accumulating retirement savings in traditional IRAs, this means that taxes will be due on all distributions at the individual's ordinary income tax rate. Each taxpayer has options when it comes to how those taxes will be paid, however. The individual may choose to make estimated income tax payments, which are due by April 15, June 15, September 15 and

---

1. Notice 2018-14.
2. Notice 2020-03.
3. Prop. Treas Reg. §31.3405(a)-1. See also Notice 2020-3.

January 15 each year, or the account owner can choose to have his or her IRA custodian with-hold taxes from each distribution (similarly to how the employer withholds from an employee paycheck).

If the taxpayer chooses withholding, he or she does not have to determine the proper level of estimated payments, but should continue to calculate anticipated income each year in order to avoid under or over-withholding. The taxpayer is able to specify the exact percentage that he or she wishes to be withheld from each distribution, so the risk remains that the taxpayer will over or under pay throughout the year. Further, the IRS will assume that the amount withheld by the taxpayer was paid in equal installments over the year, but the taxpayer is able to make a single lump sum payment if advantageous. Taxpayers are also able to have a certain percentage withheld from each IRA distribution, but also make estimated payments in order to avoid the year-end tax hit.

When an account owner converts traditional IRA funds to a Roth account, he or she is again liable for ordinary income tax on the amount converted. The taxpayer has the option of specifying the amount that should be withheld from the conversion (because each individual will have to anticipate income from other sources in order to determine his or her tax liability for the year). If the taxpayer fails to specify the percentage that should be withheld from the converted amount, the IRA custodian will withhold 10 percent as a default.

Unfortunately, for taxpayers who convert to Roth accounts, the amount that is withdrawn to cover the amount that must be withheld will also be subject to tax—at ordinary income tax rates. This requires the taxpayer to take this into consideration when determining the withholding amount, which can be complex. In the case of a Roth conversion, therefore, it is generally in the taxpayer's best interest to pay their tax liability on the distribution using funds outside of the IRA—potentially making the estimated payment route the more attractive option.

3677. What penalties apply to early distributions from an IRA?

Except as noted below, amounts distributed from a traditional IRA or a Roth IRA to the individual for whom the plan is maintained before such individual reaches age 59½ are early (premature) distributions. To the extent such distributions are taxable, they are subject to an additional tax equal to 10 percent of the amount of the distribution that is includable in gross income for that particular tax year.[1] The tax is increased to 25 percent in the case of distributions from SIMPLE IRAs (Q 3706) during the first two years of participation.[2]

The 10 percent penalty tax does not apply to the following:

(1)   Distributions made to a beneficiary or the individual's estate on or after the death of the individual.[3]

---

1.   IRC Sec. 72(t).
2.   IRC Sec. 72(t)(6).
3.   IRC Sec. 72(t)(2)(A)(ii).

Planning Point: If a surviving spouse is under age 59½ and elects to be treated as the owner of a decedent spouse's IRA (generally, for required minimum distribution purposes), distributions may be subject to the early distribution penalty unless an exception applies. The early distribution penalty would not apply to distributions after the death of the original owner in the absence of the spouse making the election to be treated as owner.

(2)   Distributions attributable to the individual's disability.[1]

(3)   Distributions made for medical care, but only to the extent allowable as a medical expense deduction for amounts paid during the taxable year for medical care (determined without regard to whether the individual itemizes).[2] Thus, only amounts in excess of 10 percent of the individual's adjusted gross income ("AGI") escape the 10 percent penalty. (The threshold amount was 7.5 percent for tax years prior to 2013, and is again 7.5 percent for 2017-2020.)

(4)   Distributions made to unemployed individuals for the payment of health insurance premiums. The AGI floor, described above, does not have to be met if the individual has received unemployment compensation for at least twelve weeks and the withdrawal is made in either the year such unemployment compensation was received or the year immediately following the year in which the unemployment compensation was received. This exception also applies to self-employed individuals whose sole reason for not receiving unemployment compensation is that they were self-employed. The exception ceases to apply once the individual has been reemployed for a period of 60 days.[3]

Planning Point: If an IRA owner pays health insurance premiums in a year of unemployment, and the owner expects to need an IRA distribution within the next few years at a time when the owner does not anticipate that any other exception will apply, the owner should consider taking an IRA distribution in the year of unemployment to avoid a future penalty tax on that amount. *Martin Silfen, J.D., Brown Brothers, Harriman Trust Co., LLC.*

(5)   Distributions made to pay "qualified higher education expenses" during the taxable year for the taxpayer, the taxpayer's spouse, or the child or grandchild of the taxpayer or the taxpayer's spouse.[4] "Qualified higher education expenses" means tuition, fees, books, supplies, and equipment required for the enrollment or attendance of the student at any "eligible educational institution." For tax years beginning after 2001, this includes expenses for special needs services in the case of a special needs beneficiary that are incurred in connection with such enrollment or attendance. Room and board (up to a certain amount) also is included if the student is enrolled at least half-time.[5] "Qualified higher education expenses" must be incurred for the taxable year of the distribution.[6] These expenses must be

1.   IRC Sec. 72(t)(2)(A)(iii).
2.   IRC Sec. 72(t)(2)(B).
3.   IRC Sec. 72(t)(2)(D).
4.   IRC Sec. 72(t)(2)(E).
5.   IRC Secs. 72(t)(7), 529(e)(3).
6.   *Lodder-Beckert v. Comm.*, TC Memo 2005-162 (2005).

reduced by any scholarships received by the individual, any educational assistance provided to the individual, or any payment for such expenses (other than a gift, devise, bequest, or inheritance) that is excludable from gross income.[1] An "eligible educational institution" is any college, university, vocational school, or other post-secondary educational institution described in Section 481 of the Higher Education Act of 1965.[2] Thus, virtually all accredited public, nonprofit, and proprietary postsecondary institutions are considered eligible educational institutions.[3] This exception to the 10 percent penalty is not available if the withdrawal qualifies for one of the other exceptions provided under IRC Section 72(t)(2) (other than the following exception for "qualified first-time homebuyers").[4]

Planning Point: If an IRA owner has higher education expenses in a given year and he or she expects to need an IRA distribution within the next few years at a time when he or she does not anticipate that any other exception will apply, the IRA owner should consider taking an IRA distribution in the year of the higher education expenses to avoid a future penalty tax on that amount. *Martin Silfen, J.D., Brown Brothers, Harriman Trust Co., LLC.*

---

(6)   Distributions that are "qualified first-time homebuyer distributions" (Q 3673). This exception to the 10 percent penalty is not available if the withdrawal qualifies for one of the other exceptions provided under IRC Section 72(t)(2).[5]

(7)   Distributions that are part of a series of substantially equal periodic payments made (at least annually) for the life or life expectancy of the individual or the joint lives or joint life expectancy of the individual and his or her designated beneficiary (Q 3679).[6]

(8)   Distributions that are "qualified hurricane distributions" (these distributions may not exceed $100,000).[7] See Q 3799.

(9)   Distributions that are "qualified reservist distributions." Qualified reservist distributions are those made to reserve members of the U.S. military called to active duty for 180 days or more at any time after September 11, 2001. Reservists have the right to return the amount of any distributions to the retirement plan for two years following the end of active duty.[8]

The penalty tax has been held not to apply to compulsory distributions where the IRS levied on a taxpayer's IRA and where the federal government seized a taxpayer's IRA as part of a plea agreement.[9]

---

1.   IRC Sec. 72(t)(7)(B).
2.   See IRC Sec. 529(e)(5).
3.   Notice 97-60, 1997-2 CB 310, at 14 (Sec. 3, A16).
4.   IRC Sec. 72(t)(2)(E).
5.   IRC Sec. 72(t)(2)(F).
6.   IRC Sec. 72(t)(2)(A)(iv).
7.   IRC Sec. 1400Q; Notice 2005-92, 2005-2 CB 1165.
8.   IRC Sec. 72(t)(2)(G).
9.   *Larotonda v. Comm.*, 89 TC 287 (1987), nonacq.; *Murillo v. Comm.*, TC Memo 1998-13, *aff'd.* 166 F.3d 1201 (2nd Cir. 1998).

Where a taxpayer withdrew from his IRA to satisfy a court order to pay alimony and child support, the penalty tax did apply.[1]

No early distribution occurs where accumulation units in an individual retirement annuity are surrendered to purchase a disability waiver of premium feature.[2] Ineligibility to set up an individual retirement plan does not prevent imposition of this penalty.[3] The fact that an IRA distribution was mandated by the insolvency of the financial institution issuing the IRA did not prevent the application of the 10 percent penalty tax when the funds were received and not rolled over.[4]

The amount reportable as an early distribution from a time deposit (such as a certificate of deposit) that is subject to an early withdrawal penalty of the trustee is the net amount of the distribution after deduction of any early withdrawal penalty imposed by the trustee.[5]

It appears that amounts includable in income as a result of a prohibited transaction, borrowing on an annuity contract, or using an account as security for a loan would be subject to the 10 percent penalty.[6]

3678. What strategies should a taxpayer consider when determining the level of distributions from retirement accounts during retirement?

Depending on a taxpayer's unique circumstances, there are many different approaches that an advisor may take to help determine an appropriate or advantageous distribution level. Two traditional strategies that are commonly used are the "4 percent rule" (see below) and the RMD method, which uses the IRS's required minimum distribution rules to make the determination.

The RMD rules (Q 3682) require that taxpayers begin withdrawing funds from tax-deferred retirement accounts, such as IRAs and 401(k)s, when they reach age 72. The minimum amounts that must be withdrawn are calculated based on the taxpayer's life expectancy, determined using IRS actuarial data.[7]

The IRS provides tables specifying the percentage of current account assets that must be withdrawn each year based on the life expectancy of the taxpayer in any given year after reaching age 72 (tables are also available for taxpayers beginning withdrawals at younger ages). In the case of a married couple where one spouse is more than 10 years younger than the other, the joint life expectancy of the couple is used in the calculation to provide a more realistic estimate of the combined life expectancy of the couple.[8]

---

1.   *Baas v. Comm.*, TC Memo 2002-130. See also *Czepiel v. Comm.*, TC Memo 1999-289, *aff'd.* by order (1st Cir. 2000).
2.   See Let. Rul. 7851087.
3.   *Orzechowski v. Comm.*, 69 TC 750 (1978), *aff'd* 79-1 USTC ¶7220 (2nd Cir. 1979).
4.   *Aronson v. Comm.*, 98 TC 283 (1992).
5.   Let. Ruls. 8643070 and 8642061.
6.   IRS Pub. 590-A (2019).
7.   IRC Secs. 408(a)(6), 408(b)(3), 401(a)(9).
8.   Treas. Reg. §1.401(a)(9)-9.

The RMD requirements are generally not meant to provide retirees with guidance on the optimal withdrawal rate, but are meant to ensure that the funds in these tax-deferred accounts are used for retirement income, rather than as estate planning vehicles. Because the requirements seek to ensure that the assets are spent during life, they are a viable alternative to the so-called "4 percent rule," even though this was not the original IRS intent in formulating the rules.

As the name suggests, under the 4 percent rule, the taxpayer withdraws 4 percent of the beginning balance of retirement savings each year during retirement. While the rule is very simple, it can have unintended consequences. For example, the rigid 4 percent-per-year require-ment tends to encourage taxpayers to seek out dividend-heavy investments to supplement their otherwise fixed income, regardless of whether those investments are otherwise appropriate.

Further, the 4 percent rule has taxpayers withdraw 4 percent even in years when their assets may have severely underperformed. The converse is also true, as the rule limits taxpayers to 4 percent withdrawals even if they could afford much more.

Some advisors find that the RMD method should be considered as a potential alternative to the traditional 4 percent rule for determining retirement account withdrawal rates. Not only is the RMD approach almost as simple as the 4 percent rule—rather than withdrawing 4 percent each year, the taxpayer would consult the IRS tables to determine the applicable percentage—but it offers much more flexibility.

The RMD rule may be, in many ways, much more realistic than the 4 percent rule because it bases withdrawals on the current value of the taxpayer's retirement assets. While this requires determining the account values each year, it also allows taxpayers to modify their consumption levels based on actual account performance. Because the percentages are based on life expectancy and vary with age, it is still unlikely that the taxpayer will outlive his assets.

3679. How are substantially equal periodic payments from an IRA calcu-lated for purposes of IRC Section 72(t)?

The 10 percent early (premature) distribution tax (Q 3677) does not apply to distributions that are part of a series of substantially equal periodic payments made at least annually for the life or life expectancy of the individual or the joint lives or joint life expectancy of the individual and his or her designated beneficiary.[1]

The IRS has approved three methods, explained below, under which payments will be con-sidered to be "substantially equal periodic payments."[2] Regardless of which method is used, the series of payments must continue for the longer of five years or until the individual reaches age 59½. Ordinarily, a "modification" (see Q 3680) that occurs before this duration requirement is satisfied will result in the penalty and interest being imposed on the entire series of payments, in the year the modification occurs.[3] However, a participant can (see Q 3680) change methods

---

1.   IRC Sec. 72(t)(2)(A)(iv).
2.   Rev. Rul. 2002-62, 2002-2 CB 710, modifying Notice 89-25, 1989-1 CB 662, A-12.
3.   IRC Sec. 72(t)(4).

one time if certain requirements are met.[1] A change in the payment series as a result of disability or death also does not trigger the penalty.[2]

The three approved methods are as follows:

1.   *The Required Minimum Distribution ("RMD") method:* requires use of a calculation that would be acceptable for purposes of calculating the required minimum distributions under IRC Section 401(a)(9). Consequently, annual payments are determined each year by dividing the account balance by the owner's current life expectancy obtained from one of three IRS tables (see below). Under this method, the account balance, the life expectancy, and the resulting annual payments are redetermined each year and can cause a variation in the payment from year to year. Such annual fluctuations will not be considered modifications.[3] Under this method, the same life expectancy table used for the first distribution year must be used for each following year.[4] Although the Worker, Retiree and Employer Recovery Act of 2008 ("WRERA 2008") waived RMDs for 2009, this did not apply for purposes of the substantially equal periodic payment exception to the early distribution penalty.[5]

2.   *The fixed amortization method:* requires annual payments determined by amortizing the individual's account balance in level amounts over a specified number of years determined using the chosen life expectancy and interest rate as explained below.[6] The account balance, life expectancy, and resulting annual payment are determined once for the first distribution year, and the annual payment is the same amount in each year thereafter.[7] The ability to recalculate the amount of the payment each year by using the taxpayer's life expectancy with the amortization method was approved in a letter ruling.[8]

3.   *The fixed annuitization method* requires annual payments determined by dividing the individual's account balance by an annuity factor that is the present value of an annuity of $1 per year beginning at the individual's age attained in the first distribution year and continuing for the life of the individual (or the joint lives of the individual and a beneficiary). The annuity factor is derived using the mortality table provided in a 2002 IRS guidance and an interest rate chosen as explained below. The account balance, annuity factor, interest rate, and resulting annual payment all are determined once for the first distribution year and the annual payment is the same amount each year thereafter.[9] The ability to recalculate the amount of the

1.   Rev. Rul. 2002-62, 2002-2 CB 710.
2.   IRC Sec. 72(t)(4).
3.   Rev. Rul. 2002-62, 2002-2 CB 710, Sec. 2.01(a).
4.   Rev. Rul. 2002-62, 2002-4 CB 710, Sec. 2.02(a).
5.   Notice 2009-82, 2009-2 CB 491.
6.   Rev. Rul. 2002-62, 2002-2 CB 710, Sec. 2.01(b).
7.   Rev. Rul. 2002-62, 2002-2 CB 710, Sec. 2.01(b).
8.   Let. Rul. 200432021.
9.   Rev. Rul. 2002-62, 2002-2 CB 710, Sec. 2.01(c).

payment each year by using the taxpayer's life expectancy with the annuitization method was approved in a letter ruling.[1]

The three life expectancy tables that may be used to calculate substantially equal periodic payments are: the single life expectancy table, the joint and last survivor life expectancy table, and the uniform lifetime table. [2] (Because the uniform lifetime table in the RMD regulations begins at age 70, the IRS included an expanded version covering a broader range of ages.)[3] All three tables are reproduced in Appendix F.

For the amortization method, an interest rate must be used that does not exceed 120 percent of the federal mid-term rate (determined in accordance with IRC Section 1274(d)) for either of the two months immediately preceding the month in which the distribution begins.[4]

Planning Point: The RMD method is the simplest calculation, but will need to be recalculated every year. The amortization and annuitization calculations are more complex, but only need to be performed once.

The IRS has stated that individual retirement plans do not have to be aggregated for purposes of calculating a series of substantially equal periodic payments.[5] If a taxpayer owns more than one IRA, any combination of the IRAs may be taken into account in determining the distributions by aggregating the account balances of those IRAs. But a portion of one or more of the IRAs may not be excluded to limit the periodic payment to a predetermined amount.[6]

Planning Point: The ability to split up or aggregate IRAs in advance of a payout makes the calculation extremely flexible. Furthermore, creating separate accounts is a good way to avoid tying up any more IRA funds than is absolutely necessary to support the needed payout.

If an individual with more than one IRA chooses to base a series of substantially equal periodic payments on the total of all of his or her IRAs, the annual distribution may be received from any or all of the accounts.[7]

Planning Point: It generally is useful to select the substantially equal periodic payment method that comes closest to withdrawing the amount that is desired. Under the amortization or annuitization methods, higher interest rates result in higher payments; lower interest rates result in lower payments. In general, having a designated beneficiary can reduce the amount of the payments (calculations can be based on two lives rather than one); a younger beneficiary results in lower payments, an older beneficiary results in higher payments. Selecting IRA accounts with a lower aggregate account balance results in lower payments; selecting IRA accounts with a higher aggregate account balance results in higher payments.

---

1.   Let. Rul. 200432023.
2.   See Rev. Rul. 2002-62 and Treas. Reg. §1.401(a)(9)-9.
3.   Rev. Rul. 2002-62, 2002-2 CB 710, Sec. 2.02(a).
4.   Rev. Rul. 2002-62, 2002-2 CB 710, Sec. 2.02(c).
5.   See Let. Ruls. 200309028, 9050030.
6.   Let. Rul. 9705033.
7.   See Let. Rul. 9705033.

3680. When is a series of substantially equal periodic payments from an IRA "modified" and what are the results?

Except in the event of death or disability, a change in payouts after the series has begun generally will constitute a "modification" and will trigger the early distribution penalties discussed in Q 3677.[1]

A modification to the series of payments generally will occur if the taxpayer makes any of the following: (1) any addition to the account balance (other than gains or losses); (2) any non-taxable transfer of a portion of the account balance to another retirement plan; or (3) a rollover of the amount received, resulting in such amount not being taxable.[2]

The IRS has determined that a change that does not alter the annual payout (such as a change from quarterly to monthly payments) is not a modification for this purpose.[3] The receipt of a qualified hurricane distribution (Q 3671) also will not be treated as a change in a series of substantially equal periodic payments.[4] However, once a change to the RMD method has been elected, no further changes may be made to the method of payment.

The IRS has stated that an individual who begins distributions using either the amortization method or the annuitization method may, in any subsequent year, switch to the RMD method to determine the payment for the year of the switch and all subsequent years. Regardless of when the payments began, a taxpayer making such a change will not be treated as having made a "modification."[5]

Planning Point: The ability to switch to the RMD method makes the amortization and annuity methods more attractive, particularly for a participant who has a short term need for larger distributions which he or she expects will diminish in a few years. *Martin Silfen, J.D., Brown Brothers, Harriman Trust Co., LLC, New York, New York.*

A taxpayer who made the one-time RMD method change late in 2002 was permitted to roll over amounts in excess of the RMD amount back to the IRA in early 2003 even though the 60 day limit (Q 4015) had elapsed.[6] The IRS determined that an inadvertent rollover of a small IRA balance into a large IRA from which a series of substantially equal periodic payments was in progress was not a modification.[7]

The IRS has also ruled that a series of substantially equal periodic payments was not modified where, as a result of an error made by the entity distributing the funds, additional distributions were made by the entity from a second account maintained by the taxpayer before the funds from the first account were exhausted. This resulted in two additional, unrequested distributions. The taxpayer was able to provide proof that the error was made after the entity maintaining the account was acquired by another entity. She further certified that she had not requested the

---

1.   IRC Sec. 72(t)(4).
2.   Rev. Rul. 2002-62, 2002-2 CB 710, Sec. 2.02(e).
3.   See Let. Rul. 8919052.
4.   Notice 2005-92, 2005-2 CB 1165, Sec. 4H.
5.   Rev. Rul. 2002-62, 2002-2 CB 710, Sec. 2.03(b).
6.   Let. Rul. 200419031.
7.   See Let. Rul. 200616046.

additional distributions and did not intend to modify the series of substantially equal periodic payments. As a result, the IRS found that the additional distributions were not a modification of the series of substantially equal periodic payments.[1]

Planning Point: Qualified plans often make a trailing distribution subsequent to making a lump sum distribution to a former employee's IRA. The IRS currently holds the position that if the participant has started a 72(t) payout from the receiving IRA, the trailing distribution will trigger a modification. Participants starting a 72(t) payout following a lump sum distribution should consider moving the funds to a different IRA prior to beginning the payout. *Robert S. Keebler, CPA, MST, Virchow, Krause & Company, LLP, Green Bay, Wisconsin.*

The commencement of another series of substantially equal periodic payments (i.e., from a different IRA) does not constitute a modification of an existing payout, and the IRS has stated privately that nothing in the IRC or regulations prevents a subsequent payout series.[2] One case determined that a distribution from an IRA that satisfied the early distribution penalty exception for qualified higher education expenses was not a modification of a series of substantially equal periodic payments from the same IRA.[3]

3681. What are the results if an IRA account owner depletes the IRA account through properly pre-determined substantially equal periodic payments?

The penalty under IRC Section 72(t) will not be applied if, as a result of applying an acceptable method of determining substantially equal periodic payments, an individual depletes his or her account and is unable to complete the payouts for the required duration period under IRC Section 72(t)(4).[4]

Required Minimum Distributions

3682. What are the minimum distribution requirements for individual retirement plans?

Editor's Note: The 2020 CARES Act waived all RMD requirements for 2020.

Amounts accumulated in an individual retirement account or annuity ("IRA") must be distributed in compliance with the minimum distribution requirements.[5] The amount that must be distributed each year according to these rules is commonly referred to as the "required minimum distribution" (or RMD). For the calculation of lifetime distributions, see Q 3686; for after-death distributions, see Q 3687. Reporting requirements pertaining to IRA required minimum distributions are explained in Q 3597.

Roth IRAs are not subject to the lifetime minimum distribution requirements, but are subject to the after-death distribution requirements explained in Q 3687.

---

1. Let. Rul. 201510060.
2. See Let. Rul. 200033048.
3. *Benz v. Comm.*, 132 TC 330 (2009).
4. Rev. Rul. 2002-62, 2002-2 CB 710, Secs. 2.03(a) and 3.
5. IRC Secs. 408(a)(6), 408(b)(3), 401(a)(9).

Traditional IRAs, SEP IRAs, and SIMPLE IRAs (non-Roth IRAs) generally are subject to the same minimum distribution requirements that apply to qualified plans, with some variations (Q 3891 to Q 3909).[1] The required beginning date for lifetime distributions from non-Roth IRAs is April 1 of the calendar year following the calendar year in which the individual attains age 72 (70½ prior to 2020) (Q 3686).[2] Under pre-SECURE Act law, an individual reached age 70½ on the date that is six calendar months after his or her 70th birthday.[3]

Planning Point: The 2020 CARES Act waived RMDs from IRAs and other defined contribution plans for calendar year 2020. The five-year rule is also determined without regard to 2020.

While the CARES Act waived all RMDs for 2020, the law was enacted after some taxpayers had already taken their 2020 RMDs early in the year. For those who took RMDs early in the year, the 60-day rollover period had already expired. In response, the IRS announced that anyone who took a 2020 RMD was eligible to roll the funds back into their account penalty-free. The 60-day rollover period was extended through August 31, 2020. Further, the rollover does not count toward the otherwise applicable "one rollover per 12-month period" rule or the restriction on rollovers for inherited IRAs.[4]

3683. What can be done before the IRA required beginning date in order to minimize required minimum distributions?

The required minimum distribution (RMD) rules essentially require taxpayers to begin withdrawing funds from IRAs when they reach age 72. The minimum amounts that must be withdrawn are calculated based on the account value and the taxpayer's life expectancy, determined using IRS actuarial data.[5] Despite this, there are ways that individuals can minimize their RMDs in the year prior to attaining age 72 if they will have no immediate need for the funds at that time.

Many individuals can reduce their RMDs by converting a portion of their traditional IRA funds into Roth funds. Roth IRAs have no minimum distribution requirements, so converting traditional IRA funds to Roth accounts will reduce the owner's RMDs. Unfortunately, if the taxpayer is still working, the taxpayer may still be in a high enough income tax bracket that the taxes generated by the rollover can be substantial (all amounts rolled over from a traditional IRA to a Roth IRA are taxed at the owner's ordinary income tax rate).

If the individual is still working, the taxpayer can also consider rolling the funds into a qualified plan (such as a profit-sharing or 401(k) plan) where distributions are not required until the later of the year the taxpayer turns 72 *or* the year the taxpayer retires. In this case, it becomes important that the taxpayer learn the rules of the qualified plan before making the rollover. Some plans do not accept rollovers, and others require that distributions begin at 72 regardless of the option to postpone until retirement.

---

1.   Treas. Reg. §1.408-8, A-1, A-2.
2.   Treas. Reg. §1.408-8, A-3.
3.   Treas. Reg. §1.401(a)(9)-2, A-3.
4.   Notice 2020-51.
5.   Treas. Reg. §1.408-8.

Importantly, both of these rollover moves must be made before the RMD requirements kick in—otherwise the individual will have to pay both the taxes associated with the RMD (which cannot be rolled over) and those generated by the rollover itself.[1]

A taxpayer can also reduce RMDs by purchasing a qualified longevity annuity contract (QLAC, see Q 554)—which is a relatively new annuity product that is purchased within the IRA, deferring annuity payouts until the taxpayer reaches old age. The value of the QLAC is excluded from the account value when calculating the RMDs, though the taxpayer is limited to purchasing a QLAC with an annuity premium value equal to the lesser of 25 percent of the account value or $135,000 (in 2020 and 2021, up from $130,000 in 2019).[2]

3684. How are minimum distribution requirements calculated if an individual owns more than one IRA?

If an individual owns more than one IRA, the required minimum distribution (RMD) must be calculated separately for each IRA, but the total for a category (Roth or non-Roth) may be taken from any one or more of the IRAs within the same category. This rule requires aggregation of amounts that an individual is required to take as the IRA owner and a separate aggregation for amounts that an individual is required to take as the designated beneficiary of a decedent's IRA. Amounts taken as an IRA owner may not be aggregated with amounts taken as a beneficiary for purposes of meeting the minimum distribution requirements. Similarly, distributions from 403(b) contracts or annuities may not be aggregated with IRA distributions to meet the distribution requirements for either type of account.[3]

> *Example:* Mark, who is 73 years old, has two IRA accounts that he contributed to during his working years and an IRA that he inherited from his deceased father. One of his IRA balances equals $50,000 (IRA 1) and the other equals $75,000 (IRA 2); the inherited IRA has a balance of $25,000. Mark's required minimum distribution from these accounts is as follows:
>
> IRA 1 = $1887   IRA 2 = $2830
>
> Inherited IRA = $943.
>
> Mark must take, in total, $4717 ($1887+ 2830) from his IRAs. But he could take this amount from either IRA 1 or IRA 2 (or a combination of the two). The $943 required from the inherited IRA, however, must be taken only from that account.

When an RMD is required during a calendar year, any amount distributed or withdrawn from the account will first be treated as the required distribution amount until the total required distribution has been satisfied. Consequently, such a distribution is not eligible for rollover.[4] However, the minimum distribution requirement may be satisfied by a distribution from another IRA owned by the same individual.[5]

---

1.   Treas. Reg. §1.408-8.
2.   IRC Sec. 401(a)(9); Treas. Reg. §1.401(a)(9)-6.
3.   Treas. Reg. §1.408-8, A-9.
4.   Treas. Reg. §1.408-8, A-4.
5.   Treas. Reg. §1.408-8, A-9.

In the event of a transfer from one IRA to another, the transferor IRA must distribute any amount required under these minimum distribution rules in the year of transfer—i.e. the transfer itself will not count as a distribution that satisfies these minimum distribution rules.[1]

3685. Is there a penalty imposed for failure to comply with IRA required minimum distribution requirements?

A penalty tax is imposed on the participant (IRA owner) if the amount distributed under an IRA for a calendar year is less than the required minimum distribution for the year. The penalty is equal to 50 percent of the amount by which the distribution made in the calendar year falls short of the required amount.[2] The penalty generally will be imposed in the calendar year in which the amount was required to be distributed. If the distribution was the first required distribution, and thus was due by April 1 following the calendar year in which the IRA owner reached 72 years old (the required beginning date), the penalty will be imposed in the calendar year when distributions were to begin even though the required distribution was technically for the preceding year.[3]

> *Example:* Joan turned 72 on October 26 of 2020. Her first required minimum distribution for 2020 was due by April 1, 2021. Joan did not receive such amount by the April 1 due date. Consequently, Joan will owe a penalty equal to 50 percent of the amount that should have been distributed, which will be imposed on her 2021 tax return.

The penalty tax may be waived if the payee establishes to the satisfaction of the IRS that the shortfall was due to reasonable error and that reasonable steps are being taken to remedy the shortfall.[4]

The minimum distribution requirements will not be treated as violated, and, the 50 percent excise tax will not apply, where a shortfall occurs because assets are invested in a contract issued by an insurance company in state insurer delinquency proceedings.[5]

Planning Point: To request a waiver of all or part of the 50 percent penalty tax imposed on RMD amounts not distributed on time, a statement of explanation should be filed with Form 5329 for each tax year there is or was a failure to properly take RMDs. The letter must explain the "reasonable error" that caused the failure and the reasonable steps that were taken to correct the error. Although the IRS has not issued guidance on what is a "reasonable error," possible examples *may* include illness, death in the family, and notification of RMD not received from the financial institution.

3686. How are the minimum distribution requirements met during an IRA owner's lifetime?

Distributions from a non-Roth Individual Retirement Account ("IRA") or annuity must begin by April 1 of the year after the year in which the owner reaches age 72, whether or not

---

1.   Treas. Reg. §1.408-8, A-8.
2.   IRC Sec. 4974(a); Treas. Reg. §54.4974-1.
3.   Treas. Reg. §§54.4974-2, A-1, 54.4974-2, A-6.
4.   IRC Sec. 4974; Treas. Reg. §54.4974-2, A-7(a).
5.   Treas. Reg. §1.401(a)(9)-8, A-8.

the owner has retired.[1] Non-Roth IRA owners working beyond age 72 are not permitted to delay distributions until after retirement, even under an employer-sponsored plan such as a SEP or SIMPLE IRA. Unless the owner's entire interest is distributed on or before the required beginning date, distributions of the balance must begin by that date and must, at a minimum, be distributed over the time period explained below.

No minimum distribution is required during life from a Roth IRA.

Planning Point: RMDs were waived for 2020 under the CARES Act.

Uniform Lifetime Table

Required minimum distributions from a non-Roth IRA during the owner's lifetime are calculated by dividing the owner's account balance by the applicable distribution period determined from the RMD Uniform Lifetime Table found in Appendix F.[2] The amount of an individual's lifetime required distribution is calculated without regard to the beneficiary's age, except in the case of a spouse who is the sole beneficiary and who is more than 10 years younger than the owner.[3]

Planning Point: The IRS released new proposed life expectancy tables that would be used in calculating required minimum distributions from both IRAs and employer-sponsored retirement plans. The new tables generally assume longer life expectancies and provide information needed to calculate RMDs for participants living to 120 (the current tables stop at 115). For most clients, the primary impact will be seen in lower required distributions (beginning in 2021, 2020 RMDs will not be impacted because the new tables are still in proposed form). The new factor for clients aged 70 is 29.1 (up from 27.4) and for clients who are age 71, the factor increases to 28.2 (up from 26.5). Individuals taking RMDs from inherited accounts will also be entitled to switch to the new life expectancy tables under a proposed transition rule, as will those clients currently receiving substantially equal periodic payments. It is expected that the IRS will modify these tables in response to the SECURE Act.

The distribution required by April 1 is actually the distribution required for the year in which the owner attains age 72. Distributions for each calendar year after the year the owner becomes age 72 (including the year of the required beginning date) must be made by December 31 of that year.[4]

For purposes of calculating minimum distributions from an IRA for a calendar year, the account balance is determined as of December 31 of the immediately preceding calendar year (i.e., the valuation calendar year).[5]

Example: Ms. Getman is an IRA owner born on July 1, 1947. She reached age 72 on July 1, 2019. Consequently, Ms. Getman's required beginning date is April 1, 2020 (the year following the calendar year in which she turned 72). Assume that as of December 31, 2018, the value of Ms. Getman's IRA was $265,000. Because Ms. Getman's age in 2019 (the year for which her first distribution will be made) is 72, the applicable distribution period from the Uniform Lifetime Table is 25.6 years. Thus, the required distribution for

---

1.   Treas. Reg. §1.408-8, A-3.
2.   Treas. Reg. §1.401(a)(9)-9, A-2.
3.   Treas. Reg. §1.401(a)(9)-5, A-4.
4.   Treas. Reg. §1.401(a)(9)-5, A-1(b).
5.   Treas. Reg. §1.408-8, A-6.

calendar year 2019 is $10,352 ($265,000 ÷ 25.6). Assume that Ms. Getman receives this amount in 2020 shortly before her required beginning date of April 1, 2020.

Assume that the value of Ms. Getman's account balance as of December 31, 2019 is $254,648. This account balance is not reduced by the distribution received in early 2020. As a result, Ms. Getman's required minimum distribution for 2020 (when she is 73, which is due by December 31, 2020, would be $10,309.64 ($254,648 ÷ 24.7). Receiving a distribution of more than the required minimum will not reduce the amount Ms. Getman is required to take in a subsequent year.[1]

Spouse Beneficiary

If the IRA owner's spouse is the only designated beneficiary of the owner's entire interest at all times during the distribution year, the owner may receive distributions over the longer of the distribution period determined from the Uniform Lifetime Table or the joint and survivor life expectancy of the owner and spouse.[2] The joint and survivor life expectancy will provide a longer payout period only if the spouse is more than 10 years younger than the IRA owner. For details on the definition of "designated beneficiary," see Q 3696.

Charitable IRA Rollover

For tax years beginning in 2006 and thereafter, an IRA owner's required minimum distribution can be reduced, within limits, by the amount of a qualified charitable distribution of up to $100,000, transferred directly from the taxpayer's IRA to a qualified charity.[3] This provision does not apply to SEP IRAs or SIMPLE IRAs (Q 3996). This charitable rollover provision was made permanent by the Protecting Americans Against Tax Hikes Act of 2015 (PATH Act).

Distributions as Annuity Payments

IRA required minimum distributions that are made as annuity payments are calculated in the same manner as required minimum distributions from defined benefit plans (Q 3896).[4]

3687. How are the minimum distribution requirements met after the death of an IRA owner?

Editor's Note: See Q3691 for a discussion of the substantial changes the SECURE Act made to the distribution rules governing IRAs inherited by non-spouse beneficiaries. The rules below apply to tax years beginning before 2020.

Prior to 2020, the minimum distribution requirements that applied after the death of an IRA owner depended on whether the IRA owner died before (see Q 3688) or after (see Q 3689) the required beginning date.

Distributions generally were treated as having begun in accordance with the minimum distribution requirements under IRC Section 401(a)(9)(A)(ii). If distributions irrevocably (except for acceleration) began prior to the required beginning date in the form of an annuity

---

1.   Treas. Reg. §§1.408-8, A-6, 1.401(a)(9)-5, A-3.
2.   Treas. Reg. §1.401(a)(9)-5, A-4(b).
3.   IRC Sec. 408(d)(8).
4.   Treas. Reg. §§1.408-8, A-1, 1.401(a)(9)-6.

that meets the minimum distribution rules, the annuity starting date would be treated as the required beginning date for purposes of calculating lifetime and after death minimum distribution requirements.[1]

3688. How are the minimum distribution requirements met when an IRA owner dies before the required beginning date?

Editor's Note: See Q 3691 for a discussion of the substantial changes the SECURE Act made to the distribution rules governing IRAs inherited by non-spouse beneficiaries. The rules below apply to IRAs whose owners died in tax years beginning before 2020. Beginning in 2020, most non-spouse beneficiaries will be required to deplete the account value within 10 years of the original owner's death.

Pre-SECURE Act Rules

If an IRA owner dies before the required beginning date, distributions must be made under either a life expectancy method or the five year rule.[2] After-death distributions from a Roth IRA will also be determined under these rules because the Roth IRA owner is treated as having died before the required beginning date.[3]

Life Expectancy Method

Under the life expectancy rule, if any portion of the interest is payable to, or for the benefit of, a designated beneficiary, that portion must be distributed over the life (or life expectancy) of the designated beneficiary (Q 3696).[4]

To the extent that the interest is payable to a nonspouse beneficiary, distributions must begin by December 31 of the calendar year immediately following the year in which the IRA owner died.[5] The nonspouse beneficiary's life expectancy for this purpose is measured as of his or her birthday in the year following the year of the owner's death and is determined using the Single Life Table (see Appendix F).[6] In subsequent years, this amount is reduced by one for each calendar year that has elapsed since the year of the owner's death.[7] After the death of a nonspouse beneficiary, the payout period to the successor beneficiary will be determined using the deceased beneficiary's remaining life expectancy (based on the age of the beneficiary in the calendar year of death) reduced by one for each calendar year that elapses thereafter.[8]

For the treatment of multiple beneficiaries, see Q 3696.

---

1.   Treas. Reg. §1.401(a)(9)-6, A-10; Treas. Reg. §1.408-8, A-1.
2.   Treas. Reg. §1.401(a)(9)-3, A-1(a).
3.   Treas. Reg. §1.408A-6, A-14(b).
4.   IRC Sec. 401(a)(9)(B)(iii), Treas. Reg. §1.401(a)(9)-3, A-1(a).
5.   Treas. Reg. §1.401(a)(9)-3, A-3.
6.   Treas. Reg. §1.401(a)(9)-9.
7.   Treas. Reg. §1.401(a)(9)-5, A-5(c)(1).
8.   Treas. Reg. §1.401(a)(9)-5, A-7(c)(2).

Planning Point: The term "stretch IRA" does not appear in the Internal Revenue Code, but describes the practice of IRA distribution planning that successfully permits the beneficiaries (e.g., a surviving spouse and a child of the owner) to receive (or "stretch") distributions over their individual life expectancies under the foregoing rules.

Prior to the SECURE Act's change, a younger beneficiary allowed for greater stretching given the longer life expectancy. When there are multiple beneficiaries, separate account rules must be followed for each designated beneficiary to use his or her own life expectancy for calculating RMDs.

A surviving spouse who is the sole designated beneficiary of an IRA generally may elect to treat the IRA as his or her own (see Q 3690). Unless this election is made, distributions to a surviving spouse beneficiary must begin by the later of the end of the calendar year immediately following the calendar year in which the owner died, or the end of the calendar year in which the owner would have reached age 70½.[1] The payout period is the surviving spouse's life expectancy, based on his or her attained age in each calendar year for which a minimum distribution is required.[2] After the surviving spouse dies, the payout period is that spouse's remaining life expectancy, based on the age of the spouse in the calendar year of death, reduced by one for each calendar year that elapses thereafter.[3]

A designated beneficiary who does not elect the five year method but fails to timely start distributions under the life expectancy method may be able to make up the missed RMDs and pay the 50 percent penalty on the missed distributions, rather than receive the entire balance within five years.[4]

Five Year Method

Under the five year rule, the entire interest must be distributed within five years after the death of the IRA owner (regardless of who or what entity receives the distribution).[5] To satisfy this rule, the entire interest must be distributed by the end of the calendar year that contains the fifth anniversary of the date of the IRA owner's death.[6]

Planning Point: The five year period was expanded to six years if 2009 was one of the five years.[7]

3689. How are the minimum distribution requirements met when an IRA owner dies on or after the required beginning date?

Editor's Note: See Q 3691 for a discussion of the substantial changes the SECURE Act made to the distribution rules governing IRAs inherited by non-spouse beneficiaries. The rules below apply to IRAs whose owners died in tax years beginning before 2020.

---

1. IRC Sec. 401(a)(9)(B)(iv); Treas. Reg. §1.401(a)(9)-3, A-3.
2. Treas. Reg. §1.401(a)(9)-5, A-5(c)(2).
3. Treas. Reg. §1.401(a)(9)-5, A-5(c)(2).
4. Let. Rul. 200811028.
5. IRC Sec. 401(a)(9)(B)(ii); Treas. Reg. §1.401(a)(9)-3, A-1(a).
6. Treas. Reg. §1.401(a)(9)-3, A-2.
7. IRC Sec. 401(a)(9)(H)(ii).

Prior to 2020, if the owner of an IRA died on or after the date minimum distributions have begun (i.e., the required beginning date), but before the entire interest in the IRA has been distributed, the entire remaining balance generally must be distributed at least as rapidly as under the method of distribution in effect at the owner's date of death.[1]

If the IRA owner does not have a designated beneficiary as of the date on which the designated beneficiary is determined (the "determination date;" i.e., September 30th of the year after death, see Q 3696), the IRA owner's interest was distributed over his or her remaining life expectancy, using the age of the owner in the calendar year of his or her death, reduced by one for each calendar year that elapses thereafter.[2]

If the owner does have a designated beneficiary as of the determination date, the beneficiary's interest was distributed over the longer of (1) the beneficiary's life expectancy, calculated as described under the "Life Expectancy Method," in Q 3688 or (2) the remaining life expectancy of the owner, determined using the age of the owner in the calendar year of his or her death, reduced by one for each calendar year that elapses thereafter.[3]

For the treatment of multiple beneficiaries and separate accounts, see Q 3696.

3690. What distribution requirements apply to an IRA that is inherited by a surviving spouse?

Editor's Note: See Q 3691 for a discussion of the substantial changes the SECURE Act made to the distribution rules governing IRAs inherited by non-spouse beneficiaries.

While a surviving spouse may elect to treat an inherited IRA in the same manner as a non-spousal beneficiary (see Q 3691), a surviving spouse of an IRA owner who is the sole beneficiary of an IRA and who has an unlimited right to make withdrawals from the IRA may also elect to treat the entire account as his or her own IRA. This election can be made at any time after the IRA owner's death.[4] Post-SECURE Act, surviving spouses qualify as eligible designated beneficiaries (EDBs), so the pre-SECURE Act distribution rules continue to apply.

Any minimum distribution that was required to be made to the deceased owner, but had not been made before the owner's death, must be made to the surviving spouse in the year of death, but in all other respects, required distributions after the owner's death are determined as if the surviving spouse were the owner.[5]

The surviving spouse will be deemed to have made the election to treat the IRA as his or her own if any required amounts in the account have not been distributed under the requirements for after-death required minimum distributions, or any additional amounts are contributed to the account or to an account or annuity to which the surviving spouse has rolled over the amounts.[6]

---

1.   IRC Sec. 401(a)(9)(B)(i).
2.   Treas. Reg. §1.401(a)(9)-5, A-5(c)(3).
3.   Treas. Reg. §1.401(a)(9)-5, A-5(c)(3); Treas. Reg. §1.401(a)(9)-5, A-5(a)(1).
4.   Treas. Reg. §1.408-8, A-5(a).
5.   Treas. Reg. §1.408-8, A-5(a).
6.   Treas. Reg. §1.408-8, A-5(b).

The result of a surviving spouse making the election to treat an IRA as his or her own is that the surviving spouse then will be considered the IRA owner for all other income tax purposes (for example, for purposes of the 10 percent penalty on early distributions).[1]

In the event that a surviving spouse beneficiary dies after the IRA owner, but before distributions to the spouse have begun, the 10-year rule, five-year rule and the life expectancy rule described in Q 3688 and Q 3691 will be applied as though the surviving spouse were the IRA owner.[2] As a result, the distribution period is determined depending upon the identity of the surviving spouse's designated beneficiary, determined as of the date of the surviving spouse's death.[3] This provision does not allow a new spouse of the deceased IRA owner's surviving spouse to delay distributions under the surviving spouse rules of IRC 401(a)(9)(B)(iv).[4]

Planning Point: A surviving spouse who is younger than 59½ years old and needs money should consider remaining a named beneficiary of the inherited IRA. As a named beneficiary, the surviving spouse can access the inherited IRA without incurring penalties–as compared to rolling the account into the spouse's own IRA, where a distribution prior to 59½ could be subject to the 10 percent penalty.

A surviving spouse who is younger than 72 years old and does not need money from the IRA should consider rolling the money into the spouse's own IRA to delay RMDs until the spouse is 72, which allows the account to continue growing tax-deferred.

3691. What distribution requirements apply to an inherited IRA where the beneficiary is not the surviving spouse?

Distribution requirements for an inherited IRA for a nonspouse beneficiary will depend on whether the IRA owner died before, on or after the required beginning date. The SECURE Act made substantial changes that eliminate the "life expectancy method" and "five-year method", discussed under the heading below, for most account beneficiaries. Under the new law, most nonspouse account beneficiaries will be required to take distributions over a 10-year period following the original account owner's death (the 10-year rule).

The law did not change the rules applicable to surviving spouses who inherit retirement accounts. Exceptions also exist for disabled beneficiaries, chronically ill beneficiaries and children who have not reached "the age of majority". A child who inherits may not be treated as reaching the age of majority (even upon reaching age 18 or 21) if that child has not completed a specified course of education (further guidance is expected as to what exactly qualifies as a "specified course of education"). A trust may be used to secure payments from the inherited account over the life expectancy of a disabled or chronically ill beneficiary. The new 10-year rule also does not apply to an account beneficiary who is not more than 10 years younger than the original account owner.

1.   Treas. Reg. §1.408-8, A-5(c); see *Gee v. Comm.*, 127 TC 1 (2006).
2.   IRC Sec. 401(a)(9)(B)(iv)(II); Treas. Reg. §1.401(a)(9)-4, A-4(b); see Let. Rul. 200436017.
3.   Treas. Reg. §1.401(a)(9)-4,A-4(b).
4.   Treas. Reg. §1.401(a)(9)-4,A-4(b).

The new rule applies for IRAs whose owners died in tax years beginning after December 31, 2019 and applies to all defined contribution-type plans (the rules governing distributions from Roth IRAs were not changed).

Pre-SECURE Act Law: Death Before Required Beginning Date

Prior to 2020, if an IRA owner died before the required beginning date, distributions were required to be made under either a life expectancy method or the five-year rule (Q 3688).[1] After-death distributions from a Roth IRA also will be determined under these rules because the Roth IRA owner is treated as having died before the required beginning date.[2]

Planning Point: The CARES Act provided relief to IRA owners by eliminating the need to take 2020 RMDs. This relief also extends to beneficiaries of inherited accounts. For account beneficiaries subject to the five-year rule, the CARES Act provides that if 2020 is one of those five years, it is not counted--essentially extending the distribution period to six years.

Under the life expectancy rule, if any portion of the interest was payable to, or for the benefit of, a designated beneficiary, that portion could be distributed over the life (or life expectancy) of the designated beneficiary, beginning within one year of the owner's death.[3] To the extent that the interest is payable to a nonspouse beneficiary, distributions had to begin by the end of the calendar year immediately following the calendar year in which the IRA owner died.[4] The nonspouse beneficiary's life expectancy for this purpose was measured as of the beneficiary's birthday in the year following the year of the owner's death. In subsequent years, this amount was reduced by one for each calendar year that has elapsed since the year of the owner's death.[5]

A person who wishes to use the life expectancy method and failed to timely start distributions could make up the missed RMDs and pay the 50 percent penalty on the missed distributions.[6]

Under the five-year rule, the entire interest had to be distributed within five years after the death of the IRA owner (regardless of who or what entity receives the distribution).[7] To satisfy this rule, the entire interest must be distributed by the end of the calendar year that contains the fifth anniversary of the date of the IRA owner's death.[8]

Pre-SECURE Act Law: Death On or After Required Beginning Date

If the owner of an IRA dies on or after the date distributions have begun (i.e., generally the required beginning date), but before the entire interest in the IRA has been distributed, the entire remaining balance generally must be distributed at least as rapidly as under the method of distribution in effect as of the owner's date of death (Q 3689).[9]

1.   Treas. Reg. §1.401(a)(9)-3, A-1(a).
2.   Treas. Reg. §1.408A-6, A-14(b).
3.   IRC Sec. 401(a)(9)(B)(iii), Treas. Reg. §1.401(a)(9)-3, A-1(a).
4.   Treas. Reg. §1.401(a)(9)-3, A-3.
5.   Treas. Reg. §1.401(a)(9)-5, A-5(c)(1).
6.   Let. Rul. 200811028.
7.   IRC Sec. 401(a)(9)(B)(ii); Treas. Reg. §1.401(a)(9)-3, A-1(a).
8.   Treas. Reg. §1.401(a)(9)-3, A-2.
9.   IRC Sec. 401(a)(9)(B)(i).

If the IRA owner does not have a designated beneficiary as of the date on which the designated beneficiary is determined (i.e., September 30 of the year after death) the IRA owner's interest is distributed over the remaining life expectancy, using the age of the owner in the calendar year of death, reduced by one for each calendar year that elapses thereafter.[1]

If the owner does have a designated beneficiary as of the determination date, the beneficiary's interest is distributed over the longer of (1) the beneficiary's life expectancy, calculated as described in Q 3688[2] or (2) the remaining life expectancy of the owner, determined using the age of the owner in the calendar year of his or her death, reduced by one for each calendar year that elapses thereafter.[3]

See Q 3690 for the treatment of an IRA that is inherited by a surviving spouse.

3692. How could an IRA be used to stretch the tax benefits of funds held within an inherited 401(k) over a beneficiary's lifetime prior to 2020?

Editor's Note: Beginning in 2020, most inherited IRAs inherited by non-spouse beneficiaries must be depleted within 10 years of the original account owner's death under the SECURE Act.

Inherited IRAs generally allowed an individual to "stretch" the tax-deferral associated with these accounts by providing for distribution of the account value over a period of years following the original account owner's death. Typically, the account beneficiary will take distributions over his or her lifetime or exhaust the account funds within five years of the original owner's death, which allows the account value to continue to grow and stretches the tax liability that accompanies the distributions over a period of years.[4] See Q 3687 to Q 3689 for a discussion of the distribution rules that apply following the original account owner's death.

Qualified plans (such as 401(k)s and profit-sharing plans), however, have always been subject to a different set of rules that do not allow the funds to be distributed over time. As a result, when a 401(k) is inherited, the funds will usually be distributed immediately in a single lump sum payment, resulting in an immediate tax liability for the beneficiary.

If the designated beneficiary of an inherited 401(k) is an individual, prior to 2020, he or she had the option of rolling the inherited account funds into an IRA that would be treated as an inherited IRA, thus allowing the individual to stretch distributions over his or her life expectancy (or over a five-year period). The rollover had to be accomplished through a trustee-to-trustee transfer whereby the 401(k) plan administrator transfers the funds directly into a new IRA account that only holds the inherited 401(k) funds.

If the original account owner has failed to name a beneficiary, the IRA will likely be paid out to his or her estate upon death—which will cause a loss of the tax-deferral benefits that can otherwise be realized with an inherited IRA. This is because the favorable rules that allow the

1. Treas. Reg. §1.401(a)(9)-5, A-5(c)(3).
2. Treas. Reg. §1.401(a)(9)-5, A-5(c)(1), (2).
3. Treas. Reg. §§1.401(a)(9)-5, A-5(c)(3); 1.401(a)(9)-5, A-5(a)(1).
4. See Treas. Reg. §§1.401(a)(9)-6, 1.408-8.

account value to be distributed over time only apply if the account's designated beneficiary is an individual (or a trust, the beneficiary of which is an individual) that actually has a life expectancy.[1]

Further, if the estate is the beneficiary of an inherited qualified plan (401(k)), the taxpayer loses the option of rolling the funds into an inherited IRA in order to maximize the tax-deferral potential.

3693. What is the difference between a spousal inherited IRA and a non-spousal inherited IRA? What do taxpayers need to be aware of with respect to the differences between these types of accounts?

The primary difference between a spousal inherited IRA and a non-spousal inherited IRA lies in the requirements that apply with respect to required minimum distributions (RMDs) after the original account owner's death. A spouse who inherits his or her deceased spouse's IRA is essentially entitled to treat the IRA as though it was the surviving spouse's own IRA.[2] This can potentially allow a younger beneficiary to delay taking RMDs until that individual reaches age 72.

A non-spouse IRA beneficiary will be required to close the account within 10 years, or use the beneficiary's life expectancy if the beneficiary qualifies as an eligible designated beneficiary under the SECURE Act rules. Non-spouse beneficiaries subject to the 10-year rule are not required to take distributions every year. But depending on the tax bracket of the beneficiary that may be wise to ensure the beneficiary is not put into a higher tax bracket if a large lump sum is taken in the 10th year.

Unlike in the case of an IRA that is inherited by a surviving spouse, non-spouse beneficiaries of inherited accounts are not entitled to complete 60-day tax-free rollovers to another account, so that the only way of moving the funds without the entire amount being deemed a taxable transaction is through a trustee-to-trustee transfer. The account to which the funds are moved must be properly titled, with an indication that the account is an inherited account, and both the names of the original owner and beneficiary.

If multiple beneficiaries exist, the account should first be split into separate accounts so that each beneficiary's distributions can be determined based on the beneficiary's status.

3694. What differences exist between the treatment of inherited IRAs and inherited 401(k)s?

While inherited IRAs often may be distributed over time (potentially spreading the associated tax liability over 10 years or the beneficiary's lifetime), qualified plans (such as 401(k)s and profit sharing plans) are subject to a different set of rules that do not allow the funds to be distributed over time. As a result, when a taxpayer inherits a 401(k), the funds typically must be distributed immediately in a single lump sum payment, resulting in an immediate tax liability for the beneficiary. Most plans will specifically require lump sum distribution treatment because of the administrative burdens associated with allowing stretched out distributions.

---

1.   See Treas. Reg. §1.401(a)(9)-4.
2.   Treas. Reg. §1.408-8, A-5(a).

Despite this, certain beneficiaries can roll those funds into an inherited IRA. Once the funds are in the inherited IRA, they must be distributed according to the same rules that govern inherited IRAs. While this option is now generally mandatory (under IRC Section 402; prior to 2010, a plan only had the option of allowing an inherited 401(k)-to-inherited IRA rollover), not all beneficiaries are eligible to roll inherited 401(k) funds into an inherited IRA.

Note that after 2020, once rolled into an IRA, the funds must be withdrawn within 10 years unless the beneficiary is an eligible designated beneficiary.

Only a designated beneficiary is entitled to take advantage of the option of rolling the inherited 401(k) funds into an inherited IRA. A designated beneficiary for this purpose means an individual, or certain trusts that qualify as "see through" or "look through" trusts. This means that the trust is an irrevocable trust that is valid under state law and identifies the beneficiaries of the trust as individuals (the trustee also must provide a copy of the trust document). The rollover must be accomplished in a trustee-to-trustee transfer (i.e., directly between the relevant financial institutions).

Planning Point: Estates and other trusts that inherit a 401(k) are generally not designated beneficiaries for purposes of the distribution rules, so their distribution rights will be limited to those provided in the plan document itself.

3695. Are inherited IRA funds exempt from the claims of a taxpayer's creditors in bankruptcy?

Whether or not the funds in an inherited IRA are exempt from the claims of a taxpayer's creditors in bankruptcy has been an issue that many have disagreed upon in the past, but that the Supreme Court resolved in 2014.[1] Under current law, the funds in an inherited IRA are subject to the claims of a beneficiary-debtor's creditors in bankruptcy *if* the account is inherited by a beneficiary *who is not the original account owner's surviving spouse.*

Traditional and Roth IRAs that are not inherited accounts are typically exempt from bankruptcy claims up to an inflation-adjusted $1 million limit (which is adjusted every three years; the new exemption, updated April 1, 2019, is $1,362,800, and between April 1, 2016 and April 1, 2019, the exemption was $1,283,025) (Q 3653).[2]

Prior to the Supreme Court's review of the issue, in some jurisdictions (the Eighth Circuit, for example), inherited IRAs were exempt from bankruptcy claims based on the premise that the funds are retirement funds contained in otherwise tax-exempt vehicles. However, other courts had held that inherited IRAs lack the requisite retirement purpose. The rationale behind this line of decisions (most prominently found in the Seventh Circuit) was that inherited IRAs are subject to an entirely different set of rules than IRAs held by their original owners.

Importantly, while a penalty is imposed on any non-inherited IRA funds that are withdrawn by the owner prior to a certain age, inherited IRA assets are liquid assets that can be accessed

---

1.   *Clark v. Rameker,* 134 S. Ct. 2242 (2014).
2.   11 U.S.C. §522.

by the beneficiary at any time and without penalty. Further, the rules actually require that the inherited IRA funds be withdrawn within a relatively short time frame (either within five years, 10 years, or over the beneficiary's life expectancy, see Q 3690 and Q 3691) set without regard to the typical retirement age.

This split among the circuits prompted the Supreme Court's review of the issue. Though the rule is now settled with respect to *nonspouse* beneficiaries, taxpayers should note that the Supreme Court decision did not specifically address the issue of IRAs that are inherited by a surviving spouse (see Q 3690).

Planning Point: To provide beneficiaries of an inherited IRA with creditor protection, an IRA owner should consider naming a trust (or trusts) as a beneficiary of the IRA. In order to preserve the "stretch" options (Q 3688), a "see-through" trust should be used (Q 3906).

3696. Who is a "designated beneficiary" for purposes of required minimum distributions from an IRA?

A designated beneficiary is an individual (or a trust meeting certain requirements, see Q 3903) designated as a beneficiary, either by the terms of the IRA plan document or by an affirmative election of the IRA owner (or such owner's surviving spouse).[1]

The designated beneficiary need not be specified by name to be a designated beneficiary so long as that beneficiary is identifiable under the terms of the IRA as of the determination date.[2] For special rules governing contingent and successor beneficiaries, see Q 3903.

For lifetime distributions, the identity and age of the designated beneficiary does not affect the IRA owner's distributions unless the sole designated beneficiary is a spouse more than 10 years younger than the owner (Q 3686). After 2020, the beneficiary's status is determined as of the date of death.

Under pre-2020 law, for purposes of after-death minimum distribution requirements, the final regulations required that a beneficiary determination be made as of September 30 of the year after the year of the IRA owner's death (i.e., the determination date).[3] This date was designed to provide ample time following the determination of the designated beneficiary(ies) to calculate and make the required distribution prior to the distribution deadline (i.e., the end of the calendar year following the owner's death).[4] Exceptions to the September 30 deadline applied if the account was payable as an annuity, or if a surviving spouse beneficiary died after the IRA owner but before distributions had begun.

An individual who was a beneficiary as of the date of the owner's death, but who is not a beneficiary as of September 30 of the following year (e.g., because the individual disclaims entitlement to the benefit or because the individual receives the entire benefit to which the

---

1.   Treas. Reg. §1.401(a)(9)-4, A-1.
2.   Treas. Reg. §1.401(a)(9)-4, A-1.
3.   Treas. Reg. §1.401(a)(9)-4, A-4(a).
4.   Treas. Reg. §1.401(a)(9)-3, A-3(a).

individual is entitled before that date) is not taken into account for purposes of determining the distribution period for required minimum distributions after the owner's death.[1]

A disclaiming beneficiary's receipt of a required distribution, prior to disclaiming the benefit, in the year after death, will not result in the beneficiary being treated as a designated beneficiary for subsequent years.[2] In a private letter ruling, the IRS also determined that a post death reformation of a beneficiary designation form that had inadvertently excluded a decedent's children was effective to create a "designated beneficiary."[3] The children had been omitted as contingent beneficiaries on their father's beneficiary designation due to a mistake by a bank employee, and not due to their fault. The children were therefore allowed to set up inherited IRAs after their father's death.

If a beneficiary is not an individual or a permitted trust, the IRA owner will be treated as having no designated beneficiary and the five year rule will apply (Q 3688). An IRA owner's estate may not be a designated beneficiary.[4] This rule continues to apply even after the SECURE Act became effective in 2020.

Generally, only an individual (not an estate or a trust) may be a designated beneficiary for required minimum distribution purposes. For example, if an IRA owner fails to name a beneficiary on the beneficiary designation form and the IRA plan document provides that in such a case benefits are paid to the owner's estate, the estate beneficiaries will be barred from using the 10-year or life expectancy method, and the five year rule will apply.[5] However, when a trust is named as a beneficiary and the special requirements for a "see-through" trust are met (Q 3906), the beneficiaries of a trust may be treated as if they had been designated as the beneficiaries of the IRA for required minimum distribution purposes (but not for purposes of "separate account treatment," see Q 3697).

In general, a valid see-through trust must satisfy the following four requirements: (1) the trust must be valid under state law, (2) the trust must be irrevocable, or must become irrevocable upon the death of the original account owner, (3) the beneficiaries of the trust who are to be beneficiaries of the IRA must be identifiable from the trust instrument itself, and (4) relevant documentation must have been provided to the plan administrator in a timely manner.[6] In this case, the life expectancy of the oldest of all trust beneficiaries will be used to determine the minimum distribution requirements that apply after the death of the original account owner.[7]

Planning Point: Prior to 2020, when multiple beneficiaries are involved, there may have been a benefit to establishing separate accounts (Q 3697), when available, or removing certain beneficiaries (via a disclaimer or lump sum distribution) between the date of the owner's death and the determination date (i.e. September 30 of the year following owner's death), as the minimum distribution requirements were determined based on the beneficiaries who still held an interest in the account as of the September 30th date.

---

1.   Treas. Reg. §1.401(a)(9)-4, A-4(a).
2.   Rev. Rul. 2005-36, 2005-1 CB 1368.
3.   Let. Rul. 200616039.
4.   Treas. Reg. §1.401(a)(9)-4, A-3.
5.   Treas. Reg. §1.401(a)(9)-4, A-3.
6.   Treas. Reg. §1.401(a)(9)-4, A-5.
7.   Treas. Reg. §1.401(a)(9)-5, A-7.

For example, prior to 2020, if an IRA owner died naming a charity and owner's son as equal beneficiaries, the son would have been prevented from using his own life expectancy to determine required minimum distributions if the charity (a non-individual) still held an interest in the IRA as of the determination date. However, if the charity received a distribution from the IRA in full satisfaction of its interest prior to September 30, son would be considered a sole designated beneficiary and could use his own life expectancy to determine required minimum distributions.

3697. Prior to the SECURE Act, what were the rules for determining required minimum distributions when there were multiple beneficiaries and separate accounts?

Editor's Note: Beginning in 2020, non-spouse beneficiaries who do not qualify as eligible designated beneficiaries must generally deplete the account within 10 years of the original account owner's death. Therefore, the life expectancy rules discussed below are no longer relevant unless the beneficiary qualifies as an eligible designated beneficiary.

If more than one beneficiary is designated as of the determination date (Q 3696), the beneficiary with the shortest life expectancy (i.e., generally the oldest) will be the designated beneficiary for purposes of determining the distribution period.[1]

As an exception to the "oldest beneficiary" rule, if an individual account (including an IRA)[2] is divided into separate accounts (as defined below) with different beneficiaries, the separate accounts do not have to be aggregated for purposes of determining the required minimum distributions for years subsequent to the calendar year in which the separate accounts were established (or date of death, if later).[3]

For purposes of Section 401(a)(9), "separate accounts" are portions of an employee's benefit (or IRA) representing the separate interests of the employee's beneficiaries under the plan as of his date of death. The separate accounting must allocate all post-death investment gains and losses, contributions, and forfeitures for the period prior to the establishment of the separate accounts on a pro rata basis in a reasonable and consistent manner among the accounts. Once separate accounts have been established, the separate accounting can provide for separate investments in each account, with gains and losses attributable to such investments allocable only to that account. A separate accounting also must allocate any post-death distribution to the separate account of the beneficiary receiving it.[4]

Planning Point: When leaving an IRA to multiple beneficiaries, an owner may leave a fixed dollar ("pecuniary") amount to one or more of them, with a "residual" gift to one or more other beneficiaries, or use "fractional"-type gifts for all beneficiaries. Although both methods are legal and acceptable, fractional gifts usually are preferable, for two reasons.

---

1.   Treas. Reg. §1.401(a)(9)-5, A-7(a).
2.   Treas. Reg. §1.408-8, A-1(a).
3.   Treas. Reg. §1.401(a)(9)-8, A-2(a)(2).
4.   Treas. Reg. §1.401(a)(9)-8, A-3.

First, if the owner uses a pecuniary gift (such as "pay $10,000 to Beneficiary A and the balance of the account to Beneficiary B"), the IRA provider may not know whether to give the "pecuniary" beneficiary just the flat dollar amount or to give that beneficiary the dollar amount plus or minus gains or losses that accrue after the date of death. The IRA provider's documents and policies should spell this out, but many do not.

Second, if the gift is truly a flat dollar amount, not adjusted for gains or losses occurring after the date of death, then that gift cannot qualify under the regulations as a "separate account" (see above) for minimum distribution purposes. Thus, the beneficiary of the flat dollar gift and the beneficiaries of the "residuary" gift will be considered beneficiaries of the same account. *Natalie B. Choate, Esq., Bingham McCutchen.*

When separate accounts are established with different beneficiaries, the "applicable distribution period" is determined for each separate account disregarding the other beneficiaries only if the separate account is established no later than December 31 of the year following the decedent's death.[1] If this deadline is not met, separate accounts can be established at any time, but the distribution period in effect prior to the separation of the accounts (generally the life expectancy of the oldest beneficiary) will continue to be applied.[2]

Planning Point: If the foregoing requirements are not met (i.e., if separate accounts are not established by the deadline or to the extent the IRA proceeds were payable to one trust benefiting more than one individual), the IRA nonetheless may be segregated into separate IRA accounts, but the "applicable distribution period" will be the life expectancy of the beneficiary with the shortest life expectancy.[3]

If a trust is the beneficiary, separate account treatment is not available to the beneficiaries of the trust.[4] Using the pre-2020 rules, the IRS has determined repeatedly that the establishment of separate IRA shares (i.e., creating separate IRAs titled in the name of the decedent for the benefit of the trust beneficiaries) did not entitle multiple beneficiaries of the same trust to use their own life expectancies as the distribution period.[5] Where the trust established by the decedent to receive IRA proceeds included provisions for a subtrust benefiting the surviving spouse, the surviving spouse's life expectancy was found to be controlling for all beneficiaries.[6] In another instance, the IRS determined that where a father had failed to designate an IRA beneficiary, making his estate, which was left to his three children, the beneficiary, the decedent's remaining life expectancy was controlling, although a subdivision of the IRA was permitted.[7] The fact that the trust meets the requirements for a "see-through trust" (Q 3899) does not change this result.[8]

The IRS has privately ruled, however, that where separate individual trusts were named as beneficiaries, the ability of each beneficiary to use his or her life expectancy was preserved even though the trusts were governed by a single "master trust."[9]

1.   Treas. Reg. §1.401(a)(9)-8, A-2(a)(2).
2.   TD 8987, 67 Fed. Reg. 18988 (4-17-02).
3.   Treas. Reg. §1.401(a)(9)-8, A-2(a)(2).
4.   Treas. Reg. §1.401(a)(9)-4, A-5(c).
5.   Let. Ruls. 200307095, 200317043, 200444033, 200432027, 200528031, 201503024.
6.   Let. Ruls. 200410019, 200438044.
7.   Let. Rul. 200343030.
8.   Let. Rul. 200317044.
9.   Let. Rul. 200537044.

For details regarding contingent and successor beneficiaries, as well as other special rules, see Q 3899.

3698. What are an IRA trustee's reporting requirements with respect to required minimum distributions?

Two reporting requirements are imposed on IRA trustees: one to the IRA owner, and one to the IRS.[1] For IRA owners, "[i]f a minimum distribution is required with respect to an IRA for a calendar year and the IRA owner is alive at the beginning of the year, the trustee that held the IRA as of December 31 of the prior year must provide a statement to the IRA owner by January 31 of the calendar year." The statement must satisfy one of the following alternatives:

(1)   It must inform the IRA owner of the amount of the required minimum distribution and the date by which it is required. The amount is permitted to be calculated assuming that the sole beneficiary of the IRA is not a spouse more than 10 years younger than the IRA owner, and that no amounts received by the IRA after December 31 of the prior year are required to be taken into account to adjust the value of the IRA as of December 31 of the prior year for purposes of determining the required minimum distribution.[2]

(2)   It must inform the IRA owner that a minimum distribution is required with respect to the IRA, and offer to calculate the amount of the distribution on request by the owner.[3]

The IRS has clarified that a trustee may use either of these two alternatives, or may use one alternative for some IRA owners and the other for other IRA owners.[4]

The reporting requirements apply only to lifetime distributions. The IRA owner is presumed not to have a spouse more than 10 years younger than the owner.[5]

No reporting is required for after death distributions (i.e. inherited IRAs) or for Roth IRAs.[6]

3699. What IRS filing requirements does an individual retirement plan participant have to meet?

An individual who establishes an individual retirement plan does not have a filing requirement (other than what is reported on the individual's 1040) for any year in which there is no plan activity other than a recharacterization or the making of contributions (other than rollover contributions) and permissible distributions.

---

1.   Notice 2002-27, 2002-1 CB 814.
2.   See Treas. Reg. §1.408-8, A-7 or A-8.
3.   Notice 2002-27, clarified by Notice 2003-3.
4.   Notice 2003-3, 2003-1 CB 258, Notice 2009-9, 2009-5 IRB.
5.   Notice 2002-27, 2002-1 CB 814.
6.   Notice 2002-27.

However, an individual does need to file Form 5329 with their tax return if there is any tax due because of an early (premature) distribution (Q 3677), excess contribution (Q 3669), or excess accumulation (Q 3682).[1]

Moreover, a separate form also is required when nondeductible contributions are made to an IRA (see below).

Nondeductible Contributions

If an individual makes a nondeductible contribution to a traditional IRA for any year, the individual must report the following on Form 8606:

(1)   The amount of the nondeductible contributions for the taxable year

(2)   The amount of distributions from individual retirement plans for the taxable year

(3)   The excess of the aggregate amount of nondeductible contributions for all preceding years over the aggregate amount of distributions that were excludable from income for such taxable years

(4)   The aggregate balance of all individual retirement plans as of the close of the year in which the taxable year begins

(5)   The amount of a traditional IRA that is converted into and recharacterized as a Roth IRA, or the amount in the same Roth IRA that is then converted back into and recharacterized as a traditional IRA (prior to 2018, the Roth recharacterization rules were generally eliminated for tax years beginning after 2017)

(6)   Any other information as prescribed by the Secretary of the Treasury[2]

Failure to file Form 8606 will result in a $50 penalty per failure unless it is shown that the failure was due to reasonable cause.[3] In one case, a failure to file a Form 8606 resulted in the taxpayer's inability to appropriately document his basis in his nondeductible IRA; contributions were taxed a second time on distribution (Q 3671).[4] Overstatement of a nondeductible contribution is subject to a penalty tax of $100 per occurrence.[5]

3700. May an employer contribute to an IRA on behalf of an employee? May an employer or union establish an IRA for its employees or members?

Yes.

An employer may contribute to a traditional or Roth IRA on behalf of any eligible employee (or an eligible spouse in some cases). Any contribution made by the employer must be included

---

1.   IRC Secs. 6058(d), 6058(e).
2.   IRC Sec. 408(o).
3.   IRC Sec. 6693(b)(2).
4.   *Alpern v. Comm.*, TC Memo 2000-246.
5.   IRC Sec. 6693(b)(1).

in the employee's gross income as compensation for the year for which the contribution was made.[1] The employer's contribution is treated as though made by the employee and subject to the maximum contribution limits applicable to individual retirement plans (Q 3656, Q 3659). If the contribution is made to a traditional IRA and the employee is eligible, the employee may take a deduction subject to the limits in Q 3656. The employer deducts the contribution as salary or other compensation and not as a contribution to a retirement plan.[2] Because amounts contributed by an employer are compensation to the employee, they are subject to FICA (Social Security tax), FUTA (federal unemployment tax), and income tax withholding.[3]

A trust that will be treated as an individual retirement account may be set up by an employer or association of employees for the benefit of employees, members, or employees of members (or the eligible spouses of any of the foregoing) if the trust meets all the requirements of an IRA (Q 3641) and there is a separate accounting maintained for each employee, member, or spouse. A contribution made by an employer to a trust on behalf of an employee will be treated as a contribution to an individual retirement plan by such employee. The assets of an employer or association trust may be held in a common fund for the account of all individuals who have an interest in the trust. A trust may include amounts held for former employees or members and employees temporarily on leave. To qualify as an "association of employees" there must initially have been some nexus between the employees (e.g., a common employer, a common industry, etc.). An association may include members who are self-employed.[4]

Employer contributions to an IRA (or employer or association trust that is treated as an individual retirement account) do not need to meet the nondiscrimination rules associated with qualified plans. An employer generally cannot satisfy the coverage requirement for a qualified plan by contributing to an individual retirement account (including an employer or association trust treated as an individual retirement account) or individual retirement annuity on behalf of employees not covered under the qualified plan.[5]

The use of a payroll deduction program to fund employee IRAs will not subject the employer to Title I of ERISA (reporting and disclosure, participation, and vesting, etc.) where employer involvement is limited. The employer's involvement is so limited where the employer maintains neutrality with respect to an IRA sponsor in its communications with its employees and so is not considered to have "endorsed" an IRA payroll deduction program. The employer must also make clear that its involvement in the program is limited to collecting the deducted amounts and remitting them promptly to the IRA sponsor, and that it does not provide any additional benefit or promise any particular investment return on the employee's savings.[6]

An employer also may establish "deemed IRAs" for employees under a qualified plan (Q 3645). An employer may contribute amounts higher than the usual individual retirement

---

1.   IRC Sec. 219(f)(5); see Prop. Treas. Reg. §1.219(a)-2(c)(4).
2.   IRC Sec. 162; Prop. Treas. Reg. §1.219-1(c)(4).
3.   H. R. Conf. Rep. 93-1280 (ERISA '74) *reprinted in* 1974-3 CB 500; H. Rep. 93-807, *reprinted in* 1974-3 Supp. CB 367; IRC Sec. 3401(a)(12)(C).
4.   IRC Sec. 408(c); Treas. Reg. §1.408-2(c).
5.   H. R. Conf. Rep. 93-1280 (ERISA '74) *reprinted in* 1974-3 CB 499.
6.   Labor Reg. §2510.3-2(d); see IB 99-1, 64 Fed. Reg. 32999 (6-18-99).

plan limits by establishing a simplified employee pension program (Q 3701) or a SIMPLE IRA (see Q 3706).

Simplified Employee Pension (SEP)

3701. What is a simplified employee pension?

A simplified employee pension (SEP) is a traditional individual retirement account or individual retirement annuity (Q 3641) that is adopted by a business to provide retirement benefits for the business owners and employees and may accept an expanded rate of contributions over traditional IRAs.[1] The SEP IRA is owned by the employee.

The SEP rules permit an employer to contribute a limited amount of money each year on behalf of its employees. A self-employed individual may contribute to his/her own SEP. All contributions must be in the form of money; property cannot be contributed. Although contributions are not required every year, any contributions made by an employer in a given year must be based on a written formula and must not discriminate in favor of highly-compensated employees.

More specifically, in order for an IRA to qualify as a SEP, certain requirements must be satisfied:

(1) **Participation:** The employer must contribute to the SEP of each employee (including certain "leased" employees, see Q 3928) who is at least 21 years old, has performed services for the employer during the year for which the contribution is made (including any such employee who, because of death or termination of employment, is no longer employed on the date contributions are actually made), *and* for at least three of the immediately preceding five years has received at least $650 in compensation for 2021[2] ($600 in 2015-2020, $550 in 2010-2014) from the employer for the year.[3] (See Appendix E for earlier years.) These participation rules also apply to employees over age 72, who are subject to the minimum distribution requirements (Q 3686). The employer may not require that an employee be employed as of a particular date in the year.[4]

Employees covered by a collective bargaining agreement may be excluded from participation if retirement benefits have been the subject of good faith bargaining. Similarly, nonresident aliens may be excluded if they received no income from the employer that is considered to be from U.S. sources.[5]

(2) **Nondiscrimination requirement:** Employer contributions must not discriminate in favor of any highly compensated employee (Q 3929). Employees who are excluded from participation as nonresident aliens, or because they are covered by

---

1. IRC Sec. 408(k).
2. Notice 2017-64, Notice 2018-83, Notice 2019-59, Notice 2020-79.
3. IRC Sec. 408(k)(2)(C); IR-2009-94, IR-2014-99, IR-2015-118.
4. Prop. Treas. Reg. §1.408-7(d)(3).
5. IRC Sec. 408(k)(2).

a collective bargaining agreement, are not considered for purposes of determining whether there is discrimination.[1]

Unless employer contributions bear a uniform relationship to total compensation (or earned income in the case of self-employed individuals) they are considered discriminatory. But compensation or earned income in excess of $290,000 for 2021 ($285,000 in 2020, $280,000 in 2019, and $275,000 in 2018)[2] is not to be taken into account for these purposes.[3] This compensation limit is indexed for inflation. (See Appendix E for the indexed amounts for earlier years.)[4] Presumably, a constant percentage of compensation would meet the nondiscrimination requirement. A rate of contribution that decreases as compensation increases will be considered uniform.[5] The IRS has informally approved a method of contribution that in effect requires that an identical dollar amount be contributed on behalf of all participants.[6]

SEPs can be integrated under the rules applicable to qualified plans (Q 3862).[7]

(3)   **Contributions based on written allocation formula:** Employer contributions must be determined under a definite written allocation formula that specifies the manner in which the allocation is computed and what requirements an employee must satisfy to share in the allocation. But the employer may vary the allocation formula from year to year so long as there is a timely amendment to the plan that indicates the new formula.[8] No minimum funding standards are imposed.

Planning Point: The allocation formula may be written to provide that contributions be based on a fixed percentage of the employee's compensation, a fixed dollar amount for all participants, or that contributions be determined each year by the employer (a discretionary contribution). Discretionary contribution formulas are the most common. The employer may uniformly vary the percentage of compensation contributed year by year or contribute nothing for a particular year, but the SEP document must state how the employer contribution will be allocated. An employer may vary the formula or percentage from year to year (for example, to change from a fixed contribution to a discretionary contribution), provided the SEP is timely amended.[9]

---

(4)   **No withdrawal restrictions:** The employer contribution may not be conditioned on the employee's keeping any part of it in the pension and the employer may not prohibit withdrawals from the plan.[10]

---

1.   IRC Sec. 408(k)(3).
2.   Notice 2017-64, Notice 2018-83, Notice 2019-59, Notice 2020-79.
3.   IRC Sec. 408(k)(3)(C).
4.   IRC Secs. 408(k)(8), 401(a)(17).
5.   Prop. Treas. Reg. §1.408-8(c).
6.   See Let. Rul. 8824019.
7.   IRC Sec. 408(k)(3)(D); TAMRA '88, Sec. 1011(f)(7).
8.   Prop. Treas. Reg. §1.408-7(e).
9.   IRS Examining Process Guide (Chapter 72, Section 17).
10.   IRC Sec. 408(k)(4).

(5)   **Top heavy plans:** If the SEP is top-heavy plan (Q 3916), it is subject to the minimum contribution rules applicable to such plans (Q 3921).[1] Employer contributions to a SEP may be taken into account in determining whether qualified plans of the employer are top-heavy (Q 3916).

Should an eligible employee or former employee not have an IRA on the date contributions are made, the employer is required to establish one on the employee's behalf.[2] A SEP plan need not be established until the contribution is made for the year (*i.e.,* it may be established after the end of the year, see Q 3704).

A controlled group of corporations or employers under common control or employers composing an "affiliated service group" (Q 3932, Q 3934) are treated as a single employer. Thus, if contributions are made to SEPs for employees in one business, they may have to be made for employees of another business if the two are under common control or constitute an affiliated service group.[3]

SEPs are treated as defined contribution plans for purposes of the overall limits on employer contributions (Q 3867).[4] For plan years beginning in 2021, the annual additions limit for defined contribution plans as a whole is the lesser of $58,000[5] ($57,000 in 2020, $56,000 in 2019, and $55,000 in 2018, see Appendix E for earlier years) or 100 percent of compensation.[6] Any contribution *by an employer* to a SEP must be aggregated with all other employer contributions by that employer to defined contribution plans for purposes of the Section 415(c) limit on annual additions. Catch-up contributions, which are available only in plans that provide for elective deferral contributions (Q 3705, Q 3706, Q 3752), are not available in SEPs but are available in grandfathered (pre-1997) salary reduction SEPs.

3702. What are the limits with respect to employee contributions to a simplified employee pension (SEP)?

While elective deferrals are not permitted to an SEP, an employee may make deductible or nondeductible contributions directly to the SEP-IRA account subject to the same general IRA rules described in Q 3654 to Q 3682. However, any dollars contributed to the SEP will reduce the amount the individual employee can contribute to other IRAs, including Roth IRAs, for the year.

> *Example 1*: Nancy's employer, JJ Handyman, contributes $5,000 to Nancy's SEP-IRA at ABC Investment Co. based on the terms of the JJ Handyman SEP plan. Nancy, age 45, is permitted to make traditional IRA contributions to her SEP-IRA account at ABC Investment Co., and she contributes $3,000 in 2020. If Nancy also wants to contribute to her Roth IRA at XYZ Investment Co. for 2020, she can contribute $3,000 ($6,000 maximum contribution less the $3,000 already contributed to her SEP-IRA) by April 15, 2021.

The amount contributed by the employer to a SEP plan does not affect the amount the employee can contribute on his or her own behalf.

---

1.   IRC Secs. 408(k)(1)(B), 416(c)(2).
2.   See Prop. Treas. Reg. §1.408-7(d)(2).
3.   IRC Secs. 414(b), 414(c), 414(m); Let. Rul. 8041045.
4.   IRC Sec. 415(a)(2)(C).
5.   Notice 2020-79.
6.   IRC Sec. 415(c)(2).

Salary deferrals are only allowed to Salary Deferral SEPs, known as SAR-SEP, and no new SAR-SEPs are permitted as of 1997 (Q 3705).

3703. What are the limits with respect to employer contributions to a simplified employee pension (SEP)?

Contributions made by an employer to an employee's SEP are excludable from the employee's income to the extent that they do not exceed *the lesser of:* (1) 25 percent of compensation from the employer (determined without regard to that employer's contribution to the SEP) or (2) $58,000 in 2021.[1] Compensation is capped by the limits in effect under IRC Sec 414(s) ($290,000 for 2021, $285,000 for 2020, $280,000 for 2019) (Q 3866). Despite the $290,000 limit on compensation, the maximum permitted SEP contribution is capped at $58,000 for 2021[2] (where $58,000 is less than $290,000 x 25 percent).

Planning Point: Interestingly, "compensation" is defined for these purposes as amounts actually includible in the employee's gross income; consequently, "elective deferrals" by an employee (i.e. amounts contributed to a qualified retirement plan) would not be considered in the "lesser of" calculation above as compensation.[3] This definition of compensation, however, differs from the definition of compensation used to determine the employer's deduction when contributing to an employee's SEP, which does consider elective deferrals when determining income (Q 3704).

When determining the contribution limits of a "self-employed" individual, "compensation" is the individual's net earnings from self-employment.

If an individual is employed by more than one employer (other than employers who are under common control or compose a controlled or affiliated service group) during the tax year, the 25 percent limit is applied separately to each employer.[4] Under proposed regulations, contributions by (and compensation received from) employers who are under common control or who are members of a controlled group must be aggregated for purposes of this limit.[5] It would seem that the IRS may also require such aggregation where the employers are members of an affiliated service group.

If an individual is self-employed with respect to more than one trade or business, the maximum contribution will be the lesser of the amount determined by applying the limit separately to each trade or business *or* the amount determined by applying the limit as if the trades or businesses constituted one employer.[6] In an integrated plan, the Section 415 dollar limit must be reduced in the case of a highly compensated employee (Q 3929).[7]

Contributions are not included in an employee's gross income tax and are not subject to income tax withholding, FICA, or FUTA, unless they are excess contributions.[8]

---

1.   IRC Secs. 402(h)(2), 415(c)(1)(A); Notice 2020-79.
2.   Notice 2017-64, Notice 2018-83, Notice 2020-79.
3.   IRC Sec. 402(h)(2)(B).
4.   See IRC Sec. 219(b)(2).
5.   See Prop. Treas. Reg. §1.219-3(c).
6.   See Prop. Treas. Reg. §1.219-3(c)(2).
7.   IRC Sec. 402(h)(2)(B).
8.   IRC Secs. 3401(a)(12)(C), 3121(a)(5)(C), 3306(b)(5)(C), 408(k)(6)(C). See also Rev. Rul. 65-209, 1965-2 CB 414.

3704. Can an employer deduct contributions made to a simplified employee pension?

Employer contributions for a calendar year are deductible for the tax year in which the calendar year ends. An employer may elect to use its taxable year instead of the calendar year for purposes of determining contributions to a SEP.[1] Employer contributions made on account of a calendar year or an employer's taxable year may be made as late as the due date (plus extensions) of the employer's tax return for such year and be treated as if contributed on the last day of that year.[2] The due date for C corporations is March 15th following the close of such year and for self-employed individuals is April 15th following the close of such year.[3] For tax years beginning after December 31, 2015, returns of partnerships and S corporations made on the basis of a calendar year are due March 15, and those made on the basis of a fiscal year are due on or before the 15th day of the third month following the close of the fiscal year.

> *Example 1.* Employer is a sole proprietor whose tax year is the calendar year. Contributions made to a SEP IRA for calendar year 2020 (including contributions made in 2021 by the 2020 tax filing deadline) are deductible for the 2020 tax year.

> *Example 2.* Employer is a fiscal year taxpayer whose tax year ends June 30. The SEP IRA it maintains is on a calendar year. If employer makes contributions to the SEP IRA for calendar year 2020, employer may deduct such contributions on its tax return for tax year ending June 30, 2021.

The maximum employer deduction amount is 25 percent of compensation for the calendar year (or, if applicable, the taxable year).[4] "Compensation," for this purpose, *includes* elective deferrals of the employee and certain other contributions made on a pre-tax basis.[5]

Contributions in excess of the 25 percent deductible limit may be carried over and deducted in succeeding years.[6] However, the employer is subject to an excise tax on nondeductible contributions (Q 3938). If the employer also contributes to a qualified profit sharing or stock bonus plan, the 25 percent deductible limit for that plan is reduced by the amount of the allowable deduction for contributions to the SEPs with respect to participants in the stock bonus or profit sharing plan.[7] If the employer also contributes to any other type of qualified plan, the SEP is treated as a separate profit sharing or stock bonus plan for purposes of applying the combination deduction limit of IRC Section 404(a)(7) (Q 3937).[8]

3705. What is a SAR-SEP? What requirements must be met if a simplified employee pension is offered on a cash or a deferred basis?

A SAR-SEP is a simplified employee pension that is offered on a salary reduction (i.e., a cash or deferred) basis. In other words, the plan permits individual employees to elect to have contributions made to the SEP or to receive the contribution in cash. A SEP must otherwise meet

1. IRC Sec. 404(h)(1)(A).
2. IRC Sec. 404(h)(1)(B).
3. IRC Secs. 6012(a), 6072.
4. IRC Sec. 404(h)(1)(C).
5. See IRC Sec. 404(a)(12), 404(n).
6. See IRC Sec. 404(h)(1)(C).
7. IRC Sec. 404(h)(2).
8. IRC Sec. 404(h)(3).

the requirements in Q 3701, as well as those explained below, and the plan had to be established before 1997. No new SAR-SEPs are permitted after 1996, but those in effect prior to 1997 may continue to operate, receive contributions, and add new employees.[1]

A SAR-SEP may be maintained by an employer who had 25 or fewer employees who were eligible to participate in the plan at any time during the prior taxable year. The amount that an employee chooses to defer and contribute to the SEP is referred to as an elective deferral. Elective deferrals (Q 3760) are subject to the same cap ($19,500 in 2020-2021, $19,000 in 2019, and $18,500 in 2018) as elective deferrals to IRC Section 401(k) plans.[2] Elective deferrals also are subject to FICA and FUTA withholding.[3] Certain lower income taxpayers may be eligible to claim the saver's credit for elective deferrals to a SAR-SEP (Q 3648).

In addition to the elective deferrals described above, a SAR-SEP may permit additional elective deferrals by individuals age 50 or over, referred to as "catch-up contributions."[4] The dollar limit on catch-up contributions to a SAR-SEP is $6,500 in 2020-2021, $6,000 in 2017-2019 (see Appendix E for earlier years).[5] For details on the requirements for catch-up contributions, see Q 3761.

Contributions made by an employer on behalf of an employee to a SAR-SEP are excludable from the employee's income to the extent that they do not exceed the lesser of 25 percent of "compensation" from the employer, or $58,000 (for 2021, see Appendix E for earlier years).[6] As a result of an apparent oversight by Congress, "compensation," for this purpose only, is includable compensation (i.e., does not include elective deferrals).[7]

The election to defer salary into a SAR-SEP account is available only if (1) at least 50 percent of the employees of the employer eligible to participate elect to have amounts contributed to the SEP; and (2) the deferral percentage for each highly compensated eligible employee does not exceed the average deferral percentage for all nonhighly compensated eligible employees multiplied by 125 percent.[8] Catch-up contributions are not taken into account for this purpose.[9] Compensation or earned income in excess of $290,000 (in 2021) is not to be taken into account in determining an employee's deferral percentage.[10] This amount is indexed for inflation. (See Appendix E for the amounts in earlier years.)

A SAR-SEP will not be treated as failing to meet the deferral percentage requirement if, before the end of the following plan year, any excess contribution (i.e., in excess of 125 percent), plus any income attributable to such excess, is distributed or treated as distributed

1.   See IRC Sec. 408(k)(6)(H).
2.   IRC Sec. 402(g)(1); Notice 2018-83, Notice 2019-59, Notice 2020-79.
3.   IRC Secs. 3121(a)(5)(C), 3306(b)(5)(C).
4.   See IRC Secs. 414(v)(1), 414(v)(6)(A)(iv).
5.   IRC Sec. 414(v)(2)(B)(i); Notice 2016-62, Notice 2017-64, Notice 2018-83, Notice 2019-59, Notice 2020-79.
6.   IRC Secs. 402(h)(2)(A), 415(c)(1)(A); Notice 2020-79.
7.   See IRC Sec. 402(h)(2)(A).
8.   IRC Sec. 408(k)(6).
9.   IRC Sec. 414(v)(3)(A).
10.   IRC Sec. 408(k)(6)(D); Notice 2020-79.

and then contributed by the employee to the plan.[1] Such a recharacterization of contributions is not permitted in the absence of regulations.[2]

Unless the excess is distributed within two and one-half months after the end of the plan year, the employer will be subject to a 10 percent excise tax.[3] Any excess amounts so distributed generally are treated as received by the recipient in the taxable year for which the original contribution was made; if total excess contributions distributed to a recipient under the plan for a plan year are less than $100, the distributions will be treated as received in the taxable year of distribution.[4]

Since an employer may not force an employee to take a distribution of excess deferrals because the contributions are held in an individual retirement plan controlled by the employee, the Secretary of Treasury has the authority to prescribe necessary rules to ensure that excess contributions are distributed, including reporting requirements and the requirement that contributions may not be withdrawn until a determination is made that the deferral percentage test has been satisfied.[5] Any distribution or transfer before such a determination has been made will be subject to ordinary income tax as well as to the early distribution penalty, regardless of whether the penalty tax would otherwise apply.[6]

A plan will not be treated as violating any applicable limit of IRC Section 408(k) merely on account of the making of (or right to make) catch-up contributions by participants age 50 or over under the provisions of IRC Section 414(v), so long as a universal availability requirement is met.[7] In addition, catch-up contributions are not taken into account for purposes of the employer deduction limitation explained in Q 3701.[8] See Q 3761 for details on the requirements for catch-up contributions.

State or local governments and other tax-exempt organizations may not offer SAR-SEPs.[9]

SIMPLE IRA

3706. What is a SIMPLE IRA plan?

A SIMPLE (which stands for Savings Incentive Match Plan for Employees) IRA plan is a simplified, tax-favored retirement plan offered by small employers that provides employees with a simplified method to contribute toward their retirement savings. Employees may choose to make salary reduction contributions (aka elective deferrals) and the employer is required to make either matching or nonelective contributions. Contributions are made to an IRA set up

---

1.   IRC Secs. 408(k)(6)(C), 401(k)(8).
2.   General Explanation of TRA '86, p. 639.
3.   IRC Sec. 4979.
4.   IRC Sec. 4979(f)(2).
5.   IRC Sec. 408(k)(6)(F).
6.   IRC Sec. 408(d)(7).
7.   IRC Sec. 414(v)(3)(B).
8.   IRC Sec. 414(v)(3)(A).
9.   IRC Sec. 408(k)(6)(E).

for each employee that meets certain vesting, participation, and administrative requirements described below.[1]

A SIMPLE IRA plan may permit contributions only under a *qualified salary reduction arrangement*, which is defined as a written arrangement of an "eligible employer" (defined below) under which:

(1)   employees eligible to participate may elect to receive payments in cash or contribute them directly to a SIMPLE IRA per a salary deferral;

(2)   the amount to which such an election applies must be expressed as either a percentage of compensation or as a dollar amount, but in any case cannot exceed $13,500 per year (for 2020-2021, up from $13,000 in 2019[2]);

(3)   the employer must make matching contributions or nonelective contributions to the account according to one of the formulas described in Q 3707; and

(4)   no contributions other than those described in (1) and (3) may be made to the account.[3]

Certain lower income taxpayers may be eligible to claim the saver's credit for elective deferrals to a SIMPLE IRA (Q 3648).

Elective Deferral and Catch-up Contributions

The amount contributed via an elective deferral cannot exceed $13,500 for 2020 or 2021.[4] A SIMPLE IRA plan, however, may permit catch-up contributions by participants who reach age 50 (or over) by the end of the plan year.[5] The limit on catch-up contributions to SIMPLE IRAs is the lesser of (a) a specified dollar limit, or (b) the excess (if any) of the participant's compensation over any other elective deferrals for the year made without regard to the catch-up limits.[6] The dollar limit is $3,000 in 2016-2021[7] (see Appendix E for earlier years).

A SIMPLE IRA will not be treated as violating any of the applicable limitations of Section 408(p) merely on account of the making of (or right to make) catch-up contributions, provided a universal availability requirement is met.[8] See Q 3761 for details on the requirements for catch-up contributions.

Elective contribution amounts made under a SIMPLE IRA plan are counted in the overall limit ($19,500 in 2020-2021, $19,000 in 2019, and $18,500 in 2018) on elective deferrals by

---

1.   IRC Sec. 408(p)(1); Notice 98-4, 1998-1 CB 269; General Explanation of Tax Legislation Enacted in the 104th Congress (JCT-12-96), p. 140 (the "1996 Blue Book").

2.   Notice 2018-83, Notice 2019-59, Notice 2020-79.

3.   IRC Sec. 408(p)(2); Notice 98-4; IR-2011-103, IR-2013-86, IR-2014-99, IR-2015-118.

4.   IRC Secs. 408(p)(2)(A)(ii), 408(p)(2)(E); Notice 2019-59.

5.   See IRC Sec. 414(v).

6.   IRC Sec. 414(v)(2)(A).

7.   IR-2015-118, Notice 2016-62, Notice 2017-64, Notice 2018-83, Notice 2019-59, 2020-79.

8.   IRC Sec. 414(v)(3); see Prop. Treas. Reg. §1.414(v)-1(d).

any individual.[1] See Q 3760 for the definition of "elective deferral." Thus, for example, an individual under age 50 who defers the maximum of $13,500 to a SIMPLE IRA of one employer and participates in a 401(k) plan of another employer would be limited to an elective deferral of $6,000 in 2021 ($19,500 - $13,500) to the 401(k) plan.[2] Catch-up contributions are not subject to the limits of IRC Section 402(g) and do not reduce an individual's otherwise applicable deferral limit under any other plan.[3]

Definitions

An arrangement will not be treated as a *qualified salary reduction arrangement* if the employer, or a predecessor employer, maintained another qualified plan (including a 403(a) annuity, a 403(b) tax sheltered annuity, a SEP, or a governmental plan other than an IRC Section 457 plan) under which contributions were made or benefits accrued for service during any year in which the SIMPLE IRA plan was in effect. But if only employees *other than* those covered under a collectively bargained agreement are eligible to participate in the SIMPLE IRA plan, this rule will be applied without regard to a collectively bargained plan.[4] Also, for purposes of this rule, transfers, rollovers, or forfeitures are disregarded except to the extent that forfeitures replace otherwise required contributions.[5]

Only an *eligible employer* may adopt a SIMPLE IRA plan. An "eligible employer" is defined as an employer who employed no more than 100 employees earning at least $5,000 from the employer during the preceding year.[6] For purposes of this limitation, *all* employees employed at any time during the calendar year are taken into account, even those who are excludable or are ineligible to participate. Furthermore, certain self-employed individuals who receive earned income from the employer during the year must be counted for purposes of the 100-employee limitation.[7] An employer who maintains a plan in which only collectively bargained employees may participate is not precluded from offering a SIMPLE IRA to its noncollectively bargained employees.[8]

Generally, an eligible employer who ceases to be eligible after having established and maintained a SIMPLE IRA plan for at least one year will, nonetheless, continue to be treated as eligible for the following two years.[9] But special rules apply where a failure to remain eligible (or to meet any other requirement of IRC Section 408(p)) was due to an acquisition, disposition, or similar transaction involving another eligible employer.[10]

Compensation, for purposes of most of the SIMPLE IRA provisions, includes wages (as defined for income tax withholding purposes), elective contributions made under a

---

1. IRC Sec. 402(g)(3)(D); Notice 2016-62, Notice 2017-64, Notice 2018-83, Notice 2019-59, Notice 2020-79.
2. Notice 2020-79.
3. IRC Sec. 414(v)(3)(A).
4. IRC Sec. 408(p)(2)(D).
5. Notice 98-4, 1998-1 CB 269.
6. IRC Sec. 408(p)(2)(C)(i).
7. Notice 98-4, 1998-1 CB 269.
8. IRC Sec. 408(p)(2)(D)(i).
9. IRC Sec. 408(p)(2)(C)(i)(II).
10. See IRC Sec. 408(p)(10).

SIMPLE IRA plan, and elective deferrals, including compensation deferred under an IRC Section 457 plan.[1] A self-employed individual who is treated as an employee may be a participant in a SIMPLE IRA plan; for this purpose, "compensation" means net earnings from self-employment, prior to subtracting the SIMPLE IRA plan contribution.[2] An employee's elective deferrals under a 401(k) plan, a SAR-SEP, and a Section 403(b) annuity contract are also included in the meaning of compensation for purposes of the 100-employee limitation (i.e., the $5,000 threshold) and the eligibility requirements.[3]

3707. What requirements apply to employer contributions to a SIMPLE IRA plan?

An employer who has set up a SIMPLE IRA must make either a matching contribution or a nonelective contribution each year on behalf of all participating employees.

Matching contribution: Under this option, the employer is generally required to match employee contributions dollar-for-dollar up to 3 percent of the employee's compensation.[4] (Matching of catch-up contributions is not required.[5]) The employer may elect to reduce the matching percentage in a calendar year for all eligible employees, but such reduced percentage cannot be below 1 percent. To get the lower percentage, the employer must notify the employees of the election within a reasonable period of time before the 60-day election period for electing to participate in the plan.[6] Also, the employer may not use the lower percentage if the election would result in the percentage being lower than 3 percent in more than two out of the five years ending with the current year. If the employer (or a predecessor employer) has maintained the plan for less than five years, the employer will be treated as if the percentage was 3 percent in the prior years during which the arrangement was not in effect.[7] Also, if the employer made nonelective contributions for a year (instead of matching contributions) under the formula described below, it will be treated as having a percentage of 3 percent in that year.[8]

The compensation limits under IRC Section 401(a)(17) do not apply for purposes of the matching formula; thus, the 3 percent match would reach the maximum employer contribution limit of $13,500 (in 2020-2021) for an employee with compensation of $433,333 in a year.[9]

A matching contribution made to a SIMPLE IRA on behalf of a self-employed individual is not treated as an elective employer contribution for purposes of the limit on such contributions.[10] The purpose of this provision is to treat self-employed individuals in the same manner as employees for purposes of the limit on elective contributions.

---

1.   IRC Sec. 408(p)(6)(A).
2.   IRC Sec. 408(p)(6)(A)(ii).
3.   Notice 98-4, 1998-1 CB 269.
4.   IRC Sec. 408(p)(2)(A)(iii).
5.   See REG-142499-01, 66 Fed. Reg. 53555 (Oct. 23, 2001).
6.   IRS Sec. 408(p)(5)(C).
7.   IRC Sec. 408(p)(2)(C)(ii).
8.   Notice 98-4, 1998-1 CB 269.
9.   See Notice 98-4, 1998-1 CB 269; IRC Sec. 401(a)(17), Notice 2019-59, Notice 2020-79.
10. IRC Sec. 408(p)(9).

Nonelective contribution formula: As an alternative to making a matching contribution, an employer can make a nonelective contribution equal to 2 percent of a participating employee's compensation. If this option is chosen, the employer must make this 2 percent contribution for all eligible employees whether or not the employee has made a contribution to the SIMPLE IRA for the calendar year.

Compensation for the purposes of this rule is capped at the annual limit of $290,000 for 2021. The employer may, but is not required to, limit nonelective contributions to eligible employees who have at least $5,000 (or some lower amount selected by the employer) of compensation for the year.

If the employer chooses the nonelective option, it must notify the employees within a reasonable time before the 60-day election period for electing to participate in the plan or make elective deferrals.[1] The compensation limit under IRC Section 401(a)(17) does apply for purposes of this formula; thus, the maximum amount that could be contributed in nonelective contributions for an employee would be $5,800 (i.e., 2 percent of $290,000 (in 2021)).[2]

A SIMPLE IRA is not subject to the nondiscrimination or top-heavy rules associated with other plans, and the reporting requirements it must meet are simplified.[3]

3708. Do any special rules apply to a SIMPLE IRA plan?

Contributions under a SIMPLE IRA plan may be made only to a SIMPLE IRA. Prior to 2016, a SIMPLE IRA could receive only contributions under a SIMPLE IRA plan and rollovers or transfers from another SIMPLE IRA account.[4] However, the Protecting Americans Against Tax Hikes Act of 2015 (PATH) eliminated this prohibition, so that a SIMPLE IRA may now accept rollover contributions from traditional IRAs, SEP-IRAs, 401(k)s, 457(b) plans and 403(b) plans so long as the SIMPLE IRA has been open for at least two years.[5]

All contributions to a SIMPLE IRA account must be fully vested and may not be subject to any prohibition on withdrawals, nor conditioned on their retention in the account.[6] The early distribution penalty on withdrawals, however, is increased to 25 percent during the first two years of participation (see Q 3709).[7]

The *participation* requirements for SIMPLE IRAs state that all nonexcludable employees who received at least $5,000 in compensation from the employer during any two preceding years and are reasonably expected to receive at least $5,000 in compensation during the year must be eligible to make the cash or deferred election (if the matching formula is used) or to receive nonelective contributions (if the nonelective formula is used).[8] Of course, employers

1.   IRC Sec. 408(p)(2)(B).
2.   See IRC Sec. 408(p)(2)(B)(ii), Notice 2020-79.
3.   See IRC Secs. 408(p)(1), 416(g)(4), 408(l)(2).
4.   Notice 98-4, 1998-1 CB 269, A-2.
5.   P.L. 114-113; see IRC Sec. 408(p)(1)(B).
6.   IRC Secs. 408(p)(3), 408(k)(4).
7.   IRC Sec. 72(t)(6).
8.   IRC Sec. 408(p)(4)(A).

are free to impose less restrictive eligibility requirements, such as a $3,000 compensation threshold, but they may not impose more restrictive ones.[1] The $5,000 threshold compensation amount is not indexed for inflation. Nonresident aliens who received no U.S. income and employees subject to a collective bargaining agreement generally are excludable employees for purposes of the participation requirement.[2] An employee who participates in another plan of a different employer may participate in a SIMPLE IRA plan, but will be subject to the aggregate limit of $19,500 (in 2020-2021) on elective deferrals.[3] An employer who establishes a SIMPLE IRA plan is not responsible for monitoring compliance with this limitation.[4]

Tax-exempt employers and governmental entities are permitted to maintain SIMPLE IRA plans. Excludable contributions may be made to the SIMPLE IRA of employees of tax-exempt employers and governmental entities on the same basis as contributions may be made to employees of other eligible employers.[5] Related employers (i.e., controlled groups, partnerships or sole proprietorships under common control, and affiliated service groups) must be treated as a single employer for purposes of the SIMPLE IRA rules, and leased employees will be treated as employed by the employer. Consequently, all employees (and leased employees) of an employer who satisfy the eligibility requirements (see below) must be permitted to participate in the SIMPLE IRA of a related employer.[6]

The administrative requirements for SIMPLE IRA plans state that an employer must deposit elective employee contributions (elective deferrals) within 30 days after the last day of the month in which the amounts would otherwise be payable to the employee in cash, and that employer's matching and nonelective contributions must be made no later than the filing date for the return for the taxable year (including extensions).[7]

Planning Point: While the IRS requires elective employer contributions within 30 days after the month with respect to which the contributions are made, the Department of Labor requires that employee deferrals be made *as soon as practicable* after the deferral, but in no event later than 15 days after the deferral was made. *Ward Anderson, CLU, ChFC, MassMutual Financial Group, Denver, Colorado.*

Employees must have the right to terminate participation at any time during the year; but the plan may preclude the employee from resuming participation thereafter until the beginning of the next year.[8]

Generally, each employee must have 60 days before the first day of any year (and 60 days before the first day the employee is eligible to participate) to elect whether to participate in the plan, or to modify his deferral amount.[9] A SIMPLE IRA plan must be maintained on a

---

1.   Notice 98-4, 1998-1 CB 269.
2.   IRC Sec. 408(p)(4)(B).
3.   Notice 2019-59, Notice 2020-79.
4.   Notice 98-4, 1998-1 CB 269.
5.   Notice 98-4, 1998-1 CB 269.
6.   Notice 98-4, 1998-1 CB 269.
7.   IRC Secs. 408(p)(5)(A), 404(m)(2)(B).
8.   IRC Sec. 408(p)(5)(B).
9.   IRC Sec. 408(p)(5)(C).

calendar year basis.[1] The IRS apparently has adopted a requirement that a plan be adopted not later than October 1 of the year for which the plan is established, but states that the October 1 requirement "does not apply to a new employer that comes into existence after October 1 of the year the SIMPLE IRA Plan is established if the employer establishes the SIMPLE IRA Plan as soon as administratively feasible after the employer comes into existence."[2]

See Q 3709 regarding the tax treatment of SIMPLE IRA plan contributions, distributions, and rollovers. See Q 3777 regarding SIMPLE 401(k) plans.

3709. How are SIMPLE IRA plan contributions taxed?

There are four permissible types of contributions to a SIMPLE IRA plan:

(1)   Salary reduction contributions

(2)   Catch-up contributions

(3)   Matching contributions

(4)   Nonelective contributions[3]

Salary reduction and catch-up contributions are made by the employee, and the employer is responsible for making either a matching or nonelective contribution.

Catch-up contributions are additional elective deferrals for individuals age 50 or over, which are not subject to the general contribution ceiling of $13,500 in 2020-2021 (Q 3706, Q 3761). All SIMPLE IRA contributions are excludable from the employee's income, provided they meet certain design requirements set forth in the IRC.[4] Moreover, certain lower income taxpayers may be eligible to claim the saver's credit for salary reduction contributions to a SIMPLE IRA (Q 3648).

Contributions to a SIMPLE IRA are not subject to income tax withholding, but salary reduction contributions are included in wages for purposes of the Social Security and federal unemployment taxes (i.e., FICA and FUTA). Consequently, salary deferrals are subject to FICA and FUTA withholding. It appears that "salary deferrals," for this purpose, would include catch-up contributions.[5] By contrast, matching contributions and nonelective contributions made by the employer are excluded from wages for purposes of Social Security tax and federal unemployment tax; they are not subject to FICA or FUTA withholding.[6]

Employer contributions to a SIMPLE IRA generally are deductible by the employer.[7] Matching and nonelective contributions can be made after the close of the tax year to which they are

1.   See Notice 98-4, 1998-1 CB 269.
2.   See Notice 98-4, 1998-1 CB 269, at K-1.
3.   See IRC Secs. 408(p)(2), 414(v).
4.   See IRC Secs. 402(k), 402(h)(1), 402(e)(3); see IRC Sec. 414(v); Notice 98-4, 1998-1 CB 25.
5.   See IRC Secs. 414(v)(1), 414(v)(6)(B).
6.   See IRC Secs. 3121(a), 3306(a), 3401(a)(12); Notice 98-4, 1998-1 CB 25.
7.   IRC Sec. 404(m)(1).

attributable, provided they are made before the due date for filing the employer's federal income tax return for the taxable year (including extensions).[1] Contributions to a SIMPLE IRA are not subject to the annual dollar limit for traditional or Roth IRAs.[2] Nondeductible contributions are subject to a 10 percent penalty.[3]

SIMPLE IRA accounts themselves are not subject to tax. The taxation of distributions from a SIMPLE IRA is the same as under a traditional IRA; thus, contributions generally are not taxable until withdrawn.[4] The early distribution penalty (Q 3677) is increased to 25 percent during the first two years of participation in a SIMPLE IRA; after the two year period has elapsed, the penalty is 10 percent.[5]

A SIMPLE IRA may not be designated as a Roth IRA.[6]

3710. Are rollovers permitted from SIMPLE IRA plans?

Tax-free rollovers (Q 4007) may be made from one SIMPLE IRA to another SIMPLE IRA at any time, but a rollover from a SIMPLE IRA to a traditional IRA is permitted only in the case of distributions to which the 25 percent early distribution penalty does not apply (Q 3709).[7] During the two year period that the 25 percent penalty is imposed, such a transfer would be treated as a distribution from the SIMPLE IRA and a contribution to the other IRA that does not qualify as a rollover contribution.[8] To the extent that an employee is no longer participating in a SIMPLE IRA plan and two years have expired since the employee first participated in the plan, the employee may treat the SIMPLE IRA account as a traditional IRA.[9]

3711. What are the differences between a simplified employee pension (SEP) and a SIMPLE IRA?

Simplified employee pensions (SEP) and SIMPLE IRAs are both types of retirement accounts designed to help small business owners offer retirement benefits to employees (as well as to provide for themselves). Contributions to both types of accounts are (within limits) tax deductible by the employer and earnings accumulate on a tax-deferred basis, but permitted contribution levels vary based on the type of account chosen (see below). Penalties on early withdrawals also vary as discussed below.

Both SEP IRAs and SIMPLE IRAs must meet certain vesting, participation, nondiscrimination and other administrative requirements (see Q 3701 and Q 3706).

1.   IRC Sec. 404(m)(2)(B).
2.   IRC Sec. 408(p)(8).
3.   IRC Sec. 4972(d)(1)(A)(iv).
4.   IRC Secs. 402(k), 402(h)(3); General Explanation of Tax Legislation Enacted in the 104th Congress (JCT-12-96), p. 141 (the 1996 Blue Book).
5.   IRC Sec. 72(t)(6).
6.   IRC Sec. 408A(f)(1).
7.   IRC Sec. 408(d)(3)(G).
8.   Notice 98-4, 1998-1 CB 25.
9.   General Explanation of Tax Legislation Enacted in the 104th Congress (JCT-12-96), p. 141 (the 1996 Blue Book).

Generally, a SEP IRA is a traditional individual retirement account or individual retirement annuity that is adopted by a business to provide retirement benefits for the business owners and employees and may accept a higher rate of contributions than traditional IRAs.[1] The SEP IRA is owned by the employee. The SEP rules permit an employer to contribute a limited amount of money each year on behalf of its employees. A self-employed individual may contribute to his or her own SEP. All contributions must be in the form of money; property cannot be contributed. Although contributions are not required every year, any contributions made by an employer in a given year must be based on a written formula and must not discriminate in favor of highly-compensated employees.

A SIMPLE (which stands for Savings Incentive Match Plan for Employees) IRA plan is a simplified, tax-favored retirement plan offered by small employers that provides employees with a simplified method to contribute toward their retirement savings. Employees may choose to make salary reduction contributions (aka elective deferrals) and the employer is *required* to make either matching or nonelective contributions.[2] A SIMPLE IRA plan may permit contributions only under a *qualified salary reduction arrangement* (see Q 3706).

Both SEP IRAs and SIMPLE IRAs are attractive retirement savings vehicles for small businesses, but SIMPLE IRA sponsors should keep in mind that the accounts must be funded each year (i.e., a contribution must always be made for employees who earn $5,000 or more per year, see Q 3708). SIMPLE IRAs have lower contribution limits than SEP IRAs, as discussed below.

SEP IRAs tend to be more popular among self-employed individuals because there is no annual funding requirement. However, if a SEP IRA is funded in any year, contributions must be made to the accounts of certain employees (i.e., those who are 21, have at least $600 in compensation and performed services for the employer during the year in question, see Q 3701).

Contributions

SEPs are treated as defined contribution plans for purposes of the overall limits on employer contributions (see Q 3867).[3] For plan years beginning in 2021, the annual additions limit for defined contribution plans as a whole is the lesser of $58,000[4] ($57,000 for 2020, $56,000 for 2019) or 100 percent of compensation.[5] Any contribution *by an employer* to a SEP must be aggregated with all other employer contributions by that employer to defined contribution plans for purposes of the Section 415(c) limit on annual additions. Catch-up contributions to a SEP IRA are only permitted in grandfathered plans established prior to 1997.

Contributions to a SIMPLE IRA cannot exceed $13,500 per year in 2020-2021 ($13,000 in 2019), but may provide for catch-up contributions in the amount of $3,000 per year (as indexed) for participants who have reached age 50 by the end of the plan year.[6] Elective contribution

---

1.   IRC Sec. 408(k).
2.   IRC Sec. 408(p)(1); Notice 98-4, 1998-1 CB 269.
3.   IRC Sec. 415(a)(2)(C).
4.   Notice 2017-64, Notice 2019-59, Notice 2020-79.
5.   IRC Sec. 415(c)(2).
6.   IRC Sec. 414(v).

amounts made under a SIMPLE IRA plan are counted in the overall limit ($19,500 in 2020-2021) on elective deferrals by any individual.[1]

Early Withdrawals

Early withdrawals (prior to age 59½) from a SEP IRA may subject the participant to an additional 10 percent penalty tax (plus ordinary income tax). Participants in a SIMPLE IRA will be subject to a 25 percent tax on early withdrawals if the withdrawal is made within two years of participating in a SIMPLE IRA. After the two-year period has expired, a 10 percent additional penalty tax will apply to early withdrawals.[2]

Estate Tax Issues

3712. Is the value of an IRA includable in the decedent's gross estate?

Yes, in general, an IRA is includible in the gross estate of decedents dying after 1984. Benefits payable to a surviving spouse, however, generally will qualify for the marital deduction (Q 3713). Additionally, benefits payable to a qualified charity should qualify for a charitable deduction at the time of death.[3]

The value of an IRA account is not discounted for income tax payable by beneficiaries or for lack of marketability. An income tax deduction may be available for federal estate tax attributable to the IRA.[4]

The value of an annuity or other payment receivable under an individual retirement plan or arrangement by the beneficiary of a deceased individual is includable in the decedent's gross estate under the rules discussed in Q 618 to Q 627. In reading those rules, be aware that any contribution for the purchase of an annuity made by the decedent's employer or former employer, as under an SEP (Q 3701), is considered to be contributed by the decedent if made by reason of his or her employment.[5]

For estates of decedents dying after 1984, the Tax Reform Act of 1984 generally repealed the previously existing estate tax exclusion; special rules may apply for decedents dying after 1984 who separated from service before January 1, 1985. Qualified plan benefits rolled over to an IRA after 1984 are treated as subject to the transitional rules for IRAs rather than those for qualified plans (Q 3992).[6]

---

1.   IRC Sec. 402(g)(3)(D); Notice 2019-59, Notice 2020-79.
2.   IRC Sec. 72(t)(6).
3.   See Let. Rul. 199939039.
4.   IRC Sec. 691(c); *Est. of Smith v. U.S.*, 198 F. 3d 515 (5th Cir. 1999), nonacq.; *Est. of Kahn v. Comm.*, 125 TC 227 (2005); TAM 200247001.
5.   IRC Sec. 2039(b).
6.   Rev. Rul. 92-22, 1992-1 CB 313; *Sherrill v. U.S.*, 415 F. Supp. 2d 953 (N.D. Ind. 2006).

3713. Is a marital deduction available for the value of a survivor benefit payable under an individual retirement plan that is includable in the decedent's gross estate?

Yes, if benefits pass to the surviving spouse in a form that qualifies for the marital deduction.[1] Thus, an outright transfer of the IRA account balance to the surviving spouse should qualify for the marital deduction. A marital deduction also should be available if any income or principal distributed while the surviving spouse is alive is distributed to the surviving spouse and remaining principal and income, if any, is distributed to the surviving spouse's estate at death.

A marital deduction also should be available if all income from the IRA is distributed at least annually to the surviving spouse and the surviving spouse is given a general power to appoint the IRA to himself or herself or to his or her estate.[2] Additionally, a marital deduction should be available if all income from the IRA is distributed at least annually to the surviving spouse, no one has the power to distribute any part of the IRA to anyone other than the surviving spouse, and the executor makes a qualified terminable interest property ("QTIP") election.[3] If the surviving spouse is given a survivor annuity where only the spouse has the right to receive payments during such spouse's lifetime, such interest would qualify for the QTIP marital deduction.[4] In the case of a surviving spouse who is not a U.S. citizen, a qualified domestic trust generally would be required to obtain the marital deduction.[5]

Planning Point: All of the QTIP trust income must be received by the surviving spouse for life. Such income is sometimes defined by state law as unitrust interest.

An executor can elect to treat an IRA and a trust as QTIP if the trustee of the trust is the beneficiary of the IRA, the surviving spouse can compel the trustee to withdraw all income earned by the IRA at least annually and distribute that amount to the spouse, and no person has the power to appoint any part of the trust to any person other than the spouse.[6]

Prior to Revenue Ruling 2000-2, where IRA proceeds were to be distributed to a trust benefiting the survivor spouse, marital deduction requirements generally had to be met at both the IRA and the trust level.

Thus, in Revenue Ruling 89-89,[7] a decedent's executor was permitted to elect to treat a decedent's IRA as eligible for the QTIP marital deduction where (1) the distribution option elected by the decedent for the IRA required the principal balance of the IRA to be distributed in annual installments to a testamentary QTIP trust and the income earned on the undistributed balance of the IRA to be distributed annually to the trust, and (2) all trust income was payable annually to the decedent's spouse.

---

1.   IRC Sec. 2056.
2.   IRC Sec. 2056(b)(5).
3.   IRC Sec. 2056(b)(7).
4.   IRC Sec. 2056(b)(7)(C).
5.   IRC Secs. 2056(d), 2056A; Let. Ruls. 9544038, 9322005.
6.   Rev. Rul. 2000-2, 2000-1 CB 305, superseded by Rev. Rul. 2006-26; 2006-1 CB 939.
7.   1989-2 CB 231, superseded by Revenue Ruling 2000-2.

A QTIP marital deduction was not available for an IRA with distributions payable to a marital trust where none of the IRA options provided that all income would be distributed at least annually to the marital trust.[1]

In determining if a spouse has been given an income interest, allocations between income and principal will be respected if state law provides that reasonable apportionments can be made between income and remainder beneficiaries of the total return of the trust (e.g., a unitrust interest in the range of 3 percent to 5 percent could be treated as an income interest).[2] Revenue Ruling 2006-26[3] provides that various means of determining income under state law are permitted under the QTIP marital deduction. Thus, income generally can be determined under state laws based on the Uniform Principal and Income Act or under general traditional statutory or common law rules that provide for allocations between income and principal.

A marital deduction also may be available if IRA proceeds are paid to a charitable remainder annuity trust or unitrust and the surviving spouse is the only noncharitable beneficiary (other than certain ESOP remainder beneficiaries).[4] Presumably, the IRA would have to incorporate all the charitable deduction requirements for such a trust.

For the income tax implications of distributions from a traditional IRA, see Q 3671, from a Roth IRA, see Q 3673.

1.   TAM 9220007.
2.   Treas. Reg. §1.643(b)-1.
3.   2006-1 CB 939.
4.   IRC Sec. 2056(b)(8).

PART XVI: PENSION AND PROFIT SHARING

Defined Plans

3714. What are the qualification requirements that apply to various types of qualified retirement plans?

Although qualification requirements (Q 3837 to Q 3934) and deduction limits (Q 3936 to Q 3942) generally affect all qualified plans, there are additional qualification requirements and deduction limits that are specific to certain types of plans.

As a general rule, qualification requirements can be divided between: (1) defined benefit plans (Q 3715 to Q 3724) and defined contribution plans (Q 3725 to Q 3731), and (2) pension (Q 3733 to Q 3748) and profit sharing plans (Q 3749 to Q 3751).

To some degree, these categories overlap. For example, all defined benefit plans are pensions, but not all pensions are defined benefit plans (Q 3733). Similarly, all profit sharing plans are defined contribution plans, but not all defined contribution plans are profit sharing plans; some are pensions.

Furthermore, special qualification, design, and nondiscrimination requirements apply to 401(k) plans (Q 3752 to Q 3807). Section 412(i)[1] insurance contract plans, although subject to the general requirements for defined benefit plans, must meet special requirements (Q 3811 and Q 3812) to be exempt from certain funding standards (Q 3742 to Q 3748). Stock bonus plans and ESOPs are subject to their own special requirements (Q 3815 to Q 3824). There also are special rules for Keogh and S corporations plans (Q 3825 to Q 3828).

Limitations on an employer's deduction for plan contributions generally are based on whether the plan is a pension (Q 3735) or a profit sharing plan (Q 3750).

Plans that offer insurance benefits are subject to the special rules explained in Q 3829 (for plans that offer life or health insurance to participants) and Q 3835 (for plans that transfer pension assets to Section 401(h) accounts).

3715. What is a defined benefit plan?

The IRC permits two types of qualified plans: defined benefit plans and defined contribution plans (Q 3725). All defined benefit pension plans are structured as pension plans (Q 3733), while defined contribution plans may be structured as pension or profit sharing plans. A defined benefit plan is a qualified retirement plan that expresses the participant's benefit as a certain amount, either as an exact dollar amount or a formula that determines the amount that will be paid at retirement. The benefit is defined by the formula, but the contribution is determined by an actuary. The IRC states that the term "defined benefit plan" means any plan that is not a defined contribution plan.[2]

---

1. 412(i) plans are now governed by Section 412(e)(3).
2. IRC Sec. 414(j).

Variations on the traditional defined benefit plan include Section 412(i)[1] insurance contract plans (Q 3811) and cash balance plans (Q 3720). See Q 3728 for the application of the Section 415 requirements to defined benefit plans, and Q 3716 for special qualification requirements. The IRS has even approved a rather unique adjustable pension plan (APP) or variable defined benefit plan (VDB) that seems to be gaining popularity in union situations.[2]

3716. What special qualification requirements apply to defined benefit pension plans?

Limitation on Benefits

A defined benefit plan must contain a limit on the projected "annual benefit" under the plan or under all such plans aggregated if the employer has more than one defined benefit plan (Q 3867, Q 3719).

Accrued Benefit Requirements

A defined benefit pension plan may not exclude from participation employees who are beyond a specified age, but the benefit of an employee who is within five years of normal retirement age when employment begins is computed using a retirement age that is the fifth anniversary of the time that plan participation begins for that employee.[3] A defined benefit plan must benefit a minimum number or percentage of employees (i.e., the 50/40 test) as explained in Q 3717.

Accrued Benefit Requirements for Not Fully Insured Plans

A defined benefit plan, other than a fully insured plan, must satisfy one of the following three accrued benefit tests:

The 3 percent test. The accrued benefit to which a participant is entitled upon separation from service must be not less than 3 percent of the normal retirement benefit to which the participant would have been entitled if the participant commenced participation at the earliest entry age under the plan and served continuously until the earlier of age 65 or the normal retirement age specified under the plan, multiplied by the number of years (not in excess of 33⅓) of participation in the plan.[4]

The 133⅓ percent test. In any particular plan year when qualification of the plan is tested, the plan must not allow for the annual rate of accrual of a participant's normal retirement benefit in any later plan year to exceed 133⅓ percent of the annual rate of accrual in any previous year.[5]

1.   412(i) insurance contract plans are now governed by IRC Sec. 412(e)(3).
2.   Let. Rul. 45-4227067, Jul. 20, 2017 given to United Workers & Hospitality Employers VDB Pension Trust. A similar IRS approval was given to the Guild-Times (New York Times) APP back in June 2014.
3.   IRC Secs. 410(a)(2), 411(a)(8).
4.   IRC Sec. 411(b)(1)(A); Treas. Reg. §1.411(b)-1(b)(1).
5.   IRC Sec. 411(b)(1)(B); Treas. Reg. §1.411(b)-1(b)(2).

The fractional (or pro rata) test. The accrued benefit to which a participant is entitled upon his or her separation from service must be not less than a fraction of the participant's assumed retirement benefit, the numerator of which is the participant's total number of years of participation in the plan and the denominator of which is the total number of years the participant would have participated in the plan had the participant separated from service at normal retirement age.[1] The participant's assumed retirement benefit is computed as though the participant had continued to earn the same rate of compensation annually that he or she had earned during the years that would have been taken into account under the plan (but not in excess of 10 years of service immediately preceding separation) had the participant reached normal retirement age at the date of his or her separation. For the calculation method (and examples) that will produce the lowest accrued benefit satisfying the fractional test where benefits are accrued following a break in service, see Revenue Ruling 81-11.[2]

A defined benefit plan that provides a stated benefit offset by the benefits of a profit sharing plan will satisfy the benefit accrual requirements if the benefit determined without the offset satisfies the requirements and if the offset is equal to the amount deemed provided by the vested portion of the account balance in the profit sharing plan on the date the amount of the offset is determined.[3]

A defined benefit plan must require separate accounting for the portion of each employee's accrued benefit derived from any voluntary employee contributions permitted under the plan.[4] Revenue Ruling 78-202[5] discusses the rules relating to calculation of accrued benefits derived from mandatory employee contributions.[6] A plan generally may not be amended to reduce a participant's accrued benefit.[7] Procedures for obtaining approval of a retroactive plan amendment reducing a participant's accrued benefit are specified in Revenue Procedure 94-42.[8]

In addition, if a defined benefit plan subject to the minimum funding rules adopts an amendment that would increase current liability under the plan, and the funded current liability percentage under the plan (the ratio of the value of the plan's assets to its current liability) is less than 60 percent, the plan must require that the amendment will not become effective until the employer (or a member of the employer's controlled group) provides adequate security in favor of the plan.[9] See also Q 3837 to Q 3935 and Q 3736 for other qualification requirements.

In plan years beginning after December 31, 2007, defined benefit plans that are "at risk" (Q 3744) became subject to a qualification requirement that suspends many benefit increases, plan amendments, and accruals in single-employer plans when funding falls below specified levels ranging from 60 percent to 80 percent.[10] Notice must be provided to participants and beneficiaries

---

1. IRC Sec. 411(b)(1)(C); Treas. Reg. §1.411(b)-1(b)(3).
2. 1981-1 CB 227.
3. Rev. Rul. 76-259, 1976-2 CB 111.
4. IRC Sec. 411(b)(2).
5. 1978-1 CB 124.
6. See also Rev. Rul. 89-60, 1989-1 C.B. 113 (amplifying Rev. Rul. 78-202); Rev. Rul. 79-259, 1979-2 CB 197.
7. Treas. Reg. §1.411(d)-4, A-1.
8. 1994-1 CB 717.
9. IRC Sec. 401(a)(29).
10. See IRC Secs. 401(a)(29), 436. See Treas. Reg. §1.436-1.

when funding falls below 60 percent.[1] If a single employer plan in bankruptcy is funded at or above 80 percent, the plan may adopt an amendment, after November 8, 2012, to eliminate an option or form of benefit that includes a prohibited payment under IRC Section 436(d)(5), if certain conditions are met.[2] See Q 3743 for the funding requirements applicable in plan years beginning after 2007 through date of publication including MAP-21 and HATFA 2014. There was a special relief provision in the WRERA 2008 just for plan years beginning after September 2008 and before October 2009.[3] Final regulations on minimum required contributions, effective January 1, 2016, are specified in Treasury Regulation Section 1.430(a)-1.[4]

Planning Point: There are also prohibitions for transferring company general reserve assets in connection with a Section 409A-covered "nonqualified deferred compensation plan" during the period a defined benefit plan is "at risk" (see Q 3564 and Q 3568).

Accrued Benefit Requirements for Fully Insured Plans

An insurance contract plan (formerly a Section 412(i) plan, but now governed by IRC section 412(e)(3)) automatically satisfies any of the foregoing accrued benefit tests if (1) the plan is funded exclusively by insurance contracts calling for level annual premiums from the date the insured becomes a participant in the plan to not later than retirement age, (2) benefits provided by the plan are equal to the benefits provided under each contract at normal retirement age and are guaranteed by the insurer, and (3) an employee's accrued benefit at any time is not less than the cash surrender value his or her insurance contracts would have assuming that all premiums currently due are paid and there is no indebtedness against the contracts.[5] See Q 3811 and Q 3812 for details on fully insured plans.

A plan is considered a fully insured 412(i) plan when funded exclusively by group insurance or group annuity contracts if the group contract has the requisite characteristics of individual contracts.[6] The IRS has taken the position that, for example, amounts received by an insurer under a group contract must be allocated to purchase individual benefits for participants: "A plan which maintains unallocated funds in an auxiliary trust fund or which provides that an insurance company will maintain unallocated funds in a separate account, such as a group deposit administration contract, does not satisfy the requirements of … [a fully insured insurance contract plan]."[7]

If at the time an employee separates from service the value of his or her employee contributions exceeds the cash surrender value of the insurance contract(s) funding the employee's retirement benefit, the plan could supplement the cash surrender value or values to satisfy the minimum vesting standard and the plan would not fail to be a fully insured plan.[8]

---

1.   Notice 2012-46, 2012-30 IRB 86.
2.   77 F.R. 66915 (Nov. 8, 2012) (adding Treas. Reg. §1.411(d)-4 A-2(b)(2)(xii)).
3.   WRERA 2008, Sec. 203.
4.   80 FR 54373 (Sept. 9, 2015).
5.   IRC Sec. 411(b)(1)(F).
6.   IRC Sec. 412(e)(3), as redesignated by PPA 2006.
7.   Treas. Reg. §1.412(i)-1(c)(2)(v).
8.   Treas. Reg. §1.412(i)-1(b).

3717. What is the minimum participation (50/40) test that applies to defined benefit pension plans?

A defined benefit plan also must benefit the lesser of (a) 50 employees or (b) the greater of (i) 40 percent of all employees or (ii) two employees (or if there is only one employee, that employee).[1] Governmental plans are not subject to this 50/40 test.[2]

Defined benefit plans must meet the minimum participation test on each day of the plan year. Under a simplified testing method, a plan is treated as satisfying this test if it satisfies it on any single day during the plan year so long as that day is reasonably representative of the employer's workforce and the plan's coverage. A plan does not have to be tested on the same day each plan year.[3] Final regulations provide that a plan that does not satisfy the test for a plan year may be amended by the 15th day of the 10th month after the close of the plan year to satisfy the test retroactively.[4] Comparable plans may not be aggregated for purposes of meeting this test.[5]

The 50/40 test may be applied separately with respect to each separate line of business if an employer makes an election to which the Secretary of the Treasury consents.[6] Furthermore, the requirement that a separate line of business have at least 50 employees generally does not apply in determining whether a plan satisfies the 50/40 test on a separate line of business basis.[7]

A defined benefit plan's prior benefit structure also must satisfy the minimum participation rule.[8] The prior benefit structure under a defined benefit plan for a plan year includes all benefits accrued to date under the plan, and each defined benefit plan has only one prior benefit structure. A prior benefit structure satisfies the minimum participation rule if the plan provides meaningful benefits to a group of employees that includes the lesser of 50 employees or 40 percent of the employer's employees. Whether a plan is providing meaningful benefits, or whether the employees have meaningful accrued benefits under a plan, is determined on the basis of all the facts and circumstances.[9]

The same employees who are excludable under the coverage tests (Q 3841) generally may be excluded from consideration in meeting the 50/40 participation test.[10] If employees who do not meet a plan's minimum age and service requirements are covered under a plan that meets the 50/40 test separately with respect to such employees, those employees may be excluded from consideration in determining whether other plans of the employer meet the 50/40 test, but only if (1) the benefits for excluded employees are provided under the same plan as benefits for other employees, (2) the benefits provided to excluded employees are not greater than comparable

1.   IRC Sec. 401(a)(26).
2.   See IRC Sec. 401(a)(26)(G).
3.   Treas. Reg. §1.401(a)(26)-7(b).
4.   Treas. Reg. §1.401(a)(26)-7(c), Treas. Reg. §1.401(a)(4)-11(g).
5.   General Explanation—TRA '86, p. 683.
6.   IRC Sec. 401(a)(26)(A).
7.   IRC Sec. 401(a)(26)(F).
8.   Treas. Reg. §1.401(a)(26)-1(a).
9.   Treas. Reg. §§1.401(a)(26)-3(b), 1.401(a)(26)-3(c).
10. IRC Sec. 401(a)(26)(B)(i); Treas. Reg. §1.401(a)(26)-6.

benefits provided to other employees under the plan, and (3) no highly compensated employee is included in the group of excluded employees for more than one year.[1]

An employee generally is treated as benefiting under a plan for a plan year if the employee actually accrues a benefit for the plan year. An employee who fails to accrue a benefit merely because of the IRC Section 415 limits (Q 3867, Q 3719) or a uniformly applicable benefit limit under the plan's structure is treated as benefiting under a plan for the plan year.[2]

As to which individuals must be treated as "employees" and which organizations make up an employer, see Q 3927, Q 3928, Q 3932, and Q 3934.

3718. How does the SECURE Act impact nondiscrimination testing rules for closed defined benefit plans?

The SECURE Act made changes that would make it easier for certain sponsors of closed defined benefit plans to satisfy their nondiscrimination testing requirements.

Many employers who have closed defined benefit plans to new participants have continued to allow groups of "grandfathered" employees to earn benefits under the closed defined benefit plans. Because of this, many of these plans have had difficulties meeting the applicable nondiscrimination requirements as more of these grandfathered employees become "highly compensated" over time. For a number of years, the IRS has released relief from the nondiscrimination rules for closed defined benefit plans. The SECURE Act essentially codifies a number of these relief provisions.

Generally, a defined benefit plan cannot discriminate in favor of highly compensated employees with respect to any plan benefit, right or feature. Under the SECURE Act, defined benefit plans will be treated as passing nondiscrimination testing with respect to benefits, rights and features if:

(1)   the plan passes nondiscrimination testing in the plan year during which the plan closure takes place, and the two subsequent plan years,

(2)   the plan was not amended after closure to discriminate in favor of highly compensated employees, either by modifying the closed class or the benefits, rights and features provided to that class and

(3)   the plan was closed before April 5, 2017 or there was no substantial increase in value of either coverage or value of the benefits, rights and features for the five-year period before the plan was closed.

A plan is treated as having had a "substantial increase" in coverage or value of the benefits, rights, or features during the applicable five-year period only if, during that period:

"(i) the number of participants covered by such benefits, rights, or features on the date the five-year period ends is more than 50 percent greater than the number of such participants on the first day of the plan year in which the period began, or

---

1.   IRC Sec. 401(a)(26)(B)(ii); Treas. Reg. §1.401(a)(26)-6(b)(1).
2.   Treas. Reg. §§1.401(a)(26)-5(a), 1.410(b)-3(a)(2)(iii).

"(ii) the benefits, rights, and features have been modified by plan amendments in such a way that, as of the date the class is closed, the value of the benefits, rights, and features to the closed class as a whole is substantially greater than the value as of the first day of such five-year period, solely as a result of the amendments.

Additionally, closed defined benefit plans can be aggregated with the employer's defined contribution plans for purposes of compliance testing if:

(1)   the defined benefit plan provides benefits to a closed group of participants,

(2)   the defined benefit plan passes nondiscrimination and coverage testing in the plan year during which the plan closure takes place, and the two subsequent plan years,

(3)   no amendments that discriminate in favor of highly compensated employees were made after the plan closed, and

(4)   the plan was closed before April 5, 2017 or there was no "substantial increase" in value of either coverage or value of the benefits, rights and features for the five-year period before the plan was closed (see above).

If the defined benefit plan is aggregated with a plan that provides matching contributions, the defined benefit plan must also be aggregated with the portion of the DC plan that provides elective deferrals and the matching contributions must be treated in the same way as nonelective contributions for purposes of nondiscrimination and coverage testing.

The nondiscrimination relief is effective immediately, but plans have the option of applying this relief retroactively to plan years beginning after December 31, 2013.

3719. How are Section 415 limits applied to defined benefit plans?

In a defined benefit plan, the highest annual benefit payable under the plan must not exceed the lesser of (a) 100 percent of the participant's average compensation in the high three years of service or (b) $230,000 in 2020-2021 ($225,000 in 2019, as indexed).[1] Regulations specify that this limit also applies to the annual benefit payable to a participant.[2] The regulations referenced throughout this question were issued April 5, 2007, and generally are effective for limitation years beginning after June 30, 2007.[3] For general rules affecting the application of the Section 415 limits, see Q 3867; for the defined contribution plan limits, see Q 3728.

In plan years beginning after 2005, a participant's high three years of service is the period of three consecutive calendar years during which the participant had the greatest aggregate compensation from the employer.[4] Regulations state that a plan may not base accruals on compensation in excess of the Section 401(a)(17) limit ($290,000 in 2021, $285,000 in 2020, $280,000

---

1.   Notice 2018-83, Notice 2019-59, Notice 2020-79.
2.   See Treas. Reg. §1.415(b)-1(a)(1).
3.   T.D. 9319; 72 Fed. Reg. 16878 (April 5, 2007).
4.   IRC Sec. 415(b)(3).

in 2019, as indexed).[1] For plan years beginning prior to January 1, 2006, a participant's high three years of service had to be three consecutive years in which he or she was both an active participant in the plan and had the greatest aggregate compensation from the employer.

For purposes of defined benefit limits, "annual benefit" means a benefit that is payable annually in the form of a straight life annuity. If the benefit is payable in a form other than a straight life annuity, the annual benefit is determined as the straight life annuity that is actuarially equivalent to the form in which the benefit is paid.[2] The application of the Section 415(b) limit to a benefit that is not payable in the form of an annual straight life annuity is explained in Treasury Regulation Section 1.415(b)-1(c). Earlier guidance appeared in Revenue Ruling 2001-51.[3] The "annual benefit" does not include employee contributions and rollover contributions.[4]

Planning Point: In Revenue Ruling 2012-4,[5] the IRS ruled that a qualified defined benefit plan that accepts a direct rollover of an employee's or former employee's benefit from a qualified defined contribution plan maintained by the same employer does not violate Sections 411 or 415 if the defined benefit plan provides an annuity resulting from the direct rollover that is determined by converting the amount directly rolled over into an actuarially equivalent immediate annuity using the applicable interest rate and applicable mortality table under Section 417(e). If the plan were to provide an annuity using a more favorable actuarial basis than required under Section 411(c), the portion of the benefit resulting from this more favorable treatment would be included in the annual benefit. This interpretation applies to rollovers made on or after January 1, 2013.

The annual benefit does not include employer contributions to an individual medical account under IRC Section 401(h) (Q 3835) of any individual under a defined benefit pension plan. Such amounts are treated as annual additions to a separate defined contribution plan (Q 3728).[6]

There are special rules requiring an adjustment of the annual benefit where a participant has more than one annuity starting date (for example, where benefits under one plan are aggregated with benefits under another plan from which distributions have already commenced, or where benefits are increased under a cost of living adjustment).[7]

The $230,000 limit (as indexed for 2020-2021) is adjusted downward if the annuity starting date occurs before the participant reaches age 62.[8] If the annuity starting date occurs after the participant reaches age 65, the limit is adjusted upward.[9] The calculation of the adjustments is explained at IRC Section 415(b)(2)(E) and Treasury Regulation Section 1.415(b)-1(d) and (e). Earlier guidance on implementing these adjustments was provided in Revenue Ruling 2001-51.[10]

An adjustment also is required for certain other forms of benefit, as well as for employee contributions and rollover contributions (Q 3995 to Q 4018), so that such benefits are converted

---

1. See Treas. Reg. §1.415(b)-1(a)(1); Notice 2018-83, Notice 2019-59, Notice 2020-79.
2. See Treas. Reg. §1.415(b)-1(b)(1).
3. 2001-2 CB 427, A-3.
4. See Treas. Reg. §1.415(b)-1(b)(1)(ii).
5. 2012-1 CB 386 (Feb. 2, 2012). Still current as of March 2020 at www.IRS.gov/retirement-plans/revenue-rulings.
6. See IRC Sec. 415(l).
7. See Treas. Reg. §1.415(b)-1(b)(1)(iii).
8. IRC Sec. 415(b)(2)(C); Treas. Reg. §1.415(b)-1(a)(4); Notice 2019-59, Notice 2020-79.
9. IRC Sec. 415(b)(2)(D); Treas. Reg. §1.415(b)-1(a)(4).
10. 2001-2 CB 427, A-4.

to the actuarial equivalent of a straight life annuity.[1] Under earlier guidance this adjustment was more complex, generally following the manner in which Social Security benefits are reduced for Social Security purposes. The interest rate assumption used for making this adjustment must be no less than the greater of 5.5 percent or the rate specified in the plan.[2] In the case of benefits subject to IRC Section 417(e)(3), the interest rate must be the rate set forth in IRC Section 417(e)(3).[3] Guidance and detailed rules for making this calculation appear in Notice 2004-78[4] and in Treasury Regulation Section 1.415(b)-1(c)(3). Simplification for amounts not subject to minimum present value rules of IRC Section 417(e)(3) is set forth in Treasury Regulation Section 1.415(b)-1(c)(2).

Adjustments to the ceiling do not need to be made for ancillary benefits not directly related to retirement benefits (such as preretirement death and disability benefits and postretirement medical benefits).[5] If the benefit is paid in the form of a joint and survivor annuity for the benefit of the participant and the participant's spouse, the value of the feature will not be taken into consideration in reducing the ceiling unless the survivor benefit is greater than the joint benefit.[6]

The 100 percent of compensation limit generally does not apply to governmental plans, multiemployer plans, or certain collectively bargained plans.[7]

The dollar limit and 100 percent compensation limit are subject to a 10-year phase-in rule. The $230,000 limit (as indexed for 2020-2021)[8] is reduced by multiplying it by the following fraction: the numerator is the participant's years of participation in the defined benefit plan, and the denominator is 10.[9] The 100 percent of compensation limit is reduced in the same manner, but based on years of service, rather than years of participation.[10] "Years of service," for this purpose, includes employment with a predecessor employer, including affiliated employers.[11] Neither reduction will reduce the limitation to less than 10 percent of the otherwise applicable limitation amount.[12]

A benefit of up to $10,000 in any limitation year may be provided to a participant without violating the IRC Section 415 limits, notwithstanding the 100 percent limit or required adjustments for ancillary benefits. This benefit, however, is subject to the 10 year phase-in rule described above, based on years of service. The participant must not at any time also have participated in a defined contribution plan maintained by the employer.[13]

---

1.   IRC Sec. 415(b)(2)(B); see Treas. Reg. §1.415(b)-1(b)(2).
2.   Notice 2009-98, 2009-2 CB 974.
3.   IRC Sec. 415(b)(2)(E)(i); IRC Sec. 415(b)(2)(E)(ii).
4.   2004-48 IRB 879.
5.   Treas. Reg. §1.415(b)-1(c)(4). See also, IRS Information Letter, 18 Pens. Rep. (BNA) 1552 (1991); Let. Rul. 9636030.
6.   IRC Sec. 415(b)(2)(B).
7.   Treas. Reg. §1.415(b)-1(a)(6).
8.   Notice 2019-59, Notice 2020-79.
9.   IRC Sec. 415(b)(5)(A).
10. IRC Sec. 415(b)(5)(B).
11. See Treas. Reg. §§1.415(b)-1(g)(2)(ii)(B), 1.415(f)-1(c), 1.415(a)-1(f); see also *Lear Eye Clinic, Ltd. v. Comm.*, 106 TC 418 (1996).
12. IRC Sec. 415(b)(5)(C).
13. IRC Secs. 415(b)(4), 415(b)(5)(B).

A plan may incorporate by reference the automatic adjustments of plan benefits to the extent of the annual cost-of-living increases provided under the IRC. The scheduled benefit increases may not take effect earlier than the year in which the dollar limit adjustment becomes effective.[1] Regulations state that the annual increase does not apply in limitation years beginning after the annuity starting date to a participant who previously has commenced receiving benefits unless the plan so specifies.[2] Earlier regulations stated that a plan could provide for automatic freezing or reduction of the rate of benefit accrual to prevent the limitations from being exceeded.[3]

A defined benefit plan may maintain a qualified cost-of-living arrangement under which employer and employee contributions may be applied to provide cost-of-living increases to the primary benefit under the plan. This kind of arrangement is qualified if the adjustment is based on increases in the cost-of-living after the annuity starting date, determined by reference to one or more indexes prescribed by the IRS (or a minimum of 3 percent). The arrangement must:

(1)   be elective;

(2)   be available to all participants under the same terms;

(3)   provide for such election at least in the year the participant attains the earliest retirement age under the plan (determined without regard to any requirement of separation from service) or separates from service; and

(4)   exclude key employees.[4]

Toward the end of 2016, the IRS released two significant sets of proposed regulations on issues important to defined benefit plans. In November, 2016, the IRS proposed a regulation[5] that would update minimum present value requirements applicable to certain distributions and also to take account of final IRS regulations[6] released earlier in the fall addressing the minimum present value requirements for pension benefits payable partly as an annuity and partly in an accelerated amount.

The second set of proposed regulations[7] would update the mortality tables to be used for single employer defined benefit plans.[8] The proposed effective date is for plan years on or after January 1, 2018.

---

1.   Treas. Reg. §§1.415(a)-1(d)(3)(v), 1.415(d)-1.
2.   See Treas. Reg. §1.415(a)-1(d)(3)(v)(C).
3.   Treas. Reg. §1.415-1(d)(1).
4.   IRC Sec. 415(k)(2).
5.   REG 107424-12, IRB 2016-51, published 2016-12 IRB (Dec. 19. 2016).
6.   TD 9783, IRB 2016-39 (Sept. 26, 2016) finalizing REG 110980-10.
7.   REG 112324-15, published 81 Fed. Reg. 95911 (Dec. 29, 2016).
8.   These proposed regulations are a response to the Society of Actuaries released RP-2014 Mortality Tables Report and Mortality Improvement Scale MP-2014 in October, 2014 containing recommendations of new mortality assumptions for private sector pension plans.

Planning Point: The change in required mortality tables is expected to increase plan funding liabilities;[1] hence PBGC variable rate premiums and also lump sum distributions. Plan sponsors had only until the end of 2017 to offer lump sum distributions utilizing the old mortality assumptions, and also avoid future PBGC premium increases based upon increased plan liabilities.

3720. What is a cash balance plan?

A cash balance plan is a defined benefit plan that calculates benefits and contributions in a manner similar to the way that defined contribution plans make those calculations. The similarity ends in that a cash balance plan's calculations require an actuary. A cash balance plan resembles a defined contribution plan in that each employee has a hypothetical account, or "cash balance," to which contributions and interest payments are credited. In a typical cash balance plan, the employee's benefit accrues evenly over the years of service, with annual pay credits to the hypothetical account. There is no separate account. These pay credits usually are a fixed percentage of pay that is stated in the plan document, such as 4 percent.

With no separate account, there is no directed investing available. As with other defined benefit plans, the employer bears both the risk and the benefits of investment performance. That is, losses in the plan's investments generally require additional employer funding. The actual amount that must be contributed is determined actuarially. This ensures that the plan has sufficient funds to provide the promised benefits.

For plan years beginning in 2012, the interest credit (or the equivalent amount) for any plan year must be at a rate that is not greater than a "market rate" of return. The term "market rate" of return is defined in regulations issued in 2010.[2] A plan will not fail this requirement merely because it provides for a reasonable minimum guaranteed rate of return or for a rate of return equal to the greater of a fixed or variable rate.[3] An interest credit of less than zero may not result in the account balance being less than the aggregate amount of contributions credited to the account.[4] This legislative change eliminates the possibility of "whipsaw," in which disparate interest rates used for crediting and discounting purposes resulted in the discounted present value of employees' accounts being higher than the theoretical account's value.

Planning Point: IRS Revenue Procedure 2018-21 allows certain preapproved defined benefit plans containing a cash benefit formula to use the actual rate of return on plan assets to determine interest crediting. Many expect that this move will encourage more plans to move to the preapproved plan structure, as the IRS has eliminated its determination letter program for many individually designed plans.[5] The IRS also provided that while the rate used to determine

---

1. Note that this impact would also extend to any nonqualified supplemental pension plan ("excess benefit") liabilities as well for accounting purposes, but of course, not PBGC premium purposes.
2. Treas. Reg. §1.411(b)(5)-1(d).
3. 29 U.S.C. §623(i)(1)(B)(i)(I).
4. IRC Sec. 411(b)(5)(B)(i)(II); Treas. Reg. §1.411(b)(5)-1.
5. In recent years, the IRS has been reconsidering the extent of its letter determination program elimination in light of comments requesting more situations where determination letters might be requested. However, full restoration of the program seems unlike as of the date of this publication.

investment credits cannot be based on the rate of return for regulated investment companies (RICs), the actual rate of return can be used even if the plan assets contain RIC returns.

Planning Point: The Moving Ahead for Progress in the 21st Century Act (MAP-21)[1] enacted on July 6, 2012, contained interest-rate stabilization provisions for defined benefit plans. In August 2012, the IRS issued Notice 2012-55,[2] which outlined the MAP-21 segment rates to be used for plan years beginning in 2012.[3] MAP-21 revises the three segment rates used under the single employer funding rules. The Highway and Transportation Funding Act of 2014 amended the MAP-21 segment rates effective for plan years beginning on or after January 1, 2013;[4] however, the plan sponsor could elect to defer use of the HAFTA segment rates until the plan year beginning in 2014. Guidance for making the election to defer is found in Notice 2015-42.[5]

IRS Notice 2012-61[6] provides guidance on pension funding stabilization under MAP-21. The guidance gives flexibility to plan administrators of plans that use the third segment rate by allowing the administrator to interpret the plan terms as requiring either the pre-MAP-21 third segment rate or the MAP-21 third segment rate, as long as the interpretation is applied for interest credited after the first plan year to which MAP-21 is applied for purposes of funding. An amendment to reflect that interpretation will not be considered a plan cutback.

In 2014, the IRS amended Treasury Regulation Section 1.411(b)(5)-1(d)(1)(iii), which provides guidance on the definition of "market rate," to expand the definition of "market rate" and to clarify that the definition is effective for plan years beginning on or after January 1, 2016.[7] Transitional rules were issued in 2015.[8]

In 2017, an IRS internal guidance memo[9] to its plan examiners provided guidance on whether a cash balance plan meets the definitely determinable benefits requirement when the formula is based upon partial compensation. The memo indicates that the benefits formula will be determinable if the plan terms provide a formula under which the pay credit is arrived at by looking at compensation information otherwise available, even if outside the terms of the plan (e.g., W-2 compensation documentation).

3721. What rules apply for converting a traditional defined benefit plan to a cash balance plan?

The recent history of cash balance plans began with the IRS directive released on September 15, 1999 instructing field offices to stop reviewing determination letters applications for cash balance plans. The Economic and Tax Relief Reconciliation Act of 2001 (EGTRRA) added additional disclosure requirements in situations involving the conversion of a traditional defined benefit plan to a cash balance plan and imposed an excise tax on plan sponsors failing

---

1. Pub. L. No. 112-141.
2. 2012-36 IRB 332 (Aug. 16, 2012). See also Notice 2014-43, 2014-31 IRB 249 (July 9, 2014).
3. Notice 2013-11, 2013-11 IRB 610 (Feb. 12, 2013). The 25-year segment rates for 2012 - 2015 were published in Notice 2012-55, 2012-36 IRB 332 (Aug. 16, 2012), Notice 2013-11, 2013-11 IRB 610 (Feb. 12, 2013), Notice 2013-58, 2013-40 IRB 294 (Sept. 11, 2013), and Notice 2014-50, 2014-40 IRB 590 (Sept. 11, 2014).
4. Notice 2015-42, 2015-26 IRB 1137 (June 10, 2015). See Notice 2014-53, 2014-2 C.B. 737 (Sept. 11, 2014).
5. 2015-26 IRB 1137 (June 10, 2015).
6. 2012-2 C.B. 479 (Sept. 11, 2012), at H-1.
7. Preamble, Additional Rules Regarding to Hybrid Retirement Plans, Part II, 79 F.R. 56442 (Sept. 19, 2014), at Effective Date.
8. 80 Fed. Reg. 70680 (Nov. 16, 2015).
9. TE/GE Memo 04-0417-0014 (Apr. 7, 2017).

to comply with these disclosure requirements. The law also imposed an excise tax if the plan sponsor specifically fails to notify participants of a plan benefit reduction in accruals, which often occurs for older plan participants in a conversion and created much of the early controversy around such plans. IRS Notice 2007-6[1] was then issued in 2007 providing additional detailed guidance on the creation of cash balance plans, and reopening the letter determination programs for such plans then being held for review. This plan design has flourished since.

A traditional defined benefit plan that is converting to a cash balance plan is currently subject to certain rules on the crediting of participant benefits. The plan's benefit after conversion must not be less than the sum of the participant's accrued benefit for years of service before the conversion under the prior formula, plus the benefit the participant earns under the new formula for service after the conversion.[2] This formula is known by actuaries as an "A+B" approach.

The A+B approach is designed to eliminate a plan issue referred to as "wearaway," which refers to situations where certain participants in the plan do not accrue any additional benefits until benefits under the prior plan are worn away to equal benefits under the new plan. This occurred in some conversions where older employees might not accrue additional benefits under the cash balance formula until their new hypothetical account balance caught up with their prior accrued benefit. Requirements for calculation of the present value of a participant's accrued benefit in such cases are set forth in IRC Section 411(a)(13)(A) (effective for distributions made after August 17, 2006).

3722. What vesting requirements apply to cash balance plans?

For plan years beginning after 2007, benefits in cash balance plans must be 100 percent vested after three years of service.[3]

3723. What requirements must a cash balance plan meet in order to avoid discriminating based on age under the Pension Protection Act of 2006?

The Pension Protection Act of 2006 ended a long period of uncertainty for cash balance plans by amending the IRC, ERISA, and the Age Discrimination in Employment Act of 1967. The effect of the legislative changes provides that cash balance plans will not be age discriminatory if certain requirements are met.

A preexisting IRC requirement under which cash balance plans had been attacked stated that an employee's benefit accruals may not cease, and the rate accrual may not be reduced, because of the attainment of any age.[4] Three parallel amendments provide that a plan will not be treated as failing this requirement if a participant's accrued benefit, determined as of any date under the terms of the plan, would be equal to or greater than that of any similarly situated, younger individual who is or could be a participant.[5] Except as otherwise indicated below, the provisions of PPA 2006 applicable to cash balance plans are effective for periods after June 28, 2005.[6]

---

1. 2007-1 CB 272.
2. IRC Secs. 411(b)(5)(B)(ii), 411(b)(5)(B)(iii), effective for conversions occurring after June 29, 2005.
3. See IRC Sec. 411(a)(13)(B); Pub. L. 109-280, Sec. 701(e)(3).
4. IRC Sec. 411(b)(1)(H)(i).
5. IRC Sec. 411(b)(5)(A)(i).
6. Pub. L. 109-280, Sec. 701(e).

A participant is "similarly situated" if he or she is identical to another individual in every respect except for age; in other words, in circumstances such as period of service, compensation, date of hire, work history.[1]

Planning Point: When modifying a pension plan to become a cash balance plans even if all the assumptions may be reasonable, the communications to the participants are extremely important and care should be taken with their preparation to accurately state the impact of the changes on those participants... It must not be in any respect either misleading or, of course, false.[2]

"Accrued benefit" is defined by the plan terms; it may be expressed as an annuity payable at normal retirement age, the balance of the participant's cash balance plan account, or some other means. Early retirement subsidies, permitted disparity, and certain other plan features are disregarded for this purpose.[3]

Prior to the passage of the PPA, the Seventh Circuit Court of Appeals held that a cash balance plan formula that was age neutral did not give rise to age discrimination under ERISA, and that an employer's choice to convert from a defined benefit plan (which tends to favor older employees) to a cash balance plan (which does not) is not per se age discrimination.[4]

3724. How are the required annual and quarterly payments to single employer defined benefit plans determined?

Editor's Note: The CARES Act gives sponsors the option of using the adjusted funding target attainment percentage for the last plan year ending before January 1, 2020.

Contributions to certain defined benefit plans (other than multiemployer or CSEC plans) subject to the minimum funding standard (Q 3742 to Q 3748) must be made, on an estimated basis, at least quarterly, and the new mortality tables released by the IRS on October 3, 2017 will impact these calculations. The quarterly contribution requirement is imposed on plans with a funding shortfall in the prior year.[5]

The required amount for each quarterly installment is 25 percent of the Required Annual Payment ("RAP").[6] The RAP is the lesser of the following:

(1)   90 percent of the minimum required contribution amount the employer is required to contribute for the plan year under the minimum funding requirements; and

(2)   100 percent of the minimum required contribution for the preceding plan year (determined without regard to a Section 412(c) waiver), but only if the preceding plan year consisted of twelve months.[7]

---

1.   See IRC Sec. 411(b)(5)(A)(ii).
2.   *See generally, Osberg v. Foot Locker, Inc.*, No. 15-3602 (2nd Cir. July 6, 2017), cert. filed Nov. 8, 2017 aff'g Dist. Ct. decision granting equitable relief to plaintiff-participants based upon misleading and false communications.
3.   See IRC Sec. 411(b)(5)(A)(iv).
4.   See *Cooper v. IBM Personal Pension Plan*, 457 F.3d 636 (7th Cir. 2006), *rev'g* 274 F. Supp. 2d (S.D. Ill. 2003).
5.   IRC Sec. 430(j)(3).
6.   IRC Sec. 430(j)(3)(D)(ii).
7.   IRC Sec. 430(j)(3)(D) (ii).

Quarterly contributions are determined without regard to increased contributions.

Defined benefit plans subject to the quarterly contributions requirement also must meet a liquidity requirement[1] and generally must maintain liquid plan assets. A plan will be deemed to have a liquidity shortfall if, with respect to a quarter, the plan does not have liquid assets in an amount approximately equal to three times the total adjusted disbursements from the plan trust during the twelve month period ending on the last day of each quarter for which the plan must pay a required quarterly installment.[2] A special rule permits this amount to be determined without regard to nonrecurring circumstances, under certain conditions.[3]

The minimum funding requirement for a plan year generally is determined without regard to any credit balance or prefunding balance as of the beginning of the plan year. A credit balance in the plan's funding standard account may not be treated as a contribution to satisfy the liquidity requirement.

If a required installment is not paid to the plan by its due date, the funding standard account is charged with interest on the amount by which the required installment exceeds the amount, if any, paid on or before such due date. This interest is charged for the period from the due date until the date when the installment actually is paid.[4] The installment due dates are April 15, July 15, October 15, and January 15 of the following year,[5] or, if the plan year is not a calendar year, the 15th of each corresponding month in the plan year.[6] The rate of interest charged is the rate of interest used to determine liability plus 5 percent.[7] Additional payments necessary to satisfy the minimum funding requirement are due within 8.5 months after the end of the plan year.

A statutory lien may be imposed on an employer, determined on a controlled group basis (Q 3932), for failure to make a required installment or any other payment required by the minimum funding rules if the aggregate unpaid balance of the contributions or payments (including interest) exceeds $1,000,000.[8]

Defined Contribution Plans

3725. What is a defined contribution plan?

The IRC permits two types of tax qualified plans: defined contribution plans, and defined benefit plans.

A defined contribution plan is characterized by two elements: 1) each participant has an individual account, and 2) all benefits are provided solely from the accumulated value of those accounts based on amounts contributed by employee and employer, forfeiture reallocation and

---

1.   IRC Sec. 430(j)(4).
2.   IRC Sec. 430(j)(4)(E)(ii)(I).
3.   IRC Sec. 430(j)(4)(E)(ii)(II).
4.   IRC Sec. 430(j)(3)(B)(ii).
5.   IRC Sec. 430(j)(3)(C)(ii).
6.   IRC Sec. 430(j)(3)(E).
7.   IRC Sec. 430(j)(3)(A).
8.   IRC Sec. 430(k)(1).

accruals, plus income, expenses, gains and losses (e.g., 401(k) plan).[1] Defined contribution plans contain a formula for determining the amount of the contribution or how a discretionary contribution to the plan is allocated to each participant's account.

A defined contribution plan can be either a pension (Q 3733) or a profit sharing plan (Q 3749). Profit sharing, age weighted and cross-tested profit sharing plans include 401(k) plans (Q 3752), stock bonus plans (Q 3815), and employee stock ownership plans (Q 3816). Pension plans include money purchase and target benefit plans (Q 3734).

See Q 3728 for the application of the Section 415 limits to defined contribution plans and Q 3726 for special qualification requirements.

3726. What special qualification requirements apply to defined contribution plans?

A defined contribution plan must contain a limitation on the amount of "annual additions" that may be credited to a participant's account each year, or, if an employer has more than one plan, to all accounts of all defined contribution plans of the employer (Q 3728, Q 3867). The plan must require a separate accounting for each employee's benefit under the plan.[2]

A defined contribution plan may not exclude from participation in the plan employees who are beyond a specified age.[3]

Hybrid plans, which combine the features of defined contribution plans and defined benefit plans, are treated as defined contribution plans to the extent that benefits are based on the individual account. One type of hybrid plan is the target benefit plan (Q 3734). The participant's target benefit is calculated according to a formula, and an actuary determines the contribution necessary to reach this target by retirement age. This amount is allocated to the participant's account.

A defined contribution plan must provide for (1) allocation of contributions and trust earnings to participants in accordance with a definite formula, (2) distributions in accordance with an amount stated or otherwise ascertainable and credited to participants, and (3) a valuation of investments held by the trust, at least once a year, on a specified inventory date, in accordance with a method consistently followed and uniformly applied.[4] The third requirement may be satisfied in a plan where contributions are invested solely in insurance contracts or in mutual fund shares even if there is no provision in the plan for periodic valuation of assets.[5]

A defined contribution plan will not fail to satisfy the participation, coverage, and vesting requirements merely because it does not unconditionally provide for an allocation to a participant with respect to a computation period in which he or she completes 1,000 hours of service (Q 3840, Q 3868). Thus, for example, a plan may require that a participant be employed as of

---

1.   IRC Sec. 414(i).
2.   IRC Sec. 411(b)(2)(A).
3.   IRC Sec. 410(a)(2).
4.   Rev. Rul. 80-155, 1980-1 CB 84.
5.   Rev. Rul. 73-435, 1973-2 CB 126; Rev. Rul. 73-554, 1973-2 CB 130.

the last day of a computation period to receive an allocation.[1] This provision will not violate nondiscrimination requirements (Q 3847).

A money purchase pension plan or a profit sharing plan will not be qualified unless the plan designates the type of plan it is.[2] The IRS has ruled that amounts transferred or directly rolled over from a money purchase pension plan to an otherwise qualified profit sharing plan must continue to be subject to the restrictions on money purchase pension plans. In the absence of such restrictions, the profit sharing plan would fail to qualify under IRC Section 401(a).[3]

3727. What diversification and vesting requirements apply to defined contribution plans that provide for acquisition of employer stock?

For plan years beginning after December 31, 2006, a diversification requirement applies to certain defined contribution plans that hold publicly-traded employer securities (Q 3732).[4]

A qualified defined contribution plan, other than a profit sharing plan, that is established by an employer whose stock is not readily tradable on an established market and that holds more than 10 percent of its assets in employer securities must provide that plan participants are entitled to exercise voting rights with respect to employer stock held by the plan with respect to approval of corporate mergers, consolidations, recapitalizations, reclassifications, liquidation, dissolution, sales of substantially all of the business's assets, and similar transactions as provided in future regulations. Each participant must be given one vote with respect to an issue, and the trustee must vote the shares held by the plan in a proportion that takes into account the one participant/one vote requirement.[5]

Planning Point: There has been significant litigation in recent years, with a resurgence in 2016-2017 against employers who allow or continue to allow investment in company stock, especially companies experiencing financial difficulties. Sears became the subject of such a class action lawsuit as of August 1, 2017.[6] Companies that have defeated such litigation include Eaton Corp., IBM, JP Morgan Chase, Lehman Brothers, RadioShack Corp., and Whole Foods Corp just to name some of the more prominent companies sued by employees. Moreover, even good performance of company stock has not prevented employee lawsuits against companies like Chesapeake Energy Corp., General Cable and Seventy Seven Energy Inc., based upon complaints involving company stock accounts in their plans. For this reason, an employer should have significant business reasons for including company stock in the plan's portfolio in the present litigious environment. In addition, the Plan Committee should monitor company financial affairs closely for changes in investment policy when company stock is included.

3728. How are Section 415 limits applied to defined contribution plans?

Annual additions include employee contributions, employer contributions, and forfeitures. The annual additions to a participant's account (or all such accounts aggregated, if the employer has more than one defined contribution plan) must not exceed the lesser of 100 percent of the

---

1.   See Treas. Reg. §§1.410(b)-3(a)(1), 1.410(b)-6(f)(3), 1.401(a)(26)-5(a)(1).
2.   IRC Sec. 401(a)(27)(B).
3.   Rev. Rul. 94-76, 1994-2 CB 46; amplified by Rev. Rul, 2002-42, 2002-2 CB 76.
4.   IRC Sec. 401(a)(35).
5.   IRC Secs. 401(a)(22), 409(e).
6.   See e.g., *Catafalmo v. Sears Holdings Corp.*, N.D. Ill., No. 1:17-CV-05230 (complaint filed Jul.14, 2017).

participant's compensation or $58,000 (as indexed for 2021, up from $57,000 in 2020, $56,000 in 2019).[1] This limit is indexed for inflation in increments of $1,000.[2]

Planning Point: When an HSA is available in a company and a viable option for an individual in his or her circumstances (e.g., spouse's company medical plan is more attractive than the individual's plan), it can allow that individual to defer amounts above the limit to the 401(k), grow it tax-free and to the extent not used for valid health care expenses, eventually withdraw it take-free. Moreover, Congress is discussing reducing the limits on the use of HSAs so that it may become available to some individuals regardless and become an attractive supplement to 401(k) deferrals for employees who are above the 401(k) limit.

Limitations applicable when an individual is a participant in one or more elective deferral plans (including 401(k) plans, SIMPLE IRAs, SAR-SEPs, and tax sheltered annuities) are explained in Q 3760. For general rules affecting the application of the Section 415 limits, see Q 3867; for defined benefit plan limits, see Q 3719. The regulations referenced throughout this question were issued April 5, 2007 and are effective for limitation years beginning after June 30, 2007.[3]

The following amounts are not annual additions:

(1)   Catch-up contributions (Q 3761)

(2)   Payments made to restore losses resulting from a breach of fiduciary duty

(3)   Excess deferrals that are distributed as required in regulations (Q 3760)

(4)   Certain restorations of accrued benefits[4]

Earlier regulations provide for corrective measures when contributions in excess of the Section 415 limits (i.e., excess annual additions) are made due to the allocation of forfeitures, due to reasonable error in estimating a participant's compensation, or under certain other limited circumstances.[5] The preamble to the 2007 regulations states that guidance on this subject is in the Employee Plans Compliance Resolution System (EPCRS).[6]

Any amount allocated to a separate account that is required to be established in a welfare benefit fund (Q 4102) to provide postretirement medical or life insurance benefits to a key employee (Q 3930) must be treated as an annual addition to a separate defined contribution plan for purposes of calculating the annual additions to defined contribution plans of an employer.[7] Such amounts are not subject to the 100 percent of compensation limit under IRC Section 415(c)(1)(B) discussed above.

---

1.   IRC Sec. 415(c); Notice 2018-83, Notice 2019-59, Notice 2020-79.
2.   IRC Sec. 415(d)(4)(B).
3.   T.D. 9319, 72 Fed. Reg. 16878 (April 5, 2007).
4.   Treas. Reg. §1.415(c)-1(b)(2)(ii); IRC Sec. 414(v)(3)(A). See also Rev. Rul. 2002-45, 2002-2 CB 116.
5.   Treas. Reg. §1.415-6(b)(6) (removed effective April 5, 2007).
6.   72 Fed. Reg. 16878 (April 5, 2007) (preamble). The current EPCRS program is described in Rev. Proc. 2016-51, 2016-42 IRB 465 *modifying and superseding* Rev. Proc. 2013-12, 2013-4 IRB 313, as modified by Rev. Proc. 2015-28, 2015-16 IRB 920 and by Rev. Proc. 2015-27, 2015-16 IRB 914. Rev. Proc. 2013-12 had superseded Rev. Proc. 2008-50 as of April 1, 2013.
7.   IRC Sec. 419A(d)(2).

While annual additions are the sum credited to a participant's account for any limitation year, of (1) employer contributions, (2) employee contributions, and (3) forfeitures, "employee contributions" do not include rollovers from another qualified plan or from an IRA (Q 3995), contributions under IRC Section 457(e)(6), or employee contributions to a SAR-SEP (Q 3701) that are excludable from the employee's gross income.[1] A direct transfer of funds or employee contributions from one defined contribution plan to another will not be considered an annual addition for the limitation year in which the transfer occurs.[2]

A corrective allocation to a participant's account because of an erroneous forfeiture or a failure to make a required allocation in a prior limitation year will not be considered an annual addition for the limitation year in which the allocation is made, but will be considered an annual addition for the limitation year to which the corrective allocation relates.[3]

Restorative payments made to a defined contribution plan, to the extent they restore plan losses that result from a fiduciary breach (or a reasonable risk of liability for a fiduciary breach), are not contributions for purposes of IRC Section 415(c). In contrast, payments made to a plan to make up for losses due to market fluctuations, but not due to a fiduciary breach, *will* be treated as contributions, not as restorative payments.[4]

Earlier regulations stated that if an allocation of forfeitures or a reasonable error in estimating a participant's annual compensation would cause additions to exceed the limit, they may, under certain circumstances, be held in suspense, be used to reduce employer contributions for that participant or be returned to the participant.[5] (A return of mandatory contributions could result in discrimination.) Certain other transactions between a plan and an employer, or certain allocations to participants' accounts, could be treated as giving rise to annual additions.[6]

Generally, an employer may elect to continue contributions under a profit sharing or stock bonus plan on behalf of permanently and totally disabled participants.[7] For the purpose of determining whether such contributions comply with the limitation on contributions, the disabled participant's compensation is deemed to be the amount of compensation he would have received for the year if paid at the rate of compensation he received immediately before becoming permanently and totally disabled. Contributions made under this provision *must* be nonforfeitable when made.[8] The IRS has privately ruled that a 401(k) plan that purchased a group long-term disability income policy to insure the continuation of benefit accumulation for disabled employees would not be required to include amounts paid under the policy as annual additions.[9]

---

1. See IRC Sec. 415(c)(2).
2. See Treas. Reg. §1.415(c)-1(b)(1); Let. Ruls. 9111046, 9052058.
3. See Rev. Proc. 2013-12, above; Treas. Reg. §1.415(c)-1(b)(6)(ii)(A).
4. Rev. Rul. 2002-45, 2002-2 CB 116; Treas. Reg. §1.415(c)-1(b)(2)(ii)(C). See also Let. Ruls. 9506048, 9628031.
5. Treas. Reg. §1.415-6(b)(6), prior to removal by T.D. 9319. See also Rev. Proc. 2015-27, 2015-16 IRB 914 §4.15.
6. Treas. Reg. §1.415-6(b)(2)(i), prior to removal by T.D. 9319.
7. IRC Sec. 415(c)(3)(C).
8. IRC Sec. 415(c)(3)(C).
9. Let. Ruls. 200031060, 200235043.

A defined contribution plan may provide for an automatic adjustment which reflects the cost-of-living increases in the limit on annual additions.[1] Like defined benefit plans, the plan may provide for automatic freezing or reduction in the rate of annual additions to prevent exceeding the limitation.[2]

In the case of an ESOP, if no more than one-third of the deductible employer contributions applied by the plan to the repayment of principal and interest on loans incurred to acquire qualifying employer securities are allocated to highly compensated employees (Q 3929), forfeitures of employer securities acquired with such loans and deductible employer contributions applied by the plan to the payment of interest on such loans may be excluded for purposes of the limitations on contributions.[3] Where an employer reversion is transferred to an ESOP, amounts in excess of the Section 415 limit which are held in a reversion suspense account are not deemed to be annual additions until the limitation year in which they are allocated to the participants' accounts.[4]

3729. What is counted as compensation for purposes of applying the Section 415 limits to defined contribution plans?

Compensation to which the limit is applied is the compensation for the limitation year from the employer maintaining the plan.[5] It includes wages, salaries, fees for professional services, and other amounts for services actually rendered (such as commissions, percentage of profits, tips, and bonuses).[6] Compensation also includes (i) elective deferrals to 401(k) plans, SAR-SEPs, SIMPLE IRAs, and Section 457(b) plans to the extent not includable in the employee's income and (ii) any amounts contributed or deferred by the election of the employee and excluded from gross income of the employee under IRC Sections 125 (cafeteria plans), 132(f) (qualified transportation fringe benefit plans), or 457 (deferred compensation plan of a government or tax-exempt organization).[7] The foregoing items may be used as a simplified safe harbor definition of compensation.[8]

The regulations also permit the following to be included as compensation to the extent they are includable in the gross income of the employee: certain payments received under an employer's accident and health plan, certain moving expense reimbursements, the value of nonqualified options in the year granted, and certain property transferred in connection with the performance of services.[9]

In the case of a self-employed person, his earned income is compensation.[10]

---

1.   Treas. Reg. §1.415(a)-1(d)(3).
2.   Treas. Reg. §1.415(a)-1(d)(1).
3.   IRC Sec. 415(c)(6). See Treas. Reg. §1.415(c)-1(f).
4.   IRC Sec. 4980(c)(3)(C); Let. Ruls. 8935056, 8925096.
5.   IRC Sec. 415(c)(3)(A).
6.   Treas. Reg. §1.415(c)-2(b)(1).
7.   See IRC Secs. 415(c)(3), 402(g).
8.   Treas. Reg. §1.415(c)-2(d)(2).
9.   Treas. Reg. §1.415(c)-2(b)(3) to (6). See also Treas. Reg. §1.415(c)-2(d)(2).
10. IRC Sec. 415(c)(3)(B).

The SECURE Act also modified the definition of compensation so that certain stipends provided to graduate students can be counted as compensation for IRA contribution purposes after December 31, 2019. Similarly, qualified foster care payments (excluded from income) can be treated as compensation for plan years effective after December 31, 2015 (retroactively) for defined contribution plans and after 2019 for IRAs.[1]

Except as noted above, compensation does not include nontaxable employer contributions toward deferred compensation plans, qualified or nonqualified, in the year in which they were contributed. Furthermore, deferred compensation distributions are not compensation when received whether or not excludable from gross income, except that distributions of unfunded nonqualified deferred compensation may be considered compensation in the year in which they are includable in gross income.[2] Excludable premiums for group term life insurance are not compensation.[3] Foreign source income generally will be treated as compensation even though excluded from gross income.[4]

The compensation must be *actually paid or made available* to be taken into account within the limitation year.[5] Compensation includes compensation from all employers that are members of a controlled group of corporations or a group of trades or businesses under common control.[6] Regulations also provide for safe harbors based on wages for income tax withholding or wages as reported in Box 1 on Form W-2.[7]

Post-severance compensation of the following amounts is included as compensation if paid within 2½ months following severance from employment: (1) payment for unused sick or vacation leave the employee could have used had employment continued or (b) amounts that would have been paid had employment continued, such as compensation and overtime, commissions, bonuses, or similar compensation. It should be noted that this treatment will not apply to other types of post-severance packages, such as parachute payments under IRC Section 280G and unfunded nonqualified deferred compensation.[8]

3730. What are savings and thrift plans, and "side car" accounts?

Savings and thrift plans are defined contribution plans that have employee contributions. The terms generally refer to plans where the employee contributions are made with under-tax employee contributions. These plans were more common before 401(k) plans were introduced, and the Roth after-tax employee contribution to a 401(k) design was added.

Today, some practitioners use these terms also to describe plans where employees make contributions on a pre-tax basis (i.e., 401(k) plans). These plans typically feature

---

1.   SECURE Act, Sec. 106, Sec. 116.
2.   Treas. Reg. §1.415(c)-2(c)(1). Note: Failure to follow the plan's definition of "compensation" continues to be one of the top 10 mistakes the
      IRS has identified in plan audits as of the date of this publication. See https://www.irs.gov/retirement-plans/top-ten-failures-found-in-
      voluntary-correction-program, last updated December 21, 2019; last visited March 22, 2020.
3.   Treas. Reg. §1.415(c)-2(c)(4).
4.   Treas. Reg. §1.415(c)-2(g)(5).
5.   Treas. Reg. §1.415(c)-2(e)(1)(i).
6.   Treas. Reg. §1.415(c)-2(g)(2).
7.   Treas. Reg. §1.415(c)-2(d).
8.   Treas. Reg. §1.415(c)-2(e)(3).

employer-matching contributions. The IRC makes no specific provision for these plans, but they may be tax qualified if they meet the requirements for a pension, profit sharing, or stock bonus plan. A savings or thrift plan may qualify as a pension plan unless there are preretirement privileges to withdraw benefits. They frequently qualify as profit sharing plans by providing for employer contributions out of current or accumulated profits.

Note: There is currently some sponsor and vendor focus to find ways to include, administer and encourage so-called after-tax "side car" accounts in connection with their plan structure. Such accounts would allow participants to specifically payroll reduce to save for financial emergencies as well as retirement and thereby avoid making hardship and loan invasions on their retirement savings.

3731. What special rules apply to the sale of employer securities to a defined contribution plan?

The IRC permits employers to make contributions to certain qualified plans in the form of employer stock, if the plan permits.[1] The restrictions on prohibited transactions normally limit these contributions to certain profit sharing plans and plans established as employee stock ownership plans ("ESOPs").[2] ESOPs also are permitted to purchase stock from the employer under a complex set of ERISA and IRC provisions.

Planning Point: No employer should consider such a transfer or sale unless the decision is coordinated with ERISA-qualified legal counsel.

3732. What is the diversification requirement for defined contribution plans?

In plan years beginning after December 31, 2006, defined contribution plans (other than certain ESOPs) that hold publicly traded employer securities must satisfy a diversification requirement to be qualified.[3] In May 2010, the IRS issued final regulations on the diversification requirement.[4] The final regulations are effective for plan years beginning on or after January 1, 2011.[5] Until that effective date, a plan was required to comply with the diversification requirement, but could rely on the proposed regulations, or the final regulations for purposes of satisfying the requirements of IRC Section 401(a)(35).

Defined contribution plans subject to this requirement must permit participants to direct the plan to divest the portion of their account attributable to employee contributions and elective deferrals invested in employer securities, and reinvest an equivalent amount in other investment options.[6] With respect to employer contributions only, the diversification feature

1.   IRC Sec. 409.
2.   IRC Sec. 4975.
3.   IRC Sec. 401(a)(35), ERISA Sec. 204(j).
4.   Treas. Reg. §1.401(a)(35)-1.
5.   Treas. Reg. §1.401(a)(35)-1.
6.   IRC Sec. 401(a)(35)(B); Treas. Reg. §1.401(a)(35)-1(b).

may be restricted to participants with at least three years of service, their beneficiaries, and the beneficiaries of deceased participants.[1]

The plan must offer at least three investment options (other than employer securities) to which an employee affected by this provision may direct the proceeds from the divestment of the employer securities. Each investment option must be diversified and have materially different risk and return characteristics.[2] A plan may limit the time for divestment and reinvestment to periodic, reasonable opportunities, provided they occur at least quarterly. If the plan places restrictions or conditions (other than the application of securities laws) with respect to the investment of employer securities that are not imposed on the investment of other assets in the plan, it will not satisfy the provisions of the diversification requirement.[3]

A transition rule, applicable only to securities acquired before January 1, 2007,[4] allowed the plan to phase in the diversification requirement ratably over three years. The phase-in did not apply to participants who reached age 55 and completed three years of service before the first plan year beginning after December 31, 2005. Under the phase-in, an "applicable percentage" of the portion of an account attributable to employer contributions (other than elective deferrals) invested in employer securities is subject to the requirement as follows: 33 percent after the first plan year, 66 percent after the second plan year, and 100 percent after the third and subsequent plan years.

Planning Point: A significant amount of litigation has been directed at plan sponsors' failure to satisfy their fiduciary obligations based on poor investment decisions. In the closely-watched *Intel* case, participants alleged that the plan over-invested in hedge funds and private equity investments. *Intel* countered by alleging that the participants had received "actual knowledge" of the potential violation, thereby triggering the running of a three-year limitations period for filing suit. The case made it all the way to the Supreme Court, which ruled in favor of the plaintiffs that the generally applicable six-year limitations period for fiduciary breach applied. This was the case even though the plan sponsor mailed information about the investments that may have been sufficient to inform them of the violation—because the plaintiffs did not recall ever reading the information.[5] While the decision leaves much unanswered, plan sponsors should exercise extreme caution in providing notice of investments to participants.

The diversification requirement does not apply to certain ESOPs. If an ESOP does not hold any 401(k) contributions, Section 401(m) match amounts, or earnings attributable to them and the plan is a separate plan for purposes of the merger and consolidation requirements of IRC Section 414(l) with respect to any other defined benefit or defined contribution plan of the same employer or employers, then the diversification requirement does not apply.[6]

Planning Point: The IRS has issued relief from the anti-cutback rules of Section 411(d)((6) for a plan sponsor who amends a non-exempt ESOP to eliminate a distribution option that had previously satisfied the diversification requirements of Section 401(a)(28)(B) if the amendment occurs

---

1.   IRC Sec. 401(a)(35)(C); Treas. Reg. §1.401(a)(35)-1(e).
2.   IRC Sec. 401(a)(35)(D)(i); Treas. Reg. §1.401(a)(35)-1(d).
3.   IRC Sec. 401(a)(35)(D)(ii); Treas. Reg. §1.401(a)(35)-1(e).
4.   IRC Sec. 401(a)(35)(H); Treas. Reg. §1.401(a)(35)-1(g)(3).
5.   *Intel Corp. Inv. Policy Comm. vs Sulyma*, U.S. No. 18-116 (February 26, 2020).
6.   IRC Sec. 401(a)(35)(E)(ii); Treas. Reg. §1.401(a)(35)-1(f)(2)(ii).

no later than the last day of the first plan year beginning on or after January 1, 2013 or by the deadline for the plan to satisfy Section 401(a)(35), if later.[1]

Publicly traded employer securities for purposes of this requirement means employer securities that are readily tradable on an established securities market.[2]

Employer security means a security issued by an employer of employees covered by the plan or by an affiliate of such an employer. Life insurance, health insurance, and annuity contracts are not securities for this purpose.[3]

If an employer corporation, or any member of a controlled group that includes the employer corporation, has issued a class of stock that is publicly traded, the employer may be treated as holding publicly traded employer securities even if its securities are not otherwise publicly traded. Controlled group status is determined using a 50 percent test instead of an 80 percent test for this purpose.[4]

The diversification requirement does not apply to plans that meet the definition of a one-participant plan.[5] This definition has the following five criteria:

(1)   On the first day of the plan year, the plan covered only one individual or that individual and his or her spouse, and the individual owns 100 percent of the plan sponsor (whether incorporated or not), or it covered only one or more partners and their spouses in the plan sponsor.

(2)   It meets the minimum coverage requirements of IRC Section 410(b) (Q 3841) without being combined with any other plan of the business that covers its employees.

(3)   It does not provide benefits to anyone except the individual or the partners and their spouses.

(4)   It does not cover a business that is a member of an affiliated service group, a controlled group or a group of businesses under common control (Q 3932, Q 3934).

(5)   It does not cover a business that uses the services of leased employees as defined in IRC Section 414(n) (Q 3928).

A partner, for purposes of this definition, also includes a 2 percent shareholder of an S corporation.[6]

ERISA applies this requirement to applicable individual account plans. An applicable individual account plan is "a pension plan which provides for an individual account for each participant and for benefits based solely upon the amount contributed to the participant's account, and any

1.   Notice 2013-17, 2013-20 IRB 1082 (Apr. 18, 2013).
2.   IRC Sec. 401(a)(35)(G)(v); Treas. Reg. §1.401(a)(35)-1(f)(5).
3.   IRC Sec. 401(a)(35)(G)(iii); ERISA Sec. 407(d)(1); Treas. Reg. §1.401(a)(35)-1(f)(3).
4.   IRC Sec. 401(a)(35)(F); Treas. Reg. §1.401(a)(35)-1(f)(2)(iv).
5.   Treas. Reg. §1.401(a)(35)-1(f)(3)(iii).
6.   IRC Sec. 401(a)(35)(E)(iv).

income, expenses, gains and losses, and any forfeitures of accounts of other participants which may be allocated to such participant's account."[1]

Pensions

3733. What is a pension plan?

A pension plan is a qualified plan established and maintained by an employer primarily to provide systematically for the payment of definitely determinable benefits (Q 3736) to its employees over a period of years, usually for life, after retirement. A plan can and must meet the requirement that the benefits be definitely determinable by providing for fixed benefits or fixed contributions.[2] Thus, a pension plan either can be a defined benefit plan or a defined contribution plan (Q 3734).

Under a plan that provides fixed benefits (a "defined benefit" plan), the amount of the pension, or a formula to determine that amount, is set in advance; an actuary determines the annual contributions that are required to accumulate a fund sufficient to provide each employee's pension when he or she retires. The size of an employee's pension is usually related to the employee's compensation, years of service, or both.

Under a plan that provides for fixed contributions (a "defined contribution" or "money purchase" plan), the annual contribution to an employee's account (rather than his or her future pension) is fixed or definitely determinable, and the employee receives whatever retirement benefit can be purchased with the funds accumulated in the employee's account. Usually the annual contribution is a fixed percentage of the employee's compensation; in any event, it must not be related to the employer's profits.[3] Contributions are not considered "fixed" where an employer intentionally overfunds a money purchase pension plan.[4]

A pension plan cannot provide regular temporary disability income or medical expense benefits (except medical expense benefits for retired employees). A pension plan may provide incidental death benefits, through life insurance or otherwise (Q 3829), and disability pensions.[5]

The employer deduction limit for pension plans is explained in Q 3801. For the minimum funding standard that applies to pension plans, see Q 3742 to Q 3746.

3734. What is a target benefit plan?

A target benefit plan is a money purchase pension plan under which contributions to an employee's account are determined by reference to the amounts necessary to fund the employee's stated benefit under the plan.[6] Consequently, allocations under a target plan are generally weighted

---

1. ERISA Secs. 204(j)(5), 3(34).
2. The IRS has recently indicated that this requirement can be satisfied in the case of a cash balance pension plan by looking outside the plan document to a another document, such as to a W-2, for the definition of "compensation".
3. IRC Sec. 401; Treas. Reg. §1.401-1.
4. *William Bryen Co., Inc. v. Comm.*, 89 TC 689 (1987).
5. IRC Sec. 401(h); Treas. Reg. §§1.401-1(a)(2)(i), 1.401-1(b)(1)(i), 1.401-14.
6. Treas. Reg. §1.401(a)(4)-8(b)(3)(i).

for both age and compensation. Although a target benefit plan is a type of defined contribution plan, it is subject to certain minimum funding requirements (Q 3742 to Q 3746).

Safe harbor requirements for target plans are set forth in the cross testing regulations under IRC Section 401(a)(4), under which a target plan will be deemed to be nondiscriminatory.[1]

Special rules apply to target plans for meeting the requirements of IRC Section 411(b)(2), which states that a plan may not discontinue or reduce a participant's benefit accruals or allocations because the participant reaches a particular age.[2]

3735. What is the maximum amount that an employer may deduct annually for contributions on behalf of employees to a qualified defined benefit pension plan?

The maximum annual limit on deductions by an employer, including a self-employed person, for contributions to a defined benefit pension plan is determined by an actuary who follows regulations that are structured to provide level funding over an employee's tenure with the employer. An overview of the rules that an actuary follows appears below.

(1)   The employer may deduct the amount needed to fund each employee's past and current service credits distributed as a level amount or level percentage of compensation over the remaining period of his or her anticipated future service. If more than one-half of the remaining unfunded cost is attributable to three or fewer participants, the deduction of such 412(c) unfunded cost for them must be spread over at least five years.[3]

(2)   The employer may deduct the plan's normal cost for the year, plus an amount necessary to amortize the past service credits equally over 10 years.[4] The "normal cost" is the level annual amount that would be required to fund the employee's pension from his or her date of employment to his or her retirement date.[5] The amortizable base is limited to the unfunded costs attributable to past service liability.

(3)   In plan years beginning in 2006 or 2007, the employer could deduct a maximum of 150 percent of the plan's unfunded current liability for the plan year (Q 3742).[6] In the case of a plan that has 100 or fewer participants, unfunded current liability does not include liability attributable to benefit increases for highly compensated employees (Q 3929) resulting from a plan amendment that is made or that becomes effective, whichever is later, within the last two years.[7]

---

1.   See Treas. Reg. §1.401(a)(4)-8(b)(3).
2.   See Prop. Treas. Reg. §1.411(b)-2(c)(2)(iii).
3.   IRC Sec. 404(a)(1)(A)(ii).
4.   IRC Sec. 404(a)(1)(A)(iii); Treas. Reg. §1.412(c)(3)-1(e)(3).
5.   For an illustration, see Rev. Rul. 84-62, 1984-1 CB 121.
6.   See IRC Secs. 404(a)(1)(A)(i), 404(a)(1)(D).
7.   IRC Sec. 404(a)(1)(D), as in effect for plan years beginning *before* January 1, 2008.

(4)   In plan years beginning after December 31, 2007, the employer deduction may be determined by calculating the excess, if any, of (1) the funding target for the plan year plus (2) the target normal cost for the plan year and (3) a cushion amount, over (4) the value of plan assets (determined under IRC Section 430(g)(2)). The deduction limit will be the greater of this amount or the sum of the minimum required contributions under IRC Section 430 (Q 3743).[1]

(5)   A defined contribution plan that is subject to the funding standards of IRC Section 412 (e.g., a money purchase plan) is treated as a stock bonus or profit sharing plan for purposes of the deduction limits; thus, it is generally subject to a deduction limit of 25 percent of compensation.[2]

Planning Point: Note that an employer is not entitled to a current deduction for defined benefit plan contributions where those contributions are comprised of the employer's own debt securities. When the employer makes a payment on the debt, the employer is entitled to deduct the amount paid at that time.[3]

In computing the deduction for a contribution to a defined benefit plan, no benefit in excess of the Section 415 limit may be taken into consideration. Note that, similarly, in computing the deduction for a contribution to a defined contribution plan, the contribution taken into account must be reduced by any annual additions in excess of the Section 415 limit for the year.[4]

In determining the deductible amount, the same funding method and actuarial assumptions must be used as those that are used for the minimum funding standard.[5] The IRS has denied the deduction where it believes contributions are based on unreasonable actuarial assumptions.[6] The question of what constitutes a reasonable actuarial assumption was once the subject of extensive litigation; after a steady stream of losses in the Tax Court and federal courts, the IRS announced its concession on the issues on which it lost in those cases.[7]

In computing the deduction under (1), (2), or (3) above, a plan may not take into consideration any adjustments to the Section 415 limits before the year in which the adjustment takes effect.[8]

If the employer contributes more than the maximum deductible amount in any year, the excess amount may be carried over and deducted in succeeding years within the same limitations, even if the plan is no longer qualified in those succeeding years.[9] (See Q 3713 for an excise tax on employer contributions that exceed the deduction limits.)

---

1.   See IRC Sec. 404(o).
2.   See IRC Sec. 404(a)(3)(A)(v).
3.   See IRS CCM 201935011.
4.   IRC Sec. 404(j)(1).
5.   IRC Sec. 404(a)(1)(A); Treas. Reg. §1.404(a)-14(d).
6.   See TAM 9250002.
7.   See IR-95-43 (June 7, 1995); *Vinson & Elkins v. Comm.*, 7 F.3d 1235 (5th Cir. 1993); *Wachtell, Lipton, Rosen & Katz v. Comm.*, 26 F.3d 291 (2d Cir. 1994).
8.   IRC Sec. 404(j)(2); Treas. Reg. §1.412(c)(3)-1(d)(i).
9.   IRC Secs. 404(a)(1)(E), 404(a)(2).

Note that in contrast, a contribution to a defined contribution plan in excess of the Section 415 limits (Q 3867, Q 3728) may not be carried over and deducted in a subsequent year, even if the contribution is required under the minimum funding rules.[1]

If, in the case of a defined benefit plan, more than one plan year is associated with the taxable year of the employer due to a change in plan years, then the deductible limit for the employer's taxable year must be adjusted as described in Revenue Procedure 87-27.[2] If an employer transfers funds from one pension plan to another, the employer realizes income if the previous deduction resulted in a tax benefit.[3]

Fully insured defined benefit pension plans. In guidance for fully insured (Section 412(i)) plans (Q 3811, Q 3812), the IRS also has stated that the portion of contributions attributable to "excess life insurance coverage" does not constitute "normal cost" and thus is not deductible.

Similarly, contributions to pay premiums for the disability waiver of a premium feature with respect to such excess coverage are not deductible. Instead, such amounts are carried over to later years, although they may be subject to a nondeductible contribution penalty (Q 3942).

"Excess" coverage generally refers to contracts held on behalf of a participant whose benefit payable at normal retirement age is not equal to the amount provided at normal retirement age with respect to the contracts held on behalf of that participant, or contracts providing for a death benefit with respect to a participant in excess of the death benefit provided to that participant under that plan.[4]

3736. What special qualification requirements regarding the payment of definitely determinable benefits apply to pension plans but not to profit sharing plans?

A pension plan must provide for the payment of definitely determinable benefits to employees upon retirement or over a period of years after their retirement or to their beneficiaries. Benefits must be determined without regard to the employer's profits.[5] Benefits actually payable need not be definitely determinable, provided the contributions can be determined actuarially on the basis of definitely determinable benefits. This is the theoretical basis for defined benefit plans of the "assumed benefit" or "variable benefit" type (so-called "target" plans). Benefits are "definitely determinable" under a money purchase pension plan that calls for contributions of a fixed percentage of each employee's compensation.[6]

Benefits that vary with the increase or decrease in the market value of the assets from which such benefits are payable or that vary with the fluctuations of a specified and generally recognized cost-of-living index are consistent with a plan providing for definitely determinable benefits.[7]

---

1.   Notice 83-10, 1983-1 CB 536, F-1, F-3.
2.   1987-1 CB 769.
3.   Rev. Rul. 73-528, 1973-2 CB 13.
4.   See Rev. Rul. 2004-20, 2004-10 IRB 546.
5.   Treas. Reg. §§1.401-1(a)(2)(i), 1.401-1(b)(1)(i).
6.   Treas. Reg. §1.401-1(b)(1)(i).
7.   Rev. Rul. 185, 1953-2 CB 202.

A plan provides a definitely determinable benefit if, in the case of an insured plan, the practice of the insurer is to provide a retirement annuity that is the higher of an annuity bought at an annuity rate guaranteed in the contract surrendered in exchange for the same type of annuity purchased at current annuity rates.[1]

The IRS determined that a governmental cash balance plan in which the interest rate credited on contributions was set by a board appointed under state law nonetheless provided a definitely determinable benefit.[2] In a TE/GE Memo to plan examiners, the IRS indicated that a cash balance plan can meet the definitely determinable requirement when the formula under which a credit is determined by looking at compensation, if the compensation information is otherwise available outside the terms of the plan, like in a W-2.[3]

Planning Point: The IRS has directed its examination staff to focus on the issue of "definitely determinable benefits" in audits since compliance with this requirement is a precondition to qualification. Hence, plan sponsors may wish to have legal counsel to periodically review their plan for compliance under current IRS guidance in order to assure themselves of continuing plan qualification in the event of an audit.

To be definitely determinable, a plan that credits interest must specify how the plan determines interest and must specify how and when interest is credited. Interest must be credited at least annually.

Regulations specify two methods that a plan can use to determine the plan's interest crediting rate: the applicable periodic interest crediting rate that applies over the current period or the rate that applied in a specified lookback month with respect to a stability period.[4] A plan is permitted to round the calculated interest rate or rate of return in accordance with regulations issued in 2015.[5]

A defined benefit plan will not be treated as providing definitely determinable benefits unless the actuarial assumptions used to determine the amount of any benefit (including any optional or early retirement benefit) are specified in the plan in a way that precludes employer discretion.[6]

Under certain plans, a participant receives not only a defined benefit specified in the plan but also amounts that have been credited to individual accounts each year based on excess earnings; in other words, actual trust earnings in excess of the investment yield assumption used in the valuation of the cost of providing the defined benefit (an excess earnings plan). Where contributions to these plans are discretionary, the amount of excess interest allocations to the defined contribution portion of the plan is not definitely determinable, and the plan will not qualify.[7]

Retirement benefits are not definitely determinable under a plan that permits the withdrawal of employer contributions. Hence, a pension plan may not permit the withdrawal of employer

---

1.   Rev. Rul. 78-56, 1978-1 CB 116.
2.   Let. Rul. 9645031.
3.   TE/GE 04-0417-0014 (4-7-2017). The memo contains some useful examples to review.
4.   Treas. Reg. §1.411(b)(5)-1.
5.   . 80 FR 70680 (Nov. 16, 2015).
6.   IRC Sec. 401(a)(25); Rev. Rul. 79-90, 1979-1 CB 155.
7.   Rev. Rul. 78-403, 1978-2 CB 153.

contributions or earnings thereon, even in the case of financial need, before death, retirement, disability, severance of employment, or termination of the plan.[1] Withdrawals may be made once the employee has reached normal retirement age even if the employee has not actually retired.[2]

A pension plan may permit withdrawal of all or part of an employee's own contributions plus interest actually earned thereon when the employee discontinues participation in the plan, even though the employee continues to work for the employer.[3]

In addition, a pension plan may permit an employee to withdraw his or her nondeductible voluntary contributions without terminating his or her participation in the plan, provided the withdrawal will not affect the employee's participation in the plan, the employer's past or future contributions on his or her behalf, or the basic benefits provided by both the employee's and the employer's mandatory contributions, and no interest is allowable with respect to the contributions withdrawn either at the time of withdrawal or in computing benefits at retirement.[4]

The IRS takes the position that all benefits payable under a plan, including early retirement, disability pension, and preretirement death benefits, must be definitely determinable. Thus, a pension plan funded by a combination of life insurance and an auxiliary fund, which provided a pension on early retirement or disability, the amount of which was based in part on the participant's interest in the auxiliary fund, failed to qualify because the employer was not required to maintain the fund at a particular level or to make contributions at any particular time.[5]

Similarly, a defined benefit pension plan that provided a preretirement death benefit equal to the amount of the pension benefit funded for a participant as of the date of the participant's death failed to qualify.[6]

Likewise, a change in actuarial factors that affects the calculation of a participant's optional or early retirement benefit would result in plan disqualification.[7]

Benefits under a defined benefit plan will be considered definitely determinable even if they are offset by benefits provided by a profit sharing plan, if determination of the amount of the offset is not subject to the employer's discretion. The actuarial basis and the time for determining the offset must be specified in the defined benefit plan to preclude employer discretion.[8]

Pension benefits will not fail to be definitely determinable because a factor or condition, determinable only after retirement, is used to compute benefits in accordance with an express provision in the plan if the factor or condition is not subject to the discretion of the employer.[9]

---

1.   Rev. Rul. 69-277, 1969-1 CB 116; Rev. Rul. 74-417, 1974-2 CB 131.
2.   Rev. Rul. 71-24, 1971-1 CB 114; Rev. Rul. 73-448, 1973-2 CB 136, superseded by GCM 38002 which republished Rev. Rul. 73-448.
3.   Rev. Rul. 60-281, 1960-2 CB 146.
4.   Rev. Rul. 60-323, 1960-2 CB 148; Rev. Rul. 69-277, 1969-1 CB 116.
5.   Rev. Rul. 69-427, 1969-2 CB 87.
6.   Rev. Rul. 72-97, 1972-1 CB 106.
7.   Rev. Rul. 81-12, 1981-1 CB 228.
8.   Rev. Rul. 76-259, 1976-2 CB 111.
9.   Rev. Rul. 80-122, 1980-1 CB 84.

Forfeitures

Related to the definitely determinable benefits rule is the requirement that a pension plan provide that forfeitures must not be applied to increase the benefits any employee would otherwise receive under the plan.[1]

3737. What special qualification requirements regarding retirement age apply to pension plans but not to profit sharing plans?

Pension and annuity plans are retirement plans; thus, they must be established primarily to provide definitely determinable benefits at normal retirement age.

The normal retirement age in a pension or annuity plan is the lowest age specified in the plan at which the employee has the right to retire without the consent of the employer and receive retirement benefits based on service to date at the full rate set forth in the plan (i.e., without actuarial or similar reduction because of retirement before some later specified age). Normal retirement age must be an age that is not earlier than the earliest age that is reasonably representative of the typical retirement age for the industry in which the covered workforce is employed.[2] The following table describes the standard by which the IRS will determine whether a normal retirement age is reasonable:

Normal Retirement Age	Standard Applied
62 or above	Deemed reasonable
Between ages 55 and 62	Depends on facts and circumstances or workforce
Under age 55	Deemed unreasonable unless Commissioner determines otherwise
Age 50 and later	Reasonable, if substantially all of participants are public safety workers[3]

The IRS has announced its intention to modify this rule to eliminate the requirement that substantially all of the public safety workers be covered by a separate plan.[4]

The IRS has issued proposed regulations that modify the normal retirement regulations to clarify that governmental plans that do not permit in-service distributions before age 62 are not required to meet a standard that otherwise requires that the normal retirement age be reasonably representative of the retirement age that is typical in the industry in question.[5] Further, if a plan covers both public safety and nonpublic safety employees, it is acceptable for the plan to have different normal retirement ages for each group. The regulations, as proposed, became effective January 1, 2017, and apply only for covered employees hired after the effective date.

1.   IRC Sec. 401(a)(8).
2.   Treas. Reg. §1.401(a)-1(b)(2).
3.   Treas. Reg. §1.401(a)-1(b)(2).
4.   Notice 2012-29, 2012 IRB 872.
5.   Prop. Treas. Reg. §1.401(a)-1(b)(2), 81 Fed. Reg. 4599 (Jan. 26, 2016).

If normal retirement age is less than age 62 and benefits begin before that age, the defined benefit dollar limit must be actuarially reduced for purposes of the Section 415 limits on benefits (Q 3728, Q 3867).[1]

The IRC also requires that the accrued benefit of an employee who retires after age 70½ be actuarially increased to take into account any period after age 70½ in which the employee was not receiving any benefits under the plan.[2] Guidance for implementing this requirement is set forth in regulations finalized in 2004 (Q 3896).[3]

An actuarial assumption that employees will retire at a normal retirement age specified in the plan that is a lower age than they normally retire could result in computation of amounts that are not currently deductible if the assumption causes the actuarial assumptions in the aggregate to be unreasonable.[4] The IRS has challenged the use of normal retirement ages under age 65 in small defined benefit plans (i.e., plans covering from one to five employees) (Q 3735). A pension plan may permit early retirement, and any reasonable optional early retirement age generally will be acceptable.

3738. Can a pension plan allow participants to retire in phases and still remain qualified?

In plan years beginning after December 31, 2006, a pension will not fail to be qualified solely because it permits distributions to be made to an employee who has attained age 59½ (62 prior to 2020) and has not separated from employment at the time of the distribution.[5]

In addition, proposed regulations addressing phased retirement were issued in late 2004, setting forth provisions that would allow pension plan participants other than key employees (Q 3930) at least 59½ years of age to voluntarily reduce their hours (at least 20 percent) and receive a pro rata portion of their pension annuity. Under the proposal, all early retirement benefits, retirement type subsidies, and optional forms of benefit available on full retirement would have to be offered in the event of a phased retirement, except that payment could not be made in the form of a single-sum distribution or other eligible rollover distribution. An employee engaged in phased retirement essentially would have a "dual status." The employee would remain an employee for purposes of plan participation, with full-time status imputed, except for the proportionate reduction in compensation for the lower number of hours worked, but the employee would receive a portion of his or her pension annuity corresponding to the reduction in his or her hours.

However, the phased retirement regulations do not take effect and may not be relied on until they are finalized.[6] Earlier rulings supported the determination that a plan could provide

---

1. IRC Sec. 415(b)(2)(C).
2. IRC Sec. 401(a)(9)(C)(ii).
3. Treas. Reg. §1.401(a)(9)-6, A-7.
4. Rev. Rul. 78-331, 1978-2 CB 158.
5. IRC Sec. 401(a)(36); Notice 2007-8; 2007-1 C.B. 276.
6. See REG-114726-04, 69 Fed. Reg. 65108 (Nov. 10, 2004); Prop. Treas. Reg. §1.401(a)-3. This remains the status of the proposed phased retirement regulations as of the date of publication even though nearly 15 years have passed since their release.

for a lump sum distribution to an employee who has reached both 59½ and normal retirement age, even if the employee continued to work for the employer.[1]

A pension plan may provide for payment of the balance to the credit of an employee on plan termination.[2] A plan that permits an employee to elect death benefits to the exclusion of retirement benefits will not qualify.[3] This rule does not prevent a plan from providing "incidental" death benefits (Q 3829, Q 3908).

3739. Under the Multiemployer Pension Reform Act of 2014, can a plan reduce a participant's benefit levels?

In some cases, a plan may reduce the benefits of plan participants and beneficiaries. The Multiemployer Pension Reform Act of 2014[4] (MPRA) created a new type of plan status, known as "critical and declining status" that applies to plans that are projected to become insolvent within either:

(1)   the current plan year, or within 14 subsequent plan years, or

(2)   the current year, or within 19 subsequent plan years if:

(a)   the ratio of inactive to active participants exceeds two to one *or*

(b)   the plan is less than 80 percent funded.[5]

If a plan is in critical and declining status, the plan may temporarily or permanently reduce any current or future payment obligations to plan participants or beneficiaries, whether or not those benefits are in pay status at the time of the reduction.[6] Once benefits are suspended, the plan has no future liability for payment of benefits that were reduced while in critical and declining status.[7]

In order to reduce benefits, however, the plan actuary must certify that the plan is projected to avoid insolvency, assuming that the reductions remain in place either indefinitely or until the expiration date set by the plan's own terms. The plan sponsor must also determine that the plan is projected to remain insolvent unless benefits are reduced, despite the fact that the plan has taken all reasonable measures to avoid insolvency.[8]

Planning Point: There has been increasing activity to reduce plan benefits under the 2014 law in recent years, so much of an an increase that the U.S. Chamber of Commerce described the situation as a "crisis".[9] The multiemployer Central States Pension Fund applied to the PBGC to

---

1.   Special ruling, 10-29-76; Let. Rul. 7740031.
2.   IRC Sec. 401(a)(20).
3.   Rev. Rul. 56-656, 1956-2 CB 280.
4.   Consolidated and Further Continuing Appropriations Act, 2015, Pub. Law. No. 113-235.
5.   IRC Sec. 432(b)(5).
6.   IRC Sec. 432(e)(9)(B)(i).
7.   IRC Sec. 432(e)(9)(B)(iii).
8.   IRC Sec. 432(e)(9)(C)(ii).
9.   *See generally,* "The Multi-Employer Pension Plan Crisis: The History, Legislation and What's Next," U.S. Chamber of Commerce (December 2017)

approve benefit reductions but was rejected on the basis the cuts would be insufficient to save the fund. However, the request of the Ironworks Union Local No. 17 Pension Fund was approved by the PBGC and by its members in 2017 to become the first to reduce retiree pension benefits under the law.[1] More plans have now followed. [2]

The problem of insolvent multi-employer pension plans recently received study from the GAO as part of its "High Risk Series." In the report, the GAO assessed the risks of these pension liabilities and made recommendations to Congress in February of 2017. In addition, the head of the PBGC has predicted that based upon current trends the PBGC's fund could be expended by 2025. This has become a priority for Congress and new legislation, allowing loans to plans and consolidation of plans to increase solvency, might be expected as a consequence.[3] In light of the rapidly evolving guidance and perhaps new law in this area, practitioners will need to check the status of any legislation and all new PBGC guidance before proceeding to formally request a reduction in benefits for a plan.

3740. Are there any limitations on a pension plan's ability to reduce participant benefit levels under the Multiemployer Pension Reform Act of 2014?

Benefit levels cannot be reduced to below 110 percent of the monthly benefit that the PBGC guarantees at the time of the reduction. Further, if the participant or beneficiary has reached age 75 at the time of the reduction, the amount of the benefit reduction is phased out until the individual reaches age 80. Benefits that are payable to participants or beneficiaries that have reached age 80 at the time of reduction, as well as benefits that are payable based upon disability, may not be reduced.[4] All benefit reductions must be distributed equitably among plan participants and beneficiaries.

The MPRA also contains limitations on how a suspension of benefits must be applied in the case of a plan where benefits are attributable to a participant's service for an employer that has withdrawn from the plan, paid the full amount of its withdrawal liability and, pursuant to a collective bargaining agreement, assumed liability for providing benefits under a separate single-employer plan.

The IRS has released proposed and temporary regulations that provide that the reduction must first be applied to reduce benefits attributable to participant's service with an employer that has withdrawn from the plan, but failed to pay the full amount of its withdrawal liability. A reduction must then be applied to reduce any other benefits before any reduction is applied to reduce benefits attributable to a participant's service with an employer that has withdrawn, paid the full amount of its withdrawal liability and, pursuant to a collective bargaining agreement, assumed liability for paying benefits under a separate single-employer plan in an amount equal to any amount of benefits for such participants and beneficiaries reduced as a result of the financial status of the multiemployer plan.[5] Guidance on application procedures for approval of

---

1.   *See generally*, www.PBGC.gov for more detail on recent plan terminations and benefit reductions actions and activities on multiemployer as well as single employer pension plans.
2.   *See e.g.*, letter to Ironworkers Local 16 Pension Funds trustees with preliminary approval of benefits reduction proposals, dated August 1, 2018.
3.   See GAO-17-317, High-Risk Series, *Progress on Many High Risk Areas, While Substantial Efforts Needed on Others*, GAO, Feb. 2017.
4.   IRC Sec. 432(e)(9)(D).
5.   80 Fed. Reg. 35207 (June 19, 2015); .80 Fed. Reg. 35262 (June 19, 2015).

benefit suspensions under IRC Section 432(e)(9) is provided in Revenue Procedure 2016-27.[1] See also Q 3739 for more information.

3741. What procedures and notices are required in order for a pension plan to reduce participant benefit levels under the Multiemployer Pension Reform Act of 2014?

In order to reduce benefits, the plan sponsor must first apply to the Secretary of the Treasury. The proposed reduction must then be approved by a vote of the plan participants and union representatives. If the reduction is rejected, however, the Treasury and Department of Labor have the authority to override the negative vote if the plan is determined to be systemically important.[2] A systemically important plan is a plan with respect to which the PBGC projects will increase its liabilities by $1 billion or more if benefit reductions are not made.[3]

The plan must also provide certain notices to plan participants and beneficiaries that are sufficient to allow the individual to understand the effect of the reduction, including an estimate of the effect on the individual participant or beneficiary. The notice must also include a description of the factors considered in reducing the benefits, a statement that the application for approval will be available on the Secretary of the Treasury website, information on the individual's rights, a statement describing appointment of a retiree representative (if applicable) and information on how to contact the Treasury for more information.[4] See also Q 3739 and Q 3740 for more information.

3742. What is the minimum funding standard that applied in plan years before 2008?

The Pension Protection Act of 2006 (PPA 2006) replaced the minimum funding standard with a single minimum required contribution (Q 3743). The PPA 2006 funding provisions generally took effect for plan years beginning after 2007. For plan years beginning before 2008, the IRC provided for a minimum funding standard requiring at least a minimum level of funding for qualified defined benefit plans. A second "deficit reduction contribution" applied in the case of certain plans with over 100 participants.

The minimum amount that an employer is required to contribute to fund a money purchase pension plan (both before and after PPA 2006) is the contribution amount required under the terms of the plan for each year, as stated in the plan formula.[5]

Profit sharing and stock bonus plans (Q 3749 to Q 3815), certain government and church plans, certain employee-pay-all plans, and fully insured plans (known as 412(i) plans) (Q 3812) are exempt from the minimum funding requirements, both before and after PPAPPA 2006.[6]

---

1.   2016-19 IRB 725 (May 9, 2016).
2.   Temp. Treas. Reg. § 1.432(e)(9)-1T(h)(5).
3.   Temp. Treas. Reg. § 1.432(e)(9)-1T(h)(5)(iv).
4.   Temp. Treas. Reg. § 1.432(e)(9)-1T(f).
5.   See IRC Sec. 412(a)(2)(B).
6.   IRC Sec. 412(e)(2).

The minimum funding requirements are not qualification requirements.[1] Waiver of the minimum funding standard because of hardship may be available in some circumstances (Q 3747).[2]

Under the minimum funding standard, the employer must contribute at least a minimum amount to its qualified defined benefit, money purchase pension, or annuity plan.[3]

To determine its minimum contribution, an employer must establish a separate funding standard account for each plan.[4] A plan that has a funding method requiring contributions at least equal to those required under the entry age normal cost method also may maintain an alternative minimum funding standard account.[5]

Under the regular funding rules, the funding standard account (and the alternative account, if one is maintained) is to be charged with certain liabilities and credited with certain amounts each plan year. If the charges to the funding standard account for all plan years beginning after the standard is first applicable to the plan exceed the credits (or, if less, the excess of the charges to the alternative minimum funding standard account for the same years over the credits), the plan has an "accumulated funding deficiency" to the extent of the excess. The minimum funding standard is satisfied when there is no accumulated funding deficiency; that is, when the balance in the funding standard account (or the alternative minimum funding standard account) at the end of the year is zero.[6]

Charges

The liabilities that must be currently funded and charged to the funding standard account under the regular funding rules are the "normal cost" (the level annual amount that would be required to fund the employee's pension from his date of employment to his retirement), and the amounts required to amortize, in equal installments, until fully amortized:

(1)   the unfunded past service liability that existed on the first day the section applied to the plan over a period of 30 years (40 years if the plan was in existence on January 1, 1974);

(2)   any net increase in unfunded past service liability because of plan amendments in the year over a period of 30 years;

(3)   any net experience loss over a period of five years (15 years if a multiemployer plan);

(4)   any net loss from changes in actuarial assumptions over a period of 10 years (30 years if a multiemployer plan);

---

1.   See *Anthes v. Comm.*, 81 TC 1 (1983), *aff'd*, 740 F.2d 953 (1st Cir. 1984).
2.   IRC Sec. 412(c)(2).
3.   See IRC Sec. 412, prior to amendment by PPA 2006.
4.   IRC Sec. 412(b).
5.   IRC Sec. 412(g).
6.   IRC Sec. 412(a).

    (5)   each previously waived funding deficiency over a period of five years (15 years if a multiemployer plan); and

    (6)   any amount previously credited to the account as a result of using the alternative minimum funding standard account as the funding standard over a period of five years.[1]

Employers generally must amortize the amount that they would have been required to contribute, but for the increase, over 20 years (Q 3724).[2] Special rules apply to funding methods that do not provide for amortization bases.[3]

Planning Point: In October, 2017 the IRS released final regulations regarding new official mortality tables and the application of mortality to the computation of plan liabilities to all plans subject to minimum funding standards. These new mortality tables for 2018 will generally increase plan liabilities because of greater longevity reflected in the tables. At the same time, the IRS released Rev. Proc. 2017-55 that allows for integrating the tables to specific plans, and Rev. Proc 2017-60 that allows for application of the new tables for about one year. Plan sponsors will wish to explore the potential to delay application for one year and to reduce the application impact by review its application to specific plans, especially if derisking or termination of a plan is under consideration since the tables will increase the liabilities of the plan and make derisking and termination more expensive.

Credits

Amounts that are credited to the funding standard account under the regular funding rules include:

    (1)   employer contributions;

    (2)   amounts necessary to amortize, in equal installments (1) any net decrease in unfunded past service liability arising from amendments over a period of 30 years, (2) any net experience gain over a period of five years (15 years if a multiemployer plan), and (3) any gain from changes in actuarial assumptions over a period of 10 years (30 years if a multiemployer plan);

    (3)   the amount of the funding standard that has been waived by the Secretary of Treasury because of substantial business hardship; and

    (4)   an adjustment, if the alternative minimum funding standard was used in a previous year.[4]

Amortization periods may be longer in certain circumstances.[5]

---

1.   See IRC Sec. 412(b)(2).
2.   IRC Sec. 412(b)(2)(E).
3.   Rev. Rul. 2000-20, 2000-1 CB 880.
4.   IRC Sec. 412(b)(3).
5.   See IRC Secs. 412(e), 412(b)(6).

Guidelines for determining experience gains and losses are set forth in Revenue Ruling 81-213.[1] Dividends, rate credits, and forfeitures are treated as experience gains if:

(1)   the plan is funded solely through a group deferred annuity contract;

(2)   the annual single premium is treated as the normal cost; and

(3)   an amount necessary to pay, in equal annual installments over the amortization period, the single premium necessary to provide all past service benefits not initially funded, is treated as the annual amortization amount.[2]

Alternative Minimum Funding Standard Account

The alternative minimum funding standard account is charged only with the lesser of (1) normal cost under the plan's funding method or under the unit credit method, any excess of the value of accrued benefits over the fair market value of plan assets, and any excess of credits over charges to the account in all prior years. The alternative funding standard account is credited with the employer's contribution and is also charged or credited with interest.[3]

Interest

The funding standard account also is charged or credited with interest at a rate consistent with that used to determine plan costs. For plan years beginning in 2006 and 2007, the interest rate was based on a yield curve derived from a two year weighted average of interest rates on investment grade corporate bonds. This amendment extended the relief implemented by PFEA 2004.[4]

Deficit Reduction Contributions

An additional charge to the funding standard account (and, thus, an increased contribution) is required for certain defined benefit plans (other than multiemployer plans) that have more than 100 participants and have a funded current liability percentage for any plan year below certain limits.[5] Relief from this requirement is available for certain airlines and steel manufacturers.[6]

3743. What is the funding requirement for defined benefit plans beginning after PPA 2006, MAP-21 and HATFA 2014?

The Pension Protection Act of 2006 (PPA 2006) replaced the minimum funding standard account and the deficit reduction contribution for single-employer defined benefit plans (Q 3742) with a single basic "minimum required contribution."[7]

---

1.   1981-2 CB 101.
2.   Treas. Reg. §1.412(b)-2.
3.   Former IRC Sec. 412(g)(2); Prop. Treas. Reg. §1.412(g)-1.
4.   See IRC Sec. 412(b)(5); see also IRC Sec. 412(l)(7)(C)(i)(IV); Notice 2004-34, 2004-18 IRB 848; Notice 2013-2, 2013-6 IRB 473.
5.   See IRC Secs. 412(l)(1), 412(l)(6).
6.   See IRC Sec. 412(i)(12).
7.   IRC Secs. 412(a)(2)(A), 430.

The minimum required contribution for a defined benefit plan (other than multiemployer plans) is determined in the following manner:

(1)   If the value of a plan's assets (reduced as described below) equals or exceeds the funding target of the plan for the plan year, the minimum required contribution is the target normal cost reduced (but not below zero) by such excess.[1]

(2)   If the value of the plan's assets (reduced as described below) is less than the funding target of the plan for the plan year, the minimum required contribution is the sum of: (a) the target normal cost, (b) the shortfall amortization charge (if any) for the plan for the plan year, and (c) the waiver amortization charge (if any) for the plan for the plan year.[2]

Target Normal Cost. With the exception of plans in "at-risk" status (Q 3744), a plan's target normal cost means the present value of all benefits that are expected to accrue or to be earned under the plan during the plan year. If any benefit attributable to services performed in a preceding plan year is increased by reason of any increase in compensation during the current plan year, the benefit increase will be treated as having accrued during the current plan year.[3]

Shortfall Amortization Charge. The shortfall amortization charge for a plan for any plan year is the aggregate total (not below zero) of the shortfall amortization installments for the plan year with respect to any shortfall amortization base that has not been fully amortized.[4] The shortfall amortization installments are the amounts necessary to amortize the shortfall amortization base of the plan for any plan year in level annual installments over the seven-plan-year period beginning with such plan year.[5] For this purpose, the use of segmented interest rates derived from a yield curve will be phased in under rules set forth in IRC Section 430(h)(2)(C).

The shortfall amortization base for a plan year is the funding shortfall (if any) of the plan for that plan year, minus the present value of the total of the shortfall amortization installments and waiver amortization installments that have been determined for the plan year and any succeeding plan year with respect to the shortfall amortization bases and waiver amortization bases of the plan for any previous plan year.[6]

The funding shortfall of a plan for any plan year is the excess (if any) of the funding target for the plan year over the value of the plan assets (reduced as described below) for the plan year that are held by the plan on the valuation date.[7] If the value of a plan's assets (reduced as described below) is equal to or greater than the funding target of the plan for the plan year, the shortfall amortization base of the plan for the plan year is zero.[8]

---

1.   IRC Sec. 430(a)(2).
2.   IRC Sec. 430(a)(1).
3.   IRC Sec. 430(b).
4.   IRC Sec. 430(c)(1).
5.   IRC Sec. 430(c)(2).
6.   IRC Sec. 430(c)(3).
7.   IRC Sec. 430(c)(5).
8.   IRC Sec. 430(c)(5)(A).

Under special transition rules, the determination of the funding shortfall for certain plans was to be calculated using only an applicable percentage of the funding target, as follows:

Plan year beginning in calendar year	The applicable percentage
2008	92
2009	94
2010	96

This phase-in transition relief was available only to plans for which the shortfall amortization base for each of the plan years beginning after 2007 was zero. The transition relief was unavailable for plans that were not in effect for a plan year beginning in 2007.[1]

Waiver amortization charge. The waiver amortization charge (if any) for the plan year is the total of the plan's waiver amortization installments for the plan year with respect to the waiver amortization bases for each of the five preceding plan years.[2] The waiver amortization installments are the amounts necessary to amortize the waiver amortization base of the plan for any plan year in level annual installments over a period of five plan years, beginning with the succeeding plan year. The waiver amortization installment for any plan year in this five-year period with respect to any waiver amortization base is the annual installment determined for that year for that base.[3]

Reduction of plan asset values. In the case of a plan that maintains a prefunding balance or a funding standard carryover balance, the amount that is treated as the value of plan assets is subject to reduction for purposes of determining the minimum required contribution and any excess assets, funding shortfall, and funding target attainment percentage. The value of plan assets is deemed to be that amount reduced by the amount of the prefunding balance, but only if the employer has elected to apply a portion of the prefunding balance to reduce the minimum required contribution for the plan year. In turn, this affects the availability of the transition relief described above.[4]

Preservation of Access to Care for Medicare Beneficiaries & Pension Relief Act of 2010. To address the hardship produced by the PPA 2006 funding requirements during the severe economic downturn in 2007-2008, Congress began a series of pension funding relief laws that continue to the date of this publication. The first step of relief was the Preservation of Access to Care for Medicare Beneficiaries and Pension Relief Act of 2010. It allowed a plan sponsor to elect one of two alternative extensions of the seven-year period otherwise required for amortizing the shortfall amortization base under PPA 2006. Special rules were also applied with respect to alternate required installments in cases of excess compensation or extraordinary dividends or stock redemptions.[5]

---

1. IRC Sec. 430(c)(5)(B) (transition rule removed by §221(a)(57)(C)(i) of the Tax Increase Protection Act of 2014).
2. IRC Sec. 430(e).
3. IRC Sec. 430(e)(2).
4. IRC Sec. 430(f)(4); Treas. Reg. §1.430(i)-1(e).
5. IRC Sec. 430(c)(7); Notice 2011-3, 2011-2 IRB 263.

This first extension was available until the latest of 1) the last day of the first plan year beginning on or after January 1, 2013, 2) the last day of the plan year for which Section 436 is effective, or 3) the due date (including extensions) of the employer's tax return for the tax year that contains the first day of the plan year for which Section 436 is first effective for the plan.[1]

Plan sponsors that elected this extension were required to give notice to participants and beneficiaries and notify the PBGC of the election.[2]

MAP-21 (Moving Ahead for Progress in the 21st Century Act of 2012). In 2012, MAP-21 sought to reduce minimum required funding contributions for single employer plans by providing a method to stabilize the interest rate assumption used in the minimum contribution calculations. MAP-21 took the required method for calculating the interest rate assumption used in the calculation, based upon the IRS monthly published "segment rates" (which are based upon investment quality corporate bonds), and stabilized the allowable required rate assumption by establishing an allowable floor and a ceiling for variable rates substituting the average annual segment rates over a 25 year time period. MAP-21 established the floor and ceiling for 2012 calculations as 90 percent and 110 percent of the 25-year historical average. However, this floor/ceiling corridor was designed to widen each year for four years ending with a 70 percent floor and 130 percent ceiling by 2016. MAP-21 gave plan sponsors the option to defer use of these new calculation rules to the 2013 plan year and even allowed for certain revocations of a prior election of interest rate assumption use without IRS consent in order to help smooth the transition. Certain disclosure requirements of the impact of the use of this interest rate assumption stabilization in annual funding notices to participants and beneficiaries was also a part of the law.[3]

In addition, MAP-21 made adjustments to PBGC governance abilities; and increased PBGC flat and variable premiums for single employers and the rate for multiemployer plans.[4] It also allowed certain over-funded plans to use the excess pension funds to fund retiree health and life insurance benefits.[5]

Planning Point: The CARES Act extended the deadline for making a 2019 defined benefit contribution until January 1, 2021. However, according to initial guidance, these contributions had to be made by the original deadline in order to be included in calculating the variable portion of the plan sponsor's PBGC premium. Contributions paid before January 1, 2021 were not considered late, so the plan sponsor did not have to worry about incurring any additional filing obligations. The IRS and Treasury have provided additional relief. Announcement 2020-17 extends the due date for reporting and paying excise taxes related to minimum required contributions to correspond to the CARES Act delay. The new deadline is January 15, 2021.

HATFA 2014 (Highway & Transportation Funding Act of 2014). Passed into law in August 2014, HATFA sought to continue pension "funding stabilization" started with MAP-21 by retroactively extending the MAP-21 so-called "phase down percentage" used to calculate the floor of the

---

1.   Notice 2011-96, 2011-52 IRB 915; Notice 2012-70, 2012-51 IRB 712.
2.   Notice 2011-3, 2011-2 IRB 263, at N.
3.   See generally, Moving Ahead for Progress in the 21st Century Act- MAP-21 (P.L. 112-141), Jul. 6, 2012.
4.   Note that the calculation of variable PBGC premiums is based upon unfunded vested benefits and these are determined without application of MAP-21 (and now HATFA 2014 as well). For all practical purposes, the variable rate premiums act as a kind of tax on a plan's underfunding.
5.   See generally, Moving Ahead for Progress in the 21st Century Act- MAP-21 (P.L. 112-141), Jul. 6, 2012.

corridor for valuation interest rates in calculating the minimum required contribution. Under HATFA 2014, the corridor, compared with MAP-21 looks as follows:

% Phase Down	Current Rules/Year	HATFA/Year
90	2012	2012-2017
85	2013	2018
80	2014	2019
75	2015	2020
70	2016 and later	2021 and after

Note that for 2018, HAFTA would allow for use of an 85 percent floor while under MAP-21 it would be 70 percent.

HATFA 2014 also allowed plan sponsors to ignore the MAP-21 extension for 2013 as to funding or benefit restrictions or just for purposes of benefit restrictions if they were required under MAP-21 to impose benefit restrictions in 2013 because of the plan's funded status.[1]

3744. What requirements apply to defined benefit plans that are "at risk" beginning after 2007?

In plan years beginning after December 31, 2007, a defined benefit plan with more than 500 participants (determined on a controlled group basis) will be considered "at-risk" if the funding target attainment percentage determined under IRC Section 430 (Q 3743), but without regard to the at-risk rules, is less than 80 percent and the funding target attainment percentage for the preceding plan year determined under IRC Section 430 and using the more aggressive assumptions described below to compute the funding target, is less than 70 percent.[2]

Under transition rules, the 80 percent funding target attainment percentage is reduced to 65 percent in 2008, 70 percent in 2009, and 75 percent in 2010. For plan years beginning in 2008, the determination of the 70 percent threshold for the preceding year may be estimated under guidance to be provided in the future.[3]

If a plan is "at risk" for a plan year, its funding target is the present value of all the benefits accrued or earned under the plan as of the beginning of the plan year, using more aggressive actuarial assumptions, as follows: (1) all employees who are not otherwise assumed to retire as of the valuation date, but who will be eligible to elect benefits during the plan year and the 10 succeeding plan years, will be assumed to retire at the earliest retirement date under the plan year after the end of the year for which the at-risk funding target and target normal cost are being determined, and (2) all employees will be assumed to elect the retirement benefit with the highest present value of benefits at the assumed retirement age determined in (1).[4]

---

1. See generally, Highway and Transportation & Funding Act of 2014 –HATFA 2014 (PL 113-159), Aug. 8, 2014.
2. IRC Secs. 430(i)(4)(A), 430(i)(6).
3. IRC Sec. 430(i)(4)(B); Treas. Reg. §1.430(i)-1.
4. IRC Sec. 430(i)(1).

In addition, plans that have been at-risk for at least two of the preceding four years will be subject to a loading factor.[1] The loading factor is $700 times the number of participants in the plan, plus 4 percent of the funding target, determined without regard to this provision, of the plan for the plan year.[2]

At-risk plans also may be subject to a qualification requirement that suspends many benefit increases, plan amendments, and accruals in single-employer plans when funding falls below specified levels ranging from 60 percent to 80 percent (Q 3716).[3] These rules were subject to certain modifications in keeping with certain funding relief provisions under MAP-21 and HATFA 2014, but generally remain applicable for underfunded plans as defined (Q 3743).

3745. When are pension plan contributions credited for funding standard account purposes?

For plan years beginning before 2008, the funding standard account is credited with the contributions for the plan year.[4] The employer had a grace period of 8½ months after the plan year ended to make contributions for that plan year.[5] This is true even with respect to the plan year in which the plan terminates.[6]

A contribution was not considered timely made when, prior to the expiration of the 8½ months, an employer merely segregated a sum sufficient to fund its plan contributions in an extra checking account in the name of the employer, not in the name of the plan.[7]

The rules governing the time when a contribution is deemed made for the purposes of crediting the funding standard account generally are independent of the rules governing the time when a contribution is deemed made for deduction purposes.[8] Thus, contributions made for one plan year but carried over to a later tax year for deduction purposes may not be credited to the account as a contribution for the later year.[9] A contribution made during the grace period on account of the preceding tax year may be made for and credited to the account for the current plan year.[10] Likewise, a contribution made in and deducted for the current plan year may be credited for the previous year for purposes of the funding rules if made during the grace period.[11] See Q 3743 for overview information on calculating a plan sponsor's required minimum contribution for the years from 2007-2021 applying the relief in MAP-21 and HATFA 2014.

1.   IRC Sec. 430(i)(1)(A)(ii).
2.   IRC Sec. 430(i)(1)(C).
3.   See IRC Sec. 436.
4.   IRC Sec. 412(b)(3)(A), prior to amendment by PPA 2006.
5.   IRC Sec. 412(c)(10), prior to amendment by PPA 2006; Temp. Treas. Reg. §11.412(c)-12(b).
6.   Rev. Rul. 79-237, 1979-2 CB 190, *as modified by* Rev. Rul. 89-87, 1989-2 CB 81.
7.   *D.J. Lee, M.D., Inc. v. Comm.*, 92 TC 291 (1989), *aff'd on other grounds*, 91-1 USTC 87,881 (6th Cir. 1991).
8.   Temp. Treas. Reg. §11.412(c)-12(b)(2); Prop. Treas. Reg. §1.412(c)(10)-1(c).
9.   Rev. Rul. 77-151, 1977-1 CB 121.
10. Rev. Rul. 77-82, 1977-1 CB 121.
11. Let. Rul. 9107033.

3746. What other special requirements applied in plan years prior to 2008 when a qualified plan was subject to the minimum funding standard?

Under the full funding limitation, a plan generally was required to fund for certain expected increases due to benefits accruing during the plan year.[1] Any resulting increase in unfunded liability must be amortized over 30 years. Although a change in benefit provisions of a plan may not be assumed under a reasonable funding method, future salary may be assumed to change without being considered a benefit change. Thus, funding was to be based on projected benefits reflecting expected salary history, but only to the extent that the projected benefits do not exceed the maximum benefit permitted under the current plan provisions. For example, funding for a benefit of 90 percent of the participant's salary for his or her high three consecutive years may be based on 90 percent of the participant's projected salary, but not in excess of the maximum dollar benefit provided under the plan for the current year.[2]

Experience gains and losses were to be determined and plan liability valued at least once a year.[3] Normal costs, accrued liabilities, and experience gains and losses were to be determined under the funding method used to determine costs under the plan. Plan assets were to be valued by any reasonable actuarial method that takes into account fair market value and is permitted under regulations.[4] Asset valuations were not to be based on a range of 85 percent to 115 percent of average value.[5]

Ordinarily, the annual valuation was to be made during the plan year or within one month prior to the beginning of the plan year. A valuation date from the immediately preceding plan year could be used provided that, as of that date, the plan assets were not less than 100 percent of the plan's current liability.[6] A change to a prior year valuation could not be made unless plan assets were not less than 125 percent of the plan's current liability.[7]

Each actuarial assumption must be reasonable or, when aggregated, result in a total contribution equal to the amount that would be determined if each were reasonable. In the case of multiemployer plans, actuarial assumptions only need be reasonable in the aggregate. Of course, all actuarial assumptions must offer the actuary's best estimate of anticipated experience.[8]

Automatic approval is available for certain changes in a plan's funding method. Examples of such automatic approvals include:

(1)   to remedy unreasonable allocation of costs;

(2)   for fully funded terminated plans;

---

1.   See IRC Sec. 412(c)(7)(E)(i)(I).
2.   Rev. Rul. 81-195, 1981-2 CB 104.
3.   IRC Sec. 412(c)(9).
4.   See Treas. Reg. §1.412(c)(2)-1(b)(6).
5.   OBRA '87, Sec. 9303(c).
6.   IRC Sec. 412(c)(9)(B).
7.   IRC Sec. 412(c)(9)(B)(iv).
8.   IRC Sec. 412(c)(3).

(3)   for takeover plans;

(4)   for changes in valuation software;

(5)   for *de minimis* mergers;

(6)   for certain mergers with the same plan year and a merger date of first or last day of plan year; and

(7)   for certain mergers involving a designated transition period.[1]

Defined benefit pension plans generally are not permitted to anticipate amendments (even if adopted within the remedial amendment period) in determining funding, except as specifically required by IRC Section 412(c)(12).[2]

For a multiemployer plan maintained pursuant to a collective bargaining agreement, the minimum funding standard is determined as if all participants in the plan were employed by a single employer.[3] Projected benefit increases scheduled to take effect during the term of the agreement must be taken into account.[4] In contrast, each employer in a multiple employer plan generally is treated as maintaining a separate plan for purposes of the minimum funding rules, unless the plan uses a method for determining required contributions under which each employer contributes at least the amount that would be required if each employer maintained a separate plan.[5]

If the employer maintaining the plan is a member of a group treated as a single employer under the controlled group, common control, or affiliated service provisions (Q 3932, Q 3934), then each member of the group is jointly and severally liable for the amount of any contributions required under the minimum funding standard or the amount of any required installments to the plan.[6]

The minimum funding standard continues to apply even if the plan later becomes non-qualified. It does not apply in years after the end of the plan year in which the plan terminates completely. For guidelines as to the application of the minimum funding standard to the plan year in which a plan terminates, see Revenue Ruling 89-87[7] and Proposed Treasury Regulation §1.412(b)-4. The minimum funding standard must be re-established if the terminated plan is restored to the sponsoring employer by the PBGC.[8]

1.   See Rev. Proc. 2000-40, 2000-2 CB 357.
2.   Rev. Proc. 98-42, 1998-2 CB 55.
3.   IRC Sec. 413(b)(5).
4.   IRC Sec. 412(c)(12).
5.   IRC Sec. 413(c)(4).
6.   IRC Sec. 412(c)(11).
7.   1989-2 CB 81.
8.   See Treas. Reg. §1.412(c)(1)-3, TD 8494, 1993-2 CB 203.

3747. What is the penalty for underfunding a qualified plan that is subject to the minimum funding standard?

If a plan subject to the minimum funding standard (Q 3742 to Q 3746) fails to meet it, the employer sponsoring the plan is penalized by an excise tax, but the plan will not be disqualified.[1] Imposition of the tax is automatic; there is no exception for unintentionally or inadvertently failing to meet the standard or for having intended to terminate the plan.[2]

For a single employer plan, the tax is 10 percent of the aggregate unpaid minimum required contributions for all plan years (Q 3742 to Q 3746) remaining unpaid as of the end of any plan year ending with or within the taxable year.[3] (In the case of a multiemployer plan, the tax is 5 percent of any accumulated funding deficiency; in the case of a CSEC plan, 10 percent of such deficiency.) In one case, an employer was liable for the 10 percent tax where a contribution was made on time according to the terms of the plan, but not within the period specified in IRC Section 412.[4]

If the 10 percent tax is imposed on any unpaid minimum required contributions and if it remains unpaid as of the close of the taxable period, or if the 10 percent tax is imposed on a multiemployer plan's accumulated funding deficiency, an additional tax of 100 percent will be imposed on the employer to the extent that the minimum required contribution or accumulated funding deficiency is not corrected within the taxable period.[5] This additional 100 percent tax will be abated if the deficiency is corrected within 90 days after the date when the notice of deficiency is mailed. This period may be extended by the Secretary of the Treasury.[6]

An additional tax is applied to certain defined benefit plans with a funded current liability percentage of less than 100 percent that have a "liquidity shortfall" for any quarter during a plan year.[7] Such a plan may be subject to a tax of 10 percent of the excess of the amount of the liquidity shortfall for any quarter over the amount of such shortfall paid by the required installment for the quarter.[8] If the shortfall was due to reasonable cause and not willful neglect, and if reasonable steps have been taken to remedy the liquidity shortfall, the Secretary of the Treasury has the discretion to waive part or all of the penalty.[9]

An uncorrected deficiency will continue in later years and will be increased by interest charges until it is paid.[10] When an employer fails to contribute a plan's normal cost in any year, that amount will not, thereafter, become a past service cost to be amortized. The funding standard account will show the amount as a deficiency subject to tax each year until corrected.

---

1.   TIR 1334 (1/8/75), M-5.
2.   See *D.J. Lee, M.D., Inc. v. Comm.*, 931 F. 2d 418, 91-1 USTC ¶50,218 (6th Cir. 1991); *Lee Eng'g Supply Co., Inc. v. Comm.*, 101 TC 189 (1993).
3.   IRC Sec. 4971(a).
4.   *Wenger v. Comm.*, TC Memo 2000-156 (2000).
5.   IRC Sec. 4971(b).
6.   IRC Secs. 4961, 4963(e).
7.   IRC Secs. 4971(f), 430(j).
8.   IRC Sec. 4971(f).
9.   IRC Sec. 4971(f)(4).
10.   See IRC Sec. 412(b)(5).

If the employer is a member of a group that is treated as a single employer under the controlled group, common control, or affiliated services group provisions (Q 3932, Q 3934), then each member of the group is jointly and severally liable for any tax payable under IRC Section 4971.[1] The tax is due for the tax year in which (or with which) the plan year ends. The IRS has determined that general partners were jointly and severally liable for a partnership's excise tax obligation resulting from failure to satisfy the minimum funding standard.[2]

Where a plan chooses to keep both a funding standard account and an alternative minimum funding standard account, the tax will be based on the lower minimum funding requirement.[3]

None of the excise taxes payable under IRC Section 4971 are deductible.[4]

Note that neither MAP-21 nor HATFA 2014 changed the definition or calculation of unfunded vested benefits upon which the tax is calculated. See Q 3743 for more information on the important changes that were made by MAP-21 and HATFA 2014.

If a plan is maintained pursuant to a collective bargaining agreement or by more than one employer, the liability of each employer will be based first on the employers' respective delinquencies in meeting their required contributions, and then on the basis of the employers' respective liabilities for contributions.[5]

The tax does not apply in years after the end of the plan year in which the plan terminates. If the accumulated funding deficiency has not been reduced to zero as of the end of that plan year, then the 100 percent tax is due for the plan year in which the plan terminates.[6]

For further guidance on the tax penalty for underfunding, see Treasury Regulation Section 54.4971-1 and Proposed Treasury Regulation Sections 54.4971-2 to 54.4971-3. Also see Q 3743 regarding HATFA 2014 limitations on executive compensation as a consequence of selecting deferred funding of qualified plans.

3748. Can the minimum funding standard for qualified plans be waived?

Under limited circumstances, the IRS may grant a waiver of the minimum funding standard. To obtain such a waiver, the employer sponsoring the plan must demonstrate that imposition of the 100 percent tax would be a substantial business hardship and adverse to the interest of plan participants in the aggregate.[7] Updated procedures for requesting a waiver of the 100 percent tax are set forth in Revenue Procedure 2004-15.[8] In 2017, the IRS issued Revenue Procedure 2017-4, which eliminated the alternative of requesting a determination letter in conjunction with a minimum funding waiver.[9] The IRS may still grant a waiver contingent on certain conditions

---

1. IRC Sec. 4971(e).
2. Let. Rul. 9414001.
3. IRC Secs. 4971(c)(1), 412(a).
4. IRC Sec. 275(a)(6).
5. IRC Secs. 413(b)(6), 413(c)(5).
6. Rev. Rul. 79-237, 1979-2 CB 190, *as modified by* Rev. Rul. 89-87, 1989-2 CB 81.
7. See IRC Sec. 412(d).
8. 2004-7 IRB 490. See, e.g., Let. Ruls. 200349005, 9849024.
9. Rev. Proc. 2017-4, 2017-1 IRB 146.

being met. If they are not met, the waiver is void retroactively. An employer sponsoring a plan may request a modification of a conditional waiver of the minimum funding requirements by private letter ruling request.[1] The IRS has privately ruled that waiver is appropriate where the hardship is likely to be temporary,[2] but not where the hardship is of a permanent nature.[3] Under certain circumstances, the IRS may approve a retroactive plan amendment reducing plan liabilities due to substantial business hardship.[4]

Employers sponsoring certain terminated single-employer defined benefit plans may obtain a waiver of the 100 percent tax imposed on an accumulated funding deficiency. To obtain the waiver, these conditions must be met:

(1)   the plan must be subject to Title IV of ERISA,

(2)   the plan must be terminated in a standard termination under ERISA Section 4041,

(3)   plan participants must not be entitled to any portion of residual assets remaining after all liabilities of the plan to participants and their beneficiaries have been satisfied,

(4)   excise taxes that have been (or could be) imposed under IRC Section 4971(a) must have been paid for all taxable years (including the taxable year related to the year of plan termination), and

(5)   the plan must have filed all applicable forms in the 5500 series (including Schedule B) for all plan years (including the year of plan termination).[5]

See Q 3743 for overview information on the relief as to the required minimum contribution by MAP-21 and HAFTA 2014.

Profit Sharing Plans

3749. What is a profit sharing plan?

A profit sharing plan is a plan for sharing company profits with employees. A profit sharing plan need not provide a definite, predetermined formula for determining the amount of profits to be shared. In the absence of a definite formula, there must be recurring and substantial contributions, and contributions must not be made at such times and in such amounts that the plan in operation discriminates in favor of highly compensated employees.[6] A profit sharing plan may explicitly provide for investment primarily in qualifying employer securities (Q 3817).[7]

---

1.   See, e.g., Let. Ruls. 9852051, 9849031.
2.   Let Rul. 9846047.
3.   Let. Rul. 9846049.
4.   See Let. Rul. 9736044.
5.   See Rev. Proc. 2000-17, 2000-1 CB 766.
6.   Treas. Reg. §1.401-1(b)(1)(ii).
7.   ERISA Secs. 407(b)(1), 407(d)(3).

For an explanation of specific qualification requirements applicable to profit sharing plans, see Q 3751. There are qualification requirements that apply to 401(k) plans (Q 3752 to Q 3807) and an employer deduction limit for profit sharing contributions (Q 3750).

A profit sharing plan must provide a definite, predetermined formula for allocating contributions among participants and for distributing accumulated funds to the employees after a fixed number of years (at least two), the attainment of a stated age, or on prior occurrence of some event such as layoff, illness, disability, retirement, death, or severance of employment. The allocation formula generally is related to compensation, although age, service, and other factors may be given consideration (Q 3861). A profit sharing plan cannot provide for allocations or distributions based on predetermined benefits, because such a plan would be a pension plan. Although a profit sharing plan is primarily a plan of deferred compensation, the plan may use funds in an employee's account to provide incidental life or health insurance for the employee or the employee's family (Q 3829).[1]

Planning Point: In a private letter ruling,[2] the IRS blessed amendment to a profit sharing plan covering collectively bargained employees to allow participants to allocate contributions between HRAs and the plan based on an annual election (a default would apply in the absence of an election). The IRS found that the proposed amendment would not cause the plan to be treated as a 401(k), because it would not create an opportunity for participants to elect cash or to use the contributions to pay for taxable benefits. Therefore, the profit sharing plan would not offer a cash or deferred arrangement under IRC Section 401. The IRS also found that the arrangement would not violate the HRA rules.

A tax-exempt "non-profit" charitable organization may maintain a profit sharing plan, including a 401(k) plan.[3]

3750. How much may an employer deduct for its contributions to a qualified profit sharing or stock bonus plan?

An employer's deduction for contributions to a profit sharing or stock bonus plan is the greater of (1) 25 percent of the compensation otherwise paid or accrued during the employer's taxable year to the beneficiaries of the plan, or (2) the amount the employer is required to contribute under Section 401(k) for the year.[4]

The amount of annual compensation of each employee taken into account for purposes of this limitation may not exceed $290,000 (in 2021, as indexed. The amount was $285,000 in 2020 and $280,000 in 2019).[5] Compensation for this purpose is Section 415(c)(3) compensation, which includes elective deferrals under 401(k) and Section 457 plans, salary reduction contributions to Section 125 cafeteria plans, and qualified transportation fringe benefits under IRC Section 132(f).[6] In the case of a self-employed person, "earned income" is used instead of "compensation" (Q 3826).

1. Treas. Reg. §1.401-1(b)(1)(ii).
2. Let. Rul. 202023001.
3. IRC Sec. 401(k)(4)(B)(i); GCM 38283 (2-15-80).
4. IRC Sec. 404(a)(3)(A)(i)(II).
5. IRC Sec. 404(l); Notice 2018-83, Notice 2019-59, Notice 2020-79.
6. IRC Sec. 404(a)(12).

Contributions, for purposes of the deduction limit, do not include elective deferrals (Q 3760), and elective deferrals are not themselves subject to any limitation contained in IRC Section 404.[1]

Contributions allocated to life and health insurance are included in the 25 percent limit. A terminating employee's compensation for the final year is included in the 25 percent only if the employee shares in profits for the final year.[2] Compensation paid to seasonal and part-time employees who are not eligible to participate in the plan may not be included in calculating the 25 percent limit; neither can compensation paid to employees who terminate before any alloca- tion is made and whose allocations made after termination would be immediately forfeitable.[3]

Where contributions are made to the trusts of two or more profit sharing or stock bonus plans, the trusts are considered a single trust for purposes of the 25 percent limit.[4] The limit is applied by aggregating all contributions to such plans and limiting the total to 25 percent of the aggregate compensation of the employees covered by the plans.[5]

Amounts in excess of the 25 percent limit contributed in any year (called a contribution carry-over) may be deducted in succeeding years. Nondeductible contributions are generally subject to a 10 percent excise tax (Q 3942). For any succeeding year, the deduction for current contributions and contribution carry-overs cannot exceed 25 percent of participating payroll for the taxable year.[6] Excess contributions made in a year when the trust is exempt may be car- ried over and deducted in a succeeding year even though the trust is no longer exempt in the succeeding year.[7]

The amount of contributions taken into account by profit sharing or stock bonus plans must be reduced by any annual additions in excess of the Section 415 limits.[8] The excess amount may not be carried over and deducted in a later year.[9]

Contributions do not need to be made from current or accumulated profits to be deductible.[10]

Restorative payments. Amounts paid to a defined contribution plan as restoration for plan losses that result from a fiduciary breach (or a reasonable risk of liability for a fiduciary breach), are not contributions for purposes of the deduction limit.[11] The same reasoning was applied in a 1998 private ruling where an employer made a restorative contribution to replace plan losses in derivatives to avoid litigation with plan participants.[12] In contrast, payments that are made to a plan to make up for losses due to market fluctuations, but not due to a fiduciary breach, will

---

1.   IRC Secs. 404(a)(3), 404(a)(7), 404(a)(9).
2.   See Rev. Rul. 65-295, 1965-2 CB 148.
3.   See *Dallas Dental Labs v. Comm.*, 72 TC 117 (1979).
4.   IRC Sec. 404(a)(3)(A)(iv).
5.   Let. Rul. 9635045.
6.   Treas. Reg. §1.404(a)-9(e).
7.   Treas. Reg. §1.404(a)-9(a).
8.   IRC Sec. 404(j)(1).
9.   Notice 83-10, 1983-1 CB 536, F-1.
10. See IRC Sec. 401(a)(27).
11. Rev. Rul. 2002-45, 2002-2 CB 116. See Let. Ruls. 9506048, 9628031.
12. See Let. Rul. 9807028.

be treated as contributions subject to the limit, not as restorative payments.[1] The IRS treated payments back to a plan to offset annuity surrender charges as contributions in one ruling,[2] but as restorative payments in another.[3]

3751. What special qualification requirements apply to profit sharing plans but not to pension plans?

A profit sharing plan is a defined contribution plan that allows for discretionary employer contributions (as opposed to a money purchase pension plan with a fixed contribution as a percentage of participant compensation). Because employer contributions are discretionary, they can be a means for sharing employer profits with employees and their beneficiaries. All 401(k) plans must be profit sharing plans. A profit sharing plan must provide (1) a definite predetermined formula for allocating contributions and trust earnings among the participants, (2) for periodic valuation of trust assets, and (3) for distribution of the funds accumulated under the plan after a fixed number of years (meaning at least two years), on the attainment of a stated age, or on the prior occurrence of some event such as layoff, illness, disability, retirement, death, or severance of employment (Q 3749).[4]

Profit sharing plans (as opposed to money purchase pension plans) have few restrictions on distributions. The IRS has ruled that a plan could permit participants with at least five years of participation to withdraw all employer contributions (including those made during the last two years).[5] With respect to amounts rolled over from another qualified plan, the receiving profit sharing plan must comply with the "fixed number of years" requirement without reference to the number of years such amounts accumulated in the previous plan.[6] Where a participant's entire account balance transfers to another qualified plan, the years of participation in both plans may be aggregated.[7]

It is not necessary that the employer contributes every year, contributes the same amount every year, or contributes in accordance with the same ratio every year. Merely making a single or occasional contribution for employees, however, does not establish a profit-sharing plan. To be a profit-sharing plan, there must be recurring and substantial contributions.[8]

A provision for offsetting contributions under a profit sharing plan by contributions made to a money purchase pension plan will not prevent either plan from qualifying.[9]

In a profit sharing plan, an age lower than 65 may be specified as retirement age.[10]

---

1. Rev. Rul. 2002-45, 2002-2 CB 116.
2. Let. Rul. 200317048.
3. Let. Rul. 200337017.
4. Treas. Reg. §1.401-1(b)(1)(ii); Rev. Rul. 71-295, 1971-2 CB 184; Rev. Rul. 80-155, 1980-1 CB 84.
5. Rev. Rul. 68-24, 1968-1 CB 150.
6. Let. Rul. 8134110.
7. Let. Rul. 8825130.
8. Treas. Reg. §1.401-1(b)(2).
9. Rev. Rul. 81-201, 1981-2 CB 88.
10. Rev. Rul. 80-276, 1980-2 CB 131.

Withdrawal of Contributions

If a plan provides that employer contributions are allocated on the basis of employee contributions that may be withdrawn immediately after they are made, the plan will not qualify because such a withdrawal provision "could reasonably be expected to result in the manipulation of the allocation and contravention of the definite predetermined allocation formula requirement of Section 1.401-1(b)(1)(ii) of the regulations."[1]

If, on the other hand, the withdrawal provision imposes a "substantial limitation" on the right of a participant to withdraw his or her own contributions, so that the provision "cannot reasonably be expected to result in the manipulation of the allocation" as described above, this provision will not cause a plan to fail to qualify.[2]

Valuation of Assets

If amounts allocated or distributed to a particular participant are to be ascertainable, the plan must provide for a valuation of investments held by the trust at least once a year, on a specified inventory date, in accordance with a method consistently followed and uniformly applied. The fair market value on the inventory date is to be used for this purpose. The respective accounts of the participants are adjusted in accordance with the valuation.[3]

If a fully insured profit sharing plan provides that all trust assets are to be invested immediately in individual annuity or retirement income contracts, the cash value of which at any particular time is contained in a schedule supplied by the insurance company, the plan need not provide for the periodic valuation of trust investments.[4]

401(k) Plans
Overview
3752. What is a 401(k) plan?

A 401(k) plan generally is a profit sharing plan or stock bonus plan that provides for contributions to be made pursuant to a "cash or deferred arrangement" ("CODA", see Q 3755) under which individual participants elect to take either amounts in cash or to have the amounts deferred under the plan. With the availability of Roth contributions under 401(k) plans, the employee also may elect to have Roth deferrals made on an after-tax basis to the CODA.

In addition to the general qualification requirements (Q 3837 through Q 3935), special qualification rules apply to 401(k) plans (Q 3753 to Q 3807). Certain nondiscrimination requirements can be met by satisfying the requirements for safe harbor plans (Q 3772). There are requirements for SIMPLE 401(k) plans (Q 3777) and there are automatic enrollment plans for plan years beginning after 2007 (Q 3762).

---

1.   Rev. Rul. 72-275, 1972-1 CB 109, *as modified by* Rev. Rul. 74-55, 1974-1 CB 89.
2.   Rev. Rul. 74-56, 1974-1 CB 90. *See also* Let. Rul. 7816022.
3.   Rev. Rul. 80-155, 1980-1 CB 84.
4.   Rev. Rul. 73-435, 1973-2 CB 126.

The elective deferral limits apply to individuals participating in more than one salary reduction plan, such as a 401(k) plan and a Section 403(b) tax sheltered annuity or SIMPLE IRA (Q 3760). There also are requirements that pertain to catch-up contributions by participant's age 50 or over (Q 3761).

Amounts deferred under a 401(k) plan are referred to as elective deferrals (Q 3760). Elective deferrals generally are excluded from a participant's gross income for the year of the deferral and are treated as employer contributions to the plan.[1] In the case of contributions to a qualified Roth contribution program (Q 3778), deferrals are made on an after-tax basis (i.e., they are treated as includable in income for withholding purposes).[2]

A 401(k) plan may provide that all employer contributions are made pursuant to the election or may provide that the cash or deferred arrangement is in addition to ordinary employer contributions. Typically, the employer contributions are in the form of a percentage match for each dollar deferred by an employee. There are requirements that apply to matching contributions (Q 3803, Q 3807).

Note: On December 16, 2019, the SECURE ACT[3] was enacted that made a number of significant changes (some made effective immediately upon enactment) to retirement plan law. Many of these changes in the law impact 401(k) plans and their operations, like the need to annually communicate lifetime income to participants, expansion of mandatory participation to certain fulltime part-time employees, and a change in the "required beginning date" and allowable distribution periods for required minimum distributions. Others reduce the burden and cost for an employer to adopt or maintain a plan.

There have also been a number of law and regulatory changes prior to the SECURE Act to certain substantive 401(k) limitation rules regarding hardship, loans and other pre-59½ distributions, especially in the case of areas officially declared to be national disaster areas, as for hurricanes, floods, and fires (Q 3798). Some changes, like extension of time to repay 401(k) loans, do not require a disaster justification.

3753. What special qualification requirements apply to 401(k) plans?

To qualify, a 401(k) plan (or a plan that provides a 401(k) cash or deferred arrangement) generally must first be a qualified profit sharing or stock bonus plan.[4]

Contributions to the plan made under a cash or deferred arrangement must satisfy the nondiscrimination in amount requirement (Q 3801), be subject to withdrawal restrictions (Q 3801), and will not be included in the employee's gross income unless the employee elects to treat the contributions as designated Roth contributions (Q 3778).

---

1.   Treas. Reg. §1.401(k)-1(a).
2.   See IRC Sec. 402A.
3.   See PL 116-94
4.   IRC Sec. 401(k); Treas. Reg. §1.401(k)-1(a)(1).

3754. Are tax-exempt and governmental employers eligible to offer 401(k) plans?

Yes. Tax-exempt employers such as 501(c)(3) organizations are eligible to offer 401(k) arrangements.[1] State and local government employers (including political subdivisions and agencies thereof) generally are prohibited from offering 401(k) arrangements to their employees, but certain rural cooperatives may do so.[2]

3755. What is a cash or deferred arrangement ("CODA") in the context of a 401(k) plan?

A "cash or deferred arrangement" ("CODA") is an arrangement under which an eligible employee may make a cash or deferred election with respect to contributions, accruals, or other benefits in a qualified plan.[3] A cash or deferred election is any direct or indirect election (or modification of an earlier election) by an employee to have the employer either (1) provide an amount to the employee in the form of cash (or some other taxable benefit) that is not currently available, or (2) contribute an amount to a trust, or provide an accrual or other benefit under a plan deferring the receipt of compensation.[4]

With respect to timing, the final regulations provide that "a contribution is made pursuant to a cash or deferred election only if the contribution is made after the election is made."[5] See Q 3938 with regard to deduction timing. Under final regulations, amounts contributed in anticipation of future performance of services generally are not treated as elective contributions. A very limited exception is provided for bona fide administrative convenience (e.g., a company bookkeeper is absent the day the funds normally would be transmitted to the plan) and not for a principal purpose of accelerating deductions.[6] Special penalties and reporting requirements apply to listed transactions (Q 4106).[7]

Automatic enrollment. For purposes of determining whether an election is a cash or deferred election, it is irrelevant whether the default that applies in the absence of an affirmative election is that the employee receives cash or that the employee contributes the specified amount to the trust.[8] In plan years beginning after 2007, a safe harbor is available for plans that provide for automatic enrollment ("qualified automatic contribution arrangement" or "QACA") and satisfy certain additional requirements (Q 3762). Beginning in 2020, under the SECURE Act, the QACA safe harbor can provide for auto escalation of the automatic contribution.[9] See Q 3762 for more detail.

1.　IRC Sec. 401(k)(4)(B)(i). Of course, 403(b) plans are an option for nongovernmental tax-exempt employers and are also available to governmental tax-exempt employers, like school districts.
2.　See IRC Secs. 401(k)(1), 401(k)(2), 401(k)(4)(B)(ii).
3.　See Treas. Reg. §1.401(k)-1(a)(2).
4.　Treas. Reg. §1.401(k)-1(a)(3).
5.　Treas. Reg. §1.401(k)-1(a)(3)(iii)(B).
6.　See Treas. Reg. §1.401(k)-1(a)(3)(iii)(C)(2).
7.　See IRC Sec. 6707A.
8.　See Treas. Reg. §1.401(k)-1(a)(3)(ii).
9.　See PL 116-94, Sec. 102

A cash or deferred arrangement does not qualify as such if any other benefit provided by the employer, except for matching contributions, is conditioned on the employee's making an election under the plan. "Other benefits" is illustrated in the regulations.[1] The IRS has privately ruled that the purchase of a group long-term disability income policy that provided continuation of benefit accumulation for disabled employees did not violate this rule.[2]

The IRS repeatedly has approved 401(k) plans involving a so-called "401(k) wraparound" nonqualified deferred compensation plan arrangement[3], whereby contributions consisting of current year salary deferrals were held initially in a nonqualified deferred compensation plan (Q 3571). The IRS concluded that such deferrals were not impermissibly conditioned on the deferral election.[4] Final regulations state that a plan will not fail to be qualified merely because it includes a nonqualified cash or deferred arrangement, but special requirements will apply to its nondiscrimination testing.[5]

Elective deferral contributions to a 401(k) cash or deferred arrangement, including Roth contributions (Q 3778), are treated as employer contributions except when they are recharacterized (Q 3807).[6] Contributions need not come from employer profits.[7]

3756. What elective deferral limits are applicable to 401(k) plans?

The plan must provide that the amount any employee can elect to defer for any calendar year under the cash or deferred arrangement of any plan is limited to $19,500 in 2020-2021 (up from $19,000 in 2019, and $18,500 in 2018), and is subject to indexing for inflation thereafter (Q 3760).[8] Plans also may allow additional elective deferrals, known as catch-up contributions, by participants age 50 or over. These catch-up contributions, if made under the provisions of IRC Section 414(v), are not subject to the Section 401(a)(30) limit (Q 3761).[9]

3757. What participation and coverage requirements apply to 401(k) plans?

Editor's Note: The SECURE Act has changed the law on mandatory eligibility to include long-term part-time employees. Under prior law, employers were permitted to exclude employees who performed fewer than 1,000 hours of service per year from participation in the employer-sponsored 401(k). The SECURE Act modified this rule in order to expand access for certain part-time employees. Under the new law, nonunion employees who perform at least 500 hours of service for at least three consecutive years (and are at least 21 years old) must be allowed to participate in the employer-sponsored 401(k). These long-term, part-time employees may, however, be excluded from coverage and nondiscrimination testing requirements. This SECURE Act provision becomes effective for plan years beginning after December 31, 2020. However,

---

1. IRC Sec. 401(k)(4)(A); Treas. Reg. §1.401(k)-1(e)(6); see Let. Rul. 9250013.
2. Let. Ruls. 200235043, 200031060.
3. The IRS has also approved this design as to the nonqualified plan covered by Section 409A, but the DOL guidance governing the timeliness of plan contributions now need to be considered as well.
4. See e.g., Let. Ruls. 199924067, 9807010, 9752017, 9530038.
5. See Treas. Reg. §1.401(k)-1(a)(5)(iv).
6. Treas. Reg. §1.401(k)-1(a)(4)(ii).
7. IRC Sec. 401(a)(27).
8. IRC Secs. 401(a)(30), 402(g)(1); Notice 2017-64, Notice 2018-83, Notice 2019-59, Notice 2020-79.
9. IRC Sec. 414(v)(3)(A).

12-month periods beginning before January 1, 2021 are not taken into account for purposes of determining whether an employee qualifies.[1] Therefore, an employer need only track part time employees on a going forward basis. However, the same is not true for tracking the vesting of employer contributions, based upon Notice 2020-68.

Section 401(k)(15)(B)(iii) provides special vesting rules for an employee who becomes eligible to participate in a CODA solely by reason of having completed three consecutive 12-month periods during each of which the employee completed at least 500 hours of service (long-term, part-time employee). A long-term, part-time employee must be credited with a year of service for purposes of determining whether the employee has a nonforfeitable right to employer contributions (other than elective deferrals) for each 12-month period during which the employee completes at least 500 hours of service.[2] In addition, Section 401(k)(15)(B)(iii) modifies the break-in-service rules of Section 411(a)(6) for a long-term, part-time employee. The special vesting rules of Section 401(k)(15)(B)(iii) continue to apply to a long-term, part-time employee even if the long-term, part-time employee subsequently completes a 12-month period during which the employee completes at least 1,000 hours of service.[3]

The IRS has clarified that the rule providing that 12-month periods beginning before January 1, 2021 are not taken into account does not apply for purposes of the vesting rules. Generally, all years of service with the employer maintaining the plan must be taken into account for purposes of determining a long-term, part-time employee's nonforfeitable right to employer contributions under the special vesting rules. For purposes of determining whether a long-term, part-time employee has a nonforfeitable right to employer contributions (other than elective deferrals), each 12-month period for which the employee has at least 500 hours of service is treated as a year of service. All years of service with the employer maintaining the plan are taken into account for purposes of determining an employee's nonforfeitable right to employer contributions, subject to certain exceptions. Those exceptions include, for example, years of service before the employee attains age 18.[4]

A plan may not require, as a condition of participation in the cash or deferred arrangement, that an employee complete a period of service beyond the later of age 21 or the completion of one year of service.[5]

A cash or deferred arrangement must satisfy a nondiscriminatory coverage test (Q 3841).[6] For purposes of applying those tests, all eligible employees are treated as benefiting under the arrangement, regardless of whether they actually make elective deferrals.[7] An eligible employee is any employee who is directly or indirectly eligible to make a cash or deferred election under the plan for all or a portion of the plan year. An employee is not ineligible merely because he or she elects not to participate, is suspended from making an election under the hardship withdrawal

---

1.   P.L. 116-94, 133 Stat. 2534 (Dec. 20, 2019), Sec. 112
2.   IRC Sec. 401(k)(15)(B)(iii).
3.   IRC Sec. 401(k)(15)(B)(iv).
4.   Notice 2020-68.
5.   IRC Sec. 401(k)(2)(D).
6.   IRC Sec. 401(k)(3)(A)(i).
7.   Treas. Reg. §1.410(b)-3(a)(2)(i).

rules, is unable to make an election because his or her compensation is less than a specified dollar amount, or because he or she may receive no additional annual additions under the IRC Section 415 limits (Q 3728, Q 3867).[1]

Employers may apply an early participation test for certain younger or newer employees permitted to participate in a plan. If a plan separately satisfies the minimum coverage rules of IRC Section 410(b), taking into account only those employees who have not completed one year of service or are under age 21, an employer may elect to exclude any eligible nonhighly compensated employees who have not satisfied the age and service requirements for purposes of the ADP test (Q 3801).[2] This provision is designed to encourage employers to allow newer and younger employees to participate in a plan without having the plan's ADP results "pulled down" by their often-lower rates of deferral. By making this election, an employer will be able to apply a single ADP test comparing the highly compensated employees who are eligible to participate in the plan to the nonhighly compensated who have completed one year of service and reached age 21.

If an employer includes a tax-exempt 501(c)(3) organization and sponsors both a 401(k) (or 401(m)) plan and a Section 403(b) plan, employees eligible to participate in the Section 403(b) plan generally can be treated as excludable employees for purposes of the 401(k) plan if (1) no employee of the 501(c)(3) organization is eligible to participate in the 401(k) (or 401(m)) plan and (2) at least 95 percent of the employees who are not 501(c)(3) employees are eligible to participate in the 401(k) or 401(m) plan.[3]

Guidelines and transition rules for satisfying the coverage requirement during a merger or acquisition are set forth at Revenue Ruling 2004-11.[4]

3758. What rules regarding nonforfeitability of benefits apply to 401(k) plans?

An employee must be fully vested at all times in his or her elective contributions and cannot be subject to the forfeitures and suspensions that are permitted by the IRC for benefits derived from employer contributions (Q 3868). Furthermore, such amounts cannot be taken into consideration in applying the vesting rules to other contributions.[5]

Employer matching contributions and nonelective employer contributions that are taken into account for purposes of satisfying the special nondiscrimination rules applicable to cash or deferred arrangements (Q 3801) must be immediately nonforfeitable and subject to the withdrawal restrictions explained in Q 3796.[6] All other contributions to a plan that includes a cash or deferred arrangement also are subject to these restrictions unless a separate accounting is

---

1.   Treas. Reg. §1.401(k)-6.
2.   IRC Sec. 401(k)(3)(F); Treas. Reg. §1.401(k)-2(a)(1)(iii).
3.   Treas. Reg. §1.410(b)-6(g).
4.   2004-7 IRB 480.
5.   IRC Sec. 401(k)(2)(C); Treas. Reg. §1.401(k)-1(c); *see also* Treas. Reg. §1.401(k)-1(c).
6.   See Treas. Reg. §§1.401(k)-1(c), 1.401(k)-1(d).

maintained.[1] Contributions made under a SIMPLE 401(k) plan are subject to special nonforfeitability requirements (Q 3777).

3759. What aggregation requirements apply to 401(k) plans?

Cash or deferred arrangements included in a plan generally are treated as a single cash or deferred arrangement for purposes of meeting the requirements discussed in Q 3754 through Q 3758, and for purposes of the coverage requirements of IRC Section 410(b).[2] The deferral percentage taken into account under the ADP tests for any highly compensated employee who is a participant in two or more cash or deferred arrangements under plans of the participant's employer that are required to be aggregated (as discussed above) is the average of the deferral percentages for the employee under each of the arrangements.[3]

Restructuring may not be used to demonstrate compliance with the requirements of IRC Section 401(k).[4]

3760. What is the limit on elective deferrals to employer-sponsored plans?

The IRC limits the total amount of "elective deferrals" any individual can exclude from income in a year. Elective deferrals, for this purpose, generally include all salary deferral contributions to all 401(k) plans (Q 3752 through Q 3778), 403(b) tax sheltered annuities (Q 4046), SAR-SEPs (Q 3705), and SIMPLE IRAs (Q 3706).[5] Contributions under a Roth 401(k) feature (Q 3778) are subject to the same elective deferral limit as other 401(k) contributions.[6]

The elective deferral limit for traditional and safe harbor 401(k) plans and for Section 403(b) tax sheltered annuities is $19,500 in 2020-2021 (up from $19,000 in 2019, as indexed).[7]

Elective deferral contributions to SIMPLE IRAs (Q 3706) and SIMPLE 401(k) plans (Q 3777) are subject to a limit of $13,500 in 2020-2021, up from $13,000 in 2019.[8] The limit on elective deferrals to tax sheltered annuity plans may be further increased in the case of certain long term employees of certain organizations (Q 4046).[9]

The IRC Section 402(g)(1)(B) elective deferral limit is not required to be coordinated with the limit on Section 457 plans. As a result, an individual participating in both a 401(k) plan (or 403(b) plan) and a Section 457 plan in 2020-2021 may defer as much as $39,000 (Q 3584).[10]

1.　　Treas. Reg. §1.401(k)-1(e)(3).
2.　　See Treas. Reg. §1.401(k)-1(b)(4)(ii).
3.　　IRC Sec. 401(k)(3)(B).
4.　　Treas. Reg. §1.401(k)-1(b)(4)(iv)(B).
5.　　IRC Sec. 402(g)(3); Treas. Reg. §1.402(g)-1(b).
6.　　See IRC Sec. 402A(a)(1). Similar rules have recently been adopted with respect to the federal Thrift Savings Plan. 77 Fed. Reg. 26417 (May 4, 2012).
7.　　IRC Sec. 402(g)(1); Notice 2018-83, Notice 2019-59, Notice 2020-79.
8.　　Notice 2018-83, Notice 2019-59, Notice 2020-79.
9.　　Treas. Reg. §1.402(g)-1(c).
10.　　See IRC Sec. 457(c), Notice 2019-59, Notice 2020-79.

Matching contributions made on behalf of self-employed individuals generally are not treated as elective deferrals for purposes of IRC Section 402(g)(1)(B). This treatment does not apply to qualified matching contributions that are treated as elective contributions for purposes of the ADP test (Q 3801).[1]

Excess deferrals. Amounts deferred in excess of the ceiling (i.e., excess deferrals) are not excludable and, therefore, must be included in the individual's gross income for the taxable year.[2] In the case of participants age 50 or over, catch-up contributions permitted under IRC Section 414(v) are not treated as excess elective deferrals under IRC Section 402(g)(1)(C) (Q 3761).[3]

If any amount is included in an individual's income under these rules and plan language permits distributions of excess deferrals, the individual, prior to the first April 15 following the close of the individual's taxable year, may allocate the excess deferrals among the plans under which the deferrals were made and the plans may distribute the excess deferrals (including any income allocated thereto, provided the plan uses a reasonable method of allocating income) not later than the first April 15 after the close of the plan's taxable year.[4] The amount of excess deferrals distributed under these rules is not included in income a second time as a distribution, but any income on the excess deferral is treated as earned and received, and includable in income in the taxable year in which distributed.[5] If the plan so provides, distributions of excess deferrals may be made during the taxable year of the deferral if the individual and the plan designate the distribution as an excess deferral and the correcting distribution is made after the date on which the plan received the excess deferral.[6]

Excess amounts that are not timely distributed are not included in the cost basis of plan distributions, even though they have previously been included in income.[7] Thus, such amounts will be subjected to a second tax when distributed in the future. Any corrective distribution of less than the entire amount of the excess deferral is treated as a pro rata distribution of excess deferrals and income.[8]

Planning Point: Due to the potential for double taxation, excess elective deferrals should be avoided, and, if they inadvertently occur, should be corrected by the applicable deadline. One common trap for the unwary may occur where an individual participates in more than one plan that allows elective deferrals. Perhaps he or she participates in a 401(k) plan at his or her regular place of employment, and also participates in a SIMPLE IRA plan sponsored by a side business. The limits on elective deferrals are applied to the individual and not just to the plan, so the individual easily might stay within the terms of the two plans and still violate the elective deferral limits by contributing the maximum amount to both plans. *Martin Silfen, J.D., Brown Brothers Harriman Trust Co., LLC.*

---

1.   See IRC Sec. 402(g)(8).
2.   IRC Sec. 402(g)(1); Treas. Reg. §1.402(g)-1(a).
3.   Treas. Reg. §1.414(v)-1(g).
4.   Treas. Reg. §§1.402(g)-1(e)(2), 1.402(g)-1(e)(5).
5.   IRC Sec. 402(g)(2)(C); Treas. Reg. §1.402(g)-1(e)(8).
6.   Treas. Reg. §1.402(g)-1(e)(3).
7.   IRC Sec. 402(g)(2); Treas. Reg. §1.402(g)-1(e)(8).
8.   IRC Sec. 402(g)(2)(D); Treas. Reg. §1.402(g)-1(e)(10).

See Q 3807 for rules on coordinating distributions of excess contributions and excess deferrals.[1]

3761. What are the rules for catch-up contributions to employer sponsored retirement plans?

Catch-up contributions are defined as additional elective deferrals by an eligible participant in an applicable employer plan, as defined in IRC Section 414(v) and regulations thereunder. Elective deferral for this purpose refers to the amounts described in IRC Section 402(g)(3) (Q 3760), but also includes amounts deferred to eligible Section 457 governmental plans.[2] The provisions allowing catch-up contributions are among the retirement amendments of EGTRRA 2001 that became permanent under the Pension Protection Act of 2006 ("PPA 2006").[3]

For purposes of IRC Section 414(v), an applicable employer plan means:

(1)   employer plans qualified under IRC Section 401(a) (Q 3837);

(2)   Section 403(b) tax sheltered annuities (Q 4046);

(3)   eligible Section 457 governmental plans (457(b) plans);

(4)   salary reduction simplified employee pensions (i.e., SAR-SEPs (Q 3705)); and

(5)   SIMPLE IRAs (Q 3706).[4]

For this purpose, qualified plans, Section 403(b) plans, SAR-SEPs, and SIMPLE IRAs that are maintained by a controlled group of corporations, a group of trades or businesses under common control, or members of an affiliated service group (Q 3934) are considered one plan. In addition, if more than one eligible Section 457 governmental plan is maintained by the same employer, the plans will be treated as one plan.[5]

Catch-up contributions permitted under IRC Section 414(v) do not apply to a catch-up eligible participant for any taxable year in which a higher catch-up amount is permitted under IRC Section 457(b)(3) during the last three years prior to the plan's normal retirement year (Q 3584).[6]

Dollar limit. A plan may not permit additional elective deferrals for any year in an amount greater than the lesser of (1) the indexed amount listed below or (2) the excess (if any) of the participant's compensation as defined in IRC Section 415(c)(3) (Q 3867, Q 3728) over any other elective deferrals for the year made without regard to the catch-up limits.[7] An employer that sponsors more than one plan must aggregate the elective deferrals treated as catch-up

---

1.   See Treas. Reg. §1.401(k)-1(f)(5)(i).
2.   IRC Secs. 414(v)(5)(B), 414(u)(2)(C) (USERRA rights); Treas. Reg. §1.414(v)-1(g)(2).
3.   See P.L. 109-280, Sec. 811.
4.   IRC Sec. 414(v)(6).
5.   IRC Sec. 414(v)(2)(D).
6.   IRC Sec. 414(v)(6)(C); Treas. Reg. §1.414(v)-1(a)(3).
7.   IRC Sec. 414(v)(2)(A).

contributions for purposes of the dollar limit.[1] An individual participating in more than one plan is subject to one annual dollar limit for all catch-up contributions during the taxable year.[2]

The indexed dollar limit on catch-up contributions to SIMPLE IRAs and SIMPLE 401(k) plans is $3,000 in 2015-2021.[3] The indexed dollar limit on catch-up contributions to all other 401(k) plans and to Section 403(b) plans, eligible Section 457 plans, and SAR-SEPs is $6,500 in 2020-2021 (up from $6,000 for 2015-2019 plan years).[4]

Eligible participant. An eligible participant with respect to any plan year is a plan participant who would attain age 50 before the end of the taxable year and with respect to whom no other elective deferrals may be made to the plan for the plan (or other applicable) year as a result of any limit or other restriction.[5] For this purpose, every participant who will reach age 50 during a plan year is treated as having reached age 50 on the first day of the plan year, regardless of the employer's choice of plan year and regardless of whether the participant survives to age 50 or terminates employment prior to his or her birthday.[6]

Universal availability. A plan will not satisfy the nondiscrimination requirements of IRC Section 401(a)(4) unless all catch-up eligible participants who participate in any applicable plan maintained by the employer are provided with the effective opportunity to make the same election with respect to the dollar limits described above.[7] This is known as the universal availability requirement. A plan will not fail to satisfy this requirement merely because it allows participants to defer an amount equal to a specified percentage of compensation for each payroll period and permits each catch-up eligible participant to defer a pro rata share of the dollar catch-up limit in addition to that amount.[8]

For purposes of the universal availability requirement, all plans maintained by employers that are treated as a single employer under the controlled group, common control, or affiliated service group rules (Q 3932, Q 3934) generally must be aggregated.[9] Exceptions to the aggregation rule apply to Section 457 plans and certain newly acquired plans.[10]

Catch-up contributions are excluded from income in the same manner as elective deferrals.[11] The calculation of the elective deferrals that will be considered catch-up contributions generally is made as of the end of the plan year by comparing the total elective deferrals for the plan year with the applicable plan year limit.[12] Elective deferrals in excess of the plan, ADP, or IRC

---

1.   Treas. Reg. §1.414(v)-1(f)(1).
2.   Treas. Reg. §§1.402(g)-2(b), 1.414(v)-1(f)(3).
3.   IR-2015-118 (Oct. 21, 2015), Notice 2016-62, Notice 2017-64, Notice 2018-83, Notice 2019-59, Notice 2020-79.
4.   IR-2015-118 (Oct. 21, 2015), Notice 2016-62, Notice 2017-64, Notice 2018-83, Notice 2019-59, Notice 2020-79.
5.   IRC Sec. 414(v)(5).
6.   See Treas. Reg. §1.414(v)-1(g)(3).
7.   IRC Sec. 414(v)(4)(A); Treas. Reg. §1.414(v)-1(e).
8.   Treas. Reg. §1.414(v)-1(e).
9.   IRC Sec. 414(v)(4)(B).
10.   See Treas. Reg. §1.414(v)-1(e)(2) and (3).
11.   See IRC Sec. 402(g)(1)(C).
12.   Treas. Reg. §1.414(v)-1(b)(2).

limits, but not in excess of the amount limitations described above, will be treated as catch-up contributions as determined on the last day of the plan year.[1]

An employer may make, but is not required to make, matching contributions on catch-up contributions. If an employer does so, the contributions must satisfy the ACP test of IRC Section 402(m) (Q 3803).[2] Reporting requirements for catch-up contributions are set forth in Announcement 2001-93.[3]

3762. What is a solo 401(k) plan?

A solo 401(k) plan refers to any 401(k) plan that covers only the business owner or the business owner and his or her spouse. These plans are subject to the same rules and requirements as any other 401(k) plan. Nondiscrimination testing is not required since the business does not have any common law employees who could have received disparate benefits. Solo 401(k) plans are a product of qualified plan reforms implemented by EGTRRA 2001, which substantially improved the tax favored treatment for employers sponsoring 401(k) plans. These changes were designed to encourage greater savings for retirement and to provide more incentive to businesses funding 401(k) plans.

The first of these changes increased the deduction limit for profit sharing and stock bonus plans (which includes 401(k) plans) to 25 percent of compensation.[4] Before 2002, profit sharing and stock bonus plans were subject to a deduction limit of 15 percent of compensation.

Planning Point: For self-employed individuals, compensation is defined as net earnings less a deduction of 50 percent of self-employment tax and employee contributions. The IRS publishes a separate deduction and rate worksheet for self-employed individuals in Publication 560.

Second, the definition of compensation for purposes of the 25 percent limit includes elective deferrals to a qualified plan, Section 403(b) plan, Section 457 plan, SEP, SIMPLE, or Section 125 FSA plan.[5] This means that the payroll on which the 25 percent is based became higher than it was in earlier years, resulting in a higher deduction limit for employer contributions to the plan.

Planning Point: If a self-employed individual also participates as an employee in another 401(k) plan, the limits on elective contributions are per individual, not per plan, so the aggregate contributions into all the plans cannot exceed the limit.

After the EGTRRA 2001 amendments, elective deferrals no longer reduce the amount of employer contributions for purposes of calculating the 25 percent deduction limit.[6] This means that a higher amount could be attributable to matching contributions, nonelective contributions or other amounts paid by the employer. The elective deferral limits increased as well: the limit

---

1.   Treas. Reg. §1.414(v)-1(c).
2.   See T.D. 9072, 2003-2 C.B. 527.
3.   2001-44 IRB 416.
4.   See IRC Sec. 404(a)(3)(A).
5.   See IRC Sec. 404(a)(12).
6.   See IRC Sec. 404(n).

is $19,500 for 2020-2021, up from $19,000 in 2019 (Q 3760), and, for individuals age 50 or older, catch-up contributions are permitted ($6,500 in 2020-2021 (Q 3761)).[1]

Planning Point: These changes to the calculation of the employer deduction for all profit sharing plans, including 401(k) plans, led to a proliferation of solo 401(k) plans. Although the advantages to a sole proprietor or one person corporation can be significant, it is important to note that the plan is subject to the same minimum participation, coverage, nondiscrimination, and other requirements that apply to any other qualified defined contribution plan, in the event one or more employees are later added to the sponsoring employer.

Third, total contributions to an employee's account (excluding catch-up contributions) cannot exceed $58,000 in 2021, $57,000 in 2020 and $56,000 in 2019.[2]

Multiple Employer Plan (MEP)

3763. What are the basic qualification requirements for forming a multiple employer plan (MEP) under the final DOL regulations?

The DOL released final rules governing MEPs on July 31, 2019, which become applicable as of September 30, 2019. In general, to quality as a multiple employer plan (MEP) under the final regulations, a plan must satisfy five basic requirements:[3]

(1)   Under the DOL guidance, the association must have at least one substantial business purpose that is not related to offering the plan.

(2)   The employer-members of the association must control the MEP's activities and any employers that participate in the MEP must control the MEP both in substance and in form, whether directly or indirectly.

(3)   The association must adopt a formal organizational structure, which includes bylaws, a governing body and other organizational aspects where relevant.

(4)   Only employees of the association's employer-members and certain working owners may participate in the MEP.

(5)   Under the DOL rules, some "commonality" of interest must exist between the employers participating in the MEP, such as the same industry or geographic location—a substantial expansion over prior rules, which required a more concrete nexus between participating MEP employers.

This means that participating employers can be located in the same city, county, state or even multi-state region. Companies operating in the same industry can join together even if they operate in entirely different regions.[4] Financial services firms, however, cannot qualify under the expanded MEP regulations.

---

1.   See IRC Secs. 402(g)(1), 414(v)(2)(B); Notice 2018-83, Notice 2019-59, Notice 2020-79.
2.   Notice 2018-83, Notice 2019-59, Notice 2020-79.
3.   See DOL Reg. 2510.3-55(b)(1).
4.   DOL Reg. 2510.3-55(b)(2).

Of course, one of the intended primary objectives of a MEP is to achieve lower costs of administration for the participating employers, and by extension, their participating employees. Failure to do so may carry risks for a MEP and its administrator. In September 2020, a lawsuit was filed against the MEP administrator by several plan participants of one participating employer alleging excessive fees by the administrator.[1] If the allegations should prove to be true, it will be interesting to see if a MEP and its administrators will be held to a higher standard of performance than single employer plans as to plan administration costs.

For plan years beginning after December 31, 2019, the SECURE Act eliminated the "one bad apple" "unified plan" rule, which could result in the entire plan being disqualified because of the bad actions of a single employer in the MEP.[2] The Act also directs the IRS and DOL for provided for a consolidated, simplified Form 5500 for similar plans. Plans must be defined contribution plans, has the same trustee, the same named fiduciary (or fiduciaries) under ERISA, the same administrator, use the same plan year, and provide the same set of investment or investment options.[3] The SECURE Act went even further in eliminating the common nexus rule all-together for certain MEPs, and created another category of MEP, referred to as a to as "pooled employer plans" ("PEP").

3764. What is a multiple employer plan (MEP)? Why might the MEP structure be attractive to small and mid-sized business owners?

A multiple employer plan (MEP), also known as an association retirement plan, is essentially a defined contribution plan that is open to employees of multiple employers.

The DOL expanded the rules to allow more employers to participate in MEPs, which is especially valuable for small business owners who can now join with other entities to share in the costs and administrative burdens of providing a qualified retirement plan option for employees. The MEP structure can also encourage small business owners to offer a retirement savings option by limiting the fiduciary liability that can attach to the employer itself. While these benefits can be significant, see Q 3768 for a discussion of the "one bad apple rule" that small business owners should understand before adopting the MEP.

Under previous law, the MEP structure was limited to small business owners with a strong connection, such as a common industry.

Importantly, the SECURE Act also simplifies filing requirements for certain related defined contribution plans and individual account plans[4] by allowing them to file a single Form 5500. This would further simplify some of the administrative burdens and costs associated with providing a retirement savings option through MEPs. To be eligible, the plans must share:

- the same trustee;

---

1.   See *Khan v. Directors of the Pentegra Defined Contribution Plan*, No, 7:20-cv-07651 (SDNY 9-15-2020).
2.   PL 116-94, Sec. 101
3.   PL 116-94, Sec. 202
4.   As defined under IRC Sec. 414(i) or ERISA Section 3(34).

- one or more of the same named fiduciaries;

- the same administrator;

- plan years beginning on the same date; and

- the same investments or investment options for participants and beneficiaries.[1]

3765. Can working owners with no employees participate in MEPs?

Sole proprietors and other self-employed workers are entitled to participate in the MEP as both employer and employee.[2] To qualify, the owner must have an ownership right in a trade or business (partners in partnerships also qualify). The owner must earn wages or self-employment income from the trade or business by providing personal services to the business. Additionally, the working owner must meet one of two additional criteria:

1.   the owner must work at least an average of 20 hours per week or at least 80 hours per month in the business; or

2.   in the case of an MEP offered via a bona fide group or association of employers (i.e., not a PEO, see Q 3766), the owner must have wages or self-employment income from the business that at least covers the working owner's cost of coverage for participation by the working owner (and any covered beneficiaries) in any group health plan sponsored by the association in which the individual participates.[3]

For purposes of determining the working owner's eligibility to participate in the MEP, the relevant date is when the individual first becomes eligible to participate, but verification of continuing eligibility must also be made over time. The DOL rule specifies only that reasonable monitoring procedures must be developed to ensure continued eligibility.[4]

3766. Can a professional employer organization (PEO) offer the MEP option? Are there any safe harbors for PEOs that choose to offer MEPs?

Professional employer organizations (PEOs) are permitted to offer MEPs under the final DOL regulations—effectively acting as the employer and "plan sponsor" under a contractual arrangement with the actual employer-members of the MEP.[5] The regulations also provided a safe harbor under which PEOs can offer MEPs by satisfying four criteria. To qualify, the PEO must:

- assume responsibility for and pay wages to employees of the clients (employers) who join the MEP without regard to the receipt of payment from those clients (or the adequacy of any payments that are received);

---

1.   PL 116-94 (SECURE Act), Sec. 202.
2.   DOL Reg. 2510.3-55(d)(1).
3.   DOL Reg. 2510.3-55(d)(2)(iii).
4.   DOL Reg. 2510.3-55(d)(3).
5.   DOL Reg. 2510.3-55(c)(1).

- assume responsibility for paying and performing reporting and withholding for all federal employment taxes for clients who adopt the MEP without regard to the receipt of payment from those clients (or the adequacy of any payments that are received);

- play a definite and contractually specified role in recruiting, hiring and firing employees of the client adopting the MEP (in addition to the employer's similar responsibilities) and

- assume responsibility for and have substantial control over the functions and activities of any employee benefits that the contract with the client (employer) requires the PEO to provide without regard to the receipt of payment from those clients (or the adequacy of any payments that are received) with respect to the benefits.[1]

3767. If employers use a PEO to provide the MEP option, do the participating employees have any fiduciary responsibilities with respect to the plan?

According to the preamble to the final regulations, participating employers retain some degree of fiduciary responsibility even if they use a PEO to administer the MEP. Although the guidance is not extensive, the preamble provides that the employer would be responsible for acting prudently in monitoring and selecting the relevant service provider. The employer would also be responsible for ensuring that employee contributions to the MEP are transferred in a timely manner.

3768. What is the "one bad apple rule" and why do business owners interested in the MEP structure need to be aware of it?

Prior to 2019, under the "one bad apple rule," (or "unitary plan rule") the entire MEP could be disqualified based upon the actions of only one employer that participated in the plan—based upon the assumption that the MEP is to be treated a single unified plan.

In 2019, the IRS and Treasury proposed rules that would mitigate the potential impact of the rule.[2] The SECURE Act finalized those rules by eliminating the one bad apple rule in certain situations.[3]

The SECURE Act essentially provides that if one employer's actions would disqualify the plan, only that employer's portion of the MEP will be disqualified. Under the new rules, in the case of one participating employer's failure to act in accordance with the qualification rules:

(1)   the assets of the plan attributable to employees of the employer will be transferred to a plan maintained only by that employer (or successor), to an eligible retirement plan under Section 402(c)(8)(B) for each person whose account is transferred (unless the Treasury determines that it is in the best interests of the participant for the assets to remain in the plan), and

---

1.   DOL Reg. 2510.3-55(c)(2).
2.   See REG-121508-18, proposed July 3, 2019.
3.   IRC Sec. 413(e)(1), added by the SECURE Act, Sec. 101

(2)   the employer (and not the plan in which the failure occurred) will be held liable for any liabilities with respect to such plan attributable to the employees of the employer.[1]

Under the IRS proposal, to continue as a qualified MEP after a single member-employer has taken action that would otherwise disqualify the entire plan, the plan must have established practices and procedures in place that are designed to ensure compliance with the qualification rules by all MEP participants.

Presumably, future IRS guidance on the SECURE Act's elimination of the one bad apple rule will mirror the previous 2019 IRS proposal. Essentially, under these rules, the MEP would continue as a qualified plan so long as the qualification failure is isolated to a single employer, rather than a reflection of a widespread issue across the employers participating in the MEP. The plan administrator should have a process in place that would provide notice to the employer responsible for the failure, and such notice, as proposed, would include a description of the failure, actions necessary to remedy the failure, and notice that the relevant employer has only 90 days from the notice date to take remedial action.

In addition, the plan should also provide a description of the consequences if the noncompliant employer fails to take the remedial action necessary and notice of the plan's right to spin off the non-compliant employer's portion of the plan and assets. After providing the initial notice and two subsequent notices containing additional information about the potential consequences of failing to take remedial action, the MEP will likely be required to notify all participants and the DOL, stop accepting contributions from the noncompliant party and implement the spin off procedures designed to terminate the noncompliant employer's interests in the MEP.

3769. What do employers evaluating the MEP options have to know about various plan options after passage of the SECURE Act?

Beginning in 2021, under the SECURE Act, employers will be able to offer MEPs, association retirement plans (ARPs) and pooled employer plans (PEPs). Clients should know the difference between the type of MEP available pre-2019, the MEP structure created by the 2019 DOL regulations and the different MEP rules that apply beginning in 2021 under the SECURE Act. Technically, these are all different types of plans with different requirements that must be evaluated. The DOL-created plans have been called "association retirement plans" (ARPs) to differentiate from the original "closed" MEP, and to clarify that ARPs must satisfy additional criteria in order to be treated as qualified plans. Under the SECURE Act, MEPs are also called pooled employer plans (PEPs)—another name for a type of MEP that meets certain additional requirements to avoid the commonality of interest requirement and one bad apple rule.

Pre-2019, to participate in MEPs, all participating employers were required to share some strong type of common interest separate and apart from the retirement plan itself. The need to share some type of affiliation or participate in the same industry sharply limited the availability of the "original" MEP—also called a "closed" MEP.

---

1.   IRC Sec. 413(e)(2), added by the SECURE Act, Sec. 101

The basic premise behind the idea of MEPs has remained the same—multiple small businesses join together to reduce the administrative burden and potential fiduciary responsibilities of offering a 401(k)-type retirement plan. The DOL 2019 regulations expand MEP availability if certain criteria are satisfied. Some in the industry began referring to these new MEPs as association retirement plans (ARPs) to differentiate from the original "closed" MEP, and to clarify that ARPs must satisfy additional criteria in order to be treated as qualified plans. Essentially, the ARP is a type of MEP, and the terms have mostly been used interchangeably.

Under the ARP structure, employers that share only the same geographic location or industry are permitted to join together in the MEP-ARP. The participating employers can be located in the same city, county, state or even multi-state region. Companies operating in the same industry can join together even if they operate in entirely different regions. The ARP can be sponsored by a permitted group of employers if certain formalities are satisfied (the organization of employers must be bona fide, with organizational documents and control over the ARP in substance and in form, directly or indirectly, among other requirements).

In the alternative, ARP members can now join together in a plan sponsored by a professional employer organization (PEO). See Q 3766 and Q 3767.

While the 2019 regulations were broadly seen as beneficial to interested small business owners, employers who choose this type of plan structure may continue to be subject to the "one bad apple" rule, absent further guidance from the IRS or DOL.

Congress enacted the SECURE Act to even further ease the restrictions on the types of employers who can join together, assuming additional criteria are satisfied, and eliminate some of the risks associated with MEPs. The SECURE Act permits MEP participation for employers who share no common interest apart from the desire to offer a retirement plan and eliminates the one bad apple rule.

Under the SECURE Act, these types of MEPs are also called pooled employer plans (PEPs)—another name for a type of MEP that meets certain additional requirements to avoid the commonality of interest requirement and one bad apple rule. The MEP-PEP, or open MEP, will be treated as a single retirement plan, so that the group will only be required to file a single Form 5500 to further reduce the administrative burdens for each of the individual employer-participants.

This type of "open MEP" must be administered by a pooled plan provider (generally, a financial services firm). Use of the pooled plan provider to act as both plan administrator and a fiduciary with respect to the plan is intended to ease both the administrative burden and fear of fiduciary liability for small business owners.

The pooled plan provider must register as a fiduciary with the Treasury Department and the DOL. The pooled plan provider also must have a trustee responsible for monitoring contributions and dealing with subsequent issues that arise.

Small business clients should understand that, as employer, they continue to bear fiduciary responsibility with respect to selecting and monitoring the pooled plan provider. Pooled plan providers can outsource investment decisions to another fiduciary (likely what is known as a "3(38) fiduciary"). This arrangement does spread the costs of investment advice among the MEP participants to reduce expenses, but the extent of the employer's fiduciary exposure still remains unclear under the law.

Safe Harbor Plans

3770. What is an automatic enrollment safe harbor 401(k) plan?

The Pension Protection Act of 2006 created a new safe harbor plan under Section 401(k) called a "qualified automatic contribution arrangement," available for plan years beginning after 2007.[1]

Plans that provide for automatic enrollment and meet certain other requirements for the safe harbor will satisfy the ADP/ACP requirements (Q 3753, Q 3801) and be excluded from the top heavy requirements (Q 3915 to Q 3921). For this treatment to apply, a plan must satisfy an automatic deferral requirement, an employer contribution requirement, and a notice requirement.[2]

The automatic deferral requirement states that each employee eligible to participate in the plan must be treated as having elected to have the employer make elective contributions equal to a "qualified percentage." The threshold amount of the automatic deferral percentage may not be less than 3 percent for the first year the employee's deemed election applies. Employees may affirmatively elect out of the plan or elect a different deferral percentage. In the second year, this default percentage must increase to 4 percent, then 5 percent in the third year, and 6 percent in the fourth year and thereafter.[3] A plan may provide for a higher percentage so long as it is applied uniformly, although the percentage may not exceed 15 percent. The SECURE Act increased the default percentage from 10 percent to 15 percent for tax years beginning after 2019 for any year after the first plan year when the employee's compensation is automatically deferred into the plan.[4] The contributions generally must continue until the last day of the plan year that begins after the date on which the first elective contribution under the automatic deferral requirement is made with respect to the employee.[5]

An employer also must provide either a matching or a nonselective contribution. The match amount must be 100 percent of the first 1 percent of compensation deferred, plus 50 percent of the amount of elective contributions over 1 percent but not exceeding 6 percent of compensation deferred. If an employer provides a nonselective contribution, it must be an amount equal to 3 percent of compensation for each employee eligible to participate in the arrangement.[6] The plan may impose a two year vesting requirement with respect to employer contributions, but employees then must be 100 percent vested after two years.[7]

1.   See IRC Sec. 401(k)(13); P.L. 109-280, Sec. 902(g).
2.   See IRC Sec. 401(k)(13)(B).
3.   IRC Sec 401(k)(13)(C).
4.   PL 116-94, Sec. 102.
5.   See IRC Sec. 401(k)(13)(C)(iii).
6.   See IRC Sec. 401(k)(13)(D)(i).
7.   See IRC Sec. 401(k)(13)(D)(iii)(I).

The written notice requirement is met if within a reasonable period before each plan year, each employee who is eligible to participate in the plan receives a written notice of his or her rights and obligations under the plan. The notice must be sufficiently accurate and comprehensive to apprise the employee of those rights and obligations, and it must be written in a manner that is calculated to be understood by the average employee to whom the plan applies. The notice must explain the employee's right to elect not to have elective contributions made under the plan, or to have contributions made at a different percentage. If the plan allows the employee to choose from among two or more investment options, the notice must inform the employee how the account will be invested in the absence of any investment election. The employee also must have a reasonable period of time after receipt of the notice and before the first elective contribution to make one of the foregoing elections.[1]

Planning Point: Further, under the SECURE Act, the notice requirements for safe harbor nonelective contributions of at least 3 percent of employer compensation has been eliminated (notice requirements for plans that provide only for an employer match remain in place).

Relief Provisions

Effective August 17, 2006, ERISA preempts any state laws that would "directly or indirectly prohibit or restrict the inclusion in any plan of an automatic contribution arrangement."[2] This provision is designed to resolve the problem of state laws that treat automatic withholding by a 401(k) arrangement as a prohibited garnishment of wages. The DOL is authorized to issue regulations establishing minimum standards that an arrangement would have to satisfy to qualify for the application of this provision.[3]

For plan years beginning after 2007, relief from the 401(k) distribution restrictions (Q 3796) and the 10 percent penalty (Q 3968) is available during the first 90 days following the start of automatic deferrals, in the event that contributions are withheld erroneously. This relief applies not only to automatic enrollment safe harbor plans, but to other automatic enrollment plans that meet the definition of an "eligible automatic contribution arrangement."[4]

An eligible automatic contribution arrangement is a plan:

(1)　　Under which a participant may elect to have the employer make payment as contributions under the plan on behalf of the participant, or to the participant directly in cash;

(2)　　under which the participant is treated as having elected to have the employer make such contributions in an amount equal to a uniform percentage of compensation provided under the plan until the participant specifically elects not to have such contributions made or elects a different percentage;

1.　　See IRC Sec. 401(k)(13)(E).
2.　　See ERISA Sec. 514(e).
3.　　PPA 2006, Sec. 902(f)(1).
4.　　See IRC Sec. 414(w)(1).

(3)   under which, in the absence of an investment election by the participant, the contributions are invested under the provisions of new ERISA Section 404(c)(5), in accordance with regulations described in Q 3771; and

(4)   that meets certain notice requirements.[1]

The timing and content of the notice requirement is virtually identical to that of the automatic enrollment safe harbor, set forth above.[2]

Refunds of excess contributions and excess aggregate contributions (Q 3807) from eligible automatic contribution arrangements will be subject to an extended time deadline. Instead of 2½ months, the plans will have six months to make refunds of such distributions.[3]

3771. When are default investments permitted under a 401(k) plan?

For plan years beginning after 2006, participants in individual account plans that meet specific notice requirements will be deemed to have exercised control over the assets in their accounts with respect to the amount of contributions and earnings that, in the absence of an investment election by the participants, are invested by the plan in accordance with regulations.[4] Final regulations offer fiduciaries relief from liability for losses resulting from automatically investing participant accounts in a qualified default investment alternative (QDIA). In addition, the fiduciary would not be liable for the decisions made by the entity managing the QDIA. Fiduciaries, however, remain liable for prudently selecting and monitoring any QDIA under the plan.[5]

For the regulatory relief to apply:

(1)   the assets must be invested in a QDIA, as defined below;

(2)   the participant or beneficiary on whose behalf the account is maintained must have had the opportunity to direct the investment of the assets in his or her account but did not do so;

(3)   the participant or beneficiary must be provided with a notice meeting requirements set forth in regulations, a summary plan description, and a summary of material modification at least 30 days before the first investment and at least 30 days before each plan year begins;

(4)   any material relating to the investment, such as account statements, prospectuses, and proxy voting material must be provided to the participant or beneficiary;

(5)   the participant or beneficiary must be permitted to make transfers to other investment alternatives at least once in any three month period without financial penalty; and

---

1.   See IRC Sec. 414(w)(3).
2.   See IRC Sec. 414(w)(4).
3.   See IRC Sec. 4979(f).
4.   ERISA Section 404(c)(5).
5.   Labor Reg. §2550.404c-5(b).

(6)   the plan must offer a "broad range of investment alternatives," as defined in DOL Regulation Section 2550.404c-1(b)(3).[1]

The notice required for a QDIA must:

(1)   describe the circumstances under which assets in the individual account of an individual or beneficiary may be invested on behalf of a participant or beneficiary in a QDIA;

(2)   explain the right of participants and beneficiaries to direct the investment of assets in their individual accounts;

(3)   describe the QDIA, including its investment objectives, risk and return characteristics (if applicable), and fees and expenses;

(4)   describe the right of the participants and beneficiaries on whose behalf assets are invested in a QDIA to direct the investment of those assets to any other investment alternative under the plan, without financial penalty, and

(5)   explain where the participants and beneficiaries can obtain investment information concerning the other investment alternatives available under the plan.[2]

A qualified default investment alternative means an investment alternative that meets five requirements:

(1)   it does not hold or permit the acquisition of employer securities except as provided below;

(2)   it does not impose financial penalties or otherwise restrict the ability of the participant or beneficiary to make transfers from the default investment to another plan investment;

(3)   it is managed by an investment manager, a registered investment company, or a plan sponsor that is a named fiduciary;

(4)   it is diversified, to minimize the risk of large losses; and

(5)   it constitutes one of three investment products (for example, a life cycle fund, a balanced fund, and a managed account) described in the regulations, each of which offers long-term appreciation and capital preservation through a mix of equity and fixed income exposures.[3]

Final regulations permit the use of capital preservation funds (money market or stable value funds) only for a limited duration of not more than 120 days after a participant's initial elective

---

1.   Labor Reg. §2550.404c-5(c).
2.   Labor Reg. §2550.404c-5(d).
3.   Labor Reg. §2550.404c-5(e).

deferral. After 120 days, funds must be redirected to one of the three regular qualified default investment alternatives.[1]

The regulations set forth two exceptions for the holding of employer securities:

(1)   The first is for the acquisition of employer securities held or acquired by a registered investment company (or similar pooled investment vehicle that is subject to state or federal examination) with respect to which such investments are in accordance with the stated investment objectives of the investment vehicle and are independent of the plan sponsor or its affiliate.[2] In the preamble to the proposed regulations, the DOL explained that this exception should accommodate large publicly traded employers whose default investment alternatives may include pooled investment vehicles that invest in such companies.[3]

(2)   A second exception is provided with respect to accounts managed by an investment management service for employer securities acquired as a matching contribution from the employer/plan sponsor or for employer securities acquired prior to management by the investment management service.[4]

3772. What are the requirements for a 401(k) safe harbor plan?

The IRC requires that deferrals, matching, and after-tax employee contributions to 401(k) or 401(m) plans satisfy certain nondiscrimination tests. A plan that is designed to meet certain safe harbors is deemed to have met those testing requirements. These tests are referred to as the ADP test for salary deferrals and the ACP test for employee after-tax and matching employer contributions. The requirements for meeting the safe harbors of 401(k) and 401(m) plans include specific plan provisions that generally require a fully vested employer contribution, one or more advance notice requirements (but see the Editor's Note below), and certain restrictions on the level of discretionary matching contributions.

A plan may be designed to satisfy safe harbors for deferrals but not for the matching employer contribution.

The safe harbor plan requirements prohibit placing restrictions on a participant's right to receive the match or 3 percent of pay employer contribution. Thus, the contribution must be given to employees who terminate employment in the plan year (Q 3801, Q 3803). The safe harbor does not eliminate the requirement of ACP testing for employee after-tax contributions.[5] In addition, 401(k) plans that meet the safe harbor of 401(k) and 401(m) generally are exempt from the top-heavy requirements (Q 3915 to Q 3921), except as explained below.[6]

---

1.   Labor Reg. §2550.404c-5(e).
2.   Labor Reg. §2550.404c-5(e)(1)(ii)(A).
3.   See 29 CFR Part 2550, 71 Fed. Reg. 56806 (Sept. 27, 2006).
4.   Labor Reg. §2550.404c-5(e)(1)(ii)(B).
5.   See IRC Secs. 401(k)(12), 401(m)(11); Treas. Reg. §1.401(k)-3(a).
6.   IRC Sec. 416(g)(4)(H).

Regulations permit the required safe harbor contributions to be made to the 401(k) plan or other defined contribution plans of the employer.[1] Except for the provisions described below, a safe harbor plan generally is subject to the same qualification requirements of IRC Section 401(a) as a traditional 401(k) plan.

The fact that a plan is a safe harbor 401(k) does not prevent certain lower income taxpayers from being eligible to claim the saver's credit for elective deferrals (Q 3648).

The dollar limit on elective deferrals to a safe harbor plan is the same as for a traditional 401(k) plan (Q 3760).

A safe harbor plan generally may also permit catch-up contributions by participants who are at least age 50 by the end of the plan year.[2] The limit on catch-up contributions (Q 3761) to safe harbor plans is calculated in the same manner as if made to a nonsafe harbor 401(k) plan.[3] The dollar limit for salary deferrals is $19,500 in 2020-2021 ($19,000 in 2019, $18,500 in 2018) and the catch-up contribution limit is $6,500 for 2020-2021.[4]

Safe harbor 401(k) and 401(m) plans generally are exempt from the top-heavy requirements; where additional employer contributions are made (e.g., profit sharing), that exemption is lost.[5]

Editor's Note: Under the SECURE Act, beginning in tax years after December 31, 2019, a plan sponsor may switch an existing 401(k) plan to a Safe harbor 401(k) with nonelective contributions at any time prior to 30 days before the close of a plan year. An amendment to do this can even be made later than this deadline if it provides (i) a nonelective contribution of at least 4 percent of compensation (versus 3 percent) for all eligible employees for the plan year; and (ii) the plan is amended no later than the last day for distributing plan excess contributions for the plan year, which is the close of the following plan year.

The SECURE Act also eliminates the safe harbor notice requirement for nonelective contributions. However, it retains the requirement to allow employees to make or change a deferral election at least once per year.[6] In addition, there is a new tax credit for certain small employers that include an automatic enrollment feature (a QACA) in their plan, whether new or existing.[7] See Q 3775.

3773. What notice must be provided to participants in a 401(k) safe harbor plan?

Editor's Note: Under the law prior to January 1, 2020, a safe harbor 401(k) plan was required to provide an annual participant notice prior to each plan year alerting them to their plan rights and obligations. This notice was required whether the employer safe harbor contribution was

---

1.   IRC Sec. 401(k)(12)(F); see Treas. Reg. §1.401(k)-3(h)(4).
2.   See IRC Sec. 414(v).
3.   IRC Sec. 414(v)(2)(A).
4.   IRC Sec. 414(v)(2)(B)(i); Notice 2017-64, Notice 2018-83, Notice 2019-59, Notice 2020-79.
5.   See IRC Sec. 416(g)(4)(H); Rev. Rul. 2004-13, 2004-7 IRB 485.
6.   PL 116-94, Sec. 103
7.   PL 116-94, Sec. 105

provided by a non-elective (i.e., profit-sharing) or matching employer contribution. Under the SECURE Act for plan years beginning after December 31, 2019, the annual safe harbor notice has been eliminated for 401(k) plans that are based upon nonelective employer contributions. See Q 3775.

The notice requirement remains for plans based upon employer matching contributions. In addition, under the SECURE Act, a nonelective contribution 401(k) plan can be adopted on any date prior to 30 days before the end of the plan year still using the 3 percent of compensation nonelective contribution. However, if the noncontribution plan is adopted within the last 30 days of a plan year, the required nonelective contribution rises to 4 percent of compensation. Regardless, the ability to adopt a nonelective plan midyear is not available if the plan was a matching contribution safe harbor 401(k) plan at any time during a year.[1]

Every year, an employer must provide certain written notices to each employee eligible to participate in a plan. This notice must be provided prior to the start of the plan year. The written notice must include a statement as to which type of safe harbor contribution will be made to the plan (i.e., the safe harbor match or safe harbor nonelective contribution). The statement must explain:

(1) how the contribution is calculated and whether any conditions exist to be eligible to use it, including a description of the levels of safe harbor matching contributions;

(2) whether any other contributions may be made under the plan or to another plan on account of elective contributions or after-tax employee contributions made to the plan;

(3) the plan to which safe harbor contributions will be made if it is different from the plan containing the cash or deferred arrangement;

(4) the type and amount of compensation that may be deferred under the plan;

(5) how to make cash or deferred elections, including any administrative requirements that apply to such elections;

(6) the periods available under the plan for making cash or deferred elections;

(7) withdrawal and vesting provisions applicable to contributions under the plan; and

(8) information that makes it easy to obtain additional information about the plan, including an additional copy of the summary plan description and telephone numbers, addresses, and, if applicable, electronic addresses, of individuals or offices from whom employees can obtain such plan information.[2]

---

1.   PL 116-94, Sec. 103.
2.   Treas. Reg. §1.401(k)-3(d)(2)(ii).

A plan that fails to meet any of these requirements will fail to be a safe harbor plan and will require the ADP and/or ACP testing of the plan year.

The timing requirement for the notice requirement is satisfied if the notice is provided within a reasonable period before the beginning of the plan year. This requirement is deemed met if the notice is provided to each eligible employee at least 30 days, and not more than 90 days, prior to the end of the plan year (i.e., by December 1 for a calendar year).[1]

Contingent Notice

There is one type of 401(k) safe harbor plan that requires a contingent notice. This plan design allows the employer to wait until 30 days before the close of the plan year to decide if the plan will be a safe harbor plan by making the fully-vested 3 percent of compensation, nonelective safe harbor. This type of plan must provide a contingent notice before the start of the plan year and a second notice when the employer decides to make the safe harbor contribution. The contingent notice must set forth the same information as above, and also state that the plan may be amended during the plan year to include the 3 percent safe harbor contribution. If the employer elects to make the contribution, the plan must be amended to reflect the contribution. Both the amendment and the follow-up notice are required to be provided to each eligible employee at least 30 days prior to the end of the plan year (i.e., by December 1 for a calendar year plan).[2]

Much of the information in the summary plan description can be cross referenced rather than set forth again in the notice.[3] In either case, the notice must be sufficiently accurate and comprehensive to inform the employee of his or her rights and obligations and must be written in a manner calculated to be understood by the average employee eligible to participate.[4]

3774. What requirements apply to matching contributions in the context of a 401(k) safe harbor plan?

Editor's Note: The SECURE Act, enacted December 20, 2019, has eliminated the annual safe harbor notice to participants of their rights and obligations for 401(k) safe harbor plans in the case of nonelective safe harbor plans. In addition, the SECURE Act also allows a nonelective plan to be adopted any time before the 30th day prior to the close of the end of the plan year, and even after until as late as the end of the following plan year; provided, the sponsor makes a 4 percent of compensation rather than the usual 3 percent nonelective contribution, and the plan was not a matching safe harbor 401(k) at any time during the year. These new rules apply for plan years after December 31, 2019.[5]

The safe harbor matching contribution requirement is met if a matching contribution is made to each nonhighly compensated employee in one of two ways: the basic match or the enhanced match. Both become an obligation of the employer for the plan year (with certain exceptions).

---

1.   See Treas. Reg. §1.401(k)-3(d)(3).
2.   See Treas. Reg. §1.401(k)-3(f).
3.   Treas. Reg. §1.401(k)-3(d)(2)(iii).
4.   IRC Secs. 401(k)(12)(D), 401(m)(11)(A)(ii); see Treas. Reg. §1.401(k)-3(d)(2)(i).
5.   PL 116-94, Sec 103.

The basic match is an employer contribution equal to 100 percent of the salary deferrals to the extent they do not exceed 3 percent of compensation, plus a match equal to 50 percent of the salary deferrals that exceed 3 percent but do not exceed 5 percent of the compensation.[1]

The enhanced match is a matching contribution under a formula that provides matching contributions that are at least the total matching contributions made under the basic match, regardless of the employee's rate of elective contributions.[2]

The safe harbor match must be fully vested at all times. Matching of catch-up contributions is not required; if done, they must be provided for all participants.[3]

In no event may the rate of matching contributions for a highly compensated employee exceed that for a nonhighly compensated employee.[4] The IRC allows some variation on the basic formula described above, but the end result essentially must be the same as under these percentages and the rate of the match cannot go up with the rate of contributions.[5]

Matching contributions may be offered on both elective deferrals and employee after-tax contributions, provided that the match on elective deferrals is not affected by the amount of employee contributions, or matching contributions are made with respect to the sum of an employee's elective deferrals and employee contributions under the same terms as they are made with respect to elective deferrals.[6]

The IRS has stated that matching contributions may be made on the basis of compensation paid for a payroll period, a month, a quarter, or at year-end.[7] The selection of a pay period basis means that if the employee contributes more than is necessary to receive a match for the pay period, there is no requirement to increase the match in other periods when the employee defers less than enough to receive the maximum match. If an employee has restrictions placed on other deferrals (for example, takes an in-service hardship distribution), the plan will impose a six month suspension on participation to the same extent as required by a traditional 401(k) plan (Q 3794).[8] Note, however, that the six month suspension requirement was eliminated under the Bipartisan Budget Act of 2018 (BBA 2018) for tax years beginning after 2018.[9] While some changes made by the BBA 2018 are optional, this change is mandatory for plans.

A plan that satisfies the ADP test through safe harbor matching contributions automatically will satisfy the ACP test for certain discretionary contributions and the safe harbor match. The discretionary match cannot exceed 40 percent of compensation and cannot be based on deferrals exceeding 6 percent of compensation (Q 3798).

1. IRC Secs. 401(k)(12)(B)(i), 401(m)(11)(A)(i).
2. Treas. Reg. § 1.401(k)-2(c)(3)..
3. See Reg-142499-01, 66 Fed. Reg. 53555 (Oct. 23, 2001).
4. IRC Secs. 401(k)(12)(B)(ii), 401(m)(11)(A)(i).
5. See IRC Secs. 401(k)(12)(B)(iii), 401(m)(11)(A)(i); see Treas. Reg. §1.401(k)-3(c)(3).
6. Treas. Reg. §1.401(k)-3(c)(5)(i).
7. Treas. Reg. §1.401(k)-3(c)(5)(ii).
8. See Treas. Reg. §1.401(k)-3(c)(6)(v)(B).
9. Bipartisan Budget Act of 2018, P.L. 115-123, §41113.

Likewise, a plan that satisfies the ADP test through the nonelective contribution safe harbor under Treasury Regulation Section 1.401(k)-3(b) automatically will satisfy the corresponding ACP test safe harbor as long as the same restrictions on matching contributions exist.[1] If the plan provides for additional matching contributions, then the ACP must be prepared.[2]

Nonelective Safe Harbor

The nonelective safe harbor contribution requirement is met if an employer contribution is made on behalf of all eligible nonhighly compensated employees in an amount equal to at least 3 percent of the employee's compensation(However, see *Editor's Note above*).[3] This contribution is made to the accounts of all participants who are eligible, not just those making salary deferrals.

The nonelective contributions must be fully vested and subject to the withdrawal restrictions on IRC Section 401(k) plans (Q 3793).[4]

One important advantage of the 3 percent safe harbor contribution is that it may be used to satisfy the nondiscrimination requirements of IRC Section 401(c)(4). It is not subject to the limitations that apply to QNECs for use in such testing (Q 3796). Contributions used to satisfy the 3 percent safe harbor contribution may not be taken into account in determining whether a plan satisfies the permitted disparity rules (i.e., Social Security integration) (Q 3859).[5]

Discretionary Match to Safe Harbor Plan

Safe harbor plans retain their ability to satisfy the ACP test for discretionary matching contributions if the contributions are limited in amount. Those limits require that discretionary matching contributions may be made where: (1) based on salary deferrals that are not in excess of 6 percent of the employee's compensation and limited to no more than 4 percent of the participant's compensation, (2) the rate of the employer's matching contribution does not increase with the rate of the employee's elective deferral or contribution, and (3) the matching contribution with respect to any highly compensated employee at any rate of employee contribution or rate of elective deferral is not greater than that made with respect to a nonhighly compensated employee.[6]

If matching contributions are made in excess of this limitation, the ACP test will be required for the plan year.[7]

1.   Treas. Reg. §§1.401(m)-3(b), 1.401(m)-3(c).
2.   See IRC Sec. 401(m)(11)(B).
3.   IRC Secs. 401(k)(12)(C), 401(m)(11)(A)(i).
4.   IRC Sec. 401(k)(12)(E)(i).
5.   IRC Sec. 401(k)(12)(E)(ii); Treas. Reg. §1.401(k)-3(h)(2).
6.   IRC Sec. 401(m)(11)(B).
7.   See 1996 Blue Book, p. 153.

3775. Can an employer reduce or suspend 401(k) safe harbor nonelective contributions mid-year?

The IRS has issued final regulations that permit a safe harbor nonelective 401(k) plan to reduce or suspend safe harbor contributions mid-year if the plan contains a statement that such action is a possibility and the amendment does not become effective until 30 days after participants receive a supplemental notice of the mid-year amendment.[1]

The IRS has provided COVID-19 relief for safe harbor plan sponsors who act by August 31, 2020. COVID-19 has placed a strain on many business owners, making it difficult for these employers to keep up with mandatory employer matching contributions. Notice 2020-52 allows plan amendments that reduce or suspend safe harbor contributions to non-highly compensated employees so long as they are made by August 31, 2020. The plan would then become subject to nondiscrimination testing for the plan year.

If the safe harbor contributions being suspended or reduced are nonelective employer contributions (as opposed to matching contributions), the 30-day requirement for supplemental notice is satisfied if the notice is provided by August 31, 2020 and the amendment is adopted no later than the effective date of the suspension or reduction. If matching contributions are being reduced or suspended there is no relief from the 30-day requirement (to give employees time to decide whether to change their own elective contributions).

The IRS also clarified that contributions for highly-compensated employees are not safe harbor contributions—so they can always be reduced or suspended.[2]

In Notice 2016-16[3], the IRS provided guidance on the safe harbor notice that must be provided to participants. The Notice also states that if it is not practicable for the revised safe harbor notice to be provided before the effective date of the change, the notice is considered to be provided timely if it is provided as soon as practicable, but not later than 30 days after the date the change is adopted. Notice 2016-16 also specifies changes to safe harbor plans that cannot be made mid-year unless required by applicable law to be made mid-year, such as a change mandated by a law change or court decision.

Previously, an employer was only permitted to exit a safe harbor nonelective 401(k) plan if the employer was experiencing a substantial business hardship. Factors to be considered in making this determination included whether the employer was operating at an economic loss, general industry conditions and whether the employer would be able to continue the plan without eliminating the safe harbor contributions.

As a result of the new regulations, an employer is able to design its plan to provide the option of reducing or eliminating safe harbor nonelective contributions regardless of profitability. The regulations are retroactively effective and apply to plan years beginning after May 18, 2009.[4]

---

1. Treas. Reg. §§1.401(k)–3(d), 1.401(k)–3(g), and 1.401(m)-3(h).
2. Notice 2020-52.
3. Notice 2016-16, 2016-7 I.R.B. 318, January 29, 2016.
4. TD 9641.

Finally, note that the annual participant notice requirements for nonelective contribution 401(k) safe harbor plans has been eliminated for plan years beginning after December 31, 2019 under the SECURE Act.[1]

3776. How does a SIMPLE 401(k) plan differ from a 401(k) safe harbor plan?

SIMPLE 401(k) plans (Q 3777) also provide a design-based alternative to the use of a safe harbor plan. Some of the differences between safe harbor plans and SIMPLE 401(k) plans are as follows:

(1)   Employees covered by a SIMPLE 401(k) plan may not be participants in any other plan offered by the employer, although employees participating in a safe harbor plan may be covered by more than one plan.

(2)   SIMPLE 401(k) plans are subject to the lower dollar limits on elective deferrals and catch-up contributions that apply to SIMPLE IRAs, rather than those applicable to traditional 401(k) plans.

(3)   Employers offering a SIMPLE 401(k) plan may not offer any contributions other than those provided under the SIMPLE 401(k) requirements, although employers maintaining a safe harbor plan may do so within the limitations described in Q 3774.

(4)   Safe harbor plans may be offered by any employer, although SIMPLE 401(k) plans are available only to employers with 100 or fewer employees earning $5,000 or more in the preceding year.

(5)   Contributions required under a safe harbor design may be made to a separate plan of the employer, although contributions required under a SIMPLE 401(k) design must be made to the SIMPLE 401(k) plan.

(6)   A SIMPLE 401(k) plan must provide the required notice to employees at least 60 days before the beginning of the plan year while safe harbor 401(k) plans must provide notice at least 30 days before the beginning of the plan year, except in the case of certain nonelective contribution safe harbor plans.[2]

(7)   A SIMPLE 401(k) plan cannot be established by completing IRS Form 5304-SIMPLE or IRS Form 5305-SIMPLE. It requires a formal written plan document.

Planning Point: A SIMPLE 401(k) must file a Form 5500 but SIMPLE IRAs do not. Anyone considering a SIMPLE 401(k) plan can do the same funding in a SIMPLE IRA. Note that the penalties for failing to file a Form 5500 are steep and increase with every day the filing is late. Pre-SECURE Act, the IRS could assess a penalty of up to $25 per day with a cap of $15,000 per year. Effective for years beginning after December 31, 2019, the penalty has increased to $250 per day for late

---

1.   PL 116-94, Sec. 103.
2.   Per the SECURE ACT, Sec. 103, the annual participant notice has been eliminated for nonelective contribution safe harbor plans.

filers and up to $150,000 per plan year (note that the additional DOL penalty exceeds $2,000 per day with no annual cap).[1]

401(k) Requirements

3777. What are the requirements for a SIMPLE 401(k) plan?

Of all the types of qualified plans that are permitted under the IRC, the SIMPLE 401(k) may be the least attractive to a plan sponsor. These plans retain all the eligibility, documentation, and reporting requirements of a qualified plan but are subject to the lower limits and other restrictions of a SIMPLE IRA. A SIMPLE 401(k) plan allows an eligible employer to satisfy the actual deferral percentage test for 401(k) plans (Q 3801) by meeting the plan design requirements described below, instead of performing annual ADP testing.[2] For a comparison of the features of a SIMPLE 401(k) plan to those of a safe harbor 401(k) plan, see Q 3776.

An eligible employer is one that had no more than 100 employees earning at least $5,000 of compensation from the employer for the preceding year.[3] An eligible employer that establishes a SIMPLE 401(k) plan for a plan year and later ceases to be eligible generally will be treated as eligible for the following two years. If the failure to remain eligible was due to an acquisition, disposition, or similar transaction, special rules apply.[4]

In addition to all the requirements of IRC Section 401(k), a SIMPLE 401(k) plan must meet the contribution and other requirements of SIMPLE IRAs. Those requirements include a contribution requirement, an exclusive plan requirement, and a vesting requirement (Q 3706, Q 3709).[5]

The SIMPLE 401(k) contribution requirement includes the following: (1) eligible employees must be able to make salary deferral contributions to the plan, (2) the amount to which the election applies may not exceed $13,500 (in 2020-2021), and (3) the employer must make matching contributions or nonelective contributions under one of the formulas described below.[6]

A SIMPLE 401(k) plan also may permit catch-up salary deferral contributions by participants who have attained age 50 by the end of the plan year.[7] The limit on catch-up contributions to SIMPLE 401(k) plans is the same as for SIMPLE IRAs. The maximum catch-up contribution is the lesser of $3,000 (in 2015-2021) or the excess (if any) of the participant's compensation over any other elective deferrals for the year made without regard to the catch-up limits.[8]

A SIMPLE 401(k) plan must satisfy a universal availability requirement for availability of catch-up contributions (Q 3761).[9]

---

1. IRC Sec. 6652(e). See PL 116-94 (SECURE Act), Sec. 403.
2. See IRC Sec. 401(k)(11); Treas. Reg. §1.401(k)-4(a).
3. IRC Secs. 401(k)(11)(D)(i), 408(p)(2)(C)(i).
4. See IRC Secs. 408(p)(10), 401(k)(11)(D)(i), 408(p)(2)(C)(i)(II); Treas. Reg. §1.401(k)-4(b)(2).
5. IRC Secs. 401(k)(11)(A), 401(k)(11)(D)(i).
6. IRC Sec. 401(k)(11)(B); Notice 2019-59, Notice 2020-79.
7. See IRC Sec. 414(v).
8. IRC Sec. 414(v)(2)(A); Notice 2017-64, Notice 2018-83, Notice 2019-59, Notice 2020-79.
9. IRC Sec. 414(v)(3)(B); Treas. Reg. §1.414(v)-1(e).

Under the matching formula option for SIMPLE 401(k) plans, the employer must match employee salary deferral contributions dollar-for-dollar up to 3 percent of the employee's compensation.[1] (Earlier guidance stated that matching of catch-up contributions was not required.)[2]

Under the second option, the employer makes a contribution of 2 percent of compensation on behalf of each employee who is eligible to participate and who has at least $5,000 in compensation from the employer for the year, provided notice of the election is given prior to the 60 day election period.[3]

The plan also must provide that no other contributions (other than rollover contributions) may be made to the plan other than those described above.[4] This is the "exclusive plan requirement." This requirement is met if no contributions were made, or no benefits accrued, for services during the year under any qualified plan of the employer on behalf of any employee eligible to participate in the cash or deferred arrangement, other than the contributions made to the SIMPLE 401(k) plans.[5] The receipt of a reallocation of forfeitures under another plan of the employer will not cause a SIMPLE 401(k) participant to violate this requirement.[6]

All contributions to a SIMPLE 401(k) plan must be nonforfeitable.[7]

Employees generally must have the right to terminate participation at any time during the year, although the plan may preclude the employee from resuming participation until the beginning of the next year.[8] Furthermore, each employee eligible to participate must have 60 days before the first day of any year (and 60 days before the first day the employee is eligible to participate) to elect whether to participate in the plan or to modify his or her deferral amount. The foregoing requirements are met only if the employer notifies each eligible employee of such rights within a reasonable time before the 60 day election period.[9]

A SIMPLE 401(k) plan that meets the requirements set forth in IRC Section 401(k)(11) is not subject to the top-heavy rules (Q 3916) provided that the plan allows only the contributions required under IRC Section 401(k)(11).[10] SIMPLE 401(k) plans are subject to the other qualification requirements of a 401(k) plan, including the $290,000 compensation limit (as indexed for 2021, $285,000 in 2020, $280,000 in 2019, $275,000 in 2018), the IRC Section 415 limits (Q 3728, Q 3867), and the prohibition on state and local governments operating a 401(k) plan (Q 3753).[11] The IRC Section 404(a) limit on the deductibility of contributions to 25 percent of compensation (Q 3750) is increased in the case of SIMPLE 401(k) plans to the

1.   Treas. Reg. §1.401(k)-4(e)(3).
2.   See REG-142499-01, 66 Fed. Reg. 53555 (Oct. 23, 2001).
3.   IRC Sec. 401(k)(11)(B)(ii); Treas. Reg. §1.401(k)-4(e)(4).
4.   IRC Sec. 401(k)(11)(B)(i)(III); Treas. Reg. §1.401(k)-4(e)(1).
5.   IRC Sec. 401(k)(11)(C); Treas. Reg. §1.401(k)-4(c).
6.   Treas. Reg. §1.401(k)-4(c)(2).
7.   IRC Sec. 401(k)(11)(A)(iii).
8.   Treas. Reg. §1.401(k)-4(d)(2)(iii).
9.   IRC Secs. 401(k)(11)(B)(iii), 408(p)(5)(B), 408(p)(5)(C); Treas. Reg. §1.401(k)-4(d)(3).
10.   IRC Sec. 401(k)(11)(D)(ii); Treas. Reg. §1.401(k)-4(h).
11.   Rev. Proc. 97-9, 1997-1 CB 624; Notice 2017-64, Notice 2018-83, Notice 2019-59, Notice 2020-79.

greater of 25 percent of compensation or the amount of contributions required under IRC Section 401(k)(11)(B).[1]

3778. What are the requirements of a Roth 401(k)?

A Roth 401(k) feature combines certain advantages of the Roth IRA with the convenience of 401(k) plan elective deferral-style contributions. The IRC states that if a qualified plan trust or a Section 403(b) annuity includes a qualified Roth contribution program, contributions to it that the employee designates to the Roth account, although not being excluded from the employee's taxable income, will be treated as an elective deferral for plan qualification purposes.[2] A qualified plan or Section 403(b) plan will not be treated as failing to meet any qualification requirement merely on account of including a qualified Roth contribution program.[3]

A qualified Roth contribution program means a program under which an employee may elect to make designated Roth contributions in lieu of all or a portion of elective deferrals that the employee is otherwise eligible to make.[4] For this purpose, a designated Roth contribution is any elective deferral that would otherwise be excludable from the gross income of the employee, but that the employee designates as not being excludable.[5] Final regulations set forth the following requirements for designated Roth contributions:

(1)   The contribution must be designated irrevocably by the employee at the time of the cash or deferred election as a designated Roth contribution that is being made in lieu of all or a portion of the pre-tax elective contributions the employee is otherwise eligible to make under the plan.

(2)   The contribution must be treated by the employer as includable in the employee's gross income at the time the employee would have received the amount in cash, if the employee had not made the cash or deferred election (i.e., it must be treated as wages subject to applicable withholding requirements).

(3)   The contribution must be maintained by the plan in a separate account, as provided under additional requirements set forth below.[6]

A plan with a Roth contribution feature must provide for separate accounts for the designated Roth contributions of each employee and any earnings allocable to the account.[7] Gains, losses, and other credits and charges associated with the Roth accounts must be separately allocated on a reasonable and consistent basis to the designated Roth account and other accounts under the plan. Forfeitures of any accounts may not be reallocated to the designated Roth account. No contributions other than designated Roth contributions and rollover Roth contributions (as described below) may be allocated to the Roth account. The separate accounting require-

---

1.   IRC Sec. 404(a)(3)(A)(ii).
2.   As defined in IRC Sec. 402(g).
3.   IRC Secs. 402A(a), 402A(e)(1).
4.   IRC Sec. 402A(b)(1).
5.   IRC Sec. 402A(c)(1).
6.   Treas. Reg. §1.401(k)-1(f)(1).
7.   IRC Sec. 402A(b)(2).

ment applies from the time the designated Roth contribution is made until the designated Roth contribution account is completely distributed.[1]

The maximum amount an employee may claim as a designated Roth contribution is limited to the maximum amount of elective deferrals permitted for the tax year, reduced by the aggregate amount of elective deferrals for the tax year for which no designation is made.[2] Only one limit can be split between the Roth and salary deferrals of the employee each calendar year.

Designated Roth contributions generally must satisfy the rules applicable to elective deferral contributions. Thus, for example, the nonforfeitability requirements and distribution limitations of Treasury Regulation Sections 1.401(k)-1(c) and (d) must be satisfied for Roth contributions. Designated Roth contributions are treated as elective deferral contributions for purposes of the Actual Deferral Percentage ("ADP") test.[3]

A designated Roth account is subject to the minimum distribution requirements of IRC Section 401(a)(9) (Q 3890 to Q 3908).[4] A payment or distribution otherwise allowable from a designated Roth account may be rolled over to another designated Roth account of the individual from whose account the payment or distribution was made or to a Roth IRA of the individual.[5] Rollover contributions to a designated Roth account under this provision are not taken into account for purposes of the limit on designated Roth contributions.[6] Funds in a Roth IRA are not subject to the lifetime minimum distribution requirements that apply to Roth accounts in a qualified plan (Q 3686).

The IRC states that any qualified distribution from a designated Roth account is excluded from gross income.[7] A qualified distribution for this purpose is defined in the same manner as for Roth IRAs except that the provision for "qualified special purpose distributions" is disregarded (Q 3673).[8] The term qualified distribution does not include distributions of excess deferrals (amounts in excess of the IRC Section 402(g) limit) or excess contributions (under IRC Section 401(k)(8)), or any income on them.[9]

Nonexclusion period. A payment or distribution from a designated Roth account will not be treated as a qualified distribution if it is made within the five-year nonexclusion period. This period begins with the earlier of (1) the first taxable year for which the individual made a designated Roth contribution to any designated Roth account established for that individual under the same retirement plan, or (2) if a rollover contribution was made to the designated Roth account from another designated Roth account previously established for the individual under

1.   Treas. Reg. §1.401(k)-1(f)(2).
2.   IRC Sec. 402A(c)(2).
3.   See Treas. Reg. §1.401(k)-1(f)(3).
4.   Treas. Reg. §1.401(k)-1(f)(3).
5.   IRC Sec. 402A(c)(3).
6.   See IRC Sec. 402(A(c)(3)(B).
7.   IRC Sec. 402A(d)(1).
8.   IRC Sec. 402A(d)(2)(A). See IRC Sec. 408A(d)(2)(A)(iv).
9.   IRC Sec. 402A(d)(2)(C).

another retirement plan, the first taxable year for which the individual made a designated Roth contribution to the previously established account.[1]

The IRC states that notwithstanding IRC Section 72, if any excess deferral attributable to a designated Roth contribution is not distributed on or before the first April 15 after the close of the taxable year in which the excess deferral was made, the excess deferral will not be treated as investment in the contract and will be included in gross income for the taxable year in which such excess is distributed.[2] Furthermore, it adds that "Section 72 shall be applied separately with respect to distributions and payments from a designated Roth account and other distributions and payments from the plan."[3]

Planning Point: Even though designated Roth contributions are not excluded from income when contributed, they are treated as elective deferrals for purposes of IRC Section 402(g). Thus, to the extent total elective deferrals for the year exceed the 402(g) limit for the year, the excess amount can be distributed by April 15 of the year following the year of the excess without adverse tax consequences. However, if the excess deferrals are not distributed by that time, any distribution attributable to an excess deferral that is a designated Roth contribution is includible in gross income (with no exclusion from income for amounts attributable to basis under Section 72) and is not eligible for rollover. If there are any excess deferrals that are designated Roth contributions that are not corrected prior to April 15 of the year following the excess, the first amounts distributed from the designated Roth account are treated as distributions of excess deferrals and earnings until the full amount of those excess deferrals (and attributable earnings) are distributed.[4]

3779. How are qualified distributions from a designated Roth 401(k) or 403(b) account taxed?

A designated Roth account is an option that is available under a 401(k) or a 403(b) plan to which designated Roth contributions (Q 3778) are made.[5] Where a distribution from the designated Roth account satisfies certain requirements (referred to as a "qualified distribution," see below), distributions from the account are free of income tax, even if not rolled over. For details on the requirements of a Roth 401(k) feature, see Q 3778.

Qualified distributions. The taxation of a distribution from a designated Roth account depends on whether the distribution constitutes a qualified distribution. A qualified distribution generally is a distribution received after a five-taxable-year period and that meets any of the following qualified purposes for this rule:

(1)   It is made after the employee reaches age 59½.

(2)   It is attributable to the employee's being disabled within the meaning of IRC Section 72(m)(7).

(3)   It is made after the employee's death.[6]

1.   IRC Sec. 402A(d)(2)(B).
2.   IRC Sec. 402A(d)(3).
3.   IRC Secs. 402A(d)(3), 402A(d)(4).
4.   TD 9324, 2007-2 IRB (May 29, 2007).
5.   See IRC Sec. 402A(b)(2)(A); Treas. Reg. §1.402A-1, A-1.
6.   See IRC Sec. 402A(d)(1), Treas. Reg. §1.402A-1, A-2.

This definition is the same as that used for Roth IRAs except that the provision for "qualified special purpose distributions" is disregarded (Q 3673).[1]

The term qualified distribution does not include distributions of excess deferrals that arise in correction of either an excess deferral under the IRC Section 402(g) limit or an excess contribution under IRC Section 401(k)(8), or any income attributable to such a distribution.[2]

3780. How are nonqualified distributions from a designated Roth 401(k) or 403(b) account taxed?

A nonqualified distribution from a designated Roth account generally is partially nontaxable. The portion of the distribution that constitutes the employee contribution is not taxable, and the portion that relates to earnings on those contributions is taxable.[3] A nonqualified distribution may be rolled over to a Roth IRA. The funds in a designated Roth account are not subject to the ordering rules that determine the tax treatment of Roth IRA distributions (Q 3673) unless they are rolled over to a Roth IRA.[4]

The preamble to the proposed regulations illustrated the pro rata treatment of nonqualified distributions as follows: If a nonqualified distribution of $5,000 is made from an employee's designated Roth account when the account consists of $9,400 of designated Roth contributions and $600 of earnings, the distribution consists of $4,700 of designated Roth contributions (that are not includible in the employee's gross income) and $300 of earnings (that are includible in the employee's gross income).

Amounts not treated as qualified. Certain amounts that are not eligible rollover distributions never can be treated as qualified distributions, and always will be currently includible in income. These include corrective distributions of excess deferrals, excess contributions and attributable income (Q 3807), deemed distributions resulting from violations of the plan loan requirements (Q 3953), and the cost of current life insurance protection (Q 3947).[5]

3781. How is the five-year holding period of qualified distributions from designated Roth 401(k) or 403(b) accounts determined?

A Roth contribution is deemed to be made on the first day of the first taxable year for which the employee first made any designated Roth contributions. Thus, for a calendar year plan, all contributions in the first year would be deemed made on January 1 of that year. Starting with that date, the five-year period ends at the end of the fifth consecutive taxable year following that date. The beginning of the five-year period for a designated Roth account does not change even if the employee receives a distribution of the entire account during the five-year holding period and subsequently makes additional designated Roth contributions under the plan.

1.   IRC Sec. 402A(d)(2)(A). See IRC Sec. 408A(d)(2)(A)(iv).
2.   IRC Sec. 402A(d)(2)(C).
3.   See Treas. Reg. §1.402A-1, A-3; IRC Sec. 72(e)(8).
4.   See Treas. Reg. §1.408A-10, A-1.
5.   See Treas. Reg. §§1.402(g)-1(e)(8)(iv), 1.402A-1, A-2(c), 1.402A-1, A-11.

If an employee makes deferrals to designated Roth accounts under more than one plan, the employee will have two or more separate five-year periods of participation that are calculated independently of one another unless the employee makes a direct rollover of a Roth distribution from one plan to another plan.[1] If a direct rollover occurs, the five-year holding period for the receiving plan is deemed to begin on the earlier of beginning of the five-year holding period for the distributing plan or the beginning of the five-year holding period for the receiving plan. This calculation differs from the five-year period calculation under a Roth IRA in which the five year period starts with the date a Roth contribution was made to any Roth IRA (Q 3673).

Planning Point: A client planning to make deferrals to a designated Roth account for the next year should begin deferrals in the current year. This will begin the five-year period one year earlier, so qualified distributions can be made one year earlier.

3782. Can the owner of a designated Roth 401(k) or 403(b) account roll those funds into another retirement account?

A rollover of a designated Roth account distribution that is not includable in income may be made only to another designated Roth account of the individual from whose account the payment or distribution was made or to a Roth IRA of the individual either through a 60-day rollover or a direct rollover. A plan receiving a designated Roth account rollover must agree to separately account for the amount that is not includable in income. Furthermore, if such a rollover is made to another plan, it must be made as a direct rollover to assure that there is proper accounting in the recipient plan. In other words, a rollover to a plan is not available if the distribution has been made directly to the employee. In that case, however, an employee would have the option of rolling over the distribution to a Roth IRA within 60 days.[2]

If a rollover is made from a designated Roth account under another plan, the five-year period for the receiving plan begins on the first day that the employee made designated Roth contributions to the other plan, if earlier.[3]

If a rollover is made from a designated Roth account to a Roth IRA, the period that the rolled over funds were in the designated Roth account does not count toward the five taxable year period for determining qualified distributions from the Roth IRA. If the Roth IRA was established in an earlier year, the five-year period for determining qualified distributions from the Roth IRA applies to distributions of rolled over amounts.[4] Furthermore, the entire amount of any qualified distribution rolled over to a Roth IRA is treated as basis in the Roth IRA. As a result, a subsequent distribution from the Roth IRA of that amount would not be includable in the owner's gross income.[5]

Planning Point: A client who does not have a Roth IRA and anticipates rolling over an amount from a designated Roth account to a Roth IRA should consider establishing a Roth IRA before the year the rollover is anticipated. This will start the five-year holding period.

1. Treas. Reg. §1.402A-1, A-4.
2. See IRC Sec. 402A(c)(3); Treas. Reg. §1.402A-1, A-5.
3. Treas. Reg. §1.402A-1, A-4(b).
4. Treas. Reg. §1.408A-10, A-4.
5. See Treas. Reg. §1.408A-10, A-3(a).

3783. What should a taxpayer consider when deciding whether to roll funds from an employer-sponsored 401(k) into an IRA?

For a taxpayer who has reached age 55, but has not yet reached age 59½, the tax advantages of allowing the funds to remain in the 401(k) are clear. If the taxpayer were to roll the funds into an IRA, a 10 percent penalty tax would apply to any withdrawals made before the taxpayer reaches age 59½ (in addition to the otherwise applicable ordinary income tax rate), unless another exception such as disability or a series of substantially equal periodic payments applies. A taxpayer who leaves employment once reaching age 55 can withdraw funds from the 401(k) without incurring the 10 percent penalty for early withdrawals.[1]

If a taxpayer plans to work past the age when distributions become mandatory (age 72), the taxpayer can avoid the required distributions by leaving the funds in the employer-sponsored 401(k). Unless the plan requires earlier distributions, as long as the taxpayer continues to work and does not own 5 percent or more of the company, he or she can avoid taking distributions from a 401(k). Distributions from an IRA are required to begin when the taxpayer turns 72, regardless of whether he or she has actually retired.[2]

Further, if a taxpayer holds stock in the employer within the 401(k) plan, the taxpayer may qualify for favorable tax treatment if the stock is left in the 401(k). After distribution from the 401(k) to a non-qualified account, a sale of the employer stock may qualify for taxation at the taxpayer's long-term capital gains tax rate under the net unrealized appreciation rules, rather than the ordinary income tax rate that would apply to the appreciation on the stock if it was rolled into the IRA and later sold and the sales proceeds distributed. (See Q 3971.)

Taxpayers may wish to keep funds in an employer-sponsored 401(k) after leaving employment because it may be possible to borrow against those funds, though these loans are limited and must be repaid relatively quickly. A loan against an IRA balance is not an option (penalties and taxes would apply to the IRA as though it were a distribution). Using an IRA as collateral for a loan is also treated as a distribution, subject to taxes and penalties.

If the 401(k) offers attractive investment options, the taxpayer may wish to keep the funds invested in the 401(k). Further, if the 401(k) has lower fees than available in an IRA, the taxpayer may benefit from leaving the funds in the 401(k). Because recently enacted disclosure rules require 401(k) plan sponsors to disclose administrative expenses and fees to participants, there is evidence to suggest that 401(k) fees may be decreasing.

3784. What is the separate accounting requirement applicable to a designated Roth 401(k) or 403(b) account?

For a designated Roth account, the plan must maintain separate accounts and recordkeeping for each employee's designated Roth contributions and any earnings that are allocated to the contributions.[3] The separate accounting requirement is violated by "any transaction or accounting

---

1.   IRC Sec. 72(t).
2.   Treas. Reg. §1.408-8, A-3.
3.   IRC Sec. 402A(b)(2).

methodology involving an employee's designated Roth account and any other accounts under the plan or plans of an employer that has the effect of directly or indirectly transferring value from another account into the designated Roth account." A transaction that merely exchanges investments between accounts at fair market value will not violate the separate accounting requirement.[1]

3785. What in-plan rollovers are permitted with respect to designated Roth 401(k) or 403(b) accounts?

Section 402A(c)(4) allows plans to permit rollovers from Section 401(k) plans to designated Roth accounts in the same plan ("in-plan Roth rollovers"). The rollover may be accomplished by a direct rollover or a 60 day rollover.[2] Amounts can be rolled over even if they would not otherwise be distributable.[3]

In-plan Roth direct rollovers simply change the plan account in which the amount is held and the tax character. They are not treated as a distribution for situations involving plan loans, spousal annuities, participant consent before an immediate distribution of an accrued benefit in excess of $5,000, and elimination of optional forms of benefit.[4]

A qualified distribution is included in gross income as if it were not rolled over to a designated Roth account. The taxable amount of the in-plan Roth rollover is the amount that would be includible in a participant's gross income if the rollover were made to a Roth IRA. This amount is equal to the fair market value of the distribution reduced by any basis the participant has in the distribution.[5] The taxable amount of a distribution that an individual rolls over in an in-plan Roth rollover generally is includible in gross income in the taxable year in which the distribution occurs.

Prior to 2018, a rollover to a Roth IRA could be unwound. This option was eliminated by the 2017 Tax Act. An in-plan rollover could never be unwound (recharacterized) because the recharacterization rule in Section 408A(d)(6) applied only to contributions to IRAs.[6] In-plan Roth direct rollovers are not subject to the otherwise mandatory 20 percent withholding and cannot be withheld for voluntary withholding.[7]

A written explanation of the in-plan Roth feature must be provided to the participant with the written explanation that the plan provides to individuals receiving an eligible rollover distribution.[8]

1.   Treas. Reg. 1.402A-1, A-13(a).
2.   Notice 2010-84, Q&A-1.
3.   Notice 2013-74, Q&A -1.
4.   Notice 2010-84, Q&A-4.
5.   See Notice 2009-75, 2009-35 I.R.B. 436.
6.   Notice 2010-84, Q&A-6.
7.   Notice 2013-74, Q&A-4.
8.   Notice 2010-84, Q&A-5.

3786. What rules apply to 401(k) to Roth 401(k) rollovers?

Since 2013, funds from traditional 401(k) accounts may be rolled over into Roth 401(k) accounts without a penalty tax (even if they are not otherwise distributable without penalty).

The amount that a plan participant can roll over is not limited. Any amount rolled over pursuant to this provision is treated as a distribution that was contributed in a qualified rollover contribution within the meaning of IRC Section 408A. This provision applies to 401(k) plans, 403(b) plans and governmental 457(b) plans.[1]

As under prior law, the amount that is rolled over from a traditional 401(k) into a Roth 401(k) is included in gross income. The taxable amount of the Roth rollover must be included in the participant's gross income. The taxable amount of an in-plan Roth rollover is the amount that would be includible in a participant's gross income if the rollover were made to a Roth IRA. This amount is equal to the fair market value of the distribution reduced by any basis the participant has in the distribution.[2] The taxable amount of a distribution that an individual rolls over in an in-plan Roth rollover generally is includible in gross income in the taxable year in which the rollover occurs.

The expanded rollover treatment is optional, so that plan administrators have discretion as to whether to adopt an amendment permitting expanded use of this type of rollover. The amendment must be made no later than the last day of the first plan year in which the amendment is to be effective.

See Q 3788 for distribution restrictions that apply following a 401(k) to Roth 401(k) rollover.

3787. What is the difference between an after-tax 401(k) contribution and a Roth contribution? What should individuals understand when deciding whether to allocate their retirement funds to after-tax or Roth contributions?

Each year, individuals have the ability to defer up to the traditional annual pre-tax contribution limit to a 401(k) plan ($19,500 in 2020-2021, or $26,000 for clients age 50 and over) and up to the individual limit to IRAs and Roth IRAs ($6,000 or $7,000 with the catch-up). The after-tax contribution rules allow the individual to defer more than the annual pre-tax limit (for a total of up to $58,000 in 2021 or 100 percent of compensation) to their traditional 401(k). While these contributions are made with after-tax dollars, they are not the same as Roth contributions (which also come from after-tax funds and are discussed below). Like pre-tax contributions, after-tax contributions cannot be withdrawn from the 401(k) without penalty except according to the terms of the plan (which will typically allow for penalty-free distributions only in the event of the client reaching age 59½, dying, retiring, becoming disabled or upon the occurrence of certain hardships).

The primary difference between the after-tax 401(k) contribution and the Roth contribution is the tax treatment of earnings on the investment. While all Roth contributions are permitted

---

1.   American Taxpayer Relief Act of 2012, Pub. Law No. 112-240, Sec. 902.
2.   Notice 2009-75, 2009-35 IRB 436; Notice 2010-84, 2010-51 IRB 872.

to grow on a tax-free basis (i.e., the entire amount of the withdrawal will generally be tax-free), earnings on after-tax contributions will eventually be taxed at ordinary income tax rates. As a result, only individuals who are already contributing the maximum pre-tax and Roth amounts to their retirement accounts should consider the after-tax contribution option (generally, these will be high net worth clients seeking to amass a larger retirement nest egg).

Individuals should also consider maximizing their Health Savings Account (HSA) contributions (which are contributed on a pre-tax basis, grow tax-free and can be withdrawn tax-free to cover medical expenses) before considering after-tax 401(k) contributions. This is because the actual benefit of the after-tax contribution is tax-deferred investing and the eventual ability to move the after-tax funds into a Roth account, from which point they will grow tax-free. Both Roth accounts and HSAs allow the funds to grow tax-free from the beginning, which will maximize the value of the contribution through compounded earnings over time. For high net worth clients, however, the after-tax 401(k) option can be valuable because all of the earnings are tax-deferred—conversely, with traditional taxable accounts (such as a mutual fund), the individual will have to pay taxes on appreciation each year, albeit usually at the lower capital gains rate. This group of taxpayers may benefit from the ability to allow all of their investment and earnings to grow tax-deferred over a period of many years. These individuals must keep in mind that they may not be able to withdraw their after-tax 401(k) contributions freely and without penalty, however.

Importantly, under relatively new IRS regulations, at retirement the taxpayer can now bifurcate the funds in his or her 401(k), transferring after-tax funds into a Roth IRA (from that point, the after-tax funds grow tax-free) and the earnings into a traditional IRA (because those earnings had never been taxed, they will eventually be subject to ordinary income tax rates).

3788. Are amounts rolled over to a Roth 401(k) subject to distribution restrictions after the rollover?

Yes. Although the American Taxpayer Relief Act of 2012 expanded the rules to allow rollovers from traditional 401(k) accounts to Roth 401(k) accounts of otherwise nondistributable amounts, the IRS has issued guidance providing that distribution restrictions will still apply after such amounts are rolled over.

Any amount that is rolled over from a traditional 401(k) to a Roth 401(k) remains subject to the same distribution restrictions that applied to the amounts before the rollover.[1] As a result, if an individual makes a rollover from a traditional 401(k) to a Roth 401(k) before reaching age 59½, for example, the rolled over amounts cannot be withdrawn from the Roth 401(k) on a penalty-free basis unless one of the other events described in IRC Section 401(k)(2)(B) has occurred (i.e., unless he or she reaches age 59½ or there has been a separation from service, death or disability).

---

1.   Notice 2013-74, 2013-52 IRB 819.

3789. Are otherwise nondistributable amounts that are rolled over from a 401(k) to a Roth 401(k) subject to withholding?

The withholding requirements of IRC Section 3405 do not apply to otherwise nondistributable amounts that are rolled over from a traditional 401(k) into a Roth 401(k) because such a rollover must be accomplished through a direct rollover.[1]

Further, because a nondistributable rollover cannot, by definition, be distributed to the taxpayer, a taxpayer is not permitted to voluntarily elect that a portion of the distribution be subject to withholding for purposes of meeting the taxpayer's tax obligations with respect to the rollover. As a result, IRS guidance specifically advises that a taxpayer who elects to roll 401(k) funds into a Roth 401(k) may wish to increase withholding or make estimated payments in order to avoid an underpayment penalty.[2]

3790. What is the exception to the 401(k) required minimum distribution (RMD) rules that can apply when a plan participant has reached age 72, but continues to work?

While the general rules governing retirement accounts require nearly every individual account owner to begin taking RMDs by April 1 of the year following the year in which he or she turns 72 (70½ prior to 2020), an exception exists for employer-sponsored 401(k) accounts owned by employees who continue working past age 72. If the plan allows, a participant who leaves funds in the 401(k) can avoid RMDs if he or she remains employed with the employer who sponsors the plan (the participant can also continue to make contributions to the 401(k)).

Importantly, the current employer must sponsor the 401(k)—a participant cannot change employers and defer RMDs beyond age 72 if a former employer sponsors the relevant 401(k). However, it does not appear that the IRS provides a concrete definition of what it means to continue working past age 72, so it may be possible for the participant to continue working on a reduced hours basis and still defer his or her RMDs past the traditional required beginning date.

The exception does not apply if the plan is an IRA (whether a traditional, SEP or SIMPLE IRA (RMDs do not apply to Roth IRAs during the original account owner's lifetime)). Additionally, because not all 401(k) plans permit this exception, the individual must be careful to ensure that his or her plan actually does allow the funds to remain in the plan to avoid steep 50 percent penalty that applies to missed RMDs.

If the individual has more than one 401(k) and the plans allow for rollovers, it may be possible for he or she to roll all 401(k) funds into the 401(k) of a current employer and delay RMDs on all of the funds if the still working exception applies. Combining accounts will also simplify RMD planning once the participant stops working, because the RMD on each account would otherwise have to be determined separately.

---

1.   Notice 2013-74, Q&A-4, 2013-52 IRB 819.
2.   IRC Sec. 3402(p); Notice 2013-74, Q&A-4, 2013-52 IRB 819.

While a plan participant may generally avoid taking RMDs from his or her 401(k) as long as he or she continues working past age 72, many small business owners will not be able to take advantage of this exception. This is because the exception does not apply to participants who are five percent owners of the business sponsoring the retirement plan. Individuals who own a portion of the business sponsoring the 401(k) must also be aware of the constructive owner-ship rules that apply when determining whether he or she is a five percent owner. Ownership interests held by certain members of the participant's family (i.e., a spouse, children, parents, etc.) and by certain entities in which the participant holds a controlling stake will be added to the ownership interest that the participant holds directly in determining whether the five percent threshold has been crossed.

3791. Can a plan restrict the types of 401(k) contributions that can be converted to a Roth 401(k)?

Yes. A plan that adopts an amendment permitting in-plan rollovers from traditional 401(k) accounts to Roth 401(k) accounts can, subject to otherwise applicable nondiscrimination require-ments, restrict the types of contributions that can be rolled over. Further, the plan amendment can limit the frequency of these rollovers.[1]

For example, otherwise nondistributable amounts may be permissibly rolled over, it is up to the plan itself to determine whether it will allow these rollovers. For administrative conve-nience, a plan may provide that it will only permit rollovers of otherwise distributable amounts or that nondistributable amounts can only be rolled over at certain intervals.

3792. What is an eligible investment advice arrangement?

ERISA contains a general prohibition against providing services to a plan for a fee. It is a prohibited transaction unless exempted either in the law or by regulations. There is a statutory exemption for investment advice rendered by a fiduciary advisor under an "eligible investment advice arrangement." These requirements are designed to allow the plan fiduciary to meet the obligations under ERISA in the hiring of an investment advisor.[2] The provisions discussed here generally are effective with respect to advice provided after December 31, 2006.

On October 25, 2011, the Employee Benefits Security Administration of the U.S. Department of Labor issued final regulations implementing a statutory exemption from ERISA's prohibited transaction rules that allows fiduciary advisors to offer plan participants and beneficiaries invest-ment advice for a fee under eligible investment advice arrangements.[3] The exemption, discussed below, was mandated by the Pension Protection Act of 2006 and is available for transactions occurring on or after December 27, 2011 that provide sufficient safeguards to ensure there is no conflict of interest.

---

1.   Notice 2013-74, Q&A-6, 2013-52 IRB 819.
2.   IRC Secs. 4975(d)(17), 4975(f)(8).
3.   DOL Reg. §2550.408g-1.

The final rules do not affect the applicability of the DOL's prior guidance on the application of the prohibited transaction rules and existing prohibited transaction exemptions to investment advice arrangements.

The Final Regulations

The statutory exemption allows fiduciary investment advisors to receive compensation from investment vehicles that they recommend if either (1) the investment advice is based on a computer model certified as unbiased which applies generally accepted investment theories, or (2) the advisor is compensated on a "level-fee" basis (i.e., fees do not vary based on investments selected by the participant). The final regulations provide detailed guidance to advisors on compliance with these conditions.

The regulations also show advisors how to comply with other conditions and safeguards in the statutory exemption, including:

- requiring that a plan fiduciary (independent of the investment advisor or its affiliates) authorize the advice arrangement;

- imposing recordkeeping requirements for investment advisors relying on the exemption;

- requiring that computer models be certified in advance as unbiased and meeting the exemption's requirements by an independent expert;

- establishing qualifications and a selection process for the investment expert who must perform the above certification;

- clarifying that the level-fee requirement does not permit investment advisors (including their employees) to receive compensation from any party (including affiliates) that varies on the basis of the investments that participants select;

- establishing an annual audit of both computer model and level-fee advice arrangements, including the requirement that the auditor be independent from the investment advice provider;

- requiring disclosures by advisors to plan participants.[1]

Fee Disclosures

In February 2012, the DOL issued final regulations on fee disclosure[2] and provided a Sample Guide to Initial Disclosures.[3] In its final rule, the DOL extended the deadline for disclosures to

---

1.   DOL Reg. §2550.408g-1.
2.   DOL Reg. §2550.408b-2.
3.   Available at https://www.dol.gov/sites/dolgov/files/EBSA/employers-and-advisers/plan-administration-and-compliance/retirement/sample-guide-for-service-provider-disclosures-under-408b2.pdf.

July 1, 2012. In May 2012, the DOL issued a Field Assistance Bulletin providing guidance on frequently asked questions about participant-level disclosure requirements.[1]

See Q 3793 for information about establishing an eligible investment advice arrangement and Q 3794 for a detailed discussion of who is a fiduciary advisor for purposes of an eligible investment advice arrangement.

3793. How is an eligible investment advice arrangement established?

An eligible investment advice arrangement may be established in either of two ways: (1) the arrangement may provide that any fees (including commissions or other compensation) received by the fiduciary for investment advice, or with respect to the sale, holding, or acquisition of any security or other property for purposes of investment of plan assets, do not vary depending on the basis of any investment option selected, or (2) the arrangement may use a computer model that meets specified criteria, described below, in connection with the provision of investment advice by a fiduciary advisor to a participant or beneficiary.[2]

The use of either method requires the plan fiduciary to comply with the statutory requirements of this exemption. Those requirements include:

(1)   that the advisor must act as an independent fiduciary;

(2)   proper authorization to provide the services;

(3)   compliance with an audit requirement;

(4)   disclosure of all relevant information including meeting certain standards for presentation of information;

(5)   the maintenance of proper records; and

(6)   that the fees charged the plan are reasonable.[3]

The fee leveling requirement is met if the fees, commissions, or any revenue sharing by the advisor do not vary based upon the recommendations provided. This applies to the affiliate of the advisor.[4]

Computer Model

The computer model must:

(1)   apply generally accepted investment theories that take into account the historic returns of different asset classes over defined periods of time;

---

1.   Field Assistance Bulletin 2012-2 (May 7, 2012).
2.   IRC Sec. 4975(f)(8)(B).
3.   IRC Sec. 4975(f)(8)(D) through (I).
4.   IRC Sec. 4975(f)(8)(B)(i)(I).

(2)   use relevant information about the participant, such as age, life expectancy, retirement age, risk tolerance, other assets or sources of income, and preferences as to certain types of investments;

(3)   use prescribed objective criteria to provide asset allocation portfolios comprised of investment options offered under the plan;

(4)   operate in a manner that is not biased toward investments offered by the fiduciary advisor, or a person in material affiliation or contractual relationship with the fiduciary advisor; and

(5)   take into account all investment options under the plan in specifying how a participant's account should be invested and not be inappropriately weighted with respect to any investment option.[1]

The person who develops or markets the computer model or investment advice program may be treated as a fiduciary advisor under certain circumstances.[2]

The utilization of the computer model must be certified by an "eligible investment expert" as meeting the foregoing criteria, and the only advice provided under the arrangement can be that generated by the computer model and any transaction requested by the participant.[3] The arrangement also must be audited annually and must meet detailed written disclosure requirements. Records of compliance must be maintained for six years.[4]

An eligible investment advice arrangement must be expressly authorized by a plan fiduciary other than the person offering the investment advice. Notifications required for participants and beneficiaries must be written in a clear and conspicuous manner, calculated to be understood by the average plan participant.[5] The DOL is directed to issue a model form for this purpose.[6]

3794. Who is a fiduciary advisor for purposes of an eligible investment advice arrangement?

A "fiduciary advisor" for purposes of this provision is a person who provides investment advice to the participant or beneficiary and is one of the following:

(1)   a Registered Investment Advisor ("RIA") under the Investment Advisers Act of 1940 or state law in which the fiduciary maintains its principal office and place of business;

---

1.   IRC Sec. 4975(f)(8)(C)(ii); DOL Reg. §2550.408g-1(b)(4).
2.   IRC Sec. 4975(f)(8)(J)(i).
3.   IRC Sec. 4975(f)(8)(C)(iii), 4975(f)(8)(C)(iv).
4.   IRC Sec. 4975(f)(8)(I).
5.   IRC Sec. 4975(f)(8)(H)(i).
6.   IRC Sec. 4975(f)(8)(H)(ii).

(2)   a bank or similar financial institution, but only if the advice is provided through a trust department that is subject to periodic examination and review by federal or state banking authorities;

(3)   an insurance company qualified to do business under the laws of a state;

4)   a person registered as a broker or dealer under the Securities Exchange Act of 1934;

(5)   an affiliate of any of the persons described in (1) through (4); or

(6)   an employee, agent, or registered representative of a person described in (1) through (5) who satisfies the requirements of applicable insurance, banking, and securities laws relating to the provision of the advice.[1]

3795. What is a combination defined benefit/401(k) plan?

For plan years beginning after December 31, 2009, an "eligible combined plan" (i.e., a combination defined benefit/401(k) plan) is available to employers with two to 500 employees.[2]

The assets of the plan will be held in a single trust, and the defined benefit and 401(k) components generally will be subject to their already-existing qualification requirements. The plan will be required to file only one Form 5500[3] and will have a single plan document.[4] The top heavy rules (Q 3915 to Q 3921) will be deemed satisfied for a combined defined benefit/401(k) plan, and the 401(k) portion will be exempt from ADP/ACP testing (Q 3753, Q 3801).[5]

The plan's design generally will be subject to the following requirements:

(1)   The benefit requirement for the defined benefit portion will be satisfied if the annual accrued benefit of each participant is not less than 1 percent of final average pay times up to 20 years of service, or if the plan is a cash balance plan providing pay credits not less than the percentage of compensation determined under the following formula:

Participant's age as of beginning of year	Cash balance pay credit percentage of compensation
30 or less	2
30 or over, less than 40	4
40 or over, less than 50	6
50 or over	8

---

1.   IRC Sec. 4975(f)(8)(J)(i); DOL Reg. §2550.408g-1(c)(2)(i).
2.   IRC Secs. 414(x)(2)(A), 4980D(d)(2).
3.   Regulations proposed in July 2016 (RIN 1210-AB63) are designed to modernize and improve the Form 5500 reporting procedures, and will generally be effective for the 2019 plan year, presumptively once they have been finalized.
4.   See IRC Secs. 414(x)(2), 414(x)(6).
5.   IRC Secs. 414(x)(3), 414(x)(4).

For this purpose, "final average pay" is determined using up to five years during which the participant had the highest aggregate compensation from the employer.[1]

(2)   The contribution requirement will be met if the 401(k) plan provides for an automatic contribution arrangement (see below) and requires the employer to match 50 percent of elective deferrals of up to 4 percent of compensation.[2] Non-elective contributions are not precluded but will not count toward satisfying this requirement.[3]

(3)   Employees must be 100 percent vested after three years of service with respect to the defined benefit portion of the plan. Matching contributions under the defined contribution portion must be nonforfeitable, including those in excess of the required match. Any nonelective contributions may be subject to a maximum three-year cliff vesting schedule.[4]

(4)   All contributions, benefits, rights, and features must be provided uniformly to all participants.[5]

(5)   The foregoing requirements must be met without taking into account permitted disparity and amounts under other plans.[6]

These criteria are the only circumstances under which a combination defined benefit/401(k) plan may constitute a single plan and trust.

A 401(k) plan will be treated as an automatic contribution arrangement if it provides a default elective contribution percentage of 4 percent and meets specific notice requirements. Employees must receive a notice explaining their right not to have contributions withheld, or to have them made at a different rate, and they must have a reasonable period of time after receipt of the notice to make such elections.[7]

3796. What restrictions apply to distributions from 401(k) plans?

Amounts held by the trust that are attributable to employer contributions made pursuant to the election to defer may not be distributed to participants or beneficiaries prior to:

(1)   the employee's death, disability, or severance from employment;

(2)   certain plan terminations, without the establishment or maintenance of another defined contribution plan;

---

1.   IRC Sec. 414(x)(2)(B).
2.   IRC Sec. 414(x)(2)(C).
3.   IRC Sec. 414(x)(2)(C)(ii).
4.   IRC Sec. 414(x)(2)(D).
5.   IRC Sec. 414(x)(2)(E).
6.   See IRC Sec. 414(x)(2)(F).
7.   See IRC Sec. 414(x)(5).

(3)   in the case of a profit sharing or stock bonus plan, the employee's reaching age 59½;

(4)   experiencing financial hardship (Q 3797) (for years beginning before January 1, 2019, limited to distributions from a profit sharing or stock bonus plan and not permitted from other plans);

(5)   in the case of a qualified reservist distribution, the date of the reservist's order or call;[1] or

(6)   Under the SECURE Act, withdrawals of up to $5,000 for up to one year following the birth or legal adoption of a child. Adopted children generally include children under age 18, but can also include someone who has reached age 18 but is physically or mentally disabled and incapable of self-support.[2]

These occurrences are referred to as "distributable events." Amounts may not be distributable merely by reason of completion of a stated period of participation or the lapse of a fixed number of years.[3]

The cost of life insurance protection as per Table 2001 or the insurer's qualifying lower published term rates (Q 3947) provided under the plan is not treated as a distribution for purposes of these rules. Neither is the making of a loan that is treated as a deemed distribution even if the loan is secured by the employee's elective contributions or is includable in the employee's income under IRC Section 72(p).

The reduction of an employee's accrued benefit derived from elective contributions (i.e., an offset distribution) by reason of a default on a loan is treated as a distribution (Q 3952).[4] The IRS has privately ruled that a transfer of 401(k) elective deferrals or rollovers to purchase service credits would not constitute an impermissible distribution from the plan and are not a violation of the separate accounting requirement.[5]

Restrictions on distributions of elective contributions generally continue to apply even if the amounts are transferred to another qualified plan of any employer.[6] Amounts transferred to a 401(k) plan by a direct rollover from another plan do not have to be subject to these restrictions.[7] See Q 3779 for discussion of in-plan Roth distributions. See Q 3786 for a discussion of penalty-free rollovers from 401(k) plan accounts into Roth 401(k) accounts. Final regulations state that rollover amounts may be excepted from the timing restrictions on distributions applicable to a receiving plan, provided there is a separate accounting for such amounts.[8]

---

1.   See IRC Sec. 72(t)(2)(G)(iii); Q 3677. See IRC Sec. 401(k)(2)(B)(1); Treas. Reg. §1.401(k)-1(d)(1).
2.   IRC Sec. 72(t)(2)(H)(iii)(II).
3.   IRC Sec. 401(k)(2)(B).
4.   Treas. Reg. §1.401(k)-1(d)(5)(ii).
5.   Let. Ruls. 200335035, 199914055.
6.   Treas. Reg. §1.401(k)-1(d)(2).
7.   Treas. Reg. §1.401(k)-1(d)(5)(iv).
8.   Treas. Reg. §1.401(k)-1(d)(5)(iv); see also Rev. Rul. 2004-12, 2004-7 IRB 478.

If an eligible retirement plan separately accounts for amounts attributable to rollover contributions to the plan, distributions of those amounts are not subject to the restrictions on permissible timing that apply, under the applicable requirements of the Internal Revenue Code, to distributions of other amounts from the plan. Accordingly, the plan may permit the distribution of amounts attributable to rollover contributions at any time pursuant to an individual's request.

Thus, for example, if the receiving plan is a money purchase pension plan and the plan separately accounts for amounts attributable to rollover contributions, a plan provision permitting the in-service distribution of those amounts will not disqualify the plan.[1]

3797. What requirements apply to hardship withdrawals from a 401(k) plan?

Editor's Note: The 2017 Tax Act created new rules governing hardship distributions made because of qualified 2016 disasters. See Q 3798 for details. The CARES Act further expanded hardship distribution eligibility in response to the COVID-19 pandemic in 2020. See Q 3800.

Hardship withdrawals may be made from a 401(k) plan only if the distribution is made on account of an immediate and heavy financial need and the distribution is necessary to satisfy the financial need.[2] The distribution may not exceed the employee's maximum distributable amount. Hardship withdrawals generally may not be rolled over (Q 3997).[3] Not all plans provide for hardship withdrawals, and plan sponsors must first look to the plan documents before determining whether a hardship distribution can be made. The final regulations cited here took effect for plan years beginning on or after January 1, 2006.[4]

The Pension Protection Act of 2006 called for regulations modifying the hardship requirements to state that if an event constitutes a hardship with respect to a participant's spouse or dependent, it constitutes a hardship with respect to the participant, to the extent permitted under the plan.[5]

An employee's maximum distributable amount generally is equal to the employee's total elective contributions as of the date of distribution reduced by the amount of previous distributions on account of hardship.[6] Early in 2018, Congress passed the Bipartisan Budget Act of 2018 (BBA 2018), which modified this rule to expand the amounts that may be withdrawn as hardship distributions. Beginning in tax years that begin after December 31, 2018, the following amounts may also be distributed as hardship distributions (1) amounts contributed by the employer to a profit sharing or stock bonus plan, (2) qualified nonelective contributions (QNECs), (3) qualified matching contributions (QMACs) and (3) earnings on any of these types of contribution.[7]

---

1.   Rev. Rul. 2004-12, 2004-7 IRB.
2.   Treas. Reg. §1.401(k)-1(d)(3)(i).
3.   IRC Sec. 402(c)(4). See also IRC Sec. 401(k)(2)(B).
4.   See Treas. Reg. §1.401(k)-1(g).
5.   See Pub. L. 109-280, Sec. 826.
6.   Treas. Reg. §1.401(k)-1(d)(3)(ii).
7.   IRC Sec. 401(k)(14)(A).

Planning Point: The changes enacted by BBA 2018 are not all mandatory, meaning that plan sponsors have the option of modifying their plans to implement the new rules. Plan sponsors operating safe harbor 401(k)s may wish to proceed with caution in implementing the changes, as Treasury has yet to issue guidance on whether the regulatory safe harbor will be satisfied if the plan retains (1) the six-month waiting period for contributions following a hardship distribution or (2) the requirement that the participant first take a plan loan before a hardship distribution is available. Plans must also consider the "leakage" problem in allowing participants to withdraw QNECs or QMACs, or in permitting hardship distributions before plan loans (which must be repaid).

The determinations of whether the participant has "an immediate and heavy financial need" and whether other resources are "reasonably available" to meet the need are to be made on the basis of all relevant facts and circumstances. Beginning for hardship distributions taken on or after January 1, 2020, the employee must provide a written representation stating that the employee does not have cash or other liquid assets reasonably available to satisfy the need (under BBA 2018). An example of "an immediate and heavy financial need" is the need to pay funeral expenses of a family member. A financial need will not fail to qualify as an immediate and heavy financial need merely because it was foreseeable or voluntarily incurred by the employee.[1]

A distribution will be deemed to be made on account of "an immediate and heavy financial need" if it is made on account of any of the following:

(1)   "medical expenses" incurred by the employee, spouse, or dependents that would be deductible as itemized deductions under section 213(d) without regard to the 10 percent (7.5 percent for 2017-2020[2]) of AGI floor;

(2)   the purchase (excluding mortgage payments) of the employee's principal residence;

(3)   payment of tuition, related educational fees, and room and board expenses for the next twelve months of post-secondary education for the employee, spouse, children, or dependents (note that the educational expenses must be for education incurred in the following twelve months, the IRS has ruled that a participant cannot take a hardship distribution to repay student loans incurred for past education);

(4)   payments necessary to prevent eviction of the employee from his or her principal residence or foreclosure on the mortgage on his or her principal residence;

(5)   funeral or burial expenses for the employee's parent, spouse, children, or other dependents (as defined prior to 2005); and

(6)   expenses for the repair or damage to the employee's principal residence that would qualify for the casualty deduction under IRC Section 165 (without regard to the 10 percent floor).[3]

---

1.   Treas. Reg. §1.401(k)-1(d)(3)(iii)(A).
2.   The year-end spending package that became law late in 2019 extended the 7.5% threshold through 2020.
3.   Treas. Reg. §1.401(k)-1(d)(3)(iii)(B).

This list may be expanded by the IRS but only by publication of documents of general applicability.[1] Apparently, to be the taxpayer's "principal residence" for this purpose, the home must be the residence of the employee, not merely that of his or her family.[2]

Planning Point: While the rules governing plan hardship distributions were not directly changed by the 2017 Tax Act, many plans that follow safe harbor standards and allow participants to withdraw funds to cover losses that are deductible as casualty losses may need to reevaluate their plan provisions. This is because, for 2018-2025, individuals may only treat losses sustained in a federal disaster area as deductible casualty losses under IRC Section 165. Unless subsequent guidance is released to change the safe harbor rules governing hardship distributions, plans may need to change the terms of their plan to comply with the new Section 165 rules.

A distribution is not necessary to satisfy such an immediate and heavy financial need (and will not qualify as a hardship withdrawal) to the extent the amount of the distribution exceeds the amount required to relieve the financial need. The amount of an immediate and heavy financial need may include any amounts necessary to pay any federal, state, or local income taxes or penalties reasonably anticipated to result from the distribution.[3]

The distribution also will not be treated as necessary to satisfy an immediate and heavy financial need to the extent the need can be satisfied from other resources that are reasonably available. However, the BBA 2018 eliminated the requirement that a plan participant first take any available plan loan before the distribution could qualify as a hardship distribution.[4]

A distribution may be treated as necessary if the employer reasonably relies on the employee's representation that the need cannot be relieved:

(1)   through reimbursement or compensation by insurance or otherwise,

(2)   by reasonable liquidation of the employee's assets,

(3)   by cessation of elective contributions or employee contributions,

(4)   by other distributions or nontaxable loans from any plans (the requirement that a participant first take any available plan loan was eliminated by the BBA 2018, but the requirement that the employee consider any ESOP dividend distributions was retained), or

(5)   by loans from commercial sources.

Notwithstanding these provisions, an employee need not "take counterproductive actions" (such as a plan loan that might disqualify the employee from obtaining other financing) if the effect would be to increase the amount of the need.[5]

---

1.   Treas. Reg. §1.401(k)-1(d)(3)(v).
2.   See ABA Joint Committee on Employee Benefits, Meeting with IRS and Department of Treasury Officials, May 7, 2004 (Q&A-18).
3.   Treas. Reg. §1.401(k)-1(d)(3)(iv)(A).
4.   IRC Sec. 401(k)(14)(B).
5.   Treas. Reg. §1.401(k)-1(d)(3)(iv)(C), (D).

The final regulations governing hardship distributions also provide that with respect to employee representations of financial hardship, the employee can reasonably represent that he or she has no cash or liquid assets reasonably available to satisfy the relevant financial need if the only cash or liquid assets available to that employee are necessary to pay some other expense (such as rent) in the near future.[1] Employees can also make representations of financial need over the phone if the employer records the call.[2] Plan documents must be amended by December 31, 2021 to provide for the new written representation provision, although the rule is effective beginning in 2020.[3]

Plan sponsors are also entitled to impose a minimum distribution amount for hardship distributions so long as the requirement is not found to be discriminatory.[4]

Regulations state that a distribution will be deemed to be "necessary" to meet a financial need (deemed or otherwise) if the employee has obtained all other distributions and nontaxable loans (prior to 2019) currently available under all of the employer's plans and, prior to 2019, the employee is prohibited from making elective contributions and employee contributions to the plan and all other plans of the employer for a period of at least six months after receipt of the hardship distribution.[5] The regulations have been modified to eliminate the prohibition on contributions during the six month period following receipt of a hardship distribution, although the final regulations have clarified that the new rule applies only to contributions to qualified plans. Plan documents must be amended by December 31, 2021 to account for this new rule, which became effective beginning in 2020.[6] Nonqualified plans, including those subject to IRC Section 409A, may continue to suspend deferrals for six months following the hardship distribution.[7]

The IRS has released internal guidance that it will use when examining a 401(k) plan to evaluate whether hardship distributions have been properly substantiated. The new guidance clarifies that, as part of the verification process for determining whether the participant has an immediate and heavy financial need, the employer or plan sponsor must review either the source documents supporting that need (such as contracts or foreclosure notices), or a summary of those documents. If only a summary is provided, an IRS agent reviewing the case will look to whether a notice was provided to the withdrawing participant before he or she is entitled to the hardship withdrawal. The notice must contain a statement that provides the following information:

(1)   the distribution is taxable,

(2)   additional taxes could apply,

(3)   the amount of the distribution cannot exceed the participant's "immediate and heavy financial need",

1.   See Preamble to the Final Regulations, 84 FR 49651.
2.   See Preamble to the Final Regulations, 84 FR 49651.
3.   Rev. Proc. 2020-9.
4.   See Preamble to the Final Regulations, 84 FR 49651. See also Treas. Reg. 1.401(k)-1(d)(3)(iv).
5.   Treas. Reg. §1.401(k)-1(d)(3)(iv)(E).
6.   Rev. Proc. 2020-9.
7.   P.L. 115-123 (Bipartisan Budget Act), Section 41113.

(4)   the distribution cannot be made from earnings on elective contributions or qualified nonelective contributions or matching contributions (QNECs and QMACs) (the prohibition on making the distribution from QNECs, QMACs, and earnings was eliminated for tax years beginning after December 31, 2018)[1], and

(5)   all source documents must be retained and provided to the employer or administrator upon request at any time.

The guidance also provides that specific information should be obtained by the plan administrator to substantiate a summary. If the summary is incomplete or inconsistent on its face, the IRS examining agent may ask for source documents.[2]

3798. What special rules governing retirement plan distributions were implemented for 2016 and 2017 disaster areas?

Editor's Note: The 2019 Tax Certainty and Disaster Relief Act extended the rules governing qualified disaster distributions from retirement accounts, discussed below for victims of disasters that occurred in 2018 through 60 days after enactment of the bill (December 20, 2019). The distribution itself must be made within 180 days after enactment of the law to qualify. See Q 3799. Also, see Q 3800 for a discussion of how the CARES Act expanded the retirement plan distribution rules for 2020 in response to the COVID-19 pandemic.

The 2017 Tax Act[3], the 2017 Disaster Tax Relief and Airport and Airway Extension Act,[4] and the Bipartisan Budget Act of 2018[5], include special tax relief for taxpayers affected by certain presidentially declared disasters that occurred in 2016 and 2017.

A 2016 qualified disaster is a major disaster that was declared in 2016 by the president. A 2016 qualified disaster distribution is any distribution received from an eligible retirement plan in 2016 or 2017 if the recipient's main home was located in a 2016 qualified disaster area and the recipient sustained an economic loss from the disaster.

A 2017 qualified disaster is limited to Hurricane Harvey and Tropical Storm Harvey, Hurricane Irma, Hurricane Maria, and the California wildfires. To be a 2017 qualified disaster distribution, the following requirements must be met:

1.   The distribution was made:

a.   After August 22, 2017, and before January 1, 2019, for Hurricane Harvey or Tropical Storm Harvey (both referred to as Hurricane Harvey);

b.   After September 3, 2017, and before January 1, 2019, for Hurricane Irma;

---

1.   P.L. 115-123 (Bipartisan Budget Act), Section 41114.
2.   The substantiation guidelines are available at https://www.irs.gov/pub/foia/ig/spder/tege-04-0217-0008.pdf (last accessed September 16, 2020).
3.   Section 11028, 2017 Tax Act, P.L. 115-97.
4.   Title V, Disaster Tax Relief and Airport and Airway Extension Act of 2017, P.L. 115-63.
5.   Subdivision 2, Title I, Bipartisan Budget Act of 2018, P.L. 115-123.

    c.   After September 15, 2017, and before January 1, 2019, for Hurricane Maria; or

    d.   After October 7, 2017, and before January 1, 2019, for California wildfires.

2.   The recipient's main home was located in a disaster area listed below on the date or any date in the period shown for that area.

    a.   August 23, 2017, for the Hurricane Harvey disaster area.

    b.   September 4, 2017, for the Hurricane Irma disaster area.

    c.   September 16, 2017, for the Hurricane Maria disaster area.

    d.   October 8, 2017 to December 31, 2017, for the California wildfire disaster area.

3.   The recipient sustained an economic loss because of Hurricane Harvey, Hurricane Irma, Hurricane Maria, or the California wildfires

None of the Acts define economic loss. Examples of economic loss include loss, damage, or destruction of real or personal property; loss related to displacement from a home; and loss of livelihood due to temporary or permanent layoff.[1] There is no requirement that the amount of the qualified disaster distribution relate to the amount of the taxpayer's economic loss from the disaster or be made on account of the disaster.

The Acts provide special rules for distributions from retirement accounts (qualified plans, 403(a)s, 403(b)s, governmental 457(b)s, and traditional, SEP, SIMPLE, and Roth IRAs). Distributions from retirement accounts made because of a qualified disaster are exempt from the 10 percent early distribution penalty (or 25 percent early distribution penalty for certain SIMPLE IRA distributions) if the penalty would otherwise be imposed under IRC Section 72(t). Qualified disaster distributions are treated as meeting the applicable plan's distribution requirements. The amount that may be treated as a qualified disaster area distribution is limited to $100,000 (the amount for any given year must be reduced by the amounts treated as 2016 disaster area distributions in prior years).

If a taxpayer is affected by multiple qualifying disasters, the $100,000 limit is applied separately to each disaster distribution. Taxpayers may recognize income attributable to a qualified disaster distribution over a three-year period beginning with the year the qualified disaster distribution was made (unless an election to the contrary is made).

In addition, taxpayers are also permitted a three-year period from the day after the distribution is received to make a repayment of qualified disaster distributions that is eligible for tax-free rollover treatment to an eligible retirement plan or made on account of a hardship. These repayments may be made at once or via a series of payments and will essentially be treated as though

---

1.   2017 IRS Publication 976, Disaster Relief.

they were rollovers made within the 60-day window. A repayment to an IRA is not considered a rollover for purposes of the one-rollover-per year limitation for IRAs. The following types of distributions cannot be repaid:

- Qualified disaster distributions received as a beneficiary other than as a surviving spouse

- Required minimum distributions

- Periodic payments other than from an IRA that are for 10 years or more, the recipient's life or life expectancy or the joint lives or life expectancies of the recipient and their beneficiary.

Plans that make such a distribution also are protected against potential disqualification. Plans that permit qualified 2016 disaster distributions must be amended by the last day of the plan year beginning on or after January 1, 2018. Plans that permit qualified 2017 disaster distributions must be amended by the last day of the plan year beginning on or after January 1, 2019.

Taxpayers who received certain distributions from retirement plans to buy or construct a principal residence but did not buy or construct the residence because of Hurricane or Tropical Storm Harvey, Hurricane Irma, Hurricane Maria, or the California wildfires had the opportunity to recontribute the distributions to an eligible retirement plan. The distributions had to be repaid before March 1, 2018 for repayments as a result of a hurricane or July 1, 2018 for repayments due to the California wildfires. A distribution that was not repaid before the applicable date may be taxable for 2017 and subject to the 10 percent additional tax on early distributions (or the 25 percent additional tax on certain SIMPLE IRA distributions).

Individuals affected by a qualified disaster (as extended by the 2019 law) qualify for relaxed rules on loans from qualified plans. The plan administrator may increase the regular $50,000 limit on plan loans to $100,000 and the 50 percent of vested benefit limit to 100 percent. For individuals affected by a hurricane, the loan must have been made between September 29, 2017 and December 31, 2018. For someone affected by the California wildfires, the loan must have been made during the period beginning February 9, 2018 and ending on December 31, 2018. In addition, loan payments due during a specified period ending on December 31, 2018 may be suspended for one year by the plan administrator. The period begins on:

- August 23, 2017 if the recipient's home was located in the Hurricane Harvey disaster area

- September 4, 2017 if the recipient's home was located in the Hurricane Irma disaster area

- September 16, 2017 if the recipient's home was located in the Hurricane Maria disaster area; or

- October 8, 2017 if the recipient's home was located in the California wildfire disaster area.

Casualty losses associated with a qualified 2016 or 2017 disaster are deductible regardless of whether total losses exceed 10 percent of the taxpayer's adjusted gross income (AGI), so long as the loss exceeds $500 per casualty. Taxpayers who do not itemize their deductions may increase their standard deduction by the net qualified disaster loss.

3799. What special rules governing retirement plan distributions were implemented for 2018 and 2019 disaster areas?

The 2019 Tax Certainty and Disaster Relief Act extended the rules governing qualified disaster distributions from retirement accounts, discussed below for victims of disasters that occurred in 2018 through 60 days after enactment of the bill (December 20, 2019). Qualified disaster areas generally include any area the President declares as such. The term "qualified disaster area" does not include the California wildfire disaster area, as defined in the 2018 Bipartisan Budget Act.

The distribution itself must be made within 180 days after enactment of the law to qualify. In general, the benefits of taking a distribution under the SECURE Act's expansion of the disaster relief option are:

- The taxpayer is exempt from the penalty on early distributions,

- The taxpayer is exempt from withholding requirements on the distribution,

- The taxpayer can elect to treat the distribution as having been distributed over a three-year period (or within the single year of distribution, and

- The taxpayer is able to repay the distribution within three years of receiving the distribution.[1]

Individuals affected by a qualified disaster qualify for relaxed rules on loans from qualified plans. The plan administrator may increase the regular $50,000 limit on plan loans to $100,000 and the 50 percent of vested benefit limit to 100 percent.

3800. What special rules governing retirement plan distributions were implemented for distributions related to the COVID-19 impact?

The Coronavirus Aid, Relief, and Economic Security Act (CARES Act) allows taxpayers to take up to $100,000 in distributions from an employer-sponsored retirement plan (401(k), 403(b) or defined benefit plan) or an IRA without the distribution becoming subject to the 10 percent early distribution penalty (the 25 percent early distribution penalty that applies to early distributions from SIMPLE IRAs is also waived). Unless the participant elects otherwise, the coronavirus-related distribution (CRD) is included income ratably over three years, beginning with the tax year of distribution.

The actual amount of the CRD does not need to be tied to the amount the participant requires to satisfy the COVID-19-related financial need. The amount is also a per-taxpayer

---

1.   The Taxpayer Certainty and Disaster Relief Act of 2019, Sec. 202.

rule, not a per-plan rule, meaning that distributions from all plans must be considered when determining whether they qualify for favorable tax treatment.[1]

Planning Point: Plan sponsors have discretion as to whether they choose to implement any of these CARES Act relief provisions. However, the employee can elect favorable tax relief on a personal tax return regardless of whether the employer chooses to implement these options.

Note, however, that plans are not required to accept rollover contributions, which could create problems for participants who wish to take advantage of the three-year repayment option.

The CARES Act also provides for repayment options to allow employees to repay CRDs during the three-year tax period beginning with the tax year of distribution (whether in a lump sum or installments over time). Although unclear from the law as written, the repayment seems to be repayable to any type of plan that will accept the repayment, in which case it will be treated as a nontaxable rollover via direct transfer. Only distributions that qualify for penalty-free distribution relief (i.e., amounts up to $100,000) are eligible for repayment. Distributions paid to account beneficiaries (except for surviving spouses) are not eligible for recontribution (although these distributions *can* be treated as qualifying coronavirus-related distributions).[2]

Planning Point: Employer-sponsored plans, however, are only able to accept rollovers from participants (and sometimes new hires). Therefore, if an employee takes their entire account balance as a CRD and later stops working for the employer, the person is no longer a participant or new hire. That former employee would, therefore, be required to re-contribute the funds to an IRA or to a plan sponsored by a new employer that accepts rollovers.

When the employee takes only part of the balance, employers should exercise more caution—because it's unclear whether that former employee would continue to be treated as a plan participant. It's important for the plan to have a non-discriminatory policy in place when deciding whether or not to accept these re-contributions (for example, by not accepting any rollovers from non-employees).

The penalty waiver is effective for distributions made on or after January 1, 2020 and before December 31, 2020.

The waiver is available for any "coronavirus affected individual", which includes both those who have been diagnosed (or had a spouse diagnosed) with the virus and those who have suffered financial consequences caused by layoffs, work reduction or being unable to work because of the need to provide child care.

Later IRS guidance expanded the list of qualifying individuals to include:

1.   A plan participant whose pay was reduced due to COVID-19 (regardless of whether hours were reduced or whether the individual was laid off).

2.   A plan participant who was planning to start a new job and the start date was pushed back (or the offer was rescinded entirely) due to COVID-19.

---

1.   Notice 2020-50.
2.   Notice 2020-50, see Section 2(D).

3. A plan participant whose spouse or member of the plan participant's household has suffered a qualifying effect.[1]

"Members of the participant's household" should include roommates or anyone who shares the participant's primary residence. For example, if the participant's live-in partner owned a business that was shut down due to COVID-19, the participant would be eligible for the plan distribution relief.

Employers can rely upon employees' certifications that they satisfy conditions related to the hardship distribution unless the employer has actual knowledge to the contrary. The IRS provided a sample employee certification document in Notice 2020-50.

Similarly, plan loan rules are expanded to increase the available loan limit from $50,000 to $100,000 during the 180-day period beginning March 27, 2020. The due date for repaying loans taken before December 31, 2020 is delayed one year. RMDs for the 2020 tax year have also been waived.[2]

Nondiscrimination

3801. How does a 401(k) plan satisfy the nondiscrimination in amount requirement?

A cash or deferred arrangement will be treated as meeting the nondiscrimination require-ment of IRC Section 401(a)(4) if it satisfies the Actual Deferral Percentage ("ADP") test (Q 3802).[3] A plan can satisfy the ADP test by annually meeting the requirements of the ADP test itself, by satisfying the design-based requirements for a SIMPLE 401(k) plan (Q 3777), or by satisfying the design-based requirements for a safe harbor plan (Q 3772).[4]

In plan years beginning after December 31, 2007, a "qualified automatic contribution arrangement" will satisfy the ADP test requirement (Q 3762).[5] The final regulations cited here took effect for plan years beginning on or after January 1, 2006.[6]

A plan will not be treated as violating the ADP test merely on account of the making of (or right to make) catch-up contributions by participants age 50 or over under the provisions of IRC Section 414(v) so long as a universal availability requirement is met (Q 3761).[7]

Salary reductions that give rise to the saver's credit (Q 3648) may be taken into account for purposes of satisfying the ADP test.[8] If the plan provides for employee after-tax contributions or employer matching contributions, those contributions must meet the requirements of IRC Section 401(m) (Q 3803). If the plan includes a profit sharing component (i.e., nonelective

---

1. Notice 2020-50.
2. Pub. Law 116-136.
3. IRC Sec. 401(k)(3)(C).
4. IRC Secs. 401(k)(3)(A)(ii), 401(k)(11)(A), 401(k)(12)(A); Treas. Reg. §1.401(k)-1(b)(1).
5. IRC Sec. 401(k)(13).
6. Treas. Reg. §1.401(k)-1(g).
7. IRC Sec. 414(v)(3)(B).
8. Ann. 2001-106, 2001-44 IRB 416, A-10.

contributions that are not QNECs, other than as part of one of the designs explained in Q 3777 and Q 3772), that portion of the plan will be subject to nondiscrimination in amount testing (Q 3847).

A cash or deferred arrangement in which all of the eligible employees for a plan year are highly compensated employees (Q 3929) will be deemed to satisfy the ADP test for the plan year.[1] A 401(k) plan also is subject to age and service, coverage, and other requirements (Q 3753).

Final regulations treat all governmental plans (within the meaning of IRC Section 414(d)) as meeting the coverage and nondiscrimination requirements.[2] The IRC states that state and local governmental plans, to the limited extent that they are eligible to offer a cash or deferred arrangement (Q 3753), meet the requirements of IRC Section 401(k)(3).[3] Under earlier guidance, plans established and maintained for its employees by the federal government or by any agency or instrumentality of it, are treated as meeting the requirements of IRC Section 401(k)(3) until the first day of the first plan year beginning on or after the date final regulations were issued (December 29, 2004).[4]

3802. What is the Actual Deferral Percentage (ADP) test? How is the ADP test satisfied?

The actual deferral percentage test requires that the Actual Deferral Percentage ("ADP") of eligible highly compensated employees (Q 3929) be compared to the ADP of all other eligible employees, and that it satisfy one of the following tests:

Test 1: The actual deferral percentage for eligible highly compensated employees (Q 3929) for the plan year does not exceed the actual deferral percentage of all other eligible employees for the preceding plan year, multiplied by 1.25.

Test 2: The actual deferral percentage for eligible highly compensated employees for the plan year does not exceed by more than 2 percent that of all other eligible employees for the preceding plan year and the actual deferral percentage for highly compensated employees for the plan year is not more than the actual deferral percentage of all other eligible employees for the preceding plan year multiplied by two.

The IRC provides two methods of applying the ADP test: a prior year testing method, and a current year testing method. The method described above is the prior year testing method (as set forth in the IRC), but the current year method is available by election.[5] Under the current year testing method, the ADP results of nonhighly compensated employees for the current year (instead of the preceding year) are used in each test. The ability of plan sponsors to switch

1.   Treas. Reg. §1.401(k)-2(a)(1)(ii).
2.   Treas. Reg. §1.401(k)-1(b)(2).
3.   IRC Sec. 401(k)(3)(G); see Notice 2001-46, 2001-2 CB 122, as modified by Notice 2003-6, 2003-3 IRB 298.
4.   Notice 2003-6, above; T.D. 9169, 69 FR 78154.
5.   See IRC Sec. 401(k)(3)(A).

between the current and prior year testing methods is limited.[1] The plan document must reflect which testing method the plan is using for a testing year.[2]

Qualified Matching Contributions ("QMACs") and Qualified Nonelective Contributions ("QNECs") are employer matching contributions and nonelective contributions, respectively, that are subject to the same nonforfeitability (Q 3753) and withdrawal restrictions (Q 3796) as elective deferral contributions. Under certain circumstances, elective contributions used to pass the ADP test may include QMACs and QNECs that are made with respect to employees eligible under the cash or deferred arrangement.[3] Specific requirements for such use are set forth in regulations.[4]

QMACs and QNECs may be used only once. In other words, contributions that are treated as elective contributions for purposes of the ADP test may not be taken into account for purposes of the ACP test under IRC Section 401(m) and are not otherwise taken into account in determining whether any other contributions or benefits are nondiscriminatory under IRC Section 401(a)(4). Similarly, QNECs that are treated as matching contributions for purposes of the ACP test may not be used to satisfy the ADP test.[5]

Calculation of Actual Deferral Percentage

The actual deferral percentage for a group of eligible employees is the average of the actual deferral ratios of employees in the group for the plan year as calculated separately for each employee and to the nearest 1/100 of 1 percent.[6]

An employee's actual deferral ratio is determined by dividing the amount of elective contributions (including amounts treated as elective contributions) made to the trust on his or her behalf for the plan year by his or her compensation for the plan year, calculated to the nearest 1/100 of 1 percent.[7] Only contributions allocated to the employee's account for the plan year and related to compensation that, but for the election to defer, would have been received during the plan year (or, if attributable to services performed during the plan year, within 2½ months after the close of the plan year) are considered in applying the ADP test. Designated Roth contributions (Q 3778) are treated as elective deferral contributions for purposes of the ADP test.[8]

Compensation, for purposes of calculating actual deferral percentages, generally means compensation for services performed for an employer, which is includable in gross income (Q 3866). An employer may limit the period taken into account to that portion of the plan year (or calendar year) in which the employee was an eligible employee, provided that this limit is applied uniformly to all eligible employees.[9]

---

1.   See IRC Sec. 401(k)(3)(A); Treas. Reg. §1.401(k)-2(c)(1)(ii).
2.   Treas. Reg. §1.401(k)-1(e)(7).
3.   IRC Sec. 401(k)(3)(D)(ii).
4.   See Treas. Reg. §1.401(k)-2(a)(6).
5.   See Treas. Reg. §1.401(k)-2(a)(6)(vi).
6.   Treas. Reg. §1.401(k)-2(a)(2)(i).
7.   Treas. Reg. §1.401(k)-2(a)(3).
8.   See Treas. Reg. §1.401(k)-1(f)(4).
9.   Treas. Reg. §1.401(k)-6.

Miscellaneous Provisions

Although a plan must, by its terms, provide that the ADP test will be met; it may incorporate by reference the 401(k) nondiscrimination provisions of the IRC and regulations.[1]

3803. What special rules apply to employer matching contributions? What rules apply to employee contributions?

A defined contribution plan that provides for employee contributions or matching contributions, typically a 401(k) plan (Q 3753), must satisfy the Actual Contribution Percentage ("ACP") test or one of the alternatives to it (see Q 3804) to meet the nondiscrimination in amount requirement of IRC Section 401(a)(4).[2] With respect to matching contributions only, two alternative plan designs are available that are deemed to satisfy the ACP test: a SIMPLE 401(k) plan (Q 3777), or a safe harbor design (Q 3772).[3] In plan years beginning after December 31, 2007, a "qualified automatic contribution arrangement" will satisfy the ACP test requirement with respect to matching contributions (Q 3762).[4]

Matching contributions are subject to a three year cliff or five year graduated vesting schedule (Q 3868).

A plan will not be treated as violating the ACP test merely on account of the making of, or the right to make, catch-up contributions by participants age 50 or over under the provisions of IRC Section 414(v) so long as a universal availability requirement is met (Q 3761).[5]

All after-tax employee contributions are subject to ACP testing even if one of the design-based alternatives is used. After-tax employee contributions for this purpose do not include designated Roth contributions (Q 3778). The term also does not include rollover amounts, repayment of loans, or any other amounts transferred from another plan.[6]

The contributions that are required under a safe harbor plan (Q 3772) may not be used to satisfy the ACP test for after-tax employee contributions. Any employer matching or nonelective contributions in excess of the amount required to satisfy the safe harbor rules for a qualified cash or deferred arrangement can be taken into account for purposes of satisfying the ACP test.[7] Voluntary after-tax employee contributions that give rise to the Saver's Credit (Q 3648) may be taken into account for purposes of satisfying the ACP test.[8]

Of course, the plan must satisfy the general nondiscrimination requirements applicable to all qualified plans (Q 3847). In particular, the availability of matching and employee contributions,

---

1.　Treas. Reg. §1.401(k)-1(e)(7).
2.　IRC Sec. 401(m)(1).
3.　IRC Secs. 401(m)(10), 401(m)(11).
4.　IRC Sec. 401(m)(12).
5.　IRC Sec. 414(v)(3)(B).
6.　Treas. Reg. §1.401(m)-1(a)(3)(ii).
7.　See General Explanation of Tax Legislation Enacted in the 104th Congress (JCT-12-96), p. 153 (the 1996 Blue Book).
8.　Ann. 2001-106, 2001-44 IRB 416, A-10.

as well as any other benefits, rights, and features under the plan, must be nondiscriminatory (Q 3859).[1]

3804. What is the actual contribution percentage (ACP) test that must be satisfied by defined contribution plans that provide for employee contributions or employer matching contributions?

The IRC provides two methods of applying the ACP test: a prior year testing method, and a current year testing method.[2] The prior year method is specified in the IRC and the current year method is available by election.[3] A plan generally must specify which of these two methods it is using.[4]

Prior year testing method. Under the prior year testing method, a defined contribution plan that provides for employee or matching contributions meets the ACP test if the contribution percentage for eligible highly compensated employees for the plan year does not exceed the greater of (1) 125 percent of the contribution percentage for all other eligible employees for the preceding plan year, or (2) the lesser of (i) 200 percent of the contribution percentage for all other eligible employees for the preceding plan year or (ii) such contribution percentage for all other employees for the preceding plan year plus two percentage points.[5]

Current year testing method. Under the current year testing method, the ACP results of nonhighly compensated employees for the current year, also known as the "testing year," are compared with those of highly compensated employees for the current year. The plan satisfies the ACP test if the contribution percentage for eligible highly compensated employees for the plan year does not exceed the greater of (1) 125 percent of the contribution percentage for all other eligible employees for the plan year or (2) the lesser of (x) 200 percent of the contribution percentage for all other eligible employees for the plan year or (y) such contribution percentage for all other employees for the plan year plus two percentage points.[6]

A plan is not required to use the same method under the ACP test as it uses under the ADP test (Q 3801), but special rules must be followed if different methods are used.[7]

Planning Point: Make sure to accurately count highly compensated employees using the family aggregation rules, which treat the spouse, child, grandparent, or parent of a 5 percent owner as a 5 percent owner. Remember that family members may have different last names.[8]

---

1. Treas. Reg. §1.401(m)-1(a)(1)(ii).
2. IRC Sec. 401(m)(2)(A).
3. IRC Sec. 401(m)(2)(A); Treas. Reg. §1.401(m)-2(a)(2)(ii).
4. Treas. Reg. §1.401(m)-1(c)(2).
5. IRC Sec. 401(m)(2)(A); Treas. Reg. §1.401(m)-2(a)(2)(ii).
6. IRC Sec. 401(m)(2)(A); Treas. Reg. §§1.401(m)-2(a)(1), 401(m)-2(a)(2)(ii).
7. Treas. Reg. §1.401(m)-2(c)(3).
8. See 401(k) Plan Fix-It Guide, at http://www.irs.gov/Retirement-Plans/401k-Plan-Fix-It-Guide-The-Plan-Failed-The-401k-ADP-and-ACP-Nondiscrimination-Tests.

Changes in Testing Method

Change from current year testing method to prior year testing method. A plan that elects to continue using the current year testing method may be subject to certain restrictions if an employer wants to change to the prior year testing method: one governs the revocability of the election, and a second limits the "double counting" of certain contributions.

The election to use the current year testing method ordinarily will not be revocable except with the permission of the IRS.[1] Regulations provide for limited circumstances under which a plan will be permitted to change from the current year testing method to the prior year testing method.[2] A plan that changes from the current year testing method to the prior year testing method also is subject to limitations designed to prevent double counting of certain contributions.[3] Plans using the prior year testing method may change back to the current year method for any subsequent testing year.[4]

Special rules apply in the first plan year; essentially a plan other than a successor plan may designate the ACP of nonhighly compensated employees at 3 percent in the first plan year that the plan uses the prior year testing method. The employer may elect to use the plan's first year ACP results instead.[5] The plan document must specify the method that will be used.[6]

Miscellaneous Rules

Plans that accept rollover contributions generally assume the risk that the contributions qualify for rollover treatment (Q 3995). The IRS has determined that where a plan accepted a rollover contribution that, in fact, did not qualify for rollover, the amount involved was received by the plan as a voluntary employee contribution, which had to be considered for purposes of the ACP test.[7]

Matching contributions, other than QMACs (Q 3801), on behalf of self-employed individuals are not treated as an elective employer contribution for purposes of the limit on elective deferrals under IRC Section 402(g).[8]

See Q 3805 for information on qualified nonelective contributions (QNECs) and Q 3806 for information on calculating the actual contribution percentage.

---

1.   IRC Sec. 401(m)(2)(A).
2.   Treas. Reg. §§1.401(m)-2(c)(1), 1.401(k)-2(c)(1)(ii).
3.   Treas. Reg. §1.401(m)-2(a)(6)(vi).
4.   IRC Sec. 401(m)(2)(A). See Treas. Reg. §1.401(m)-2(c)(1).
5.   Treas. Reg. §1.401(m)-2(c)(2)(i).
6.   Treas. Reg. §1.401(m)-1(c)(2).
7.   See Let. Rul. 8044030.
8.   IRC Sec. 402(g)(8).

3805. What is a qualified nonelective contribution (QNEC)? Can QNECs be taken into account in determining whether a defined contribution plan satisfies the ACP test?

A "QNEC" is any employer contribution (other than elective contributions and matching contributions) with respect to which the employee does not have an election to receive the amount in cash and that satisfies the nonforfeitability and withdrawal restrictions applicable to elective deferrals to qualified cash or deferred (401(k)) arrangements (Q 3753 and Q 3796).[1] Elective and qualified nonelective contributions ("QNECs") may be taken into account in determining whether a plan satisfies the ACP test, provided certain requirements are met.[2]

Employer matching contributions that are treated as elective contributions for purposes of the actual deferral percentage ("ADP") test applicable to cash or deferred arrangements (Q 3801) are not subject to the ACP test above and may not be used to help employee contributions or other matching contributions to satisfy this test. Similarly, a QNEC that is treated as an elective contribution is subject to the ADP test and is not considered as a matching contribution for purposes of the ACP test.[3] Essentially, a QNEC is a supplemental employer contribution that is tested as if it were an elective deferral for purposes of the ADP test.

Under limited circumstances set forth in regulations, an employer may elect to include certain elective contributions and QNECs in computing the contribution percentage.[4] To be considered in the calculation of the ACP for a year under the prior year testing method, a QNEC must be contributed no later than the end of the twelve month period following the applicable year, even though that year is different than the plan year being tested.[5]

On July 20, 2018, the IRS published regulations that modify the definitions of QNEC to allow employers to use forfeitures in order to pass nondiscrimination testing that applies to qualified plans. This amendment generally broadens the definition of contributions that qualify as QNECs and permits plan sponsors that allow the use of forfeiture accounts to offset future employer contributions under the plan. Therefore, the final regulations would require that QNECs be fully vested and subject to certain distribution restrictions only when they are allocated to the participant's account, rather than when they are first contributed to the plan. The changes apply to taxable years ending on or after July 20, 2018.[6]

3806. How is the actual contribution percentage (ACP) calculated in determining whether the ACP test is satisfied?

The ACP for a group of eligible employees is the average of their actual contribution ratios ("ACRs") for the year, computed separately for each employee and to the nearest one-hundredth of one percent. An employee's ACR is (1) the sum of matching contributions and employee

---

1.   IRC Sec. 401(m)(4); Treas. Reg. §§1.401(m)-5, 1.401(k)-1(c)-(d).
2.   See Treas. Reg. §1.401(m)-2(a)(6).
3.   Treas. Reg. §1.401(m)-2(a)(6)(vi).
4.   IRC Sec. 401(m)(3); Treas. Reg. §1.401(m)-2(a)(6).
5.   Treas. Reg. §1.401(m)-2(a)(6)(i).
6.   REG-131643-15.

contributions (including any QNECs taken into account) divided by (2) the employee's compensation (Q 3890).[1] Special rules apply for the first year a plan, other than a successor plan, is in existence.[2]

Compensation for this purpose generally is the same as under IRC Section 414(s) (Q 3866), based on the plan year or the calendar year ending within the plan year; the period selected must be applied uniformly for every eligible employee under the plan.[3]

A matching contribution is (1) any employer contribution, including a discretionary contribution, to a defined contribution plan on account of an employee contribution to a plan maintained by the employer, (2) any employer contribution, including a discretionary contribution, to a defined contribution plan on account of an elective deferral (Q 3760),[4] and (3) any forfeiture allocated on the basis of employee contributions, matching contributions, or elective contributions.[5]

For purposes of the ACP test, employee contributions generally are contributions that are designated or treated at the time of contribution as after-tax employee contributions, and are allocated to an individual account for each eligible employee.[6]

Matching contributions are taken into account for a plan year only if such contributions are (1) allocated to the employee's account under the terms of the plan as of a date within the plan year, (2) made on behalf of an employee on account of the employee's contributions (elective or otherwise) for the plan year, and (3) actually paid to the trust no later than the end of the twelve month period immediately following the close of the plan year.[7]

Matching contributions that do not satisfy these requirements may not be considered in applying the ACP test for any plan year, but instead must meet the general test for the nondiscriminatory amount requirement (Q 3847) by treating them as if they were nonelective contributions and were the only nonelective employer contributions for the year.[8]

An eligible employee generally is any employee who is directly or indirectly eligible to make a contribution or to receive a matching contribution (including those derived from forfeitures) for all or a portion of the plan year. Employees who would be eligible to make contributions were it not for a suspension or an election not to participate also are considered eligible.[9]

Under a special rule for early participation, a plan that separately satisfies the minimum coverage rules (Q 3841), taking into account only those employees who have not completed one year of service or are under age 21, may ignore, for purposes of the ACP test, eligible nonhighly

---

1.   Treas. Reg. §1.401(m)-2(a)(3)(i).
2.   IRC Secs. 401(m)(3), 401(k)(3)(E).
3.   Treas. Reg. §1.401(m)-5.
4.   As defined in Treas. Reg. §1.402(g)-1(b).
5.   IRC Sec. 401(m)(4)(A); Treas. Reg. §1.401(m)-1(a)(2).
6.   See Treas. Reg. §1.401(m)-1(a)(3) for details.
7.   Treas. Reg. §1.401(m)-2(a)(4)(iii).
8.   Treas. Reg. §1.401(m)-2(a)(5).
9.   See IRC Sec. 401(m)(5); Treas. Reg. §1.401(m)-5.

compensated employees who have not met the age and service requirements in applying the ACP test.[1] This provision is designed to encourage employers to include younger employees in the plan without the concern that they will "pull down" the ACP test results.

Although a plan must, by its terms, provide that the ACP test will be met, it may incorporate by reference the IRC Section 401(m) nondiscrimination provisions.[2]

3807. What happens if a 401(k) plan fails its nondiscrimination testing?

A plan's continued tax qualification is conditioned on its meeting the operational requirements of IRC Section 401(c). For a 401(k) plan, that includes passage of annual ADP and ACP testing. When that testing fails, a plan is required either to make certain additional contributions for the nonhighly compensated employees (Q 3809) or certain distributions to the highly compensated employees (Q 3808).[3] Thus, a failure to make these corrections for a failed test is an operational failure that could lead to a loss of the plan's tax qualification.

When a 401(k) plan fails the ADP testing and elects to distribute certain deferrals to highly compensated employees, those deferrals are referred to as excess contributions.

When a plan's matching contributions fail the ACP testing and the plan elects to distribute certain matching contributions to highly compensated employees, those matching contributions are referred to as excess aggregate contributions (Q 3810). The complexity of the ADP and ACP tests, as well as that of the rules that follow, have led many employers to implement design-based plans that are deemed to satisfy these tests (Q 3772, Q 3777).[4]

3808. What are the rules that apply when a 401(k) plan fails its nondiscrimination testing and elects to distribute excess contributions in order to correct the failure?

An otherwise qualified 401(k) plan with a failed ADP test will not be disqualified if, before the end of the following plan year, any excess contributions are distributed along with any allocable income. Additional contributions ("QNECs") may be made to the plan by the employer to the accounts of the nonhighly compensated employees sufficient to pass ADP testing.[5] Another seldom-used option permits recharacterization of these deferrals by treating them as if they had been distributed to the employee and then contributed by the employee to the plan on an after-tax basis. These after-tax employee contributions then are included in the ACP testing. Excess contributions may not remain unallocated in the plan or held in a suspense account for allocation in future years.[6]

---

1. IRC Sec. 401(m)(5)(C); Treas. Reg. §1.401(m)-3(j)(3).
2. Treas. Reg. §1.401(m)-1(c)(2).
3. See Rev. Proc. 2013-12 Appendices A (section 3) and B (section 2), as modified by Rev. Proc. 2015-28, 2015-16 IRB 920 and Rev. Proc. 2016-51, 2016-42 IRB 465.
4. See Treas. Reg. §§1.401(k)-1(g), 1.401(m)-1(d).
5. Treas. Reg. §54.4979-1(c)(4); Rev. Proc. 2013-12 Appendices A (section 3), as modified by Rev. Proc. 2015-28, 2015-16 IRB 920 and Rev. Proc. 2016-51, 2016-42 IRB 465.
6. IRC Sec. 401(k)(8); Treas. Reg. §1.401(k)-2(b)(1).

Excess contributions are to be distributed (or otherwise corrected) within 2½ months after the end of the plan year to avoid the employer being subject to a 10 percent excise tax on the amount distributed.[1] A plan that contains an automatic enrollment (even if not an "eligible automatic contribution arrangement") is subject to an extended time period for distributing refunds of excess contributions of six months rather than 2½ months.[2]

An excess contribution may consist of elective salary deferrals, Roth employee contributions, QNECs and QMACs, and certain employer contributions, all of which are included in ADP testing.[3] A plan will specify whether an ordering of the distributions is required (Q 3737). Salary deferrals and Roth contributions that exceed $19,500 in 2020-2021 are referred to as "excess deferrals" (Q 3760) and should not be confused with excess contributions. Special rules apply for coordinating distributions of excess contributions and excess deferrals.[4]

Excess contributions and income thereon distributed to an employee are treated as earned and received by the employee in the year in which the distributions are made.[5]

Where the plan specifies, or where the employer elects to make corrective distributions of excess contributions and the distribution is not made within 2½ months after the close of the plan year (or six months if the plan has an automatic enrollment feature), two requirements are triggered. The employer pays a penalty of 10 percent of the excess distribution,[6] and a statutory twelve month period applies. If the distribution occurs more than twelve months after the close of the plan year, the plan has an operational failure that must be corrected under EPCRS to avoid the plan's disqualification.[7]

Corrective distributions of excess contributions may be made without regard to the spousal consent rules (Q 3881).[8] Corrective distributions may not be considered for purposes of satisfying the minimum distribution requirements (Q 3890 to Q 3908).[9]

3809. What is a QNEC and how can a 401(k) plan that has failed its non-discrimination testing use QNECs to correct the failure?

A plan may provide for an employer to make fully vested contributions for certain nonhighly compensated employees. These contributions then are included as deferrals in the ADP testing and, if sufficiently significant, can cause the plan to satisfy the ADP testing.

Recharacterization. Excess contributions of highly compensated employees may be recharacterized as after-tax employee contributions only to the extent that the recharacterized amount, together with the amount of any actual after-tax contributions, satisfies the ACP testing.[10] This

---

1.   IRC Sec. 4979; Treas. Reg. §§1.401(k)-2(b)(5), 54.4979-1.
2.   Treas. Reg. §1.401(k)-2(b)(5)(iii).
3.   IRC Sec. 401(k)(8)(B). See Treas. Reg. §§1.401(k)-6, 1.401(k)-2(b)(2)(iii).
4.   See Treas. Reg. §1.401(k)-2(b)(4)(i).
5.   IRC Sec. 4979(f)(2).
6.   Treas. Reg. §§1.401(k)-2(b)(5), 54.4979-1(a)(4).
7.   Treas. Reg. §1.401(k)-2(b)(5).
8.   Treas. Reg. §1.401(k)-2(b)(2)(vii)(A).
9.   Treas. Reg. §1.401(k)-2(b)(2)(vii)(C).
10. Treas. Reg. §1.401(k)-2(b)(3)(i).

amount is treated the same as a match in that testing.[1] Note that these recharacterization rules are different than the recharacterization of Roth IRA conversions eliminated under the 2017 tax reform legislation.

Recharacterized excess contributions must be included in an employee's gross income on the earliest date any elective contributions made on behalf of the employee during the plan year would have been received. The payor or plan administrator must report such amounts as employee contributions to the IRS and the employee.[2] These recharacterized contributions continue to be treated as employer contributions that are elective contributions for all other purposes under the IRC (for example, they remain subject to the nonforfeitability and withdrawal requirements applicable to elective contributions).[3]

On July 20, 2018, the IRS published final regulations that modify the definitions of QNEC to allow employers to use forfeitures in order to pass nondiscrimination testing that applies to qualified plans. Under the proposal, QNECs need to be nonforfeitable and subject to certain distribution restrictions when they are allocated to participants' accounts, rather than when they are first contributed to the plan. This amendment generally broadens the definition of contributions that qualify as QNECs and permits plan sponsors that allow the use of forfeiture accounts to offset future employer contributions under the plan. Therefore, the final regulations would require that QNECs be fully vested only when they are allocated to the participant's account. The changes apply to taxable years ending on or after July 20, 2018.[4]

3810. What are excess aggregate contributions and how can a 401(k) plan that has failed its nondiscrimination testing use them to correct the failure?

Excess aggregate contributions are the excess of the aggregate amount of employee contributions and employer matching contributions (including any QNECs or elective deferrals treated as matching contributions) made on behalf of highly compensated employees over the maximum amount permitted under the ACP test (Q 3803).[5] Distributions or forfeitures of excess aggregate contributions must be made to highly compensated employees under a process identified in regulations.[6]

A plan will not be disqualified for a failed ACP test for any plan year if, within the twelve month period following the close of that plan year, the excess aggregate contributions (including any income thereon) are distributed (or forfeited) by the plan.[7]

Any corrective distribution of less than the entire amount of the excess aggregate contributions is treated as a pro rata distribution of excess aggregate contributions and income.[8] No early

---

1.   Treas. Reg. §1.401(k)-2(b)(3)(ii).
2.   See Treas. Reg. §1.401(k)-2(b)(3)(ii).
3.   See Treas. Reg. §1.401(k)-2(b)(3)(iii)(C).
4.   T.D. 9835.
5.   IRC Sec. 401(m)(6)(B); Treas. Reg. §1.401(m)-5.
6.   IRC Sec. 401(m)(6)(C). For an example of this allocation, see Treas. Reg. §1.401(m)-2(b)(3)(ii). See also Rev. Proc. 2013-12, Appendix B.
7.   IRC Sec. 401(m)(6); Treas. Reg. §1.401(m)-2(b)(1).
8.   Treas. Reg. §1.401(m)-2(b)(3)(iv).

(premature) distribution penalty tax is imposed on the distribution.[1] Corrective distributions may be made without regard to the spousal consent rules (Q 3881).[2] Furthermore, corrective distributions may not be considered for purposes of satisfying the required minimum distribution rules (Q 3890 to Q 3908).[3]

If the total amount of excess aggregate contributions (and income) is not distributed within the twelve month period following the close of the plan year, the plan will be treated as having an operational failure and will need to be corrected under EPCRS to retain its tax qualification.[4]

A penalty will be imposed on the employer unless the excess is distributed within 2½ months after the end of the plan year. The employer will be subject to a 10 percent excise tax.[5] For plan years beginning after 2007, a plan that satisfies the definition of any automatic contribution feature (Q 3762) is permitted an extended time period for distributing refunds of excess contributions. The extension for making the correction is from 2½ months to six months.[6]

Distributions of excess aggregate contributions (and income) are treated as received by the recipient in the taxable year of the employee ending with or within the plan year for which the original contribution was made. If the total excess amount, including any excess contributions to a 401(k) plan as discussed above, that is distributed to the recipient under the plan for the plan year is less than $100, it is includable in the taxable year distributed.[7] Amounts distributed more than 2½ months after the plan year are includable in gross income for the taxable year of the employee in which distributed.[8]

Instead of distributing excess aggregate contributions, an employer may, to the extent permitted by the terms of the plan, correct the excess by making additional QNECs that, when combined (Q 3803) with employee contributions and matching contributions, satisfy the ACP test. Excess aggregate contributions may not be corrected by forfeiting vested matching contributions, by recharacterization, by failing to make matching contributions required under the plan, by refusing to allocate the excess aggregate contributions, or by holding contributions in a suspense account for allocation in future years.[9]

In the case of a plan that includes a cash or deferred arrangement, the determination of excess aggregate contributions is made after determining excess deferrals (Q 3760) and excess contributions to the cash or deferred arrangement (Q 3801).[10]

---

1.   Treas. Reg. §1.401(m)-2(b)(2)(vi).
2.   Treas. Reg. §1.401(m)-2(b)(3)(i).
3.   Treas. Reg. §1.401(m)-2(b)(3)(iii).
4.   Treas. Reg. §1.401(m)-2(b)(4)(ii).
5.   IRC Sec. 4979; Treas. Reg. §1.401(m)-2(b)(4)(i).
6.   IRC Secs. 401(k)(13), 401(m)(12), 414(w), Treas. Reg. §1.401(m)-2(b)(4)(iii).
7.   Treas. Reg. §1.401(m)-2(b)(2)(vi)(B).
8.   Treas. Reg. §1.401(m)-2(b)(2)(vi)(A).
9.   Treas. Reg. §1.401(m)-2(b)(1)(iii).
10.   IRC Sec. 401(m)(6)(D).

Fully Insured Plans (412(i))

3811. What is a fully insured, or 412(i) plan?

A "fully insured" defined benefit pension plan was originally subject to IRC Section 412(i). These are defined benefit plans that are entirely funded by life insurance and annuity contracts. After the passage of the Pension Protection Act of 2006, the term 412(i) became a misnomer because that legislation restructured the IRC and these plans are now governed by IRC Sections 404(o) and 412(e)(3). No substantive changes were made to the law.[1]

These plans have found favor in the advisor community because they offer the ability to deduct contributions similar to other defined benefit pension plans but are not subject to the funding that requires certification by an actuary each year with the filing of a Schedule B. This exemption requires that the status and operation of the plan follow very strict rules; if violated, these rules require the plan to operate as a traditional defined benefit pension plan including the filing of Schedule B. When a Schedule B is required to be filed and is not, the Form 5500 that was filed becomes delinquent, triggering a possible $1,000 a day fine.[2]

A fully insured plan is also subject to all of the qualification requirements that apply to any other defined benefit plan, although it should be noted that the funding arrangement is not a qualification requirement. The general qualification requirements are explained at Q 3837 to Q 3934 and plan-specific qualification requirements are explained at Q 3715 to Q 3716, Q 3733 and Q 3736.

The IRS has issued extensive guidance designed to target three potentially abusive issues: (1) the valuation of life contracts held by and distributed out of such plans, (2) discrimination in the types of contracts provided to highly compensated employees, versus the rank and file, and (3) the ability of employers to purchase and deduct premiums paid for amounts of life insurance the IRS views as excessive. For details on the application of these standards in the fully insured (Section 412(i)) or 412(e)(3) plan context, see Q 3812.[3]

Planning Point: Certain abusive 412(i) plans are treated as a listed transaction that, if not properly reported on the employer's (and employee's) tax filing, can result in violation with flat penalties of $100,000 to $200,000 for each non filing.[4] The IRC currently provides for no relief on this penalty. Thus, any individual with a 412(i) plan should confirm annually with the provider of the plan whether the plan is operating as a plan that is treated as a listed transaction.

3812. What requirements must a fully insured plan (a "412(i) plan") meet to be exempt from the minimum funding requirements?

A fully insured plan, known as a "Section 412(i) plan" or a "412(e)(3) plan" and governed by IRC Section 412(e)(3), is a defined benefit plan that is funded entirely by a combination of life insurance and annuity contracts. This plan can avoid the funding requirements and certain

---

1.   See Pub. L. 109-280, Sec. 111.
2.   29 U.S.C. §1132(c)(2).
3.   See TD 9223, 70 Fed. Reg. 50967 (Aug. 29, 2005); Rev. Proc. 2005-25, 2005-17 IRB 962; Rev. Rul. 2004-20, 2004-10 IRB 546; Rev. Rul. 2004-21, 2004-10 IRB 544.
4.   IRC Sec. 6707A(b)(2)(A).

reporting requirements of other defined benefit plans or plans when certain requirements are met initially and annually:

(1)   The plan must be funded exclusively with individual insurance or annuity contracts (or a combination of both);

(2)   The contracts must provide for payment of level annual or more frequent premiums over a period ending no later than the normal retirement age of each participant, or the date when the participant ceases participation in the plan, if earlier, and beginning on the date (or the first payment date occurring thereafter) when the individual became a participant, or the time an increase in benefits became effective;

(3)   The benefits provided each individual under the terms of the plan must equal the benefits provided under each contract at normal retirement age and must be guaranteed by an insurance carrier to the extent premiums have been paid;

(4)   All premiums must have been paid before the policy due date. In the case of a lapse of policy for late payment, the reinstatement of the policy must occur during the plan year of the lapse and before benefits commence to any participant whose benefits are impacted by the lapse;

(5)   No rights under the contract may have been subject to a security interest at any time during the plan year; and

(6)   There are no policy loans on the insurance (including loans to individual participants) at any time.[1]

A plan funded exclusively with group contracts, which has the same characteristics as described above, also will be exempt.[2] A plan may be funded by a combination of individual contracts and a group contract, if the combination, in the aggregate, satisfies the requirements.[3]

Regulations finalized in 2005 require that life insurance contracts distributed from any qualified plan be valued at their fair market value (Q 610).[4] Abuse in this area has been subject to a rigorous audit program by the IRS.

As any other qualified plan, a fully insured plan is subject to IRC requirements prohibiting discrimination against nonhighly compensated employees. This requirement applies to contributions and benefits (Q 3847), as well as the availability of any other benefits, rights and features (Q 3859). Plans providing uniform benefits and meeting the safe harbor requirements will satisfy the "nondiscriminatory in amount" requirement of IRC Section 401(a)(4) (Q 3847).[5] The IRS has stated that a plan that provides highly compensated employees the right to purchase life insurance

1.   IRC Sec. 412(e)(3).
2.   IRC Sec. 412(e)(3); Treas. Reg. §1.412(i)-1(c).
3.   Treas. Reg. §1.412(i)-1(d).
4.   2005-2 C.B. 591, T.D. 9223.
5.   Treas. Reg. §1.401(a)(4)-3(b)(5).

contracts from the plan at cash surrender value, but does not provide that right (or rights of equal value) to nonhighly compensated employees, violates the nondiscrimination requirement.[1]

The IRS also has ruled that differences in cash value growth terms or different exchange features among life insurance contracts can create an optional form of benefit, or distinctly different rights and features (Q 3859), even if the terms under which the contracts can be purchased from the plan are the same. The IRS noted that one benefit right or feature is of inherently equal or greater value than another benefit, right, or feature (i.e., it is nondiscriminatory) only if, at any time and under any conditions, it is impossible for any employee to receive a smaller amount or a less valuable right under the first benefit, right, or feature than under the second benefit, right, or feature. If this "inherently equal to or greater than" standard is not met, when comparing the benefits, rights and features available to nonhighly versus highly compensated employees, the plan is discriminatory.[2]

Miscellaneous Rules

Premium payments will be considered level even though experience gains and dividends are applied against premiums.[3] The requirement that a plan be funded exclusively by insurance contracts does not prevent an employer from making payments to satisfy minimum vesting requirements with respect to accrued benefits derived from employee contributions. For example, an employer may pay the "load factor" on insurance contracts to meet requirements that an employee be 100 percent vested in the accrued benefit derived from his or her own contributions.[4] Furthermore, if certain conditions are met, a side fund may be used to fund the additional benefits required when a plan is top-heavy (Q 3916, Q 3921).[5]

3813. Are there any limits on the amount of life insurance that a fully insured (412(i)) plan can purchase to fund the plan?

A 412(i) plan must limit the amount of life insurance that can be provided under the plan. A failure to meet this requirement is a qualification failure that could lead to a disqualification; it also may result in the plan becoming a listed transaction.

The IRS has provided guidance illustrating two circumstances under which fully insured (Section 412(i)) plans have purchased excessive amounts of life insurance.[6] In the first example, the participant's benefit payable at normal retirement age was not equal to the amount provided at normal retirement age with respect to the contracts held on behalf of that participant. The IRS ruled that such a plan fails to satisfy the requirements of IRC Section 412(e)(3)(C), as redesignated by PPA 2006. Accordingly, although the plan still can be a qualified defined benefit plan, it must satisfy the other requirements of IRC Section 412, including reasonableness of actuarial assumptions.

1.   See Rev. Rul. 2004-21, 2004-10 IRB 544.
2.   Rev. Rul. 2004-21, 2004-10 IRB 544.
3.   Treas. Reg. §1.412(i)-1(b)(2)(ii).
4.   Treas. Reg. §§1.412(i)-1(b)(2)(i), 1.412(i)-1(c)(2)(i).
5.   See Treas. Reg. §1.416-1, M-17.
6.   See Rev. Rul. 2004-20, 2004-10 IRB 546.

In the second example, the life insurance contracts on the life of a participant provided for death benefits in excess of the death benefit provided to that participant under the plan. In the example, on the employee's death, proceeds in excess of the death benefit payable to the employee's beneficiary were applied to the payment of premiums with respect to other participants.

The IRS ruled that the portion of contributions attributable to excess coverage did not constitute "normal cost" and thus, was not deductible. Similarly, contributions to pay premiums for the disability waiver of premium feature with respect to such excess coverage were not deductible. Instead, such amounts are carried over to later years.

With respect to the excess coverage, the IRS stated that such premiums could be carried over and treated as contributions in later years. They are deductible in years when excess death benefits are used to satisfy the employer's obligation to pay future premiums on other participants. It should be noted that nondeductible contributions are subject to a 10 percent excise tax under IRC Section 4972 (Q 3942).

Transactions that are the same as or substantially similar to the second example (in which excessive death benefit coverage is held) are classified as "listed transactions" if the employer has deducted amounts used to pay premiums on a life insurance contract with a death benefit exceeding the participant's death benefit under the plan by more than $100,000.[1]

3814. Can an existing defined benefit plan be converted into a fully insured (412(i)) plan?

An existing defined benefit plan can be converted to a fully insured plan, and the requirement that payment of level annual premiums commence with the beginning of plan participation will be considered satisfied, if:

(1)   the plan otherwise satisfies the requirements under IRC Sections 412(e)(3), 403(a), and 404(a)(2) for the plan year containing the conversion date;

(2)   all benefits accruing for each participant on and after the conversion date are funded by level annual premium contracts under which payments begin at the time when the increased accrual becomes effective and end not later than the individual's normal retirement age;

(3)   all benefits accrued for each participant prior to the conversion date are guaranteed through insurance or annuity contracts, the purchase price of which equals the minimum amount required by the life insurance company for a contract that guarantees to provide the accrued benefits, including any optional forms of benefit;

(4)   there are meaningful continuing benefit accruals under the plan after the conversion date (i.e., for at least three years); and

---

1.   See Rev. Rul. 2004-20, 2004-10 IRB 546; *Zarrella v. Pac. Life Ins. Co.*, 820 F. Supp. 2d 1371 (S.D. Fla. 2011), *aff'd*, 498 Fed. Appx. 945 (11th Cir. 2012).

(5)   the following are accomplished before the conversion date: (x) the contracts are purchased guaranteeing the benefits, (y) any remaining plan assets are applied to the payment or prepayment of premiums described in (2) above, and (z) any necessary plan amendments are adopted and made effective.[1]

The IRS determined that where a defined benefit plan was terminated and plan assets were used to purchase fully insured annuity contracts for participants, no "meaningful benefit accruals" would occur after the date of the conversion; thus, the plan could not meet the requirements for conversion.[2]

Final nondiscrimination regulations under IRC Section 401(a)(4) include a safe harbor for fully insured insurance contract plans.[3]

Employee Stock Ownership Plans

3815. What is a stock bonus plan?

A stock bonus plan is a profit sharing plan that holds employer securities and generally distributes those securities to participants when benefits are paid.[4] These plans can be funded through contribution of employer securities, cash, or both. Traditionally, the IRS has taken the position that the distribution must be in the form of employer stock (except for the value of a fractional share).[5] The Tax Court has upheld this requirement.[6] A stock bonus plan may provide for payment of benefits in cash if certain conditions are met (Q 3818). For the purpose of allocating contributions and distributing benefits, the plan is subject to the same requirements as a profit sharing plan.

3816. What is an Employee Stock Ownership Plan ("ESOP")?

An Employee Stock Ownership Plan ("ESOP") is a defined contribution plan and can be either a qualified stock bonus plan or a profit sharing or money purchase pension plan, or any combination.[7] The unique feature of this type of plan that distinguishes it from stock bonus plans is that an ESOP is permitted to purchase employer securities through a loan. A similar purchase under any other plan would be a prohibited transaction.[8] The loan can be from the employer or another party, such as a bank. Although an ESOP is designed to invest primarily in employer securities, the trustee of the ESOP must make a determination as to whether the purchase of employer securities for the plan is prudent. In *Fifth Third Bancorp v. Dudenhoeffer*,[9] the Supreme Court held that a trustee is not entitled to a presumption of prudence in making this determination.

---

1.   Rev. Rul. 94-75, 1994-2 CB 59.
2.   TAM 9234004.
3.   Treas. Reg. §1.401(a)(4)-3(b)(5).
4.   Treas. Reg. §1.401-1(a)(2)(iii).
5.   Rev. Rul. 71-256, 1971-1 CB 118.
6.   *Miller v. Comm.*, 76 TC 433 (1981).
7.   IRC Sec. 4975(e)(7).
8.   IRC Sec. 4975(d)(3).
9.   134 S. Ct. 2459 (2014).

The IRC specifies that an ESOP must be designed to invest primarily in "qualifying employer securities."[1] Qualifying employer securities are shares of common stock issued by the employer (or a member of the same controlled group) that are (1) readily tradable on an established securities market or, in case there is no such readily tradable stock and (2) have a combination of voting power and dividend rights at least equal to the class of common stock having the greatest voting power and the class of common stock having the greatest dividend rights.

Noncallable preferred shares also qualify if they are convertible into stock meeting the requirements of (1) or (2), above, (as appropriate) and if the conversion price is reasonable at the time the shares are acquired by the plan.[2] The IRS determined that the common stock of a corporation did not constitute employer securities with respect to employees of a partnership owned by the corporation's subsidiary because a partnership is not a corporate entity. As a result, the employees of the partnership could not participate in the corporation's ESOP.[3]

Certain tax-exempt entities (such as a qualified retirement plan trust) are eligible to be shareholders of S corporations; consequently, S corporations may adopt ESOPs.[4] Rigorous restrictions apply when the employer is an S corporation (Q 3731, Q 3823, Q 3824).

An ESOP is an "eligible individual account plan" (Q 3817) subject to additional, stricter requirements. The significant tax advantages of meeting the stricter requirements for an ESOP are that certain loan transactions, including a loan guarantee, between the plan and the employer are exempt from the prohibited transaction rules against loans between plans and parties-in-interest,[5] certain forfeitures and contributions are excluded from the annual additions limit (Q 3867, Q 3728), and increased deductions by a C corporation employer are permitted on loan repayments (Q 3823).

For loans made prior to August 21, 1996, certain lenders were permitted to exclude from income 50 percent of the interest received on certain loans to an ESOP or sponsoring corporation used to purchase employer securities.[6] This exclusion was repealed, but certain refinancings and loans pursuant to a written contract in effect on June 10, 1996, are treated as having been made prior to the effective date of the repeal.[7]

3817. May plans other than stock bonus and employee stock ownership plans hold investments in employer securities?

Yes, but under limited circumstances and normally only under a profit sharing plan.

If, immediately after the acquisition, the aggregate fair market value of the employer securities and of employer real property held by the plan exceeds 10 percent of the fair market value

---

1.   IRC Sec. 4975(e)(7).
2.   IRC Secs. 4975(e)(8), 409(l).
3.   GCM 39880 (10-8-92).
4.   See IRC Sec. 1361(c)(6); Senate Committee Report for SBJPA '96.
5.   IRC Sec. 4975(d)(3); ERISA Sec. 408(b)(3).
6.   IRC Sec. 133, prior to repeal by SBJPA '96.
7.   SBJPA '96, Sec. 1602(c).

of the plan's assets, then only an "eligible individual account plan" that explicitly provides for the acquisition and holding of "qualifying employer securities" may acquire the employer securities.[1]

An eligible individual account plan is an individual account plan that is a profit sharing, stock bonus, thrift, or savings plan, or an employee stock ownership plan (Q 3816). A money purchase plan (a defined contribution pension plan) that was in existence on September 2, 1974, and that on that date invested primarily in qualifying employer securities, has certain grandfathered rights as to employer securities. Qualifying employer securities are employer stock and certain marketable obligations.[2]

S corporation stock generally may be held by an exempt plan or a tax-exempt organization; thus, S corporations may establish a plan designed to invest primarily in employer securities, including an ESOP (Q 3816, Q 3818, Q 3824).[3] These plans also may be installed by other small closely held corporations, as well as by corporations with shares that are publicly traded. The transfer of stock to such a plan by the employer is exempt from the prohibited transaction restrictions if the transfer is for an adequate value and no commission is charged.[4]

An investment in employer securities must satisfy ERISA's fiduciary standards, which require that an investment in employer stock be prudent. An individual account plan (whether profit sharing, stock bonus, thrift, or savings, and whether qualified or not) designed to invest in more than 10 percent of qualifying employer securities is exempt from the requirement that a plan trustee diversify the trust's investments.[5]

Investments in employer securities by qualified plans must satisfy IRS requirements that the plan be for the exclusive benefit of employees or their beneficiaries.[6] The Conference Committee Report on ERISA indicates that to the extent a fiduciary meets the prudent investment rules of ERISA, it will be deemed to meet the exclusive benefit requirements of Revenue Ruling 69-494.[7]

To qualify, a plan must meet the applicable requirements set forth in Q 3726, Q 3751, and Q 3837. Notice that Q 3726 explains that profit sharing plans are not required to pass through voting rights. If a plan is not qualified, it is subject to the rules in Q 3532 to Q 3539.

3818. What special qualification requirements apply to stock bonus plans and employee stock ownership plans?

In addition to meeting all of the requirements of IRC Section 401(a), stock bonus plans and employee stock ownership plans ("ESOPs") (Q 3819) must meet certain additional requirements as to employer stock that is held by the plan. There are requirements concerning distribution of employer securities, diversification, and certain pass-through voting requirements.[8]

---

1.   ERISA Secs. 407(a)(2), 407(b).
2.   ERISA Secs. 407(a)(2), 407(b)(1), 407(d)(5).
3.   IRC Sec. 1361(b)(1)(B).
4.   IRC Sec. 4975(d)(3).
5.   ERISA Sec. 404(a)(2).
6.   Rev. Rul. 69-494, 1969-2 CB 88.
7.   1969-2 CB 88.
8.   IRC Secs. 401(a)(23), 4975(e)(7).

Furthermore, an ESOP that holds stock in an S corporation must provide that no "prohibited allocation" will take place with respect to any portion of the assets of the plan attributable to such securities.[1]

Where employer securities are not readily traded on a public market, any transactions involving stock require an independent valuation of the stock for that transaction.

A stock bonus plan or ESOP generally is required to give participants the right to demand benefits in the form of employer securities. If employer securities are not readily tradable on an established market, the participant must have the right to require the employer (not the plan) to repurchase employer securities under a fair valuation formula (a "put option").[2]

The requirement that participants have the right to demand benefits in the form of employer securities does not apply to the portion of a participant's ESOP account that has been reinvested under applicable diversification rules (Q 3732, Q 3819).[3] The requirement also does not apply in the case of an employer whose charter or bylaws restrict the ownership of substantially all outstanding employer securities to employees, to a qualified plan trust, or to an S corporation (Q 3825).[4] Anti-cutback relief generally is available for ESOPs that are amended to eliminate the right of participants to demand benefits in the form of employer securities (Q 3875).[5]

The put option must be available for at least 60 days following distribution of the stock and, if not exercised within that time, for another 60 day period (at a minimum) in the following year.[6]

Planning Point: Regulations have not yet been issued governing when the second option period should begin. One realistic approach is for the second 60 day period to begin after the next plan year's appraisal has been obtained by the plan trustee. *Martin Silfen, J.D., Brown Brothers Harriman Trust Co., LLC.*

The plan may repurchase the stock instead of the employer, but the plan cannot be required to do so. Banks prohibited by law from redeeming or purchasing their own shares are excused from the requirement that they give participants a put option.[7]

If, pursuant to a put option, an employer is required to repurchase securities distributed to an employee as part of a "total distribution," the amount paid for the securities must be paid in substantially equal periodic payments (at least annually), over a period beginning within 30 days after the exercise of the put option, and not exceeding five years. Adequate security must be provided, and a reasonable interest paid on unpaid amounts. A total distribution is a distribution to the recipient within one taxable year of the balance to the credit in his or her account.[8] If an employer is required to repurchase securities distributed to an employee as part

---

1.   IRC Secs. 409(p), 4975(e)(7).
2.   IRC Sec. 409(h).
3.   IRC Sec. 409(h)(7).
4.   IRC Sec. 409(h)(2)(B).
5.   Treas. Reg. §1.411(d)-4, A-2(d)(2)(ii), A-11.
6.   IRC Sec. 409(h)(4).
7.   IRC Sec. 409(h)(3).
8.   IRC Sec. 409(h)(5).

of an "installment distribution," the amount paid for the securities must be paid within 30 days after the put option is exercised.[1]

Distributions are subject to mandatory 20 percent withholding, unless the employee elects a direct rollover.[2] The mandatory withholding requirement does not apply to any distribution that consists only of securities of the employer corporation and cash of up to $200 in lieu of stock. The maximum amount to be withheld under the mandatory withholding rules may not exceed the sum of the amount of money received and the fair market value of property other than securities of the employer corporation received in the distribution.[3]

The plan must provide that if a participant with the consent of his or her spouse so elects, the distribution of the account balance will commence within one year after the plan year (1) in which the participant separates from service by reason of attainment of the normal retirement age under the plan, disability, or death, or (2) which is the fifth plan year following the plan year in which the participant otherwise separated from service. Distribution under (2) will not be required if the participant is re-employed by the employer before distributions actually begin.[4] Special rules, explained below, apply to leveraged ESOPs where the loan or loans used to acquire the employer securities remain outstanding.[5]

The plan also must provide that, unless the participant elects otherwise, distribution of the account balance will be in substantially equal periodic payments (at least annually) over a period not longer than the greater of (1) five years, or (2) in the case of a participant with an account balance in excess of $1,165,000 as indexed for 2021 (up from $1,150,000 in 2020 and $1,130,000 in 2019), five years plus one additional year (not to exceed five additional years) for each $230,000 in 2020-2021 (up from $225,000 in 2019), or fraction thereof, by which the employee's account balance exceeds $1,165,000.[6]

If employer securities in an ESOP are acquired with the proceeds of a loan and repayments of principal are deductible under IRC Section 404(a)(9) (Q 3823), the securities are not considered to be part of a participant's account balance for purposes of these rules until the close of the plan year in which the loan is fully repaid.[7]

Planning Point: An employer whose stock is not publicly traded, and therefore is subject to the employer's potential obligation to repurchase its stock from terminating plan participants, should be concerned about the impact that obligation could have on its cash flow. The employer should consider writing its plan to take the maximum time allowed, generally five years, to begin the process of distributing stock from the plan and then repurchasing that stock from former employees. *Martin Silfen, J.D., Brown Brothers Harriman Trust Co., LLC.*

---

1. IRC Sec. 409(h)(6).
2. IRC Sec. 3405(c).
3. IRC Sec. 3405(e)(8).
4. IRC Sec. 409(o)(1)(A).
5. See IRC Sec. 409(o)(1)(B).
6. IRC Sec. 409(o)(1)(C); Notice 2017-64, Notice 2018-83, Notice 2019-59, Notice 2020-79.
7. IRC Sec. 409(o)(1)(B).

Notwithstanding these requirements, if the general rules for commencement of distributions from qualified plans (Q 3890) require distributions to begin at an earlier date, those general rules control.[1]

A stock bonus plan or ESOP must pass through certain voting rights to participants or beneficiaries. If an employer's securities are "registration-type," each participant or beneficiary generally must be entitled to direct the plan as to how securities allocated to him are to be voted.[2] "Registration-type" securities are securities that must be registered under Section 12 of the Securities and Exchange Act of 1934 or that would be required to be registered except for an exemption in that law.[3]

If securities are not "registration-type" and more than 10 percent of a plan's assets are invested in securities of the employer, each participant (or beneficiary) must be permitted to direct voting rights under securities allocated to his or her account with respect to approval of corporate mergers, consolidations, recapitalizations, reclassifications, liquidations, dissolutions, sales of substantially all of the business' assets, and similar transactions as provided in future regulations.[4]

A plan meets this requirement in the case of nonregistration-type securities if each participant is given one vote with respect to an issue and the trustee votes the shares held by the plan in a proportion that takes this vote into account.[5] The IRS has ruled that an ESOP will not fail to comply in operation with these pass-through voting requirements merely because the trustee of the ESOP votes the shares of stock allocated to participants' accounts for which no voting directions are timely received, whether the securities are registration type or nonregistration-type.[6]

3819. What special qualification requirements apply to employee stock ownership plans ("ESOPs")?

Stock bonus plans and employee stock ownership plans ("ESOPs") must meet the requirements set forth in Q 3818; S corporation ESOPs must meet the special requirements described in Q 3824. ESOPs also must meet the requirements discussed below.

Qualified Sales

Provisions of the plan must ensure that, in the case of certain "qualified sales" of employer securities by a participant or executor to the ESOP, no portion of the assets of the plan (or any other qualified plan of the employer) attributable to the securities purchased by the plan may accrue or be allocated for the benefit of any of the following persons:

(1)　　a taxpayer who has elected to have the gain on the sale and replacement of employer securities deferred under the qualified sales rules of IRC Section 1042 (Q 3731);

1.　　See General Explanation of TRA '86, p. 840.
2.　　IRC Secs. 401(a)(28), 4975(e)(7), 409(e)(2).
3.　　15 U.S.C. Sec. 12(g)(2)(H).
4.　　IRC Sec. 409(e)(3).
5.　　IRC Secs. 401(a)(22), 409(e)(3), 409(e)(5).
6.　　Rev. Rul. 95-57, 1995-2 CB 62.

(2)   any individual who is a member of the family (brothers, sisters, spouse, ancestors, lineal descendants) or is related under the other rules of IRC Section 267(b) to the taxpayer described in (1);

(3)   any person not described in (1) or (2) who owns, or is considered as owning under the attribution rules of IRC Section 318(a), more than 25 percent (by number or value) of any class of outstanding stock of the employer or of any corporation which is a member of the same controlled group of corporations as is the employer (Q 3932).[1] For purposes of determining whether this limitation applies, an individual is treated as owning any securities he owned during the one-year period ending on the date of the sale to the plan, or as of the date the securities are allocated to participants in the plan.[2]

No employer securities acquired by the plan in any transaction to which IRC Section 1042 applied can be allocated to such persons. Thus, an employee who sold his employer securities to an ESOP and elected nonrecognition under IRC Section 1042 could not receive allocations based on other employer securities acquired by the plan in a different IRC Section 1042 transaction.[3]

Nonallocation Period

After the later of the date that is 10 years after the date of the sale of securities or the date of the plan allocation attributable to the final payment on indebtedness incurred in connection with the sale, a plan may permit accruals or allocations for individuals described in (1) or (2), above, but not individuals described in (3). This 10 year period is referred to as the "nonallocation period."[4] This time period should not be confused with the "nonallocation year" (Q 3824).

A special rule provides that the prohibition under (2) does not apply to a lineal descendant of the taxpayer if the aggregate amount allocated for the benefit of all lineal descendants of the taxpayer during the nonallocation period is not more than 5 percent of the employer securities (or amounts allocated in lieu thereof) held by the plan which are attributable to a qualified sale by a member of any of the descendants' families (brothers, sisters, spouse, ancestors, lineal descendants).[5]

If a plan fails to meet these requirements, not only is the plan likely to be disqualified, but a penalty tax equal to 50 percent of the amount of any prohibited accrual or allocation will generally be levied against the plan. Also, the amount of any prohibited accrual or allocation will be treated as if distributed to the individual involved and taxed as such.[6]

---

1.   IRC Secs. 409(n)(1)(B).
2.   IRC Sec. 409(n)(3)(B).
3.   Let. Rul. 9041071.
4.   IRC Secs. 409(n)(1)(A), 409(n)(3)(C).
5.   IRC Sec. 409(n)(3)(A).
6.   IRC Secs. 409(n)(2), 4979A.

Regulations

An ESOP must meet requirements set forth in applicable regulations.[1] The regulations require that an exempt loan be primarily for the benefit of participants and their beneficiaries. The proceeds of an exempt loan may not be used to buy life insurance; otherwise, the general rules applicable to the purchase of life insurance by qualified plans apply (Q 3829). The plan or employer may have a right of first refusal if the stock is not publicly traded.

Stock that is acquired after September 30, 1976, with the proceeds of an exempt loan and that is not publicly traded or that is subject to a trading restriction must be subject to a put option exercisable only by a plan participant or by the participant's donees or successors. The option must permit a participant to "put" the security to the employer but must not bind the plan. Nonetheless, the plan may have the right to assume the employer's obligation when the put option is exercised. An ESOP may not otherwise obligate itself to a put option or to acquire securities from a particular security holder on the happening of an event such as the death of the holder (e.g., a buy-sell agreement). Regulations provide rules for the current distribution of income. ESOPs generally may not be integrated with Social Security.[2]

3820. What requirements regarding diversification of investments apply to Employee Stock Ownership Plans ("ESOPs")?

An ESOP generally must provide for diversification of investments by permitting a plan participant (including one who has already separated from service with the employer) who has completed 10 years of participation in the plan and attained age 55 to elect to direct the investment (allowing at least three investment options) of a portion of his account balance. (This requirement does not apply to plans subject to the diversification requirement explained at Q 3732.)[3]

Planning Point: The IRS has issued relief from the anticutback rules of Section 411(d)(6) for a plan sponsor who amends a nonexempt ESOP to eliminate a distribution option that had previously satisfied the diversification requirements of Section 401(a)(28)(B) if the amendment occurs no later than the last day of the first plan year beginning on or after January 1, 2013 or by the deadline for the plan to satisfy Section 401(a)(35), if later.[4]

Planning Point: An employer sponsoring an ESOP that does not otherwise offer directed investments complying with these diversification requirements may wish to design the ESOP to offer a distribution election in lieu of a diversification election, rather than make the administration of the plan needlessly complex. *Martin Silfen, J.D., Brown Brothers Harriman Trust Co., LLC.*

In the case of an ESOP that had not existed for 10 years, the IRS permitted a plan participant to count years of participation in a terminated predecessor ESOP to meet the 10 years of participation requirement.[5]

1.　IRC Sec. 4975(e)(7); ERISA Sec. 407(d)(6).
2.　Treas. Reg. §§54.4975-7, 54.4975-11.
3.　IRC Sec. 401(a)(28).
4.　Notice 2013-17, 2013-20 IRB 1082 (Apr. 18, 2013).
5.　Let. Rul. 9213006.

The diversification election must be made within 90 days after the close of each plan year in the six-plan-year period, which begins with the plan year in which the employee becomes eligible to make the election. Generally, at least 25 percent of the account balance attributable to employer securities acquired by or contributed to an ESOP must be subject to the election; but in the last year of the six-plan-year period the 25 percent is increased to 50 percent.[1]

The amount that must be subject to the election at the end of a given year is generally equal to (1) 25 percent (or 50 percent in the last year) of the total number of shares of employer securities acquired by or contributed to the plan that have ever been allocated to the participant's account on or before the most recent plan allocation date, minus (2) the number of shares previously diversified.[2] Employer securities may not be one of the three investment options.[3]

A plan may meet this diversification requirement by distributing the portion of an account for which an election is made.[4] The diversification requirement can also be satisfied by allowing a participant to transfer that portion of an account for which an election is made into a qualified defined contribution plan which provides for employee directed investment and in which the required diversification options are available.[5]

Any form of diversification elected (i.e., the distribution, transfer, or implementation of an investment option) must be completed within 90 days after the close of the election period.[6] An election to diversify may be revoked or amended, or a new election made, at any time during the 90 day election period.[7]

3821. What valuation requirements apply for employer securities held in employee stock ownership plans ("ESOPs")?

With respect to plan activities, all valuations of employer securities that are not readily tradable on an established securities market must be made by an independent appraiser whose name is reported to the IRS. For this purpose, an independent appraiser is an appraiser who meets requirements similar to those imposed under the charitable deduction rules of Section 170(a)(1).[8]

Planning Point: If the company hires an appraiser and decides the appraised value is too high, that information is discoverable in any subsequent legal dispute, such as with the IRS. But if the company's attorney hires the appraiser, the appraisal remains in the files of the law firm and is subject to attorney-work product privilege. This allows the attorney to seek a lower appraisal, without fear that the appraisal for the higher amount will be discoverable and will create support for a finding of undervaluation. *Lawrence Brody, J.D., LL.M, Bryan Cave LLP.*

---

1. IRC Sec. 401(a)(28)(B)(i).
2. Notice 88-56, 1988-1 C.B. 540, A-9.
3. See General Explanation of TRA '86, p. 838.
4. IRC Sec. 401(a)(28)(B)(ii); Notice 88-56, 1988-1 C.B. 540.
5. Notice 88-56, 1988-1 C.B. 540, A-13.
6. IRC Sec. 401(a)(28)(B)(i); Notice 88-56, 1988-1 C.B. 540, A-13.
7. See General Explanation of TRA '86, p. 835.
8. IRC Sec. 401(a)(28)(C). See General Explanation of TRA '86, p. 840. See IRC Sec. 170(f)(11) and Prop. Reg. § 1.170A-17 for appraiser requirements.

3822. What is a Section 1042 election? What rules apply to qualified sales to an ESOP?

A taxpayer or executor who sells qualified securities to an Employee Stock Ownership Plan ("ESOP") (Q 3816) and purchases qualified replacement property may be able to elect to defer recognition of long-term capital gain on the sale.[1] This is referred to as a Section 1042 election. If the election is made, the taxpayer or estate recognizes gain on the sale only to the extent that the amount realized on the sale exceeds the cost of the securities purchased to replace the stock sold to the ESOP.[2]

The election must be made in a written "statement of election" and filed with the taxpayer's return for the year of sale by the due date for that year, including extensions.[3] The statement of election must contain specific information set forth in the regulations.[4] The election cannot be made on an amended return, and, once made, is irrevocable.[5] In the absence of such an election, the Tax Court denied the deferral of gain to a taxpayer whose estate argued that he had "substantially complied" with the election requirements.[6] Similarly, where a taxpayer failed, through his accountant's error, to make a timely election, the IRS strictly construed the statutory deadline.[7]

A taxpayer must file a statement from the employer whose employees are covered by the ESOP consenting to the application of an excise tax[8] if the transferred securities are disposed of prematurely (see below) and a tax[9] on prohibited allocations of securities acquired in the sale.[10] Failure to substantially comply with the statement of election and statement of consent requirements has resulted in denial of nonrecognition treatment.[11]

The qualified replacement property must be purchased during the period that begins three months before the sale of qualified securities and ends twelve months after the sale.[12] If the replacement property has not yet been purchased when the statement of election is required, the taxpayer must file a notarized statement of purchase with his or her income tax return for the tax year following the year for which the election was made. The statement of purchase must contain specific information and must be notarized within 30 days of the purchase.[13] The IRS has found that taxpayers had substantially complied with the election requirement where they had relied on tax professionals concerning the election requirements and immediately acted to correct the noncompliance.[14]

---

1.   See IRC Sec. 1042(a).
2.   IRC Secs. 1042(a), 1042(b)(3).
3.   IRC Sec. 1042(c)(6); Temp. Treas. Reg. §1.1042-1T, A-3(a).
4.   See Temp. Treas. Reg. §1.1042-1T, A-3(b).
5.   Temp. Treas. Reg. §1.1042-1T, A-3(a).
6.   *Estate of J.W. Clause*, 122 TC 115 (2004).
7.   See Let. Rul. 9438016.
8.   Under IRC Sec. 4978.
9.   Under IRC Sec. 4979A.
10.   IRC Sec. 1042(b)(3).
11.   Let. Rul. 9733001.
12.   IRC Sec. 1042(c)(3).
13.   See Temp. Treas. Reg. §1.1042-1T, A-3.
14.   See Let. Ruls. 200234003, 200246027, 200151008, 200019002.

Qualified securities, for purposes of a Section 1042 exchange, means stock (1) in a domestic C corporation (i.e., not an S corporation) that has no stock outstanding that is readily tradable on an established securities market, and (2) that was not (x) acquired from a qualified pension, profit sharing, or stock bonus plan, (y) acquired under an employer stock option plan or an employee stock purchase plan, or (z) transferred to the individual in connection with his or her performance of services to the corporation.[1] In addition, the taxpayer must have held the qualified securities for at least three years before the sale to the ESOP.[2] Nonrecognition does not apply to any gain on the sale of any qualified securities that is includable in the gross income of any C corporation.[3]

Qualified replacement property means securities issued by a domestic operating corporation that (1) did not have more than 25 percent of its gross receipts in certain passive investment income (including, generally, receipts from rents, royalties, dividends, interest, annuities, and sales and exchanges of stock or securities) for the taxable year preceding the tax year in which the security was purchased, and (2) is not the corporation or a member of its controlled group (Q 3932) that issued the qualified securities being replaced.[4]

If a taxpayer does not intend to reinvest the total amount required, under IRC Section 1042, to completely defer the gain on the sale in replacement securities, the installment method may be available for the gain that does not qualify for nonrecognition, provided that the sale otherwise qualifies as an installment sale. The amount of gain is the same proportion of the installment payment actually received in such year that the total gain to be recognized under IRC Section 1042 bears to the total amount realized. The gain is recognized in the taxable year in which the installment payment is made.[5]

A taxpayer's basis in his or her replacement securities is reduced by the amount of gain not recognized. If more than one item is purchased, the unrecognized gain is apportioned among them.[6] If a taxpayer dies while still holding replacement securities, the basis provisions of IRC Section 1014 prevail and the replacement securities receive a stepped-up basis.[7] The holding period of the replacement property includes the holding period of the securities sold.[8]

To qualify for nonrecognition, the sale must meet certain additional requirements. The ESOP generally must own, immediately after the sale, at least 30 percent of each class of outstanding stock of the corporation that issued the qualified securities, or the total value of outstanding employer securities.[9]

1.   IRC Sec. 1042(c)(1).
2.   IRC Sec. 1042(b)(4).
3.   IRC Sec. 1042(c)(7).
4.   IRC Sec. 1042(c)(4)(A).
5.   Let. Ruls. 9102021, 9102017.
6.   IRC Sec. 1042(d).
7.   Let. Rul. 9109024.
8.   IRC Sec. 1223(11).
9.   IRC Sec. 1042(b)(2).

The IRS has determined that where a note acquired by a company's owners from an ESOP in exchange for stock was a cash equivalent for tax purposes, the stock in a separate corporation acquired in exchange for the note constituted qualified replacement property.[1]

If a taxpayer disposes of any qualified replacement property, he or she generally will recognize gain (if any) to the extent that it was not recognized when the replacement property was acquired.[2] If a taxpayer owns stock representing control of a corporation that issued the replacement property, he or she will be treated as having disposed of his or her qualified replacement property if that corporation disposes of a substantial portion of its assets other than in the ordinary course of its trade or business.

The recapture rules do not apply if the transfer of the qualified replacement property is:

(1)   in a reorganization (if certain requirements are met);

(2)   by reason of the death of the person making the original election;

(3)   by gift (even if a charitable deduction is obtained);[3] or

(4)   in a subsequent transfer that is eligible for an election not to recognize gain under the rules discussed above.[4]

A transfer to a revocable trust by a taxpayer will not trigger recapture where the grantor (i.e., the taxpayer) will continue to be treated as the owner of the property transferred to the grantor trust.[5]

The IRS also has determined that the distribution of qualified replacement property by a trust to its beneficiary was not a disposition for purposes of IRC Section 1042(e); thus, the recapture rules did not apply.[6]

Although the transfer of qualified replacement property to a charitable remainder unitrust technically was a "disposition," it did not result in recapture of the deferred gain, because the donors did not realize gain on the transaction.[7]

Subsequent Dispositions by the ESOP

If, within three years, an ESOP disposes of stock acquired in a sale in which the seller was permitted to defer the recognition of income (as discussed above) and, as a result, the number of the ESOP's shares falls below the number of employer securities held immediately after the sale, or the value is less than 30 percent of the total value of all employer securities, the disposition will be subject to a tax equal to 10 percent of the amount realized on the disposition, unless

---

1.   Let. Rul. 9321067.
2.   IRC Sec. 1042(e).
3.   See TAM 9515002.
4.   IRC Sec. 1042(e)(3).
5.   Let. Ruls. 9141046, 9130027.
6.   Let. Rul. 9226027.
7.   Let. Rul. 9234023. See also Let. Ruls. 9438012 and 9438021.

the disposition is a distribution made by reason of (1) the death or disability of an employee, (2) retirement of the employee after age 59½, or (3) separation of the employee from service for any period that results in a one year break in service.[1]

3823. How much may an employer deduct for its contributions to an ESOP?

The deduction rules that apply to profit sharing, stock bonus, and money purchase pension plans (Q 3750) generally apply to Employee Stock Ownership Plans ("ESOPs") (Q 3816) with a few exceptions that expand how much can be deducted. A C corporation with an ESOP is permitted to deduct additional amounts without regard to the deduction limits for profit sharing, stock bonus, and pension plans to the extent such additional amounts do not exceed the IRC Section 415 limits. The rules that follow generally are not available to ESOPs maintained by an S corporation.[2]

An employer's ESOP contributions that are used to repay the principal of a loan incurred to acquire employer securities are deductible up to 25 percent of the compensation paid to covered employees. This deduction limit is measured based on compensation paid in the employer's tax year for which the deduction is taken. To be deductible, the contribution must have been both paid to the trust and applied by the trust to the repayment of the principal by the due date (including extensions) of the tax return for that year. For contributions exceeding 25 percent of compensation, a contribution carryover is permitted in succeeding years in which the 25 percent limit is not fully used (but contributions to a defined contribution plan in excess of the IRC Section 415 limits may not be carried over).[3]

In addition, contributions applied by the plan to the repayment of interest on a loan used to acquire employer securities may be deducted without limit in the tax year for which it is contributed if the contribution is paid by the due date (including extensions) for filing the tax return for that year.[4]

Pass Through Dividends

An employer sponsoring an ESOP also may deduct the amount of any dividend paid on stock held by the ESOP on the record date when the dividend is:

(1)   paid in cash to the plan participants or their beneficiaries;

(2)   paid to the plan and distributed in cash to the participants or their beneficiaries within 90 days after the close of the plan year;

(3)   at the election of the participants or their beneficiaries (x) payable as provided in (1) or (2), or (y) paid to the plan and reinvested in qualifying employer securities (in which case the amounts must be fully vested);[5] or

---

1.   IRC Sec. 4978.
2.   IRC Secs. 404(a)(9)(C), 404(k)(1).
3.   Notice 83-10, 1983-1 C.B. 536, F-1, as modified by Notice 99-44; 1999-2 C.B. 326. See IRC Sec. 404(a)(9)(A).
4.   IRC Sec. 404(a)(9)(B).
5.   See IRC Sec. 404(k)(7).

(4)   used to make payments on an ESOP loan used to acquire the employer securities with respect to which the dividend is paid.[1]

Dividend payments described in IRC Section 404(k)(2) are not treated as distributions subject to withholding.[2]

Planning Point: Dividends on Section 404(k) stock are not subject to the lower income tax rates enacted in 2003 for other types of dividend payments.[3]

The IRS has issued guidance on numerous issues related to the election that employers can offer participants or their beneficiaries, as described in (3) above.[4]

The deduction for dividends that a participant elects to reinvest in qualifying employer securities, as described in (3) above, is allowable for the taxable year in which the reinvestment occurs or the election is made, whichever is later.[5]

The IRS may disallow the deduction for a dividend under IRC Section 404(k)(1) if the dividend constitutes, in substance, an avoidance or evasion of taxation.[6]

The authority of the IRS to recharacterize excessive dividends paid on ESOP stock as employer contributions was upheld by the Court of Appeals for the Eighth Circuit in a ruling that resulted in disqualification of the ESOP for its resulting failure to meet the IRC Section 415 limits.[7]

3824. What requirements apply when an S corporation maintains an ESOP?

The IRC permits certain qualified retirement plan trusts to be shareholders of S corporations; thus, an S corporation can adopt an ESOP.[8] When a tax-exempt entity (e.g., an ESOP) holds an ownership interest in an S corporation, the distributions from the S corporation received by the tax-exempt entity are not subject to income tax. This unique tax benefit is available to S corporation ESOPs only when certain requirements are met.

First, the IRC restricts the type of entities that can own an interest in an S corporation.

Second, the IRC places certain restrictions on the operation of the ESOP. These operational rules apply to the allocation of S corporation stock within the ESOP to certain individuals, and limit certain tax benefits otherwise available to ESOP sponsors. Those limits apply to the deductions for employer contributions to the plan and for dividends paid on employer securities, and do not permit the rollover of gain on the sale of stock to an ESOP (Q 3731, Q 3823).

---

1.   IRC Sec. 404(k)(2)(A). See also Let. Ruls. 9840048, 9523034, 9439019.
2.   IRC Sec. 3405(e)(1)(B)(iv).
3.   See IRC Sec. 1(h)(11)(B)(ii)(III).
4.   See Notice 2002-2, 2002-1 CB 285.
5.   IRC Sec. 404(k)(4)(B).
6.   IRC Sec. 404(k)(5)(A); see also Let. Rul. 9304003.
7.   *Steel Balls, Inc. v. Comm.* 89 F.3d 841, 96-1 USTC ¶50,309 (8th Cir. 1996), *aff'g* TC Memo 1995-266. See also *Hollen v. Comm.*, TC Memo 2011-2 (2011), *aff'd*, 437 Fed. Appx. 525 (8th Cir. 2011), *cert. denied*, 132 S. Ct. 2443 (2012).
8.   See IRC Sec. 1361(c)(6); Senate Committee Report for SBJPA '96.

Planning Point: Because there is a possibility for abuse of this benefit, the IRS has targeted S corporation ESOPs for special attention.[1]

The IRS has stated that an ESOP may direct certain rollovers of distributions of S corporation stock to an IRA, in accordance with a distributee's election, without terminating the corporation's S election, provided certain requirements are met. The effect of these requirements is that either the S corporation or the ESOP repurchases the S corporation stock immediately upon the distribution to the IRA and that no income, loss, deduction, or credit attributable to the distributed S corporation is allocated to the IRA.[2]

An S corporation that maintains an ESOP also generally is exempt from the requirement that employees be able to demand distribution of employer securities.[3] To do otherwise could violate the IRC limit on the number of shareholders in an S corporation (Q 3818). An ESOP maintained by an S corporation will not be treated as receiving unrelated business income on items of income or loss of the S corporation in which it holds an interest.[4]

Prohibited Allocations of Stock

An ESOP that holds securities consisting of stock in an S corporation also must provide that no portion of the assets of the plan attributable to such securities will accrue or be allocated, directly or indirectly, to a "disqualified person" during a "nonallocation year."[5] Such an allocation is referred to as a prohibited allocation.

A disqualified person is any person for whom:

(1)   the number of the person's deemed-owned ESOP shares is at least 10 percent of the number of deemed-owned ESOP shares of the S corporation;

(2)   the aggregate number of the person's deemed-owned ESOP shares and synthetic equity shares is at least 10 percent of the aggregate number of deemed-owned ESOP shares and synthetic equity shares of the S corporation;[6]

(3)   the aggregate number of deemed-owned ESOP shares of the person and his or her family is at least 20 percent of the number of deemed-owned ESOP shares of stock in the S corporation; or

(4)   the aggregate number of deemed-owned ESOP shares and synthetic equity shares of the person and his or her family is at least 20 percent of the aggregate number of deemed-owned ESOP shares and synthetic equity shares of the S corporation.[7]

---

1.   Rev. Rul. 2004-4, 2004-1 C.B. 414.
2.   See Rev. Proc. 2004-14, 2004-7 IRB 489.
3.   See IRC Sec. 409(h)(2)(B).
4.   IRC Sec. 512(e)(3).
5.   IRC Secs. 409(p), 4975(f)(7); Treas. Reg. §1.409(p)-1(b)(1).
6.   *Ries Enters., Inc. v. Comm.*, TC Memo 2014-14, aff'd, No. 14-2094 (8th Cir. 2014).
7.   Treas. Reg. §1.409(p)-1(d)(1); see IRC Secs. 409(p)(4)(A), 409(p)(4)(B).

Family member means the individual's spouse, an ancestor or lineal descendant of the individual or spouse, a sibling of the individual or spouse, and lineal descendants of any siblings, as well as spouses of the aforementioned individuals (except in the case of a legal separation or divorce).[1]

Deemed-owned shares with respect to any person are the stock in the S corporation constituting employer securities of an ESOP that is allocated to such person's account under the plan, and the person's share (based on the same proportions as of the most recent allocation) of the stock in the corporation that is held by the ESOP but that is not allocated under the plan to participants.[2]

A nonallocation year means any plan year of the ESOP if, at any time during the year, the ESOP holds any employer securities that are shares in an S corporation and disqualified persons own at least 50 percent of the number of outstanding shares in the S corporation (including deemed owned shares) or the aggregate number of outstanding shares of stock (including deemed owned shares) and synthetic equity in the S corporation.[3] For purposes of determining whether there is a nonallocation year, the attribution rules of IRC Section 318(a) apply in determining stock ownership (except that the broader "family member" rules above apply), the IRC Section 318(a) rules regarding options do not apply, and an individual is treated as owning "deemed-owned" shares.[4]

In the event that a prohibited allocation is made in a nonallocation year to a disqualified person, the plan will be treated as having distributed the amount of the allocation to the disqualified person on the date of the allocation.[5] In other words, the allocation is a taxable distribution to the individual.[6] Furthermore, an excise tax of 50 percent of the amount involved is imposed on the allocation, and a 50 percent excise tax is imposed on any synthetic equity owned by a disqualified person.[7] The 50 percent excise taxes are imposed against the employer sponsoring the plan.[8]

Planning Point: The IRS has released "snapshot" guidance to help S corporations avoid a non-allocation year for employee stock ownership plan (ESOP) purposes. Pursuant to the snapshot, which is not precedential but can be helpful in understanding the IRS' position on an issue, ESOPs may incorporate a "transfer method" into the plan document, pursuant to which the plan can transfer employee stock from a participant's ESOP account if that participant is a disqualified person into a non-ESOP account of that same person. Alternative methods are also available, including excluding allocations for participants who may potentially be disqualified persons or increasing allocations to certain employees who are not highly compensated. These methods must also comply with all other qualification rules. Importantly, to use the transfer method, the method must be included in the ESOP plan document prior to the occurrence of a nonallocation year.[9]

---

1.   IRC Sec. 409(p)(4)(D); Treas. Reg. §1.409(p)-1(d)(2).
2.   IRC Sec. 409(p)(4)(C), Treas. Reg. §1.409(p)-1(e).
3.   IRC Sec. 409(p)(3)(A); Treas. Reg. §1.409(p)-1(c)(1).
4.   IRC Sec. 409(p)(3)(B); Treas. Reg. §1.409(p)-1(c)(2).
5.   IRC Sec. 409(p)(2)(A).
6.   For details on the application of this rule, see Treas. Reg. §1.409(p)-1(b).
7.   IRC Sec. 4979A(a).
8.   IRC Sec. 4979A(c).
9.   The snapshot guidance can be accessed at: https://www.irs.gov/retirement-plans/issue-snapshot-preventing-the-occurrence-of-a-nonallocation-year-under-section-409p

Synthetic equity includes any stock option, warrant, restricted stock, deferred issuance stock right, stock appreciation right payable in stock, or similar interest or right that gives the holder the right to acquire or receive stock of the S corporation in the future. Synthetic equity also includes a right to a future payment (payable in cash or any other form other than stock of the S corporation) that is based on the value of the stock of the S corporation or appreciation in such value, or a phantom stock unit.[1]

Synthetic equity also includes any remuneration under certain nonqualified deferred compensation arrangements for services rendered to the S corporation or a related entity.[2] The stock upon which synthetic equity is based will be treated as outstanding stock of the S corporation and deemed-owned shares of the person owning the synthetic equity, if such treatment results in the treatment of any person as a disqualified person or the treatment of any year as a nonallocation year.[3]

Final regulations explaining the prohibited allocation rules of the IRC apply to plan years beginning on or after January 1, 2016.[4] For plan years beginning before January 1, 2016, temporary regulations explain the prohibited allocation rules.[5]

3825. What special requirements apply to plans covering shareholder-employees of S corporations?

With respect to qualification, plans of an S corporation (whether defined benefit or defined contribution) generally must meet the same requirements applicable to other corporate plans (Q 3837). The special rules that apply to S corporation ESOPs are explained at Q 3824.

Probably the only significant difference from other entities is in the way that the owner's compensation is treated for plan purposes. Only wages paid to an S corporation employee-shareholder generally may be included in compensation for purposes of determining contributions, nondiscrimination testing, and classification of key or highly compensated employees. That is, S corporation distributions are not included. In contrast, the K-1 income paid to a member in an LLC taxed as a partnership or a partner in a partnership is treated as contributions for plan purposes. Certain abusive S corporation ESOPs will not be treated as qualified plans, will be subject to prohibited transaction penalties (Q 3979), and are among the "listed transactions" treated as corporate tax shelters (subject to additional penalties).[6]

Keogh Plans

3826. What special qualification rules apply to Keogh plans?

A Keogh plan, which at one time was called an HR-10 plan, is a qualified plan that covers self-employed individuals such as partners in a partnership or sole proprietors. Since the

---

1.   IRC Sec. 409(p)(6)(C); Treas. Reg. §1.409(p)-1(f)(2).
2.   See Temp. Treas. Reg. §1.409(p)-1T(f)(2)(iv); TD 9082, 2003-2 C.B. 420.
3.   IRC Sec. 409(p)(5).
4.   For details see Treas. Reg. §1.409(p)-1(i)(2).
5.   See Temp. Reg. §1.409(p)-1T(i)(2).
6.   See Rev. Rul. 2003-6, 2003-3 IRB 286.

enactment of the Economic Growth and Tax Relief Reconciliation Act of 2001, the qualified plan rules have not distinguished between plans sponsored by a corporation and plans sponsored by other types of entities so the terms "Keogh" and "HR-10" are not used frequently. The only difference is in determining the earned income of self-employed individuals and common law employees. As a general rule, a qualified trust must be established by an employer for the exclusive benefit of the employer's employees or their beneficiaries.[1] Self-employed individuals (sole proprietors, partners in a partnership, or members in an LLC taxed as a partnership) are not common law employees (Q 3927). For the purpose of allowing such individuals to participate in qualified plans and to enjoy the tax advantages available to other participants in such plans, the law confers employee status on these individuals. The IRC says that for purposes of IRC Section 401, the term "employee" includes for any taxable year an individual who has "earned income."[2]

The term earned income means, in general, net earnings from self-employment in a trade or business in which personal services of the individual are a material income-producing factor.[3] Thus, a partner who has contributed capital to the firm but renders no personal services for it has no "earned income" from the firm and cannot participate in a qualified plan of the partnership.[4]

In arriving at the net earnings that are used to determine a self-employed individual's own contribution, business expenses, including contributions to the plan on behalf of regular employees, are deducted. The definition of earned income of a self-employed person (which is reported on Schedule K-1 for a partner) does not include a deduction for the contributions to the plan on behalf of the self-employed individual. The self-employed individual reports contributions on a Form 1040 individual income tax return.[5] A partner's earned income is the share of partnership net income, including any draw or "salary" the partner receives (other than separately stated items, such as rental income, capital gains and losses, most dividends, and most interest).[6]

All of the requirements for qualified retirement plans covering common law employees apply equally to plans that cover self-employed individuals. A plan covering only a sole proprietor, or a sole proprietor and his or her spouse, or partners in partnerships (and their spouses) generally is exempt from ERISA requirements.[7]

3827. How is the amount of a self-employed individual's contribution to a Keogh plan calculated?

The calculation of the contribution for the self-employed individual involves two unique calculations that do not apply to common law employees: the calculation of the deduction for self-employment taxes, and the contribution calculation.

The individual's earned income from a business is used to calculate the self-employment taxes that are due on the earned income. These taxes are similar to FICA taxes. A self-employed

1.   IRC Sec. 401(a)(2).
2.   IRC Sec. 401(c)(1).
3.   IRC Sec. 401(c)(2).
4.   Treas. Reg. §1.401-10(c)(3).
5.   IRC Secs. 401(c)(2)(A)(v), 404(a)(8)(C).
6.   IRC Secs. 401(c)(2), 1402(a).
7.   ERISA Reg. §2510.3-3(b).

individual may deduct one-half of his or her self-employment taxes[1] in computing adjusted gross income but not in computing the earned income subject to self-employment tax.

This reduces the amount of earned income available to calculate the self-employed individual's own contribution. The net amount is referred to as net earnings from self-employment.

Contributions on behalf of a self-employed individual are based on his or her "net earnings from self-employment reduced by the contribution itself. That is, the earned income that is used to determine the individual's contributions is reduced by the contribution made to the plan on the individual's own behalf. Thus, for example, a common law employee would need only $232,000 of compensation to support a deductible contribution of $58,000 to a defined contribution plan in 2021 ($232,000 × 25% = $58,000) (Q 3750). A self-employed individual would need net earnings from self-employment of $290,000 ($232,000 plus $58,000) or more in 2021 to receive a contribution of the same amount.[2] This produces an effective maximum contribution percentage of 20 percent for self-employed individuals.

Matching contributions that are in effect made by the partner, other than QMACs (Q 3859), are not treated as elective deferrals for purposes of the limit on such deferrals under IRC Section 402(g) (Q 3760, Q 3801).[3] Rather, they are treated as employer contributions for all plan purposes.

3828. What rules govern the deduction for contributions by a self-employed individual to a Keogh plan?

The deduction for any employee being paid on a W-2 basis is the same whether to a plan of a corporation or to a Keogh plan. The calculation of deductible contributions for a self-employed individual to a Keogh plan works in a backward way. "Compensation" for all purposes of meeting the IRC's qualification requirements, as applied to a self-employed individual, is based on earned income after a deduction for one-half self-employment taxes and the self-employed individual's own contribution. Each self-employed individual will require a separate contribution calculation. The contribution is not reported as an employer contribution on the partnership's tax return or a sole proprietor's Schedule C. Each self-employed individual's contribution to a profit sharing plan can be determined without respect to what the other participants are doing or what the plan requires. This means that it is not possible to know what the self-employed individual's compensation is for meeting the various IRC limits until after the individual's contribution is determined. Thus, although a W-2 employee may receive up to 25 percent of compensation as a contribution, the self-employed individual has a 20 percent gross earned income limit. The 20 percent of gross earned income results in a 25 percent of net earned income calculation.[4]

In determining his or her adjusted gross income, a self-employed person deducts his or her plan contributions directly from gross income; the deduction is allowable whether or not the person itemizes deductions. A self-employed individual deducts the portion of the contribution

---

1.   IRC Sec. 162(f).
2.   IRC Sec. 401(d); IR-2016-141, Notice 2018-83, Notice 2019-59.
3.   IRC Sec. 402(g)(8).
4.   IRC Sec. 404(a)(8)(D).

made by the business on his or her behalf on his or her own individual return; the contributions are not treated as expenses of the business.[1]

Contributions on behalf of a self-employed individual may not be used to create or increase a net operating loss.[2]

Employer contributions allocable to the purchase of life, accident, health, or other insurance on behalf of self-employed persons are not deductible. The cost of such coverage (Q 3947) is subtracted from the full contribution to determine the amount deductible.[3]

If life insurance protection is provided under a plan, the amount to be subtracted is the Table 2001 (or P.S. 58) cost (Q 3947) plus the cost of any contract extras, such as a waiver of premium. This produces a result for self-employed individuals similar to the result for employees – the value of the life insurance protection and contract extras is taxable. If amounts attributable to deductible employee contributions are used to purchase life insurance, the amount to be subtracted is the amount so used.

Insurance Benefits

3829. To what extent can a qualified plan provide life or health insurance benefits for its participants?

According to Treasury regulations, life and health insurance benefits must be merely "incidental" to the primary purpose of a plan. A pension plan exists primarily to provide retirement benefits but it "may also provide for the payment of incidental death benefits through insurance or otherwise."[4] A profit sharing plan is "primarily a plan of deferred compensation, but the amounts allocated to the account of a participant may be used to provide for the participant or family incidental life or accident or health insurance."[5]

The IRS has ruled that a profit sharing plan containing a medical reimbursement account does not satisfy the qualification requirements where distributions from the medical reimbursement account are available only for reimbursement of substantiated medical expenses of the participant, spouse, or dependents. The IRS noted that the plan would violate the nonforfeitability requirement of IRC Section 401(a)(7) and may violate other qualification requirements. The fact that only 25 percent of the plan contributions were used to fund the medical reimbursement account did not change this result.[6]

In 2004 guidance, the IRS specifically described as "excessive" life insurance coverage on a participant that provided for death benefits in excess of the death benefit provided to the participant under the plan (Q 3812).[7] The IRS added that transactions that are the same as,

---

1.   IRC Sec. 62(a)(6); Temp. Treas. Reg. §1.62-1T; Treas. Reg. 1.404(e)-1A(f).
2.   IRC Sec. 172(d)(4)(D).
3.   IRC Sec. 404(e); Treas. Reg. §1.404(e)-1A(g).
4.   Treas. Reg. §1.401-1(b)(1)(i).
5.   Treas. Reg. §1.401-1(b)(1)(ii).
6.   See Rev. Rul. 2005-55, 2005-33 IRB 284.
7.   See Rev. Rul. 2004-20, 2004-10 IRB 546.

or substantially similar, to the example are classified as "listed transactions" if the employer has deducted amounts used to pay premiums on a life insurance contract with a death benefit exceeding the participant's death benefit under the plan by more than $100,000.[1]

Applicability of Limitation

A profit sharing plan may provide for distribution of funds accumulated under a plan after a fixed number of years (no fewer than two), the attainment of a stated age, or on the prior occurrence of some event such as layoff, illness, disability, retirement, death, or severance of employment.[2] The IRS also has ruled that a plan could permit participants with at least five years of participation to withdraw all employer contributions, including those made during the last two years.[3]

If life or health insurance may be purchased only with funds that have been accumulated for the period required by the plan for the deferment of distributions, there is no limit on the amount of such funds that can be used to purchase life or health insurance. The "incidental" limitation applies if the plan permits the use of funds that have not been so accumulated to purchase such insurance.[4]

The incidental limitation does not apply to life or health insurance bought with nondeductible voluntary employee contributions.[5] Furthermore, the IRS determined that where the demutualization of a company that had been placed in rehabilitation resulted in traditional whole life contracts being restructured into flexible adjustable life contracts, the restructuring would not result, in and of itself, in a violation of the incidental death benefit requirements.[6]

Aside from the foregoing exceptions, the incidental limitation applies to insurance when it is purchased by a qualified plan on the life of a participant and benefits are payable to or for the participant, the participant's estate, or the participant's named beneficiary. The limitation also applies to contracts purchased under a qualified annuity plan.[7]

It would seem a reasonable inference from this regulation that the incidental rule would not be applied to the purchase of insurance bought by a profit sharing plan on the life of a key individual to indemnify the plan for the premature loss by death of the insured.

3830. What tests are used to determine whether life or health insurance benefits provided by a qualified plan to participants are "incidental"?

The basic approach taken by the IRS in determining whether life insurance benefits in a pension plan, or life or health insurance benefits in a profit sharing plan, are incidental begins by determining what proportion the cost of providing such benefits bears to the cost of providing

---

1.   See Rev. Rul. 2004-20, 2004-10 IRB 546.
2.   Rev. Rul. 71-295, 1971-2 CB 184.
3.   Rev. Rul. 68-24, 1968-1 CB 150.
4.   Rev. Rul. 61-164, 1961-2 CB 99; Rev. Rul. 66-143, 1966-1 CB 79, clarified by Rev. Rul. 68-31.
5.   Rev. Rul. 69-408, 1969-2 CB 58.
6.   See Let. Rul. 9339024.
7.   Treas. Reg. §1.403(a)-1(d).

all benefits under the plan. If the cost of providing current life and health insurance benefits generally is less than 25 percent of the cost of providing all the benefits under the plan (both deferred and current), the incidental limitation is satisfied.

Despite the fact that an element of savings is involved in universal life coverage, the IRS has taken the position that universal life coverage must be treated under the rules applicable to term coverage and thus is subject to the 25 percent rule.[1] For purposes of the incidental rule, the IRS defines permanent insurance as insurance on which the premium does not increase and the death benefit does not decrease.[2]

The IRS has ruled privately that a variable contract in which the death benefit might decrease as a result of a decline in cash values and the operation of IRC Section 7702 (Q 65), and unscheduled extra premiums were permitted, would be treated as permanent insurance.[3]

The IRS also ruled for an insurer where an adjustable life contract was to be used as a funding vehicle for a defined contribution plan. The IRS stated that it would apply the incidental rule applied in Revenue Ruling 61-164, below. In other words, one-half the premiums paid while the contract was providing lifetime protection plus the whole premium paid while the policy was providing term protection must total less than 25 percent of the total plan contributions to date.[4]

In the case of a plan that provides life insurance benefits, the 25 percent rule is applied to the portion of the premium used to provide current life insurance protection (the cost of the "amount at risk"). In the case of a profit sharing plan that provides health insurance benefits, the 25 percent rule is applied to the entire cost of providing current health insurance protection for participants and their families. Rulings discussed and cited below illustrate the application of the 25 percent requirement in various circumstances.

Profit Sharing Plans—The 50 Percent Test

A profit sharing plan that provides that less than one-half the amount allocated annually to each participant's account will be used to purchase ordinary life insurance on his or her life meets the 25 percent requirement (assuming the plan provides no other current benefits purchased with nondeferred funds). The reason is that by IRS reckoning, on the average, during an employee's working years, about one-half of each annual premium on ordinary life contracts bought by the plan on his or her life is required to pay the cost of current life insurance protection.

In a profit sharing plan funded by a combination of ordinary life policies and a side fund, the aggregate premiums that have been paid (with nonaccumulated funds) for insurance on a participant's life must be at all times less than 50 percent of the aggregate employer contributions and forfeitures (without regard to trust earnings and capital gains and losses) that have been allocated to the participant. The plan also must require the trustee, at or before each employee's

1.   FSA 1999-633.
2.   Ira Cohen, Director, Employee Plans Technical and Actuarial Division, Internal Revenue Service, in response to a question asked at the 29th Annual Meeting of the AALU, 3-4-86.
3.   See Let. Rul. 9014068.
4.   Let. Rul. 8725088.

retirement, either to convert the employee's policies into cash to provide income (without life insurance protection that continues past the employee's retirement) or to distribute the policies to the employee.[1]

Thus, where at all times cash values under a whole life insurance policy equaled or exceeded the minimum cash values under an ordinary whole life insurance policy and less than 50 percent of the total contributions allocated to the participant were applied to premiums, the IRS determined that the death benefits were incidental.[2]

If the 25 percent requirement is met with respect to insurance purchased by a plan, the plan may pay as a death benefit both the face amount of the insurance and the amount accumulated in the side fund allocated to the participant.[3] There appears to be no reason a profit sharing plan could not provide for the purchase of term insurance (individual or group) rather than ordinary life, so long as aggregate premiums paid for insurance on each participant are less than 25 percent of aggregate employer contributions and forfeitures allocated to him. The IRS has applied the 25 percent limitation in the manner just described to an ordinary life contract to which was added a 10 year decreasing term rider in a ratio of one-to-one (i.e., $1,000 initial face amount of term for each $1,000 face amount of ordinary life).[4]

The IRS also has applied the 25 percent limitation as described to a policy combining 70 percent participating whole life and 30 percent one year term insurance under which dividends are used to purchase paid-up additions; as the additions total increases, the amount of term insurance is reduced, so that a level death benefit is provided.[5]

If a profit sharing plan provides for the purchase of both ordinary life and health insurance for participants from funds that have not been accumulated for the period required by the plan for deferment of distributions, the amount expended on health insurance premiums plus one-half the amount expended on ordinary life premiums must not exceed 25 percent of such accumulated funds. For example, assume the account of an employee has been allocated $1,000, no part of which has been accumulated for the requisite period. If $300 is expended for the purchase of ordinary life, not more than $100 may be expended on health insurance.[6]

The "100-to-1" Test

In a pension plan of any type, and in a profit sharing plan, on the assumption that there is no other current benefit to be considered, the incidental limitation automatically is satisfied if a death benefit is provided that does not exceed the amount of (1) the death benefit that would be paid if all benefits under the plan were funded by retirement income endowment policies that have a death benefit of $1,000, or (2) the reserve, if greater, for each $10 per month of life

---

1. Rev. Rul. 60-84, 1960-1 CB 159; Rev. Rul. 57-213, 1957-1 CB 157; Rev. Rul. 54-51, 1954-1 CB 147; Letter Ruling, 3-14-66, signed by I. Goodman, Chief, Pension Trust Div. of IRS, Spencer's RPS 241-2.
2. Let. Rul. 201043048.
3. Rev. Rul. 73-501, 1973-2 CB 128.
4. Rev. Rul. 76-353, 1976-2 CB 112.
5. Let. Rul. 8029100.
6. 25% × $1000 (total allocation) = $250. $250 - (50% × $300) (the amount paid for ordinary life insurance premiums) = $100. See Rev. Rul. 61-164, 1961-2 CB 99.

annuity the policy guarantees at retirement age. The reason is that the IRS has determined that the cost of providing such a death benefit will not in any case exceed 25 percent of the cost of providing all benefits under the plan.[1] This so-called 100-to-1 ratio test therefore is merely a "safe harbor" rule; it is not a limitation on the amount of death benefit that may be provided.

Miscellaneous Rulings

Postretirement death benefits in a pension plan are subject to the incidental limitation, presumably in the same way preretirement death benefits are subject to the limitation.[2] These benefits are to be distinguished from post-death payments derived from amounts accumulated under a plan for payment to a retired employee or his or her beneficiaries (e.g., the annuity paid to the survivor under a joint and survivor annuity). These latter type payments are subject to entirely different rules (Q 3908).

A plan providing only such benefits as are afforded through the purchase of ordinary life contracts, which are converted to annuities at retirement, is not a pension plan within the meaning of the regulations and will not qualify.[3] A prototype pension plan providing for funding solely through ordinary life contracts will not qualify even if it requires the adopting employer to maintain a second plan containing provisions such that, when the two plans are considered as one, the death benefit does not exceed 100 times the monthly retirement annuity.[4]

A pension plan that permits a participant to invest a portion of his or her account in life insurance on the life of anyone in whom he or she has an insurable interest will not qualify because it would provide a benefit that is not "definitely determinable" (Q 3736).[5]

3831. To what extent can an employee stock ownership plan (ESOP) provide life or health insurance benefits for its participants?

The rules applicable to purchases of life insurance by qualified plans (Q 3829 and Q 3830) generally apply to employee stock ownership plans (Q 3816).[6] Thus, if assets are invested primarily in qualifying employer securities, life insurance may be purchased on the lives of participants for the benefit of their estates or named beneficiaries within the limits of the 25 percent "incidental" rule described in Q 3830. Proceeds of an exempt loan (Q 3816) may not be used by an employee stock ownership plan to purchase life insurance.[7]

Planning Point: There appears to be no reason, so long as assets are invested primarily in qualifying employer securities, that an employee stock ownership plan may not purchase key person life insurance in the same way profit sharing plans do, and for essentially the same purpose. Also,

1.   Rev. Rul. 60-83, 1960-1 CB 157 (profit sharing plan funded by single premium endowment policies maturing at retirement age); Rev. Rul. 61-121, 1961-2 CB 65 (pension plan death benefits based on employee's anticipated retirement income and the past service credits); Rev. Rul. 68-31, 1968-1 CB 151 (money purchase pension plan funded by retirement income policies); Rev. Rul. 68-453, 1968-2 CB 163 (pension plan funded by ordinary life contracts with face amount equaling 100 times anticipated monthly retirement benefit, plus side fund); Rev. Rul. 74-307, 1974-2 CB 126.
2.   Rev. Rul. 60-59, 1960-1 CB 154.
3.   Rev. Rul. 81-162, 1981-1 CB 169; Rev. Rul. 65-25, 1965-1 CB 173.
4.   Rev. Rul. 71-25, 1971-1 CB 115.
5.   Rev. Rul. 69-523, 1969-2 CB 90.
6.   TD 7506, 1977-2 CB 449.
7.   TD 7506, 1977-2 CB 449 (Major Revision (9)); Treas. Reg. §54.4975-7(b)(4).

should a key person insured be a shareholder, there appears to be no reason death proceeds could not be used to purchase employer stock from his or her estate.

An employee stock ownership plan must not obligate itself to acquire securities from a particular security holder at an indefinite time determined on the happening of an event such as the death of the holder.[1]

3832. To what extent can a money purchase pension plan provide life or health insurance benefits for its participants?

Where life insurance is purchased on the lives of participants in a money purchase pension plan, the 25 percent rule is applied in basically the same way as if the plan were a profit sharing plan (Q 3829 and Q 3830). The incidental limitation applies regardless of whether the plan provides that funds used to purchase insurance must have been accumulated for at least two years.[2]

In a plan funded by a combination of life insurance and a side fund, if the 25 percent requirement is met with respect to the premiums, the plan may provide for a death benefit consisting of both the face amount of the insurance and the amount credited to the participant's account at death.[3]

3833. To what extent can a defined benefit pension plan provide life or health insurance benefits for its participants?

Death benefits under a pension plan of any type will be considered incidental if either (1) less than 50 percent of the employer contribution credited to each participant's account is used to purchase ordinary life insurance even if the total death benefit consists of both the face amount of the insurance and the amount credited to the participant's account at time of death, or (2) such death benefits would be incidental under the "100-to-1" test described in Q 3830.[4]

It is clear, therefore, not only from the foregoing but also from dicta in prior rulings that the 25 percent rule (Q 3830) is intended to apply to life insurance benefits provided in defined benefit pension plans as well as in defined contribution plans. Because in a pension plan "death benefits" must be incidental, it would seem that the 25 percent rule would be applied to the cost of providing the entire death benefit the plan actually pays.

In the case where a plan purchases life insurance on participants' lives and participants have separate accounts, it appears that the 25 percent rule is applied only to the cost of providing current life insurance protection (i.e., the portion of premium paying for the "amount at risk").[5]

1.   Treas. Reg. §54.4975-11(a)(7)(i).
2.   Rev. Rul. 66-143, 1966-1 CB 79, clarified by Rev. Rul. 68-31, 1968-1 CB 151.
3.   Rev. Rul. 74-307, 1974-2 CB 126.
4.   Rev. Rul. 74-307, 1974-2 CB 126.
5.   See also Rev. Rul. 61-164, 1961-2 CB 99; Rev. Rul. 66-143, 1966-1 CB 79, clarified by Rev. Rul. 68-31, 1968-1 C.B. 151; Rev. Rul. 70-611, 1970-2 CB 89, modified by Rev. Rul. 85-15, 1985-1 C.B. 132; Rev. Rul. 76-353, 1976-2 C.B. 112.

3834. When can health insurance benefits be provided under a pension plan?

A pension plan may provide for the payment of a pension due to disability, but it may not provide benefits for sickness, accident, hospitalization, or medical expenses for active plan participants or their beneficiaries.[1] These benefits may be provided for retired employees, their spouses, and their dependents, but only if:

(1)   the benefits are subordinate to the retirement benefits provided by the plan,

(2)   a separate account is established and maintained for the benefits,

(3)   the employer's contributions to the separate account are reasonable and ascertainable,

(4)   no part of the account may be diverted to any other purpose,

(5)   the plan calls for return to the employer of any amounts remaining after satisfaction of all liabilities, and

(6)   in the case of an employee who is a key employee (Q 3930) at any time during the plan year (or any preceding plan year when contributions were made on behalf of such employee), a separate account is established and maintained for the benefits payable to the employee, spouse, and dependents (Q 3835).[2]

Medical benefits generally are considered subordinate to retirement benefits as required under (1) above if, at all times, the aggregate of employer contributions made (after the date on which the plan first includes such medical benefits) to provide such medical benefits and any life insurance protection does not exceed 25 percent of the aggregate pension contributions made after that date (other than contributions to fund past service credits).[3] The IRS has provided guidance on the calculation of this limit, as well as the coordination of benefits between an IRC Section 401(h) account and a VEBA.[4]

See Q 3944 for a discussion of the tax aspects of IRC Section 401(h) contributions and benefits; and see Q 3719 for the effect of IRC Section 401(h) contributions on behalf of key employees on the IRC Section 415 limitation on benefits in a defined benefit plan.

3835. May excess pension assets be transferred to Section 401(h) accounts?

Yes, under certain circumstances.

A "qualified transfer" of "excess pension assets" (see below) from a defined benefit plan to a Section 401(h) account of the same plan will not violate the qualification rules of IRC

---

1.   Treas. Reg. §1.401-1(b)(1)(i).
2.   IRC Sec. 401(h).
3.   IRC Sec. 401(h); Treas. Reg. §1.401-14(c)(1).
4.   See Let. Rul. 9834037.

Section 401(a). This kind of transfer will not be treated as an employer reversion (Q 3978) or as a prohibited transaction (Q 3979).[1]

A "qualified transfer" is one that does not contravene any other provision of law (e.g., a collective bargaining agreement under relevant law) and that meets the use, vesting, and minimum cost requirements described below.[2] The rules permitting qualified transfers to Section 401(h) accounts apply for taxable years beginning before January 1, 2026.[3]

If an employer elects to make a qualified transfer, the amount transferred may not exceed an amount that reasonably is estimated to be the amount the employer maintaining the plan will pay (directly or through reimbursement) out of the Section 401(h) account during the taxable year for qualified current retiree health liabilities.[4] The amount of the qualified transfer may be based on amounts the employer paid during the taxable year before the date of the transfer and prior to the establishment of the Section 401(h) account as long as the account is established prior to the transfer and before the end of such taxable year.[5] In addition, no more than one transfer per plan per taxable year may be treated as a qualified transfer.[6] Section 420 qualified transfers (but not qualified future transfers) are available to multiemployer plans in plan years beginning after 2006.[7]

A qualified transfer must meet the following three requirements:

(1)   Use requirement—Assets transferred to a Section 401(h) account may be used only to pay qualified current retiree health liabilities for the taxable year of the transfer.[8] Qualified current retiree health liabilities do not include amounts provided for health benefits to retired key employees.[9] Amounts not used to pay for health benefits or life insurance must be transferred back to the transferor plan and are not includable in the gross income of the employer for such taxable year, but are treated as an employer reversion and subject to the 20 percent penalty.[10] Any amounts paid out of a health benefits account or an applicable life insurance account are treated as being paid first out of the transferred assets and income allocable to those assets.[11]

(2)   Vesting requirement—The plan generally must provide that the accrued pension benefits of any participant or beneficiary under the plan become nonforfeitable as if the plan had terminated immediately before the qualified transfer (or in the case

1.   IRC Sec. 420(a).
2.   See IRC Sec. 420(b)(1)(C).
3.   IRC Sec. 420(b)(4), as amended by P.L. 114-41, Sec. 2007(a). Note that the sunset of January 1, 2026 was enacted in 2015 and not part of the changes made by the 2017 Tax Act. Any changes to the sunset provisions of the 2017 Tax Act will not automatically affect this sunset.
4.   IRC Sec. 420(b)(3).
5.   See IRS General Information Letter, 5 Pens. Pl. Guide (CCH) ¶17,381I (July 5, 1991).
6.   IRC Sec. 420(b)(2).
7.   See IRC Sec. 420(f)(2)(E).
8.   IRC Sec. 420(c)(1).
9.   IRC Sec. 420(e)(1)(D), (E).
10.   IRC Sec. 420(c)(1)(B).
11.   IRC Sec. 420(c)(1)(C).

of a participant who separated from service during the one year period ending on the date of the transfer, immediately before the separation).[1]

(3)   Minimum cost requirement—Each group health plan or arrangement under which applicable health benefits or life insurance benefits are provided must provide that the applicable employer cost (see below) for each taxable year during the "cost maintenance period" will not be less than the higher of the applicable employer cost for each of the two taxable years immediately preceding the taxable year of the qualified transfer. The "cost maintenance period" means the period of five taxable years beginning with the taxable year in which the qualified transfer occurs. If a taxable year is in two or more overlapping cost maintenance periods, the highest applicable employer cost required during the taxable year will be taken into account for purposes of this rule.[2]

Regulations state that an employer who significantly reduces retiree health coverage during the cost maintenance period will not satisfy the minimum cost requirement.[3] A retiree health coverage reduction is significant if, for any taxable year during the cost maintenance period, either the employer-initiated reduction percentage for the taxable year exceeds 10 percent or the sum of such percentages for that taxable year and all prior taxable years during the cost maintenance period exceeds 20 percent.[4]

The term "excess pension assets" generally means the excess of the lesser of the fair market value of the plan's assets or the value of such assets determined under the minimum funding rules over 125 percent of the current liability of the plan (as determined for purposes of the full funding limitation) (Q 3744).[5]

Applicable employer cost means the amount determined by dividing the qualified current retiree health liabilities of the employer for the taxable year by the number of individuals to whom coverage for applicable health benefits was provided during the taxable year. For this purpose, the amount of qualified current retiree health liabilities is determined without regard to reductions for amounts previously set aside. If there was no qualified transfer during the taxable year, the qualified current retiree health liabilities amount is determined as though there had been such a transfer at the end of the taxable year.[6]

For transfers made after August 17, 2006, an employer maintaining a defined benefit plan other than a multiemployer plan may elect to make a qualified future transfer or qualified collectively bargained transfer in lieu of a qualified transfer. Excess pension assets, for purposes of qualified future transfers, are calculated by substituting 120 percent for 125 percent of plan liability, and the amount of excess pension assets that may be transferred is increased to the sum of the qualified retiree health liabilities for all the taxable years during the transfer period.

1.   IRC Sec. 420(c)(2).
2.   IRC Sec. 420(c)(3).
3.   Treas. Reg. §1.420-1(a).
4.   See Treas. Reg. §1.420-1(b).
5.   IRC Sec. 420(e)(2).
6.   IRC Sec. 420(c)(3)(B).

The transfer period must not be less than two and not more than 10 consecutive taxable years, beginning with the taxable year of the transfer.[1]

An employer generally may not contribute to a Section 401(h) account or a welfare benefit fund with respect to qualified current retiree health liabilities for which transferred assets are required to be used.[2] In addition, the amount that can be transferred in a qualified transfer is reduced if the employer previously has made a contribution to a Section 401(h) account or welfare benefit fund for the same liabilities.[3]

The Moving Ahead for Progress in the 21st Century Act (MAP-21), enacted in 2012, also permits the transfer of excess pension assets for retiree group-term life insurance benefits (up to $50,000 per participant).[4]

In addition, ERISA requires that notice of any qualified transfer be given to plan participants, the DOL, and the IRS at least 60 days before the date of the qualified transfer;[5] the DOL and Treasury have agreed that one notice filed with the DOL within the requisite period will satisfy the requirement to file with the IRS.[6] Penalties of up to $110 a day may be imposed on any plan administrator or employer for failure to provide the required notice.[7]

Qualification

Overview

3836. What are the advantages of a qualified pension, annuity, profit sharing, or stock bonus plan?

The term "qualified plan" refers to an employer sponsored retirement plan meeting the requirements of IRC Section 401. Section 401 not only provides for an extensive list of requirements incorporating additional IRC sections, but it also conveys uniquely favorable tax treatment to employers and covered employees and their beneficiaries as long as those requirements continue to be met. This section (Q 3836 to Q 3935) explains the basic qualification requirements that apply to all qualified plans. The additional plan-specific qualification requirements that apply only to certain types of plans are explained beginning at Q 3714.

Assuming the qualification requirements set forth in the IRC are met, the following tax advantages are available for qualified plans:

(1)   An employer can take a current business expense deduction (within limits) for its contributions to the plan even though employees are not currently taxed on these contributions (Q 3936 to Q 3941);

---

1.   See IRC Secs. 420(f)(2)(B); 420(f)(5).
2.   IRC Sec. 420(d)(2).
3.   See IRC Sec. 420(e)(1)(B); see also, IRS General Information Letter, 5 Pens. Pl. Guide (CCH) ¶17,381I (July 5, 1991).
4.   Public Law 112-141, §40242; IRC Secs. 420(e)(1)(D), 420(e)(4)
5.   ERISA Sec. 101(e).
6.   Ann. 92-54, 1992-13 IRB 35.
7.   ERISA Sec. 502(c).

(2)   An employee pays no tax until benefits are distributed regardless of whether he or she has a forfeitable or non-forfeitable right to the contributions made on his or her behalf unless the plan offers a designated Roth account option and the employee makes contributions to that account (Q 3944);

(3)   Distributions meeting certain requirements may be eligible for rollover or special tax treatment (Q 3967 to Q 3971);

(4)   Annuity and installment payments are taxable only as received (Q 3967 to Q 3968, Q 3974);

(5)   The fund within the plan earns and compounds income on a tax deferred basis (Q 3977); and

(6)   Certain small employers (i.e., employers with fewer than 100 employees earning compensation over $5,000 per year) may be able to claim a business tax credit equal to 50 percent of qualified start-up costs of up to $500 per year for three years of an eligible employer plan.[1]

In addition, ERISA provides creditor protection to accounts, even in the case of bankruptcy, though levies and fines may be chargeable against a participant's account.[2]

For owners of pass-through entities, the deduction for contributions to qualified plans passed through from the entity may assist in reducing taxable income below the $329,800 (joint returns)/$164,900 (other taxpayers) thresholds for 2021 to qualify for the qualified business income (QBI) deduction under section 199A.[3] If an owner's taxable income exceeds those limits, the QBI deduction may be subject to additional limits. For the owner of a specified service trade or business,[4] no QBI deduction is available if the owner's taxable income exceeds the annual threshold level for the year, plus $50,000 for single filers or $100,000 for joint returns.

Self-employed persons (i.e., sole proprietors and partners) (Q 3931) may participate in qualified plans as "employees." There are special rules applicable to self-employed individuals (Q 3825 to Q 3828).

3837. What requirements must be met for a plan to be qualified?

A retirement plan is tax qualified when the plan document complies with the requirements under IRC Section 401(a). The document must be updated periodically to meet this section's changing requirements, and the plan must be operated in compliance with the IRC and the document. A plan that fails to meet these requirements, either in its document or operation, has a document failure or an operational failure, respectively. A plan that does not correct either failure could be disqualified by the IRS. An IRS disqualification strips the plan of its tax benefits.

---

1.   For details, see IRC Sec. 45E.
2.   ERISA Sec. 206(d).
3.   IRC Sec. 199A, Rev. Proc. 2020-45.
4.   See IRC Sec. 199(d)(2), Rev. Proc. 2020-45.

Most document or operational failures can be corrected through one of the IRS' voluntary correction programs under the Employee Plans Compliance Resolution System ("EPCRS").[1]

To meet the basic qualification requirements of IRC Section 401(a), a plan must:

(1) Be established in the United States by an employer for the exclusive benefit of employees or their beneficiaries (Q 3838).

(2) Prohibit the use of plan assets for purposes other than the exclusive benefit of the employees or their beneficiaries until such time as all liabilities to employees and their beneficiaries have been satisfied (Q 3838).

(3) Meet minimum age and service standards (Q 3840), and minimum coverage requirements (Q 3841).

(4) Provide for contributions or benefits that are not discriminatory (Q 3847 to Q 3862 in general, and Q 3801 to Q 3803 with respect to 401(k) plans).

(5) Provide for contributions or benefits that do not exceed the IRC Section 415 limitations (Q 3867, Q 3719, and Q 3728).

(6) Meet minimum vesting standards (Q 3868 to Q 3875).

(7) Provide for distributions that satisfy both the commencement rules and the minimum distribution requirements (Q 3890 to Q 3909).

(8) Provide for automatic survivor benefits under certain circumstances (Q 3880 to Q 3889).

(9) Contain provisions that meet the requirements for "top-heavy" plans and provide that these provisions will become effective should the plan become top-heavy (Q 3915 to Q 3921).

(10) Prohibit the assignment or alienation of benefits (Q 3911 to Q 3914).

(11) Meet the miscellaneous requirements described in Q 3926.

(12) Meet the plan-specific requirements that are based on the type of plan (e.g., profit sharing) (Q 3714 to Q 3826).

(13) Provide that if the distributee of an eligible rollover distribution elects to have the distribution as permitted under IRC Section 401(a)(31)(A) paid as a direct rollover, the distribution will be made in the form of a direct rollover.

---

1. For details, see Rev. Proc. 2013-12, 2013-4 IRB 313, as modified by Rev. Proc. 2015-27, 2015-16 IRB 914, Rev. Proc. 2015-28, 2015-16 IRB 920 and Rev. Proc. 2016-51, 2016-42 IRB 465.

(14) Provide that if the plan uses the forced distribution provision of IRC Section 401(a)(31)(B) for distributions of vested benefits that do not exceed $5,000, the plan also must notify the distributee in writing of the rollover (Q 4000).[1]

(15) Provide to each recipient of a plan distribution a written explanation of his or her right to elect a direct rollover and the withholding consequences of not making the election prior to making the distribution (Q 3997).[2]

(16) Be established through a written plan document that is communicated to employees prior to the first day of the plan year for which it is to be effective. This document must satisfy the requirements of 401(b). In most cases, plan sponsors rely on either a determination letter or other IRS approval to confirm that the form of the document is in compliance. Prototype and volume submitter documents have a form or preapproval by the IRS.[3]

(17) If the plan holds assets in a custodial account, that account must be with a bank or other entity that demonstrates to the satisfaction of the IRS that assets will be properly held.

(18) If the plan covers employees who are covered under a collectively bargained plan, the requirements of IRC Section 413 must be met.

(19) If the plan covers self-employed individuals, it must meet the requirements discussed under Q 3825, Q 3826, and Q 3931.

Although a document must fully satisfy the provisions of 401(a) on the date of adoption, changing legislation and Treasury regulations may require amendments prior to the close of a specific plan year. Almost every plan needs some required plan amendments every year. The IRS regularly releases a list of required amendments for qualified retirement plans.[4]

Failure to timely amend a plan to meet newly enacted or modified qualification requirements can result in revocation of a plan's qualified status,[5] even if the plan has been terminated.[6] Nonetheless, a terminated plan must meet the IRC's qualification rules until such time as all the assets are distributed in satisfaction of its liabilities.

3838. What is the exclusive benefit rule of plan qualification?

A plan must be established in the United States by an employer for the exclusive benefit of employees or their beneficiaries.[7]

---

1. IRC Sec. 401(a)(31)(B).
2. IRC Sec. 402(f).
3. *Engineered Timber Sales, Inc. v. Comm.*, 74 TC 808 (1980), appeal dismissed (5th Cir. 1981); *G&W Leach Co. v. Comm.*, TC Memo 1981-91.
4. See Notice 2019-64 for the 2019 list.
5. *Christy & Swan Profit Sharing Plan v. Comm.*, TC Memo 2011-62.
6. See *Basch Eng'g, Inc. v. Comm.*, TC Memo 1990-212; *Fazi v. Comm.*, 102 TC 695 (1994).
7. IRC Sec. 401(a).

A plan will not qualify if it includes participants who are not employees of the employer that established and maintains the plan except in the case of "leased employees" (Q 3928).[1] An individual generally is an employee for the purpose of participating in a qualified plan if he or she is an employee under common law rules (Q 3927); however, under IRC Section 3508, certain real estate agents and direct sellers of consumer products are specifically defined as non-employees. An individual is an employee under the common law rules if the person or organization for whom he or she performs services has the right to control and direct his or her work, not only as to the result to be accomplished but also as to the details and means by which the result is accomplished.[2]

Self-employed individuals are eligible to participate in their own qualified plans under the same rules applicable to common law employees, although some special rules apply (Q 3826, Q 3931). Participation by independent contractors who are not employees of a corporation in a corporation's plan generally would be a violation of the exclusive benefit rule; however, the IRS has not been inclined to disqualify plans on this ground alone.[3]

Stockholders, even sole owners of corporations, who are bona fide employees of corporations (including professional corporations and associations and S corporations) are eligible to participate in a qualified plan of the corporation as regular employees, not as self-employed individuals.[4] A full-time life insurance salesperson who is an employee for Social Security purposes can participate in a qualified plan as a regular employee.[5] He or she cannot set up a plan as a self-employed individual.[6]

The primary purpose of benefiting employees or their beneficiaries must be maintained with respect to investment of trust funds as well as with respect to other activities of the trust.[7]

The use of the exclusive benefit rule to disqualify a plan where trust funds have been misappropriated generally occurs only under egregious circumstances. For example, the Tax Court held that where a plan loaned out almost all of its assets to the company president without seeking adequate security, a fair return, or prompt repayment, the plan was not operated for the exclusive benefit of the employees and the plan was disqualified.[8]

Likewise, where a corporation's sole shareholder and plan trustee caused the plan to make 22 unsecured loans to himself and none of the loans bore a reasonable rate of interest or were adequately secured, the exclusive benefit rule was violated and the plan disqualified.[9]

---

1. Rev. Rul. 69-493, 1969-2 CB 88.
2. Treas. Reg. §31.3121(d)-1(c)(2); *Packard v. Comm.*, 63 TC 621 (1975).
3. See e.g., *Lozon v. Comm.*, TC Memo 1997-250.
4. Treas. Reg. §1.401-1(b)(3); Rev. Rul. 63-108, 1963-1 CB 87; Rev. Rul. 55-81, 1955-1 CB 392 as amplified by Rev. Rul. 72-4, 1972-1 C.B. 105; *Thomas Kiddie, M.D., Inc. v. Comm.*, 69 TC 1055 (1978).
5. See IRC Sec. 7701(a)(20).
6. Treas. Reg. §1.401-10(b)(3).
7. Rev. Rul. 73-380, 1973-2 CB 124; Rev. Rul. 73-282, 1973-2 CB 123; Rev. Rul. 73-532, 1973-2 CB 128; Rev. Rul. 69-494, 1969-2 CB 88; *Feroleto Steel Co. v. Comm.*, 69 TC 97 (1977); *Bing Management Co., Inc. v. Comm.*, TC Memo 1977-403.
8. *Winger's Dept. Store, Inc. v. Comm.*, 82 TC 869 (1984).
9. TAM 9145006; see also TAM 9701001.

A loan made by a plan to an employer from excess funds that would have been returned to the employer did not violate the exclusive benefit requirement despite the imposition of the excise tax on prohibited transactions.[1]

The Tax Court has held that a violation of the prudent investor rule (i.e., a failure to diversify) did not violate the exclusive benefit rule.[2]

The IRS has decided that where an ESOP trust contained a provision permitting the trustee to consider nonfinancial, employment-related factors in evaluating tender offers for company stock, the exclusive benefit rule was violated.[3]

The garnishment of an individual's plan interest under the Federal Debt Collections Procedures Act ("FDCPA") to pay a judgment for restitution or fines will not violate the exclusive benefit rule.[4]

3839. Can a qualified plan permit reversion of plan funds to the employer and still satisfy the exclusive benefit rule?

It must be impossible under a plan at any time prior to the satisfaction of all liabilities with respect to employees and their beneficiaries for any part of the funds to be used for or diverted to purposes other than for the exclusive benefit of the employees or their beneficiaries.[5] (See Q 3838.)

As a rule, therefore, no sums may be refunded to the employer. A plan may provide for the return of a contribution (and any earnings) where the contribution is conditioned on the initial qualification of the plan, the plan receives an adverse determination with respect to its qualification, and the application for determination is made within the time prescribed by law for filing the employer's return for the taxable year in which the plan was adopted or a later date as the Secretary of Treasury may prescribe.[6]

A plan also may provide for return to the employer of contributions made on a good faith mistake of fact and of contributions conditioned on deductibility where there has been a good faith mistake in determining deductibility.[7] Earnings attributable to any excess contribution based on a good faith mistake may not be returned to the employer, but losses attributable to such contributions must reduce the amount returned.[8]

Employer contributions made to satisfy the quarterly contribution requirements (Q 3724) may revert to the employer if the contribution depends on its deductibility, a requested letter ruling disallows the deduction, and the contribution is returned to the employer within one year

1.　See TAM 9430002.
2.　See *Shedco, Inc v. Comm.*, TC Memo 1998-295.
3.　GCM 39870 (4-17-92).
4.　Let. Rul. 200426027.
5.　IRC Sec. 401(a)(2).
6.　Rev. Rul. 91-4, 1991-1 CB 54; see also ERISA Sec. 403(c)(2)(B).
7.　Let Rul. 201208043.
8.　Rev. Rul. 91-4, above; see also ERISA Secs. 403(c)(2)(A), 403(c)(2)(C).

from the date of the disallowance of the deduction.[1] Documentation must be provided showing that the contribution was conditioned on deductibility at the time it was made; board resolutions dated after the contribution is made are not sufficient.[2] A letter ruling request may not be needed if the employer contribution is less than $25,000 and certain other requirements are met.[3]

If, on termination of a pension plan (other than a profit sharing plan), all fixed and contingent liabilities to employees and their beneficiaries have been satisfied, the employer may recover any surplus existing because of actuarial "error."[4] The plan must specifically provide for such a reversion.[5] Thus, where a plan had no such provision, the employer was required to distribute surplus assets to the former employees (or their surviving spouses) covered by the plan.[6] Furthermore, the calculation of the employees' share of residual assets must result in an equitable distribution before the surplus assets may revert to the employer.[7] An excise tax may apply to any employer reversion (Q 3978).

If a pension or annuity plan maintains a separate account that provides for the payment of medical benefits to retired employees, their spouses, and their dependents, any amount remaining in such an account following the satisfaction of all liabilities to provide the benefits must be returned to the employer even though liabilities exist with respect to other portions of the plan.[8]

Minimum Participation and Coverage

3840. What are the age and service requirements that can be used for qualified plans?

Editor's Note: The SECURE Act modified the service requirements to expand access for certain part-time employees. Under the new law, employees who perform at least 500 hours of service for at least three consecutive years (and are at least 21 years old[9]) also must be allowed to participate in the employer-sponsored 401(k).[10] These long-term, part-time employees may, however, be excluded from coverage and nondiscrimination testing requirements.[11] The new rule also does not apply to employees covered under collectively bargained plans.[12]

A plan document need not set any threshold for employees to meet before becoming eligible to participate in the plan. That is, every employee could be eligible on being hired.

Most employers, however, favor requiring a new employee to work for a period of time and to attain a specific age before he or she is eligible to participate. The longest period and oldest

1.   Rev. Proc. 90-49, 1990-2 CB 620.
2.   Let. Ruls. 9021049, 8948056.
3.   See Rev. Proc. 90-49, above, Sec. 4.
4.   Treas. Reg. §1.401-2(b); Rev. Rul. 70-421, 1970-2 CB 85; Rev. Rul. 83-52; 1983-1 CB 87, modified by Rev. Rul. 85-6; 1985-1 C.B. 133.
5.   See ERISA Sec. 4044(d)(1).
6.   *Rinard v. Eastern Co.*, 978 F.2d 265 (6th Cir. 1992).
7.   See *Holland v. Amalgamated Sugar Co.*, 787 F. Supp. 996 (D.C. Utah 1992), *rev. & remanded*, 22 F.3d 968 (10th Cir. 1994).
8.   IRC Sec. 401(h)(5).
9.   IRC Sec. 401(k)(15)(A).
10.   IRC Sec. 401(k)(2)(D).
11.   IRC Sec. 401(k)(15)(B).
12.   IRC Sec. 401(k)(15)(C).

age that may be set in a plan document is established by the IRC and is referred to as minimum age and service.

Under the rules, a plan generally may not require that an employee complete a period of service extending beyond the later of age 21 or, under pre-SECURE Act law, the completion of one year of service.[1] The one year period could extended to two years if the plan provided that after not more than two years of service each participant has a non-forfeitable right to 100 percent of the accrued benefit.

Under the SECURE Act, employees must be eligible to participate in a 401(k) upon the earlier of (1) the plan's eligibility requirements as established under pre-SECURE Act law, or (2) the end of the first period of three consecutive 12-month periods where the employee has provided at least 500 hours of service. Plans are permitted to allow part-time employees to participate earlier, however.

Planning Point: While the SECURE Act rule requires employers to allow certain long-term, part-time employees to participate in the 401(k), it does not require employers to contribute on behalf of those employees (although employers are free to do so). The law only requires that these employees be permitted to make their own contributions to the 401(k).

Planning Point: The new applies to 401(k) plans, but absent future guidance to the contrary, does not change the rules for part-time participants in 403(b) plans.

Planning Point: Part-time employees will not be eligible to participate under the new rules until 2024. However, employers should act in advance to create a method for tracking employee hours this year (as hours will begin to be counted in 2021 for calendar-year plans).

This SECURE Act provision is effective for plan years beginning after December 31, 2020. However, 12-month periods beginning before January 1, 2021 are not taken into account for purposes of determining whether an employee qualifies.

In the case of a plan maintained exclusively for employees of a tax-exempt (under IRC Section 501(a)) educational institution, the minimum age limitation can be 26 instead of 21, but only if the plan provides that each participant having at least one year of service has a non-forfeitable right to 100 percent of the accrued benefit.[2]

A plan must provide that any employee who has satisfied the IRC's minimum age and service requirements specified above (and who is not otherwise excluded as a class) is eligible to participate in the plan no later than the earlier of the first day of the first plan year beginning after the date on which the employee satisfied such requirements, or the date six months after the date on which the employee satisfied such requirements.[3] Special rules apply to calculation of service for this purpose.[4]

---

1.   IRC Sec. 410(a)(1)(2).
2.   IRC Secs. 401(a)(3), 410(a)(1). See Temp. Treas. Reg. §1.410(a)-3T.
3.   IRC Sec. 410(a)(4).
4.   IRC Sec. 410(a)(3).

Plans can use shorter periods and younger ages, and some designs favoring highly paid owners have every employee enter the plan, even those who, by the nature of their job, would never obtain a vested benefit. In a 2004 memorandum to its staff, the IRS expressed disapproval with these and other plan designs that attempt to satisfy various IRC requirements by opening participation to rank and file employees with very short periods of service. These plans may be the subject of adverse rulings or other action.[1]

Not all employees meeting a plan's age and service requirements will be eligible for plan participation. Other requirements not related to age or service may be imposed by a plan as a condition of participation.[2] These individuals are referred to as excluded employees. For example, it is possible to structure a plan that is limited only to salaried employees, although additional testing will generally be required (Q 3841). Nevertheless, if the effect of a plan provision is to impose an additional age or service requirement, that provision will be treated as an age or service requirement even if it does not specifically refer to age or service.[3] The IRS has stated that this problem exists when a plan document excludes "part-time" employees from the plan. These provisions are treated as violating the minimum age and service rules under IRC Section 410(a) even if they otherwise would satisfy minimum coverage under IRC Section 410(b).[4]

The year of service for determining eligibility generally meant a 12-month period, measured from the date the employee became employed, during which the employee has worked at least 1,000 hours. This is referred to as the hours of service method of determining years of service.

A plan could require less, but not more, than 1,000 hours in a 12-month period to determine the threshold for being credited with a year of service.

Another method that may be used to calculate a year of service looked at the period from hire to a "separation of service" to see if the 12-month period has passed. This was referred to as the elapsed time method.[5]

In addition, special rules apply where there are breaks-in-service and where there is absence from work due to pregnancy, childbirth, or adoption of a child.[6] Special rules also apply in the cases of seasonal industries and maritime industries.[7]

Service with former employers may be credited for the purpose of determining eligibility to participate in a plan provided the former employers are specified in the plan or trust, all employees having such past service are treated uniformly, and the use of the past service factor does not produce discrimination in favor of highly compensated employees (Q 3847).[8] The IRS also has permitted individuals to be credited for services performed as partners or sole

1. Memorandum dated October 22, 2004, Carol D. Gold, Director Employee Plans.
2. Treas. Reg. §1.410(a)-3(d).
3. Treas. Reg. §1.410(a)-3(e)(1).
4. IRS Field Directive (November 22, 1994), CCH Pension Plan Guide ¶23,902F; see also TAM 9508003; 1995 FSA LEXIS 8.
5. Treas. Reg. §§ 1.410(a)-7, Temp. Treas. Reg. 1.410(a)-9T.
6. IRC Secs. 410(a)(3), 410(a)(5)(E); Treas. Reg. §§1.410(a)-5, 1.410(a)-6. See Temp. Treas. Reg. §1.410(a)-8T, Treas. Reg. §1.410(a)-9.
7. IRC Secs. 410(a)(3)(B), 410(a)(3)(D); Treas. Reg. §1.410(a)-5.
8. See Rev. Rul. 72-5, 1972-1 CB 106.

proprietors before becoming employees in a successor corporation for this purpose.[1] Companies working with the Defense Department frequently will credit service within the armed forces for eligibility or vesting.

3841. What is the minimum coverage requirement for qualified plans?

Understanding how a plan can meet the IRC's minimum coverage requirements may be one of the more difficult concepts to master in regard to qualified plans.

Satisfying the minimum coverage requirements of IRC Section 410(b) differs from satisfying the age and service requirements of IRC Section 410(a) because coverage looks to see if individuals who have met the plan's age and service requirement in fact receive benefits.

A plan demonstrates that it satisfies minimum coverage each year by satisfying either a ratio percentage test (Q 3842) or an average benefit test (Q 3843). Governmental plans, whether maintained by a state or local government, or the federal government, are exempt from this requirement and implementing regulations.[2] Salary deferrals to Section 401(k) plans are subject to certain modifications of the coverage requirements (Q 3753).

A plan will not be treated as violating the coverage requirements of Section 410(b) merely on account of the making of, or the right to make, catch-up contributions by participants age 50 or over under the provisions of IRC Section 414(v), so long as a universal availability requirement for access to the catch-up contribution is met (Q 3761).[3]

3842. What is the ratio percentage test that can be used to determine whether a qualified plan satisfies the minimum coverage requirement?

A plan satisfies the ratio percentage test when benefits apply to either 70 percent of all non-highly compensated employees (i.e., the percentage test) or a percentage of the non-highly compensated employees that is at least 70 percent of the percentage of highly compensated employees benefiting under the plan.[4] A participant generally is treated as benefiting if he or she receives an allocation under a defined contribution plan or who has an increase in a benefit accrued or treated as an accrued benefit.[5] Individuals are treated as benefiting for deferral purposes if they are eligible to defer, even if they choose not to do so.[6]

> *Example:* Smith Steel Company has a profit sharing plan that allocates a contribution to cover nine of its 10 non-excludable highly compensated employees and 160 of its 200 non-excludable non-highly compensated employees. Under its plan, otherwise eligible participants do not receive a contribution unless they are employed at year-end. One of the highly compensated participants and 40 of its non-highly compensated terminated and did not receive an allocation. The plan's ratio percentage is determined by dividing the percentage of the non-highly compensated employees who benefit under the plan (160/200, or 80 percent)

---

1.   See Let. Rul. 7742003.
2.   IRC Sec. 410(c)(1)(A); See IRC Sec 401(a)(5)(G).
3.   IRC Sec. 414(v)(3)(B).
4.   IRC Sec. 410(b)(1)(A), (B).
5.   Treas. Reg. §1.410(b)-3(a).
6.   Treas. Reg. §1.401(k)-6.

by the percentage of the highly compensated employees who benefit under the plan (9/10, or 90 percent). Smith Steel's ratio percentage is 80/90, or 89 percent; thus, it passes the 70 percent ratio percentage test.[1]

3843. What is the average benefit test that can be used to determine whether a qualified plan satisfies the minimum coverage requirement?

A plan that cannot satisfy the ratio percentage test (Q 3842) still may satisfy the coverage requirement by passing the average benefit test.[2] The average benefits test may allow a plan with a ratio percentage of less than 70 percent to satisfy minimum coverage. It has two parts: the "non-discriminatory classification" test and the "average benefit percentage" test. Both of these requirements must be met for a plan to satisfy the average benefit test.[3] Note that the non-discriminatory classification test has two separate requirements that must be met.

A plan passes the non-discriminatory classification test when the plan benefits "such employees as qualify under a classification set up by the employer and found by the Secretary not to be discriminatory in favor of highly compensated employees."[4] Regulations state that this requirement has two parts: (1) the classification of employees must be reasonable and established under objective business criteria identifying the category of employees who benefit under the plan; that is, it must reflect a bona fide business classification of employees,[5] and (2) the classification must be non-discriminatory based on a threshold of coverage specified in regulations. Theoretically it is possible to demonstrate that a classification not satisfying the mathematical threshold of part (2) may satisfy the requirement through a facts and circumstances demonstration or a safe harbor percentage test as explained below.[6]

To determine whether a classification is non-discriminatory, the plan's ratio percentage (as defined above) is compared to a table (described below) that is set forth in the regulations. This table contains a range of "safe harbor" and "unsafe harbor" percentages determined based on the percentage of non-highly compensated employees participating in the plan (a concentration level).[7] This comparison produces one of three results: (1) if the plan's ratio percentage falls below the unsafe harbor percentage, it is discriminatory; (2) if the plan's ratio percentage falls between the safe harbor and unsafe harbor amounts, it must satisfy a facts and circumstances test; or (3) if the plan's ratio percentage falls at or above the safe harbor amount, the classification is non-discriminatory.[8]

The table for the concentration percentage begins with a non-highly compensated employee concentration of zero to 60 percent, and for that level provides a safe harbor percentage of 50 percent and an unsafe harbor percentage of 40 percent. In other words, for an employer with 100 employees, of whom 40 are highly compensated and only 60 are non-highly compensated, the classification would automatically be non-discriminatory under the safe harbor if its ratio

---

1. See generally Treas. Reg. §1.410(b)-4.
2. IRC Sec. 410(b)(2).
3. Treas. Reg. §1.410(b)-2(b)(3); see IRC Sec. 410(b)(2).
4. IRC Sec. 410(b)(2)(A)(i).
5. Treas. Reg. §1.410(b)-4(b).
6. Treas. Reg. §1.410(b)-4(c).
7. Treas. Reg. §1.410(b)-4(c)(4)(iv).
8. Treas. Reg. §1.410(b)-4(c).

percentage were 50 percent or higher. For each 1 percent that the non-highly compensated employee concentration increases above 60 percent, the safe harbor percentage and unsafe harbor percentage are reduced by three-fourths of a percentage point. The unsafe harbor percentage cannot be reduced below 20 percent.[1] If the non-highly compensated employee concentration percentage were 70 percent, the safe harbor percentage and unsafe harbor percentage are each reduced by 7.5 percentage points, to 42.5 percent and 32.5, respectively.

Average benefit percentage test. The second part of the average benefit test requires that the average benefit percentage for non-highly compensated employees be at least 70 percent of the average benefit percentage for highly compensated employees.[2] An employee's benefit percentage is the employee's employer-provided contributions, including forfeitures and elective deferrals, or benefits under all qualified plans maintained by the employer, expressed as a percentage of the employee's compensation.[3] Employee contributions and benefits attributable to employee contributions are not taken into account in calculating employee benefit percentages.[4] Regulations permit benefit percentages to be determined on either a contributions or a benefits basis.[5]

The final component of the average benefit test is calculating the average benefit percentage for the plan. This is a separate calculation from the rate group percentages in the previous step. Here, a benefit percentage is calculated for participants taking into account the total of all benefits, including deferrals, employee contributions and forfeiture reallocations, divided by compensation. Then, the average for the non-highly compensated employees is compared to the average of the highly compensated employees. This component is passed only when that ratio is 70 percent or more. All plans of an employer, with certain exceptions, are used in determining the benefit percentages, even if another plan satisfies the ratio percentage test or is a safe harbor design. When an employer maintains separate lines of business or where certain plans for union employees exist, the benefit percentage for any plan year is computed on the basis of contributions or benefits for that year or, at the election of the employer, any consecutive plan year period, up to three years, ending with the plan year and specified in the election. An election under this provision cannot be revoked or modified without the consent of the Secretary of the Treasury.[6]

A plan maintained by an employer that has no employees other than highly compensated employees for any year or that benefits no highly compensated active employees for any year is treated as meeting the minimum coverage requirements.[7]

---

1.   Treas. Reg. §1.410(b)-4(c)(4).
2.   IRC Sec. 410(b)(2)(A)(ii); Treas. Reg. §1.410(b)-5(a).
3.   IRC Sec. 410(b)(2)(C)(i).
4.   Treas. Reg. §1.410(b)-5(d)(2).
5.   See Treas. Reg. §1.410(b)-5(d)(4).
6.   IRC Sec. 410(b)(2)(C).
7.   IRC Sec. 410(b)(6)(F); Treas. Reg. §§1.410(b)-2(b)(5), 1.410(b)-2(b)(6).

3844. What are the miscellaneous rules associated with the minimum coverage requirement for qualified plans?

Separate Lines of Business

Employers that operate separate lines of business may apply the tests discussed in Q 3842 and Q 3843 separately with respect to employees in each line of business, so long as any such plan benefits a class of employees that is determined, on a company wide basis, not to be discriminatory in favor of highly compensated employees.[1]

A separate line of business exists if the employer, for bona fide business reasons, maintains separate lines of business or operating units. A separate line of business, however, cannot have fewer than 50 employees, disregarding any employees excluded from the top-paid group when determining the employees who are highly compensated (Q 3929). A separate line of business also must meet either a statutory safe harbor with respect to ratios of highly compensated employees provided in the IRC, meet one of the administrative safe harbors provided in final regulations, or request and receive an individual determination from the IRS that the separate line of business satisfies administrative scrutiny.[2]

Former Employees

Active and former employees are tested separately for purposes of the rules.[3] A plan satisfies the coverage requirement with respect to former employees only if, under all the relevant facts and circumstances, the group of former employees' plan does not discriminate significantly in favor of highly compensated former employees.[4]

Excludable Employees

Certain otherwise eligible employees can be excluded from coverage testing. They include (1) employees covered by a collective bargaining agreement, provided that retirement benefits were the subject of good faith bargaining between the employee representatives and the employer, and (2) nonresident aliens who receive no U.S. earned income.[5] Although a plan may permit an otherwise eligible employee to waive his or her right to participate, such a waiver may, under some circumstances, result in discriminatory coverage.[6] Employees who have not satisfied the plan's minimum age and service requirements and are not participants are excluded from consideration in meeting the above tests.[7]

Other employees who meet the plan's age and service requirements may be excluded under the terms of the plan. Such excluded employees include, but are not limited to, employees who, once eligible for the plan, are required to be employed on the last day of the plan year, similar

---

1. IRC Sec. 410(b)(5).
2. IRC Sec. 414(r); Treas. Reg. §§1.414(r)-5, 1.414(r)-6.
3. Treas. Reg. §1.410(b)-2(c)(1).
4. Treas. Reg. §1.410(b)-2(c)(2).
5. IRC Sec. 410(b)(3); Treas. Reg. §§1.410(b)-6(d), 1.410(b)-9.
6. See Rev. Rul. 80-351, 1980-2 CB 152. But see *Olmo v. Comm.*, TC Memo 1979-286, nonacq., 1980 AOD LEXIS 135.
7. IRC Sec. 410(b)(2)(D).

employees who are required to have been credited with at least 1,000 hours in the plan year, and employees who are excluded as a class such as hourly or salaried employees.[1]

Employees Treated as Benefiting

An employee benefits under a plan for a year only if the employee accrues a benefit or receives an allocation under the plan for that year.[2] An employee is treated as "benefiting" under a plan for a plan year if the employee satisfies all of the applicable conditions for accruing a benefit for the year but fails to accrue a benefit solely because of the IRC Section 415 limits or some other uniformly applicable plan benefit limit.[3]

Certain Terminating Employees Excluded from Testing

Many plans require an employee to be employed on the last day of the plan year to be eligible to receive a contribution or benefit. A terminated employee who fails to satisfy the minimum hours of service or a last-day requirement may be excluded from consideration in meeting the coverage test if the employee had accrued no more than 500 hours, terminated service during the plan year, and did not receive a benefit in the plan year.[4]

Mandatory Disaggregation

Some plans or portions of plans must be disaggregated to meet the minimum coverage rules. The mandatory disaggregation requirement specifies that certain single plans must be treated as comprising separate plans, each of which is subject to the minimum coverage requirements.

Some of the plans that generally have to be disaggregated for coverage purposes are:[5]

(1)   the portion of a plan that includes a cash or deferred arrangement subject to IRC Section 401(k) (or matching and employee after-tax contributions subject to IRC Section 401(m)), and the portion that does not;

(2)   the portion of a plan that is an ESOP, and the portion that is a non-ESOP (this varies from the disaggregation rules that would apply under regulations for ADP/ACP testing purposes only (Q 3801, Q 3803));[6]

(3)   the portion of a plan that benefits otherwise excludable employees, and the portion that does not;

(4)   a plan that benefits the employees of a separate line of business, and any plan maintained by any other line of business if the employer elects to use the separate line of business rules; and

---

1.   Treas. Reg. §1.410(b)-6(b).
2.   Treas. Reg. §1.410(b)-3(a).
3.   Treas. Reg. §§1.410(b)-3(a)(2)(ii), 1.410(b)-3(a)(2)(iii).
4.   Treas. Reg. 1.410(b)-6(f).
5.   Treas. Reg. §1.410(b)-7(c).
6.   See Treas. Reg. §1.401(k)-1(b)(4)(v).

(5)   the portion of a plan that benefits employees under a collective bargaining arrangement, and the portion that benefits nonunion employees.[1]

For testing the benefits of employees who change from one qualified separate line of business to another, a reasonable treatment must be used.[2] A multiple employer plan (a plan covering two or more unrelated employers) also is treated as comprising separate plans each of which is maintained by a separate employer and generally must satisfy the minimum coverage requirements by reference only to such employer's employees.[3]

Permissive Aggregation

For purposes of applying the ratio percentage test and the nondiscriminatory classification test, an employer may elect to designate two or more of its plans as a single plan, but only if the plans have the same plan years.[4] If plans are aggregated under this rule, they must be treated as a single plan for all purposes under IRC Sections 410(b) and 401(a)(4).[5]

Of course, plans that are required to be disaggregated under the rules described above cannot be aggregated under this rule. Furthermore, for purposes of applying these tests, the following plans also must be disaggregated: the portion of a plan that is an ESOP, and the portion that is a non-ESOP; and the portion of a plan that includes a cash or deferred arrangement subject to IRC Section 401(k) (or matching and employee after-tax contributions subject to IRC Section 401(m)), and the portion that does not.[6]

For purposes of applying the average benefit percentage test, all plans that may be aggregated under the permissive aggregation rules must be aggregated and treated as a single plan. In addition, plans (or portions of plans) that are ESOPs or that are subject to IRC Section 401(k) or 401(m) also must be aggregated with all other qualified plans of the employer.[7]

A special rule in the final regulations permits benefits provided to collectively bargained employees and noncollectively bargained employees to be considered together, for purposes of the average benefit percentage test only, if certain requirements are met.[8]

Snapshot Testing

The IRC states that a plan will be considered as meeting the minimum coverage requirement during the whole of any taxable year of the plan if on one day in each quarter it satisfied that requirement.[9] Employers may demonstrate compliance with the coverage requirement using

---

1.   Treas. Reg. §1.410(b)-7(c)(4)(ii)(B).
2.   Treas. Reg. §1.410(b)-7(c)(4)(i)(D).
3.   Treas. Reg. §1.410(b)-7(c)(4)(ii)(C).
4.   Treas. Reg. §§1.410(b)-7(d)(1), 1.410(b)-7(d)(5).
5.   Treas. Reg. §1.410(b)-7(d).
6.   Treas. Reg. §§1.410(b)-7(c), 1.410(b)-7(d)(2).
7.   IRC Sec. 401(k)(4)(C); Treas. Reg. §1.410(b)-7(e).
8.   See Treas. Reg. §1.410(b)-5(f).
9.   IRC Sec. 401(a)(6).

"snapshot" testing on a single day during the plan year, provided that that day is representative of the employer's work force and the plan's coverage throughout the plan year.[1]

Corrective Amendments

A plan that does not satisfy the minimum coverage requirement during a plan year may be retroactively amended by the 15th day of the 10th month after the close of the plan year to satisfy one of the tests.[2] This amendment would have the effect of including individuals who had been excluded by the plan. A retroactive amendment must separately satisfy the nondiscrimination and minimum coverage requirements, and cannot violate the anticutback rule of IRC Section 411(d)(6) (Q 3860, Q 3875).[3]

Merger or Acquisition

The IRC provides certain transition relief from the coverage rules in the event of a merger or acquisition.[4] The IRS has provided guidance for certain changes in a plan sponsors' controlled group, offering temporary relief from the coverage requirements provided that each plan has satisfied the coverage requirements prior to the change in the controlled group and no significant change in the plan or its coverage takes place during the transition period, other than the change resulting from the merger or acquisition itself.[5]

3845. What effect does noncompliance with the minimum coverage requirements have upon a qualified plan?

Special rules apply to prevent a loss of tax qualification when a plan fails to qualify solely because it does not meet one of the coverage tests. In this case, contributions on behalf of nonhighly compensated employees will not be taxed under the rules for nonqualified plans. (Presumably, all other complications arising from plan disqualification would apply.) Instead, highly compensated employees will be required to include in income the amount of their vested accrued benefits, other than their investment in the contract.[6]

The minimum coverage requirement generally is inapplicable to church plans, governmental plans, and plans that have not provided for employer contributions at any time after September 2, 1974. The coverage regulations generally apply to tax-exempt organizations; however, and plans maintained by certain tax-exempt organizations (i.e., a society, order, or association described in IRC Sections 501(c)(8) or 501(c)(9)) are not subject to the coverage requirements.[7] Other than governmental plans, these plans are treated as meeting the coverage provisions only if they meet the coverage requirements of IRC Section 401(a)(3) as in effect on September 1, 1974.[8]

---

1.   Rev. Proc. 93-42, 1993-2 CB 540.
2.   Treas. Reg. §§1.401(a)(4)-11(g)(2), 1.401(a)(4)-11(g)(3)(iv).
3.   Treas. Reg. §1.401(a)(4)-11(g)(3).
4.   See IRC Sec. 410(b)(6)(C).
5.   For details, see Rev. Rul. 2004-11, 2004-7 IRB 480.
6.   IRC Sec. 402(b)(2).
7.   IRC Sec. 410(c)(1)(D).
8.   See IRC Secs. 410(c)(1)(B), 410(c)(2).

3846. Can a qualified plan be established for the sole shareholder of a corporation?

A corporation may establish a qualified plan even though it has only one permanent employee and that employee owns all the stock of the corporation. If the plan is either designed or operated so that only the shareholder-employee can ever benefit, however, it will not qualify. Provision must be made for participation of future employees if any are hired.[1]

A pension plan will not fail to qualify merely because it is established by a corporation that is operated for the purpose of selling the services, abilities, or talents of its only employee, who is also its principal or sole shareholder.[2] The plan of a corporation's sole shareholder was disqualified for violating the coverage requirement after it was shown that the only two hired personnel of the company, who had been excluded from the plan as independent contractors, in fact were employees.[3]

As to which individuals must be treated as employees and what organizations make up an employer, see Q 3927, Q 3928, Q 3932, and Q 3934.

Nondiscrimination

3847. When is a plan nondiscriminatory?

Editor's Note: See below for information on the relief provided by the IRS for closed defined benefit plans.

The IRC has established requirements that prohibit a plan from providing benefits that discriminate in favor of highly compensated employees. A plan will demonstrate that it is not discriminatory by passing certain annual nondiscrimination testing under IRC Section 401(a)(4) or through using a plan that has a safe harbor design. A plan demonstrates that it does not discriminate in favor of highly compensated employees by satisfying, on an annual basis, three basic requirements:

(1) contributions or benefits must not discriminate in favor of "highly compensated employees" as defined in IRC Section 414(q) (Q 3929); the annual testing to meet this requirement is described in Q 3849;

(2) benefits, rights, and features available to employees do not discriminate in favor of highly compensated employees (Q 3859); and

(3) the effect of plan amendments, including grants of past service credit, and plan terminations cannot discriminate in favor of highly compensated employees (Q 3860).[4]

---

1. Rev. Rul. 63-108, 1963-1 CB 87; Rev. Rul. 55-81, 1955-1 CB 392.
2. Rev. Rul. 72-4, 1972-1 CB 105 (amplifying Rev. Rul. 55-81).
3. See *Kenney v. Comm.*, TC Memo 1995-431.
4. Treas. Reg. §1.401(a)(4)-1(b)(1).

Employees not included in the plan but who are covered by a collective bargaining agreement can be excluded from consideration in meeting the nondiscrimination requirement if there is evidence that retirement benefits were the subject of good faith bargaining between the employee representatives and the employer. If union employees are covered under the plan, benefits or contributions must be provided for them on a nondiscriminatory basis.[1] Nonresident aliens with no U.S. earned income also may be excluded.

Governmental plans generally are not subject to the requirements of IRC Section 401(a)(4).[2]

Regulations under IRC Section 401(a)(4) provide the exclusive rules for determining whether a plan satisfies the nondiscrimination requirements of IRC Section 401(a)(4).[3] A plan may satisfy the nondiscrimination requirement on the basis of either measuring the employer's contributions or the benefits attributable to those contributions (benefits testing). Both options are available regardless of whether the plan is a defined benefit plan or a defined contribution plan. The process of testing defined benefit plans on the basis of contributions or defined contribution plans on the basis of benefits is referred to as "cross testing" (Q 3861).

A plan will not be considered discriminatory merely because contributions or benefits bear a uniform relationship to the employees' compensation (Q 3866).[4] A plan will satisfy IRC Section 401(a)(4) only if it complies both in form and in actual operation with the regulations that provide for nondiscrimination testing methods and safe harbor designs. Intent is irrelevant in making this determination.[5]

A plan also will not be treated as discriminatory merely on account of the making of, or the right to make, catch-up contributions (Q 3761) by participants age 50 or over under the provisions of IRC Section 414(v), so long as a universal availability requirement is met.[6]

There are two basic options for satisfying the IRC's nondiscrimination requirements. The plan can use one of the safe harbor formulas (Q 3848, Q 3850) stated in the regulations or it can satisfy certain testing annually. Thus, plans that do not meet the requirements for one of the safe harbors must use the general nondiscrimination test. The safe harbor compliance methods are design-based. Essentially, they require the plan to have uniform provisions that reduce the potential for prohibited discrimination and, therefore, annual testing is unnecessary. As a result, the safe harbors avoid costly testing, which focuses on actual plan results and requires annual review.

Planning Point: Whether an employer decides to structure its plan to meet a safe harbor or to favor owners and higher paid employees often depends on whether the employer expects to satisfy the general non-discrimination test and if it wants the simpler administration offered by a safe harbor plan.

---

1.   IRC Secs. 401(a)(4), 410(b)(3). See, e.g., Let. Rul. 8419001.
2.   See IRC Sec. 401(a)(5)(G).
3.   Treas. Reg. §1.401(a)(4)-1(a).
4.   IRC Sec. 401(a)(5)(B).
5.   Treas. Reg. §1.401(a)(4)-1(a).
6.   IRC Sec. 414(v)(3)(B).

Nondiscrimination Relief for Closed Plans

Many employers who have closed defined benefit plans to new participants have continued to allow groups of "grandfathered" employees to earn benefits under the closed defined benefit plans. Because of this, many of these plans have had difficulties meeting the applicable nondiscrimination requirements as more of these grandfathered employees become "highly compensated" over time. Proposed regulations published in 2016 contain special rules to make it easier for these plans to satisfy the nondiscrimination requirements and Notice 2014-5 was released to provide temporary relief if certain conditions are satisfied.

The proposed regulations modify the rules applicable to defined benefit replacement allocations (DBRAs) that allow some allocations to be disregarded when determining whether a defined contribution plan has a broadly available allocation rate in order to allow more allocations to satisfy the rules. Further, the regulations provide a special nondiscrimination testing rule that can apply if a benefit or plan feature is only made available to grandfathered employees in a closed plan. In anticipation of the finalization of these regulations, Notice 2019-49 expands the nondiscrimination relief to plan years beginning before 2021, so long as the conditions in Notice 2014-5 are satisfied.

Although the IRS has previously extended the nondiscrimination relief for closed DB plans in Notice 2014-5, newly released Notice 2019-60 also expands the relief to include relief from benefits, rights and features testing for closed plans. To qualify, the plan must have closed via amendments adopted before December 13, 2013. Notice 2019-60 does not change prior relief, but adds additional relief. Closed plans' benefits, rights and features are treated as satisfying testing if the benefits, rights and features were provided at the time of the amendment closing the plan and one of two conditions are satisfied: (1) no amendments were adopted after January 29, 2016 that expanded or restricted eligibility for the benefits, rights and features or (2) if there was such an amendment, the benefit, right or feature does not benefit a relatively larger proportion of highly compensated employees (measured using the plan's ratio percentage) than before the amendment. This relief is available for plan years ending after November 13, 2019 and before January 1, 2021.

3848. What safe harbor designs allow a defined contribution plan to satisfy the nondiscrimination requirements?

The regulations set forth two safe harbor designs for defined contribution plans.

Under the first safe harbor, referred to as a uniform allocation formula, a defined contribution plan will be nondiscriminatory if it allocates employer contributions and forfeitures for the year under an allocation formula that allocates to each employee the same percentage of plan year compensation, the same dollar amount, or the same dollar amount for each uniform unit of service (not exceeding one week) performed by the employee during the year.[1]

---

1.   Treas. Reg. §1.401(a)(4)-2(b)(2).

The second safe harbor design is referred to as a uniform points allocation formula. This formula allows a defined contribution plan other than an ESOP to be nondiscriminatory even though contributions are weighted for age, service, or compensation.[1] It unfortunately imposes restrictions that limit its ability to favor higher paid employees with larger contributions and for that reason is seldom found outside the not-for-profit world.

A plan with a non-uniform allocation formula may retain its safe harbor status if the effect of the non-uniform allocation is to provide lower benefits to highly compensated employees.[2]

3849. How can a defined contribution plan that does not satisfy one of the safe harbor designs show that it does not discriminate in favor of highly compensated employees?

A defined contribution plan other than plans subject to IRC Section 401(k) or 401(m) that does not satisfy one of the safe harbor designs will meet the "nondiscrimination in amount" requirement if it meets a general test. First, the employer calculates a benefit percentage ratio for each employee and sets up rate groups based upon these benefit percentages.

The next step is to compare the rate groups for highly compensated employees to the rate groups for non-highly compensated employees. It is such a complicated process that this discussion is just an overview of the process. If each "rate group" satisfies the minimum coverage requirements of IRC Section 410(b), the plan will have passed the general test. For this purpose, a "rate group" exists for each highly compensated employee in the plan, and consists of highly compensated employees ("HCEs") and all other employees in the plan (whether highly compensated or non-highly compensated) who have an allocation rate greater than or equal to the highly compensated employee's allocation rate. An employee's allocation ratio equals the sum of the allocations to the employee's account for the plan year, expressed either as a percentage of plan year compensation or as a dollar amount.[3] In other words, each employee, regardless of compensation level, is included in the rate group for every HCE who has an allocation rate less than or equal to that employee's allocation rate.[4]

3850. What safe harbors exist that allow a defined benefit plan to satisfy the nondiscrimination requirements?

The final regulations provide a set of uniformity requirements that apply to all defined benefit safe harbors. A plan generally must provide a uniform normal retirement benefit in the same form for all employees, using a uniform normal retirement age. For purposes of this requirement, Social Security retirement age will be treated as a uniform retirement age.[5] The regulations provide for three safe harbors: one for unit credit plans, one for fractional accrual plans (including flat benefit plans), and one for insurance contract plans.[6]

1.　　See Treas. Reg. §1.401(a)(4)-2(b)(3).
2.　　Treas. Reg. §1.401(a)(4)-2(b)(4)(v).
3.　　Treas. Reg. §1.401(a)(4)-2(c)(2).
4.　　Treas. Reg. §1.401(a)(4)-2(c)(1).
5.　　IRC Sec. 401(a)(5)(F).
6.　　Treas. Reg. §1.401(a)(4)-3(b).

3851. How can a defined benefit plan that does not satisfy one of the safe harbors show that it does not discriminate in favor of highly compensated employees?

Defined benefit plans that do not satisfy any of the safe harbors will satisfy the "nondiscriminatory in amount" requirement only if they satisfy the general test, which requires the calculation of accrual rates and an analysis of their distribution. The general test will be satisfied if each "rate group" satisfies the minimum coverage requirements of IRC Section 410(b). For this purpose, a "rate group" exists for each highly compensated employee in the plan, and consists of the highly compensated employee and all other employees in the plan (whether highly compensated or non-highly compensated) who have a normal accrual rate greater than or equal to the highly compensated employee's normal accrual rate, *and* who also have a most valuable accrual rate greater than or equal to the highly compensated employee's most valuable accrual rate.

Planning Point: In other words, an employee is in the rate group for each highly compensated employee who has a normal accrual rate less than or equal to the employee's normal accrual rate and who also has a most valuable accrual rate less than or equal to the employee's most valuable accrual rate.[1]

The regulations provide a facts and circumstances "safety valve" for certain defined benefit plans that would pass the general test if no more than 5 percent of the highly compensated employees were disregarded. If the IRS determines on the basis of all the relevant facts and circumstances that such a plan does not discriminate with respect to the amount of employer-provided benefits, the plan will pass the general test. For purposes of calculating the 5 percent, the number of highly compensated employees may be rounded to the nearest whole number.[2]

3852. Can a plan satisfy the nondiscrimination requirements by limiting participation to highly compensated employees and nonhighly compensated employees with very short periods of service?

The IRS released guidance expressing disapproval of plans that attempt to satisfy the non-discrimination requirements by limiting participation to highly compensated employees and to rank and file employees with very short periods of service. The IRS noted that sponsors of such plans use "plan designs and hiring practices that limit who receives a benefit to the nonhighly compensated employees and to other employees with very small amounts of compensation" and whose tenure with the company never results in their benefits being vested. These plans are targeted for adverse rulings, possible disqualification, or other actions.[3]

---

1.   Treas. Reg. §1.401(a)(4)-3(c)(1).
2.   Treas. Reg. §1.401(a)(4)-3(c)(3).
3.   Memorandum dated October 22, 2004, Carol D. Gold, Director Employee Plans.

3853. What safe harbor designs allow a target benefit plan to satisfy the nondiscrimination requirements?

The regulations provide a safe harbor testing method for target benefit plans. Because target benefit plans are defined contribution plans that determine allocations based on a defined benefit funding approach, the safe harbor is included in the rules for cross testing.

A target benefit plan generally will be deemed to meet the "nondiscrimination in amount" requirement if:

(1)   it satisfies uniformity requirements with respect to normal retirement age and the allocation formula (the Social Security retirement age will be treated as a uniform retirement age);[1]

(2)   it provides a stated benefit formula that complies with one of the defined benefit plan safe harbors that uses the fractional accrual rule;

(3)   employer contributions are determined under an individual level premium funding method specified in the regulations, based on an employee's stated benefit and "theoretical reserve;"

(4)   employee contributions, if any, are not used to fund the stated benefit; and

(5)   the stated benefit formula satisfies Treasury Regulation Section 1.401(l)-3, if permitted disparity is taken into account.[2]

3854. How do 401(k) plans satisfy the IRC nondiscrimination requirements?

These plans may not use the general test of IRC Section 401(a)(4). The plans must satisfy the IRC's nondiscrimination requirements following the requirements that are specified under IRC Sections 401(k) and 401(m). Those sections also allow several safe harbor designs that can eliminate a requirement to complete a mathematical test for deferrals and matching contributions (Q 3801 to Q 3807).[3]

3855. Can a plan satisfy the IRC nondiscrimination requirements through aggregating multiple plans or restructuring the plan?

Under certain circumstances, a plan may be aggregated or combined with other plans or restructured (i.e., treated as two or more separate plans) for purposes of meeting the nondiscrimination in amount requirement. Where plans are restructured, each component plan must separately satisfy the nondiscrimination requirements and the coverage requirements (Q 3841).[4]

If two or more plans are permissively aggregated and treated as a single plan for purposes of satisfying the minimum coverage requirements (Q 3841), the aggregated plans also must be treated

---

1.   IRC Sec. 401(a)(5)(F).
2.   Treas. Reg. §1.401(a)(4)-8(b)(3).
3.   IRC Secs. 401(k), 401(m); Treas. Reg. §1.401(a)(4)-1(b)(2)(ii)(B).
4.   See Treas. Reg. §1.401(a)(4)-9(c).

as a single plan for purposes of meeting the nondiscrimination requirements.[1] The regulations include guidelines for determining whether several of these plans, when considered as a unit, provide contributions and benefits that discriminate in favor of highly compensated employees.

A disability plan that is not a pension, profit sharing, stock bonus, or annuity plan may not be aggregated with these plans for this purpose.[2]

Special rules are provided for applying the nondiscrimination requirements to an aggregated plan that includes both a defined benefit plan and a defined contribution plan.[3] Special rules apply where an aggregated plan includes a new comparability plan (Q 3861).[4]

3856. Will a plan be considered discriminatory if it is integrated with Social Security?

An integrated plan will not be considered discriminatory merely because the plan is integrated with Social Security (i.e., the plan uses the permitted disparity rules).[5] As a result, if a plan is integrated in a way that satisfies the permitted disparity rules, the disparity is disregarded in determining whether the plan satisfies the applicable defined contribution or defined benefit safe harbor.[6] For details on Social Security integration, see Q 3862.

3857. What substantiation requirements must an employer follow to show compliance with the IRC nondiscrimination requirement?

Employers may demonstrate compliance with the "nondiscrimination in amount" requirement by using "snapshot" testing on a single day during the plan year, provided that that day is representative of the employer's work force and the plan's coverage throughout the plan year.[7]

3858. Is a plan that offers credits for past service considered discriminatory?

The effect of plan provisions with respect to grants of past service must be non-discriminatory. The determination of whether credit for past service causes discrimination is made on a facts and circumstances basis. A plan provision that credits pre-participation service or imputed service to any highly compensated employee will be considered non-discriminatory if, based on all the facts and circumstances, the provision applies on the same terms to all similarly-situated non-highly compensated employees, there is a legitimate business purpose for crediting the service, and the crediting of the service does not by design or operation discriminate significantly in favor of highly compensated employees. Relevant facts and circumstances used to determine if a plan discriminates significantly in favor of highly compensated employees include (1) whether the service credit merely prevents the employee from being disadvantaged with respect to benefits by a change in job or employer or provides the employee with benefits comparable to those of other employees; (2) the business ties between the current employer and prior employer;

---

1.   Treas. Reg. §1.401(a)(4)-9(a).
2.   See Rev. Rul. 81-33, 1981-1 CB 173.
3.   See Treas. Reg. §1.401(a)(4)-9(b).
4.   See Treas. Reg. §1.401(a)(4)-9(c)(3)(ii).
5.   See IRC Sec. 401(a)(5)(D).
6.   See Treas. Reg. §1.401(l)-1(a)(1).
7.   Rev. Proc. 93-42, 1993-2 CB 540, modified by Rev. Proc. 95-34, 1995-2 CB 385.

(3) the degree of excess coverage under section 410(b) of non-highly compensated employees for the plan crediting the service, considering employees who are credited with pre-participation service; (4) the circumstances of the employee's transfer into the group of employees covered by the plan; and (5) the type of service being credited.[1] For an explanation of the nondiscrimination requirements for plan amendments granting past service credit, see Q 3860.

As to which individuals must be treated as employees and what organizations constitute the employer in the IRC's nondiscrimination testing, see Q 3927, Q 3928, Q 3932, and Q 3934.

3859. What are the requirements with respect to the nondiscriminatory availability of plan benefits, rights, and features?

Editor's Note: The SECURE Act made changes that would make it easier for certain sponsors of closed defined benefit plans to satisfy their nondiscrimination testing requirements.[2] See heading below for details.

The benefits, rights, and features provided under a plan (i.e., all optional forms of benefit, ancillary benefits, and other rights and features available to any employee under a plan) must be made available in a nondiscriminatory manner. Benefits, rights, and features generally will meet this requirement only if each benefit, right, and feature satisfies a "current availability" requirement and an "effective availability" requirement.[3]

The current availability requirement generally is satisfied if the group of employees to whom the benefit, right, or feature is currently available during the plan year satisfies the minimum coverage test of section 410(b) (Q 3841) without regard to the average benefit percentage test.[4]

Current availability is based on the current facts and circumstances of the employee; the fact that an employee may satisfy an eligibility condition in the future does not make the benefit option currently available to that employee. Conditions based on termination of employment, disability, hardship, or conditions based on age or length of service may be disregarded in determining current availability.[5]

To satisfy the effective availability requirement, the group of employees to whom a benefit, right, or feature is effectively available must not substantially favor highly compensated employees, based on all the facts and circumstances.[6] Thus, for example, a matching contribution that is available only to employees deferring a relatively high percentage of income would fail this requirement if the level of deferral required makes the match effectively unavailable to most non-highly compensated employees.

---

1.   Treas. Reg. §1.401(a)(4)-11(d)(3)(iii).
2.   IRC Sec. 401(o).
3.   Treas. Reg. §§1.401(a)(4)-1(b)(3), 1.401(a)(4)-4(a).
4.   Treas. Reg. §1.401(a)(4)-4(b)(1).
5.   Treas. Reg. §1.401(a)(4)-4(b)(2).
6.   Treas. Reg. §1.401(a)(4)-4(c)(1).

A plan that offers catch-up contributions will not be treated as violating these requirements merely because participants age 50 or over make, or have the right to make, catch-up contributions under the provisions of IRC Section 414(v), so long as a universal availability requirement is met (Q 3761).[1]

The IRS has issued guidance under which two optional forms of benefit that differ only with respect to the timing of their commencement generally may be aggregated and treated as a single optional form of benefit for purposes of satisfying the nondiscriminatory current and effective availability requirements.[2] For example, a preretirement age 72 (70½ pre-2020) distribution option that is available only to 5 percent owners, as required under IRC Section 401(a)(9) (Q 3894), may be aggregated with another optional form of benefit that differs only in the timing of the commencement of payments, provided certain requirements are met.[3]

The fact that subsidized early retirement benefits and joint and survivor annuities are based on an employee's Social Security retirement age generally will not result in their being treated as unavailable to employees on the same terms.[4]

Employers may demonstrate compliance with the current availability requirement by using snapshot testing on a single day during the plan year, provided that that day is representative of the employer's work force and the plan's coverage throughout the plan year.[5]

The IRS determined that a plan, in operation, violated IRC Section 401(a)(4) when it permitted highly compensated employees to direct their own investments, which resulted in their earning a substantially higher return than that earned on contributions by rank and file employees. The IRS commented that even if the investment decisions had resulted in a lower return or a loss, the opportunity for only highly compensated employees to make their own investment decisions still would result in discrimination.[6]

SECURE Act Changes

Many employers who have closed defined benefit plans to new participants have continued to allow groups of "grandfathered" employees to earn benefits under the closed defined benefit plans. Because of this, many of these plans have had difficulties meeting the applicable nondiscrimination requirements as more of these grandfathered employees become "highly compensated" over time. For a number of years, the IRS has released relief from the nondiscrimination rules for closed defined benefit plans. The SECURE Act essentially codifies a number of these relief provisions.

---

1.   IRC Sec. 414(v)(3)(B).
2.   See Notice 97-75, 1997-2 CB 337.
3.   Notice 97-75, 1997-2 CB 337, A-5.
4.   IRC Sec. 401(a)(5)(F)(ii).
5.   Rev. Proc. 93-42, 1993-2 CB 540.
6.   TAM 9137001.

Generally, a defined benefit plan cannot discriminate in favor of highly compensated employees with respect to any plan benefit, right or feature. Under the SECURE Act, defined benefit plans will be treated as passing nondiscrimination testing with respect to benefits, rights and features if:

(1)   the plan passes nondiscrimination testing in the plan year during which the plan closure takes place, and the two subsequent plan years,

(2)   the plan was not amended after closure to discriminate in favor of highly compensated employees, either by modifying the closed class or the benefits, rights and features provided to that class and

(3)   the plan was closed before April 5, 2017 or there was no substantial increase in value of either coverage or value of the benefits, rights and features for the five-year period before the plan was closed.[1]

A plan is treated as having had a "substantial increase" in coverage or value of the benefits, rights, or features during the applicable five-year period only if, during that period:

"(i) the number of participants covered by such benefits, rights, or features on the date the five-year period ends is more than 50 percent greater than the number of such participants on the first day of the plan year in which the period began, or

"(ii) the benefits, rights, and features have been modified by plan amendments in such a way that, as of the date the class is closed, the value of the benefits, rights, and features to the closed class as a whole is substantially greater than the value as of the first day of such five-year period, solely as a result of the amendments.[2]

Additionally, closed defined benefit plans can be aggregated with the employer's defined contribution plans for purposes of compliance testing if

(1)   the defined benefit plan provides benefits to a closed group of participants,

(2)   the defined benefit plan passes nondiscrimination and coverage testing in the plan year during which the plan closure takes place, and the two subsequent plan years,

(3)   no amendments that discriminate in favor of highly compensated employees were made after the plan closed, and

(4)   the plan was closed before April 5, 2017 or there was no "substantial increase" in value of either coverage or value of the benefits, rights and features for the five-year period before the plan was closed (see above).[3]

If the defined benefit plan is aggregated with a plan that provides matching contributions, the defined benefit plan must also be aggregated with the portion of the DC plan that provides

---

1.   IRC Sec. 401(o)(1)(A), (C).
2.   IRC Sec. 401(o)(1)(D).
3.   IRC Sec. 401(o)(1)(B).

elective deferrals and the matching contributions must be treated in the same way as nonelective contributions for purposes of nondiscrimination and coverage testing.[1]

The nondiscrimination relief is effective immediately, but plans have the option of applying this relief retroactively to plan years beginning after December 31, 2013.

3860. What nondiscrimination requirements must a plan meet with respect to plan amendments and terminations?

The timing of plan amendments must not have the effect of discriminating significantly in favor of highly compensated employees.[2] For this purpose, a plan amendment includes the establishment or termination of the plan, as well as any change in the benefits, rights, or features, benefit formulas, or allocation formulas under the plan.[3]

Regulations provide a facts and circumstances test for determining whether a plan amendment or series of amendments has the effect of discriminating significantly in favor of current or former highly compensated employees.[4]

The timing of a plan amendment that grants past service credit or increases benefits attributable to years of service for a period in the past will be deemed to be nondiscriminatory if the following four safe harbor requirements are met:

(1)   the period for which the credit is granted does not exceed the five years preceding the current year,

(2)   the past service credit is granted on a reasonably uniform basis to all employees,

(3)   benefits attributable to the period are determined by applying the current plan formula, and

(4)   the service credited is service, including pre-participation or imputed service (Q 3847), with the employer or a previous employer.[5]

Guidelines for nondiscriminatory allocation of assets on termination of a defined benefit plan are set forth in Revenue Ruling 80-229.[6]

3861. What are the requirements for cross tested plans?

Editor's Note: The SECURE Act made changes that would make it easier for certain sponsors of closed defined benefit plans to satisfy their nondiscrimination testing requirements.[7] See Q 3859 for details.

---

1.   IRC Sec. 401(o)(1)(B)(ii).
2.   Treas. Reg. §1.401(a)(4)-1(b)(4).
3.   Treas. Reg. §1.401(a)(4)-5(a).
4.   Treas. Reg. §1.401(a)(4)-5(a)(2).
5.   Treas. Reg. §1.401(a)(4)-5(a)(3).
6.   1980-2 CB 133.
7.   IRC Sec. 401(o).

Cross testing is the process by which defined contribution plans are tested for prohibited discrimination on the basis of benefits and defined benefit plans are tested on the basis of contributions. The general rules for converting allocations under a defined contribution plan to equal benefits and for converting benefits under a defined benefit plan to equal allocation rates are explained at Treasury Regulation Section 1.401(a)(4)-8.

The most common form of cross testing is comparability testing of profit sharing plans. That is because it is normally more advantageous for older and more highly compensated participants to have contributions to a defined contribution plan tested on the basis of equivalent benefits than it is to have benefits in a defined benefit plan tested on the basis of allocations. The comparability feature uses cross testing to show that contributions under a plan provide nondiscriminatory benefits. Cross testing also can involve aggregating a defined benefit plan with a defined contribution plan, and testing plans together on the basis of the benefits they provide.

Cross-testing requires that a defined contribution plan pass two tests: the gateway test and the non-discrimination test.

The Gateway Test

The gateway test requires that even a cross-tested plan must provide a minimum level of benefits to all participants and is a precondition to moving on to the nondiscrimination test.

The minimum allocation gateway test sets forth two standards for comparability plans. First, if the allocation rate for each Nonhighly Compensated Employee ("NHCE") in the plan is at least one-third of the allocation rate of the Highly Compensated Employee ("HCE") with the highest allocation rate under the plan, the gateway will be satisfied. In the alternative, if the allocation rate for each NHCE is at least 5 percent of his or her plan year compensation, within the meaning of IRC Section 415(c)(3) (Q 3866), the gateway will be satisfied.[1]

In lieu of the gateway contribution test, a comparability plan may pass through the gateway if it provides for "broadly available allocation rates."[2] To be broadly available, each allocation rate must be available to a group of employees that satisfies IRC Section 410(b), without regard to the average benefit percentage test (Q 3841).[3] Final regulations liberalized this determination somewhat by allowing groups receiving two different allocation rates to be aggregated for purposes of determining whether allocation rates are "broadly available." Thus, for example, a group receiving a 3 percent allocation rate could be aggregated with a group receiving a 10 percent allocation rate if each group passes the coverage test (not counting the average benefit percentage test).[4] Differences in allocation rates resulting from permitted disparity under the Section 1.401(l) regulations may be disregarded.[5]

---

1.   Treas. Reg. §1.401(a)(4)-8(b)(1)(vi)(A).
2.   Treas. Reg. §1.401(a)(4)-8(b)(1)(i)(B).
3.   Treas. Reg. §1.401(a)(4)-8(b)(1)(iii)(A).
4.   Rev. Rul. 2001-30, 2001-1 CB 46.
5.   Treas. Reg. §1.401(a)(4)-8(b)(1)(vii).

A plan that provides for age-based allocation rates also will be excepted from the minimum allocation gateway if it has a gradual age or service schedule. A plan has a gradual age or service schedule if the allocation formula for all employees under the plan provides for a single schedule of allocation rates that (1) defines a series of bands based solely on age, years of service, or points representing the sum of age and years of service that applies to all employees whose age, years of service, or points are within each band, and (2) the allocation rates under the schedule increase smoothly at regular intervals (as defined in the regulations).

Samples of smoothly-increasing allocation schedules, based on the sum of age and service, are included in the final regulations.[1] Certain plans that fail the safe harbor for target benefit plans[2] may satisfy the requirements for age-based allocation rates if the plan's allocation rates are based on a uniform target benefit allocation.[3]

The Nondiscrimination Test

Once the gateway test is passed, the equivalent benefit rate groups are subject to nondiscrimination testing. To pass nondiscrimination testing, every rate group must satisfy the coverage requirements of IRC Section 410(b) (Q 3859). Both the ratio percentage test and average benefit test are available for this purpose.

A defined benefit plan, benefitting primarily HCEs, may be aggregated with a defined contribution plan benefitting primarily NHCEs (sometimes referred to as a "DB/DC plan") if a gateway similar to the one described above is met, with the 5 percent safe harbor contribution being increased to 7.5 percent.[4]

In the alternative, if the combined plan is primarily defined benefit in character or consists of broadly available separate plans, as defined in regulations, it may be nondiscriminatory without satisfying the gateway.[5]

The IRS recently advised that a DB/DC plan was not primarily defined benefit in character because the non-highly compensated employees participating in the arrangement received no meaningful benefit from the DB portion of the plan. In this case, a "floor offset arrangement" was created so that DB plan (cash balance plan) benefits were offset by DC plan (profit-sharing plan) benefits only for non-highly compensated, non-owner employees, and the arrangement essentially eliminated the DB plan benefits for these employees. The IRS found that in order to satisfy the minimum aggregate allocation gateway, non-highly compensated employees must receive sufficient allocations under the profit-sharing plan in order to demonstrate that the plans were nondiscriminatory based on equivalent benefits.[6]

---

1.   Treas. Reg. §1.401(a)(4)-8(b)(1)(iv)(B).
2.   See Treas. Reg. §1.401(a)(4)-8(b)(3).
3.   See Treas. Reg. §1.401(a)(4)-8(b)(1)(v).
4.   Treas. Reg. §1.401(a)(4)-9(b)(2)(v)(A) and (D).
5.   See Treas. Reg. §1.401(a)(4)-9(b)(1)(v)(B) and (C).
6.   CCA 201810008.

The IRS released guidance expressing disapproval with plans that attempt to satisfy the nondiscrimination requirements by limiting participation to highly compensated employees and to rank and file employees with very short periods of service. By way of example, the IRS stated that a plan cross tested under the forgoing provisions violates the nondiscrimination requirements of IRC Section 401(a)(4) (Q 3847) where:

(1)   the plan excludes most or all permanent NHCEs;

(2)   the plan covers a group of NHCEs who were hired temporarily for short periods of time;

(3)   the plan allocates a higher percentage of compensation to the accounts of the HCEs than to those of the NHCEs covered by the plan; and

(4)   compensation earned by the NHCEs covered by the plan is significantly less than the compensation earned by the NHCEs not covered by the plan.[1]

3862. What is permitted disparity and how does it work?

Permitted disparity, also called Social Security integration, describes a contribution allocation formula or a benefit accrual formula that has two tiers of benefits. Under this formula, higher paid participants receive a slightly larger employer-provided benefit than employees whose contribution is below a level specified in the plan (i.e., the integration level in a defined contribution plan).

Permitted disparity rules are an exception to the general nondiscrimination requirement. Thus, a plan may use permitted disparity and still be classified as a safe-harbor design. The two-tier formula is based on the principle that employer-paid Social Security benefits will fund a greater portion of the replacement income of lower paid workers than of those whose earnings are above the Social Security wage base. The rules for permitted disparity are found under IRC Section 401(l).

An integrated plan will not be considered discriminatory merely because plan contributions or benefits favor the highly compensated employees if certain disparity thresholds are met.[2] If the requirements of IRC Section 401(l) are met, the disparity will be disregarded in determining whether the plan satisfies the nondiscrimination rules (Q 3847).[3] The regulations under IRC Section 401(l) provide the exclusive means for a plan to satisfy IRC Sections 401(l) and 401(a)(5)(C).[4]

Disparity formulas are not permitted for ESOPs, salary deferrals under a 401(k) plan, or employee or matching contributions to a 401(m) plan (Q 3753 to Q 3797).

---

1.   Memorandum dated October 22, 2004, Carol D. Gold, Director Employee Plans.
2.   IRC Sec. 401(a)(5)(C).
3.   Treas. Reg. §1.401(l)-1(a)(1).
4.   Treas. Reg. §1.401(l)-1(a)(3).

3863. What are the permitted disparity requirements applicable to defined contribution plans?

A defined contribution plan may provide for disparity in the rates of employer contributions allocated to employees' accounts if the contribution allocation formula meets the following requirements:

(1)   The disparity between contributions above the integration level (and contributions below the integration level)[1] must not exceed the maximum excess allowance. The maximum excess allowance is the lesser of (1) the base contribution percentage, or (2) the greater of (x) 5.7 percentage points or (y) the percentage equal to the portion of the rate of Social Security tax in effect for the year that is attributable to old-age insurance.[2] When the integration level in the plan document is less than the Social Security wage base, the percentages reflected above will need to be reduced as specified in regulations. The IRS will publish the percentage rate of the portion attributable to old-age insurance when it exceeds 5.7 percent.[3] Currently, the Social Security tax rate for old-age, survivors, and disability insurance combined is 6.2 percent.

(2)   The integration level, which determines the two levels of contributions, can be either equal to the taxable wage base in effect as of the beginning of the plan year, or a lower amount. If lower, then the contribution percentages must be reduced to satisfy one of two alternative tests.[4] The integration level is the amount of compensation specified under the plan at or below which the rate of contributions, expressed as a percentage, is less than the rate of contribution above that level.[5]

Special rules apply to target benefit plans (Q 3847).[6] Cash balance plans (Q 3720) that meet the safe harbor requirements provided in final regulations under IRC Section 401(a)(4) may satisfy the permitted disparity rules on the basis of the defined contribution plan rules.[7]

3864. What are the permitted disparity requirements applicable to defined benefit plans?

A defined benefit plan may be structured to use permitted disparity and satisfy the safe harbor provided by the Treasury regulations under IRC Section 401(a)(4). A defined benefit plan will not be considered discriminatory merely because the plan provides that a participant's retirement benefit may not exceed the excess of (1) the participant's final pay with the employer, over (2) the retirement benefit, under Social Security law, derived from employer contributions attributable to service by the participant with the employer.[8] The participant's final pay is the

1.   Treas. Reg. §§1.401(l)-2(a)(2), 1.401(l)-1(c)(16)(ii).
2.   IRC Sec. 401(l)(2).
3.   Treas. Reg. §§1.401(l)-2(a)(3), 1.401(l)-2(b).
4.   Treas. Reg. §§1.401(l)-2(a)(5), 1.401(l)-2(d).
5.   IRC Sec. 401(l)(5)(A).
6.   See Treas. Reg. §1.401(a)(4)-8(b)(3)(i)(C).
7.   Treas. Reg. §1.401(a)(4)-8(c)(3)(iii)(B).
8.   IRC Sec. 401(a)(5)(D)(i); Treas. Reg. §1.401(a)(5)-1(d)(2).

highest compensation paid to the participant by the employer for any year that ends during the five year period ending with the year in which the participant separated from service.[1] Compensation in excess of $290,000 (for 2021) may not be taken into account.[2]

A defined benefit plan may provide for disparity in the rates of employer-provided benefits if it meets all of the following requirements:

(1)   The disparity in benefit accruals for all employees under the plan must not exceed the maximum excess allowance (in the case of an excess plan) or the maximum offset allowance (in the case of an offset plan).[3]

The maximum excess allowance is the lesser of .75 percent (subject to reduction as described below) or the base benefit percentage for the plan year.[4] The maximum excess allowance cannot exceed the base benefit percentage.[5]

The maximum offset allowance is the lesser of (1) .75 percent (reduced as described below) or (2) one-half of the gross benefit percentage multiplied by a fraction (not to exceed one) of which the numerator is the employee's average annual compensation and the denominator is the employee's final average compensation up to the offset level.[6] The maximum offset allowance may not exceed 50 percent of the benefit that otherwise would have accrued.[7] For plans meeting the maximum offset allowance limitation, the "PIA Offset" safe harbor described below may be available.

(2)   The disparity for all employees under the plan must be uniform.[8] To be uniform, an excess plan must use the same base benefit percentage and the same excess benefit percentage for all employees with the same number of years of service. An offset plan is uniform only if it uses the same gross benefit percentage and the same offset percentage for all employees with the same number of years of service. The disparity provided under a plan that determines each employee's accrued benefit under the fractional accrual method in IRC Section 411(b)(1)(C) is subject to special uniformity requirements.[9]

(3)   The integration level under an excess plan or the offset level under an offset plan for each participant must be the participant's "covered compensation" (see below), a uniform percentage above 100 percent of covered compensation, a uniform dollar amount, or one of two intermediate amounts specified in the regulations.[10]

---

1.   IRC Sec. 401(a)(5)(D)(ii).
2.   Treas. Reg. §1.401(a)(5)-1(e)(2); IRC Sec. 401(a)(17); Notice 2020-79.
3.   Treas. Reg. §§1.401(l)-3(a)(3), 1.401(l)-3(b)(1).
4.   Treas. Reg. §1.401(l)-3(b)(2).
5.   IRC Sec. 401(l)(4)(A).
6.   Treas. Reg. §1.401(l)-3(b)(3).
7.   IRC Sec. 401(l)(4)(B).
8.   Treas. Reg. §1.401(1)-3(b)(1).
9.   Treas. Reg. §§1.401(l)-3(a)(4), 1.401(l)-3(c)(1).
10.   Treas. Reg. §1.401(l)-3(d). See IRC Sec. 401(l)(5)(A).

Regulations under IRC Sections 401(a)(4) and 401(l) provide a "PIA offset" safe harbor for those defined benefit plans that limit the offset to the maximum offset allowance described above. Under the safe harbor, a defined benefit plan that satisfies any of the existing safe harbors provided in the regulations under IRC Section 401(a)(4) will not fail to be a safe harbor plan merely because it offsets benefits by a percentage of PIA.[1]

Covered compensation, which is similar to the integration level in defined contribution plans and only applies to permitted disparity in defined benefit plans, means the average of the taxable wage bases for the 35 calendar years ending with the last day of the calendar year an individual attains Social Security retirement age.[2] The IRS publishes tables annually for determining employees' covered compensation.[3]

Average annual compensation is the participant's highest average annual compensation for any period of at least three consecutive years or, if shorter, the participant's full period of service.[4]

Final annual compensation is the participant's average annual compensation for the three consecutive year period ending with the current year, or, if shorter, the participant's full period of service, but not exceeding the contribution and benefit base in effect for Social Security purposes for the year.[5]

Final regulations require certain reductions in the .75 percent factor if the integration or offset level exceeds covered compensation or if benefits begin at an age other than Social Security retirement age. These reductions may be determined on an individual basis by comparing each employee's final average compensation to the employee's covered compensation.[6]

3865. What are the permitted disparity requirements when an employee is covered by two or more plans of any employer?

The IRC specifies that in the case of an employee covered by two or more plans of an employer, regulations are to provide rules preventing the multiple use of the disparity otherwise permitted under IRC Section 401(l).[7] Consequently, final regulations provide both an annual overall limit and a cumulative overall limit.[8]

The annual overall permitted disparity limit requires the determination of a fraction based on the disparity provided to an employee for the plan year under each plan. The annual overall limit is met if the sum of those fractions does not exceed one.[9]

---

1.   Treas. Reg. §1.401(l)-3(c)(2)(ix).
2.   Treas. Reg. §1.401(l)-1(c)(7)(i).
3.   See Rev. Rul. 2020-02 for the 2020 covered compensation table. See Rev. Rul. 2019-06, Rev. Rul. 2018-04 and Rev. Rul. 2017-05 for earlier years.
4.   IRC Sec. 401(l)(5)(C). Treas. Reg. §§1.401(l)-1(c)(2), 1.401(a)(4)-3(e)(2).
5.   IRC Sec. 401(l)(5)(D); Treas. Reg. §1.401(l)-1(c)(17).
6.   Treas. Reg. §§1.401(l)-3(d)(9), 1.401(l)-3(e).
7.   IRC Sec. 401(l)(5)(F)(ii).
8.   Treas. Reg. §1.401(l)-5.
9.   Treas. Reg. §1.401(l)-5(b)(1).

The cumulative permitted disparity limit generally is satisfied for an employee who has benefited from a defined benefit if the total of an employee's annual disparity fractions under all plans for all years of service does not exceed 35. In the case of an employee who has not benefited under a defined benefit plan for any plan year described in paragraph (c)(1)(v) of this section, the cumulative permitted disparity limit is satisfied.[1]

3866. What is compensation for purposes of nondiscrimination in a qualified plan?

Compensation applies in at least three different ways under the IRC when addressing nondiscrimination requirements for qualified plans.

First, when plans are tested for prohibited discrimination in favor of highly compensated employees, one element of the test is the participant's compensation. IRC Section 401(a)(4) sets the definition of what constitutes compensation for this purpose.

Second, plans must specify the types of compensation that are used to determine benefits or contributions under the plan.

Third, compensation is used to determine if certain employees are to be treated as highly compensated employees in the nondiscrimination testing.

The nondiscrimination rules of the IRC generally refer to nondiscriminatory compensation as compensation meeting the requirement of IRC Section 414(s). That definition then is tied to the definition of compensation under IRC Section 415(c)(3) and allows for certain modifications.

That listing is not all inclusive, and other definitions of compensation may be used in various testing. For, example, plans must limit the maximum amount of compensation used to determine benefits or to test for prohibited nondiscrimination. No compensation in excess of $290,000 in 2021 $285,000 in 2020, and $280,000 in 2019) may be taken into account for these purposes (Q 3926F).[2] The limit is indexd for inflation in increments of $5,000.[3]

IRC Section 415(c)(3) compensation is the compensation of the participant from the employer for the year.

IRC Section 415(c)(3) compensation is determined under one of the following definitions: currently includible compensation,[4] W-2 compensation[5] or wages for income tax withholding.[6] The regulations provide a degree of latitude in modifying each of these definitions of compensation.

Compensation generally includes elective deferrals as well as any amounts contributed or deferred by the employer at the election of the employee that are excluded from income under

---

1. Treas. Reg. §§1.401(l)-5(c)(1)(i), 1.401(l)-5(c)(2).
2. IRC Secs. 401(a)(17), 414(s)(1); Notice 2018-83, Notice 2019-59, Notice 2020-79.
3. IRC Sec. 401(a)(17); see Treas. Reg. §1.401(a)(17)-1(a).
4. See Treas. Reg. §1.415(c)-2(b)(1).
5. See Treas. Reg. §1.415(c)-2(d)(4).
6. See Treas. Reg. §1.415(c)-2(d)(3).

a cafeteria plan, a qualified transportation fringe benefit plan, or an IRC Section 457 plan.[1] IRC Section 414(s) permits an employer to either exclude or include such deferrals, as described below.

Employers may demonstrate that a definition of compensation is nondiscriminatory using snapshot testing on a single day during the plan year, provided that that day is representative of the employer's work force and the plan's coverage throughout the plan year.[2] This is seldom used in a small plan.

Planning Point: The definition of "compensation" is important for many reasons in the retirement planning arena, but has gained new importance in light of suspended deductions and exclusions post-tax reform. Retirement plans generally must use the IRC definition of compensation for non-discrimination testing purposes, which includes, for example, nondeductible moving expenses (but excludes deductible moving expenses). Post-reform, however, all moving expenses are nondeductible. Despite this, the moving expense deduction was only suspended, not eliminated. This is one example of how tax reform has created a level of uncertainty regarding the appropriate definition of compensation while all tax reform provisions remain (at least temporarily) in effect, making it important for plan administrators to evaluate their definition of compensation and consult with qualified tax counsel in determining how to proceed.

A definition of compensation other than IRC Section 415(c)(3) compensation still can satisfy IRC Section 414(s) if it meets the safe harbor definition or meets one of the alternative definitions plus a nondiscrimination test.[3] The safe harbor definition is IRC Section 415(c)(3) compensation, reduced by:

(1)   reimbursements or other expense allowances;

(2)   cash and non-cash fringe benefits;

(3)   moving expenses;

(4)   deferred compensation; and

(5)   welfare benefits.[4]

An alternative definition that defines compensation based on the rate of pay of each employee satisfies IRC Section 414(s) if the definition is nondiscriminatory and meets certain other requirements specified in the regulations.[5]

An employer generally may elect not to treat as compensation any of the following items: (1) elective contributions to a cafeteria plan, a qualified transportation fringe benefit plan (note that these amounts are no longer deductible for 2018-2025), an IRC Section 401(k) arrangement, a cash or deferred SEP, or a tax sheltered annuity; (2) compensation deferred under a Section 457 plan; and (3) employee contributions to a government employer pick-up plan.[6]

---

1.   IRC Sec. 415(c)(3)(D).
2.   Rev. Proc. 93-42, 1993-2 CB 540, modified by Rev. Proc. 95-34, 1995-2 CB 385.
3.   IRC Sec. 414(s)(3).
4.   Treas. Reg. §1.414(s)-1(c)(3).
5.   Treas. Reg. §1.414(s)-1(e).
6.   IRC Sec. 414(s)(2); Treas. Reg. §1.414(s)-1(c)(4).

Any other reasonable alternative definition of compensation can satisfy IRC Section 414(s) if it does not favor, by design, highly compensated employees and if it meets a nondiscriminatory requirement. An alternative definition of compensation meets the nondiscriminatory require-ment if the average percentage of total compensation included under the alternative definition for the employer's highly compensated employees as a group does not exceed, by more than a *de minimis* amount, the average percentage of total compensation included under the alternative definition for the employer's other employees as a group.[1] Self-employed individuals are subject to special rules for purposes of using an alternative definition.[2]

Compensation may have a slightly different definition for other purposes of the IRC.

Planning Point: Currently, certain employees are exempt from overtime requirements based on compensation, including employees who are paid a minimum salary of $455 per week and employees who perform certain types of duties and earn at least $100,000 per year (and so are considered highly compensated for overtime exemption purposes). The DOL has proposed to increase those amounts to $679 per week and $147,414 per year, respectively, for certain types of employees (these amounts would not become subject to cost-of-living increases). If these rules become effective, they would change the calculus for many retirement plans that base contribu-tions on compensation definitions that include overtime. The DOL compensation limit that applies to highly compensated employees would also be higher than the Section 414(q) limit ($130,000 for 2021), which could create issues with respect to nondiscrimination testing in qualified plans. Because of these changes, it may be valuable for qualified plan sponsors to follow closely and calculate the potential impact in order to avoid qualification problems.

3867. What are the Section 415 limits for qualified plans?

IRC Section 415 sets maximum levels for the annual contributions that may be made for any one participant under a defined contribution plan and the maximum accruals for participants under a defined benefit plan. A plan is qualified only if the plan document pre-cludes the possibility that benefits or contributions will exceed the limitations set forth in IRC Section 415 for any limitation year.[3]

For limitation years beginning in 2021, the highest annual benefit payable that may be paid under a defined benefit plan or under all such plans aggregated, if the employer has more than one, at the plan's normal retirement age (that is, at least 62) must not exceed the lesser of 100 percent of the participant's average compensation during his or her high three years of service, or $230,000 (in 2020).[4] See Q 3719 for further discussion on the application of the Section 415 limits to defined benefit plans.

The contribution limits applicable to defined contribution plans generally are referred to as the "annual additions limit." The annual additions limit is the maximum total allocation permitted to a participant's account (this calculation includes all such accounts in any defined contribution plan of the employer). The annual additions for any participant under a defined contribution plan must not exceed the lesser of 100 percent of the participant's compensation or $58,000

1.   Treas. Reg. §1.414(s)-1(d).
2.   See Treas. Reg. §§1.414(s)-1(d)(3)(iii)(B), 1.414(s)-1(g).
3.   See IRC Sec. 401(a)(16); Treas. Reg. §1.415(a)-1(d).
4.   IRC Sec. 415(b)(1); Notice 2020-79.

(as indexed in 2021, up from $57,000 in 2019).[1] See Q 3728 for details on the application of the Section 415 limits to defined contribution plans. All allocations to the account (other than "catch-up" contributions to a 401(k) plan and investment earnings) including salary deferrals, employer match, employer profit sharing contributions, employee contributions, and forfeiture reallocations are included as an annual addition in applying this limit.

Unless the plan document provides otherwise, a limitation year is the calendar year.[2] Contributions in excess of the Section 415 limits disqualify a plan for the year made and all subsequent years until such excess is corrected.[3] The regulations referenced here are effective for limitation years beginning on or after July 1, 2007.[4]

For purposes of the Section 415 limits, a benefit provided to an alternate payee of a participant pursuant to a qualified domestic relations order ("QDRO") (Q 3914) is treated as if it were provided to the participant.[5]

A controlled group of corporations or a group of trades or businesses under common control (Q 3932) or all members of an affiliated service group (Q 3934) are considered one employer for purposes of applying the limitations on contributions or benefits.[6] Thus, annual additions to any plan of the group are treated as made to a single plan.

A plan may incorporate the Section 415 limits by reference and will not fail to meet the definitely determinable benefit requirement (for defined benefit plans) or the definite predetermined allocation formula requirement (for defined contribution plans) merely because it incorporates the limits of IRC Section 415 by reference.[7]

Vesting

3868. What vesting standards must a qualified plan meet?

A plan must meet certain minimum standards regarding the non-forfeitability of retirement accounts or accrued benefits.[8] This is determined by the plan's vesting schedule. Defined benefit plans that are top heavy may be subject to an accelerated vesting schedule (Q 3921).

Five basic requirements generally apply to the vesting of participant benefits:

(1)   full vesting at the plan's retirement age,

(2)   full vesting at the termination of the plan,

(3)   full vesting of salary deferrals and employee contributions,

---

1.   IRC Sec. 415(c); Notice 2019-59, Notice 2020-79.
2.   Treas. Reg. §1.415(j)-1(a).
3.   Treas. Reg. §1.415(a)-1(a)(3); *Martin Fireproofing Profit Sharing Plan and Trust v. Comm.*, 92 TC 1173 (1989); *Hollen v. Comm.*, TC Memo 2011-2, 437 Fed. App'x 525 (8th Cir. 2011), *cert. denied*, 132 S. Ct. 2443 (2012).
4.   72 Fed. Reg. 16878 (April 15, 2007).
5.   Treas. Reg. §1.415(a)-1(f)(6).
6.   IRC Secs. 415(g), 415(h), 414(m); see Treas. Reg. §1.415(a)-1(f)(2).
7.   Treas. Reg. §1.415(a)-1(d)(3).
8.   IRC Sec. 401(a)(7).

(4)   a plan must meet either the cliff vesting or the scheduled vesting requirements under all other circumstances, and

(5)   a plan amendment may not reduce a participant's vested benefit.

An employee's right to normal retirement benefits must be non-forfeitable on the attainment of normal retirement age.[1] Normal retirement age is defined in the IRC as the earlier of normal retirement age under the plan, or the later of age 65 or the fifth anniversary of the date participation commenced.[2] Plans may, under certain circumstances, define normal retirement age as the earlier of normal retirement age as defined above or the age at which the participant completes the number of years of service (not less than 30) required by the plan.[3] An employee's rights in accrued benefits derived from the employee's own contributions must be non-forfeitable.[4]

Vesting can be determined based on all accounts in the plan or may provide separate schedules for various types of accounts (e.g., match, deferral, profit sharing account). It generally is not permissible for one group of employees to be subject to one vesting schedule and another group subject to another schedule in the same plan.[5] Where there is a pattern of abuse relating to vesting or changes in vesting (such as dismissing employees to prevent vesting), a more rapid rate of vesting may be required.[6] The determination of whether there is a pattern of abuse depends solely on the facts and circumstances in each case.[7]

Specific vesting requirements that apply to defined benefit plans are discussed in Q 3870, and those applicable to defined contribution plans and certain top heavy defined benefit plans are discussed in Q 3871.

Planning Point: Firing an employee to prevent vesting is also a violation of ERISA Section 510.

Rate of Benefit Accruals or Allocations

If an employee's benefit accruals or allocations (in the case of a defined contribution plan) cease, or if the rate of an employee's benefit accrual or rate of allocation is reduced because of the attainment of any age, the plan will not satisfy the IRC's vesting requirements.[8] Special rules apply to reductions of benefit accruals in statutory hybrid plans effective plan years beginning on or after January 1, 2016.[9]

Definitions

"Normal retirement benefit" means the employee's accrued benefit without regard to whether it is vested; thus, a plan cannot qualify if it provides no retirement benefits for employees who

---

1.   IRC Sec. 411(a).
2.   IRC Sec. 411(a)(8).
3.   IRC Sec. 411(f)(2).
4.   IRC Sec. 411(a)(1).
5.   Temp. Treas. Reg. §1.411(a)-3T(a)(2).
6.   ERISA Conf. Comm. Report, 1974-3 CB 437.
7.   Treas. Reg. §1.411(b)-1; News Release IR 80-85.
8.   IRC Secs. 411(b)(1)(H), 411(b)(2).
9.   Treas. Reg. §1.411(b)(5)-1.

reach normal retirement age with fewer than five years of vesting service.[1] A plan that provides that an employee's right to normal retirement benefits becomes non-forfeitable on the normal retirement date will fail to meet this requirement if the normal retirement date, as defined in the plan, may occur after the employee's "normal retirement age" as defined in IRC Section 411 (e.g., where normal retirement date is defined in the plan to be the first day of the calendar month following the employee's 65 birthday).[2]

"Accrued benefit" means, in the case of a defined benefit plan, the employee's accrued benefit determined under the plan (Q 3716) expressed in the form of an annual benefit commencing at normal retirement age, or, in the case of any other kind of plan, the balance of the employee's account.[3] The accrued benefit of a participant generally may not be decreased by an amendment to the plan (Q 3875).

The term "year of service" generally means a twelve month period, typically the plan year, designated by the plan during which an employee has worked at least 1,000 hours (although that amount may be less). It also may be measured using an elapsed time method.[4] All years of an employee's service with the employer are taken into account for purposes of computing the non-forfeitable percentages specified above except those years specifically excluded in IRC Section 411(a).[5] That section permits a plan to exclude service before age 18, and service prior to the effective date of the plan.

A right to an accrued benefit is considered to be non-forfeitable at a particular time if, at that time and thereafter, it is an unconditional right.[6] Some courts have made a distinction between vesting and non-forfeitability. A participant is vested when he or she has an immediate, fixed right of present or future enjoyment of his or her accrued benefit. A plan may provide that a vested benefit will be forfeited in whole or in part if, for example, the participant terminates his or her employment and goes to work for a competitor of the employer or commits a crime against the employer.[7] Thus, for example, a participant could be offered immediate 100 percent vesting of his or her benefit under a plan, but the benefit could be forfeitable (to the extent the benefit would not be vested under the closest IRC and ERISA schedules) if the employee commits certain forbidden acts. These are called "bad boy" clauses. Several circuit courts have held that forfeiture provisions are enforceable only to the extent that the accrued benefit forfeited by commission of the forbidden act is in excess of the non-forfeitable accrued benefit derived from employer contributions to which the participant was entitled under the nearest equivalent

1.   See Rev. Rul. 84-69, 1984-1 CB 125. See also *Board of Trustees of N.Y. Hotel Trades Council & Hotel Assoc. of N.Y. City, Inc. Pension Fund v. Comm.*, TC Memo 1981-597; *Trustees of the Taxicab Indus. Pension Fund v. Comm.*, TC Memo 1981-651; *Caterpillar Tractor Co. v. Comm.*, 72 TC 1088 (1979).
2.   Rev. Rul. 81-211, 1981-2 CB 98.
3.   IRC Sec. 411(a); Treas. Reg. §1.411(a)-7.
4.   IRC Sec. 411(a)(5).
5.   Treas. Reg. §§1.411(a)-5, 1.411(a)-6.
6.   Temp. Treas. Reg. §1.411(a)-4T(a).
7.   Rev. Rul. 85-31, 1985-1 CB 153.

ERISA vesting schedule at the time the forfeiture occurred.[1] The temporary regulations generally follow this reasoning.[2]

3869. What vesting standards apply to defined benefit plans?

A defined benefit plan (Q 3715) that is not structured as a cash balance plan or that is not top heavy, as determined under IRC Section 416, must provide vesting based on credited service that is at least as favorable as one of two schedules (IRC Section 411(a)(1)):

(1)   Under the five year cliff vesting schedule, an employee who has at least five years of credited service must have a nonforfeitable right to 100 percent of his or her accrued benefit derived from employer contributions.[3]

(2)   Under the three to seven year vesting schedule, an employee who has completed at least three years of credited service must have a nonforfeitable right to at least the following percentages of his or her accrued benefit derived from employer contributions: 20 percent after three years of service, 40 percent after four years of service, 60 percent after five years of service, 80 percent after six years of service, and 100 percent after seven years of service.[4]

A defined benefit plan structured as a cash balance plan must provide full vesting at the completion of three years of creditable service.

3870. What vesting standards apply to defined contribution and top heavy defined benefit plans?

All defined contribution plans and top-heavy defined benefit plans are required to provide vesting based on a participant's credited years of service that are at least as favorable as one of the following two schedules (Q 3725):

(1)   Under the three year cliff vesting schedule, an employee who has at least three years of service must have a non-forfeitable right to 100 percent of his or her accrued benefit derived from employer contributions.[5]

(2)   Under the two to six year vesting schedule, an employee who has completed at least two years of service must have a non-forfeitable right to at least the following percentages of his or her accrued benefit derived from employer contributions: 20 percent after two years of service, 40 percent after three years of service, 60 percent after four years of service, 80 percent after five years of service, and 100 percent after six years of service.[6]

---

1.   *Clark v. Lauren Young Tire Center Profit Sharing Trust*, 816 F.2d 480 (9th Cir. 1987); *Noell v. American Design, Inc.*, 764 F.2d 827 (11th Cir. 1985); *Fremont v. McGraw Edison*, 606 F.2d 752 (7th Cir. 1979); *Hepple v. Roberts & Dybdahl, Inc.*, 622 F.2d 962 (8th Cir. 1980); *Hummell v. S.E. Rykoff & Co.*, 634 F.2d 446 (9th Cir. 1980).

2.   See Temp. Treas. Reg. §1.411(a)-4T.

3.   IRC Sec. 411(a)(2)(A)(ii); see Temp. Treas. Reg. §1.411(a)-3T(b).

4.   IRC Sec. 411(a)(2)(A)(iii); see Temp. Treas. Reg. §1.411(a)-3T(c).

5.   IRC Sec. 411(a)(2)(B)(ii).

6.   IRC Sec. 411(a)(2)(B)(iii).

3871. Can a qualified plan's vesting schedule be changed?

Generally, yes. If a plan's vesting schedule is modified by a plan amendment, the general rule is that the plan does not comply with the vesting schedule requirement if the nonforfeitable percentage of the percentage of the accrued benefit derived from employer contributions, (determined as of the later of the date the amendment was adopted or became effective) of any plan participant is less than the nonforfeitable percentage computed without regard to the amendment. In addition, a plan amendment that changes the vesting schedule must permit each participant with at least three years of service to elect to have the non-forfeitable percentage computed under the plan without regard to the amendment.[1]

3872. What are the rules with respect to permitted forfeitures provided by the vesting requirements applicable to qualified plans?

The vesting rules do not require a plan to provide a preretirement death benefit aside from the employee's accrued benefit derived from his or her own contributions. The IRC provides that, "A right to an accrued benefit derived from employer contributions shall not be treated as forfeitable solely because the plan provides that it is not payable if the participant dies," except as required by the survivor annuity provisions (Q 3881).[2]

A reversion to the employer of contributions made under a mistake of fact or a mistake as to deductibility is not a forfeiture even if it results in adjustment of an entirely or partially non-forfeitable account, provided the return is limited to an amount that does not reduce a participant's balance below what it would have been had the mistaken amount not been contributed.[3]

Without violating the nonforfeitability rules, a plan may provide that payment of benefits to a retired employee is suspended for any period during which the retired employee resumes active employment with the employer who maintains the plan or, in the case of a multiemployer plan, in the same industry, the same trade or craft, and the same geographic area covered by the plan as when his or her benefits commenced.[4] The provision must be carefully drafted and administered to comply with applicable regulations and rulings.[5]

3873. What impact does a plan termination or discontinuance of contributions have on the vesting of qualified plan benefits?

A plan must provide that on its termination or partial termination (or, in the case of a profit sharing plan, also on complete discontinuance of contributions), benefits accrued to the date of termination or to the date of discontinuance of contributions become nonforfeitable to the extent funded at such date.[6]

---

1. IRC Sec. 411(a)(10); see Temp. Treas. Reg. §1.411(a)-8T(b).
2. IRC Sec. 411(a)(3)(A).
3. Rev. Rul. 91-4, 1991-1 CB 54.
4. IRC Sec. 411(a)(3)(B).
5. See Labor Reg. §2530.203-3; Rev. Rul. 81-140, 1981-1 CB 180; Notice 82-23, 1982-2 CB 752.
6. IRC Sec. 411(d)(3); Treas. Reg. §1.411(d)-2.

The merger or conversion of a money purchase pension plan into a profit sharing plan generally does not result in a partial termination and accelerated vesting provided that all employees who are covered by the money purchase plan remain covered under the continuing profit sharing plan, the money purchase plan assets and liabilities retain their characterization under the profit sharing plan, and employees vest in the profit sharing plan under the same vesting schedule that existed under the money purchase plan.[1]

A complete discontinuance may be deemed to have occurred when amounts contributed by an employer are not substantial enough to reflect an intent to continue to maintain the plan. Failure to make substantial and recurring contributions generally is regarded as a discontinuance of the plan. If this occurs solely because there are no current or accumulated profits, it may not constitute discontinuance as long as it is reasonable to expect contributions in future years.[2]

Whether partial termination or complete discontinuance has occurred depends on all the facts and circumstances. If a partial termination occurs, the vesting requirements that result from a partial termination apply only to the part of the plan that is terminated. Thus, a plan provision that states discontinuance will occur only when the ratio of aggregate contributions to compensation falls below a predetermined figure does not meet this qualification requirement and would need to be removed from the document.[3]

3874. What impact does the reduction of benefits by offset have upon whether a qualified plan satisfies the applicable vesting requirements?

Vesting requirements are not violated by a provision requiring pension payments to be reduced, or offset, by amounts received by the pensioner under a state workers' compensation law. Furthermore, state laws prohibiting offset of retirement benefits by workers' compensation benefits are preempted by ERISA.[4]

Vesting requirements were not violated where, under a severance pay plan, an employee's severance pay was reduced by the actuarial value, at discharge, of the employee's vested interest in a qualified pension plan. The severance pay plan was not a pension plan under ERISA subject to vesting standards.[5]

A pension plan whose benefits may be offset by benefits under a profit sharing plan will be considered to satisfy benefit accrual requirements if the accrued benefit, determined without regard to the offset, satisfies the vesting requirements and the offset is equal to the vested portion of the account balance in the profit sharing plan (or to a specified portion of the vested account balance).[6]

---

1.   Rev. Rul. 2002-42, 2002-2 CB 76.
2.   Rev. Rul. 80-146, 1980-1 CB 90.
3.   Rev. Rul. 80-277, 1980-2 CB 153.
4.   *Alessi v. Raybestos-Manhattan, Inc.*, 451 U.S. 504 (1981).
5.   *Spitzler v. New York Post Corp.*, 620 F.2d 19 (2d Cir. 1980).
6.   Rev. Rul. 76-259, 1976-2 CB 111.

Anti-Cutback Rule

3875. What is the anti-cutback rule and to which benefits does it apply?

ERISA and the Code contain provisions that protect participants and beneficiaries. The anti-cutback rule prohibits a plan amendment that decreases, directly or indirectly, the accrued benefit of a participant.[1] An exception may be available in certain cases of substantial business hardship described below.

Except as otherwise provided below, a plan amendment that has the effect of eliminating or reducing an early retirement benefit or a retirement-type subsidy, or eliminating certain optional forms of benefit attributable to service before the amendment is treated as impermissibly reducing accrued benefits.[2] Regulations include a list of benefits that are not protected in Treasury Regulation Section 1.411(a)-4, A-1(d).

The anti-cutback rule does not prohibit any plan amendment that reduces or eliminates benefits or subsidies that create significant burdens or complexities for the plan and plan participants unless the amendment adversely affects the rights of any participant in a more than *de minimis* manner.[3] If a series of plan amendments made at different times have the effect, when taken together, of reducing or eliminating a protected benefit in a more than *de minimis* manner, the amendment will violate IRC Section 411(d)(6).[4]

Employee stock ownership plans ("ESOPs") (Q 3819) will not be treated as failing to meet the anti-cutback requirement merely on account of modifying distribution options in a nondiscriminatory manner.[5]

Transfers between Plans

Benefits that are protected under IRC Section 411(d)(6) may not be eliminated by reason of a transfer or any transaction amending or having the effect of amending a plan to transfer benefits. A defined contribution "transferee" plan (e.g., in a merger, acquisition, consolidation, or similar transaction) will not be treated as failing the anti-cutback rule merely because the transferee plan does not provide some or all of the forms of distribution previously available under a transferor plan, if certain requirements are met.[6]

Elimination of a Form of Distribution

Except to the extent provided in regulations, a defined contribution plan will not be treated as failing the anti-cutback rule merely because of the elimination of a form of distribution previously available under the plan, provided that, with respect to any participant, a single sum payment is available to the participant at the same time or times as the form of distribution

1.   IRC Sec. 411(d)(6)(A); ERISA Sec. 204(g).
2.   IRC Sec. 411(d)(6)(B); see Treas. Reg. §1.411(d)-4, A-1(a).
3.   IRC Sec. 411(d)(6)(B).
4.   Treas. Reg. §1.411(d)-4, A-2(c).
5.   IRC Sec. 411(d)(6)(C); Treas. Reg. §1.411(d)-4, A-2(d); Notice 2013-17, 2013-20 IRB 1082.
6.   IRC Sec. 411(d)(6)(D); see Treas. Reg. §1.411(d)-4, A-3(b).

being eliminated and the single sum payment is based on the same or greater portion of the participant's account as the form of distribution being eliminated.[1]

3876. Are there any circumstances where a plan may be amended to eliminate an optional form of benefit? What is the redundancy rule?

A plan generally may be amended to eliminate an optional form of benefit with respect to benefits accrued before the amendment date if the optional form of benefit is redundant with a retained optional form of benefit.[2] For this purpose, the regulations identify six basic "families" of optional forms of benefit:

(1)   the 50 percent or more joint and contingent family;

(2)   the below 50 percent joint and contingent family;

(3)   the 10 years or less term certain and life annuity family;

(4)   the greater than 10 years term certain and life annuity family;

(5)   the 10 years or less level installment family; and

(6)   the greater than 10 years level installment family.[3]

The redundancy rule does not apply to certain "core options" unless the retained optional form of benefit and the eliminated option are identical except for differences described in the regulations.[4]

As an alternative to the redundancy rule, an employer is permitted to eliminate a protected benefit if the amendment does not apply to participants with annuity starting dates less than four years after the date the amendment is adopted and certain "core options" are retained.[5]

The core options generally mean:

(1)   a straight life annuity;

(2)   a 75 percent joint and contingent annuity;

(3)   a 10 year certain and life annuity; and

(4)   the most valuable option for a participant with a short life expectancy.[6]

---

1.   IRC Sec. 411(d)(6)(E).
2.   Treas. Reg. §1.411(d)-3(c)(1)(ii).
3.   Treas. Reg. §1.411(d)-3(c)(4).
4.   See Treas. Reg. §1.411(d)-3(c)(2)(ii).
5.   Treas. Reg. §1.411(d)-3(d).
6.   Treas. Reg. §1.411(d)-3(g)(5).

Special rules apply to plans in bankruptcy that allow the plan to eliminate optional forms of benefits that violate IRC Section 436 without violating IRC Section 411(d)(6).[1]

3877. What benefits are protected by the anti-cutback rule?

An employee's accrued benefit under a defined contribution plan is the value of the employee's account plus amounts to which the participant is entitled under the terms of the plan. These additional amounts include contributions that have accrued but have not been credited to the account due to a delay in the bookkeeping process.[2] Thus, a retroactive amendment to a defined contribution plan's allocation formula after the contribution for the year had been made but before the allocation to a participant's account had occurred violated IRC Section 411(d)(6) because it reduced the amounts allocated to some of the participants.[3]

The basic rule followed by most professionals is that once a participant has accrued a right to a contribution (for example, once the participant has met a 1,000 hours of credited service plan requirement) the formula cannot be modified to lower benefits to any employee, although this is not a bright line threshold.

The elimination of a cost-of-living adjustment ("COLA") provision through termination of a plan violated the ERISA prohibition against the reduction of accrued benefits.[4] But see Q 3878.

It also been held that a company's elimination of a lump sum distribution option, resulting in a decrease in former employees' accrued benefits, violated the ERISA provision and IRC Section 411(d)(6).[5]

The U.S. Supreme Court has determined that the plan sponsor violated the rule prohibiting cutbacks of early retirement benefits or retirement-type subsidies when it adopted a plan amendment expanding the range of post-retirement employment that would disqualify retired construction workers from receiving pension benefits.[6] The IRS followed with guidance limiting the retroactive application of this provision.[7] Final regulations take the position that a plan amendment may not impose new restrictions on a participant's rights to benefits that are protected under IRC Section 411(d)(6), whether or not the amendment would otherwise be permitted under the IRC.[8]

A change in actuarial factors may result in a violation of the anti-cutback rule. A cash balance plan (Q 3720) violated the rule where its use of a lower interest rate than was guaranteed by the plan resulted in a taxpayer receiving less than the actuarial equivalent of the taxpayer's normal retirement benefit.[9]

---

1. TD 9601 (Mar. 4, 2013) (adding 1.411(d)-4, A-2(b)(2)(xii)).
2. TAM 9735001.
3. See TAM 9735001.
4. *Hickey v. Chicago Truck Drivers, Helpers and Warehouse Workers Union*, 980 F.2d 465 (7th Cir. 1992).
5. *Auwarter v. Donohue Paper Sales Corp. Defined Benefit Pension Plan*, 802 F. Supp. 830 (E.D.NY 1992).
6. *Central Laborers' Pension Fund v. Heinz*, 124 S.Ct. 2230 (2004).
7. See Rev. Proc. 2005-23, 2005-18 IRB 991, as modified by Rev. Proc. 2005-76, 2005-2 C.B. 1139.
8. See TD 9280, 71 Fed. Reg. 45379 (Aug. 9, 2006).
9. See *Edsen v. Bank of Boston*, 229 F.3d 154 (2d Cir. 2000).

The IRS has provided guidance as to when a change in actuarial factors will indirectly affect accrued benefits, as well as acceptable methods for preventing a violation of the vesting rules as a result of such a change.[1]

3878. What benefits are not protected by the anti-cutback rule?

Despite the fact that a COLA provision may constitute an essential element of an accrued benefit,[2] a COLA provision was not an accrued benefit with respect to retirees who retired before the provision was adopted, even though it was made available to them.[3]

Regulations permit profit sharing or stock bonus plans (as well as cash or deferred arrangements) to be amended to eliminate hardship withdrawal provisions without violating IRC Section 411(d)(6).[4]

Plan amendments adopted within the remedial amendment period that are necessary to bring a plan into compliance with the IRC or to prevent unintended benefit increases as a result of an IRC amendment generally are afforded relief from IRC Section 411(d)(6).[5] Thus, for example, the elimination of the right to receive employer securities from an S corporation ESOP does not violate IRC Section 411(d)(6).[6] The elimination of the right to receive a distribution prior to retirement after age 70½ (Q 3894) also does not do so, if certain conditions are met.[7]

The following benefits are not protected under IRC Section 411(d)(6) and may be reduced or otherwise amended:

(1)   ancillary life insurance protection,

(2)   accident or health insurance benefits,

(3)   availability of loans,

(4)   the right to make after-tax contributions or elective deferrals, and

(5)   the right to direct investments.[8]

Ancillary benefits, other rights or features, and any other benefits not described in IRC Section 411(d)(6) are not protected under IRC Section 411(d)(6).[9]

Despite the protection provided to early retirement benefits, the IRS determined that where an employer offered an early retirement window benefit repeatedly for substantially

1.   See Rev. Rul. 81-12, 1981-1 CB 228.
2.   See *Hickey v. Chicago Truck Drivers, Helpers and Warehouse Workers Union*, 980 F.2d 465 (7th Cir. 1992).
3.   *Sheet Metal Workers' Nat'l Pension Fund Bd. of Trustees v. Comm.*, 117 TC 220 (2001), *aff'd*, 318 F.3d 599 (4th Cir. 2003).
4.   Treas. Reg. §1.411(d)-4, A-2(b)(2)(x).
5.   See, e.g., Rev. Proc. 94-13, 1994-1 CB 566 (reduction of compensation limit under IRC Sec. 401(a)(17)); Notice 99-44, 1999-2 CB 326 (repeal of combined plan limit).
6.   See Treas. Reg. §1.411(d)-4, A-2(d).
7.   See Treas. Reg. §1.411(d)-4, A-10.
8.   Treas. Reg. §1.411(d)-4, A-1(d); see Rev. Rul. 96-47, 1996-2 CB 35.
9.   See Treas. Reg. §1.411(d)-4, A-1(d).

consecutive, limited periods of time, its failure to offer the benefit permanently did not violate IRC Section 411(d)(6).[1]

3879. What special rules are related to the anti-cutback rule? When can a plan reduce benefits in the case of a substantial business hardship?

Plans subject to the funding standards of ERISA Section 302 (generally, defined benefit plans, money purchase pensions and target benefit plans), must meet a notice requirement if the plan is amended in a manner that significantly reduces the participants' rate of future benefit accruals.[2]

Under limited circumstances, a retroactive plan amendment reducing benefits may be available in the case of a substantial business hardship where it is determined that a waiver of the minimum funding standard (Q 3747) is unavailable or inadequate.[3] Among the factors the IRS will consider in determining whether a substantial business hardship exists are whether:

(1)   the employer is operating at an economic loss,

(2)   there is substantial unemployment or underemployment in the trade or business and the industry concerned,

(3)   the sales and profits of the industry are depressed or declining, and

(4)   it is reasonable to expect that the plan will be continued only if the waiver is granted.[4]

The IRS permitted such an amendment to a plan whose sponsor was insolvent and expected no additional revenues, but the plan's only participants and the sponsor's only employees were the five owners of the business.[5]

Automatic Survivor Benefits

3880. What plans are subject to the automatic survivor benefit (QJSA and QPSA) requirements?

The requirement that a plan provide the qualified joint and survivor annuity ("QJSA") and qualified preretirement survivor annuity ("QPSA") forms of benefit (Q 3881) applies to all defined benefit plans, to all defined contribution plans that are subject to minimum funding standards (e.g., target benefit and money purchase pensions), and to profit sharing plans that include annuity provisions as the normal form of benefit.[6]

---

1.   Rev. Rul. 92-66, 1992-2 CB 92.
2.   ERISA Sec. 204(h).
3.   IRC Sec. 412(d)(2).
4.   IRC Sec. 412(c)(2).
5.   See Let. Rul. 9736044.
6.   IRC Sec. 401(a)(11)(B).

The automatic survivor benefit requirements also may apply to any participant under any other defined contribution plans unless, (1) the plan provides that in the event of the participant's death, his or her non-forfeitable accrued benefit will be paid in full to his or her surviving spouse or to another designated beneficiary if the spouse consents or if there is no surviving spouse; (2) the participant does not elect payment of benefits in the form of a life annuity; and (3) with respect to such participant, the plan is not a direct or an indirect transferee of a plan to which the automatic survivor annuity requirements apply.[1]

The automatic survivor benefit requirements will not apply to the portion of benefits accrued under a tax credit ESOP or leveraged ESOP if the participant has the right to demand distribution in the form of employer securities or to require repurchase by the employer of non-publicly traded securities.[2]

3881. What survivor benefits must be provided under a qualified plan?

Plans that are subject to the automatic survivor benefit requirements (Q 3880), sometimes referred to as the QJSA requirements, must provide that, unless waived by the participant with the consent of the spouse (Q 3889), retirement benefits will be paid in the form of a "qualified joint and survivor annuity."[3]

An unmarried participant must be provided with a life annuity, unless he or she elects another form of benefit.[4]

Furthermore, such plans must provide that if a vested participant dies prior to the annuity starting date, benefits will be paid to a surviving spouse in the form of a "qualified preretirement survivor annuity."

This benefit requirement may be waived by the participant with the consent of his or her spouse (Q 3889).

These requirements apply to all pension plans but only to certain profit sharing plans. This requirement only applies to profit sharing plans where the document specifies the normal form of benefit is payable as an annuity or where the profit sharing plan contains pension plan assets of a plan of the employer that were merged into the profit sharing plan. Most profit sharing plans do not specify that benefits be paid in the form of an annuity.[5]

When a plan is subject to these requirements, notices are required advising the participant and spouse of their benefits. Thus, benefits other than the required QJSA or QPSA cannot be paid from a pension plan unless the participant (and spouse, if married) elects not to receive the annuity payment.

---

1. IRC Sec. 401(a)(11)(B); Treas. Reg. §1.401(a)-20, A-3.
2. IRC Secs. 401(a)(11)(C), 409(h).
3. IRC Sec. 401(a)(11); Treas. Reg. §1.401(a)-20.
4. Treas. Reg. §1.401(a)-20, A-25.
5. Treas. Reg. §1.401(a)-20, A-11.

An exception to these general rules applies if the present value of the participant's benefit does not exceed $5,000 and the plan specifies that a lump sum payout will be paid without need for consent of either the participant or spouse. If the payment is after the participant's annuity starting date, the participant and the participants' spouse (or surviving spouse) must consent in writing.[1]

The annuity starting date is the first day of the first period for which an amount is payable as an annuity regardless of when or whether payment is actually made or, in the case of benefits not payable in the form of an annuity, the date on which all events have occurred that entitle the participant to the benefit.[2] This requirement applies only to those benefits in which a participant was vested immediately prior to his or her death under a defined benefit plan and to all non-forfeitable benefits that are payable under a defined contribution plan.[3]

3882. What is a qualified joint and survivor annuity ("QJSA")?

A qualified joint and survivor annuity ("QJSA") is an annuity (1) for the life of the participant, with a survivor annuity for the life of his or her spouse that is not less than one-half (nor greater than 100 percent) of the amount of the annuity payable during the joint lives of the participant and his or her spouse, and (2) that is the actuarial equivalent of a single annuity for the life of the participant.[4]

With respect to married participants, the qualified joint and survivor annuity must be at least as valuable as any other optional form of benefit payable under the plan at the same time. If a plan has two joint and survivor annuities that satisfy the QJSA requirements and one has a greater actuarial value than the other, the more valuable one is the QJSA. If a plan offers two actuarially equivalent joint and survivor annuities that meet the QJSA requirements, it may designate which joint and survivor annuity is the QJSA and allow a participant to elect out of the designated QJSA in favor of the equal QJSA without spousal consent.[5]

A plan subject to the QJSA requirements must permit a participant to receive a distribution under a QJSA when the participant attains the earliest retirement age under the plan. Written consent of the participant (but not the spouse) is required for a QJSA benefit to commence. The earliest retirement age is the earlier of the earliest age at which a participant could receive a distribution under the plan or the early retirement age determined under the plan (or, if no early retirement age, the normal retirement age under the plan).[6]

3883. What is a qualified preretirement survivor annuity ("QPSA")?

A qualified preretirement survivor annuity ("QPSA") is a survivor annuity for the life of the surviving spouse of the participant under which payments are to begin no later than the month

---

1.   IRC Sec. 417(e)(1); Treas. Reg. §1.417(e)-1(b)(2)(i).
2.   IRC Sec. 417(f)(2); Treas. Reg. §1.401(a)-20, A-10(b)(2).
3.   Treas. Reg. §1.401(a)-20, A-12.
4.   IRC Sec. 417(b).
5.   Treas. Reg. §1.401(a)-20, A-16.
6.   Treas. Reg. §1.401(a)-20, A-17.

in which the participant would have reached the earliest retirement age provided under the plan and that also meets the following requirements with respect to the amount of the annuity:

(1)　In the case of a defined contribution plan, the survivor annuity is the actuarial equivalent of the participant's account and must not be less than one-half of the participant's vested account balance as of the date of his or her death unless waived by the participant and spouse.[1]

(2)　In the case of all other plans, (x) if the participant died after the date the participant attained the earliest retirement age provided under the plan, the payments to the surviving spouse must not be less than the amounts that would have been payable under the survivor portion of a qualified joint and survivor annuity had the participant retired with an immediate qualified joint and survivor annuity on the day before he died, or (y) if the participant died on or before the date the participant would have reached the earliest retirement age, the payments to the surviving spouse must not be less than the amounts that would have been paid under the survivor portion of a QJSA had the participant separated from service on the earlier of the actual time of separation or death, survived to the earliest retirement age, retired with an immediate qualified joint and survivor annuity at the earliest retirement age, and died on the day after he or she reached the earliest retirement age.[2] In any case, payments to the surviving spouse must not violate the incidental benefit rule (Q 3829).[3]

A defined benefit plan must permit the surviving spouse to receive distributions under the QPSA no later than the month in which the participant would have attained the earliest retirement age. In the case of a defined contribution plan, the spouse must be permitted to elect to begin receiving payments under the QPSA within a reasonable time after the participant's death.[4]

3884. What is a qualified optional survivor annuity and how can it be used to satisfy the QJSA requirements for qualified plans?

In plan years beginning after December 31, 2007, a plan will satisfy the QJSA requirements only if a participant who has waived the QJSA may elect a qualified optional survivor annuity.[5] Spousal consent is not required to elect a qualified optional survivor annuity.

Generally, spousal consent is subject to a physical presence requirement so that the spouse granting consent must do so in person, before a notary public. When a plan participant requests a distribution or loan (the availability of which were expanded by the 2020 CARES Act), the spouse must grant a waiver. Notice 2020-42 provides relief in permitting remote electronic notarization executed via live auto-video technology that satisfies any state-level requirements that apply to a notary public. The relief in Notice 2020-42 applies to any participant election

---

1.　Treas. Reg. §1.401(a)-20, A-20.
2.　IRC Sec. 417(c); Treas. Reg. §1.401(a)-20, A-18.
3.　Sen. Fin. Comm. Rep. to P.L. 98-397. See Rev. Rul. 85-15, 1985-1 CB 132.
4.　Treas. Reg. §1.401(a)-20, A-22.
5.　IRC Sec. 417(a)(1)(A).

that requires a signature to be witnessed in the physical presence of a plan representative or notary before January 1, 2020.

The term qualified optional survivor annuity means an annuity for the life of the participant with a survivor annuity for the life of the spouse that is equal to an "applicable percentage" of the amount of the annuity that is payable during the joint lives of the participant and spouse and is the actuarial equivalent of a single annuity for the participant's life. For this purpose, if the survivor annuity percentage is less than 75 percent, the qualified optional survivor annuity percentage must be at least 75 percent. If the survivor annuity percentage is equal to or greater than 75 percent, the qualified optional survivor annuity percentage must be at least 50 percent.[1]

3885. Does a plan participant have to be married for a certain length of time before QJSA and QPSA requirements apply?

A plan generally is not required to provide either the QJSA or the QPSA (but may do so) if the participant and the spouse were not married throughout the one year period ending on the earlier of the participant's annuity starting date (see Q 3881) or the date of the participant's death. If a participant marries within one year before the annuity starting date and the participant and the participant's spouse were married for at least a one year period ending on or before the date of the participant's death, the participant and the spouse are treated as though they had been married throughout the one year period ending on the participant's annuity starting date.[2] Special rules may apply where there is a Qualified Domestic Relations Order ("QDRO") in effect that applies to plan benefits (Q 3914).

Planning Point: Because of the administrative difficulties involved, plan sponsors should consider whether the costs of imposing a one year of marriage requirement outweigh any potential savings. Where possible, plan sponsors should design plans to minimize the administrative processes for profit sharing plans.

Planning Point: In *United States v. Windsor*,[3] the Supreme Court found unconstitutional the Defense of Marriage Act, which defines marriage as a legal union between one man and one woman and spouse as a person of the opposite sex. Revenue Ruling 2013-17[4] provides that for federal tax purposes, spouse means a person of the same sex if lawfully married under state law and marriage includes marriage between persons of the same sex. Notice 2014-19[5] provides further guidance on the application of *Windsor* and Revenue Ruling 2013-17 to qualified plans. The Supreme Court's decision in *Obergefell v. Hodges*[6] requires states to recognize same sex marriages performed in other states. This ruling will simplify plan administration, as administrators will no longer have to apply the place of celebration rule to determine whether the marriage was lawful. Notice 2015-86 provides guidance on the application of *Obergefell* to plans.[7]

---

1.   See IRC Sec. 417(g).
2.   IRC Sec. 417(d); Treas. Reg. §1.401(a)-20, A-25(b)(2).
3.   33 S.Ct. 2645 (2013).
4.   2013-38 IRB 201.
5.   2014-17 IRB 979.
6.   135 S.Ct. 2584 (2015).
7.   Notice 2015-86, 2015-52 I.R.B. 887.

3886. When is a profit sharing plan not subject to QJSA and QPSA requirements?

As noted in Q 3880, unless a profit sharing plan document is written to provide an annuity as the normal form of benefit, or if the plan contains pension assets that were merged into the profit sharing plan, QJSA and QPSA annuity rules do not apply. Another requirement, however, mandates that at least 50 percent of the benefit be paid to a surviving spouse. Under waiver rules similar to those discussed in Q 3889, a spouse may agree to waive these rights and have the benefit paid to another beneficiary.

In 2012, the IRS issued Revenue Ruling 2012-3, which describes how the QJSA and QPSA rules apply when a deferred annuity contract is purchased under a profit-sharing plan.[1] Qualified joint and survivor annuity (QJSA) and qualified preretirement survivor annuity (QPSA) rules generally impose a series of spousal consent, notice, and election requirements upon certain lifetime income options. While the rules regarding whether a defined contribution plan is subject to QJSA and QPSA requirements are relatively clear, it has been much more difficult to determine when these requirements would apply to a plan that contains a deferred annuity contract.

Revenue Ruling 2012-3 outlines the QJSA and QPSA requirements in situations involving defined contribution plans that contain deferred annuity contracts.

If a defined contribution plan contains a deferred annuity contract, QJSA requirements are not triggered until the plan participant irrevocably elects to receive the retirement funds in the form of an annuity. As a result, even in a situation where a life annuity may be the default payment under a deferred annuity, if the participant has the option to choose another investment option or receive a lump-sum payment, the plan will not be subject to the QJSA and QPSA requirements until the annuity actually starts making payments (or until the participant can no longer change his or her investment options). Further, if the participant does not affirmatively elect a life annuity during the 180 days before the annuity starting date, he or she is not considered to have elected the life annuity until the starting date.

QPSA requirements will not be triggered if the annuity contract gives the plan participant's surviving spouse a nonwaivable right to the QPSA benefit. If it is not certain that the surviving spouse will receive the benefit, then the QPSA requirements apply.

3887. What notice requirements apply to qualified plans subject to QJSA rules?

A plan subject to the QJSA rules generally must provide, within certain specified periods, each participant (vested and nonvested, married or unmarried) with a written explanation of the automatic survivor annuity forms of benefit, certain optional forms of benefit, and their relative values. The notice must explain the participant's (and his or her spouse's) rights with respect

---

1.   2012-1 CB 383 (Feb. 2, 2012).

to waiving such benefits.[1] Notices of automatic survivor benefits generally may be provided in electronic form provided certain requirements are met.[2]

The explanation may be provided after the annuity starting date, but the applicable election period for waiving the benefit (Q 3889) may not end before the thirtieth day after the explanation is provided.[3] Under certain circumstances, a "retroactive annuity starting date" may be permitted (Q 3889).[4] The plan may allow the participant with any applicable spousal consent to waive the 30 day requirement if the distribution begins more than seven days after the explanation is provided.[5]

The explanation must include information on the financial effect and relative value comparisons of any optional forms of benefit compared to the value of the QJSA. This may be offered in the form of generally applicable information or as information that is specific to the participant to whom it is provided. Details and procedures for making the required disclosures, as well as a sample disclosure, are set forth in final regulations. These requirements generally are effective for QJSAs with annuity starting dates after February 1, 2006.[6]

A defined benefit pension plan that fully subsidizes a qualified survivor annuity is not required to provide an explanation unless it offers participants an election to waive the benefit or designate a beneficiary.[7]

3888. What special rules apply to plans that are subject to QJSA and QPSA requirements?

For plan years beginning before January 1, 2008, the present value of the accrued benefit generally was required to be determined using the annual interest rate on 30-year Treasury securities for the month before the date of distribution. Temporary regulations permitted the employer to base the determination on a monthly, quarterly, or annual interest rate. The rate could have been determined using any month during a "stability period" of up to five months, provided the plan specified the month that will be used. In any event, the interest rate had to be determined in a consistent manner that is applied uniformly to all plan participants.[8]

In plan years beginning after December 31, 2007, the present value of the accrued benefit generally must be determined using a mortality table specified in regulations and an interest rate derived from a three-segment yield curve, phased in over five years.[9]

1.   IRC Sec. 417(a)(3); see TD 9256, 71 Fed. Reg. 14798.
2.   See Treas. Reg. §1.401(a)-21.
3.   IRC Sec. 417(a)(7).
4.   See Treas. Reg. §1.417(e)-1(b)(3)(iv).
5.   IRC Sec. 417(a)(7)(B); TD 8796, 1999-1 CB 344.
6.   See Treas. Reg. §1.417(a)(3)-1(f)(1).
7.   IRC Secs. 417(a)(3), 417(a)(5); See Treas. Reg. §1.401(a)-20, A-37.
8.   IRC Sec. 417(e)(3), prior to amendment by PPA 2006; Treas. Reg. §1.417(e)-1(d)(4).
9.   See IRC Sec. 417(e)(3).

Corrective distributions of excess deferrals, excess contributions, and excess aggregate contributions (Q 3760, Q 3807) from a 401(k) plan are not subject to the QJSA or spousal consent rules.[1]

Plans that offer plan loans (Q 3952 to Q 3959) and are subject to the QJSA requirements generally must provide that no portion of the accrued benefit of the participant may be used as security for any loan unless, at the time the security agreement is entered into, the participant's spouse consents to the use of the accrued benefit as security.[2] If spousal consent is not obtained or is not required at the time benefits are used as security, it is not required at the time of any setoff of the loan against the accrued benefit, even if the participant is married to a different spouse at the time of the setoff.[3]

The IRS audits plans to determine if the consent rules have been met. Revenue Procedure 2016-51[4] explains the procedure to follow if distributions are made without spousal consent.

The automatic survivor benefit rules generally do not apply to a beneficiary who murders his or her participant spouse.[5] An employee's widow convicted of his murder was held entitled to receive the preretirement annuity where applicable state law made her a constructive trustee of the annuity.[6]

3889. When may survivor benefits required under a qualified plan be waived?

A qualified plan that is subject to the automatic survivor benefit rules generally must provide that participants may elect (or revoke an election) to waive the qualified joint and survivor annuity ("QJSA") or the qualified preretirement survivor annuity ("QPSA") forms of benefit (Q 3881) at any time during the applicable election period.[7] The participant may elect the qualified optional survivor annuity ("QOSA") at any time during the applicable election period.[8]

The plan also must provide that such an election will not be effective unless (1) the spouse of the participant, if any, consents in writing to the election, (2) the election designates a beneficiary or a form of benefits that may not be changed without spousal consent (unless the consent expressly permits future designations by the participant without further spousal consent), and (3) the consent acknowledges the effect of the election and is witnessed by a plan representative or notary public.[9] See Q 3885, which explains the use of the term spouse to apply to same sex couples.

---

1.   Treas. Reg. §1.401(k)-2(b)(2)(vii)(A).
2.   IRC Secs. 417(a)(1), 417(a)(4); Treas. Reg. §1.401(a)-20, A-24.
3.   Treas. Reg. §1.401(a)-20, A-24(b).
4.   2016-42 IRB 465.
5.   See *Mendez-Bellido v. Board of Trustees of Div. 1181*, 709 F. Supp. 329 (E.D.N.Y. 1989). See also, Let. Ruls. 8908063, 8905058.
6.   *George Pfau's Sons Co. v. Neal*, 665 NE 2d 68 (Ct. App. Ind. 1996).
7.   IRC Sec. 417(a)(1)(a).
8.   See IRC Sec. 417(a)(1)(a).
9.   IRC Sec. 417(a)(2); Treas. Reg. §1.401(a)-20, A-31.

An election made without the consent of the spouse is effective only if it is established to the satisfaction of a plan representative that there is no spouse, that the spouse cannot be located, or that certain other specified circumstances prevent securing such consent.[1] Caution should be exercised when following any of these exceptions as a missing spouse who suddenly resurfaces may be entitled to benefits that already have been fully paid to another beneficiary. Any consent by the spouse of a participant, or proof that consent cannot be obtained from the spouse, is effective only with respect to that spouse and not to any subsequent spouse except in the case of plan benefits securing a loan (Q 3881).[2]

A spousal waiver that had not been properly witnessed or notarized was struck down despite the wife's acknowledgement that she had signed the form because the waiver did not meet the requirements clearly set forth in the IRC and ERISA.[3]

In an earlier district court ruling, the lack of a written, notarized spousal consent did not render the designation of a non-spouse beneficiary completely ineffective; the designation remained effective to the extent the benefits exceeded what was required to be paid to the spouse.[4] In another case, the Seventh Circuit held that where the husband was also the plan representative, his wife's consent was valid even though he did not witness it on behalf of the plan, because he knew the person who signed it was his wife.[5]

Prior consent to waive a benefit is not invalid simply because the benefit increased after the consent was given.[6]

A prenuptial agreement or similar contract entered into prior to marriage is not, by itself, effective to waive a widow's surviving spouse benefits,[7] based on parallel provisions found in ERISA Section 205(c) and IRC Section 417(a).[8] For a valid waiver to occur, ERISA requires a notarized waiver containing specific language by a spouse who actually is entitled, by marriage, to the statutory benefits being waived. In addition, the spouse executing the waiver must designate an alternative beneficiary.[9]

Planning Pointer: If the parties intend that the surviving spouse's right to benefits be waived after the marriage, the agreement should provide that the waiver be executed in conformance with the waiver requirements after the marriage.

The Court of Appeals for the Eighth Circuit held that neither a prenuptial agreement with a participant's second wife, nor a separation agreement in which his first wife had "relinquished

---

1. See Treas. Reg. §1.401(a)-20, A-27.
2. IRC Sec. 417(a)(2); Treas. Reg. §1.401(a)-20, A-29.
3. See *Lasche v. George W. Lasche Basic Profit Sharing Plan*, 111 F.3d 863 (11th Cir. 1997).
4. *Profit Sharing Plan for Employees of Republic Fin. Services, Inc. v. MBank Dallas, N.A.*, 683 F. Supp. 592 (N.D. Tex. 1988). But see *United Parcel Service, Inc. v. Riley*, 532 N.Y.S.2d 473 (1988).
5. *Burns v. Orthotek, Inc. Employees' Pension Plan & Trust*, 657 F.3d 571 (7th Cir. 2011).
6. *Kifafi v. Hilton Hotels Ret. Plan*, 826 F. Supp. 2d 25 (D.D.C. 2011).
7. Treas. Reg. §1.401(a)-20, A-28; *Hurwitz v. Sher*, 982 F.2d 778 (2d Cir. 1992), *cert. denied*, 113 S.Ct. 2345; *Nellis v. Boeing*, 1992 U.S. Dist. Lexis 8510 (D.C. Kan. 1992).
8. See also, *Pedro Enter., Inc. v. Perdue*, 998 F.2d 491 (7th Cir. 1993).
9. See *Hagwood v. Newton*, 282 F.3d 285 (4th Cir. 2002).

any right, title or interest in and to any … pension plans," constituted a valid waiver; thus, the court divided the benefit equally between them on his death.[1]

The Court of Appeals for the Fourth Circuit found that a valid waiver was executed where the separation agreement specified the plan in which the interest was waived, even though the ex-spouse was still named as beneficiary.[2]

A plan is not required to permit a waiver of the QJSA or QPSA form of benefit if it fully subsidizes the cost of such benefit and does not permit a participant to waive the benefit or designate another beneficiary. A plan fully subsidizes the cost of a benefit if the failure to waive the benefit would not result in a decrease of any plan benefits to the waiving participant and would not result in increased contributions from that participant.[3]

Applicable Election Period

With respect to the QJSA form of benefit, the applicable election period is the 180 day period ending on the annuity starting date (the 90 day period, in the case of plan years beginning before 2007).[4] The plan generally may not commence the distribution of any portion of a participant's accrued benefit to which these requirements apply unless the applicable consent requirements are satisfied.[5]

A plan must provide participants with written notice of the QJSA requirement no less than 30 days and no more than 180 days (90 days for plan years prior to 2007) before the annuity starting date.[6] If a participant, after receiving the written explanation of the QJSA, affirmatively elects a form of distribution with spousal consent, the plan will not fail to satisfy the requirements of IRC Section 417(a) merely because the annuity starting date is less than 30 days after the written explanation was provided to the participant, provided four requirements are met:

(1)   the plan administrator must provide information to the participant clearly indicating that the participant has a right to at least 30 days to consider whether to waive the QJSA and consent to another form of distribution;

(2)   the participant must be permitted to revoke an affirmative distribution election at least until the annuity starting date, or, if later, at any time prior to the expiration of the seven day period that begins the day the explanation of the QJSA is provided to the participant;

(3)   the annuity starting date must be after the date the explanation of the QJSA is provided, except as provided in IRC Section 417(a)(7) (Q 3881); and

1.   *National Auto. Dealers and Assoc. Retirement Trust v. Arbeitman*, 89 F.3d 496 (8th Cir. 1996).
2.   *Estate of Altobelli v. IBM*, 77 F.3d 78 (4th Cir. 1996), overruled in part by *Kennedy v. Plan Administrator for DuPont Savings & Inv. Plan*, 555 U.S. 285 (2009).
3.   IRC Sec. 417(a)(5).
4.   See IRC Sec. 417(a)(6)(A).
5.   Treas. Reg. §1.417(e)-1(b)(1).
6.   See Treas. Reg. §1.417(e)-1(b)(3); IRC Sec 417(a)(6)(A).

(4)   distribution in accordance with the affirmative election must not begin before the expiration of the seven day period that begins the day the explanation of the QJSA is provided to the participant.[1]

With respect to the QPSA form of benefit, the applicable election period begins on the first day of the plan year in which the participant attains age 35 and ends on the date of his or her death. Where a participant has separated from service with the employer, the election period with respect to previously accrued benefits may begin no later than the date of separation.[2]

The applicable election period may not end before the thirtieth day after the plan provides the explanation required under IRC Section 417(a)(3).[3] Under that rule, a plan generally must, within certain specified periods, provide each participant (vested and non-vested, married or unmarried) with a written explanation of the automatic survivor annuity forms of benefit and of the participant's (and his or her spouse's) rights with respect to waiving the benefits (Q 3881).

Required Minimum Distributions

3890. What is the latest date that benefits under a qualified plan can be paid?

A qualified plan must meet two separate sets of rules with regard to commencement of benefits: (i) The plan cannot delay the payment of benefits to a date beyond that which is set by statute, and (ii) the plan must meet the minimum distribution requirements of the Code. (See Q 3891 to Q 3907.) As to the first element of this rule, a plan must provide that, unless a participant elects otherwise, payments of benefits to the participant will begin within 60 days after the close of the latest of (1) the plan year in which the participant attains the earlier of age 65 or the normal retirement age specified under the plan, (2) the plan year in which the 10th anniversary of the participant's plan participation occurs, or (3) the plan year in which the participant terminates his or her service with the employer.[4]

A qualified plan also must meet the minimum distribution requirements set forth at IRC Section 401(a)(9). The SECURE Act, enacted December 20, 2019, generally set back the late start date for required minimum distributions (RMDs) from age 70½ to age 72 for distributions to participants turning age 70½ beginning in 2020.[5] It also made other major changes to these requirements, including substantially eliminating so-called "stretch" beneficiary distributions from defined contribution plans (including IRAs), and generally replace it with a 10-year fixed period, including for IRAs, unless the beneficiary is an "eligible designated beneficiary". The change in the stretch distribution rules apply only to plan participants who die after December 31, 2019[6] (See Q 3891 to Q 3907). In light of the COVID-19 pandemic, the CARES Act[7] was passed waiving most RMDs from defined contribution plans for 2020. The IRS released Notice 2020-51

---

1.   Treas. Reg. §1.417(e)-1(b)(3)(ii).
2.   IRC Sec. 417(a)(6)(B).
3.   See Treas. Reg. §1.417(e)-1(b)(3)(ii).
4.   IRC Sec. 401(a)(14).
5.   See generally PL 116-94, Sec 114. Note that it did not set back the Section 401(a)(9)(C)(iii) actuarial adjustment rule to age 72.
6.   See generally PL 116-94, Sec. 401
7.   PL 116-136; also see Notice 2020-51 reference transition relief for certain non-COVID RMDs in 2020.

to allow a waiver of or repayment of RMD distributions made in early 2020 that would have otherwise not have been required as a consequence of enactment of the SECURE Act.

TEFRA 242(b)(2) Election

Notwithstanding the general requirements above, the plan may be subject to a grandfathered TEFRA Section 242(b)(2) election. This election was permitted at the time the minimum distribution requirements of Section 401(a)(9) were enacted. Basically, a participant is not subject to the minimum distribution requirements if the participant designated, before January 1, 1984, a method of distribution that would have been permissible under pre-TEFRA law.[1] The final regulations stated that the transitional election rule in TEFRA Section 242(b)(2) was preserved and that a plan will not be disqualified merely because it pays benefits in accordance with this election. The plan must provide for the continuation of the election when it is restated or the election is lost.

3891. What are the minimum distribution requirements for qualified plans?

Editor's Note: The SECURE Act, enacted on December 20, 2019, made significant changes in required minimum distribution (RMD) rules for all qualified plans. It did so by the addition of a new subsection (H) to 26 USC 401(a)(9) that provides for a change of the mandatory start date for RMDs from age 70½ to age 72 for distributions made after December 31, 2019 to individuals who attain age 70½ after that date. It also eliminates for defined contribution plans (including IRAs) so-called "stretch" distributions upon the participant's death, based upon the life expectancy of the designated beneficiary. It generally replaces life expectancy with a 10-year fixed period, including for IRAs, unless the beneficiary is an "eligible designated beneficiary".[2] The change in the stretch distribution rules apply only to plan participants who die after December 31, 2019.[3]

To be qualified, a plan must meet all the statutory rules of IRC Section 401(a)(9), including the incidental death benefit requirement in IRC Section 401(a)(9)(G), and now IRC Section 409(a)(9)(H). The plan must also provide that distributions will be made in accordance with the minimum distribution requirements set forth by IRS statute as amended and modified by the SECURE Act, as well as available in regulations and other guidance. This compliance is require except to the extent of grandfathering for certain pre-2020 distributions under existing plans for participants who died prior to 2020. In addition, a qualified plan must provide that the minimum distribution rules override any distribution options offered under the plan that are inconsistent with these requirements.[4]

Planning Point: Although the plan participant is subject to significant 50 percent penalty for failure to properly take RMDs on a timely basis, the employer and plan sponsor itself must also ensure that RMDs are properly calculated and distributed. Failure to do so can result in an operational error that could result in disqualification. The plan document itself must provide that the RMD rules contained in the IRC will control, and that they will override any inconsistent terms in the plan

---

1.   TEFRA, Sec. 242(b)(2); TRA '84, Sec. 521(d)(3).
2.   See generally PL 116-94, Sec.114.
3.   See generally PL 116-94, Sec. 401
4.   IRC Sec. 401(a)(9); Treas. Reg. §1.401(a)(9)-1, A-3(a).

document; importantly, the enactment of the SECURE Act.[1] The changes, plus the grandfathering, makes compliance more complicated. Because of the SECURE Act (and CARES Act), amendments to plans will be necessary to plan documents as well, although the IRS has provided two sample amendments in Notice 2020-51, addressing 2020 waiver of mandatory RMDs.

For tax years before 2020, 409(A)(9) regulations made governmental plans subject only to a "reasonable, good faith interpretation" of the minimum distribution requirements.[2] This does not appear to have changed by the SECURE Act.

Unless otherwise noted, the questions that follow explain the rules set forth in 409(a)(9), as modified and amended by the SECURE Act, the pre 2020 final regulations and any new guidance, to the extent it exits, in light of SECURE ACT changes . The pre-2020 regulations themselves were complex, and the changes made by the SECURE Act have only magnified this complexity. Therefore, all current authority should be reviewed carefully with respect to any specific case, including the required beginning date (Q 3894), the minimum distribution requirements from individual accounts during the employee's lifetime (Q 3895), annuity payouts from defined benefit plans (Q 3896), after-death distribution requirements (Q 3899), designated beneficiaries (Q 3903), and the effect of a qualified domestic relations order on required distributions (Q 3907). All these questions, take account of the impact of the SECURE Act to the extent it is understood as of the date of publication.

3892. What penalties are imposed on a qualified plan that fails to satisfy the minimum distribution requirements?

Editor's Note: The SECURE Act, enacted on December 20, 2019, made significant changes in required minimum distribution (RMD) rules for all qualified plans. It did so by the addition of a new subsection (H) to 26 USC 401(a)(9) that provides for a change of the mandatory start date for RMDs from age 70½ to age 72 for distributions made after December 31, 2019 to individuals who attain age 70½ after that date. It also eliminates so-called "stretch" distributions for defined contribution plans, including IRAs, upon the participant's death, based upon the life expectancy of the designated beneficiary. It generally replaces it with a 10-year fixed period, including for IRAs, unless the beneficiary is an "eligible designated beneficiary".[3] The change in the stretch distribution rules apply only to plan participants who die after December 31, 2019.[4]

Failure to make minimum distributions. Although a plan that fails to meet the minimum distribution requirements with respect to all required distributions is technically subject to disqualification, Rev. Proc. 2016-51 states such failures can be corrected through the Employee Plans Compliance Resolution System ("EPCRS").[5]

For a defined contribution plan, the correction prescribed is to distribute the required minimum distributions, including earnings from the date of the failure to the date of distribution.

---

1.   See PL 116-94, Sec. 114.
2.   Treas. Reg. §1.401(a)(9)-1, A-2(d).
3.   See generally PL 116-94, Sec.114.
4.   See generally PL 116-94, Sec. 401
5.   2016-42 IRB 465.

The amount that must be distributed for each year a required minimum distribution was not made is determined by dividing the adjusted account balance on the applicable valuation date by the application distribution period. The adjusted account balance is the actual account balance on the applicable valuation date, reduced by the total missed distributions for prior years.

For a defined benefit plan, the correction prescribed is to distribute the required minimum distribution plus an interest payment based on the plan's actuarial equivalence factors in effect on the date the distribution should have been made.

If the plan is subject to a restriction on single-sum payments under section 436(d), the plan sponsor must contribute an amount to the plan determined according to the rules set out in Rev. Proc. 2016-51.[1]

Planning Point: Plan sponsors and administrators should establish a system to monitor the ages of all participants. As a result of the SECURED Act, the employment status of participants who are approaching both age 70 and 72 will need to be reviewed to determine if the exception for participants who are less than 5 percent owners are still working for the plan sponsor applies.[2] Those who do not qualify for the exception or who no longer qualify should be notified that they are nearing their required beginning date and when their required minimum distributions must begin.

3893. What penalties are imposed on an individual who fails to satisfy the minimum distribution requirements?

Editor's Note: The SECURE Act, enacted on December 20, 2019, made significant changes in required minimum distribution (RMD) rules for all qualified plans. It did so by the addition of a new subsection (H) to 26 USC 401(a)(9) that provides for a change of the mandatory start date for RMDs from age 70½ to age 72 for distributions made after December 31, 2019 to individuals who attain age 70½ after that date. It also eliminates so-called "stretch" distributions for defined contribution plans (including IRAs) upon the participant's death, based upon the life expectancy of the designated beneficiary. It generally replaces it with a 10-year fixed period, including for IRAs, unless the beneficiary is an "eligible designated beneficiary"[3] The change in the stretch distribution rules apply only to plan participants who die after December 31, 2019.[4]

In 2020, the IRS released transition guidance permitting rollbacks of RMDs already taken for 2020 into retirement accounts (excluding defined benefit plans) by August 31, 2020 for any individual who would have had to take a distribution by April 1, 2020. In that same guidance, the IRS also provides relief to beneficiaries or IRA owners who have received a distribution if the RMD is repaid by August 31, 2020. The IRS Notice also provided two sample amendments for defined contribution plan documents that employers may adopt to give participants and beneficiaries, whose RMDs were waived, a choice as to whether or not to receive the waived RMD.[5]

---

1.   Rev. Proc. 2016-51, Appendix A, section .06.
2.   PL 116-94, Sec. 114(b)
3.   See generally PL 116-94, Sec.114.
4.   See generally PL 116-94, Sec. 401.
5.   Notice 2020-51

In addition to the qualification implications, if an amount distributed from a plan is less than the RMD, an excise tax equal to 50 percent of the shortfall generally is levied against the individual (Q 3908).[1] The tax may be waived if the payee establishes to the satisfaction of the IRS that the shortfall is due to reasonable error and that reasonable steps are being taken to remedy the shortfall.[2] The excise tax will be waived automatically if the beneficiary is an individual whose minimum distribution amount is determined under the life expectancy rule for after-death distributions, and the entire benefit to which that beneficiary is entitled is distributed under the five year rule.[3] It is to be hoped that this automatic waiver will continue for the five categories of eligible designated beneficiaries whose distributions may still be eligible for use of the life expectancy rule as provided in the SECURE Act.[4]

Historical Note: WRERA 2008 waived the RMD requirement from defined contribution plans and IRAs for calendar year 2009. Also, the five year rule is determined without regard to 2009. A person who received an RMD for 2009, including a distribution for 2009 made as late as April 1, 2010, had until the later of 60 days of receiving the RMD or November 30, 2009, to roll over the RMD to an IRA or other retirement plan (assuming the rollover would otherwise qualify).[5]

The minimum distribution requirements will also not be treated as violated and, thus, the 50 percent excise tax will not apply where a shortfall occurs because assets are invested in a contract issued by an insurance company that is in state insurer delinquency proceedings. To the extent that a distribution otherwise required under IRC Section 401(a)(9) is not made during the state insurer delinquency proceedings, this amount and any additional amount accrued during this period will be treated as though it is not vested.[6]

3894. What is the beginning date for required minimum distributions from a qualified plan?

Editor's Note: The SECURE Act, enacted on December 20, 2019, made significant changes in required minimum distribution (RMD) rules for all qualified plans. It did so by the addition of a new subsection (H) to 26 USC 401(a)(9) that provides for a change of the mandatory start date for RMDs from age 70½ to age 72 for distributions made after December 31, 2019 to individuals who attain age 70½ after that date. It also eliminates so-called "stretch" distributions upon the participant's death, based upon the life expectancy of the designated beneficiary, and generally replace it with a 10-year fixed period, including for IRAs, unless the beneficiary is an "eligible designated beneficiary".[7] The change in the stretch distribution rules apply only to plan participants who die after December 31, 2019.[8]

---

1. IRC Sec. 4974.
2. Treas. Reg. §54.4974-2, A-7(a).
3. Treas. Reg. §54.4974-2, A-7(b).
4. See 409A(a)(9)(H)(ii) as added by PL 116-94, Sec. 401.
5. Notice 2009-82, 2009-41 IRB 491.
6. Treas. Reg. §1.401(a)(9)-8, A-8.
7. See generally PL 116-94, Sec.114.
8. See generally PL 116-94, Sec. 401

In order to be qualified, a plan must provide that the entire interest of each employee will be distributed not later than his required beginning date, or will be distributed beginning not later than the required beginning date over certain prescribed time periods.[1]

For purposes of the minimum distribution rules (Q 3891 to Q 3907) and the minimum distribution incidental benefit rule (Q 3908), the term required beginning date means April 1 of the calendar year following the later of the year in which the employee attains age 72 or the year in which the employee (other than a 5 percent owner) retires from the employer maintaining the plan.[2]

In the case of a 5 percent owner, there is only one required beginning date: April 1 of the calendar year following the year in which the employee attains age 72.[3] Under pre-SECURE Act law, the IRS determined that where a 5 percent owner rolls the account balance over to the plan of another employer in which the 5 percent owner was not a 5 percent owner (after receiving the required distribution for the year in question), the individual could delay distributions from the new plan until retiring after age 70½.[4]

Under pre-SECURE Act regulations, a plan was permitted to provide that the required beginning date for all employees was April 1 of the calendar year following the calendar year in which the employee attained age 70½ regardless of whether the employee is a 5 percent owner.[5] Presumably, this ability to mandate distribution will be available even though the SECURE Act has changed the attained age from 70½ to 72.

If distributions began irrevocably (except for acceleration) prior to the required beginning date in the form of an annuity that meets the minimum distribution rules, the annuity starting date will be treated as the required beginning date for purposes of calculating lifetime and after death minimum distribution requirements (Q 3896).[6]

Pre SECURE Act, if, for example, an employee's date of birth is June 30, 1939, the employee would reach age 70 on June 30, 2009, and would reach age 70½ on December 30, 2009. Consequently, assuming the employee is retired or a 5 percent owner, the employee's required beginning date would be April 1, 2010. Because distributions from a defined contribution plan are waived for 2009, a distribution from a defined contribution plan would not be required until December 31, 2010. (See Q 3891.) If the same employee's birthday were July 1, 1948, the employee would reach age 70½ on January 1, 2019, and the employee's required beginning date would be April 1, 2020.[7] Post 2019, if for example, the employee's date of birth is July 1, 1949, the employee would reach age 70½ on January 1, 2020. Pre-SECURE Act under prior law, the calendar year for the first required distribution for the employee would be 2020. But, because the employee will have reached age 70½ after December 31, 2019, the new law will

---

1.   IRC Sec. 401(a)(9)(A).
2.   IRC Sec. 401(a)(9)(C).
3.   IRC Sec. 401(a)(9)(C)(ii)(I).
4.   Let. Rul. 200453015.
5.   Treas. Reg. §1.401(a)(9)-2, A-2(e).
6.   Treas. Reg. §1.401(a)(9)-6, A-10.
7.   Treas. Reg. §1.401(a)(9)-2, A-3; Notice 2009-82; 2009-2 CB 491.

apply, and the first calendar year of distribution to the employee will be 2022. Unfortunately, any employee born a day earlier (June 30, 1949) or more is stuck with the first distribution in calendar year 2020 (See Q 3891.)

3895. What minimum distribution requirements apply to individual account plans during the lifetime of the employee?

Editor's Note:Editor's Note: The SECURE Act, enacted on December 20, 2019, made significant changes in required minimum distribution (RMD) rules for all qualified plans. It did so by the addition of a new subsection (H) to 26 USC 401(a)(9) that provides for a change of the mandatory start date for RMDs from age 70½ to age 72 for distributions made after December 31, 2019 to individuals who attain age 70½ after that date.[1] It also eliminates so-called "stretch" distributions for defined contribution plans, including IRAs, upon the participant's death, based upon the life expectancy of the designated beneficiary. It generally replaces it with a 10-year fixed period, including for IRAs, unless the beneficiary is an "eligible designated beneficiary". The change in the stretch distribution rules apply only to plan participants who die after December 31, 2019.[2] IRS Notice 2020-51 provides certain transition relief for 2020 since the new rule applies to distributions made after December 31, 2019 for individuals who attain age 70½ after that date.

To satisfy IRC Section 401(a)(9)(A), the entire interest of each employee either must be distributed to the employee in its entirety not later than the required beginning date or must be distributed starting not later than the required beginning date over the life (or life expectancy) of the employee (or the employee and a beneficiary).[3]

Uniform Lifetime Table. Required minimum distributions from an individual account under a defined contribution plan during the owner's lifetime are calculated by dividing the employee's account balance by the applicable distribution period determined from the RMD Uniform Lifetime Table found in Appendix F.[4] See Q 3686 for an example showing the calculation under this rule. As a consequence of an Executive Order issued in August 2018, the IRS has issued proposed updated life expectancy tables reflecting longer life spans.[5] For example, the table divisor for a 72-year-old in the proposed regulations is 27.3, while the divisor in the current regulations for that age is 25.6. The updated tables are expected to become effective in 2021. The amount of an individual's lifetime required distribution is calculated without respect to the beneficiary's age, except in the case of a spouse beneficiary who is more than 10 years younger than the employee.[6]

If the sole designated beneficiary is the employee's spouse, the distribution period during the employee's lifetime is the longer of the uniform lifetime table or the joint and survivor life expectancy of the employee and spouse using their attained ages in the distribution calendar year.[7]

---

1. See generally PL 116-94, Sec.114.
2. See generally PL 116-94, Sec. 401
3. IRC Sec. 401(a)(9)(A).
4. Treas. Reg. §1.401(a)(9)-9, A-2.
5. See Prop Reg. 132210-18, Nov.7, 2019.
6. Treas. Reg. §1.401(a)(9)-5, A-4.
7. Treas. Reg. §1.401(a)(9)-5, A-4(b).

As a practical matter, the joint and survivor life expectancy table will produce a longer (and thus, lower) payout only if the spouse beneficiary is more than 10 years younger than the employee.

Account balance. For purposes of calculating minimum distributions, the account balance is determined as of the last valuation date in the immediately preceding calendar year (i.e., the valuation calendar year).[1] The account balance is increased by the amount of any contributions or forfeitures allocated to the employee's account as of dates in the valuation calendar year after the valuation date. Contributions include contributions made after the close of the valuation calendar year that are allocated as of a date in the valuation calendar year.[2] The account balance is decreased by any distributions made during the valuation calendar year, after the valuation date.[3] The account balance does not include the value of a qualifying longevity annuity contract purchased after July 2, 2014.[4]

Employee not fully vested. If a portion of an employee's individual account is not vested as of the employee's required beginning date, the benefit used to calculate the required minimum distribution for any year is determined without regard to whether all of the benefit is vested, and distributions will be treated as being paid from the vested portion of the benefit first. If the required minimum distribution amount is greater than the vested benefit, only the vested portion is required to be distributed.[5] In any event, the required minimum distribution amount will never exceed the entire vested account balance on the date of distribution.[6] The required minimum distribution for subsequent years, however, must be increased by the sum of amounts not distributed in prior calendar years because the employee's vested benefit was less than the required minimum distribution amount.[7]

Distributions made prior to an individual's required beginning date are not subject to these rules. If distributions begin under a distribution option (such as an annuity) that provides for payments after the individual's required beginning date, distributions that will be made under the option on and after that date must satisfy these rules or the entire option fails from the beginning.[8]

Distributions in excess of the amounts required under these rules do not reduce the amount required in subsequent years.[9] Rollovers and transfers among plans during years in which distributions are required under these rules can have a significant effect on the application of the minimum distribution rules.[10] For rules that apply to distributions when a QDRO is in effect, see Q 3907. Rules pertaining to separate accounts or segregated shares under a single plan, to employees participating in more than one plan, and other special rules affecting the application of the minimum distribution requirements are set forth in Treasury Regulation Section 1.401(a)(9)-8.

---

1.   Treas. Reg. §1.401(a)(9)-5, A-3(a).
2.   Treas. Reg. §1.401(a)(9)-5, A-3(b).
3.   Treas. Reg. §1.401(a)(9)-5, A-3(c)(1).
4.   Treas. Reg. §1.401(a)(9)-5, A-3(d). See Treas. Reg. §1.401(a)(9)-6, A-17 for definition of QLAC.
5.   Treas. Reg. §1.401(a)(9)-5, A-8.
6.   Treas. Reg. §1.401(a)(9)-5, A-1(a).
7.   Treas. Reg. §1.401(a)(9)-5, A-8.
8.   Treas. Reg. §1.401(a)(9)-2, A-4.
9.   Treas. Reg. §1.401(a)(9)-5, A-2.
10.   Treas. Reg. §1.401(a)(9)-7.

Distributions made in accordance with the provisions set forth in Treasury Regulation Section 1.401(a)(9)-5, as explained above, will satisfy the minimum distribution incidental benefit requirement (Q 3908).[1]

3896. What minimum distribution requirements apply to annuity payouts from a defined benefit plan?

Editor's Note: The SECURE Act, enacted December 20, 2019, generally set back the late start date for required minimum distributions (RMDs) from age 70½ to age 72 for distributions to participants attaining age 70½ beginning in 2020.[2] It also made other major changes to these requirements, including substantially eliminating so-called "stretch" beneficiary distributions from defined contribution plans (including IRAs). It generally replaces it with a 10-year fixed period, including for IRAs, unless the beneficiary is an "eligible designated beneficiary". The change in the stretch distribution rules apply only to plan participants who die after December 31, 2019[3] (see Q 3891 to Q 3907). In light of the COVID-19 pandemic, the CARES Act[4] was passed waiving most RMDs from defined contribution plans for 2020. The IRS released Notice 2020-51 to allow a waiver of or repayment of RMD distributions made in early 2020 that would have otherwise not have been required as a consequence of enactment of the SECURE Act.

Annuity distributions from a defined benefit plan must be paid in periodic payments at least annually for the employee's life (or for the joint lives of an employee and beneficiary), or over a period certain that is not longer than the life expectancy (or joint and survivor life expectancy) of the employee (or the employee and a beneficiary), as set forth in the IRC's provisions for lifetime and after death distributions.[5] The annuity also may be a life annuity (or joint and survivor annuity) with a period certain, as long as the life (or lives) and period certain each meet the foregoing requirements.[6]

Regulations state that qualifying longevity annuity distributions from defined benefit plans must meet new requirements in Treasury Regulation Sections 1.401(a)(9)-6, A-17(b) and (d)(1) rather than the rules in Sections 1.408-8, A-12(b) and (c).[7]

Regulations set forth requirements that annuity distributions under a defined benefit plan must meet to satisfy IRC Section 401(a)(9)(A).[8] Although the regulations do not address annuity distributions from defined contribution plans, the IRS has ruled privately that a fixed or variable annuity could be used to satisfy the minimum distribution requirements from a profit sharing or money purchase plan.[9]

---

1.   Treas. Reg. §1.401(a)(9)-5, A-1(d). Under the proposed rules, (d) becomes (e).
2.   See generally PL 116-94, Sec. 114
3.   See generally PL 116-94, Sec 401.
4.   PL 116-136; also see Notice 2020-51 reference transition relief for certain non-COVID RMDs.
5.   Treas. Reg. §§1.401(a)(9)-6, A-1(a); 1.401(a)(9)-6, A-3; see IRC Sec. 401(a)(9)(A).
6.   Treas. Reg. §1.401(a)(9)-6, A-1(b).
7.   79 FR 37633.
8.   TD 9130, 2004-26 IRB 1082.
9.   Let. Rul. 200635013.

Distributions from an annuity contract must commence on or before the employee's required beginning date. The first payment must be the payment that is required for one payment interval. The second payment need not be made until the end of the next payment interval, even if the interval ends in the next calendar year.[1] Examples of payment intervals include monthly, bimonthly, semi-annually, and annually. All benefit accruals as of the last day of the first distribution calendar year must be included in the calculation of the amount of the life annuity payments for payment intervals ending on or after the employee's required beginning date.[2]

Period Certain Limits

The period certain for annuity distributions commencing during the life of an employee, with an annuity starting date on or after the required beginning date, may not exceed the amount set forth in the Uniform Lifetime Table in Appendix F. If an employee's spouse is the sole beneficiary as of the annuity starting date and the annuity provides only a period certain and no life annuity, the period certain may be as long as the joint and survivor life expectancy of the employee and spouse based on their ages as of their birthdays in the calendar year that contains the annuity starting date.[3]

Employee Not Fully Vested

If any portion of an employee's benefit is not fully vested as of his or her required beginning date, the employee's required minimum distribution will be calculated as though the portion that is not vested has not yet accrued. As additional vesting occurs, the amounts will be treated as additional accruals.[4] If additional benefits accrue after the participant's required beginning date, the amounts will be treated separately for purposes of the minimum distribution rules.[5]

Changes in Form of Distribution

In addition to the permitted increases discussed in Q 3898, the final regulations permit the employee or beneficiary to change the form of distributions in response to various changes in circumstances. The annuity stream must otherwise satisfy the regulations, and certain other requirements must be met (e.g., the new payout must satisfy IRC Section 401(a)(9)) and the modification must be treated as a new annuity starting date under Sections 415 and 417.[6]

If these conditions are met, the annuity payment period may be changed and the payments may be modified if: (1) the modification occurs at the time the employee retires, or in connection with a plan termination, (2) the annuity payments prior to modification are annuity payments paid over a period certain without life contingencies, or (3) the employee marries and the annuity payments after modification are paid under a qualified joint and survivor annuity over the joint lives of the employee and spouse.[7]

---

1.   Treas. Reg. §1.401(a)(9)-6, A-1(c).
2.   Treas. Reg. §1.401(a)(9)-6, A-1(c)(1).
3.   Treas. Reg. §1.401(a)(9)-6, A-3(a).
4.   Treas. Reg. §1.401(a)(9)-6, A-6.
5.   Treas. Reg. §1.401(a)(9)-6, A-5.
6.   Treas. Reg. §1.401(a)(9)-6, A-13(c).
7.   Treas. Reg. §1.401(a)(9)-6, A-13(b).

Special Rules

The distribution of an annuity contract is not a distribution for purposes of meeting the required minimum distribution requirements of IRC Section 401(a)(9).[1] If the employee's entire accrued benefit is paid in the form of a lump sum distribution, the portion that is a required minimum distribution will be determined by treating the distribution either as if it were from an individual account plan (Q 3895) or as if it were an annuity that would satisfy the regulations with an annuity starting date on the first day of the distribution calendar year for which the required minimum distribution is being determined, and one year of annuity payments constitutes the required minimum distribution.[2]

In the case of an annuity contract under an individual account plan that has not yet been annuitized, the required minimum distribution for the period prior to the date annuity payments commence is determined by treating the value of an employee's entire interest under an annuity contract as an individual account. Thus, the required minimum distribution would be determined under Treasury Regulation Section 1.401(a)(9)-5; for the rules for individual account plans, see Q 3895.

Regulations making governmental plans subject to only a "reasonable, good faith interpretation" of the minimum distribution requirements under Section 401(a)(9) have been adopted.[3]

3897. How are defined benefit plan annuity payments to children treated for purposes of the minimum distribution requirements?

Editor's Note: The SECURE Act, enacted December 20, 2019, generally set back the late start date for required minimum distributions (RMDs) from age 70½ to age 72 for distributions to participants attaining age 70½ beginning in 2020.[4] It also made other major changes to these requirements, including substantially eliminating so-called "stretch" beneficiary distributions from defined contribution plans (including IRAs). It generally replaces it with a 10-year fixed period, including for IRAs, unless the beneficiary is an "eligible designated beneficiary". The change in the stretch distribution rules apply only to plan participants who die after December 31, 2019[5] (see Q 3891 to Q 3907). In light of the COVID-19 pandemic, the CARES Act[6] was passed waiving most RMDs from defined contribution plans for 2020. The IRS released Notice 2020-51 to allow a waiver of or repayment of RMD distributions made in early 2020 that would have otherwise not have been required as a consequence of enactment of the SECURE Act.

Payments under a defined benefit plan or annuity contract that are made to an employee's surviving child[7] until the child reaches the age of majority may be treated (for required minimum distribution purposes) as having been paid to the surviving spouse, provided that they are

---

1. Treas. Reg. §1.401(a)(9)-8, A-10.
2. Treas. Reg. §1.401(a)(9)-6, A-1(d).
3. Treas. Reg. §§1.401(a)(9)-1, A-2(d),
4. See generally PL 116-94, Sec. 114
5. See generally PL 116-94, Sec 401.
6. PL 116-136; also see Notice 2020-51 reference transition relief for certain non-COVID RMDs.
7. Pursuant to IRC Sec. 401(a)(9)(F).

payable to the surviving spouse once the child reaches the age of majority. For this purpose, a child under age 26 who has not completed "a specified course of education" may be treated as not having reached the age of majority.

Furthermore, a child who is disabled may be treated as not having reached the age of majority as long as the child continues to be disabled. The child will not be taken into consideration for purposes of the Minimum Distribution Incidental Benefit (MDIB) requirement and the increase in payments to the surviving spouse that results when the child recovers or reaches the age of majority will not be considered an increase for purposes of the non-increasing annuity requirement.[1]

3898. Are there any situations in which a defined benefit plan participant's benefit must, or may, be increased?

Editor's Note: The SECURE Act, enacted December 20, 2019, amended IRC Sections 401(a) (9)(C)(i) and (ii) to change the "required beginning date" from age 70½ to age 72. These changes are effective for those turning age 70½ in 2020. However, the SECURE Act did not change Section 401(a)(9)(C)(iii) requiring an actuarial increase for a pension benefit under a defined benefit plan starting later than age 70½. Since subsections (i) and (ii) in the same subparagraph were amended to age 72, this failure to change the required actuarial increase provision to age 72 does not appear to be an accidental legislative oversight. However, practitioners dealing with a required actuarial increase should check for the most current status of this rule. If the failure to change the age is a legislative error, a change would likely occur in a technical corrections act to the SECURE Act.[2]

Actuarial Increase Requirement

Per the Editor's Note above, if an employee (other than a 5 percent owner) retires after the calendar year in which the employee reaches age 70½, a defined benefit plan must actuarially increase the employee's accrued benefit to take into account any period after age 70½ during which the employee was not receiving benefits under the plan.[3] The increase must be provided starting on April 1 of the year after the employee reaches age 70½ and ending on the date when required minimum distributions commence in an amount sufficient to satisfy IRC requirements.[4] This actuarial increase requirement does not apply to (1) plans that provide the same required beginning date (i.e., April 1 of the year after the employee reaches age 70½) for all employees, regardless of whether they are 5 percent owners and make distributions accordingly, and (2) governmental or church plans.[5]

---

1.   Treas. Reg. §1.401(a)(9)-6, A-15.
2.   IRC Sec. 401(a)(9)(C)(iii) after modification by PL 116-94, Sec. 114. The American Retirement Association in its comment letter to the IRS as to the Act said: "This appears to require a technical correction, unless Treasury and IRS find sufficient statutory authority to clarify in regulations." See HYPERLINK "https://www.asppa.org/sites/asppa.org/files/PDFs/Comment%20Letters/20.02.12%20ARA%20Comment%20Letter%20to%20Treasury%20-%20SECURE%20Act%20guidance.pdf" \t "_blank" https://www.asppa.org/sites/asppa.org/files/PDFs/Comment Letters/20.02.12 ARA Comment Letter to Treasury - SECURE Act guidance.pdf
3.   IRC Sec. 401(a)(9)(C)(iii) after modification by PL 116-94, Sec. 114.
4.   Treas. Reg. §1.401(a)(9)-6, A-7(a).
5.   Treas. Reg. §§1.401(a)(9)-6, A-7(c), 1.401(a)(9)-6, A-7(d).

Non-increasing Annuity Requirement

Except as otherwise provided below, annuity payments must be non-increasing, or must increase only:

(1) in accordance with an annual percentage not exceeding that of an eligible cost-of-living index (e.g., one issued by the Bureau of Labor Statistics or certain others defined in the regulations);

(2) in accordance with a percentage increase that occurs at specified times (e.g., at specified ages) and does not exceed the cumulative total of annual percentage increases in an eligible cost of living index (see (1)) since the annuity starting date;

(3) in accordance with the extent of the reduction in the amount of the employee's payments to provide for a survivor benefit upon death but only if there is no longer a survivor's benefit (because the beneficiary dies or is no longer the employee's beneficiary subject to a QDRO);

(4) in accordance with a plan amendment; or

(5) to allow a beneficiary to convert the survivor portion of a joint and survivor annuity into a single sum distribution upon the employee's death.[1]

Additional Permitted Increases

If the total future expected payments from an annuity purchased from an insurance company exceed the total value being annuitized, payments under the annuity will not fail to satisfy the non-increasing payment requirement merely because the payments are increased in accordance with one or more of the following:

(1) by a constant percentage, applied not less frequently than annually;

(2) to provide a final payment on the employee's death that does not exceed the excess of the total value being annuitized over the total of payments before the death of the employee;

(3) as a result of dividend payments or other payments resulting from certain actuarial gains; and

(4) an acceleration of payments under the annuity (as defined in the regulations).[2]

In the case of annuity payments made by a qualified defined benefit plan (i.e., paid directly from the trust rather than a commercial annuity), payments will not fail to satisfy the non-increasing payment requirement merely because the payments are increased in accordance with one or more of the following: (1) by a constant percentage, applied not less frequently than

---

1.   Treas. Reg. §1.401(a)(9)-6, A-14(a).
2.   Treas. Reg. §§1.401(a)(9)-6, A-14(c), 1.401(a)(9)-6, A-14(e).

annually, at a rate that is less than 5 percent per year; (2) to provide a final payment on the death of the employee that does not exceed the excess of the actuarial present value of the employee's accrued benefit (as defined in the regulations) over the total of payments before the death of the employee; or (3) as a result of dividend payments or other payments resulting from actuarial gain (measured and paid as specified in the regulations).[1]

An annuity contract purchased with an employee's plan benefit from an insurance company will not fail to satisfy the rules of Section 401(a)(9) merely because of the purchase, provided the payments meet the foregoing requirements.[2] If the annuity contract is purchased after the required beginning date, the first payment interval must begin on or before the purchase date and the payment amount required for one interval must be made no later than the end of that payment interval.[3]

3899. How are the minimum distribution requirements met after the death of an employee?

Editor's Note: The SECURE Act, enacted December 20, 2019, generally set back the late start date for required minimum distributions (RMDs) from age 70½ to age 72 for distributions to participants attaining age 70½ beginning in 2020.[4] It also made other major changes to these requirements, including substantially eliminating so-called "stretch" beneficiary distributions from defined contribution plans (including IRAs). It generally replaces it with a 10-year fixed period, including for IRAs, unless the beneficiary is an "eligible designated beneficiary". The change in the stretch distribution rules apply only to plan participants who die after December 31, 2019[5] (see Q 3891 to Q 3907). In light of the COVID-19 pandemic, the CARES Act[6] was passed waiving most RMDs from defined contribution plans for 2020. The IRS released Notice 2020-51 to allow a waiver of or repayment of RMD distributions made in early 2020 that would have otherwise not have been required as a consequence of enactment of the SECURE Act.

The minimum distribution requirements that apply after the death of an employee depend on whether the employee died before(Q 3900) or after (Q 3901) his or her required beginning date. For this purpose, distributions are treated as having begun in accordance with the minimum distribution requirements under IRC Section 401(a)(9)(A)(ii) without regard to whether payments have been made before that date.[7]

If distributions irrevocably (except for acceleration) began prior to the required beginning date in the form of an annuity that satisfies the minimum distribution rules (Q 3896), the annuity starting date will be treated as the required beginning date (Q 3894) for purposes of calculating lifetime and after death minimum distribution requirements.[8] For details on the

---

1.   Treas. Reg. §§1.401(a)(9)-6, A-14(d), 1.401(a)(9)-6, A-14(e).
2.   Treas. Reg. §1.401(a)(9)-6, A-4.
3.   Treas. Reg. §1.401(a)(9)-6, A-4.
4.   See generally PL 116-94, Sec. 114
5.   See generally PL 116-94, Sec 401.
6.   PL 116-136; also see Notice 2020-51 reference transition relief for certain non-COVID RMDs.
7.   Treas. Reg. §1.401(a)(9)-2, A-6(a).
8.   Treas. Reg. §1.401(a)(9)-6, A-10, A-11.

ability of a non-spouse designated beneficiary to rollover funds from a qualified plan account to an inherited IRA, see Q 4013.

3900. How are the minimum distribution requirements met if an employee died before the required beginning date?

Editor's Note: The SECURE Act, enacted December 20, 2019, generally set back the late start date for required minimum distributions (RMDs) from age 70½ to age 72 for distributions to participants attaining age 70½ beginning in 2020.[1] It also made other major changes to these requirements, including substantially eliminating so-called "stretch" beneficiary distributions from defined contribution plans (including IRAs) only. It generally replaces it with a 10-year fixed period, unless the beneficiary is an "eligible designated beneficiary".

The change in the stretch distribution rules apply only to plan participants, of defined contribution plans and IRAs, who die after December 31, 2019.[2] In light of the COVID-19 pandemic, the CARES Act[3] was passed waiving most RMDs from defined contribution plans for 2020. The IRS released Notice 2020-51 to allow a waiver or repayment of RMD distributions made in early 2020 that would otherwise not have been required as a consequence of enactment of the SECURE Act. See below for more details on these changes.

Pre-SECURE ACT Distribution Rules for Employees of All Qualified Plans

Under the pre-SECURE Act rules, if an employee dies before his or her required beginning date, distributions must be made under one of two methods:

(1)   Under the life expectancy rule, if any portion of the interest is payable to, or for the benefit of, a designated beneficiary, that portion must be distributed over the life (or life expectancy) of the beneficiary, beginning within one year of the employee's death or later date prescribed by regulations.[4] As described below, regulations do provide a later date.

To the extent that the interest is payable to a non-spouse beneficiary, distributions must begin by the end of the calendar year immediately following the calendar year in which the employee died.[5] The nonspouse beneficiary's life expectancy for this purpose is measured as of his or her birthday in the year following the year of the employee's death. In subsequent years, this amount is reduced by one for each calendar year that has elapsed since the year immediately following the year of the employee's death.[6]

(2)   Under the five year rule, if there is no designated beneficiary, or if the foregoing rule is not satisfied, the entire interest must be distributed within five years after the

---

1.   See generally PL 116-94, Sec. 114
2.   See generally PL 116-94, Sec 401.
3.   PL 116-136; also see Notice 2020-51 reference transition relief for certain non-COVID RMDs.
4.   IRC Sec. 401(a)(9)(B)(iii); Treas. Reg. §1.401(a)(9)-3, A-1(a).
5.   Treas. Reg. §1.401(a)(9)-3, A-3(a).
6.   Treas. Reg. §1.401(a)(9)-5, A-5(c)(1).

death of the employee (regardless of who or what entity receives the distribution).[1] To satisfy this rule, the entire interest must be distributed by the end of the calendar year that contains the fifth anniversary of the date of the employee's death.[2]

Surviving spouse beneficiary. If the sole designated beneficiary is the employee's surviving spouse, distributions must begin by the later of the end of the calendar year immediately following the calendar year in which the employee died or the end of the calendar year in which the employee would have reached age 70½.[3]

In the event that a surviving spouse beneficiary dies after the employee, but before distributions to the spouse have begun, the five year rule and the life expectancy rule for surviving spouses will be applied as though the surviving spouse were the employee.[4] The payout period during the surviving spouse's life is measured by the surviving spouse's life expectancy as of his or her birthday in each distribution calendar year for which a minimum distribution is required after the year of the employee's death.[5] The provision that treats a surviving spouse as though the surviving spouse were the employee (i.e., the surviving spouse rules of IRC Section 401(a)(9)(B)(iv)) will not allow a new spouse of the deceased employee's spouse to continue delaying distributions.[6]

Life expectancy tables. There are tables with single and joint and survivor life expectancies for calculating required minimum distributions, as well as a "Uniform Lifetime Table," for determining the appropriate distribution periods.[7] See Appendix F. The Single Life Table must be used to calculate the required minimum distributions after the death of the employee.

Plan provisions. Unless a plan adopts a provision specifying otherwise, if distributions to an employee have not begun prior to his or her death, they must commence automatically—either under the life expectancy rule described above or, if there is no designated beneficiary, under the five year rule.[8] A plan may adopt a provision specifying that the five year rule will apply after the death of an employee, or a provision allowing employees (or beneficiaries) to elect whether the five year rule or the life expectancy rule will be applied.[9]

Post-SECURE ACT Distribution Rules for Employees after December 31, 2019

For all qualified plans (defined benefit and defined contribution), the "required beginning date" for RMDs must be no later than April 1 of the calendar year immediately following the year in which the participant attains age 72, or, if the participant is not a 5 percent owner of the employer, April 1 of the calendar year following the year in which the participant's employment terminates (retires), if later.

---

1.   IRC Sec. 401(a)(9)(B)(ii), Treas. Reg. §1.401(a)(9)-3, A-1(a).
2.   Treas. Reg. §1.401(a)(9)-3, A-2.
3.   IRC Sec. 401(a)(9)(B)(iv); Treas. Reg. §1.401(a)(9)-3, A-3(b).
4.   IRC Sec. 401(a)(9)(B)(iv)(II); Treas. Reg. §1.401(a)(9)-3, A-5.
5.   Treas. Reg. §1.401(a)(9)-5, A-5(c)(2).
6.   Treas. Reg. §1.401(a)(9)-3, A-5.
7.   Treas. Reg. §1.401(a)(9)-9.
8.   Treas. Reg. §§1.401(a)(9)-1, A-3(c), 1.401(a)(9)-3, A-4(a).
9.   Treas. Reg. §§1.401(a)(9)-3, A-4(b), 1.401(a)(9)-3, A-4(c).

For IRAs, the "required beginning date" is April 1 of the calendar year immediately following the calendar year in which the IRA account owner attains age 72.

Note: Roth accounts in qualified plans continue to be subject to RMD requirements, while Roth IRAs continue to be exempt from RMD requirements during an IRA account owner's lifetime. These new delayed required beginning dates are applicable for distributions made after December 31, 2019 to qualified plan participants and IRA account owners who attain age 70½ after December 31, 2019.[1] Hence, this new beginning start date will apply to those born after June 30, 1949, and the prior law will continue to apply to those born on or before June 30, 1949.

Actuarial Adjustment: The SECURE Act did not amend Section 409(a)(9)(C)(iii) to change the age 70½ to age 72, although it did amend subsections (C)(i) and (C)(ii) to modify the age. Subsection (C)(iii) deals with required actuarial adjustments of benefits under defined benefit plans to participants that retire after the "require beginning date" (still age 70½ and not age 72), and begins to receive his or her pension benefit. This subsection requires the plan to provide an actuarially increased benefit that has the same value as a benefit beginning at age 70½ (not age 72). This could be an error, but may be intentional, since the other two subsections were addressed and leaving the age unchanged at 70½ effectively provides cutback protection for pension benefits to older workers who remain working.[2] We will need clarification or Congressional correction in a likely technical corrections act if this failure to change the age is an error in legislative drafting.

Note: The IRS recently proposed regulations that will change the actuarial tables to better reflect longer life expectancy and thus allow qualified plan distributions to be taken more slowly when they are finalized and made effective. For instance, the divisor for a 72-year-old is 25.6 and the prosed revised divisor is 27.3 for an RMD.[3] The combined effectiveness of the SECURE Act changes and the proposed regulations for revised actuarial tables is a delay in the start of an RMD to age 72 and a reduced RMD when finally taken.

Distributions Beginning When Death Occurs after a Participant's "Required Beginning Date". See Q 3901 and Q 3902 for the new rules that imposes the 10-year rule on distributions to a designated beneficiary when death occurs after a participant's required beginning date.

3901. How are the minimum distribution requirements met if an employee died on or after the required beginning date?

Editor's Note: After enactment of the SECURE Act, minimum distribution requirements after death are the same regardless of whether the death occurred before or after the required beginning date. Generally, the value of an inherited account must now be depleted within 10 years

---

1. IRC, Sec 401(a)(9)(C) as amended by PL 116-94, Sec. 114.
2. IRC, Sec. 401(a)(9)(C)(iii) reads:
    "(iii) Actuarial adjustment In the case of an employee to whom clause (i)(II) applies who retires in a calendar year after the calendar year in which the employee attains age 70½, the employee's accrued benefit shall be actuarially increased to take into account the period after age 70½ in which the employee was not receiving any benefits under the plan."
3. See Prop. Reg. §132210-18, Nov. 7, 2019 with target effective date of January 1, 2021.

of the account owner's death unless the beneficiary is an eligible designated beneficiary (see Q 3902).[1] The 10-year rule applies to all defined contribution retirement plans, including IRAs.[2]

The SECURE Act

Under the new law, most non-spouse account beneficiaries will be required to take distributions over a 10-year period.[3] However, the law also eliminates the requirement that inherited account beneficiaries must take a distribution each year. Practically, this means that all beneficiaries can stretch the tax deferral potential of the inherited account over 10 years, taking the entire value as a distribution at the end of year 10 if they choose. The law did not change the rules applicable to surviving spouses who inherit the account.

Planning Point: Prior to enactment of the SECURE Act, financial institutions were required to notify account owners who turned 70½ in 2020 of their RMD obligations by January 31. Post-SECURE Act, taxpayers are not required to begin taking RMDs until age 72. Therefore, sponsors currently have two groups of employees to notify—those who are still subject to the age 70½ rule and those subject to the age 72 rules. However, some taxpayers turning 70½ in 2020 may have already received a notice of their 2020 RMD obligations, which would now be incorrect. Under relief provided in Notice 2020-06, the IRS has provided that it will not consider statements that have already been mailed incorrect as long as corrected forms are sent by April 15, 2020 (corrected forms would notify these taxpayers that no RMD Is due for 2020 under the new law).

Pre-SECURE Act Rules

The entire remaining balance generally had to be distributed at least as rapidly as under the method of distribution in effect as of an employee's date of death.[4] If an employee died after distributions have begun, (i.e., generally on or after his or her required beginning date), but before the employee's entire interest in the plan has been distributed, the method of distribution will depend on whether the distribution was in the form of distributions from an individual account under a defined contribution plan or annuity payments from a defined benefit plan.[5] If the distributions are annuity payments from a defined benefit plan, they will be determined as explained in Q 3896.

The beneficiary must be determined as of September 30 of the year after the year of the employee's death.[6] In the case of an individual account plan, if the employee does not have a "designated beneficiary" (Q 3903) as of that date, the employee's interest is distributed over the employee's remaining life expectancy, using the age of the employee in the calendar year of his or her death, reduced by one for each calendar year that elapses thereafter.[7]

If the employee does have a designated beneficiary as of the determination date, the beneficiary's interest is distributed over the longer of the beneficiary's life expectancy, calculated as

---

1.　IRC Sec. 401(a)(9)(H)(i)(II), as added by PL 116-94, Sec. 114.
2.　IRC Sec. 401(a)(9)(H)(vi), as added by PL 116-94, Sec. 114.
3.　IRC Sec. 401(a)(9)(H)(i)(I), as added by PL 116-94, Sec. 114.
4.　IRC Sec. 401(a)(9)(B)(i).
5.　Treas. Reg. §1.401(a)(9)-2, A-5.
6.　Treas. Reg. §1.401(a)(9)-4, A-4(a).
7.　Treas. Reg. §1.401(a)(9)-5, A-5(c)(3).

described above under the life expectancy rule[1] or the remaining life expectancy of the employee determined using the age of the employee in the calendar year of his or her death, reduced by one for each calendar year that elapses thereafter.[2] In both situations, the life expectancy is calculated using the IRS Single Life Table.[3]

3902. What is an eligible designated beneficiary? How does this designation impact the rules governing retirement plan distributions after an account owner's death?

Exceptions to the 10-year distribution rule (see Q 3900 and Q 3901) created by the SECURE Act exist for a newly created class of beneficiaries called "eligible designated beneficiaries". Eligible designated beneficiaries who are not required to use the "ten-year rule" for distributions (and who may continue to use the pre-SECURE Act life expectancy rules) include:[4]

- Surviving spouses,

- Disabled beneficiaries,

- Chronically ill beneficiaries,

- The account owner's children who have not reached "the age of majority", and

- Individuals who are not more than 10 years younger than the account owner.

Whether an individual is an eligible designated beneficiary is determined as of the date of the original account owner's death.[5]

A child who inherits may be treated as *not* reaching the "age of majority" if that child has not yet finished a specified course of education (further guidance is expected as to what exactly qualifies as a "specified course of education"). Otherwise, once the child reaches age 18,[6] the child becomes subject to the 10-year rule beginning at that point, rather than beginning with the account owner's death.[7]

Planning Point: Note that only the account owner's minor children qualify as eligible designated beneficiaries. Grandchildren and other minor children become subject to the 10-year rule beginning with the account owner's death regardless of their age.

Whether a beneficiary is disabled is determined using the definition in IRC Section 72(m)(7). Disabled beneficiaries include those who are unable to engage in any substantial gainful activity by reason of any medically determinable physical or mental impairment which can be expected to (1) result in death or (2) create the need for long-term care for an indefinite duration.

---

1. Treas. Reg. §1.401(a)(9)-5, A-5(c)(1) or (2).
2. Treas. Reg. §§1.401(a)(9)-5, A-5(c)(3), 1.401(a)(9)-5, A-5(a)(1).
3. Treas. Reg. §1.401(a)(9)-9, A-1.
4. IRC Sec. 401(a)(9)(E)(ii), as added by PL 116-94, Sec. 401
5. IRC Sec. 401(a)(9)(E)(ii) (flush language).
6. What constitutes the "age of majority" is defined by state law, which is 18 in all but three states.
7. IRC Sec. 401(a)(9)(E)(iii).

"Chronically ill beneficiaries" include those who are unable to perform (without substantial assistance) at least two activities of daily living for a period of 90 days due to a loss of a functional capacity or those who require substantial supervision to protect them from threats to health and safety because of severe cognitive impairment.[1]

A trust may be used to secure payments from the inherited account over the life expectancy of a disabled or chronically ill beneficiary (See Q 3900 for requirements when a trust for the benefit of multiple disabled or chronically-ill beneficiaries is desired).

Upon the death of the eligible designated beneficiary, the 10-year rule applies regardless of whether that individual's beneficiary is also an eligible designated beneficiary.[2]

The SECURE Act modifications apply to all defined contribution plans. These new rules apply to distributions as to employees who die after December 31, 2019 (note that the rules governing distributions from Roth IRAs were not changed).

3903. How is the designated beneficiary determined for purposes of the minimum distribution requirements?

Editor's Note: The SECURE Act, enacted December 20, 2019, generally set back the late start date for required minimum distributions (RMDs) from age 70½ to age 72 for distributions to participants attaining age 70½ beginning in 2020.[3] It also made other major changes to these requirements, including substantially eliminating so-called "stretch" beneficiary distributions from defined contribution plans (including IRAs) only. It generally replaces it with a 10-year fixed period, unless the beneficiary is an "eligible designated beneficiary". The change in the stretch distribution rules apply only to plan participants, of defined contribution plans and IRAs, who die after December 31, 2019[4]. In light of the COVID-19 pandemic, the CARES Act[5] was passed waiving most RMDs from defined contribution plans for 2020. The IRS released Notice 2020-51 to allow a waiver of or repayment of RMD distributions made in early 2020 that would otherwise not have been required as a consequence of enactment of the SECURE Act. See Q 3900 for more details on these changes.

A designated beneficiary means any individual designated as a beneficiary by the employee.[6] An individual may be designated as a beneficiary under a plan either by the terms of the plan or, if the plan so provides, by an affirmative election by the employee (or the employee's surviving spouse) specifying the beneficiary.[7]

The fact that an employee's interest under a plan passes to a certain individual under applicable state law, however, does not make that individual a designated beneficiary unless the individual is

---

1.   I.e., the standard of IRC Sect. 7702B(c)(2).
2.   IRC Sec. 401(a)(9)(H)(iii), as added by PL 116-94, Sec. 401
3.   See generally PL 116-94, Sec. 114
4.   See generally PL 116-94, Sec 401.
5.   PL 116-136; also see Notice 2020-51 reference transition relief for certain non-COVID RMDs.
6.   IRC Sec. 401(a)(9)(E).
7.   Treas. Reg. §1.401(a)(9)-4, A-1.

designated as a beneficiary under the plan.[1] For details on the ability of a non-spouse designated beneficiary to rollover funds from a qualified plan account to an inherited IRA, see Q 4013.

A beneficiary designated under a plan is an individual (or certain trusts (see below)) who is entitled to a portion of an employee's benefit, contingent on the employee's death or another specified event. A designated beneficiary need not be specified by name in the plan or by the employee to the plan to be a designated beneficiary so long as the individual who is to be the beneficiary is identifiable under the plan as of the date the beneficiary is determined.

Planning Point: To be a QDRO, the beneficiary should be named or otherwise be clearly identified (see Q 3907).

The choice of beneficiary is subject to the IRC's provisions for joint and survivor annuities, QDROs, and consent requirements (Q 3881, Q 3889, and Q 3914).[2] For an explanation of the effect of a QDRO on the minimum distribution requirements, see Q 3907.

To be a designated beneficiary for purposes of minimum distributions, an individual first must be a beneficiary on the date of the employee's death. The determination of the existence and identity of a designated beneficiary for purposes of minimum distributions is made on September 30 of the calendar year following the year of the employee's death.[3] Post-SECURE Act, it is the date of the employee's death.

Exceptions may apply if the account is payable as an annuity, or if a surviving spouse beneficiary dies after the employee but before distributions have begun. This is so a distribution may be calculated and made by the deadline of December 31 following the year of the employee's death.

Consequently, pre-SECURE Act, an individual who was a beneficiary as of the date of the employee's death, but is not a beneficiary as of September 30 of the following year (e.g., because the individual disclaims entitlement to the benefit or because the individual receives the entire benefit to which he or she is entitled before that date) was not considered for purposes of determining the distribution period for required minimum distributions after the employee's death.[4]

A disclaiming beneficiary's receipt (prior to disclaiming the benefit) of a required distribution in the year after death will not result in the beneficiary being treated as a designated beneficiary for subsequent years.[5]

An entity other than an individual or a trust meeting certain requirements (see Q 3906) cannot be a designated beneficiary for required minimum distribution purposes. Thus, for example, an employee's estate cannot be a designated beneficiary.[6]

See Q 3904 for a discussion of the impact of multiple, contingent and successor beneficiaries.

---

1.   Treas. Reg. §1.401(a)(9)-4, A-1. See e.g. *Kennedy v. Plan Adm'r for DuPont Sav. & Inv. Plan*, 555 U.S. 285 (2009).
2.   Treas. Reg. §1.401(a)(9)-4, A-2.
3.   Treas. Reg. §1.401(a)(9)-4, A-4(a).
4.   Treas. Reg. §1.401(a)(9)-4, A-4(a).
5.   Rev. Rul. 2005-36, 2005-26 IRB 1368; Let. Rul. 201125009; Let. Rul. 201245004.
6.   Treas. Reg. §1.401(a)(9)-4, A-3.

3904. How does the presence of multiple, contingent or successor beneficiaries impact the minimum distribution requirements?

Editor's Note: The SECURE Act, enacted December 20, 2019, generally set back the late start date for required minimum distributions (RMDs) from age 70½ to age 72 for distributions to participants attaining age 70½ beginning in 2020.[1] It also made other major changes to these requirements, including substantially eliminating so-called "stretch" beneficiary distributions from defined contribution plans (including IRAs) only. It generally replaces it with a 10-year fixed period, unless the beneficiary is an "eligible designated beneficiary". The change in the stretch distribution rules apply only to plan participants, of defined contribution plans and IRAs, who die after December 31, 2019[2]. In light of the COVID-19 pandemic, the CARES Act[3] was passed waiving most RMDs from defined contribution plans for 2020. The IRS released Notice 2020-51 to allow a waiver of or repayment of RMD distributions made in early 2020 that would otherwise not have been required as a consequence of enactment of the SECURE Act. See Q. 3900 for more detail on these changes.

Multiple Beneficiaries

If more than one beneficiary is designated with respect to an employee as of the date on which the designated beneficiary is to be determined, the designated beneficiary with the shortest life expectancy is the measuring life for purposes of determining the distribution period.[4] Special rules apply if the employee's benefit is divided into separate accounts, or segregated shares, and the beneficiaries of each account differ.

If an employee has designated multiple beneficiaries, and as of the date on which the designated beneficiary is to be determined, one of the beneficiaries is an entity (such as a trust not meeting applicable requirements or a charitable organization), the employee will be treated as having no beneficiaries.[5]

Contingent and Successor Beneficiaries

If a beneficiary's entitlement to an employee's benefit is contingent on an event other than the employee's death or the death of another beneficiary, the contingent beneficiary will be considered a designated beneficiary for purposes of determining whether an entity is designated as a beneficiary and the designated beneficiary who has the shortest life expectancy.[6] The fact that the contingency may be extremely remote (e.g., two children predeceasing a 67-year-old relative) does not appear to affect this outcome.[7]

In contrast, if a "successor beneficiary's" entitlement is contingent on the death of another beneficiary, the successor beneficiary's life expectancy will not be counted for purposes of

---

1.   See generally PL 116-94, Sec. 114
2.   See generally PL 116-94, Sec 401.
3.   PL 116-136; also see Notice 2020-51 reference transition relief for certain non-COVID RMDs.
4.   Treas. Reg. §1.401(a)(9)-5, A-7(a)(1).
5.   Treas. Reg. §1.401(a)(9)-4, A-3.
6.   Treas. Reg. §1.401(a)(9)-5, A-7(b).
7.   See Let. Rul. 200228025.

determining the designated beneficiary who has the shortest life expectancy unless the other beneficiary dies prior to the date on which the beneficiary is determined.[1]

3905. What are the separate account rules for purposes of the minimum distribution requirements?

Editor's Note: The SECURE Act, enacted December 20, 2019, generally set back the late start date for required minimum distributions (RMDs) from age 70½ to age 72 for distributions to participants attaining age 70½ beginning in 2020.[2] It also made other major changes to these requirements, including substantially eliminating so-called "stretch" beneficiary distributions from defined contribution plans (including IRAs) only. It generally replaces it with a 10-year fixed period, unless the beneficiary is an "eligible designated beneficiary". The change in the stretch distribution rules apply only to plan participants, of defined contribution plans and IRAs, who die after December 31, 2019[3]. In light of the COVID-19 pandemic, the CARES Act[4] was passed waiving most RMDs from defined contribution plans for 2020. The IRS released Notice 2020-51 to allow a waiver of or repayment of RMD distributions made in early 2020 that would otherwise not have been required as a consequence of enactment of the SECURE Act. See Q. 3900 for more detail on these changes.

If an employee's benefit is divided into separate accounts under a defined contribution plan (or in the case of a defined benefit plan, into segregated shares) and the separate accounts have different beneficiaries, the accounts do not have to be aggregated for purposes of determining the required minimum distributions for years subsequent to the calendar year in which they were established (or date of death, if later).[5] Separate account treatment is permitted for the year following the year of death, provided the separate accounts are actually established by the end of the calendar year following death.

For purposes of Section 401(a)(9), separate accounts are portions of an employee's benefit representing the separate interests of the employee's beneficiaries under the plan as of the employee's date of death for which separate accounting is maintained. The separate accounting must allocate all post-death investment gains and losses, contributions, and forfeitures for the period prior to the establishment of the separate accounts on a pro rata basis in a reasonable and consistent manner among the accounts.

Once separate accounts actually are established, the separate accounting can provide for separate investments in each account, with gains and losses attributable to such investments allocable only to that account. A separate accounting also must allocate any post-death distribution to the separate account of the beneficiary receiving it.[6]

---

1.   Treas. Reg. §1.401(a)(9)-5, A-7(c)(1).
2.   See generally PL 116-94, Sec. 114
3.   See generally PL 116-94, Sec 401.
4.   PL 116-136; also see Notice 2020-51 reference transition relief for certain non-COVID RMDs.
5.   Treas. Reg. §1.401(a)(9)-8, A-2(a)(2).
6.   Treas. Reg. §1.401(a)(9)-8, A-3.

The applicable distribution period is determined for each separate account disregarding the other beneficiaries (i.e., allowing each beneficiary to use his or her own life expectancy) only if the separate account is established no later than December 31 of the year following the decedent's death.[1]

If a trust is the beneficiary of an employee's plan interest, separate account treatment is not available to the beneficiaries of the trust.[2] The IRS has determined repeatedly that the establishment of separate shares under the trust did not entitle multiple beneficiaries of the same trust to use their own life expectancies as the distribution period.[3] The IRS has privately ruled that where separate individual trusts were named as beneficiaries, the ability of each beneficiary to use his or her life expectancy was preserved even though the trusts were governed by a single "master trust."[4]

If the December 31 deadline is missed, or if the plan beneficiary is a trust with multiple beneficiaries, separate accounts still may be established (e.g., for administrative convenience); however, the applicable distribution period will be the shortest life expectancy of the various beneficiaries.[5] The fact that the trust meets the requirements for a "see-through trust" does not change this result.[6]

3906. When may a trust be a designated beneficiary for purposes of the minimum distribution requirements?

Editor's Note: The SECURE Act, enacted December 20, 2019, generally set back the late start date for required minimum distributions (RMDs) from age 70½ to age 72 for distributions to participants attaining age 70½ beginning in 2020.[7] It also made other major changes to these requirements, including substantially eliminating so-called "stretch" beneficiary distributions from defined contribution plans (including IRAs). It generally replaces it with a 10-year fixed period, including for IRAs, unless the beneficiary is an "eligible designated beneficiary". The change in the stretch distribution rules apply only to plan participants who die after December 31, 2019[8] (See Q 3891 to Q 3907). In light of the COVID-19 pandemic, the CARES Act[9] was passed waiving most RMDs from defined contribution plans for 2020. The IRS released Notice 2020-51 to allow a waiver of or repayment of RMD distributions made in early 2020 that would have otherwise not have been required as a consequence of enactment of the SECURE Act.

---

1. Treas. Reg. §1.401(a)(9)-8, A-2(a)(2).
2. Treas. Reg. §1.401(a)(9)-4, A-5(c).
3. See, e.g., Let. Ruls. 200307095, 200444033, 200528031.
4. See Let. Rul. 200537044.
5. Treas. Reg. §1.401(a)(9)-8, A-2(a)(2).
6. See Let. Rul. 200317044.
7. See generally PL 116-94, Sec. 114
8. See generally PL 116-94, Sec 401.
9. PL 116-136; also see Notice 2020-51 reference transition relief for certain non-COVID RMDs.

General Rule Documentation Requirements for Trust Beneficiaries of Employees Dying Prior to January 1, 2020

The general rule prior to 2020, only an individual could be a designated beneficiary for required minimum distribution purposes. However, if special requirements are met, beneficiaries of a trust could be treated as having been designated as beneficiaries of the employee under the plan for purposes of determining the period over which required minimum distributions must be made.

During any period in which required minimum distributions are being determined by treating the beneficiaries of the trust as designated beneficiaries of the employee, the requirements could be met if:

(1)   the trust is a valid trust under state law, or would be but for the fact that there is no corpus;

(2)   the trust is irrevocable or will, by its terms, become irrevocable upon the death of the employee;

(3)   the beneficiaries of the trust who are beneficiaries with respect to the trust's interest in the employee's benefit are identifiable from the trust instrument, as described below; and

(4)   the documentation described below has been provided to the plan administrator.[1]

General Rule Documentation Requirements for Trust Beneficiaries of Employees Dying Prior to January 1, 2020

Under Pre SECURE Act law, the IRS privately ruled that a see-through trust's provision for payment of expenses such as funeral and burial costs, probate administration expenses, and estate costs, whether before or after September 30 of the year after the decedent's death, did not preclude the trust from meeting the foregoing requirements.[2]

A designated beneficiary did not need to be specified by name in a plan or by an employee to a plan to be a designated beneficiary, so long as the individual who is to be the beneficiary is identifiable under the plan as of the date the beneficiary is determined (see above). The members of a class of beneficiaries capable of expansion or contraction will be treated as identifiable if it is possible, as of the date the beneficiary is determined, to identify the class member with the shortest life expectancy.[3]

---

1.   Treas. Reg. §1.401(a)(9)-4, A-5(b); Let. Rul. 201320021.
2.   See Let. Rul. 200432027.
3.   Treas. Reg. §1.401(a)(9)-4, A-1.

Pre-SECURE Act Documentation Requirements for Distributions before Death

To satisfy the documentation requirement for trust beneficiaries to be treated as designated beneficiaries for purposes of lifetime distributions, an employee must meet one of two requirements:

(1) the employee must provide to the plan administrator a copy of the trust and agree that if the trust instrument is amended at any time in the future, the employee will, within a reasonable time, provide the plan administrator with a copy of any such amendment, or

(2) the employee must provide the plan administrator with a list of all the beneficiaries (including contingent and remainder beneficiaries, as well as a description of the conditions on their entitlement) of the trust. If the spouse is the sole beneficiary, the employee must provide a description of the conditions of the remainder beneficiaries' entitlement sufficient to establish that fact. The employee must certify that to the best of the employee's knowledge, the list is correct and complete, and that the other requirements for the beneficiaries of the trust to be treated as designated beneficiaries have been satisfied. The employee also must agree to provide a copy of the trust instrument on demand. In any event, if the trust is amended, the employee must provide a copy of any such amendment or provide a corrected certification to the extent that the amendment changes the information previously certified.[1]

Pre-SECURE Act Documentation Requirements for After-Death Distributions

To satisfy the documentation requirements for required minimum distributions after the death of an employee (or after the death of an employee's surviving spouse, if the spouse dies after the employee but before distributions have begun), the trustee must meet following requirements by October 31 of the calendar year after the year of the employee's death:

(1) the trustee must:

    a. provide the plan administrator with a final list of all the beneficiaries (including contingent and remainder beneficiaries, as well as a description of the conditions on their entitlement) as of September 30 of the calendar year following the calendar year of the employee's death;

    b. certify that to the best of the trustee's knowledge the list is correct and complete and that the trust meets the general requirements listed above for all trust beneficiaries; and

    c. agree to provide a copy of the trust instrument to the plan administrator on demand; or

---

1.   Treas. Reg. §1.401(a)(9)-4, A-6.

(2)   the trustee must provide the plan administrator with a copy of the actual trust document for the trust that is named as a beneficiary of the employee under the plan as of the employee's date of death.[1]

If the foregoing requirements were met, a plan would not fail to satisfy Section 401(a)(9) merely because the actual terms of the trust instrument were inconsistent with the information in the certifications or trust instruments previously provided. This relief applied, however, only if the plan administrator reasonably relied on the information provided and the required minimum distributions for calendar years after the discrepancy was discovered are determined based on the actual terms of the trust instrument.[2] The actual trust terms would govern for purposes of determining the amount of any excise tax under Section 4974 for failure to take the RMD for the year (Q 3909).[3]

General Rule Documentation Requirements for Trust Beneficiaries of Employees Dying After December 31, 2019

The general rule for employees dying on or after January 1, 2020, allows beneficiaries of a trust to still be treated as having been designated as beneficiaries of the employee under a qualified plan for purposes of determining the period over which RMDs must be made. The SECURE Act did not eliminate the Code Sections governing designated beneficiaries when there is a trust, but further limited the applicability of who are eligible to receive distributions based upon the life expectancy of the designated beneficiary (so-called "stretch distributions"). There are now three classes of beneficiaries: (1) nondesignated beneficiaries, (2) designated beneficiaries, and (3) eligible designated beneficiaries.

Under the SECURE Act, distributions based upon life expectancy of the beneficiary are limited an individual who falls into one of five categories of the new class referred to as "eligible designated beneficiaries" (See Q 9008), who are a new subset of those who are "designated beneficiaries" as defined by pre-SECURE Act law.[4] Therefore, it appears as of the date of this publication, and in the absence of further guidance, that the pre-SECURE Act documentation requirements discussed above for creating a "see-through trust" to obtain the advantage of the lifetime stretch distribution will generally continue to apply. There is the possible exception that the IRS could require that the only eligible designated beneficiaries receive distributions from the trust during their lifetimes. For a more detailed discussion of eligible designated beneficiaries and the new rules governing distributions from trusts of employees dying after December 31, 2019, see Q 9008.

3907. Who is the employee's spouse or surviving spouse for purposes of the minimum distribution requirements? What is the effect of a QDRO?

Editor's Note: The SECURE Act, enacted December 20, 2019, generally set back the late start date for required minimum distributions (RMDs) from age 70½ to age 72 for distributions

---

1.   Treas. Reg. §1.401(a)(9)-4, A-6(b).
2.   Treas. Reg. §1.401(a)(9)-4, A-6(c)(1).
3.   Treas. Reg. §1.401(a)(9)-4, A-6(c)(2).
4.   See IRC Sec. 401(a)(9)(H)(ii) as added by PL 116-94, Sec. 401 and IRC 401(a)(9)(E) as amended by PL 116-94, Sec. 401.

to participants attaining age 70½ beginning in 2020.[1] It also made other major changes to these requirements, including substantially eliminating so-called "stretch" beneficiary distributions from defined contribution plans (including IRAs). It generally replaces it with a 10-year fixed period, including for IRAs, unless the beneficiary is an "eligible designated beneficiary". The change in the stretch distribution rules apply only to plan participants who die after December 31, 2019[2] (See Q 3891 to Q 3907). In light of the COVID-19 pandemic, the CARES Act[3] was passed waiving most RMDs from defined contribution plans for 2020. The IRS released Notice 2020-51 to allow a waiver of or repayment of RMD distributions made in early 2020 that would otherwise not have been required as a consequence of enactment of the SECURE Act. See Q. 3900 for more details on these changes.

For purposes of the minimum distribution requirements under IRC Section 401(a)(9), unless a Qualified Domestic Relations Order ("QDRO") is in effect (see below), an individual will be considered a spouse or surviving spouse of an employee if that individual is treated under applicable state law as the spouse or surviving spouse of the employee.

Planning Point: Since the federal Defense of Marriage Act was successfully challenged in front of the Supreme Court in the *U.S. v. Windsor*[4] decision, same sex spouses have the same rights as opposite sex spouses for purposes of these rules.

For purposes of the life expectancy rule applied after an employee's death, the spouse of the employee is determined as of the employee's date of death.[5]

If a portion of an employee's benefit is payable to a former spouse pursuant to a QDRO (Q 3914), the former spouse will be treated as a spouse or surviving spouse, as the case may be, of the employee for purposes of the minimum distribution and minimum distribution incidental benefit requirements. This treatment applies even if the QDRO does not specifically provide that the former spouse is treated as the spouse for purposes of the rules governing qualified joint spousal annuities and qualified preretirement spousal annuities.[6]

If a QDRO provides that an employee's benefit is to be divided and a portion is to be allocated to an alternate payee, that portion will be treated as a separate account or as a segregated share for purposes of satisfying the minimum distribution requirements. For example, distributions from the account generally will satisfy IRC Section 401(a)(9) if required minimum distributions begin not later than the employee's required beginning date, using the rules for individual accounts.[7]

A distribution of a separate account allocated to an alternate payee will satisfy the lifetime distribution requirements if the distribution begins no later than the employee's required beginning date (Q 3894) and is made over the life or life expectancy of the payee.

1.   See generally PL 116-94, Sec. 114
2.   See generally PL 116-94, Sec 401.
3.   PL 116-136; also see Notice 2020-51 reference transition relief for certain non-COVID RMDs.
4.   *U.S. v. Windsor*, 570 U.S. 744, 133 S.Ct. 2675 (2013).
5.   Treas. Reg. §1.401(a)(9)-8, A-5.
6.   Treas. Reg. §1.401(a)(9)-8, A-6(a).
7.   Treas. Reg. §1.401(a)(9)-8, A-6(b)(1).

Planning Point: Because of these rules, distributions to a child pursuant to a QDRO can be stretched out over a greater period than otherwise would be allowed under the minimum distribution rules to a spousal alternate payee. Under the SECURE Act, the 10-year distribution period begins to run when the account owner's minor child reaches the age of majority.

If an alternate payee dies after distributions have begun but before the employee dies, distribution of the remaining portion of the benefit allocated to the alternate payee must be made in accordance with the lifetime distribution rules for individual accounts (Q 3895) or annuity payouts (Q 3896).[1]

If a QDRO provides that a portion of the employee's benefit is to be paid to an alternate payee but does not provide for the benefit to be divided, the alternate payee's portion will not be treated as a separate account (or segregated share) of the employee. Instead, the alternate payee's portion will be aggregated with any amount distributed to the employee and will be treated, for purposes of meeting the minimum distribution requirement, as if it had been distributed to the employee.[2]

A plan will not fail to satisfy IRC Section 401(a)(9) merely because it fails to distribute a required amount during the period in which the qualified status of a domestic relations order is being determined provided it does not extend beyond the 18-month period described in the IRC and ERISA. Any distributions delayed under this rule will be treated as though they had not been vested at the time distribution was required.[3]

3908. What is the incidental benefit rule for qualified plans?

Editor's Note: The SECURE Act, enacted December 20, 2019, generally set back the late start date for required minimum distributions (RMDs) from age 70½ to age 72 for distributions to participants attaining age 70½ beginning in 2020.[4] It also made other major changes to these requirements, including substantially eliminating so-called "stretch" beneficiary distributions from defined contribution plans (including IRAs) only. It generally replaces it with a 10-year fixed period, unless the beneficiary is an "eligible designated beneficiary". The change in the stretch distribution rules apply only to plan participants, of defined contribution plans and IRAs, who die after December 31, 2019[5]. In light of the COVID-19 pandemic, the CARES Act[6] was passed waiving most RMDs from defined contribution plans for 2020. The IRS released Notice 2020-51 to allow a waiver of or repayment of RMD distributions made in early 2020 that would have otherwise not have been required as a consequence of enactment of the SECURE Act. See Q. 3900 for more detail on these changes.

Qualified retirement plans exist primarily for payment of retirement benefits, although certain other benefits (e.g., death benefits) may be provided through the "incidental benefit

---

1.   Treas. Reg. §1.401(a)(9)-8, A-6(b)(2).
2.   Treas. Reg. §1.401(a)(9)-8, A-6(c).
3.   Treas. Reg. §1.401(a)(9)-8, A-7.
4.   See generally PL 116-94, Sec. 114
5.   See generally PL 116-94, Sec 401.
6.   PL 116-136; also see Notice 2020-51 reference transition relief for certain non-COVID RMDs.

rule" or "incidental death benefit rule." This restriction commonly refers to two similar, but separate, rules.

One limits pre-retirement distributions in the form of nonretirement benefits such as life, accident, or health insurance (Q 3829).

The second is a rule more properly referred to as the "minimum distribution incidental benefit ("MDIB") rule." The purpose of the MDIB rule is to ensure that funds are accumulated under a qualified plan primarily for distribution to employee participants as retirement benefits, and that payments to their beneficiaries are merely "incidental."[1]

The MDIB requirement applies only during an employee's life.[2] The MDIB requirement will be met if:

(1)   non-annuity distributions are made in accordance with the individual account rules of IRC Section 401(a)(9) (Q 3895);[3]

(2)   the employee's benefit is payable in the form of a life annuity for the life of the employee that satisfies the requirements of IRC Section 401(a)(9) without regard to the MDIB requirement (Q 3896);[4] or

(3)   the employee's sole beneficiary as of the annuity starting date is the employee's spouse, and the distributions otherwise satisfy IRC Section 401(a)(9).

Payments under the annuity must be non-increasing, except for the exceptions explained at Q 3898.[5]

If distributions begin under a particular distribution option that is in the form of a joint and survivor annuity for the joint lives of the employee and a non-spouse beneficiary, the MDIB requirement will not be satisfied as of the date distributions begin unless the distribution option provides that annuity payments to be made to the employee on and after the employee's required beginning date will satisfy the conditions set forth in regulations.[6] Under those provisions, the periodic annuity payment payable to the survivor must not at any time on and after the employee's required beginning date exceed the applicable percentage of the annuity payment payable to the employee using the RMD MDIB Joint and Survivor Annuity Table found in Appendix F.[7]

The applicable percentage is based on how much older the participant is than the beneficiary as of their attained ages on their birthdays in the first calendar year for which distributions to the participant are required. For example, if the beneficiary is 10 or fewer years younger, the survivor annuity may be 100 percent. If the age difference is greater than 10 years, the maximum

---

1.   Cf. Rev. Rul. 56-656, 1956-2 CB 280; Rev. Rul. 60-59, 1960-1 CB 154.
2.   IRC Sec. 401(a)(9)(G); Treas. Reg. §1.401(a)(9)-2, A-1(b).
3.   Treas. Reg. §1.401(a)(9)-5, A-1(d).
4.   Treas. Reg. §1.401(a)(9)-6, A-2(a).
5.   Treas. Reg. §1.401(a)(9)-6, A-2(b).
6.   Treas. Reg. §1.401(a)(9)-6, A-2(c).
7.   Treas. Reg. §1.401(a)(9)-6, A-2(c)(2).

survivor annuity permitted is less than 100 percent. If there is more than one beneficiary, the age of the youngest beneficiary is used.[1]

If a distribution form includes a life annuity and a period certain, the amount of the annuity payments payable to the beneficiary need not be reduced during the period certain, but in the case of a joint and survivor annuity with a period certain, the amount of the annuity payments payable to the beneficiary must satisfy the foregoing requirements after the expiration of the period certain.[2]

Period Certain Limitations

The period certain for annuity distributions commencing during the life of the employee with an annuity starting date on or after his required beginning date generally may not exceed the applicable distribution period for the employee for the calendar year that contains the annuity starting date.

If the employee's spouse is the employee's sole beneficiary and if the annuity provides only a period certain and no life annuity, the period certain may last as long as the joint and survivor life expectancy of the employee and spouse, if that period is longer than the applicable distribution period for the employee.[3]

If distributions commence after the death of the employee under the life expectancy rule explained in Q 3899, the period certain for any distributions commencing after death cannot exceed the distribution period determined under the life expectancy provisions of Treasury Regulation Section 1.401(a)(9)-5, A-5(b).

3909. How is an individual taxed when a qualified plan distribution fails to meet the minimum distribution requirements?

Editor's Note: The SECURE Act, enacted December 20, 2019, generally set back the late start date for required minimum distributions (RMDs) from age 70½ to age 72 for distributions to participants attaining age 70½ beginning in 2020.[4] It also made other major changes to these requirements, including substantially eliminating so-called "stretch" beneficiary distributions from defined contribution plans (including IRAs) only. It generally replaces it with a 10-year fixed period, unless the beneficiary is an "eligible designated beneficiary". The change in the stretch distribution rules apply only to plan participants, of defined contribution plans and IRAs, who die after December 31, 2019[5]. In light of the COVID-19 pandemic, the CARES Act[6] was passed waiving most RMDs from defined contribution plans for 2020. The IRS released Notice 2020-51 to allow a waiver of or repayment of RMD distributions made in early 2020 that would otherwise not have been required as a consequence of enactment of the SECURE Act. See Q. 3900 for more detail on these changes.

---

1.   Treas. Reg. §1.401(a)(9)-6, A-2(c).
2.   Treas. Reg. §1.401(a)(9)-6, A-2(d).
3.   Treas. Reg. §1.401(a)(9)-6, A-3(a).
4.   See generally PL 116-94, Sec. 114
5.   See generally PL 116-94, Sec 401.
6.   PL 116-136; also see Notice 2020-51 reference transition relief for certain non-COVID RMDs.

An individual who is required to take a minimum distribution is subject to an excise tax equal to 50 percent of the amount that should have been distributed as a minimum distribution but was not.[1]

The amount that must be distributed from a plan for a calendar year is the greater of (1) the amount that must be distributed for that year under the required minimum distribution ("RMD") rules (Q 3891 to Q 3907), or (2) the amount required to be distributed for that year under the minimum distribution incidental benefit ("MDIB") rule (Q 3908).

The excise tax is imposed on the recipient of the distribution for the taxable year beginning with or within the calendar year for which the distribution is required.[2] For purposes of the excise tax, a distribution for a participant's first distribution year is not required until April 1 of the following year (i.e., the required beginning date) (Q 3894).[3]

The excise tax may be waived if the IRS is satisfied that the shortfall was due to reasonable error and reasonable steps are being taken to remedy it.[4]

Planning Point: Form 5329 should be filed to request that the IRS waive the penalty. If a waiver is requested, the penalty should not be paid unless the IRS denies the waiver request.

In addition, if an employee dies before his or her required beginning date, the excise tax will be automatically waived if the recipient is the sole beneficiary, the RMD amount for a calendar year is determined under the life expectancy rule (Q 3899), and the entire distribution is completed by the end of the fifth calendar year following the calendar year of the employee's date of death.[5]

Individual Accounts

If distributions are being made in a form other than an annuity under a contract purchased from a life insurance company or directly from a defined benefit plan, the rules for individual accounts apply and the shortfall is determined by subtracting the actual amount of the distribution from the amount required under the RMD rules or the MDIB rule, whichever is greater.

For this purpose, if there is more than one permissible method for determining a required distribution, the default method provided by the regulations is used unless the plan provides otherwise (Q 3895 to Q 3907).

If distributions following the death of a participant are to be made under a method that complies with the five-year rule (Q 3899), no amounts need be distributed, and thus there can be no excise tax, until the fifth calendar year following the participant's death. In that year, the recipient must take a distribution of the entire remaining balance. Presumably, this rule will also apply with respect to the new 10-year rule under the SECURE Act.

1.   IRC Sec. 4974(a).
2.   IRC Sec. 4974; Treas. Reg. §54.4974-2, A-6.
3.   Treas. Reg. §54.4974-2, A-6.
4.   IRC Sec. 4974(d); Treas. Reg. §54.4974-2, A-7.
5.   Treas. Reg. §54.4974-2, A-7.

State Insurer Delinquency Proceedings

There is no violation of the minimum distribution requirements and thus no excise tax if a shortfall occurs because assets are invested in a contract issued by an insurance company that is in the midst of state insurer delinquency proceedings. The RMD rules are not violated merely because payments were reduced or suspended by reason of state insurer delinquency proceedings against the life insurance company issuing the annuity. This amount and any additional amount accrued during this period will be treated as though it is not vested during such proceedings. Any distributions with respect to such amounts must be made under the relevant rules for non-vested benefits described in Treasury Regulations Sections 1.401(a)(9)-5, A-8 or 1.401(a)(9)-6, A-6 (Q 3895, Q 3896).

3910. How is an individual taxed when a qualified plan distribution made under an annuity contract or defined benefit plan annuity option fails to meet the minimum distribution requirements?

Editor's Note: The SECURE Act, enacted December 20, 2019, generally set back the late start date for required minimum distributions (RMDs) from age 70½ to age 72 for distributions to participants attaining age 70½ beginning in 2020.[1] It also made other major changes to these requirements, including substantially eliminating so-called "stretch" beneficiary distributions from defined contribution plans (including IRAs) only. It generally replaces it with a 10-year fixed period, unless the beneficiary is an "eligible designated beneficiary". The change in the stretch distribution rules apply only to plan participants, of defined contribution plans and IRAs, who die after December 31, 2019[2]. In light of the COVID-19 pandemic, the CARES Act[3] was passed waiving most RMDs from defined contribution plans for 2020. The IRS released Notice 2020-51 to allow a waiver of or repayment of RMD distributions made in early 2020 that would have otherwise not have been required as a consequence of enactment of the SECURE Act. See Q. 3900 for more detail on these changes.

For purposes of the following rules, determinations as to whether there is a designated beneficiary and the designated beneficiary's life expectancy that is controlling are made under the rules explained in Q 3903 and Q 3904.[4]

If distributions are being made under an annuity contract purchased from a life insurance company or under an annuity option of a defined benefit plan, and that annuity contract or option would meet the requirements of both the RMD rules and the MDIB rule, the shortfall is determined by subtracting the actual amount of distributions for the calendar year from the amount that should have been made for that calendar year under the provisions of the contract or option.[5]

---

1. See generally PL 116-94, Sec. 114
2. See generally PL 116-94, Sec 401.
3. PL 116-136; also see Notice 2020-51 reference transition relief for certain non-COVID RMDs.
4. Treas. Reg. §54.4974-2, A-4(b)(1)(ii).
5. Treas. Reg. §54.4974-2, A-4(a).

If the annuity contract or option is an impermissible contract or option (i.e., one that fails to meet either the RMD rules or the MDIB rule), the shortfall is determined by subtracting the actual amount distributed for the calendar year from the minimum distribution determined under the following rules:

(1)   In the case of a defined benefit plan, if distributions commence before the death of the participant, the minimum distribution is the amount that would have been distributed under the plan's joint and survivor annuity option for the lives of the participant and designated beneficiary, which is permissible under both the RMD rules and the MDIB rule, and provides the greatest level amount payable to the participant on an annual basis. If the plan does not provide such an option, or there is no designated beneficiary, the minimum distribution is the amount that would have been distributed under the plan's life annuity option payable in a level amount for the life of the participant with no survivor benefit.[1]

(2)   In the case of a defined benefit plan, if distributions commence after the death of the participant and a designated beneficiary is named under the impermissible annuity option, the minimum distribution is the amount that would have been distributed under the plan's life annuity option payable in a level amount for the life of the beneficiary. If there is no designated beneficiary, no amount need be distributed until the fifth calendar year following the participant's death, at which time the entire interest must be distributed.[2]

(3)   In the case of a defined contribution plan, if distributions commence before the death of the participant, the minimum distribution is the amount that would have been distributed from an annuity contract purchased under the plan's joint and survivor annuity option for the lives of the participant and designated beneficiary, which is both permissible under the RMD rules and the MDIB rule, and provides the greatest level amount payable to the participant on an annual basis. If there is no designated beneficiary, the minimum distribution is the amount that would have been distributed from a contract purchased under the plan's life annuity option providing level payments for the life of the participant with no survivor benefit.[3]

If a plan does not provide a permissible annuity distribution option, the minimum distribution is the amount that would have been distributed under a theoretical annuity contract purchased with the amount used to purchase the impermissible annuity. If there is a designated beneficiary, this theoretical contract is a joint and survivor annuity, which (1) provides level annual payments, (2) would be permissible under the RMD rules, and (3) provides the maximum survivor benefit permissible under the MDIB rule. If there is no designated beneficiary, the theoretical contract

---

1.   Treas. Reg. §54.4974-2, A-4(b)(1)(i).
2.   Treas. Reg. §§54.4974-2, A-4(b)(1)(ii), 54.4974-2, A-4(b)(3).
3.   Treas. Reg. §54.4974-2, A-4(b)(2).

is a life annuity for the life of the participant, which provides level annual payments and which is permissible under the RMD rules and the MDIB rule.[1]

(4)   In the case of a defined contribution plan, if distributions commence after the death of the participant and a designated beneficiary is named under the impermissible annuity option, the minimum distribution is the amount that would have been distributed under a theoretical life annuity for the life of the designated beneficiary, which provides level annual payments and which would be permissible under the RMD rules. If there is no designated beneficiary, no amount need be distributed until the fifth calendar year following the participant's death, at which time the entire interest must be distributed.[2]

The amount of the payments will be determined using the interest rate and mortality tables prescribed under IRC Section 7520 using the distribution commencement date determined under Treasury Regulation Section 1.401(a)(9)-3, A-3 and using the age of the beneficiary as of his or her birthday in the calendar year that contains that date.[3]

3911. What restrictions apply to the assignment or alienation of a participant's qualified plan benefit?

A qualified plan must provide that benefits under the plan generally may not be assigned, alienated, or subject to garnishment or execution.[4] Limited exceptions are provided, including a Qualified Domestic Relations Order ("QDRO," see Q 3914), for collection of taxes or certain federal judgments (see Q 3912), or when a participant has committed a breach of fiduciary duty, or a criminal act, against the plan (see Q 3913).[5]

The U.S. Supreme Court has held that, for purposes of the anti-alienation provision, a working business owner and the owner's spouse are ERISA-protected participants, provided the plan covers one or more employees other than the owner and spouse.[6]

Bankruptcy Protection

The Supreme Court has held that qualified plan interests generally are protected from the reach of plan participants' creditors in bankruptcy.[7] The Supreme Court also has extended the protection offered to qualified plan assets under the federal Bankruptcy Code to an IRA containing a rolled over lump sum distribution from a qualified plan.[8] Even where it is unclear whether a plan was tax qualified, lower courts have allowed anti-alienation provisions to stand.[9]

---

1.   Treas. Reg. §54.4974-2, A-4(b)(2).
2.   Treas. Reg. §§54.4974-2, A-4(b)(2), 54.4974-2, A-4(b)(3).
3.   Treas. Reg. §54.4974-2, A-4(b)(2)(ii).
4.   IRC Sec. 401(a)(13), ERISA Sec. 206(d).
5.   IRC Sec. 401(a)(13)(C).
6.   *Yates v. Hendon*, 124 S. Ct. 1330 (2004).
7.   *Patterson v. Shumate*, 112 S.Ct. 2242 (1992).
8.   See *Rousey v. Jacoway*, 125 S. Ct. 1561 (2005).
9.   *Traina v. Sewell*, 180 F.3d 707 (5th Cir. 1999) (citing *Baker v. LaSalle*, 114 F.3d 636 (7th Cir. 1997)). See also *United States v. Wofford*, 560 F.3d 341 (5th Cir. 2009).

Payment of a participant's accrued benefit to a bankruptcy trustee pursuant to a bankruptcy court order, even with the participant's consent, is a prohibited alienation for qualification purposes.[1] If the plan permits and the participant consents, however, a plan administrator may draw a loan check or a hardship withdrawal check payable to the participant and send such checks directly to the bankruptcy trustee, to be endorsed over to the trustee by the participant, without violating the anti-alienation prohibition.[2]

A Bankruptcy Code requirement that debtors apply all "projected disposable income to be received … to make payments under the [bankruptcy] plan" does not require a plan participant to take out a plan loan to pay toward his or her debt, because plan loans are not "income" for bankruptcy purposes.[3] If a participant has already taken a plan loan and subsequently files for bankruptcy, amounts used to repay the loan do not receive preferential treatment merely because the loans are secured by plan assets. In at least two rulings, the payments were not deemed necessary for the participant's "maintenance and support."[4]

QDRO Exception

A plan may not distribute, segregate, or otherwise recognize the attachment of any portion of a participant's benefits in favor of the participant's spouse, former spouse, or dependents unless such action is mandated by a QDRO (Q 3914).[5] The voluntary partition of a participant's vested account balance between the participant's spouse and the participant in a community property state is an alienation of benefits.[6] The Tax Court ruled that a participant's voluntary waiver of benefits was a prohibited alienation, despite the PBGC's approval of the plan's termination. The waiver resulted in the plan's disqualification and the participant, who was the sole shareholder, was taxed on benefits the participant did not receive.[7]

Other Exceptions

A plan may provide that, after a benefit is in pay status, the participant or beneficiary receiving such benefit may make a voluntary and revocable assignment not to exceed 10 percent of any benefit payment, provided the assignment is not for the purpose of defraying plan administrative costs.[8]

Payment, pursuant to a court order that is the result of a judicial determination that benefits cannot be paid to a beneficiary who murdered the plan participant, is permitted if the order conforms to the terms of the plan for directing payments when there is an ineligible beneficiary.[9]

---

1.   Let. Ruls. 9011037, 8910035, 8829009.
2.   Let. Rul. 9109051.
3.   *In re Stones*, 157 BR 669 (Bankr. S.D.Cal. 1993).
4.   *In re Cohen*, 246 BR 658 (Bankr. D. Colo. 2000); *In re Estes*, 254 BR 261 (Bankr. D. Idaho 2000).
5.   IRC Secs. 401(a)(13)(B), 414(p).
6.   Let. Rul. 8735032.
7.   *Gallade v. Comm.*, 106 TC 355 (1996).
8.   IRC Sec. 401(a)(13)(A); Treas. Reg. §1.401(a)-13(d)(1).
9.   Let. Rul. 8905058.

Planning Point: Courts sometimes hold that ERISA preempts state slayer statutes. The U.S. Supreme Court has not yet decided the issue. If faced with this issue, the plan can argue that federal common law precludes payment to a beneficiary who murders the participant.[1]

A disclaimer of qualified plan benefits that satisfies the requirements of state law and IRC Section 2518(b) is not a prohibited assignment or alienation.[2]

An anti-alienation provision also will not prevent a plan from holding a rolled over distribution from another plan subject to an agreement to repay a part of the distribution in the event of early termination of the other plan.[3]

A loan from a plan made to a participant or beneficiary and secured by a participant's accrued nonforfeitable benefit is not treated as an assignment or alienation if the loan is exempt from the excise tax on prohibited transactions or would be exempt if the participant or beneficiary were a disqualified person.[4]

A participant or beneficiary may direct payment of his or her plan benefit payment to a third party, including the employer, if the arrangement is revocable and the third party files with the plan administrator a written acknowledgement stating that he or she has no enforceable right to any plan benefit other than payments actually received. The written acknowledgement must be filed within 90 days after the arrangement is entered into.[5] After the death of a participant, an assignment made pursuant to a bona fide settlement between good faith adverse claimants to the participant's pension plan benefits was not invalidated by ERISA's anti-alienation provision.[6]

3912. Do anti-alienation rules prevent collections of federal taxes or judgments from qualified plan assets?

An anti-alienation provision will not prevent collection of federal taxes from the plan benefits.[7] The IRS determined that a retirement plan was not obligated to honor an IRS levy on the benefits of a participant who was not yet entitled to receive a distribution; instead, the levy could be ignored until such time as the participant was eligible for a distribution.[8] Similarly, when a participant dies, pension benefits no longer are "property" of the deceased participant; consequently, the IRS cannot attach benefits payable to a participant's son as beneficiary for the participant's tax debts if the participant's only rights under the plan were to collect lifetime benefits and designate a beneficiary but could not obtain or alienate the funds.[9]

In some cases, the IRS has permitted the collection of criminal fines and restitution against plan assets.[10] The IRS has privately ruled that benefits of individuals already in "pay status" may

---

1. See *Standard Ins. Co. v. Coons*, 1998 U.S. App. LEXIS 5333 (9th Cir. 1998); see also dicta in *Egelhoff v. Egelhoff*, 532 U.S. 141 (2000).
2. GCM 39858 (9-9-91).
3. *Francis Jungers, Sole Proprietorship v. Comm.*, 78 TC 326 (1982), *acq.* 1983-1 CB 1.
4. Treas. Reg. §1.401(a)-13(d)(2); Rev. Rul. 89-14, 1989-1 CB 111.
5. Treas. Reg. §§1.401(a)-13(d), 1.401(a)-13(e); TD 7534.
6. *Stobnicki v. Textron, Inc.*, 868 F.2d 1460 (5th Cir. 1989).
7. Treas. Reg. §1.401(a)-13(b)(2); *Iannone v. Comm.*, 122 TC 287 (2004).
8. FSA 199930039.
9. *Asbestos Workers Local No. 23 Pension Fund v. U.S.*, 303 F. Supp. 2d 551 (D.C. Pa. 2004).
10. See Let. Rul. 200342007.

be subject to garnishment under the Federal Debt Collection Procedures Act regardless of whether the defendant is a plan participant or a beneficiary. The IRS noted that such collections could be made whether the recipient was a government entity or a private party; the government, in effect, "steps into the shoes of the taxpayer," receiving funds the taxpayer would have received and applying them toward a valid debt of the taxpayer. These collections did not extend to individuals not yet in pay status, because they were not yet eligible for a distribution under the terms of the plan.[1]

3913. Do anti-alienation rules prevent collections of payments from qualified plan assets if the payment is required because the participant committed a crime or violated his or her fiduciary duties?

A plan generally may offset a participant's benefit under a qualified plan to recover certain amounts that the participant is ordered or required to pay.[2] For this exception to apply, the order or requirement to pay must arise under a judgment of conviction for a crime involving the plan, under a civil judgment entered by a court in an action brought in connection with a violation of the fiduciary responsibility provisions of ERISA, or pursuant to a settlement agreement between the Department of Labor or the Pension Benefit Guaranty Corporation and the participant in connection with a fiduciary violation. The judgment, order, decree, or settlement specifically must provide for the offset of all or part of the amount required to be paid to the plan.

If a plan is subject to survivor annuity rules (Q 3880), the offset will be permitted if the spouse has consented to the offset or signed a waiver of the survivor annuity rules, the spouse is ordered or required to pay an amount to the plan in connection with a fiduciary violation (e.g., the spouse is held responsible for the fiduciary violation), or the judgment, order, decree, or settlement provides that the spouse retains the right to the minimum survivor annuity.[3] Special rules are provided for determining the amount of the minimum survivor annuity.[4]

3914. What is a qualified domestic relations order?

A Qualified Domestic Relations Order ("QDRO") is a judgment, decree, or order (including an approval of a property settlement agreement) that awards all or a portion of a participant's benefits to an alternate payee and that meets all the requirements under the IRC for being qualified.

A plan may distribute, segregate, or otherwise recognize the attachment of any portion of a participant's benefits in favor of the participant's spouse, former spouse, or dependents without violating the restrictions on alienation of benefits (Q 3911) only if such action is mandated by a QDRO.[5] Only a spouse, former spouse, child, or other dependent of a participant may be classified as an alternate payee under a QDRO.

---

1.   Let. Rul. 200426027.
2.   IRC Sec. 401(a)(13).
3.   IRC Sec. 401(a)(13)(C)(iii).
4.   See IRC Sec. 401(a)(13)(D).
5.   IRC Secs. 401(a)(13)(B), 414(p).

The following requirements must be met for a domestic relations order ("DRO") to be qualified:

(1)   it must relate to the provision of child support, alimony, or property rights to a spouse, former spouse, child, or other dependent;

(2)   it must be made under a state's community property or other domestic relations law;

(3)   it must create, recognize, or assign to the spouse, former spouse, child, or other dependent of the participant the right to receive all or a portion of a participant's plan benefits;

(4)   it must clearly specify the names and, unless the plan administrator has reason to know them, the addresses of the participant and each alternate payee, the amount or percentage of the participant's benefit to be paid to each alternate payee (or a method for determining the amount), the number of payments or the period to which the order applies, and each plan to which the order applies; and

(5)   it may not require the plan to provide any type or form of benefit or benefit option increased benefits to an alternate payee that are required to be paid to another alternate payee under another previously ordered qualified DRO.[1]

A distribution from a governmental plan, a church plan, or an eligible Section 457 governmental plan (Q 3584) will be treated as made pursuant to a QDRO as long as the domestic relations order meets requirements (1) through (3).[2]

Note: The plan sponsors of unfunded nonqualified deferred compensation plan subject to Section 409A are optionally permitted, but not required, to make distribution under a DRO as defined in Section 414(p)(i)(B) and not the full set of requirements imposed in a QDRO by Section 414(p) on "qualified" plans, and it will not be treated as a 409A prohibited acceleration[3] (See Q 3547 and Q 3575).[4]

Model language for a QDRO is set forth in Notice 97-11.[5]

A marital settlement agreement that was incorporated into a divorcing couple's dissolution agreement constituted a QDRO, not merely a property settlement.[6]

An amendment to a divorce decree did not constitute a QDRO, and thus could not confer on the ex-wife a 50 percent interest in the participant's preretirement survivor annuity because

---

1.   IRC Sec. 414(p)(1).
2.   IRC Sec. 414(p)(11).
3.   Treas. Reg., Sec. 1.409A-3(j)(4)(ii); also see 1.409A-6(a)(4)(i)(C) as to grandfathered plans.
4.   There are important key differences between qualified plans and nonqualified deferred compensation plans. For instance there are no RERISA "plan assets" for the DRO to direct; all asset connected to a nonqualified plan belong to the employer, even if held in a "rabbi" grantor trust.
5.   1997-1 CB 379.
6.   *Hawkins v. Comm.* 86 F.3d 982 (10th Cir. 1996), *rev'g* 102 TC 61.

prior to the amendment the participant had died and the benefits had lapsed. As a result, the amendment impermissibly provided for increased benefits.[1]

In a private ruling, the IRS approved the use of a second QDRO to secure other marital obligations. The second QDRO ordered the segregation of a portion of the husband's retirement plan benefit for the wife's benefit.[2]

Most federal circuit courts hold that a QDRO is enforceable after a participant's death.[3] The Department of Labor has issued regulations under which a QDRO will not fail to be treated as valid merely because it revises, or is issued after, another QDRO. The regulations also provide that a QDRO will not be treated as invalid solely because of the time it was issued.[4]

The applicability of the QDRO provisions to benefits other than those provided by qualified plans is not fully clear. After having ruled in 1992 that they were inapplicable to nonqualified deferred compensation plans and welfare benefit plans, a Michigan district court reversed itself in 1996, holding that a QDRO provision should be followed with respect to the disposition of a welfare plan, such as life insurance.[5]

The Court of Appeals for the Seventh Circuit has ruled that the QDRO provisions of ERISA were applicable to group term life insurance and other welfare plans.[6]

Final regulations governing Section 403(b) plans extend the application of the QDRO rules to tax-sheltered annuity contracts, at least with respect to taxable years beginning after 2005.[7]

A QDRO generally may not require that the plan provide any form of benefit not otherwise provided under the plan and may not require that the plan provide increased benefits. Within certain limits, it is permissible for a QDRO to require that payments to an alternate payee begin on or after the participant's earliest retirement age, even though the participant has not separated from service at that time. For these purposes, a participant's earliest retirement age is the earlier of (1) the date that the participant is entitled to a distribution under the plan or (2) the later of (i) the date the participant reaches age 50 or (ii) the earliest date on which the participant could begin receiving benefits under the plan if the participant separated from service.[8] A plan may provide for payment to an alternate payee prior to the earliest retirement age as defined in the IRC.[9]

Planning Point: Employers should consider drafting their retirement plans to offer in-service distributions to alternate payees so as not to be burdened with administering the benefits of

---

1.   *Samaroo v. Samaroo*, 193 F.3d 185 (3d Cir. 1999).
2.   See Let. Rul. 200252097.
3.   See *Hogan v. Raytheon*, 302 F.3d 854 (8th Cir. 2002); *Trustees of the Directors Guild of America-Producer Pension Benefits Plans v. Tise*, 234 F.3d 415 (9th Cir. 2000); see also IRC Sec. 414(p)(7), ERISA Sec. 206(d)(3)(H).
4.   29 CF.R. §2530.206(b) and (c).
5.   See *Metropolitan Life Ins. Co. v. Fowler*, 922 F. Supp. 8 (E.D. Mich. 1996), rev'g *Metropolitan Life Ins. Co. v. Person*, 805 F. Supp. 1411 (E.D. Mich. 1992).
6.   See *Metropolitan Life Ins. Co. v. Wheaton*, 42 F.3d 1080 (7th Cir. 1994).
7.   See Treas. Reg. §§1.403(b)-10(c); 1.403(b)-11(a).
8.   IRC Sec. 414(p)(4)(B).
9.   Treas. Reg. §1.401(a)-13(g)(3).

employees' ex-spouses, a group that by its nature may be hostile to the employer. *Martin Silfen, J.D., Brown Brothers Harriman Trust Co., LLC.*

A domestic relations order requiring payment of benefits to an alternate payee is not qualified if the benefits are required to be paid to another alternate payee under a previous QDRO. The IRS has determined that the assignment of or placement of a lien on a participant's retirement account to secure payment of obligations under the terms of a QDRO was not a prohibited alienation.[1]

The IRC provides that, to the extent specified in a QDRO, the former spouse of a participant (and not the current spouse) may be treated as a surviving spouse for purposes of the survivor benefit requirements and, for that purpose, a former spouse will be treated as married to the participant for the requisite one year period if the former spouse and the participant had been married for at least one year (Q 3881).[2] In the absence of this provision, a former spouse was not entitled to receive any benefits where the husband died before becoming entitled to receive retirement benefits and the preretirement survivor annuity was payable to the current spouse.[3]

A recent case addressed an issue that may arise when the nonparticipant spouse dies prior to the participant spouse's retirement (so that benefits have yet to commence). In this case, the plan argued that the nonparticipant spouse's benefit reverted to the plan, so that the participant spouse was only entitled to receive 50 percent of his pension benefit. The court disagreed, finding that an amended QDRO obtained by the participant spouse was valid, but also that the non-participant spouse's benefit reverted to the *plan participant* upon her death. Therefore, the plan participant was entitled to receive the full amount of his pension benefit.[4]

The plan administrator is required to make the determination as to whether an order is a QDRO. All plans must establish reasonable procedures for making such determinations.[5] In addition, a plan administrator who has reason to believe an order is a sham or is questionable in nature must take reasonable steps to determine its credibility.[6]

A plan administrator is not required under the IRC or ERISA to review the correctness of the determination that an individual is a surviving spouse under state domestic relations law.[7] A plan administrator is not required to, and should not, "look beneath the face" of a state court order to determine whether amounts to which it relates were properly awarded.[8]

---

1. Let. Ruls. 9234014, 200252093.
2. IRC Sec. 414(p)(5); Treas. Reg. §1.401(a)-13(g)(4).
3. *Dugan v. Clinton*, 1987 U.S. Dist. LEXIS 4276 (N.D. Ill. 1987).
4. *Cingrani v. Sheet Metal Workers' Local No. 73 Pension Fund*, No. 15-c-6430.
5. IRC Secs. 414(p)(6), 414(p)(7).
6. DOL Adv. Op. 99-13A.
7. DOL Adv. Op. 92-17A.
8. *Joint Trs. of the Int'l Longshore & Warehouse Union-Pacific Mar. Ass'n Pension Plan v. Pritchow*, 2012 U.S. Dist. LEXIS 179633 (W.D. Wash. Dec. 19, 2012); *Brown v. Cont'l Airlines, Inc.*, 647 F.3d 221 (5th Cir. 2011); *Blue v. UAL Corp.*, 160 F.3d 383 (7th Cir. 1998).

Final DOL regulations effective August 9, 2010 make it clear that a plan administrator cannot disqualify a QDRO solely because it is issued after, or revises, another domestic relations order or QDRO, or because it is issued after the participant's death, divorce, or annuity starting date.[1]

The DOL has stated that nothing in ERISA Section 206(d)(3) precludes a state court from altering or modifying an earlier QDRO of a couple petitioning the court for such a change, provided the new order satisfies the requirements of a QDRO. In such a case, the DOL noted that the new order would operate on a prospective basis only.[2]

A plan may provide for a "hold" to be placed on a participant's account while the determination is being made as to whether an order is a QDRO; however, where a plan with such a provision went beyond its written procedures and placed a hold on an account before the order was received but after the divorce was final, the hold violated ERISA.[3] The Department of Labor also has stated that plans are not permitted to impose separate fees for the costs of these procedures to individual participants or alternate payees.[4]

For the taxation of payments made pursuant to a QDRO, see Q 3943 and Q 3968. For an explanation of the effect of a QDRO on the minimum distribution requirements, see Q 3907.

Top-Heavy Plan Requirements

3915. What do the top-heavy rules require with respect to a qualified plan?

In any plan year in which a plan is a top-heavy plan (Q 3916), additional qualification requirements must be met.[5]

Moreover, except to the extent provided in the regulations, all non-exempt plans, whether or not actually top-heavy, must contain provisions that meet the additional top-heavy qualification requirements and that will become effective should a plan become top-heavy.[6]

Plans established and maintained by the United States, by state governments and political subdivisions thereof, and by agencies and instrumentalities of any of these, are exempt from the top-heavy requirements.[7] Also, the top-heavy rules are not applicable to SIMPLE IRA plans (Q 3706), SIMPLE 401(k) plans (Q 3777), safe harbor 401(k) plans (Q 3772), or automatic enrollment safe harbor 401(k) plans (Q 3762).[8] PPA '06 Section 902(c) amended IRC Section 416(g)(4)(H) to exempt from the top-heavy rules plans consisting solely of (1) cash or deferred arrangements that meet the requirements of Section 401(k)(12) or 401(k)(13) and (2) matching contributions which meet the requirements of Section 401(m)(11) or 401(m)(12).

1.   29 CFR 2530.206.
2.   DOL Adv. Op. 2004-02A.
3.   *Schoonmaker v. The Employee Sav. Plan of Amoco Corp.*, 987 F.2d 410 (7th Cir. 1993).
4.   DOL Adv. Op. 94-32A.
5.   IRC Sec. 401(a)(10)(B).
6.   For rules and exemptions, see Treas. Reg. §§1.416-1, T-35 to 1.416-1, T-38.
7.   IRC Sec. 401(a)(10)(B).
8.   IRC Secs. 416(g)(4)(G), 401(k)(11)(D)(ii); IRC Sec. 416(g)(4)(H).

As to when a participant is a key employee for purposes of the top-heavy rules, see Q 3930. For the additional qualification requirements applicable to top-heavy plans, see Q 3921.

3916. When is a single plan top-heavy?

Where an employer maintains only one qualified plan, that plan is a top-heavy plan with respect to a plan year if the present value of the cumulative accrued benefits under the plan, or the aggregate account balances if the plan is a defined contribution plan, for key employees (Q 3930) exceeds 60 percent of the present value of the cumulative accrued benefits under the plan, or the aggregate account balances, for all employees.[1]

For purposes of determining the present values of accrued benefits, or the sums of account balances, benefits derived from both employer contributions and nondeductible employee contributions are considered; benefits derived from deductible employee contributions are disregarded. Deductible employee contributions are certain contributions made before 1987; the term does not refer to salary reductions or employee deferrals.

Any reasonable interest rate assumption may be used to calculate these present values, but the IRS automatically will accept as reasonable a rate that is not less than 5 percent or greater than 6 percent. The interest rate used need not be the same as other assumptions used in the plan (e.g., the rate assumed for funding purposes). Where an aggregation group consists of two or more defined benefit plans, the interest rate assumptions used to calculate the present values must be the same in all plans.[2]

Present values and account balances generally are determined on the last day of the prior plan year, but when testing for top-heaviness with respect to the first plan year (as well as the second) of a new plan, the determination date is the last day of the first plan year.[3]

In the case of a defined contribution plan, the balance in each account on the determination date is calculated by adjusting the balance of each account as of the most recent valuation date occurring within twelve months prior to the determination date for contributions due as of the determination date.[4]

For defined benefit plans, the present value of an accrued benefit as of the determination date generally is determined as of the most recent valuation date occurring in the previous twelve months. Special rules apply in the case of a new defined benefit plan in its first and second plan years.[5]

The cumulative accrued benefit of non-key employees must be determined under the method used for accrual purposes for all plans of the employer or, if there is no such method, as if such benefit accrued not more rapidly than under the fractional method (Q 3716).[6]

---

1.   IRC Sec. 416(g)(1)(A).
2.   Treas. Reg. §§1.416-1, T-26, 1.416-1, T-28.
3.   IRC Sec. 416(g)(4)(C).
4.   Treas. Reg. §1.416-1, T-24.
5.   Treas. Reg. §1.416-1, T-25.
6.   IRC Sec. 416(g)(4)(F).

In determining these present values and account balances, any distribution (generally including death benefits) made from the plan with respect to any employee during the one-year period ending on the determination date, and that is not already reflected in the present value or account balance, must be added back to the present value of that employee's accrued benefit or to his or her account balance, whichever is applicable.[1] In the case of a distribution made for a reason other than severance from employment, death, or disability, a five-year look-back period applies for this purpose.[2]

If an individual has not performed any services for his or her employer during the one-year period ending on the determination date, the individual's accrued benefit and account are not to be taken into account for purposes of determining whether the plan is top-heavy.[3] If an individual was a key employee in a previous plan year but currently is a non-key employee for purposes of the top-heavy test, the individual's cumulative accrued benefit (or account balance) is totally disregarded.

The terms "key employee" (Q 3930) and "employee" include their beneficiaries, so that the beneficiary of a key employee is treated as a key employee and the beneficiary of a former key employee is treated as a former key employee.[4] This apparently means that for purposes of testing top-heaviness, an individual's accrued benefit or account balance must be considered in its entirety and not allocated between the individual and his or her beneficiaries. For plan years beginning before January 1, 2002, it also meant that the accrued benefit or account balance of a deceased key employee, even though payable (or paid) to his or her beneficiary, was treated as that of a key employee for four years.[5]

A plan will not be treated as violating the top-heavy rules merely on account of the making of, or the right to make, catch-up contributions (Q 3761) by participants age 50 or over, under the provisions of IRC Section 414(v), so long as a universal availability requirement is met.[6]

3917. When are multiple plans top-heavy?

Where an employer maintains more than one qualified plan, some or all of those plans will be aggregated and tested as a group for top-heaviness.

Specifically, all qualified plans (including collectively-bargained plans) of an employer that cover at least one key employee (i.e., key employee plans) and any qualified plans that enable an otherwise discriminatory key employee plan to satisfy the nondiscrimination requirements of IRC Sections 401(a)(4) or 410 (Q 3840 to Q 3862, Q 3772 to Q 3801) are required to be aggregated into a single group.

In addition, an employer may designate any other qualified plan or plans (including collectively-bargained plans) not required to be aggregated under the above rules to be included in an

---

1.   IRC Sec. 416(g)(3)(A); Treas. Reg. §1.416-1, T-30, T-31.
2.   IRC Sec. 416(g)(3)(B).
3.   IRC Sec. 416(g)(4)(E).
4.   IRC Sec. 416(i)(5); Treas. Reg. §1.416-1, T-12.
5.   See IRC Sec. 416(i)(1)(A), prior to amendment by EGTRRA 2001.
6.   IRC Sec. 414(v)(3)(B).

existing aggregation group, provided that the resulting group, taken as a whole, would continue to satisfy IRC Sections 401(a)(4) and 410.

If an aggregation group is top-heavy, all plans required to be included in the group under the above rules will be considered top-heavy plans; any plan included in the group solely because of the employer's designation will not be treated as top-heavy. Even though a collectively-bargained plan covering a key employee might be part of a top-heavy aggregation group because it was required to be aggregated, that collectively-bargained plan will be excepted from the faster vesting, minimum benefits, and maximum compensation requirements discussed in Q 3921.[1] If an aggregation group is not top-heavy, no plan in the group will be considered top-heavy, even though one or more plans composing the group would be top-heavy if tested alone.[2]

The procedure for testing top-heaviness of an aggregation group is the same as that discussed in Q 3916 for a single plan, except that the values tested are the sums of the respective present values and account balances determined for each plan, as of its determination date, composing the group. When plans composing the aggregation group have different plan years, the test is carried out using the determination dates that fall within the same calendar year.[3]

If only one of the employer's plans is a key employee plan and that plan, by itself, satisfies the nondiscrimination requirements of IRC Sections 401(a)(4) and 410, that plan will be tested as a single plan unless the employer elects to designate another plan for aggregation with the key employee plan.

3918. How do the top-heavy rules apply to simplified employee pension plans?

For purposes of testing for top-heaviness, a simplified employee pension plan (SEP), including a SAR-SEP (Q 3705), is treated as a defined contribution plan. An employer may elect to use aggregate employer contributions to the simplified employee pension plan, rather than aggregate account balances, for purposes of the top-heavy test.[4]

3919. Are rollover plans subject to the top-heavy rules?

How amounts rolled over (or otherwise transferred) to or from a qualified plan are treated for purposes of determining whether a plan is top-heavy depends on the surrounding circumstances.

A related rollover or transfer is initiated other than by the employee, as in the case of a merger or division of plans, or is made between plans of the same employer, or related employers required to be aggregated under IRC Section 414. For a related rollover or transfer, the amount rolled over is counted as part of an employee's accrued benefits by the receiving plan but is disregarded by the distributing plan.

---

1. See Treas. Reg. §1.416-1, T-3.
2. Treas. Reg. §1.416-1, T-9.
3. Treas. Reg. §1.416-1, T-23.
4. IRC Sec. 416(i)(6).

An unrelated rollover or transfer is initiated by an employee, regardless of who initiated the distribution, and made between plans of unrelated employers. For unrelated rollovers or transfers, the rollover or distribution generally must be added back to the distributing plan for a one year period and generally is disregarded by the receiving plan.[1]

Notice 2013-74[2] provides that an in-plan Roth rollover is considered a "related rollover" and so the accepting plan must include the rollover in determining the present value of accrued benefits for top-heavy status.

3920. Are there simplified calculation methods for a top-heavy plan?

Precise top-heavy ratios need not be computed every year so long as the plan administrator knows whether or not the plan is top-heavy. For this purpose, and for the purpose of demonstrating to the IRS that a plan is not top-heavy, an employer may use computations that are not precisely in accordance with the top-heavy rules but that mathematically prove that the plan is not top-heavy. Several such methods are provided in the regulations.[3]

3921. What special qualification requirements apply to top-heavy plans?

In addition to the qualification requirements that apply to qualified plans generally (Q 3837), special requirements are imposed by the IRC on top-heavy plans. In addition, top-heavy simplified employee pension plans are required to meet certain minimum contribution requirements (Q 3923). In meeting these requirements the common control, controlled group, and affiliated service group aggregation rules apply (Q 3932, Q 3934). Under some circumstances, "leased" employees may be imputed to an employer (Q 3928).[4]

The requirements discussed in Q 3922 and Q 3923 must be met by top-heavy plans in general; top-heavy simplified employee pensions must meet only the minimum contribution requirements discussed in Q 3923.

3922. What vesting requirements apply to top-heavy plans?

A top-heavy plan must provide that an employee has a non-forfeitable right to his or her accrued benefit derived from employer contributions in accordance with one of the two following requirements:

1.   *Three-year vesting.* An employee who has completed at least three years of service with the employer must have a non-forfeitable right to 100 percent of his or her accrued benefit.[5]

2.   *Six-year graded vesting.* An employee who has completed at least two years of service must have a non-forfeitable right to at least the following: 20 percent of his or her accrued benefit after two years of service, and 20 percent additional for each of

---

1.   IRC Sec. 416(g)(4)(A); Treas. Reg. §1.416-1, T-32.
2.   2013-52 IRB 819.
3.   Treas. Reg. §1.416-1, T-39.
4.   Guidelines for applying the top-heavy rules may be found in Treas. Reg. §1.416-1.
5.   IRC Sec. 416(b)(1)(A).

the following years of service, reaching 100 percent after six years of service with the employer.[1]

Except to the extent that they are inconsistent with these fast vesting schedules, the rules that pertain to vesting in qualified plans generally (including years of service and breaks in service, etc.) apply for purposes of the fast vesting requirements.[2] Thus, the fast vesting schedules are not safe harbors; even faster vesting may be required by IRC Section 411(d) where there is a pattern of abuse (Q 3868).

When a plan becomes top-heavy, fast vesting under one of the two schedules generally must be applied to all benefits accrued under the plan for the current plan year and all prior plan years (including benefits accrued in years before the plan became top-heavy and benefits accrued before the effective date of the top-heavy rules). The accrued benefit of any employee who does not have an hour of service after the plan became top-heavy, and any accrued benefits that were forfeited before the plan became top-heavy, need not be covered by the fast vesting schedule.[3]

Although the IRC does not require that fast vesting be applied to benefits accrued in future plan years in which a plan is not top-heavy, a return to the plan's slower vesting when the plan ceases to be top-heavy in many cases may be impractical or impossible. For example, IRC Section 411(a)(10) requires that a change in vesting schedules not reduce a participant's non-forfeitable percentage in his or her accrued benefit and that participants with at least three years of service be allowed to elect to be covered by the previous vesting schedule (Q 3868).[4]

Integration

Although the IRC does not prohibit integration in a top-heavy plan, the fast vesting and minimum benefit (and contribution) requirements must be satisfied without considering employer payments of FICA taxes or contributions or benefits made or received under any other federal or state law.[5]

3923. What requirements with respect to minimum benefits and contributions apply to top-heavy defined benefit plans?

For any top-heavy plan year, a plan generally must provide a minimum benefit or contribution for each non-key employee who is a participant.[6] Integration (i.e., permitted disparity) must be disregarded for purposes of determining a minimum benefit or contribution.

Defined benefit plans. A top-heavy defined benefit plan generally must provide an accrued benefit derived from employer contributions for each non-key employee participant that, when

---

1.   IRC Sec. 416(b)(1)(B).
2.   IRC Sec. 416(b)(2); see Treas. Reg. §§1.416-1, V-1; 1.416-1, V-2.
3.   Treas. Reg. §1.416-1, V-3.
4.   See IRC Sec. 411(a)(10)(b) and Treas. Reg. §1.416-1, V-7. For additional rules regarding vesting in a top-heavy plan, see Treas. Reg. §§1.416-1, V-5 and 1.416-1, V-6.
5.   IRC Sec. 416(e).
6.   IRC Sec. 416(c); Treas. Reg. §1.416-1, M-1.

expressed as an annual retirement benefit, is not less than the participant's average compensation multiplied by the lesser of 2 percent for each year of service with the employer or 20 percent.[1]

Years of service are the same as the "years of service" taken into account for the ordinary vesting rules (Q 3868), but years of service in which non-top-heavy plan years end are not counted for this purpose; years in which no key employee or former key employee benefits under the plan also are not counted.[2]

Average compensation is a participant's average annual compensation for the period of consecutive years (not exceeding five) during which the participant had the greatest aggregate compensation from the employer.[3] Compensation for any year that is not a year of service is disregarded.[4]

Similarly, unless the plan provides otherwise, compensation (Q 3866) for any year beginning after a plan has ceased forever to be top-heavy, is not counted.[5] Annual retirement benefit means a benefit payable annually in the form of a single life annuity (with no ancillary benefits) beginning at the normal retirement age under the plan.[6] If a benefit other than a single life annuity without ancillary benefits is provided, the employee must receive an amount that is the actuarial equivalent of a single life annuity commencing at normal retirement age. Similarly, if the benefit starts at a date other than normal retirement age, the employee must receive an amount that is at least the actuarial equivalent of the minimum single life annuity benefit starting at normal retirement age.[7]

For the application of the minimum benefit requirement to a defined benefit plan funded exclusively by level premium insurance contracts, see Treasury Regulation Section 1.416-1.[8]

Collective bargaining units. The minimum contribution and minimum benefit requirements do not apply in the case of any employee covered by a collective bargaining agreement if there is evidence that retirement benefits were the subject of good faith bargaining.[9]

3924. What requirements with respect to minimum benefits and contributions apply to top-heavy defined contribution plans?

For any top-heavy plan year, a plan generally must provide a minimum benefit or contribution for each non-key employee who is a participant.[10] Integration (i.e., permitted disparity) must be disregarded for purposes of determining a minimum benefit or contribution.

---

1. For the non-key employees for which a minimum benefit is not required, see Treas. Reg. §1.416-1, M-4.
2. IRC Sec. 416(c)(1)(C)(iii).
3. IRC Sec. 416(c)(1)(D)(i).
4. IRC Sec. 416(c)(1)(D)(ii).
5. IRC Sec. 416(c)(1)(D)(iii).
6. IRC Sec. 416(c)(1)(E); Treas. Reg. §§1.416-1, M-2, 1.416-1, M-3.
7. Treas. Reg. §1.416-1, M-3.
8. Treas. Reg. §1.416-1, M-17.
9. IRC Sec. 416(i)(4).
10. IRC Sec. 416(c); Treas. Reg. §1.416-1, M-1.

Defined contribution plans. For each plan year in which a defined contribution plan or simplified employee pension plan is top-heavy, employer contributions and forfeitures allocated to the account of each non-key employee participant must not be less than the amount that is calculated by multiplying the participant's compensation by the lesser of 3 percent or the percentage that is the highest contribution rate made for a key employee.[1]

For purposes of determining the highest contribution rate received by a key employee, employer contributions and forfeitures made on behalf of each key employee under the plan or, if the plan is part of a required aggregation group (Q 3916), all defined contribution plans included in the group, are divided by total compensation for the year (but not more than $290,000, as indexed in 2021, up from $285,000 in 2020 and $280,000 in 2019).[2]

Although employer contributions attributable to salary reduction or similar arrangements may not be disregarded when calculating the minimum contribution requirement for a top-heavy defined contribution plan, these contributions may not be used to satisfy the top-heavy minimum contribution requirement.[3] Non-elective contributions and employer matching contributions may be used to satisfy the minimum contribution requirement, but such amounts generally cannot then be used in the ACP or ADP test (Q 3801, Q 3803).[4] For application of the minimum contribution requirement in the case of a plan that has received a waiver of the minimum funding requirements, see Treasury Regulation Section 1.416-1.[5]

If a top-heavy defined contribution plan required to be included in an aggregation group (Q 3916) with a discriminatory defined benefit plan enables that defined benefit plan to satisfy the nondiscrimination requirements of IRC Sections 401(a)(4) and 410, the minimum contribution is 3 percent of the participant's compensation, and the highest contribution rate for key employees is disregarded.[6]

3925. What requirements with respect to minimum benefits and contributions apply to top-heavy plans if the employer has both a top-heavy defined contribution plan and a top-heavy defined benefit plan?

For any top-heavy plan year, a plan generally must provide a minimum benefit or contribution for each non-key employee who is a participant.[7] Integration (i.e., permitted disparity) must be disregarded for purposes of determining a minimum benefit or contribution.

Defined benefit and defined contribution plans. Although an employer that maintains both a top-heavy defined benefit plan and a top-heavy defined contribution plan is not required by the top-heavy rules to provide a non-key employee who participates in both plans with a minimum contribution and a minimum benefit, the non-key employee may not receive less under

---

1.   IRC Sec. 416(c)(2); Treas. Reg. §1.416-1, M-7 to M-9.
2.   IRC Sec. 401(a)(17); Treas. Reg. §1.416-1, M-7; Notice 2018-83, Notice 2019-59, Notice 2020-79.
3.   Treas. Reg. §1.416-1, M-20.
4.   Treas. Reg. §§1.416-1, M-18, 1.416-1, M-19.
5.   Treas. Reg. §1.416-1, M-9.
6.   IRC Sec. 416(c)(2)(B)(ii)(II).
7.   IRC Sec. 416(c); Treas. Reg. §1.416-1, M-1.

the combined plans than he or she would if he or she participated in only one of the plans.[1] The regulations provide four safe harbor rules a plan may use to determine the minimum an employee must receive.[2]

Collective bargaining units. The minimum contribution and minimum benefit requirements do not apply in the case of any employee covered by a collective bargaining agreement if there is evidence that retirement benefits were the subject of good faith bargaining.[3]

3926. What miscellaneous qualification requirements must be met in order for a plan to be qualified?

A. *Permanence.* A qualified plan must be a permanent program. Thus, although an employer may reserve the right to amend or terminate the plan, the abandonment of the plan for any reason other than business necessity within a few years after its establishment will be evidence that the plan from its inception was not a bona fide program for the exclusive benefit of employees in general. This will especially be true if, for example, a pension plan is abandoned soon after pensions have been funded for the highly-paid or stockholder employees. The permanency of a plan will be indicated by all of the surrounding facts and circumstances, including the likelihood of the employer's ability to continue contributions as provided under the plan. In the case of a profit-sharing plan, other than a profit-sharing plan which covers employees and owner-employees (see section 401(d)(2)(B)), it is not necessary that the employer contribute every year or that he contribute the same amount or contribute in accordance with the same ratio every year. However, merely making a single or occasional contribution out of profits for employees does not establish a plan of profit-sharing. Since 1985, plan sponsors no longer must have profits to make contributions to profit-sharing plans.[4] In the event a plan is abandoned, the employer should promptly notify the district director, stating the circumstances which led to the discontinuance of the plan.[5]

B. *Benefits after merger.* The plan must provide that in the case of any merger or consolidation with, or transfer of assets or liabilities to, any other plan, each participant in the plan would (if the plan then terminated) receive a benefit immediately after the merger, consolidation, or transfer which is equal to or greater than the benefit the participant would have been entitled to receive immediately before the merger, consolidation, or transfer (if the plan had then terminated).[6] (This requirement does not apply to certain multiemployer plans.) Shifting assets between funding media used for a single plan (e.g., between trusts and annuity contracts) is not a transfer of assets or liabilities.[7]

C. *Early retirement benefit.* If a plan provides for payment of an early retirement benefit, a vested participant who terminates employment after having satisfied the service requirements,

---

1.   See TEFRA Conf. Rep., 1982-2 CB 677; see IRC Sec. 416(f).
2.   See Treas. Reg. §1.416-1, M-12.
3.   IRC Sec. 416(i)(4).
4.   IRC Sec. 401(a)(27), added by P.L.99-514.
5.   Treas. Reg. §1.401-1(b)(2). This regulation has not been amended to reflect the addition of section 401(a)(27), eliminating the requirement that contributions be made from profits.
6.   IRC Sec. 401(a)(12).
7.   Treas. Reg. §1.414(l)-1.

but not the age requirement for the early benefit, must be entitled, upon satisfaction of the age requirement, to receive a benefit not less than the benefit to which the participant would be entitled at normal retirement age, actuarially reduced in accordance with reasonable actuarial assumptions.[1] In the case of a defined contribution plan, the employee, upon reaching early retirement age following termination after having satisfied service requirements, must be entitled to receive a benefit equal in value to the vested portion of his account balance at early retirement age.[2]

D. *Social Security offset.* The plan must not permit benefits to be reduced by reason of any increase in Social Security benefit levels or wage base occurring (1) after separation from service, in the case of a participant who has separated from service with nonforfeitable rights to benefits, or (if earlier) (2) after first receipt of benefits, in the case of a participant or beneficiary who is receiving benefits under the plan.[3] This requirement also applies to plans that supplement benefits provided under state or federal laws other than the Social Security Act, such as the Railroad Retirement Act of 1937.[4]

E. *Withdrawal of employee contributions.* The plan must preclude forfeitures of accrued benefits derived from employer contributions (whether forfeitable or nonforfeitable) solely because a benefit derived from the participant's contributions is voluntarily withdrawn by him after the participant has a nonforfeitable right to 50 percent of the accrued benefit derived from employer contributions.[5]

F. *Compensation.* Generally, a plan will not be qualified unless (for the purpose of any of the qualification rules) not more than $290,000 (as indexed for 2021) of annual compensation of any employee is taken into account under the plan for any plan year.[6] (See Appendix E for the amounts for earlier plan years.) This amount is indexed for inflation in increments of $5,000.[7]

3927. Who is an employee for purposes of meeting the requirements applicable to qualified plans?

"Employee" generally includes any individual who performs services for a person or entity that has the right to control and direct the individual's work, not only as to the result to be accomplished but also as to the details and means by which the result is accomplished.[8] These individuals are referred to as common law employees. The U.S. Supreme Court has set forth a 20-factor test for determining whether an individual is a common law employee.[9] Self-employed individuals, including sole proprietors, partners, and members of LLCs taxed as partnerships

1.   IRC Sec. 401(a)(14); Treas. Reg. §1.401(a)-14(c).
2.   TIR 1334 (1/8/75), M-3.
3.   IRC Sec. 401(a)(15).
4.   Treas. Reg. §1.401(a)-15(b).
5.   IRC Sec. 401(a)(19); Treas. Reg. §1.401(a)-19(b).
6.   IRC Sec. 401(a)(17)(A); Notice 2019-59.
7.   See IRC Sec. 401(a)(17)(B); Treas. Reg. §1.401(a)(17)-1(a).
8.   Treas. Reg. §31.3121(d)-1(c)(2); *Packard v. Comm.*, 63 TC 621 (1975).
9.   See *Nationwide Mutual Ins. Co. v. Darden*, 503 U.S. 318 (1992).

operating trades, businesses, or professions, are treated as employees for purposes of partici-pating in qualified plans even though they clearly are not common law employees (Q 3931).[1]

To prevent abuses of the tax advantages of qualified retirement plans through the manipula-tion of separate employer entities, the IRC provides several special rules that generally must be applied when testing plan qualification, as follows:

(1)   All employees of all corporations that are members of a controlled group of cor-porations and all employees of trades or businesses under common control must be treated as employed by a single employer (Q 3932).[2]

(2)   All employees of the members of an affiliated service group must be treated as employed by a single employer (Q 3934).[3]

(3)   Leased employees must be treated as employees (Q 3928).[4]

The aggregation rules for controlled groups and trades and businesses under common control also appear in ERISA; the aggregation rules for affiliated service groups do not. Except in the case of employees of an affiliated service group or certain leased employees, employees of a partnership need not be treated as employees of any partner who does not own more than a 50 percent interest in the capital or profits of the partnership.[5]

3928. What special rules apply to leased employees for purposes of the requirements that apply to qualified plans?

For the IRC's qualification requirements, an employer generally treats any individual who is a leased employee as though that individual were the employer's own employee. To the extent that contributions or benefits provided for a leased employee by the organization from which the employee is leased are attributable to services performed for the employer, these contributions or benefits are treated as if they were provided by the employer under a qualified plan.[6] These two requirements have the effect of requiring most leased employees who have met a recipient plan's eligibility provisions to be included in the recipient's plan as an employee of the recipient.

A leased employee is an individual who is not an employee of the recipient employer and who performs services for a recipient employer, if (1) the individual's services are provided to the recipient under one or more agreements with a leasing organization, (2) the individual has performed services for the recipient or related employer on a substantially full-time basis for a period of at least one year, and (3) the services are performed under the primary direction or control of the recipient employer.[7] For purposes of this definition, the term employee means a common law employee as determined under the 20 factor test set forth in *Nationwide Mutual Ins.*

---

1.   IRC Sec. 401(c)(1).
2.   IRC Secs. 414(b), 414(c); Treas. Reg. §§1.414(b)-1, 1.414(c)-1 to 1.414(c)-5.
3.   IRC Sec. 414(m); Prop. Treas. Reg. §1.414(m)-1.
4.   IRC Sec. 414(n).
5.   See *Garland v. Comm.*, 73 TC 5 (1979); *Thomas Kiddie, M.D., Inc. v. Comm.*, 69 TC 1055 (1978).
6.   IRC Sec. 414(n)(1).
7.   IRC Sec. 414(n)(2).

Co. v. Darden,[1] which must be applied before it can be determined whether an individual meets the definition of a "leased employee."[2]

The fact that an individual is a leased employee does not automatically mean he or she must be a participant in a plan maintained by the employer. A plan may exclude a leased employee from participation in the plan when the plan can satisfy coverage and nondiscrimination testing by including the leased employee with no benefits or the benefits provided by the leasing company plan. At least two circuit courts have held that ERISA does not *per se* require the inclusion of leased employees in an employer's plan.[3] In addition, the IRS addressed this issue in Notice 84-11,[4] stating that leased employees should be treated as employees, but the plan's failure to include them as participants in the plan does not result in disqualification of the plan. Despite its issuance prior to TRA '86, Notice 84-11 was cited favorably in *Bronk v. Mountain States Tel. & Tel., Inc.*,[5] as controlling authority on this issue.

The determination of whether services are performed under the primary direction or control of the recipient is based on the facts and circumstances. A finding will be made if the service recipient exercises the majority of direction and control over the individual; for example, whether the individual is required to comply with the recipient's instructions as to when, where, and how the services are to be performed; whether the services will be performed by a particular person; whether the individual is subject to the recipient's supervision; and whether the services must be performed in a particular order or sequence set by the recipient.

The recipient may be a single employer or a group consisting of employers required to be aggregated under the controlled group, common control, or affiliated service group rules (Q 3932, Q 3934).[6] Employers are related if a loss on a sale of property between them would be disallowed as a deduction under IRC Sections 267 or 707(b) or they are members of the same controlled group of corporations, using a 50 percent rather than 80 percent ownership test.[7]

Safe Harbor

Even though an individual is a leased employee, he or she may be disregarded by the employer for purposes of determining qualification if the individual is covered by a qualified money purchase pension plan maintained by the leasing organization and the following requirements are satisfied:

(1)   The plan provides for employer contributions by the leasing organization at a nonintegrated rate which is not less than 10 percent.

---

1.   503 U.S. 318 (1992).
2.   *Burrey v. Pacific Gas and Elect. Co.*, 1998 U.S. App. Lexis 26594 (9th Cir. 1998); General Explanation of Tax Legislation Enacted in the 104th Congress (JCT-12-96), p. 173 (the 1996 Blue Book).
3.   See *Abraham v. Exxon Corp.*, 85 F.3d 1126 (5th Cir. 1996); *Bronk v. Mountain States Tel. & Tel., Inc.*, 140 F.3d 1335 (10th Cir. 1998), *aff'd*, 2000 U.S. App. LEXIS 14677 (10th Cir. 2000).
4.   1984-2 CB 469, A-14.
5.   140 F.3d 1335 (10th Cir. 1998).
6.   IRC Sec. 414(n)(6)(B).
7.   IRC Secs. 414(n)(6)(A), 414(a)(3).

(2)   The plan provides for immediate participation on the first day an individual becomes an employee of the leasing organization unless (x) the individual's compensation from the leasing organization in each plan year during the four year period ending with the plan year is less than $1,000, or (y) the individual performs substantially all of his or her services for the leasing organization.

(3)   The plan provides for full and immediate vesting of all contributions under the plan.

(4)   Leased employees do not constitute more than 20 percent of the recipient's non-highly compensated work force.[1]

This safe harbor applies only for purposes of the leased employee provision; it does not permit an employer to disregard a common law employee who otherwise meets the definition of a leased employee.[2]

A recipient's nonhighly compensated work force is the aggregate number of individuals who are not highly compensated (Q 3929) but who are common law employees of the recipient and have performed services for the recipient on a substantially full-time period of at least one year or who are leased employees with respect to the recipient.[3]

A money purchase pension plan of a leasing organization is not qualified if it covers any individuals who are leased by the leasing organization to the recipient but who are not themselves employees of the leasing organization. That is because the plan would not meet the "exclusive benefit" rule (Q 3838).[4]

3929. Who are highly compensated employees for purposes of the requirements that apply to qualified plans?

Status as a highly compensated employee is determined by focusing on the determination year (i.e., the plan year for which the determination is being made) and the immediately preceding twelve month period (the "look-back" year).

An employee is a highly compensated active employee with respect to a plan year (i.e., the determination year) if the employee (1) was a 5 percent owner, as defined for top-heavy purposes (Q 3930), at any time during either the determination year or look-back year, or (2) received compensation for the preceding year in excess of $130,000 in 2021 from the employer.[5]

The compensation element of this determination can be limited to the top 20 percent of employees ranked by compensation (the "top-paid group").[6] The income threshold ($130,000

---

1.   IRC Sec. 414(n)(5).
2.   IRC Sec. 414(n)(2). See *Burnetta v. Comm.*, 68 TC 387 (1977), *acq.* 1978-2 C.B. 1.
3.   IRC Sec. 414(n)(5)(C)(ii).
4.   See *Professional & Executive Leasing, Inc. v. Comm.*, 89 TC 225 (1987), *aff'd*, 862 F.2d 751 (9th Cir. 1988).
5.   Notice 2019-59.
6.   IRC Sec. 414(q)(1).

for 2021) is indexed at the same time and in the same manner as the Section 415 defined benefit dollar limitation.[1]

The applicable dollar amount for a particular determination or look-back year is the dollar amount for the calendar year in which the determination year or look-back year begins.[2]

Employers may identify the employees who are highly compensated employees under IRC Section 414(q) using the same snapshot testing that is used for the nondiscrimination requirements (i.e., test results for a single day during the plan year, provided that that day is representative of the employer's workforce and the plan's coverage throughout the plan year).[3]

The IRS has stated that a fiscal year plan may make a calendar year data election. If the election is made, the calendar year beginning with or within the look-back year will be treated as the employer's look-back year for purposes of determining whether an individual is a highly compensated employee on account of his or her compensation. This election will not apply in determining whether a 5 percent owner is highly compensated. The effect of this election is that even though an employer maintains a plan on a fiscal year basis, it uses calendar year data. Once made, the election applies for all subsequent years unless changed by the employer.[4]

Planning Point: For a plan that is maintained on a fiscal year basis, making a calendar year data election can simplify plan administration. Calendar year compensation information is easily available because Form W-2 requires the use of calendar year information. Using fiscal year information would require the employer to make a special calculation to determine if an individual is highly compensated.

Top-Paid Group

An alternative way to determine highly compensated employees is to make a "top-paid group" election. The top-paid group election must be made in the plan document. The top-paid group of employees for a year is the group of employees in the top 20 percent, ranked on the basis of compensation paid for the year.[5]

Once made, a top-paid group election remains in effect until the employer changes it via plan amendment.[6] Former employees are not included in the top-paid group. Also, employees who are excluded under the collective bargaining agreement exclusion in determining the number of employees in the top-paid group also are excluded for purposes of identifying the members of the top-paid group.[7]

---

1. IRC Sec. 414(q)(1). See Temp. Treas. Reg. §1.414(q)-1T, A-3(c)(1); Notice 2020-79.
2. Temp. Treas. Reg. §1.414(q)-1T, A-3(c)(2); Information Letter to Kyle N. Brown dated December 9, 1999.
3. Rev. Proc. 93-42, 1993-2 CB 540, as modified by Rev. Proc. 95-34, 1995-2 CB 385.
4. Notice 97-45, 1997-2 CB 296.
5. IRC Sec. 414(q)(3).
6. Notice 97-45, 1997-2 CB 296.
7. Temp. Treas. Reg. §1.414(q)-1T, A-9(c).

In determining the number of employees in the top-paid group (but not for the purpose of identifying the particular employees in the group), the following employees may be excluded:[1]

(1)   employees with less than six months of service, including any service in the immediately preceding year;

(2)   employees who normally work fewer than 17½ hours per week, if certain requirements are met;[2]

(3)   employees who normally work during not more than six months in any year, determined on the basis of the facts and circumstances as evidenced by the employer's customary experience in the years preceding the determination year;[3]

(4)   employees under the age of 21 at the end of the year; and

(5)   employees covered by a collective bargaining agreement if 90 percent or more of the employees of the employer are covered under the agreement and the plan being tested covers only employees who are not covered under the agreement.[4]

An employer may elect to use a shorter period of service, smaller number of hours or months, or lower age than those specified above (including no age or service requirement exclusion).[5] Also, an employer may elect not to exclude members under the collective bargaining exclusion.[6]

No special notification or filing of a top-paid group election or a calendar year data election is required, although certain plan amendments may be necessary to incorporate a definition of highly compensated employees that reflects the election.[7] Furthermore, a consistency requirement states generally that an election made by an employer operating more than one plan must apply consistently to all plans of the employer that begin with or within the same calendar year.[8]

Nonresident aliens who receive no earned income from sources within the United States are disregarded for all purposes in determining the identity of highly compensated employees.[9] An employer may adopt any rounding or tie-breaking method that is reasonable, nondiscriminatory, and uniformly and consistently applied.[10] An employee who is highly compensated as a result of meeting two or more of the tests above is not disregarded for the purpose of applying any of those tests to other individuals.[11]

1.   IRC Sec. 414(q)(5); Temp. Treas. Reg. §1.414(q)-1T, A-9(b).
2.   See Temp. Treas. Reg. §1.414(q)-1T, A-9(e).
3.   See Temp. Treas. Reg. §1.414(q)-1T, A-9(f).
4.   Temp. Treas. Reg. §1.414(q)-1T, A-9(b).
5.   IRC Sec. 414(q)(5). See Temp. Treas. Reg. §1.414(q)-1T, A-9(b)(2)(i).
6.   Temp. Treas. Reg. §1.414(q)-1T, A-9(b)(2)(ii).
7.   Notice 97-45, 1997-2 CB 296.
8.   Notice 97-45, 1997-2 CB 296.
9.   IRC Sec. 414(q)(8).
10.   Temp. Treas. Reg. §1.414(q)-1T, A-3(b).
11.   Temp. Treas. Reg. §1.414(q)-1T, A-3(d).

Compensation is the compensation received by the participant from the employer for the year, including elective or salary reduction contributions to a cafeteria plan, cash or deferred arrangement, or a tax sheltered annuity.[1]

A highly compensated former employee for a determination year is any employee who had a separation year prior to the determination year and was a highly compensated active employee for either his or her separation year or any determination year ending on or after his or her 55th birthday.[2]

A separation year is any year during which the employee separates from service with the employer. For purposes of this rule, an employee who performs no services for the employer during a determination year is treated as having separated from service with the employer in the year that he or she last performed services for the employer. An employee will be deemed to have a separation year if, in a determination year prior to attainment of age 55, the employee receives compensation in an amount less than 50 percent of his or her average annual compensation for the three consecutive calendar years preceding the determination year in which the employee received the greatest amount of compensation from the employer (or the total period of the employee's service with the employer, if less).

Because an employee who is deemed to have a separation is still performing services for the employer during the determination year, the employee is treated as an active employee and the deemed separation year is relevant only for purposes of determining whether the employee will be a highly compensated former employee after he or she actually separates from service. An employee with a deemed separation year will not be treated as a highly compensated former employee by reason of the deemed separation year if the employee later has a significant increase in services and compensation and, thus, is deemed to have a resumption of employment.[3]

The controlled group, common control, and affiliated service group aggregation rules, as well as the employee leasing provisions, are applied before applying the highly compensated employee rules (Q 3928, Q 3932, and Q 3934).[4] The entity aggregation rules are not taken into account for purposes of determining who is a 5 percent owner. The separate lines of business rules also are not applicable in determining the highly compensated group.[5]

3930. Who is a key employee for purposes of the top-heavy rules for qualified plans?

A key employee for purposes of the top-heavy rules is any employee or, in some cases, a former or deceased employee who, at any time during the plan year containing the determination date for the plan year to be tested, is:

---

1.   IRC Sec. 414(q)(4); Temp. Treas. Reg. §1.414(q)-1T, A-13.
2.   Temp. Treas. Reg. §1.414(q)-1T, A-4.
3.   Temp. Treas. Reg. §1.414(q)-1T, A-5.
4.   IRC Sec. 414(q)(7).
5.   Temp. Treas. Reg. §1.414(q)-1T, A-6, A-8.

(1)   an officer of the employer whose annual compensation from the employer exceeds $185,000 (as indexed for 2020-2021, $180,000 for 2019,[1] this amount is indexed for inflation in increments of $5,000);

(2)   a more-than-5 percent owner of the employer; or

(3)   a more-than-1 percent owner of the employer having annual compensation from the employer for a plan year in excess of $150,000; this amount is not indexed for inflation.[2] (As to when the determination date occurs, see Q 3916.)

The determination as to whether an individual is an officer is made on the basis of all facts and circumstances; job titles are disregarded. An officer is an administrative executive who is in regular and continuous service, not a nominal officer whose administrative duties are limited to special and single transactions. A partner of a partnership will not be treated as an officer for purposes of the key employee test merely because he owns a capital or profits interest in the partnership, exercises his voting rights as a partner, and may, for limited purposes, be authorized and does in fact act as an agent of the partnership.[3] Unincorporated associations, including partnerships and sole proprietorships, may have officers.[4]

In any case, the number of individuals treated as key employees because of their officer status is limited to the greater of three individuals or 10 percent of all employees, but in any event, not more than 50.[5]

Those employees who can be excluded when determining the number of employees in the top-paid group for purposes of identifying an employer's highly compensated employees (Q 3929) also can be disregarded in determining the number of officers to be taken into account in identifying key employees.[6] It is unclear how ties in compensation should be resolved. Whether an individual is a key employee because of his or her officer status is determined without regard to whether the individual is a key employee for any other reason.[7]

An individual owns more than 5 percent of a corporate employer if the individual owns more than 5 percent of the outstanding stock of the corporation by value or stock possessing more than 5 percent of the total combined voting power of all stock of the corporation. In determining stock ownership, the attribution rules of IRC Section 318 apply, but stock is attributed from a corporation if a 5 percent rather than 50 percent ownership test is met. Only ownership in the particular employer is considered; the controlled group, common control, and affiliated service group aggregation rules of IRC Section 414 are disregarded. An individual owns more than 5 percent of a noncorporate employer if he or she owns more than 5 percent of the capital or profits interest in that employer. Rules similar to the attribution rules of IRC

---

1.   Notice 2018-83, Notice 2020-79.
2.   IRC Sec. 416(i); Notice 2012-67 (Dec. 10, 2012); Treas. Reg. §1.416-1, T-12.
3.   Treas. Reg. §1.416-1, T-13; Rev. Rul. 80-314, 1980-2 CB 152.
4.   Treas. Reg. §1.416-1, T-15.
5.   IRC Sec. 416(i), flush language.
6.   IRC Secs. 416(i)(1), 414(q)(5).
7.   Treas. Reg. §1.416-1, T-14.

Section 318 apply for purposes of determining ownership in a noncorporate employer.[1] The aggregation rules of IRC Section 414 are disregarded.[2]

The rules discussed in the previous paragraph also apply to determine whether an individual is a more-than-1-percent owner of the employer.[3] All employers who are under common control or who are members of a controlled or affiliated service group (Q 3932, Q 3934) are treated as one employer for the purpose of determining whether a more-than-1-percent owner has annual compensation from the employer in excess of $185,000 (as indexed for 2021).

Compensation, for purposes of identifying key employees generally, is the compensation considered for purposes of the IRC Section 415 limits on contributions and benefits. Any elective or salary reductions contributions made on behalf of an employee to a 401(k) cash or deferred plan, simplified employee pension, 403(b) tax sheltered annuity, or cafeteria plan are included as compensation for purposes of IRC Section 415.[4]

For purposes of determining an employee's ownership in the employer, the attribution rules of IRC Section 318 and the aggregation rules of IRC Section 414 apply. If two employees have the same ownership interest in the employer, the employee who has the greater annual compensation from that employer will be treated as owning the larger interest.[5]

The terms employee and key employee include their respective beneficiaries.[6]

The term key employee is applied under various provisions of the IRC (e.g., IRC Sections 401(h), 415(l), and 419A). For these purposes, the term does not include any officer or employee covered by a governmental plan.[7] Thus, the separate accounting and nondiscrimination rules under those provisions do not apply to employees covered by governmental plans.

3931. Who is an owner-employee for purposes of the requirements that apply to qualified plans?

An owner-employee is an employee (Q 3826) who owns the entire interest in an unincorporated trade or business or, in the case of a partnership, owns more than 10 percent of either the capital interest or the profits interest in the partnership.[8] Even if a partnership agreement does not specify a more than 10 percent interest in profits for any partner, if the formula for dividing profits (e.g., based on a partner's earnings productivity during the year) in operation produced a distribution at the end of the year of more than 10 percent of profits to a partner, the Tax Court has ruled that he or she is an owner-employee for the year.[9]

1.   IRC Sec. 416(i)(1)(C).
2.   IRC Sec. 416(i)(1)(B); Treas. Reg. §§1.416-1, T-17; 1.416-1, T-8.
3.   Treas. Reg. §1.416-1, T-16.
4.   IRC Secs. 416(i)(1)(D), 414(q)(4), 415(c)(3).
5.   Treas. Reg. §1.416-1, T-19.
6.   IRC Sec. 416(i)(5). Treas. Reg. §1.416-1, T-12.
7.   IRC Sec. 416(i).
8.   IRC Sec. 401(c)(3).
9.   *Hill, Farrer & Burrill v. Comm.*, 67 TC 411 (1976), *aff'd*, 594 F.2d 1282 (9th Cir. 1979).

An individual who owns the entire interest in an unincorporated trade or business is treated as his or her own employer.[1] Thus, a proprietor or sole practitioner who has earned income (Q 3826) can establish a qualified plan under which he or she is both employer and employee.

A partnership is treated as the employer of each partner who is an employee (Q 3826).[2] Thus, partners individually cannot establish a qualified plan for a firm or solely for themselves, but the partnership can establish a plan in which the partners can participate.

Persons who are shareholder-employees in professional corporations or associations or in business corporations (including S corporations) are not self-employed individuals. These people participate in a qualified plan of the corporation as regular employees of the corporation.[3] This is true even of a shareholder-employee who is sole owner of the corporation. S corporation pass-through income may not be treated as self-employment earnings for purposes of a Keogh plan deduction, even where the shareholder performed services for the corporation.[4]

A common law employee is an employee under common law rules, as distinguished from a self-employed individual who is considered an employee only for qualified plan purposes. An individual generally is considered an employee under common law rules if the person or organization for whom the individual performs services has the right to control and direct his or her work not only as to the result to be accomplished, but also as to the details and means by which the result is accomplished (Q 3927).[5]

The common law rules also apply generally in determining whether an individual is an employee for Social Security purposes. Ordinarily, therefore, an individual who is an employee under Social Security is a common law employee for self-employed plan purposes.

A person's status for self-employed plan purposes is determined by the definition of employee under the Social Security law, irrespective of whether or how the person's earnings are covered under Social Security.

Thus, if a person is an employee under the common law rules, it is immaterial that his or her earnings are treated as self-employment income under the Social Security law. For example, a minister or other clergy who is employed by a congregation on a salaried basis is a common law employee, and not a self-employed individual, even though for Social Security purposes the person's compensation is treated as net earnings from self-employment. Amounts received by the minister directly from members of the congregation, such as fees for performing marriages, baptisms, or other personal services, represent earnings from self-employment.

Full-time life insurance salespersons are treated as common law employees for both Social Security and qualified retirement plan purposes even though, under the common law rules, they are self-employed. This is because of special statutory provisions in the Social Security Act and

---

1.   IRC Sec. 401(c)(4).
2.   IRC Sec. 401(c)(4).
3.   Treas. Reg. §1.401-1(b)(3).
4.   See *Durando v. U.S.*, 70 F.3d 548 (9th Cir. 1995).
5.   Treas. Reg. §31.3121(d)-1(c)(2).

the IRC. Thus, a full-time life insurance salesperson under the Social Security law is prohibited from establishing a qualified plan for himself or for herself.[1] Depending on the salesperson's contractual arrangements, he or she may be considered a self-employed individual for some sales or services, allowing them to establish a qualified plan. These provisions do not appear to apply to general agents and most general lines insurance agents and brokers. As a result, based on their situation, they may be considered self-employed individuals and are eligible to establish qualified plans for themselves and their employees.

Attorneys with a law firm, depending on the circumstances, can either be self-employed or have the status of an "employee" of the firm.[2]

An individual may participate in a qualified plan as a self-employed person even though the individual performs work as a common law employee for another employer. For example, an attorney who is a common law employee of a corporation and who in the evenings maintains an office in which he or she practices law is eligible to establish a plan as a self-employed person with respect to the law practice.

An individual may be self-employed with respect to some services the individual sells to a business even though he or she also provides other services to the same business as an employee. In either case, the individual may participate in a qualified plan as a self-employed person with respect to his or her self-employed earnings, even though the employer maintains a qualified plan under which the individual is covered as a common law employee.[3] A tenured university professor who conducted seminars in a separate capacity at the university with which he was employed was determined by the Tax Court to be self-employed, despite objections by the IRS. As a result, he was permitted to establish a Keogh plan with amounts earned from his self-employment.[4]

3932. What is a controlled group of corporations?

The term controlled group is used to determine who makes up the group of employees that will be subject to the IRC's coverage, nondiscrimination testing, and most qualification requirements that apply to qualified retirement plans. All employees of a single employer generally are included in this testing. The controlled group rules aggregate several entities (e.g., partnerships, sole proprietorships, and corporations) into a single employer for purposes of meeting various qualification requirements of the IRC. All employees of a group of employers that are members of a controlled group of corporations or, in the case of partnerships and proprietorships, are under common control will be treated as employed by a single employer.[5] In general, the determination of whether a group is a controlled group of corporations or under common control is based on stock ownership by value or voting power.

---

1.   Treas. Reg. §1.401-10(b)(3). See also IRC Sec. 7701(a)(20); IRS Pub. 560.
2.   See Rev. Rul. 68-324, 1968-1 CB 433.
3.   *Pulver v. Comm.*, TC Memo 1982-437; Treas. Reg. §1.401-10(b)(3)(ii).
4.   *Reece v. Comm.*, TC Memo 1992-335.
5.   IRC Secs. 414(b), 414(c).

A controlled group may be a parent-subsidiary controlled group, a brother-sister controlled group, or a combined group.[1]

A parent-subsidiary controlled group is composed of one or more chains of subsidiary corporations connected through stock ownership with a common parent corporation. A parent-subsidiary group exists if at least 80 percent of the stock of each subsidiary corporation is owned by one or more of the other corporations in the group and the parent corporation owns at least 80 percent of the stock of at least one of the subsidiary corporations. When determining whether a parent owns 80 percent of the stock of a subsidiary corporation, all stock of that corporation owned directly by other subsidiaries is disregarded.

A brother-sister controlled group consists of two or more corporations in which five or fewer persons, individuals, estates, or trusts own stock consisting of 80 percent or more of each corporation and more than 50 percent of each corporation when taking into account each stockholder's interest only to the extent he or she has identical interests in each corporation. For purposes of the 80 percent test, a stockholder's interest is considered only if he or she owns some interest in each corporation of the group.[2]

A combined group consists of three or more corporations, each of which is a member of a parent-subsidiary group or a brother-sister group and one of which is both a parent of a parent-subsidiary group and a member of a brother-sister group.[3]

Special rules apply for determining stock ownership, including special constructive ownership rules, when determining the existence of a controlled group.[4] Community property rules, where present, also apply.[5] For purposes of qualification, the test for a controlled group is strictly mechanical; once the existence of a group is established, aggregation of employees is required and will not be negated by showing that the controlled group and plans were not created or manipulated for the purpose of avoiding the qualification requirements.[6]

3933. When are trades or businesses under common control?

Under the regulations, trades or businesses are under common control if they constitute a parent-subsidiary group of trades or businesses, a brother-sister group of trades or businesses, or a combined group of trades or businesses. The existence of these groups is determined under rules similar to those discussed in Q 3932 for controlled groups of corporations. "Trades or businesses" include sole proprietorships, partnerships, estates, trusts, and corporations.[7]

1.　Treas. Reg. §1.414(b)-1; IRC Sec. 1563(a).
2.　*U.S. v. Vogel Fertilizer Co.*, 455 U.S. 16 (1982); Treas. Reg. §1.1563-1(a)(3).
3.　IRC Secs. 414(b), 1563; Treas. Reg. §1.414(b)-1.
4.　IRC Sec. 1563(d); Treas. Reg. §1.414(b)-1.
5.　*Aero Indus. Co., Inc. v. Comm.*, TC Memo 1980-116.
6.　*Fujinon Optical, Inc. v. Comm.*, 76 TC 499 (1981).
7.　IRC Sec. 414(c); Treas. Reg. §§1.414(c)-1, 1.414(c)-2, 1.414(c)-3, 1.414(c)-4.

3934. What is an affiliated service group?

For purposes of certain qualification requirements, as well as for the vesting requirements, top-heavy rules, Section 415 limits and the requirements for SEPs, all employees of the members of an affiliated service group generally are treated as employed by a single employer.[1]

An affiliated service group is a group consisting of a service organization (referred to as "FSO" for "first service organization") and:

(1)   an additional service organization (referred to as an "A" organization) that is a shareholder or partner in an FSO and that regularly performs services for the FSO or that is regularly associated with the FSO in the performance of services for third parties, or

(2)   an organization (referred to as a "B" organization) if a significant portion of the organization's business is the performance of services for an FSO or for an A organization (or both) and the services are of a type historically performed by employees in the service field of the FSO or A organization; and

(3)   10 percent or more (in the aggregate) of the interests in the B organization is held by highly compensated employees of an FSO or an A organization or certain common owners.[2]

The term affiliated service group also includes a group consisting of (1) an organization the principal business of which is performing management functions for another organization on a regular and continuing basis, and (2) the organization for which the functions are performed.[3]

An organization is a service organization if its principal business is the performance of services in one of the fields enumerated in the regulations (e.g., health, law, etc.) or if capital is not a material income-producing factor for the organization.[4]

The performance of services for a first service organization or for an A organization (or both) will be assumed to constitute a significant portion of a B organization's business if 10 percent or more of its total gross receipts from all sources during the current year, or two preceding years, was derived from performing services for such organization or organizations. It will be assumed that the performance of services for such organization or organizations is not a significant portion of a B organization's business if less than 5 percent of its gross receipts derived from performing services during the current year and two preceding years was derived from performing services for such organizations.[5] Services are of a type historically performed by employees in a particular field if it was not unusual for the services to be performed by employees of organizations in that service field in the United States on December 13, 1980.[6]

---

1.   IRC Sec. 414(m)(1).
2.   IRC Sec. 414(m); Prop. Treas. Reg. §1.414(m)-2(c)(1).
3.   IRC Sec. 414(m)(5).
4.   IRC Sec. 414(m)(3); Prop. Treas. Reg. §1.414(m)-2(f). See Rev. Rul. 81-105, 1981-1 CB 256.
5.   Prop. Treas. Reg. §1.414(m)-2(c)(2).
6.   Prop. Treas. Reg. §1.414(m)-2(c)(3).

The principles of the constructive stock ownership rules of IRC Section 318(a) apply. Thus, ownership generally will be attributed to an individual from the individual's spouse, children, grandchildren and parents, between a partner and the partnership, between a trust or estate and its beneficiaries, and between a corporation and a more-than-50 percent shareholder, including a corporate shareholder.[1]

Two or more affiliated service groups will not be aggregated merely because an organization is an A organization or a B organization with respect to each affiliated service group. All organizations that are A organizations or B organizations with respect to a single FSO, together with that FSO, must be treated as a single affiliated service group.[2]

Taxpayers may rely on the proposed regulations covering service-type affiliated groups until final rules are published. Examples explaining the tests for a service-type affiliated service group can be found in Revenue Ruling 81-105.[3]

3935. Can the IRS retroactively apply a finding that a plan does not meet qualification requirements?

Yes. The IRS may retroactively revoke a plan's determination letter by notice to the taxpayer if:

(1)   there has been a change in the applicable law;

(2)   the organization omitted or misstated a material fact;

(3)   the organization has operated in a manner materially different from that originally represented; or

(4)   in the case of organizations to which IRC Section 503 applies (which includes qualified plan trusts), the organization engaged in a prohibited transaction with the purpose of diverting corpus or income of the organization from its exempt purpose, and such transaction involved a substantial part of the corpus or income of such organization.[4]

The IRS has broad discretion to determine the extent to which rulings and regulations will be given retroactive effect.[5] The wide array of correction procedures established by the IRS in the past decade offers a choice of less severe remedies, however, and suggests that the IRS is reluctant to disqualify plans except under the most egregious circumstances.

The IRS also may retroactively correct its own mistaken application of law, even where a taxpayer may have relied to the taxpayer's detriment on the IRS's mistake.[6] Concerning determination letters, the IRS has voluntarily limited its authority by the issuance of revenue procedures

---

1.   IRC Sec. 414(m)(6)(B).
2.   Prop. Treas. Reg. §1.414(m)-2(g).
3.   1981-1 CB 256.
4.   Rev. Proc. 2017-5. See also Tax Consequences of Plan Disqualification at http://www.irs.gov/Retirement-Plans/Tax-Consequences-of-Plan-Disqualification.
5.   *Automobile Club of Mich. v. Comm.*, 353 U.S. 180 (1957); IRC Sec. 7805(b).
6.   *Dixon v. U.S.*, 381 U.S. 68 (1965).

stating the standards by which the continuing effect of a determination letter will be judged. In substance, there are two standards.

First, if a published revenue ruling is issued that is applicable to a previously approved plan, to retain its qualified status the plan must be amended to conform with that ruling before the end (and effective at least as of the beginning) of the first plan year following the one in which the ruling was published.[1] Thus, with respect to the approved plan, the revenue ruling is not given retroactive effect and becomes effective only at the beginning of the next plan year.[2]

Second, if no applicable published ruling affecting the qualification of the plan has intervened between the approval and the revocation of the approval, the revocation ordinarily will not have retroactive effect with respect to the taxpayer to whom the ruling was originally issued or to a taxpayer whose tax liability was directly involved in such ruling if:

(1)   there has been no misstatement or omission of material facts;

(2)   the facts subsequently developed are not materially different from the facts on which the ruling was based;

(3)   there has been no change in the applicable law;

(4)   the ruling originally was issued with respect to a prospective or proposed transaction; and

(5)   the taxpayer directly involved in the ruling acted in good faith in reliance on the ruling and a retroactive revocation would be to the taxpayer's detriment.[3]

Employer Deduction

3936. How is an employer's deduction limited for qualified plan contributions?

The amount of an employer's deduction for contributions to a qualified plan depends on the type of plan being maintained. The maximum amounts an employer may deduct are explained at Q 3735 for pension plans, Q 3750 for profit sharing or stock bonus plans, and Q 3823 for employee stock ownership plans ("ESOPs"). If an employer contributes to two or more plans covering any common participants, it is subject to the limits explained in Q 3941.

Rules that govern the timing of an employer's deduction are explained at Q 3938. Other more specific requirements that may affect an employer's ability to deduct contributions or plan expenses are explained at Q 3939.

---

1.   See generally Rev. Proc. 2016-37, 2016-29 IRB 136.
2.   See also *Wisconsin Nipple and Fabricating Corp. v. Comm.*, 581 F.2d 1235 (7th Cir. 1978).
3.   Rev. Proc. 2016-6, 2016-1 IRB 200 at 21.03. See also *Churchill, Ltd. Emple. Stock Ownership Plan & Trust v. Comm.*, TC Memo 2012-300 (2012), *pet. denied*, 2013 U.S. App. LEXIS 11046 (8th Cir. May 29, 2013); *Lansons, Inc. v. Comm.*, 622 F.2d 774 (5th Cir. 1980); *Oakton Distributors, Inc. v. Comm.*, 73 TC 182 (1979); *Pittman Construction v. U.S.*, 436 F. Supp. 1215 (E.D. La. 1977).

Special rules governing contributions of property are explained at Q 3937. The 10 percent penalty on nondeductible contributions is explained at Q 3942.

3937. Can an employer contribute property other than money to a qualified plan trust?

The U.S. Supreme Court has held that an employer's transfer of unencumbered property to a defined benefit plan in satisfaction of a funding obligation is a prohibited transaction.[1] The Court left open the question of whether a transfer of unencumbered property that is not in satisfaction of a funding obligation might be permissible without violating prohibited transaction rules.

The Department of Labor has expressed the view that a contribution of property other than cash that reduces a sponsor's funding obligation would be a prohibited transaction in the absence of a statutory or administrative exemption, whether it is made to a defined benefit or a defined contribution plan; a contribution in excess of amounts needed to meet a plan's funding requirements may be permissible, provided that acceptance of the contribution is consistent with the general standards of fiduciary conduct under ERISA.[2]

Certain contributions of employer stock and employer real property are exempt from the prohibited transaction rules (Q 3979). Furthermore, there is an administrative exemption for the contribution of a life insurance policy to a plan if certain conditions are met (Q 3973). This exemption also protects self-employed owner-employees and more-than-5-percent shareholder-employees of S corporations from the prohibited transaction rules of Title I of ERISA (Q 3979).[3] If only a sole proprietor or partners and their spouses participate in the plan, Title I of ERISA does not apply.[4]

A contribution of an employer's promissory note to a trust does not constitute payment and no deduction is allowable until the note is paid.[5] The IRS has taken the position that the contribution of an employer's own term promissory note is a prohibited transaction.[6]

Planning Point: One way to deal with a plan's inability to distribute illiquid assets may be for the plan to contribute the illiquid assets to a separate trust and distribute certificates of interest in that trust to its participants as part of their lump sum distributions. *Martin Silfen, J.D., Brown Brothers Harriman Trust Co., LLC.*

A sale by plan fiduciaries of some of their customers' promissory notes to a plan was a prohibited transaction, notwithstanding the fact that the notes generated a competitive rate of return.[7] An earlier letter ruling indicated that a contribution of a third party promissory note

---

1. *Keystone Consol. Indus., Inc. v. Comm.*, 113 S.Ct. 2006 (1993).
2. DOL Interpretive Bulletin 94-3, 59 Fed. Reg. 66735 (Dec. 28, 1994).
3. PTE 92-5, 57 Fed. Reg. 5019, (formerly PTE 77-7, 1977-2 CB 423).
4. See Labor Reg. §2510.3-3.
5. Rev. Rul. 55-608, 1955-2 CB 546; Rev. Rul. 80-140, 1980-1 CB 89; *Don E. Williams Co. v. U.S.*, 429 U.S. 569 (1977).
6. Rev. Rul. 80-140, 1980-1 CB 89.
7. See *Westoak Realty and Inv. Co., Inc. v. Comm.*, 999 F. 2d 308, 93-2 USTC ¶50,395 (8th Cir. 1993).

was payment and that its fair market value could be deducted.[1] Contribution of a check is only conditional payment; if the check is not paid, the deduction will be disallowed.[2]

The fair market value of contributed property is considered to be the amount contributed for purposes of calculating annual additions within the overall Section 415 limits (Q 3867, Q 3719, and Q 3728).[3]

For special rules applying to the sale of employer securities to a defined contribution plan, see Q 3731. The requirements for a Section 1042 election upon the sale of employer stock to an ESOP are explained at Q 3819.

3938. When may an employer take a deduction for contributions made to a pension, profit sharing, or stock bonus plan?

An employer's contribution generally is deductible only in the taxable year it is paid, except for certain carry-forwards (Q 3735).[4] Both cash and accrual basis employers, including self-employed individuals, are deemed to have made a contribution in the preceding tax year if the payment is on account of that year and is made no later than the due date, including extensions, of the employer's tax return.[5]

In contrast, minimum funding rules may require that a contribution be made earlier than the time at which it is deductible (Q 3742).

A payment will be considered made on account of the preceding tax year if the plan treats it as if received on the last day of that year and either the employer designates, in writing, that the payment is made on account of the previous year or the employer claims it as a deduction on its tax return for the preceding tax year. This kind of designation is irrevocable.[6] See Q 3724 for requirements of quarterly estimated contribution payments applicable to certain plans.

A delayed payment is deductible for the prior year only if the payment would have been deductible had it actually been made on the last day of the prior taxable year.[7] Thus, where an employer's taxable year ended June 30 and the plan year ended December 31, the employer could not deduct elective deferrals and matching contributions attributable to compensation earned by plan participants after June 30 because the contributions were not compensation for services rendered in the prior taxable year of the employer (Q 3939).[8]

Where an employer's taxable year ended January 31, 1998, and the plan year was the calendar year, the employer could deduct elective deferrals and matching contributions attributable

---

1.   Let. Rul. 7852116.
2.   *Springfield Prod., Inc., v. Comm.*, TC Memo 1979-23.
3.   Treas. Reg. §1.415(c)-1(b)(4).
4.   IRC Sec. 404(a).
5.   IRC Sec. 404(a)(6). See, e.g., Let. Rul. 199935062.
6.   Rev. Rul. 76-28, 1976-1 CB 106, as modified by Rev. Rul. 76-77, 1976-1 CB 107.
7.   Rev. Rul. 90-105, 1990-2 CB 69; *Lucky Stores, Inc. v. Comm.*, 153 F.3d 964 (9th Cir. 1998).
8.   Rev. Rul. 90-105, 1990-2 CB 69. See also *American Stores Co. v. Comm.* 108 TC 178 (1997), *aff'd*, 170 F.3d 1267 (10th Cir. 1999).

to compensation earned by plan participants during January 1998 on its return for its fiscal year ending January 31, 1998, even though that was the first month of the 1998 plan year.[1]

Regulations under IRC Section 401(k) provide that contributions made in anticipation of future performance of services generally will not be treated as elective contributions; thus, no deduction is available for these amounts. The regulations essentially make it clear that contributions made pursuant to a cash or deferred election must be made after the employee's performance of services with respect to which the compensation is payable (Q 3753).[2]

The liability to make a contribution need not have accrued in the preceding year, but the plan must have been in existence before the end of the preceding tax year.[3] Likewise, the trust must be in existence within the taxable year for which deductions for contributions are claimed (Q 3837).[4] If a plan trust is complete in all respects on the last day of the taxable year except that it has no corpus, the trust is deemed to have been in existence in the taxable year if the initial contribution is made within the grace period.[5]

In the case of a nontrusteed annuity plan evidenced only by a contract with an insurance company, the plan is not in effect until the contract is executed and issued. Where the plan is separate from the insurance contract, the plan will be considered in effect by the close of the taxable year if:

(1)   the contract has been applied for and the application accepted by the insurance company;

(2)   a contract or abstract has been prepared outlining the terms of the plan;

(3)   a part payment of premium has been made; and

(4)   the plan has been communicated to the employees.[6]

If the plan year of a defined benefit plan and the employer's tax year are not the same, the employer may claim a deduction for a contribution made for the plan year that either ends or begins in the tax year or may use a weighted average such as the number of months in each plan year falling in the tax year. The same method must be used consistently.[7]

Where a short taxable year with no plan year beginning or ending within it resulted when an employer changed its taxable year to a calendar year, the IRS approved a method giving the employer a prorated deduction for the length of the short year.[8]

---

1.   CCA 200038004, 2000 IRS CCA LEXIS 101.
2.   See Treas. Reg. §1.401(k)-1(a)(3)(iii).
3.   Rev. Rul. 76-28, as modified by 76-77, 1976-1 CB 107; *Engineered Timber Sales, Inc. v. Comm.*, 74 TC 808 (1980), *appeal dismissed* (5th Cir. 1981).
4.   *Catawba Indus. Rubber Co. v. Comm.*, 64 TC 1011 (1975); *Attardo v. Comm.*, TC Memo 1991-357.
5.   Rev. Rul. 81-114, 1981-1 CB 207.
6.   Rev. Rul. 59-402, 1959-2 CB 122; *Becker v. Comm.*, TC Memo 1966-55.
7.   Treas. Reg. §1.404(a)-14(c).
8.   See Let. Rul. 8806053.

3939. What other specific rules affect an employer's deduction for its contributions to a qualified plan?

If a plan is qualified, an employer may deduct its contributions currently, regardless of whether the rights of the individual participants are forfeitable or nonforfeitable.[1] To be deductible, a contribution on behalf of a participant must qualify as reasonable compensation for services actually rendered to the contributing employer by the participant as an employee.[2] The IRS has discussed the limitations on deductions and carryovers for contributions to a qualified profit sharing plan when an employee's total compensation is unreasonable.[3]

Where reasonableness of compensation was not in question, the Tax Court ruled that a newly formed corporation could deduct its full contribution to a defined benefit plan for the plan year that began in the corporation's short first tax year and it rejected the IRS argument that only 4.5/12 of the contribution should be deductible because the short year was only 4.5 months long.[4]

Deductions with respect to a multiemployer plan maintained pursuant to a collective bargaining agreement are determined as if all participants were employed by a single employer.[5] In the case of a multiple employer plan, the deduction limit generally is applied as if each employer maintained a separate plan.[6] Different rules apply to a plan adopted by two or more corporations that are members of the same controlled group (Q 3932); in that case, the deduction limits are determined as if all such employers were a single employer.[7]

Deductions with respect to a CSEC (Cooperative and Small Employer Charity) plan are determined as if all participants were employed by a single employer.[8]

Certain employer liability to the Pension Benefit Guaranty Corporation ("PBGC") as a result of plan termination or withdrawal from a multiemployer plan will be treated as a contribution to be deducted when paid without regard to the usual limits on the deduction of employer contributions to qualified plans.[9]

Contributions to fund post-retirement medical benefits under IRC Section 401(h) for common law employees may be deducted currently by an employer if they are reasonable, ascertainable, and distinct from contributions to fund retirement benefits, provided the benefits are subordinate to the retirement benefits provided by the plan (Q 3829).[10] Contributions to fund postretirement

---

1. IRC Sec. 404.
2. IRC Sec. 404(a); *Thousand Oaks Residential Care Home I, Inc. v. Comm.*, TC Memo 2013-10; *Bianchi v. Comm.*, 66 TC 324 (1976), *aff'd*, 553 F.2d 93 (2d Cir. 1977); *La Mastro v. Comm.*, 72 TC 377 (1979); *Edwin's Inc. v. U.S.*, 501 F.2d 675 (7th Cir. 1974); *Chas. E. Smith & Sons Co. v. Comm.*, 184 F.2d 1011 (6th Cir. 1950); *Bardahl Mfg. Co. v. Comm.*, TC Memo 1960-223; *Acme Pie Co. v. Comm.*, 10 TCM (CCH) 97 (1951).
3. Rev. Rul. 67-341, 1967-2 CB 156.
4. *Plastic Eng'g & Mfg. Co. v. Comm.*, 78 TC 1187 (1982).
5. IRC Sec. 413(b)(7); see Let. Rul. 8743077.
6. IRC Sec. 413(c)(6).
7. IRC Sec. 414(b).
8. IRC Sec. 413(d)(2).
9. IRC Sec. 404(g).
10. IRC Sec. 404(a)(2); Treas. Reg. §1.404(a)-3(f).

medical benefits are not taken into account in determining the amount deductible with respect to contributions for retirement benefits. The amount of any excess pension assets transferred in a "qualified transfer" (Q 3835) to an IRC Section 401(h) account is not deductible.[1]

Any allocable portion of past service and current pension costs that must be included in the basis of property produced by an employer or held for resale by the employer under the uniform capitalization rules is not deductible by the employer.[2]

3940. Are plan expenses deductible by an employer?

Broker fees paid by a qualified plan are not separately deductible by an employer and are subject to the deduction limits of IRC Section 404(a) (Q 3735, Q 3750).[3] Amounts that an employer reimburses a plan trustee for amounts paid to an investment manager to manage and invest plan assets also are not deductible under IRC Sections 162 or 212.

Amounts that an employer pays directly to an investment manager in connection with the management of a plan's assets apparently are deductible and are not treated as plan contributions under IRC Section 404.[4] The distinction appears to be that brokers' fees are directly related to the purchase of an asset and thus are part of the cost of the securities, but that investment managers' fees, as well as legal, accounting, and trustee fees, are recurring administrative expenses that do not vary with the number or volume of investment transactions.[5]

Some plans allocate plan expenses to the accounts of participants. The IRS has issued guidance permitting such plans to pay these expenses on behalf of active employees while charging the accounts of former employees their proportionate share of such expenses.[6]

3941. How much may an employer deduct if it contributes to more than one kind of qualified plan?

An employer that sponsors both a defined benefit and defined contribution plan covering any common participants may deduct no more than the greater of 25 percent of participant payroll paid in the employer's tax year or the contribution necessary to satisfy the minimum funding requirements for the plan year for any of the defined benefit plans.[7] In the case of employer contributions to one or more defined contribution plans, this limitation applies only to the extent contributions exceed 6 percent of the compensation paid or accrued during the taxable year.[8]

This combined limit does not apply if the only amounts contributed to the defined contribution plan are elective deferrals (Q 3752, Q 3753, Q 3760).[9] Nonetheless, contributions or benefits may not be deducted in the year of contribution to the extent that they exceed the

---

1.   IRC Sec. 420(d)(1)(A).
2.   OBRA '87, Sec. 10204. See also Notice 88-86, 1988-2 CB 401, obsoleted by TD 8897, 2000-2 CB 234.
3.   Rev. Rul. 86-142, 1986-2 CB 60.
4.   See Let. Ruls. 9124036, 9124035, 8941009, 8940013.
5.   Let. Rul. 9252029.
6.   See Rev. Rul. 2004-10, 2004-7 IRB 484.
7.   IRC Sec. 404(a)(7)(A).
8.   See IRC Sec. 404(a)(7)(C)(iii).
9.   IRC Sec. 404(a)(7)(C)(ii).

Section 415 limits (Q 3719, Q 3728, Q 3867), even if they are required by the minimum funding requirements.[1] The excess may be deducted in succeeding years as a contribution carry-over, but see Q 3942 for an excise tax on nondeductible contributions. The deduction for current contributions and carryovers in a tax year cannot exceed 25 percent of aggregate compensation (Q 3750).[2]

For purposes of the deduction limitations, a Section 412(e)(3) (formerly 412(i)) fully insured plan (Q 3811, Q 3812) is treated as a defined benefit plan (Q 3735).[3] In plan years beginning after December 31, 2007, contributions to defined benefit plans insured by the PBGC are excluded from the combined plan limit.[4]

If no employee or former employee benefits under both plans, then the limits that would apply to such plans separately (Q 3735, Q 3750) are not reduced by this overall limit.[5]

Under earlier provisions, a simplified employee pension plan was treated as if it were a separate profit sharing or stock bonus plan for purposes of the overall 25 percent limit.[6] If an employer maintains both a simplified employee pension plan and a profit sharing or stock bonus plan, the 25 percent deductible limit applicable to qualified profit sharing and stock bonus plans must be reduced by the amount of any employer deduction for contributions to the simplified employee pension plan on behalf of a participant also covered under the profit sharing or stock bonus plan.[7] An employer sponsoring both a stock bonus and a profit sharing plan is considered to have a single plan.[8]

3942. Is there a penalty if an employer contributes more to its qualified plan than it can deduct in a year?

Yes, if the plan is a defined contribution plan.

The penalty for making nondeductible contributions also applied to defined benefit plans until 2008. The employer is subject to a tax equal to 10 percent of the nondeductible amount (determined as of the close of the employer's tax year) made to a defined contribution plan (e.g., a pension, profit sharing, or stock bonus plan, a simplified employee pension plan, or a SIMPLE IRA plan).[9]

Nondeductible contributions are the sum of the amounts that the employer contributes to these plans in excess of the deduction limit for the taxable year plus the total amount of employer contributions for each preceding year that were not allowable as a deduction (Q 3735, Q 3750, Q 3938, Q 3941).

---

1.   IRC Sec. 404(j); Notice 83-10, 1983-1 CB 536, F-3.
2.   IRC Sec. 404(a)(7)(B).
3.   IRC Sec. 404(a)(7)(D).
4.   See IRC Sec. 404(a)(7)(C)(iv).
5.   IRC Sec. 404(a)(7)(C).
6.   IRC Sec. 404(h)(3).
7.   IRC Sec. 404(h)(2).
8.   Let. Rul. 7916102.
9.   IRC Sec. 4972(a).

Regulations provide two exceptions to this penalty, although they have little practical application. They reduce the nondeductible amounts by the sum of the portion of the amounts returned to the employer during the taxable year and the portion of the amounts that became deductible for a preceding taxable year or for the current year.[1] The amount allowable as a deduction for any taxable year is treated as coming first from carry-forwards from preceding taxable years, in chronological order, and then from contributions made during the taxable year.[2]

Defined benefit plan contributions generally are disregarded in determining whether an employer has made nondeductible contributions.[3] Contributions that are nondeductible solely because of the combined plan deduction limits are exempt from the excise tax to the extent of the greater of (1) the amount of contributions not exceeding 6 percent of compensation or (2) the sum of matching contributions under IRC Section 401(m)(4)(A) plus elective deferrals under IRC Section 402(g)(3)(A) (Q 3760).[4]

Where amounts contributed in one year to satisfy the preceding year's funding requirement under a conditional waiver would exceed the deductible limit for that prior year, the employer was permitted to report some of those contributions as contributions for the current year for deduction purposes and avoid the nondeductible contributions penalty.[5]

Although the IRC allows the amount of excess contributions to be reduced by the withdrawal of the excess contribution, there are several restrictions for the return of employer contributions to the employer (Q 3838). Apparently, the penalty applicable to an excess contribution also is eliminated on plan termination because the plan no longer exists.

The excise tax does not apply in the case of a governmental plan or an employer that is exempt from income tax.[6] To the extent that an employer has been subject to unrelated business income tax, this exception is inapplicable.[7] Contributions by a tax-exempt employer that was part of a controlled group including at least one non-exempt employer were subject to the excise tax.[8]

If a self-employed individual contributes more than he or she is permitted to deduct in a year, the individual is subject to a tax penalty equal to 10 percent of nondeductible contributions under the plan determined as of the close of the individual's tax year. In the case of a plan that provides contributions or benefits for self-employed individuals, this tax is payable by the employer, which is the sole proprietor or the partnership.[9] Contributions required to meet the minimum funding standards are not subject to this tax even if the self-employed individual cannot deduct them because they exceed his or her earned income.[10]

---

1.   IRC Sec. 4972(c)(1).
2.   IRC Sec. 4972(c)(2).
3.   IRC Secs. 4972(c)(6), 4972(c)(7).
4.   IRC Sec. 4972(c)(6)(A).
5.   Let. Rul. 9107033.
6.   IRC Sec. 4972(d)(1)(B).
7.   See Let. Ruls. 9622037; 9304033.
8.   See Let. Rul. 9236026.
9.   IRC Sec. 4972.
10.   IRC Sec. 4972(c)(4).

3943. How are distributions from a qualified plan taxed?

Benefits distributed from a plan generally are included in the participant's income as ordinary income in the year received. Certain exceptions to the general rule apply based on the timing and nature (e.g., lump sum or periodic) of the distribution. These exceptions include:

(1)   the taxation of certain lump sum distributions (Q 3970);

(2)   distribution of an annuity contract (Q 610);

(3)   distribution of certain employer securities that are distributed as a lump sum distribution (Q 3971);

(4)   distributions that are made as qualified Roth distributions;

(5)   distributions that consist in part of nontaxable basis (e.g., a participant loan in default that was treated as a deemed distribution, or the total employee after-tax contributions made to a plan); and

(6)   distributions that constitute eligible rollover distributions and that are rolled over to another plan or IRA.

The ordinary income taxation of plan distributions is discussed as follows:

(1)   the taxation of periodic retirement payments (Q 611 and Q 3972);

(2)   the taxation of disability payments (Q 383);

(3)   the taxation of payments to beneficiaries (Q 3973 to Q 3975);

(4)   the taxation of amounts received preretirement (Q 3967);

(5)   certain early or premature distributions that are subject to a 10 percent penalty (Q 3968);

(6)   the treatment of amounts received postretirement (Q 3969);

(7)   distribution of corrective distributions of excess contributions and excess aggregate contributions (Q 3807);

(8)   corrective distributions of excess deferrals (Q 3760).

Participant loans meeting certain IRC requirements are not treated as taxable distributions. Loans to employees that do not meet certain requirements (Q 3952 to Q 3959) will be taxed as deemed distributions.

Distribution to alternate payee. A spouse or other alternate payee under a qualified domestic relations order (QDRO, see Q 3914) is treated as a distributee for most purposes under rules relating to the taxation of distributions from qualified plans (Q 3970, Q 621).[1]

---

1.   IRC Secs. 402(e)(1); 402(e)(4). See Let. Ruls. 8751040, 8744023.

Planning Point: A divorcing or separating spouse who is negotiating a qualified domestic relations order and who has not attained age 59½ should weigh the relative advantages and disadvantages of a lump sum distribution that can be rolled over to an IRA in his or her own name and a series of distributions directly from his or her spouse's plan, if available. Distributions from a spouse's plan pursuant to a QDRO would be exempt from the 10 percent tax, whereas distributions from his or her own IRA made before age 59½ would not be exempt unless another exception, such as the substantially equal periodic payment exception, applies.

If any assets of an individually directed account under a qualified plan are used to purchase collectibles, including works of art, gems, antiques, metals, and certain coins, the amount so used will be treated as distributed from the account.[1]

3944. Is an employee generally taxed on the employer's current contributions to a qualified plan?

No, unless the contributions are designated Roth contributions under a 401(k) plan.

A participant does not have to include contributions made by the employer in gross income when the participant's rights in the plan become fully vested or when benefits can be paid, if elected by the participant (i.e., if the benefits are constructively received). Rather, there is no taxation until benefits actually are distributed to a participant. Delaying distribution will postpone taxation unless it is delayed too long and minimum distribution requirements are not met (Q 3890 to Q 3908).[2]

Another exception to the general rule that employer contributions are not taxable when contributed is when the plan uses some of those contributions to purchase life insurance on the participant that is payable to a beneficiary of the participant. Basically, the participant reports as income the cost of the pure death benefit under the contract. This cost is determined based on a table referred to as Table 2001. For the method of determining the "cost" of such insurance protection taxable to the employee, see Q 3947.

Effective January 1, 2015, premiums paid by a pension, profit sharing trust, stock bonus plan, 401(h) plan, pension plan, or annuity plan on accident or health insurance for an employee are currently taxable to the employee as distributions from the trust.[3] Final regulations effective May 12, 2014 clarify that amounts used to pay accident or health insurance premiums (but not disability insurance that replaces contributions) are taxable distributions, with some exceptions, regardless of whether the employer pays the premium from a current year contribution or forfeitures.[4] Thus, if a trustee of a qualified trust uses employer contributions or trust earnings to purchase insurance to provide postretirement medical benefits in an IRC Section 401(h) account or to pay accident or medical benefits, the amounts applied are not taxable income to the employee for whom the insurance is purchased.[5]

---

1. IRC Sec. 408(m).
2. IRC Secs. 402(a), 403(a); Treas. Reg. §§1.402(a)-1(a), 1.403(a)-1.
3. Rev. Rul. 61-164, 1961-2 CB 99; Treas. Reg. §1.402(a)-1(e)(1)(i).
4. 79 FR 26838 (May 12, 2014), amending §1.401(a)-1(e)).
5. Treas. Reg. §1.402(a)-1(e)(iii)(2).

In contrast, a direct distribution from a pension, profit sharing trust, stock bonus plan, 401(h) plan, pension plan, or annuity plan to reimburse an employee for medical expenses is not a taxable distribution to the employee.[1]

Regulations also clarify that with respect to pension, annuity, profit sharing and stock bonus plans, the payment of disability premiums for insurance that replaces retirement contributions are not distributions.[2]

Where a governmental employer "picks up" plan contributions otherwise designated as employee contributions, the contributions are treated as employer contributions.[3] These contributions are excluded from the employee's income and are not subject to withholding.[4] A state law authorizing various retirement systems to "pick up" contributions is not sufficient to effectuate a "pick up" of employee contributions.[5] A governmental employer must specify that contributions designated as employee contributions are being paid by the employer in lieu of employee contributions, and the employee must not have the option of choosing to receive the contribution directly.[6] The required specification of payment of designated employee contributions by the employer must be completed before the period to which the contributions relate; retroactive "pick up" is not permitted.[7] An employer may "pick up" either pre-tax or after-tax contributions used to repurchase service credit.[8]

Where a governmental employer's plan explicitly stated that mandatory employee contributions, although designated as the participants' contributions, would be "picked up" by the employer and treated as employer contributions, those contributions were excluded from the employee's income until the time that they were distributed. Further, the contributions were excluded from wages for income tax withholding purposes. Importantly, the IRS noted that the plan did not give the plan participant the right to choose cash or a deferred election right with respect to the picked up contributions.[9]

3945. Is an employee taxed on current contributions to a plan that has lost its tax qualification?

Contributions to a plan that has ceased to be tax qualified are taxed to an employee in the first year in which his or her right to such amounts is no longer subject to a substantial risk of forfeiture.[10] Thus, an employee is taxed on these contributions to the extent that the employee is vested.

---

1.   Treas. Reg. §1.402(a)-1(e)(1)(ii).
2.   Treas. Reg. §1.402(a)-1(e)(1)(iii).
3.   IRC Sec. 414(h)(2).
4.   Rev. Rul. 77-462, 1977-2 CB 358; Let. Ruls. 201317025; 201143032.
5.   *Foil v. Comm.*, 92 TC 376 (1989), *aff'd*, 920 F.2d 1196 (5th Cir. 1990).
6.   Rev. Rul. 81-35, 1981-1 CB 255; Rev. Rul. 81-36, 1981-1 CB 255; Rev. Rul. 2006-43, 2006-35 IRB 329; Let. Ruls. 201317025; 9441042.
7.   Rev. Rul. 87-10, 1987-1 CB 136, modified by Rev. Rul. 2006-43, 2006-35 IRB 329; *Alderman v. Comm.*, TC Memo 1988-49.
8.   Let. Rul. 200035033.
9.   Treas. Reg. §1.401(k)-1(a)(3); Let. Rul. 201509069.
10. IRC Secs. 402(b)(1).

If a plan fails to be tax qualified solely because it does not satisfy either the minimum participation rule (in the case of a defined benefit plan, see Q 3716) or the coverage requirements (Q 3841), then contributions on behalf of non-highly compensated employees will not be includable in their income. Highly compensated employees must include in income their vested accrued benefits (other than their basis in the account).[1]

3946. Are contributions to a qualified plan subject to Social Security taxes?

Amounts that a regular (i.e., common law) employee elects to contribute under a cash or deferred arrangement under IRC Section 401(k), a section 403(b) plan (Q 3760), and SIMPLE IRA plans are treated as wages subject to Social Security tax.[2] Payments to, from, or under a qualified retirement plan are specifically excluded from the definition of wages under the Social Security law. Consequently, neither employer contributions to, nor distributions from, a qualified retirement plan are subject to Social Security taxes.[3]

Taxation of Distributions

3947. What method is used to determine the cost of current life insurance protection provided in a qualified plan and taxed to employee participants?

The cost of life insurance protection provided under a qualified pension, annuity, or profit sharing plan must be included in an employee's gross income for the year in which deductible employer contributions (whether deducted in the current year or a prior year) or trust income is applied to purchase life insurance protection.[4] This rule applies whether the insurance is provided under group permanent or individual cash value life insurance policies or term insurance, and whether it is provided under a trusteed or non-trusteed plan.[5] According to letter rulings, the rule applies as well to the protection under a life insurance policy on a third party if proceeds are allocable to an employee's account, as can occur with the funding of a buy-sell arrangement.[6]

An employee is taxed currently on the cost of life insurance protection if the proceeds either are (1) payable to the employee's estate or beneficiary, or (2) payable to the plan's trustee, if the plan requires the trustee to pay them to the employee's estate or beneficiary.[7]

On the other hand, an insured is not taxed on the insurance cost if the trustee has the right to retain any part of the death proceeds.[8] Thus, an insured is not taxed on the cost of key person insurance purchased by the trustee as a trust investment. Likewise, participants are not taxed on the cost of a group indemnity policy purchased to indemnify the trust against excessive death benefit payments.[9]

---

1. IRC Sec. 402(b)(4).
2. IRC Secs. 3121(v)(1); 3121(a)(5)(H).
3. IRC Sec. 3121(a)(5).
4. IRC Sec. 72(m)(3)(B); Treas. Reg. §1.72-16(b).
5. Treas. Reg. §§1.402(a)-1(a)(3), 1.403(a)-1(d).
6. See Let. Ruls. 8426090, 8108110.
7. Treas. Reg. §1.72-16(b)(1).
8. Treas. Reg. §1.72-16(b)(6).
9. Rev. Rul. 66-138, 1966-1 CB 25.

The insured does not avoid tax on the current cost of the insurance protection merely because, under the terms of the plan, his or her interest in the policy may be forfeited before his or her death and the trust may receive the cash surrender value of the contract.[1]

3948. How is the amount of taxable income determined when cash value insurance is provided under a qualified plan?

Only the cost of the pure amount at risk is treated as a currently taxable distribution. This cost, the amount of taxable income, is determined by applying the one year premium term rate at the insured's age to the difference between the face amount of insurance and the cash surrender value at the end of the year.[2] The applicable rate is the rate for the insured's age on his or her birthday nearest the beginning of the policy year, although the insured's age on his or her last birthday probably would be acceptable to the IRS, if used consistently.

For many years, P.S. 58 rates were used to calculate the value of the protection.[3] The IRS, however, revoked Revenue Ruling 55-747 for most purposes.[4]

The manner in which the value of current life insurance provided under a qualified plan must be determined is not entirely clear. Guidance issued in 2001 and revised in 2002 provided Table 2001, which sets forth premium rates that replaced the earlier P.S. 58 Table.[5] This table is reproduced in Appendix G. Table 2001 will be used until additional guidance, which was authorized by final regulations in 2003, is published in the Internal Revenue Bulletin.[6]

Until future guidance takes effect, taxpayers are permitted to use the insurer's lower published premium rates that are available to all standard risks for initial issue one-year term insurance.[7] The IRS does not consider an insurer's published premium rates to be available to all standard risks who apply for term insurance unless (1) the insurer generally makes the availability of these rates known to persons who apply for term insurance coverage from the insurer, and (2) the insurer regularly sells term insurance at these rates to individuals who apply for term insurance coverage through the insurer's normal distribution channels.[8]

Earlier guidance stated that if an insurer published rates for individual, initial issue, and one-year term policies available to all standard risks, and these rates were lower than the then-applicable P.S. 58 (now Table 2001) rates, these insurer rates could be substituted to the extent provided by Revenue Ruling 66-110.[9] The ability to use the insurer's lower published rates was limited to arrangements entered into before the effective date of the final regulations (i.e., generally, September 17, 2003).[10]

---

1. *Funkhouser v. Comm.*, 58 TC 940 (1972).
2. Treas. Reg. §§ 1.72-16(b), 1.402(a)-1(a)(3); 1.403(a)-1(d).
3. Rev. Rul. 55-747, 1955-2 CB 228, amplified by Rev. Rul. 67-154, 1967-1 CB 11 and Rev. Rul. 78-420, 1978-2 C.B. 67.
4. See Notice 2002-8, 2002-1 CB 398.
5. See Notice 2002-8, 2002-1 CB 398.
6. See Treas. Reg. §1.61-22(d)(3).
7. See Notice 2002-8, 2002-1 CB 398.
8. See Notice 2002-8, 2002-1 CB 398.
9. 1966-1 CB 12, as amplified by Rev. Rul. 67-154, 1967-1 CB 11 and Rev. Rul. 78-420, 1978-2 C.B. 67.
10. See Notice 2002-8, 2002-1 CB 398; *Neff v. Comm.*, TC Memo 2012-244.

If a profit sharing plan permits a participant to direct a trustee to purchase term insurance riders on either the participant's spouse or dependent children, the cost of the rider must be measured using the P.S. 58 rates (now Table 2001), not the actual cost of the rider.[1]

The premium paid during an employee's taxable year may cover a period extending into the following year. An employee will not be permitted to apportion the cost between the two years; the employee must include the entire P.S. 58 (now Table 2001) cost in his or her gross income for the taxable year during which the premium is paid.

If only a portion of the premium is paid during the taxable year, the cost may be apportioned for that year.[2]

An employee who leaves before the end of the year for which a premium has been paid must include in gross income the annual term cost reduced by the unearned premium credit reallocated to pay premiums for remaining employee-participants.[3]

3949. How is the amount of taxable income determined when term insurance is provided under a qualified plan?

Where individual or group term life insurance is provided under a qualified plan, the cost of the entire amount of protection is taxable to employees. No part of the coverage of group term insurance is exempt under IRC Section 79 (Q 246).[4] Moreover, the cost of the insurance protection cannot be determined by use of the special group term rates that are applicable to taxing excess group term life insurance purchased directly by an employer.[5] It is not settled whether the taxable amount is the actual premium or the P.S. 58 (now Table 2001) cost.

3950. How is the amount of taxable income determined when life insurance protection is purchased under a contributory plan?

Life insurance protection purchased under a contributory plan is considered to have been paid first from employer contributions and trust earnings, unless the plan provides otherwise. Thus, the P.S. 58 (currently Table 2001) costs are taxed to the employee unless the plan provides that employee contributions are to be applied to the insurance cost.[6]

If amounts attributable to deductible employee contributions, including net earnings allocable to them, are used to purchase life insurance, the amount used, not the P.S. 58 (currently Table 2001) cost, is included in the employee's gross income.[7] It is unclear whether such amounts are subject to a premature distribution penalty; the IRS has specifically exempted P.S. 58 (currently Table 2001) costs of life insurance protection included in income from such a penalty (Q 3968). Although the deduction for any contribution used to purchase life

---

1. See Let. Rul. 9023044.
2. See Special Ruling, 1946, Pension Plan Guide (CCH), Pre-1986 IRS Tax Releases, ¶17,303.
3. Rev. Rul. 69-490, 1969-2 CB 11.
4. IRC Sec. 79(b)(3).
5. Treas. Reg. §§1.79-1(a)(3), 1.79-3(d)(3).
6. Rev. Rul. 68-390, 1968-2 CB 175.
7. IRC Sec. 72(o)(3)(B).

insurance is not disallowed, it is, in effect, offset. Loans under the policy would be considered a distribution, including automatic premium loans on default of payment of a premium.

3951. May the cost of life insurance protection provided under a qualified plan be recovered tax-free when benefits are paid?

If life insurance protection under a plan is provided by a cash value policy and the employee has reported the pure death benefit each year, then the total amount reported will be the basis in the contract (Q 3947, Q 3948). That basis may be recovered tax-free if it is paid as a death benefit directly to the beneficiary of the participant.

If a contract is distributed to a participant as a benefit, then the basis in that contract is not taxable.[1] It does not matter whether the contract is distributed or is cashed in and that amount is distributed. It would seem that deductible employee contributions that have been applied to purchase life insurance and taxed to the employee also would be recovered tax-free from benefits received under the policy.[2] The amount recoverable is the total amount of income that has been reported, and not just the taxes paid on that income.[3]

Regulations say that "each separate program of the employer consisting of interrelated contributions and benefits" is a single contract. Where retirement benefits and life insurance are separately provided (e.g., through retirement income contracts and a side fund), they generally are separate programs. Thus, if insurance is provided under a separate term policy, the taxable cost cannot be recovered from the retirement benefits.[4]

Where a plan was amended to eliminate death benefits for employees dying prior to age 65 and its trustees redeemed the whole life insurance policies and invested the proceeds in various securities, the plan became a single program of interrelated contributions and benefits; the employees then could recover their taxable insurance cost from distributions from the plan.[5]

Where, under a combination plan, the trustee surrendered the life insurance policy and used both the policy's cash surrender value and the auxiliary fund to purchase an immediate annuity for a retiring employee, the employee could not recover the taxable insurance costs from the annuity payments; the result would have been different had the auxiliary fund been applied to a settlement under the life insurance policy.[6]

Similarly, where life insurance policies were surrendered and the value used to provide a cash lump sum distribution, the costs taxed to the employee under Table 2001 or P.S. 58 (Q 3947) were not part of the employee's cost recoverable from the distribution. Thus, they could be included in the amount rolled over (Q 3999).[7]

---

1.   Treas. Reg. §1.72-16(b).
2.   See IRC Sec. 72(o)(3)(B).
3.   Treas. Reg. §1.72-16(b)(4). See Let. Rul. 8539066.
4.   Treas. Reg. §1.72-2(a)(3), Ex. 6.
5.   Let. Rul. 8721083.
6.   Rev. Rul. 67-336, 1967-2 CB 66.
7.   Let. Ruls. 7902083, 7830082.

Where nondeductible employee contributions have been earmarked under plan provisions for payment of the cost of life insurance protection, a letter ruling provided the following guidelines: (1) if the life insurance contracts are surrendered by the trustee and payment is made as a lump sum distribution or otherwise, the employee's basis is the amount of the employee's nondeductible contributions to the plan that were not applied to the cost of life insurance protection, and (2) if the life insurance contract is distributed as part of the distribution, the employee's basis is (x) the amount of the employee's nondeductible contributions to the plan, including those applied to the cost of life insurance protection, plus (y) any additional amounts taxed to the employee as the cost of life insurance protection under Table 2001 or P.S. 58 (Q 3952).[1] For estate tax results, see Q 3992.

Keogh Plans

A self-employed individual does not include any costs the individual paid for life insurance protection (Q 3947, Q 3948) in the individual's cost basis of benefits received under the contract.[2] Rather, a self-employed individual loses the tax deduction for the part of the employer's contribution that is allocable to the cost of pure insurance protection for himself or herself.

In other words, the income tax deduction must be based on the balance of the premium after subtracting the one year term cost of the current life insurance protection.[3]

The premium attributable to a waiver of premium provision may not be deducted.[4] If any trust earnings are applied to purchase life insurance protection under a trusteed plan, however, a self-employed individual must include the cost, (Q 3947, Q 3948) in gross income.[5] The life insurance cost is determined in the same manner as for regular employees (Q 3947, Q 3948). The cost of life insurance protection included in income may not be included in an owner-employee's cost basis.[6]

3952. What are the tax consequences and requirements for a loan from a qualified plan?

Editor's Note: See Q 3958 for a discussion of how the CARES Act changed the plan loan rules for 2020.

Qualified plans may permit participants to borrow from their accounts, but are not required to permit loans. A loan from a plan to a participant or to a beneficiary will be treated as a taxable distribution unless it meets certain requirements regarding:

    (1)   the enforceability of the agreement,

    (2)   the term of the loan,

---

1.   Let. Rul. 7922109.
2.   Treas. Reg. §1.72-16(b)(4).
3.   IRC Sec. 404(e); Treas. Reg. §1.404(e)-1(b)(1).
4.   Treas. Reg. §1.404(e)-1(b)(1).
5.   IRC Sec. 72(m)(3)(B); Treas. Reg. §1.72-16(b)(2).
6.   Treas. Reg. §1.72-16(b)(4).

(3)   repayment, and

(4)   a limitation on the maximum loan that may be made (Q 3953).[1]

In certain situations, a violation of one of these requirements will not result in taxation to the participant if the violation is corrected under EPCRS. The IRS expanded the EPCRS program with respect to plan loans in Revenue Procedure 2019-19. Plans may now use the self-correction program to correct errors with respect to defaulted loans, failure to obtain spousal consent if necessary and situations where the plan issues more loans than are permitted under the plan. With respect to defaulted loans, the participant will generally be responsible for making a corrective payment, although the employer will be required to pay interest in certain circumstances. For corrections for failure to obtain spousal consent, the spouse must be notified so that he or she can provide consent. The revenue procedure also permits plans to be amended retroactively to allow for the number of plans loans that were actually permitted.[2]

Repayment of a loan treated as a distribution will be considered a nondeductible employee contribution for tax purposes.[3] When a recipient's benefit is later distributed to the recipient, the amount already taxed will not be taxed again. Repayments constitute investment in the contract (i.e., basis)[4] and are not considered annual additions subject to the IRC Section 415 limits.[5]

Plan Qualification

A qualified plan generally can provide for loans to participants if they are adequately secured, bear a reasonable rate of interest, have a reasonable repayment schedule, and are made available on a nondiscriminatory basis.[6] If a plan is subject to automatic survivor benefit requirements, the loan may require spousal consent (Q 3881).

Treatment of a loan as a distribution for tax purposes generally does not affect the plan's tax qualification. A bona fide loan that is not a prohibited transaction (Q 3979) will not cause a pension plan to fail to satisfy the requirement that a pension plan primarily provide benefits for employees or their beneficiaries over a period of years or for life after retirement.[7] When a plan loaned out almost all of its assets to the company president, without seeking adequate security, a fair return, or prompt repayment, the plan was held not to have been operated for the exclusive benefit of the employees and plan disqualification was justified.[8]

A deemed distribution under IRC Section 72(p) will not be treated as an actual distribution for purposes of the qualification requirements of IRC Section 401; thus, plan qualification will not be affected by reason of a deemed distribution. If a participant's accrued benefit is reduced or offset to repay a plan loan, an actual distribution occurs for purposes of IRC Section 401. This

---

1.   IRC Sec. 72(p)(2); Treas. Reg. §1.72(p)-1, A-3.
2.   Rev. Proc. 2019-19.
3.   Sen. Rept. 97-494, 97th Cong. 2nd Sess.
4.   Let. Rul. 9122059.
5.   Notice 82-22, 1982-2 CB 751.
6.   IRC Sec. 4975(d)(1); Notice 82-22, 1982-2 CB 751; Rev. Rul. 71-437, 1971-2 CB 185; Rev. Rul. 67-288, 1967-2 CB 151.
7.   Notice 82-22, 1982-2 CB 751.
8.   *Winger's Dept. Store, Inc. v. Comm.*, 82 TC 869 (1984).

occurs generally when a participant with a loan terminates employment with the employer, if so specified in the loan agreement. An offset distribution from a 401(k) plan or a pension plan at a time when the plan is not otherwise permitted to make a distribution would result in plan disqualification.[1]

Planning Point: Under prior law, if a loan from a qualified plan had not been repaid when the participant left employment or the plan was terminated (among other reasons), the outstanding loan balance would be offset against his or her account balance and would become taxable if not rolled over to another retirement account within 60 days. Under the 2017 Tax Act, the 60-day deadline is extended to the participant's tax filing deadline for the tax year in which the offset occurs if the amount is treated as distributed from the participant's qualified plan because either: (1) the plan was terminated, or (2) the participant failed to meet the loan repayment terms because of a separation from employment (if the plan provides that the accrued unpaid loan amount must be offset at this time).

A plan loan that is secured by a participant's or a beneficiary's interest in the plan but that is not a prohibited transaction generally will not be an assignment or alienation of plan benefits that would disqualify a plan.[2] If there is a tacit understanding that collection of a loan is not intended, however, the loan may be treated as a disqualifying distribution if made at a time when the plan is not permitted to make distributions.[3]

When an actual distribution follows a deemed distribution, a plan must treat the loan transition amount as an outstanding loan that is taxable on actual distribution. The loan transition amount is the amount by which the initial default amount, attributed as tax basis, exceeds the tax basis immediately preceding the transition date, plus any increase in tax basis thereafter. The plan may not attribute investment in the contract as a loan repayment (Q 3972). The tax basis in the distribution is determined based on the initial default amount and, to the extent that a tax basis has been attributed, it must be reduced by the initial default amount.

Cash repayments made after a loan is deemed to have been distributed will increase the participant's tax basis as if they were after-tax contributions, although they are not treated as after-tax contributions for other purposes.[4]

Prohibited transactions. Plan loans that do not meet any of the requirements for a prohibited transaction exemption (Q 3979) could result in excise taxes and possible plan disqualification. The prohibited transaction rules apply to a loan that does not meet the exemption requirements, even if it is treated as (and taxed as) a distribution (Q 3979). Loans from a qualified plan to certain S corporation shareholders, partners, and sole proprietors also may qualify for the prohibited transaction exemption (Q 3979).[5]

Investments in residential mortgages. Plan investments in residential mortgages of employees, other than officers, directors, or owners, or their beneficiaries, are permitted but are subject to

---

1.	See Treas. Reg. §1.72(p)-1, A-12, A-13.
2.	Treas. Reg. §1.401(a)-13(d)(2). See Q 3911. See also Notice 82-22, 1982-2 CB 751.
3.	See Rev. Rul. 71-437, 1971-2 CB 185.
4.	Treas. Reg. §1.72(p)-1, A-19 through A-21. See also Treas. Reg. §1.72(p)-1, A-1 through A-18.
5.	IRC Sec. 4975(f)(6)(B)(iii).

limitations of IRC Section 72(p) unless they are made in the ordinary course of a plan investment program that is not limited to participants and their beneficiaries.[1] A longer term than the five years allowed for other plan loans may be permitted (Q 3953).

Mandatory Withholding

Distributions that constitute eligible rollover distributions from a qualified plan generally are subject to mandatory income tax withholding at the rate of 20 percent, unless the participant elects a direct rollover.[2] The IRS has stated that a deemed distribution attributable to a plan loan that does not meet the requirements of IRC Section 72(p) will not be subject to the 20 percent mandatory withholding requirement because such a distribution cannot be an eligible rollover distribution.

Where a participant's accrued benefit is reduced or offset to repay a plan loan, such as when employment is terminated, the offset amount may constitute an eligible rollover distribution.[3] Mandatory withholding is required on a deemed distribution of a loan, or a loan repayment by benefit offset, to the extent that a transfer included cash or property other than employer securities at the same time.[4]

3953. What requirements must a qualified plan loan meet to avoid taxation as a distribution?

To avoid being taxed as a distribution, a loan made from a plan to a participant or beneficiary must be made pursuant to an enforceable agreement (Q 3954) that meets certain requirements with respect to the term of the loan (Q 3955), its repayment (Q 3956), and the dollar amount loaned (Q 3957).[5] Under the SECURE Act, plan loans cannot be repaid via credit card or similar arrangements.[6]

3954. Must a qualified plan loan be evidenced by a loan agreement to avoid taxation as a distribution?

A plan loan must be evidenced by a legally enforceable agreement, which may consist of more than one document. The agreement must specify the date, amount, and term of the loan, as well as the repayment schedule. The agreement need not be signed if it is enforceable without a signature under applicable law.[7] The date of the loan is the date the loan is funded (i.e., the date of delivery of the check to the participant).[8]

An agreement must be set forth in a written paper document, an electronic medium, or any other form approved by the IRS.[9] If a loan agreement is in the form of an electronic medium, the

1.   Treas. Reg. §1.72(p)-1, A-18.
2.   IRC Sec. 3405(c).
3.   See Notice 93-3, 1993-1 CB 293.
4.   Treas. Reg. §1.72(p)-1, A-15.
5.   IRC Sec. 72(p)(2); Treas. Reg. §1.72(p)-1, A-3(a).
6.   IRC Sec. 72(p)(2)(D).
7.   Treas. Reg. §1.72(p)-1, A-3(b).
8.   ABA Joint Committee on Employee Benefits, Meeting with IRS and Department of Treasury Officials, May 7, 2004 (Q&A-4).
9.   Treas. Reg. §1.72(p)-1, A-3(b).

medium must be reasonably accessible to the participant or beneficiary and must be provided under a system that is reasonably designed to preclude any individual other than the participant or beneficiary from requesting a loan.[1]

The system also must provide the participant or beneficiary with a reasonable opportunity to review the terms of the loan, and to confirm, modify, or rescind the terms of the loan before it is made.[2] Finally, the system must provide a confirmation to the participant or beneficiary within a reasonable time after the loan is made. The confirmation may be made on a written paper document or through an electronic medium that meets the accessibility requirements above. The electronic confirmation must be no less understandable than a written paper document and must inform the participant or beneficiary of his or her right to receive confirmation via a written paper document at no charge.[3]

3955. How long can a qualified plan loan remain outstanding in order to avoid being taxed as a distribution?

Editor's Note: See Q 3958 for a discussion of how the CARES Act changed the plan loan rules for 2020.

The term of a loan must be no longer than five years. If a loan does not meet the term requirement, the entire loan is a distribution.[4] A distribution is deemed to occur the first time the term requirement is not met in form or operation; thus, it may occur at the time the loan is made, or at a later date.[5]

If a loan initially satisfies the term requirement but payments are not made under the terms of the loan, a deemed distribution occurs as a result of the failure to make the payments.[6] Although such a failure will constitute an immediate violation of the loan provisions, the plan may allow for a cure period of up to three months beyond the calendar quarter in which the payment was due. A distribution in the amount of the entire outstanding balance of the loan will be deemed to have occurred on the last day of the cure period.[7] Legislative history suggests that a loan treated as a distribution because its repayment period was not limited to five years cannot be corrected by renegotiation or repayment.[8] If a loan is outstanding when a total distribution is made to a participant, the loan is treated as repaid (and the amount included in the distribution) on the date of distribution; thus, inclusion in income cannot be deferred until the end of the five year period.[9]

The IRS has released guidance explaining situations in which a cure period may apply to prevent missed installment payments on a retirement plan loan from causing the loan to be

---

1.   Treas. Reg. §1.401(a)-21(d).
2.   Treas. Reg. §1.401(a)-21(f), Example 3.
3.   Treas. Reg. §1.401(a)-21(d)(5), §1.401(a)-21(b)(3)(i).
4.   IRC Sec. 72(p)(2)(B)(i).
5.   Treas. Reg. §1.72(p)-1, A-4.
6.   Treas. Reg. §1.72(p)-1, A-4.
7.   Treas. Reg. §1.72(p)-1, A-10.
8.   Sen. Rept. 97-760, 97th Cong. 2nd Sess.
9.   Let. Rul. 8433065.

treated as a deemed distribution. Generally, a plan loan is treated as a taxable deemed distribution unless it is paid in installment payments over a five-year period. A cure period that lasts up until the last day of the calendar quarter following the quarter when the missed installment payment was due may apply to prevent deemed distribution treatment. Pursuant to the guidance, the IRS uses the example of payments missed on March 31, 2020 and April 30, 2020, followed by on-time payments on May 31, 2020 and June 30, 2020 where a cure period ending June 30 applies. The May and June payments apply to "cure" the missed March and April payments, but then the normal May and June payments are treated as though they were missed because they were applied to cure the missed payments. As a result, the borrower is required to make an installment payment equal to three normal payments to bring the account up to date.[1]

An exception to the five-year rule exists for residence loans used to acquire a dwelling unit that is to be, within a reasonable time, the principal residence of the participant (Q 3959).[2]

3956. What repayment requirements must apply to qualified plan loans?

Editor's Note: The 2017 Tax Act modified the plan loan rules for tax years beginning after 2017 by permitting an extended period of time for repaying or rolling over "plan loan offset amounts". See below. See Q 3958 for a discussion of how the CARES Act changed the plan loan rules for 2020.

The loan agreement must specify the amount and term of the loan and the repayment schedule.[3] Failure to make a timely payment of a plan loan installment when due generally will result in a deemed distribution, but the agreement may provide for a cure period so long as the cure period does not extend beyond the end of the calendar quarter following the quarter in which the payment was due.[4]

A loan that was not repayable in full within five years and that had a balloon payment at the end was held to be a premature distribution subject to the 10 percent penalty (Q 3968) because it violated both the term requirement and the level amortization requirement. The participant was not subject to the substantial understatement or negligence components of the accuracy-related penalty because the participant relied in good faith on the plan administrator's representations that the plan loan was in compliance.[5]

It should be noted that U.S. bankruptcy courts have held that a debtor's repayment of a participant loan from a 401(k) plan is not necessary for support and thus is not exempt from the bankruptcy estate (Q 3911).[6]

---

1. ILM 201736022.
2. IRC Sec. 72(p)(2)(B)(ii).
3. Treas. Reg. §1.72(p)-1, A-3(b).
4. Treas. Reg. §1.72(p)-1, A-10.
5. *Plotkin v. Comm.*, TC Memo 2001-71.
6. *In re Darcy I. Estes*, 254 BR 261 (2000); *In re Cohen*, 246 BR 658 (2000).

The 2017 Tax Act

The 2017 Tax Act modified the plan loan rules for tax years beginning after 2017. Under prior law, if a loan from a qualified plan (including 403(b) plans) had not been repaid when the participant left employment or the plan was terminated (among other reasons), the outstanding loan balance would be offset against his or her account balance and would become taxable if not rolled over to another retirement account within 60 days.

Under the 2017 Tax Act, the 60-day deadline is extended to the participant's tax filing deadline (including extensions) for the tax year in which the offset occurs if the amount is treated as distributed from the participant's qualified plan 401(k) plan, 403(b) plan or 457(b) plan because either (1) the plan was terminated or (2) because the participant failed to meet the loan repayment terms because of a separation from employment (if the plan provides that the accrued unpaid loan amount must be offset at this time).[1] The 2017 Tax Act does not extend the 60-day deadline for plan loan offset amounts that arise for other reasons.

Under IRS proposed regulations, if the participant files a federal tax return on time, an additional six-month window to complete the rollover will apply even if the taxpayer does not request the extension. The automatic six-month extension applies if the taxpayer files his or her tax return by the normal due date of the return (without extensions) and then rolls over the plan loan offset amount within the six-month period and amends the return by that due date to reflect the rollover.[2]

Planning Point: This provision applies to defaulted loans that are actually offset against the retirement account that provided security for the loan and treated as an actual distribution, rather than a deemed distribution. If an actual distribution does not occur by the end of the year in which the default occurs, the tax liability for the deemed distribution accrues in the year of the default. Plan sponsors and administrators should consider how to best meet their fiduciary obligations and achieve the purpose of the retirement plan if a plan loan goes into default.

This extended time period does not apply to loans that have already been deemed taxable distributions (whether because the loan installment payment remained unpaid beyond the applicable cure period or because the loan's terms did not comply with the IRC requirements).

Repayment during Military Service

A participant may suspend repayment of a loan during any period that he or she serves in the military.[3] This rule applies regardless of whether the service performed is "qualified military service" under the Uniformed Services Employment and Reemployment Rights Act of 1994. The suspension of repayment under these circumstances may extend beyond one year, unlike the suspension rules for other leaves of absence.[4]

A participant must resume loan repayment once the participant completes his or her service with the uniformed services, at which time payments must be made as frequently and in

---

1. IRC Sec. 402(c)(3)(C).
2. See Treas. Reg. §301.9100-2.
3. IRC Sec. 414(u)(4).
4. Treas. Reg. §1.72(p)-1, A-9(b).

an amount no less than was made before the suspension. The latest permissible term of the loan is five years from the date of the original loan, plus any period during which repayment was suspended due to military service.[1]

3957. Are there limits on the amount that can be borrowed under a qualified plan loan?

Editor's Note: The CARES Act relaxed the rules to provide relief for qualified plan participants with existing plan loans. See Q 3958.

The amount of the loan, when added to the outstanding balance of all other loans, whenever made, from all plans of the employer, may not exceed the lesser of (1) $50,000 (reduced by the excess of the highest outstanding balance of plan loans during the one-year period ending on the day before the date when the loan is made over the outstanding balance of plan loans on the date when the loan is made), or (2) one-half of the present value of the employee's non-forfeitable accrued benefit under the plans, determined without regard to any accumulated deductible employee contributions. A plan may provide that a minimum loan amount of up to $10,000 may be borrowed, even if it is more than one-half of the present value of the employee's non-forfeitable accrued benefit.[2] For valuation purposes, a valuation within the prior twelve months may be used, if it is the latest available.[3]

If a loan does not meet the dollar limitation, distribution of the amount in excess of the dollar limit is deemed to occur when the loan is made.[4] If the outstanding loan balance meets the dollar limitation immediately after the date when the loan is made, the loan will not be treated as a distribution merely because the present value of the employee's non-forfeitable accrued benefit subsequently decreases.[5]

In determining the outstanding balance and the present value of the non-forfeitable accrued benefit under a plan, an employer's plans include plans of all members of a controlled group of employers, of trades and businesses under common control, and of members of an affiliated service group (Q 3932, Q 3934).[6] The plans include all qualified pension, profit sharing, and stock bonus plans, all Section 403(b) tax sheltered annuities, and all Section 457 deferred compensation plans of aggregated employers.[7]

3958. What relief did the CARES Act provide to expand the qualified plan loan rules post COVID-19?

The CARES Act relaxed the rules to provide relief for qualified plan participants with existing plan loans. If a participant had an existing plan loan with a repayment obligation falling between March 27 and December 31, 2020, that repayment obligation was extended for one

---

1. Treas. Reg. §1.72(p)-1, A-9.
2. IRC Sec. 72(p)(2)(A).
3. Notice 82-22, 1982-2 CB 751.
4. Treas. Reg. §1.72(p)-1, A-4(a).
5. General Explanation—TEFRA, p. 296.
6. IRC Sec. 72(p)(2)(E)(i).
7. IRC Sec. 72(p)(2)(E)(ii).

year. Any subsequent repayment obligations are to be adjusted to reflect this extension. For plan participants who are "qualifying individuals," the plan loan limits were increased to the greater of $100,000 or 100 percent of the vested balance in the participant's account.

Qualifying individuals are those (1) diagnosed with COVID-19, (2) whose spouse or dependent are diagnosed with COVID-19 or (3) who experiences adverse financial consequences as a result of being quarantined, furloughed or laid off (or having work hours reduced) due to COVID-19, being unable to work due to lack of child care due to COVID-19, closing or reducing hours of a business owned or operated by the individual due to COVID-19, or other factors as determined by the Treasury.[1]

Later IRS guidance expanded the list of qualifying individuals to include anyone whose pay was reduced due to COVID-19 (regardless of whether hours were reduced or whether the individual was laid off). If a taxpayer was planning to start a new job and the start date was pushed back (or the offer was rescinded entirely) due to COVID-19, that taxpayer also qualifies for relief. Further, if a spouse or member of the plan participant's household has suffered one of the effects described above, the participant becomes eligible for the expanded retirement account access.[2] "Members of the participant's household" presumably include roommates or anyone who shares the participant's primary residence. For example, if the participant's live-in partner owned a business that was shut down due to COVID-19, the participant would be eligible for the plan distribution relief.

Planning Point: Despite the increased loan limits, plan sponsors need to remember the one-year lookback rule. In reality, the $100,000 limit is reduced by (a) the excess of the employee's highest outstanding plan loan balance during the one-year period ending on the day before the loan is made, over (b) the employee's outstanding balance of any plan loan on the date the loan is made (this calculation also includes loans from any other plans maintained by the employer or member of a controlled group). See below for more details.

The IRS has also released the first Q&A in what is likely to be a series of guidance on the CARES Act retirement-related provisions. One overarching issue is the IRS confirmation that plan sponsors can look to past guidance issued in response to Hurricane Katrina in 2005 and the RMD waiver in 2009 for help implementing the CARES Act provisions.

IRS Q&A clarifies that increased loan limits are currently available between March 27, 2020 and December 31, 2020. Further, the guidance confirms that the loan and distribution relief is optional for plan sponsors—and sponsors can elect to adopt one provision and not another (including the loan repayment option). Plan sponsors can rely on the participant's certifications that they are eligible for the relief. COVID-19 related distributions are reported on Form 1099-R (even if the distribution is repaid in the same year).[3]

The IRS has confirmed that the plan loan or hardship distribution amount does not have to directly correspond to the financial loss the participant has suffered. As a result, plan sponsors

---

1.　Pub. Law No. 116-36, CARES Act, Sec. 2202(b).
2.　Notice 2020-50.
3.　IRS FAQ, which are expected to be updated on a rolling basis, available at: https://www.irs.gov/newsroom/coronavirus-related-relief-for-retirement-plans-and-iras-questions-and-answers

will not have to obtain documentation to substantiate the amount of the financial hardship and plan participants will not have to prove the amount of their loss.[1]

The expanded plan loan and hardship withdrawal options are completely optional for plan sponsors. However, Notice 2020-50 clarifies that plan participants are eligible for the tax benefits regardless of whether the plan sponsor chooses to amend the plan in accordance with the CARES Act relief options.

Plan administrators are also entitled to rely upon plan participants' certifications that they are qualifying individuals absent actual knowledge to the contrary (there is no duty to investigate)—but the participant must be a qualifying individual to reap the tax benefits.

If the plan permits a delayed repayment for outstanding loans as of March 27, 2020, the payments can be deferred until 2021 with the remaining amounts re-amortized beginning with the first payment date after January 1, 2021. The re-amortization period will begin January 1, 2021 and run through the date that is one year after the loan was originally due. The guidance also notes that there may be other reasonable methods to handle the loan repayment deferral.

3959. What special rules apply to residence loans from a qualified plan?

If a plan has a program to invest in residential mortgage loans, loans made in the ordinary course of the program are not subject to the rules that apply to plan loans. Loans that benefit an officer, director, or owner of the employer maintaining the plan or their beneficiaries are not treated as made under an investment program and are subject to the limitations of IRC Section 72(p) (Q 3953). An investment program exists if the plan has established that a certain percentage or amount of plan assets will be invested in residential mortgages available to persons who satisfy commercially customary financial criteria.[2]

If a loan is to acquire a dwelling unit that is to be, within a reasonable time, the principal residence of the participant, it will not be subject to the otherwise applicable 5-year term requirement (Q 3953).[3] The determination of whether the unit is to be used, within a reasonable time, as the participant's principal residence is made when the loan is made. Legislative history indicates that a dwelling unit includes a house, apartment, condominium, or mobile home not used on a transient basis. The determination of whether plan loan proceeds are used for the purchase or improvement of a principal residence is made using the tracing rules under IRC Section 163(h)(3)(B).[4]

A principal residence loan can include a plan loan used to repay a third-party loan used to pay a portion of the purchase price if the plan loan would qualify as a principal residence loan without regard to the third-party loan.[5] For example, on July 1, 2020, a participant requests a plan loan to acquire a principal residence to be paid in level monthly installments over

---

1. Notice 2020-50.
2. Treas. Reg. §1.72(p)-1, A-18.
3. See IRC Sec. 72(p)(2)(B)(ii).
4. Treas. Reg. §1.72(p)-1, A-7.
5. Treas. Reg. §1.72(p)-1, A-8(a).

15 years. On August 1, 2020, the participant acquires a principal residence, paying a portion of the purchase price with a bank loan. On September 1, 2020, the plan makes the loan and the participant uses it to repay the bank loan. The regulations state that the plan loan qualifies as a principal residence loan, considering the IRC Section 163(h)(3) tracing rules.[1]

Interest paid on residence loans may be deductible if the general requirements for deducting mortgage interest are met and the deduction is not denied based on the participant's status as a key employee or the loan is secured by amounts attributable to elective deferrals. (Q 3964)

Planning Point: Although a mortgage is not required for this purpose,[2] a participant may want to give the trustee a mortgage to qualify the interest as deductible interest. Treasury Department regulations require that for interest to be deductible as qualified residence interest the borrower must give the lender a mortgage and the lender actually must take the step of recording the mortgage. *Martin Silfen, J.D., Brown Brothers Harriman Trust Co., LLC.*

Planning Point: If a participant wants to give the plan a mortgage to qualify for the mortgage interest deduction, the participant should verify with the plan that the plan will record the mortgage and that the mortgage in favor of the plan will not violate the terms of any other mortgage secured by the residence.

Planning Point: Because the 2017 tax reform legislation increased the standard deduction and limited the state and local tax deduction to $10,000 through 2025, many people will no longer be able to deduct mortgage interest, even if the interest otherwise qualifies.

No specific time limit is placed on residential loans, but the loans must provide for substantially level amortization, with payments to be made at least quarterly.[3] This requirement does not preclude repayment or acceleration of the loan prior to the loan period, or the use of a variable interest rate.[4] All loans, regardless of when made, must provide for a reasonable repayment schedule to qualify as a loan exempt from the prohibited transaction rules (Q 3979). A loan need not be secured by the residence to be considered a principal residence plan loan.[5]

Assuming that a loan is otherwise a bona fide debt and the other requirements for deducting the plan loan interest as mortgage interest are met, a taxpayer may deduct interest paid on a mortgage loan from his or her qualified plan, even though the amount by which the loan exceeded the $50,000 limit of IRC Section 72(p) was deemed to be a taxable distribution. (Q 3964).[6]

3960. How did the 2017 tax reform legislation change the rules governing loans from 401(k) plans and other types of qualified plans?

Generally, If a qualified plan participant leaves his job (or is fired), the loan must be repaid within 60 days in order to avoid taxes and penalties (the 10 percent excise tax for early distributions will apply in addition to ordinary income taxes if the individual is under 59½). Typically,

---

1. Treas. Reg. §1.72(p)-1, A-8(b).
2. See Treas. Reg. §1.72(p)-1, A-6.
3. See IRC Sec. 72(p)(2)(C).
4. General Explanation — TRA '86, p. 728.
5. Treas. Reg. §1.72(p)-1, A-6.
6. FSA 200047022.

the participant would roll the required funds into another tax-preferred retirement account within the 60-day period to avoid taxes and penalties.

This is known as a "plan loan offset" (or the part of the taxpayer's remaining 401(k) account balance that would have to be reduced in order to repay the loan). Prior to tax reform, the participant had only 60 days to come up with the funds necessary to satisfy this requirement, which could, in many cases, present a problem for an individual who may have recently lost his or her primary source of income. The otherwise applicable five-year time frame does not apply to plan participants in this situation. These rules applied for any qualified plan, including 403(b) and 457 plans as well as 401(k)s.

Under the 2017 tax reform legislation, the 60-day deadline is extended to the participant's tax filing deadline for the tax year in which the offset occurs if the amount is treated as distributed from the participant's qualified 401(k) plan because either: (1) the plan was terminated, or (2) the participant failed to meet the loan repayment terms because of a separation from employment (if the plan provides that the accrued unpaid loan amount must be offset at this time). This generally means that individuals will have until April 15 of the following tax year (or October 15 if they take advantage of the ability to extend the deadline) to gather the funds necessary to satisfy the offset.

Planning Point: This extended time period does not apply to loans that have already been deemed taxable distributions (whether because the loan installment payment remained unpaid beyond the applicable cure period or because the loan's terms did not comply with the IRC requirements). If the default occurred while the individual remained employed with the employer and continued to have the ability to participate in the plan, the 60-day limit continues to apply.

3961. How can a plan participant who has taken a loan from his or her 401(k) plan cure a default on repayments?

The IRS has guidance explaining situations in which a cure period may apply to prevent missed installment payments on a 401(k) plan loan from causing the loan to be treated as a deemed distribution. Generally, a plan loan will be treated as a taxable deemed distribution unless it is paid in installment payments over the applicable five-year period.

A cure period that lasts up until the last day of the calendar quarter following the quarter when the missed installment payment was due may apply to prevent deemed distribution treatment. Pursuant to the guidance, the IRS allowed taxpayers to apply a later payment to an earlier missed payment in order to prevent deemed distribution treatment. The IRS uses the example of payments missed on March 31, 2020 and April 30, 2020, followed by on-time payments on May 31, 2020 and June 30, 2020 where a cure period ending June 30 applies. The May and June payments apply to "cure" the missed March and April payments, but then the normal May and June payments are treated as though they were missed because they were applied to cure the missed payments. As a result, the borrower is required to make an installment payment equal to three normal payments to bring the account up to date.[1]

---

1.   IRS CCA 201736022.

Further, a taxpayer who misses payments may also be permitted to refinance the plan loan in order to include the missed payments, but the refinancing must occur before the end of the applicable cure period.

3962. What miscellaneous rules apply to loans from a qualified plan?

Both direct and indirect loans are considered loans. A participant's or beneficiary's assignment, agreement to assign, pledge, or agreement to pledge any portion of his or her interest in the plan is considered to be a loan of that portion. If a participant's interest in a plan is pledged or assigned as security for a loan, only the amount of the loan, not the amount assigned or pledged, is treated as a loan.[1]

Any amount received as a loan under a contract purchased under a plan, and any assignment or pledge with respect to such a contract, is treated as a loan under the plan.[2] This would appear to treat a policy loan by a trustee as a loan to the participant. If a premium that is otherwise in default is paid in the form of a loan against the contract, the loan is not considered made to the participant unless the contract has been distributed to the participant.[3]

The IRS has stated, in a general information letter, that where plan participants received mortgage loans from a bank that were contingent on the plan making deposits equal to the loan amounts, the loans were indirect plan loans for purposes of IRC Section 72(p).[4]

A loan received by a beneficiary is treated as received by the participant if he or she is alive at the time the loan is treated as a distribution.[5]

3963. How do renegotiations, extensions, renewals, or revisions work in the context of qualified plan loans?

Any loan balance outstanding on August 13, 1982 (September 3, 1982, in the case of certain government plans) that is renegotiated, extended, renewed, or revised is treated as a loan made on the date it is renegotiated, extended, renewed, or revised.[6]

A consolidation of two qualified plans is not a renegotiation, extension, renewal, or revision that would subject a loan to the provisions of IRC Section 72(p).[7]

Similarly, the transfer of a participant's account balance, including an outstanding loan, in a trustee-to-trustee transfer is not treated as such a renegotiation, extension, renewal, or revision.[8]

A plan loan offset against the participant's account balance when the plan terminated was treated as a constructive distribution, subject to income tax and penalties.[9]

---

1. Treas. Reg. §1.72(p)-1, A-1.
2. Treas. Reg. §1.72(p)-1, A-1.
3. General Explanation – TEFRA, p. 295.
4. See IRS General Information Letter, 5 Pens. Pl. Guide (CCH) ¶17,383J (August 12, 1992).
5. General Explanation – TEFRA, p. 295.
6. TRA '86, Sec. 1134(e). See e.g., TAM 9344001.
7. Let. Rul. 8542081.
8. Let. Rul. 8950008.
9. *Caton v. Comm.*, TC Memo 1995-80.

Planning Point: A qualified plan may not allow modifications to an existing plan loan. A new plan loan can be used to pay off an existing plan loan if the total of all plan loans does not exceed the maximum loan permitted (generally, the lesser of $50,000 or 50 percent of the account balance. See Q 3957.) Refinancing of a plan loan used to acquire the participant's principal residence will be subject to the five year term. Because the loan is not used to acquire the residence, it does not qualify for an extended term. However, a plan loan used to repay a loan from a third party can qualify as a principal residence loan. (See Q 3959.)

3964. How does the interest deduction apply to qualified plan loans?

An employee is not allowed an interest deduction with respect to a loan (otherwise meeting the requirements explained in Q 3953) made after 1986 during the period on or after the first day on which the borrower is a key employee (Q 3930) or in which the loan is secured by elective contributions made to a 401(k) plan or tax sheltered annuity.[1] Loans from a qualified retirement plan do not qualify as a qualified education loan for which an interest deduction is available.[2]

3965. How do refinancing transactions work in the context of qualified plan loans?

A refinancing transaction is any transaction in which one loan replaces another. For example, a refinancing may exist if the outstanding loan amount is increased or if the interest rate or the repayment term of the loan is renegotiated.[3]

If the term of a replacement loan ends later than the term of the loan it replaces, then both loans are treated as outstanding on the date of the refinancing transaction. This generally means that the loans must collectively satisfy the requirements of IRC Section 72(p).[4] There is an exception where the replacement loan would satisfy IRC Section 72(p)(2) if it were treated as two separate loans. Under this exception, the amount of the replaced loan, amortized over a period ending no later than the end of the original term of the replaced loan or five years, if later, is treated as one loan. The other loan is for an amount equal to the difference between the amount of the replacement loan and the outstanding balance of the replaced loan.[5]

The IRS will not view the transaction as circumventing IRC Section 72(p) if a replacement loan effectively amortizes an amount equal to the replaced loan within the original term of the replaced loan or within five years, if later. For this reason, the outstanding balance of a replaced loan need not be taken into account in determining whether the limitations of IRC Section 72(p)(2) have been met; only the amount of the replacement loan plus any existing loans that are not being replaced is considered.[6] If the term of a replacement loan does not end later than the term of the replaced loan, then only the amount of the replacement loan plus the outstanding balance of any existing loans that are not being replaced must be taken into account in determining whether IRC Section 72(p) has been satisfied.[7]

---

1. IRC Sec. 72(p)(3).
2. Treas. Reg. §1.221-1(e)(3)(iii).
3. Treas. Reg. §1.72(p)-1, A-20(a).
4. Treas. Reg. §1.72(p)-1, A-20(a)(2).
5. Treas. Reg. §1.72(p)-1, A-20(a)(2).
6. Treas. Reg. §1.72(p)-1, A-20(a)(2).
7. Treas. Reg. §1.72(p)-1, A-20(a)(1).

Multiple Loans

Where a participant receives multiple loans from a qualified retirement plan, each loan must separately satisfy IRC Section 72(p), taking into account the outstanding balance of each existing loan. The refinancing rules do not apply because the new loan is not used to replace any existing loan.[1] Earlier proposed regulations set a limit of two loans per participant within a single year, but final regulations contain no such limit.[2]

3966. Are deemed distributions treated as outstanding loans?

Yes. For purposes of the dollar limitation on loans under IRC Section 72(p) (Q 3953), a loan treated as a deemed distribution is considered an outstanding loan until it is repaid.[3]

Regulations place two conditions on loans made while a deemed distribution loan remains unpaid.

First, the subsequent loan must satisfy the rules for qualifying plan loans.

Second, the loan must either be repayable under a payroll withholding arrangement enforceable under applicable law or the participant must provide the plan with adequate collateral for the loan in addition to the participant's accrued benefit.

The payroll withholding arrangement may be revocable, but should the participant revoke it, the outstanding loan balance is treated as a deemed distribution. If, for any reason, the additional collateral ceases to be in force before the subsequent loan is repaid, the outstanding balance of the subsequent loan is treated as a deemed distribution.

If these conditions are not satisfied, the entire subsequent loan is treated as a deemed distribution under IRC Section 72(p).[4]

3967. How is an employee taxed on preretirement distributions from a qualified plan?

Preretirement distributions, meaning those received before the annuity starting date, that are made to an employee from a qualified plan are fully included in gross income except to the extent allocated to investment in the contract, as described below.[5] Early or premature distributions generally are subject to an additional tax (Q 3968).

A participant who has an investment or cost basis (Q 3972) in a contract under a pension, profit sharing, or stock bonus plan, or under an annuity contract purchased by any such plan, is taxed under a rule that provides for pro rata recovery of cost.[6] The employee excludes the portion of the distribution that bears the same ratio to the total distribution as his or her investment

---

1. Treas. Reg. §1.72(p)-1, A-20(a)(1).
2. Treas. Reg. §1.72(p)-1, A-20(a)(2).
3. Treas. Reg. §1.72(p)-1, A-19(b)(1).
4. Treas. Reg. §1.72(p)-1, A-19.
5. IRC Secs. 72(e)(8), 72(e)(2)(B).
6. See IRC Sec. 72(e)(8).

in the contract bears to the total value of the employee's accrued benefit on the date of the distribution. The IRS has released guidance providing that amounts received under a defined benefit plan during phased retirement are not taxed as annuity payments if (1) the employee who has begun to receive phased benefits will not receive a full benefit until he or she stops working and begins receiving full benefits at an indeterminate future time (i.e., if his or her date of full retirement could change), (2) the plan's obligations to the employee are based in part on the employee's continued part-time employment and (3) the employee does not have an election as to the form of phased retirement benefit, but elects a distribution option at full retirement that applies to his or her entire benefit (including the phased benefits).[1]

The total value of an employee's account balance generally is the fair market value of the total assets under the account, excluding any net unrealized appreciation attributable to employee contributions, whether or not all of such securities are distributed.[2] The annuity starting date is the first day of the first period for which an amount is received as an annuity under the plan or contract (Q 534).[3]

Employee contributions under a defined contribution plan may be treated as a separate contract for purposes of these rules.[4] A defined benefit plan is treated as a defined contribution plan to the extent that employee contributions and earnings thereon are credited to a separate account to which actual earnings and losses are allocated.[5]

Conversely, the IRS privately ruled that there was a single contract in the case of a defined benefit plan that did not credit earnings on employee after-tax contributions and allowed single sum withdrawal of such contributions at retirement, in exchange for actuarially reduced lifetime pension payments. The withdrawn amounts were taxed as preretirement distributions under IRC Section 72(e)(8)(B) and the investment in the contract with respect to the remaining benefit was reduced by the amount of such distribution.[6]

A lump sum distribution received under the alternative form of the Civil Service Retirement System annuity did not qualify as a defined contribution plan or a hybrid plan under these rules; thus it was not subject to separate contract treatment.[7]

Grandfather Rule

If, on May 5, 1986, a plan permitted in-service withdrawal of employee contributions, the pro rata recovery rules do not apply to investment in the contract prior to 1987. Instead, investment in the contract prior to 1987 will be recovered first, and the pro rata recovery rules will apply only to the extent that amounts received before the annuity starting date, when added to all other amounts previously received under the contract after 1986, exceed the employee's

---

1.   Notice 2016-39.
2.   Notice 87-13, 1987-1 CB 432, A-11, as modified by Notice 2000-30, 2000-1 CB 1266; Rev. Rul. 2002-62, 2002-2 CB 710.
3.   IRC Sec. 72(c)(4).
4.   IRC Sec. 72(d)(2).
5.   IRC Sec. 414(k)(2); Notice 87-13, 1987-1 CB 432, A-14. See also, Let. Ruls. 9618028, 8916081.
6.   Let. Rul. 9847032.
7.   *George v. U.S.*, 96-2 USTC ¶50,389 (Fed. Cir. 1996); *Logsdon v. Comm.*, TC Memo 1997-8.

investment in the contract as of December 31, 1986.[1] If employee contributions are transferred after May 5, 1986 from a plan that permitted in-service withdrawals to another plan permitting such withdrawals, the pre-1987 investment in the contract under both plans continues to qualify for this grandfather treatment. If the transferor plan did not permit such in-service withdrawals, only the pre-1987 investment in the contract under the transferee plan qualifies.[2]

An employee who cashed out prior to 1986 and buys back after 1986 cannot use the grandfather rule because there is no pre-1987 investment in the contract. Even if the cash-out occurs after 1986 and there was investment in the contract as of December 31, 1986, the cash-out causes a permanent reduction in the grandfathered investment that may not be restored by a later buy-back.[3]

Where an employer amended its plan to provide that employees could receive distributions at their request, but not less than the minimum amounts that must be distributed by the applicable distribution date under IRC Section 401(a)(9), distributions were not annuity payments and there was no annuity starting date, so distributions were treated as amounts received before the annuity starting date and were subject to the grandfather rule of IRC Section 72(e)(8)(D).[4]

Where a state's defined benefit plan allowed eligible participants to elect optional retirement with Partial Lump Sum Distributions ("PLSDs") and PLSDs were received within the window of eligibility specified in TAMRA '88, Section 1011A(b)(11), the PLSDs were taxable, on a pro-rata basis under IRC Section 72(e), to the extent that they exceeded the recipient's investment in the plan.[5]

3968. What is an early distribution from a qualified plan, and what penalties relate to it?

Except as noted below, amounts distributed from qualified retirement plans before the participant reaches age 59½ are early or premature distributions subject to an additional tax equal to 10 percent of the amount of the distribution includable in gross income.[6]

To the extent that they are attributable to rollovers from a qualified retirement plan or a Section 403(b) plan, amounts distributed from Section 457 plans (Q 3584) generally will be treated as distributed from a qualified plan, for purposes of the early distribution penalty.[7]

The 10 percent penalty tax does not apply to distributions:

    (1)   made to a beneficiary, or the employee's estate, on or after the death of the employee;

    (2)   attributable to the employee's disability;[8]

---

1.   IRC Sec. 72(e)(8)(D); see also Let. Ruls. 9652031, 8747061.
2.   Notice 87-13, 1987-1 CB 432, A-13. See also, Let. Ruls. 8829017, 8829006.
3.   Notice 89-25, 1989-1 CB 662, A-5, modified by Notice 2002-62.
4.   Let. Ruls. 200117044, 200117045.
5.   Let. Rul. 200114040.
6.   IRC Sec. 72(t).
7.   IRC Sec. 72(t)(9).
8.   As defined in IRC Section 72(m)(7).

(3)   that are part of a series of substantially equal periodic payments made at least annually for the life or life expectancy of the employee or the joint lives or joint life expectancies of the employee and his or her designated beneficiary, and beginning after the employee separates from the service of the employer (Q 3679);

(4)   made to an employee after separation from service during or after the year in which the employee attained age 55, or age 50 for distributions to qualified public safety employees from a governmental plan as defined in IRC Section 414(d);[1]

(5)   made to an alternate payee under a qualified domestic relations order (Q 3914);

(6)   made to an employee for medical care, but not in excess of the amount allowable as a deduction to the employee under IRC Section 213 for amounts paid during the year for medical care, determined without regard to whether the employee itemizes deductions for the year;

(7)   made to reduce an excess contribution under a 401(k) plan (Q 3807);

(8)   made to reduce an excess employee or matching employer contribution, that is, an excess aggregate contribution (Q 3807);[2]

(9)   made to reduce an excess elective deferral (Q 3760);[3]

(10)   that are dividends paid with respect to stock of a corporation described in IRC Section 404(k) (ESOPs) (Q 3823);

(11)   made on account of certain levies against a qualified plan;[4] or

(12)   that are qualified reservist distributions, which are distributions of elective deferrals made to reserve members of the U.S. military called to active duty for 180 days or more at any time after September 11, 2001. Reservists have the right to rollover the amount of any distributions to an individual retirement plan for two years following the end of active duty.[5]

(13)   made on account of qualified births or adoptions under the SECURE Act (see heading below for more details).

Planning Point: Note that many clients mistakenly believe that the penalty does not apply to certain distributions used to fund the purchase of the taxpayer's home. This exception applies only with respect to IRA distributions—the 401(k) rules do not provide for a similar exception.

Planning Point: Early distribution penalties are generally waived in the event of natural disasters, and have been waived in response to COVID-19-related distributions for 2020.

---

1.   IRC Sec. 72(t)(10) as modified by Pub. L. 114-26.
2.   See IRC Sec. 401(m)(7).
3.   IRC Sec. 402(g)(2)(C).
4.   Under IRC Sec. 6331.
5.   IRC Sec. 72(t)(2)(G).

The IRS has approved three methods for determining what constitutes a series of substantially equal periodic payments in the exception discussed in (3) above. If the series of payments is later modified, other than because of death or disability, before the employee reaches age 59½, or if after the employee reaches age 59½, within five years of the date of the first payment, the employee's tax for the year in which the modification occurs is increased by an amount equal to the tax that would have been imposed in the absence of the exception, plus interest for the deferral period. For an explanation of the calculation under each method, the definition of "modified," and related rulings, see Q 3679.

The exception for distributions pursuant to a QDRO (see (5) above) was not applicable where a participant took a distribution from the plan following a trade of other marital property rights for his or her spouse's waiver of rights in his or her plan benefits.[1]

Planning Point: A participant who separates from service during or after the year he or she attains age 55 but is not yet age 59½ should generally leave plan accounts in the plan if permitted rather than transferring or rolling the accounts to an IRA or other qualified plan. This allows the participant to take distributions from the account as permitted by the plan without being subject to the 10 percent tax. A transfer to an IRA would subject the money transferred to the 10 percent tax while a transfer to another qualified plan would subject it to the new plan's restrictions on distributions and the 10 percent tax.

A court determined that a distribution originating from an arbitration award was subject to the 10 percent penalty because the amounts attributable to the award were thoroughly integrated with benefits provided under the state retirement plan.[2] The involuntary nature of a distribution does not preclude the application of the tax, provided that the participant had an opportunity, such as by a rollover, to avoid the tax.[3]

The IRS has stated that the garnishment of an individual's plan interest under the Federal Debt Collections Procedure Act to pay a judgment for restitution or fines as discussed in (11) above, will not trigger the application of the 10 percent penalty.[4]

Planning Point: An individual who is facing an IRS levy against his or her plan benefit and who is not yet age 59½ should allow the IRS to follow through on the levy rather than voluntarily taking a plan distribution and paying it to the IRS in satisfaction of the unpaid taxes. A "voluntary" distribution would be subject to the 10 percent tax, whereas any amount distributed directly to the IRS pursuant to the levy would not. *Martin Silfen, J.D., Brown Brothers Harriman Trust Co., LLC.*

The cost of life insurance protection included in an employee's income (Q 3947) is not considered a distribution for purposes of applying the 10 percent penalty.[5] The Civil Service Retirement System is a qualified plan for purposes of the early distribution penalty.[6]

---

1. *O'Brien v. Comm.*, TC Summary Opinion 2001-148.
2. *Kute v. U.S.*, 191 F.3d 371 (3d Cir. 1999).
3. *Swihart v. Comm.*, TC Memo 1998-407.
4. See Let. Rul. 200426027.
5. Notice 89-25, 1989-1 CB 662, A-11.
6. *Roundy v. Comm.*, 122 F.3d 835, 97-2 USTC ¶50,625, *aff'g* TC Memo 1995-298; *Shimota v. U.S.*, 21 Cl. Ct. 510, 90-2 USTC ¶50,489 (Cl. Ct. 1990).

A plan is not required to withhold the amount of the additional income tax on an early withdrawal.[1] Distributions that are rolled over (Q 3995 to Q 4018) generally are not includable in income, and, thus, the 10 percent penalty does not apply. In the case of a distribution subject to 20 percent mandatory withholding, the 20 percent withheld will be includable in income, however, to the extent required by IRC Section 402(a) or IRC Section 403(b)(1), even if the participant rolls over the remaining 80 percent of the distribution within the 60-day period (Q 4015). Thus, an employee who rolls over only 80 percent of a distribution may be subject to the 10 percent penalty on the 20 percent withheld.[2]

Qualified Birth and Adoption Distributions

The SECURE Act amended the IRC to allow qualified plan participants to withdraw up to $5,000 for a qualified birth or adoption without becoming subject to the 10 percent penalty on early distributions. The distribution must be taken within the one-year period following the birth or adoption.

IRS guidance clarifies that an "eligible adoptee" does not include the child of the participant's spouse (in other words, step-parent adoptions do not count).[3] Notice 2020-68 also clarifies that each parent is entitled to take a distribution with respect to the same child. Parents are also eligible to take distributions more than once—i.e., for multiple children over time. Parents of twins are entitled to double the $5,000 limit. However, plans are not required to provide the option for qualified birth or adoption distributions. If the plan permits distributions for qualified birth or adoption, it must also permit recontribution of those amounts.

A qualified birth or adoption distribution is not treated as an eligible rollover distribution for purposes of the direct rollover rules of Section 401(a)(31), the notice requirement under Section 402(f), and the mandatory withholding rules under Section 3405. Thus, the plan is not required to offer an individual a direct rollover with respect to a qualified birth or adoption distribution. In addition, the plan administrator is not required to provide a Section 402(f) notice. Finally, the plan administrator or payor of the qualified birth or adoption distribution is not required to withhold an amount equal to 20 percent of the distribution, as generally is required in Section 3405(c)(1).

However, a qualified birth or adoption distribution is subject to the voluntary withholding requirements. If the plan does not permit qualified birth or adoption distributions and an individual receives an otherwise permissible in-service distribution that meets the requirements of a qualified birth or adoption distribution, the individual may treat the distribution as a qualified birth or adoption distribution on the individual's federal income tax return. The distribution, while includible in gross income, is not subject to the 10 percent additional tax. If the individual decides to recontribute the amount to an eligible retirement plan, the individual may recontribute the amount to an IRA.

---

1. General Explanation—TRA '86, p. 716.
2. See Treas. Reg. §§1.402(c)-2 A-11, 1.403(b)-2.
3. Notice 2020-68.

In the case of a recontribution made with respect to a qualified birth or adoption distribution from an applicable eligible retirement plan other than an IRA, an individual is treated as having received the distribution as an eligible rollover distribution (as defined in Section 402(c)(4)) and as having transferred the amount to an applicable eligible retirement plan in a direct trustee-to-trustee transfer within 60 days of the distribution.[1]

3969. How is an employee taxed on postretirement distributions from a qualified plan?

The tax treatment of distributions received at or after retirement depends on the time and manner of distribution.

If a distribution is rolled over to an IRA or other eligible retirement plan, taxation of the amounts rolled over is deferred until it is distributed in the future (Q 3995).

If a lump sum distribution is made, it is subject to the treatment explained in Q 3970 and, in the case of net unrealized appreciation on employer securities, as explained in Q 3971.

If an employee receives annuity payments, the benefits are taxed as explained in Q 611 and Q 616. The employee's cost basis, if any, is determined under the rules set forth in Q 3972.

If a distribution is received prior to age 59½, it may trigger the 10 percent penalty on early or premature distributions unless one of the exceptions applies (Q 3968).

3970. What is a lump sum distribution? What special tax treatment is available for a lump sum distribution from a qualified plan?

A distribution is a lump sum distribution if it:

(1)   is made in one taxable year;

(2)   consists of the balance to the credit of an employee;

(3)   is payable on account of the employee's death, after the employee attained age 59½, disabled or on account of the employee's separation from service; and

(4)   is made from a qualified pension, profit sharing, or stock bonus plan.[2]

The classification will be relevant to certain distributions of employer securities that consist of net unrealized appreciations.

The distinction between lump sum distributions has become less important as fewer participants are able to use the pre-ERISA grandfather provisions for capital gain treatment of pre-ERISA accounts under a plan and certain income averaging rules that were repealed in 1986 (Q 621). The following discussion applies to the grandfathered tax treatment of certain participant accounts that are conditioned on a distribution constituting a lump sum distribution.

---

1.   IRC Sec. 72(t)(2)(H)(v)(III).
2.   IRC Sec. 402(e)(4)(D).

Planning Point: The IRS has released a ruling that impacts whether pension plan sponsors are permitted to provide lump-sum distribution options to plan participants who are already receiving plan benefits via regular annuity payments. The issue was whether, under the IRS required minimum distribution (RMD) rules, a lump-sum payment would constitute an impermissible increase in the payment amounts these participants were receiving. In 2015, the IRS reversed its previous position allowing these lump-sum payments to participants in pay status and stated its intent to amend the RMD rules to prohibit the lump-sum option for participants already receiving annuity payments. Now, the IRS has once again changed course and announced that, for the time being anyway, it is no longer planning to amend the RMD rules to prohibit lump-sum payments to pension plan participants already receiving annuity payments under the plan.[1]

The same requirements apply to distributions to self-employed individuals, except that full distributions made after a self-employed person has become disabled are considered lump sum distributions, and distributions made on account of "separation from service" are not.

The balance to the credit includes all amounts in the participant's account, including nondeductible employee contributions, as of the first distribution received after the triggering event.[2]

Certain eligible employees may elect 10-year averaging of certain lump sum distributions and special treatment of certain capital gains. For this purpose, an eligible employee is an employee who attained age 50 before January 1, 1986. Earlier IRC provisions that allowed for five year averaging of lump sum distributions were repealed for tax years beginning after 1999.

Ten-year averaging. An eligible employee makes a special averaging election by filing Form 4972 with his or her tax return; the election may be revoked by filing an amended return.[3] An eligible employee can make this election only once and it must apply to all lump sum distributions the employee receives for that year.

Under 10-year averaging, the tax on the ordinary income portion of the distribution is 10 times the tax on 1 / 10 of the total taxable amount, reduced by the minimum distribution allowance. 1986 tax rates must be used, considering the prior law's zero bracket amount.[4] Generally speaking, the larger the distribution, the less likely that 10-year averaging will be advantageous.

Long-term capital gain treatment. An eligible employee also may elect capital gain treatment for the portion of a lump sum distribution allocable to his or her pre-1974 plan participation.[5] This portion is determined by multiplying the total taxable amount by a fraction, the numerator of which is the number of pre-January 1, 1974 calendar years of active plan participation and the denominator of which is the total number of calendar years of active plan participation.

For these purposes, the minimum distribution allowance is the lesser of $10,000 or one-half of the total taxable amount. This must be reduced by 20 percent of the total taxable amount in excess of $20,000. Thus, if the total taxable amount is $70,000 or more, there is no minimum

1. Notice 2019-18.
2. Let. Ruls. 9031028, 9013009.
3. Treas. Reg. §11.402(e)(4)(B)-1 (prior to removal in 2019).
4. TRA '86, Sec. 1122(h)(5); TAMRA '88, Sec. 1011A(b)(15)(B).
5. TRA '86, Sec. 1122(h)(3).

distribution allowance. The total taxable amount is the amount of the distribution that exceeds the employee's cost basis (Q 3972). The employee's cost basis is reduced by any previous distributions excludable from his or her gross income.

Planning Point: It is particularly important to pay attention to the exact terms of a lump sum offer when considering whether to accept. Many plans offer a lump sum "window", during which the participant must make a decision and may have an opportunity to revoke that decision. However, once the window is closed, courts generally will not allow the participant to change the final decision made during the window.

3971. How is net unrealized appreciation taxed when employer securities are distributed from a qualified plan?

Net unrealized appreciation ("NUA") is the excess of the fair market value of employer securities at the time of a lump sum distribution over the cost or other basis of the securities to a qualified plan trust.[1] Employer securities for this purpose include shares of a parent or subsidiary corporation.[2]

If employer securities are distributed as part of a lump sum distribution (Q 3970) from a qualified plan, the net unrealized appreciation is excluded from the employee's income at the time of distribution to the extent that the securities are attributable to employer and nondeductible employee contributions. Taxation of NUA following a lump sum distribution is deferred until the securities are sold or disposed of, unless the employee elects out of NUA treatment.[3] The election is made on the tax return for the year in which the distribution must be included in gross income and does not preclude an election for special income averaging.[4]

On a sale or other disposition of employer securities, the NUA amount is treated as long-term capital gain, regardless of the distributee's actual holding period. The taxpayer's basis in the stock is the same as the basis in the hands of the qualified plan trust; that is, it does not include the NUA amount.[5] Gain accruing after distribution of the securities and before the later disposition of them is treated as long-term or short term capital gain, depending on the holding period after distribution.[6] The distributee's holding period begins the day after the day the plan trustee delivers the stock to the transfer agent with instructions to reissue the stock in the distributee's name.[7]

Planning Point: The portion of the fair market value of the employer securities in excess of their net unrealized appreciation and the amount of the participant's after-tax contributions to the plan, if any, is included in income and potentially subject to the 10 percent tax, so that tax should be taken into account in determining whether and how much of the distribution should be rolled over to an IRA if the participant has not yet attained age 59½ and has separated from service before age 55. *Martin Silfen, J.D., Brown Brothers Harriman Trust Co., LLC.*

---

1.   See Treas. Reg. §1.402(a)-1(b)(2)(i).
2.   IRC Sec. 402(e)(4)(E).
3.   See IRC Sec. 402(e)(4)(B).
4.   IRC Sec. 402(e)(4).
5.   Treas. Reg. §1.402(a)-1(b)(1)(i).
6.   See Treas. Reg. §1.402(a)-1(b); Notice 98-24, 1998-1 CB 929; see also Rev. Rul. 81-122, 1981-1 CB 202.
7.   Rev. Rul. 82-75, 1982-1 CB 116.

An employer's shares, if acquired and credited to an employee's account, still are considered employer stock, even if later transferred to the trust of an acquiring or subsidiary corporation.[1] The basis does not change.[2] The balance of the value of the stock is taxable to the recipient under the regular rules for taxing lump sum distributions (Q 3970).[3]

Unrealized appreciation that is excluded from income is not includable in the recipient's basis in the stock for the purpose of computing gain or loss upon a later sale or other taxable disposition.[4] If part or all of the unrealized appreciation is excluded as something other than unrealized appreciation, only the part excluded as unrealized appreciation is not added to basis.[5]

Unrealized appreciation realized on sale of the stock by the recipient of a distribution on account of the death of the employee or by a person inheriting the stock from the employee is income in respect of a decedent. It is taxed as long-term capital gain and a deduction may be taken for the estate tax attributable to the inclusion of any part of the appreciation prior to distribution in the deceased employee's estate.[6]

Planning Point: In the case of divorce, be sure that the non-participant spouse has the QDRO drafted to specifically provide for an alternate payee to receive a pro-rata share of employer securities with the same cost basis; otherwise the ability to utilize NUA tax treatment may be lost. Many plans do not preserve this benefit for alternate payees in their sample QDRO language, so customized language may be required. *Helen Modly, CFP, ChFC, Focus Wealth Management, Ltd.*

Planning Point: NUA treatment may not be the best option for a distribution of employer securities. Each situation should be analyzed based on factors including the amount of unrealized appreciation, the outlook for the employer's securities, and whether the participant can pay the tax on the basis without selling some of the employer securities.

NUA in employer securities distributed in other than a lump sum distribution is excludable only to the extent that the appreciation is attributable to nondeductible employee contributions.[7] Thus, a rollover of employer securities to an IRA will preclude the taxpayer from receiving NUA treatment.

A transfer to an IRA of less than all of a participant's account under an ESOP, with a distribution of the balance to the participant, does not bar treatment as a lump sum distribution, however. The IRS determined that a participant could exclude the net unrealized appreciation on the stock distributed outright to the participant until the participant disposes of it.[8]

Similarly, a participant who had received a series of substantially equal periodic payments (Q 3679, Q 3959) from his plan account prior to retirement was not precluded from treating

---

1. Rev. Rul. 73-29, 1973-1 CB 198; Let. Rul. 201242019.
2. Rev. Rul. 80-138, 1980-1 CB 87.
3. See Rev. Rul. 57-514, 1957-2 CB 261.
4. Treas. Reg. §1.402(a)-1(b).
5. Rev. Rul. 74-398, 1974-2 CB 136.
6. Rev. Rul. 69-297, 1969-1 CB 131; Rev. Rul. 75-125, 1975-1 CB 254.
7. IRC Sec. 402(e)(4)(A).
8. Let. Ruls. 9721036, 200038057.

a distribution of the remaining amounts, including stock, in his plan account as a lump sum distribution (Q 3967), nor from excluding net unrealized appreciation on the stock.[1]

3972. How is an employee's cost basis determined for an interest in a qualified plan?

An employee normally will have no cost basis if a plan is noncontributory and does not provide life insurance protection.

If life insurance protection has been provided under a cash value policy, the employee usually will have some cost basis, namely, the aggregate one year term costs that have been taxed to the employee, even though the plan is noncontributory.[2]

A self-employed person who is an owner-employee cannot include in his or her cost basis the annual one year costs of life insurance protection under Table 2001 or previously under P.S. 58 (Q 3947), even though these costs were not deductible.[3] No self-employed person, whether or not an owner-employee, can include in cost basis the cost of any health insurance features under the plan.

A common law employee's cost basis consists of:

(1) total nondeductible contributions made by the employee if the plan is contributory and amounts contributed by an S corporation for years beginning before January 1, 1984, on behalf of a more-than-5-percent shareholder-employee in excess of the excludable amount;

(2) the sum of the annual one year term costs of life insurance protection under Table 2001 or previously P.S. 58 (Q 3947) that have been includable as taxable income if payment is being received under the contract that provided the life insurance protection(Q 3951);

(3) any other employer contributions other than excess deferrals (Q 3760) that already have been taxed to the employee, such as where a nonqualified plan was later qualified;

(4) certain employer contributions attributable to foreign services performed before 1963; and

(5) the amount of any loans included in income as taxable distributions (Q 3952).

In addition, although amounts attributable to deductible employee contributions are not part of basis, it would seem they should be included in basis if benefits are received under the contract to the extent that they have been taxable to the employee because they were used to purchase a life insurance contract (Q 3951). This cost basis must be reduced by any amounts

---

1.   See Let. Rul. 200315041.
2.   IRC Sec. 61(a)(1); Treas. Reg. §1.61-2(a)(1).
3.   IRC Sec. 72(m)(2); Treas. Reg. §1.72-16(b)(4).

previously distributed to the employee that were excludable from gross income as a return of all or part of the employee's basis.[1]

A self-employed person's cost basis consists of (1) the nondeductible 50 percent of contributions made before 1968, after subtracting the cost of incidental benefits, if any, such as waiver of premium and health insurance benefits, and, in the case of an owner-employee, the costs of life insurance protection under Table 2001 or previously P.S. 58 (Q 3947), (2) contributions on behalf of owner-employees under the three year average rule for determining contributions to level premium insurance and annuity contracts in excess of the deductible limit, in effect for years beginning before 1984, and (3) nondeductible voluntary contributions, if any, to a contributory plan.

In addition, any amounts taxed to an individual because they were attributable to deductible voluntary employee contributions used to purchase life insurance, if benefits are received under the contract, probably should be included.

3973. When an employee dies before retirement, how is the employee's beneficiary taxed on a single sum cash payment of the death benefit payable under the employee's qualified plan?

If a death benefit is payable from the proceeds of a life insurance policy, the difference between the cash surrender value and the face amount is treated as death proceeds of life insurance, and is excluded from income under IRC Section 101(a), but only if the insurance cost under Table 2001, the insurer's qualifying term rate, (or previously under P.S. 58 (Q 3947)) has been paid with nondeductible employee contributions or has been taxable to the employee.[2] The balance of the proceeds, representing the cash surrender value, is treated as a distribution from the plan.[3]

The following amounts may be subtracted from the cash surrender value and also excluded from gross income:

(1)   the sum of the annual term costs of life insurance protection previously taxed to the employee (Q 3951), but if the deceased was a self-employed owner-employee, the deceased's beneficiary cannot subtract these costs even though they were not deductible by the owner-employee;

(2)   if the plan is contributory, the employee's nondeductible contributions toward the cost of the insurance;

(3)   the amount of any loans included in the employee's income as taxable distributions (Q 3952); and

(4)   any employer contributions other than excess deferrals (Q 3760) that have been taxed to an employee, including contributions in pre-1984 years on behalf of a

1.   IRC Sec. 72(f); Treas. Reg. §§1.72-8, 1.72-16(b)(4), 1.402(a)-1(a)(6), 1.403(a)-2. See also Rev. Rul. 72-149, 1972-1 CB 218.
2.   Treas. Reg. §1.72-16(c)(4).
3.   IRC Sec. 72(m)(3)(C); Treas. Reg. §1.72-16(c).

more-than-5-percent shareholder-employee in an S corporation in excess of excludable amounts.

The balance, if any, of the cash surrender value is taxable according to the rules applicable to lump sum distributions (Q 3970).

If an employer has purchased an existing policy from an employee for contribution to the trust, or if an employee has contributed it directly to the trust, the transfer for value rule (Q 279) does not apply so long as neither the employer nor the trustee has the right to change the beneficiary. The IRS determined that there was no significant change in the beneficial ownership of the policy.[1]

Similarly, if a trustee of one plan purchases a life insurance policy from the trustee of another plan, there is no transfer for value where the beneficiary is entitled to designate the beneficiary both before and after the transfer because there has been no change in beneficial ownership.[2]

If a contract is a retirement income contract, and the cash surrender value before death equals or exceeds the face amount, no portion of the proceeds is excludable as death proceeds of life insurance.[3] The annual term costs of life insurance protection previously taxed to the employee would be excludable, except by the beneficiary of an owner-employee.

If the contract was distributed to the employee before his or her death, the IRS has previously considered the proceeds entirely tax-exempt as life insurance proceeds, although the Tax Court has considered them taxable as proceeds payable under an annuity contract, because death occurs after the element of risk has disappeared.[4]

If a contract distributed before death is subject to the definition of life insurance in IRC Section 7702 or IRC Section 101(f), the treatment of the death benefit would be as discussed in Q 65.

If a death benefit is not from life insurance proceeds, the beneficiary may subtract and receive tax-free any nondeductible employee contributions, the amount of any loans included in income, and any employer contributions other than excess deferrals (Q 3760) that have been taxed to the employee. The balance, if any, of the death benefit, other than amounts attributable to deductible employee contributions, is taxable according to the rules applicable to lump sum distributions (Q 3970).

A distribution to an employee's beneficiary on account of plan termination, rather than on account of death, may not be treated as a lump sum distribution or as payment of an employee death benefit.[5]

---

1. Rev. Rul. 73-338, 1973-2 CB 20; Rev. Rul. 74-76, 1974-1 CB 30.
2. Let. Rul. 7844032.
3. *Jeffrey v. U.S.*, 11 AFTR 2d 1401 (D. N.J. 1963).
4. See *Evans v. Comm.*, 56 TC 1142 (1971).
5. *Est. of Stefanowski v. Comm.*, 63 TC 386 (1974).

A beneficiary may be entitled to an income tax deduction for any estate tax attributable to the distribution (Q 3992).[1]

3974. How is a beneficiary taxed on life income or installment payments of a death benefit under a qualified plan when an employee dies before retirement?

If a beneficiary has no cost basis for the payments, each payment will be fully taxable as ordinary income when received. The beneficiary's cost basis generally is the same as the employee's cost basis (Q 3972). In the case of decedents dying before August 21, 1996, the $5,000 death benefit exclusion was included in the beneficiary's cost basis.[2]

If the beneficiary does have a cost basis, payments are subject to the rules that follow, depending on whether the death benefits come from life insurance proceeds.

If death benefit payments do not come from life insurance proceeds, the beneficiary is taxed as the employee would have been taxed had the employee lived and received the periodic payments (Q 3967, Q 3968). The beneficiary's cost basis, rather than the employee's cost basis, is used. Depending on the annuity starting date, an exclusion ratio may have to be determined; if so, the beneficiary's cost basis is used as the investment in the contract (for an explanation of the basic annuity rule and its application to various types of payments see Q 525 to Q 550). For annuities with a starting date on or before November 19, 1996, if a beneficiary elected the simplified safe harbor method for taxing annuity payments (Q 611) and increased the investment in the contract by any employee death benefit exclusion allowable, the beneficiary had to attach a signed statement to his or her income tax return stating that the beneficiary was entitled to such exclusion in applying the safe harbor method.[3] After such date, if the annuitant is under age 75, the simplified method is required, rather than optional.[4] When more than one beneficiary is to receive payments under a plan, the cost basis, including the $5,000 exclusion, if available, is apportioned among them according to each beneficiary's share of the total death benefit payments.

If death benefit payments do come from life insurance proceeds, the proceeds are divided into two parts: the amount at risk, which are proceeds in excess of the cash surrender value immediately before death, and the cash surrender value.[5]

The portion of the payments attributable to the amount at risk is taxable under IRC Section 101(d) as life insurance proceeds settled under a life income or installment option, as the case may be (Q 71). The amount at risk generally is prorated over the payment period, whether for a fixed number of years or for life, and the prorated amounts are excludable from the beneficiary's gross income as a return of principal.

1.   IRC Sec. 691(c).
2.   Rev. Rul. 58-153, 1958-1 CB 43.
3.   Notice 88-118, 1988-2 CB 450, obsoleted by Notice 98-2, 1998-2 I.R.B. 22 below.
4.   Notice 98-2, 1998-1 C.B. 266.
5.   Treas. Reg. §1.72-16(c).

Where payments are for life, the beneficiary's life expectancy generally is taken from IRS unisex annuity tables V and VI (Appendix A).[1]

The portion of the payments attributable to the cash surrender value is taxed in the same manner as any other periodic payments from a qualified plan.

> *Example:* The widow of an employee who died on June 1, 2021 elects to receive $25,000 of life insurance proceeds in 10 annual installments of $3,000 each. The cash surrender value of the policy immediately before the insured's death was $11,000. The employee made no contributions to the plan and the aggregate one-year term costs of life insurance protection that were taxed to the employee amounted to $940. The widow must include $1,506 of each $3,000 installment, computed in the following manner.

Face amount of insurance contract	$25,000
Cash value immediately before death	11,000
Excludable as life insurance proceeds	$14,000
Portion of each installment attributable to life insurance proceeds (14/25 of $3,000)	$ 1,680
Excludable as return of principal ($14,000 ÷ 10)	1,400
Includable in gross income	$ 280

(If the beneficiary is the surviving spouse of an employee who died before October 23, 1986, the $280 would be excludable under the $1,000 annual interest exclusion)

Portion of each installment attributable to cash surrender value of the contract (11/25 of $3,000)	$ 1,320
Beneficiary's cost basis ($940)	$ 940
Expected return (10 × $1,320)	$13,200
Exclusion ratio ($940/$13,200)	7.12%
Amount excludable each year (7.12% of $1,320)	$ 93.98
Includable in gross income ($1,320 - $93.98)	$ 1,226.02

The beneficiary may be entitled to an income tax deduction for any estate tax attributable to the decedent's interest in the plan (Q 3992).[2] It would seem that the deduction would be prorated over the beneficiary's life expectancy, in the case of life income payments, or over a fixed period, in the case of installment payments (Q 542).

3975. How is an employee's beneficiary taxed on death benefit payments from a qualified plan when the employee dies after retirement?

If an employee had no cost basis for his or her interest, or has recovered his or her cost basis from benefits received during the employee's life, all amounts received by the beneficiary will

---

1.   Treas. Reg. §1.101-7.
2.   IRC Sec. 691(c).

be fully taxable. The beneficiary may be entitled to an income tax deduction for any estate tax attributable to the employee's interest in the plan.[1]

Joint and Survivor Annuity

The method of taxing survivor annuity payments to a beneficiary depends on how the employee was taxed (Q 611).

If the employee was taxed on everything, the survivor annuitant will be taxed on everything as well.[2]

If the employee was taxed under the three year cost recovery rule in existence with respect to annuities with starting dates prior to July 1, 1986, and had not recovered his or her full cost basis, the survivor will receive the guaranteed payments tax-free until the total of the employee's and survivor's tax-free receipts equals the employee's cost basis; thereafter everything will be includable in gross income.[3]

If the employee was taxed under regular annuity rules or under the safe harbor method, the survivor will continue with the same exclusion ratio,[4] but if the employee's annuity starting date was after December 31, 1986, no amount is excludable by the employee or beneficiary after the investment in the contract has been recovered.[5]

Refund Beneficiary

If the employee had a cost basis for the employee's interest and had not recovered the full amount tax-free, a refund beneficiary under a life annuity with a refund or period-certain guarantee can exclude the balance of the cost basis from gross income (Q 611). Otherwise, everything received by the beneficiary is taxable.[6]

If the beneficiary receives the refund in a lump sum distribution, the lump sum distribution rules apply (Q 3970). If the beneficiary surrenders an annuity contract that has been previously distributed to the employee, the payment does not qualify for lump sum treatment because it is not viewed as a distribution from the trust but as a payment in settlement of the insurer's liability to make future payments.[7]

If the beneficiary receives the refund in installments, the payments are taxable as ordinary income.

1.   IRC Sec. 691(c).
2.   Treas. Reg. §1.72-4(d).
3.   Treas. Reg. §1.72-13.
4.   Treas. Reg. §§1.72-4, 1.72-5.
5.   IRC Sec. 72(b)(2).
6.   Treas. Reg. §1.72-11; Treas. Reg. §1.72-13.
7.   Rev. Rul. 68-287, 1968-1 CB 174.

If the refund beneficiary of a decedent whose annuity starting date was after July 1, 1986, does not fully recover the cost basis unrecovered at the decedent's death, the refund beneficiary may take a deduction for the remaining unrecovered amount.[1]

Installment Payments

Where payments for a fixed period or of a fixed amount, not involving a life contingency, had commenced to the employee, tax consequences to the beneficiary can differ, depending on whether the installments are continued or are commuted and paid to the beneficiary in a lump sum.

In addition, the balance, if any, of the lump sum payment is taxable under the lump sum distribution rules.

If installments are continued, the method of taxing payments then will depend on how the employee was taxed (Q 611). If the employee was taxed on everything, the beneficiary also will be.[2] If the employee was taxed under the three year cost recovery rule in existence for annuities with starting dates prior to July 1, 1986, and had not recovered his or her full cost basis tax-free, the beneficiary can exclude the balance from the first payments received. Thereafter, everything is taxable.[3]

If the employee was taxed under regular annuity rules or under the safe harbor method, the beneficiary will continue to exclude the same portion of each payment from gross income.[4]

If the annuity starting date was after December 31, 1986, the beneficiary can exclude amounts only until the investment in the contract has been fully recovered; thereafter, all amounts are included in income.[5]

3976. What general rules apply to withholding of income tax from qualified retirement plan benefits?

The withholding rules that apply to a distribution depend on whether it constitutes an eligible rollover distribution (Q 3997). An eligible rollover distribution from a qualified retirement plan is subject to mandatory income tax withholding at the rate of 20 percent unless the distribution is directly rolled over to an eligible retirement plan (Q 3999). An employee receiving an eligible rollover distribution may not otherwise elect out of this withholding requirement.[6]

On the other hand, a recipient may elect out of withholding with respect to distributions that do not qualify as eligible rollover distributions.[7] The amount to be withheld on periodic payments that are not eligible rollover distributions is determined at the rate applicable to wages.[8]

---

1. IRC Sec. 72(b)(3).
2. Treas. Reg. §1.72-4(d).
3. Treas. Reg. §1.72-13.
4. Treas. Reg. §1.72-4(a).
5. IRC Sec. 72(b)(2).
6. IRC Sec. 3405(c).
7. IRC Secs. 3405(a)(2), 3405(b)(2).
8. IRC Sec. 3405(a)(1).

Non-periodic payments that are not eligible rollover distributions are subject to income tax withholding at the rate of 10 percent.[1]

Withholding applies to amounts paid to a beneficiary of a participant as well as to the participant. Withholding does not apply to amounts that it is reasonable to believe are not includable in income.

Planning Point: The IRS has released guidance providing that when a check for a fully taxable distribution from a qualified plan is mailed to a plan participant, but not cashed, it is considered to have been "actually distributed" from the plan and is taxable to the participant in the year of distribution. The fact that the participant failed to cash the check is irrelevant. Further, the failure to cash the check does not change the plan administrator's withholding obligations with respect to the distribution and does not change the obligation to report the distribution on Form 1099-R (assuming the distribution exceeds the applicable reporting threshold). Despite these findings, the IRS was careful to note that it continues to consider the issue of uncashed distribution checks in situations involving missing participants.[2]

The maximum amount withheld cannot exceed the sum of the money plus the fair market value of property received other than employer securities.[3] Thus, a payor will not need to dispose of employer securities to meet the withholding tax liability. Loans treated as distributions (i.e., deemed distributions) continue to be subject to withholding as non-periodic distributions at a rate of 10 percent. The IRS has stated that loans deemed to be distributions are not subject to the 20 percent mandatory withholding requirement because a deemed distribution cannot be an eligible rollover distribution. Where a participant's accrued benefit is reduced or offset to repay a plan loan, such as when employment is terminated, the offset amount may constitute an eligible rollover distribution.[4] Withholding is not required on the costs of current life insurance protection taxable to plan participants under Table 2001 or previously P.S. 58 (Q 3947).

3977. When are the earnings of a qualified pension or profit sharing trust taxable to the trust or to participants? When does trust income constitute unrelated business income?

Normally, neither a participant nor a trust pays any tax on earnings on a trust because as long as the plan meets the requirements of IRC Section 401(a), the trust is tax-exempt under IRC Section 501(a). The tax exemption also applies to trusts of plans covering self-employed individuals.

Trust income may be subject to income tax when it constitutes unrelated business income.[5] For example, a plan has unrelated business income from a trade or business regularly carried on by the trust.[6] This could occur when an exempt trust is a limited partner that receives unrelated business income to the same extent as if it were a general partner.[7] A specific deduction of up

---

1.   IRC Sec. 3405(b)(1).
2.   Rev. Rul. 2019-19.
3.   IRC Sec. 3405(e)(8).
4.   See Notice 93-3, 1993-1 CB 293.
5.   IRC Sec. 511.
6.   IRC Sec. 512.
7.   *Service Bolt & Nut Co. Profit Sharing Trust v. Comm.*, 724 F.2d 519 (6th Cir. 1983).

to $1,000 is allowed against unrelated business income.[1] Thus, a trust generally will pay income taxes when its unrelated taxable income exceeds $1,000.

Income from any type of property will be taxable as unrelated business income if the property has been acquired with borrowed funds, that is, debt-financed property. Thus, income from plan assets subject to debt, such as life insurance with policyholder loans, may give rise to unrelated business taxable income.[2]

Where a pension fund, in an attempt to increase the rate of return on three certificates of deposit, borrowed funds from a savings and loan with the three old certificates as collateral and was issued a new certificate in an amount equal to the borrowed amount, the net interest earned on the new certificate was income from debt-financed property.[3]

An exempt trust or 501(c)(3) organization may be a shareholder in an S corporation (Q 3817). Ordinarily, such an interest would be treated as an interest in an unrelated trade or business; thus, items of S corporation income allocable to a plan could result in unrelated business income.

An employee stock ownership plan (Q 3816, Q 3824) maintained by an S corporation is not treated as receiving unrelated business income on items of income or loss of the S corporation in which it holds an interest.[4]

Employer securities purchased by an ESOP with borrowed funds do not give rise to unrelated business taxable income because the indebtedness that an ESOP incurs to purchase employer securities is inherent in the purpose of the trust's tax exemption.[5] Securities purchased on margin by a profit sharing trust and by a pension trust have been held to be debt-financed property.[6]

Where a trust is taxed because of its unrelated business income, the tax rate is the rate applicable to trusts.[7]

A trust's earnings are not entirely tax-free, but are merely deferred until they are distributed or made available to participants or their beneficiaries.[8]

3978. What is the tax treatment of trust assets that revert to a plan sponsor?

The fair market value of any property reverting to an employer from a qualified plan is includable in the employer's gross income and generally is subject to a nondeductible excise tax.[9] The basic rule is that the excise tax is equal to 50 percent and is imposed on the amount of

---

1.   IRC Sec. 512(b)(12).
2.   See *Siskin Memorial Found., Inc. v. U.S.*, 790 F.2d 480 (6th Cir. 1986), *aff'g* 603 F. Supp. 91 (E.D. Tenn. 1984); *Henry E. & Nancy Horton Bartels Trust v. United States*, 617 F.3d 1357 (Fed. Cir. 2010). See also Let. Rul. 7918095.
3.   *Kern County Elec. Pension Fund v. Comm.*, 96 TC 845 (1991).
4.   IRC Sec. 512(e)(3).
5.   Rev. Rul. 79-122, 1979-1 CB 204.
6.   *Elliot Knitwear Profit Sharing Plan v. Comm.*, 614 F.2d 347 (3d Cir. 1980).
7.   See IRC Sec. 511(b); *Marprowear Profit Sharing Trust v. Comm.*, 74 TC 1086 (1980), *affirmed without opinion* (3d Cir. 1981).
8.   IRC Secs. 402(a), 403(a).
9.   IRC Sec. 4980.

reversion that is subject to income taxes. The 50 percent tax rate can be reduced to 20 percent if the employer establishes or maintains a qualified replacement plan, provides for pro rata benefit increases for generally all participants and certain beneficiaries, or is in Chapter 7 bankruptcy liquidation as of the termination date of the qualified plan. Where the entire reversion is paid to a qualified replacement plan, there is no reversion to the employer, the employer pays no income taxes on the amount of the reversion, and as a result there is no excise tax.

A qualified replacement plan is any qualified plan established or maintained by the employer in connection with a qualified plan termination in which:

(1)   at least 95 percent of the active participants in the terminated plan who remain employed by the employer are active participants;

(2)   a direct transfer of assets is made from the terminated plan to the replacement plan equal to 25 percent of the maximum reversion that could have been received under prior law, reduced, dollar-for-dollar, by the present value of certain increases in participants' accrued benefits, if any, made pursuant to a plan amendment adopted during the 60 day period ending on the date of termination and taking effect on that date, before any reversion occurs; and

(3)   the portion of the reversion transferred to a defined contribution replacement plan is allocated to participants' plan accounts in the plan year in which the transfer occurs or is credited to a suspense account and allocated to participants' accounts no less rapidly than ratably over the seven year period beginning with the year of the transfer.

If any amount credited to a suspense account cannot be allocated to a participant's account within the seven year period, such amount generally must be allocated to the accounts of other participants.[1]

The IRS has determined that where the above requirements were met, amounts transferred to a replacement plan could be used to make employer matching contributions.[2] If the entire surplus is transferred to a 401(k) plan that meets the requirements of a qualified replacement plan, the employer's excise tax on the reversion will be eliminated.[3] A profit sharing plan with a 401(k) feature also has been approved as a qualified replacement plan.[4] None of the reversion, however, may be treated as employee salary deferrals.

Any amount transferred to a qualified replacement plan is not includable in the employer's gross income and is not treated as a reversion. No deduction is allowed with respect to the transferred amount.[5]

---

1.   IRC Sec. 4980(d)(2).
2.   Let. Ruls. 200045031, 9834036, 9302027.
3.   Let. Rul. 9837036.
4.   Let. Ruls. 9834036, 9252035.
5.   IRC Sec. 4980(d)(2)(B)(iii).

An employer is considered to provide for pro rata benefit increases for generally all plan participants and certain beneficiaries under the terminated plan if (1) a plan amendment is adopted in connection with the termination of the plan, (2) the pro rata benefit increases have an aggregate present value of not less than 20 percent of the maximum amount that the employer would otherwise have received as a reversion, and (3) the pro rata benefit increases take effect immediately on termination of the plan.[1]

Where a plan is amended to increase benefits in an effort to reduce the reversion, the benefits may not be increased, and amounts may not be allocated in contravention of the qualification requirements of IRC Section 401(a) or the IRC Section 415 limits (Q 3719, Q 3728, and Q 3867). Any such increases or allocations must be treated as annual benefits or annual additions under IRC Section 415.[2] The employer is determined on a controlled group basis and the Secretary of the Treasury may provide that two or more plans may be treated as one plan or that a plan of a successor may be considered.[3]

The tax applies to both direct and indirect reversions. An indirect reversion occurs where plan assets are used to satisfy an obligation of the employer.[4]

An employer maintaining a plan must pay the tax, which is due on the last day of the month following the month in which the reversion occurs.[5] Where money or property reverts to a sole proprietorship or partnership, the employer is the sole proprietor or the partners.

A distribution to any employer by reason of a contribution made in error may be permitted if one of three criteria is met: a mistake of fact has occurred, the funds are being returned because of a failure of the plan to qualify initially, or the error arose from a failure of employer contributions to be deductible and the repayment is permitted by the terms of the plan document.

A reversion from a multiemployer plan also will not be subject to the tax if made because of a mistake of law or the return of any withdrawal liability payment.[6] ERISA exempts from the prohibited transaction rules the return of contributions or withdrawal liability payments if certain requirements are met.[7]

A transfer of excess assets from a defined benefit plan to a defined contribution plan constitutes a reversion of assets to an employer if the assets were first transferred to the employer followed by a contribution to the defined contribution plan. Thus, excess assets are included in the employer's income and subject to the penalty tax.[8]

Although a qualified transfer of excess pension assets (Q 3835) from a defined benefit plan to an IRC Section 401(h) account of the plan is not treated as a reversion to the employer, any

1.   IRC Sec. 4980(d)(3).
2.   IRC Sec. 4980(d)(4).
3.   IRC Secs. 4980(d)(5)(D), 4980(d)(5)(E).
4.   See, e.g., Let. Rul. 9136017.
5.   IRC Sec. 4980(c)(4).
6.   IRC Sec. 4980(c)(2)(B). See also Treas. Reg. 1.401(a)(2)-1; IRM 4.72.11.
7.   ERISA Sec. 403(c).
8.   Notice 88-58, 1988-1 CB 546; GCM 39744 (7-14-88).

amount transferred and not used to pay for qualified current retiree health benefits must be returned to the transferor plan and generally is treated as a reversion subject to the 20 percent excise tax.[1]

Prohibited Transactions

3979. What are prohibited transactions?

Any transaction, whether direct or indirect, between a plan and a disqualified person (see Q 3980) constitutes a prohibited transaction under the IRC. These transactions include:

(1)   a sale, exchange, or lease of any property, including a transfer of property subject to a security interest assumed by the plan or placed on it within 10 years prior to the transfer;[2]

(2)   lending of money or other extension of credit;

(3)   furnishing of goods, services, or facilities; and

(4)   the transfer of plan assets or income to, or use of them by or for the benefit of, a disqualified person.

Note, however, that there are statutory and regulatory exemptions from what would ordinarily be a prohibited transaction.

Planning Point: Before a plan enters any transaction, counsel should scrutinize the transaction to determine whether it is prohibited. If the transaction is prohibited, counsel should first determine whether a statutory exemption is available under ERISA Section 408. If so, counsel should make sure that each requirement is met, that the trustees approve the transaction and document the decision-making process in the plan's minutes, and that the transaction is adequately documented in writing. If no statutory exemption is available, then counsel should check class action exemptions to determine if one applies. Finally, if no other exemptions are available, counsel can apply for an individual exemption.[3]

It is a prohibited transaction for a disqualified person who is a fiduciary to deal with income or assets of a plan in his or her own interest or to receive consideration for his or her own personal account from a party dealing with the plan in connection with a transaction involving plan income or assets.[4]

Title I of ERISA prohibits a fiduciary from acting, in any transaction involving the plan, on behalf of anyone having interests adverse to those of the plan or plan participants or beneficiaries.[5]

---

1.   IRC Sec. 420(c)(1)(B).
2.   See IRC Sec. 4975(f)(3).
3.   Final Department of Regulations on Prohibited Transaction Exemption Procedures are available at 29 CFR §§2570.30 – 2570.52.
4.   IRC Sec. 4975(c)(1).
5.   ERISA Sec. 406(b)(2).

The Department of Labor has issued final regulations on ERISA Section 408(b)(2) required fee disclosures by service providers to plan fiduciaries and participants (Q 4123).[1]

The definition of a plan for this purpose includes not only any qualified pension, profit sharing, stock bonus, or annuity plan, but also an individual retirement plan (Q 3641), health savings account ("HSA") (Q 388), Archer medical savings account ("MSA") (Q 420), or Coverdell education savings account. The term "plan" includes such plans even after they are no longer qualified. Government and church plans are excluded.[2]

3980. What is a "disqualified person" for purposes of the prohibited transaction rules?

A disqualified person is:

(1)   a fiduciary (see Q 3981);

(2)   a person providing services to the plan;

(3)   an employer or employee organization, any of whose employees or members are covered by the plan;

(4)   a 50 percent owner, directly or indirectly, of an employer or employee organization described in (3);

(5)   a family member of any person described in (1) through (4);

(6)   a corporation, partnership, trust, or estate that is 50 percent or more owned by any person described in (1), (2), (3), or (5);

(7)   an officer, director, 10 percent or more shareholder, or highly compensated employee of a person described in (3), (4), or (6); or

(8)   a 10 percent or more (in capital or profits) partner or joint venturer of a person described in (3), (4), or (6).[3]

Family Member

A family member is defined as a spouse, ancestor, lineal descendant, or any spouse of a lineal descendant.[4]

Highly Compensated Employee

A highly compensated employee is defined as any employee earning 10 percent or more of the yearly wages of an employer.[5]

---

1.   29 CFR §2550.408b-2(c).
2.   IRC Sec. 4975(e)(1).
3.   IRC Sec. 4975(e)(2).
4.   IRC Sec. 4975(e)(6).
5.   IRC Sec. 4975(e)(2)(H).

3981. Who is a fiduciary for purposes of the prohibited transaction rules?

A fiduciary is a person who has discretionary authority or control over plan management or administration or disposition of plan assets, or who renders investment advice for a fee or other compensation, direct or indirect, with respect to any money or other property of the plan.[1]

A person renders investment advice if advising trustees as to the value of property or making recommendations about the advisability of buying or selling property and, directly or indirectly (1) has discretionary authority with respect to buying or selling property, or (2) renders advice on a regular basis to the plan, pursuant to a mutual understanding that (x) the services will be the primary basis for investment decisions, and (y) he or she will render individualized advice regarding investment policies.[2] Whether advice and recommendations regarding plan purchases of insurance contracts and annuities constitute investment advice depends on the facts in each situation.[3] A fee or other compensation can include insurance sales commissions.

A final rule issued by the Department of Labor (DOL) in 2016 broadened the definition of fiduciary, effective April 10, 2017[4] to include a person who gives fiduciary investment advice to a plan, plan fiduciary, participant, beneficiary, or IRA owner. It was vacated on June 21, 2018 after the Fifth Circuit Court of Appeals issued a mandate. The DOL did not appeal, and instead proposed a new class exemption. See Q 3985.[5]

Under earlier DOL regulations, a person who develops a computer model or who markets a computer model or investment advice program used in an "eligible investment advice arrangement" is a fiduciary of a plan by reason of the provision of investment advice and is treated as a "fiduciary advisor."[6] The regulations specify the conditions that must be met for a fiduciary to elect to be the sole fiduciary advisor under the investment advice program.

ERISA does not modify the definition of a fiduciary under IRC Section 4975; consequently, an individual who is not a fiduciary under ERISA still can be a fiduciary for purposes of IRC Section 4975.[7]

3982. What exemptions to the prohibited transaction rules are provided by the Internal Revenue Code?

The IRC lists specific exemptions from the broad prohibited transaction rules. These include:

(1)   the receipt of benefits under the terms of the plan;

(2)   the distribution of the assets of the plan meeting allocation requirements;

---

1.   IRC Sec. 4975(e)(3).
2.   Treas. Reg. §54.4975-9(c).
3.   Prohibited Transaction Exemption (PTE) 77-9 (Discussion of Major Comments).
4.   29 C.F.R. 2510.3-21(a).
5.   *Chamber of Commerce v. Acosta*, No. 17-10238, (5th Cir. June 21, 2018)
6.   DOL Reg. §2550.408g–2; IRC Sec. 4975(f)(8).
7.   *Flahertys Arden Bowl, Inc. v. Comm.*, 115 TC 269 (2000), *aff'd*, 262 F. 3d 1162, 88 AFTR 2d 2001-5547 (8th Cir. 2001).

(3)   loans available to all plan participants or beneficiaries under certain circumstances (see Q 3983);

(4)   a loan to an employee stock ownership plan (ESOP, see Q 3816); and

(5)   the acquisition or sale of qualifying employer securities by an individual account profit sharing, stock bonus, thrift, savings plan, or ESOP for adequate consideration and without commission.[1]

Another statutory exemption is for the provision of office space or services necessary for the establishment or operation of the plan under a reasonable arrangement for no more than reasonable compensation.[2] This exemption shields only the provision of services that would be prohibited transactions under (1), (3), and (4) in Q 3979, not fiduciary self-dealing. Thus, if an insurance agent is not a fiduciary, the agent's sale of insurance to a plan and receipt of a commission is within this statutory exemption. If an agent is a fiduciary (for example, if the trustee relies on his or her investment advice) receipt of a commission for sale of insurance or annuities to a plan may be a prohibited transaction.[3]

Certain administrative exemptions (see Q 3984) permit receipt of fees or commissions by fiduciaries in connection with the sale of insurance and annuity contracts to plans and the transfer of insurance contracts between plan and plan participants or employers.

Final DOL regulations provide that compensation paid to certain service providers will not be considered reasonable for purposes of the prohibited transaction exemption unless the covered service provider satisfies a fee disclosure mandate.[4] Failure to comply with the disclosure mandate will mean that compensation paid to the covered service provider does not qualify for the statutory prohibited transaction exemption.

The service providers covered by the mandate are fiduciaries, registered investment advisors, platform providers for participant directed defined contribution plans, and other indirectly compensated service providers who reasonably expect $1,000 or more in direct or indirect compensation in connection with providing covered services. Indirectly compensated services include accounting, auditing, actuarial, appraisal, banking, certain consulting related to the plan or plan investments, custodial, insurance, investment advisory, legal, recordkeeping, investment brokerage, third party administration, or valuation services provided to the plan for which the covered service provider, an affiliate, or subcontractor reasonably expects to receive indirect compensation.[5]

Direct compensation is compensation received directly from the plan. Indirect compensation is compensation received from any source other than the plan, the plan sponsor, the covered

---

1.   IRC Sec. 4975(d).
2.   IRC Sec. 4975(d)(2).
3.   PTE 77-9 (Discussion of Major Comments); see also Treas. Reg. §54.4975-6(a)(5).
4.   Labor Reg. §2550.408b-2.
5.   Labor Reg. §2550.408b-2(c)(1)(iii).

service provider, or an affiliate. Compensation received from a subcontractor is generally indirect compensation.[1]

The disclosure must include the following information:

(1)   A description of the services to be provided;

(2)   If applicable, a statement that the services will be provider as a fiduciary, as a registered investment advisor, or both;

(3)   A description of all direct and indirect compensation expected to be received;

(4)   If recordkeeping services will be provided to the plan, a description of the compensation expected to be received for the services and information about any arrangement where the recordkeeping services will be provided without explicit compensation;

(5)   Information about fiduciary services provided to investment products that the plan has a direct equity investment in;

(6)   Information about investment products made available through a platform in connection with recordkeeping and brokerage services; and

(7)   A description of the manner in which the compensation will be received, such as whether the plan will be billed or the compensation will be deducted directly from the plan's accounts or investments.[2]

Except for the first two exemptions listed above, these statutory exemptions do not apply where a plan that covers owner-employees (1) lends assets or income, (2) pays any compensation for personal services rendered to the plan, or (3) except as described in the following paragraph, acquires property from or sells property to (x) an owner-employee (Q 3931) or an employee who owns more than 5 percent of the outstanding shares of an S corporation, an individual retirement plan participant, beneficiary, or sponsoring employer or association, as the case may be, (y) a family member of a person described in (x), or (z) a corporation controlled by a person described in (x) through ownership of 50 percent or more of total combined voting power of all classes of stock or 50 percent or more of total shares of all classes of stock of the corporation.[3]

A transaction consisting of a sale of employer securities to an ESOP (Q 3818) by a shareholder-employee, a member of his or her family, or a corporation in which he or she owns 50 percent or more of the stock generally will be exempt from the prohibited transaction rules. For this purpose, a shareholder-employee is an employee or officer of an S corporation who owns or is deemed to own, under the constructive ownership rules of IRC Section 318(a)(1), more than 5 percent of the outstanding stock of the corporation on any day during the corporation's

---

1.   Labor Reg. §2550.408b-2(c)(1)(viii)(B).
2.   Labor Reg. §2550.408b-2(c)(1)(iv).
3.   IRC Sec. 4975(f)(6)(A).

taxable year.[1] For special rules applying to S corporation ESOPs that the IRS views as abusive, see Q 3824.

The Pension Protection Act of 2006 created an exemption from the prohibited transaction rules for certain fiduciary advisors who provide investment advice under an eligible investment advice arrangement (Q 3792).[2]

3983. When is a plan loan exempted from the prohibited transaction rules?

Loans made to plan participants and beneficiaries generally are exempted from the prohibited transaction rules if the loans:

(1)   are made available to all participants and beneficiaries on a reasonably equivalent basis,

(2)   are not made available to highly compensated employees (Q 3929) in an amount greater than the amount made available to other employees,

(3)   are made in accordance with specific provisions regarding such loans set forth in the plan,

(4)   bear reasonable rates of interest, and

(5)   are adequately secured.[3]

A reasonable rate of interest is one that provides the plan with a return commensurate with the interest rates charged by persons in the business of lending money for loans made under similar circumstances.[4]

Security for participant loans is considered adequate if it may reasonably be anticipated that loss of principal or interest will not result if default occurs.[5] The effect of this no loss requirement varies depending on the type of plan; a plan in which the investment experience of the plan's assets is shared by all participants may require additional loan conditions, such as mandatory payroll deduction repayment on stated events or additional collateral.

No more than 50 percent of the present value of a participant's vested accrued benefit under a plan generally may be considered as security for the outstanding balance of all plan loans made to the participant.[6] Except in the case of directed investment loans, this loan exemption is not an exemption from the other fiduciary standards of ERISA. The prohibited transaction rules apply to a loan that does not meet the exemption requirements, even if it is treated and taxed as a distribution (Q 3952).[7]

1.   IRC Secs. 4975(f)(6)(B)(ii), 4975(f)(6)(C).
2.   IRC Secs. 4975(d)(17), 4975(f)(8), ERISA 408(g).
3.   ERISA Sec. 408(b)(1); IRC Sec. 4975(d)(1); Labor Reg. §2550.408b-1.
4.   Labor Reg. §2550.408b-1(e).
5.   Labor Reg. §2550.408b-1(f)(1).
6.   Labor Reg. §2550.408b-1(f)(2).
7.   Medina v. U.S., 112 TC 51 (1999).

Loans from a qualified plan to S corporation shareholders, partners, and sole proprietors generally are exempt from the prohibited transaction rules (Q 3952),[1] although there are rules applying to certain S corporation ESOPs that the IRS views as abusive (Q 3824).

The Tax Court determined that a loan between a plan and a corporation partially owned by a disqualified person did not constitute a prohibited transaction where the loan was approved by and made at the sole discretion of the plan's independent bank trustee.[2] A transfer of property to a plan in satisfaction of a participant loan was treated as a prohibited transaction where the borrower was a disqualified person.[3]

3984. What is the prohibited transaction exemption that allows life insurance agents, brokers, or pension consultants (including fiduciaries) who are disqualified persons to receive commission or effect transactions related to certain life insurance and annuities?

Administrative Exemption: 84-24

Prohibited Transaction Exemption 84-24[4] provides administrative relief in addition to the statutory provisions. It permits a life insurance agent, broker, or pension consultant and affiliates, including a fiduciary, who is a disqualified person (1) to receive sales commissions for certain insurance and annuity sales to a plan, or (2) to effect a transaction for the purchase of an insurance or annuity contract from an insurance company. The exemption also permits an investment company principal underwriter to effect a transaction for the purchase of an insurance or annuity contract. Furthermore, it allows the purchase of insurance or annuities from an insurance company that is a disqualified person. This class exemption is available only if certain conditions are met.

Planning Point: Note that the exemption was significantly changed by the Department of Labor Fiduciary Rule, which was scheduled to become effective January 1, 2018 (although the impartial conduct standards were effective June 9, 2017)).[5] However, the rule was vacated in the courts in March, 2018, and the DOL has yet to release a revised rule.

First, the transaction must be effected in the ordinary course of business of the agent, broker, or consultant on terms at least as favorable to the plan as those that would be negotiated in an arm's length transaction with an unrelated party. The total fees and commissions also must not be in excess of reasonable compensation, determined on a facts and circumstances basis.

Second, the agent, broker, consultant, or insurance company may not act as a plan trustee (other than a nondiscretionary trustee who does not render investment advice with respect to any assets of the plan), plan administrator, a fiduciary authorized to manage, acquire, or dispose of plan assets on a discretionary basis, or an employer, any of whose employees are covered by the plan. PTE 84-24, as amended, extends the same relief to situations where an affiliate of the

---

1.   IRC Sec. 4975(f)(6)(B)(iii).
2.   *Greenlee v. Comm.*, TC Memo 1996-378.
3.   *Morrissey v. Comm.*, TC Memo 1998-443.
4.   1984-2 CB 231 (formerly PTE 77-9, 1977-2 CB 428, as amended by 1979-1 CB 371).
5.   See Amendment to and Partial Revocation of PTE 84-24, 81 Fed. Reg. 21147 (April 8, 2016).

insurance agent or broker, pension consultant, or investment company principal underwriter is a trustee with investment discretion over plan assets that are not involved in the transaction.[1]

The term affiliates includes (1) any person controlled by or under common control with the agent, broker, consultant, or insurance company, (2) any officer, director, employee, or relative of or a partner in (but not of) the agent, broker, consultant, or insurance company, and (3) any corporation or partnership of which the agent, broker, consultant, or insurance company is an officer, director, or employee, or in which he or she is a partner.

The transaction must be approved, in writing, by an independent fiduciary, who may be the employer. Prior to the sale, the agent, broker, or consultant must disclose to the independent fiduciary:

(1)   the nature of the affiliation between the agent and the insurer whose contract is being recommended;

(2)   any limitations on the agent's ability to recommend insurance or annuity contracts;

(3)   the amount of sales commission, expressed as a percentage of gross annual premium payments for the first and renewal years; and

(4)   a description of any charges, fees, discounts, penalties, or adjustments that may be imposed in connection with the purchase, holding, exchange, termination, or sale of such contracts.

Finally, the agent, broker, or consultant must retain records relating to the transaction for six years, but no filing is required with either the IRS or the Department of Labor. The records must be available for examination by those two federal agencies, plan participants, beneficiaries, and any employer or employee organization whose employees or members are covered by the plan.

An insurance company that is a service provider or fiduciary solely because it sponsors a master or prototype plan need satisfy only the first set of conditions. An agent, broker, or consultant who is a fiduciary and who sells insurance in connection with the master or prototype plan must meet both sets of conditions.

The impartial conduct standards of PTE 84-24 (as amended) were effective June 9, 2017, and required written acknowledgement of fiduciary status. In addition, the advisor must act in the best interest of the plan at the time of the transaction; any statements made by the advisor may not be "materially misleading at the time they were made; and the total of all fees and compensation received cannot exceed reasonable compensation. As the status of the fiduciary rule is in flux, so are these new requirements.

Prior to the changes, PTE 84-24 applied to transactions involving variable annuities and indexed annuities. Effective January 1, 2018, PTE 84-24 is only available for life insurance and fixed annuities.

---

1.   See Amendment to PTE 84-24, 71 Fed. Reg. 5887 (Feb.1, 2006).

The changes to PTE 84-24 also require more disclosures, including the disclosure of insurance commissions in dollar amounts, rather than as a percentage of premiums as required under the previous rules, unless it is not feasible to do so. Receipt of the disclosure must be acknowledged in writing by the plan fiduciary.

3985. What requirements must be satisfied for an investment advice fiduciary to qualify under the fiduciary PTE proposed by the DOL in 2020?

Editor's Note: After the 5th Circuit vacated the 2016 DOL fiduciary rule, the DOL removed the Best Interest Contract Exemption (BICE) in 2020.[1] In June 2020, the DOL proposed a fiduciary PTE as a replacement to the 2016 rule. See the heading below for a discussion of BICE, as it would have applied under the 2016 DOL rule.

In 2020, the DOL released its long-awaited follow-up to the 5th Circuit's vacation of its 2016 fiduciary rule. The DOL proposed a new class exemption that grants relief for financial advisors and institutions who provide investment advice (including retirement-related and rollover advice, see Q 3986) if the terms of the PTE are satisfied.[2]

In creating the new exemption, the DOL's stated goal was to provide impartial conduct standards that are in line with guidance released by other regulators, including the SEC Regulation Best Interest and state-level fiduciary rules. To qualify under the new fiduciary PTE, advisors must provide advice in accordance with impartial conduct standards, which generally include standards related to: (1) acting in the client's best interests, (2) a reasonable compensation, (3) refraining from misleading statements, (4) disclosure, (5) conflict mitigation and (6) retroactive compliance review.[3]

The proposed exemption would be available to registered investment advisers, broker-dealers, banks, and insurance companies (financial institutions) and their individual employees, agents, and representatives (investment professionals) that provide fiduciary investment advice to retirement investors.

The proposal defines retirement investors as plan participants and beneficiaries, IRA owners, and plan and IRA fiduciaries. In determining whether an advisor is a fiduciary who may take advantage of the exemption, pre-2016 standards apply. The exemption's relief also specifically applies to otherwise prohibited transactions related to investment advice about retirement plan rollovers.

A person is an investment advice fiduciary to the extent he or she renders investment advice for a fee or other compensation, whether direct or indirect, with respect to any money or other property of a plan, or has any authority or responsibility to do so.

For fiduciary investment advice standards to apply, a person who is not otherwise a fiduciary must (1) render advice as to the value of securities or other property, or make recommendations

---

1.   See Amendment to and Partial Revocation of PTE 84-24, 81 Fed. Reg. 21147 (April 8, 2016).
2.   See "Improving Investment Advice for Workers & Retirees", ZRIN 1210-ZA29.
3.   Sec. II(d).

as to the advisability of investing in, purchasing, or selling securities or other property (2) on a regular basis (3) pursuant to a mutual agreement, arrangement, or understanding with the plan, plan fiduciary or IRA owner that (4) the advice will serve as a primary basis for investment decisions with respect to plan or IRA assets, and that (5) the advice will be individualized based on the particular needs of the plan or IRA. This is the five-part test that applied prior to the 2016 DOL fiduciary rule. Relief under the new exemption is conditioned on adhering to impartial conduct standards, as follows:

Best Interests Standard. The best interest standard follows longstanding legal concepts. It is generally satisfied if investment advice "reflects the care, skill, prudence, and diligence under the circumstances then prevailing that a prudent person acting in a like capacity and familiar with such matters would use in the conduct of an enterprise of a like character and with like aims, based on the investment objectives, risk tolerance, financial circumstances, and needs of the investor, and does not place the financial or other interest of the [advisor/firm] or any affiliate, related entity or other party ahead of the interests of the investor, or subordinate the investor's interests to their own." The preamble is careful to note that the PTE does not create a duty to monitor—although a duty to monitor could be generated depending upon whether an investment could prudently be recommended to the investor *absent* ongoing monitoring.[1]

Reasonable Compensation Rule. The reasonable compensation standard requires that compensation not be excessive, as measured by the market value of the particular services, rights, and benefits the advisor is delivering. The reasonableness of fees will depend on the particular facts and circumstances at the time of the recommendation. Several factors inform whether compensation is reasonable, including the market price of services provided and/or the underlying assets, the scope of monitoring, and the complexity of the product. No single factor is controlling in determining whether compensation is reasonable. The important question is whether the charges are reasonable in relation to what the investor receives. Firms and advisors have no obligation to recommend the transaction that is the lowest cost or that generates the lowest fees without regard to other factors.[2]

The exemption would also require financial firms and advisors to seek to obtain the "best execution" of the investment transaction reasonably available under the circumstances. This duty is satisfied if the advisor complies with applicable federal securities laws, including those imposed by the SEC and FINRA that are beyond the scope of this discussion.[3]

No Misleading Statements. This element would require that statements by the both the financial firm and the advisor to the investor about the recommended transaction and other relevant matters are not materially misleading at the time they are made. The preamble to the PTE states that "other relevant matters" include fees and compensation, material conflicts of interest, and any other fact that could reasonably be expected to affect the investor's investment decisions.[4]

---

1. Sec. II(a)(1).
2. Sec. II(a)(2).
3. Sec. II(a)(2)(B).
4. Sec. II(a)(3).

Disclosure Requirement. Financial firms are required to make written disclosure of their fiduciary status to investors prior to engaging in any transactions covered by the exemption. The disclosure must contain a written description of the services to be provided and material conflicts of interest arising out of the services and any recommended investment transaction. The disclosures should be in plain English, considering the investor's level of financial experience. The proposed PTE does not require specific disclosures to be tailored for each investor or each transaction as long as a compliant disclosure is provided before engaging in the particular transaction.[1]

Financial Firms' Policies & Procedures Requirement. The proposed exemption requires financial firms to establish, maintain and enforce written policies and procedures prudently designed to ensure compliance with the impartial conduct standards. These policies and procedures should be designed to mitigate conflicts of interests generally and avoid incentives to violate the impartial conduct standards.[2]

BICE: Administrative Exemption: 2016-01

Prohibited Transaction Exemption 2016-01[3] added the Best Interest Contract (BIC) Exemption as part of the Department of Labor's 2016 Fiduciary Rule (Q 4123 to Q 4159), designed to minimize conflicts of interest and provide that advisors act in the employee or participant's best interests. Under the BIC Exemption, financial institutions and advisors may receive variable compensation by acknowledging they are fiduciaries in providing investment advice and adhere to impartial conduct standards. In addition, the financial institution must have policies and procedures in place designed to ensure compliance with the impartial conduct standards, detect and record any material conflicts of interest, and designate a person responsible for compliance with the impartial conduct standard. Specified information must be disclosed to participants prior to or at the time transactions based on the advice occur. A website must be available with information required to be disclosed.

3986. When does the 2020 DOL investment advice fiduciary PTE apply to rollover transactions?

The new DOL proposed exemption for fiduciary advice specifically applies to rollover advice, assuming the circumstances qualify under the five-part test for determining whether the advisor is an investment advice fiduciary (see Q 3985). Rollovers from a 401(k) to an IRA, IRA to IRA, or one type of account to another (i.e., from a fee-based account to a commission-based account) are all potentially covered by the exemption.

However, the DOL commentary included with the proposed exemption makes clear that not every rollover triggers investment advice fiduciary status. A facts-and-circumstances analysis will be required in every case to determine whether the transaction is subject to the new standard. Specifically, the DOL notes that it does not intend to apply the guidance in DOL Advisory

---

1. Sec. II(b).
2. Sec. II(c).
3. 81 Fed. Reg. 21002, corrected by 81 Fed. Reg. 44773.

Opinion 2005-23A (the *Deseret* Letter), which would have found that rollover advice generally does not constitute investment advice.

All five prongs of the test must be satisfied for the advisor to be an investment advice fiduciary under the DOL definition. Advice to execute a rollover transaction can potentially be an isolated event that would not satisfy the "regular basis" component of the five-prong approach. On the other hand, rollover advice can be given as a part of an ongoing relationship between client and advisor, or an anticipated future ongoing relationship between the parties.

Further, determining whether there is a "mutual understanding" between the parties is based upon the reasonable understanding of both parties—even if no formal agreement is found. In fact, the DOL notes that advice to roll over plan assets is often given for the purpose of establishing an ongoing relationship where advice is provided on a regular basis outside of the plan (in return for a fee/commission). In other words, the rollover advice can be the first step in an investment advisory relationship that continues on a regular basis.

The proposed exemption requires financial firms and advisors to document the reasons for recommending the rollover, including why the rollover is in the client's best interests.

3987. What is the PTE that permits certain insurance agents or brokers who are employers (or related) maintaining a plan to sell insurance or annuity contracts to the plan and receive commission?

Administrative Exemption: 79-60

Prohibited Transaction Exemption 79-60[1] permits an insurance agent or broker who is the employer (or related, in certain ways listed below, to the employer) maintaining a plan to sell an insurance or annuity contract (including a contract providing only for the provision of administrative services) to the plan and receive a commission. A general agent who is the employer (or related to the employer in one of the listed ways) may receive override commissions on such sales by another agent.

The following three conditions must be met for a transaction to come within this exemption.

First, the agent or broker must be:

(1)   an employer with employees covered by the plan (including a sole proprietor who is the only plan participant);

(2)   a 10 percent or more partner of such an employer;

(3)   an employee, officer, or director (or an individual having powers or responsibilities similar to those of officers or directors), or a 10 percent or more stockholder of such an employer;

---

1.   44 Fed. Reg. 59018.

(4)   a 50 percent or more owner of the employer; or

(5)   a corporation or partnership that is 50 percent or more owned by a plan fiduciary, a person providing services to the plan, the employer, a 50 percent owner of the employer, or an employee organization with members covered under the plan.

Second, the plan may pay no more than adequate consideration for the policy or contract.

Finally, the total commissions received in each taxable year of the agent or broker as a result of sales under this exemption must not exceed 5 percent of the total insurance commission income received by the agent or broker in that taxable year. There are no record-keeping requirements.

3988. What is the PTE that permits disqualified persons other than a plan to make unsecured interest-free loans to a plan to pay ordinary operating expenses?

Administrative Exemption: 80-26

Prohibited Transaction Exemption 80-26[1] permits a disqualified person other than another plan to make unsecured interest-free loans to a plan to pay ordinary operating expenses (including the payment of benefits and periodic premiums under an insurance or annuity contract) or, for a period no longer than three days, for a purpose incidental to the ordinary operation of the plan. The Department of Labor adopted a temporary amendment to PTE 80-26 to include interest-free loans made to plans affected by the 9/11 terrorist attacks.[2] In 2006, the Department amended the regulation to eliminate the three-day limit, provided that if the loan is for longer than 60 days, the terms of the agreement are written.[3] An amendment proposed in 2013 would provide retroactive and temporary relief for certain guarantees of the payment of debits to plan investment accounts (including IRAs) by parties in interest to such plans as well as certain loans and loan repayments made pursuant to such guarantees.[4]

3989. What are the PTEs that establish conditions for the transfer of life insurance and annuity contracts to and from plans?

Administrative Exemptions: 92-5 and 92-6

Prohibited Transaction Exemptions 92-5 and 92-6[5] establish conditions for the transfer of life insurance and annuity contracts to and from plans. PTEs 92-5 and 92-6 extended the relief granted under PTEs 77-7 and 77-8 to owner-employees and to shareholders owning more than 5 percent of the outstanding stock in an S corporation. PTE 92-5 permits individual contracts to be transferred to a plan by participants or employers, any of whose employees participate in the plan. The plan generally must pay no more than the lesser of the cash surrender value of the contract or the value of the participant's accrued benefit at the time of the transaction

---

1.   1980-2 CB 323.
2.   Temp. Amendments to PTE 80-26. 67 Fed. Reg. 9485 (Mar. 3, 2002).
3.   67 Fed. Reg. 17917 (April 7, 2006).
4.   78 Fed. Reg. 31584.
5.   57 Fed. Reg. 5019, 5189 (formerly PTEs 77-7 and 77-8, 1977-2 CB 423, 425).

(or account balance, in the case of a defined contribution plan), and the contract must not be subject to any loan that the plan assumes. The DOL has stated that where participants transfer individual policies that have no cash surrender value, the transfer will not violate the prohibited transaction rules where the plan pays no consideration for the policies.[1]

PTE 92-6 enables a plan to sell insurance contracts and annuities to a plan participant insured under the policies, a relative of such participant who is a beneficiary under the contract, an employer whose employees are covered by the plan, or another employee benefit plan for the cash surrender value of the contracts, provided certain conditions are met. In the absence of these exemptions, these transfers would be prohibited transactions.

PTE 92-6 first was clarified in 1998 so that, if all of its other conditions are met, two or more relatives who are the sole beneficiaries under a contract may be considered a single relative and an individual life insurance contract may be read to include a contract covering the life of the participant and his or her spouse (if permitted by applicable state insurance law, other applicable law, and pertinent plan provisions). In addition, a sale of a partial interest in a life insurance contract qualifies as a sale of an individual life insurance contract if certain requirements are met with both the portion sold and the portion retained.[2]

In 2002, PTE 92-6 was retroactively amended to permit transfers of life insurance contracts directly to life insurance trusts and certain other trusts.[3] In addition, the DOL clarified that second-to-die policies covering spouses are included within the scope of PTE 92-6.[4]

Planning Point: This expansion and liberalization by the Department of Labor adds trusts to the list of those to whom life insurance owned by a qualified plan can safely be sold. It is important to note that the exemption is conditioned on the fact that, but for the sale, the plan would have surrendered the life insurance contract. Furthermore, the plan must be paid what the policy is worth at the time it is sold.

The preamble to PTE 77-8[5] (which was replaced by PTE 92-6) noted that, for federal income tax purposes, the value of an insurance policy is not the same as, and may exceed, its cash surrender value, and that a purchase of an insurance policy at its cash surrender value therefore may be a purchase of property for less than its fair market value.

In 2004 guidance, the Treasury Department clarified that under new proposed regulations, any such bargain element will be treated as a distribution under IRC Section 402(a) as well as for other purposes of the IRC, including the limitations on in-service distributions from certain qualified plans and the limitations of IRC Section 415.[6]

The DOL also has extended the application of PTE 92-6 to the transfer of a second-to-die policy owned by two spouses from a self-directed profit sharing plan account, provided certain

---

1.   DOL Adv. Op. 2002-12A.
2.   See DOL Adv. Op. 98-07A.
3.   See 67 Fed. Reg. 56313.
4.   DOL Adv. Op. 2006-03A (February 26, 2006).
5.   Citing Rev. Rul. 59-195, 1959-1 CB 18.
6.   See REG-126967-03, 69 Fed. Reg. 7384 (Feb. 17, 2004).

requirements are met. Generally, the requirements are that the participant must be the insured under the contract, the contract would be surrendered but for the sale by the plan, and the amount received by the plan as consideration must be at least equal to the amount necessary to put the plan back in the same position as if it had retained the contract, surrendered it, and made any distribution owed to the participant on his or her vested interest under the plan.[1]

3990. What is the PTE that allows banks and brokers to offer no or low cost services based on account balances in IRAs and Keogh plans?

Administrative Exemption: 93-33 and 97-11

Prohibited Transaction Exemption 93-33[2] and Prohibited Transaction Exemption 97-11[3] allow banks and brokerages, respectively, to offer no or low cost services based on account balances in IRAs and Keogh plans, if certain requirements are met:

(1)   the services offered must be those that could be offered under applicable state and federal law and that are available in the ordinary course of business to other customers who do not maintain an IRA or Keogh plan;

(2)   the eligibility requirements, based on the account value or the amount of fees incurred, must be as favorable as any such requirements imposed on any other account included in determining eligibility to receive such services;

(3)   the IRA or Keogh plan must be established for the exclusive benefit of the participant, his or her spouse, or their beneficiaries;

(4)   the investment performance of the IRA or Keogh plan must equal or exceed that of a like investment made at the same time by a customer ineligible to receive such low or no cost services.

In addition, PTE 97-11 requires that the services offered by brokerages be the same as those offered to non-IRA or non-Keogh plan customers with like account values or like fees generated and that the combined total of all fees for the provision of services to the IRA or Keogh plan may not exceed reasonable compensation within the meaning of IRC Section 4975(d)(2).

The Department of Labor subsequently adopted amendments expanding these exemptions to Coverdell education savings accounts and SIMPLE IRAs (Q 3706).[4] PTE 97-11 was similarly amended to extend its provisions to Roth IRAs, assuming they are not part of an employee benefit plan covered by Title I of ERISA, other than an SEP or a SIMPLE IRA.[5]

---

1.   DOL Adv. Op. 2006-03A (February 26, 2006).
2.   58 Fed. Reg. 31053.
3.   62 Fed. Reg. 5855.
4.   See 64 Fed. Reg. 11042 and 64 Fed. Reg. 11044 (Mar. 8, 1999).
5.   See 67 Fed. Reg. 76425 (Dec. 12, 2002).

3991. What are the penalties for engaging in a prohibited transaction?

A first tier tax equal to 15 percent of the amount involved is imposed on each prohibited transaction for each year or part thereof from the time the transaction occurs until the earliest of the date: (1) it is corrected, (2) a deficiency notice is mailed, or (3) the tax is assessed.[1] An employer fined under this provision for failing to make timely 401(k) transfer deferrals was assessed the 15 percent penalty only on the amount of interest the employer would have paid for a bank loan for the same amount, not 15 percent of the amount of the late deposit.[2]

All disqualified persons who participate in the prohibited transaction, other than a fiduciary acting only as a fiduciary, are jointly and severally liable for the full amount of the tax. A trustee was held liable for the tax even though the trustee did not vote to approve the payment that was determined to be a prohibited transaction; the Seventh Circuit Court of Appeals determined that the trustee had benefited from the payments and thus had participated in the transaction.[3]

An act of self-dealing involving the use of money or property (for example, the leasing of property) may be treated as giving rise to multiple transactions – one on the day the transaction occurs and separate ones on the first day of each taxable year within the above period – and, thus, may result in multiple penalties.[4]

Second Tier Tax

If a transaction is not corrected within the above period, there is a second tier tax of 100 percent of the amount involved. This tax will be abated if the transaction is corrected within 90 days after the notice of deficiency with respect to the additional tax is mailed. This 90-day period may be extended in certain circumstances.

To be corrected, the transaction must be undone to the extent possible, but, in any event, so as to place the plan in a financial position no worse than it would have been in had the disqualified person acted under the highest fiduciary standards.[5]

A prohibited transaction was held to be self-correcting, and thus not subject to the second tier tax (or to the first tier tax in subsequent tax years), where the extraordinary success of the investment was such that to undo the transaction would have put the plan in a worse position than if the disqualified persons had acted under the highest fiduciary standards. Essentially, the transaction involved a sale of mineral rights that were producing over a million dollars a year in royalties to an ESOP by the employees of the employer in return for a private annuity.[6] The Tax

---

1.   IRC Sec. 4975(a); IRC Sec. 4975(f)(2).
2.   See Rev. Rul. 2006-38, 2006-29 IRB 80.
3.   *O'Malley v. Comm.*, 972 F.2d 150 (7th Cir. 1992).
4.   Treas. Reg. §141.4975-13. See *Lambos v. Comm.*, 88 TC 1440 (1987).
5.   IRC Secs. 4975(b), 4961.
6.   *Zabolotny v. Comm.*, 7 F.3d 774 (8th Cir. 1993), *nonacq.* 1994-1 CB 1.

Court considers this case to be an anomaly and has stated that, in general, prohibited transactions cannot be self-correcting.[1]

If the owner of an individual retirement account, or the owner's beneficiary, engages in a prohibited transaction and, as a result, the account ceases to be an individual retirement account, the tax does not apply (Q 3649). Similar rules apply to beneficiaries of health and Archer medical savings accounts (Q 388 to Q 420) and to beneficiaries of and contributors to education savings accounts.[2]

The IRS has the authority to impose tax penalties as a result of prohibited transactions, even when the Department of Labor has entered into a consent judgment concerning the plan.[3]

Other Consequences

In addition to the potential tax penalties discussed above, there can be other consequences to a prohibited transaction. IRAs cease to qualify as IRAs as of the first day of the taxable year in which the prohibited transaction occurs and the account is treated as distributing all of its assets on that date.[4]

A self-directed IRA purchased land and contributed it and cash to a partnership with an LLC solely owned by the IRA owner and his wife that owned the adjacent property. It allowed the IRA owner to use the IRA assets for his personal benefit. Because the IRA owner was a fiduciary with regard to the IRA, this was a prohibited transaction and immediately terminated the IRA's exempt status. As a result, the IRA assets were not protected when the IRA owner filed for bankruptcy.[5]

Qualified Plans and Estate Taxes

3992. Is the value of a death benefit payable from a qualified plan includable in the employee's gross estate?

In general, yes, if the employee dies after 1984.

Estates of Decedents Dying After 1984

The present value (at the date of the decedent's death or at an alternate valuation date) of an annuity or any other benefit payable to any surviving beneficiary under a qualified plan on the death of a participant, other than death proceeds of insurance on the participant's life, is includable in the decedent's estate.[6]

The Tax Reform Act of 1984 generally repealed the estate tax exclusion discussed below for estates of decedents dying after 1984. The repeal does not apply to the estate of any decedent

---

1.   See *Morrissey v. Comm.*, TC Memo 1998-443.
2.   IRC Sec. 4975(c)(3).
3.   *Baizer v. Comm.*, 204 F.3d 1231 (9th Cir. 2000).
4.   IRC Sec. 408(e)(2).
5.   *In Re Kellerman*, 115 AFTR 2D 2015-1944 (Bktcy CT AR).
6.   IRC Secs. 2039(a), 2039(b).

who was a plan participant in pay status on December 31, 1984, and who irrevocably elected the form of the benefit before July 18, 1984.[1] The Tax Reform Act of 1986 provided that these conditions are considered met if the decedent separated from service before January 1, 1985, and does not change the form of benefit before death.[2] Qualified plan benefits rolled over to an IRA are treated as IRA benefits (Q 3712) that are not eligible for the TRA '86 separation from service rule.[3] For the meaning of the term "in pay status" and the requirements of an irrevocable election of the form of benefit, see Temporary Treasury Regulation Section 20.2039-1T.

Life insurance proceeds are includable under IRC Section 2042, assuming the participant held an incident of ownership in the insurance at his or her death or the proceeds are payable to or for the participant's estate. The right to name the beneficiary of the death proceeds is an incident of ownership (Q 86).

Estates of Decedents Dying After 1982 and Before 1985

Up to $100,000 in value of an annuity or other benefit payable to any surviving beneficiary under a qualified plan on the death of a participant, to the extent such value is attributable to employer contributions and to deductible employee contributions, is excludable from the gross estate, although special rules apply to a lump sum distribution.[4] The $100,000 limitation is an aggregate limitation applicable to survivor benefits payable under a qualified plan, a tax sheltered annuity (Q 631), an individual retirement plan (Q 3712), a Retired Serviceman's Family Protection Plan, or a Survivor Benefit Plan.

The Tax Reform Act of 1984 amended TEFRA to provide that the $100,000 limit shall not apply to the estate of any decedent who was a plan participant in pay status on December 31, 1982, and who irrevocably elected the form of benefit before January 1, 1983.[5] The Tax Reform Act of 1986 provided that these conditions are considered met if the decedent separated from service before January 1, 1983, and does not change the form of benefit before death.[6]

Estates of Decedents Dying After 1953 and Before 1983

The value of an annuity or other benefit payable to any surviving beneficiary under a qualified plan on the death of a participant, to the extent such value is attributable to employer contributions and to deductible employee contributions, is excludable from the gross estate, although special rules apply to a lump sum distribution.[7]

---

1.   TRA '84, Sec. 525.
2.   TRA '86, Sec. 1852(e)(3).
3.   Rev. Rul. 92-22, 1992-1 CB 313; *Sherrill v. U.S.*, 415 F. Supp. 2d 953 (N.D. Ind. 2006).
4.   IRC Secs. 2039(c), 2039(g), as amended and added by the Tax Equity and Fiscal Responsibility Act of 1982 (TEFRA), and before repeal by the Tax Reform Act of 1984.
5.   TRA '84, Sec. 525.
6.   TRA '86, Sec. 1852(e)(3).
7.   IRC Sec. 2039(c), before amendment by TEFRA.

3993. Is a death benefit payable under a Keogh plan includable in a self-employed individual's gross estate?

Yes, generally, as to decedents dying after 1984.

Estates of Decedents Dying After 1984

The federal estate taxation of survivor benefits payable under a Keogh plan (Q 3826) is the same in the estate of a self-employed individual/participant as in the estate of a participant covered under a corporate plan (Q 3992).

Estates of Decedents Dying After 1953 and Before 1985

The federal estate tax exclusion (Q 3992) is available to the estates of self-employed individuals covered under qualified plans. For purposes of the exclusion, contributions or payments on behalf of the decedent participant while he or she was covered as a self-employed individual (Q 3931) are treated as employer contributions to the extent they were deductible as contributions to a qualified plan (Q 3939); to the extent they were not so deductible, such contributions or payments are treated as employee contributions.[1]

The exclusion applies only to amounts that are attributable to employer contributions[2] and to deductible employee contributions. In an insured plan, for example, the cost of current life insurance protection for self-employed participants is not deductible (Q 3951H); therefore, the at risk portion of the death proceeds of life insurance payable under the plan is not eligible for the estate tax exclusion. As to common law employees, on the other hand, the entire proceeds are eligible for the exclusion where the employer pays the cost.

3994. How does community property law affect the estate taxation of qualified plan benefits?

If an employee's interest in the employer's qualified plan is community property, then the interest is considered to be owned one-half by the employee and one-half by the employee's spouse. Accordingly, if the employee were to predecease the spouse, only the employee's community interest in any death benefit would be includable in the employee's estate (Q 3992). Likewise, if the employee's spouse were to die first, only the employee's spouse's community interest in the plan would be includable in the gross estate.[3]

The extent to which employee interests in qualified plans are community property is a matter of local law. There appears to be little doubt that an employee's vested interest in a qualified plan, to the extent it is attributable to contributions made while the employee was married

---

1.   IRC Sec. 2039(c); Treas. Reg. §20.2039-2(c)(iii).
2.   Let. Rul. 8122024.
3.   IRC Sec. 2033.

and living in a community property state, is community property.[1] Moreover, there appears to be increasing support for the view that nonvested benefits in a retirement plan are not mere expectancies but are property, and thus can be community property.[2]

1.   *Herring v. Blakeley*, 385 S.W. 2d 843 (Tex. 1965); *Lynch v. Lawrence*, 293 So. 2d 598 (La. App. 1974, writs *ref'd.*); *T.L. James & Co., Inc. v. Montgomery*, 332 So. 2d 834 (La. 1976); *Everson v. Everson*, 537 P. 2d 624 (Ariz. App. 1975); *Marriage of Ward*, 50 Cal. App.3d 150, *aff'd and mod'd*, 494 Pa. 348, 431 A.2d 889 (1981) (1975); *Fox v. Smith*, 531 S.W. 2d 654 (Tex. Civ. App. 1975); 50 *Texas L. Rev.* 334 (1972); 17 *Loyola L. Rev.* 162 (1970-71); 24 *So. Calif. Tax Inst.* 469 (1972); 94 ALR3d 176.
2.   *Johnson v. Johnson*, 638 P.2d 705 (Ariz. 1981); *Re Marriage of Brown*, 544 P.2d 561 (Cal. 1976); *Cearley v. Cearley*, 544 S.W. 2d 661 (Tex. 1976).

PART XVII: ROLLOVER

3995. What is a rollover or rollover contribution and what are its tax effects?

A rollover or rollover contribution is the transfer of a distribution from a qualified plan, an IRC Section 403(b) tax sheltered annuity, an individual retirement plan, or an eligible Section 457 governmental plan. Distributions that are rolled over according to applicable IRC rules and regulations are not included in gross income until receipt at some time in the future (Q 3997). A rollover to a Roth IRA generally is a taxable event (Q 3662).

Once funds or properties are rolled over to an eligible retirement plan (Q 3999), they generally are subject to the tax treatment given that plan.[1] Different rules apply to distributions made from a traditional IRA to an eligible retirement plan other than an IRA. The portion of a distribution that is rolled over to an eligible retirement plan generally will be treated as coming first from nonafter-tax contributions and earnings in all of the IRAs of the owner.[2] This rule effectively allows the owner to rollover the maximum amount permitted (Q 3671).

A direct distribution from a traditional IRA or a Roth IRA to a charity will be tax-free if it meets the requirements of the qualified charitable distribution rules available in 2006 and thereafter (Q 3996).

It is the responsibility of a plan administrator to determine whether a rollover it accepts is an eligible rollover distribution (Q 3997) and plans that accept invalid rollovers can face disqualification. Regulations state that a receiving plan will not be disqualified for accepting a rollover that fails to meet the requirements for an eligible rollover distribution if the plan administrator reasonably concluded such requirements would be met and distributed the amount of the invalid rollover contribution, plus any earnings, to the employee within a reasonable time after the administrator determined that the contribution was an invalid rollover contribution. It is not necessary that a distributing plan have a determination letter with respect to its status as a qualified plan for the administrator of a receiving plan to reasonably conclude that a contribution is a valid rollover contribution.[3]

Although the IRS generally takes the position that the right to a rollover is personal to an employee and cannot be exercised by anyone else, except in the case of a spousal rollover (Q 4013), at least one court has held that where an employee received a qualifying rollover distribution but died before making the rollover, the employee's executor could complete the rollover, as long as the 60 day period had not expired.[4]

There are requirements for a direct rollover option (Q 4000) and rules regarding the application of a mandatory income tax withholding rate of 20 percent on rollovers not made through a direct rollover (Q 4003). In some cases, a nonparticipant in a qualified plan may roll over amounts received from a plan by reason of a divorce or separation agreement (Q 4004).

---

1. See IRC Sec. 408(d).
2. IRC Sec. 408(d)(3).
3. Treas. Reg. §1.401(a)(31)-1, A-14.
4. *Gunther v. U.S.*, 573 F. Supp. 126, 82-2 USTC ¶13,498 (W.D. Mich. 1982).

3996. What is a charitable IRA rollover or qualified charitable distribution?

A taxpayer age 70½ or older is permitted to make a qualified charitable distribution (QCD) from a traditional IRA or Roth IRA that is not includable in the gross income of the taxpayer.[1] The exclusion for qualified charitable distributions generally is available for distributions from any type of IRA (including a Roth IRA described in Section 408A and a deemed IRA described in Section 408(q)) that is neither an ongoing SEP IRA described in Section 408(k) nor an ongoing SIMPLE IRA described in Section 408(p).[2]

The provision permitting a qualified charitable distribution to be excluded from gross income was allowed to expire at the end of 2011, but the American Taxpayer Relief Act of 2012 ("ATRA 2012") retroactively revived the provision for 2012 and extended it for the 2013 tax year. The Tax Increase Prevention Act of 2014 extended the provision retroactively for 2014, and the Protecting Americans Against Tax Hikes (PATH) Act of 2015 made the provision permanent.[3]

A qualified charitable distribution is any distribution:

1. not exceeding $100,000 in the aggregate during the taxable year;

2. made directly, in a trustee-to-charity transfer (including a check from an IRA made payable to a charity and delivered by the IRA owner to the charity);[4]

3. from a traditional or Roth IRA (although distributions from ongoing SEPs and SIMPLE IRAs do not qualify);

4. to a public charity (but not a donor-advised fund or supporting organization);

5. that would otherwise qualify as a deductible charitable contribution (not including the percentage of income limits in IRC Section 170(b) (Q 737)); and

6. to the extent the distribution would otherwise be includable in gross income.[5]

No charitable income tax deduction is allowed for a qualified charitable distribution.[6]

Planning Points: Only distributions from a taxpayer's own IRA are includable to determine whether a taxpayer has met the $100,000 limit. Therefore, although married taxpayers can make qualified distributions totaling $200,000, each spouse can only make distributions of up to $100,000 from his or her own IRA.

A participant in a qualified plan, an IRC Section 403(b) tax sheltered annuity, or an eligible IRC Section 457 governmental plan is first required to perform a rollover to a traditional IRA before taking advantage of a charitable IRA rollover.

---

1.   IRC Sec. 408(d)(8), as amended.
2.   Notice 2007-7, 2007-1 C.B. 395, A-36.
3.   The American Taxpayer Relief Act of 2012, Pub. Law No. 112-240.
4.   Notice 2007-7, 2007-1 CB 395.
5.   IRC Sec. 408(d)(8).
6.   IRC Sec. 408(d)(8)(E).

Transfers to donor-advised funds, supporting organizations, private foundations, charitable remainder trusts, charitable gift annuities, and pooled income funds are not qualified charitable distributions.

Rollovers to charities by taxpayers who reside in states that tax IRA distributions and do not have a charitable deduction cannot escape tax at the state level. *Ted R. Batson, Jr., MBA, CPA, and Gregory W. Baker, JD, CFP®, CAP, Renaissance Administration, LLC.*

If a qualified charitable distribution is made from any IRA funded with nondeductible contributions, the distribution is treated as coming first from deductible contributions and earnings.[1] This is contrary to the general rule that distributions from a traditional IRA with both deductible and nondeductible contributions are deemed made on a pro-rata basis.[2]

Qualified charitable distributions count toward a taxpayer's required minimum distributions (Q 3682).[3]

The prohibition on making a qualified charitable distribution from a SEP IRA or a SIMPLE IRA only applies to "ongoing" SEP IRAs or SIMPLE IRAs. These kinds of IRAs are ongoing if a contribution is made for the taxable year of the charitable distribution.[4]

Post-SECURE Act, taxpayers who make both post-70½ (deductible) IRA contributions and take qualified charitable distributions (QCDs) are also subject to an anti-abuse rule. Future QCDs are reduced by the total amount of deductible post-70½ IRA contributions that have not offset another QCD, although the amount cannot be reduced below zero.[5] Amounts that cannot be treated as a pre-tax QCD can be treated as an itemized deduction for the taxpayer.

> *Example:* An individual who turned age 70½ before 2020 deducts $5,000 for contributions for each of 2020 and 2021 but makes no contribution for 2022. The individual makes no QCDs for 2020 and makes QCDs of $6,000 for 2021 and $6,500 for 2022.
>
> The excludable amount of QCDs for 2021 is the $6,000 of QCDs reduced by the $10,000 aggregate amount of post-age 70½ contributions for 2021 and earlier taxable years. For this individual, these amounts are $5,000 for each of 2020 and 2021, resulting in no excludable QCDs for 2021 (that is, $6,000 – $10,000 = ($4,000)).
>
> The excludable amount of the QCDs for 2022 is the $6,500 of QCDs reduced by the portion of the $10,000 aggregate amount of post-age 70½ contributions deducted that did not reduce the excludable portion of the QCDs for earlier taxable years. Thus, $6,000 of the aggregate amount of post-age 70½ contributions deducted does not apply for 2022 because that amount has reduced the excludable amount of QCDs for 2021. The remaining $4,000 of the aggregate amount of post-age 70½ contributions deducted reduces the excludable amount of any QCDs for subsequent taxable years. Accordingly, the excludable amount of the QCDs for 2022 is $2,500 ($6,500 – $4,000 = $2,500). As described above, because the $4,000 amount reduced the excludable amount of QCDs for 2022, that $4,000 amount does not apply again in later years, and no amount of post-age 70½ contributions remains to reduce the excludable amount of QCDs for later taxable years.[6]

---

1.   IRC Sec. 408(d)(8)(D).
2.   IRC Secs. 72, 408(d)(1).
3.   IRC Sec. 408(d)(8), as amended.
4.   Notice 2007-7, 2007-1 CB 395.
5.   IRC Sec. 408(d)(8)(A).
6.   Notice 2020-68.

3997. What is required to roll over a distribution received from a qualified retirement plan or an eligible Section 457 governmental plan?

If any portion of the balance to the credit of an employee in a qualified retirement plan is paid in an eligible rollover distribution and the distributee transfers any portion of the property received to an eligible retirement plan (Q 3994), then the amount of the distribution so transferred generally will not be includable in income.[1] Unless otherwise indicated, the rules that apply to qualified plans are incorporated by reference into the requirements for eligible Section 457 governmental plans.

An eligible rollover distribution is any distribution of all or any portion of the balance to the credit of the employee in a qualified trust, except that the term does not include:

(1) any distribution that is part of a series of substantially equal payments, at least annually, made over the life or life expectancy of the employee or the joint lives or life expectancies of the employee and his or her designated beneficiary,

(2) any distribution made for a specified period of 10 years or more,

(3) any distribution that is a required minimum distribution under IRC Section 401(a)(9), and

(4) any hardship distribution.[2]

Regulations specify other items that are not considered eligible rollover distributions, including any portion of a distribution excludable from gross income other than net unrealized appreciation (although this has been modified by subsequent legislation), the Table 2001 or P.S. 58 cost of life insurance (Q 3947), corrective distributions of excess contributions and excess aggregate contributions (Q 3807), excess deferrals (Q 3760), and dividends paid on employer securities under IRC Section 404(k) (Q 3823).[3] Treasury Regulations Sections 1.402(c)-2, A-9, and 1.401(a)(31)-1 provide guidance on the treatment of plan loans for purposes of the rollover and withholding rules.

If a qualified retirement plan distributes an annuity contract to a participant, amounts paid under that contract are considered to be payments of the balance to the participant's credit and may be treated as eligible rollover distributions to the extent they would otherwise qualify. Therefore, a participant may surrender the annuity contract and treat the sum received as an eligible rollover distribution to the extent that it is includable in income and is not a required distribution under IRC Section 401(a)(9).[4] The IRS determined that a separate lump sum settlement payment to the widow of a plan participant who already was receiving monthly payments under the plan was eligible for rollover treatment under IRC Section 402(c)(4).[5]

---

1. IRC Sec. 402(c)(1).
2. IRC Secs. 402(c)(4), 457(e)(16).
3. Treas. Reg. §§1.402(c)-2, A-3, 1.402(c)-2, A-4.
4. Treas. Reg. §1.402(c)-2, A-10; Let. Rul. 9338041.
5. Let. Rul. 9718037.

A distribution of property other than money is treated the same. The amount transferred equals the property distributed.[1] A taxpayer may not retain property received in a distribution and simply rollover a cash amount representing the fair market value of the property.[2] Conversely, a taxpayer may not take cash received in a distribution, convert it into stock or any other type of investment, and then contribute the converted cash investment into an IRA as a rollover.[3] This rule applies to IRA and qualified retirement plan rollovers, including rollovers into Roth IRAs.

Where a distribution includes property and exceeds the rollover contribution, the participant, following a sale, may irrevocably designate the portion of the money received, and the portion of the proceeds of the sale, that are to be treated as included in the rollover and the portions that are to be deemed attributable to nondeductible employee contributions, if any. If the taxpayer fails to make a designation, allocations will be made on a ratable basis.[4] Under the basis recovery rules of IRC Section 72(e), nondeductible employee contributions are recovered first from amounts not rolled over.[5]

The IRS determined that a mistaken transfer by a broker of an otherwise eligible rollover distribution from a qualified plan into a brokerage account and then into an IRA failed to qualify as an eligible rollover and was includable in the taxpayer's gross income.[6] Taxpayers who were defrauded by their investment advisor of IRA distributions intended to be rollovers were not permitted to replace the stolen assets from other funds and treat the replacement assets as rollover contributions.[7]

The maximum amount that may be rolled over generally is the amount that would be includable in income if not rolled over.[8] After-tax contributions can be rolled over from a qualified plan to a traditional IRA or transferred in a direct trustee-to-trustee transfer to a defined contribution plan provided the plan separately accounts for after-tax contributions. After-tax contributions, including nondeductible contributions to a traditional IRA, may not be rolled over from a traditional IRA into a qualified plan, Section 403(b) tax sheltered annuity, or eligible Section 457 governmental plan.[9] Rollover amounts will be treated as first consisting of taxable amounts.[10]

Unless a rollover is carried out by means of a direct rollover, a rollover generally must be completed within 60 days after receipt of the distribution (Q 4015).[11] The IRS has the authority to waive the 60 day requirement where failure to waive it would be against equity or good conscience, including casualty, disaster, or other events beyond the reasonable control of the

---

1. IRC Sec. 402(c)(1)(C).
2. Rev. Rul. 87-77, 1987-2 CB 115.
3. *Lemishow v. Comm.*, 110 TC 110 (1998).
4. IRC Secs. 402(c)(6), 457(e)(16)(B).
5. Notice 87-13, 1987-1 CB 432, A-18; Let. Rul. 9043056.
6. Let. Rul. 9847031.
7. FSA 199933038.
8. IRC Secs. 402(c)(2), 457(e)(16)(B).
9. IRC Secs. 402(c)(2), 457(e)(16)(B).
10. See IRC Sec. 402(c)(2).
11. IRC Sec. 402(c)(3)(A), 457(e)(16)(B).

individual subject to the requirement.[1] The IRS has provided guidance on the requirements for a hardship waiver of the 60-day requirement.[2] See Q 4016 for a discussion of the new self-certification process that may allow a taxpayer to obtain a waiver of the 60-day time limit.

Unless a rollover is carried out by means of a direct rollover, the distribution amount will be subject to a mandatory income tax withholding rate of 20 percent (Q 4000, Q 4003).[3]

Rollover contributions may be divided among several traditional IRAs.[4] These may be either existing plans or plans newly created to receive the rollover (Q 4007). A traditional IRA inherited from someone who died after 1983, other than a deceased spouse, generally is ineligible to receive a rollover. If an individual retirement annuity is used, it may not be an endowment contract. Although property may normally be rolled over, a rollover to a traditional individual retirement account may not include a retirement income, endowment, or other life insurance contract because IRC Section 408(a)(3) prohibits investment of individual retirement account funds in life insurance contracts.[5] A rollover may be made from a qualified plan even though the participant is an active participant in another plan.

See Q 3998 for the new rules that allow a taxpayer to roll pre-tax and after-tax contributions into separate accounts in a single distribution.

3998. What new rules apply to allow a taxpayer to rollover pre-tax and after-tax contributions in a qualified plan into separate accounts in a single distribution?

Notice 2014-54 allows a distribution from an employer-sponsored retirement account to be treated as a single distribution even if it contains both pre-tax and after-tax contributions, and even if those contributions are rolled over into separate accounts, so long as the amounts are scheduled to be distributed at the same time. The guidance now allows the taxpayer to allocate pre-tax and after-tax contributions among different types of accounts in order to maximize their future earnings potential—avoiding the pro-rata tax treatment discussed below.

This creates a planning opportunity for higher income taxpayers who have sufficient funds so that they are able to make contributions in excess of the pre-tax limit ($19,500 in 2021). If the specific plan allows for after-tax contributions, these taxpayers can contribute after-tax dollars with the knowledge that those funds can be separated and rolled directly into a Roth upon exiting the employer-sponsored plan, without additional tax liability.

The new rules became effective for transactions scheduled to occur on or after January 1, 2015, but the IRS guidance allowed clients to rely on the rules as of their release on September 18, 2014.[6]

---

1. IRC Sec. 402(c)(3)(B).
2. See Rev. Proc. 2003-16, 2003-1 CB 359.
3. IRC Sec. 3405(c)(1).
4. See Rev. Rul. 79-265, 1979-2 CB 186; Let. Rul. 9331055.
5. Rev. Rul. 81-275, 1981-2 CB 92.
6. Notice 2014-54, 2014-41 IRB 670.

Prior regulations permitted a distribution to be rolled partly into a traditional account and partly into a Roth, but the taxpayer was required to treat the distribution as two separate distributions—meaning that the distribution to each account would be treated as coming partly from pre-tax contributions and partly from after-tax contributions.

So, for example, if the taxpayer's distribution of $100,000 consisted of $80,000 in pre-tax contributions and $20,000 in after-tax contributions, the taxpayer could direct that $80,000 be transferred to a traditional IRA and $20,000 to a Roth. However, the amount transferred to each account would be pro-rated (80 percent-20 percent) so that 80 percent of the Roth transfer would be taxed.

3999. What is an eligible retirement plan for purposes of the rollover rules?

The definition of "eligible retirement plan" depends on the plan from which a rollover is made. The availability of rollovers between various types of plans was considerably expanded by EGTRRA 2001.

An eligible retirement plan with respect to a distribution from a qualified plan means an IRA, another qualified plan, a Section 403(a) annuity, a Section 403(b) tax sheltered annuity, and an eligible Section 457 governmental plan (provided it agrees to separately account for funds received from any eligible retirement plan except another eligible Section 457 governmental plan).[1] For taxpayers wishing to preserve any capital gains or special averaging treatment (Q 3970), a distribution can be made to a conduit IRA and rolled back to another qualified plan. For this purpose, money from a qualified plan may not be commingled with other money (Q 4007).

Non-Roth IRAs (traditional, SEP, and SIMPLE). An eligible retirement plan with respect to a distribution from a non-Roth IRA (an individual retirement account or an individual retirement annuity) means an IRA, a qualified plan, a Section 403(a) annuity, an eligible Section 457 governmental plan (provided it agrees to separately account for funds received from any eligible retirement plan except another eligible Section 457 governmental plan), and a Section 403(b) tax sheltered annuity (Q 4007).[2] Amounts paid or distributed out of a SIMPLE IRA during the first two years of participation may be rolled over only to another SIMPLE IRA.[3] Prior to 2016, the only rollover permitted to a SIMPLE IRA was from another SIMPLE IRA. The PATH Act removed this restriction so that amounts from other types of retirement plans may be rolled into a SIMPLE IRA so long as the plan has existed for at least two years.

Roth IRAs. A distribution from a Roth IRA generally can be rolled over only to another Roth IRA. A rollover or conversion from a non-Roth IRA or other retirement plan into a Roth IRA generally is a taxable event (Q 3662).[4]

Section 403(b) annuity. An eligible retirement plan with respect to a distribution from a Section 403(b) tax sheltered annuity includes a non-Roth IRA, a qualified plan, a Section 403(a)

---

1.   IRC Secs. 402(c)(8), 402(c)(10).
2.   IRC Secs. 408(d)(3)(A), 402(c)(10).
3.   IRC Sec. 408(d)(3)(G).
4.   IRC Secs. 408A(e), 402(c)(8)(B).

annuity, an eligible Section 457 governmental plan (provided it agrees to separately account for funds received from any eligible retirement plan except another eligible Section 457 governmental plan), and another Section 403(b) annuity.[1]

Eligible Section 457 governmental plan. An eligible retirement plan with respect to a distribution from an eligible Section 457 governmental plan includes a non-Roth IRA, a qualified plan, a Section 403(a) annuity, another eligible Section 457 governmental plan and a Section 403(b) annuity.[2]

See Q 3998 for the new rules that allow a taxpayer to roll pre-tax and after-tax contributions into separate accounts in a single distribution.

4000. Must a participant receiving an eligible rollover distribution have the option of making a direct rollover to another qualified plan?

Yes.

A qualified plan, a Section 403(b) tax sheltered annuity, and an eligible Section 457 governmental plan must provide a participant receiving an eligible rollover distribution the option to have the distribution transferred in the form of a direct rollover to another eligible retirement plan.[3] This direct rollover option generally must be provided to any participant receiving a distribution.[4]

A direct rollover is defined as an eligible rollover distribution (Q 3997) that is paid directly to an eligible retirement plan (Q 3999) for the benefit of the distributee. A direct rollover may be accomplished by any reasonable means of direct payment, including the use of a wire transfer or a check that is negotiable only by the trustee of the eligible retirement plan.[5] Giving the check to the distributee for delivery to the eligible retirement plan is considered reasonable provided that the check is made payable to the trustee of the eligible retirement plan for the benefit of the distributee.[6] Certain amounts may be rolled over only in the form of a trustee-to-trustee transfer.[7] Plans are not required to accept rollovers, direct or otherwise.

If a participant's total distribution is expected to be less than $200, the participant need not be offered the option of a direct rollover. While a participant must be permitted to elect a direct rollover of only a portion of the distribution, a plan administrator may require that this direct rollover portion equal at least $500. In the case of Section 403(b) tax sheltered annuities, the payor of the eligible rollover distribution is treated as the plan administrator.

A plan administrator is not required to permit a participant to make a direct rollover of only a portion of the distribution if the full amount of the distribution totals less than $500.

---

1.   IRC Secs. 403(b)(8)(A)(ii), 402(c)(10).
2.   IRC Sec. 457(e)(16).
3.   IRC Secs. 401(a)(31), 403(b)(10), 457(d)(1)(C).
4.   Treas. Reg. §1.402(c)-2, A-1.
5.   Treas. Reg. §1.401(a)(31)-1, A-3.
6.   Treas. Reg. §1.401(a)(31)-1, A-4.
7.   See IRC Sec. 402(c)(2).

A plan administrator may permit a participant to divide his or her distribution into separate distributions to be paid to two or more eligible retirement plans in direct rollovers but is not required to do so.[1]

If an eligible rollover distribution from a qualified retirement plan, tax sheltered annuity, or eligible governmental 457 plan is not handled by means of a direct rollover, the distribution will be subject to a mandatory income tax withholding rate of 20 percent (Q 4003).[2]

Automatic Rollovers

Plans subject to the direct rollover rules are required to provide that a cash-out distribution (Q 3868) in excess of $1,000 and less than $5,000 will automatically be transferred to an individual retirement plan unless the distributee affirmatively elects to have it transferred to another eligible retirement plan or elects to receive it directly.

4001. Is there a safe harbor for plans that are subject to the direct rollover rules?

DOL regulations provide a safe harbor for plan fiduciaries who comply with certain requirements outlined below.[3]

To qualify for the safe harbor, a plan fiduciary generally must meet six conditions:

(1) The distribution must not exceed $5,000, not including balances rolled into the plan from another plan or an IRA. The safe harbor applies to balances of $1,000 or less, even though those balances are not subject to the automatic rollover rules;

(2) The distribution must be to an individual retirement account or annuity pursuant to a written agreement with the individual retirement plan provider that addresses the default investments and related fees and expenses;

(3) The distribution must be invested in a manner designed "to preserve principal and provide a reasonable rate of return, whether or not such return is guaranteed, consistent with liquidity." The investment must be offered by a state or federally regulated financial institution and must seek to maintain a stable dollar value (e.g., money market funds, interest-bearing savings accounts, certificates of deposit, and stable value products);

(4) The fees and expenses charged to the IRA may not be higher than fees charged by the IRA trustee or custodian for other rollover IRAs;

(5) The summary plan description provided to plan participants must provide an explanation of the plan's automatic rollover provisions, including an explanation

---

1. Treas. Reg. §1.401(a)(31)-1, A-2, A-9 to A-11.
2. IRC Sec. 3405(c)(1).
3. Labor Reg. §2550.404a-2; IRC Sec. 401(a)(31)(B); EGTRRA 2001, Sec. 657(a).

of the expenses and default investments in the rollover IRA and a plan contact for further information; and

(6)   The selection of the IRA custodian or trustee and investment options must not result in a prohibited transaction under ERISA Section 406. The DOL has finalized a class exemption that will allow financial institutions to establish IRAs for their own employees.

4002. What notice requirements must a plan satisfy if it is subject to the direct rollover rules?

Under IRC Section 402(f), a plan administrator, within a reasonable time before a distribution is made, must provide the recipient of the distribution with a written explanation of the options available for transferring the funds. The explanation must include the provisions under which the recipient may have the funds transferred by means of a direct rollover and under which circumstances the income tax withholding requirements will apply. Where applicable, the notice must explain that the automatic rollover rules apply to certain distributions.[1]

With respect to qualified plans and eligible Section 457 governmental plans, the notice generally must be given no fewer than 30 days and no more than 90 days before the date of distribution. If the recipient elects a distribution, the plan will not fail to comply with these notice requirements merely because the distribution is made fewer than 30 days after notice is given if the plan administrator provides information to the recipient that clearly indicates that he or she has the opportunity to consider the direct rollover decision for at least 30 days after receiving notice.[2] With respect to Section 403(b) annuities, Treasury Regulation Section 1.402(f)-1, A-2, is not applicable in determining what is considered to be a reasonable time for providing the notice. The payor of a Section 403(b) annuity will be deemed to have provided the explanation within a reasonable time if it complies with the time period in this section of the regulations.[3]

The IRS has issued two safe harbor explanations that plan administrators may use to satisfy the notice requirements of IRC Section 402(f).[4]

The explanations may be provided to recipients of eligible rollover distributions from an employer plan in order to satisfy IRC Section 402(f). The first safe harbor explanation applies to a distribution not from a designated Roth account (as described in IRC Section 402A). The second safe harbor explanation applies to a distribution from a designated Roth account. These safe harbor explanations update the safe harbor explanations that were published in Notice 2002-3, 2002-1 CB 289, to reflect changes in the law. These safe harbor explanations also reorganize and simplify the presentation of the information.

The IRS recently amended the safe harbor notices to reflect recent tax law changes. The updated notice identifies several types of new distributions that are not eligible for rollover. Those

---

1.   IRC Secs. 402(f), 457(e)(16)(B).
2.   Treas. Reg. §1.402(f)-1, A-2.
3.   Treas. Reg. §1.402(f)-1, A-2.
4.   Notice 2009-68; 2009-2 CB 423, Notice 2014-74, modifying Notice 2008-68; 2009-2 CB 423.

include: (1) qualified birth or adoption distributions (newly available under the SECURE Act, (2) RMDs (now starting at age 72) and (3) CARES Act distributions taken during 2020.[1]

The IRS has issued final regulations that permit the use of electronic media to satisfy the IRC Section 402(f) notice requirements. Under the regulations, notice may be provided either in written form on paper or through an electronic medium. Any electronic notice issued must use a medium that is reasonably accessible to the participant such as email or a plan website. The participant may request the notice on a paper document that must be provided free of charge.[2]

4003. If a rollover is not made through a direct rollover, must income tax be withheld from the distribution?

Distributions from qualified retirement plans, tax sheltered annuities, and eligible Section 457 governmental plans are subject to a mandatory income tax withholding rate of 20 percent unless the transfer is handled by means of a direct rollover.[3] An employee receiving a distribution may not elect out of the withholding requirement. Distributions from traditional IRAs are not subject to mandatory 20 percent withholding (Q 3674).

If a participant's total distribution is expected to be less than $200, the participant need not be offered the option of a direct rollover.[4]

If a participant receives an eligible rollover distribution that is subject to the 20 percent withholding rate, the 20 percent withheld will be includable in income to the extent required by IRC Sections 402(a), 403(b)(1), or 457(a)(1)(A), even if the participant rolls over the remaining 80 percent of the distribution within the 60 day period (Q 4015).

Because the amount withheld is considered to be an amount distributed under those sections, the participant may add an amount equal to the 20 percent withheld to the 80 percent he or she has received, resulting in a rollover of the full distribution amount.

The 10 percent early or premature distribution penalty (Q 3677, Q 4073) may apply to the amount withheld where only the remaining 80 percent of the distribution is rolled over from a qualified plan or a Section 403(b) plan.[5]

A distribution from an eligible Section 457 governmental plan is treated as an early distribution from a qualified plan only to the extent that it represents funds rolled over from a qualified plan, a Section 403(b) plan, or a traditional IRA.[6]

Where a distributee elects to transfer a portion of the distribution by a direct rollover and receive the remainder, the 20 percent withholding requirement applies only to the portion of

1.   Notice 2020-62.
2.   Treas. Reg. §1.402(f)-1, A-5.
3.   IRC Secs. 3405(c)(1), 457(e)(16)(B).
4.   Treas. Reg. §1.401(a)(31)-1, A-11.
5.   Treas. Reg. §§1.402(c)-2, A-11, 1.403(b)-2, A-1.
6.   IRC Sec. 72(t)(9).

the distribution that the distributee actually receives. It does not apply to the portion of the distribution that is transferred directly to another eligible retirement plan.[1]

In calculating the amount to be withheld, there are special rules if the distribution includes employer stock, other property, or a deemed distribution of a plan loan balance.[2]

4004. May an individual who is not a participant in a qualified plan roll over amounts received from the plan by reason of a divorce or separation agreement?

Yes, if the agreement is a qualified domestic relations order ("QDRO") and certain requirements are met.[3]

A QDRO is a decree or judgment under state domestic relations law that recognizes or creates the right of a spouse or child to receive, or to have set aside, a portion of a participant's interest in a qualified plan, 403(b) plan, or eligible Section 457 governmental plan (Q 3914, Q 3584).[4]

If an alternate payee who is the spouse or former spouse of the participant receives a distribution by reason of a QDRO, the rollover rules apply to the alternate payee as if the alternate payee were the participant.[5] Thus, the alternate payee can avoid the requirement of including the distribution in income to the extent any portion of an eligible rollover distribution is directly rolled over or rolled over to an eligible retirement plan within 60 days.[6]

A qualified retirement plan may be an eligible retirement plan for an alternate payee who is a spouse or former spouse of the participant and who receives the distribution by reason of a QDRO.[7] This kind of rollover must be handled through a direct rollover to avoid a mandatory income tax withholding rate of 20 percent (Q 4000, Q 4003).[8] There are separate rules applicable to surviving spouses (Q 4013).

QDRO rules do not apply to IRAs. An IRA, however, can be transferred tax-free in connection with a divorce if the correct procedure is followed. In such cases, the transfer of an individual's interest in an IRA or an individual retirement annuity to a spouse or former spouse under a divorce or separation instrument is not considered a taxable transfer made by the individual, and such interest at the time of the transfer is treated as the spouse's IRA and not such individual's IRA. Thereafter the account or annuity will be treated as maintained for the benefit of the spouse.[9]

1.   Treas. Reg. §31.3405(c)-1, A-6.
2.   IRC Sec. 3405(e)(8).
3.   Let. Ruls. 9109052, 8744023, 8712066, 8608055.
4.   IRC Secs. 414(p)(1)(A), 414(p)(12).
5.   IRC Sec. 402(e)(1).
6.   IRC Sec. 402(c)(1).
7.   See IRC Sec. 402(e)(1)(B).
8.   IRC Sec. 3405(c)(1).
9.   IRC Sec. 408(d)(6).

4005. May a participant who receives a distribution of an annuity from a qualified pension or profit sharing plan surrender the annuity and roll over the proceeds?

Where a qualified pension or profit sharing plan distributes an ordinary annuity contract, deferred or otherwise, to a participant, the annuity contract or cash amount received on surrender of the contract may be rolled over if the distribution is an eligible rollover distribution and meets the requirements necessary for rollover of such a distribution (Q 3997).[1] For purposes of the 60 day rule, the distribution takes place on distribution of the annuity contract from the plan, not on its surrender or transfer to the receiving plan (Q 4015).[2]

4006. When may a participant roll over permitted distributions from a Section 403(b) tax sheltered annuity?

For distributions received from tax sheltered annuities, any portion of the balance to the credit of an employee that is paid to the employee in the form of an eligible rollover distribution (Q 3997) and transferred to an eligible retirement plan (Q 3999) is not includable in income by the employee. Rollover distributions from tax sheltered annuities may be made to another tax sheltered annuity, an IRA, a qualified plan, a Section 403(a) plan, and an eligible Section 457 governmental plan (provided the IRC Section 457 plan agrees to separately account for such funds).[3] A rollover to a Roth IRA generally is a taxable event (Q 3662).

A trustee-to-trustee transfer from a Section 403(b) plan to a defined benefit governmental plan that is used to purchase permissive service credits will be excluded from income.[4] The Tax Court has disallowed rollover treatment for such a transfer.[5] A proper rollover was not achieved where a taxpayer invested a tax sheltered annuity distribution in a certificate of deposit.[6]

Distributions excepted from the term eligible rollover distribution include any:

(1)   distribution that is part of a series of substantially equal payments made over the life or life expectancy of the employee or the joint lives or life expectancies of the employee and his or her designated beneficiary,

(2)   distribution made for a specified period of 10 years or more,

(3)   distribution that is a required minimum distribution under IRC Section 401(a)(9), and

(4)   hardship distribution.[7]

---

1.   IRC Sec. 402(c).
2.   See Let. Ruls. 8014034, 8035054.
3.   IRC Secs. 402(c)(1), 403(b)(8).
4.   IRC Sec. 403(b)(13).
5.   See *Tolliver v. Comm.*, TC Memo 1991-460.
6.   *Adamcewicz v. Comm.*, TC Memo 1994-361.
7.   IRC Secs. 402(c)(4), 408(b)(8)(B).

Regulations specify other items not considered to be eligible rollover distributions, including any portion of a distribution excludable from gross income (although this has been modified by subsequent legislation), the Table 2001 or P.S. 58 cost of life insurance (Q 4060), and corrective distributions of excess deferrals (Q 4046) and excess employer matching contributions (Q 4037).[1] Treasury Regulation Sections 1.402(c)-2, A-9, and 1.401(a)(31)-1 provide guidance on the treatment of plan loans for purposes of the rollover and withholding rules.

A distribution of property other than money is treated the same way. The amount transferred equals the value of the property distributed.[2]

The maximum amount that may be rolled over generally is the amount that would be includable in income if not rolled over.[3] After-tax contributions can be rolled over to a traditional IRA or transferred in a direct trustee-to-trustee transfer to a defined contribution plan, provided the plan separately accounts for after-tax contributions. After-tax contributions, including nondeductible contributions to a traditional IRA, may not be rolled over from a traditional IRA into a qualified plan, Section 403(b) tax sheltered annuity, or eligible Section 457 governmental plan. Rollover amounts will be treated as first consisting of taxable amounts.[4]

See Q 3998 for the new rules that allow a taxpayer to roll pre-tax and after-tax contributions into separate accounts in a single distribution.

The IRS has indicated that a direct rollover may not be made of amounts that are not eligible for distribution from a Section 403(b) annuity due to the distribution restrictions of IRC Section 403(b)(11) (i.e., distributions payable only when the employee attains age 59½, dies, or becomes disabled). These amounts may be transferred between tax sheltered annuities if the requirements of the regulations can be met.[5]

Reaching a similar conclusion, a federal district court held that funds in a tax sheltered annuity attributable to a salary reduction agreement were not eligible for rollover treatment unless the requirements of IRC Section 403(b)(11) were satisfied (Q 4034).[6]

Funds subject to distribution requirements may be transferable to another tax sheltered annuity in a direct transfer (Q 4056). A deemed distribution under IRC Section 72(p) is not eligible to be rolled over to an eligible retirement plan.[7]

If funds are not distributed in a direct rollover, a rollover generally must be completed within 60 days after the distribution is received (Q 4015).[8] The IRS has the authority to waive the 60 day requirement where failure to waive it would be against equity or good conscience,

---

1.   Treas. Reg. §§1.402(c)-2, A-3 & A-4, 1.403(b)-2, A-1.
2.   IRC Sec. 402(c)(1)(C).
3.   IRC Sec. 402(c)(2).
4.   IRC Secs. 402(c)(2), 403(b)(8)(B).
5.   Treas. Reg. §1.403(b)-10.
6.   *Frank v. Aaronson*, 1996 U.S. Dist. LEXIS 15617.
7.   Treas. Reg. §1.72(p)-1, A-12.
8.   IRC Sec. 402(c)(3).

including casualty, disaster, or other events beyond the reasonable control of the individual subject to the requirement.[1] Guidance on the requirements for this hardship waiver has been issued.[2]

Unless a rollover is done by means of a direct rollover, the distribution amount will be subject to a mandatory income tax withholding rate of 20 percent (Q 4000, Q 4003).[3]

4007. When may rollover contributions be made from an IRA by the owner of the plan?

It depends on the type of individual retirement plan owned and the source from which the funds in the plan originated.

No rollover from a traditional or Roth IRA is permitted if the individual for whose benefit the plan is maintained acquired the plan by reason of the death of another individual (i.e., in the case of an inherited plan) who died after 1983. This does not apply where the plan is maintained for the benefit of the surviving spouse of the deceased individual. This rule also does not prohibit a trustee-to-trustee transfer to an identically-titled beneficiary IRA.[4]

A qualified rollover contribution may be made from a Roth IRA to another Roth IRA or from a traditional IRA to a Roth IRA. A qualified rollover contribution means a rollover contribution to a Roth IRA from another Roth IRA or from a traditional IRA but only if the rollover contribution meets the requirements discussed in Q 4011.[5] Special rules apply to rollovers of traditional IRAs to Roth IRAs (Q 3662).

For tax years prior to 2008, no rollover contribution from a tax sheltered annuity or a qualified plan, other than a designated Roth account (Q 3778), could be made to a Roth IRA, and, thus, no rollover contribution could be made from a Roth IRA to a tax sheltered annuity or to a qualified plan other than to a designated Roth account.[6]

A distribution from a designated Roth account may be rolled over to another designated Roth account of the individual from whose account the payment or distribution was made or to a Roth IRA of the individual.[7] Beginning in 2008, a direct rollover or conversion may be made from a qualified plan, a tax sheltered annuity, or a Section 457 eligible governmental plan to a Roth IRA (Q 3662).

A rollover may be made from one SIMPLE IRA (Q 3706) to another SIMPLE IRA, but a rollover from a SIMPLE IRA to a traditional IRA or to a Roth IRA is permitted only in the case of distributions to which the 25 percent early distribution penalty does not apply; the penalty generally applies during the first two years of participation (Q 3968).[8] Prior to 2016,

---

1.   IRC Sec. 402(c)(3)(B).
2.   See Rev. Proc. 2003-16, 2003-1 CB 359.
3.   IRC Secs. 403(b)(10), 3405(c)(1).
4.   IRC Secs. 408(d)(3)(C), 408A(a).
5.   IRC Sec. 408A(e).
6.   See IRC Sec. 408A(c)(5)(A).
7.   IRC Sec. 402A(c)(3).
8.   IRC Secs. 408(d)(3)(G), 408A(a); Treas. Reg. §1.408A-4, A-4.

the only rollover permitted to a SIMPLE IRA was from another SIMPLE IRA. The PATH Act removed this restriction so that amounts from other types of retirement plans may be rolled into a SIMPLE IRA so long as the plan has existed for at least two years. To the extent that an employee is no longer participating in a SIMPLE IRA plan and two years have expired since the employee first participated in the plan, the employee may treat the SIMPLE IRA account as a traditional IRA.[1]

Once in a lifetime, a taxpayer may make a qualified HSA funding distribution (Q 411).[2]

4008. When may rollover contributions be made from an IRA to a qualified retirement plan?

An individual generally may receive a distribution from his or her traditional IRA and, to the extent that the distribution would be includable in income if not rolled over, the individual may roll it over within 60 days into a qualified pension, profit sharing, or stock bonus plan.[3] After-tax contributions including nondeductible contributions to a traditional IRA may not be rolled over from a traditional IRA into a qualified plan.[4]

The IRS may waive the 60 day rollover requirement if failure to waive it would be against equity or good conscience, including casualty, disaster, or other events beyond the reasonable control of the individual subject to the requirement (Q 4015).[5]

An IRA owner who mixes a rollover contribution from a qualified plan with funds from other sources will forfeit any capital gain or special averaging treatment that otherwise might have been available for the qualified plan money.[6]

A terminated vested employee who rolled over her account balance to an IRA and began receiving substantially equal periodic payments from the IRA was permitted to roll over the remaining IRA account balance back into her employer's plan when she returned to her former job.[7]

A surviving spouse who receives a distribution from a qualified plan and rolls it over into a traditional IRA is subject to the same treatment as would be applied to the employee (Q 4013).[8]

4009. When may rollover contributions be made from an IRA to a tax sheltered annuity?

An individual may receive a distribution from his or her traditional IRA and within 60 days roll it over into a tax sheltered annuity to the extent that the distribution would be includable

---

1.   General Explanation of Tax Legislation Enacted in the 104th Congress (JCT-12-96), p. 141 (the Blue Book).
2.   IRC Sec. 408(d)(9).
3.   IRC Sec. 408(d)(3)(A).
4.   IRC Sec. 402(c)(2).
5.   IRC Sec. 402(c)(3)(B); Rev. Proc. 2003-16, 2003-1 CB 359.
6.   See EGTRRA 2001, Secs. 641(f)(3), 642(c)(2); see Let. Rul. 8433078.
7.   Let. Rul. 9818055.
8.   IRC Sec. 402(c)(9).

in income if not rolled over.[1] After-tax contributions including nondeductible contributions to a traditional IRA may not be rolled over from a traditional IRA into a Section 403(b) tax sheltered annuity.[2]

The IRS may waive the 60-day rollover requirement if failure to waive it would be against equity or good conscience, including in the event of a casualty, disaster, or other event beyond the reasonable control of the individual subject to the requirement (Q 4015). In determining whether to grant a waiver, the IRS considers (1) certain errors committed by a financial institution; (2) inability to complete a rollover due to death, disability, hospitalization, incarceration, restrictions imposed by a foreign country, or postal error; (3) the use of the amount distributed (for example, in the case of payment by check, whether the check was cashed); and (4) the time elapsed since the distribution occurred.

See Q 4016 for a discussion of the new self-certification process that can allow a taxpayer to obtain a waiver of the 60-day time limit.

4010. When may rollover contributions be made from an IRA to an IRC Section 457 plan?

An individual may receive a distribution from his or her traditional IRA and within 60 days roll it over into an eligible Section 457 governmental plan to the extent that the distribution would be includable in income if not rolled over.[3] The Section 457 plan must agree to separately account for the funds.[4] After-tax contributions including nondeductible contributions to a traditional IRA may not be rolled over from a traditional IRA into an eligible Section 457 governmental plan.[5]

The IRS may waive the 60 day rollover requirement if failure to waive it would be against equity or good conscience, including upon the occurrence of a casualty, disaster, or other event beyond the reasonable control of the individual subject to the requirement (Q 4015).[6]

4011. When may rollover contributions be made from an IRA to another IRA?

An owner of a traditional IRA (other than a SIMPLE IRA during the first two years of participation (Q 3709)) may receive a distribution of any amount from it and within 60 days roll that amount, or any part of that amount, over into any other traditional IRA (i.e., a receiving plan).[7] Likewise, an owner of a Roth IRA may receive such a distribution from it and within 60 days roll that amount, or any part of that amount, over into any other Roth IRA.[8] Under previous rules, the only rollover permitted to a SIMPLE IRA was from another SIMPLE IRA.

1.   IRC Secs. 408(d)(3)(A), 402(c)(8)(B)(vi).
2.   IRC Secs. 402(c)(2), 403(b)(8)(B).
3.   IRC Secs. 408(d)(3)(A), 402(c)(8)(B)(v).
4.   IRC Sec. 402(c)(10).
5.   IRC Secs. 402(c)(2), 457(e)(16).
6.   IRC Sec. 402(c)(3); Rev. Proc. 2003-16, 2003-1 CB 359.
7.   IRC Sec. 408(d)(3).
8.   IRC Secs. 408(d)(3), 408A(a), 408A(e).

However, the Protecting Americans from Tax Hikes Act of 2015 (PATH) modified these rules to permit a taxpayer to roll over funds from an employer-sponsored retirement plan (such as a 401(k)) to a SIMPLE IRA as long as the taxpayer has participated in the SIMPLE IRA plan for at least two years.[1] A Roth IRA generally can be rolled over only to another Roth IRA.

The IRS is authorized to waive the 60 day rollover requirement where failure to waive it would be against equity or good conscience, including upon the occurrence of a casualty, disaster, or other event beyond the reasonable control of the individual subject to the requirement (Q 4015).[2]

The owner, for purposes of these rules, includes a spouse who has made a rollover (Q 4013). The receiving plan may be an existing plan or one newly created, but an endowment contract or an individual retirement plan inherited from a decedent who died after 1983, other than a deceased spouse, may not be used as a receiving individual retirement plan.

The distributing plan or any other eligible retirement plan (Q 3999) may receive any or all of the distribution as a rollover amount.[3] Mixing of funds from different sources in a single traditional IRA will not prevent further rollover to another eligible retirement plan, but it will prevent the owner from preserving any capital gains or special averaging treatment (Q 3970) available on a plan distribution.[4]

Only one rollover from a traditional IRA to any other traditional IRA or from a particular Roth IRA to any other Roth IRA may be made in any one-year period.[5] Trustee-to-trustee transfers are not considered rollovers for this purpose.

Until recently, the IRS applied this limitation separately to each IRA.[6] However, the Tax Court disagreed with the IRS' interpretation of the rule and found that each taxpayer is limited to one nontaxable IRA rollover contribution per one-year period, even though the taxpayer may own multiple IRAs and take only a single distribution from each IRA. The Tax Court examined the wording of IRC Section 408(d)(3)(B) and found that the prohibition against multiple nontaxable rollover transactions in a single year was not specific to any particular IRA held by a taxpayer, but instead applied to all IRAs maintained by a taxpayer.[7]

The IRS has since indicated that it will follow the Tax Court's decision in this case.[8] Therefore, the limitation will now be imposed on an aggregate basis, rather than on an IRA-by-IRA basis.

1.	See IRC Sec. 408(p)(1)(B).
2.	IRC Sec. 402(c)(3)(B); Rev. Proc. 2003-16, 2003-1 CB 359.
3.	See IRC Sec. 402(c)(8)(B).
4.	See EGTRRA 2001, Secs. 641(f)(3), 642(c)(2).
5.	See IRC Secs. 408(d)(3)(B), 408A(a).
6.	See IRS Pub. 590 (2013).
7.	*Bobrow v. Commissioner*, TC Memo 2014-21.
8.	Ann. 2014-15, 2014-16 IRB 1.

The one year lookback limitation of IRC Section 408(d)(3)(B) applies only to distributions from an individual retirement plan; a rollover from a qualified plan to an IRA is not counted.[1] Also, a rollover from a traditional IRA to a Roth IRA does not count towards this limit.[2]

Payment of an arbitration award, designed to replace wasted IRA assets, into a new individual retirement account was a valid rollover.[3] Likewise, a court-ordered payment of the diminished value of an IRA resulting from the investment company's error was eligible for rollover treatment.[4]

4012. Can a required minimum distribution (RMD) from an IRA be rolled over into another account?

A required minimum distribution from an IRA is not eligible for rollover. If a minimum distribution is required for a calendar year, any amounts distributed during a calendar year from an IRA are first treated as the required minimum distribution for the year.

Planning Point: The portion of a distribution that is a required minimum distribution from an IRA, and so not eligible for rollover, is determined in the same manner as provided for distributions from qualified plans. For example, if a minimum distribution is required under IRC Section 401(a)(9) for a calendar year, an amount distributed during a calendar year from an IRA is treated as a required minimum distribution to the extent that the total required minimum distribution for the year under Section 401(a)(9) for that IRA has not been satisfied.[5]

4013. May a surviving spouse make a rollover contribution?

Yes.

Where any portion of an eligible distribution from a qualified plan is paid to the spouse of a participant after that participant's death, the spouse may make a rollover contribution of all or any part of that portion within 60 days of receipt.[6] The IRS is authorized to waive the 60 day rule under certain circumstances (Q 4015).

A qualified plan, a traditional IRA, a Roth IRA (Q 3662), a tax sheltered annuity, or an eligible Section 457 governmental plan that agrees to separately account for funds received from any eligible retirement plan except another eligible Section 457 governmental plan is treated as an eligible retirement plan with respect to a surviving spouse.[7] In other words, a surviving spouse may roll over an eligible distribution into his or her own plan account, provided the plan accepts rollover contributions.[8]

The other rules applicable to rollovers in general apply to rollovers by a deceased participant's spouse (Q 3999, Q 4000, Q 4003, Q 4006, Q 4015).[9] Thus, unless a spouse elects the

1.   Let. Rul. 8745054.
2.   See IRC Sec. 408A(e).
3.   Let. Rul. 8739034.
4.   Let. Rul. 8814063.
5.   Treas. Reg. §1.408-8, A-4.
6.   IRC Sec. 402(c)(9).
7.   IRC Secs. 402(c)(9), 402(c)(10).
8.   See Treas. Reg. §1.402(c)-2, A-11.
9.   IRC Secs. 402(c)(9), 403(a)(4), 403(b)(8).

direct rollover option, the distribution will be subject to mandatory withholding at 20 percent (Q 4003).

Planning Point: An IRA beneficiary who is a surviving spouse has the option of rolling over a distribution to his or her own IRA. If the surviving spouse exercises the rollover option and is under age 59½, then future distributions from the IRA before the surviving spouse reaches age 59½ will be subject to the 10 percent tax, whereas distributions directly from the deceased spouse's IRA would not. The surviving spouse's need for distributions before age 59½ is one factor in the rollover decision. *Martin Silfen, J.D., Brown Brothers, Harriman Trust Co., LLC.*

Because the surviving spouse of an owner of a traditional IRA is not subject to the inherited account rules, the surviving spouse may make rollovers to and from the plan.[1] This generally has held true whether the spouse was the beneficiary designated under the plan or inherited the account as sole beneficiary of the owner's estate.[2]

Furthermore, a proper rollover was considered made by a surviving spouse who, as her deceased husband's executrix, transferred the right to receive the benefits due her husband from his profit sharing plan to herself under the residuary bequest in the husband's will and then transferred this amount into an IRA already established on her behalf.[3]

In a number of private rulings during the 1990s, the IRS stated that if a decedent's IRA or tax sheltered annuity passed through a third party, such as a trust, and then was distributed to the decedent's surviving spouse, the spouse was treated as acquiring the IRA or tax sheltered annuity from the trust rather than from the decedent; thus, no rollover was possible.[4]

The IRS also determined on several occasions that if the trustee had no discretion as to the allocation of IRA proceeds to a trust or the payment of the proceeds directly to the surviving spouse, the surviving spouse would be treated as having acquired the IRA proceeds from the decedent rather than from the trust. In other words, a rollover was possible.[5]

In numerous rulings, the IRS has treated a surviving spouse as having acquired the IRA from the decedent and not the trust where the surviving spouse had the power to revoke the trust.[6]

The preamble to the 2002 final regulations under IRC Section 401(a)(9) (Q 3891) clarifies that if a surviving spouse receives a distribution from a deceased spouse's IRA, the spouse is permitted to roll that distribution over within 60 days into an IRA in the spouse's own name to the extent that the distribution is not a required distribution, regardless of whether or not the spouse is the sole beneficiary of the IRA owner.[7] In other words, it appears that for rollover purposes, the final regulations were intended to put to rest the distinction between trusts that provide discretion to the surviving spouse and those that do not.

---

1.   See IRC Sec. 408(d)(3)(C).
2.   See e.g., Let. Ruls. 9820010, 9502042, 9402023, 8925048.
3.   Let. Rul. 9351041.
4.   See e.g., Let. Ruls. 9515041, 9427035, 9416045.
5.   See e.g., Let. Ruls. 200324059, 9813018, 9649045, 9533042, 9445029, 201430026, 201430029.
6.   Let. Ruls. 199910067, 9815050, 9721028, 9427035.
7.   See TD 8987, 67 Fed. Reg. 18988 (4-17-02).

The surviving spouse does not receive a stepped up basis with respect to the decedent's plan interest or tax sheltered annuity, as retirement benefits are treated as income in respect of a decedent.[1]

4014. May a surviving non-spouse beneficiary make a rollover contribution?

Yes.

Beginning for distributions in 2008, a non-spouse designated beneficiary of a qualified plan, a tax sheltered annuity, or an eligible Section 457 governmental plan may make a direct rollover into an inherited IRA, including a Roth IRA (Q 3662).[2] The rollover must be made by means of a trustee-to-trustee transfer. The transfer will be treated as an eligible rollover distribution.[3] Distributions to non-spouse beneficiaries prior to 2008 were not eligible rollover distributions.

An inherited IRA created under this provision must remain in the name of the owner of the original retirement account payable to the designated beneficiary. The IRA is subject to required minimum distributions as for any IRA payable to a designated beneficiary (Q 3687).

4015. How is the 60-day time limit on rollovers applied?

Once a distribution eligible for rollover treatment is received by a participant, the participant must make the rollover contribution within 60 days.[4] If more than one distribution is received by an employee from a qualified plan during a taxable year, the 60-day rule applies separately to each distribution.[5]

The IRS has the authority to waive the 60-day requirement where failure to waive it would be against equity or good conscience, including casualty, disaster, or other events beyond the reasonable control of the individual subject to the requirement.[6]

The IRS has issued guidelines for requesting a waiver of the 60-day requirement.[7] Under the guidelines, a taxpayer may request a private letter ruling from the IRS waiving a failure to meet the 60-day requirement. The IRS will consider "all relevant facts and circumstances," such as whether financial institutions committed any errors; whether an incomplete rollover was due to death, disability, hospitalization, incarceration, or postal error; how an amount distributed was used by the taxpayer, including whether a check was cashed; and how much time has elapsed since the distribution. The guidelines grant automatic waivers in cases where the failure to timely complete a rollover is "solely due to an error on the part of the financial institution." If the taxpayer followed the institution's required procedures within the 60-day rollover period, and the error is ultimately corrected within one year of the distribution, no waiver request is necessary.

1.   IRC Sec. 691; Treas. Reg. §1.691(a)-1.
2.   Notice 2008-30, 2008-1 CB 638, A-7.
3.   IRC Sec. 402(c)(11).
4.   IRC Sec. 402(c)(3).
5.   Treas. Reg. §1.402(c)-2, A-11.
6.   IRC Sec. 402(c)(3)(B).
7.   See Rev. Proc. 2003-16, 2003-1 CB 359.

The IRS has liberally applied the new guidelines, granting waivers for alcohol and drug treatment, blizzards, bank errors, dementia, health problems, hurricanes, mistakes of fact including confusing an IRA distribution for a life insurance or annuity payment, and mistakes of law including not understanding the tax consequences of the distribution.[1] The IRS has denied waivers where a taxpayer used a distribution as a short term loan and made no actual attempt to roll over the distribution within the 60-day limit.[2]

Prior to EGTRRA 2001, no waivers of the 60-day time limit were permitted, even where the failure to meet it was the result of mistake, erroneous advice, the inaction of third parties, or reliance on prior rulings by the IRS itself.[3]

Where a stock certificate representing the participant's distribution was sent by registered mail but the participant was away from home, the 60-day period did not begin until the taxpayer signed the registered mail claim check at the post office and took physical receipt of the stock distribution.[4] Likewise, the 60-day period began on the taxpayer's receipt of a distribution check even though the check had been issued 10 months earlier but delivery was delayed because of an incorrect address.[5]

The 60-day period does not include any period during which the amount transferred to the individual is a frozen deposit that cannot be withdrawn because of the bankruptcy or insolvency of the financial institution or any state-imposed requirement based on the bankruptcy or insolvency or threat of bankruptcy or insolvency of institutions in the state. Also, the 60-day period will not be considered to expire any earlier than 10 days after the account ceases to be frozen.[6]

The inclusion of a distribution as income is not deferred into another calendar year merely because the 60-day rollover period extends into the succeeding year.[7]

A timely rollover occurred where a corrective bookkeeping entry was made after the 60-day period but, based on the facts of the case; the Tax Court concluded that the transfer itself actually had occurred within the required period.[8]

A letter ruling waived the 60-day rollover period for transfers between IRAs where a financial institution was closed on the sixtieth day, a Sunday, and the rollover was completed on the following day.[9] See Q 4016 for a discussion of the new self-certification process that can allow taxpayers to obtain a waiver of the 60-day time limit.

1.   Let. Ruls. 200611038, 200610025, 200606053, 200606052.
2.   Let. Ruls. 200544027, 200544030.
3.   See e.g., *Orgera v. Comm.*, TC Memo 1995-575; Let. Ruls. 9826036, 9211035, 9145036.
4.   Let. Rul. 8804014.
5.   Let. Rul. 8833043.
6.   IRC Secs. 402(c)(7)(A), 403(a)(4)(B), 403(b)(8)(B), 408(d)(3)(F), 457(e)(16)(B).
7.   *Robinson v. Comm.*, TC Memo 1996-517.
8.   *Wood v. Comm.*, 93 TC 114 (1989).
9.   Let. Rul. 200930052.

4016. What is the self-certification process that can potentially allow individuals to obtain a waiver of the 60-day time limit on rollovers?

In the past, an individual was required to obtain a private letter ruling from the IRS in order to obtain a waiver of the 60-day time limit on retirement plan rollovers, as discussed in Q 4015. The IRS has now developed a process designed to help individuals who receive retirement plan distributions, but miss the 60-day deadline. Revenue Procedure 2016-47 contains a self-certification process that can allow these individuals to qualify for a waiver of the time limit and potential penalties if one or more of 11 potential circumstances apply.

Some of the circumstances that can qualify a taxpayer for a waiver via self-certification include the following:

(1)   An error was committed by the financial institution receiving the contribution or making the distribution to which the contribution relates.

(2)   The distribution check was misplaced and never cashed.

(3)   The taxpayer's principal residence was severely damaged.

(4)   A member of the taxpayer's family died.

(5)   The taxpayer or a member of his or her family was severely ill.

(6)   A postal error occurred.

(7)   Restrictions were imposed by a foreign country.

(8)   The distribution was deposited into and remained in an account that the taxpayer mistakenly believed was an eligible retirement plan.

(9)   The taxpayer was incarcerated.

(10)   The distribution was made on account of a levy under IRC Section 6331 and the proceeds of the levy have been returned to the taxpayer.

(11)   The party making the distribution to which the rollover relates delayed providing information that the receiving plan or IRA required in order to complete the rollover, despite the taxpayer's reasonable efforts to obtain that information.

The rollover must be made as soon as practicable after the reason that prevented the rollover no longer applies (a 30-day safe harbor period exists).

The IRS has provided a form certification letter that may be used word for word (or a substantially similar letter may be used) and provided to the plan administrator or IRA trustee. The plan administrator or IRA trustee may rely on the taxpayer's self-certification unless he or she has actual knowledge that the self-certification is false. The IRS may still determine that the taxpayer does not qualify for a waiver, but the taxpayer is entitled to report the contribution as a valid rollover unless it is informed otherwise by the IRS.[1]

---

1.   Rev. Proc. 2016-47.

4017. May an individual who has attained age 70½ make a rollover?

Editor's Note: The SECURE Act now permits taxpayers to make contributions to traditional IRAs at any age.

Although there was considerable confusion on this issue at one time, it now seems clear that rollovers may be made to traditional IRAs as long as the minimum distribution requirements are met (Q 3682 to Q 3698).[1] Rollovers, as well as contributions, may be made to Roth IRAs by individuals at any age.

It appears that the same rationale also permits rollovers to qualified plans and Section 403(b) tax sheltered annuities after age 72 if minimum distribution requirements are met (Q 3891 to Q 3907, Q 4074 to Q 4083).

4018. May a recipient of a distribution roll over the amount into another person's individual retirement plan?

No.[2]

Where a plan participant received a distribution from a qualified retirement plan and, within 60 days, the funds were placed in a traditional IRA held in the participant's wife's name only, but not pursuant to a valid QDRO (Q 4004), the Tax Court found that a valid rollover had not occurred.[3]

4019. May a taxpayer roll over amounts from a defined contribution plan into a defined benefit plan? What special rules apply to the rolled over funds?

Yes. The Pension Benefit Guaranty Corporation (PBGC) has issued rules that are designed to encourage taxpayers to roll amounts from defined contribution plans into defined benefit plans by clarifying the protection that these funds would receive should the defined benefit plan be terminated and become subject to PBGC control.

Typically, the PBGC guarantees the payment of non-forfeitable pension benefits up to a statutory maximum that is adjusted each year. Further, if the plan's benefit increase has been effective for fewer than five years, the percentage of the benefit that is guaranteed is phased-in over a five-year period, becoming fully guaranteed only after five years.

Under the PBGC's new rules, amounts rolled from a defined contribution plan into a defined benefit plan will not be subject to the maximum guaranteed benefit limitations or the otherwise applicable five-year phase-in limitations. This will provide taxpayers with greater assurance that their defined contribution plan funds will be protected if they are rolled over into a defined benefit plan.[4]

---

1. See Rev. Rul. 82-153, 1982-2 CB 86; Let. Rul. 9534027. But see Let. Rul. 8450068.
2. News Release IR-1809, Q17, 5-9-77; IRC Sec. 408(d)(3)(A).
3. *Rodoni v. Comm.*, 105 TC 29 (1995).
4. 29 CFR Parts 4001, 4022, 4044; 79 FR 70090.

4020. How does the Department of Labor fiduciary standard impact advisors who provide advice with respect to IRA rollovers?

Editor's Note: See Q 3985 and Q 3986 for a discussion of how the new proposed PTE impacts advisors, including those who offer rollover advice. The discussion below applies to the 2016 DOL fiduciary rule standards, which have been repealed.

The final Department of Labor fiduciary rule specifically provides that advisors who provide advice with respect to rollovers or transfers from a plan or IRA are providing investment advice so as to become subject to the new fiduciary standard. The advisor must also provide this advice for a fee or other commission, whether direct or indirect.

The advisor will become subject to the heightened fiduciary standard regardless of whether the advice relates to whether the rollover should be executed, the amount of the rollover, the form that the rolled over amounts will take or to what destination the rollover should be made.

The preamble to the final rules notes that decisions to engage in rollover transactions are among the most important financial decisions that an individual will make, so it is important that these individuals be protected by the heightened fiduciary standard. As such, the preamble provides that recommendations with respect to rollover decisions constitute investment advice (and are thus subject to the fiduciary standard) regardless of whether the advisor makes specific recommendations with respect to how to invest assets once they are rolled over.[1]

---

1.   Preamble to DOL Fiduciary Rule, 81 FR 20964.

PART XVIII: SPLIT DOLLAR PLAN

4021. What is a split dollar plan?

Split dollar insurance is an arrangement that often exists between an employer and an employee under which policy benefits are split and the premiums may be split. Split dollar plans also can be set up between corporations and shareholders ("shareholder split dollar") or between parents and their children ("private split dollar").

Planning Point: In early 2020, the Tax Court ruled in favor of taxpayers who used a private split-dollar strategy in estate planning. In the *Morrissette* case, a parent purchased life insurance on her sons' lives--the policies were technically purchased through revocable "dynasty" trusts—for $29.9 million (premium costs). When she died, her reimbursement rights under these "split-dollar" arrangements were valued at only $7.5 million, because the policies would not pay out until the sons died at some future date. Essentially, the strategy is valuable because the difference between the two values is a tax-free gift.

The IRS argued that a fair market valuation approach must be used in split-dollar cases, which would assign the much higher premium cost to the value of the policies using the logic typically applied to buy-sell arrangements in family businesses. The Tax Court instead found that the economic benefit theory of split-dollar could be applied, a result that favored the estate. A similar case, *Cahill v. Comm.*, was settled out of court in 2018.

For years, the premium was often split, with the employer paying the cost of annual term coverage, and the employee paying the balance. Under this arrangement, the employer received from the proceeds an amount equal to the cash value of the policy or at least its premium payments, and the employee's beneficiary received the balance of the proceeds.

From this basic concept, hybrid plans evolved. For example, there are "employer pay all" plans under which an employer pays the entire premium and "level contribution" plans under which an employee pays a level amount each year. There also are reverse split dollar plans (Q 4029) and charitable split dollar plans (Q 121).

A split dollar arrangement may be in the form of an endorsement plan where an employer owns a policy and the benefit-split is provided by endorsement, or a collateral assignment plan under which an employee owns the policy and the employer's interest is secured by collateral assignment of the policy.

The Sarbanes-Oxley Act of 2002[1] generally prohibits direct or indirect loans to certain executive officers and directors of public companies.

After passage of the Sarbanes-Oxley Act, there is now a question of whether it is legal for a publicly traded company to set up a split dollar plan or to continue paying premiums on an already existing plan. Many publicly traded companies have stopped paying premiums on split dollar plans.

---

1.   P.L. 107-204.

Planning Point: Most practitioners are comfortable that endorsement plans (whereby the employee merely rents current death benefit converge) do not violate the Sarbanes-Oxley Act's prohibition against indirect loans. However, collateral assignment arrangements are regarded as more problematic. Some companies are instead paying bonuses to employees covered by split dollar plans so that the employees can pay the premiums themselves.

Plans Entered Into After September 17, 2003

Treasury regulations issued in 2003 define a split dollar life insurance arrangement as any arrangement between an owner and a nonowner of a life insurance contract satisfying the following criteria:

(1)   either party to the arrangement pays all or a portion of the premiums on the life insurance contract, including payment by means of a loan to the other party that is secured by the life insurance contract;

(2)   at least one of the parties to the arrangement that is paying premiums is entitled to recover all or a portion of the premiums and the recovery is to be made from or secured by the proceeds of the life insurance contract; and

(3)   the arrangement is not part of a group term life insurance plan unless the plan provides permanent benefits.[1]

Certain compensatory arrangements and shareholder arrangements are treated as split dollar arrangements even if they do not meet the general definition of a split dollar arrangement. A compensatory arrangement is one where:

(1)   the arrangement is entered into in connection with the performance of services and is not part of a group term life insurance plan;

(2)   the employer pays all or a portion of the premiums; and

(3)   either (x) the beneficiary of any portion of the death benefit is designated by the employee or is a person the employee would reasonably be expected to designate as a beneficiary, or (y) the employee has any interest in the cash value of the policy.

The definition of a shareholder agreement is similar, but with corporation substituted for employer and shareholder for employee.[2]

These definitions are effective for split dollar arrangements entered into after September 17, 2003, or split dollar arrangements entered into before September 18, 2003, that are materially modified after September 17, 2003 (Q 4022).[3]

---

1.   Treas. Reg. §1.61-22(b)(1).
2.   Treas. Reg. §1.61-22(b)(2).
3.   Treas. Reg. §1.61-22(j).

Plans Entered into Before September 18, 2003

The following discussion applies to split dollar plans entered into before September 18, 2003.

If a transaction is cast in a form that results in similar benefits to an employee as in a traditional split dollar plan, it will be treated as a split dollar plan.[1] Thus, an arrangement dividing interests in a policy on an employee between the employer and the insured employee's wife was ruled a split dollar plan providing a taxable economic benefit to the employee (Q 4026, Q 576).

Similarly, where an insured was the employee's father, the plan was held to provide a benefit to the employee taxable as a split dollar plan.[2]

A split dollar plan between a corporation and an insured nonemployee shareholder was ruled to provide a taxable dividend to the shareholder.[3]

Other Considerations

A split dollar arrangement offered as a fringe benefit to employees of an S corporation in which the employer agreed to pay the total premium less the term insurance cost did not violate the one class of stock restriction applicable to S corporations under IRC Section 1361(b)(1)(D).[4]

Similarly, a split dollar arrangement for shareholders in which the employer agreed to pay the full premium and the shareholders agreed to reimburse the employer for the economic benefit amount did not violate the one class of stock restriction.[5]

The cash values of policies in an endorsement-type split dollar plan that made use of an independent fiduciary to select the policies were not considered plan assets for purposes of ERISA.[6]

The IRS has issued guidance regarding the application of IRC Section 409A to split dollar life insurance arrangements. The notice also provides that certain modifications of split dollar life insurance arrangements necessary to comply with, or avoid application of, IRC Section 409A will not be treated as a material modification.[7]

4022. What are the income tax results of a split dollar plan entered into, or materially modified, after September 17, 2003?

The tax treatment of a split dollar arrangement depends on when the arrangement is entered into. For split dollar arrangements entered into after September 17, 2003, the taxation of the arrangement generally is governed by regulations issued in 2003. Split dollar arrangements entered into before September 18, 2003, generally are governed by revenue rulings and other guidance issued by the IRS between 1964 and the issuance of the final regulations (Q 4026).

---

1.   Rev. Rul. 64-328, 1964-2 CB 11.
2.   Rev. Rul. 78-420, 1978-2 CB 67.
3.   Rev. Rul. 79-50, 1979-1 CB 138.
4.   Let. Rul. 9248019.
5.   Let. Rul. 9318007, Let. Rul. 9331009.
6.   DOL Adv. Op. 92-22A.
7.   Notice 2007-34, 2007-17 IRB 996. See, also, T.D. 9321, 73 Fed. Reg. 19234, 19249 (4-17-2007) (IRC Sec. 409A final regulations).

For split dollar arrangements entered into after September 17, 2003, the tax treatment will be governed by one of two mutually exclusive regimes. The arrangement will be treated either as (1) one in which the life insurance policy owner provides economic benefits to the non-owner (Q 4023) or (2) one in which the non-owner makes loans to the owner (Q 4024).[1] The person named on the policy as the owner generally is considered the owner of the policy. A non-owner is any person other than the owner who has an interest in a policy except for a life insurance company acting only as the issuer of the policy.[2]

4023. When is a split dollar plan that was entered into or materially modified after September 17, 2003 governed by the economic benefit theory and what are the tax consequences?

If a split dollar arrangement is not treated as a loan, the contract's owner is treated as providing economic benefits to the nonowner. For gift and employment tax purposes, the nonowner and the owner must take into account the full value of the economic benefits provided to the nonowner by the owner, reduced by any consideration paid by the nonowner. Depending on the relationship between the owner and the nonowner, the economic benefits may consist of compensation income, a dividend, a gift, or some other transfer under the IRC.[3]

The value of the economic benefits is equal to:

(1) the cost of life insurance protection provided to the nonowner;

(2) the amount of any cash value the nonowner has current access to, to the extent that these amounts were not taken into account in previous years; and

(3) the value of other benefits provided to the nonowner.

The cost of life insurance protection may be determined by a life insurance premium factor issued by the IRS.[4] Presumably, Table 2001 will be used until the IRS issues another table.[5] In addition, in Notice 2002-8, the IRS found that an insurer's renewable term rate could be used to measure the annual cost of life insurance protection if the insurer generally makes the availability of the product known to those who apply for term insurance, the insurer's product is regularly sold through normal distribution channels, and the product otherwise meets the IRS' previously stated requirements for such use.[6]

Under the economic benefit regime, a nonowner has no investment in the contract with respect to a life insurance policy subject to a split dollar arrangement. Premiums paid by the owner will be included in the owner's investment in the contract. Any amount the nonowner

---

1.　　Treas. Reg. §1.61-22(b)(3).
2.　　Treas. Reg. §1.61-22(c).
3.　　Treas. Reg. §1.61-22(d)(1).
4.　　Treas. Reg. §1.61-22(d)(2)-(3).
5.　　See Notice 2002-8, 2002-1 CB 398.
6.　　See also Rev. Rul. 66-110, 1966-1 CB 12; Let. Rul. 8547006; and Rev. Rul. 67-154, 1967-1 CB 11.

pays toward a policy will be included in the income of the owner and increase the owner's investment in the contract.[1]

Death benefits paid to a beneficiary other than the owner of the policy by reason of the death of an insured will be excluded from income to the extent that the amount of the death benefit is allocable to current life insurance protection provided to the nonowner, the cost of which was paid by the nonowner or the benefit of which the nonowner took into account for income tax purposes.[2]

Planning Point: In other words, failure to pay or recognize as taxable income the cost of the life insurance economic benefit can make the insurance death benefit taxable to the recipient.

On the transfer of a policy to a nonowner, the nonowner generally is considered to receive the cash value of the policy and the value of all other rights in the policy minus any amounts paid for the policy and any benefits that previously were included in the nonowner's income. Amounts that were previously included in income due to the value of current life insurance protection that was provided to the nonowner may not be used to reduce the amount the nonowner is considered to receive on roll-out. Thus, the taxation on the value of current life insurance protection will not provide the nonowner with any basis in the policy, although taxation for a previous increase in cash value will add basis for the nonowner.[3]

4024. When is a split dollar plan that was entered into or materially modified after September 17, 2003 treated as a loan and what are the tax consequences?

A split dollar arrangement will be treated as a loan if:

(1)   payment is made by the non-owner to the owner;

(2)   payment is a loan under general principles of federal tax law or a reasonable person would expect the payment to be repaid to the non-owner; and

(3)   repayment is made from, or secured by, either the policy's death benefit, cash value, or both.[4]

If a split dollar arrangement is treated as a loan, the owner is considered the borrower and the non-owner is considered the lender.[5] If a split dollar loan is a below market loan, then interest will be imputed at the applicable federal rate ("AFR"), with the owner and the non-owner of the policy considered to transfer imputed amounts to each other.[6]

In a split dollar arrangement between an employer and employee, the lender is the employer and the borrower is the employee. Each payment under a split dollar arrangement will be

---

1.   Treas. Reg. §1.61-22(f).
2.   Treas. Reg. §1.61-22(f)(3).
3.   Treas. Reg. §1.61-22(g).
4.   Treas. Reg. §1.7872-15(a)(2).
5.   Treas. Reg. §1.7872-15(a)(2).
6.   See IRC Sec. 7872.

treated as a separate loan. The employer is considered to transfer the imputed interest to the employee. This amount is considered taxable compensation, and generally will be deductible by the employer, although no deduction will be allowed in a corporation-shareholder arrangement. The employee then is treated as paying the imputed interest back to the employer, which will be taxable income to the employer. This imputed interest payment by the employee generally will be considered personal interest and therefore not deductible.

Planning Point: If the policy is owned by a third party, such as an irrevocable trust in a collateral assignment structure, the economic benefit is treated as a gift by the employee to the trust.

The calculation of the amount of imputed interest differs depending on the type of below market loan involved. A below market loan is either a demand loan or a term loan. A demand loan is a loan that is payable in full on the demand of the lender.[1] All other below market loans are term loans.[2] A split dollar term loan generally will cause more interest to be imputed in the early years of the arrangement, with the amount of imputed interest decreasing each year. In a split dollar demand loan, imputed interest will be smaller in the early years of the arrangement but will increase each year the arrangement is in place.

4025. When will a split dollar plan that is entered into before September 17, 2003 found to be "materially modified" so that it is governed by the 2003 regulations?

The 2003 regulations apply to split dollar arrangements entered into after September 17, 2003, and arrangements entered into on or before September 17, 2003, that are materially modified after September 17, 2003.[3] The final regulations provide a nonexclusive list of changes that will not be considered material modifications. This list includes:

(1) a change solely in premium payment method, for example, from monthly to quarterly;

(2) a change solely of beneficiary, unless the beneficiary is a party to the arrangement;

(3) a change solely in the interest rate payable on a policy loan;

(4) a change solely necessary to preserve the status of the life insurance contract under IRC Section 7702;

(5) a change solely to the ministerial provisions of the life insurance contract such as a change in the address to send premiums; and

(6) a change made solely under the terms of a split dollar agreement other than the life insurance contract if the change is dictated by the arrangement, is nondiscretionary

---

1.   IRC Sec. 7872(f)(5).
2.   IRC Sec. 7872(f)(6).
3.   Treas. Reg. §§1.61-22(j), 1.7872-15(n).

to the parties, and was made under a binding commitment in effect on or before September 17, 2003.[1]

An exchange of policies under IRC Section 1035 is not on the list of nonmaterial modifications. The IRS will not issue rulings or determination letters on whether a modification is material.[2]

The IRS has released guidance regarding the application of IRC Section 101(j) and Section 264(f) to life insurance contracts that are subject to split dollar life insurance arrangements. According to the IRS, if parties to a split dollar life insurance arrangement modify the terms of the arrangement but do not modify the terms of the life insurance contract underlying the arrangement, the modification will not be treated as a material change in the life insurance contract for purposes of IRC Section 101(j) and Section 264(f) even if the modification is treated as a material modification of the split dollar arrangement for purposes of Treasury Regulation Section 1.61-22(j). In other words, the contract will not lose its grandfathered status.[3]

The final regulations also contain rules on when a split dollar arrangement is considered to be entered into. A split dollar arrangement is entered into on the latest of the following dates:

(1)   the date the life insurance contract is issued;

(2)   the effective date of the life insurance contract under the arrangement;

(3)   the date the first premium on the life insurance contract is paid;

(4)   the date the parties to the arrangement enter into an agreement with regard to the policy; or

(5)   the date on which the arrangement satisfies the definition of a split dollar life insurance arrangement.[4]

4026. What are the income tax results of a split dollar plan entered into before September 18, 2003?

Split dollar arrangements that were entered into before September 18, 2003, are governed by various rulings and other guidance that were issued by the IRS between 1964 and the issuance of final regulations on split dollar arrangements in 2003. This guidance includes Notice 2002-8,[5] which provides transition rules for arrangements not subject to split dollar regulations. No inference is to be drawn, however, from Notice 2002-8 or the proposed or final regulations regarding the appropriate tax treatment of split dollar arrangements entered into before September 18, 2003.

---

1.   Treas. Reg. §1.61-22(j)(2).
2.   Rev. Proc. 2012-3, 2012-1 IRB 113; Sec. 3.01(2), 2007-1 IRB 108, as modified by Rev. Proc. 2019-3.
3.   Notice 2008-42, 2008-15 IRB 747.
4.   Treas. Reg. §1.61-22(j)(1)(ii).
5.   2002-1 CB 398.

For the treatment of split dollar arrangements entered into after September 17, 2003, see Q 4022 and Q 4023.

Notice 2002-8

For split dollar arrangements entered into before September 18, 2003:

(1)   The IRS will not treat an employer as having made a transfer of a portion of the cash value of a life policy to an employee for purposes of Section 83 solely because the interest or other earnings credited to the cash value of the policy cause the cash value to exceed the portion payable to an employer;

(2)   Where the value of current life insurance protection is treated as an economic benefit provided by an employer to an employee, the IRS will not treat the arrangement as having been terminated, and thus will not assert that there has been a transfer of property to the employee by reason of termination of the arrangement, as long as the parties to the arrangement continue to treat and report the value of the life insurance protection as an economic benefit provided to the employee. This treatment will be accepted without regard to the level of the remaining economic interest that the employer has in the life insurance contract; and

(3)   The parties to the arrangement may treat premium or other payments by an employer as loans. The IRS will not challenge reasonable efforts to comply with the rules regarding original issue discount and below-market loans. All payments by an employer from the beginning of the arrangement, reduced by any repayments to the employer, before the first taxable year in which payments are treated as loans for tax purposes must be treated as loans entered into at the beginning of the first year in which payments are treated as loans.

For split dollar arrangements entered into before January 28, 2002, under which an employer has made premium or other payments under the arrangement and has received or is entitled to receive full repayment, the IRS will not assert that there has been a taxable transfer of property to an employee on termination of the arrangement if (1) the arrangement is terminated before January 1, 2004, or (2) for all periods beginning on or after January 1, 2004, all payments by an employer from the beginning of the arrangement, reduced by any repayments to the employer, are treated as loans for tax purposes and the parties to the arrangement report the tax treatment in a manner consistent with this loan treatment, including the rules for original issue discount and below-market loans. Any payments by an employer before the first taxable year in which payments are treated as loans for tax purposes must be treated as loans entered into at the beginning of the first year in which payments are treated as loans.

Notice 2001-10

Notice 2001-10 was revoked by Notice 2002-8. For split dollar arrangements entered into before September 18, 2003, taxpayers may rely on the guidance contained in Notice 2001-10.

Under Notice 2001-10, the IRS generally will accept the parties' characterization of an employer's payments under a split dollar plan, provided that:

(1)   the characterization is not clearly inconsistent with the substance of the arrangement;

(2)   the characterization has been consistently followed by the parties from the inception of the agreement; and

(3)   the parties fully account for all economic benefits conferred on the employee in a manner consistent with that characterization.[1]

Under Notice 2001-10, there are three different ways that a split dollar plan may be characterized.

First, a plan can be characterized as a loan subject to the below market loan rules.

Second, a plan can be characterized so as to be governed under the traditional split dollar rules of Revenue Ruling 64-328.[2]

Finally, a plan can be characterized in such a way so that the employer's payments are treated as compensation.

Value of Economic Benefit

The employee is taxed on the value of the economic benefit he or she receives from his or her employer's participation in the split dollar arrangement.[3] One of the benefits an employee receives is current life insurance protection under the basic policy. The value of this benefit to an employee may be calculated by using government premium rates. For many years, P.S. 58 rates were used to calculate the value of the protection,[4] but the IRS revoked Revenue Ruling 55-747 and provided new Table 2001 rates. P.S. 58 rates generally may be used prior to 2002; Table 2001 rates generally may be used starting in 2001.[5] Notice 2002-8 provides for some grandfathering of P.S. 58 rates. For split dollar arrangements entered into before January 28, 2002, in which a contractual agreement between an employer and employee provides that P.S. 58 rates will be used to determine the value of current life insurance protection provided to an employee or to an employee and one or more additional persons, the employer and employee may continue to use P.S. 58 rates.[6]

If an insurer publishes rates for individual, initial issue, one year term policies (available to all standard risks) and these rates are lower than the P.S. 58 or Table 2001 rates, as applicable, these insurer rates may be substituted.[7] Only standard rates may be substituted, not preferred

---

1.   Notice 2001-10, 2001-1 CB 459.
2.   1964-2 CB 11.
3.   See Rev. Rul. 64-328, 1964-2 CB 11.
4.   See Rev. Rul. 55-747, 1955-2 CB 228.
5.   Notice 2002-8, 2002-1 CB 398.
6.   Notice 2002-8, 2002-1 CB 398.
7.   See Rev. Rul. 66-110, 1966-1 CB 12.

rates (such as those offered to non-smoking individuals).[1] The substituted rate must be a rate charged for initial issue insurance and must be available to all standard risks.[2]

For arrangements entered into before September 18, 2003, taxpayers may use an insurer's lower published premium rates available to all standard risks for initial issue one year term insurance. For arrangements entered into after January 28, 2002, and before September 18, 2003, for periods after December 31, 2003, however, an insurer's rates may not be used unless (1) the insurer generally makes the availability of the rates known to those who apply for term insurance coverage from the insurer, and (2) the insurer regularly sells term insurance at those rates to individuals who apply for term insurance coverage through the insurer's normal distribution channels.[3]

The IRS has said that taxpayers should make appropriate adjustments to premium rates if life insurance protection covers more than one life.[4] Where a policy death benefit is payable at the second death, rates for single lives should be used to measure the survivor's economic benefit (Appendix A found in volume 1).

Employer's Premiums Nondeductible

An employer cannot take a business expense deduction for its share of the annual premium because the employer is a beneficiary under the policy, within the meaning of IRC Section 264(a)(1).[5] Moreover, it appears that an employer cannot deduct the value of the economic benefit, that is, the Table 2001 or P.S. 58 cost that is taxable to an employee because the employer has not paid or incurred any expense other than nondeductible premium expense.[6]

Death Proceeds

On the death of an employee, both the portion of the proceeds received by the employer and the portion of the proceeds received by the employee's beneficiary are ordinarily exempt from federal income tax under IRC Section 101(a) as life insurance proceeds received by reason of the insured's death.[7] Death proceeds of split dollar life insurance payable to a corporation may affect the calculation of the alternative minimum tax (Q 316).

Stockholder-Employees

Although the issue was not litigated, the IRS treated the P.S. 58 benefit of a substantial stockholder-employee as a dividend in *Johnson v. Commissioner*.[8] The IRS already had ruled that in the case of a split dollar arrangement between a nonemployee stockholder and the corporation,

---

1.   Let. Rul. 8547006.
2.   Rev. Rul. 67-154, 1967-1 CB 11.
3.   Notice 2002-8, 2002-2 CB 398.
4.   Notice 2002-8, 2002-4 CB 398.
5.   See Rev. Rul. 64-328 above.
6.   See IRC Sec. 162.
7.   Rev. Rul. 64-328, supra.
8.   74 TC 1316 (1980).

the economic benefit flowing from the corporation to the insured stockholder is taxed as a corporate distribution or dividend.[1]

4027. What are the income tax consequences of the transfer or roll-out of a policy subject to a split dollar arrangement entered into after September 17, 2003?

Under the split dollar regulations, on the transfer of a policy to a nonowner, the nonowner generally is considered to receive the cash value of the policy and the value of all other rights in the policy minus any amounts paid for the policy and any benefits that were previously included in the nonowner's income. Amounts that previously were included in income due to the value of current life insurance protection that was provided to a nonowner may not be used to reduce the amount the non-owner is considered to receive on roll-out. Thus, the taxation on the value of current life insurance protection will not provide a nonowner with any basis in the policy, although taxation for a previous increase in cash value will add basis for a nonowner.[2]

No inference is to be drawn regarding the tax treatment of split dollar arrangements entered into before September 18, 2003 (Q 4026).[3]

4028. What are the income tax consequences of the transfer or rollout of a policy subject to a split dollar arrangement entered into before September 18, 2003?

The IRS considered this issue in two private letter rulings. In the first private letter ruling, the split dollar plan provided that the insured employee would be entitled to a portion of the life insurance policy's cash surrender value annual increase equal to the employee's share of the annual premium. The employee's portion of the annual premium was determined by a payment schedule which entitled the employee to a portion of the cash surrender value of the policy. The plan's rollout provision stated that if the employee remained employed for a specified time, the policy then would be transferred to the employee without cost. The net cash value of the policy transferred to the employee at that time would equal the employee's cumulative premium, or if greater, the cash surrender value less the employer's cumulative premiums.

The IRS concluded that when the policy is transferred to the employee, the employee would have taxable income to the extent the cash value in the policy exceeded the amounts the employee contributed. The IRS reasoned that the cash surrender value would be property transferred in connection with the performance of services and therefore the amount exceeding the employee's basis, that is, the employee's contributions, immediately would be taxable under IRC Section 83. Under IRC Section 83(h), the employer would be entitled to a deduction equal to the amount included in the employee's income. This deduction would be offset by the employer's recognition of a gain equal to the amount received in excess of its basis. Further,

---

1.   Rev. Rul. 79-50, 1979-1 CB 138.
2.   Treas. Reg. §1.61-22(g).
3.   See Notice 2002-8, 2002-1 CB 398.

the insured employee must include in income each year the annual P.S. 58 cost of life insurance protection the employee received, to the extent paid for by the employer.[1]

The employee was not entitled to use the employee's contributions to offset the employer-provided insurance protection. The ruling does not indicate how the amount of protection provided by the employer is calculated, but it has been suggested that the calculation should be made in a manner consistent with Revenue Ruling 64-328.[2]

The second private letter ruling involved an endorsement arrangement in which the employer owned all the cash values but was to receive death benefits limited to its premium contributions. At the eighth policy year, the employer borrowed an amount equal to its premium contribution from the policy, leaving some amount of cash value in the policy, which then was rolled out to the employee. The IRS, once again, applied IRC Section 83 and found that in the year of the rollout the employer recognized gain in the policy to the extent the cash value exceeded its cumulative premium basis.[3] The employer was entitled to an IRC Section 162 business deduction equal to the total cash value less the employee's premium contributions. The employee likewise must include under IRC Section 83 the full amount of the policy cash value less the premiums the employee paid over the first seven years.[4]

The IRS has provided little or no guidance on the more customary split dollar plan in which an employer's interest is limited to its aggregate premium outlay both during lifetime and at death. Under these circumstances an employer's contractual rights to cash values are limited to the premiums it has paid, which the amount is borrowed from or withdrawn out of the policy in the year of rollout. Typically, the employee pays premiums to offset the economic benefit and contractually owns cash values in excess of the employer's aggregate premium outlay. The 1979 ruling suggested an employee's premium outlay could not be used to offset both the economic benefits and serve as the employee's basis in mitigating the tax on the cash values. The 1983 ruling does not clearly respond to this issue. Neither ruling considered the policy loan in measuring the value transferred to the employee.

In *Neff v Commissioner*,[5] the Tax Court looked at a case involving the termination of a pre-final regulation equity collateral assignment split dollar arrangement. Unfortunately, the case provided little guidance on most issues. The opinion did confirm that at least the amount of corporate premiums was taxable income to the employee when the employment arrangement was terminated and the collateral assignment was released. The court rejected the taxpayer argument that the compensation to the employer was limited to the present value of the premiums discounted to the insured's life expectancy.

Although there are no IRS rulings on point, whether a policy has failed the seven pay test of IRC Section 7702A(b) and therefore is classified as a modified endowment contract should be considered in determining the income tax consequences of a split dollar rollout. Any policy

---

1.   Let. Rul. 7916029.
2.   1964-2 CB 11.
3.   Treas. Reg. §1.83-6(b).
4.   Let. Rul. 8310027.
5.   TC Memo 2012-244.

distributions, including policy loans, generally may be taxed less favorably if a policy is a modified endowment contract than if it is not (Q 13).

Where a split dollar arrangement provides a permanent benefit (Q 255) to a member of a group covered by group term life insurance issued by the same insurer or an affiliate, the arrangement may be considered part of a policy providing group term life insurance and its taxation subject to rules discussed in Q 254.

4029. What is reverse split dollar and how is it taxed?

Reverse split dollar is a variation on the split dollar arrangement (Q 4021) in which the ownership of the policy cash value and death proceeds is split between a corporation and an insured employee, but the traditional roles of the two parties to the arrangement are reversed. In the typical reverse split dollar plan, an employer pays a portion of the policy premium equal to the annual P.S. 58 cost or the Table 2001 cost each year while the difference between this cost and the full premium is contributed by the employee. Notice 2002-59[1] is believed to have ended the viability of reverse split dollar.

In Notice 2002-59, the IRS stated that a party to a split dollar arrangement may use Table 2001 or an insurer's rates only for the purpose of valuing current life insurance protection when the protection is conferred as an economic benefit by one party on another party, determined without regard to consideration or premiums paid by the other party. Thus, if one party has the right to current life insurance protection, neither Table 2001 nor an insurer's rates can be used to value that party's insurance protection for purposes of establishing the value of policy benefits to which another party may be entitled.

Notice 2002-59 provides one example where the premium rates are properly used and one where they are not properly used. In the first example, a donor is assumed to pay the premiums on a life insurance policy that is part of a split dollar arrangement between the donor and a trust, with the trust having the right to the current life insurance protection. The current life insurance protection has been conferred as an economic benefit by the donor on the trust and the donor is permitted to value the life insurance protection using either Table 2001 or an insurer's lower term rates.

In the second example, if the donor or the donor's estate has the right to the current life insurance protection, neither Table 2001 nor an insurer's lower term rates may be used to value the donor's current life insurance protection to establish the value of economic benefits conferred on the trust. Results will be similar if the trust pays for all or a portion of its share of benefits provided under the life insurance arrangement.

Planning Point: Notice 2002-59 does not contain an effective date, which indicates that the IRS does not consider it new guidance but a restatement by the IRS of current law. If that is the case, it will affect reverse split dollar arrangements that were in place before the notice was issued.

---

1.   2002-2 CB 481.

4030. What is private split dollar and how is it taxed?

Private split dollar is yet another variation on the traditional split dollar arrangement (Q 4021). The label of private comes from the fact that this type of split dollar arrangement does not include the participation of an employer. Rather, a private split dollar arrangement is typically between two family members or one family member and a trust. When two family members are involved the label "family split dollar" often is used. A common example of family split dollar involves a father assisting his son in setting up a policy insuring the son's life.

The IRS has said that the same principles that govern the tax treatment of employer-employee split dollar plans (Q 4022, Q 4026) also should govern arrangements that provide benefits in gift contexts, which presumably would include private split dollar plans.[1]

The regulations regarding split dollar also apply to private split dollar arrangements (Q 4022). For the estate tax consequences of private split dollar, see Q 325 (under "Non-Employer-Employee Relationship"). For gift tax implications, see Q 576.

---

1.   See Notice 2002-8, 2002-1 CB 398.

PART XIX: TAX SHELTERED ANNUITIES FOR EMPLOYEES OF SECTION 501(C)(3) ORGANIZATIONS AND PUBLIC SCHOOLS

Overview

4031. What are the tax benefits of a tax sheltered annuity?

A tax sheltered annuity is a deferred tax arrangement expressly granted by Congress in IRC Section 403(b). An employee can exclude from gross income, within limits, the contributions paid to an annuity for the employee's retirement or amounts paid to a custodian for the purchase of stock in regulated investment companies (Q 4033). The plan may be used by only certain employers (Q 4032). An employee generally must report the payments received under the contract or custodial account as taxable income (Q 4087).

A plan must meet specific requirements (Q 4034, Q 4037), although some but not all failures to meet these requirements may be subject to correction under the Employee Plans Compliance Resolution System ("EPCRS").[1]

Planning Point: Most common problems can now be corrected under EPCRS, but many corrections are slightly different than for similar problems under 401(a) plans.

Final 403(b) Regulations. Final regulations concerning tax sheltered annuity contracts were released and became effective on July 26, 2007, and generally apply for tax years beginning after December 31, 2008.[2]

4032. What organizations can make tax sheltered annuities available to their employees?

An organization must be either a tax-exempt organization of one of the types described in IRC Section 501(c)(3) or a public school system. An organization in either of these two categories may make tax sheltered annuity benefits available to one or more of its full-time or part-time employees.

A participant must be an employee; persons working for an organization in a self-employed capacity generally are not eligible.[3]

A tax sheltered annuity also may be purchased for a duly ordained, commissioned, or licensed minister of a church by the minister himself if the minister is self-employed or by an organization that employs the minister and with respect to which the minister shares common religious bonds.[4] This definition includes chaplains (Q 4051).

---

1. See Rev. Proc. 2008-50, 2008-35 IRB 464, as modified and superseded by Rev. Proc. 2013-12, 2013-4 IRB 313, and as modified by Rev. Proc. 2015-27, 2015-16 IRB 914; Rev. Proc. 2015-28, 2015-16 IRB 920 and Rev. Proc. 2016-51, 2016-42 IRB 465.
2. Treas. Reg. §1.403(b)-11(a).
3. IRC Sec. 403(b)(1).
4. IRC Secs. 403(b)(1)(A)(iii), 414(e)(5).

IRC Section 501(c)(3) organizations are nonprofit organizations that are organized and operated exclusively for religious, charitable, scientific, literary, educational, or safety testing purposes, or for the prevention of cruelty to children or animals. Organizations other than public schools that are wholly owned by a state or other local government generally are not eligible employers. Some of these organizations will qualify as 501(c)(3) organizations if they are separately organized, are not an integral part of the government, and meet the description of a 501(c)(3) organization, such as some state or city hospitals.[1]

A school or college that is operated exclusively for educational purposes by a separate educational instrumentality may qualify doubly, both as a public school and as an IRC Section 501(c)(3) organization.[2] A state department of education may qualify as a part of a public school system if its services involve the operation or direction of the state's public school program.[3] Likewise, a state agency that administers a guaranteed student loan program and is part of a state department of insurance may qualify.[4] Thus, annuities may be purchased for employees of these organizations as well as public school teachers, teachers in private and parochial schools, school superintendents, college professors, clergymen, and social workers.

A doctor who works as an employee for a hospital is eligible provided the hospital is a qualified employer. A doctor generally is not eligible, however, unless the doctor is an employee of the hospital for all purposes, such as Social Security and withholding tax purposes. If the doctor's relationship to the hospital is that of an independent contractor, the doctor is not eligible and any premiums paid on the doctor's behalf for an annuity will be currently taxable.[5]

Although teachers who are covered under a state teachers' retirement system also may participate in a tax sheltered annuity plan, the employees of the retirement system itself are not eligible.[6] The Uniformed Services University of the Health Sciences will be treated as a 501(c)(3) employer for purposes of providing tax sheltered annuities for employee members of a civilian faculty or staff with respect to service after December 31, 1979.[7]

4033. How may a tax sheltered annuity plan be funded?

Annuity Contracts. IRC Section 403(b) provides that the tax sheltered annuity rules apply if an annuity contract is purchased for an employee. Final regulations provide that an annuity contract means a contract that is issued by an insurance company qualified to issue annuities in a state and that includes payment in the form of an annuity.[8] A custodial account also is treated as an annuity contract.[9] In addition, retirement income accounts are treated as annuity contracts.[10]

---

1.   Rev. Rul. 55-319, 1955-1 CB 119, as modified by Rev. Rul. 60-384, 1960-2 CB 172; Rev. Rul. 67-290, 1967-2 CB 183.
2.   See *Est. of Johnson v. Comm.*, 56 TC 944 (1971), *acq.*, 1973-2 CB 2; Let. Rul. 7817098.
3.   Rev. Rul. 73-607, 1973-2 CB 145.
4.   See Let. Rul. 9438031.
5.   Rev. Rul. 66-274, 1966-2 CB 446; Rev. Rul. 70-136, 1970-1 CB 12; *Azad v. U.S.*, 388 F.2d 74 (8th Cir. 1968); see also Rev. Rul. 73-417, 1973-2 CB 332; *Ravel v. Comm.*, TC Memo 1967-182; *Haugen v. Comm.*, TC Memo 1971-294.
6.   Rev. Rul. 80-139, 1980-1 CB 88.
7.   P.L. 96-613 Sec. 104.
8.   Treas. Reg. §1.403(b)-2(b)(2).
9.   Treas. Reg. §1.403(b)-8(d)(1).
10.   Treas. Reg. §1.403(b)-9(a).

An individual or group insurance company annuity contract that provides fixed retirement benefits may be used. A single group annuity contract that pools the assets of an employer's tax sheltered annuity plan and defined contribution plan also may be used where the assets of each plan are separately accounted for at the plan level and at the participant level through the use of sub-accounts.[1]

The IRS has ruled that a variable annuity contract will qualify.[2] A variable annuity contract in which the contract holder directs the investments in publicly available securities (i.e., mutual funds) will be treated as an annuity contract and the contract holder will not be treated as owning the underlying assets if certain conditions are met.

For contracts intended to qualify as annuity contracts under IRC Section 403(b), that status will be granted if no additional federal tax liability would have been incurred if the employer of the contract holder had instead paid an amount into a custodial account in an arrangement under IRC Section 403(b)(7)(A).

In other words, a contract holder will receive the same favorable tax treatment whether the investment in publicly available mutual fund shares is made through a mutual fund custodial account or variable annuity contract. The diversification rules under IRC Section 817(h) for variable annuity contracts are not applicable to IRC Section 403(b) contracts. The revenue procedure, which was effective on November 16, 1999, with respect to all taxable years, will not be applied adversely to an issuer or holder of a contract issued before November 16, 1999.[3]

Face Amount Certificates. The IRC expressly provides that so-called face amount certificates are to be treated as annuity contracts.[4]

Regulated Investment Company Stock. According to the final regulations, custodial account means a plan or a separate account under a plan in which an amount attributable to 403(b) contributions or an amount rolled over to a 403(b) contract is held by a bank or certain other entities, as discussed below, if:

(1)   all of the amounts held in the account are invested in stock of a regulated investment company;

(2)   the distribution restrictions that apply to custodial accounts are satisfied with respect to the amounts held in the account;

(3)   the assets held in the account cannot be used for, or diverted to, purposes other than for the exclusive benefit of plan participants or their beneficiaries; and

(4)   the account is not part of a retirement income account.

---

1.   Let. Rul. 9422053.
2.   Rev. Rul. 68-116, 1968-1 CB 177.
3.   Rev. Proc. 99-44, 1999-48 IRB 598, *modifying* Rev. Rul. 81-225, 1981-2 CB 12.
4.   IRC Sec. 401(g). See also Treas. Reg. §1.401-9(a).

The custodial account rule is not satisfied if the account includes any assets other than regulated investment company stock.[1] The custodian must be a bank, insured federal credit union, building and loan association or other person satisfactory to the IRS.[2]

If the amounts are to be invested in regulated investment company stock to be held in that custodial account, and under the custodial account no amounts may be paid or available to any distributee (unless such amount is a distribution to which section 72(t)(2)(G) applies) before:

(1)   the employee dies,

(2)   the employee attains age 59½,

(3)   the employee has a severance from employment,

(4)   the employee becomes disabled,

(5)   in the case of contributions made pursuant to a salary reduction agreement, the employee encounters financial hardship, or

(6)   except as may be otherwise provided by regulations, with respect to amounts invested in a lifetime income investment, the date that is 90 days prior to the date that such lifetime income investment may no longer be held as an investment option under the contract, and in the case of amounts described (6), above, such amounts must be distributed only in the form of a qualified distribution or a qualified plan distribution annuity contract.

State Teachers' Retirement System. According to the final regulations, the requirement that a contract be issued by an insurance company qualified to issue annuities in a state does not apply if one of the following two conditions is, and continuously has been, satisfied since May 17, 1982:

(1)   benefits are provided from a separately funded retirement reserve that is subject to supervision of the state insurance department, or

(2)   benefits are provided from a fund that is separate from the fund used to provide statutory benefits payable under a state teachers' retirement system to purchase benefits that are unrelated to the basic benefits provided under the retirement system, and the death benefit under the contract does not at any time exceed the larger of the reserve or the contribution made for the employee.[3]

Credit Union Share Accounts. The IRS takes the position that separate nonforfeitable share accounts in a credit union may not be considered annuity contracts for purposes of IRC Section 403(b).[4]

---

1.   Treas. Reg. §1.403(b)-8(d).
2.   IRC Sec. 403(b)(7).
3.   Treas. Reg. §1.403(b)-8(c)(3).
4.   Rev. Rul. 82-102, 1982-1 CB 62. See *Corbin v. U.S.*, 760 F.2d 234 (8th Cir. 1985).

Retirement Income Accounts of Churches. Churches are permitted to maintain a retirement income account that will be treated as a tax sheltered annuity (Q 4051).[1]

According to the final regulations, a life insurance contract, endowment contract, health or accident contract, or property, casualty, or liability insurance contract do not meet the definition of an annuity contract.[2] If a contract issued by an insurance company provides death benefits as part of the contract, however, that coverage is permitted assuming that those death benefits do not cause the contract to fail to satisfy any requirement applicable to Section 403(b) contracts; that is, assuming that those benefits satisfy the incidental benefit rule under Treasury Regulation Section 1.403(b)-6(g). The special rule for life insurance contracts does not apply to a contract issued before September 24, 2007.[3]

Multiple contracts are considered a single contract for purposes of applying the 403(b) rules; consequently, separate insurance contracts may be purchased as part of a 403(b) annuity plan. These insurance contracts must meet the form requirements and all the limitations of an IRC Section 403(b) annuity contract. It does not appear to matter whether the form requirements and limitations are imposed by means of an endorsement to the insurance policy,[4] an addendum to the salary reduction agreement,[5] or a trust agreement.[6]

Planning Point: It should be noted, however, that most IRS rulings on this issue do not address whether such an insurance investment would be permissible if the amounts were invested in a custodial account.

Where an insurance policy endorsement failed to adequately restrict the premiums to meet the incidental benefit limit and the elective deferral limit and also contained conflicting provisions that rendered the agreement revocable, the IRS ruled that the life policy as endorsed did not constitute a 403(b) annuity contract.[7]

The IRS has ruled privately that it is irrelevant whether the premiums under the insurance contract are paid by contributions made by the employer on behalf of the participant under a salary reduction agreement or by dividends and interest thereon accumulated under the contract so long as the incidental benefit limit is not exceeded.[8]

Planning Point: Revenue Ruling 90-24 has been revoked, and life insurance now cannot be purchased under a 403(b) plan.

The life insurance protection contained in a retirement income or pension plan endowment type of policy comes within the incidental limitation. An endowment policy with an annuity rider that, when combined, provided in later policy years a death benefit greater than under a typical retirement income policy qualified as an annuity contract when actuarial comparison of only

---

1. Treas. Reg. §§1.403(b)-8(e), 1.403(b)-9(a).
2. Treas. Reg. §1.403(b)-8(c)(2); see also Treas. Reg. §1.401(f)-4(e).
3. Treas. Reg. §1.403(b)-8(c)(2). See also Treas. Reg. §1.403(b)-11(f).
4. See Let. Ruls. 9713022 (variable universal life policy), 9626042, 9336054, 9336053, 9327025, 9324042, 9303024.
5. See Let. Rul. 9324044.
6. See Let. Ruls. 9324043, 9106022.
7. Let. Rul. 9242022.
8. Let. Rul. 9215055.

the endowment contract with the retirement income contract indicated the cost of the death benefit under the endowment contract was less than that of the retirement income contract.[1] However, Treasury Regulation Section 1.403(b)–8(c)(2) does not permit a life insurance contract, an endowment contract, a health or accident insurance contract, or a property, casualty, or liability insurance contract to constitute an annuity contract for purposes of Section 403(b) if issued after September 23, 2007.

Contract Requirements

4034. What nine requirements must a tax sheltered annuity contract meet in order for contributions to be excluded from the employee's gross income?

Editor's Note: The remedial amendment period (RAP) applicable to tax sheltered annuities (see Q 4036) has been extended through March 31, 2020 under Revenue Procedure 2017-18. Pursuant to this new plan, employers will be required to restate their plans to reflect a new plan document by the end of the extended RAP. In response to COVID-19, the March 31 deadline was extended to June 30, 2020.

Exclusion for Contributions to Purchase 403(b) Contracts

Under final regulations (Q 4025), amounts contributed by an eligible employer for the purchase of an annuity contract for an employee are excluded from the gross income of the employee under IRC Section 403(b) only if each of the nine requirements below are satisfied.[2] The final regulations require the 403(b) plan, in both form and operation, to satisfy the applicable requirements for exclusion.[3]

(1)　*Purchase by Eligible Employer.* A tax sheltered annuity contract must be purchased by an eligible employer (Q 4026).[4] Final regulations provide that the annuity contract cannot be purchased under a qualified plan (Q 3831, Q 3933), or an eligible governmental plan (Q 3600).[5]

Thus, an employer must agree to pay premiums. Although the employer must pay premiums, the premiums may be derived either directly from the employer as additional compensation to the employee or indirectly from the employee through a reduction in his or her salary. If premiums are to come from a reduction in the employee's salary, the reduction must be made under a legally binding agreement between the employer and the employee, and the agreement must be irrevocable as to salary earned while the agreement is in effect.

An employee is permitted to enter into multiple salary reduction agreements with the same employer during any one taxable year of the employer. For purposes of IRC Section 403(b), the frequency that an employee is permitted to enter into

1.　　Rev. Rul. 74-115, 1974-1 CB 100.
2.　　Treas. Reg. §1.403(b)-3(a).
3.　　Preamble, TD 9340, 72 Fed. Reg. 41128, 41129 (7-26-2007).
4.　　IRC Sec. 403(b)(1).
5.　　Treas. Reg. §1.403(b)-3(a)(1).

a salary reduction agreement, the salary to which such an agreement may apply, and the ability to revoke such an agreement generally is determined under IRC Section 401(k).[1]

All annuity contracts, including custodial accounts and retirement income accounts, purchased by an employer on behalf of an employee are treated as a single annuity contract for purposes of applying the requirements of IRC Section 403(b).[2]

Tax deferment will be achieved only for premium payments attributable to amounts earned by an employee after the agreement becomes effective; premium payments attributable to salary earned prior to the effective date, or after termination of the agreement, are includable in the employee's gross income. For this purpose, salary is considered earned when the services for which it is compensation are performed, even though payment is deferred and subject to a risk of forfeiture.[3] After-tax contributions can be made by payroll deduction to a 403(b) plan, but will not be excludable.[4]

The final regulations specify that contributions to a 403(b) plan must be transferred to the insurance company issuing the annuity contract or the entity holding assets of any custodial or retirement income account that is treated as an annuity contract within a period that is not longer than is reasonable for the proper administration of the plan. A plan may provide for elective deferrals for a participant under the plan to be transferred to the annuity contract within a specified period after the date the amounts would otherwise have been paid to the participant,[5] although in no event may that ever be longer than as soon as reasonably possible.

If a tax sheltered annuity plan is subject to Title I of ERISA, the Department of Labor requires that amounts an employee pays to the employer or has withheld from salary by the employer for contribution to a plan become plan assets as soon as these amounts reasonably can be segregated from the employer's general assets, but in no event later than the 15th business day of the month following the month in which the contributions are received or withheld by the employer,[6] though the DOL generally takes the position that the required period is a matter of a few days following the payroll date. A tax sheltered annuity plan also can qualify for the ERISA contribution safe harbor for small plans, which is generally a seven day period.

(2)   *Nonforfeitable Rights.* An employee's rights under a 403(b) contract must be nonforfeitable except for failure to pay future premiums.[7] According to final regulations, an employee's rights under a contract are not nonforfeitable unless the participant

---

1.   SBJPA '96, Sec. 1450(a).
2.   IRC Sec. 403(b)(5); Treas. Reg. §1.403(b)-3(b)(1).
3.   GCM 39659 (9-8-87).
4.   *Bollotin v. U.S.*, 76-2 USTC ¶9604 (S.D. N.Y. 1976), *aff'd*, 77-1 USTC ¶9,450 (2d Cir. 1977).
5.   Treas. Reg. §1.403(b)-8(b).
6.   Labor Reg. §2510.3-102.
7.   See IRC Sec. 403(b)(1)(C).

for whom the contract is purchased has at all times a fully vested and nonforfeitable right to all benefits provided under the contract.[1] The effect of this requirement is that salary reduction contributions to a tax sheltered annuity must be immediately vested. Actual employer contributions can be subjected to delayed vesting by treating such nonvested contributions as being subject to 403(c) instead of 403(b).

Tax sheltered annuity plans are not subject to the vesting rules under Section 411, but may be subject to ERISA's vesting rules. PPA 2006 extended to employer nonelective contributions the faster vesting requirements that had applied to employer matching contributions since 2002. The vesting requirements are satisfied under either a three year cliff vesting schedule that reaches 100 percent after three years of service or a graduated vesting schedule, i.e., 20 percent after two years of service, 40 percent after three years, 60 percent after four years, 80 percent after five years, and 100 percent after six years. This change effectively makes all employer contributions in defined contribution plans subject to the faster vesting requirements.[2]

There are vesting rules applicable to employer contributions in plan years beginning after December 31, 2001 (Q 3862). With exceptions for governmental and certain church plans, tax sheltered annuity plans with actual employer contributions generally are subject to ERISA and must comply with ERISA's minimum vesting schedules if they delay vesting.

(3) *Participation and Coverage.* Except for contracts purchased under plans by certain churches or certain governmental plans, tax sheltered annuity contracts generally must be provided under a plan that meets minimum participation, coverage and nondiscrimination requirements if employer contributions are made to those contracts (Q 4031).[3]

(4) *Limits on Elective Deferrals.* Under final regulations, a contract must satisfy IRC Section 401(a)(30), relating to limits on elective deferrals. A contract does not satisfy this limit unless the contract requires all elective deferrals for an employee not to exceed the limits of IRC Section 402(g)(1), which include (1) elective deferrals for the employee under the contract, and (2) any other elective deferrals under the plan under which the contract is purchased and under all other plans, contracts, or arrangements of the employer.[4]

(5) *Nontransferable.* A contract must be expressly nontransferable.[5] An agreement between employer and employee that the employee will not transfer the contract is not sufficient.[6] For this purpose, an employer is considered to have purchased

1.   Treas. Reg. §1.403(b)-3(a)(2).
2.   See IRC Sec. 411(a)(11).
3.   IRC Sec. 403(b)(1)(D); Treas. Reg. §1.403(b)-3(a)(3).
4.   Treas. Reg. §1.403(b)-3(a)(4).
5.   Treas. Reg. §1.403(b)-3(a)(5).
6.   Rev. Rul. 74-458, 1974-2 CB 138.

a new contract when it pays the first premium on a previously issued contract.[1] Although the contract must be nontransferable, the employee can surrender the contract to the insurer, borrow against the loan value, transfer assets to another 403(b) annuity contract or custodial account (Q 4050) and exercise all other ownership rights. Tax results of a policy loan are discussed in Q 4056, Q 4066.

(6)   *Minimum Required Distributions.* Tax sheltered annuity contracts and custodial accounts must provide that distributions of at least a minimum amount must be made.[2] These requirements were previously permitted to be incorporated in a plan by reference (Q 4068), but now must be stated in the annuity contracts themselves.[3]

(7)   *Direct Rollover Option.* A plan generally must provide that if a distributee of any eligible rollover distribution (Q 4000) elects to have the distribution paid directly to a traditional IRA, another tax sheltered annuity (if applicable), or an eligible retirement plan (Q 3993) and specifies the plan to which the distribution is to be paid, then the distribution will be paid to that plan in a direct rollover (Q 3994).[4]

Before PPA 2006, amounts held in an annuity contract or account described in IRC Section 403(b) could not be converted directly to a Roth IRA.[5] Effective for distributions beginning after December 31, 2007, distributions from a 403(b) plan may be rolled over directly into a Roth IRA, subject to the rules that apply to rollovers from a traditional IRA into a Roth IRA. This eliminates the necessity for a conduit traditional IRA.[6]

The payor of a 403(b) annuity contract or custodial account must withhold 20 percent from any eligible rollover distribution that the distributee does not elect to have paid in a direct rollover (Q 3997).[7] A safe harbor explanation that a payor may give to recipients of eligible rollover distributions from tax sheltered annuities is provided in Notice 2002-3.[8]

(8)   *Limitation on Incidental Benefits.* The contract must satisfy the incidental benefit requirements of IRC Section 401(a) (Q 3823, Q 4027, Q 4054, and Q 4075).[9]

(9)   *Maximum Annual Additions.* The annual additions to the contract must not exceed the applicable limitations of IRC Section 415(c), treating contributions and other additions as annual additions (Q 4036, Q 4039).[10]

1.   Rev. Rul. 68-33, 1968-1 CB 175.
2.   IRC Sec. 403(b)(10); Treas. Reg. §1.403(b)-3(a)(6).
3.   TAMRA '88, Sec. 1101A(a)(3), Rev. Proc. 2017-18, 2017-5 IRB 743.
4.   IRC Secs. 403(b)(10), 401(a)(31); Treas. Reg. §1.403(b)-3(a)(7).
5.   Treas. Reg. §1.408A-4, A-5.
6.   See IRC Sec. 408A(e).
7.   IRC Sec. 3405(c).
8.   Notice 2002-3, 2002-2 IRB 289, as updated by Notice 2009-68, 2008-2 CB 423.
9.   Treas. Reg. §1.403(b)-3(a)(8).
10.   Treas. Reg. §1.403(b)-3(a)(9).

Plan in Form and Operation

According to final regulations, a contract does not satisfy the requirements for exclusion from gross income unless it is maintained pursuant to a plan. For this purpose, a plan is a written defined contribution plan that, in both form and operation, satisfies the requirements set forth in IRC Section 403(b) and Treasury regulations.[1] Thus, a plan must contain all of the material terms and conditions for eligibility, benefits, applicable limitations, the contracts available under the plan, and the time and form under which benefit distributions would be made (Q 4030).[2]

4035. What prohibited distribution requirements apply to tax-sheltered annuity plans?

A custodial account invested in mutual funds must provide that amounts will not be made available before the employee dies, attains age 59½, has a severance from employment, becomes disabled within the meaning of IRC Section 72(m)(7), encounters financial hardship or except as may be otherwise provided by regulations, with respect to amounts invested in a lifetime income investment (i) on or after the date that is 90 days prior to the date that such lifetime income investment may no longer be held as an investment option under the contract, and (ii) in the form of a qualified distribution (as defined in section 401(a)(38)(B)(i)) or a qualified plan distribution annuity contract (as defined in section 401(a)(38)(B)(iv)).[3]

Hardship withdrawals may be made only on account of an immediate and heavy financial need (Q 3797). In years beginning after December 31, 1988, financial hardship distributions may be made only from assets held as of the close of the last year beginning before 1989 and from amounts contributed thereafter under a salary reduction agreement, not including earnings on these amounts.

An annuity contract must provide that distributions attributable to salary reduction contributions, including the earnings on them, may be made only after the employee attains age 59½, has severance from employment, dies, becomes disabled, or in the case of hardship, except that the earnings on salary reduction contributions may not be distributed for financial hardship, or, for tax years beginning after 2020, with respect to amounts invested in a lifetime income investment (i) on or after the date that is 90 days prior to the date that such lifetime income investment may no longer be held as an investment option under the contract, and (ii) in the form of a qualified distribution or a qualified plan distribution annuity contract.[4] These restrictions apply for years beginning after 1988, but only with respect to distributions attributable to assets other than assets held as of the close of the last year beginning before 1989.[5] Assets held prior to that date are not subject to these restrictions.

1. Treas. Reg. §1.403(b)-3(b)(3)(i). See Treas. Reg. §§1.403(b)-1 through 1.403(b)-11. See also Preamble, TD 9340, 72 Fed. Fed. 41128, 41130 (7-26-2007).
2. Treas. Reg. §1.403(b)-3(b)(3)(i). See Treas. Reg. §§1.403(b)-1 through 1.403(b)-11.
3. IRC Sec. 403(b)(7)(A)(ii).
4. IRC Sec. 403(b)(11); Treas. Reg. §1.403(b)-6(d)(1)(ii).
5. TAMRA '88, Sec. 1011A(c)(11). See also Let. Rul. 9442030.

Planning Point: The Bipartisan Budget Act of 2018 removed the restriction on distributing earnings as hardship distributions beginning in 2019 (although the changes remain optional for plan sponsors) for qualified plans. Despite this, it is unclear whether the new rules will apply to 403(b) plans because of the way the statute itself is drafted. The Section 403(b) regulations (as well as Section 403(b) itself) clearly prohibit the distribution of earnings as hardship distributions.[1] Future IRS guidance may clarify this point, but for the time being, it appears that the newly expanded rules will not apply equally to 403(b) plans.

Timely distributions of excess elective deferrals (Q 4046) and excess aggregate contributions (Q 4037) may be made without regard to the above restrictions,[2] as they are amounts not attributable to salary reductions that are held in an annuity contract. For the restrictions affecting retirement income accounts, see Q 4051.

Amounts borrowed from a tax sheltered annuity and treated as a deemed distribution under IRC Section 72(p) (Q 4062) are not treated as actual distributions for purposes of these distribution restrictions and will not violate these restrictions.[3] If a participant's accrued benefit is reduced or offset to repay a loan, an actual distribution occurs for purposes of these distribution restrictions.[4] Accordingly, a plan may be prohibited from making such an offset to enforce its security interest in a participant's account balance attributable to salary reduction contributions until a date on which a distribution is permitted under IRC Section 403(b)(11).[5]

Similarly, it would seem that servicing a plan loan with tax sheltered annuity funds before a distribution is permitted would constitute a prohibited distribution. Even though a distribution may be permitted under these rules for hardship or after severance from employment, it may nonetheless be subject to a 10 percent tax in addition to income tax as a premature distribution (Q 4073). These rules also apply to custodial accounts.

A distribution to a former spouse pursuant to a qualified domestic relations order ("QDRO") will be permitted under certain circumstances (Q 3914) even though the distribution otherwise might be prohibited under the prohibited distribution rules.[6]

4036. What is the written plan requirement for 403(b) plans?

According to final regulations, a contract does not satisfy the requirements for exclusion from gross income (Q 4034) unless it is maintained pursuant to a plan. For this purpose, a plan is a written defined contribution plan that in both form and operation satisfies the requirements set forth in the regulations.[7] Thus, a plan must contain all of the material terms and conditions for eligibility, benefits, applicable limitations, the contracts available under the plan, and the time and form under which benefit distributions would be made.[8]

---

1. Treas. Reg. §1.403(b)-6(d)(2).
2. IRC Secs. 402(g)(2), 401(m)(6).
3. Treas. Reg. §1.72(p)-1, A-12.
4. Treas. Reg. §1.403(b)-6(g).
5. Treas. Reg. §1.72(p)-1, A-13(b).
6. IRC Sec. 414(p)(10); Treas. Reg. §1.403(b)-10(c).
7. Treas. Reg. §1.403(b)-3(b)(3)(i). See Treas. Reg. §§1.403(b)-1 through 1.403(b)-11.
8. Treas. Reg. §1.403(b)-3(b)(3)(i). See Treas. Reg. §§1.403(b)-1 through 1.403(b)-11.

A plan may contain optional features that are consistent with, but not required, under IRC Section 403(b), including features with respect to hardship withdrawal distributions, loans, plan-to-plan or annuity contract-to-annuity contract transfers, and acceptance of rollovers to the plan. If a plan contains any optional provisions, the optional provisions must meet, in both form and operation, the relevant requirements.[1]

A plan may allocate responsibility for performing administrative functions, including functions to comply with the requirements of Section 403(b) and other tax requirements. Any allocation must identify responsibility for compliance with the requirements of the IRC that apply on the basis of the aggregated contracts issued to a participant under a plan, including loans under IRC Section 72(p) and conditions for obtaining a hardship withdrawal. A plan is permitted to assign responsibilities to parties other than the eligible employer, but not to participants.[2]

The final regulations do not require that there be a single plan document.[3] To satisfy the requirement that a plan include all material provisions, the regulations permit the plan to incorporate by reference other documents including the insurance policy or custodial account, which as a result then become part of the plan. Consequently, a plan may include a wide variety of documents, but it is important for the employer that adopts the plan to ensure that there is no conflict with other documents that are incorporated by reference.[4]

Notice 2009-3 provided relief from immediate compliance with the written plan requirement in calendar year 2009. Effective January 1, 2009, sponsors of 403(b) plans generally were required to maintain a written plan that satisfies, in both form and operation, the requirements of the final regulations. In response to numerous requests for deferral of the effective date, the IRS announced in Notice 2009-3 that it will not treat a 403(b) plan as failing to satisfy the requirements of IRC Section 403(b) and the final regulations during the 2009 calendar year, provided that, (1) on or before December 31, 2009, the sponsor of the plan had adopted a written 403(b) plan that was intended to satisfy the requirements of IRC Section 403(b), including the final regulations, effective as of January 1, 2009, (2) during 2009, the sponsor operated the plan in accordance with a reasonable interpretation of IRC Section 403(b), taking into account the final regulations, and (3) before the end of 2009, the sponsor made its best efforts to retroactively correct any operational failure during the 2009 calendar year to conform to the terms of the written 403(b) plan, with such corrections based on the general principles of correction set forth in the Employee Plans Compliance Resolution System "(EPCRS").[5] The IRS makes clear that the relief provided under Notice 2009-3 applies solely with respect to the 2009 calendar year and may not be relied on with respect to the operation of the plan or correction of operational defects in any prior or subsequent year.[6]

1.   Treas. Reg. §1.403(b)-3(b)(3)(i).
2.   Preamble, TD 9340, 72 Fed. Reg. 41128, 41130 (7-26-2007).
3.   See Preamble, TD 9340, 72 Fed. Reg. 41128, 41130 (7-26-2007). See also "Retirement Plan FAQs Regarding 403(b) Tax Sheltered Annuity Plans" at: (http://www.irs.gov/Retirement-Plans/Retirement-Plans-FAQs-regarding-403%28b%29-Tax-Sheltered-Annuity-Plans).
4.   Preamble, TD 9340, 72 Fed. Reg. 41128, 41130 (7-26-2007).
5.   Section 6 of Rev. Proc. 2008-50, 2008-35 IRB 464, as modified by Rev. Proc. 2013-12, 2013-1 CB 313, and superseded and supplemented by Rev. Proc. 2016-8, 2016-1 IRB 243 and Rev. Proc. 2019-5.
6.   Notice 2009-3, 2009-2 IRB 250.

The IRS amended its EPCRS program to permit employers which have not timely adopted written plan documents under Notice 2009-3 to correct that error by submitting the document for approval of late adoption. This is done by filing under the Voluntary Compliance Program under the EPCRS, and paying a filing fee which specifically applies to nonadopters.

Remedial Amendment Period

The IRS has established an initial "Remedial Amendment Period" ("RAP") for 403(b) plans related to changes imposed by the 2007 regulations.[1] This remedial amendment period runs through March 31, 2020, under Revenue Procedure 2017-18. This deadline was delayed to June 30, 2020 in response to COVID-19.

The first day of this RAP is January 1, 2010 (though plan sponsors were permitted to amend their plans retroactively to January 1, 2009), and the last day of the period is June 30, 2020. The IRS has now approved the first pre-approved 403(b) prototype plans submitted under Revenue Procedure 2013-22, as extended by Revenue Procedure 2014-28, under Revenue Procedure 2017-18.

Any employer can also correct any plan document errors which occurred between January 1, 2009 and June 30, 2020 by adopting one of these IRS pre-approved plans by that date.

Plan document errors made after the June 30, 2020 can be corrected in accordance with the EPCRS by making a filing under the Voluntary Compliance Program.

Model Plan Language

In 2007, the IRS issued Revenue Procedure 2007-71, which provides model plan language that may be used by public schools either to adopt a written plan to reflect the requirements of IRC Section 403(b) and Treasury regulations, or to amend a 403(b) plan to reflect the requirements of IRC Section 403(b) and Treasury regulations.[2]

The revenue procedure also provides rules for when plan amendments or a written plan are required to be adopted by public schools or other eligible employers to comply with final IRC Section 403(b) regulations.

In addition, the revenue procedure addresses the use of the model plan language by employers that are not public schools.

However, the model plan language will no longer be effective after June 30, 2020, and any employer adopting such model plan will need to restate the plans to an IRS pre-approved document.

---

1.   Rev. Proc. 2013-22, 2013-18 IRB 985.
2.   Rev. Proc. 2007-71, 2007-51 IRB 1184, *as modified by* Notice 2009-3, 2009-2 IRB 250.

403(b) Prototype Plan Program

The IRS has issued a pre-approved plan program for 403(b) plans similar to the current programs offered for IRC Section 401(a) tax-qualified plans under Revenue Procedure 2013-22. The IRS is only intending to issue determination letters to these pre-approved plans, and will not issue determination letters on individually designed 403(b) plans.

The IRS program will provide pre-approved documents for 403(b) retirement plans, which means that employers will need to restate their plans to reflect a new plan document by the end of a remedial amendment period (RAP) that ended June 30, 2020. Annuity contracts and custodial agreements will need to be updated, and now the plan RMD requirements must be stated in the contracts themselves, rather than in the plan document. The employer will also need to complete an administrative appendix that will now be included with the IRS-approved plan documents.[1]

Interaction between Title I of ERISA and IRC Section 403(b)

The Department of Labor is of the view that tax-exempt employers will be able to comply with the requirements in the new IRC Section 403(b) regulations and remain within the DOL's safe harbor for TSA programs funded solely by salary deferrals. The DOL noted, however, that new IRC Section 403(b) regulations offer employers considerable flexibility in shaping the extent and nature of their involvement under a tax-sheltered annuity program. Thus, the question of whether any particular employer, in complying with the IRC Section 403(b) final regulations, has established a plan covered under Title I of ERISA must be analyzed on a case-by-case basis.[2]

4037. What nondiscrimination requirements must a tax sheltered annuity meet?

Prior to 1989, there was no requirement that all employees, or that all of any class of employees, be made eligible for participation in an employer's tax sheltered annuity plan. In years beginning after 1988, except for contracts purchased by certain churches or church-controlled organizations, tax sheltered annuities must be provided under a plan that meets certain nondiscrimination requirements.[3]

Notice 89-23 provided that a tax sheltered annuity plan would be deemed to be in compliance with these nondiscrimination requirements if the employer operated the plan in accordance with a reasonable, good faith interpretation of the requirements.[4] Notice 89-23 provided guidance for complying with the nondiscrimination rules. Also, transitional safe harbors were generally available for tax sheltered annuities to meet most of these requirements.

---

1. Rev. Proc. 2017-18, 2017-5 IRB 743.
2. Department of Labor Field Assistance Bulletin No. 2007-02 (7-24-2007).
3. IRC Secs. 403(b)(1)(D), 403(b)(12).
4. Notice 89-23, 1989-1 CB 654, as modified by Notice 90-73, 1990-2 CB 353, Notice 92-36, 1992-2 CB 364 and Notice 96-64, 1996-2 CB 229; see also Ann. 95-48, 1995-23 IRB 13.

The final 403(b) regulations do not include the Notice 89-23 good faith reasonable standard, however.[1] The final regulations provide that an annuity contract does not satisfy the nondiscrimination requirements unless the contributions are made pursuant to a plan (Q 4034), and the terms of the plan satisfy the nondiscrimination rules.[2]

In General

Various employees, including students employed by a school in which they are enrolled and regularly attending classes and employees who normally work fewer than 20 hours per week, generally may be excluded.[3] If any students or part-time employees are excluded, all must be.[4] An employee normally works fewer than 20 hours per week if (1) for the twelve month period beginning on the date the employee's employment commenced, the employer reasonably expects the employee to work fewer than 1,000 hours of service as defined in IRC Section 410(a)(3)(C) in that period, and (2) for each plan year ending after the close of the twelve month period beginning on the date the employee's employment commenced or, if the plan so provides, each subsequent twelve month period, the employee worked fewer than 1,000 hours of service in the preceding twelve month period.[5]

In the case of plans subject to ERISA, if an employer requires a minimum age or a minimum number of years of service, the employer may not require that the employee complete a period of service extending beyond the date the employee becomes 21 or, if later, completes one year of service. If an employee is given a non-forfeitable right to 100 percent of his or her accrued benefits as normally would be the case with a tax sheltered annuity, the waiting period may be as much as two years instead of one. In the case of employees of an educational institution, the age may be 26 instead of 21 if after one year of service the employee is 100 percent vested and the employee's rights are non-forfeitable.[6]

Title I of ERISA, regarding reporting, disclosure, participation, and vesting, does not apply to governmental and church plans.[7] ERISA also generally does not apply to tax sheltered annuities of other employers unless the plan is established or maintained by the employer.[8]

A salary reduction plan generally will not be considered "established or maintained" by an employer if, among other things, employee participation is voluntary, employer involvement is limited to such things as requesting and providing information and collecting and remitting premiums, and the employer permits employees at least a reasonable choice among products and annuity contractors; an employer need not seek out products and contractors.[9] An employer was found to exceed the limited involvement permitted under the regulation where the employer

---

1. Preamble, 72 Fed. Reg. 41128, 41134 (7-27-2007).
2. Treas. Reg. §§1.403(b)-5(c), 1.403(b)-5.
3. See IRC Sec. 403(b)(12)(A).
4. See IRC Sec. 403(b)(12)(A).
5. Treas. Reg. §1.403(b)-5(b)(4)(iii)(B).
6. ERISA Sec. 202.
7. ERISA Sec. 4(b).
8. See ERISA Sec. 3(2).
9. Labor Reg. §2510.3-2(f).

evaluated circumstances and exercised its judgment in determining eligibility for in-service withdrawals on account of disability or financial hardship.[1]

Planning Point: Since the issuance of the 2007 regulations, the DOL has issued extensive guidance on the circumstances when an employer may be considered establishing and maintaining a plan.[2]

4038. What nondiscrimination requirements apply to tax sheltered annuity plans offering salary reduction contributions?

Tax sheltered annuity plans offering salary reduction contributions generally are subject to a single nondiscrimination rule (the "universal availability" rule) with respect to salary reduction contributions. The requirement does not apply to contracts purchased by certain churches or church-controlled[3] organizations.[4]

If any employee may elect to have the employer make contributions to a TSA under a salary reduction agreement, then all employees of the organization other than certain excludable employees generally must be allowed to elect to have the employer make contributions of more than $200 annually pursuant to a salary reduction agreement.[5] Furthermore, the employee's right to make elective deferrals also includes the right to designate 403(b) elective deferrals as Roth contributions, if Roth contributions are otherwise permitted under the plan.[6]

The final 403(b) regulations clarify that an employee is not treated as being permitted to have 403(b) elective deferrals unless the employee is provided with an effective opportunity that satisfies certain requirements (see Q 4039).

The general thrust of this rule is to require that all employees be eligible to make salary reduction contributions if the opportunity to make salary reduction contributions is offered to any employee, as a way to prevent discrimination in favor of the highly compensated employees. The employer may, however, require a minimum annual salary reduction contribution of more than $200, and may exclude from participation in a salary reduction agreement any employee who is not willing to reduce salary by more than $200 per year.[7] The rule probably also prohibits employer efforts to cap an employee's annual salary reduction contributions at $200 or less.

In addition, the nondiscrimination rule applicable to salary reduction contributions allows an employer to exclude certain other employees, including those who are participants in an IRC Section 457(b) deferred compensation plan of a governmental employer, a qualified cash or

---

1.   DOL Adv. Op. 94-30A.
2.   DOL Adv. Op. 2012-02A; Field Assistance Bulletins 2010-01 2009-02 and 2007-02.
3.   Treas. Reg. §1.403(b)-5(b)(2).
4.   Treas. Reg. §1.403(b)-5(d).
5.   IRC Secs. 403(b)(1)(D), 403(b)(12)(A)(ii), 403(b)(12)(B). See also Treas. Reg. §1.403(b)-5(b)(1).
6.   Treas. Reg. §1.403(b)-5(b)(1).
7.   See, e.g., H.R. Rep. No. 99-426 (Tax Reform Act of 1986), at 715, *reprinted in* 1986-3 CB (vol. 2), at 715; H.R. Conf. Rep. No. 99-841 (TRA '86), at II-420, *reprinted in* 1986-3 CB (vol.4), at 420. See also Treas. Reg. §1.403(b)-5(b)(3)(i).

deferred IRC Section 401(k) arrangement of the employer, or another tax sheltered annuity.[1] Certain ministers[2] may be excluded as well.[3]

A contribution is considered not made pursuant to a salary reduction agreement if under the agreement it is made pursuant to a one time irrevocable election by the employee at the time of initial eligibility to participate.[4] The legislative history provides that if an employee has a one-time election to participate in a program that requires an employee contribution, the contribution will not be considered an elective deferral to the extent that the employee is not permitted subsequently to modify the election in any manner.[5]

An employer that historically has treated one or more of its various geographically distinct units as separate for employee benefit purposes may treat each unit as a separate organization so long as the unit is operated independently on a day-to-day basis. Units located within the same Standard Metropolitan Statistical Area generally are not geographically distinct.[6]

A plan will not be treated as violating the requirements under IRC Section 403(b)(12) merely on account of the making of, or the right to make, catch-up contributions (Q 3761) by participants age 50 or over under the provisions of IRC Section 414(v), so long as a universal availability requirement is met.[7]

4039. When does an employee participating in a tax-sheltered annuity plan have an "effective opportunity" to make elective deferrals for purposes of the nondiscrimination requirements applicable to plans that offer salary reduction contributions?

An employee is not treated as being permitted to have 403(b) elective deferrals contributed on the employee's behalf unless the employee is provided an effective opportunity that satisfies the following requirements.[8]

Whether an employee has an effective opportunity is determined based on all relevant facts and circumstances, including (1) notice of the availability of the election, (2) the period of time during which an election may be made, and (3) any other conditions on elections.

A 403(b) plan satisfies the effective opportunity requirement only if, at least once during each plan year, the plan provides an employee with an effective opportunity to make or change a cash or deferred election between cash or a contribution to the plan.

Furthermore, an effective opportunity includes the right to have 403(b) elective deferrals made on his or her behalf up to the lesser of (1) the applicable limits for 403(b) elective deferrals,

1.   IRC Sec. 403(b)(12)(A); Treas. Reg. §1.403(b)-5(b)(4)(ii).
2.   Described in IRC Sec. 414(e)(5)(C).
3.   See IRC Sec. 403(b)(12)(A).
4.   IRC Sec. 403(b)(12)(A).
5.   H.R. Conf. Rep. No. 99-841 (TRA '86), at II-420, *reprinted in* 1986-3 CB (vol. 4), at 420; General Explanation of TRA '86, p. 680.
6.   Treas. Reg. §1.403(b)-5(b)(3)(ii).
7.   IRC Sec. 414(v)(3)(B).
8.   Treas. Reg. §1.403(b)-5(b)(2).

including any permissible catch-up elective deferrals under the age 50 catch-up, and the special 403(b) catch-up for certain organizations, or (2) the applicable limits under the contract with the largest limitation, and applies to part-time as well as full-time employees.

An effective opportunity is not considered to exist if there are any other rights or benefits that are conditioned, directly or indirectly, on a participant making or failing to make a cash or deferred election with respect to a contribution to a 403(b) contract.

4040. What nondiscrimination requirements apply to a tax sheltered annuity plan that provides for contributions other than by salary reduction?

According to the final regulations, under IRC Section 403(b)(12)(A)(i), employer contributions and employee after-tax contributions must satisfy all of the following nondiscrimination requirements in the same manner as a qualified plan under IRC Section 401(a):

(1)   Section 401(a)(4), relating to nondiscrimination in contributions and benefits, taking Section 401(a)(5) into account

(2)   Section 401(a)(17), limiting the amount of compensation that can be taken into account

(3)   Section 401(m), relating to matching and after-tax employee contributions

(4)   Section 410(b), relating to minimum coverage[1]

Section 401(a)(26), although listed in IRC Section 403(b)(12)(A)(i), no longer applies to defined contribution plans.

The final regulations do not adopt the good faith reasonableness standard of Notice 89-23 for purposes of satisfying the nondiscrimination requirements of IRC Section 403(b)(12)(A)(i).[2] The Notice 89-23 standard continues to apply to state and local public schools and certain church entities for determining whether the controlled group rules apply.[3] See Q 3841 through Q 3866 for the actual requirements of IRC Section 401(a)(4), IRC Section 401(a)(5), IRC Section 401(a)(17), IRC Section 401(m), and IRC Section 410(b).

Governmental plans. A governmental plan is one established by the United States government, the government of any state or political subdivision, or any agency or instrumentality of any of them.[4] The minimum participation and coverage and nondiscrimination requirements described in IRC Section 403(b)(12)(A)(i), other than IRC Section 401(a)(17), do not apply to state and local governmental plans. In particular, the requirements of IRC Sections 401(a)(4), 401(a)(5),

---

1.   Treas. Reg. §1.403(b)-5(a).
2.   Preamble, T.D. 9340, 72 Fed. Reg. 41128, 41134 (7-26-2007).
3.   Preamble, T.D. 9340, 72 Fed. Reg. 41128, 41134 (7-26-2007).
4.   IRC Sec. 414(d).

401(m), and 410(b) do not apply to such plans.[1] Sponsors of governmental 403(b) plans must comply with regulations under IRC Section 401(a)(17).[2]

501(c)(3) tax-exempt organizations. Regulations under IRC Sections 401(a)(4), 401(a)(5), and 410(b) generally are effective for plans maintained by tax-exempt organizations. Tax-exempt sponsors of 403(b) plans must comply with regulations under Section 401(a)(17).

All employees of a group of employers that are members of a controlled group of corporations or all employees of trades or businesses that are under common control will be treated as employed by a single employer for purposes of the minimum participation, coverage, and nondiscrimination rules (Q 3932).[3] Under the final regulations, common control exists between an exempt organization and another organization if at least 80 percent of the directors or trustees of one organization either are representatives of, or are directly or indirectly controlled by, the other organization. A trustee or director is treated as a representative of another exempt organization if he or she also is a trustee, director, agent, or employee of the other exempt organization. A trustee or director is controlled by another organization if the other organization has the general power to remove the trustee or director and designate a new trustee or director. Whether a person has the power to remove or designate a trustee or director is based on facts and circumstances.[4]

Contributions

4041. What limits exist with respect to excludable contributions to a tax sheltered annuity?

An employee generally can exclude from gross income the contributions paid by the employee's IRC Section 501(c)(3) or public school employer to a retirement annuity for the employee's benefit.[5] The amount that the employee may exclude in the employee's tax year is limited.

For taxable years beginning after 2001, there are two limits to be considered. The first is the overall limit (Q 4042). The second is the limit on the amount that may be excluded under a salary reduction agreement (Q 4046).[6]

For taxable years beginning after 2001, the exclusion allowance is permanently repealed.[7]

If the entire contribution in the year is by salary reduction, only the lowest of the two limits may be excluded. If the contribution is partly salary reduction and partly additional contribution, the salary reduction portion is limited to the salary reduction limit, and the excludable

---

1. IRC Sec. 403(b)(12)(C).
2. Treas. Reg. §1.401(a)(17)-1(d)(4)(i).
3. IRC Secs. 403(b)(12)(A)(i), 414(b), 414(c).
4. Treas. Reg. §1.414(c)-5; T.D. 9340, 72 Fed. Reg. 41128, 41158 (7-26-2007).
5. IRC Sec. 403(b)(1).
6. IRC Sec. 403(b)(1).
7. Sec. 811, PPA 2006; IRC Sec. 403(b)(2), as repealed by EGTRRA 2001.

contribution may not exceed the IRC Section 415 limit.[1] The effect of contributions that exceed these limits is explained in Q 4045, Q 4046, and Q 4052.

The IRC Section 415 overall limit (see Q 4042) applies to contributions and other additions regardless of whether they are vested or not.[2]

4042. How does the Section 415 limit affect the excludable amount for a tax sheltered annuity?

The limit on contributions and benefits applicable to qualified pension plans applies to tax sheltered annuities (Q 4041).[3] For the purpose of this limit, tax sheltered annuities generally will be treated as defined contribution plans.[4] Thus, they are subject to a limit of the lesser of 100 percent of the participant's compensation (defined in Q 4043) or the applicable dollar limit. The applicable dollar limit for 2021 is $58,000.[5] This limit is indexed for inflation in increments of $1,000 (Q 3867).[6]

The limit is on the amount of annual additions that may be made in any limitation year to a participant's account.

Annual additions are employer contributions, including salary reduction amounts and employee after-tax contributions. Excess elective deferrals (Q 4046) that are correctly distributed under the regulations are not included as annual additions.[7] Excess matching employer contributions (Q 4037) are included, however, even if the excess is corrected by a distribution from the plan.[8]

Earnings attributable to distributed elective deferrals that are not themselves distributed will be treated as an employer contribution for the limitation year in which the distributed elective deferral was made.[9] A contribution made during a tax year is considered to be made on the last day of the limitation year that ends in or with the tax year.[10]

A limitation year is the calendar year or any other twelve month period that may be elected by the plan in the plan document. Contributions in excess of the overall limit are discussed in Q 4045.

1. See Treas. Reg. §1.415-6(e)(1).
2. See IRC Sec. 403(b)(1).
3. IRC Sec. 415(a)(2).
4. Treas. Reg. §1.415-6(e)(1)(i).
5. IRC Sec. 415(c); Notice 2020-79.
6. IRC Sec. 415(d)(4)(B).
7. Treas. Reg. §§1.402(g)-1(e)(1)(ii); 1.415-6(b)(1)(i).
8. Treas. Reg. §§1.401(m)-1(e)(3)(iv); 1.415-6(b)(1)(i).
9. Treas. Reg. §1.415-6(b)(6)(iv).
10. Treas. Reg. §1.415-6(e)(1)(iii).

4043. What is includable compensation for purposes of the Section 403(b) contribution limits?

In the case of a 403(b) annuity contract, "participant's compensation" means the participant's includable compensation determined under IRC Section 403(b)(3).[1] Includable compensation is based on compensation earned by the employee for the most recent period, ending not later than the close of the taxable year for which the limitation is being determined, that constitutes a full year of service and that precedes the taxable year by no more than five years.[2]

Thus, for a full time employee, includable compensation generally is the employee's salary for the current taxable year. For a part-time employee, fractional year earnings are required to be aggregated.[3] To illustrate, assume that as of the end of 2021, an employee had worked three years half-time and had the following earnings: $11,500 in 2018, $12,000 in 2019, and $12,500 in 2020-2021. In computing the employee's exclusion allowance for 2021, the employee's includable compensation would be $24,500 ($12,000 + $12,500).

The definition of includable compensation includes any elective deferrals (Q 4046) made to the plan and any amount that has been contributed or deferred by the employer at the election of the employee and that is not includable in gross income by reason of IRC Section 125, IRC Section 132(f)(4), or IRC Section 457 (see Q 3501 concerning cafeteria plans and Q 3581 concerning IRC Section 457 deferred compensation plans).[4]

Only compensation from an employer that made the contribution can be included; compensation from any other employer or any other source cannot be included. The employer is generally the common law employer.

For purposes of determining the limits on contributions under IRC Section 415(c), amounts paid to a minister as a tax-free housing allowance may not be treated as compensation under the general or alternative definitions of compensation under the regulations.[5]

Certain payments made after an employee's severance from employment will not fail to be compensation within the meaning of IRS Section 415(c) if the compensation is paid by the later of 2½ months after severance from employment with the employer maintaining the plan or the end of the limitations year that includes the date of severance from employment with the employer maintaining the plan.[6]

4044. Are contributions to a 403(b) plan aggregated with other defined contribution plan contributions to determine the Section 415 limitation?

Contributions to a 403(b) plan generally do not need to be aggregated with other 401(a) defined contribution plans of the employer in computing the Section 415 limitation. If a person

---

1. IRC Sec. 415(c)(3)(E).
2. IRC Sec. 403(b)(3).
3. IRC Sec. 403(b)(4)(B).
4. IRC Sec. 403(b)(3).
5. Let. Rul. 200135045.
6. See Treas. Reg. §§1.415(c)-2(e)(3)(ii), 1.403(b)-3(b)(4)(ii).

participates in a 401(a) defined contribution plan and also participates in a 403(b) plan of another employer, contributions to both plans must be aggregated for 415 purposes if that participant is in control of either employer.

In applying the IRC Section 415 limit to a combination of a 403(b) annuity and a defined contribution plan of an individual controlled by the employer, each plan separately must meet the limit applicable to it taking into consideration only the compensation from the employer providing the plan. In determining the combined limit, compensation from the controlled employer may be aggregated with that from the employer providing the annuity.[1]

4045. What is the effect of making contributions to a tax sheltered annuity in excess of the overall limit?

To the extent a contribution in a limitation year exceeds the overall IRC Section 415 limit, it must be included in gross income for the tax year with which or in which the limitation year ends[2] to the extent the excess is not returned in a timely manner.

As a result of excess IRC Section 415 amounts, the annuity contract or custodial account is bifurcated into a non-qualified annuity, comprised of the excess and earnings thereon, and considered a "403(c)" contract and a qualifying 403(b) annuity.[3] The entire contract fails to be a 403(b) contract if an excess annual addition is made and a separate account is not maintained with respect to the excess.[4]

An excess contribution made to a custodial account also may be subject to an excise tax (Q 4052).

4046. What is the limit on excludable amounts that may be contributed to tax sheltered annuity plans under salary reduction agreements?

The amount of elective deferrals that an individual can exclude from income for a tax year is limited. Elective deferrals are:

(1)   amounts contributed to tax sheltered annuity plans under salary reduction agreements;

(2)   amounts contributed under cash or deferred arrangements to 401(k) plans (Q 3751) and salary reduction SEPs ("SAR-SEPs") (Q 3705); and

(3)   amounts contributed under salary reductions to SIMPLE IRAs (Q 3706).[5]

Elective deferrals do not include elective contributions made pursuant to a one-time irrevocable election that is made at initial eligibility to participate in the salary reduction agreement

---

1.   IRC Sec. 415(f).
2.   Treas. Reg. §§1.415-6(e)(1)(ii), 1.403(b)-4(f)(1).
3.   See Treas. Reg. §1.403(b)-3(b)(2), referring to IRC Sec. 415(a)(2) (flush language).
4.   Treas. Reg. §1.403(b)-3(b)(2).
5.   IRC Sec. 402(g).

or pursuant to certain other one time irrevocable elections specified in regulations, or pre-tax contributions made as a condition of employment.[1]

For 2018, the aggregate limit on elective deferrals was $18,500, the limit for 2019 is $19,000, and the limit for 2020-2021 is $19,500.[2] The elective deferral limit is indexed for inflation in increments of $500.[3]

4047. What is the special increase to the limit on amounts contributed to a tax sheltered annuity plan under a salary reduction agreement for employees who have completed 15 years of service?

A special increased limit is provided for amounts contributed to 403(b) plans under a salary reduction agreement in the case of an employee who has completed 15 years of service with an educational institution, hospital, health and welfare service agency (including a home health service agency or an adoption agency), a church (or a convention or association of churches), or church-related organization.[4]

The limit for any one year is increased by the lesser of the following:

(1) $3,000;

(2) $15,000, reduced by the sum of amounts already excluded for prior taxable years by reason of this special exception and the aggregate amount of designated Roth contributions for prior taxable years; or

(3)   the excess of $5,000 multiplied by the number of years of service the employee has with the organization over all elective deferrals to 403(b) plans, 401(k) plans, SEPs, and SIMPLE IRAs.[5]

The current limit ($19,500 in 2021) is the amount subject to increase by the above amount.[6]

The 15 years of service requirement takes into account only employment with the qualified organization. Thus, an employee who has not completed at least 15 years of service taking into account only employment with the qualified organization is not a qualified employee.[7] For the rule coordinating the 15 years of service catch-up with the age 50 catch-up, see Q 4049.

---

1.   IRC Sec. 402(g)(3).
2.   IRC Sec. 402(g)(1); Notice 2017-64, Notice 2018-83, Notice 2019-59, Notice 2020-79.
3.   IRC Sec. 402(g)(4).
4.   Treas. Reg. §1.403(b)-4(c)(3). See, e.g., Let. Rul. 200934012.
5.   IRC Sec. 402(g)(7). See also IRS Publication 571, Tax Sheltered Annuity Plans (January 2019).
6.   Notice 2020-79.
7.   See Treas. Reg. §1.403(b)-4(c)(3)(iii). See Let. Rul. 200934012 ($3,000 catch-up contribution permitted where the employee had worked for the same college for 24 years).

4048. What are the consequences of exceeding the limit on elective deferrals to a tax sheltered annuity plan?

Any elective deferral in excess of the applicable limit is included in the individual's gross income for the year of deferral. If any such amount is included, the individual may, no later than April 15 of the following year, allocate the excess deferrals among the plans under which the deferrals were made and, if plan language permits it, the plans may distribute to the individual the amounts so allocated together with income allocable to the amounts no later than April 15 of that year.[1] A timely distribution may be made regardless of otherwise applicable prohibitions on distributions (Q 4034).[2]

Because an excess deferral is not excluded from gross income, the excess amount distributed under these rules by April 15 is not included in income as a distribution. Any income on the excess deferral is included in income in the taxable year in which distributed.[3]

A distribution of less than the entire amount of excess and income is treated as a pro rata distribution of deferral amount and income.[4] A distribution by April 15 of excess deferrals and income is not subject to tax as a premature distribution under IRC Section 72(t).[5] A distribution of an excess deferral is not a distribution for purposes of meeting the minimum distribution requirements.[6]

If the excess deferral is not distributed by April 15, it is subject to the regular prohibitions on withdrawals and is not included in the investment in the contract, or basis, even though it has been included in income. Thus, excess deferrals are includable in gross income when later distributed.[7] A withdrawal that occurs before the excess deferral was made does not count as a distribution of an excess deferral.[8]

The amount of salary reduction excludable in a year may actually be less than the amount permitted under the limit if the overall limit is less (Q 4041). Contributions by salary reduction are not deductible employee contributions; they are employer contributions that are excludable within limits (Q 4034, Q 4041).

4049. Can participants in a tax sheltered annuity plan who are age 50 and over contribute a "catch-up" contribution each year?

The otherwise applicable dollar limit on elective deferrals under a Section 403(b) annuity can be increased for individuals who attain age 50 by the end of the taxable year.[9]

---

1.   IRC Sec. 402(g)(2); Treas. Reg. §1.402(g)-1(e)(2). See also Treas. Reg. §§1.403(b)-4(f)(1), 1.403(b)-4(f)(4).
2.   IRC Sec. 402(g)(2).
3.   Treas. Reg. §1.402(g)-1(e)(8).
4.   Treas. Reg. §1.402(g)-1(e)(10).
5.   Treas. Reg. §1.402(g)-1(e)(8).
6.   IRC Sec. 402(g)(2)(C); Treas. Reg. §1.402(g)-1(e)(9).
7.   IRC Sec. 402(g)(6).
8.   Treas. Reg. §1.402(g)-1(e)(3).
9.   IRC Secs. 414(v)(1), 414(v)(5).

In 2021, the applicable dollar amount is \$6,500.[1] The limit is indexed for inflation in \$500 increments.[2]

Catch-up contributions by participants age 50 or over made under the provisions of IRS Section 414(v) are not subject to the elective deferral limit.[3] The elective deferral limit of \$19,500 in 2021 is increased by the special catch-up limit under IRC Section 402(g)(7) and by the catch-up limit under Treasury Regulation Section 1.414(v)-1(c)(2).[4]

According to final 403(b) regulations, any catch-up amount contributed by an employee who is eligible for both an age 50 catch-up and the special 403(b) catch-up for certain organizations is treated first as an amount contributed as a special 403(b) catch-up, to the extent that type of catch-up is permitted and second as an amount contributed as an age 50 catch-up to the extent the catch-up amount (Q 3761) exceeds the maximum special 403(b) catch-up after taking into account IRC Sections 402(g) and 415(c), the special 403(b) catch-up, and any limits on the special 403(b) catch-up that are imposed by the terms of the plan.[5]

4050. Are the elective deferral limits for tax sheltered annuity plans coordinated with the limits applicable to IRC Section 457 plans?

For taxable years beginning after 2001, the rules requiring that the contribution limits under IRC Section 457 be coordinated with elective deferral limits are permanently repealed.[6] Consequently, an individual who participates in a 403(b) and 457 plan conceivably could defer a total of \$39,000 in 2020-2021 (\$19,500 in each plan), up from \$38,000 in 2019 (\$19,000 in each plan) (Q 3584).[7]

4051. What special rules apply to tax sheltered annuities for church employees?

A duly ordained, commissioned, or licensed minister of a church or a lay person who is an employee of a church or a convention or association of churches, including a tax-exempt organization controlled by or associated with a convention or association of churches, may be able to increase excludable tax sheltered annuity contributions under the special rules explained below.

For these purposes, a duly ordained, commissioned, or licensed minister who is self-employed or who is employed by an organization other than one described in IRC Section 501(c)(3), but with respect to which the minister shares common religious bonds, is considered a church employee.[8] This definition includes chaplains.

---

1. See IRC Sec. 414(v)(2)(B)(i); Notice 2020-79.
2. See IRC Sec. 414(v)(2)(B)(ii).
3. See IRC Section 414(v)(3)(A); Treas. Reg. §1.414(v)-1(d).
4. Treas. Reg. §1.402(g)-2(a).
5. Treas. Reg. §1.403(b)-4(c)(3)(iv).
6. IRC Sec. 457(c).
7. IR-2013-86 (Oct. 31, 2013), IR-2014-99 (Oct. 23, 2014). See, e.g., Let. Rul. 200934012 (college president allowed to defer \$15,500 each to a 403(b) plan and a 457(b) plan for calendar year 2008), Notice 2018-83, Notice 2019-59, Notice 2020-79.
8. See IRC Sec. 414(e)(5).

A church employee may make an election that may provide a higher IRC Section 415 annual additions limit than discussed in Q 4042. This employee may elect an annual addition limit of as much as $10,000 in any one year. Employer contributions under this election, that is, payments in excess of the otherwise applicable annual addition limit, may not aggregate more than $40,000 over the employee's lifetime.[1]

A church employee with 15 years of service is eligible for the higher elective deferral limit explained in Q 4046.

Contributions to a defined contribution program (a "retirement income account") established or maintained by a church are considered contributions for a tax sheltered annuity contract. A program in existence on August 13, 1982, will not fail to be a tax sheltered annuity merely because it is a defined benefit plan even if it is later amended or extended to other employees.[2]

Retirement income accounts can be established for self-employed ministers and chaplains and ministers who are employed by an organization other than one described in IRC Section 501(c)(3) but with respect to which the ministers share common religious bonds. The SECURE Act clarified that employees of a non-qualified church-controlled organization may be covered under a Section 403(b) plan.

The final 403(b) regulations clarify that retirement income accounts will be expected to be maintained pursuant to a plan that affirmatively states the intent to be a retirement income account.[3]

Contributions made by a minister to a retirement income account after 2001 are allowed to the extent they do not exceed the limit on elective deferrals or the limit on annual additions.[4]

A church plan does not have to meet the participation and nondiscrimination requirements applicable to other employer tax sheltered annuity plans (Q 4037)[5] if it meets certain requirements of being a church.

In figuring the Section 415 annual additions limit, a church employee must count all years of service with organizations that are part of a particular church as years of service with one employer. Similarly, the church employee must treat contributions by the churches as made by one employer.[6] In the case of a foreign missionary, contributions and other additions for an annuity contract or retirement income contract, when expressed as an annual addition to the employee's account, are not treated as exceeding the IRC Section 415 annual additions limit if the annual addition is not in excess of the greater of $3,000 or the employee's includable compensation under IRC Section 403(b)(3).[7]

---

1.   IRC Sec. 415(c)(7).
2.   IRC Sec. 403(b)(9); Treas. Reg. §§1.403(b)-8(e), 1.403(b)-9(a)(1); TEFRA, Sec. 251(e)(5); Let. Rul. 8837061.
3.   Treas. Reg. §§1.403(b)-3(b)(3), 1.403(b)-9(a)(2)(ii).
4.   IRC Secs. 404(a)(10)(B), 414(e)(5).
5.   IRC Sec. 403(b)(1)(D); see also IRC Sec. 403(b)(12)(B).
6.   IRC Sec. 415(c)(7)(B).
7.   IRC Sec. 415(c)(7)(C).

4052. What is an excess contribution and an excess aggregate contribution to a tax sheltered annuity? What excise taxes apply to them?

There are several different limitations applicable to amounts contributed to 403(b) annuities. Contributions that exceed any of these particular limits may be thought of as excess contributions, but they are treated differently depending on the limit that is exceeded and, sometimes, depending on whether the excess amount is contributed to a custodial account or toward the purchase of an annuity contract.

When contributions that exceed the lesser of the excludable amount or the overall limit are made to a custodial account for the purchase of regulated investment company stock or a retirement income account to the extent funded through custodial accounts, they are properly called excess contributions and are subject to an excise tax.[1] The tax is 6 percent (not to exceed 6 percent of the value of the account) of the following: (1) the amount by which the contributions, other than a permissible rollover contribution (Q 4006), exceed the lesser of the amount excludable from gross income under IRC Section 403(b) or the overall limitation under IRC Section 415, or whichever is applicable if only one is applicable, plus (2) any excess carried over from the preceding tax year. An excess carried over from a previous year may be reduced by contributing in a year less than the excludable amount or the contribution limit, whichever is lower. An excess also may be reduced by taxable distributions.[2] The tax is imposed on the employee.

If contributions are made toward the purchase of an annuity contract, the excess is not subject to an excise tax.

For contributions in excess of the overall limit of IRC Section 415, see Q 4045.

Where salary reduction contributions are in excess of the limit on elective deferrals, the amount above the limit is not excludable from income when contributed and, if not timely distributed, is included in gross income for a second time when later distributed (Q 4046, Q 4041).

Discriminatory Matching Employer Contributions. If an employer makes certain discriminatory matching contributions toward an annuity contract or to a custodial account, amounts in excess of nondiscriminatory amounts are called excess aggregate contributions and are subject to a 10 percent excise tax if not timely distributed (Q 3807).[3]

4053. What are the requirements for an automatic enrollment provision in a 403(b) plan?

The safe harbor rules for automatic contribution plans with respect to 401(k) plans also apply with respect to matching contributions under a 403(b) annuity through the application of IRC Section 403(b)(12) (Q 3762). This provision is effective for years beginning after December 31, 2007.[4]

1.   IRC Sec. 4973(c).
2.   IRC Sec. 4973(c).
3.   IRC Sec. 4979.
4.   See IRC Secs. 401(k)(13), 401(m)(12), 414(w).

4054. Can an employer make post-retirement contributions to a tax sheltered annuity on behalf of a retired employee?

Yes, but time limits apply.

Under the IRC, the term includable compensation (Q 4042) means compensation earned by the employee for the most recent period, ending not later than the close of the taxable year for which the limitation is being determined, that constitutes a full year of service and that precedes the taxable year by no more than five years.[1]

A former employee is deemed to have monthly includable compensation (Q 4042) for the period through the end of the taxable year in which the employee ceases to be an employee and through the end of each of the next five taxable years. The amount of the monthly includable compensation is equal to one-twelfth of the former employee's includable compensation during the former employee's most recent year of service. Accordingly, non-elective employer contributions for a former employee must not exceed the IRC Section 415(c) limit up to the lesser of the dollar amount in IRC Section 415(c) or the former employee's annual includable compensation based on the former employee's average monthly compensation during his or her most recent year of service.[2]

4055. What is a Roth 403(b) contribution program?

Section 403(b) plans are allowed to offer a *qualified Roth contribution program*, which is basically a Roth account for elective deferrals.[3] Essentially, participants of 403(b) plans establishing these programs are able to designate all or a portion of their elective deferrals as Roth contributions. Roth contributions will be included in the participant's gross income in the year the contribution is made and then be held in a separate account with separate recordkeeping.[4] For details on Roth contribution programs under cash or deferred arrangements, see Q 3779.[5]

4056. May an employee exchange his or her tax sheltered annuity contract for another contract within the same plan?

Under the final 403(b) regulations, a non-taxable exchange or transfer is permitted for a 403(b) contract if it:

(1)   is a mere change of investment within the same plan, that is, a contract exchange;

(2)   constitutes a plan-to-plan transfer, so that there is another employer plan receiving the exchange (see Q 4057); or

(3)   it is a transfer to purchase permissive service credit (Q 4059).[6]

---

1.   IRC Sec. 403(b)(3).
2.   Treas. Reg. §1.403(b)-4(d)(1).
3.   IRC Secs. 402A(b), 402A(e).
4.   IRC Sec. 402A(b).
5.   See also Treas. Reg. §§1.403(b)-3(c), 1.403(b)-7(e), 1.403(b)-10(d)(2).
6.   Preamble, T.D. 9340, 72 Fed. Reg. 41128, 41131 (7-26-2007); Treas. Reg. §1.403(b)-10(b).

Contract Exchanges within the Same Plan

Under prior law, Revenue Ruling 90-24 provided that a direct transfer between issuers of an amount representing all or part of an individual's interest in an IRC Section 403(b) annuity or custodial account was not a distribution subject to tax or to the premature distribution penalty provided that, after the transfer, the funds transferred continued to be subject to distribution requirements at least as strict as those applicable to them before the transfer.[1] The final 403(b) regulations revoked Revenue Ruling 90-24 and any exchanges now are allowed under rules that generally are similar to those applicable to qualified plans.[2]

The final regulations provide that a 403(b) contract of a participant or beneficiary may be exchanged for another 403(b) contract of that participant or beneficiary under the same 403(b) plan if each of the following conditions is satisfied:

(1) the plan under which the contract is issued provides for the exchange;

(2) the participant or beneficiary has an accumulated benefit immediately after the exchange that is at least equal to the accumulated benefit before the exchange, taking into account the accumulated benefit under both 403(b) contracts immediately before the exchange; and

(3) the new contract is subject to distribution restrictions with respect to the participant that are no less stringent than those imposed on the contract being exchanged and the employer enters into an information sharing agreement with the issuer of the new contract.[3]

Under the information sharing agreement, the employer and the issuer agree that from time to time in the future they will provide each other with the following information:

(1) information about the participant's employment;

(2) information that takes into account other 403(b) contracts or qualified employer plans, such as whether a severance from employment has occurred for purposes of the distribution restrictions and whether the hardship withdrawal rules are satisfied; and

(3) information necessary for the resulting contract to satisfy other tax requirements, such as whether a plan loan satisfies the conditions so that the loan is not a deemed distribution under IRC Section 72(p)(1).[4]

---

1. Rev. Rul. 90-24, 1990-1 CB 97.
2. Preamble, T.D. 9340, 72 Fed. Reg. 41128, 41131 (7-26-2007).
3. Treas. Reg. §1.403(b)-10(b)(2).
4. Treas. Reg. §1.403(b)-10(b)(2).

The rule for contracts received in an exchange does not apply to a contract received in an exchange that occurred on or before September 24, 2007, if the exchange (including the contract received in the exchange) satisfied the rules applicable at the time of the exchange.[1]

4057. May an employee exchange his or her tax sheltered annuity contract for another contract in another 403(b) plan?

Under the final regulations, a plan-to-plan transfer from a 403(b) plan to another 403(b) plan is permitted if each of the following conditions is met:

(1)   the participant is an employee or former employee of the employer for the receiving plan or, in the case of a transfer for a beneficiary of a deceased participant, the participant was an employee or former employee of the employer for the receiving plan;

(2)   the transferring plan provides for transfers;

(3)   the receiving plan provides for the receipt of transfers;

(4)   the participant or beneficiary whose assets are being transferred has an accumulated benefit immediately after the transfer that is at least equal to the accumulated benefit immediately before the transfer;

(5)   the receiving plan imposes restrictions on distributions to the participant or beneficiary whose assets are being transferred that are no less stringent than those imposed on the transferring plan; and

(6)   if a plan-to-plan transfer does not constitute a complete transfer of the participant's or beneficiary's interest in the 403(b) plan, the receiving plan treats the amount transferred as a continuation of a pro rata portion of the participant's or beneficiary's interest in the Section 403(b) plan (e.g., a pro rata portion of the participant's or beneficiary's interest in any after-tax employee contributions).[2]

Planning Point: No transfers are permitted between contracts that are not part of a plan under Revenue Procedure 2007-71, because the 2007 regulations revoked Revenue Ruling 90-24 which had previously permitted such transfers.

Amounts Received Under the Plan

4058. May an employee, the employee's surviving spouse, or a non-spouse beneficiary rollover a distribution from a tax sheltered annuity?

Yes, but only certain distributions may be rolled over (Q 4006, Q 4013).[3]

---

1.   Treas. Reg. §1.403(b)-11(g).
2.   Treas. Reg. §1.403(b)-10(b)(3).
3.   See IRC Secs. 402(c)(2)(A), 402(c)(11).

4059. May an employee transfer funds from a 403(b) account to purchase past service credit?

Yes.

Plan participants may exclude from income amounts directly transferred from an IRC Section 403(b) tax sheltered annuity to a governmental defined benefit plan that are used to purchase permissive service credit. Likewise, a participant may use directly transferred amounts to repay contributions or earnings that previously were refunded because of a forfeiture of service credit under either the transferee plan or an IRC Section 403(b) tax sheltered annuity maintained by a governmental employer in the same state.[1]

PPA 2006 modifies the definition of permissive service credit. Under the new definition, "permissive service credit" means service credit that relates to benefits to which a participant is not otherwise entitled under a governmental plan, rather than service credit that a participant has not received under a plan.

Credit qualifies as permissive service credit if it is purchased to provide an increased benefit for a period of service already credited under the plan (e.g., if a lower level of benefit is converted to a higher benefit level otherwise offered under the same plan) as long as it relates to benefits to which the participant is not otherwise entitled.

PPA 2006 also allows participants to purchase credit for periods regardless of whether service is subject to the limits on nonqualified service. Under the provision, service as an employee of an educational organization providing elementary or secondary education can be determined under the law of the jurisdiction in which the service was performed. Thus, for example, permissive service credit can be granted for time spent teaching outside of the U.S. without being considered nonqualified service credit.[2]

The limits regarding nonqualified service are not applicable in determining whether a plan to plan transfer from a Section 403(b) annuity to a governmental defined benefit plan is for the purchase of permissive service credit. Thus, the failure of the transferee plan to satisfy the limits does not cause the transferred amounts to be included in the participant's income. The transferee plan must satisfy the limits in providing permissive service credit as a result of the transfer.

Plan-to-plan transfers under IRC Section 403(b)(13) may be made regardless of whether a transfer is made between plans maintained by the same employer. The provision also provides that amounts transferred from a Section 403(b) annuity to a governmental defined benefit plan to purchase permissive service credit are subject to distribution rules applicable under the IRC to the defined benefit plan.[3]

---

1. IRC Secs. 403(b)(13), 457(e)(17). See also Treas. Reg. §1.403(b)-10(b)(4).
2. See IRC Sec. 415(n)(3).
3. See IRC Sec. 415(n)(3)(d).

4060. Is an employee taxed on incidental life insurance protection and waiver of premium benefits under a tax sheltered annuity contract?

The final 403(b) regulations confirm that only certain incidental insurance benefits may be part of a 403(b) contract (Q 4033) (note that life insurance contracts can no longer be purchased under a 403(b) plan).

Under prior law, the one year term cost of pure life insurance protection provided by an employer must be included each year in an employee's gross income. This cost is computed in the same manner and with use of the same rates as under a qualified plan (Q 3947).[1] Thus, the applicable rate is applied to the amount at risk each year to determine the amount includable in gross income. The death benefit must be provided as part of an annuity contract and cannot be part of a life insurance contract purchased after September 23, 2007.

Where insurance is provided through a group contract, the insurance company issuing the group contract is responsible for reporting the one year term costs on Form 1099-R in accordance with IRC Section 6047(d).[2] The sum of the annual one year term costs that have been taxed to an employee will constitute all or part of the employee's cost basis in computing the tax on the payments the employee receives under the contract (Q 4087).[3] In other words, the aggregate cost of insurance protection, which is the amount reported by the employee as taxable income, can be recovered tax-free from annuity payments.[4]

Because a waiver of premium provision and a disability income provision are not pure annuity features, their cost is not within the overall limit provided by the IRC. The extra premiums for these provisions must be included in the employee's gross income.[5] See Q 4089 for the taxation of the death benefit.

Planning Point: Life insurance contracts can no longer be purchased under a 403(b) plan.

4061. How are dividends under a tax sheltered annuity treated for income tax purposes?

Dividends are treated as earnings on 403(b) investments. The IRS treats interest on accumulated dividends as part of a retirement fund and interest is not taxed until the participant begins to receive distributions from the fund.[6]

4062. Are amounts borrowed under a tax sheltered annuity taxable income?

Loans made after August 13, 1982, under IRC Section 403(b) tax sheltered annuity plans including IRC Section 403(b)(7) custodial accounts are subject to the same rules that apply to loans under qualified plans (Q 3952).[7] Therefore, unless certain requirements are met, amounts

---

1.   Treas. Reg. §1.72-16(b).
2.   See Let. Rul. 9007001.
3.   Treas. Reg. §1.72-16(b)(4).
4.   Rev. Rul. 68-304, 1968-1 CB 179.
5.   Let. Rul. 3-15-66, signed I. Goodman, Chief Pension Trust Branch, 1968 MDRT Proceedings, p. 221.
6.   General Information Letter, January 20, 1978.
7.   IRC Sec. 72(p)(4)(A).

borrowed from a tax sheltered annuity will be taxed as a deemed distribution under the plan. Specifically, a loan will be treated as a deemed distribution under the plan unless it satisfies the following:

    (1)   the repayment term requirement (Q 4063);

    (2)   the substantially level amortization requirement (Q 4064);

    (3)   the enforceable agreement requirement (Q 4065); and

    (4)   certain dollar limitations (Q 4066).[1]

According to the final 403(b) regulations, a facts and circumstances inquiry must be made when determining whether the availability of a loan, making of a loan, or failure to repay a loan is treated as a distribution directly or indirectly. Among the facts and circumstances to be considered are whether the loan has a fixed repayment schedule, whether it bears a reasonable rate of interest, and whether there are repayment safeguards to which a prudent lender would adhere. Thus, for example, a loan must bear a reasonable interest rate to not be treated as a distribution.[2]

If there is an express or tacit understanding that the loan will not be repaid or, for any reason, the transaction does not create a debtor-creditor relationship, then the amount transferred is treated as an actual distribution from the plan rather than as a loan or a deemed distribution.[3] If a participant pledges or assigns any portion of his or her interest in a plan as security for a loan, the amount pledged or assigned is subject to the deemed distribution rule.[4]

Other considerations. Tax sheltered annuity plans that are subject to ERISA are subject to the prohibited transaction requirements applicable to loans: they must be adequately secured, bear a reasonable rate of interest, be available to all participants or beneficiaries on a reasonably equivalent basis, be made in accordance with specific provisions regarding such loans set forth in the plan, and not discriminate in favor of a prohibited group (Q 3979).[5]

In addition, to the extent a tax sheltered annuity is not funded by salary reduction, the plan must meet nondiscrimination rules that generally would require that loans be available on a nondiscriminatory basis (Q 4037).

See Q 4072 for a discussion of the rules governing deduction of interest on a loan. See Q 4034 for a discussion of deemed distributions, plan loan offsets, and the distribution restrictions of IRC Sections 403(b)(7) and 403(b)(11).

---

1.   IRC Secs. 72(p)(1), 72(p)(2); Treas. Reg. §1.72(p)-1, A-3.
2.   Treas. Reg. §1.403(b)-6(f).
3.   Treas. Reg. §1.72(p)-1, A-17.
4.   Treas. Reg. §1.72(p)-1, A-1(b).
5.   ERISA Sec. 408(b); Labor Reg. §2550.408b-1.

4063. How long can a loan under a tax sheltered annuity remain outstanding and still avoid treatment as a deemed distribution and inclusion in the participant's taxable income?

To avoid treatment as a deemed distribution, a loan by its terms must be required to be repaid within five years. A loan used to acquire a dwelling that within a reasonable time is to be used as the participant's principal residence (as defined in IRC Section 121) is not subject to the five year repayment term requirement.[1] Although the IRC puts no specific limit on the term of principal residence loans, it is likely that the IRS will impose at least a reasonable term on the theory that a loan is not in fact a loan if there is no obligation to repay.[2] A loan need not be secured by the dwelling that is to be the participant's principal residence to qualify as a principal residence loan exempt from the five year term requirement,[3] but see Q 4072 if there is a desire to render the interest on the loan deductible as qualified residence interest.

Tracing rules under IRC Section 163(h)(3)(B) apply in determining whether a loan is treated as for the acquisition of a principal residence and, therefore, exempt from the five year term requirement.[4]

Finally, a refinancing generally cannot qualify as a principal residence loan exempt from the five year term requirement. A loan used to repay a loan from a third party will qualify as a principal residence loan if it qualifies as such a loan without regard to the loan from the third party.[5]

4064. What is the substantially level amortization requirement applicable to a loan taken under a tax sheltered annuity that seeks to avoid taxation as a deemed distribution?

To avoid treatment as a deemed distribution, a loan generally must provide for substantially level amortization over the term of the loan with loan repayments to be made at least quarterly.[6] The level amortization requirement does not apply, and payments may be suspended, for a period up to one year while a participant is on a leave of absence and the participant's pay from his or her employer is insufficient to service the debt; a participant taking advantage of a suspension still must repay the loan by the latest permissible term of the loan and the installments due after payments resume must be at least as great as those required under the terms of the original loan. The latest permissible term of the loan is the latest date permitted under IRC Section 72(p)(2)(B), that is, five years from the date of the loan subject to the exception for principal residence loans, plus any additional period of suspension permitted under a military service leave.[7]

---

1. IRC Sec. 72(p)(2)(B); Treas. Reg. §1.72(p)-1, A-5.
2. Compare Treas. Reg. §1.72(p)-1, A-17, above. But see *Dean v. Commissioner* (suggesting that the term of principal residence loans extends to maturity of the tax sheltered annuity contract; deciding treatment of principal residence loans taken out before effective date of level amortization requirement). See also the example under Treas. Reg. §1.72(p)-1, A-8 (involving the application of the tracing requirement to a 15 year loan used to repay a bank loan for the purchase of a principal residence).
3. Treas. Reg. §1.72(p)-1, A-6.
4. Treas. Reg. §1.72(p)-1, A-7.
5. Treas. Reg. §1.72(p)-1, A-8.
6. IRC Sec. 72(p)(2)(C); see *Est. of Gray v. Comm.*, TC Memo 1995-421.
7. Treas. Reg. §§1.72(p)-1, A-9(a), 1.72(p)-1, A-9(c), 1.72(p)-1, A-19(c).

With respect to a leave of absence due to military service, IRC Section 414(u)(4) allows a participant to suspend repayment of a loan during any period that he or she serves in the uniformed services. The suspension of repayment under these circumstances may extend beyond one year, unlike the suspension rules for other leaves of absence.

A participant must resume loan repayments once he or she completes military service, at which time payments must be made as frequently and in an amount no less than was made before the suspension. The full amount of the loan, including interest accrued during the suspension, must be repaid by the end of the latest permissible loan term.

The latest permissible loan term under these circumstances is the latest permissible date under IRC Section 72(p)(2)(B), that is, five years from the date of the loan, subject to the exception for principal residence loans, plus any additional period of suspension permitted for military service. For example, if a military reservist obtained a three year loan and then served two years on active duty, the officer would have up to seven years to repay the loan, calculated as the five year maximum permissible loan term plus the two year suspension period. An example in the regulations illustrates the application of a 6 percent interest rate cap under the Soldier's and Sailor's Civil Relief Act Amendments of 1942 on a reservist's monthly installments and payment period.[1]

Failure to make any installment payment when due generally results in a deemed distribution of the entire outstanding balance of the loan at the time of such failure. A plan may provide a cure period for payments so long as the cure period does not extend beyond the last day of the calendar quarter following the calendar quarter in which the required payment was due. The cure period was referred to as a grace period under the proposed regulations.[2]

4065. Does a loan taken under a tax sheltered annuity plan have to be evidenced by an enforceable agreement in order to avoid taxation as a deemed distribution?

To avoid treatment as a deemed distribution, a loan must be evidenced by a legally enforceable agreement, which may include more than one document, set forth either in writing or in an electronic medium specifying the amount of the loan, the term of the loan, and the repayment schedule.

The agreement does not have to be signed if it is enforceable under applicable law without being signed.[3]

If the agreement is set forth in an electronic medium, it must be one that is reasonably accessible to the participant and provided under a system that is reasonably designed to preclude anyone other than the participant from requesting a loan, provides the participant with a reasonable opportunity to review, confirm, modify, or rescind the terms of the loan before it is made, and provides the participant with confirmation of the loan terms within a reasonable time after

---

1. Treas. Reg. §1.72(p)-1, A-9.
2. Treas. Reg. §1.72(p)-1, A-10.
3. Treas. Reg. §1.72(p)-1, A-3(b).

it is made. The confirmation may be provided in an electronic format or in a written paper document. If it is provided electronically, it must be done in a manner that is no less understandable to a participant than a written document; at the time a confirmation is provided, a participant must be advised that he or she may request and receive a written paper document at no charge.[1]

4066. Is there a dollar limit on the amount that a participant can borrow under a tax sheltered annuity and avoid the loan being treated as a taxable distribution?

Editor's Note: The CARES Act increased the available loan amounts to $100,000 or 100 percent of the employee's account balance for 2020.

Loans made after 1986 are taxable as distributions from a plan to the extent the amount of the loan, when added to the outstanding balance of all other loans, whenever made, from all tax sheltered annuities, IRC Section 457 deferred compensation plans, and qualified pension, profit sharing, stock bonus, and bond purchase plans of the employer, exceeds the lesser of the following: (1) $50,000, reduced by the excess of the highest outstanding balance of loans from the plans during the one year period ending on the day before the date the loan is made over the outstanding balance of loans from the plans on the date the loan is made, or (2) one-half of the present value of the employee's nonforfeitable accrued benefit under the plans, of at least $10,000.[2]

Loans subject to the above dollar limits are those that by their terms require repayment within five years or, if they are "principal residence" loans, within a reasonable time and that satisfy the substantially level amortization requirement and the enforceable agreement requirement. All plans of all other members of a controlled group of employers, of an affiliated service group, or businesses under common control are counted as plans of the employer.[3]

4067. When is a loan taken under a tax sheltered annuity considered to be a deemed distribution? How does subsequent repayment of the loan, or subsequent failure to repay the loan, impact the participant's ability to receive additional loans?

The entire amount of a loan will be treated as a distribution from the outset if the terms of the loan do not satisfy the repayment term requirement or the level amortization requirement, or if the loan is not evidenced by an appropriate enforceable agreement.[4]

If a loan satisfies the other requirements but the amount loaned exceeds the applicable dollar limitation, the amount of the loan in excess of the limit is a deemed distribution at the time the loan is made.[5]

---

1.   Treas. Reg. §1.72(p)-1, A-3(b).
2.   IRC Sec. 72(p)(2)(A); see also Let. Rul. 8742008.
3.   IRC Sec. 72(p)(2)(E).
4.   Treas. Reg. §1.72(p)-1, A-4(a); see IRC Secs. 72(p)(1), 72(p)(2); *Est. of Gray v. Comm.*, above.
5.   Treas. Reg. §1.72(p)-1, A-4(a); see IRC Secs. 72(p)(1), 72(p)(2).

If a loan initially satisfies all of the requirements to avoid treatment as a deemed distribution but payments are not made in accordance with the terms of the loan, a deemed distribution of the entire outstanding balance, including accrued interest, generally results at the time of such failure.[1]

A plan may provide a cure period (referred to as a grace period under the proposed regulations) for payments so long as the cure period does not extend beyond the last day of the calendar quarter following the calendar quarter in which the required payment was due. A failure to make a payment will not trigger a deemed distribution of the outstanding balance until the end of the cure period.[2]

Once a loan is deemed distributed under IRC Section 72(p), the interest that accrues on that loan is not included in income for purposes of determining the amount that is taxable under IRC Section 72. In addition, neither the income that results from the deemed distribution nor the interest that accrues thereafter increases the participant's investment or tax basis in the contract under IRC Section 72. To the extent the deemed distribution is repaid, his or her investment in the contract will be increased.[3]

A loan that is deemed distributed under IRC Section 72(p), including interest accruing thereafter, and that has not been repaid (such as by a plan loan offset) still is considered outstanding for purposes of determining the maximum amount of any subsequent loans to the participant or the beneficiary.[4] Thus, for example, the amount limitation would be reduced by an outstanding loan even after a deemed distribution has occurred. To the extent that a participant repays by cash any portion of a loan that has been deemed distributed, the participant acquires a tax basis in the contract in the same manner as if the repayments were after-tax contributions; however, loan repayments are not treated as after-tax contributions for other purposes, including the nondiscrimination requirements and IRC Section 415 limits.[5]

Planning Point: The 2017 tax reform legislation modified the treatment of plan loan offsets in certain circumstances. Plan participants with outstanding loans now have until their tax filing deadline (rather than 60 days) to roll the plan loan offset amount into another tax-preferred retirement account and avoid taxation as a deemed distribution, if the amount would be treated as distributed because (1) the plan was terminated or (2) the participant failed to meet the loan repayment terms because of a separation from employment (if the plan provides that the accrued unpaid loan amount must be offset at this time).

The final loan regulations place two conditions on loans made while the loan treated as a distribution remains unpaid.

First, the subsequent loan must be repayable under a payroll withholding arrangement enforceable under applicable law. This arrangement may be revocable, but if the participant revokes it, the outstanding balance of the loan is treated as a deemed distribution.

---

1. Treas. Reg. §§1.72(p)-1, A-4(a), 1.72(p)-1, A-10(b).
2. Treas. Reg. §§1.72(p)-1, A-4(a), 1.72(p)-1, A-10(a).
3. See Treas. Reg. §§1.72(p)-1, A-19(a), 1.72(p)-1, A-21(a).
4. Treas. Reg. §1.72(p)-1, A-19(b)(1).
5. See Treas. Reg. §1.72(p)-1, A-21(a).

Second, the participant must provide the plan with adequate security in the form of collateral for the loan in addition to the participant's accrued benefit. If, for any reason, the additional collateral is no longer in force before the subsequent loan is repaid, the outstanding balance of the subsequent loan is treated as a deemed distribution. If these conditions are not satisfied, the entire subsequent loan is treated as a distribution under IRC Section 72(p).[1]

Where a loan fee is withheld from net loan proceeds actually received by a participant but is included in a participant's outstanding loan balance, the deemed distribution on a default may include the withheld loan fee.[2]

4068. What is the process for determining whether loans taken under a tax sheltered annuity are taxable income when the participant receives multiple loans?

Where a participant receives multiple loans, each such loan must separately satisfy IRC Section 72(p), taking into account the outstanding balance of each existing loan. Under the final loan regulations, there is no limit on the number of loans a participant is permitted to take out.[3]

4069. Can loans taken under a tax sheltered annuity be refinanced? What is the effect of a refinancing on determining whether the outstanding loans constitute deemed distributions?

A refinancing transaction is any transaction in which one loan replaces another. For example, a refinancing may exist if the outstanding loan amount is increased or if the interest rate or the repayment term of the loan is renegotiated.[4]

If the term of a replacement loan ends after the latest permissible term of the loan it replaces, then both loans are treated as outstanding on the date of the refinancing transaction. This generally means that the loans must collectively satisfy the requirements of IRC Section 72(p) when determining whether the loans will constitute deemed distributions.[5]

There is an exception where the replacement loan would satisfy IRC Section 72(p)(2) if it were treated as two separate loans. Under this exception, the amount of the replaced loan, amortized in substantially level payments over a period ending not later than the last day of the latest permissible term of the replaced loan, is treated as one loan. The other loan is for an amount equal to the difference between the amount of the replacement loan and the outstanding balance of the replaced loan.[6]

The IRS will not view the transaction as circumventing IRC Section 72(p) provided that the replacement loan effectively amortizes an amount equal to the replaced loan over a period ending not later than the last day of the latest permissible term of the replaced loan. For this

1.   Treas. Reg. §1.72(p)-1, A-19(b).
2.   See *Earnshaw v. Comm.*, TC Memo 1995-156.
3.   Treas. Reg. §1.72(p)-1, A-20(a)(3).
4.   Treas. Reg. §1.72(p)-1, A-20(a).
5.   Treas. Reg. §1.72(p)-1, A-20(a)(2).
6.   Treas. Reg. §1.72(p)-1, A-20(a)(2).

reason, the outstanding balance of the replaced loan need not be taken into account in determining whether the limitations of IRC Section 72(p)(2) have been met; only the amount of the replacement loan plus any existing loans that are not being replaced are considered.[1]

If the term of a replacement loan does not end later than the latest permissible term of the replaced loan, then only the amount of the replacement loan plus the outstanding balance of any existing loans that are not being replaced must be taken into account in determining whether IRC Section 72(p) has been satisfied.[2]

4070. When are amounts borrowed under a tax sheltered annuity taxable income as actual distributions?

Loans to participants can give rise to two kinds of taxable distributions: deemed distributions under IRC Section 72(p) and actual distributions. As noted in Q 4062, sham loans are treated as actual distributions. Even bona fide loans can result in actual distributions through distributions of plan loan offset amounts.

A distribution of a plan loan offset amount occurs when the accrued benefit of the participant is reduced or offset to repay the loan. The amount of the account balance that is offset against the loan is an actual distribution of plan benefits (see Q 3960 for a discussion of plan loan offsets post-tax reform).[3] Accordingly, a plan may be prohibited from making such an offset under the distribution restrictions of IRC Sections 403(b)(7) and 403(b)(11) (Q 4034).[4]

4071. What is the tax treatment when amounts borrowed under a tax sheltered annuity are found to constitute deemed distributions?

If a loan is treated as a deemed distribution, it is includable in gross income (Q 4087) as if it were an actual distribution.[5] A loan treated as a deemed distribution may be subject to the 10 percent tax on early distributions imposed by IRC Section 72(t) (Q 4073) as if it were an actual distribution.[6]

To the extent a loan, when made, is a deemed distribution or an account balance is reduced to repay a loan, apparently at the time a loan is made, the amount includable in income is subject to withholding. If a deemed distribution or a loan repayment by benefit offset results in income after the date the loan is made, withholding is required only if a transfer of cash or property excluding employer securities is made from the plan at the same time.[7]

Deemed distributions under IRC Section 72(p) are not eligible rollover distributions and are not subject to the mandatory 20 percent withholding applicable to certain eligible rollover

1.   Treas. Reg. §1.72(p)-1, A-20(a)(2).
2.   Treas. Reg. §1.72(p)-1, A-20(a)(1).
3.   Treas. Reg. §1.72(p)-1, A-13. See also Treas. Reg. §1.403(b)-6(f), stating that a plan loan offset is a distribution. Compare *Caton v. Comm.*, TC Memo 1995-80.
4.   Treas. Reg. §1.72(p)-1, A-13(b).
5.   See Treas. Reg. §1.72(p)-1, A-11(a).
6.   Treas. Reg. §1.72(p)-1, A-11(b); see also *Dean v. Comm.*, above.
7.   Treas. Reg. §1.72(p)-1, A-15. For further guidance on withholding rules, see Temp. Treas. Reg. §35.3405-1T, Q&A F-4 and Treas. Reg. §§31.3405(c)-1, A-9, and 31.3405(c)-1, A-11.

distributions.[1] Plan loan offset amounts can be eligible rollover distributions.[2] For withholding rules relevant to plan loan offset amounts that are eligible rollover distributions, see Treasury Regulation Section 31.3405(c)-1, especially A-11.

4072. Is interest on a loan under a tax sheltered annuity deductible?

Interest on a loan not treated as a distribution (Q 4062) made, renewed, renegotiated, modified, or extended after December 31, 1986, is not deductible. No basis is created in a participant's account with respect to nondeductible interest paid to a plan.[3]

Interest paid on amounts borrowed under a retirement plan for the purchase or improvement of a principal residence is deductible as qualified residence interest if the loan is secured by a recorded deed of trust, is not the participant's account balance,[4] and is deductible. Because custodial accounts and annuity carriers typically are unable to perfect a security interest, interest on these types of loans from 403(b) arrangements will not be deductible.

4073. What distributions from a tax sheltered annuity are subject to a penalty for early or premature distributions?

If a taxpayer receives a taxable amount from a tax sheltered annuity including any amount attributable to accumulated deductible contributions and including plan loan amounts treated as deemed distributions (Q 4062), the taxpayer will be subject to an excise tax of 10 percent on that distribution unless the distribution is:

(1)   made on or after the date on which an employee attains age 59½;[5]

(2)   made to a beneficiary or the employee's estate on or after the death of the employee;[6]

(3)   attributable to an employee's disability;[7]

(4)   part of a series of substantially equal periodic payments made not less frequently than annually for the life or life expectancy of the employee or the joint lives or joint life expectancies of the employee and the employee's beneficiary and beginning after the employee separates from the service of the employer.[8] Q 3679 discusses acceptable methods for meeting this exception. If the series of payments is later modified other than because of death or disability before the employee reaches age 59½ or, if after the employee reaches age 59½, within five years of the date of the first payment, the employee's tax for the year the modification occurs is increased

---

1.   Treas. Reg. §§1.402(c)-2, A-4, 31.3405(c)-1, A-1(a); Treas. Reg. §1.72(p)-1, A-12.
2.   Treas. Reg. §1.402(c)-2, A-9.
3.   General Explanation of TRA '86, p. 729.
4.   See Let. Ruls. 8935051, 8742025; see also *Earnshaw v. Comm.*, TC Memo 1995-156.
5.   IRC Sec. 72(t)(2)(i).
6.   IRC Sec. 72(t)(2)(ii).
7.   IRC Sec. 72(t)(2)(iii).
8.   IRC Secs. 72(t)(2)(A)(iv), 72(t)(3).

by an amount equal to the tax that, but for the exception, would have been imposed plus interest for the deferral period;[1]

(5)   made to an employee on account of separation from service after attaining age 55.[2] A distribution will be treated as falling within this exception if the distribution is made after the employee has separated from service and the separation occurs during or after the calendar year in which the employee attains age 55;[3]

(6)   properly made to an alternate payee under a qualified domestic relations order (Q 4034);[4]

(7)   made to an employee for medical care but not in excess of the amount allowable as a medical expense deduction to the employee for amounts paid during the taxable year for medical care determined without regard to whether the employee itemizes deductions for the year. Apparently, this exempts from the penalty only amounts in excess of the 10 percent floor (7.5 percent for tax years beginning before 2013, and in 2017-2020) on deductible medical expenses;[5]

(8)   timely made to correct an excess aggregate contribution[6] (Q 4037);

(9)   timely made to reduce an excess elective deferral (Q 4046);

(10)   made on account of a qualified birth or adoption for tax years in an amount up to $5,000 beginning after 2019.[7]

The costs of life insurance protection that are included in an employee's income are not considered as distributions for purposes of applying the premature distribution penalty.[8] See Q 3947 regarding the proper measure of the value of current life insurance protection.

Distributions

4074. When must distributions begin from a tax sheltered annuity?

Tax sheltered annuities, including custodial accounts and church retirement income contracts, are subject to minimum distribution rules set forth in IRC Section 401(a)(9), both in form and operation.[9] Except as described below and in Q 4077 to Q 4083, Section 403(b) contracts are treated as IRAs for purposes of applying the minimum distribution requirements.[10] Regulations

---

1.   IRC Sec. 72(t)(4).
2.   IRC Sec. 72(t)(2)(A)(v).
3.   Notice 87-13, 1987-1 CB 432, A-20.
4.   IRC Sec. 72(t)(2)(C).
5.   IRC Sec. 72(t)(2)(B); see Ann. 87-2, 1987-2 IRB 38.
6.   IRC Sec. 401(m)(7).
7.   IRC Sec. 402(g)(2)(C).
8.   Notice 89-25, 1989-1 CB 662, A-11.
9.   IRC Sec. 403(b)(10); Treas. Reg. §1.403(b)-6(e)(1).
10.   Treas. Reg. §1.403(b)-6(e)(2); see Treas. Reg. §1.408-8.

finalized in 2007 address a number of issues concerning the application of these rules to tax sheltered annuities.[1]

If a custodian has adequate records to distinguish between amounts accruing before January 1, 1987, known as the pre-1987 account balance, and amounts accruing after December 31, 1986, known as the post-1986 account balance, which includes earnings on the pre-1987 account balance, the minimum distribution requirements are imposed only on the post-1986 account balance.[2]

The issuer or custodian of the contract must be able to identify the pre-1987 balance, maintain accurate records of changes in it, and provide information on request to the participant or beneficiaries with respect to the contract. If the issuer or custodian does not keep these records, the entire balance will be treated as subject to IRC Section 401(a)(9).[3]

The characterization of distributions as coming from pre-1987 or post-1986 balances has no relevance for purposes of determining the portion of a distribution that is includable in income under Section 72.[4]

The application of IRC Section 401(a)(9) rules to tax sheltered annuities is explained in Q 4077 for lifetime distributions and Q 4083 for after-death distributions. The application of the minimum distribution incidental benefit rule is explained in Q 4081.

Guidance on the application of the minimum distribution requirements under IRC Section 401(a)(9) is found in regulations finalized in 2002 and 2004, as well as regulations under Section 403(b) finalized in 2007.[5] The 2007 regulations made minimal changes to the pre-existing requirements, but clarify the treatment of pre-1987 balances.[6]

Distributions that are required under IRC Section 401(a)(9) reduce the post-1986 balance to the extent they are necessary to meet the requirements; to the extent they exceed the minimum, they permanently reduce the pre-1987 balance.[7]

Under earlier rules that are still in effect, distributions, regardless of when the amounts accrued, also must satisfy the incidental benefit or Minimum Distribution Incidental Benefit ("MDIB") rule (Q 4081).[8]

The distribution requirements under the two sets of rules are different.

First, the MDIB requirement affects only distributions required to be made to a participant during his or her lifetime although distributions to be made after death are considered in determining the minimum required to be distributed to the participant during the participant's lifetime.

---

1.   Treas. Reg. §1.403(b)-6.
2.   Treas. Reg. §1.403(b)-6(e)(6)(i); Treas. Reg. §1.403(b)-3, A-2(a).
3.   Treas. Reg. §1.403(b)-3, A-2(b); Treas. Reg. §1.403(b)-6(e)(ii).
4.   Treas. Reg. §1.403(b)-6(e)(6)(v).
5.   TD 8987, 67 Fed. Reg. 18988 (4-17-02); TD 9130, 2004-26 IRB 1082; REG-155608-02, 69 Fed. Reg. 67075.
6.   Treas. Reg. §1.403(b)-6(e)(6).
7.   Treas. Reg. §1.403(b)-3, A-2(b); Treas. Reg. §1.403(b)-6(e)(3).
8.   IRC Sec. 403(b)(10); Treas. Reg. §§1.401-1(b)(1)(i); 1.403(b)-3, A-3.

Second, the amounts required under the two rules may be different. If the two requirements call for different minimums, the larger of the two is the amount that must be distributed.

According to both the final 2002 regulations and the 2007 regulations, distributions attributable to the pre-1987 account balance are treated as satisfying the MDIB requirement if all distributions from a Section 403(b) contract, including distributions attributable to a post-1986 account balance, satisfy the requirements of Treasury Regulation Section 1.401-1(b)(1)(i), which the regulations cite as authority for the old MDIB rule, without regard to whether distributions under the 2002 regulations and distributions from the post-1986 account satisfy the requirements of IRC Section 401(a)(9).[1]

In the alternative, distributions attributable to a pre-1987 account will be treated as satisfying the MDIB requirement if all distributions from the contract, whether pre-1987 or post-1986 amounts, satisfy the regulations under IRC Section 401(a)(9).[2]

The IRS previously has ruled privately that for purposes of determining the minimum distribution where amounts are transferred, in installments, from an insolvent insurer to another insurer pursuant to an exchange agreement between the two insurers and a court-appointed receiver, all amounts, subject to any grandfathering of unrecovered pre-1987 account balances, under all annuity contracts of the individual, must be taken into account. This includes any amounts not yet transferred under the agreement.[3]

Rollovers and transfers. If a distribution is made from a participant's pre-1987 balance and rolled over to another tax sheltered annuity, it will be treated as part of the post-1986 balance in the second contract. If a direct transfer of pre-1987 funds is made from one contract to another, the amount transferred retains its character as part of the pre-1987 balance provided the issuer of the second contract meets the recordkeeping requirements described above.[4]

4075. How are distribution requirements from a tax sheltered annuity satisfied if an individual has more than one tax sheltered annuity?

If an individual has more than one tax sheltered annuity, each must meet the requirements separately. However, after determining the required minimum for each 403(b) annuity separately, the amounts may be totaled and the total taken from any one or more of the annuities.

Only amounts that an individual holds as a participant may be aggregated under this rule. If an individual account holder is also the beneficiary of the tax sheltered annuity of a decedent, the required distribution from that account may not be aggregated with amounts required under contracts held by the individual for purposes of meeting the distribution requirements.[5]

---

1.   Treas. Reg. §1.403(b)-3, A-3; Treas. Reg. §1.403(b)-6(e)(6)(vi).
2.   Treas. Reg. §1.403(b)-3, A-3; Treas. Reg. §1.403(b)-6(e)(6)(vi).
3.   Let. Rul. 9442030.
4.   Treas. Reg. §1.403(b)-6(e)(6)(iv).
5.   Treas. Reg. §1.403(b)-3, A-4; Prop. Treas. Reg. §1.403(b)-6(e)(7).

4076. What is the effect of failure to make timely distributions from a tax sheltered annuity?

If an amount distributed from a tax sheltered annuity is not taken by the participant, or is less than the required minimum distribution, an excise tax equal to 50 percent of the shortfall is generally levied against the individual (not the plan).[1] See Q 3909. However, the tax may be waived if the payee establishes to the satisfaction of the IRS that the shortfall was due to reasonable error, and that reasonable steps are being taken to remedy the shortfall.[2] Generally, the excise tax will be waived automatically in the case of a beneficiary who receives the entire benefit to which he is entitled under the five-year rule.[3]

The minimum distribution requirements will not be treated as violated and, thus, the 50 percent excise tax will not apply, where a shortfall occurs because assets are invested in a contract issued by an insurance company in state insurer delinquency proceedings. To the extent that a distribution otherwise required under IRC Section 401(a)(9) is not made during the state insurer delinquency proceedings, this amount and any additional amount accrued during this period will be treated as though it is not vested.[4]

4077. What minimum distributions must be made under Section 401(a)(9) from a tax sheltered annuity during the life of the participant?

If a post-1986 account balance is not totally distributed to a participant by the required beginning date, distributions of the balance must begin by that date and must, at a minimum, be distributed over one of the following periods: the life of the participant, the lives of the participant and the beneficiary, or a period not extending beyond the life expectancy of the participant or the life expectancy of the participant and a designated beneficiary.[5] If the issuer or custodian of the account does not keep adequate records to distinguish between pre-1987 and post-1986 balances, the entire account will be treated as subject to IRC Section 401(a)(9).[6]

The minimum distribution requirements include regulations finalized in 2002.[7] Additional regulations finalized in 2004 govern annuity distributions under Section 403(b) plans.[8] Regulations finalized in 2007 apply to distributions after 2008.[9]

The Pension Protection Act of 2006 called for regulations that would provide that governmental plans are subject to a reasonable, good faith interpretation of the minimum distribution requirements.[10] This same standard is applicable under earlier guidance and compliance with

---

1.   IRC Sec. 4974.
2.   Treas. Reg. §54.4974-2, A-7(a).
3.   Treas. Reg. §54.4974-2, A-7(b).
4.   Treas. Reg. §1.401(a)(9)-8, A-8.
5.   IRC Secs. 403(b)(10), 401(a)(9).
6.   Treas. Reg. §1.403(b)-3, A-2(b); Treas. Reg. §1.403(b)-6(e)(6)(ii).
7.   TD 8987, 67 Fed. Reg. 18988 (4-17-02).
8.   TD 9130, 2004-26 IRB 1082.
9.   TD 9340, 72 Fed. Reg. 41128 (July 26, 2007).
10.   P.L. 109-280, Sec. 823.

the 2002 regulations, the 2001 regulations, or the 1987 regulations will be considered to meet that standard.[1]

A participant's required beginning date is April 1 of the calendar year following the later of the calendar year in which the participant attains age 72 or the calendar year in which the participant retires.[2] For any part of a Section 403(b) contract that is not part of a government plan or church plan, regulations state that the required beginning date for a 5 percent owner is April 1 of the calendar year following the calendar year in which the employee reaches age 72.[3]

Under 2002 regulations (as under earlier guidance), a plan is permitted to provide that the required beginning date for all participants is April 1 of the calendar year following the calendar year in which the participant attains age 72.[4] Governmental or church plan participants are permitted under the IRC to delay distributions until April 1 of the calendar year following the later of the year in which the participant retires or turns 72; consequently, this provision is not applicable to them.[5]

A distribution for the calendar year a participant becomes age 72 or retires, if applicable, must be made by April 1 of the following calendar year. The distribution for each calendar year after the year the participant becomes 72 or retires, if applicable, must be made by December 31 of that year. Thus, it is possible that distributions for the calendar year in which a participant becomes 72 or retires and the following calendar year will be made in the same calendar year.

Account Balance

For purposes of calculating minimum distributions, the account balance is determined as of the last valuation date in the immediately preceding calendar year, that is, the valuation calendar year. The account balance does not include the value of any QLAC held under the plan on or after July 2, 2014.[6] Distributions in excess of the amount required in one year may not be used to reduce the amount required in subsequent years.[7]

4078. What minimum distributions requirements apply under Section 401(a)(9) during the life of a tax sheltered annuity participant if distributions are not made as annuity payments?

Under 2002 regulations, if distributions are not made as annuity payments under an annuity contract, the account balance generally is distributed according to a uniform lifetime table (Appendix F).[8] The minimum required to be distributed each year is determined by dividing the post-1986 account balance as of the end of the preceding year by the applicable distribution period of the participant as found in the table. For an example of a calculation under this

---

1.   Rev. Proc. 2003-10, 2003-1 CB 259; Notice 2003-2, 2003-1 CB 257.
2.   IRC Sec. 401(a)(9)(C); Treas. Reg. §1.403(b)-6(e)(3).
3.   Treas. Reg. §1.403(b)-6(e)(3).
4.   Treas. Reg. §1.401(a)(9)-2, A-2(e).
5.   IRC Sec. 401(a)(9)(C).
6.   Treas. Reg. §1.401(a)(9)-5, A-3(a).
7.   Treas. Reg. §1.401(a)(9)-5, A-2.
8.   Treas. Reg. §1.401(a)(9)-9, A-2.

method, see Q 3686. The amount of an individual's lifetime required distribution is calculated without regard to the beneficiary's age, except in the case of a spouse beneficiary who is more than 10 years younger than the participant.[1]

If a sole designated beneficiary is a participant's spouse, the distribution period during the participant's lifetime is the longer of the uniform lifetime table or the joint and survivor life expectancy of the participant and spouse (Appendix F)[2] using their attained ages in the distribution calendar year.[3] As a practical matter, the joint and survivor life expectancy table will produce a longer and thus lower payout only if the spouse beneficiary is more than 10 years younger than the participant.

4079. What minimum distributions requirements apply under Section 401(a)(9) during the life of a tax sheltered annuity participant if distributions are made as annuity payments?

Regulations under Section 401(a)(9) govern annuity distributions from Section 403(b) plans.[4] Under those regulations, annuity distributions must be periodic payments made at least annually, for a life or lives, or over a period certain not longer than a life expectancy or a joint and survivor life expectancy of the participant or the participant and a beneficiary, as set forth in the IRC's provisions for lifetime and after death distributions (Q 3896).[5] The annuity also may be a life annuity with a period certain, as long as the life or lives and period certain each meet the foregoing requirements.[6] The distribution of an annuity contract is not a distribution for purposes of meeting the required minimum distribution requirements of IRC Section 401(a)(9).[7]

Commencement of Distributions

Distributions from an annuity contract must begin on or before the participant's required beginning date. The first payment must be the payment that is required for one payment interval. Regulations state that the second payment need not be made until the end of the next payment interval, even if the interval ends in the next calendar year. Examples of payment intervals include monthly, bimonthly, semi-annually, and annually.[8]

All benefit accruals as of the last day of the first distribution calendar year must be included in the calculation of the amount of the life annuity payments for payment intervals ending on or after the participant's required beginning date.[9]

---

1.   Treas. Reg. §1.401(a)(9)-5, A-4.
2.   Treas. Reg. §1.401(a)(9)-9, A-3.
3.   Treas. Reg. §1.401(a)(9)-5, A-4(b).
4.   TD 9130, 2004-26 IRB 1082.
5.   Treas. Reg. §§1.401(a)(9)-6, A-1(a); 1.401(a)(9)-6, A-3; IRC Sec. 401(a)(9)(A).
6.   Treas. Reg. §1.401(a)(9)-6, A-1(b).
7.   Treas. Reg. §1.401(a)(9)-8, A-10.
8.   Treas. Reg. §1.401(a)(9)-6, A-1(c).
9.   Treas. Reg. §1.401(a)(9)-6, A-1(c)(1).

Exceptions to Nonincreasing Annuity Requirement

Except as otherwise provided, annuity payments must be nonincreasing, or increase only in accordance with the following:

(1)   an annual percentage not exceeding that of an eligible cost-of-living index, for example, one issued by the Bureau of Labor Statistics or certain others defined in the regulations;

(2)   a percentage increase that occurs at specified times or specified ages and does not exceed the cumulative total of annual percentage increases in an eligible cost of living index (see (1)) since the annuity starting date;

(3)   increases to the extent of the reduction in the amount of the employee's payments to provide for a survivor benefit upon death (if a beneficiary dies or is no longer subject to a QDRO, see Q 3914);

(4)   increases that result from a plan amendment; or

(5)   increases to allow a beneficiary to convert the survivor portion of a joint and survivor annuity into a single sum distribution on the employee's death.[1]

Additional Permitted Increases

If the total future expected payments from an annuity purchased from an insurance company exceed the total value being annuitized, payments under the annuity will not fail to satisfy the nonincreasing payment requirement merely because the payments are increased in accordance with one or more of the following:

(1)   by a constant percentage, applied not less frequently than annually;

(2)   to provide a final payment on the employee's death that does not exceed the excess of the total value being annuitized over the total of payments before the death of the employee;

(3)   as a result of dividend payments or other payments resulting from certain actuarial gains; and

(4)   an acceleration of payments under the annuity (as defined in the regulations).[2]

Period Certain Limit

The period certain for annuity distributions commencing during the life of a participant, with an annuity starting date on or after the required beginning date, may not exceed the Uniform Lifetime Table. If a participant's spouse is the sole beneficiary as of the annuity starting date and

---

1.   Treas. Reg. §1.401(a)(9)-6, A-14(a).
2.   Treas. Reg. §§1.401(a)(9)-6, A-14(c), 1.401(a)(9)-6, A-14(e).

the annuity provides only a period certain and no life annuity, the period certain may be as long as the joint and survivor life expectancy of the participant and spouse based on their ages as of their birthdays in the calendar year that contains the annuity starting date.[1]

The IRS privately ruled under the 1987 Regulations that an IRC Section 403(b) annuity contract that offered a settlement option under which the retirement benefit payment was determined in accordance with the individual account rules, that is, the nonannuity payments rule, and provided for nonlevel retirement income benefits satisfied the minimum distribution rules.[2]

4080. How is the designated beneficiary under a tax sheltered annuity determined?

Editor's Note: The SECURE Act significantly changed the rules applicable to designated beneficiaries and eligible designated beneficiaries for tax years beginning in 2020. The new law generally did not change the rules applicable to surviving spouses. See Q 3901 and Q 3902 for details.

A designated beneficiary means any individual designated as a beneficiary by a participant.[3] Under the 2002 regulations, a participant's designated beneficiary is determined based on the beneficiaries designated as of September 30 of the calendar year following the year of the participant's death.[4]

Thus, for example, a beneficiary who disclaims his or her interest after the death of the participant but before the September 30 deadline would not be a considered a beneficiary for this purpose. Under the SECURE Act rules, beneficiary status is determined as of the date of the account owner's death. Exceptions apply if the account is payable as an annuity or if a surviving spouse beneficiary dies after the participant but before distributions have begun (Q 3903).

Under the 2002 regulations, a beneficiary designated as such under the plan is an individual, or certain trusts (Q 3903), who is entitled to a portion of a participant's benefit, contingent on the participant's death or another specified event. A designated beneficiary need not be specified by name in the plan or by the participant to the plan to be a designated beneficiary so long as the individual who is to be the beneficiary is identifiable under the plan as of the date the beneficiary is determined.

The 2002 regulations state that an individual may be designated as a beneficiary under the plan either by the terms of the plan or, if the plan so provides, by an affirmative election by the participant or the participant's surviving spouse specifying the beneficiary. The fact that a participant's interest under the plan passes to a certain individual under applicable state law, however, does not make that individual a designated beneficiary unless the individual is designated as a beneficiary under the plan or the plan recognizes succession under applicable state law.[5]

---

1.   Treas. Reg. §1.401(a)(9)-6, A-3(a).
2.   Let. Rul. 9128035.
3.   IRC Sec. 401(a)(9)(E).
4.   Treas. Reg. §1.401(a)(9)-4, A-4(a).
5.   Treas. Reg. §1.401(a)(9)-4, A-1.

4081. What is the minimum distribution incidental benefit requirement with respect to tax sheltered annuities?

The minimum distribution incidental benefit ("MDIB") requirement constitutes a second set of minimum distribution rules that must be considered in determining the minimum amount required to be distributed during a participant's lifetime.[1] The MDIB rules apply to the pre-1987 account balance as well as the post-1986 balance. The reason they apply to the pre-1987 account balance, while the minimum distribution rules under IRC Section 401(a)(9) do not, is that unlike those requirements, the incidental benefit rule existed in regulations for many years before it was enacted into the IRC in 1986 and amounts accumulated before 1987 were subject to its requirements. Regulations under IRC Section 403(b) required that the death benefit under a tax sheltered annuity be merely incidental to its primary purpose of providing retirement benefits.

In 2007, regulations under Section 403(b) were finalized that briefly addressed the application of the older MDIB rule. These regulations took effect after 2008.[2] They generally restated rules contained in earlier regulations, to the effect that the post-1986 balance is subject to the IRC Section 401(a)(9) regulations and that both the pre-1987 balance and the post-1986 balance are subject to the MDIB rule (Q 4074).[3]

The 2007 regulations do not interpret the old MDIB rule but describe two ways it can be satisfied. First, distributions attributable to the pre-1987 account balance are treated as satisfying the MDIB requirement if all distributions from a Section 403(b) contract, including distributions attributable to the post-1986 account balance, satisfy the requirements of Treasury Regulation Section 1.401-1(b)(1)(i) (which the regulations cite as authority for the old MDIB rule) without regard to whether distributions under the 2002 regulations and distributions from the post-1986 account satisfy the requirements of IRC Section 401(a)(9).[4]

Second, and in the alternative, distributions attributable to the pre-1987 account will be treated as satisfying the MDIB requirement if all distributions from the contract, whether pre-1987 or post-1986 amounts, satisfy the regulations under IRC Section 401(a)(9).[5]

Under much earlier rulings, the old rule generally was interpreted as requiring a distribution arrangement under which the present value of the aggregate payments to be made to the participant must be more than 50 percent of the present value of the total payments to be made to the participant and his or her beneficiaries.[6] The old rules generally required that distributions commence by age 75.[7] It would appear that the old rules may continue to apply in determining distributions required from the pre-1987 balance.[8] Of course, nothing would prevent a participant from choosing to apply the Section 401(a)(9) rules.[9]

1. IRC Sec. 403(b)(10); Treas. Reg. §1.401-1(b)(1)(i).
2. TD 9340, 72 Fed. Reg. 41128 (July 26, 2007).
3. Treas. Reg. §1.403(b)-3, A-2, A-3; Treas. Reg. §1.403(b)-6(e)(6).
4. Treas. Reg. §1.403(b)-3, A-3; Treas. Reg. §1.403(b)-6(e)(6)(vi).
5. Treas. Reg. §1.403(b)-3, A-3; Treas. Reg. §1.403(b)-6(e)(6)(vi).
6. Rev. Rul. 72-241, 1972-1 CB 108; Rev. Rul. 73-239, 1973-1 CB 201; Let. Ruls. 8642072, 7843043, 7825010.
7. Let. Ruls. 9345044, 7825010.
8. Let. Rul. 9345044.
9. Treas. Reg. §1.403(b)-3, A-3; Treas. Reg. §1.403(b)-6(e)(6)(vi).

Final 2002 regulations state that if distributions are made in accordance with the individual account rules set forth therein (Q 4077), the MDIB requirement will be satisfied.[1]

4082. How are the minimum distribution incidental benefit (MDIB) rules that apply to tax sheltered annuities satisfied if the benefit is payable as an annuity?

If a participant's benefit is payable in the form of a life annuity for the life of the participant that satisfies the requirements of IRC Section 401(a)(9), the MDIB requirement will be satisfied.[2] If a participant's sole beneficiary as of the annuity starting date is the participant's spouse, and the distributions satisfy IRC Section 401(a)(9), the MDIB requirement will be satisfied.[3] Payments under the annuity must be nonincreasing, except as explained at Q 4077.[4]

If distributions begin under a particular distribution option that is in the form of a joint and survivor annuity for the joint lives of the participant and a nonspouse beneficiary, the MDIB requirement will not be satisfied as of the date distributions begin unless the distribution option provides that annuity payments to be made to the participant on and after his or her required beginning date will satisfy the conditions set forth in Treasury Regulation Section 1.401(a)(9)-6, A-2(c). Under those provisions, the periodic annuity payment payable to the survivor must not at any time on and after the participant's required beginning date exceed the applicable percentage of the annuity payment payable to the participant using the RMD MDIB Joint and Survivor Annuity Table (Appendix F).[5]

The applicable percentage is based on how much older the participant is than the beneficiary as of their attained ages on their birthdays in the first calendar year for which distributions to the participant are required. For example, if a beneficiary is 10 or fewer years younger, the survivor annuity may be 100 percent. If the age difference is greater than 10 years, the maximum survivor annuity permitted is less than 100 percent. If there is more than one beneficiary, the age of the youngest beneficiary is used.[6]

If a distribution form includes a life annuity and a period certain, the amount of the annuity payments payable to the beneficiary need not be reduced during the period certain, but in the case of a joint and survivor annuity with a period certain, the amount of the annuity payments payable to the beneficiary must satisfy the foregoing requirements after the expiration of the period certain.[7]

The period certain for annuity distributions commencing during the life of a participant with an annuity starting date on or after his or her required beginning date generally may not

---

1.   Treas. Reg. §1.401(a)(9)-5, A-1(d).
2.   Treas. Reg. §1.401(a)(9)-6, A-2(a).
3.   Treas. Reg. §1.401(a)(9)-6, A-2(b).
4.   Rev. Proc. 2003-10, 2003-1 CB 259; Notice 2003-2, 2003-1 CB 257.
5.   Treas. Reg. §1.401(a)(9)-6, A-2(c)(2).
6.   Treas. Reg. §1.401(a)(9)-6, A-2(c)(1).
7.   Treas. Reg. §1.401(a)(9)-6, A-2(d).

exceed the applicable distribution period for the participant (Q 4077) for the calendar year that contains the annuity starting date.

If the participant's spouse is his or her sole beneficiary and the annuity provides only a period certain and no life annuity, the period certain may last as long as the joint and survivor life expectancy of the participant and spouse, if that period is longer than the applicable distribution period for the participant.[1] If distributions commence after the death of the participant under the life expectancy rule (Q 3899), the period certain for any distributions commencing after death cannot exceed the distribution period determined under the life expectancy provisions of Treasury Regulation Section 1.401(a)(9)-5, A-5(b).

The amount required to be distributed generally is the greater of the MDIB or the regular RMD amount (Q 3891 to Q 3907). If the amount required to be distributed exceeds the amount distributed, the shortfall is subject to a 50 percent excise tax, levied on the individual, not the plan (Q 3909).[2]

4083. How are the minimum distribution requirements met after the death of a tax sheltered annuity participant?

Editor's Note: Post-SECURE Act, the minimum distribution rules no longer vary based upon whether the participant dies before or after his or her required beginning date. See Q 3901 for details.

A tax sheltered annuity must satisfy the minimum distribution requirements set forth in IRC Section 401(a)(9) for qualified plans.[3] Most of the requirements were explained in regulations published in 2002.[4] Regulations governing annuity payouts from defined benefit plans were finalized in 2004 (Q 4077, Q 3754), and regulations addressing additional matters were finalized under IRC Section 403(b) in 2007.[5]

The 2002 regulations simplified the calculation process and included longer life expectancy tables (Appendix F). The final regulations took effect for required minimum distributions in 2003 and later years (Q 3896, Q 4077).

Pre-SECURE Act, after the death of a tax sheltered annuity participant, the application of the minimum distribution requirements depended on whether he or she died before or after his or her required beginning date. For this purpose, distributions generally were treated as having begun in accordance with the minimum distribution requirements under IRC Section 401(a)(9)(A)(ii), without regard to whether payments had been made before that date.[6] If distributions irrevocably, except for acceleration, began prior to the required beginning date in the form of an annuity that meets the minimum distribution rules, the

---

1. Treas. Reg. §1.401(a)(9)-6, A-3(a).
2. IRC Sec. 4974.
3. IRC Sec. 403(b)(10).
4. TD 8987, 67 Fed. Reg. 18988 (4-17-02).
5. Treas. Reg. §1.403(b)-6.
6. Treas. Reg. §1.401(a)(9)-2, A-6(a).

annuity starting date was treated as the required beginning date for purposes of calculating lifetime and after death minimum distribution requirements.[1]

4084. How are the minimum distribution requirements met after the death of a tax sheltered annuity participant who died before the required beginning date?

Editor's Note: Post-SECURE Act, the minimum distribution rules no longer vary based upon whether the participant dies before or after his or her required beginning date. See Q 3901 for details.

Pre-SECURE Act, if a participant died before his or her required beginning date, distributions were made under one of two methods:

(1)   Under the five year rule, the entire interest must be distributed within five years after the death of the participant regardless of who or what entity receives the distribution.[2] To satisfy this rule, the entire interest must be distributed by the end of the calendar year that contains the fifth anniversary of the date of the participant's death.[3]

(2)   Under the life expectancy rule, if any portion of the interest is payable to, or for the benefit of, a designated beneficiary, that portion must be distributed over the life or life expectancy of the beneficiary, beginning within one year of the participant's death.[4]

To the extent that the interest is payable to a non-spouse beneficiary, distributions must begin by the end of the calendar year immediately following the calendar year in which the participant died.[5] The non-spouse beneficiary's life expectancy for this purpose is measured as of his or her birthday in the year following the year of the participant's death. In subsequent years, this amount is reduced by one for each calendar year that has elapsed since the year immediately following the year of the participant's death.[6]

If the sole designated beneficiary is the participant's surviving spouse, distributions must begin by the later of the end of the calendar year immediately following the calendar year in which the participant died or the end of the calendar year in which the participant would have reached age 72 (70½ pre-2020).[7] The payout period during the surviving spouse's life is measured by the surviving spouse's life expectancy as of his or her birthday in each distribution calendar year for which a minimum distribution is required after the year of the participant's death.[8] After the surviving spouse's death, the distribution period is based on his or her remaining life

---

1.   Treas. Reg. §1.401(a)(9)-6, A-10, A-11.
2.   IRC Sec. 401(a)(9)(B)(ii), Treas. Reg. §1.401(a)(9)-3, A-1(a).
3.   Treas. Reg. §1.401(a)(9)-3, A-2.
4.   IRC Sec. 401(a)(9)(B)(iii); Treas. Reg. §1.401(a)(9)-3, A-1(a).
5.   Treas. Reg. §1.401(a)(9)-3, A-3(a).
6.   Treas. Reg. §1.401(a)(9)-5, A-5(c)(1).
7.   IRC Sec. 401(a)(9)(B)(iv); Treas. Reg. §1.401(a)(9)-3, A-3(b).
8.   Treas. Reg. §1.401(a)(9)-5, A-5(c)(2).

expectancy. This is determined using the age of the surviving spouse in the calendar year of his or her death, reduced by one for each calendar year that has elapsed after the calendar year of the surviving spouse's death.[1]

The 2002 regulations set forth tables containing single and joint and survivor life expectancies for calculating required minimum distributions, as well as a Uniform Lifetime Table for determining the appropriate distribution periods (Q 4077, Appendix F).[2]

Unless a plan adopts a provision specifying otherwise, if distributions to a participant have not begun prior to his or her death, they must be made automatically either under the life expectancy rule described above or, if there is no designated beneficiary, under the five year rule.[3] A plan may adopt a provision specifying that the five year rule will apply after the death of a participant, or a provision allowing participants or beneficiaries to elect whether the five year rule or the life expectancy rule will be applied.[4]

4085. How are the minimum distribution requirements met after the death of a tax sheltered annuity participant who died on or after the required beginning date?

Editor's Note: Post-SECURE Act, the minimum distribution rules no longer vary based upon whether the participant dies before or after his or her required beginning date. See Q 3901 for details.

Pre-SECURE Act

If the participant dies on or after the date distributions have begun (i.e., generally on or after the required beginning date), but before the entire interest in the plan has been distributed, the IRC states that the entire remaining balance generally must be distributed at least as rapidly as under the method of distribution in effect as of the participant's date of death.[5] This method of distribution will depend on whether the distribution was in the form of distributions from an individual account or annuity payments.[6]

Under the 2002 regulations, a beneficiary determination is made as of September 30 of the year after the year of the participant's death.[7] If the participant does not have a designated beneficiary as of that date, the participant's interest is distributed over the remaining life expectancy, using the age of the participant in the calendar year of the participant's death, reduced by one for each calendar year that elapses thereafter.[8] If the participant does have a designated beneficiary as of the determination date, the beneficiary's interest is distributed over the longer of the following: (1) the beneficiary's life expectancy, calculated as described in Q 4084 under

---

1.   Treas. Reg. §1.401(a)(9)-5, A-5(c)(2).
2.   Treas. Reg. §1.401(a)(9)-9.
3.   Treas. Reg. §§1.401(a)(9)-1, A-3(c), 1.401(a)(9)-3, A-4(a).
4.   Treas. Reg. §§1.401(a)(9)-3, A-4(b), 1.401(a)(9)-3, A-4(c).
5.   IRC Sec. 401(a)(9)(B)(i).
6.   Treas. Reg. §1.401(a)(9)-2, A-5.
7.   Treas. Reg. §1.401(a)(9)-4, A-4(a).
8.   Treas. Reg. §1.401(a)(9)-5, A-5(c)(3).

the life expectancy rule (i.e., under Treasury Regulation Section 1.401(a)(9)-5, A-5(c)(1) or (2)), or (ii) the remaining life expectancy of the participant, determined using the age of the participant in the calendar year of death, reduced by one for each calendar year that elapses thereafter (i.e., under Treasury Regulation Section 1.401(a)(9)-5, A-5(c)(3)).[1]

4086. How is the designated beneficiary of a tax sheltered annuity determined after the participant's death?

To be a designated beneficiary, an individual must be a beneficiary on the date of the participant's death. The determination of the existence and identity of a designated beneficiary for purposes of minimum distributions is made as of the date of the participant's death for tax years beginning in 2020 and thereafter. Pre-SECURE Act, the determination was made on September 30 of the calendar year following the year of the participant's death.[2] Exceptions may apply if the account is payable as an annuity, or if a surviving spouse beneficiary dies after the participant but before distributions have begun. Pre-2020, the September 30 deadline was imposed so that a distribution may be calculated and made by the deadline of December 31 following the year of the participant's death. Consequently, an individual who was a beneficiary as of the date of the participant's death, but was not a beneficiary as of September 30 of the following year, such as because he or she disclaims entitlement to the benefit or because he or she receives the entire benefit to which he or she is entitled before that date, was not taken into account for purposes of determining the distribution period for required minimum distributions after the participant's death.[3]

Note that the SECURE Act did not change the definition of designated beneficiary. Instead, the Act created a new class of beneficiaries called eligible designated beneficiaries. Post-SECURE Act, only an eligible designated beneficiary is entitled to rely upon the life expectancy method of distribution. See Q 3901 and Q 3902 for details.

Under the 2002 regulations, special rules apply if more than one beneficiary is designated as of the date on which the determination is made. Generally, the beneficiary with the shortest life expectancy will be the designated beneficiary for purposes of determining the distribution period.[4]

If a surviving spouse beneficiary dies after the participant, but before distributions to the spouse have begun, the 10 year rule, the five year rule and the life expectancy rule described above for surviving spouses will be applied as though the surviving spouse were the participant.[5] This provision will not allow a new spouse of the deceased participant's surviving spouse to delay distributions under the surviving spouse rules of IRC Section 401(a)(9)(B)(iv).[6]

1.　Treas. Reg. §1.401(a)(9)-5, A-5(a)(1).
2.　Treas. Reg. §1.401(a)(9)-4, A-4(a).
3.　Treas. Reg. §1.401(a)(9)-4, A-4(a).
4.　Treas. Reg. §1.401(a)(9)-5, A-7(a).
5.　IRC Sec. 401(a)(9)(B)(iv)(II); Treas. Reg. §1.401(a)(9)-3, A-5.
6.　Treas. Reg. §1.401(a)(9)-3, A-5.

The 2007 regulations provide that the special rule allowing a surviving spouse to treat an IRA interest as the spouse's own[1] does not apply to a Section 403(b) contract, even if the spouse is the sole beneficiary.[2]

If a beneficiary is not an individual or a permitted trust (Q 3903), the participant will be treated as having no beneficiary. A participant's estate may not be a designated beneficiary.[3]

4087. Are payments received under a tax sheltered annuity taxable income to the employee?

Yes, except to the extent the amounts are a recovery of the employee's investment in the contract including the amount of a defaulted loan or to the extent the employee rolls over an eligible distribution to another tax sheltered annuity, a qualified retirement plan, an eligible governmental 457 plan, or a traditional individual retirement plan (Q 4006).

Where an annuity contract without life insurance protection is used for funding, all payments received normally are taxable in full as ordinary income to the employee. This is the result regardless of whether contributions were made by the employer as additional compensation to the employee, were derived from a reduction in the employee's salary, or were paid in part by deductible voluntary employee contributions. Because salary reduction contributions have not been previously taxed to the employee, where they have come within the overall limit, they cannot be treated as a cost basis for the contract.[4]

In some instances, however, the employee will have a cost basis for the contract. An employee's cost basis consists of any nondeductible contributions the employee has paid and any portion of the contributions made by the employer on which the employee has paid tax, except that excess salary reduction amounts not distributed from the plan by April 15 of the year following the contribution are not included in basis even though they were included in income (Q 4046). The value of a non-distributed defaulted loan is also included in the employee's cost basis.

Where a life insurance policy is used (Q 4033), the sum of the annual one year term costs that have been taxed to the employee are included in the employee's cost basis.[5] See Q 4060 regarding the proper measure of the value of current life insurance protection.

Similarly, any portion of an employer's premiums that have been included in an employee's gross income because they exceeded the employee's overall limit are included in the employee's cost basis (Q 4041). The amount of any policy loans included in income as a taxable distribution (Q 4062) also constitutes part of the employee's cost basis.

Once a loan is deemed distributed under IRC Section 72(p), the interest that accrues thereafter on that loan is not included in income for purposes of determining the amount that

1.   Treas. Reg. §1.408-8, A-5.
2.   Treas. Reg. §1.403(b)-6(e)(4).
3.   Treas. Reg. §1.401(a)(9)-4, A-3.
4.   IRC Sec. 403(b)(1).
5.   Rev. Rul. 68-304, 1968-1 CB 179.

is taxable under IRC Section 72. In addition, neither the income that results from the deemed distribution nor the interest that accrues thereafter increases the participant's investment or cost basis in the contract under IRC Section 72. To the extent that a participant repays by cash any portion of a loan that has been deemed distributed, the participant acquires a tax basis in the contract in the same manner as if the repayments were after-tax contributions.[1]

If an employee takes an account balance in a single lump sum cash payment, the full amount received will be ordinary income to the employee in the year of receipt unless the employee has a cost basis, except as provided in Q 4056 and Q 4058. If the employee has a cost basis, the amount in excess of the cost basis will be ordinary income.[2]

Amounts received before the annuity starting date, that is, in-service distributions, by an employee who has a cost basis are taxed under a rule that provides for pro rata recovery of cost.[3] An employee excludes that portion of the distribution that bears the same ratio to the total distribution as the employee's investment in the contract bears to the total value of the employee's accrued benefit as of the date of the distribution. Amounts received prior to July 2, 1986 were taxed under a cost recovery rule permitting recovery of basis before taxing any of the distribution as interest.[4]

The annuity starting date is the first day of the first period for which an amount is received as an annuity under a contract (Q 534).[5] If a plan on May 5, 1986 permitted in-service withdrawal of employee contributions, the pro rata recovery rules do not apply to investment in the contract prior to 1987. Instead, investment in the contract prior to 1987 will be recovered first and the pro rata recovery rules will apply only to the extent that amounts received before the annuity starting date, when added to all other amounts previously received under the contract after 1986, exceed the employee's investment in the contract as of December 31, 1986.[6]

If an employee who has a cost basis for his or her contract receives life annuity or installment payments, the payments are taxed as discussed in Q 611, depending on the annuity starting date.

Where the 403(b) annuity contract or custodial account is solely liable for the payment of investment expenses, the direct payment of investment advisor fees from a participant's annuity or account is not treated as a distribution.[7] Likewise, where an annuity contract consists of different subaccounts for which a financial advisor provides asset allocation advice, if the annuity contract expenses are assessed directly against the contract value itself, those payments then are expenses of the contract itself and, therefore, are not distributions from the contract includable in gross income. Furthermore, assessing expenses against a contract in this manner does not cause the contract to lose its qualified status under IRC Section 403(b).[8]

---

1.   See Treas. Reg. §§1.72(p)-1, A-19(a), 1.72(p)-1, A-21(a).
2.   IRC Sec. 72(e)(5).
3.   IRC Sec. 72(e)(8).
4.   IRC Sec. 72(e)(5)(D).
5.   IRC Sec. 72(c)(4).
6.   IRC Sec. 72(e)(8)(D).
7.   Let. Ruls. 9332040, 9316042, 9047073.
8.   Let. Rul. 9845003.

4088. Are distributions from a tax sheltered annuity subject to withholding?

With respect to distributions other than eligible rollover distributions (Q 4006), amounts will be withheld from periodic payments at the rates applicable to wage payments and from other distributions at a 10 percent rate. An employee may elect not to have income tax withheld from these payments. Tax will not be withheld on amounts distributed where it is reasonable to believe they will not be includable in income.[1]

Any eligible rollover distribution made after December 31, 1992 is subject to mandatory income tax withholding at the rate of 20 percent unless the distributee elects to have the distribution paid by means of a direct rollover.[2] This mandatory withholding applies even if the employee's employment terminated prior to January 1, 1993, and even if the eligible rollover distribution is part of a series of payments that began before January 1, 1993.[3] For distributions after 1992 but before October 19, 1995, slightly different rules may be applicable under temporary regulations (Q 3999).

4089. How is a death benefit under a tax sheltered annuity taxed to an employee's beneficiary?

A death benefit under a tax sheltered annuity generally is taxed in the same way as a death benefit under a qualified pension, qualified plan or profit sharing plan (Q 3973 to Q 3975).

In the case of a single sum payment where no life insurance is involved, all amounts received by a beneficiary are taxable as ordinary income except that the beneficiary may exclude from gross income the employee's unrecovered cost basis, if any.

If a death benefit consists of life insurance proceeds, the amount of the proceeds in excess of the cash surrender value of the policy immediately before the insured's death is excludable from gross income under IRC Section 101(a)(1). For the rule under the final regulations restricting the availability of life insurance in 403(b) arrangements, see Q 4033.

Cash surrender value is taxable as ordinary income to the extent that it exceeds the portion of the premiums taxed to the employee as being the cost of life insurance protection (see Q 4060 regarding the proper measure of the value of current life insurance protection), and any other unrecovered cost basis of the employee.[4]

4090. Are death benefits paid to an employee's beneficiary under a tax sheltered annuity subject to withholding?

With respect to distributions other than eligible rollover distributions (Q 4006), payments to a surviving spouse or beneficiary are subject to income tax withholding unless the spouse or beneficiary elects not to have withholding apply. Amounts need not be withheld on any part of the distribution where it is reasonable to believe those amounts will not be includable in gross

1.   IRC Sec. 3405; Temp. Treas. Reg. §35.3405-1T, A-20.
2.   IRC Sec. 3405(c); Treas. Reg. §31.3405(c)-1, A-1(a).
3.   Treas. Reg. §31.3405(c)-1, A-1(c)(1)(i).
4.   IRC Secs. 403(c), 72(m)(3)(C); Treas. Reg. §1.72-16(c).

income. Annuity payments are subject to withholding at the rate applicable to wages; other payments are subject to withholding at a 10 percent rate.[1] In the case of an eligible rollover distribution, a surviving spouse or other beneficiary is subject to the same mandatory withholding rules as the employee (Q 4087).

Social Security and Other Taxes

4091. How is a reduction in salary for a tax sheltered annuity treated for Social Security tax and income tax withholding purposes?

Excludable amounts paid into a tax sheltered annuity are not wages subject to income tax withholding, even if the amounts are derived from a salary reduction agreement.[2]

The amount of salary reduction contributions to the plan is subject to Social Security taxes even though it is excludable from the employee's gross income. Employer non-salary reduction contributions are not includable in wages for Social Security purposes.[3]

Under the final regulations, salary reduction agreement means a plan or arrangement under which payment will be made by an employer on behalf of an employee or his or her beneficiary under or to an annuity contract if the employee:

(1)   elects to reduce his or her compensation under a cash or deferred election;

(2)   elects to reduce his or her compensation pursuant to a one time irrevocable election made at or before the time of initial eligibility to participate in such plan or arrangement; or

(3)   if the employee agrees as a condition of employment to make a contribution that reduces his or her compensation.[4]

The Seventh Circuit Court of Appeals concluded that Congress intended IRC Section 3121(a)(5)(D) to include salary reduction agreements, whether voluntary or mandatory, in the FICA wage base. Accordingly, the Seventh Circuit held that payments made under a salary reduction agreement include salary reductions made under voluntary and mandatory agreements.[5]

Amounts contributed by salary reduction by a minister or by church employees whose organizations have chosen to be exempt from FICA are not treated as wages subject to Social Security taxes to the extent the contributions are not more than the employer contribution limit.[6]

---

1.   IRC Sec. 3405; Temp. Treas. Reg. §§35.3405-1T, A-17; 35.3405-1T, A-28.
2.   Rev. Rul. 65-208, 1965-2 CB 414. See also IRS Pub. 571.
3.   IRC Sec. 3121(a)(5); Rev. Rul. 65-208, 1965-2 CB 383; Rev. Rul. 181, 1953-2 CB 111. See also CCA 200333003; TAM 200305006; Let. Ruls. 200318074, 200234009.
4.   Treas. Reg. §31.3121(a)(5)-2.
5.   *University of Chicago vs. United States*, 547 F.3d 773 (7th Cir. 2008).
6.   See IRS Pub. No. 517.

Amounts of salary reduction treated as wages for Social Security tax are creditable to the individual's Social Security account for benefit purposes.[1]

4092. What excise taxes and additional taxes apply to tax sheltered annuity contributions and distributions?

Excess Contributions to Custodial Accounts

Contributions to a custodial account for the purchase of regulated investment company stock and to a retirement income account to the extent funded through custodial accounts are subject to a tax of 6 percent, not to exceed 6 percent of the value of the account, on (1) the amount by which the contributions other than a permissible rollover contribution (Q 4006) exceed the lesser of the amount excludable from gross income under IRC Section 403(b) or the overall limitation under IRC Section 415, or whichever is applicable if only one is applicable, plus (2) any such excess carried over from the preceding tax year (Q 4052).[2]

Early or Premature Distributions

If a taxpayer receives a premature distribution from a tax sheltered annuity, he or she will be subject to an excise tax equal to 10 percent of the portion of the distribution includable in income (Q 4073).[3]

Minimum Required Distribution Failure

If the amount distributed during a tax year is less than the minimum required distribution for the year, there generally is a tax equal to 50 percent of the amount that the distribution made in the year falls short of the required amount. The tax is on the payee (Q 4074).[4]

Excess Aggregate Contributions

If an employee makes after-tax contributions or the employer makes contributions that match contributions under an employee's salary reduction agreement or match employee after-tax contributions and the aggregate amount of the contributions exceeds the nondiscriminatory amount (Q 3803), a tax of 10 percent of the amount in excess of the permitted, nondiscriminatory maximum is imposed on the employer to the extent the excess amount and income attributable to it is not distributed within 2½ months after the end of the plan year (Q 3807).[5]

4093. Can a 403(b) plan be frozen or terminated?

Yes, if certain conditions are met.

An employer is permitted to amend its 403(b) plan to eliminate future contributions for existing participants, or to limit participation to existing participants and employees. A 403(b)

---

1. SSR 64-59.
2. IRC Sec. 4973.
3. IRC Sec. 72(t).
4. IRC Sec. 4974.
5. IRC Sec. 4979.

plan also is permitted to contain provisions that provide for plan termination and that allow accumulated benefits to be distributed on termination.[1]

In the case of a 403(b) contract that is subject to distribution restrictions relating to custodial accounts and 403(b) elective deferrals, termination of the plan and the distribution of accumulated benefits is permitted only if the employer does not establish a successor 403(b) plan by making contributions to any 403(b) contract that is not part of the plan during the period beginning on the date of plan termination and ending twelve months after distribution of all assets from the terminated plan, taking into account all entities that are treated as the same employer under IRC Sections 414(b), 414(c), 414(m), or 414(o) on the date of the termination.

The alternative 403(b) contract will be disregarded if, at all times during the period beginning twelve months before the termination and ending twelve months after distribution of all assets from the terminated plan, fewer than 2 percent of the employees who were eligible under the 403(b) plan as of the date of plan termination are eligible under the alternative 403(b) contract.

For a 403(b) plan to be considered terminated, all accumulated benefits under the plan must be distributed to all participants and beneficiaries as soon as administratively practicable after termination of the plan. For this purpose, delivery of a fully paid individual insurance annuity contract is treated as a distribution. The mere provision for, and making of, distributions to participants or beneficiaries on plan termination does not cause a contract to cease to be a 403(b) contract. The IRS has informally taken the position that a custodial account cannot qualify for treatment as a fully paid individual annuity contract.

Employers that cease to be eligible employers. An employer that ceases to be an eligible employer may no longer contribute to a 403(b) contract for any subsequent period and the contract will fail to satisfy Treasury Regulation Section 1.403(b)-3(a), which is the exclusion for contributions to 403(b) contracts, if any further contributions are made with respect to a period after the employer ceases to be an eligible employer.[2]

Planning Point: The IRS has not recognized the distribution of custodial accounts as being terminating distributions from a plan.

---

1. Treas. Reg. §1.403(b)-10(a)(1).
2. Treas. Reg. §1.403(b)-10(a)(2).

PART XX: WELFARE BENEFIT FUNDS

4094. May an employer deduct contributions to a welfare benefit fund to provide medical, disability, and life insurance benefits, including post-retirement medical and death benefits, for employees and independent contractors?

The deduction of contributions paid by an employer to a fund under a plan to provide benefits to employees and their beneficiaries generally is limited. These limits also apply to contributions to provide benefits for independent contractors and their beneficiaries.[1]

As a general rule, the limits apply to contributions to any fund that is part of an employer plan, or a method or arrangement having the effect of a plan, and through which the employer provides welfare benefits to employees or their beneficiaries. A welfare benefit is rather cryptically defined as any benefit other than one subject to the deduction rules applicable to property transferred in connection with performance of services (so-called "IRC Section 83 property") and qualified and nonqualified deferred compensation. For tax purposes, this kind of fund is called a welfare benefit fund.[2]

A welfare benefit fund can be (1) any tax-exempt organization that is a Voluntary Employees' Beneficiary Association ("VEBA"), a trust providing for payment of Supplemental Unemployment Compensation Benefits ("SUB"), a qualified Group Legal Services Organization ("GLSO") (although the tax exemption for GLSOs is not available in taxable years beginning after June 30, 1992), or a social club, or (2) any taxable organization that is a corporation, a trust, or other organization.[3]

Certain accounts held by an insurance company for an employer also will be considered welfare benefit funds.[4]

Amounts held by an insurance company are not considered a fund subject to the limit if they are held pursuant to a contract that is (1) a life insurance contract covering the life of an officer, employee, or any person financially interested in any trade or business carried on by a policyholder if the policyholder is directly or indirectly a beneficiary, or (2) not guaranteed renewable and the only payments other than insurance protection to which the employer or employees are entitled are experience-rated refunds or policy dividends that are not guaranteed and that are determined by factors other than the amount of welfare benefits paid to or on behalf of employees or their beneficiaries. The experience refund or policy dividend in (2) also must be treated by an employer as paid or accrued in the taxable year in which the policy year ends.[5]

---

1.   See IRC Secs. 419(a), 419(b), 419(g).
2.   IRC Secs. 419(e)(1), 419(e)(2).
3.   IRC Secs. 419(e)(3), 120(e).
4.   See IRC Sec. 419(e)(3)(C); TRA '86, Sec. 1851(a)(8)(B); Temp. Treas. Reg. §1.419-1T, A-3(c); Ann. 86-45, 1986-15 IRB 52.
5.   IRC Sec. 419(e)(4).

An employer's ability to contribute to a welfare benefit fund with respect to certain retiree health liabilities may be limited if the employer has made a qualified transfer of excess pension assets to a 401(h) retiree health account.[1]

In addition, setting assets aside in a welfare benefit fund to pay for retiree health liabilities may limit an employer's ability to make a qualified transfer of excess pension assets to a 401(h) retiree health account (Q 3835).[2] The rules permitting transfers to 401(h) accounts apply for taxable years beginning before January 1, 2026.[3] Details of the coordination of benefits between an IRC Section 401(h) account and a VEBA have been explained by the IRS.[4]

4095. When may an employer deduct contributions to a welfare benefit fund?

Contributions paid or accrued by an employer to a welfare benefit fund generally will be deductible when paid to the fund, if they are otherwise deductible, subject to the limit discussed in Q 4096.[5] If contributions paid by an employer during a taxable year exceed the deduction limit, the excess is treated as paid to the fund in the next taxable year.[6]

4096. What is the limit on the amount an employer may deduct for contributions to a welfare benefit fund to provide disability, medical, death, and other benefits to employees and independent contractors?

Qualified Cost

An amount, otherwise deductible, that is contributed by an employer to a welfare benefit fund may be deducted up to the fund's qualified cost for the taxable year of the fund that ends with or within the employer's taxable year.[7] A fund's qualified cost for any taxable year generally is its (1) qualified direct cost for that taxable year, plus (2) any additions to a qualified asset account for that taxable year to the extent the additions do not cause the account to exceed its account limit for the taxable year, minus (3) the fund's after-tax income for the taxable year.[8] The deductible amount may be reduced further by additional rules.[9]

To determine whether a company's contributions to a proposed trust to fund postretirement medical benefits for union retirees under a plan would be treated as not exceeding the trust's qualified cost under IRC Section 419(b) and IRC Section 419(c) and would be deductible without regard to the limits of IRC Section 419A(b) and IRC Section 419A(c), the IRS determined that if the amount of the contribution satisfies the requirements of IRC Section 419, the deduction of the amount generally is not limited by IRC Section 162.

---

1.   IRC Sec. 420(d)(2).
2.   IRC Sec. 420(e)(1)(B).
3.   IRC Sec. 420(b)(4).
4.   See Let. Rul. 9834037.
5.   IRC Sec. 419(a).
6.   IRC Sec. 419(d).
7.   IRC Secs. 419(a), 419(b); Temp. Treas. Reg. §§1.419-1T, A-1, 1.419-1T, A-4.
8.   IRC Secs. 419(c)(1), 419(c)(2), 419A(b); Temp. Treas. Reg. §1.419-1T, A-5(a).
9.   See Temp. Treas. Reg. §1.419-1T, A-5(b).

If a contribution is such that the assets exceed the amount needed to provide postretirement benefits to all current and future retirees from current active employees, that is, the present value of future benefits, then the contribution fails to satisfy the requirements of IRC Section 162.[1]

When the taxable year of a fund is different from the taxable year of an employer, special rules determine the deduction limit for the taxable year of the employer in which the fund is established and for the employer's next taxable year.[2] Special rules also require contributions made after the close of a fund's taxable year but during the employer's taxable year to be treated as an amount in the fund as of the last taxable year of the fund that relates to the taxable year of the employer.[3] Accordingly, an employer with a differing tax year than its welfare benefit trust cannot accelerate its deduction for its contribution to the trust to an earlier tax year by making its contribution after the end of the trust's tax year but before the end of the employer's tax year and, therefore, prefunding the trust for benefits to be provided in the following tax year.[4]

A fund's qualified direct cost for a taxable year generally is the amount, including administrative expenses that a cash basis employer with the same taxable year as the fund could deduct had it provided the benefits directly instead of through an intermediary fund. Rules limiting the deduction for benefits provided directly by an employer apply even though the benefits are provided through a fund. The benefit is considered provided in the year the benefit is includable in income by the employee or would be includable except for IRC provisions excluding the benefit from income.[5]

A qualified asset account is an account consisting of assets set aside to provide for the payment of disability benefits, medical benefits, Supplemental Unemployment Benefits ("SUB"), severance pay benefits, or life insurance benefits including any other death benefits.[6] The account limit on a qualified asset account for a taxable year generally is the amount reasonably and actuarially necessary to fund claims incurred but unpaid as of the close of the fund's taxable year for the benefits, as well as the administrative costs with respect to those claims.[7]

In one case, the Tax Court concluded that assets actually must be set aside for the payment of future long-term disability benefits that were incurred but unpaid; thus, an employer could not deduct contributions for the benefits where the employer had failed to accumulate the necessary assets in a VEBA trust.

The Sixth Circuit Court of Appeals determined that the Tax Court had erroneously interpreted the term "set aside" in IRC Section 419A(a) as having the same meaning as the term "reserve" in IRC Section 419A(c)(2). The Sixth Circuit held that an employer has set aside assets

---

1.   Let. Rul. 199945066.
2.   See Temp. Treas. Reg. §1.419-1T, A-7.
3.   See Temp Treas. Reg. §1.419-1T, A-5(b).
4.   *Square D Co. v. Comm.*, 109 TC 200 (1997).
5.   IRC Sec. 419(c)(3); Temp. Treas. Reg. §§1.419-1T, A-6(a), 1.419-1T, A-6(c).
6.   IRC Sec. 419A(a).
7.   IRC Sec. 419A(c)(1).

for purposes of IRC Section 419A(a) when it has made an irrevocable contribution to a welfare benefit fund providing those benefits specified in IRC Section 419A(a).[1]

In other words, "set aside" with respect to an account for disability, medical, supplemental unemployment, severance, or life insurance benefits under IRC Section 419A(a) has a different, less restrictive meaning than "reserve" as it applies to an account for postretirement medical or life insurance benefits.[2] Apparently, the amount reasonably and actuarially necessary to fund incurred but unpaid claims in a fully insured plan is zero.[3]

Under certain circumstances, the account limit also may include an amount to fund, over their working lives, postretirement medical or life insurance benefits including any other death benefit to be provided to covered employees.[4] The reserve may not be included in the account limit, however, unless such a reserve actually is established and funded, that is, unless assets actually are accumulated in the fund to cover postretirement obligations.[5]

The present value of projected postretirement medical benefits for employees who are retired at the time a reserve is created may be deducted in the year the reserve is created. The Tax Court has approved the use of the individual level premium cost method to compute the reserve and rejected the use of the aggregate cost method.[6]

The IRS privately ruled that where a company's VEBA intended to purchase a retiree health insurance policy to fund retiree benefits under the VEBA:

(1)   the VEBA would not be taxed on any income from the policy;

(2)   the company would not be required to recognize any income on the amount of the policy; and

(3)   the benefit payments under the policy to the VEBA would be excluded from the VEBA's gross income.[7]

Whether deductions may be claimed under IRC Section 419A(c)(2) turns on the intent of the employer at the time that the reserve is established.[8] A reserve for postretirement benefits is not required to be segregated from the general assets of the fund into a separate account.[9]

---

1.   *Parker–Hannifin Corp. v. Comm.*, TC Memo 1996-337, *aff'd in part, rev'd in part*, 139 F.3d 1090 (6th Cir. 1998).
2.   Internal Revenue Service Exempt Organizations Continuing Professional Education Text for Fiscal Year 1999, Chapter F, Voluntary Employees' Beneficiary Associations.
3.   See Let. Rul. 9325050.
4.   See IRC Secs. 419A(c)(2), 419A(e)(1).
5.   *General Signal Corp. v. Comm.*, 103 TC 216 (1994), *aff'd*, 142 F.3d 546 (2nd Cir. 1998); *Parker–Hannifin Corp. v. Comm.*, TC Memo 1996-337, *aff'd in part, rev'd in part*, 139 F.3d 1090 (6th Cir. 1998). See also *Square D Co. v. Comm.*, 109 TC 200 (1997); IRS CCA 201040018.
6.   *Wells Fargo v. Comm.*, 120 TC 69 (2003).
7.   Let. Rul. 200404055.
8.   *General Signal Corp. v. Comm.*, 142 F.3d 546 (2nd Cir. 1998).
9.   See *General Signal Corp. v. Comm.*, 103 TC 216 (1994) (agreeing in dicta with IRS attorneys' argument that a postretirement reserve need not be maintained in a separate account), *aff'd*, 142 F.3d 546 (2nd Cir. 1998); *Parker–Hannifin Corp. v. Comm.*, 139 F.3d 1090 (6th. Cir. 1998).

One special rule provides that certain employee pay-all VEBAs have no account limits.[1] Another special rule provides that welfare benefit funds under collective bargaining agreements have no account limits.[2] Certain arrangements purportedly qualifying as collectively-bargained welfare benefit funds excepted from the account limits of IRC Sections 419 and 419A have been identified as listed transactions (Q 4106).[3]

The DOL has released criteria for determining when a plan is established and maintained under a collective bargaining agreement for purposes of the exception from the Multiple Employer Welfare Arrangement ("MEWA") rules under ERISA.[4]

Maintenance of a separate welfare benefit fund for union employees is required. A fund for union employees must not only be separate from the employer and its creditors, but must also be "distinct and apart from any funds provided for noncollectively bargained employees."[5]

A fund's after-tax income generally is the fund's gross income, including employee contributions but excluding employer contributions, reduced by allowable deductions directly connected with production of gross income and by the tax on the income.[6]

Employer contributions that are not deductible in one year because they exceed the limit on allowable deductions are carried over and treated as contributed in the next year.[7]

Special rules apply if a welfare benefit fund is part of a 10 or more employer plan (Q 4106).

Account Limit

Claims are incurred only on the occurrence of an event entitling the employee to benefits, such as a medical expense, a separation, a disability, or a death. The allowable reserve includes amounts for claims estimated to have been incurred but that have not yet been reported, as well as those claims that have been reported but have not yet been paid.[8]

Incurred but unpaid claims include the present value of a future stream of payments under a long-term disability or death claim, using reasonable actuarial assumptions.[9] The report of the Senate committee (TRA '86) notes that no more than twelve months of disability benefits may be deemed incurred with respect to a short term disability expected to last more than five months.[10]

The account limit to fund disability claims that have been incurred, but remain unpaid, may not take into account disability benefits to the extent they are payable at an annual rate in excess of (1) the lower of 75 percent of the individual's average high three years of compensation

---

1.   IRC Sec. 419A(f)(5)(B).
2.   IRC Sec. 419A(f)(5)(A); see Temp. Treas. Reg. §1.419A-2T, A-2.
3.   Notice 2003-24, 2003-18 IRB 853.
4.   See Labor Reg. §2510.3-40; 68 Fed. Reg. 17471 (4-9-2003).
5.   *Parker-Hannifin Corp. v. Comm.*, 139 F.3d 1090 (6th Cir. 1998). But see Let. Ruls. 200137066, 199945066.
6.   IRC Sec. 419(c)(4).
7.   IRC Sec. 419(d).
8.   H.R. Conf. Rep. 861 (TRA '84), 98th Cong., 2d Sess. 1156, *reprinted in* 1984-3 CB (vol. 2) 410.
9.   See *id.*
10. S. Rep. No. 313, 99th Cong., 2d Sess. 1006, *reprinted in* 1986-3 CB (vol. 3) 1006.

or (2) the dollar limit on an annual benefit of a defined benefit plan ($230,000 in 2020-2021, $225,000 in 2019, up from $220,000 in 2018).[1] In applying this limit, all welfare benefit funds of the employer are treated as one fund.[2]

The account limit with respect to reserves set aside to provide postretirement medical or life insurance benefits may not take into account life insurance benefits in excess of $50,000, except to the extent a higher amount may be provided tax-free under grandfathering provisions of Section 79 for certain individuals.[3] For this purpose, all welfare benefit funds of an employer are treated as one.[4] In funding for postretirement medical benefits, current cost assumptions must be used; future inflation may not be assumed.[5]

The account limit generally may not include a reserve to provide postretirement medical or death benefits under a plan that fails to meet nondiscriminatory benefit requirements (Q 4103).[6] If postretirement benefits are provided for key employees, see Q 4102.

Unless there is an actuarial certification of the account limit by a qualified actuary, the account limit for a taxable year may not exceed certain safe harbor limits.[7] The IRC's reference to safe harbor limits here is potentially confusing because these limits are not true safe harbors.[8] That is, the safe harbor limits do not establish a minimal reserve level or account limit that an employer can automatically fund on a currently deductible basis. An employer claiming an account limit equal to or less than the applicable safe harbor limit or limits still must show that its claimed reserve satisfies the generally applicable restrictions of IRC Section 419A. That is, the claimed reserve still must be reasonably and actuarially necessary to pay incurred but unpaid claims plus administrative costs.[9]

Any reserve for postretirement medical or life insurance benefits must be determined actuarially on a level basis to fund the postretirement benefits over the working lives of covered employees. Claiming an account limit at or below the applicable safe harbor limit or limits simply relieves the employer of the obligation to obtain an actuarial certification justifying its reserve computations.[10] Actuarial valuation reports do not constitute an actuarial certification for purposes of IRC Section 419A.[11]

The safe harbor limit for any taxable year for short term disability claims is 17.5 percent of the qualified direct costs other than insurance premiums for short term disability benefits for the immediately preceding taxable year.[12]

---

1.   IRC Sec. 419A(c)(4)(A); Notice 2017-64, Notice 2018-83, Notice 2019-59, Notice 2020-79.
2.   IRC Sec. 419A(h)(1)(A).
3.   IRC Sec. 419A(e)(2); TRA '86, Sec. 1851(a)(3)(B), as amended by TAMRA '88 Sec. 1018(t)(2)(D).
4.   IRC Sec. 419A(h).
5.   IRC Sec. 419A(c)(2).
6.   See IRC Sec. 419A(e)(1); TRA '86 Sec. 1851(a)(3)(B), as amended by TAMRA '88 Sec. 1018(t)(2)(D).
7.   See IRC Sec. 419A(c)(5)(A); H.R. Conf. Rep. 861 (TRA '84), above, *reprinted in* 1984-3 CB (vol. 2) 412.
8.   See *General Signal Corp. v. Comm.*, 103 TC 216 (1994), *aff'd*, 142 F.3d 546 (2nd Cir. 1998); *Square D Co. v. Comm.*, 109 TC 200 (1997); TAMs 9818001, 9446002, 9334002.
9.   See, e.g., Let. Rul. 9818001.
10.   See *General Signal*, above; *Square D Co.*, above; H.R. Conf. Rep. No. 861, above, *reprinted in* 1984-3 CB (vol. 2) 412.
11.   Let. Rul. 9818001.
12.   IRC Sec. 419A(c)(5)(B)(i).

The safe harbor limit for any taxable year for long-term disability or life insurance benefits is to be prescribed by regulations.[1]

The safe harbor limit for any taxable year for medical claims is 35 percent of the qualified direct costs other than insurance premiums for medical benefits for the immediately preceding taxable year.[2] The TRA '84 conference report explains that insurance premiums may not be taken into account because the conferees did not intend that a fund be used as a vehicle for prepayment of insurance premiums for current benefits.[3]

4097. What is the additional reserve for medical benefits of bona fide association plans?

For tax years beginning after December 31, 2006, an applicable account limit for any taxable year may include a reserve in an amount not to exceed 35 percent of the sum of the qualified direct costs and the change in claims incurred but unpaid for such taxable year with respect to medical benefits other than post-retirement medical benefits. For this purpose, applicable account limit means an account limit for a qualified asset account with respect to medical benefits provided through a plan maintained by a bona fide association as defined in Section 2791(d)(3) of the Public Health Service Act.[4]

In determining an employer's deduction, no item may be taken into account more than once.[5]

4098. How do supplemental unemployment compensation ("SUB") and severance pay benefits apply in the context of a welfare benefit fund?

Where contributions are made to a fund to provide supplemental unemployment compensation ("SUB") or severance pay benefits, the account limit for SUB or severance pay benefits is 75 percent of the average qualified direct costs for any two of the immediately preceding seven taxable years, as selected by the fund.[6] If the benefit to any individual is payable at an annual rate in excess of 150 percent of the IRC Section 415 dollar limit on contributions to defined contribution plans, the excess cannot be taken into account in determining the account limit.[7] In applying this latter limit, all welfare benefit funds of the employer are treated as one fund.[8] Treasury regulations are to provide an interim limit for new SUB or severance pay plans that do not cover key employees.[9]

The safe harbor limit for SUB or severance pay benefits is the amount as determined above.[10]

---

1.   IRC Sec. 419A(c)(5)(B)(iv).
2.   IRC Sec. 419A(c)(5)(B)(ii).
3.   H.R. Conf. Rep. 861, above, *reprinted in* 1984-3 CB (vol. 2) 412.
4.   42 USC 300gg-91(d)(3). IRC Sec. 419A(c)(6), as added by PPA 2006.
5.   IRC Sec. 419(c)(5).
6.   IRC Sec. 419A(c)(3)(A).
7.   IRC Sec. 419A(c)(4)(B).
8.   IRC Sec. 419A(h)(1)(A).
9.   IRC Sec. 419A(c)(3)(B).
10.   IRC Sec. 419A(c)(5)(B)(iii).

For an explanation of how certain severance benefits are treated in light of the deferred compensation rules set forth in IRC Section 409(A), see Q 4117.

4099. How do the aggregation rules apply to welfare benefit funds?

An employer must treat all of its welfare benefit funds as one fund for certain purposes.[1] For other purposes, an employer may elect to treat two or more of its funds as one.[2] An election to aggregate must be consistent for deduction and nondiscrimination purposes (Q 4103, Q 4112).[3] There are aggregation rules similar to those of IRC Section 414 for controlled groups of corporations, employers under common control, and affiliated service groups and there are rules similar to the employee leasing rules.[4]

4100. What are the tax consequences to an employer and to a welfare benefit fund if the employer contributes excess amounts to the fund?

First, the deduction for the excess contribution is disallowed currently, although the excess contribution may be carried over and may be deductible in a later year. This carryover appears to be unlimited in time.[5]

Second, the fund's income-based tax liability may be increased. If contributions are made to a tax-exempt fund, the fund's liability for unrelated business income tax (UBTI) may increase. Thus, to the extent that excess contributions reduce any difference between the qualified asset account and the qualified asset account limit, which is calculated with some modification, the excess contributions will limit a fund's ability to protect some of its income from treatment as UBTI. In addition, excessive contributions to a fund ultimately may increase the fund's earnings, which may cause an increased exposure to UBTI (Q 4101).

Third, any increase in a fund's after-tax income, including employee contributions but not employer contributions, reduces the amount the employer can deduct (Q 4096). Thus, the IRC forces the fund's earnings to be used to provide benefits. The amount of tax imposed on an employer attributable to income of the fund is treated as a contribution to the fund as of the last day of the employer's taxable year. The amount of tax is treated as a tax on the fund for purposes of determining the fund's after-tax income.

Finally, efforts to retrieve excessive contributions may be costly because the IRC imposes an excise tax of 100 percent on any portion of a fund that reverts to the benefit of an employer to the extent it is attributable to deductible contributions (Q 4104).[6] It is not clear whether efforts to retrieve excessive contributions to a voluntary employees' beneficiary association ("VEBA") would violate the prohibition against private inurement (Q 4112).

1.   IRC Sec. 419A(h)(1)(A).
2.   IRC Sec. 419A(h)(1)(B).
3.   H.R. Conf. Rep. 861, above, *reprinted in* 1984-3 CB (vol. 2) 413.
4.   IRC Sec. 419A(h)(2).
5.   See IRC Sec. 419(d).
6.   IRC Sec. 4976.

4101. What income of a tax-exempt welfare benefit fund is taxable as unrelated business taxable income?

A tax-exempt welfare benefit fund is subject to a tax on its unrelated business taxable income ("UBTI"); a corporate fund is taxed at corporate rates and a trust at rates applicable to trusts.[1] Income less certain deductions from an unrelated trade or business regularly carried on by the organization is taxable. Other income of a tax-exempt organization, excluding member contributions and certain deductions, is taxable except to the extent it is set aside for certain purposes and, at least in some cases, within certain limits.[2]

A VEBA or SUB may protect income from treatment as UBTI by setting it aside for the payment of life, sick, accident, or other benefits and reasonable, directly connected administrative costs.[3] The amount that may be so protected is expressly limited to the amount that may be set aside without causing the total assets set aside for such purposes to exceed the fund's account limit (Q 4096) for the taxable year.[4] This limitation applies to a fund that is part of a 10 or more employer plan. In determining the account limit for this purpose, a reserve for postretirement medical benefits generally may not be taken into consideration.[5] Income in excess of the amount properly set aside is taxable as unrelated business income. To the extent the account limit already is satisfied, a fund's income cannot be set aside tax-free.

Pre-2018, entities could aggregate income from all trades or businesses when calculating UBTI. The 2017 tax reform legislation changed the tax treatment of VEBA and SUB UBTI so that UBTI has to be calculated separately for each unrelated trade or business (called "silos").[6] The proposed regulations maintain this treatment, so that deductions from one business cannot be used to offset income from another. Under the regulations, VEBAs and SUBs must treat certain listed investment activities as separate unrelated trades or businesses (for example certain S-corporation interests). Exempt organizations are, however, entitled to identify separate trades and businesses using general NAICS two-digit codes (rather than the more specific six-digit codes). This should mitigate the burden for exempt organizations to allow for aggregation of similar activities.[7]

If any amount attributable to income set aside tax-free is used for any purpose other than one entitling the set-aside to tax-free treatment, the amount generally will be treated as UBTI.[8]

Special rules apply where there are existing reserves set aside as of the close of the last plan year ending before July 18, 1984, or, if greater, on July 18, 1984, to provide postretirement medical or life insurance benefits.[9]

---

1.   IRC Sec. 511. See, e.g., *Sherwin-Williams Co. Employee Health Plan Trust v. U.S.*, 2005-1 USTC ¶50,286 (6th Cir. 2005), *aff'g*, 2002-2 USTC ¶50,271 (ND Ohio 2002).
2.   IRC Sec. 512(a)(3).
3.   IRC Sec. 512(a)(3)(B)(ii).
4.   IRC Sec. 512(a)(3)(E)(i).
5.   IRC Sec. 512(a)(3)(E)(ii).
6.   IRC Sec. 512(a)(6).
7.   See also Notice 2018-67.
8.   IRC Sec. 512(a)(3)(B). But see Let. Ruls. 200126035, 200126034, 200023052, 9401033, 9147059.
9.   See IRC Sec. 512(a)(3)(E)(ii); Temp. Treas. Reg. §1.512(a)-5T, A-4.

Editor's Note: The IRS resolved the controversy discussed below by releasing final regulations that are effective as of December 10, 2019. The IRS regulations clarify that all investment income earned during a given tax year must be counted in calculating UBTI. If the organization's year-end assets exceed the account limit, the tax may apply regardless of whether investment income is spent on benefit payments or administrative expenses, or retained after the end of the year.[1]

In *Sherwin-Williams Co. Employee Health Plan Trust v. Comm.*, the Sixth Circuit Court of Appeals reversed the Tax Court and held that the IRC Section 512(a)(3)(E)(i) limit on accumulating set-aside income does not apply to income that was set aside and spent on the reasonable costs of administering health care benefits under IRC Section 512(a)(3)(B) over the course of the year. Instead, the limit is on the amount of income that is still set aside at the end of the year. The Sixth Circuit reasoned that the limit does not apply to such spent income because that income is exempt function income, which is not subject to tax under IRC Section 512(a)(3)(A).[2]

The IRS did not acquiesce in the decision, but did recognize its precedential effect on other cases appealed to the Sixth Circuit. Therefore, with respect to cases within the Sixth Circuit, the IRS announced that it will follow the *Sherwin-Williams* decision if the opinion cannot be meaningfully distinguished.[3]

Distinguishing *Sherwin-Williams* on its facts, and also disagreeing with the Sixth Circuit's legal interpretation of the limit set forth in IRC Section 512(a)(3)(E)(i), the Court of Federal Claims held in *CNG Transmission Management VEBA v. United States* that a VEBA may not avoid the limit on exempt function income merely by allocating investment income to the payment of welfare benefits during the course of the tax year.[4] Affirming the lower court's ruling, the Court of Appeals for the Federal Circuit flatly rejected CNG's argument that its investment income could not have resulted in any account overage because it had spent all of its investment income on member benefits during the course of the tax year. In the view of the appellate court, money is fungible. Therefore, CNG could not avoid taxation by claiming that it had spent money from investment income, rather than money from some other source, on member benefits. Furthermore, the appellate court held that there is no requirement in Section 512(a)(3)(E)(i) that a VEBA's investment income can result in a year-end account overage only to the extent that the actual dollars in the account at year end are traceable to income made on investments.[5] The Court of Federal Claims continues to follow *CNG*.[6]

In technical advice, the IRS stated that all income of a VEBA, other than income from an existing reserve, is included in computing the UBTI of a VEBA even though the VEBA consists of four separate claims reserves that are accounted for separately.

---

1. Treas. Reg. §1.512(a)-5.
2. *Sherwin-Williams Co. Employee Health Plan Trust v. Comm.*, 330 F.3d 449 (6th Cir. 2003), rev'g, 115 TC 440 (2000).
3. See Action on Decision 2005-2 (released 9-12-2005) at www.irs.gov/pub/irs-aod/aod200502.pdf.
4. *CNG Transmission Management VEBA v. United States*, 84 Fed. Cl. 327(2008).
5. *CNG Transmission Management VEBA v. United States*, 588 F.3d 1376 (CA Fed. Cir. 2009).
6. *Northrop Corp. Emple. Ins. Ben. Plans*, 99 Fed. Cl. 1 (June 28, 2011), aff'd, 467 Fed. Appx. 886 (Fed. Cir. 2012), *cert. denied*, 133 S. Ct. 756 (2012).

In computing UBTI, income from tax-exempt bonds is not treated as exempt function income of a VEBA. That income affects the amount of assets available to pay benefits and, thus, may indirectly affect the computation of UBTI.

Finally, amounts set aside in existing reserves and additional reserves for postretirement medical or life insurance benefits are taken into account in accordance with Treasury Regulation Sections 1.512(a)-5T, Q&A-4(a) and 1.512(a)-5T, Q&A-4(d) when computing the UBTI of a VEBA.[1] In other technical advice, the IRS determined that an employer could aggregate two welfare benefit funds, such as a VEBA and a non-tax exempt welfare benefit fund, for the purpose of computing UBTI.[2]

The set aside limitation does not apply to any funds to which substantially all contributions are made by employers that were tax-exempt throughout the five taxable year period ending with the taxable year in which the contributions are made.[3] Because they have no account limits, welfare benefit funds under collective bargaining agreements and certain employee pay-all VEBAs, namely those with at least 50 employees and in which no employee is entitled to a refund other than one based on the experience of the entire fund, are not subject to the IRC's express set-aside limitation.

4102. What special rules apply if postretirement medical or life insurance benefits are provided to a key employee through a welfare benefit fund?

Separate Account Required

In the first year a reserve for postretirement medical or life insurance benefits, including any other death benefits, is taken into account in determining the applicable account limit (Q 4096), a separate account must be established for any medical or life insurance benefits provided after retirement with respect to a key employee. The separate account must be maintained for all subsequent taxable years. Medical or life insurance benefits provided with respect to an employee after retirement must be paid from that separate account only.[4]

A key employee is one who at any time during the plan year or any preceding plan year is or was a key employee (Q 3930) as defined for top-heavy qualified retirement plans.[5] A separate account is to include amounts contributed to the plan with respect to service after the employee becomes a key employee as well as a reasonable allocation, determined under applicable regulations, of amounts contributed on his or her behalf before the individual became a key employee.[6]

Annual Additions

Any amount allocated to an account of a key employee for postretirement medical benefits must be counted as an annual addition for purposes of the IRC Section 415 dollar limit, but

---

1.   TAM 199932050.
2.   TAM 200317036.
3.   IRC Sec. 512(a)(3)(E)(iii).
4.   IRC Sec. 419A(d)(1).
5.   IRC Sec. 419A(d)(3).
6.   H.R. Conf. Rep. 861 (TRA '84), 98th Cong., 2d Sess. 1157, *reprinted in* 1984-3 CB (vol.2) 411.

not for determining the percentage of compensation, as if it were a contribution to a qualified defined contribution plan; all welfare benefit funds of the employer are treated as one fund for this purpose.[1]

Therefore, the amount allocated to a key employee's account can have a significant effect on the qualification of any pension, profit sharing, or stock bonus plan in which the employee is a participant. Presumably, amounts allocated for periods before the employee became a key employee can be disregarded.

4103. Must a welfare benefit fund providing postretirement life insurance or medical benefits meet nondiscrimination requirements?

The current status for the tax treatment of these benefits is awaiting regulatory guidance under IRC Section 9815 (effective after a regulation is adopted).[2]

Prior to the passage of health care reform legislation, the following applied:

A reserve for postretirement benefits generally may not be included in determining a fund's qualified asset account limit if the plan of which the fund is a part is discriminatory with respect to those benefits; thus, in effect, a deduction is not available for contributions to prefund discriminatory benefits.[3]

A plan is discriminatory with respect to postretirement medical or life insurance benefits (including any other death benefits) unless it meets the nondiscrimination requirements, if any, specifically applicable to the benefit it provides or, if none, satisfies the following two requirements: (1) each class of these benefits must be provided under a classification of employees that is set forth in the plan and that is found by the IRS not to be discriminatory in favor of highly compensated individuals, and (2) the benefits provided under each class of benefits must not discriminate in favor of highly compensated individuals.[4] These nondiscrimination requirements also apply to VEBAs (Q 4112).

4104. What is the penalty for providing certain disqualified benefits through a welfare benefit fund?

An employer will be subject to a tax equal to 100 percent of:

(1)   any postretirement medical or life insurance benefit including any other death benefit provided to a key employee other than from a separate account, if a separate account was required (Q 4102);

(2)   any postretirement medical or life insurance benefit including any other death benefit provided with respect to an individual in whose favor discrimination is

---

1.   IRC Secs. 419A(d)(2), 419A(h)(1)(A).
2.   Notice 2011-1.
3.   IRC Sec. 419A(e)(1).
4.   IRC Secs. 419A(e)(1), 505(b).

prohibited unless the plan is nondiscriminatory (Q 4103, Q 4112) with respect to this benefit, or

(3)   any portion of the fund reverting to the benefit of the employer that is attributable to contributions that were deductible in the current or any prior year.[1]

One exception provides that postretirement medical or life insurance benefits charged against amounts in a reserve up to the greater of the amount in the reserve as of the close of the last plan year ending before July 18, 1984, or on July 18, 1984, or charged against the income on such amounts, are not subject to the tax referred to in (1) and (2) above.[2]

Another exception provides that certain welfare benefit funds maintained pursuant to collective bargaining agreements are not subject to the tax described in (2) above.[3]

A loan by a VEBA to its members' employer is not necessarily a prohibited reversion, but any such transaction will be carefully reviewed to determine whether it is a genuine, commercially viable loan.[4]

4105. Must a tax-exempt welfare benefit fund apply for recognition of its tax-exempt status?

Yes.

A VEBA or SUB must give notice to the IRS, in the manner required in the regulations that it is applying for tax-exempt status.[5] An organization that fails to provide the required notice will not be tax-exempt until it gives notice. Requirements for giving notice are set forth in Temporary Treasury Regulation Section 1.505(c)-1T.

4106. What exception applies to a welfare benefit fund that is part of a 10 or more employer plan?

IRC Sections 419 and 419A do not apply to a welfare benefit fund that is part of a 10 or more employer plan that does not maintain experience rating arrangements with respect to individual employers. A 10 or more employer plan is one to which more than one employer contributes, and to which no employer normally contributes more than 10 percent of the total contributions made under the plan by all employers.[6]

A variety of multi-employer plans have been marketed to take advantage of the 10 or more employer plan exception; some of these plans were very aggressive and did not qualify for the exception. In 1995, the IRS claimed to have uncovered significant tax problems in multi-employer arrangements and warned taxpayers that arrangements claiming to qualify for the multi-employer plan exception may suffer from various defects, including:

---

1.   IRC Sec. 4976.
2.   IRC Sec. 4976(b)(4).
3.   IRC Sec. 4976(b)(2).
4.   See GCM 39884 (10-29-92).
5.   IRC Sec. 505(c).
6.   IRC Sec. 419A(f)(6).

(1)   The arrangements actually may be providing deferred compensation rather than welfare benefits. This issue seems to arise most often in connection with plans purporting to provide severance benefits.[1]

(2)   The arrangements in fact may be separate plans maintained for each employer although nominally linked together as part of multi-employer arrangements.

(3)   The arrangements may be experience-rated with respect to individual employers in form or operation because, among other things, the trusts may maintain, formally or informally, separate accounts for each employer and the employers may have reason to expect that their contributions will benefit only their employees.[2]

The IRS successfully argued before the Tax Court points (2) and (3) with respect to the multi-employer plan in question in *Booth v. Comm.*[3] The Tax Court held that the multi-employer plan did not fall within the scope of IRC Section 419A(f)(6)(A) because the plan was an aggregation of separate welfare benefit plans each having an experience-rating arrangement with the related employer.

The Tax Court stated, "We interpret the word 'plan' to mean that there must be a single pool of funds for use by the group as a whole (i.e., to pay the claims of all participants), and we interpret the phrase '10 or more employer plan' to mean that 10 or more employers must contribute to this single pool. We do not interpret the statutory language to include a program like the instant one where multiple employers have contributed funds to an independent party to hold in separate accounts until disbursed primarily for the benefit of the contributing employer's employees in accordance with unique terms established by that employer."[4] As a result, the deductions of the employers participating in the plan were subject to the deduction limitations of IRC Sections 419 and 419A.

In *Neonatology Assoc., P.A., et al. v. Comm.*,[5] the Tax Court denied deductions for the portion of VEBA contributions in excess of the cost of current year (term) life insurance under IRC Section 162. Contributions to a welfare benefit fund can be deducted only in the amount (Q 4096) and at the time permitted by IRC Section 419 (Q 4095), but they also must satisfy the requirements of IRC Section 162 or IRC Section 212.[6]

In this case, the two VEBAs were structured so that each employer established and contributed to its own plan. The premiums on the underlying insurance policies were substantially greater than the cost of conventional term life insurance because they funded both the costs of term life insurance and credits that would be applied to conversion universal life policies

---

1.   See, e.g., *Wellons v. Comm.*, 31 F.3d 569, 94-2 USTC ¶50,402 (7th Cir. 1994), *aff'g*, TC Memo 1992-704 (severance pay arrangement is more akin to deferred compensation plan than welfare benefit plan where five years of service must be given before benefits accrue, benefit amount is linked to level of compensation and length of service, and benefits can be paid at virtually any termination of employment).

2.   See Notice 95-34, 1995-1 CB 309.

3.   108 TC 524 (1997).

4.   *Id.* at 571.

5.   115 TC 43 (2000) (19 consolidated cases), *aff'd*, 299 F.3d 221 (3d Cir. 2002).

6.   See IRC Sec. 419(a), Temp. Treas. Reg. §1.419-1T, A-10.

of individual insureds. Policyholders generally could withdraw any earned amount or borrow against their policies without any out-of-pocket costs.

The Tax Court in *Neonatology* determined that the VEBAs were not designed, marketed, purchased, or sold as a means for an employer to provide welfare benefits to its employees. The Tax Court held that the VEBAs were primarily vehicles that were designed and served in operation to distribute surplus cash surreptitiously in the form of excess contributions from the medical corporations for the employee/owners' ultimate use and benefit. Although the plans provided term life insurance to the employee/owners, the excess contributions were not attributable to that current year protection. The Tax Court further held that the excess contributions were constructive distributions of cash to the employee/owners that did not constitute deductible ordinary and necessary business expenses under IRC Section 162(a).[1]

In 2009, the IRS released a lengthy background document that outlined the issues and patterns its agents would look for during audits of welfare benefit plans with respect to uncovering disguised dividend arrangements, for example as in the *Neonatology* and *DeAngelis* cases, as well as disguised deferred compensation arrangements.[2] In the audit guidance, the IRS advises its agents to place a particularly sharp focus on arrangements using cash value life insurance policies and includes several questions that agents will use to identify abusive arrangements.

Definitions

The term benefits or other amounts payable includes all amounts payable or distributable or that otherwise will be provided directly or indirectly to employers, to employees or their beneficiaries, or to another fund as a result of a spin-off or transfer, regardless of the form of the payment or distribution (i.e., whether provided as welfare benefits, cash, dividends, credits, rebates of contributions, property, promises to pay, or otherwise).[3]

Benefits experience of an employer or of an employee or a group of employers or employees means the benefits and other amounts incurred, paid, or distributed or otherwise provided, directly or indirectly, including to another fund as a result of a spin-off or transfer, with respect to the employer regardless of the form of payment or distribution.[4]

The overall experience of an employer or group of employers is the balance that would have accumulated in a welfare benefit fund if that employer were the only employer providing benefits under the plan.

The overall experience of an employee is the balance that would have accumulated in a welfare benefit fund if that employee were the only employee being provided benefits under the plan. Overall experience as of any date may be either a positive or a negative number.[5]

---

1. See also *DeAngelis et al. v. Comm.*, TC Memo 2007-360, *aff'd*, 574 F.3d 789 (2d Cir. 2009), citing *Neonatology; Curcio v. Comm.*, 2012 U.S. App. LEXIS 16645 (2d Cir. 2012).
2. See Revised Background Document No. 200931049 (Release Date 7-31-2009).
3. Treas. Reg. §1.419A(f)(6)-1(d)(1).
4. Treas. Reg. §1.419A(f)(6)-1(d)(2).
5. Treas. Reg. §1.419A(f)(6)-1(d)(3).

The term employer means the employer whose employees are participating in the plan and those employers required to be aggregated under IRC Sections 414(b), 414(c), or 414(m).[1] Rating group means a group of participating employers that includes the employer or a group of employees covered under the plan that includes one or more employees or that employer.[2]

A plan provides a fixed welfare benefit package, that is, fixed welfare benefits for a fixed coverage period for a fixed cost, if it: (1) defines one or more welfare benefits, each of which has a fixed amount that does not depend on the amount or type of assets held by the fund, (2) specifies fixed contributions to provide for those welfare benefits, and (3) specifies a coverage period during which the plan agrees to provide specified welfare benefits subject to the payment of the specified contributions by the employer.[3] For the treatment of actuarial gains or losses, see Treasury Regulation Section 1.419A(f)(6)-1(d)(5)(ii).

Plan administrator is defined the same as in Treasury Regulation Section 1.414(g)-1.[4] The plan administrator of a plan that is intended to be a 10 or more employer plan described in IRC Section 419A(f)(6) is required to maintain permanent records and other documentary evidence sufficient to substantiate that the plan satisfies the requirements of IRC Section 419A(f)(6) and the regulations.[5]

4107. What are the circumstances that will cause the IRS to classify a multi-employer welfare benefit plan as a listed transaction? What is the penalty that applies for this classification?

Certain trust arrangements under Notice 95-34[6] that are purported to qualify as multiple employer plans exempt from the IRC Section 419 and IRC Section 419A limits have been classified by the IRS as listed transactions.[7]

Reportable transaction means any transaction with respect to which information is required to be included with a return or statement because, as determined under regulations prescribed under IRC Section 6011, the transaction is of a type that the IRS determines has a potential for tax avoidance or evasion.[8] One category of reportable transactions is a listed transaction, that is, a transaction that is the same as, or substantially similar to, one of the types of transactions that the IRS has determined to be a tax avoidance transaction and has identified as such by notice, regulation, or other form of published guidance.[9] For guidance on the penalty assessed under IRC Section 6707A, see T.D. 9550.[10]

---

1.   Treas. Reg. §1.419A(f)(6)-1(d)(4).
2.   Treas. Reg. §1.419A(f)(6)-1(b)(4)(iii).
3.   Treas. Reg. §1.419A(f)(6)-1(d)(5)(i).
4.   Treas. Reg. §1.419A(f)(6)-1(a)(2).
5.   Treas. Reg. §1.419A(f)(6)-1(e).
6.   1995-1 CB 309.
7.   See Notice 2009-59; 2009-2 CB 170.
8.   IRC Sec. 6707A(c)(1).
9.   IRC Sec. 6707A(c)(2). See Treas. Reg. §1.6011-4(b)(2). Notice 2009-59; 2009-2 CB 170.
10. 2011-2 CB 785.

Generally, Section 6707A imposes a penalty for failure to disclose information related to a reportable transaction in the amount of 75 percent of the decrease in the tax shown on a tax return as a result of the reportable transaction. The maximum penalty for failing to disclose a listed transaction is $100,000 (with a minimum penalty of $5,000) in the case of a natural person and $200,000 (with a $10,000 minimum) in any other case.[1] The IRS has released proposed regulations that retain these requirements, but provide that the "decrease in tax" is the difference between the amount of tax reported on the return as filed, and the amount that would have been reported if the taxpayer had not participated in the reportable transaction. The decrease in tax is determined separately for each year that the taxpayer participates in the reportable transaction for which only one disclosure was required, and the amount of the penalty is 75 percent of the aggregate decrease in tax in all the years that disclosure was required (subject to the minimum and maximum amounts discussed above).[2]

A 20 percent penalty applies when a taxpayer has a reportable transaction understatement attributable to a listed transaction.[3] A 30 percent penalty applies to undisclosed listed transactions.[4] Guidance on the penalty assessed under IRC Section 6662A is provided in Notice 2005-12.[5]

For other tax shelter provisions, see IRC Section 6111 (disclosure of reportable transactions by material advisors), IRC Section 6112 (list maintenance requirements for material advisors) and IRC Section 6502(c) (statute of limitations). T.D. 9350[6] discusses modifications to the rules relating to the disclosure of reportable transactions affecting taxpayers and material advisors; T.D. 9351[7] discusses modifications to the rules relating to the disclosure of reportable transactions by material advisors; and T.D. 9352[8] discusses modifications to the rules relating to list maintenance requirements for material advisors. For additional guidance on material advisor reporting and exceptions to tax shelter reportable transactions, see Notice 2004-80.[9] For the final regulations outlining the requirements applicable to tax shelters, see TD 9046.[10] For the final requirements for tax shelter opinion letters, see TD 9165.[11]

4108. What regulations govern the exception for a welfare benefit fund that is part of a 10 or more employer plan?

A valid 10 or more employer plan is a single plan:

(1)   to which more than one employer contributes,

(2)   to which no employer normally contributes more than 10 percent of the total contributions of all employers under the plan, and

---

1.   IRC Sec. 6707A.
2.   REG-103033-11.
3.   IRC Secs. 6662A(a), 6662A(b).
4.   IRC Sec. 6662A(c).
5.   2005-7 IRB 494; see also IRS News Release IR-2005-10 (1-19-2005).
6.   72 Fed. Reg. 43146 (8-3-2007).
7.   72 Fed. Reg. 43157 (8-3-2007).
8.   72 Fed. Reg. 43154 (8-3-2007).
9.   2004-50 IRB 963 clarified and modified by, Notice 2005-17, 2005-8 IRB 606, and Notice 2005-22, 2005-12 IRB 756. See also Rev. Proc. 2008-20, 2008-20 IRB 980.
10.   68 Fed. Reg. 10161 (3-4-2003).
11.   2005-1 CB 357, modified by 2005-1 CB 996.

(3)　　that does not maintain an experience-rating arrangement with respect to any individual employer.[1]

To qualify as a valid 10 or more employer plan, a plan also must satisfy certain compliance requirements. It must be maintained pursuant to a written document that: (1) requires the plan administrator to maintain records sufficient for the IRS or any participating employer to readily verify the plan's compliance with the requirements of IRC Section 419A(f)(6) and Treasury Regulation Section 1.419A(f)(6)-1(a)(2), and (2) provides the IRS and each participating employer with the right on written request to the plan administrator to inspect and copy all of these records.[2]

To qualify as a valid 10 or more employer plan, a plan must satisfy the requirements of the regulations in both form and operation.[3] The term "plan" includes the totality of the arrangement and all related facts and circumstances, including any related insurance contracts. Thus, all agreements and understandings, including promotional materials, policy illustrations, and the terms of any insurance contracts, will be taken into account in determining whether the requirements are satisfied in form and in operation.[4]

Special Rules

Treatment of insurance contracts. Insurance contracts generally will be treated as assets of the fund. Thus, the value of the insurance contracts, including non-guaranteed elements, is included in the value of the fund, and amounts paid between the fund and the insurance company are disregarded, except to the extent they generate gains or losses, as explained below.[5]

Payments to and from an insurance company. Payments from a participating employer or its employees to an insurance company with respect to insurance contracts will be treated as contributions made to the fund. Amounts paid under the arrangement from an insurance company will be treated as payments from the fund.[6]

Gains and losses from insurance contracts. As of any date, if the sum of benefits paid by an insurer and the value of the insurance contract, including non-guaranteed elements, is greater than the cumulative premiums paid to the insurer, the excess is treated as a gain to the fund. As of any date, if the cumulative premiums paid to the insurer are greater than the sum of the benefits paid by the insurer and the value of the insurance contract, including non-guaranteed elements, the excess is treated as a loss to the fund.[7]

Treatment of flexible contribution arrangements. Solely for purposes of determining the cost of coverage under a plan, if contributions for any period can vary with respect to a benefit package,

---

1.　　Treas. Reg. §1.419A(f)(6)-1(a)(1).
2.　　Treas. Reg. §1.419A(f)(6)-1(a)(2).
3.　　Treas. Reg. §1.419A(f)(6)-1(a)(3)(i).
4.　　Treas. Reg. §1.419A(f)(6)-1(a)(3)(ii).
5.　　Treas. Reg. §1.419A(f)(6)-1(b)(4)(i)(A).
6.　　Treas. Reg. §1.419A(f)(6)-1(b)(4)(i)(B).
7.　　Treas. Reg. §1.419A(f)(6)-1(b)(4)(i)(C).

the IRS may treat the employer as contributing the minimum amount that would maintain the coverage for that period.[1]

Experience-rating by group of employers (or employees). A plan will not be treated as maintaining an experience-rating arrangement (Q 4109) with respect to an individual employer merely because the cost of coverage under the plan is based, in whole or in part, on the benefits experience or the overall experience of a rating group provided that no employer normally contributes more than 10 percent of all contributions with respect to that rating group.[2]

4109. What is an experience-rating arrangement and what are the results if a welfare benefit plan is found to maintain such an arrangement?

A plan maintains an experience-rating arrangement with respect to an individual employer if, for any period, the relationship of contributions under the plan to the benefits or other amounts payable under the plan, that is, the cost of coverage, is or can be expected to be based, in whole or in part, on the benefits experience or the overall experience of that employer or one or more employees of that employer.[3] According to the IRS, this determination is not intended to be purely a computational one, although actual numbers often can be used to demonstrate the existence of an experience-rating arrangement.[4]

For these purposes, an employer's contributions include all contributions made by or on behalf of the employer or the employer's employees. The prohibition against experience-rating applies under all circumstances, including employer withdrawals and plan terminations.[5]

An example of a plan that maintains an experience-rating arrangement with respect to an individual employer is a plan that entitles the employer to, or for which the employer can expect, a reduction in future contributions if that employer's overall experience is positive or an increase in future contributions if that employer's overall benefits experience is negative.[6]

Another example of a plan that maintains an experience-rating arrangement with respect to an individual employer is a plan under which benefits for an employer's employees are or can be expected to be increased if that employer's overall experience is positive or decreased if that employer's overall experience is negative.[7]

Use of insurance contracts. The IRS recognizes that if whole life insurance contracts or other insurance contracts that provide for level premiums or otherwise generate a savings element are purchased under an arrangement, the economic values reflected under those contracts, including cash values, reserves, conversion credits, high dividend rates, or the right to continue coverage at a premium that is lower than the premium that would apply in the absence of that

---

1.   Treas. Reg. §1.419A(f)(6)-1(b)(4)(ii).
2.   Treas. Reg. §1.419A(f)(6)-1(b)(4)(iii).
3.   Treas. Reg. §1.419A(f)(6)-1(b)(1).
4.   Preamble, TD 9079, 68 Fed. Reg. 42254, 42256 (7-17-2003).
5.   Treas. Reg. §1.419A(f)(6)-1(b)(1).
6.   Treas. Reg. §1.419A(f)(6)-1(b)(2).
7.   Treas. Reg. §1.419A(f)(6)-1(b)(3).

savings element, reflect the overall experience of the employers and employees who participate under the plan.[1]

The IRS also states that neither IRC Section 419A(f)(6) nor the regulations govern the investments of a welfare benefit fund, including investments by a trust in cash value policies. Instead, the IRS is concerned with the economic relationship between a fund and participating employers, and whether the pass-through of premiums based on the insurance contracts associated with an employer's employees has the effect of creating experience-rating arrangements with respect to individual employers. Furthermore, the IRS believes that the exception is still viable for many life and health benefit arrangements that are self-insured in accordance with ERISA or state law.[2]

4110. What characteristics indicate a plan is not a 10 or more employer plan?

The presence of any of the characteristics listed below generally indicates that the plan is *not* a 10 or more employer plan under IRC Section 419A(f)(6). It is important to note that a plan's lack of all of the following characteristics does not create any inference that it is a 10 or more employer plan described in IRC Section 419A(f)(6).[3] The characteristics are as follows:

(1)   Allocation of plan assets. Assets of the plan or fund are allocated to a specific employer or employers through separate accounting of contributions and expenditures for individual employers, or otherwise.[4]

(2)   Differential pricing. The amount charged under the plan is not the same for all the participating employers, and those differences are not merely reflective of differences in current risk or rating factors that are commonly taken into account in manual rates used by insurers (such as current age, gender, geographic locale, number of covered dependents, and benefit terms) for the particular benefit or benefits being provided.[5]

(3)   No fixed welfare benefit package. The plan does not provide for fixed welfare benefits for a fixed coverage period for a fixed cost.[6]

(4)   Unreasonably high cost. The plan provides for fixed welfare benefits for a fixed coverage period for a fixed cost, but that cost is unreasonably high for the covered risk for the plan as a whole.[7]

(5)   Nonstandard benefit triggers. The plan provides for benefits (or other amounts payable) that can be paid, distributed, transferred or otherwise provided from a

---

1.   Preamble, TD 9079, 68 Fed. Reg. 42254, 42256 (7-17-2003).
2.   Preamble, TD 9079, 68 Fed. Reg. 42254, 42257 (7-17-2003).
3.   Treas. Reg. §1.419A(f)(6)-1(c)(1).
4.   Treas. Reg. §1.419A(f)(6)-1(c)(2).
5.   Treas. Reg. §1.419A(f)(6)-1(c)(3).
6.   Treas. Reg. §1.419A(f)(6)-1(c)(4).
7.   Treas. Reg. §1.419A(f)(6)-1(c)(5).

fund that is part of a plan by reason of any event other than the illness, personal injury, or death of an employee or family member, or the employee's involuntary separation from employment. For example, a plan exhibits this characteristic if the plan provides for the payment of benefits to an employer's employees on the occasion of the employer's withdrawal from the plan. A plan will not be treated as having this characteristic merely because upon cessation of participation in the plan, an employee is provided with the right to convert coverage under a group life insurance contract to coverage under an individual life insurance contract without demonstrating evidence of insurability, but only if there is an additional economic value association with the conversion right.[1]

For examples of arrangements classified as experience-rating arrangements, see Treasury Regulation Section 1.419A(f)(6)-1(f).

4111. What is an abusive 419(e) plan, and how is it taxed?

A 419(e) plan is a welfare benefit fund that is sponsored by an employer to provide welfare benefits to its employees. When a 419(e) plan meets all of the IRC's requirements, the employer's contributions are fully deductible with no taxation to the employee then or when benefits are provided. When these plans operate consistently with the IRC, they generally are unattractive to smaller employers.[2] These plans may involve a taxable welfare benefit fund or a tax-exempt VEBA (Q 4112). Different deduction limits apply to 10 or more employer plans (Q 4106) and collectively bargained plans (Q 4096).

Abusive Arrangements in Single Employer Plans

The IRS cautions taxpayers about participating in certain trust arrangements being sold to professional corporations and other small businesses as welfare benefit funds.[3] Some of the arrangements have been identified as listed transactions (see Notice 2007-83, IR 2007-170, below).

Revenue Ruling 2007-65 addresses situations where an arrangement is considered a welfare benefit fund, but the employer's deduction for its contributions to the fund is denied in whole or part for premiums paid by the trust on cash value life insurance policies.[4] For purposes of determining the limitations on an employer's deduction for contributions to a welfare benefit fund under Section 419 and Section 419A, the IRS concluded that regardless of whether the benefit provided through the fund is life insurance coverage, premiums paid on cash value life insurance policies by the fund are not included in the fund's qualified direct cost whenever the fund is directly or indirectly a beneficiary under the policy within the meaning of Section 264(a). The fund's qualified direct cost includes amounts paid as welfare benefits by the fund during the taxable year for claims incurred during the year.[5]

---

1. Treas. Reg. §1.419A(f)(6)-1(c)(6).
2. See IRC Sec. 419(e).
3. IRS News Release IR-2007-170 (10-17-2007).
4. Rev. Rul. 2007-65, 2007-45 IRB 949.
5. IRC Section 264(a) provides that no deduction is allowable for premiums on any life insurance policy, or endowment or annuity contract, if the taxpayer is directly or indirectly a beneficiary under the policy or contract.

Some of the arrangements described above and substantially similar arrangements, as well as certain other arrangements using cash value life insurance policies for which an employer has deducted amounts as contributions to a welfare benefit fund, may be transactions that have been designated as listed transactions. If a transaction is designated as a listed transaction, affected persons may be subject to additional penalties and disclosure responsibilities (Q 4106).

The IRS has identified certain trust arrangements involving cash value life insurance policies and substantially similar arrangements as listed transactions.[1] If a transaction is designated as a listed transaction, affected persons have disclosure obligations and may be subject to applicable penalties.

The IRS cautions taxpayers that the tax treatment of trusts that, in form, provide post-retirement medical and life insurance benefits to owners and other key employees may vary from the treatment claimed.[2] The IRS may issue further guidance to address these arrangements, and taxpayers should not assume that the guidance will be applied prospectively only.

The IRS and Treasury released a warning on certain trust arrangements being sold as welfare benefit plans to professional employers and small employers. The announcement discussed certain welfare plan arrangements using life insurance contracts that constitute listed transactions.

In 2009, the IRS released a lengthy background document that outlines the issues and patterns its agents will look for during audits of welfare benefit plans with respect to uncovering disguised dividend arrangements, for example, as in the *Neonatology* and *DeAngelis* cases (Q 4106), as well as disguised deferred compensation arrangements.[3] In the audit guidance, the IRS advises its agents to place a particularly sharp focus on arrangements using cash value life insurance policies and includes several questions that agents will use to identify abusive arrangements.

4112. What is a 501(c)(9) trust ("VEBA")?

A Voluntary Employees' Beneficiary Association ("VEBA") is a tax-exempt entity created to fund life, sick, accident, or certain other benefits (Q 4117) for members, their dependents, or their designated beneficiaries. A VEBA may be established by an employer or through collective bargaining. A trust created to provide benefits to one employee does not qualify as an employees' association for purposes of exemption from federal income tax under IRC Section 501(c)(9).[4] Some of the requirements for tax-exempt VEBA status include:

(1)   Membership eligibility (Q 4113);

(2)   Nondiscrimination (Q 4114);

(3)   Entities and individuals entitled to maintain control over the VEBA (Q 4115); and

---

1.   Notice 2007-83, 2007-45 IRB 960.
2.   Notice 2007-84, 2007-45 IRB 963.
3.   See Revised Background Document 200931049 (Release Date 7-31-2009).
4.   Rev. Rul. 85-199, 1985-2 CB 163.

(4)   Prohibition on inurement of earnings for the benefit of private shareholders or individuals (Q 4116).

4113. What are the membership eligibility restrictions that apply to a 501(c)(9) trust ("VEBA")?

Membership in a VEBA generally must be limited to employees, including certain former employees.[1] Membership may include some non-employees, as long as they share an employment-related bond with the employee-members and as long as at least 90 percent of the members are employees.[2]

Eligibility for membership must be defined by reference to objective standards that constitute an employment-related common bond. A common bond could be a common employer or common coverage under a collective bargaining agreement.[3] The IRS has ruled that employees whose only connection is that their employers are engaged in the same line of business will have the requisite common bond only if their employers are in the same geographic locale.[4] The IRS has maintained this position despite *Water Quality Assoc'n Employees' Benefit Corp. v. U.S.*,[5] which held a geographic locale restriction invalid.[6]

Currently, the IRS holds that an area is a single geographic locale if it does not exceed the boundaries of three contiguous states. The IRS also has found that larger areas can be considered a single geographic locale under appropriate facts and circumstances.[7]

Membership may be limited by objective criteria reasonably related to employment, such as a limitation based on a reasonable minimum period of service or a requirement that members be full time employees. Any criteria used to restrict membership may not be used to limit membership to officers, shareholders, or highly compensated employees.[8]

4114. What nondiscrimination requirements apply to a 501(c)(9) trust ("VEBA")?

Although eligibility for membership and benefits generally may be restricted by objective conditions (Q 4113), any objective criteria used to restrict eligibility for membership or for benefits may not limit membership or benefits to officers, shareholders, or highly compensated employees of a contributing employer and may not entitle any member of that prohibited group to disproportionate benefits.[9] A plan will not run afoul of the prohibition against disproportionate benefits by basing life or disability income benefits on a uniform percentage of compensation.[10] In the context of associations with a small number of members receiving disparate levels of

---

1.   See Treas. Reg. §§1.501(c)(9)-2(a)(1), 1.501(c)(9)-2(b)(2), 1.501(c)(9)-2(b)(3).
2.   Treas. Reg. §1.501(c)(9)-2(a)(1); GCM 39834 (12-26-90). See, e.g., Let. Rul. 200137066.
3.   Treas. Reg. §1.501(c)(9)-2(a)(1).
4.   See, e.g., GCM 39817 (5-9-90).
5.   795 F.2d 1303 (7th Cir. 1986).
6.   See, e.g., the preamble to Prop. Treas. Reg. §1.501(c)(9)-2(d), 57 Fed. Reg. 34886 (8-7-92).
7.   See Treas. Reg. §1.501(c)(9)-2(d).
8.   Treas. Reg. §1.501(c)(9)-2(a)(2).
9.   Treas. Reg. §1.501(c)(9)-2(a)(2)(i).
10. Treas. Reg. §§1.501(c)(9)-2(a)(2)(ii)(F), 1.501(c)(9)-2(a)(2)(ii)(G).

compensation, general counsel memoranda have concluded that severance benefits may be based on a uniform percentage of compensation; these memoranda also have concluded that severance benefits may be based on length of service requirements as long as those requirements do not limit benefits to members of the prohibited group.[1]

The association may violate the prohibition against inurement if, by virtue of basing death and disability benefits on uniform percentages of compensation or by basing severance benefits on a percentage of compensation and determining that percentage by reference to length of service, (1) an association provides a dominant share of benefits to a member of a prohibited group, (2) the association provides that on termination of the association members will be entitled to their allocable share of the association's assets and (3) the member of the prohibited group effectively controls the association.[2] For further important information, see the inurement discussion in Q 4116, especially the references to the *Lima Surgical* litigation. Courts have pointed to the basing of severance benefits on both level of compensation and length of service in ruling that benefits really were impermissible retirement benefits.[3]

A VEBA generally will not be tax-exempt unless the plan meets the nondiscrimination rules applicable to the particular benefits provided or, if none, the following nondiscrimination requirements: (1) each class of benefits under the plan must be provided under a classification of employees that is set forth in the plan and that is found by the IRS not to be discriminatory in favor of employees who are highly compensated individuals, and (2) benefits provided under each class of benefits must not discriminate in favor of employees who are highly compensated individuals.[4] IRC Section 505(a)(2) provides an exception for certain collectively bargained VEBAs.[5]

A highly compensated individual is similar to a highly compensated employee for qualified plan purposes (Q 3929).

To apply the nondiscrimination standards, certain employees may be excluded from consideration.[6] For purposes of testing for discrimination, an employer may elect to treat two or more plans as one plan.[7] An election to aggregate must be consistent for deduction and discrimination purposes (Q 4096).[8]

Employers related under the common control, controlled group, and affiliated service group aggregation rules (Q 3932, Q 3934) must be treated as a single employer, and the employee leasing provision, other than the safe harbor rule, must be applied (Q 3928).[9]

1.　GCMs 39818 (5-10-90), 39300 (10-30-84).
2.　See *id.* See also GCM 39801 (10-26-89).
3.　See *Lima Surgical Assoc., Inc. v. U.S.*, 20 Cl. Ct. 674, 90-1 USTC ¶50,329 (U.S. Claims Court 1990), *aff'd*, 944 F.2d 885, 91-2 USTC ¶50,473 (Fed. Cir. 1991). See Q 4111..
4.　See IRC Secs. 505(a)(1), 505(b)(1).
5.　See Let. Ruls. 200119064, 199920044 (VEBA maintained pursuant to a collective bargaining agreement, which was the subject of good faith bargaining between the company and the union, not subject to the nondiscrimination requirements).
6.　See IRC Sec. 505(b)(2); H.R. Conf. Rep. 861 (TRA '84), 98th Cong., 2d Sess. 1164, *reprinted in* 1984-3 CB (vol. 2) 418; the General Explanation of TRA '84, p. 800.
7.　IRC Sec. 505(b)(4).
8.　H.R. Conf. Rep. 861 (TRA '84), above, *reprinted in* 1984-3 CB (vol. 2) 413.
9.　IRC Secs. 414(n)(3)(C), 414(t).

A life insurance, disability, severance, or supplemental unemployment compensation benefit is not considered discriminatory merely because the benefits bear a uniform relationship to total (or basic, or regular rate of) compensation of employees covered by the plan.[1]

A plan generally will not satisfy the nondiscrimination requirements of IRC Section 505(b) unless the annual compensation of each employee taken into consideration for any year does not exceed $290,000 in 2021.[2] This limit does not apply in determining whether the nondiscrimination rules of IRC Section 79 are met.[3]

If a VEBA plan provides postretirement medical or group term life insurance benefits, see Q 4102 and Q 4103.

4115. Who may control a 501(c)(9) trust ("VEBA") in order for it to maintain its tax-exempt status?

The association must be controlled by (1) its membership, that is, by its participants, (2) independent trustees, or (3) trustees, some of whom are designated by or on behalf of members.[4] Requisite control was held lacking where trustees were appointed by a self-perpetuating board of directors, new members of which were appointed by current members from among a group only indirectly selected by employees.[5] A bank may not necessarily be considered an independent trustee.[6]

4116. What is the prohibition on inurement of earnings to private individuals that is applicable to a 501(c)(9) trust ("VEBA")?

Except in payment of permissible benefits, no part of the earnings of a VEBA may inure to the benefit of any private shareholder or individual.[7] A return of excess insurance premiums to the payor, based on mortality or morbidity experience, is not prohibited.[8] In addition, the refund of contributions to an employer, which had been paid after a collective bargaining agreement had ended but during the pendency of a labor dispute with a union, did not constitute inurement.[9]

On termination of a plan, there is no prohibited inurement if, after satisfaction of all liabilities to existing beneficiaries, remaining assets are applied to provide permitted benefits pursuant to criteria that do not provide for disproportionate benefits to officers, shareholders, or highly compensated employees.

---

1. IRC Sec. 505(b)(1).
2. IRC Sec. 401(a)(17)); Notice 2020-79.
3. IRC Sec. 505(b)(7).
4. Treas. Reg. §1.501(c)(9)-2(c)(3).
5. *American Assn. of Christian Schools v. U.S.*, 663 F. Supp. 275, 87-1 USTC ¶9328 (M.D. Ala. 1987), *aff'd*, 850 F.2d 1510, 88-2 USTC ¶9452 (11th Cir. 1988).
6. See *Lima Surgical Assoc., Inc. v. U.S.*, 20 Cl. Ct. 674, 90-1 USTC ¶50,329 (U.S. Claims Court 1990), *aff'd on other grounds*, 944 F.2d 885, 91-2 USTC ¶50,473 (Fed. Cir. 1991).
7. Treas. Reg. §§1.501(c)(9)-1(d), 1.501(c)(9)-4(a).
8. Treas. Reg. §1.501(c)(9)-4(c); Let. Rul. 9006051. See also Let. Rul. 9214030 (the rebate of excess insurance premiums to professional associations whose members contributed premiums to the VEBA for disability protection and agreed that any excess funds in the VEBA could go to the professional associations was not prohibited inurement as long as the professional associations could use the money to provide VEBA benefits to their members).
9. Let. Rul. 199930040.

A distribution to members on dissolution of a VEBA made on an objective and reasonable basis not resulting in unequal payments to similarly situated employees or disproportionate distributions to officers, shareholders, or highly compensated employees will not be prohibited inurement.

Assets of a VEBA may not be distributable to contributing employers on dissolution, either under the trust document or by operation of law, unless the distribution is applied to provide permissible benefits in a manner that does not result in disproportionate benefits for officers, shareholders, or highly compensated employees of the employers.[1]

A transfer of assets from a VEBA to a separate nonexempt trust resulting from the termination of a sick leave/severance plan component of the VEBA and then to a bank account to be distributed to employees who participated in the terminated trust was not considered prohibited inurement as funds apparently were used to pay qualifying Section 501(c)(9) benefits.[2]

In terminating a VEBA, use of the assets in a postretirement medical reserve to pay health care claims of employees who had retired prior to the effective date of the VEBA did not constitute prohibited inurement or a reversion of plan assets to the employer because the use of the reserves for an additional class of retirees was consistent with the purpose of the reserve.[3]

The termination of the life insurance portion (the retiree life plan) of a welfare benefit plan that was a non-exempt trust and the subsequent transfer to a VEBA of the assets remaining after the purchase of individual paid-up policies to satisfy the obligation of the retiree life plan and the subsequent use of those remaining assets to provide payment of permitted benefits other than life insurance did not result in prohibited inurement to the employer.[4]

Where an employer intended to reactivate a previously inactive VEBA by using the remaining assets to purchase one or more insurance policies that would provide accidental death, disability, and long-term care benefits to current employees and then terminate the VEBA on exhaustion of such assets, the proposed use of the net assets would not affect the tax-exempt status, that is, there was no prohibited inurement, because the assets would be used to provide benefits contemplated by IRC Section 501(c)(9).[5]

A general counsel memorandum concluded that a transfer of assets from an employer's VEBA to a 401(h) arrangement under a qualified pension plan of the same employer, providing retiree health benefits, would result in inurement of earnings from the VEBA to the employer, inasmuch as a 401(h) arrangement is required to provide for return to the employer of assets remaining in the account after satisfaction of all liabilities under the plan (Q 3941).[6]

1.   Treas. Reg. §1.501(c)(9)-4(d).
2.   TAM 9647001.
3.   Let. Rul. 9720034.
4.   Let. Rul. 9740024.
5.   See Let. Rul. 9446036, Treas. Reg. §1.501(c)(9)-4(d).
6.   GCM 39785 (3-24-89).

The transfer of excess assets from a terminating VEBA to a successor VEBA to fund permissible VEBA benefits for the employer's employees generally should not result in prohibited inurement.[1]

The transfer of a terminated VEBA's remaining assets to an exempt educational trust fund did not result in prohibited inurement.[2] No inurement resulted from the termination of a VEBA and transfer of assets back to its original tax-exempt sponsor, which had operated as a charity hospital and was operating as a charity only, because the assets were to be distributed by the charity for charitable purposes, with the remaining assets to be distributed to the charity's former employees who were currently working for the new hospital.[3]

The termination of a VEBA and distribution of remaining assets to a 501(c)(3) private foundation did not result in a reversion because the foundation was not an employer with respect to the trust, nor was it an organization that otherwise was merely an alter ego of the employer; instead, the foundation was a charitable organization whose assets were dedicated to charitable purposes and that could not be used for the private benefit of the employer.[4]

The substitution of a successor company for the original company in a VEBA trust document did not constitute prohibited inurement.[5]

The IRS has indicated tax-exempt status may be denied where principal shareholders receive a dominant share of aggregate benefits and effectively control the organization.[6]

In administrative proceedings prior to litigation in the *Lima Surgical* case, the IRS found a violation of the inurement proscription because the owner-employees were entitled to a dominant share of severance benefits and controlled the corporation. The court found a violation of the prohibition against private inurement because the dominant benefits were based on both level of compensation and length of service but did not explicitly analyze whether owner-employees also effectively controlled the plan trust.[7] On appeal, the circuit court did not address the lower court's inurement ruling, but the IRS conceded that the arrangement did not violate the prohibition against inurement.[8]

The IRS disqualified a VEBA because it failed to satisfy the requirement of no prohibited inurement. The IRS concluded that the plan, in substance, was not adopted or operated as an employee benefit plan, but was merely a separate fund controlled by the controlling family for the

---

1. See, e.g., Let. Ruls. 200122051, 200122047 (assets transferred from a terminated VEBA to another VEBA would be used to provide permissible welfare benefits in a nondiscriminatory manner, a common employment-related bond was present, and the transfer was not being used to avoid any of the statutory VEBA requirements). In each situation, the IRS ruled that the transfer did not result in inurement or trigger excise tax. See also Let. Ruls. 200024054, 200009051, 9812035, 9551007, 9505019, 9438017, 9414011, 9322041, 9115035, and 9014065.
2. Let. Rul. 200136028.
3. Let. Rul. 200003054.
4. Let. Rul. 199908054.
5. Let. Rul. 200041035.
6. See, e.g., GCMs 39818 (5-10-90), 39801 (10-26-89), 39300 (10-30-84).
7. 20 Cl. Ct. 674, 90-1 USTC ¶50,329, at pp. 84,145-84,146.
8. 944 F.2d 885, 91-2 USTC ¶50,473, at p. 89,800.

primary benefit of two members of the controlling family, with the incidental coverage of other employees of the corporation being merely a cost of attempting to secure tax-exempt status.[1]

In another disqualification due to prohibited inurement, the IRS privately ruled that the trust was established for the personal and private benefit of the company president and his wife, the universal life policies in the plan were not eligible for inclusion in a Section 501(c) (9) trust because they allowed for periodic payments and loans, and the trust was disqualified because it was not controlled by an independent trustee as required in the Treasury regulations.[2]

A loan from a VEBA to its members' employer might violate the prohibition against private inurement.[3]

4117. What benefits can a 501(c)(9) trust ("VEBA") provide?

A VEBA trust may provide for the payment of life, sick, accident, or other benefits to members, their dependents or their designated beneficiaries. A dependent can be, among others, a spouse, a child of the member or the member's spouse who is a minor or a student for income tax dependent exemption purposes, or any other minor child residing with the member.[4] Provision of an insubstantial or de minimis amount of impermissible benefits will not disqualify an arrangement from tax-exempt VEBA status.[5]

A life benefit is one payable by reason of the death of a member or dependent; it may be provided directly or through insurance. It generally must consist of current protection, but it may include a permanent benefit as defined in, and subject to the conditions in, regulations under Section 79 (Q 254, Q 255).[6] In addition, the IRS has indicated that life benefits may be provided through employer-funded whole-life policies that are not group-permanent policies under IRC Section 79 if:

(1)   the policies are owned by a VEBA,

(2)   the policies are purchased through level premiums over the expected lives or working lives of the individual members, and

(3)   the accumulated cash reserves accrue to a VEBA.[7]

The purchase of individual whole life insurance by VEBAs funding ERISA plans may violate ERISA.[8]

---

1.   Let. Rul. 200836041.
2.   Let. Rul. 200950049.
3.   See GCM 39884 (10-29-92) (whether loan violated prohibition was not an issue in the memorandum, but IRS noted that the loan might have been a sham transaction for employer's benefit and was "tainted by the type of economic domination by a controlling person … that [has been] found to constitute private inurement").
4.   Treas. Reg. §1.501(c)(9)-3(a).
5.   See, e.g., GCM 39817 (5-9-90); TAM 9139003.
6.   Treas. Reg. §1.501(c)(9)-3(b).
7.   GCM 39440 (11-7-85).
8.   Compare *Reich v. Lancaster*, 55 F.3d 1034 (5th Cir. 1995), *aff'g*, 843 F. Supp. 194 (N.D. Tex. 1993) (purchases of individual whole life insurance by self-funded welfare benefit plan violated various provisions of ERISA) with *Reich v. McDonough*, Civ. Action No. 91-12025 H (D. Mass. Dec. 10, 1993) (in part recognizing that individual whole life insurance can be an appropriate investment for ERISA plans).

A reserve for future retirees' life insurance held by a postretirement trust was found to provide an impermissible benefit similar to deferred compensation and the trust was not tax-exempt under 501(c)(9).[1]

Also, consider the conference report to TRA '84, which admonishes that a plan providing medical or life insurance benefits exclusively for retirees would be considered a deferred compensation plan rather than a welfare benefit plan.[2]

The payment of self-funded, paid-up life insurance constituted a qualifying benefit for purposes of IRC Section 501(c)(9) regardless of how self-funded, paid-up life insurance was characterized under state law where (1) payment of the benefit only came due on the occurrence of an unanticipated event (i.e., the death of the insured) and protected a member and the member's family or beneficiary against a contingency that interrupted or impaired the member's earning power, and (2) it was clear that unlike an annuity or retirement benefit, the self-funded, paid-up life insurance benefit was not payable merely by reason of passage of time.[3]

Sick and accident benefits may be reimbursement for medical expenses. They may be amounts paid in lieu of income during a period a member is unable to work because of sickness or injury. Sick benefits include benefits designed to safeguard or improve the health of members and their dependents. They may be provided directly, through payment of premiums to an insurance company, or to another program providing medical services.[4]

Home health care benefits provided under a VEBA qualified as medical care benefits and, thus, were excludable from gross income.[5] Supplemental medical benefits qualified as sick and accident benefits.[6] Reimbursement of union members' health insurance premiums constituted a permitted benefit where benefits would be paid only as reimbursement for health premiums, and under no circumstances could employees take the contributions as unrestricted cash.[7]

Paid sick days and short term disability wage replacement benefits have been considered sick and accident benefits.[8] Health benefits provided by a VEBA to nondependent, nonspousal domestic partners of participants did not adversely affect the VEBA's tax-exempt status because the coverage and benefits would constitute no more than a de minimis amount of the VEBA's total benefits under Treasury Regulation Section 1.501(c)(9)-3(a).[9]

Other benefits are limited to those similar to life, sick or accident benefits. A benefit is similar if it is intended to safeguard or improve the health of a member or a member's dependents or if it protects against a contingency that interrupts or impairs a member's earning

---

1.   Let. Rul. dated May 25, 1982.
2.   H.R. Conf. Rep. 861, 98th Cong., 2d Sess. 1157, *reprinted* in 1984-3 CB (vol. 2) 411. But consider Let. Rul. 9151027 (Q 4094).
3.   Let. Rul. 199930040.
4.   Treas. Reg. §1.501(c)(9)-3(c).
5.   Let. Rul. 200028007.
6.   Let. Rul. 200003053.
7.   Let. Rul. 199902016.
8.   See TAM 9126004.
9.   Let. Rul. 200108010.

power.[1] The IRS understands a contingency to be an unanticipated event beyond the control of the beneficiary.[2]

Other benefits may include vacation benefits, child care facilities, supplemental unemployment compensation benefits, severance benefits (but see Q 4118), and education benefits.[3]

Holiday pay and paid personal days have been considered other benefits.[4] Social, recreational, and cultural benefits provided to retirees, designed to promote their physical, mental or emotional well-being or to provide them with information relating to retirement and asset management, constituted permissible benefits.[5]

Other benefits do not include, among other things, any benefit that is similar to a pension or annuity payable at the time of mandatory or voluntary retirement, or a benefit that is similar to a benefit provided under a stock bonus or profit-sharing plan. In other words, other benefits do not include deferred compensation payable by reason of the passage of time rather than because of an unanticipated event.[6]

Plans that provide medical and death benefits, but that require participants to contribute a portion of the cost, may violate Treasury Regulation Section 1.501(c)(9)-3(f).[7]

A benefit payable by reason of death may be settled in the form of an annuity to the beneficiary.[8]

4118. What requirements apply to a 501(c)(9) trust ("VEBA") that provides severance pay arrangements?

IRC Section 409A creates requirements governing whether and when employees are to be taxed on deferred compensation. Under the general rule, if a nonqualified deferred compensation plan fails to meet certain requirements regarding distributions, acceleration of benefits, and interest on tax liability payments (Q 3541) or is not operated in accordance with such requirements, all compensation deferred under the plan for the taxable year and all preceding taxable years is includible in gross income for the taxable year to the extent not subject to a substantial risk of forfeiture and not previously included in gross income.[9]

---

1. Treas. Reg. §1.501(c)(9)-3(d).
2. See GCM 39879 (9-15-92).
3. Treas. Reg. §1.501(c)(9)-3(e).
4. See TAM 9126004.
5. Let. Rul. 9802038.
6. Treas. Reg. §1.501(c)(9)-3(f). See also *Lima Surgical Assoc., Inc. v. U.S.*, 20 Cl. Ct. 674, 90-1 USTC ¶50,329 (U.S. Claims Court 1990)(severance benefits based on length of service and level of compensation and payable upon retirement were impermissible deferred compensation), *aff'd*, 944 F.2d 885, 91-2 USTC ¶50,473 (Fed. Cir. 1991); Let. Rul. 9249027 (severance benefits payable upon any voluntary or involuntary termination, including retirement, are deferred compensation or retirement benefits and are not qualifying other benefits). Compare *Wellons v. Comm.*, 31 F.3d 569, 94-2 USTC ¶50,402 (7th Cir. 1994)(severance pay arrangement is more akin to deferred compensation plan than welfare benefit plan where five years of service must be given before benefits accrue, benefit amount is linked to level of compensation and length of service, and benefits can be paid at virtually any termination of employment), *aff'g*, TC Memo 1992-704.
7. See *Internal Revenue Service Exempt Organizations Continuing Professional Education Text for Fiscal Year 1999*, Chapter F, Voluntary Employees' Beneficiary Associations.
8. Treas. Reg. §1.501(c)(9)-3(b).
9. IRC Sec. 409A(a)(1).

Plans providing for severance pay, or for separation pay, as it officially is labeled by the IRS, are not excluded from the definition of nonqualified deferred compensation plan (unlike bona fide vacation leave, sick leave, compensatory time, disability pay, or death benefits).[1] Final 409A regulations state that a separation pay plan does not provide for a deferral of compensation to the extent the plan is:

(1)   a collectively bargained separation pay plan;

(2)   separation pay due to an involuntary separation from service or participation in a window program;

(3)   a foreign separation pay plan; or

(4)   a reimbursement or certain other separation payments.[2]

A plan that provides separation pay only due to an involuntary separation does not provide for a deferral of compensation under 409A if the plan meets the following requirements:

(1)   The separation pay does not exceed two times the lesser of (x) the sum of the employee's annualized compensation based on the annual pay rate for services provided to the employer for the taxable year preceding the taxable year in which the employee had a separation from service, or (y) the maximum amount that may be taken into account under a qualified plan under IRC Section 401(a)(17) ($290,000 in 2021) for the year in which the employee had a separation from service.[3]

(2)   The plan provides that the separation pay must be paid no later than the last day of the second taxable year following the taxable year in which the separation from service occurred.[4]

A window program is a program established by an employer, in connection with an impending separation from service, to provide separation pay where it is made available by the employer for a limited period of time (no longer than twelve months) to employees who separate from service during that period or to service providers who separate from service during the period under specified circumstances.[5]

Final regulations became effective April 17, 2007, with transition relief extended to December 31, 2008.[6] For further explanation of IRC Section 409A, see Q 3541.

---

1.   See IRC Sec. 409A(d). See also Treas. Reg. §§1.409A-1(a)(5), 1.409A-1(b)(9)(i).
2.   See Treas. Reg. §§1.409A-1(b)(9)(ii), 1.409A-1(b)(9)(iii), 1.409A-1(b)(9)(iv), 1.409A-1(b)(9)(v). See also Treas. Reg. §§1.409A-1(m), 1.409A-1(n).
3.   Notice 2020-79.
4.   Treas. Reg. §1.409A-1(b)(9)(iii).
5.   Treas. Reg. §1.409A-1(b)(9)(vi).
6.   See Notice 2007-86, 2007-46 IRB 990.

4119. Are an employer's contributions to a 501(c)(9) trust ("VEBA") deductible?

As a general rule, contributions to an employer-funded VEBA are deductible to the extent contributions to an employee welfare benefit fund are deductible (Q 4094 to Q 4100).[1]

4120. How are contributions to 501(c)(9) trusts ("VEBAs") taxed to participants?

Whether an employer's contributions to a VEBA to provide particular benefits are taxable to participants would seem to be determined under generally applicable tax rules. The presence of the VEBA would not seem to require special treatment. For example, the IRS has privately ruled that employer contributions to trusts providing accident and health benefits are excludable from participants' gross income as provided in IRC Section 106.[2]

Similarly, whether contributions to a VEBA are wages for FICA, FUTA, and federal income tax withholding purposes generally is determined under the FICA, FUTA, and withholding rules applicable to the kind of benefit or kinds of benefits at issue.[3]

Planning Point: Rules governing the taxation of employer-owned life insurance (i.e., COLI) were enacted under PPA 2006.[4] Whether these rules might apply to a VEBA, if the VEBA were considered to be engaged in a trade or business, is unclear.

4121. How are benefits payable under 501(c)(9) trusts ("VEBAs") taxed to participants?

Both cash and noncash benefits provided through the association are included in or excluded from income under general tax rules. They are not given special tax treatment simply because they are provided by a 501(c)(9) association.[5]

Medical expense benefits and dismemberment and disability benefits appear to be tax-free or taxable to the participant under rules applicable to employer-provided health insurance (Q 332, Q 334) to the extent such benefits are attributable to employer contributions. These benefits appear to be excludable from gross income to the extent allowed under the rules applicable to personal health insurance (Q 343) to the extent they are attributable to participant contributions.[6]

Fully insured group term life insurance coverage provided by an employer through a VEBA has been privately ruled to be excludable from the employee's gross income to the extent permitted by IRC Section 79 (Q 246).[7]

---

1.   See, e.g, *National Presto Indus., Inc. v. Comm.*, 104 TC 559 (1995); Let. Ruls. 9401033, 9351042, 9322041.
2.   See e.g., Let. Ruls. 9513007, 9340054, 9151017, 9046023, 8534048, 8507024, 8445019.
3.   See e.g., Let. Ruls. 9340054, 8824030, 8534048.
4.   See IRC Sec. 101(j), as discussed in Q 276.
5.   Treas. Reg. §1.501(c)(9)-6.
6.   See, e.g., Let. Ruls. 9340054, 9151017, 9046023, 8534048, 8507024, 8445019, 8352022, 8344069. See also Let. Rul. 199930015 (long-term disability coverage purchased under either of two options would be attributable to employee contributions for purposes of IRC Section 104(a)(3); accordingly, if union employees could be treated as a separate class of employees, the long-term disability benefits received by participants in new plans created under two different options would be excludable from participants' gross income under IRC Section 104(a)(3)).
7.   See Let. Ruls. 8302034, 8248108, 8226062, 8225147.

Fully insured group term life insurance coverage provided by employees to themselves through a VEBA has been considered not to be subject to the inclusion rules of IRC Section 79 where the insurance is not carried directly or indirectly by the employer.[1]

Employees who purchased fully insured group term life insurance for their dependents through a VEBA were not required to include the cost of that coverage in their income as a fringe benefit where the employer's involvement with the arrangement was limited to providing reimbursed administrative services and the insurance was arranged and financed on an after-tax basis entirely by the employees.[2]

Fully insured group term life insurance death benefits payable by reason of an employee's death are excludable under IRC Section 101(a), at least where the benefits are paid directly from the insurance company to the beneficiary.[3]

After "extensive study," the IRS announced it would issue rulings on whether a death benefit under self-insured life insurance provided through a 501(c)(9) trust will be tax-exempt under IRC Section 101(a).[4]

Uninsured death benefits payable under a private plan created under federal law constituted amounts received under a life insurance contract and were excludable from gross income under IRC Section 101(a).[5]

Reimbursement of health insurance premiums under a collectively bargained Retiree Premium Reimbursement Plan would be excludable from gross income of members under IRC Section 106.[6]

Whether benefits provided through a VEBA are wages for FICA, FUTA, and federal income tax withholding purposes generally is determined under the FICA, FUTA, and withholding rules applicable to the kind of benefit or kinds of benefits at issue.[7]

4122. How are rebates and termination distributions taxed to participants in 501(c)(9) trusts ("VEBAs")?

The IRS has privately ruled that payments made by a company to its employees from its general assets to reimburse employees for excess pre-tax and after-tax contributions to a VEBA were wages for FICA, FUTA, and income tax withholding purposes. If the employer had made the payments on behalf of the VEBA and then received reimbursement from the VEBA,

1.   See Let. Ruls. 9549029, 8906023.
2.   See Let. Ruls. 9549029, 9151033.
3.   See Let. Ruls. 8507024, 8352022, 8248108, 8226062, 8225147.
4.   Rev. Proc. 90-3, 1990-1 CB 402. See, e.g., Let. Rul. 199921036 (general and accidental death benefits paid by a self-insured VEBA constituted amounts received under a life insurance contract and, therefore, were excludable from gross income under IRC Section 101(a); the arrangement was found to possess the requisite risk-shifting and risk-distributing elements necessary to establish the existence of a life insurance arrangement under *Helvering v. LeGierse*, 312 U.S. 531 (1941)). See also Let. Rul. 200002030.
5.   Let. Rul. 9840040 (as corrected by Let. Rul. 199903026).
6.   Let. Rul. 199902016.
7.   See e.g., Let. Ruls. 200043007, 9340054, 8824030, 8534048.

the portion of the rebate attributable to employee after-tax contributions would have escaped that treatment.[1]

Participants in an employee pay-all VEBA who were receiving disability benefits were not required to recognize income when, on termination of the VEBA, they received disability insurance policies purchased with VEBA assets providing precisely the same benefits. Further, disability benefits under the policies were ruled excludable from income under IRC Section 104(a)(3) to the extent that disability benefits from the VEBA were excludable under that section.[2]

On the termination of employee pay-all VEBAs and the distribution of their assets in cash, all participants were considered to have received income to the extent the distributions exceeded their contributions; those who had taken deductions for their contributions were considered to have received additional income in the amount of any contributions for which they had taken a deduction that reduced their tax liability in earlier years.[3] Where the distributions did not exceed the employees' contributions, the distributions were not wages for FICA or FUTA purposes.[4]

---

1. Let. Rul. 9203033.
2. E.g., Let. Ruls. 9244035, 9219016, 9219014, 9219013.
3. Let. Ruls. 9147059, 9039009. See also 200023052.
4. Let. Rul. 9039009. Compare *Sheet Metal Workers Local 141 Supplemental Unemployment Benefit Trust Fund v. U.S.*, 64 F.3d 245 (6th Cir. 1995)(distributions at termination of supplemental unemployment benefit fund of amounts representing earnings on contributions to the fund were wages for FICA and FUTA purposes where the distributions derived solely from employer contributions and where eligibility for distribution payments was based on satisfaction of work requirements or their equivalents).

PART XXI: DISCLOSURE REQUIREMENTS

Disclosure Regulations for
Retirement Plan Service Providers

4123. What are the fee disclosure requirements imposed by the Department of Labor ("DOL")?

The DOL has taken a three pronged approach in educating plan sponsors and participants about fees related to qualified retirement plans.

The first prong of the DOL's approach to fee education requires all large plan filers to complete a Schedule C with their annual 5500 series report. Schedule C reports compensation exceeding $5,000 that has been paid to plan service providers in the reporting year. The compensation reported must be categorized as either direct or indirect compensation. Payments received directly from the covered plan are direct compensation. Compensation received from sources other than directly from the plan or plan sponsor is indirect compensation.

The second prong of the DOL's disclosure initiatives are promulgated under ERISA Section 408(b)(2). The regulation requires covered service providers to disclose compensation in excess of $1,000 to responsible plan fiduciaries. The initial disclosures were due by July 1, 2012. Providing these disclosures is the responsibility of the covered service provider; however, if the covered service provider does not provide the disclosures, the responsible plan fiduciary must request them or risk having the contract between the service provider and plan deemed a "prohibited transaction."

The third and final prong of the DOL's fee disclosure initiative requires disclosure to plan participants in individually directed account plans. For calendar year plans, the deadline for initial participant fee disclosures was August 30, 2012. Following the initial disclosures, plans are required to make ongoing disclosures to participants and beneficiaries in participant-directed individual account plans on an annual basis, with quarterly disclosures identifying fees and expenses deducted from the participant's account in the prior quarter.

4124. What is the purpose of the Department of Labor ("DOL") 408(b)(2) covered service provider disclosure regulations?

The DOL believes that the fee and cost structures associated with retirement plans can be complicated and difficult for retirement plans sponsors to understand. In an effort to bring clarity to the often confusing world of fees and expenses associated with retirement plans, the DOL has promulgated disclosure regulations intended to help shine a light on the costs of operating a retirement plan.

When selecting and monitoring service providers, ERISA requires plan fiduciaries to act prudently and solely in the interest of the plan's participants and beneficiaries. Responsible plan fiduciaries must ensure that arrangements with service providers are "reasonable" and that only "reasonable compensation" is paid for services. Unfortunately, there is no bright line rule defining what constitutes "reasonable compensation." In the 408(b)(2) regulations, the DOL delineates that "No contract or arrangement for services between a covered plan and a covered service provider, nor any extension or renewal, is reasonable" unless appropriate fee disclosures are made.

Thus, for any contract or arrangement between a covered service provider and an ERISA retirement plan to be considered "reasonable," the covered service provider must make certain disclosures to the responsible plan fiduciary. Even if the service provided and the compensation received is fair and comparable with industry standards, if the disclosures are not made, the agreement will be considered unreasonable. The disclosures must be sufficiently detailed to allow a responsible plan fiduciary to evaluate the prudence of the agreement and must be made reasonably in advance of entering into the contract. The responsibility for making appropriate disclosures initially falls on the service provider, however, when required disclosures are not made, the plan sponsor must request the disclosures from the service provider. If the disclosures are still not made after the disclosure request, the responsible plan fiduciary must report the covered service provider to the DOL and seek out a new service provider. If the disclosures are not made or the reporting procedure is not followed, the arrangement will constitute a prohibited transaction subject to monetary penalties reportable to the DOL, and require correction.[1]

Of course, merely making the required disclosures does not automatically make a contract or arrangement reasonable under ERISA. The compensation paid for the services provided must also be reasonable.

The disclosures were required to be in place for all existing service arrangements by July 1, 2012. New service provider arrangements on or after that date require these disclosures reasonably in advance of the entry into the contract.

All ERISA-covered retirement plans are treated as covered plans for purposes of these regulations. The DOL has specifically exempted non-ERISA retirement plans from the requirements of this regulation. Non-ERISA retirement plans include Simplified Employer Plans ("SEPs"), salary reduction SEPs ("SAR-SEPs"), SIMPLE IRAs, government plans, non-ERISA 403(b) plans, most church plans, top hat nonqualified deferred compensation plans and 457 plans.

Other types of qualified retirement plans that cover only a proprietor and spouse, or partners of a partnership and their spouses, are exempt from ERISA as well. On the date any common law employee becomes a participant in either of these plan types, the disclosures are required.

4125. What disclosures are required under the 408(b)(2) regulations?

Required disclosures under 408(b)(2) include the following:

(1)   the services to be provided;

(2)   fees associated with those services;

(3)   whether the fees will be paid directly or indirectly from the plan;

---

1.   Preamble to Final and Interim Reg. §2550.408b-2(c), July 16, 2010.

(4)   certain financial information on investment options;

(5)   identification of any termination penalties; and

(6)   an explanation of how any prepaid amounts will be handled at termination.

The required disclosures are triggered when covered services may be provided by a covered service provider and the covered service provider (or its affiliate or subcontractor) reasonably expects to receive payments in excess of $1,000 over the life of the contract.

An interesting note is that the regulations do not specify what the plan's fiduciary is to do with the disclosures, other than to ask for them and to take certain actions to correct a deficiency where a deficiency is discovered in the disclosures that were provided. Presumably the plan fiduciaries will evaluate the content of the disclosures and document for their own records why they engaged the service provider.

Planning Point: Because the disclosures are required in advance, and the purpose of the disclosures is to provide information on fees to be paid by a plan, the new regulations establish a minimum standard of care in evaluating all service provider arrangements. That is, plan fiduciaries will need to document what they did with the disclosures. Just filing them away will not be enough, as fiduciaries can expect that savvy participants will ask for these disclosures and all follow-up assessments. Participants suing a plan fiduciary over excessive fees will also ask for the disclosures and any documentation of what the fiduciary did with them. Thus, fiduciaries will want to confirm that they did in fact evaluate the information in the disclosure and document why they deemed the agreement to be prudent for the services provided. They also will want to retain the disclosures for proposed services from the service providers they did not hire.

4126. When does a service provider arrangement result in a prohibited transaction?

Plan fiduciaries are required to make prudent decisions regarding the use of a plan's assets to pay a plan's service providers. ERISA and the IRC impose this obligation on plan fiduciaries by creating a classification of individuals and entities known as parties-in-interest. Parties-in-interest include, but are not limited to, individuals and entities such as plan fiduciaries, service providers, the employer (and 50 percent owners of the employer) whose employees are covered by the plan and other related parties. Both ERISA and the IRC state that transactions between parties-in-interest and a plan constitute prohibited transactions unless exempted under either statute or regulations. An agreement between a service provider and plan to do enrollments, calculation of vesting, brokerage, recordkeeping, allocation of contributions, or filing of Form 5500 are prohibited transactions unless an exemption is available.[1] ERISA and the IRC are clear that neither a plan sponsor nor a fiduciary need to show that the transaction results in adverse consequences to the plan to be considered prohibited.

Planning Point: The requirements regarding parties-in-interest and prohibited transactions are found in ERISA Sections 406(a)(1)(C) and 408(b)(2) and IRC Sections 4975(c)(1) and 4975(c)(1)(C). These laws have been modified over the years by various regulations. The exemptions that are available cover most of the normal services that are offered to retirement plans. These

---

1.   Labor Reg. §2550.408b-2(c)(1)(i).

regulations do not replace any of those exemptions but focus on a process to document that the fees being paid are reasonable.[1]

A prohibited transaction exemption is generally available to a service provider arrangement when the services are necessary for the proper administration of the plan and no more than "reasonable" compensation is paid to the provider.

The regulations establish one criterion for what constitutes an arrangement where reasonable compensation is paid. The regulations refer to such an arrangement as a reasonable arrangement. To be classified as a reasonable arrangement, the disclosures identified in the regulations must be timely provided. Otherwise, the arrangement is not reasonable and the arrangement is not exempt from being treated as a prohibited transaction.

The regulations provide a way for a responsible plan fiduciary to bring deficient disclosures back into compliance. If these procedures are followed, the responsible plan fiduciary is exempted from the penalties associated with the prohibited transaction.

There is specific relief in the regulations for covered service providers who, acting in good faith and using reasonable diligence, make an error or omission in disclosing the required information. A service provider can provide the corrected disclosures within 30 days of discovery without the arrangement being treated as failing to be reasonable.

If the responsible plan fiduciary discovers that disclosures have not been made, they must request appropriate disclosure from the covered service provider within 30 days of discovery. If the covered service provider actively refuses to disclose the required information, the responsible plan fiduciary must notify the DOL within 30 days of the refusal. If the covered service provider simply does not respond to the request, the covered service provider must notify the DOL within 90 days of the request. The notice must contain the following information:

(1)   The name of the covered plan and its plan number

(2)   The plan sponsor's name, address and EIN

(3)   The name, address and phone number of the responsible plan fiduciary

(4)   The name, address, phone number and, if known, the EIN of the covered service provider

(5)   A description of the services provided to the covered plan

(6)   A description of the information the covered service provider failed to disclose

(7)   The date on which such information was requested in writing from the covered service provider

---

1.   ERISA Secs. 406(a)(1)(c); 408(b)(2); IRC Secs. 4975(c)(1); 4975(c)(1)(C).

(8)   A statement as to whether the covered service provider continues to provide services to the plan

The DOL has made a fee disclosure reporting failure notice available online at: http://www.dol.gov/ebsa/regs/feedisclosurefailurenotice.html.

4127. Does a plan fiduciary still have to evaluate the reasonableness of compensation paid under a service provider's arrangement?

Yes.

This evaluation is done on a facts and circumstances basis following the basic requirements of ERISA that apply to all fiduciary decisions. The disclosures under these regulations are designed to provide the appropriate information to enable a responsible plan fiduciary to determine whether the fees paid for the services provider are reasonable. Best practices indicate that fiduciaries will document receipt of the disclosures and why they deemed the arrangements reasonable and prudent.

There is no bright line guidance in these regulations or in ERISA as to when a specified level of fees being paid to a service provider is unreasonable for the services being provided. The DOL, through the Employee Benefits Security Administration ("EBSA"), has provided on its website (http://www.dol.gov/ebsa/) numerous documents that discuss a fiduciary's responsibility regarding the selection of service providers. Those documents contain work sheets that may be used by a plan fiduciary to help evaluate the reasonableness of the amount of the fees being paid to a covered service provider.

Although this guidance replaces Section (c) of DOL Regulation Section 2550.408b-2, these regulatory changes should be read in conjunction with the full regulations under this section. In particular, see comments under termination compensation from subsection (a) and (d).[1]

4128. How can a covered service provider correct a prohibited transaction arising from a failure to timely disclose required information?

The answer to this question assumes that the service provider did not make the appropriate corrections within 30 days and that a prohibited transaction occurred. There are no IRS regulations that specify how to correct a prohibited transaction under IRC Section 4975. The IRS generally applies the prohibited transaction rules that apply to private foundations under IRC Section 4941 for which regulations have been issued. A correction under those rules generally requires that the transaction be undone to the fullest extent possible, and that the plan participants be restored to the position they would have been in had the prohibited transaction not occurred. Penalties typically apply to a prohibited transaction.[2]

The 408(b)(2) regulations provide a process for a responsible plan fiduciary to request a correction of a deficient disclosure and a process for notifying the DOL if those deficiencies are

---

1.   Preamble to Final and Interim Reg. §2550.408b-2(c), July 16, 2010.
2.   IRC Sec. 4975.

not timely corrected. The regulations also state that a plan fiduciary should, on discovery of a disclosure failure, make a determination as to whether to terminate or continue the arrangement. The plan fiduciary should take into account the adverse consequences of a termination on the plan's participants as part of that determination.

It is unclear at this point as to how much, if any, of the fees received by the service provider would need to be refunded to restore the participants' accounts when the disclosures are not provided. Where payments are accelerated in the early months of the contract, it is likely that some repayment of that amount would be required if the contract is terminated. A refund of fees paid also may be required to correct the failure if the disclosure failure related directly to undisclosed fees.

4129. What penalties typically apply if there has been a prohibited transaction?

The IRS imposes both a first tier excise tax (15 percent) and a second tier excise tax (100 percent) on a prohibited transaction. The tax is applied to the amount involved in the transaction. Here, the excise tax would be applied to the payment of the fees to the service provider. The DOL likely will be providing future guidance on how and when a penalty would be imposed on prohibited transactions arising from a failure to make the proper disclosures.

The regulations provide relief to covered service providers who, acting in good faith and applying reasonable diligence, made an error or omission in disclosing the required information. A service provider that meets these conditions can provide the correct disclosures within 30 days of its discovery without the arrangement being treated as failing to be reasonable due to failure to provide adequate disclosures.

A provider whose actions do not meet this criterion may be able to take advantage of the general 14 day correction period that applies to private foundations. Under this rule, certain prohibited transactions that are corrected within 14 days of discovery are exempt from the penalties associated with prohibited transactions. The 14 day correction period generally is only available if the transactions do not relate to self-dealing by plan fiduciaries. It should be available for violations arising from:

(1)   sale, exchange or leasing of plan assets;

(2)   lending of plan assets;

(3)   furnishing of goods, services and facilities; and

(4)   use of plan assets by a disqualified party.

A failure to adequately provide a required disclosure that is corrected within 14 days of discovery would appear to be eligible for this treatment and should not become a prohibited transaction.

The final 408(b)(2) regulations identify a process that a responsible plan fiduciary can follow when a disclosure failure has been discovered. That process, if followed, provides an exemption to a responsible plan fiduciary from the penalties of engaging in a prohibited transaction. This process does not exempt the arrangement from being a prohibited transaction.

The IRS tax qualification correction program, generally referred to as EPCRS, is not available to reduce any excise taxes such as those arising from a prohibited transaction. EPCRS is available only for correcting IRC Section 401(a) qualification failures. A prohibited transaction in and of itself is not a qualification issue.[1]

The DOL provides a correction process under its VFC Program that is available to correct a breach of fiduciary duty. This correction generally provides relief to a plan fiduciary from investigation and penalties under ERISA Sections 502(l) and 502(i). This option would be available to any plan fiduciary that did not meet the exemptions from certain prohibited transactions penalties that are provided for in the final 408(b)(2) regulations.

4130. What does a responsible plan fiduciary need to do to avoid the penalties of a prohibited transaction from a disclosure failure?

Assuming a responsible plan fiduciary was not aware of a disclosure failure, the responsible plan fiduciary will not be subject to sanctions under the prohibited transaction rules.

On discovery of the failure, however, the responsible plan fiduciary must take several actions to ensure that the proper disclosures are received. First, within 30 days of the discovery of the failure, the responsible plan fiduciary must request in writing that the service provider correct the deficiency. If the service provider does not provide the proper disclosures within 90 days of the request, the responsible plan fiduciary must provide a notice to the DOL of that failure within 30 days following the lapse of the 90 day request period. If the service provider affirmatively refuses to provide the requested information, the responsible plan fiduciary must notify the DOL within 30 days of that refusal.[2] The notice can be filed in paper format with the DOL, or by using the DOL's online fee disclosure failure notice website located at http://www.dol.gov/ebsa/regs/feedisclosurefailurenotice.html.

The notice sent to the DOL must contain certain information, including:

(1)   the name of the plan and plan number listed on Form 5500;

(2)   the plan sponsor's name, address and phone number;

(3)   the name, address and telephone number of the responsible plan fiduciary;

(4)   the name, address, phone number, and, if known, the EIN of the service provider;

(5)   a description of the services provided to the plan;

(6)   a description of the deficiency in the disclosure failure;

---

1.   Rev. Proc. 2008-50, Sept. 2, 2008, as modified and superseded by Rev. Proc. 2013-12 and Rev. Proc. 2016-51.
2.   Labor Reg. §2550.408b-2(c)(1)(ix).

(7)   the date the written request for the correction was made by the plan fiduciary; and

(8)   a statement as to whether the service provider is continuing to provide services to the plan.

Planning Point: If the covered service provider does not provide appropriate disclosures within the 90 day period, and the requested disclosures relate to future services to be provided to the plan, the responsible plan fiduciary must take action to terminate the contract as quickly as prudently possible.

4131. Are new fiduciary responsibilities imposed upon plan fiduciaries under the DOL 408(b)(2) regulations?

Other than requiring a responsible plan fiduciary to ask for appropriate disclosures from each covered service provider as well as follow specific procedures for correcting disclosure failures, the regulations do not impose any new requirements on a plan fiduciary. The receipt of the disclosure information implies that a plan fiduciary will need to review those disclosures and document an evaluation of the services and fees disclosed to ensure that they are reasonable and prudent.[1]

These regulations focus on the disclosure requirements that a covered service provider must provide for the arrangement to qualify as an exemption from a prohibited transaction. A plan fiduciary generally can rely on a service provider's representation that proper disclosures were made; assuming that the responsible plan fiduciary makes a good faith effort to ensure that the disclosures are proper. When a responsible plan fiduciary receives proper disclosures, the arrangement will be treated as meeting the requirements for the reasonable arrangement component of the exemption, provided the compensation paid is reasonable. The regulations include an exemption for a plan fiduciary being subject to prohibited transaction penalties, provided that the plan fiduciary had no reason to suspect that the disclosures were incorrect. If a plan fiduciary discovers a deficiency in the disclosures, it must request correct and accurate disclosures. If the plan does not receive the correct disclosures, the plan fiduciary then must report the service provider to the Department of Labor.

4132. What is a responsible plan fiduciary?

The final regulations define a responsible plan fiduciary as a fiduciary who has the authority to cause a plan to enter into or extend a contract or agreement with a service provider. Most plan documents assign this responsibility to the plan administrator, which, under the terms of the plan, may be the employer. The regulations do not appear to provide any special protections for fiduciaries other than a responsible plan fiduciary.[2]

---

1.   Labor Reg. §2550.408b-2(c)(1)(ix).
2.   Labor Reg. §2550.408b-2(c)(1)(viii).

4133. How can a qualified plan loan impact the analysis of the plan sponsor's fiduciary status? What new considerations did tax reform create?

The 2017 tax legislation changed the treatment of qualified plan participant loan offsets, delaying the offset when default on the loan is caused by employment or plan termination. In the fiduciary context, plan sponsors should note that loans to plan participants are treated as investments that are subject to ERISA's fiduciary standards (in other words, the potential elimination of the DOL fiduciary rule itself should not impact these obligations). The DOL requires that loan programs be prudently established and administered, which includes a duty to assess and monitor these programs.

Although loan provisions may be necessary in order to encourage retirement savings in these plans (many would not contribute absent the knowledge that they could access those funds if the need arose), the plan sponsor must carefully monitor the loan fund. Any changes to the plan loan rules brought about by the new loan offset rules must be considered taking the relevant fiduciary obligations into consideration.

In order to be considered a fiduciary under the ERISA rules, the old five-part test that applied before the imposition of the DOL rule is again relevant. Under this test, an advisor would be considered a fiduciary if (1) the advisor provided advice for compensation about the advisability of investing in, purchasing, or selling a security or other property, (2) on a regular basis, (3) pursuant to a mutual understanding, whether written or not, (4) that the advice would form the primary basis for the client's investment decision, and (5) the advice was individualized based upon the client's needs.

4134. What is a reasonable service provider agreement?

The stated purpose of the regulations is to address the reasonableness of a service provider's arrangement with a plan. The regulations state "no contract or arrangement for services between a 'covered' plan and a 'covered service provider' is reasonable within the meaning of ERISA Section 408(b)(2) unless the requirements of the regulation are satisfied." A reasonable arrangement, for purposes of these regulations, is one where a covered service provider provides certain required disclosures to a plan fiduciary. If the disclosures are not provided, the arrangement is not reasonable and will constitute a prohibited transaction unless properly corrected.[1] The actual details of the fees paid for the services provided must also be considered when determining whether a service provider agreement is reasonable.

4135. What are covered service providers?

A covered service provider is a service provider that enters into a contract or arrangement with a covered plan, and reasonably expects to receive $1,000 or more from the plan in either direct or indirect compensation for covered services.

For the purposes of the 408(b)(2) regulations, covered services include fiduciary services provided to the plan, fiduciary services provided to the investments held by the plan, services of

---

1.   Labor Reg. §2550.408b-2(c)(1)(i).

registered investment advisors ("RIAs"), accounting, certain third party administrative services, record keeping services, brokerage services, and basically any service for which the service provider receives indirect compensation from a plan.[1]

4136. What plan services are impacted by the 408(b)(2) regulations?

The 408(b)(2) disclosures apply only to covered services provided to ERISA retirement plans. The regulations set a *de minimis* exception that excludes providers expecting to collect less than $1,000 over the lifetime of the arrangement. The $1,000 threshold includes both direct and indirect compensation, so as a practical matter, this exception is of limited use.[2]

Just about any type of service relating to a typical 401(k) plan will be subject to the new disclosures. Certain types of services require disclosures in addition to the general disclosures required of all covered service providers. The regulations specifically discuss fiduciary (including RIA services) and nonfiduciary services.

Fiduciary Services

The two types of fiduciary services addressed in the regulations are:

(1)   Fiduciary services provided directly to a plan as an ERISA fiduciary. This class of service provider generally includes organizations with discretionary control or authority concerning the plan's benefits or investments. These services are described under ERISA Section 21(2).

Planning Point: There is a trend among certain independent investment advisors to agree to be fiduciaries to a plan. This kind of service provider falls under this first category. These individuals generally refer to their services as being a cofiduciary with a responsible plan fiduciary. These services are being promoted as a way for a plan sponsor to be relieved of certain fiduciary responsibilities relating to a plan. In some situations, these cofiduciary arrangements actually may increase the liability for a plan sponsor that, in effect, becomes responsible for the prudent hiring and monitoring of the cofiduciary, especially when the advisor/fiduciary has discretion over some aspect of the plan's investment or management. These fiduciary service arrangements require careful consideration of the advisor's net worth, liability insurance, and licensing history. Any agreement to share fiduciary duties with an outside party should be clearly spelled out in a contract drafted by ERISA counsel representing the plan sponsor and responsible plan fiduciary, not the service provider.

---

(2)   The second category covers fiduciary services provided to an investment contract, product, or entity that holds plan assets or in which the plan has a direct equity investment. This group of service providers includes those who provide fiduciary services to collective trusts and certain hedge funds and private equity partnerships (except mutual fund managers) held by the plan.

---

1.   Labor Reg. §2550.408b-2(c)(1)(iii).
2.   Labor Reg. §2550.408b-2(c)(1)(iii).

RIA Services

RIA services include services provided directly to a plan by an individual or entity that is an investment advisor registered under a state law or the Investment Advisors Act of 1940. This includes all RIAs who are providing services, including those who are not doing so in a fiduciary role. RIAs providing fiduciary services to a plan are also included in the first group of fiduciary service providers above.

Nonfiduciary Services

There are two categories of nonfiduciary services that are covered services.

First are certain recordkeeping and brokerage services. This class of service provider includes recordkeeping or brokerage services that meet two requirements: (1) the services are provided to an individual account plan that permits participants or beneficiaries to direct the investment of their accounts, and (2) there is at least one designated investment option available to participants.

A designated investment alternative is any investment alternative selected by a fiduciary into which participants and beneficiaries may direct the investment of assets held in, or contributed to, their individual accounts. The term designated investment alternative generally does not include a plan in which the only options available to participants are a brokerage window, self-directed brokerage accounts, or similar plan arrangements that enable participants and beneficiaries to select investments. This classification applies to the plan itself and not the specific services offered by the service provider. Thus, a broker working with a plan that offers a brokerage window in addition to a core of investments available to the plan fiduciary will be required to provide disclosures for the broker's service under the brokerage window.

A broker providing services to defined contribution plans who only offers access to individual brokerage accounts generally would not fall under this classification. Nonetheless, the broker's services would require disclosure if the plan fiduciary uses a Designated Investment Alternative ("DIA"). DIAs are a way to limit a fiduciary's liability when participants are given the right to direct the investment of their accounts.

When recordkeeping services are provided under any of the covered service classifications, certain additional disclosures are required relating to the fees paid and the costs of the recordkeeping services. If any indirect compensation is paid to a service provider that offers recordkeeping services, additional disclosures are required as to the cost and fees associated with each investment option.

The second category of nonfiduciary services includes service providers receiving indirect compensation. This category of covered services includes a broad range of other plan services, but only applies if the service provider reasonably expects to receive indirect compensation. The covered services for this purpose are accounting, auditing, actuarial, appraisal, banking, legal, valuation services, consulting (related to the development or implementation of investment policies or objectives or the selection or monitoring of service providers or plan investments), custodial, insurance, investment advisory services (for plan or participants), recordkeeping, securities or other investment brokerage services, or third party administration. The determination as to whether a service provider is in this category is based solely on whether the service provider receives indirect compensation. Most record keepers and brokerage firms receive indirect compensation and thus will be included in this class of nonfiduciary service provider as well as the other nonfiduciary classification.

The regulations define covered services to include services offered by affiliates and subcontractors of a service provider. Thus, when affiliates of service providers or subcontractors meet one of the thresholds requiring disclosure, the service provider then will be required to make specified disclosures to the responsible plan fiduciary.

4137. Are any service providers exempt from providing Section 408(b)(2) disclosures to a covered plan?

Yes.

The regulations establish only five specific classes of service providers that are required to provide disclosures based on their services offered or their receipt of indirect compensation. Any service provider not falling into one of these five classifications will not be required to provide a disclosure under these regulations. However, a service provider that is not classified under one of the categories of covered provider based on the services it provides may become a covered provider if it accepts indirect compensation.

An example of a service organization that would not be a covered service provider is a law firm that drafts or amends a plan document and receives payment only directly from the plan sponsor. Another is the CPA who either audits or assembles the Form 5500 filing for the plan and whose fees are directly paid by the plan sponsor. If either of these service providers receives any indirect compensation from the plan, such as a referral fee or a disguised consulting fee, then they become a covered service provider. The general disclosures are still required if that referral fee or other indirect payment is paid to an affiliate or a subcontractor of the service provider.[1]

The disclosure requirements get more complex when a single service provider offers an array of services where some relate to plan activities that trigger a required disclosure and some are not related to any plan activities. Payroll processing or human resources services are examples of unrelated services and can occur with a payroll provider offering 401(k) services or a professional employee leasing company offering 401(k) recordkeeping services for a single monthly fee. Entities that offer a combination of services must provide the general disclosures required under the 408(b)(2) regulations. These organizations frequently receive revenue, or indirect compensation, from a plan's assets or from the investment managers on their 401(k) platform. This compensation is typically used to offset the costs of providing their 401(k) plan services. These multiservice providers are required to separate their plan and nonplan activities, although that may be difficult. The regulations identify "services related to plan administration and monitoring of plan activities (e.g., payroll deductions and contributions)" as recordkeeping

---

1.   Labor Reg. §2550.408b-2(c)(1)(iii).

services requiring disclosure. Normally, one would not expect payroll services to constitute covered recordkeeping services.

Payroll-processing firms and some financial advisors who are covered providers frequently pay referral fees to accountants who provide services that might fall into one of the covered services classifications (for example, preparation of Form 5500). The payment of that referral fee from the payroll company or the financial advisor may constitute an indirect payment that would trigger a disclosure obligation for these accounting services that would not otherwise create a disclosure obligation.

4138. What disclosures will a bundled service provider need to provide under the 408(b)(2) regulations?

Bundled service providers typically charge a single fee to a plan that is a combination of transaction charges, per-account charges and basis-points charges. Bundled service providers typically receive indirect compensation from the investment options offered under their bundled services. The bundled charge imposed on a plan or a plan's assets pays for a group of services such as plan documents, enrollment supports, investment material, recordkeeping, plan distributions, vesting calculations, and annual reporting.[1]

Assuming that a bundled service provider either receives indirect compensation from a plan or a plan is a participant-directed plan with at least one designated investment alternative, the bundled provider will need to provide the general disclosures and certain additional disclosures as to fees and charges associated with each investment option.

Where a bundled service provider's fees for participant recordkeeping are not explicit or are offset by indirect compensation, the provider will need to provide "a good faith estimate of the cost of such recordkeeping services, including a disclosure of the methodology and assumptions used to prepare the estimate." The provider is required to provide a statement describing how they developed the good faith estimate.

Regulations require this good faith estimate for recordkeeping services, but the term "recordkeeping services" covers a multitude of activities. Under the regulations, recordkeeping services include services related to plan administration and monitoring of plan and participant and beneficiary transactions (e.g., enrollment, payroll deductions and contributions, offering designated investment alternatives and other covered plan investments, loans, withdrawals, and distributions) and the maintenance of covered plan and participant and beneficiary accounts, records, and statements.

Planning Point: Because the regulations allow a responsible plan fiduciary to request additional information on the disclosures required, several businesses have been created to help plan fiduciaries determine whether they have received information sufficient to make prudent decisions regarding the service provider's fee and services. The regulations do not limit the information that a responsible plan fiduciary could request, and if those requests are denied or are just late in arriving, the responsible plan fiduciary may need to report the service provider arrangement

---

1.   Labor Reg. §2550.408b-2(c)(1)(iv)(D)(2).

to the DOL. Thus, covered service providers will need to take appropriate steps to assure that any requests are answered in a timely manner.

4139. What are the general (or "initial") required 408(b)(2) disclosures?

All covered service providers must provide certain general disclosures that are referred to in the regulations as the "initial disclosures." There are four categories of initial disclosures. These disclosures are provided to a responsible plan fiduciary. There also are three classes of covered services requiring certain additional disclosures.

The four disclosures required of all covered service providers are a description of services provided, fiduciary status, compensation, and a description of how the compensation will be received.

(1)   The first disclosure is a description of the services to be provided to the plan pursuant to the contract or arrangement. The regulations provide no bright line guidance other than that the description should be sufficient for the responsible plan fiduciary to understand what is to be done so that the responsible plan fiduciary can evaluate the reasonableness of the arrangement's fees and services.

(2)   The second disclosure is fiduciary status. If applicable, the disclosure must state whether the service provider will provide or expects to provide services as a fiduciary. This notice is required if the services are to be provided directly to a plan or to an investment or entity in which the plan has a direct investment. A separate, additional statement is required if a provider expects to provide services directly to a plan as an investment advisor registered under either the Investment Advisors Act of 1940 or any state law.[1]

Planning Point: There have been several appeals court decisions on breach-of-fiduciary-duty lawsuits relating to fees paid by a plan. In some of the cases, the court looked to the agreements between the service provider and the plan to help determine if the service provider was a fiduciary. Almost all agreements today between service providers and plans have statements where the responsible plan fiduciary recognizes that the service provider is not a fiduciary to the plan. In at least one lawsuit involving a covered service provider, the court relied in part on that statement to dismiss the suit. In light of that, individuals and service organizations not acting in a fiduciary role generally will want to include in the contractual arrangement a statement that they are not acting as fiduciaries. Where a service organization is acting as a fiduciary, the disclosures in these regulations are required, including a statement that the service provider is a fiduciary.

(3)   The third disclosure is a statement that describes all of the compensation the service provider expects to receive as either direct compensation, indirect compensation, compensation paid among related parties, or compensation payable on termination of the arrangement. For purposes of meeting this threshold, compensation is defined to mean anything of monetary value. A *de minimis* exception applies to non-monetary items of $250 or less received during the term of the contract or

---

1.   Labor Reg. §2550.408b-2(c)(1)(iv).

arrangement, and to total payments including direct and indirect compensation of less than $1,000.

Certain disclosures are required of specific types of compensation as described below.

With respect to direct compensation, the disclosure must describe all direct compensation, either in the aggregate or by service that the service provider reasonably expects to receive. In general, direct payments include payments made directly from a plan to a service provider in any form.

With respect to indirect compensation, the disclosure must describe the indirect compensation that the service provider expects to receive. This includes both an identification of the services for which the indirect compensation will be received and the identification of the payer of the indirect compensation. Indirect compensation is compensation that is received from any source other than the plan, the plan sponsor, the covered service provider, an affiliate of the service provider, or a subcontractor of the covered service provider.

With respect to compensation paid among related parties, the disclosure must describe all compensation that will be paid to the service provider or an affiliate or subcontractor if it is set on a transaction basis or charged directly against the plan's investments and reflected in the net value of the investments (for example, 12b-1 fees). Compensation paid on a transaction basis includes commissions, soft dollars, finder's fees, or other similar incentive compensation based on business placed or retained. This description must include an identification of the services for which such compensation will be paid and identification of the payers and recipients of such compensation. The latter must include the status of a payer or recipient as an affiliate or a subcontractor.

Bundled providers that provide multiple services under one arrangement will be able to disclose their revenues on a bundled, or aggregate, basis. As described below, however, if a service provider agreement includes recordkeeping as part of its bundled services and the expected cost of those services is not part of the disclosure agreement, additional disclosures must be made, including a good faith estimate of the explicit cost to provide those services and a description of how that estimate was developed.

With respect to termination compensation, the disclosure must describe any compensation that the service provider reasonably expects to receive in connection with termination of the contract or arrangement. The statement must include a description of how any prepaid amounts will be calculated and refunded on termination. The regulations go on to say that "[a] provision that reasonably compensates the service provider for loss of early termination of the contract is not a penalty."

Planning Point: At the end of the regulations is a statement that "no contract or agreement is reasonable within the meaning of ERISA [S]ections 408(b)(2) and DOL regulations 2550.408b-2(a)(2) if it does not permit termination by the plan without penalty to the plan on reasonably short notice under the circumstances to prevent the plan from becoming locked into an arrangement that has become disadvantageous." These provisions could have a significant impact on certain insurance contracts and mutual funds that impose back end charges that are triggered on termination or early sale of an investment. Look for additional guidance on the application of this component of the regulations.

(4)   The fourth disclosure is a description of how the expected compensation will be received by the service provider. For example, the disclosure must explain whether revenues will be billed directly to the plan, whether amounts will be deducted directly from the plan's investments, or whether the service provider will impose a basis point charge on assets under its direction.

4140. How is a service provider's expected compensation to be disclosed under the DOL 408(b)(2) regulations?

The regulations give service providers latitude in how they disclose the compensation they receive. A fiduciary who needs more information to ascertain the reasonableness of an agreement would request such information in accordance with the notification process in the regulations. The fee disclosures may be an estimate of the compensation and can be expressed as a monetary amount, formula, percentage of the covered plan's assets, a per capita charge for each participant or beneficiary, or, if the compensation cannot reasonably be expressed in these terms, by any other reasonable method. This disclosure, in whatever form it is provided, must contain sufficient information to permit evaluation of the reasonableness of the compensation by the responsible plan fiduciary.[1]

Planning Point: Since the effective date of the final 408(b)(2) regulations, the Department of Labor has been reviewing service provider's disclosures and has proposed an amendment to the regulations which would now require that plan sponsors issue a "guide" to their disclosure packages. The guide is designed to allow plan fiduciaries to quickly and easily find their specific disclosures in what has proven to be voluminous pages of paperwork plan service providers have used as their disclosure packages.

4141. Under the DOL 408(b)(2) regulations, what additional disclosures are required for fiduciaries and covered service providers who provide investment and recordkeeping services?

Investment Disclosure

Fiduciaries providing services to an investment or entity into which the plan invests must disclose the following types of information:[2]

(1)   a description of all compensation that will be charged directly against the amount invested in connection with the acquisition, sale, transfer of, or withdrawal from the investment contract, product, or entity, for example, sales loads, sales charges, deferred sales charges, redemption fees, surrender charges, exchange fees, account fees, and purchase fees;

---

1.   Labor Reg. §2550.408b-2(c)(1)(iv)(E).
2.   Labor Reg. §2550.408(b)-2(c)(1)(iv)(F).

(2)   a description of the annual operating expenses (for example, the expense ratio), but only if the return on the investment is not fixed; and

(3)   a description of any ongoing expenses in addition to annual operating expenses (for example, wrap fees, mortality, and expense fees). In most cases these disclosures will be met through another service provider that will be providing the information to the responsible plan fiduciary. Organizations providing this type of information include fiduciaries for entities such as collective trusts, partnerships, and hedge funds.

Recordkeeping Services

When a covered service provider provides any recordkeeping services, certain additional disclosures are required. The regulations define recordkeeping services to include any "services related to plan administration and monitoring of plan and participant and beneficiary transactions (e.g., enrollment, payroll deductions and contributions, offering designated investment alternatives and other covered plan investments, loans, withdrawals and distributions); and the maintenance of covered plan and participant and beneficiary accounts, records, and statements."[1]

These disclosures must include:

(1)   A description of all direct and indirect compensation that the service provider, an affiliate, or a subcontractor reasonably expects to receive in connection with the recordkeeping services.

(2)   If the service provider reasonably expects the recordkeeping services to be provided, in whole or in part, without explicit compensation for such recordkeeping services or when compensation for recordkeeping services is offset or rebated based on other compensation received, an additional disclosure is to be provided. The service provider must provide a reasonable and good faith estimate of the cost to the plan of such recordkeeping services without offset that includes both an explanation of the methodology and assumptions used to prepare the estimate. This estimate shall take into account either (1) the rates that the covered service provider would charge to perform these services or the rates that would be charged for a third party, or (2) the prevailing market rates charged for similar recordkeeping services for a similar plan with similar number of participants.

Planning Point: These specific disclosures will be required for most bundled service providers that provide multiple services and are paid in whole or in part through indirect compensation (for example, 12b-1 fees and subtransfer agency fees). Under this disclosure requirement, a recordkeeper that receives indirect compensation and then offsets the amount received against the provider's stated fee, or that gives credits against its recordkeeping fees, must disclose the reasonable charge for those services as if there was no revenue sharing being paid.

Planning Point: This level of disclosure will impact bundled providers that have provided certain settlor services on a no charge basis while at the same time collecting indirect compensation

---

1.   Labor Reg. §2550.408(b)-2(c)(1)(iv)(G).

for other plan services. These regulations seem to be prohibiting such a provider from offering any free services when the provider receives indirect compensation. An interesting fallout may be that plan sponsors will need to start paying for their document services when a plan is set up. A plan sponsor may not offset the cost to perform settlor services with any revenue sharing because a plan cannot pay settlor costs. Settlor services include drafting the initial plan document and making plan amendments that primarily benefit the employer.

Investment Disclosure for Certain Participant Directed Plans

Where recordkeeping and brokerage services are provided to a plan in which the participants have at least one designated investment option available to them, or where indirect compensation is being paid by the plan, a separate disclosure is required for each designated investment option available. This disclosure must include the same investment information that is required for fiduciaries that provide services to investments in which the plan invests, as explained above.[1]

4142. What is the required format for the disclosures that service providers must make under the DOL 408(b)(2) regulations?

The regulations do not require a service provider to follow a specific format in how it discloses required information. One document or several may be involved, especially when a prospectus is available for certain of the investment disclosures.

All disclosures must provide the information in a manner that can be understood by the responsible plan fiduciary and participants.[2]

Planning Point: In March of 2014, the Department of Labor released a proposed amendment to the IRC Section 408(b)(2) regulations which, if finalized, will require plan service providers to provide a "guide" to their 408(b)(2) disclosures if the service provider discloses the appropriate information through "multiple or lengthy documents." The DOL does not give an exact number of pages that would constitute a "lengthy" document, but it is assumed that any final amendment to the regulations would specify an exact number.

The guide to the disclosures would need to be provided with the initial 408(b)(2) disclosures and would act as an index to the longer disclosures, allowing plan fiduciaries to quickly identify the information required by the regulations. The guide must include specific lookup references by identifying the page number and document in which the following information can be found:

1) description of the services to be provided;

2) statement concerning services to be provided as a fiduciary and/or as a registered investment provider;

3) description of all direct and indirect compensation, any compensation that will be paid among related parties, compensation for termination of the contract or arrangement, as well as compensation for recordkeeping services; and

4) the required investment disclosures for fiduciary services and recordkeeping and brokerage services, including annual operating expenses and ongoing expenses, or if applicable, total annual operating expenses.

---

1.   Labor Reg. §2550.408b-2(c)(1)(iv)(G).
2.   Labor Reg. §2550.408b-2(c)(1)(iv)(E).

4143. What filing method must be used for Section 408(b)(2) disclosures required of plan administrators who are required to file at least 250 returns?

Final regulations require that plan administrators who are required to file at least 250 returns file certain reports electronically. These reports include statements, returns and reports under IRC Section 6057 (relating to deferred vested retirement benefits, IRC Section 6058 (filings required in connection with deferred compensation plans), and IRC Section 6059 (filing requirements for periodic actuary reports).

With respect to IRC Section 6057 filings, the new requirements apply for filings required for plan years that began on or after January 1, 2014, but only if the filing deadline was on or after July 31, 2015. With respect to filings required under IRC Sections 6058 and 6059, the new requirements apply for plan years that began on or after January 1, 2015, but only for filings with a deadline after December 31, 2015.[1]

4144. When must covered service providers make the 408(b)(2) disclosures required under the DOL regulations?

A service provider must deliver the required information before the agreement or contract is consummated. Provider relationships in existence on July 1, 2012 were required to deliver the appropriate disclosures by that date. That is, there is no grace period for meeting these requirements where contracts already were in place on the effective date of the regulations.[2]

4145. Are covered service providers required by the DOL 408(b)(2) regulations to make any subsequent disclosures after the initial disclosure is provided?

A covered service provider is required to disclose any change to a responsible plan fiduciary as soon as is practicable but not later than 60 days from the date the service provider is aware of the change. Where such disclosures are late due to circumstances beyond the control of the service provider, the information must be disclosed as soon as practicable.[3]

In addition, if a responsible plan fiduciary requests information that is necessary to comply with a reporting requirement or is required for its own evaluation of the arrangement, a service provider must furnish that information. The preamble to the regulations discusses the additional information a responsible plan fiduciary may need to acquire to carry out the required duties. The regulations discuss the need for a service provider to promptly provide information that is requested. In this regard, a service provider must disclose the information no later than 30 days following receipt of a written request from a responsible plan fiduciary unless the disclosure is delayed due to extraordinary circumstances beyond the service provider's control, in which case the information must be provided as soon as practicable.[4]

---

1. TD 9695.
2. Labor Reg. §2550.408b-2(c)(1)(iv)(E).
3. Labor Reg. §2550.408b-2(c)(1)(v)(B).
4. Labor Reg. §2550.408b-2(c)(1)(v)(A).

4146. Do the final DOL 408(b)(2) regulations provide any protection for a responsible plan fiduciary if a covered service provider does not provide the required disclosures?

In addition to requiring covered service providers to disclose their compensation and service arrangements, a responsible plan fiduciary is responsible for collecting these disclosures from service providers. The regulations provide an exemption permitting a responsible plan fiduciary to escape prohibited transaction liability if a covered service provider does not provide the required disclosures.

For a responsible plan fiduciary to be exempt from the prohibited transaction rules under these disclosure regulations, a plan fiduciary must not know that a covered service provider failed to provide complete disclosure. If a fiduciary discovers that a covered service provider has not fully disclosed its compensation arrangements, a responsible plan fiduciary must request that the covered service provider make full and complete disclosures. If, after 90 days after the date of the request, the service provider has failed to comply with the disclosure request, the responsible plan fiduciary then is required to report the failure to comply with the disclosure requirements to the DOL within 30 days of the service provider's refusal to comply with the request, or 90 days after the request for complete disclosure was made.

On the failure or refusal to respond to the request for disclosure, the responsible plan fiduciary must evaluate the nature of the failure, the availability, qualifications, and cost of replacement service providers, and the covered service provider's response to notification of the failure.

Planning Point: If the requested information relates to future services and is not disclosed promptly after the end of the 90 day period, the responsible plan fiduciary is required to terminate the arrangement with the covered service provider prudently and as soon as practically possible.

4147. What 408(b)(2) disclosures are required of a broker who sells a security to a defined benefit pension plan?

Whether a disclosure is required in any factual situation will be based on whether a plan is a covered plan and whether brokerage services fall into one of the covered categories of services. If a broker is selling a security to a covered plan with no participant direction, such as a defined benefit pension plan, and the broker or an affiliate is not receiving any indirect compensation, then the broker's services do not fall into any of the five categories identified in the regulations. So long as a broker is not acting as a fiduciary to a plan, no disclosure is required.[1]

If a broker also provides assistance on enrollments, distributions, and participant loans, then the broker could be providing a service classified as recordkeeping services. There still are no disclosures assuming the factors above and that the plan is a defined benefit pension plan. The triggering event for disclosure of recordkeeping services occurs when a plan has a designated investment alternative or a broker, affiliate, or subcontractor of a broker receives indirect income. The same results would apply if a plan was a profit sharing plan without participant

---

1.   Labor Reg. §2550.408b-2(c)(1)(ii).

directed investment, so long as there is no payment of indirect income to a broker, affiliate, or subcontractor.

If a broker instead sells a mutual fund to a defined benefit pension plan and the mutual fund pays indirect compensation to the broker or the brokerage firm, then the broker falls into the category triggered by receipt of indirect compensation and certain disclosures relating to the indirect compensation are required. If a broker also provides recordkeeping services, then the broker must provide the disclosures for recordkeeping services.

4148. What disclosures are required under the DOL 408(b)(2) regulations if a broker sells securities to a 401(k) plan?

Brokerage services are covered services so that the broker is required to disclose compensation arrangements under Section 408(b)(2) if the services are provided to an individually directed plan where one or more designated investment alternatives are made available. Essentially, if a plan offers a menu of investments in which participants must invest, then the services would be covered services that trigger the disclosure obligations under the regulations. If a plan permits individually directed accounts but does not have designated investment alternatives, the plan may not be required to provide disclosures under the recordkeeping and brokerage sections of the DOL regulations.

The disclosure requirements apply even if a broker is not selling the designated investment alternative to a plan. This situation could arise in the case of a broker working with a single participant who has elected to use a window allowing the participant to buy securities outside the plan's core funds available to other participants. Because the plan has a core group of investments, it is treated as having a designated investment alternative. If a broker also assists with distributions, loans, calculation of vesting, or enrollments, additional disclosures will be required for these recordkeeping services.[1]

4149. What disclosures are required of a CPA who reconciles a plan's participant records under the DOL 408(b)(2) regulations?

No disclosures are required if the plan does not allow for investment direction by participants, the CPA is paid by the employer, and the CPA does not have a subcontractor or affiliate who receives indirect compensation from the plan.

If this CPA makes a referral to a payroll provider that provides 401(k) recordkeeping services, and the payroll provider that then handles the 401(k) plan pays a referral fee or a disguised consulting fee to the CPA, then the CPA will need to report as a service provider who receives indirect compensation.

If a plan has participant direction and has at least one designated investment alternative or a QDIA, a CPA will be treated as providing recordkeeping services. Then, the general disclosures are required under the covered service classification of recordkeeper. A CPA also may need to provide certain other disclosures based on how it gets paid and the services provided.

---

1.   Labor Reg. §2550.408b-2(c)(1)(ii).

Some CPAs have staff that are investment advisors and are registered under state law or the Investment Advisor's Act of 1940. If these advisors provide services to a plan, then they must provide both the general disclosures and certain additional disclosures based on the type of services that are provided to the plan and the structure of the plan.

If a CPA firm has an affiliate such as an investment advisory group that receives indirect compensation from the plan, then the general disclosures will be required.

4150. What disclosures are required of a 401(k) plan's third party record-keeper under the DOL 408(b)(2) regulations?

A recordkeeper is required to provide disclosures if it receives indirect compensation or if the plan has a designated investment alternative. Most recordkeepers that work with mutual fund investments receive indirect compensation from the funds in the form of sub-transfer agency fees and other revenue sharing or indirect compensation, as well as direct compensation in the form of fees for participant transactions such as loan maintenance or distributions.

If a covered service provider is offering recordkeeping services for free or expects the services to be provided without explicit compensation, the recordkeeper is required to provide the responsible plan fiduciary with a good faith estimate as to the cost of the recordkeeping services that will be provided. The estimate for recordkeeping services must take into account the rates that a covered service provider would normally charge to a plan to perform the recordkeeping or the prevailing market rates charged for similar recordkeeping services for a similar plan with a similar number of covered participants and beneficiaries.

Planning Point: Practically, this disclosure requirement will most affect bundled providers that sell their recordkeeping services as free to be made up with higher investment costs in other places.

4151. What is the purpose of the Department of Labor ("DOL") Section 404(a)(5) participant disclosure regulations?

With the proliferation of 401(k) and profit sharing plans that permit plan participants to individually direct their retirement plan assets, the DOL has grown exceedingly concerned about plan participants being required to make investment decisions without having access to information concerning the account fees and expenses.

When a plan permits participants to direct their investments, the regulations require that the plan administrator take action to inform the plan participants of the rights and responsibilities afforded to each participant with the ability to direct their investments. These disclosures must be provided prior to the date on which a participant or beneficiary can first direct the investments in their account and on a regular and periodic basis thereafter. Information required includes, but is not limited to, fees and expenses, voting rights, and rights associated with the direction of investments. For calendar year plans, the initial participant disclosures were required to be distributed by August 30, 2012, and at least annually thereafter. In addition, the first quarterly disclosures under these regulations were required to be distributed by November 14, 2012, as well as quarterly thereafter.

In contrast to the 408(b)(2) covered service provider disclosures, a plan that does not comply with the plan participant disclosure requirements does not run the risk of violating the prohibited transaction rules, but may be found to be in breach of its fiduciary duty. Since the plan participant disclosure requirements do not run up against the prohibited transaction rules, the participants will first need to suffer losses before liability for failure to comply accrues.

4152. To what plans do the 404(a)(5) participant fee disclosures apply?

To meet their fiduciary duties, the plan administrator of "covered individual account plans" must comply with the disclosure requirements of Section 404(a)(5).

Covered individual account plans include any defined contribution plan (as defined by Section 3(34) of ERISA) which permits plan participants or beneficiaries to direct investment of their plan assets. If a plan participant or beneficiary is permitted to direct only a portion of their account balance, while another portion of the account balance is trustee directed, the plan fiduciary need only comply with the disclosure requirements with respect to the assets that the plan participant has the right to direct.

SEPs, SIMPLEs, and defined benefit plans are not subject to these disclosure requirements.

The disclosures must be made to the plan participants or beneficiaries who have the right to direct their investments under the plan.

4153. What information must be disclosed to plan participants under the 404(a)(5) regulations?

The disclosures required under these regulations can be broken down into two over-arching categories: *plan-related information* and *investment-related information*.

Plan-related information must include disclosures describing:

(1)   "General Information" consisting of information concerning the structure and mechanics of the plan;

(2)   "Administrative Expenses" consisting of any fees and expenses for general plan administrative services that may be charged against all individual accounts; and

(3)   "Individual Expense Information" consisting of any fees and expenses that may be charged to each individual participant's account due to actions taken by that participant.

The plan-related information disclosures must be provided to plan participants on or before the date they are first eligible to direct their investments, and then annually thereafter. On a quarterly basis, plan participants must receive notice of the actual charges relating to these plan-related fees and expenses charged to their account in the preceding quarter.

Investment-related information must include disclosures regarding any default investment option under the plan and describing:

(1)   performance data concerning historical investment performance for one, five, and ten-year returns for investment options that do not have fixed rates of return;

(2)   benchmarking against an appropriate broad-based securities index over one, five, and ten years for investment options without a fixed rate of return.

(3)   fee and expense information for investments without a fixed rate of return must be expressed as both a percentage of assets and as a dollar amount for each $1,000 invested, as well as fees and restrictions on the ability to purchase or withdraw from the investments. For fixed rate of return investments, only shareholder-type fees or restrictions on the purchase or withdrawal from the investment need be disclosed;

(4)   a website address where participants can access information that is sufficiently specific to provide participants with additional information about the investments; and

(5)   a glossary of terms that will assist participants in understanding the plan's investment options. Plan administrators can provide this information in the form of a website address that is sufficiently specific to provide access to such a glossary.

Investment-related return information must be furnished to participants in a chart or similar format designed to encourage a comparison of each investment option available under the plan. The information that must be disclosed pursuant to these disclosure requirements is discussed in detail in Q 4157.

4154. What information must be included in the "general disclosures" section of a 404(a)(5) disclosure?

On or before the date that a plan participant or beneficiary can first direct their investments, and annually thereafter, the plan administrator must provide them with "General Disclosures" describing:

(1)   an explanation of the circumstances under which participants and beneficiaries may give investment instructions;

(2)   an explanation of any specified limitations on such instructions under the terms of the plan, including any restrictions on transfer to or from a designated investment alternative;

(3)   a description of or reference to plan provisions relating to the exercise of voting, tender, and similar rights appurtenant to an investment in a designated investment alternative as well as any restrictions on such rights;

(4)   an identification of any designated investment alternatives offered under the plan;

(5)   an identification of any designated investment managers; and

(6)   a description of any "brokerage windows," "self-directed brokerage accounts," or similar plan arrangements that enable participants and beneficiaries to select investments beyond those designated by the plan.

If there are any changes to the disclosed information, the participant or beneficiary must be given notice of the change at least 30, but no more than 90 days, before the effective date of the change. However, if circumstances present themselves to prevent disclosing changes to this information within the appropriate time frame, the plan administrator must issue a notice describing the changes as soon as practicable.

4155. What information relating to administrative expenses must be included in a 404(a)(5) disclosure?

On or before the date on which a participant or beneficiary can first direct their investments, and on an annual basis thereafter, the administrative expenses of the plan that may be charged against a participant or beneficiary's account must be disclosed to the extent that the charge is not included in the annual operating expense of any designated investment alternative. Recordkeeping, accounting, or legal services are examples of expenses that may need to be disclosed relating to administrative expenses. The plan administrator must also disclose the method in which the amount for services will be deducted from the participants' account balance, whether it is on a pro-rata, per capita, or a flat dollar basis.

The disclosures must be written in such a manner as to be understood by the average plan participant. If the fees for a service are known at the time of the disclosure, the plan administrator must identify the service provided, the cost of the services, and the allocation method used. In DOL Field Assistance Bulletin 2012-02R, the following examples of fee disclosures were found to be consistent with the DOL's disclosure requirements:

Example 1: The plan divides total recordkeeping costs equally among all individual accounts so that each participant or beneficiary with a plan account will pay $25.00 per year. One fourth of this amount is subtracted from each individual plan account each quarter.

Example 2: An annual recordkeeping fee of .12 percent of the account balance will be charged to each individual plan account. Each month, an amount equal to .01 percent of the account's ending balance for the month will be deducted from your individual account.

Example 3: An annual recordkeeping fee of .12 percent of the account balance will be charged to each individual plan account. Each month, an amount equal to .01 percent of the account's ending balance for the month will be deducted from your individual account. For example, if your ending account balance for a month is $55,000, then $5.50 will be deducted for that month.

If the actual fees or services are not known at the time of disclosure, and the plan administration reasonably expects the fees for services to be incurred and paid out of plan assets, the disclosures must describe the services that it expects to be provided and how the charges will be allocated to each participant's account. As an example, "if the plan incurs any legal expenses, such expenses will be paid from the plan's assets and deducted from individual plan accounts on a pro-rata basis" would be an appropriate disclosure for this scenario.

On a quarterly basis, the plan administrator must provide the plan participant or beneficiary with the actual dollar amount of the fees and expenses deducted from the participant's account for the provision of administrative services for the prior quarter, as well as a description of the services to which the charges relate. If applicable, the plan administrator must also disclose whether some of the plan's administrative expenses from the preceding quarter were paid from the total annual operating expenses of one or more of the plan's designated investment alternatives (e.g. revenue sharing arrangements, 12b-1 fees, subtransfer agent fees).

If there are any changes to the disclosed information, the participant or beneficiary must be given notice of the change at least 30 but no more than 90 days before the effective date of the change. However, if circumstances present themselves to prevent disclosing changes to this information within the appropriate time frame, the plan administrator must issue a notice describing the changes as soon as practicable.

4156. What information must be disclosed relating to individual expenses under the 404(a)(5) disclosure regulations?

On or before the date on which a participant or beneficiary can first direct plan investments, and annually thereafter, the plan administrator must disclose any fees and expenses that can be charged against the participant's investment account for services provided on an individual basis. Examples for which this disclosure would apply include loan fees, QDRO processing, or distribution fees.

On a quarterly basis, the plan administrator must provide the participants or beneficiaries an accounting of the dollar amount of the fees and expenses charged against the account for individual services deducted in the preceding quarter, as well as a description of the services provided.

If there are any changes to the disclosed information, the participant or beneficiary must be given notice of the change at least 30 but no more than 90 days before the effective date of the change. However, if circumstances present themselves to prevent disclosing changes to this information within the appropriate time frame, the plan administrator must issue a notice describing the changes as soon as practicable.

4157. What disclosures must be made with respect to investment-related information under the 404(a)(5) disclosure regulations?

Editor's Note: Note that the SECURE Act mandated new disclosure requirements with respect to lifetime income options for qualified plan participants. See Q 560.

Automatic Disclosures

On or before the date on which a participant or beneficiary can first direct their investments, and on an annual basis thereafter, the plan administrator must disclose certain investment-related information concerning each designated investment alternative offered under the plan.

For each designated investment alternative offered (see Q 4128), the plan administrator must disclose the following items in a comparative chart format designed to facilitate a comparison of such information for each designated investment:

(1)   The name of the investment,

(2)   The type or category of the investment (e.g., money market fund, balanced fund (stocks and bonds), large-cap stock fund, employer stock fund, employer securities), and

(3)   Performance data.

For designated investment alternatives with a variable rate of return, the plan administrator must disclose the average annual total return of the investment for one, five, and ten-year calendar periods ending on the date of the most recently ended calendar year. The plan administrator must also disclose that an investment's performance is not necessarily an indication of how the investment will perform.

For designated investment alternatives with a fixed rate of return, the plan administrator must disclose both the fixed or stated annual rate of return and the term of the investment. If the issuer of the fixed rate of return investment reserves the right to adjust the fixed or stated rate of return prospectively during the term of the contract, the disclosure must include the current rate of return, the minimum guaranteed rate under the contract, and a statement advising participants and beneficiaries that the issuer may adjust the rate of return prospectively along with information on how to obtain the most recent rate of return.

(1)   *Benchmarks.* For each designated investment alternative with a variable rate of return, the plan administrator must disclose the name and return of an appropriate broad-based security market indexed over the one, five, and ten-year periods comparable to the performance data of the designated investment alternative. The broad-based index fund used as a benchmark must not be administered by an affiliate of the designated investment alternative issuer, its investment advisor, or a principal underwriter, unless the index is widely recognized and used. If the designated investment alternative is a balanced fund that blends multiple appropriate broad-based securities market indexes, the plan administrator may use benchmark returns that are also a blend of index funds, provided they match the target blend of the designated investment alternative if the target blend of the investment is representative of the investment's actual holdings.

Note that there are no benchmarking requirements for designated investment alternatives that have fixed rates of return.

(2)   *Fee and expense information.* For each designated investment alternative with a variable rate of return, the plan administrator must disclose: (a) the amount and a description of each shareholder-type fee (fees charged directly against a participant's or beneficiary's investment, such as commissions, sales loads, sales

charges, deferred sales charges, redemption fees, surrender charges, exchange fees, account fees, and purchase fees, which are not included in the total annual operating expenses of any designated investment alternative) and a description of any restriction or limitation that may be applicable to a purchase, transfer, or withdrawal of the investment in whole or in part (such as round trip, equity wash, or other restrictions); (b) the total annual operating expenses of the investment expressed as a percentage (expense ratio); (c) the total annual operating expenses of the investment for a one-year period expressed as a dollar amount per $1,000 investment; (d) a statement indicating that the fees and expenses are only one of several factors that participants and beneficiaries should consider when making investment decisions; and (e) a statement that the cumulative effect of fees and expenses can substantially reduce the growth of a participant's or beneficiary's retirement account, and that participants and beneficiaries can visit the Employee Benefit Security Administration's website for an example demonstrating the long-term effect of fees and expenses.

(3)   *Internet website address*. The plan administrator must disclose an Internet website address that is sufficiently specific to provide participants and beneficiaries access to (a) the name of the designated investment alternative's issuer; (b) the investment alternative's objectives or goals, (c) the alternative's principal strategies and principal risks; (d) the alternative's portfolio turnover rate; (e) the alternative's performance data updated on a quarterly or more frequent basis; and (f) the alternative's fee and expense information.

(4)   *Glossary*. The glossary must include terms that assist the participants and beneficiaries in understanding the designated investment alternatives. The glossary may be provided at an internet web address if the address contains information that is sufficiently specific to provide access to such a glossary as well as a general explanation of the purpose of the address.

(5)   *Annuity Options*. If the designated investment alternative is part of a contract, fund, or product that permits participants or beneficiaries to allocate contributions toward the future purchase of a stream of retirement income payments guaranteed by an insurance company, the information provided must include the (a) name of the annuity contract, fund or product; (b) the annuity's objectives or goals (e.g., to provide a stream of fixed retirement income payments for life); (c) the benefits and factors that determine the price of the guaranteed income payments; (d) limitations placed upon the participant or beneficiary's ability to withdraw or transfer amounts allocated to the option, as well as a description of any fees or charges applicable to such withdrawal or transfers; (e) fees that will reduce the value of amounts allocated by participants or beneficiaries to the option (e.g. surrender charges, market value adjustments, administrative fees); (f) a statement that the guarantees of an insurance company are subject to its long-term financial strength and claims-paying ability; and (g) a website address sufficiently specific to provide the information contained in items (a) through (f) above.

Information to be Provided Subsequent to Investment

Subsequent to investment in any designated investment alternative, to the extent that voting, tender and similar rights are passed through to a participant or beneficiary of the plan, the plan administrator must furnish to the participant and beneficiary any materials provided to the plan relating to the exercise of voting, tender and similar rights.

Information to be Provided upon Request

Upon request of the participant or beneficiary, the plan administrator must provide a copy of any prospectuses (or short-form or summary prospectus), a copy of any financial statement or report relating to the designated investment alternative to the extent they were provided to the plan as well as a statement of the value of a share or unit of each designated investment alternative on the date of valuation.

4158. What are the electronic disclosure safe harbor rules for ERISA-required disclosures that retirement plan providers can rely upon beginning in 2020?

The DOL finalized its e-disclosure safe harbor proposal in 2020, allowing electronic distribution of certain notices and disclosures required by ERISA. Under the safe harbor rules, retirement plans can deliver documents electronically by posting required documents on the plan sponsor's website and furnishing notice of internet availability to participants via email. The sponsor can also send the documents directly via email to plan participants, whether in an attachment or in the body of the email.

These safe harbors are voluntary and are limited to ERISA-mandated retirement plan disclosures. Notices required for health and welfare plans and notices required by the IRS are not covered.

Participants are permitted to request paper copies of the documents or opt out of electronic delivery altogether and receive paper documents at no cost. The initial notice advising participants that documents will be delivered electronically, and advising of their right to opt out of e-delivery, must be provided on paper. The initial paper notice must specifically outline the electronic delivery method the plan will be using (direct email or website posting), including the email address to which future disclosures and notices of website availability will be sent.

Documents posted on the website must remain posted until superseded by a subsequent version and in no event for less than one year. The sponsor must also put into place a system designed to alert the administrator if the email address is invalid or undeliverable.

4159. What is a designated investment alternative?

A designated investment alternative is any investment alternative designated by the plan into which participants and beneficiaries may direct the investment of assets held in, or contributed to, their individual accounts. Designated investment alternatives do not include "brokerage windows," "self-directed brokerage accounts," or similar plan arrangements that permit plan participants and beneficiaries to select investments beyond those designated by the plans.

Generally, a model portfolio is not considered a designated investment alternative if it is clearly presented to the participants and beneficiaries as merely a means of allocating account assets among specific designated investment alternatives. However, if in choosing a model portfolio, the plan participant acquires an equity security, unit participation, or similar interest in an entity that invests in some combination of the plan's designated investment alternatives, the model portfolio would then be considered a designated investment alternative.

SEC Regulation Best Interest

4160. What is the new Form CRS that would be required under the SEC best interest proposal?

The SEC version of a fiduciary standard (known as regulation best interest) creates a new Form CRS, which will function as a client relationship summary to avoid confusion among clients as to the relationship between the parties and the duties of the advisor.

The final version of Form CRS was modified to contain less information which, according to the SEC, was deemed appropriate in order to avoid "information overload" for retail clients. The form will be required for investment advisors and broker dealers, and will contain the following information, in addition to a standardized introductory paragraph:

1.   description of relationship and services offered by the firm and advisors,

2.   information about fees and costs, as well as information regarding any conflicts of interest and the standard of conduct associated with services provided by the advisor,

3.   whether the firm and advisors have a reportable legal or disciplinary history,

4.   where the client can find additional information about the firm, and contact information for clients to register complaints, and

The relationship summary will also be required to link to Investor.gov/CRS on the SEC website, where the client can obtain educational information. Form CRS will follow a question-and-answer format, and is limited in length to two pages for investment advisors and broker-dealers, and four pages for dual registrants.

The Form CRS must be filed with the SEC, and clients would be allowed to access any firm's Form CRS, which are available to the public at investor.gov.

4161. How does the SEC Regulation Best Interest impact advisors who provide rollover advice to clients?

The SEC's Regulation Best Interest, which prohibits broker-dealers and certain other advisors from providing conflicted advice, among other things, also applies to transactions involving rollovers between retirement accounts. The rule clearly states that the best interest standard will now apply to rollovers from employer-sponsored plans into IRAs.

Because of this, advisors who make recommendations regarding rollover of retirement assets will now be required to establish that the rollover was in the client's best interest. Establishing that the rollover transaction was in the client's best interests can be accomplished in a number of ways, including by showing that the advisory services provided by the advisor with respect to the IRA add value as a tool for meeting the client's goals. This may be the case even if the fees associated with the IRA are higher than those in the employer plan. In other situations, investment options and investment mix in the rollover IRA may better suit the client's goals. Generally, broker-dealers who make rollover recommendations must consider:

- fees and expenses,

- available services in both plans,

- available investment options,

- availability of penalty-free withdrawals from the accounts,

- how required minimum distribution (RMD) rules can impact the client's goals,

- whether the plan provides any level of creditor protection,

- whether the plan permits holding of employer stock, and

- any additional special features of the initial account.

Ultimately, the SEC may provide additional guidance on the best interest standard with respect to rollovers. In the alternative, its eventual enforcement of the rule may provide clarity for advisors.

APPENDIX A

Actuarial Tables for Taxing Annuities

Gender based Tables I, II, IIA, and III, and Unisex Tables V, VI, VIA and VII for the taxing of annuities, appear on the following pages. (The IRS has provided a simplified method of taxing annuity payments from qualified plans and tax sheltered annuities, see Q 611.)

Gender based Tables I-III are to be used if the investment in the contract does not include a post-June 30, 1986 investment in the contract. Unisex Tables V-VII are to be used if the investment in the contract includes a post-June 30, 1986 investment in the contract.

However, even if there is no investment in the contract after June 30, 1986, an annuitant receiving annuity payments after June 30, 1986 (regardless of when they first began) may elect to treat his entire investment in the contract as post-June 30, 1986 and apply Tables V-VIII. This election may be made for any taxable year in which such amounts are received by the taxpayer; it is irrevocable and applies with respect to all amounts the taxpayer receives as an annuity under the contract in the taxable year for which the election is made or in any subsequent tax year. The election is made by the taxpayer's attaching to his return for that year a statement that he is making the election under Treasury Regulation §1.72-9 to treat the entire investment in the contract as post-June 1986 investment.[1]

If investment in the contract includes both a pre-July 1986 investment and a post-June 1986 investment, an election may be made to make separate computations with respect to each portion of the aggregate investment in the contract using with respect to each portion the tables applicable to it. The amount excludable is the sum of the amounts determined under the separate computations. However, the election is not available (i.e., the entire investment must be treated as post-June 1986 investment) if the annuity starting date is after June 30, 1986 and the contract provides an option (whether or not it is exercised) to receive amounts under the contract other than in the form of a life annuity. Thus, the election is not available if the contract provides: an option to receive a lump sum in full discharge of the obligation under the contract; an option to receive an amount under the contract after June 30, 1986 and before the annuity starting date; an option to receive an annuity for a period certain; an option to receive payments under a refund feature that is substantially equivalent to an annuity for a period certain (i.e., if its value determined under Table VII exceeds 50 percent); an option to receive a temporary life annuity that is substantially equivalent to an annuity for a period certain (i.e., if the multiple determined under Table VIII exceeds 50 percent of the maximum duration of the annuity).[2]

Treasury regulations extend some of the Tables to higher and lower ages, but the partial Tables are adequate for all practical purposes. The multiples in Tables I, II, and IIA, or V, VI and VIA need not be adjusted for monthly payments. For quarterly, semi-annual or annual payments, they must be adjusted according to the Frequency of Payment Adjustment Table, below. Table III and Table VII multiples, giving the percentage value of refund features, are never adjusted.

---

1. Treas. Reg. §1.72-9.
2. Treas. Reg. §1.72-6(d).

ALL TABLES ARE ENTERED WITH AGE OF ANNUITANT AT BIRTHDAY NEAREST ANNUITY STARTING DATE.

Frequency of Payment Adjustment Table

If the number of whole months from the annuity starting date to the first payment date is	0-1	2	3	4	5	6	7	8	9	10	11	12
And payments under the contract are to be made:												
Annually	+ .5	+ .4	+ .3	+ .2	+ .1	0	0	− .1	− .2	− .3	− .4	− .5
Semiannually	+ .2	+ .1	0	0	− .1	− .2	....	....	....	....	....	....
Quarterly	+ .1	0	− .1	....	....	....	....	....	....	....	....	....

Example. Ed Black bought an annuity contract on January 1 which provides him with an *annual* payment of $4,000 payable on December 31st of each year. His age on birthday nearest the annuity starting date (January 1) is sixty-six. The multiple from Table V for male age 66, is 19.2. This multiple must be adjusted for annual payment by subtracting .5 (19.2 − .5 = 18.7). Thus, his total expected return is $74,800 (18.7 × $4,000). See Treas. Reg. §1.72-5(a)(2).

Table I – Ordinary Life Annuities – One Life – Expected Return Multiples

Ages			Ages		
Male	Female	Multiples	Male	Female	Multiples
6	11	65.0	46	51	28.7
7	12	64.1	47	52	27.9
8	13	63.2	48	53	27.1
9	14	62.3	49	54	26.3
10	15	61.4	50	55	25.5
11	16	60.4	51	56	24.7
12	17	59.5	52	57	24.0
13	18	58.6	53	58	23.2
14	19	57.7	54	59	22.4
15	20	56.7	55	60	21.7
16	21	55.8	56	61	21.0
17	22	54.9	57	62	20.3
18	23	53.9	58	63	19.6
19	24	53.0	59	64	18.9
20	25	52.1	60	65	18.2
21	26	51.1	61	66	17.5
22	27	50.2	62	67	16.9
23	28	49.3	63	68	16.2
24	29	48.3	64	69	15.6
25	30	47.4	65	70	15.0
26	31	46.5	66	71	14.4
27	32	45.6	67	72	13.8
28	33	44.6	68	73	13.2
29	34	43.7	69	74	12.6
30	35	42.8	70	75	12.1
31	36	41.9	71	76	11.6
32	37	41.0	72	77	11.0
33	38	40.0	73	78	10.5
34	39	39.1	74	79	10.1
35	40	38.2	75	80	9.6
36	41	37.3	76	81	9.1
37	42	36.5	77	82	8.7
38	43	35.6	78	83	8.3
39	44	34.7	79	84	7.8
40	45	33.8	80	85	7.5
41	46	33.0	81	86	7.1
42	47	32.1	82	87	6.7
43	48	31.2	83	88	6.3
44	49	30.4	84	89	6.0
45	50	29.6	85	90	5.7

Table I – Ordinary Life Annuities – One Life –
Expected Return Multiples (cont'd)

Ages				Ages		
Male	Female	Multiples		Male	Female	Multiples
86	91	5.4		101	106	1.9
87	92	5.1		102	107	1.7
88	93	4.8		103	108	1.5
89	94	4.5		104	109	1.3
90	95	4.2		105	110	1.2
91	96	4.0		106	111	1.0
92	97	3.7		107	112	.8
93	98	3.5		108	113	.7
94	99	3.3		109	114	.6
95	100	3.1		110	115	.5
96	101	2.9		111	116	.0
97	102	2.7				
98	103	2.5				
99	104	2.3				
100	105	2.1				

Table II – Ordinary Joint Life and Last Survivor Annuities – Two Lives – Expected Return Multiples

Ages													
	Male	35	36	37	38	39	40	41	42	43	44	45	46	47
Male	Female	40	41	42	43	44	45	46	47	48	49	50	51	52
35	40	46.2	45.7	45.3	44.8	44.4	44.0	43.6	43.3	43.0	42.6	42.3	42.0	41.8
36	41	...	45.2	44.8	44.3	43.9	43.5	43.1	42.7	42.3	42.0	41.7	41.4	41.1
37	42	...	...	44.3	43.8	43.4	42.9	42.5	42.1	41.8	41.4	41.1	40.7	40.4
38	43	...	...	...	43.3	42.9	42.4	42.0	41.6	41.2	40.8	40.5	40.1	39.8
39	44	...	...	...	...	42.4	41.9	41.5	41.0	40.6	40.2	39.9	39.5	39.2
40	45	...	...	...	...	...	41.4	41.0	40.5	40.1	39.7	39.3	38.9	38.6
41	46	...	...	...	...	...	...	40.5	40.0	39.6	39.2	38.8	38.4	38.0
42	47	...	...	...	...	...	...	...	39.6	39.1	38.7	38.2	37.8	37.5
43	48	...	...	...	...	...	...	...	...	38.6	38.2	37.7	37.3	36.9
44	49	...	...	...	...	...	...	...	...	...	37.7	37.2	36.8	36.4
45	50	...	...	...	...	...	...	...	...	...	...	36.8	36.3	35.9
46	51	...	...	...	...	...	...	...	...	...	...	...	35.9	35.4
47	52	...	...	...	...	...	...	...	...	...	...	...	...	35.0

Ages													
	Male	48	49	50	51	52	53	54	55	56	57	58	59	60
Male	Female	53	54	55	56	57	58	59	60	61	62	63	64	65
35	40	41.5	41.3	41.0	40.8	40.6	40.4	40.3	40.1	40.0	39.8	39.7	39.6	39.5
36	41	40.8	40.6	40.3	40.1	39.9	39.7	39.5	39.3	39.2	39.0	38.9	38.8	38.6
37	42	40.2	39.9	39.6	39.4	39.2	39.0	38.8	38.6	38.4	38.3	38.1	38.0	37.9
38	43	39.5	39.2	39.0	38.7	38.5	38.3	38.1	37.9	37.7	37.5	37.3	37.2	37.1
39	44	38.9	38.6	38.3	38.0	37.8	37.6	37.3	37.1	36.9	36.8	36.6	36.4	36.3
40	45	38.3	38.0	37.7	37.4	37.1	36.9	36.6	36.4	36.2	36.0	35.9	35.7	35.5
41	46	37.7	37.3	37.0	36.7	36.5	36.2	36.0	35.7	35.5	35.3	35.1	35.0	34.8
42	47	37.1	36.8	36.4	36.1	35.8	35.6	35.3	35.1	34.8	34.6	34.4	34.2	34.1
43	48	36.5	36.2	35.8	35.5	35.2	34.9	34.7	34.4	34.2	33.9	33.7	33.5	33.3
44	49	36.0	35.6	35.3	34.9	34.6	34.3	34.0	33.8	33.5	33.3	33.0	32.8	32.6
45	50	35.5	35.1	34.7	34.4	34.0	33.7	33.4	33.1	32.9	32.6	32.4	32.2	31.9
46	51	35.0	34.6	34.2	33.8	33.5	33.1	32.8	32.5	32.2	32.0	31.7	31.5	31.3
47	52	34.5	34.1	33.7	33.3	32.9	32.6	32.2	31.4	31.6	31.9	31.1	30.9	30.6
48	53	34.0	33.6	33.2	32.8	32.4	32.0	31.7	31.4	31.1	30.8	30.5	30.2	30.0
49	54	...	33.1	32.7	32.3	31.9	31.5	31.2	30.8	30.5	30.2	29.9	29.6	29.4
50	55	...	...	32.3	31.8	31.4	31.0	30.6	30.3	29.9	29.6	29.3	29.0	28.8
51	56	...	...	...	31.4	30.9	30.5	30.1	29.8	29.4	29.1	28.8	28.5	28.2
52	57	...	...	...	...	30.5	30.1	29.7	29.3	28.9	28.6	28.2	27.9	27.6
53	58	...	...	...	...	...	29.6	29.2	28.8	28.4	28.1	27.7	27.4	27.1
54	59	...	...	...	...	...	...	28.8	28.3	27.9	27.6	27.2	26.9	26.5
55	60	...	...	...	...	...	...	...	27.9	27.5	27.1	26.7	26.4	26.0
56	61	...	...	...	...	...	...	...	...	27.1	26.7	26.3	25.9	25.5
57	62	...	...	...	...	...	...	...	...	...	26.2	25.8	25.4	25.1
58	63	...	...	...	...	...	...	...	...	...	...	25.4	25.0	24.6
59	64	...	...	...	...	...	...	...	...	...	...	...	24.6	24.2
60	65	...	...	...	...	...	...	...	...	...	...	...	...	23.8

Table II – Ordinary Joint Life and Last Survivor Annuities – Two Lives – Expected Return Multiples (cont'd)

Ages													
	Male	61	62	63	64	65	66	67	68	69	70	71	72	73
Male	Female	66	67	68	69	70	71	72	73	74	75	76	77	78
35	40	39.4	39.3	39.2	39.1	39.0	38.9	38.9	38.8	38.8	38.7	38.7	38.6	38.6
36	41	38.5	38.4	38.3	38.2	38.2	38.1	38.0	38.0	37.9	37.9	37.8	37.8	37.7
37	42	37.7	37.6	37.5	37.4	37.3	37.3	37.2	37.1	37.1	37.0	36.9	36.9	36.9
38	43	36.9	36.8	36.7	36.6	36.5	36.4	36.4	36.3	36.2	36.2	36.1	36.0	36.0
39	44	36.2	36.0	35.9	35.8	35.7	35.6	35.5	35.5	35.4	35.3	35.3	35.2	35.2
40	45	35.4	35.3	35.1	35.0	34.9	34.8	34.7	34.6	34.6	34.5	34.4	34.4	34.3
41	46	34.6	34.5	34.4	34.2	34.1	34.0	33.9	33.8	33.8	33.7	33.6	33.5	33.5
42	47	33.9	33.7	33.6	33.5	33.4	33.2	33.1	33.0	33.0	32.9	32.8	32.7	32.7
43	48	33.2	33.0	32.9	32.7	32.6	32.5	32.4	32.3	32.2	32.1	32.0	31.9	31.9
44	49	32.5	32.3	32.1	32.0	31.8	31.7	31.6	31.5	31.4	31.3	31.2	31.1	31.1
45	50	31.8	31.6	31.4	31.3	31.1	31.0	30.8	30.7	30.6	30.5	30.4	30.4	30.3
46	51	31.1	30.9	30.7	30.5	30.4	30.2	30.1	30.0	29.9	29.8	29.7	29.6	29.5
47	52	30.4	30.2	30.0	29.8	29.7	29.5	29.4	29.3	29.1	29.0	28.9	28.8	28.7
48	53	29.8	29.5	29.3	29.2	29.0	28.8	28.7	28.5	28.4	28.3	28.2	28.1	28.0
49	54	29.1	28.9	28.7	28.5	28.3	28.1	28.0	27.8	27.7	27.6	27.5	27.4	27.3
50	55	28.5	28.3	28.1	27.8	27.6	27.5	27.3	27.1	27.0	26.9	26.7	26.6	26.5
51	56	27.9	27.7	27.4	27.2	27.0	26.8	26.6	26.5	26.3	26.2	26.0	25.9	25.8
52	57	27.3	27.1	26.8	26.6	26.4	26.2	26.0	25.8	25.7	25.5	25.4	25.2	25.1
53	58	26.8	26.5	26.2	26.0	25.8	25.6	25.4	25.2	25.0	24.8	24.7	24.6	24.4
54	59	26.2	25.9	25.7	25.4	25.2	25.0	24.7	24.6	24.4	24.2	24.0	23.9	23.8
55	60	25.7	25.4	25.1	24.9	24.6	24.4	24.1	23.9	23.8	23.6	23.4	23.3	23.1
56	61	25.2	24.9	24.6	24.3	24.1	23.8	23.6	23.4	23.2	23.0	22.8	22.6	22.5
57	62	24.7	24.4	24.1	23.8	23.5	23.3	23.0	22.8	22.6	22.4	22.2	22.0	21.9
58	63	24.3	23.9	23.6	23.3	23.0	22.7	22.5	22.2	22.0	21.8	21.6	21.4	21.3
59	64	23.8	23.5	23.1	22.8	22.5	22.2	21.9	21.7	21.5	21.2	21.0	20.9	20.7
60	65	23.4	23.0	22.7	22.3	22.0	21.7	21.4	21.2	20.9	20.7	20.5	20.3	20.1
61	66	23.0	22.6	22.2	21.9	21.6	21.3	21.0	20.7	20.4	20.2	20.0	19.8	19.6
62	67	...	22.2	21.8	21.5	21.1	20.8	20.5	20.2	19.9	19.7	19.5	19.2	19.0
63	68	...	...	21.4	21.1	20.7	20.4	20.1	19.8	19.5	19.2	19.0	18.7	18.5
64	69	...	...	...	20.7	20.3	20.0	19.6	19.3	19.0	18.7	18.5	18.2	18.0
65	70	...	...	...	...	19.9	19.6	19.2	18.9	18.6	18.3	18.0	17.8	17.5
66	71	...	...	...	...	...	19.2	18.8	18.5	18.2	17.9	17.6	17.3	17.1
67	72	...	...	...	...	...	...	18.5	18.1	17.8	17.5	17.2	16.9	16.7
68	73	...	...	...	...	...	...	...	17.8	17.4	17.1	16.8	16.5	16.2
69	74	...	...	...	...	...	...	...	...	17.1	16.7	16.4	16.1	15.8
70	75	...	...	...	...	...	...	...	...	...	16.4	16.1	15.8	15.5
71	76	...	...	...	...	...	...	...	...	...	...	15.7	15.4	15.1
72	77	...	...	...	...	...	...	...	...	...	...	...	15.1	14.8
73	78	...	...	...	...	...	...	...	...	...	...	...	...	14.4

Table II – Ordinary Joint Life and Last Survivor Annuities – Two Lives – Expected Return Multiples (cont'd)

Ages													
	Male	74	75	76	77	78	79	80	81	82	83	84	85
Male	Female	79	80	81	82	83	84	85	86	87	88	89	90
35	40	38.6	38.5	38.5	38.5	38.4	38.4	38.4	38.4	38.4	38.4	38.3	38.3
36	41	37.7	37.6	37.6	37.6	37.6	37.5	37.5	37.5	37.5	37.5	37.5	37.4
37	42	36.8	36.8	36.7	36.7	36.7	36.7	36.6	36.6	36.6	36.6	36.6	36.6
38	43	36.0	35.9	35.9	35.8	35.8	35.8	35.8	35.8	35.8	35.7	35.7	35.7
39	44	35.1	35.1	35.0	35.0	35.0	34.9	34.9	34.9	34.9	34.8	34.8	34.8
40	45	34.3	34.2	34.2	34.1	34.1	34.1	34.1	34.0	34.0	34.0	34.0	34.0
41	46	33.4	33.4	33.3	33.3	33.3	33.2	33.2	33.2	33.2	33.1	33.1	33.1
42	47	32.6	32.6	32.5	32.5	32.4	32.4	32.4	32.3	32.3	32.3	32.3	32.3
43	48	31.8	31.8	31.7	31.7	31.6	31.6	31.5	31.5	31.5	31.5	31.4	31.4
44	49	31.0	30.9	30.9	30.8	30.8	30.8	30.7	30.7	30.7	30.6	30.6	30.6
45	50	30.2	30.1	30.1	30.0	30.0	29.9	29.9	29.9	29.8	29.8	29.8	29.8
46	51	29.4	29.4	29.3	29.2	29.2	29.2	29.1	29.1	29.0	29.0	29.0	28.9
47	52	28.7	28.6	28.5	28.5	28.4	28.4	28.3	28.3	28.2	28.2	28.2	28.1
48	53	27.9	27.8	27.8	27.7	27.6	27.6	27.5	27.5	27.5	27.4	27.4	27.4
49	54	27.2	27.1	27.0	26.9	26.9	26.8	26.8	26.7	26.7	26.6	26.6	26.6
50	55	26.4	26.3	26.3	26.2	26.1	26.1	26.0	26.0	25.9	25.9	25.8	25.8
51	56	25.7	25.6	25.5	25.5	25.4	25.3	25.3	25.2	25.2	25.1	25.1	25.0
52	57	25.0	24.9	24.8	24.7	24.7	24.6	24.5	24.5	24.4	24.4	24.3	24.3
53	58	24.3	24.2	24.1	24.0	23.9	23.9	23.8	23.7	23.7	23.6	23.6	23.5
54	59	23.6	23.5	23.4	23.3	23.2	23.2	23.1	23.0	23.0	22.9	22.9	22.8
55	60	23.0	22.9	22.8	22.7	22.6	22.5	22.4	22.3	22.3	22.2	22.2	22.1
56	61	22.3	22.2	22.1	22.0	21.9	21.8	21.7	21.6	21.6	21.5	21.5	21.4
57	62	21.7	21.6	21.5	21.3	21.2	21.1	21.1	21.0	20.9	20.8	20.8	20.7
58	63	21.1	21.0	20.8	20.7	20.6	20.5	20.4	20.3	20.2	20.2	20.1	20.0
59	64	20.5	20.4	20.2	20.1	20.0	19.9	19.8	19.7	19.6	19.5	19.4	19.4
60	65	19.9	19.8	19.6	19.5	19.4	19.3	19.1	19.0	19.0	18.9	18.8	18.7
61	66	19.4	19.2	19.1	18.9	18.8	18.7	18.5	18.4	18.3	18.3	18.2	18.1
62	67	18.8	18.7	18.5	18.3	18.2	18.1	18.0	17.8	17.7	17.7	17.6	17.5
63	68	18.3	18.1	18.0	17.8	17.6	17.5	17.4	17.3	17.2	17.1	17.0	16.9
64	69	17.8	17.6	17.4	17.3	17.1	17.0	16.8	16.7	16.6	16.5	16.4	16.3
65	70	17.3	17.1	16.9	16.7	16.6	16.4	16.3	16.2	16.0	15.9	15.8	15.8
66	71	16.9	16.6	16.4	16.3	16.1	15.9	15.8	15.6	15.5	15.3	15.3	15.2
67	72	16.4	16.2	16.0	15.8	15.6	15.4	15.3	15.1	15.0	14.9	14.8	14.7
68	73	16.0	15.7	15.5	15.3	15.1	15.0	14.8	14.6	14.5	14.4	14.3	14.2
69	74	15.6	15.3	15.1	14.9	14.7	14.5	14.3	14.2	14.0	13.9	13.8	13.7
70	75	15.2	14.9	14.7	14.5	14.3	14.1	13.9	13.7	13.6	13.4	13.3	13.2
71	76	14.8	14.5	14.3	14.1	13.8	13.6	13.5	13.3	13.1	13.0	12.8	12.7
72	77	14.5	14.2	13.9	13.7	13.5	13.2	13.0	12.9	12.7	12.5	12.4	12.3
73	78	14.1	13.8	13.6	13.3	13.1	12.9	12.7	12.5	12.3	12.1	12.0	11.8
74	79	13.8	13.5	13.2	13.0	12.7	12.5	12.3	12.1	11.9	11.7	11.6	11.4
75	80	...	13.2	12.9	12.6	12.4	12.2	11.9	11.7	11.5	11.4	11.2	11.0
76	81	...	...	12.6	12.3	12.1	11.8	11.6	11.4	11.2	11.0	10.8	10.7
77	82	...	...	...	12.1	11.8	11.5	11.3	11.1	10.8	10.7	10.5	10.3
78	83	...	...	...	...	11.5	11.2	11.0	10.7	10.5	10.3	10.1	10.0
79	84	...	...	...	...	...	11.0	10.7	10.5	10.2	10.0	9.8	9.6
80	85	...	...	...	...	...	...	10.4	10.2	10.0	9.7	9.5	9.3
81	86	...	...	...	...	...	...	...	9.9	9.7	9.5	9.3	9.1
82	87	...	...	...	...	...	...	...	...	9.4	9.2	9.0	8.8
83	88	...	...	...	...	...	...	...	...	...	9.0	8.7	8.5
84	89	...	...	...	...	...	...	...	...	...	...	8.5	8.3
85	90	...	...	...	...	...	...	...	...	...	...	...	8.1

Table IIA–Annuities for Joint Life Only – Two Lives – Expected Return Multiples (cont'd)

Ages													
	Male	35	36	37	38	39	40	41	42	43	44	45	46	47
Male	Female	40	41	42	43	44	45	46	47	48	49	50	51	52
35	40	30.3	29.9	29.4	29.0	28.5	28.0	27.5	27.0	26.5	26.0	25.5	24.9	24.4
36	41	...	29.5	29.0	28.6	28.2	27.7	27.2	26.7	26.2	25.7	25.2	24.7	24.2
37	42	...	...	28.6	28.2	27.8	27.3	26.9	26.4	25.9	25.5	25.0	24.4	23.9
38	43	...	...	...	27.8	27.4	27.0	26.5	26.1	25.6	25.2	24.7	24.2	23.7
39	44	...	...	...	...	27.0	26.6	26.2	25.8	25.3	24.8	24.4	23.9	23.4
40	45	...	...	...	...	...	26.2	25.8	25.4	25.0	24.5	24.1	23.6	23.1
41	46	...	...	...	...	...	...	25.4	25.0	24.6	24.2	23.8	23.3	22.9
42	47	...	...	...	...	...	...	...	24.6	24.2	23.8	23.4	23.0	22.6
43	48	...	...	...	...	...	...	...	...	23.9	23.5	23.1	22.7	22.2
44	49	...	...	...	...	...	...	...	...	...	23.1	22.7	22.3	21.9
45	50	...	...	...	...	...	...	...	...	...	...	22.4	22.0	21.6
46	51	...	...	...	...	...	...	...	...	...	...	...	21.6	21.2
47	52	...	...	...	...	...	...	...	...	...	...	...	...	20.9

Ages													
	Male	48	49	50	51	52	53	54	55	56	57	58	59	60
Male	Female	53	54	55	56	57	58	59	60	61	62	63	64	65
35	40	23.8	23.3	22.7	22.1	21.6	21.0	20.4	19.8	19.3	18.7	18.1	17.5	17.0
36	41	23.6	23.1	22.5	22.0	21.4	20.8	20.3	19.7	19.1	18.6	18.0	17.4	16.9
37	42	23.4	22.9	22.3	21.8	21.2	20.7	20.1	19.6	19.0	18.4	17.9	17.3	16.8
38	43	23.2	22.6	22.1	21.6	21.1	20.5	20.0	19.4	18.9	18.3	17.8	17.2	16.7
39	44	22.9	22.4	21.9	21.4	20.9	20.3	19.8	19.3	18.7	18.2	17.7	17.1	16.6
40	45	22.7	22.2	21.7	21.2	20.7	20.1	19.6	19.1	18.6	18.0	17.5	17.0	16.5
41	46	22.4	21.9	21.4	20.9	20.4	19.9	19.4	18.9	18.4	17.9	17.4	16.9	16.3
42	47	22.1	21.6	21.2	20.7	20.2	19.7	19.2	18.7	18.2	17.7	17.2	16.7	16.2
43	48	21.8	21.4	20.9	20.5	20.0	19.5	19.0	18.6	18.1	17.6	17.1	16.6	16.1
44	49	21.5	21.1	20.6	20.2	19.8	19.3	18.8	18.4	17.9	17.4	16.9	16.4	15.9
45	50	21.2	20.8	20.4	19.9	19.5	19.1	18.6	18.1	17.7	17.2	16.7	16.3	15.8
46	51	20.9	20.5	20.1	19.7	19.2	18.8	18.4	17.9	17.5	17.0	16.6	16.1	15.6
47	52	20.5	20.1	19.8	19.4	19.0	18.5	18.1	17.7	17.3	16.8	16.4	15.9	15.5
48	53	20.2	19.8	19.4	19.1	18.7	18.3	17.9	17.5	17.0	16.6	16.2	15.7	15.3
49	54	...	19.5	19.1	18.8	18.4	18.0	17.6	17.2	16.8	16.4	16.0	15.5	15.1
50	55	...	...	18.8	18.4	18.1	17.7	17.3	16.9	16.6	16.2	15.8	15.3	14.9
51	56	...	...	...	18.1	17.8	17.4	17.0	16.7	16.3	15.9	15.5	15.1	14.7
52	57	...	...	...	...	17.4	17.1	16.8	16.4	16.0	15.7	15.3	14.9	14.5
53	58	...	...	...	...	...	16.8	16.4	16.1	15.8	15.4	15.1	14.7	14.3
54	59	...	...	...	...	...	...	16.1	15.8	15.5	15.1	14.8	14.4	14.1
55	60	...	...	...	...	...	...	...	15.5	15.2	14.9	14.5	14.2	13.9
56	61	...	...	...	...	...	...	...	...	14.9	14.6	14.3	13.9	13.6
57	62	...	...	...	...	...	...	...	...	...	14.3	14.0	13.7	13.4
58	63	...	...	...	...	...	...	...	...	...	...	13.7	13.4	13.1
59	64	...	...	...	...	...	...	...	...	...	...	...	13.1	12.8
60	65	...	...	...	...	...	...	...	...	...	...	...	...	12.6

Table IIA – Annuities for Joint Life Only –
Two Lives – Expected Return Multiples (cont'd)

Ages													
	Male	61	62	63	64	65	66	67	68	69	70	71	72	73
Male	Female	66	67	68	69	70	71	72	73	74	75	76	77	78
35	40	16.4	15.8	15.3	14.7	14.2	13.7	13.1	12.6	12.1	11.6	11.1	10.7	10.2
36	41	16.3	15.8	15.2	14.7	14.1	13.6	13.1	12.6	12.1	11.6	11.1	10.6	10.2
37	42	16.2	15.7	15.1	14.6	14.1	13.6	13.0	12.5	12.0	11.5	11.1	10.6	10.1
38	43	16.1	15.6	15.1	14.5	14.0	13.5	13.0	12.5	12.0	11.5	11.0	10.6	10.1
39	44	16.0	15.5	15.0	14.5	13.9	13.4	12.9	12.4	11.9	11.5	11.0	10.5	10.1
40	45	15.9	15.4	14.9	14.4	13.9	13.4	12.9	12.4	11.9	11.4	11.0	10.5	10.0
41	46	15.8	15.3	14.8	14.3	13.8	13.3	12.8	12.3	11.8	11.4	10.9	10.5	10.0
42	47	15.7	15.2	14.7	14.2	13.7	13.2	12.7	12.3	11.8	11.3	10.9	10.4	10.0
43	48	15.6	15.1	14.6	14.1	13.6	13.1	12.7	12.2	11.7	11.3	10.8	10.4	9.9
44	49	15.5	15.0	14.5	14.0	13.5	13.1	12.6	12.1	11.7	11.2	10.8	10.3	9.9
45	50	15.3	14.8	14.4	13.9	13.4	13.0	12.5	12.0	11.6	11.1	10.7	10.3	9.8
46	51	15.2	14.7	14.2	13.8	13.3	12.9	12.4	12.0	11.5	11.1	10.6	10.2	9.8
47	52	15.0	14.6	14.1	13.7	13.2	12.8	12.3	11.9	11.4	11.0	10.6	10.1	9.7
48	53	14.9	14.4	14.0	13.5	13.1	12.6	12.2	11.8	11.3	10.9	10.5	10.1	9.7
49	54	14.7	14.3	13.8	13.4	13.0	12.5	12.1	11.7	11.3	10.8	10.4	10.0	9.6
50	55	14.5	14.1	13.7	13.3	12.8	12.4	12.0	11.6	11.2	10.7	10.3	9.9	9.5
51	56	14.3	13.9	13.5	13.1	12.7	12.3	11.9	11.5	11.1	10.7	10.3	9.9	9.5
52	57	14.1	13.7	13.3	12.9	12.5	12.1	11.7	11.3	10.9	10.6	10.2	9.8	9.4
53	58	13.9	13.6	13.2	12.8	12.4	12.0	11.6	11.2	10.8	10.5	10.1	9.7	9.3
54	59	13.7	13.4	13.0	12.6	12.2	11.9	11.5	11.1	10.7	10.3	10.0	9.6	9.2
55	60	13.5	13.2	12.8	12.4	12.1	11.7	11.3	11.0	10.6	10.2	9.9	9.5	9.1
56	61	13.3	12.9	12.6	12.2	11.9	11.5	11.2	10.8	10.5	10.1	9.8	9.4	9.0
57	62	13.0	12.7	12.4	12.1	11.7	11.4	11.0	10.7	10.3	10.0	9.6	9.3	8.9
58	63	12.8	12.5	12.2	11.8	11.5	11.2	10.9	10.5	10.2	9.8	9.5	9.2	8.8
59	64	12.6	12.3	11.9	11.6	11.3	11.0	10.7	10.4	10.0	9.7	9.4	9.1	8.7
60	65	12.3	12.0	11.7	11.4	11.1	10.8	10.5	10.2	9.9	9.6	9.3	8.9	8.6
61	66	12.0	11.8	11.5	11.2	10.9	10.6	10.3	10.0	9.7	9.4	9.1	8.8	8.5
62	67	...	11.5	11.2	11.0	10.7	10.4	10.1	9.8	9.6	9.3	9.0	8.7	8.4
63	68	...	...	11.0	10.7	10.5	10.2	9.9	9.7	9.4	9.1	8.8	8.5	8.2
64	69	...	...	...	10.5	10.2	10.0	9.7	9.5	9.2	8.9	8.7	8.4	8.1
65	70	...	...	...	...	10.0	9.8	9.5	9.3	9.0	8.8	8.5	8.2	8.0
66	71	...	...	...	...	...	9.5	9.3	9.1	8.8	8.6	8.3	8.1	7.8
67	72	...	...	...	...	...	...	9.1	8.9	8.6	8.4	8.1	7.9	7.7
68	73	...	...	...	...	...	...	...	8.6	8.4	8.2	8.0	7.7	7.5
69	74	...	...	...	...	...	...	...	...	8.2	8.0	7.8	7.6	7.3
70	75	...	...	...	...	...	...	...	...	...	7.8	7.6	7.4	7.2
71	76	...	...	...	...	...	...	...	...	...	...	7.4	7.2	7.0
72	77	...	...	...	...	...	...	...	...	...	...	...	7.0	6.8
73	78	...	...	...	...	...	...	...	...	...	...	...	...	6.7

Table IIA – Annuities for Joint Life Only – Two Lives – Expected Return Multiples (cont'd)

Ages													
	Male	74	75	76	77	78	79	80	81	82	83	84	85	86
Male	Female	79	80	81	82	83	84	85	86	87	88	89	90	91
35	40	9.7	9.3	8.9	8.5	8.1	7.7	7.3	6.9	6.6	6.2	5.9	5.6	5.3
36	41	9.7	9.3	8.9	8.4	8.0	7.7	7.3	6.9	6.6	6.2	5.9	5.6	5.3
37	42	9.7	9.3	8.8	8.4	8.0	7.6	7.3	6.9	6.5	6.2	5.9	5.6	5.3
38	43	9.7	9.2	8.8	8.4	8.0	7.6	7.2	6.9	6.5	6.2	5.9	5.6	5.3
39	44	9.6	9.2	8.8	8.4	8.0	7.6	7.2	6.9	6.5	6.2	5.9	5.6	5.3
40	45	9.6	9.2	8.8	8.4	8.0	7.6	7.2	6.9	6.5	6.2	5.9	5.5	5.2
41	46	9.6	9.2	8.7	8.3	7.9	7.6	7.2	6.8	6.5	6.2	5.8	5.5	5.2
42	47	9.5	9.1	8.7	8.3	7.9	7.5	7.2	6.8	6.5	6.2	5.8	5.5	5.2
43	48	9.5	9.1	8.7	8.3	7.9	7.5	7.2	6.8	6.5	6.1	5.8	5.5	5.2
44	49	9.5	9.0	8.6	8.2	7.9	7.5	7.1	6.8	6.4	6.1	5.8	5.5	5.2
45	50	9.4	9.0	8.6	8.2	7.8	7.5	7.1	6.8	6.4	6.1	5.8	5.5	5.2
46	51	9.4	9.0	8.6	8.2	7.8	7.4	7.1	6.7	6.4	6.1	5.8	5.5	5.2
47	52	9.3	8.9	8.5	8.1	7.8	7.4	7.1	6.7	6.4	6.1	5.8	5.5	5.2
48	53	9.3	8.9	8.5	8.1	7.7	7.4	7.0	6.7	6.4	6.0	5.7	5.4	5.1
49	54	9.2	8.8	8.4	8.1	7.7	7.3	7.0	6.7	6.3	6.0	5.7	5.4	5.1
50	55	9.1	8.8	8.4	8.0	7.7	7.3	7.0	6.6	6.3	6.0	5.7	5.4	5.1
51	56	9.1	8.7	8.3	8.0	7.6	7.3	6.9	6.6	6.3	6.0	5.7	5.4	5.1
52	57	9.0	8.6	8.3	7.9	7.6	7.2	6.9	6.6	6.2	5.9	5.6	5.4	5.1
53	58	8.9	8.6	8.2	7.9	7.5	7.2	6.9	6.5	6.2	5.9	5.6	5.3	5.1
54	59	8.9	8.5	8.2	7.8	7.5	7.1	6.8	6.5	6.2	5.9	5.6	5.3	5.0
55	60	8.8	8.4	8.1	7.7	7.4	7.1	6.8	6.4	6.1	5.8	5.6	5.3	5.0
56	61	8.7	8.4	8.0	7.7	7.3	7.0	6.7	6.4	6.1	5.8	5.5	5.3	5.0
57	62	8.6	8.3	7.9	7.6	7.3	7.0	6.7	6.4	6.1	5.8	5.5	5.2	5.0
58	63	8.5	8.2	7.9	7.5	7.2	6.9	6.6	6.3	6.0	5.7	5.5	5.2	4.9
59	64	8.4	8.1	7.8	7.5	7.1	6.8	6.5	6.3	6.0	5.7	5.4	5.2	4.9
60	65	8.3	8.0	7.7	7.4	7.1	6.8	6.5	6.2	5.9	5.6	5.4	5.1	4.9
61	66	8.2	7.9	7.6	7.3	7.0	6.7	6.4	6.1	5.9	5.6	5.3	5.1	4.8
62	67	8.1	7.8	7.5	7.2	6.9	6.6	6.4	6.1	5.8	5.5	5.3	5.0	4.8
63	68	8.0	7.7	7.4	7.1	6.8	6.6	6.3	6.0	5.7	5.5	5.2	5.0	4.7
64	69	7.8	7.6	7.3	7.0	6.7	6.5	6.2	5.9	5.7	5.4	5.2	4.9	4.7
65	70	7.7	7.4	7.2	6.9	6.6	6.4	6.1	5.9	5.6	5.4	5.1	4.9	4.7
66	71	7.6	7.3	7.1	6.8	6.5	6.3	6.0	5.8	5.5	5.3	5.1	4.8	4.6
67	72	7.4	7.2	6.9	6.7	6.4	6.2	6.0	5.7	5.5	5.2	5.0	4.8	4.6
68	73	7.3	7.0	6.8	6.6	6.3	6.1	5.9	5.6	5.4	5.2	4.9	4.7	4.5
69	74	7.1	6.9	6.7	6.4	6.2	6.0	5.8	5.5	5.3	5.1	4.9	4.7	4.5
70	75	7.0	6.8	6.5	6.3	6.1	5.9	5.7	5.4	5.2	5.0	4.8	4.6	4.4
71	76	6.8	6.6	6.4	6.2	6.0	5.8	5.6	5.3	5.1	4.9	4.7	4.5	4.3
72	77	6.6	6.4	6.3	6.1	5.9	5.7	5.5	5.3	5.0	4.9	4.7	4.5	4.3
73	78	6.5	6.3	6.1	5.9	5.7	5.5	5.3	5.1	5.0	4.8	4.6	4.4	4.2
74	79	6.3	6.1	6.0	5.8	5.6	5.4	5.2	5.0	4.9	4.7	4.5	4.3	4.1
75	80	..	6.0	5.8	5.6	5.5	5.3	5.1	4.9	4.8	4.6	4.4	4.2	4.1
76	81	..	..	5.6	5.5	5.3	5.2	5.0	4.8	4.7	4.5	4.3	4.1	4.0
77	82	..	..	..	5.3	5.2	5.0	4.9	4.7	4.5	4.4	4.2	4.1	3.9
78	83	..	..	..	..	5.0	4.9	4.7	4.6	4.4	4.3	4.1	4.0	3.8
79	84	..	..	..	..	..	4.7	4.6	4.5	4.3	4.2	4.0	3.9	3.7
80	85	..	..	..	..	..	..	4.5	4.3	4.2	4.1	3.9	3.8	3.6
81	86	..	..	..	..	..	..	..	4.2	4.1	3.9	3.8	3.7	3.6
82	87	..	..	..	..	..	..	..	..	4.0	3.8	3.7	3.6	3.5
83	88	..	..	..	..	..	..	..	..	..	3.7	3.6	3.5	3.4
84	89	..	..	..	..	..	..	..	..	..	..	3.5	3.4	3.3
85	90	..	..	..	..	..	..	..	..	..	..	..	3.3	3.2
86	91	..	..	..	..	..	..	..	..	..	..	..	..	3.1

Table III – Percent Value of Refund Feature

Ages		Duration of guaranteed amount											
Male	Female	1 Yr %	2 Yrs %	3 Yrs %	4 Yrs %	5 Yrs %	6 Yrs %	7 Yrs %	8 Yrs %	9 Yrs %	10 Yrs %	11 Yrs %	12 Yrs %
6	11	..	..	..	..	..	..	..	..	1	1	1	1
7	12	..	..	..	..	..	..	..	..	1	1	1	1
8	13	..	..	..	..	..	..	..	1	1	1	1	1
9	14	..	..	..	..	..	..	..	1	1	1	1	1
10	15	..	..	..	..	..	..	..	1	1	1	1	1
11	16	..	..	..	..	..	..	..	1	1	1	1	1
12	17	..	..	..	..	..	..	..	1	1	1	1	1
13	18	..	..	..	..	..	..	..	1	1	1	1	1
14	19	..	..	..	..	..	..	..	1	1	1	1	1
15	20	..	..	..	..	..	..	..	1	1	1	1	1
16	21	..	..	..	..	..	..	..	1	1	1	1	1
17	22	..	..	..	..	..	..	..	1	1	1	1	1
18	23	..	..	..	..	..	..	..	1	1	1	1	1
19	24	..	..	..	..	..	..	..	1	1	1	1	1
20	25	..	..	..	..	..	..	..	1	1	1	1	1
21	26	..	..	..	..	..	..	..	1	1	1	1	1
22	27	..	..	..	..	..	..	1	1	1	1	1	1
23	28	..	..	..	..	..	..	1	1	1	1	1	1
24	29	..	..	..	..	..	..	1	1	1	1	1	1
25	30	..	..	..	..	..	..	1	1	1	1	1	1
26	31	..	..	..	..	..	1	1	1	1	1	1	1
27	32	..	..	..	..	..	1	1	1	1	1	1	1
28	33	..	..	..	..	..	1	1	1	1	1	1	1
29	34	..	..	..	..	..	1	1	1	1	1	1	1
30	35	..	..	..	..	1	1	1	1	1	1	1	2
31	36	..	..	..	..	1	1	1	1	1	1	1	2
32	37	..	..	..	..	1	1	1	1	1	1	2	2
33	38	..	..	..	1	1	1	1	1	1	1	2	2
34	39	..	..	..	1	1	1	1	1	1	2	2	2
35	40	..	..	..	1	1	1	1	1	2	2	2	2
36	41	..	..	..	1	1	1	1	1	2	2	2	2
37	42	..	..	1	1	1	1	1	2	2	2	2	3
38	43	..	..	1	1	1	1	1	2	2	2	2	3
39	44	..	..	1	1	1	1	2	2	2	2	3	3
40	45	..	..	1	1	1	1	2	2	2	3	3	3
41	46	..	..	1	1	1	1	2	2	2	3	3	3
42	47	..	..	1	1	1	2	2	2	3	3	3	4
43	48	..	1	1	1	1	2	2	2	3	3	4	4
44	49	..	1	1	1	1	2	2	3	3	3	4	4
45	50	..	1	1	1	2	2	2	3	3	4	4	5

Table III – Percent Value of Refund Feature (cont'd)

		Duration of guaranteed amount											
Ages		1 Yr	2 Yrs	3 Yrs	4 Yrs	5 Yrs	6 Yrs	7 Yrs	8 Yrs	9 Yrs	10 Yrs	11 Yrs	12 Yrs
Male	Female	%	%	%	%	%	%	%	%	%	%	%	%
46	51	..	1	1	1	2	2	3	3	3	4	4	5
47	52	..	1	1	1	2	2	3	3	4	4	5	5
48	53	..	1	1	2	2	2	3	3	4	5	5	6
49	54	..	1	1	2	2	3	3	4	4	5	5	6
50	55	..	1	1	2	2	3	3	4	5	5	6	7
51	56	..	1	1	2	3	3	4	4	5	6	6	7
52	57	1	1	2	2	3	3	4	5	5	6	7	8
53	58	1	1	2	2	3	4	4	5	6	7	7	8
54	59	1	1	2	2	3	4	5	5	6	7	8	9
55	60	1	1	2	3	3	4	5	6	7	8	8	9
56	61	1	1	2	3	4	4	5	6	7	8	9	10
57	62	1	1	2	3	4	5	6	7	8	9	10	11
58	63	1	2	2	3	4	5	6	7	8	9	10	12
59	64	1	2	3	4	5	6	7	8	9	10	11	12
60	65	1	2	3	4	5	6	7	8	10	11	12	13
61	66	1	2	3	4	5	6	8	9	10	12	13	14
62	67	1	2	3	4	6	7	8	10	11	12	14	15
63	68	1	2	4	5	6	7	9	10	12	13	15	16
64	69	1	3	4	5	7	8	9	11	13	14	16	17
65	70	1	3	4	6	7	9	10	12	13	15	17	19
66	71	1	3	4	6	8	9	11	13	14	16	18	20
67	72	2	3	5	6	8	10	12	14	15	17	19	21
68	73	2	3	5	7	9	11	13	14	16	18	21	23
69	74	2	4	6	7	9	11	13	16	18	20	22	24
70	75	2	4	6	8	10	12	14	17	19	21	23	26
71	76	2	4	6	9	11	13	15	18	20	22	25	27
72	77	2	5	7	9	12	14	16	19	21	24	26	29
73	78	2	5	7	10	12	15	18	20	23	25	28	30
74	79	3	5	8	11	13	16	19	22	24	27	30	32
75	80	3	6	8	11	14	17	20	23	26	29	31	34
76	81	3	6	9	12	15	18	21	24	27	30	33	36
77	82	3	7	10	13	16	20	23	26	29	32	35	38
78	83	4	7	11	14	17	21	24	28	31	34	37	40
79	84	4	8	11	15	19	22	26	29	33	36	39	42
80	85	4	8	12	16	20	24	27	31	34	38	41	44
81	86	4	9	13	17	21	25	29	33	36	40	43	46
82	87	5	9	14	18	23	27	31	35	38	42	45	48
83	88	5	10	15	19	24	28	33	37	40	44	47	50
84	89	5	11	16	21	26	30	34	38	42	46	49	52
85	90	6	11	17	22	27	32	36	41	44	48	51	55

Table III – Percent Value of Refund Feature (cont'd)

		Duration of guaranteed amount										
Ages		13 Yrs	14 Yrs	15 Yrs	16 Yrs	17 Yrs	18 Yrs	19 Yrs	20 Yrs	21 Yrs	22 Yrs	23 Yrs	24 Yrs
Male	Female	%	%	%	%	%	%	%	%	%	%	%	%
6	11	1	1	1	1	1	1	1	1	1	1	1	2
7	12	1	1	1	1	1	1	1	1	1	1	1	2
8	13	1	1	1	1	1	1	1	1	1	1	1	2
9	14	1	1	1	1	1	1	1	1	1	1	1	2
10	15	1	1	1	1	1	1	1	1	1	1	2	2
11	16	1	1	1	1	1	1	1	1	1	1	2	2
12	17	1	1	1	1	1	1	1	1	1	1	2	2
13	18	1	1	1	1	1	1	1	1	1	2	2	2
14	19	1	1	1	1	1	1	1	1	1	2	2	2
15	20	1	1	1	1	1	1	1	1	1	2	2	2
16	21	1	1	1	1	1	1	1	1	2	2	2	2
17	22	1	1	1	1	1	1	1	1	2	2	2	2
18	23	1	1	1	1	1	1	1	2	2	2	2	2
19	24	1	1	1	1	1	1	2	2	2	2	2	2
20	25	1	1	1	1	1	1	2	2	2	2	2	2
21	26	1	1	1	1	1	2	2	2	2	2	2	2
22	27	1	1	1	1	1	2	2	2	2	2	2	3
23	28	1	1	1	1	2	2	2	2	2	2	2	3
24	29	1	1	1	2	2	2	2	2	2	2	3	3
25	30	1	1	1	2	2	2	2	2	2	3	3	3
26	31	1	1	2	2	2	2	2	2	3	3	3	3
27	32	1	2	2	2	2	2	2	3	3	3	3	3
28	33	1	2	2	2	2	2	3	3	3	3	3	4
29	34	2	2	2	2	2	2	3	3	3	3	4	4
30	35	2	2	2	2	2	3	3	3	3	4	4	4
31	36	2	2	2	2	3	3	3	3	4	4	4	5
32	37	2	2	2	3	3	3	3	4	4	4	5	5
33	38	2	2	3	3	3	3	4	4	4	5	5	5
34	39	2	3	3	3	3	4	4	4	5	5	5	6
35	40	2	3	3	3	4	4	4	5	5	5	6	6
36	41	3	3	3	4	4	4	5	5	5	6	6	7
37	42	3	3	3	4	4	4	5	5	6	6	7	7
38	43	3	3	4	4	4	5	5	6	6	7	7	8
39	44	3	4	4	4	5	5	6	6	7	7	8	8
40	45	4	4	4	5	5	6	6	7	7	8	8	9
41	46	4	4	4	5	6	6	7	7	8	8	9	9
42	47	4	5	5	5	6	6	7	8	8	9	9	10
43	48	4	5	5	6	6	7	8	8	9	9	10	11
44	49	5	5	6	6	7	7	8	9	9	10	11	12
45	50	5	6	6	7	7	8	9	9	10	11	12	12

Table III – Percent Value of Refund Feature (cont'd)

Ages		Duration of guaranteed amount											
Male	Female	13 Yrs %	14 Yrs %	15 Yrs %	16 Yrs %	17 Yrs %	18 Yrs %	19 Yrs %	20 Yrs %	21 Yrs %	22 Yrs %	23 Yrs %	24 Yrs %
46	51	5	6	7	7	8	9	9	10	11	12	12	13
47	52	6	7	7	8	9	9	10	11	12	12	13	14
48	53	6	7	8	8	9	10	11	12	12	13	14	15
49	54	7	8	8	9	10	11	11	12	13	14	15	16
50	55	7	8	9	10	11	11	12	13	14	15	16	17
51	56	8	9	10	10	11	12	13	14	15	16	17	18
52	57	8	9	10	11	12	13	14	15	16	17	18	20
53	58	9	10	11	12	13	14	15	16	17	19	20	21
54	59	10	11	12	13	14	15	16	17	18	20	21	22
55	60	10	11	13	14	15	16	17	18	20	21	22	24
56	61	11	12	13	15	16	17	18	20	21	22	24	25
57	62	12	13	14	16	17	18	20	21	22	24	25	27
58	63	13	14	15	17	18	19	21	22	24	25	27	28
59	64	14	15	16	18	19	21	22	24	25	27	28	30
60	65	15	16	18	19	20	22	24	25	27	28	30	32
61	66	16	17	19	20	22	23	25	27	28	30	32	33
62	67	17	18	20	22	23	25	27	28	30	32	33	35
63	68	18	20	21	23	25	26	28	30	32	33	35	37
64	69	19	21	23	24	26	28	30	32	33	35	37	39
65	70	20	22	24	26	28	30	32	33	35	37	39	41
66	71	22	24	26	28	29	31	33	35	37	39	41	43
67	72	23	25	27	29	31	33	35	37	39	41	43	45
68	73	25	27	29	31	33	35	37	39	41	43	45	47
69	74	26	28	30	33	35	37	39	41	43	45	47	48
70	75	28	30	32	34	37	39	41	43	45	47	49	50
71	76	29	32	34	36	39	41	43	45	47	49	51	52
72	77	31	34	36	38	41	43	45	47	49	51	53	54
73	78	33	35	38	40	43	45	47	49	51	53	55	56
74	79	35	37	40	42	45	47	49	51	53	55	57	58
75	80	37	39	42	44	47	49	51	53	55	57	58	60
76	81	39	41	44	46	49	51	53	55	57	59	60	62
77	82	41	43	46	48	51	53	55	57	59	61	62	64
78	83	43	45	48	50	53	55	57	59	61	62	64	65
79	84	45	48	50	53	55	57	59	61	63	64	66	67
80	85	47	50	52	55	57	59	61	63	64	66	67	69
81	86	49	52	54	57	59	61	63	65	66	68	69	70
82	87	51	54	56	59	61	63	65	66	68	69	71	72
83	88	53	56	58	61	63	65	66	68	70	71	72	73
84	89	55	58	60	63	65	67	68	70	71	73	74	75
85	90	57	60	62	65	67	68	70	71	73	74	75	76

Table III – Percent Value of Refund Feature (cont'd)

		Duration of guaranteed amount										
Ages		25 Yrs	26 Yrs	27 Yrs	28 Yrs	29 Yrs	30 Yrs	31 Yrs	32 Yrs	33 Yrs	34 Yrs	35 Yrs
Male	Female	%	%	%	%	%	%	%	%	%	%	%
6	11	2	2	2	2	2	2	2	2	2	2	2
7	12	2	2	2	2	2	2	2	2	2	2	3
8	13	2	2	2	2	2	2	2	2	2	2	3
9	14	2	2	2	2	2	2	2	2	2	3	3
10	15	2	2	2	2	2	2	2	2	3	3	3
11	16	2	2	2	2	2	2	2	2	3	3	3
12	17	2	2	2	2	2	2	2	3	3	3	3
13	18	2	2	2	2	2	2	2	3	3	3	3
14	19	2	2	2	2	2	2	3	3	3	3	3
15	20	2	2	2	2	2	3	3	3	3	3	3
16	21	2	2	2	2	3	3	3	3	3	3	4
17	22	2	2	2	2	3	3	3	3	3	4	4
18	23	2	2	2	3	3	3	3	3	4	4	4
19	24	2	2	3	3	3	3	3	4	4	4	4
20	23	2	3	3	3	3	3	4	4	4	4	5
21	26	3	3	3	3	3	4	4	4	4	5	5
22	27	3	3	3	3	4	4	4	4	5	5	5
23	28	3	3	3	3	4	4	4	5	5	5	5
24	29	3	3	3	4	4	4	5	5	5	5	6
25	30	3	3	4	4	4	5	5	5	6	6	6
26	31	3	4	4	4	5	5	5	6	6	6	7
27	32	4	4	4	5	5	5	6	6	6	7	7
28	33	4	4	5	5	5	6	6	6	7	7	8
29	34	4	5	5	5	6	6	6	7	7	8	8
30	35	5	5	5	6	6	6	7	7	8	8	9
31	36	5	5	6	6	6	7	7	8	8	9	9
32	37	5	6	6	7	7	7	8	8	9	10	10
33	38	6	6	7	7	7	8	8	9	10	10	11
34	39	6	7	7	8	8	9	9	10	10	11	12
35	40	7	7	8	8	9	9	10	10	11	12	12
36	41	7	8	8	9	9	10	10	11	12	13	13
37	42	8	8	9	9	10	11	11	12	13	13	14
38	43	8	9	9	10	11	11	12	13	13	14	15
39	44	9	9	10	11	11	12	13	14	14	15	16
40	45	9	10	11	11	12	13	14	15	15	16	17
41	46	10	11	11	12	13	14	15	16	16	17	18
42	47	11	12	12	13	14	15	16	17	18	18	19
43	46	12	12	13	14	15	16	17	18	19	20	21
44	49	12	13	14	15	16	17	18	19	20	21	22
45	50	13	14	15	16	17	18	19	20	21	22	23

Table III – Percent Value of Refund Feature (cont'd)

		Duration of guaranteed amount										
		25	26	27	28	29	30	31	32	33	34	35
Ages		Yrs	Yrs	Yrs	Yrs	Yrs	Yrs	Yrs	Yrs	Yrs	Yrs	Yrs
Male	Female	%	%	%	%	%	%	%	%	%	%	%
46	51	14	15	16	17	18	19	20	21	22	24	25
47	52	15	16	17	18	19	20	21	23	24	25	26
48	53	16	17	18	19	20	22	23	24	25	26	28
49	54	17	18	19	21	22	23	24	25	27	28	29
50	55	18	20	21	22	23	24	26	27	28	29	31
51	56	20	21	22	23	25	26	27	28	30	31	32
52	57	21	22	23	25	26	27	29	30	31	33	34
53	58	22	24	25	26	28	29	30	32	33	34	36
54	59	24	25	26	28	29	31	32	33	35	36	38
55	60	25	26	28	29	31	32	34	35	36	38	39
56	61	27	28	29	31	32	34	35	37	38	40	41
57	62	28	30	31	33	34	36	37	39	40	41	43
58	63	30	31	33	34	36	37	39	40	42	43	45
59	61	31	33	35	36	38	39	41	42	44	45	47
60	65	33	35	36	38	40	41	43	44	46	47	48
61	66	35	37	38	40	41	43	44	46	47	49	50
62	67	37	38	40	42	43	45	46	48	49	51	52
63	68	39	40	42	44	45	47	48	50	51	52	54
64	69	41	42	44	46	47	49	50	52	53	54	55
65	70	42	44	46	47	49	50	52	53	55	56	57
66	71	44	46	48	49	51	52	54	55	56	58	59
67	72	46	48	50	51	53	54	56	57	58	59	61
68	73	48	50	52	53	55	56	57	59	60	61	62
69	74	50	52	53	55	56	58	59	60	62	63	64
70	75	52	54	55	57	58	60	61	62	63	64	65
71	76	54	56	57	59	60	61	63	64	65	66	67
72	77	56	58	59	60	62	63	64	65	66	67	68
73	78	58	59	61	62	64	65	66	67	68	68	70
74	79	60	61	63	64	65	66	67	68	69	70	71
75	80	62	63	64	66	67	68	69	70	71	72	72
76	81	63	65	66	67	68	69	70	71	72	73	..
77	82	65	66	68	69	70	71	72	73	74	..	..
78	83	67	68	69	70	71	72	73	74	..	..	..
79	84	68	70	71	72	73	74	75	..	..	..	..
80	85	70	71	72	73	74	75	..	..	..	..	..
81	86	72	73	74	75	75	..	..	..	..	..	..
82	87	73	74	75	76	..	..	..	..	..	..	..
83	88	74	75	76	..	..	..	..	..	..	..	..
84	89	76	77	..	..	..	..	..	..	..	..	..
85	90	77	..	..	..	..	..	..	..	..	..	..

Table V – Ordinary Life Annuities – One Life – Expected Return Multiples

Age	Multiple	Age	Multiple	Age	Multiple
5	76.6	42	40.6	79	10.0
6	75.6	43	39.6	80	9.5
7	74.7	44	38.7	81	8.9
8	73.7	45	37.7	82	8.4
9	72.7	46	36.8	63	7.9
10	71.7	47	35.9	84	7.4
11	70.7	48	34.9	85	6.9
12	69.7	49	34.0	86	6.5
13	68.8	50	33.1	87	6.1
14	67.8	51	32.2	88	5.7
15	66.8	52	31.3	89	5.3
16	65.8	53	30.4	90	5.0
17	64.8	54	29.5	91	4.7
18	63.9	55	28.6	92	4.4
19	62.9	56	27.7	93	4.1
20	61.9	57	26.8	94	3.9
21	60.9	58	25.9	95	3.7
22	59.9	59	25.0	96	3.4
23	59.0	60	24.2	97	3.2
24	58.0	61	23.3	98	3.0
25	57.0	62	22.5	99	2.8
26	56.0	63	21.6	100	2.7
27	55.1	64	20.8	101	2.5
28	54.1	65	20.0	102	2.3
29	53.1	66	19.2	103	2.1
30	52.2	67	18.4	104	1.9
31	51.2	68	17.6	105	1.8
32	50.2	69	16.8	106	1.6
33	49.3	70	16.0	107	1.4
34	48.3	71	15.3	108	1.3
35	47.3	72	14.6	109	1.1
36	46.4	73	13.9	110	1.0
37	45.4	74	13.2	111	.9
38	44.4	75	12.5	112	.8
39	43.5	76	11.9	113	.7
40	42.5	77	11.2	114	.6
41	41.5	78	10.6	115	.5

Table VI – Ordinary Joint Life and Last Survivor Annuities – Two Lives – Expected Return Multiples

AGES	35	36	37	38	39	40	41	42	43	44	45	46	47	48	49	50
35	54.0	...	...	...	...	...	...	...	...	...	...	...	...	...	...	...
36	53.5	53.0	...	...	...	...	...	...	...	...	...	...	...	...	...	...
37	53.0	52.5	52.0	...	...	...	...	...	...	...	...	...	...	...	...	...
38	52.6	52.0	51.5	51.0	...	...	...	...	...	...	...	...	...	...	...	...
39	52.2	51.6	51.0	50.5	50.0	...	...	...	...	...	...	...	...	...	...	...
40	51.8	51.2	50.6	50.0	49.5	49.0	...	...	...	...	...	...	...	...	...	...
41	51.4	50.8	50.2	49.6	49.1	48.5	48.0	...	...	...	...	...	...	...	...	...
42	51.1	50.4	49.8	49.2	48.6	48.1	47.5	47.0	...	...	...	...	...	...	...	...
43	50.8	50.1	49.5	48.8	48.2	47.6	47.1	46.6	46.0	...	...	...	...	...	...	...
44	50.5	49.8	49.1	48.5	47.8	47.2	46.7	46.1	45.6	45.1	...	...	...	...	...	...
45	50.2	49.5	48.8	48.1	47.5	46.9	46.3	45.7	45.1	44.6	44.1	...	...	...	...	...
46	50.0	49.2	48.5	47.8	47.2	46.5	45.9	45.3	44.7	44.1	43.6	43.1	...	...	...	...
47	49.7	49.0	48.3	47.5	46.8	46.2	45.5	44.9	44.3	43.7	43.2	42.6	42.1	...	...	...
48	49.5	48.8	48.0	47.3	46.6	45.9	45.2	44.5	43.9	43.3	42.7	42.2	41.7	41.2	...	...
49	49.3	48.5	47.8	47.0	46.3	45.6	44.9	44.2	43.6	42.9	42.3	41.8	41.2	40.7	40.2	...
50	49.2	48.4	47.6	46.8	46.0	45.3	44.6	43.9	43.2	42.6	42.0	41.4	40.8	40.2	39.7	39.2
51	49.0	48.2	47.4	46.6	45.8	45.1	44.3	43.6	42.9	42.2	41.6	41.0	40.4	39.8	39.3	38.7
52	48.8	48.0	47.2	46.4	45.6	44.8	44.1	43.3	42.6	41.9	41.3	40.6	40.0	39.4	38.8	38.3
53	48.7	47.9	47.0	46.2	45.4	44.6	43.9	43.1	42.4	41.7	41.0	40.3	39.7	39.0	38.4	37.9
54	48.6	47.7	46.9	46.0	45.2	44.4	43.6	42.9	42.1	41.4	40.7	40.0	39.3	38.7	38.1	37.5
55	48.5	47.6	46.7	45.9	45.1	44.2	43.4	42.7	41.9	41.2	40.4	39.7	39.0	38.4	37.7	37.1
56	48.3	47.5	46.6	45.8	44.9	44.1	43.3	42.5	41.7	40.9	40.2	39.5	38.7	38.1	37.4	36.8
57	48.3	47.4	46.5	45.6	44.8	43.9	43.1	42.3	41.5	40.7	40.0	39.2	38.5	37.8	37.1	36.4
58	48.2	47.3	46.4	45.5	44.7	43.8	43.0	42.1	41.3	40.5	39.7	39.0	38.2	37.5	36.8	36.1
59	48.1	47.2	46.3	45.4	44.5	43.7	42.8	42.0	41.2	40.4	39.6	38.8	38.0	37.3	36.6	35.9
60	48.0	47.1	46.2	45.3	44.4	43.6	42.7	41.9	41.0	40.2	39.4	38.6	37.8	37.1	36.3	35.6
61	47.9	47.0	46.1	45.2	44.3	43.5	42.6	41.7	40.9	40.0	39.2	38.4	37.6	36.9	36.1	35.4
62	47.9	47.0	46.0	45.1	44.2	43.4	42.5	41.6	40.8	39.9	39.1	38.3	37.5	36.7	35.9	35.1
63	47.8	46.9	46.0	45.1	44.2	43.3	42.4	41.5	40.6	39.8	38.9	38.1	37.3	36.5	35.7	34.9
64	47.8	46.8	45.9	45.0	44.1	43.2	42.3	41.4	40.5	39.7	38.8	38.0	37.2	36.3	35.5	34.8
65	47.7	46.8	45.9	44.9	44.0	43.1	42.2	41.3	40.4	39.6	38.7	37.9	37.0	36.2	35.4	34.6
66	47.7	46.7	45.8	44.9	44.0	43.1	42.2	41.3	40.4	39.5	38.6	37.8	36.9	36.1	35.2	34.4
67	47.6	46.7	45.8	44.8	43.9	43.0	42.1	41.2	40.3	39.4	38.5	37.7	36.8	36.0	35.1	34.3
68	47.6	46.7	45.7	44.8	43.9	42.9	42.0	41.1	40.2	39.3	38.4	37.6	36.7	35.8	35.0	34.2
69	47.6	46.6	45.7	44.8	43.8	42.9	42.0	41.1	40.2	39.3	38.4	37.5	36.6	35.7	34.9	34.1
70	47.5	46.6	45.7	44.7	43.8	42.9	41.9	41.0	40.1	39.2	38.3	37.4	36.5	35.7	34.8	34.0
71	47.5	46.6	45.6	44.7	43.8	42.8	41.9	41.0	40.1	39.1	38.2	37.3	36.5	35.6	34.7	33.9
72	47.5	46.6	45.6	44.7	43.7	42.8	41.9	40.9	40.0	39.1	38.2	37.3	36.4	35.5	34.6	33.8
73	47.5	46.5	45.6	44.7	43.7	42.8	41.8	40.9	40.0	39.0	38.1	37.2	36.3	35.4	34.6	33.7
74	47.5	46.5	45.6	44.7	43.7	42.7	41.8	40.9	39.9	39.0	38.1	37.2	36.3	35.4	34.5	33.6
75	47.4	46.5	45.5	44.7	43.6	42.7	41.8	40.8	39.9	39.0	38.1	37.1	36.2	35.3	34.5	33.6
76	47.4	46.5	45.5	44.7	43.6	42.7	41.7	40.8	39.9	38.9	38.0	37.1	36.2	35.3	34.4	33.5
77	47.4	46.5	45.5	44.7	43.6	42.7	41.7	40.8	39.8	38.9	38.0	37.1	36.2	35.3	34.4	33.5
78	47.4	46.4	45.5	44.5	43.6	42.6	41.7	40.7	39.8	38.9	38.0	37.0	36.1	35.2	34.3	33.4
79	47.4	46.4	45.5	44.5	43.6	42.6	41.7	40.7	39.8	38.9	37.9	37.0	36.1	35.2	34.3	33.4

Table VI – Ordinary Joint Life and Last Survivor Annuities – Two Lives – Expected Return Multiples (cont'd)

AGES	35	36	37	38	39	40	41	42	43	44	45	46	47	48	49	50
80	47.4	46.4	45.5	44.5	43.6	42.6	41.7	40.7	39.8	38.8	37.9	37.0	36.1	35.2	34.2	33.4
81	47.4	46.4	45.5	44.5	43.5	42.6	41.6	40.7	39.8	38.8	37.9	37.0	36.0	35.1	34.2	33.3
82	47.4	46.4	45.4	44.5	43.5	42.6	41.6	40.7	39.7	38.8	37.9	36.9	36.0	35.1	34.2	33.3
83	47.4	46.4	45.4	44.5	43.5	42.6	41.6	40.7	39.7	38.8	37.9	36.9	36.0	35.1	34.2	33.3
84	47.4	46.4	45.4	44.5	43.5	42.6	41.6	40.7	39.7	38.8	37.8	36.9	36.0	35.0	34.1	33.2
85	47.4	46.4	45.4	44.5	43.5	42.6	41.6	40.7	39.7	38.8	37.8	36.9	36.0	35.0	34.1	33.2
86	47.3	46.4	45.4	44.5	43.5	42.5	41.6	40.6	39.7	38.8	37.8	36.9	36.0	35.0	34.1	33.2
87	47.3	46.4	45.4	44.5	43.5	42.5	41.6	40.6	39.7	38.7	37.8	36.9	35.9	35.0	34.1	33.2
88	47.3	46.4	45.4	44.5	43.5	42.5	41.6	40.6	39.7	38.7	37.8	36.9	35.9	35.0	34.1	33.2
89	47.3	46.4	45.4	44.4	43.5	42.5	41.6	40.6	39.7	38.7	37.8	36.9	35.9	35.0	34.1	33.2
90	47.3	46.4	45.4	44.4	43.5	42.5	41.6	40.6	39.7	38.7	37.8	36.9	35.9	35.0	34.1	33.2

AGES	51	52	53	54	55	56	57	58	59	60	61	62	63	64	65	66
51	38.2	...	...	...	...	...	...	...	...	...	...	...	...	...	...	...
52	37.8	37.3	...	...	...	...	...	...	...	...	...	...	...	...	...	...
53	37.3	36.8	36.3	...	...	...	...	...	...	...	...	...	...	...	...	...
54	36.9	36.4	35.8	35.3	...	...	...	...	...	...	...	...	...	...	...	...
55	36.5	55.9	35.4	34.9	34.4	...	...	...	...	...	...	...	...	...	...	...
56	36.1	35.6	35.0	34.4	33.9	33.4	...	...	...	...	...	...	...	...	...	...
57	35.8	35.2	34.6	34.0	33.5	33.0	32.5	...	...	...	...	...	...	...	...	...
58	35.5	34.8	34.2	33.6	33.1	32.5	32.0	31.5	...	...	...	...	...	...	...	...
59	35.2	34.5	33.9	33.3	32.7	32.1	31.6	31.1	30.6	...	...	...	...	...	...	...
60	34.9	34.2	33.6	32.9	32.3	31.7	31.2	30.6	30.1	29.7	...	...	...	...	...	...
61	34.6	33.9	33.3	32.6	32.0	31.4	30.8	30.2	29.7	29.2	28.7	...	...	...	...	...
62	34.4	33.7	33.0	32.3	31.7	31.0	30.4	29.9	29.3	28.8	28.3	27.8	...	...	...	...
63	34.2	33.5	32.7	32.0	31.4	30.7	30.1	29.5	28.9	28.4	27.8	27.3	26.9	...	...	...
64	34.0	33.2	32.5	31.8	31.1	30.4	29.8	29.2	28.6	28.0	27.4	26.9	26.4	25.9	...	...
65	33.8	33.0	32.3	31.6	30.9	30.2	29.5	28.9	28.2	27.6	27.1	26.5	26.0	25.5	25.0	...
66	33.6	32.9	32.1	31.4	30.6	29.9	29.2	28.6	27.9	27.3	26.7	26.1	25.6	25.1	24.6	24.1
67	33.5	32.7	31.9	31.2	30.4	29.7	29.0	28.3	27.6	27.0	26.4	25.8	25.2	24.7	24.2	23.7
68	33.4	32.5	31.8	31.0	30.2	29.5	28.8	28.1	27.4	26.7	26.1	25.5	24.9	24.3	23.8	23.3
69	33.2	32.4	31.6	30.8	30.1	29.3	28.6	27.8	27.1	26.5	25.8	25.2	24.6	24.0	23.4	22.9
70	33.1	32.3	31.5	30.7	29.9	29.1	28.4	27.6	26.9	26.2	25.6	24.9	24.3	23.7	23.1	22.5
71	33.0	32.2	31.4	30.5	29.7	29.0	28.2	27.5	26.7	26.0	25.3	24.7	24.0	23.4	22.8	22.2
72	32.9	32.1	31.2	30.4	29.6	28.8	28.1	27.3	26.5	25.8	25.1	24.4	23.8	23.1	22.5	21.9
73	32.8	32.0	31.1	30.3	29.5	28.7	27.9	27.1	26.4	25.6	24.9	24.2	23.5	22.9	22.2	21.6
74	32.8	31.9	31.1	30.2	29.4	28.6	27.8	27.0	26.2	25.5	24.7	24.0	23.3	22.7	22.0	21.4
75	32.7	31.8	31.0	30.1	29.3	28.5	27.7	26.9	26.1	25.3	24.6	23.8	23.1	22.4	21.8	21.1
76	32.6	31.8	30.9	30.1	29.2	28.4	27.6	26.8	26.0	25.2	24.4	23.7	23.0	22.3	21.6	20.9
77	32.6	31.7	30.8	30.0	29.1	28.3	27.5	26.7	25.9	25.1	24.3	23.6	22.8	22.1	21.4	20.7
78	32.5	31.7	30.8	29.9	29.1	28.2	27.4	26.6	25.8	25.0	24.2	23.4	22.7	21.9	21.2	20.5
79	32.5	31.6	30.7	29.9	29.0	28.2	27.3	26.5	25.7	24.9	24.1	23.3	22.6	21.8	21.1	20.4
80	32.5	31.6	30.7	29.8	29.0	28.1	27.3	26.4	25.6	24.8	24.0	23.2	22.4	21.7	21.0	20.2

Table VI – Ordinary Joint Life and Last Survivor Annuities – Two Lives – Expected Return Multiples (cont'd)

AGES	51	52	53	54	55	56	57	58	59	60	61	62	63	64	65	66
81	32.4	31.5	30.7	29.8	28.9	28.1	27.2	26.4	25.5	24.7	23.9	23.1	22.3	21.6	20.8	20.1
82	32.4	31.5	30.6	29.7	28.9	28.0	27.2	26.3	25.5	24.6	23.8	23.0	22.3	21.5	20.7	20.0
83	32.4	31.5	30.6	29.7	28.8	28.0	27.1	26.3	25.4	24.6	23.8	23.0	22.2	21.4	20.6	19.9
84	32.3	31.4	30.6	29.7	28.8	27.9	27.1	26.2	25.4	24.5	23.7	22.9	22.1	21.3	20.5	19.8
85	32.3	31.4	30.5	29.6	28.8	27.9	27.0	26.2	25.3	24.5	23.7	22.8	22.0	21.3	20.5	19.7
86	32.3	31.4	30.5	29.6	28.7	27.9	27.0	26.1	25.3	24.5	23.6	22.8	22.0	21.2	20.4	19.6
87	32.3	31.4	30.5	29.6	28.7	27.8	27.0	26.1	25.3	24.4	23.6	22.8	21.9	21.1	20.4	19.6
88	32.3	31.4	30.5	29.6	28.7	27.8	27.0	26.1	25.2	24.4	23.5	22.7	21.9	21.1	20.3	19.5
89	32.3	31.4	30.5	29.6	28.7	27.8	26.9	26.1	25.2	24.4	23.5	22.7	21.9	21.1	20.3	19.5
90	32.3	31.3	30.5	29.5	28.7	27.8	26.9	26.1	25.2	24.3	23.5	22.7	21.8	21.0	20.2	19.4

AGES	67	68	69	70	71	72	73	74	75	76	77	78	79	80	81	82
67	23.2	...	...	...	...	...	...	...	...	...	...	...	...	...	...	...
68	22.8	22.3	...	...	...	...	...	...	...	...	...	...	...	...	...	...
69	22.4	21.9	21.5	...	...	...	...	...	...	...	...	...	...	...	...	...
70	22.0	21.5	21.1	20.6	...	...	...	...	...	...	...	...	...	...	...	...
71	21.7	21.2	20.7	20.2	19.8	...	...	...	...	...	...	...	...	...	...	...
72	21.3	20.8	20.3	19.8	19.4	18.9	...	...	...	...	...	...	...	...	...	...
73	21.0	20.5	20.0	19.4	19.0	18.5	18.1	...	...	...	...	...	...	...	...	...
74	20.8	20.2	19.6	19.1	18.6	18.2	17.7	17.3	...	...	...	...	...	...	...	...
75	20.5	19.9	19.3	18.8	18.3	17.8	17.3	16.9	16.5	...	...	...	...	...	...	...
76	20.3	19.7	19.1	18.5	18.0	17.5	17.0	16.5	16.1	15.7	...	...	...	...	...	...
77	20.1	19.4	18.8	18.3	17.7	17.2	16.7	16.2	15.8	15.4	15.0	...	...	...	...	...
78	19.9	19.2	18.6	18.0	17.5	16.9	16.4	15.9	15.4	15.0	14.6	14.2	...	...	...	...
79	19.7	19.0	18.4	17.8	17.2	16.7	16.1	15.6	15.1	14.7	14.3	13.9	13.5	...	...	...
80	19.5	18.9	18.2	17.6	17.0	16.4	15.9	15.4	14.9	14.4	14.0	13.5	13.2	12.8	...	...
81	19.4	18.7	18.1	17.4	16.8	16.2	15.7	15.1	14.6	14.1	13.7	13.2	12.8	12.5	12.1	...
82	19.3	18.6	17.9	17.3	16.6	16.0	15.5	14.9	14.4	13.9	13.4	13.0	12.5	12.2	11.8	11.5
83	19.2	18.5	17.8	17.1	16.5	15.9	15.3	14.7	14.2	13.7	13.2	12.7	12.3	11.9	11.5	11.1
84	19.1	18.4	17.7	17.0	16.3	15.7	15.1	14.5	14.0	13.5	13.0	12.5	12.0	11.6	11.2	10.9
85	19.0	18.3	17.6	16.9	16.2	15.6	15.0	14.4	13.8	13.3	12.8	12.3	11.8	11.4	11.0	10.6
86	18.9	18.2	17.5	16.8	16.1	15.5	14.8	14.2	13.7	13.1	12.6	12.1	11.6	11.2	10.8	10.4
87	18.8	18.1	17.4	16.7	16.0	15.4	14.7	14.1	13.5	13.0	12.4	11.9	11.4	11.0	10.6	10.1
88	18.8	18.0	17.3	16.6	15.9	15.3	14.6	14.0	13.4	12.8	12.3	11.8	11.3	10.8	10.4	10.0
89	18.7	18.0	17.2	16.5	15.8	15.2	14.5	13.9	13.3	12.7	12.2	11.6	11.1	10.7	10.2	9.8
90	18.7	17.9	17.2	16.5	15.8	15.1	14.5	13.8	13.2	12.6	12.1	11.5	11.0	10.5	10.1	9.6

AGES	83	84	85	86	87	88	89	90
83	10.8	...	...	...	...	...	...	...
84	10.5	10.2	...	...	...	...	...	...
85	10.2	9.9	9.6	...	...	...	...	...
86	10.0	9.7	9.3	9.1	...	...	...	...
87	9.8	9.4	9.1	8.8	8.5	...	...	...
88	9.6	9.2	8.9	8.6	8.3	8.0	...	...
89	9.4	9.0	8.7	8.3	8.1	7.8	7.5	...
90	9.2	8.8	8.5	8.2	7.9	7.6	7.3	7.1

Table VIA – Annuities for Joint Life Only –
Two Lives – Expected Return Multiples

AGES	35	36	37	38	39	40	41	42	43	44	45	46	47	48	49	50
35	40.7	...	...	...	...	...	...	...	...	...	...	...	...	...	...	...
36	40.2	39.7	...	...	...	...	...	...	...	...	...	...	...	...	...	...
37	39.7	39.3	38.8	...	...	...	...	...	...	...	...	...	...	...	...	...
38	39.2	38.7	38.3	37.9	...	...	...	...	...	...	...	...	...	...	...	...
39	38.6	38.2	37.8	37.4	36.9	...	...	...	...	...	...	...	...	...	...	...
40	38.0	37.7	37.3	36.9	36.4	36.0	...	...	...	...	...	...	...	...	...	...
41	37.4	37.1	36.7	36.3	35.9	35.5	35.1	...	...	...	...	...	...	...	...	...
42	36.8	36.5	36.2	35.8	35.4	35.0	34.6	34.1	...	...	...	...	...	...	...	...
43	36.2	35.9	35.6	35.2	34.9	34.5	34.1	33.7	33.2	...	...	...	...	...	...	...
44	35.5	35.2	34.9	34.6	34.3	34.0	33.6	33.2	32.8	32.3	...	...	...	...	...	...
45	34.8	34.6	34.3	34.0	33.7	33.4	33.0	32.7	32.3	31.8	31.4	...	...	...	...	...
46	34.1	33.9	33.7	33.4	33.1	32.8	32.5	32.1	31.8	31.4	30.9	30.5	...	...	...	...
47	33.4	33.2	33.0	32.8	32.5	32.2	31.9	31.6	31.2	30.8	30.5	30.0	29.6	...	...	...
48	32.7	32.5	32.3	32.1	31.8	31.6	31.3	31.0	30.7	30.3	30.0	29.6	29.2	28.7	...	...
49	32.0	31.8	31.6	31.4	31.2	30.9	30.7	30.4	30.1	29.8	29.4	29.1	28.7	28.3	27.9	...
50	31.3	31.1	30.9	30.7	30.5	30.3	30.0	29.8	29.5	29.2	28.9	28.5	28.2	27.4	27.4	27.0
51	30.5	30.4	30.2	30.0	29.8	29.6	29.4	29.2	28.9	28.6	28.3	28.0	27.7	27.3	26.9	26.5
52	29.7	29.6	29.5	29.3	29.1	28.9	28.7	28.5	28.3	28.0	27.7	27.4	27.1	26.8	26.5	26.1
53	29.0	28.9	28.7	28.6	28.4	28.2	28.1	27.9	27.6	27.4	27.1	26.9	26.6	26.3	25.9	25.6
54	28.2	28.1	28.0	27.8	27.7	27.5	27.4	27.2	27.0	26.8	26.5	26.3	26.0	25.7	25.4	25.1
55	27.4	27.3	27.2	27.1	27.0	26.8	26.7	26.5	26.3	26.1	25.9	25.7	25.4	25.1	24.9	24.6
56	26.7	26.6	26.5	26.3	26.2	26.1	26.0	25.8	25.6	25.4	25.2	25.0	24.8	24.6	24.3	24.0
57	25.9	25.8	25.7	25.6	25.3	25.4	25.2	25.1	24.9	24.8	24.6	24.4	24.2	24.0	23.7	23.5
58	25.1	25.0	24.9	24.8	24.7	24.6	24.5	24.4	24.2	24.1	23.9	23.7	23.5	23.3	23.1	22.9
59	24.3	24.2	24.1	24.1	24.0	23.9	23.8	23.6	23.3	23.4	23.2	23.1	22.9	22.7	22.5	22.3
60	23.5	23.4	23.4	23.3	23.2	23.1	23.0	22.9	22.8	22.7	22.5	22.4	22.2	22.1	21.9	21.7
61	22.7	22.6	22.6	22.5	22.4	22.4	22.3	22.2	22.1	22.0	21.8	21.7	21.6	21.4	21.2	21.1
62	21.9	21.9	21.8	21.7	21.7	21.6	21.5	21.4	21.3	21.2	21.1	21.0	20.9	20.7	20.6	20.4
63	21.1	21.1	21.0	21.0	20.9	20.8	20.8	20.7	20.6	20.5	20.4	20.3	20.2	20.1	19.9	19.8
64	20.3	20.3	20.2	20.2	20.1	20.1	20.0	20.0	19.9	19.8	19.7	19.6	19.5	19.4	19.3	19.1
65	19.6	19.5	19.5	19.4	19.4	19.3	19.3	19.2	19.1	19.1	19.0	18.9	18.8	18.7	18.6	18.5
66	18.8	18.8	18.7	18.7	18.6	18.6	18.5	18.5	18.4	18.4	18.3	18.2	18.1	18.0	17.9	17.8
67	18.0	18.0	18.0	17.9	17.9	17.9	17.8	17.8	17.7	17.6	17.6	17.5	17.4	17.3	17.3	17.2
68	17.3	17.3	17.2	17.2	17.2	17.1	17.1	17.0	17.0	16.9	16.9	16.8	16.7	16.7	16.6	16.5
69	16.5	16.5	16.5	16.5	16.4	16.4	16.4	16.3	16.3	16.2	16.2	16.1	16.1	16.0	15.9	15.8
70	15.8	15.8	15.8	15.7	15.7	15.7	15.6	15.6	15.6	15.5	15.5	15.4	15.4	15.3	15.3	15.2
71	15.1	15.1	15.1	15.0	15.0	15.0	15.0	14.9	14.9	14.9	14.8	14.8	14.7	14.7	14.6	14.5
72	14.4	14.4	14.4	14.3	14.3	14.3	14.3	14.2	14.2	14.2	14.1	14.1	14.1	14.0	14.0	13.9
73	13.7	13.7	13.7	13.7	13.7	13.6	13.6	13.6	13.6	13.5	13.5	13.5	13.4	13.4	13.3	13.3
74	13.1	13.0	13.0	13.0	13.0	13.0	13.0	12.9	12.9	12.9	12.8	12.8	12.8	12.7	12.7	12.7

Table VIA – Annuities for Joint Life Only – Two Lives – Expected Return Multiples (cont'd)

AGES	35	36	37	38	39	40	41	42	43	44	45	46	47	48	49	50
75	12.4	12.4	12.4	12.4	12.3	12.3	12.3	12.3	12.3	12.2	12.2	12.2	12.2	12.1	12.1	12.1
76	11.8	11.8	11.7	11.7	11.7	11.7	11.7	11.7	11.6	11.6	11.6	11.6	11.6	11.5	11.5	11.5
77	11.1	11.1	11.1	11.1	11.1	11.1	11.1	11.1	11.0	11.0	11.0	11.0	11.0	10.9	10.9	10.9
78	10.5	10.5	10.5	10.5	10.5	10.5	10.5	10.5	10.5	10.4	10.4	10.4	10.4	10.4	10.3	10.3
79	10.0	10.0	9.9	9.9	9.9	9.9	9.9	9.9	9.9	9.9	9.9	9.8	9.8	9.8	9.8	9.8
80	9.4	9.4	9.4	9.4	9.4	9.4	9.4	9.3	9.3	9.3	9.3	9.3	9.3	9.3	9.2	9.2
81	8.9	8.8	8.8	8.8	8.8	8.8	8.8	8.8	8.8	8.8	8.8	8.8	8.7	8.7	8.7	8.7
82	8.3	8.3	8.3	8.3	8.3	8.3	8.3	8.3	8.3	8.3	8.3	8.2	8.2	8.2	8.2	8.2
83	7.8	7.8	7.8	7.8	7.8	7.8	7.8	7.8	7.6	7.8	7.8	7.8	7.7	7.7	7.7	7.7
84	7.3	7.3	7.3	7.3	7.3	7.3	7.3	7.3	7.3	7.3	7.3	7.3	7.3	7.3	7.3	7.2
85	6.9	6.9	6.9	6.9	6.9	6.9	6.9	6.9	6.9	6.9	6.8	6.8	6.8	6.8	6.8	6.8
86	6.5	6.5	6.5	6.5	6.4	6.4	6.4	6.4	6.4	6.4	6.4	6.4	6.4	6.4	6.4	6.4
87	6.1	6.0	6.0	6.0	6.0	6.0	6.0	6.0	6.0	6.0	6.0	6.0	6.0	6.0	6.0	6.0
88	5.7	5.7	5.7	5.7	5.7	5.7	5.7	5.6	5.6	5.6	5.6	5.6	5.6	5.6	5.6	5.6
89	5.3	5.3	5.3	5.3	5.3	5.3	5.3	5.3	5.3	5.3	5.3	5.3	5.3	5.3	5.3	5.3
90	5.0	5.0	5.0	5.0	5.0	5.0	5.0	5.0	5.0	5.0	5.0	4.9	4.9	4.9	4.9	4.9

AGES	51	52	53	54	55	56	57	58	59	60	61	62	63	64	65	66
51	26.1	...	...	...	...	...	...	...	...	...	...	...	...	...	...	...
52	25.7	25.3	...	...	...	...	...	...	...	...	...	...	...	...	...	...
53	25.2	24.8	24.4	...	...	...	...	...	...	...	...	...	...	...	...	...
54	24.7	24.4	24.0	23.6	...	...	...	...	...	...	...	...	...	...	...	...
55	24.2	23.9	23.5	23.2	22.7	...	...	...	...	...	...	...	...	...	...	...
56	23.7	23.4	23.1	22.7	22.3	21.9	...	...	...	...	...	...	...	...	...	...
57	23.2	22.9	22.6	22.2	21.9	21.5	21.1	...	...	...	...	...	...	...	...	...
58	22.6	22.4	22.1	21.7	21.4	21.1	20.7	20.3	...	...	...	...	...	...	...	...
59	22.1	21.8	21.5	21.2	20.9	20.6	20.3	19.9	19.5	...	...	...	...	...	...	...
60	21.5	21.2	21.0	20.7	20.4	20.1	19.8	19.5	19.1	18.7	...	...	...	...	...	...
61	20.9	20.6	20.4	20.2	19.9	19.6	19.3	19.0	18.7	18.3	17.9	...	...	...	...	...
62	20.2	20.0	19.8	19.6	19.4	19.1	18.8	18.5	18.2	17.9	17.5	17.1	...	...	...	...
63	19.6	19.4	19.2	19.0	18.8	18.6	18.3	18.0	17.7	17.4	17.1	16.8	16.4	...	...	...
64	19.0	18.8	18.6	18.5	18.3	18.0	17.8	17.5	17.3	17.0	16.7	16.3	16.0	15.6	...	...
65	18.3	18.2	18.0	17.9	17.7	17.5	17.3	17.0	16.8	16.5	16.2	15.9	15.6	15.3	14.9	...
66	17.7	17.6	17.4	17.3	17.1	16.9	16.7	16.5	16.3	16.0	15.8	15.5	15.2	14.9	14.5	14.2
67	17.1	16.9	16.8	16.7	16.5	16.3	16.2	16.0	15.8	15.5	15.3	15.0	14.7	14.5	14.1	13.8
68	16.4	16.3	16.2	16.1	15.9	15.8	15.6	15.4	15.2	15.0	14.8	14.6	14.3	14.0	13.7	13.4
69	15.8	15.7	15.6	15.4	15.3	15.2	15.0	14.9	14.7	14.5	14.3	14.1	13.9	13.6	13.3	13.1
70	15.1	15.0	14.9	14.8	14.7	14.6	14.5	14.3	14.2	14.0	13.8	13.6	13.4	13.2	12.9	12.6
71	14.5	14.4	14.3	14.2	14.1	14.0	13.9	13.8	13.6	13.5	13.3	13.1	12.9	12.7	12.5	12.2
72	13.8	13.8	13.7	13.6	13.5	13.4	13.3	13.2	13.1	12.9	12.8	12.6	12.4	12.3	12.0	11.8
73	13.2	13.2	13.1	13.0	13.0	12.9	12.8	12.7	12.5	12.4	12.3	12.1	12.0	11.8	11.6	11.4
74	12.6	12.6	12.5	12.4	12.4	12.3	12.2	12.1	12.0	11.9	11.8	11.6	11.5	11.3	11.2	11.0
75	12.0	12.0	11.9	11.9	11.8	11.7	11.7	11.6	11.5	11.4	11.3	11.1	11.0	10.9	10.7	10.5

Table VIA – Annuities for Joint Life Only – Two Lives – Expected Return Multiples (cont'd)

AGES	51	52	53	54	55	56	57	58	59	60	61	62	63	64	65	66
76	11.4	11.4	11.3	11.3	11.2	11.2	11.1	11.0	10.9	10.9	10.8	10.6	10.5	10.4	10.3	10.1
77	10.8	10.8	10.8	10.7	10.7	10.6	10.6	10.5	10.4	10.3	10.3	10.2	10.0	9.9	9.8	9.7
78	10.3	10.2	10.2	10.2	10.1	10.1	10.0	10.0	9.9	9.8	9.8	9.7	9.6	9.5	9.4	9.2
79	9.7	9.7	9.7	9.6	9.6	9.6	9.5	9.5	9.4	9.3	9.3	9.2	9.1	9.0	8.9	8.8
80	9.2	9.2	9.1	9.1	9.1	9.0	9.0	9.0	8.9	8.9	8.8	8.7	8.7	8.6	8.5	8.4
81	8.7	8.7	8.6	8.6	8.6	8.5	8.5	8.5	8.4	8.4	8.3	8.3	8.2	8.1	8.0	8.0
82	8.2	8.2	8.1	8.1	8.1	8.1	8.0	8.0	8.0	7.9	7.9	7.8	7.8	7.7	7.6	7.5
83	7.7	7.7	7.7	7.6	7.6	7.6	7.6	7.5	7.5	7.5	7.4	7.4	7.3	7.3	7.2	7.1
84	7.2	7.2	7.2	7.2	7.2	7.1	7.1	7.1	7.1	7.0	7.0	7.0	6.9	6.9	6.8	6.7
85	6.8	6.8	6.8	6.7	6.7	6.7	6.7	6.7	6.6	6.6	6.6	6.5	6.5	6.5	6.4	6.4
86	6.4	6.4	6.3	6.3	6.3	6.3	6.3	6.3	6.2	6.2	6.2	6.2	6.1	6.1	6.0	6.0
87	6.0	6.0	6.0	5.9	5.9	5.9	5.9	5.9	5.9	5.8	5.8	5.8	5.8	5.7	5.7	5.6
88	5.6	5.6	5.6	5.6	5.6	5.5	5.5	5.5	5.5	5.5	5.5	5.5	5.4	5.4	5.3	5.3
89	5.2	5.2	5.2	5.2	5.2	5.2	5.2	5.2	5.2	5.1	5.1	5.1	5.1	5.1	5.0	5.0
90	4.9	4.9	4.9	4.9	4.9	4.9	4.9	4.9	4.9	4.8	4.8	4.8	4.8	4.8	4.7	4.7

AGES	67	68	69	70	71	72	73	74	75	76	77	78	79	80	81	82
67	13.5	...	...	...	...	...	...	...	...	...	...	...	...	...	...	...
68	13.1	12.8	...	...	...	...	...	...	...	...	...	...	...	...	...	...
69	12.8	12.5	12.1	...	...	...	...	...	...	...	...	...	...	...	...	...
70	12.4	12.1	11.8	11.5	...	...	...	...	...	...	...	...	...	...	...	...
71	12.0	11.7	11.4	11.2	10.9	...	...	...	...	...	...	...	...	...	...	...
72	11.6	11.4	11.1	10.8	10.5	10.2	...	...	...	...	...	...	...	...	...	...
73	11.2	11.0	10.7	10.5	10.2	9.9	9.7	...	...	...	...	...	...	...	...	...
74	10.8	10.6	10.4	10.1	9.9	9.6	9.4	9.1	...	...	...	...	...	...	...	...
75	10.4	10.2	10.0	9.8	9.5	9.3	9.1	8.8	8.6	...	...	...	...	...	...	...
76	9.9	9.8	9.6	9.4	9.2	9.0	8.8	8.5	8.3	8.0	...	...	...	...	...	...
77	9.5	9.4	9.2	9.0	8.8	8.6	8.4	8.2	8.0	7.8	7.5	...	...	...	...	...
78	9.1	9.0	8.8	8.7	8.5	8.3	8.1	7.9	7.7	7.5	7.3	7.0	...	...	...	...
79	8.7	8.6	8.4	8.3	8.1	8.0	7.8	7.6	7.4	7.2	7.0	6.8	6.6	...	...	...
80	8.3	8.2	8.0	7.9	7.8	7.6	7.5	7.3	7.1	6.9	6.8	6.6	6.3	6.1	...	...
81	7.9	7.9	7.7	7.5	7.4	7.3	7.1	7.0	6.8	6.7	6.5	6.3	6.1	5.9	5.7	...
82	7.5	7.4	7.3	7.2	7.1	6.9	6.6	6.7	6.5	6.4	6.2	6.0	5.9	5.7	5.5	5.3
83	7.1	7.0	6.9	6.8	6.7	6.6	6.5	6.4	6.2	6.1	5.9	5.8	5.6	5.5	5.3	5.1
84	6.7	6.6	6.5	6.4	6.4	6.3	6.2	6.0	5.9	5.8	5.7	5.5	5.4	5.2	5.1	4.9
85	6.3	6.2	6.2	6.1	6.0	5.9	5.8	5.7	5.6	5.5	5.4	5.3	5.2	5.0	4.9	4.7
86	5.9	5.9	5.8	5.8	5.7	5.6	5.5	5.4	5.4	5.3	5.1	5.0	4.9	4.8	4.7	4.5
87	5.6	5.6	5.5	5.4	5.4	5.3	5.2	5.2	5.1	5.0	4.9	4.8	4.7	4.6	4.4	4.3
88	5.3	5.2	5.2	5.1	5.1	5.0	5.0	4.9	4.8	4.7	4.6	4.5	4.4	4.3	4.2	4.1
89	5.0	4.9	4.9	4.8	4.8	4.7	4.7	4.6	4.5	4.5	4.4	4.3	4.2	4.1	4.0	3.9
90	4.7	4.6	4.6	4.6	4.5	4.5	4.4	4.4	4.3	4.2	4.2	4.1	4.0	3.9	3.8	3.8

Table VIA – Annuities for Joint Life Only – Two Lives – Expected Return Multiples (cont'd)

AGES	83	84	85	86	87	88	89	90
83	4.9	...	...	...	...	...	...	...
84	4.7	4.6	...	...	...	...	...	...
85	4.6	4.4	4.2	...	...	...	...	...
86	4.4	4.2	4.1	3.9	...	...	...	...
87	4.2	4.1	3.9	3.8	3.6	...	...	...
88	4.0	3.9	3.8	3.6	3.5	3.4	...	...
89	3.8	3.7	3.6	3.5	3.4	3.2	3.1	...
90	3.7	3.5	3.4	3.3	3.2	3.1	3.0	2.9

Table VII – Percent Value of Refund Feature
Duration of Guaranteed Amount

Age	1 Yr.	2 Yrs.	3 Yrs.	4 Yrs.	5 Yrs.	6 Yrs.	7 Yrs.	8 Yrs.	9 Yrs.	10 Yrs.	11 Yrs.	12 Yrs.	13 Yrs.	14 Yrs.	15 Yrs.	16 Yrs.	17 Yrs.	18 Yrs.	19 Yrs.	20 Yrs.
19	...	...	...	...	...	...	...	...	...	...	...	...	...	...	...	...	...	...	...	...
20	...	...	...	...	...	...	...	...	...	...	...	...	...	...	...	...	...	...	...	1
21	...	...	...	...	...	...	...	...	...	...	...	...	...	...	...	...	...	...	...	1
22	...	...	...	...	...	...	...	...	...	...	...	...	...	...	...	...	...	...	...	1
23	...	...	...	...	...	...	...	...	...	...	...	...	...	...	...	...	...	1	1	1
24	...	...	...	...	...	...	...	...	...	...	...	...	...	...	...	...	...	1	1	1
25	...	...	...	...	...	...	...	...	...	...	...	...	...	...	...	...	1	1	1	1
26	...	...	...	...	...	...	...	...	...	...	...	...	...	...	...	...	1	1	1	1
27	...	...	...	...	...	...	...	...	...	...	...	...	...	...	...	1	1	1	1	1
28	...	...	...	...	...	...	...	...	...	...	...	...	...	...	...	1	1	1	1	1
29	...	...	...	...	...	...	...	...	...	...	...	...	...	...	1	1	1	1	1	1
30	...	...	...	...	...	...	...	...	...	...	...	...	...	1	1	1	1	1	1	1
31	...	...	...	...	...	...	...	...	...	...	...	...	...	1	1	1	1	1	1	1
32	...	...	...	...	...	...	...	...	...	...	...	...	...	1	1	1	1	1	1	1
33	...	...	...	...	...	...	...	...	...	...	...	...	1	1	1	1	1	1	1	1
34	...	...	...	...	...	...	...	...	...	...	...	1	1	1	1	1	1	1	1	1
35	...	...	...	...	...	...	...	...	...	...	...	1	1	1	1	1	1	1	1	1
36	...	...	...	...	...	...	...	...	...	...	1	1	1	1	1	1	1	1	1	1
37	...	...	...	...	...	...	...	...	...	1	1	1	1	1	1	1	1	1	1	1
38	...	...	...	...	...	...	...	...	1	1	1	1	1	1	1	1	1	1	1	2
39	...	...	...	...	...	...	...	...	1	1	1	1	1	1	1	1	1	1	2	2
40	...	...	...	...	...	...	...	1	1	1	1	1	1	1	1	1	1	1	2	2
41	...	...	...	...	...	...	...	1	1	1	1	1	1	1	1	1	1	2	2	2
42	...	...	...	...	...	...	1	1	1	1	1	1	1	1	1	1	1	2	2	2
43	...	...	...	...	...	...	1	1	1	1	1	1	1	1	1	1	2	2	2	3
44	...	...	...	...	...	1	1	1	1	1	1	1	1	1	1	2	2	2	3	3
45	...	...	...	...	...	1	1	1	1	1	1	1	1	1	2	2	2	3	3	3
46	...	...	...	...	1	1	1	1	1	1	1	1	1	2	2	2	3	3	3	3
47	...	...	...	...	1	1	1	1	1	1	1	1	1	2	2	2	3	3	3	4
48	...	...	...	...	1	1	1	1	1	1	1	1	2	2	2	2	3	3	4	4

Table VII – Percent Value of Refund Feature
Duration of Guaranteed Amount (cont'd)

Age	1 Yr.	2 Yrs.	3 Yrs.	4 Yrs.	5 Yrs.	6 Yrs.	7 Yrs.	8 Yrs.	9 Yrs.	10 Yrs.	11 Yrs.	12 Yrs.	13 Yrs.	14 Yrs.	15 Yrs.	16 Yrs.	17 Yrs.	18 Yrs.	19 Yrs.	20 Yrs.
49	...	...	...	1	1	1	1	1	1	2	2	2	2	2	3	3	3	4	4	4
50	...	...	...	1	1	1	1	1	1	2	2	2	2	3	3	3	3	4	4	5
51	...	...	...	1	1	1	1	1	2	2	2	2	3	3	3	3	4	4	5	5
52	...	...	...	1	1	1	1	1	2	2	2	2	3	3	3	4	4	5	5	5
53	...	...	1	1	1	1	1	2	2	2	2	3	3	3	4	4	5	5	5	6
54	...	...	1	1	1	1	2	2	2	3	3	3	4	4	4	5	5	5	6	7
55	...	...	1	1	1	2	2	2	3	3	3	4	4	4	5	5	6	6	7	7
56	...	...	1	1	1	1	2	2	2	3	3	3	4	4	5	5	6	7	7	8
57	...	...	1	1	1	2	2	2	3	3	3	4	4	5	5	6	6	7	8	9
58	...	1	1	1	1	2	2	2	3	3	4	4	5	5	6	6	7	8	9	9
59	...	1	1	1	1	2	2	3	3	4	4	5	5	6	6	7	8	9	9	10
60	...	1	1	1	2	2	2	3	3	4	4	5	6	6	7	8	9	10	10	11
61	...	1	1	1	2	2	3	3	4	4	5	6	6	7	8	9	10	10	11	13
62	...	1	1	2	2	2	3	4	4	5	5	6	7	8	9	10	11	12	13	14
63	...	1	1	2	2	3	3	4	5	5	6	7	8	9	10	11	12	13	14	15
64	...	1	1	2	2	3	4	4	5	6	7	8	8	9	10	12	13	14	15	17
65	...	1	2	2	3	3	4	5	6	6	7	8	9	10	12	13	14	15	17	18
66	1	1	2	2	3	4	5	5	6	7	8	9	10	12	13	14	15	17	18	20
67	1	1	2	3	3	4	5	6	7	8	9	10	11	13	14	15	17	18	20	22
68	1	1	2	3	4	5	6	7	8	9	10	11	13	14	15	17	19	20	22	24
69	1	1	2	3	4	5	6	7	8	10	11	12	14	15	17	19	20	22	24	26
70	1	2	3	4	5	6	7	8	9	11	12	14	15	17	19	20	22	24	26	28
71	1	2	3	4	5	6	8	9	10	12	13	15	17	18	20	22	24	26	28	30
72	1	2	3	4	6	7	8	10	11	13	15	17	18	20	22	24	26	28	30	32
73	1	2	4	5	6	8	9	11	13	14	16	18	20	22	24	26	28	31	33	35
74	1	3	4	5	7	9	10	12	14	16	18	20	22	24	26	28	31	33	35	37
75	1	3	4	6	8	9	11	13	15	17	19	22	24	26	28	31	33	35	38	40
76	2	3	5	7	9	10	12	15	17	19	21	24	26	28	31	33	36	38	40	43
77	2	4	5	7	9	12	14	16	18	21	23	26	28	31	33	36	38	41	43	45
78	2	4	6	8	10	13	15	18	20	23	25	28	31	33	36	38	41	43	46	48
79	2	4	7	9	11	14	17	19	22	25	28	30	33	36	38	41	44	46	48	51
80	2	5	7	10	13	15	18	21	24	27	30	33	36	38	41	44	46	49	51	53
81	3	5	8	11	14	17	20	23	26	29	32	35	38	41	44	47	48	51	54	56
82	3	6	9	12	15	19	22	25	28	32	35	38	41	44	47	49	52	54	56	58
83	3	7	10	13	17	20	24	27	31	34	38	41	44	47	49	52	54	57	59	61
84	4	7	11	15	19	22	26	30	33	37	40	44	47	49	52	55	57	59	61	63
85	4	8	12	16	20	24	28	32	36	40	43	46	49	52	55	57	59	62	63	65
86	4	9	13	18	22	27	31	35	39	42	46	49	52	55	57	60	62	64	66	67
87	5	10	15	20	24	29	33	37	41	45	48	52	55	57	60	62	64	66	68	69
88	5	11	16	21	26	31	36	40	44	48	51	54	57	60	62	64	66	68	70	71
89	6	12	18	23	28	33	38	43	47	50	54	57	60	62	65	67	68	70	72	73
90	7	13	19	25	31	36	41	45	49	53	56	59	62	64	67	69	70	72	74	75

Table VII – Percent Value of Refund Feature
Duration of Guaranteed Amount (cont'd)

Age	21 Yr.	22 Yrs.	23 Yrs.	24 Yrs.	25 Yrs.	26 Yrs.	27 Yrs.	28 Yrs.	29 Yrs.	30 Yrs.	31 Yrs.	32 Yrs.	33 Yrs.	34 Yrs.	35 Yrs.	36 Yrs.	37 Yrs.	38 Yrs.	39 Yrs.	40 Yrs.
5	…	…	…	…	…	…	…	…	…	…	…	1	1	1	1	1	1	1	1	1
6	…	…	…	…	…	…	…	…	…	…	…	1	1	1	1	1	1	1	1	1
7	…	…	…	…	…	…	…	…	…	…	1	1	1	1	1	1	1	1	1	1
8	…	…	…	…	…	…	…	…	…	1	1	1	1	1	1	1	1	1	1	1
9	…	…	…	…	…	…	…	…	…	1	1	1	1	1	1	1	1	1	1	1
10	…	…	…	…	…	…	…	1	1	1	1	1	1	1	1	1	1	1	1	1
11	…	…	…	…	…	…	1	1	1	1	1	1	1	1	1	1	1	1	1	1
12	…	…	…	…	…	…	1	1	1	1	1	1	1	1	1	1	1	1	1	1
13	…	…	…	…	…	1	1	1	1	1	1	1	1	1	1	1	1	1	1	1
14	…	…	…	…	1	1	1	1	1	1	1	1	1	1	1	1	1	1	1	1
15	…	…	…	1	1	1	1	1	1	1	1	1	1	1	1	1	1	1	1	1
16	…	…	1	1	1	1	1	1	1	1	1	1	1	1	1	1	1	1	1	1
17	…	…	1	1	1	1	1	1	1	1	1	1	1	1	1	1	1	1	1	1
18	…	1	1	1	1	1	1	1	1	1	1	1	1	1	1	1	1	1	1	2
19	1	1	1	1	1	1	1	1	1	1	1	1	1	1	1	1	1	1	2	2
20	1	1	1	1	1	1	1	1	1	1	1	1	1	1	1	1	1	2	2	2
21	1	1	1	1	1	1	1	1	1	1	1	1	1	1	1	1	2	2	2	2
22	1	1	1	1	1	1	1	1	1	1	1	1	1	1	2	2	2	2	2	2
23	1	1	1	1	1	1	1	1	1	1	1	1	1	2	2	2	2	2	2	2
24	1	1	1	1	1	1	1	1	1	1	1	1	2	2	2	2	2	2	2	2
25	1	1	1	1	1	1	1	1	1	1	1	2	2	2	2	2	2	2	3	3
26	1	1	1	1	1	1	1	1	1	1	2	2	2	2	2	2	2	3	3	3
27	1	1	1	1	1	1	1	1	1	2	2	2	2	2	2	2	3	3	3	3
28	1	1	1	1	1	1	1	1	2	2	2	2	2	2	2	3	3	3	3	3
29	1	1	1	1	1	1	1	2	2	2	2	2	2	2	3	3	3	3	3	4
30	1	1	1	1	1	1	2	2	2	2	2	2	2	3	3	3	3	3	4	4
31	1	1	1	1	1	2	2	2	2	2	2	2	3	3	3	3	3	4	4	4
32	1	1	1	1	2	2	2	2	2	2	2	3	3	3	3	3	4	4	4	5
33	1	1	1	2	2	2	2	2	2	2	3	3	3	3	3	4	4	4	5	5
34	1	1	2	2	2	2	2	2	2	3	3	3	3	3	4	4	4	5	5	5
35	1	2	2	2	2	2	2	2	3	3	3	3	3	4	4	4	5	5	5	6
36	2	2	2	2	2	2	2	3	3	3	3	4	4	4	4	5	5	5	6	6
37	2	2	2	2	2	2	3	3	3	3	4	4	4	4	5	5	6	6	6	7
38	2	2	2	2	2	3	3	3	3	4	4	4	5	5	5	6	6	7	7	8
39	2	2	2	2	3	3	3	3	4	4	4	5	5	5	6	6	7	7	8	8
40	2	2	3	3	3	3	3	4	4	4	5	5	5	6	6	7	7	8	8	9
41	2	3	3	3	3	3	4	4	4	5	5	5	6	6	7	7	8	9	9	10
42	3	3	3	3	3	4	4	4	5	5	6	6	6	7	7	8	9	9	10	11
43	3	3	3	4	4	4	4	5	5	6	6	7	7	8	8	9	9	10	11	12
44	3	3	4	4	4	4	5	5	6	6	7	7	8	8	9	10	10	11	12	13
45	3	4	4	4	5	5	5	6	6	7	7	8	8	9	10	10	11	12	13	14
46	4	4	4	5	5	5	6	6	7	7	8	9	9	10	11	11	12	13	14	15
47	4	4	5	5	5	6	6	7	7	8	9	9	10	11	12	12	13	14	15	16
48	4	5	5	5	6	6	7	7	8	9	9	10	11	12	13	14	15	16	17	18
49	5	5	5	6	6	7	8	8	9	10	10	11	12	13	14	15	16	17	18	19

Table VII – Percent Value of Refund Feature
Duration of Guaranteed Amount (cont'd)

Age	21 Yr.	22 Yrs.	23 Yrs.	24 Yrs.	25 Yrs.	26 Yrs.	27 Yrs.	28 Yrs.	29 Yrs.	30 Yrs.	31 Yrs.	32 Yrs.	33 Yrs.	34 Yrs.	35 Yrs.	36 Yrs.	37 Yrs.	38 Yrs.	39 Yrs.	40 Yrs.
50	5	5	6	6	7	8	8	9	10	10	11	12	13	14	15	16	17	18	20	21
51	5	6	6	7	8	8	9	10	11	11	12	13	14	15	16	17	19	20	21	22
52	6	7	7	8	8	9	10	11	11	12	13	14	15	17	18	19	20	21	23	24
53	7	7	8	8	9	10	11	12	13	14	15	16	17	18	19	20	22	23	24	26
54	7	8	8	9	10	11	12	13	14	15	16	17	18	19	21	22	23	25	26	28
55	8	9	9	10	11	12	13	14	15	16	17	18	20	21	22	24	25	27	28	30
56	9	9	10	11	12	13	14	15	16	18	19	20	21	23	24	26	27	29	30	32
57	9	10	11	12	13	14	15	17	18	19	20	22	23	25	26	28	29	31	32	34
58	10	11	12	13	14	16	17	18	19	21	22	24	25	27	28	30	31	33	34	36
59	11	12	13	15	16	17	18	20	21	22	24	25	27	28	30	32	33	35	36	38
60	12	14	15	16	17	19	20	21	23	24	26	27	29	31	32	34	35	37	38	40
61	14	15	16	17	19	20	22	23	25	26	28	29	31	33	34	36	37	39	40	42
62	15	16	18	19	20	22	23	25	27	28	30	32	33	35	36	38	40	41	42	44
63	16	18	19	21	22	24	25	27	29	30	32	34	35	37	39	40	42	43	45	46
64	18	19	21	23	24	26	28	29	31	33	34	36	38	39	41	42	44	45	47	48
65	20	21	23	25	26	28	30	31	33	35	37	38	40	42	43	45	46	47	49	50
66	21	23	25	27	28	30	32	34	35	37	39	41	42	44	45	47	48	50	51	52
67	23	25	27	29	31	32	34	36	38	40	41	43	45	46	48	49	50	52	53	54
68	25	27	29	31	33	35	37	38	40	42	44	45	47	48	50	51	52	54	55	56
69	28	29	31	33	35	37	39	41	43	44	46	48	49	51	52	53	54	56	57	58
70	30	32	34	36	38	40	42	43	45	47	48	50	51	53	54	55	57	58	59	60
71	32	34	36	38	40	42	44	46	47	49	51	52	54	55	56	57	59	60	61	62
72	35	37	39	41	43	45	46	48	50	51	53	54	56	57	58	59	60	62	62	63
73	37	39	41	43	45	47	49	51	52	54	55	57	58	59	60	61	62	63	64	65
74	40	42	44	46	48	50	51	53	54	56	57	59	60	61	62	63	64	65	66	67
75	42	44	46	48	50	52	54	55	57	58	59	61	62	63	64	65	66	67	68	69
76	45	47	49	51	53	54	56	58	59	60	62	63	64	65	66	67	68	69	69	70
77	47	50	51	53	55	57	58	60	61	62	64	65	66	67	68	69	70	70	71	72
78	50	52	54	56	57	59	61	62	63	64	66	67	68	69	70	70	71	72	73	73
79	53	55	56	58	60	61	63	64	65	66	67	68	69	70	71	72	73	73	74	75
80	55	57	59	60	62	63	65	66	67	68	69	70	71	72	73	74	74	75	76	76
81	58	59	61	63	64	66	67	68	69	70	71	72	73	74	74	75	76	76	77	78
82	60	62	63	65	66	68	69	70	71	72	73	74	74	75	76	77	77	78	78	79
83	62	64	66	67	68	70	71	72	73	74	74	75	76	77	77	78	79	79	80	80
84	65	66	68	69	70	71	72	73	74	75	76	77	77	78	79	79	80	80	81	81
85	67	68	70	71	72	73	74	75	76	77	78	78	79	79	80	81	81	82	82	83
86	69	70	72	73	74	75	76	77	77	78	79	80	80	81	81	82	82	83	83	84
87	71	72	73	75	76	76	77	78	79	80	80	81	81	82	83	83	83	84	84	85
88	73	74	75	76	77	78	79	80	80	81	82	82	83	83	84	84	85	85	85	86
89	74	76	77	78	79	79	80	81	81	82	83	83	84	84	85	85	85	86	86	87
90	76	77	78	79	80	81	81	82	83	83	84	84	85	85	86	86	86	87	87	87

Suggested Charitable Gift Annuity Rates—Single Life

Approved by the American Council on Gift Annuities on May 7, 2020
Rates effective as of July 1, 2020

Age	Rate	Age	Rate
5-8	1.5	64-65	4.2
9-13	1.6	66	4.3
14-17	1.7	67	4.4
18-21	1.8	68	4.5
22-24	1.9	69	4.6
25-28	2.0	70	4.7
29-30	2.1	71	4.8
31-33	2.2	72	4.9
34-35	2.3	73	5.1
36-37	2.4	74	5.2
38-39	2.5	75	5.4
40-41	2.6	76	5.6
42	2.7	77	5.8
43-44	2.8	78	6.0
45	2.9	79	6.2
46-47	3.0	80	6.5
48	3.1	81	6.7
49	3.2	82	7.0
50	3.3	83	7.2
51	3.4	84	7.4
52	3.5	85	7.6
53-54	3.6	86	7.8
55-56	3.7	87	8.0
57-58	3.8	88	8.2
59-60	3.9	89	8.4
61-62	4.0	90+	8.6
63	4.1		

1. The rates are for ages at the nearest birthday.
2. For immediate gift annuities, these rates will result in a charitable deduction of more than 10% if the CFMR is 0.6% or higher, whatever the payment frequency. If the CFMR is less than 0.6%, the deduction will be less than 10% when annuitants are below certain ages.
3. For deferred gift annuities with longer deferral periods, the rates may not pass the 10% test when the CFMR is low.
4. To avoid adverse tax consequences, the charity should reduce the gift annuity rate to whatever level is necessary to generate a charitable deduction in excess of 10%.

See Q 605 regarding charitable gift annuities.

Source: American Council on Gift Annuities

Suggested Charitable Gift Annuity Rates—
Two Lives – Joint and Survivor

Younger Age	Older Age	Rate	Younger Age	Older Age	Rate
5	5 - 95+	1.3	49	49 - 95+	2.7
6	6 - 95+	1.3	50	50 - 95+	2.7
7	7 - 95+	1.3	51	51 - 52	2.8
8	8 - 95+	1.3	51	53 - 95+	2.9
9	9 - 95+	1.4	52	52 - 56	2.9
10	10 - 95+	1.4	52	57 - 95+	3.0
11	11 - 95+	1.4	53	53 - 55	2.9
12	12 - 95+	1.4	53	56 - 60	3
13	13 - 95+	1.4	53	61 - 95+	3.1
14	14 - 95+	1.5	54	54 - 58	3.0
15	15 - 95+	1.5	54	59 - 95+	3.1
16	16 - 95+	1.5	55	55 - 57	3.1
17	17 - 95+	1.5	55	58 - 62	3.2
18	18 - 95+	1.6	55	63 - 95+	3.3
19	19 - 95+	1.6	56	56 - 60	3.2
20	20 - 95+	1.6	56	61 - 95+	3.3
21	21 - 95+	1.6	57	57 - 58	3.3
22	22 - 95+	1.7	57	59 - 63	3.4
23	23 - 95+	1.7	57	64 - 95+	3.5
24	24 - 95+	1.7	58	58 - 61	3.4
25	25 - 95+	1.7	58	62 - 95+	3.5
26	26 - 95+	1.8	59	59 - 60	3.5
27	27 - 95+	1.8	59	61 - 64	3.6
28	28 - 95+	1.8	59	65 - 95+	3.7
29	29 - 95+	1.8	60	60 - 62	3.6
30	30 - 95+	1.9	60	63 - 95+	3.7
31	31 - 95+	1.9	61	61	3.6
32	32 - 95+	1.9	61	62 - 66	3.7
33	33 - 95+	1.9	61	67 - 95+	3.8
34	34 - 95+	2.0	62	62 - 64	3.7
35	35 - 95+	2.0	62	65 - 95+	3.8
36	36 - 95+	2.0	63	63	3.7
37	37 - 95+	2.1	63	64 - 68	3.8
38	38 - 95+	2.1	63	69 - 95+	3.9
39	39 - 95+	2.2	64	64 - 66	3.8
40	40 - 95+	2.2	64	67 - 71	3.9
41	41 - 95+	2.2	64	72 - 95+	4.0
42	42 - 95+	2.3	65	65	3.8
43	43 - 95+	2.3	65	66 - 69	3.9
44	44 - 95+	2.4	65	70 - 95+	4.0
45	45 - 95+	2.4	66	66 - 67	3.9
46	46 - 95+	2.5	66	68 - 71	4.0
47	47 - 95+	2.5	66	72 - 95+	4.1
48	48 - 95+	2.6	67	67 - 70	4.0

Suggested Charitable Gift Annuity Rates—
Two Lives – Joint and Survivor (cont'd)

Younger Age	Older Age	Rate	Younger Age	Older Age	Rate
67	71 - 74	4.1	76	76 - 77	4.8
67	75 - 95+	4.2	76	78 - 79	4.9
68	68	4.0	76	80	5.0
68	69 - 72	4.1	76	81 - 82	5.1
68	73 - 75	4.2	76	83 - 85	5.2
68	76 - 95+	4.3	76	86 - 88	5.3
69	69 - 70	4.1	76	89 - 95+	5.4
69	71 - 73	4.2	77	77	4.9
69	74 - 77	4.3	77	78 - 79	5.0
69	78 - 95+	4.4	77	80	5.1
70	70 - 72	4.2	77	81 - 82	5.2
70	73 - 75	4.3	77	83 - 84	5.3
70	76 - 78	4.4	77	85 - 86	5.4
70	79 - 95+	4.5	77	87 - 90	5.5
71	71	4.2	77	91 - 95+	5.6
71	72 - 73	4.3	78	78	5.0
71	74 - 76	4.4	78	79	5.1
71	77 - 79	4.5	78	80	5.2
71	80 - 95+	4.6	78	81 - 82	5.3
72	72	4.3	78	83 - 84	5.4
72	73 - 74	4.4	78	85	5.5
72	75 -77	4.5	78	86 - 88	5.6
72	78 - 80	4.6	78	89 - 91	5.7
72	81 - 95+	4.7	78	92 - 95+	5.8
73	73	4.4	79	79	5.2
73	74 - 75	4.5	79	80	5.3
73	76 - 77	4.6	79	81 - 82	5.4
73	78 - 80	4.7	79	83	5.5
73	81 - 83	4.8	79	84 - 85	5.6
73	84 - 95+	4.9	79	86	5.7
74	74	4.5	79	87 - 89	5.8
74	75 - 76	4.6	79	90 - 91	5.9
74	77 - 78	4.7	79	92 - 95+	6.0
74	79 - 80	4.8	80	80	5.4
74	81 - 83	4.9	80	81 - 82	5.5
74	84 - 95+	5.0	80	83	5.6
75	75	4.6	80	84	5.7
75	76	4.7	80	85 - 86	5.8
75	77 - 78	4.8	80	87	5.9
75	79 - 80	4.9	80	88 - 89	6.0
75	81 - 83	5.0	80	90 - 91	6.1
75	84 - 86	5.1	80	92 - 94	6.2
75	87 - 95+	5.2	80	95+	6.3

Suggested Charitable Gift Annuity Rates—
Two Lives – Joint and Survivor (cont'd)

Younger Age	Older Age	Rate	Younger Age	Older Age	Rate
81	81	5.6	84	90	6.9
81	82 - 83	5.7	84	91	7.0
81	84	5.8	84	92	7.1
81	85	5.9	84	93 - 95+	7.2
81	86	6.0	85	85	6.5
81	87	6.1	85	86	6.6
81	88 - 89	6.2	85	87	6.8
81	90 -91	6.3	85	88	6.9
81	92 - 93	6.4	85	89	7.0
81	94 - 95+	6.5	85	90	7.1
82	82	5.8	85	91	7.2
82	83	5.9	85	92	7.3
82	84	6.0	85	93 - 95+	7.4
82	85	6.1	86	86	6.8
82	86 - 87	6.2	86	87	6.9
82	88	6.3	86	88	7.1
82	89	6.4	86	89	7.2
82	90 - 91	6.5	86	90	7.4
82	92	6.6	86	91	7.5
82	93 - 95+	6.7	86	92 - 95+	7.6
83	83	6.0	87	87	7.1
83	84	6.1	87	88	7.3
83	85	6.2	87	89	7.4
83	86	6.3	87	90	7.6
83	87	6.4	87	91	7.7
83	88	6.5	87	92 - 95+	7.8
83	89	6.6	88	88	7.5
83	90	6.7	88	89	7.6
83	91 - 92	6.8	88	90	7.8
83	93	6.9	88	91 - 95+	8.0
83	94 - 95+	7.0	89	89	7.8
84	84	6.2	89	90	8.0
84	85	6.4	89	91 - 95+	8.2
84	86	6.5	90	90	8.2
84	87	6.6	90	91 - 95+	8.4
84	88	6.7	91+	91+	8.4
84	89	6.8			

APPENDIX B

Income Tax Tables

(Tax Years Beginning in 2016 and beyond)

The American Taxpayer Relief Act of 2012 (ATRA) made the income tax brackets put into place under the Economic Growth and Tax Relief Reconciliation Act (EGTRRA) permanent and added a new top tax bracket for certain high income taxpayers. The permanence of the ATRA provisions eliminated much of the uncertainty faced by taxpayers in previous years.

Under ATRA, for tax years beginning after 2012 and before 2018, individual income tax rates are set at 10 percent, 15 percent, 25 percent, 28 percent, 33 percent, 35 percent and 39.6 percent. Under the 2017 Tax Act (Pub. Law No. 115-97), individual income tax rates are set at 10 percent, 12 percent, 22 percent, 24 percent, 32 percent, 35 percent and 37 percent for tax years beginning after 2017 and before 2026.

Individual 2021 Tax Rates

	Taxable Income			
Tax Rate	Single	Married Filing Jointly Including Qualifying Widow(er) with Dependent Child	Married Filing Separately	Head of Household
10%	$0 to $9,950	$0 to $19,900	$0 to $9,950	$0 to $14,200
12%	$9,950-$40,525	$19,900-$81,050	$9,950-$40,525	$14,200-$54,200
22%	$40,525-$86,375	$81,050-$172,750	$40,525-$86,375	$54,200-$86,350
24%	$86,375-$164,925	$172,750-$329,850	$86,375-$164,925	$86,350-$164,900
32%	$164,925-$209,425	$329,850-$418,850	$164,925-$209,425	$164,900-$209,400
35%	$209,425-$523,600	$418,850-$628,300	$209,425-$314,150	$209,400-$523,600
37%	Over $523,600	Over $628,300	Over $314,150	Over $523,600

Estates and Trusts 2021 Tax Rates

Tax Rate	Trusts and Estate Income
10%	$0 to $2,650
$265 plus 24% of the excess over $2,650	$2,650-$9,550
$1,921 plus 35% of the excess over $9,550	$9,550-$13,050
$3,146 plus 37% of the excess over $13,050	Over $13,050

Individual 2020 Tax Rates

Tax Rate	Taxable Income			
	Single	Married Filing Jointly Including Qualifying Widow(er) with Dependent Child	Married Filing Separately	Head of Household
10%	$0 to $9,875	$0 to $19,750	$0 to $9,875	$0 to $14,100
12%	$9,875-$40,100	$19,750-$80,200	$9,875 -$40,100	$14,100-$53,700
22%	$40,100-$85,525	$80,200-$171,050	$40,100-$85,525	$53,700-$85,500
24%	$85,525-$163,300	$171,050-$326,600	$85,525-$163,300	$85,500-$163,300
32%	$163,300-$207,350	$326,600-$414,700	$163,300-$207,350	$163,300-$207,350
35%	$207,350-$518,400	$414,700-$622,050	$207,230-$311,025	$207,350-$518,400
37%	Over $518,400	Over $622,050	Over $311,025	Over $518,400

Estates and Trusts 2020 Tax Rates

Tax Rate	Trusts and Estate Income
10%	$0 to $2,600
$260 plus 24% of the excess over $2,600	$2,600-$9,450
$1,868 plus 35% of the excess over $9,300	$9,450-$12,950
$3,075.50 plus 37% of the excess over $12,750	Over $12,950

Individual 2019 Tax Rates

Tax Rate	Taxable Income			
	Single	Married Filing Jointly Including Qualifying Widow(er) with Dependent Child	Married Filing Separately	Head of Household
10%	$0 to $9,700	$0 to $19,400	$0 to $9,700	$0 to $13,850
12%	$9,700-$39,475	$19,400-$78,950	$9,700-$39,475	$13,850-$52,850
22%	$39,475-$84,200	$78,950-$168,400	$39,475-$84,200	$52,850-$84,200
24%	$84,200-$160,725	$168,400-$321,450	$84,200-$160,725	$84,200-$160,700
32%	$160,725-$204,100	$321,450-$408,200	$160,725-$204,100	$160,700-$204,100
35%	$204,100-$510,300	$408,200-$612,350	$204,100-$306,175	$204,100-$510,300
37%	Over $510,300	Over $612,350	Over $306,175	Over $510,300

Estates and Trusts 2019 Tax Rates

Tax Rate	Trusts and Estate Income
10%	$0 to $2,600
$260 plus 24% of the excess over $2,600	$2,600-$9,300
$1,868 plus 35% of the excess over $9,300	$9,300-$12,750
$3,075.50 plus 37% of the excess over $12,750	Over $12,750

Individual 2018 Tax Rates

		Taxable Income		
Tax Rate	Single	Married Filing Jointly Including Qualifying Widow(er) with Dependent Child	Married Filing Separately	Head of Household
10%	$0 to $9,525	$0 to $19,050	$0 to $9,525	$0 to $13,600
12%	$9,525-$38,700	$19,050-$77,400	$9,525-$38,700	$13,600-$51,800
22%	$38,700-$82,500	$77,400-$165,000	$38,700-$82,500	$51,800-$82,500
24%	$82,500-$157,500	$165,000-$315,000	$82,500-$157,500	$82,500-$157,500
32%	$157,500-$200,000	$315,000-$400,000	$157,500-$200,000	$157,500-$200,000
35%	$200,000-$500,000	$400,000-$600,000	$200,000-$300,000	$200,000-$500,000
37%	Over $500,000	Over $600,000	Over $300,000	Over $500,000

Estates and Trusts 2018 Tax Rates

Tax Rate	Trusts and Estate Income
10%	$0 to $2,550
$255 plus 24% of the excess over $2,550	$2,550-$9,150
$1,839 plus 35% of the excess over $9,150	$9,150-$12,500
$3,011.50 plus 37% of the excess over $12,500	Over $12,500

Corporations

Beginning in 2018, all corporations have a 21percent tax.

2021 Inflation Indexed Amounts

In May, 2020, the IRS announced, in Revenue Procedure 2020-32, these 2021 inflation indexed amounts:

Health Savings Accounts. An HDHP has annual deductible of not less than $1,400 for self-only coverage, $2,800 for family coverage, annual out-of-pocket expenses not exceeding $7,000 for self-only coverage, or $14,000 for family coverage. The maximum annual HSA contribution is $3,600 for self-only coverage and $7,200 for family coverage.

APPENDIX C

Valuation Tables

Note: New valuation tables were issued in 2009. See heading below for effective date and transitional rules.

The value of an annuity, an interest for life or term of years, or a remainder or a reversionary interest, is valued for most income, estate, gift, and generation-skipping transfer tax purposes using the following valuation tables and the current interest rate for the month in which the valuation date occurs. See Q 920. For purposes of these tables, round the age of any person whose life is used to measure an interest to the age of such person on his birthday nearest the valuation date.

Selected single life and term certain factors are provided here. [See Appendix A in *Tax Facts on Investments* for selected unitrust tables.] Both the single life and term certain tables provide factors for remainder interests that can be converted into an income factor or an annuity factor. A remainder interest is converted into an income factor by subtracting the remainder factor from 1. An income factor is converted into an annuity factor by dividing the income factor by the appropriate interest rate for the month.

The value of a remainder or income interest is equal to the principal amount multiplied by the appropriate remainder or income factor.

The value of an annuity payable *annually at the end of each year* is equal to the aggregate payment received during the year multiplied by the annuity factor. If the annuity is payable *other than annually at the end of each period*, the value of an annuity payable annually at the end of each year is adjusted to reflect the more frequent payments by multiplying such value by the appropriate Table A annuity adjustment factor. If an annuity is payable at the *beginning of each period during the life of one individual* (or *until the death of the survivor of two persons*), add the amount of one additional payment to the calculation of the value of an annuity payable at the end of each period. If the annuity is payable at the *beginning of each period during a term certain*, the value of an annuity payable annually at the end of each year is adjusted to reflect the more frequent payments by multiplying such value by the appropriate Table B annuity adjustment factor.

2009 Change in Valuation Tables

The valuation tables underlying Section 7520 were updated with new valuation factors based on Mortality Table 2000CM. The most recent valuation tables are generally effective for valuation dates after April 2009. However, May and June 2009 were transitional months. A person with a valuation date in May or June 2009 could elect to use either the new or the prior valuation tables (based on Table 90CM). If a person was mentally incompetent on May 1, 2009, such person's executor may be able to elect later to use either the new or the prior valuation tables.

If a charitable deduction is involved, a person can use the Section 7520 interest rate for either of the two preceding months or the current month. If a person made a charitable gift during May or June 2009 and elected to use a Section 7520 rate for a month before May 2009, the prior valuation tables must be used. If a person made a charitable gift during May or June 2009 and elected to use a Section 7520 rate for May or June 2009, the person can elect to use either the new or the prior valuation tables. If a person makes a charitable gift after June 2009, the person must use the new valuation tables.

Example Calculations

Example 1. Jack Jones set up a trust funded with $100,000 to provide income to his mother (age 70) for life with remainder to his son, Tom. Assume the valuation table interest rate for the month is 3.0 percent. The factor for the present value of the remainder interest which follows a life estate given to a person age 70 at a 3.0 percent interest rate is .67291 (Single Life Remainder Factors Table). Consequently, Jack has made a gift of $67,291 to Tom ($100,000 × .67291).

The factor for the present value of the income interest given to Jack's mother is .32709 (1 − .67291). Consequently, Jack has made a gift of $32,709 to his mother ($100,000 × .32709). The gift to Jack's mother is a gift of a present interest which may qualify for the annual exclusion.

Example 2. Bob Martin (age 66) transferred property in exchange for a private annuity of $12,000 a year, payable annually at the end of each year for life. Assume the valuation table interest rate for the month is 3.0 percent. The present value of an annuity payable at the end of each year for the life of a person 66 years of age at an interest rate of 3.0 percent is calculated as follows. (1) The remainder factor is .62383 (Single Life Factors Table). (2) The income factor is .37617 (1 − .62383). (3) The annuity factor is 12.5391 (.37617 ÷ 3.0 percent). (4) The present value of the private annuity is $150,469 (12.5391 × $12,000).

If the annuity is payable monthly (i.e., $1,000 per month) at the end of each period, the annuity payable annually at the end of each year as calculated above is adjusted as follows. Multiply the value of the annuity payable annually at the end of each year ($150,469) by an annuity adjustment factor of 1.0137 (Annuity Adjustment Factors Table A). Thus, the value of such an annuity is equal to $152,531 ($150,469 × 1.0137).

If the annuity in either of the two preceding paragraphs is payable at the beginning of the period, add one payment to the value of the annuity calculated above. The value of the $12,000 annual annuity payable at the end of each year is increased to $162,469 ($150,469 + $12,000) if made payable at the beginning of the year. The value of the $1,000 monthly annuity payable at the end of each period is increased to $153,531 ($152,531 + $1,000) if made payable at the beginning of the period.

Example 3. Kim Brown (age 40) transferred property worth $100,000 in exchange for a private annuity payable for her life. Assume the valuation table interest rate for the month is 3.0 percent. To calculate what quarterly payments payable at the beginning of each period should be, the following steps are taken.

1. Calculate the annuity factor for an annuity payable annually at the end of each year during the life of a person 40 years of age at a 3.0 percent interest rate. This factor, 21.9370, is obtained by (a) locating the remainder factor of .34189 in the Single Life Remainder Factors Table, (b) subtracting (a) from 1, and (c) dividing (b) by the interest rate of 3.0 percent.

2. Locate the annuity adjustment factor of 1.0112 from the Annuity Adjustment Factors Table A.

3. Multiply (1) by (2) to obtain a product of 22.1827 (21.9370 × 1.0112).

4. Divide 1 by the number of periodic payments per year (i.e., 1/4, or .25) [if payments at end of period, equals 0].

5.   The sum of (3) and (4) is equal to 22.4327 (22.1827 + .25).

6.   Annuity payments should be $4,458 per year ($100,000 ÷ 22.4327).

7.   Quarterly payments should be $1,114 ($4,458 ÷ 4).

ANNUITY ADJUSTMENT FACTORS TABLE A*

FREQUENCY OF PAYMENTS

INTEREST RATE	ANNUALLY	SEMI ANNUALLY	QUARTERLY	MONTHLY	WEEKLY
1.0%	1.0000	1.0025	1.0037	1.0046	1.0049
1.2%	1.0000	1.0030	1.0045	1.0055	1.0059
1.4%	1.0000	1.0035	1.0052	1.0064	1.0068
1.6%	1.0000	1.0040	1.0060	1.0073	1.0078
1.8%	1.0000	1.0045	1.0067	1.0082	1.0088
2.0%	1.0000	1.0050	1.0075	1.0091	1.0098
2.2%	1.0000	1.0055	1.0082	1.0100	1.0107
2.4%	1.0000	1.0060	1.0090	1.0110	1.0117
2.6%	1.0000	1.0065	1.0097	1.0119	1.0127
2.8%	1.0000	1.0070	1.0104	1.0128	1.0137
3.0%	1.0000	1.0074	1.0112	1.0137	1.0146
3.2%	1.0000	1.0079	1.0119	1.0146	1.0156
3.4%	1.0000	1.0084	1.0127	1.0155	1.0166
3.6%	1.0000	1.0089	1.0134	1.0164	1.0175
3.8%	1.0000	1.0094	1.0141	1.0173	1.0185
4.0%	1.0000	1.0099	1.0149	1.0182	1.0195
4.2%	1.0000	1.0104	1.0156	1.0191	1.0205
4.4%	1.0000	1.0109	1.0164	1.0200	1.0214
4.6%	1.0000	1.0114	1.0171	1.0209	1.0224
4.8%	1.0000	1.0119	1.0178	1.0218	1.0234

*For use in calculating the value of an annuity payable at the end of each period or, if the term of the annuity is determined with respect to one or more lives, an annuity payable at the beginning of each period.

ANNUITY ADJUSTMENT FACTORS TABLE B*

FREQUENCY OF PAYMENTS

INTEREST RATE	ANNUALLY	SEMI ANNUALLY	QUARTERLY	MONTHLY	WEEKLY
1.0%	1.0100	1.0075	1.0062	1.0054	1.0051
1.2%	1.0120	1.0090	1.0075	1.0065	1.0061
1.4%	1.0140	1.0105	1.0087	1.0076	1.0071
1.6%	1.0160	1.0120	1.0100	1.0086	1.0081
1.8%	1.0180	1.0135	1.0112	1.0097	1.0091
2.0%	1.0200	1.0150	1.0125	1.0108	1.0102
2.2%	1.0220	1.0165	1.0137	1.0119	1.0112
2.4%	1.0240	1.0180	1.0150	1.0130	1.0122
2.6%	1.0260	1.0195	1.0162	1.0140	1.0132
2.8%	1.0280	1.0210	1.0174	1.0151	1.0142
3.0%	1.0300	1.0224	1.0187	1.0162	1.0152
3.2%	1.0320	1.0239	1.0199	1.0172	1.0162
3.4%	1.0340	1.0254	1.0212	1.0183	1.0172
3.6%	1.0360	1.0269	1.0224	1.0194	1.0182
3.8%	1.0380	1.0284	1.0236	1.0205	1.0192
4.0%	1.0400	1.0299	1.0249	1.0215	1.0203
4.2%	1.0420	1.0314	1.0261	1.0226	1.0213
4.4%	1.0440	1.0329	1.0274	1.0237	1.0223
4.6%	1.0460	1.0344	1.0286	1.0247	1.0233
4.8%	1.0480	1.0359	1.0298	1.0258	1.0243

*For use in calculating the value of a term certain annuity payable at the beginning of each period.

TERM CERTAIN REMAINDER FACTORS

INTEREST RATE

YEARS	1.0%	1.2%	1.4%	1.6%	1.8%	2.0%	2.2%	2.4%	2.6%	2.8%
1	0.990099	0.988142	.986193	.984252	.982318	.980392	.978474	.976562	.974659	.972763
2	0.980296	0.976425	.972577	.968752	.964949	.961169	.957411	.953674	.949960	.946267
3	0.970590	0.964847	.959149	.953496	.947887	.942322	.936801	.931323	.925887	.920493
4	0.960980	0.953406	.945906	.938480	.931127	.923845	.916635	.909495	.902424	.895422
5	0.951466	0.942101	.932847	.923701	.914663	.905731	.896903	.888178	.879555	.871033
6	0.942045	0.930930	.919967	.909155	.898490	.887971	.877596	.867362	.857266	.847308
7	0.932718	0.919891	.907265	.894837	.882603	.870560	.858705	.847033	.835542	.824230
8	0.923483	0.908983	.894739	.880745	.866997	.853490	.840220	.827181	.814369	.801780
9	0.914340	0.898205	.882386	.866875	.851667	.836755	.822133	.807794	.793732	.779941
10	0.905287	0.887554	.870203	.853224	.836608	.820348	.804435	.788861	.773618	.758698
11	0.896324	0.877030	.858188	.839787	.821816	.804263	.787119	.770372	.754013	.738033
12	0.887449	0.866630	.846339	.826562	.807285	.788493	.770175	.752316	.734906	.717931
13	0.878663	0.856354	.834654	.813545	.793010	.773033	.753596	.734684	.716282	.698376
14	0.869963	0.846200	.823130	.800734	.778989	.757875	.737373	.717465	.698131	.679354
15	0.861349	0.836166	.811766	.788124	.765215	.743015	.721500	.700649	.680440	.660851
16	0.852821	0.826251	.800558	.775712	.751684	.728446	.705969	.684228	.663196	.642851
17	0.844377	0.816453	.789505	.763496	.738393	.714163	.690772	.668191	.646390	.625341
18	0.836017	0.806772	.778604	.751473	.725337	.700159	.675902	.652530	.630010	.608309
19	0.827740	0.797205	.767854	.739639	.712512	.686431	.661352	.637237	.614045	.591740
20	0.819544	0.787752	.757253	.727991	.699914	.672971	.647116	.622302	.598484	.575622
21	0.811430	0.778411	.746798	.716526	.687538	.659776	.633186	.607716	.583318	.559944
22	0.803396	0.769181	.736487	.705242	.675381	.646839	.619556	.593473	.568536	.544693
23	0.795442	0.760061	.726318	.694136	.663439	.634156	.606219	.579563	.554129	.529857
24	0.787566	0.751048	.716290	.683205	.651708	.621722	.593169	.565980	.540087	.515425
25	0.779768	0.742142	.706401	.672446	.640185	.609531	.580400	.552715	.526400	.501386
26	0.772048	0.733342	.696648	.661856	.628866	.597579	.567906	.539761	.513061	.487729
27	0.764404	0.724646	.687029	.651433	.617746	.585862	.555681	.527110	.500059	.474445
28	0.756836	0.716054	.677544	.641174	.606823	.574375	.543720	.514756	.487387	.461522
29	0.749342	0.707563	.668189	.631077	.596094	.563112	.532015	.502691	.475036	.448952
30	0.741923	0.699173	.658964	.621139	.585554	.552071	.520563	.490909	.462998	.436724
31	0.734577	0.690882	.649865	.611357	.575200	.541246	.509357	.479404	.451265	.424828
32	0.727304	0.682690	.640893	.601730	.565029	.530633	.498392	.468168	.439830	.413257
33	0.720103	0.674595	.632044	.592254	.555039	.520229	.487664	.457195	.428684	.402001
34	0.712973	0.666596	.623318	.582927	.545225	.510028	.477166	.446479	.417820	.391052
35	0.705914	0.658692	.614712	.573747	.535584	.500028	.466894	.436015	.407232	.380400
36	0.698925	0.650881	.606225	.564711	.526114	.490223	.456844	.425796	.396913	.370039
37	0.692005	0.643163	.597855	.555818	.516812	.480611	.447010	.415816	.386854	.359960
38	0.685153	0.635537	.589600	.547065	.507673	.471187	.437387	.406071	.377051	.350156
39	0.678370	0.628001	.581460	.538450	.498697	.461948	.427972	.396553	.367496	.340619
40	0.671653	0.620554	.573432	.529970	.489879	.452890	.418759	.387259	.358183	.331341
41	0.665003	0.613196	.565515	.521624	.481217	.444010	.409745	.378183	.349107	.322316
42	0.658419	0.605924	.557707	.513410	.472708	.435304	.400924	.369319	.340260	.313537
43	0.651900	0.598740	.550007	.505325	.464350	.426769	.392294	.360663	.331637	.304997
44	0.645445	0.591640	.542413	.497367	.456140	.418401	.383849	.352210	.323233	.296690
45	0.639055	0.584624	.534924	.489534	.448074	.410197	.375586	.343955	.315042	.288609
46	0.632728	0.577692	.527538	.481825	.440152	.402154	.367501	.335894	.307059	.280748
47	0.626463	0.570842	.520255	.474237	.432369	.394268	.359590	.328021	.299277	.273101
48	0.620260	0.564073	.513072	.466769	.424724	.386538	.351850	.320333	.291693	.265663
49	0.614119	0.557384	.505988	.459418	.417214	.378958	.344276	.312825	.284302	.258427
50	0.608039	0.550775	.499002	.452183	.409837	.371528	.336864	.305494	.277097	.251388

TERM CERTAIN REMAINDER FACTORS

INTEREST RATE

YEARS	3.0%	3.2%	3.4%	3.6%	3.8%	4.0%	4.2%	4.4%	4.6%	4.8%
1	.970874	.968992	.967118	.965251	.963391	.961538	.959693	.957854	.956023	.954199
2	.942596	.938946	.935317	.931709	.928122	.924556	.921010	.917485	.913980	.910495
3	.915142	.909831	.904562	.899333	.894145	.888996	.883887	.878817	.873786	.868793
4	.888487	.881620	.874818	.868082	.861411	.854804	.848260	.841779	.835359	.829001
5	.862609	.854282	.846052	.837917	.829876	.821927	.814069	.806302	.798623	.791031
6	.837484	.827793	.818233	.808801	.799495	.790315	.781257	.772320	.763502	.754801
7	.813091	.802125	.791327	.780696	.770227	.759918	.749766	.739770	.729925	.720230
8	.789409	.777253	.765307	.753567	.742029	.730690	.719545	.708592	.697825	.687242
9	.766417	.753152	.740142	.727381	.714865	.702587	.690543	.678728	.667137	.655765
10	.744094	.729799	.715805	.702106	.688694	.675564	.662709	.650122	.637798	.625730
11	.722421	.707169	.692268	.677708	.663482	.649581	.635997	.622722	.609749	.597071
12	.701380	.685241	.669505	.654158	.639193	.624597	.610362	.596477	.582935	.569724
13	.680951	.663994	.647490	.631427	.615792	.600574	.585760	.571339	.557299	.543630
14	.661118	.643405	.626199	.609486	.593249	.577475	.562150	.547259	.532790	.518731
15	.641862	.623454	.605608	.588307	.571531	.555265	.539491	.524195	.509360	.494972
16	.623167	.604122	.585695	.567863	.550608	.533908	.517746	.502102	.486960	.472302
17	.605016	.585390	.566436	.548131	.530451	.513373	.496877	.480941	.465545	.450670
18	.587395	.567238	.547810	.529084	.511031	.493628	.476849	.460671	.445071	.430028
19	.570286	.549649	.529797	.510699	.492323	.474642	.457629	.441256	.425498	.410332
20	.553676	.532606	.512376	.492952	.474300	.456387	.439183	.422659	.406786	.391538
21	.537549	.516091	.495529	.475823	.456936	.438834	.421481	.404846	.388897	.373605
22	.521892	.500088	.479235	.459288	.440208	.421955	.404492	.387783	.371794	.356494
23	.506692	.484582	.463476	.443329	.424093	.405726	.388188	.371440	.355444	.340166
24	.491934	.469556	.448236	.427923	.408567	.390121	.372542	.355785	.339813	.324586
25	.477606	.454996	.433497	.413053	.393610	.375117	.357526	.340791	.324869	.309719
26	.463695	.440888	.419243	.398700	.379200	.360689	.343115	.326428	.310582	.295533
27	.450189	.427217	.405458	.384846	.365318	.346817	.329285	.312670	.296923	.281998
28	.437077	.413970	.392125	.371473	.351944	.333477	.316012	.299493	.283866	.269082
29	.424346	.401133	.379231	.358564	.339060	.320651	.303275	.286870	.271382	.256757
30	.411987	.388695	.366762	.346105	.326648	.308319	.291051	.274780	.259447	.244997
31	.399987	.376643	.354702	.334078	.314689	.296460	.279319	.263199	.248038	.233776
32	.388337	.364964	.343038	.322469	.303169	.285058	.268061	.252106	.237130	.223069
33	.377026	.353647	.331759	.311263	.292070	.274094	.257256	.241481	.226702	.212852
34	.366045	.342681	.320850	.300447	.281378	.263552	.246887	.231304	.216732	.203103
35	.355383	.332055	.310300	.290007	.271077	.253415	.236935	.221556	.207201	.193801
36	.345032	.321759	.300096	.279930	.261153	.243669	.227385	.212218	.198089	.184924
37	.334983	.311782	.290228	.270202	.251593	.234297	.218220	.203274	.189377	.176454
38	.325226	.302114	.280685	.260813	.242382	.225285	.209424	.194707	.181049	.168373
39	.315754	.292747	.271456	.251750	.233509	.216621	.200983	.186501	.173087	.160661
40	.306557	.283669	.262530	.243002	.224960	.208289	.192882	.178641	.165475	.153302
41	.297628	.274873	.253897	.234558	.216725	.200278	.185107	.171112	.158198	.146281
42	.288959	.266350	.245549	.226407	.208791	.192575	.177646	.163900	.151241	.139581
43	.280543	.258091	.237474	.218540	.201147	.185168	.170486	.156992	.144590	.133188
44	.272372	.250088	.229666	.210946	.193783	.178046	.163614	.150376	.138231	.127088
45	.264439	.242334	.222114	.203616	.186689	.171198	.157019	.144038	.132152	.121267
46	.256737	.234819	.214810	.196540	.179855	.164614	.150690	.137968	.126340	:115713
47	.249259	.227538	.207747	.189711	.173270	.158283	.144616	.132153	.120784	.110413
48	.241999	.220483	.200916	.183118	.166927	.152195	.138787	.126583	.115473	.105356
49	.234950	.213646	.194309	.176755	.160816	.146341	.133193	.121248	.110395	.100530
50	.228107	.207021	.187920	.170613	.154929	.140713	.127824	.116138	.105540	.095926

SINGLE LIFE REMAINDER FACTORS

(For valuation dates occurring after April 30, 2009)

INTEREST RATE

AGE	1.0%	1.2%	1.4%	1.6%	1.8%	2.0%	2.2%	2.4%	2.6%	2.8%
35	.65414	.60253	.55549	.51261	.47347	.43774	.40509	.37523	.34792	.32290
36	.66021	.60921	.56266	.52014	.48127	.44572	.41318	.38337	.35606	.33100
37	.66631	.61594	.56989	.52774	.48916	.45381	.42139	.39165	.36435	.33927
38	.67244	.62272	.57718	.53544	.49715	.46201	.42974	.40008	.37281	.34771
39	.67860	.62955	.58453	.54320	.50523	.47032	.43821	.40864	.38141	.35631
40	.68479	.63641	.59194	.55104	.51340	.47873	.44679	.41734	.39016	.36507
41	.69100	.64331	.59940	.55894	.52165	.48724	.45549	.42616	.39906	.37399
42	.69723	.65024	.60690	.56691	.52998	.49585	.46430	.43511	.40809	.38307
43	.70348	.65721	.61447	.57495	.53840	.50457	.47324	.44421	.41729	.39232
44	.70976	.66422	.62208	.58305	.54690	.51338	.48229	.45343	.42663	.40172
45	.71605	.67125	.62973	.59122	.55547	.52228	.49144	.46277	.43611	.41128
46	.72236	.67832	.63743	.59945	.56413	.53129	.50072	.47225	.44574	.42101
47	.72867	.68541	.64517	.60773	.57286	.54037	.51009	.48185	.45550	.43089
48	.73501	.69253	.65295	.61606	.58166	.54955	.51958	.49158	.46540	.44093
49	.74135	.69967	.66077	.62446	.59053	.55882	.52917	.50143	.47545	.45113
50	.74771	.70684	.66864	.63292	.59949	.56819	.53888	.51141	.48566	.46150
51	.75409	.71404	.67655	.64143	.60852	.57766	.54871	.52153	.49602	.47204
52	.76048	.72127	.68450	.65001	.61763	.58722	.55865	.53179	.50653	.48276
53	.76687	.72852	.69249	.65863	.62680	.59687	.56869	.54217	.51718	.49363
54	.77326	.73577	.70050	.66730	.63603	.60658	.57882	.55265	.52796	.50465
55	.77964	.74302	.70851	.67598	.64530	.61635	.58902	.56322	.53884	.51579
56	.78599	.75024	.71651	.68465	.65457	.62613	.59926	.57383	.54978	.52701
57	.79230	.75744	.72448	.69332	.66384	.63593	.60951	.58449	.56078	.53830
58	.79857	.76459	.73242	.70195	.67309	.64573	.61978	.59517	.57182	.54964
59	.80479	.77170	.74033	.71057	.68233	.65553	.63007	.60589	.58290	.56105
60	.81098	.77879	.74822	.71918	.69158	.66534	.64039	.61665	.59405	.57254
61	.81713	.78584	.75608	.72776	.70081	.67515	.65072	.62743	.60524	.58409
62	.82323	.79283	.76388	.73630	.71001	.68494	.66104	.63822	.61645	.59566
63	.82926	.79977	.77164	.74479	.71917	.69470	.67133	.64900	.62766	.60726
64	.83524	.80665	.77933	.75323	.72828	.70443	.68161	.65977	.63887	.61887
65	.84116	.81346	.78697	.76162	.73735	.71411	.69186	.67053	.65009	.63049
66	.84706	.82027	.79461	.77002	.74645	.72385	.70216	.68136	.66140	.64223
67	.85292	.82705	.80223	.77841	.75554	.73359	.71250	.69224	.67277	.65405
68	.85874	.83378	.80980	.78676	.76461	.74331	.72283	.70312	.68416	.66590
69	.86449	.84044	.81731	.79504	.77362	.75299	.73312	.71398	.69553	.67776
70	.87016	.84702	.82473	.80326	.78256	.76260	.74335	.72479	.70688	.68959
71	.87577	.85353	.83209	.81140	.79143	.77215	.75353	.73556	.71819	.70141
72	.88129	.85996	.83935	.81945	.80021	.78162	.76364	.74626	.72945	.71318
73	.88671	.86627	.84651	.82739	.80888	.79098	.77365	.75686	.74061	.72487
74	.89202	.87247	.85353	.83518	.81741	.80019	.78350	.76733	.75164	.73643
75	.89720	.87851	.86039	.84281	.82577	.80923	.79318	.77761	.76249	.74781
76	.90224	.88440	.86708	.85026	.83393	.81807	.80266	.78769	.77314	.75899
77	.90715	.89013	.87360	.85753	.84191	.82671	.81194	.79756	.78358	.76997
78	.91190	.89571	.87995	.86461	.84968	.83515	.82100	.80722	.79380	.78072
79	.91652	.90112	.88611	.87149	.85725	.84337	.82984	.81664	.80378	.79124
80	.92098	.90635	.89208	.87817	.86460	.85135	.83843	.82582	.81351	.80149
81	.92529	.91141	.89786	.88463	.87172	.85910	.84678	.83474	.82298	.81148
82	.92944	.91629	.90344	.89088	.87861	.86660	.85487	.84339	.83217	.82119
83	.93343	.92099	.90882	.89691	.88526	.87385	.86269	.85177	.84107	.83060
84	.93727	.92551	.91399	.90271	.89166	.88084	.87024	.85986	.84968	.83970

SINGLE LIFE REMAINDER FACTORS

(For valuation dates occurring after April 30, 2009)

INTEREST RATE

AGE	3.0%	3.2%	3.4%	3.6%	3.8%	4.0%	4.2%	4.4%	4.6%	4.8%
35	.29998	.27896	.25967	.24195	.22567	.21070	.19692	.18423	.17253	.16174
36	.30800	.28688	.26746	.24961	.23317	.21803	.20407	.19119	.17931	.16833
37	.31621	.29499	.27546	.25746	.24087	.22557	.21144	.19838	.18631	.17515
38	.32460	.30330	.28366	.26554	.24880	.23334	.21904	.20582	.19357	.18222
39	.33316	.31179	.29205	.27381	.25694	.24133	.22687	.21348	.20105	.18952
40	.34189	.32046	.30064	.28229	.26529	.24954	.23493	.22137	.20878	.19707
41	.35080	.32932	.30942	.29097	.27386	.25797	.24322	.22950	.21674	.20487
42	.35987	.33836	.31840	.29986	.28264	.26662	.25173	.23786	.22494	.21290
43	.36913	.34760	.32758	.30897	.29165	.27552	.26049	.24648	.23342	.22122
44	.37857	.35702	.33697	.31829	.30088	.28465	.26950	.25535	.24214	.22979
45	.38817	.36663	.34655	.32782	.31033	.29400	.27874	.26447	.25112	.23862
46	.39796	.37644	.35634	.33757	.32002	.30360	.28824	.27385	.26038	.24774
47	.40791	.38642	.36633	.34753	.32992	.31343	.29798	.28349	.26989	.25712
48	.41803	.39660	.37652	.35770	.34006	.32351	.30797	.29338	.27967	.26678
49	.42833	.40696	.38691	.36810	.35043	.33383	.31822	.30355	.28974	.27674
50	.43883	.41754	.39754	.37874	.36106	.34442	.32876	.31401	.30011	.28701
51	.44951	.42832	.40838	.38961	.37194	.35528	.33958	.32477	.31079	.29759
52	.46038	.43931	.41945	.40073	.38307	.36641	.35068	.33582	.32178	.30851
53	.47143	.45050	.43074	.41208	.39446	.37781	.36206	.34717	.33308	.31974
54	.48265	.46186	.44222	.42364	.40607	.38945	.37371	.35880	.34467	.33127
55	.49400	.47338	.45387	.43540	.41789	.40131	.38559	.37067	.35652	.34308
56	.50544	.48501	.46565	.44729	.42987	.41335	.39765	.38275	.36859	.35512
57	.51698	.49675	.47755	.45932	.44201	.42555	.40990	.39502	.38086	.36739
58	.52858	.50858	.48956	.47147	.45427	.43790	.42231	.40747	.39333	.37985
59	.54027	.52050	.50167	.48375	.46668	.45041	.43490	.42011	.40600	.39253
60	.55205	.53253	.51392	.49617	.47925	.46310	.44768	.43296	.41890	.40546
61	.56390	.54465	.52627	.50872	.49196	.47595	.46064	.44600	.43200	.41860
62	.57581	.55683	.53870	.52136	.50478	.48892	.47373	.45920	.44527	.43194
63	.58774	.56907	.55120	.53409	.51770	.50200	.48696	.47253	.45870	.44544
64	.59970	.58134	.56375	.54688	.53071	.51519	.50030	.48601	.47229	.45911
65	.61170	.59367	.57637	.55976	.54381	.52849	.51377	.49963	.48603	.47295
66	.62383	.60615	.58916	.57283	.55713	.54203	.52750	.51352	.50007	.48711
67	.63605	.61874	.60208	.58605	.57062	.55575	.54144	.52765	.51436	.50154
68	.64833	.63140	.61509	.59938	.58423	.56963	.55554	.54196	.52885	.51619
69	.66062	.64409	.62815	.61277	.59793	.58360	.56976	.55640	.54349	.53102
70	.67291	.65680	.64124	.62621	.61168	.59764	.58407	.57095	.55826	.54598
71	.68519	.66951	.65434	.63968	.62549	.61176	.59848	.58561	.57316	.56109
72	.69744	.68220	.66745	.65317	.63933	.62593	.61294	.60035	.58815	.57632
73	.70962	.69484	.68051	.66662	.65315	.64009	.62741	.61512	.60318	.59160
74	.72167	.70735	.69346	.67997	.66688	.65417	.64183	.62983	.61818	.60686
75	.73355	.71971	.70625	.69318	.68048	.66813	.65612	.64444	.63309	.62204
76	.74524	.73187	.71886	.70621	.69390	.68192	.67026	.65891	.64786	.63710
77	.75672	.74382	.73127	.71904	.70713	.69553	.68423	.67321	.66248	.65201
78	.76798	.75556	.74346	.73166	.72016	.70894	.69800	.68733	.67692	.66676
79	.77900	.76706	.75542	.74405	.73296	.72213	.71156	.70124	.69116	.68132
80	.78976	.77830	.76711	.75618	.74550	.73507	.72487	.71490	.70516	.69563
81	.80025	.78927	.77853	.76803	.75777	.74773	.73791	.72830	.71890	.70970
82	.81045	.79994	.78966	.77959	.76974	.76009	.75065	.74140	.73235	.72348
83	.82035	.81030	.80047	.79083	.78139	.77214	.76308	.75419	.74548	.73695
84	.82993	.82035	.81095	.80174	.79271	.78385	.77516	.76664	.75828	.75008

APPENDIX C-1

Static Mortality Tables Determined under Former §1.430(h)(3)-1(c) and (d)

(Applicable for Valuation Dates in 2018 for Plan Years Beginning in 2017 or if the Option under §1.430(h)(3)-1(f)(2) is Used)

Age	MALE 2018 Non-Annuitant Mortality Rate	MALE 2018 Annuitant Mortality Rate	MALE 2018 Optional Combined Table for Small Plans	FEMALE 2018 Non-Annuitant Mortality Rate	FEMALE 2018 Annuitant Mortality Rate	FEMALE 2018 Optional Combined Table for Small Plans
1	0.000327	0.000327	0.000327	0.000293	0.000293	0.000293
2	0.000221	0.000221	0.000221	0.000191	0.000191	0.000191
3	0.000183	0.000183	0.000183	0.000143	0.000143	0.000143
4	0.000143	0.000143	0.000143	0.000107	0.000107	0.000107
5	0.000131	0.000131	0.000131	0.000097	0.000097	0.000097
6	0.000125	0.000125	0.000125	0.000090	0.000090	0.000090
7	0.000120	0.000120	0.000120	0.000085	0.000085	0.000085
8	0.000111	0.000111	0.000111	0.000075	0.000075	0.000075
9	0.000107	0.000107	0.000107	0.000072	0.000072	0.000072
10	0.000109	0.000109	0.000109	0.000072	0.000072	0.000072
11	0.000112	0.000112	0.000112	0.000073	0.000073	0.000073
12	0.000117	0.000117	0.000117	0.000076	0.000076	0.000076
13	0.000123	0.000123	0.000123	0.000080	0.000080	0.000080
14	0.000135	0.000135	0.000135	0.000089	0.000089	0.000089
15	0.000143	0.000143	0.000143	0.000100	0.000100	0.000100
16	0.000151	0.000151	0.000151	0.000107	0.000107	0.000107
17	0.000160	0.000160	0.000160	0.000116	0.000116	0.000116
18	0.000168	0.000168	0.000168	0.000118	0.000118	0.000118
19	0.000176	0.000176	0.000176	0.000115	0.000115	0.000115
20	0.000183	0.000183	0.000183	0.000112	0.000112	0.000112
21	0.000196	0.000196	0.000196	0.000109	0.000109	0.000109
22	0.000208	0.000208	0.000208	0.000110	0.000110	0.000110
23	0.000227	0.000227	0.000227	0.000116	0.000116	0.000116
24	0.000244	0.000244	0.000244	0.000122	0.000122	0.000122
25	0.000270	0.000270	0.000270	0.000130	0.000130	0.000130
26	0.000310	0.000310	0.000310	0.000144	0.000144	0.000144

Age	MALE 2018 Non-Annuitant Mortality Rate	MALE 2018 Annuitant Mortality Rate	MALE 2018 Optional Combined Table for Small Plans	FEMALE 2018 Non-Annuitant Mortality Rate	FEMALE 2018 Annuitant Mortality Rate	FEMALE 2018 Optional Combined Table for Small Plans
27	0.000324	0.000324	0.000324	0.000150	0.000150	0.000150
28	0.000333	0.000333	0.000333	0.000158	0.000158	0.000158
29	0.000349	0.000349	0.000349	0.000167	0.000167	0.000167
30	0.000376	0.000376	0.000376	0.000189	0.000189	0.000189
31	0.000423	0.000423	0.000423	0.000236	0.000236	0.000236
32	0.000476	0.000476	0.000476	0.000269	0.000269	0.000269
33	0.000535	0.000535	0.000535	0.000292	0.000292	0.000292
34	0.000595	0.000595	0.000595	0.000312	0.000312	0.000312
35	0.000655	0.000655	0.000655	0.000330	0.000330	0.000330
36	0.000713	0.000713	0.000713	0.000345	0.000345	0.000345
37	0.000766	0.000766	0.000766	0.000360	0.000360	0.000360
38	0.000790	0.000790	0.000790	0.000376	0.000376	0.000376
39	0.000810	0.000810	0.000810	0.000394	0.000394	0.000394
40	0.000828	0.000828	0.000828	0.000429	0.000429	0.000429
41	0.000847	0.000875	0.000847	0.000470	0.000470	0.000470
42	0.000872	0.000968	0.000873	0.000517	0.000517	0.000517
43	0.000902	0.001108	0.000905	0.000569	0.000569	0.000569
44	0.000938	0.001295	0.000944	0.000625	0.000625	0.000625
45	0.000979	0.001528	0.000991	0.000660	0.000668	0.000660
46	0.001015	0.001808	0.001037	0.000695	0.000754	0.000696
47	0.001053	0.002135	0.001087	0.000728	0.000883	0.000732
48	0.001092	0.002508	0.001143	0.000787	0.001055	0.000796
49	0.001133	0.002928	0.001206	0.000851	0.00127	0.000869
50	0.001174	0.003395	0.001275	0.000952	0.001527	0.000981
51	0.001215	0.003422	0.001325	0.001065	0.001643	0.001099
52	0.001257	0.003406	0.001404	0.001235	0.001861	0.001282
53	0.001346	0.003453	0.001547	0.001433	0.002141	0.001500
54	0.001444	0.003498	0.001709	0.001666	0.002481	0.001763
55	0.001608	0.003655	0.002031	0.001938	0.002889	0.002118
56	0.001815	0.003889	0.002473	0.002260	0.003377	0.002579
57	0.002060	0.004198	0.002868	0.002551	0.003869	0.003000

Age	MALE 2018 Non-Annuitant Mortality Rate	MALE 2018 Annuitant Mortality Rate	MALE 2018 Optional Combined Table for Small Plans	FEMALE 2018 Non-Annuitant Mortality Rate	FEMALE 2018 Annuitant Mortality Rate	FEMALE 2018 Optional Combined Table for Small Plans
58	0.002347	0.004607	0.003342	0.002789	0.004341	0.003391
59	0.002592	0.005001	0.003793	0.003050	0.004880	0.003848
60	0.002865	0.005476	0.004336	0.003332	0.005470	0.004391
61	0.003268	0.006169	0.005107	0.003632	0.006104	0.005067
62	0.003594	0.006795	0.005868	0.003946	0.006783	0.005818
63	0.004064	0.007698	0.006936	0.004271	0.007507	0.006704
64	0.004413	0.008518	0.007843	0.004601	0.008288	0.007566
65	0.004756	0.009433	0.008887	0.004934	0.009143	0.008534
66	0.005259	0.010720	0.010349	0.005261	0.010069	0.009645
67	0.005583	0.011867	0.011559	0.005579	0.011063	0.010716
68	0.005695	0.012794	0.012538	0.005886	0.012149	0.011850
69	0.005972	0.014133	0.013900	0.006178	0.013368	0.013100
70	0.006026	0.015219	0.014980	0.006452	0.014770	0.014488
71	0.006827	0.016839	0.016605	0.007035	0.015984	0.015711
72	0.008428	0.018697	0.018483	0.008200	0.017778	0.017518
73	0.010830	0.020825	0.020643	0.009948	0.019270	0.019049
74	0.014033	0.023233	0.023089	0.012278	0.021358	0.021174
75	0.018037	0.026595	0.026484	0.015191	0.022993	0.022860
76	0.022841	0.029643	0.029572	0.018686	0.025332	0.025242
77	0.028446	0.033819	0.033777	0.022764	0.028612	0.028552
78	0.034852	0.038544	0.038525	0.027424	0.031540	0.031512
79	0.042059	0.043933	0.043928	0.032667	0.034821	0.034814
80	0.050067	0.050067	0.050067	0.038490	0.038490	0.038490
81	0.057467	0.057467	0.057467	0.042601	0.042601	0.042601
82	0.065843	0.065843	0.065843	0.047227	0.047227	0.047227
83	0.073396	0.073396	0.073396	0.052439	0.052439	0.052439
84	0.083709	0.083709	0.083709	0.058321	0.058321	0.058321
85	0.092919	0.092919	0.092919	0.066628	0.066628	0.066628
86	0.103019	0.103019	0.103019	0.076203	0.076203	0.076203
87	0.117040	0.117040	0.117040	0.087152	0.087152	0.087152
88	0.132854	0.132854	0.132854	0.097072	0.097072	0.097072

Age	MALE 2018 Non-Annuitant Mortality Rate	MALE 2018 Annuitant Mortality Rate	MALE 2018 Optional Combined Table for Small Plans	FEMALE 2018 Non-Annuitant Mortality Rate	FEMALE 2018 Annuitant Mortality Rate	FEMALE 2018 Optional Combined Table for Small Plans
89	0.146819	0.146819	0.146819	0.110532	0.110532	0.110532
90	0.165921	0.165921	0.165921	0.122153	0.122153	0.122153
91	0.180722	0.180722	0.180722	0.134140	0.134140	0.134140
92	0.200931	0.200931	0.200931	0.146213	0.146213	0.146213
93	0.216754	0.216754	0.216754	0.162113	0.162113	0.162113
94	0.232553	0.232553	0.232553	0.173875	0.173875	0.173875
95	0.254433	0.254433	0.254433	0.185013	0.185013	0.185013
96	0.270045	0.270045	0.270045	0.195353	0.195353	0.195353
97	0.285214	0.285214	0.285214	0.209923	0.209923	0.209923
98	0.307507	0.307507	0.307507	0.218415	0.218415	0.218415
99	0.322050	0.322050	0.322050	0.225671	0.225671	0.225671
100	0.336045	0.336045	0.336045	0.231601	0.231601	0.231601
101	0.358628	0.358628	0.358628	0.244834	0.244834	0.244834
102	0.371685	0.371685	0.371685	0.254498	0.254498	0.254498
103	0.383040	0.383040	0.383040	0.266044	0.266044	0.266044
104	0.392003	0.392003	0.392003	0.279055	0.279055	0.279055
105	0.397886	0.397886	0.397886	0.293116	0.293116	0.293116
106	0.400000	0.400000	0.400000	0.307811	0.307811	0.307811
107	0.400000	0.400000	0.400000	0.322725	0.322725	0.322725
108	0.400000	0.400000	0.400000	0.337441	0.337441	0.337441
109	0.400000	0.400000	0.400000	0.351544	0.351544	0.351544
110	0.400000	0.400000	0.400000	0.364617	0.364617	0.364617
111	0.400000	0.400000	0.400000	0.376246	0.376246	0.376246
112	0.400000	0.400000	0.400000	0.386015	0.386015	0.386015
113	0.400000	0.400000	0.400000	0.393507	0.393507	0.393507
114	0.400000	0.400000	0.400000	0.398308	0.398308	0.398308
115	0.400000	0.400000	0.400000	0.400000	0.400000	0.400000
116	0.400000	0.400000	0.400000	0.400000	0.400000	0.400000
117	0.400000	0.400000	0.400000	0.400000	0.400000	0.400000
118	0.400000	0.400000	0.400000	0.400000	0.400000	0.400000
119	0.400000	0.400000	0.400000	0.400000	0.400000	0.400000
120	1.000000	1.000000	1.000000	1.000000	1.000000	1.000000

APPENDIX C-2

Applicable Mortality Table for Distributions Subject to §417(e)(3) with Annuity Starting Dates Occurring in Stability Periods Beginning in 2018

Age	Mortality Rate	Age	Mortality Rate	Age	Mortality Rate
0	0.002327	41	0.000368	81	0.042142
1	0.000141	42	0.000400	82	0.047336
2	0.000095	43	0.000439	83	0.053242
3	0.000076	44	0.000486	84	0.059995
4	0.000059	45	0.000541	85	0.067626
5	0.000052	46	0.000608	86	0.076267
6	0.000048	47	0.000685	87	0.086016
7	0.000044	48	0.000775	88	0.096873
8	0.000039	49	0.000877	89	0.108929
9	0.000035	50	0.000995	90	0.122286
10	0.000031	51	0.001116	91	0.136576
11	0.000033	52	0.001267	92	0.151466
12	0.000043	53	0.001442	93	0.166679
13	0.000053	54	0.001645	94	0.182208
14	0.000063	55	0.001951	95	0.197901
15	0.000073	56	0.002348	96	0.215845
16	0.000083	57	0.002701	97	0.234417
17	0.000093	58	0.003092	98	0.253767
18	0.000104	59	0.003526	99	0.273753
19	0.000114	60	0.004029	100	0.294309
20	0.000123	61	0.004629	101	0.315174
21	0.000135	62	0.005297	102	0.336021
22	0.000147	63	0.006056	103	0.356761
23	0.000157	64	0.006793	104	0.377020
24	0.000163	65	0.007601	105	0.396564
25	0.000160	66	0.008513	106	0.415512
26	0.000160	67	0.009419	107	0.433450
27	0.000163	68	0.010399	108	0.450441
28	0.000168	69	0.011477	109	0.466489
29	0.000175	70	0.012664	110	0.481504
30	0.000185	71	0.013995	111	0.491560
31	0.000197	72	0.015486	112	0.498309
32	0.000210	73	0.017176	113	0.501231
33	0.000225	74	0.019081	114	0.500577
34	0.000239	75	0.021243	115	0.500000
35	0.000253	76	0.023707	116	0.500000
36	0.000266	77	0.026500	117	0.500000
37	0.000282	78	0.029713	118	0.500000
38	0.000299	79	0.033373	119	0.500000
39	0.000318	80	0.037591	120	1.000000
40	0.000342				

APPENDIX D

Transfer Tax Tables

Though the American Taxpayer Relief Act of 2012 made transfer tax rates permanent for tax years beginning after 2012, in an effort to keep you informed, we have inserted material throughout the text to explain the status of the information and changes that have occurred.

2010 Estate and Gift Tax Table

Taxable Gift/Estate		Tax on	Rate on
From	To	Col. 1	Excess
$0	$10,000	$0	18%
10,001	20,000	1,800	20%
20,001	40,000	3,800	22%
40,001	60,000	8,200	24%
60,001	80,000	13,000	26%
80,001	100,000	18,200	28%
100,001	150,000	23,800	30%
150,001	250,000	38,800	32%
250,001	500,000	70,800	34%
500,001	…….	155,800	35%

2011-2012 Gift and Estate Tax Table

Taxable Gift/Estate		Tax on	Rate on
From	To	Col. 1	Excess
$0	$10,000	$0	18%
10,001	20,000	1,800	20%
20,001	40,000	3,800	22%
40,001	60,000	8,200	24%
60,001	80,000	13,000	26%
80,001	100,000	18,200	28%
100,001	150,000	23,800	30%
150,001	250,000	38,800	32%
250,001	500,000	70,800	34%
500,001	750,000	155,800	35%

IRC Secs. 2001(c), 2502(a), 2210, as amended by EGTRRA 2001.

2013-2021 Gift and Estate Tax Table

Taxable Gift/Estate		Tax on	Rate on
From	To	Col. 1	Excess
$0	$10,000	$0	18%
10,001	20,000	1,800	20%
20,001	40,000	3,800	22%
40,001	60,000	8,200	24%
60,001	80,000	13,000	26%
80,001	100,000	18,200	28%
100,001	150,000	23,800	30%
150,001	250,000	38,800	32%
250,001	500,000	70,800	34%
500,001	750,000	155,800	37%
750,000	1,000,000	248,300	39%
1,000,000		345,800	40%

IRC Secs. 2001(c), 2502(a), 2210, as amended by EGTRRA 2001 and ATRA.

2020 State Estate and Inheritance Tax Table

State	Estate Tax (Rate)	Inheritance Tax (Rate)	Exemption
Alabama	None	None	
Alaska	None	None	
Arizona	None	None	
Arkansas	None	None	
California	None	None	
Colorado	None	None	
Connecticut[1]	10%-12%	None	$5.1 million
Delaware	None	None	
District of Columbia	12%-16%	None	$5.8 million
Florida	None	None	
Georgia	None	None	
Hawaii	10%-20%	None	$5.5 million
Idaho	None	None	
Illinois	0.8%-16%	None	$4 million
Indiana	None	None	
Iowa	None	0%-15%	
Kansas	None	None	
Kentucky[2]	None	0%-16%	$500/$1,000/$0
Louisiana	None	None	
Maine	8%-12%	None	$5.7 million
Maryland[3]	0.8%-16%	0%-10%	$5 million (estate)
Massachusetts	0.8%-16%	None	$1 million

State	Estate Tax (Rate)	Inheritance Tax (Rate)	Exemption
Michigan	None	None	
Minnesota	13%-16%	None	$3 million
Mississippi	None	None	
Missouri	None	None	
Montana	None	None	
Nebraska	None	1%-18%	$10,000
Nevada	None	None	
New Hampshire	None	None	
New Jersey[4]	None	0%-16%	
New Mexico	None	None	
New York	3.06%-16%	None	$5.9 million
North Carolina	None	None	
North Dakota	None	None	
Ohio	None	None	
Oklahoma	None	None	
Oregon	10%-16%	None	$1 million
Pennsylvania[5]	None	0%-15%	
Rhode Island[6]	0.8%-16%	None	$1.6 million
South Carolina	None	None	
South Dakota	None	None	
Tennessee	None	None	
Texas	None	None	
Utah	None	None	
Vermont	16%	None	$2.8 million
Virginia	None	None	
Washington[7]	10%-20%	None	$2.2 million
West Virginia	None	None	
Wisconsin	None	None	
Wyoming	None	None	

[1] In Connecticut, the top estate tax rate is 12 percent and is capped at $15 million (*exemption threshold: $3.6 million; the exemption amount will rise to $5.1 million in 2020, $7.1 million in 2021, $9.1 million in 2022, and is scheduled to match the federal amount in 2023.*).

[2] In Kentucky, The top inheritance tax rate is 16 percent (*exemption threshold for Class C beneficiaries: $500; exemption threshold for Class B beneficiaries: $1,000; Class A beneficiaries, which is the majority, pay no inheritance tax*).

[3] Maryland passed a new law in 2014 that gradually increased the estate tax exemption. Beginning in 2019, the exemption will be equal to the federal exemption amount. Maryland's inheritance tax does not apply to surviving spouses, children, grandchildren, parents, grandparents, brothers or sisters of the decedent, among others.

[4] Spouses, domestic partners, civil union partners, parents, grandparents, children (including stepchildren), grandchildren (but not step grandchildren) are exempt from the inheritance tax. The $25,000 inheritance tax exemption applies to brothers, sisters, spouses or civil union partners of the decedent's child, and surviving spouses or civil union partners of the decedent's child. There is no exemption for any other person who inherits.

[5] In Pennsylvania, the inheritance tax does not apply to surviving spouses, parents, stepparents (if the decedent was 21 or younger), charitable organizations and government entities that inherit. The Pennsylvania inheritance tax rates differ depending upon who inherits (children, grandchildren and spouses of children pay a 4.5% rate, while brothers and sisters pay a 12% rate, and all others pay a 15% rate).

[6] The Rhode Island exemption is indexed annually for inflation.

[7] The Washington exemption amount is indexed annually for inflation.

Estate Tax Unified Credit

Year	Exclusion Equivalent	Unified Credit
2000-2001	$675,000	$220,550
2002-2003	$1,000,000	$345,800
2004-2005	$1,500,000	$555,800
2006-2008	$2,000,000	$780,800
2009	$3,500,000	$1,455,800
2010-2011	$5,000,000	$1,730,800
2012	$5,120,000	$1,772,800
2013	$5,250,000	$2,045,800
2014	$5,340,000	$2,081,800
2015	$5,430,000	$2,117,800
2016	$5,450,000	$2,125,800
2017	$5,490,000	$2,141,800
2018	$11,180,000	$4,419,800
2019	$11,400,000	$4,505,800
2020	$11,580,000	$4,577,800
2021	$11,700,000	$4,625,800

IRC Sec. 2010(c), as amended by EGTRRA 2001 and ATRA. Pub. Law No. 115-97 (2017 Tax Act).

Gift Tax Unified Credit

Year	Exclusion Equivalent	Unified Credit
1977 (1-1 to 6-30)	$30,000	$6,000
1977 (7-1 to 12-31)	120,667	30,000
1978	134,000	34,000
1979	147,333	38,000
1980	161,563	42,500
1981	175,625	47,000
1982	225,000	62,800
1983	275,000	79,300
1984	325,000	96,300
1985	400,000	121,800
1986	500,000	155,800
1987-1997	600,000	192,800
1998	625,000	202,050
1999	650,000	211,300
2000-2001	675,000	220,550

Year	Exclusion Equivalent	Unified Credit
2002-2009	1,000,000	345,800
2010-2011	$5,000,000	$1,730,800
2012	$5,120,000	$1,772,800
2013	$5,250,000	$2,045,800
2014	$5,340,000	$2,081,800
2015	$5,430,000	$2,117,800
2016	$5,450,000	$2,125,800
2017	$5,490,000	$2,141,800
2018	$11,180,000	$4,419,800
2019	$11,400,000	$4,505,800
2020	$11,580,000	$4,577,800
2021	$11,700,000	$4,625,800

IRC Secs. 2505(a), 2010(c), as amended by EGTRRA 2001 and ATRA. Pub. Law No. 115-97 (2017 Tax Act).

Maximum State Death Tax Credit (SDTC)

Adjusted Taxable Estate		Credit on Col. 1	Rate on Excess
From	To		
$40,000	$90,000	$0	0.8%
90,001	140,000	400	1.6%
140,001	240,000	1,200	2.4%
240,001	440,000	3,600	3.2%
440,001	640,000	10,000	4.0%
640,001	840,000	18,000	4.8%
840,001	1,040,000	27,600	5.6%
1,040,001	1,540,000	38,800	6.4%
1,540,001	2,040,000	70,800	7.2%
2,040,001	2,540,000	106,800	8.0%
2,540,001	3,040,000	146,800	8.8%
3,040,001	3,540,000	190,800	9.6%
3,540,001	4,040,000	238,800	10.4%
4,040,001	5,040,000	290,800	11.2%
5,040,001	6,040,000	402,800	12.0%
6,040,001	7,040,000	522,800	12.8%
7,040,001	8,040,000	650,800	13.6%
8,040,001	9,040,000	786,800	14.4%
9,040,001	10,040,000	930,800	15.2%
10,040,001	....	1,082,800	16.0%

For this purpose, the term "adjusted taxable estate" means the taxable estate reduced by $60,000.

Reduction in Maximum SDTC

Year	Multiply Maximum SDTC Above By
2002	75%
2003	50%
2004	25%
2005-2009	NA*
2010	NA*
2011-2018	NA*

*deduction for state death taxes paid replaces credit
IRC Secs. 2011(b), 2011(g), 2058, as amended by EGTRRA 2001 and ATRA.

Qualified Family-Owned Business Deduction

Year	Deduction Limitation
1998-2003	$675,000
2004-2018	NA

IRC Secs. 2057(a)(2), 2057(j), as amended by EGTRRA 2001 and ATRA.

Estate Tax Deferral: Closely Held Business

Year	2% Interest Limitation
1998	$410,000
1999	$416,500
2000	$427,500
2001	$441,000
2002	$484,000
2003	$493,800
2004	$532,200
2005	$539,900
2006	$552,000
2007	$562,500
2008	$576,000
2009	$598,500
2010	($603,000)
2011	$601,600
2012	$486,500
2013	$572,000
2014	$580,000

Year	2% Interest Limitation
2015	$588,000
2016	$592,000
2017	$596,000
2018	$608,000
2019	$620,000
2020	$628,000
2021	$636,000

Special Use Valuation Limitation

Year	Limitation
1997-1998	$750,000
1999	$760,000
2000	$770,000
2001	$800,000
2002	$820,000
2003	$840,000
2004	$850,000
2005	$870,000
2006	$900,000
2007	$940,000
2008	$960,000
2009	$1,000,000
2010	$1,000,000
2011	$1,020,000
2012	$1,040,000
2013	$1,070,000
2014	$1,090,000
2015	$1,100,000
2016	$1,110,000
2017	$1,120,000
2018	$1,140,000
2019	$1,160,000
2020	$1,180,000
2021	$1,190,000

IRC Sec. 2032A(a). As updated by Rev. Proc. 2020-45.

Qualified Conservation Easement Exclusion

Year	Exclusion Limitation
1998	$100,000
1999	$200,000
2000	$300,000
2001	$400,000
2002 and thereafter	$500,000

IRC Sec. 2031(c)(3).

Gift (and GST) Tax Annual Exclusion

Year	Annual Exclusion
1997-2001	$10,000
2002-2005	$11,000
2006-2008	$12,000
2009-2010	$13,000
2011-2012	$13,000
2013-2017	$14,000
2018-2021	$15,000

IRC Sec. 2503(b). As updated by Rev. Proc. 2020-45.

Gift Tax Annual Exclusion
(Donee Spouse not U.S. Citizen)

Year	Annual Exclusion
1997-1998	$100,000
1999	$101,000
2000	$103,000
2001	$106,000
2002	$110,000
2003	$112,000
2004	$114,000
2005	$117,000
2006	$120,000
2007	$125,000
2008	$128,000
2009	$133,000
2010	$134,000
2011	$136,000

Year	Annual Exclusion
2012	$139,000
2013	$143,000
2014	$145,000
2015	$147,000
2016	$148,000
2017	$149,000
2018	$152,000
2019	$155,000
2020	$157,000
2021	$159,000

IRC Sec. 2523(i). As updated by Rev. Proc. 2020-45.

Generation-Skipping Transfer Tax Table

Year	Tax Rate
2001	55%
2002	50%
2003	49%
2004	48%
2005	47%
2006	46%
2007-2009	45%
2010	0%
2011-2012	35%
2013-2021	40%

IRC Secs. 2641, 2001(c), 2664, as amended by EGTRRA 2001 and ATRA.

Generation-Skipping Transfer Tax Exemption

Year	GST Exemption
1997-1998	$1,000,000
1999	$1,010,000
2000	$1,030,000
2001	$1,060,000
2002	$1,100,000
2003	$1,120,000
2004-2005	$1,500,000
2006-2008	$2,000,000
2009	$3,500,000

Year	GST Exemption
2010-2011	$5,000,000
2012	$5,120,000
2013	$5,250,000
2014	$5,340,000
2015	$5,430,000
2016	$5,450,000
2017	$5,490,000
2018	$11,180,000
2019	$11,400,000
2020	$11,580,000
2021	$11,700,000

*Plus increases for indexing for inflation after 2012.
IRC Secs. 2631, 2010(c), as amended by EGTRRA 2001 and ATRA, Rev. Proc. 2020-45, Pub. Law No. 115-97 (2017 Tax Act).

Indexed Amounts Source

Year	Rev. Proc.
1999	98-61, 1998-2 CB 811
2000	99-42, 1999-46 IRB 568
2001	2001-13, 2001-3 IRB 337
2002	2001-59, 2001-52 IRB 623
2003	2002-70, 2002-46 IRB 845
2004	2003-85, 2003-49 IRB 1184
2005	2004-71, 2004-50 IRB 970
2006	2005-70, 2005-47 IRB 979
2007	2006-53, 2006-48 IRB 996
2008	2007-66, 2007-45 IRB 970
2009	2008-66, 2008-45 IRB 1107
2010	2009-50, 2009-45 IRB 617
2011	2010-40, 2010-46 IRB 663
2012	2011-52, 2011-45 IRB 701
2013	2013-15, 2013-5 IRB 444
2014	2013-35, 2013 -47 IRB 537
2015	2014-61, 2014-47 IRB 860
2016	2015-53, 2015-44 IRB 1
2017	2016-55, 2016-45 IRB 1
2018	2017-58, 2017-42 IRB 1; Pub. Law No. 115-97 (2017 Tax Act)
2019	2018-57, 2018-49, IRB 1
2020	2019-44, 2019-47, IRB 1
2021	2020-45, 2020-46, IRB 1

APPENDIX E

Employee Benefit Limits: 2015-2021

The employee benefit limits that follow are indexed annually for inflation, rounded to the increment levels set forth below.

Type of Limit	2015 (Rev. Proc. 2014-61)	2016 (IR-2015-118)	2017 (Rev. Proc. 2016-55)	2018 (Notice 2017-64)	2019 (Notice 2018-83)	2020 (2019-59)	2021 (Notice 2020-79)	Increment
Defined Benefit Plans Q 3867	$210,000	$210,000	$215,000	$220,000	$225,000	$230,000	$230,000	$5,000
Defined Contribution Plans Q 3867	$53,000 or 100% of pay	$53,000 or 100% of pay	$54,000 or 100% of pay	$55,000 or 100% of pay	$56,000 or 100% of pay	$57,000 or 100% of pay	$58,000 or 100% of pay	$1,000
Elective Deferral Limit for 401(k) Plans and SAR-SEPs Q 3705, Q 3760	$18,000	$18,000	$18,000	$18,500	$19,000	$19,500	$19,500	$500
Elective Deferral Limit for SIMPLE IRAs and SIMPLE 401(k) Plans Q 3706, Q 3760	$12,500	$12,500	$12,500	$12,500	$13,000	$13,500	$13,500	$500
Elective Deferral Limit for 457 Plans Q 3584	$18,000	$18,000	$18,000	$18,500	$19,000	$19,500	$19,500	$500
Minimum Compensation Amount for SEPs Q 3701	$600	$600	$600	$600	$600	$600	$650	$50
Maximum Compensation Amount for VEBAs Q 4102; SEPs Q 3701; TSAs Q 4032; Qualified Plans Q 3866, Q 3926F	$265,000	$265,000	$270,000	$275,000	$280,000	$285,000	$290,000	$5,000
Catch-up for 401(k) Plans Q 3761	$6,000	$6,000	$6,000	$6,000	$6,000	$6,500	$6,500	$500
Catch-up for SIMPLE IRAs and SIMPLE 401(k) Plans Q 3706, Q 3761	$3,000	$3,000	$3,000	$3,000	$3,000	$3,000	$3,000	$500
Highly Compensated Employee Definition Limit Q 3929	$120,000	$120,000	$120,000	$120,000	$125,000	$130,000	$130,000	$5,000
ESOP Payout Limits Q 3818	$210,000 $1,070,000	$210,000 $1,070,000	$215,000- $1,080,000	$220,000 $1,105,000	$225,000 $1,130,000	$230,000 $1,150,000	$230,000 $1,165,000	$5,000
Key Employee Definition Q 3930	$170,000	$170,000	$175,000	$175,000	$180,000	$185,000	$185,000	$5,000

Indexed IRA Limits: 2015-2021

Individual Retirement Account Limit	2015 (Rev. Proc. 2014-61)	2016 (IR 2015-118)	2017 (Rev. Proc. 2016-55)	2018 (Notice 2017-64)	2019 (Notice 2018-83)	2020 (2019-59)	2021 (2020-79)	Increment
Total Contributions to Traditional and Roth IRAs – see Q 3656, Q 3659	$5,500	$5,500	$5,500	$5,500	$6,000	$6,000	$6,000	$500
Total Catch-up Contributions to Traditional and Roth IRAs – see Q 3656, Q 3659	$1,000	$1,000	$1,000	$1,000	$1,000	$1,000	$1,000	NA
Traditional IRA Deductible Contribution Limit: MAGI- see Q 3656								
Joint Return (Active Participant Spouse)	$98,000-$118,000	$98,000-$118,000	$99,000-$119,000	$101,000-$121,000	$103,000-$123,000	$104,000-$124,000	$105,000-$125,000	$1,000
Joint Return (Non Active Participant Spouse)	$183,000-$193,000	$184,000-$194,000	$186,000-$196,000	$189,000-$199,000	$193,000-$203,000	$196,000-$206,000	$198,000-$208,000	$1,000
Single/Head of Household	$61,000-$71,000	$61,000-$71,000	$62,000-$72,000	$63,000-$73,000	$64,000-$74,000	$65,000-$75,000	$66,000-$76,000	$1,000
Roth IRA Contribution Limit: MAGI- see Q 3659								
Joint Return	$183,000-$193,000	$184,000-$194,000	$186,000-$196,000	$189,000-$199,000	$193,000-$203,000	$196,000-$206,000	$198,000-$208,000	$1,000
Single/Head of Household	$116,000-$131,000	$117,000-$132,000	$118,000-$133,000	$120,000-$135,000	$122,000-$137,000	$124,000-$139,000	$125,000-$140,000	$1,000

APPENDIX F

Required Minimum Distribution (RMD) Tables

RMD Uniform Lifetime Table – Distribution Period

Age	Factor	Age	Factor	Age	Factor
10	86.2	45	51.5	80	18.7
11	85.2	46	50.5	81	17.9
12	84.2	47	49.5	82	17.1
13	83.2	48	48.5	83	16.3
14	82.2	49	47.5	84	15.5
15	81.2	50	46.5	85	14.8
16	80.2	51	45.5	86	14.1
17	79.2	52	44.6	87	13.4
18	78.2	53	43.6	88	12.7
19	77.3	54	42.6	89	12.0
20	76.3	55	41.6	90	11.4
21	75.3	56	40.7	91	10.8
22	74.3	57	39.7	92	10.2
23	73.3	58	38.7	93	9.6
24	72.3	59	37.8	94	9.1
25	71.3	60	36.8	95	8.6
26	70.3	61	35.8	96	8.1
27	69.3	62	34.9	97	7.6
28	68.3	63	33.9	98	7.1
29	67.3	64	33.0	99	6.7
30	66.3	65	32.0	100	6.3
31	65.3	66	31.1	101	5.9
32	64.3	67	30.2	102	5.5
33	63.3	68	29.2	103	5.2
34	62.3	69	28.3	104	4.9
35	61.4	70	27.4	105	4.5
36	60.4	71	26.5	106	4.2
37	59.4	72	25.6	107	3.9
38	58.4	73	24.7	108	3.7
39	57.4	74	23.8	109	3.4
40	56.4	75	22.9	110	3.1
41	55.4	76	22.0	111	2.9
42	54.4	77	21.2	112	2.6
43	53.4	78	20.3	113	2.4
44	52.4	79	19.5	114	2.1
				115	1.9

Treas. Reg. Sec. 1.401(a)(9)-9

RMD Single Life Table – Life Expectancy

Age	Factor	Age	Factor	Age	Factor
0	82.4	40	43.6	80	10.2
1	81.6	41	42.7	81	9.7
2	80.6	42	41.7	82	9.1
3	79.7	43	40.7	83	8.6
4	78.7	44	39.8	84	8.1
5	77.7	45	38.8	85	7.6
6	76.7	46	37.9	86	7.1
7	75.8	47	37.0	87	6.7
8	74.8	48	36.0	88	6.3
9	73.8	49	35.1	89	5.9
10	72.8	50	34.2	90	5.5
11	71.8	51	33.3	91	5.2
12	70.8	52	32.3	92	4.9
13	69.9	53	31.4	93	4.6
14	68.9	54	30.5	94	4.3
15	67.9	55	29.6	95	4.1
16	66.9	56	28.7	96	3.8
17	66.0	57	27.9	97	3.6
18	65.0	58	27.0	98	3.4
19	64.0	59	26.1	99	3.1
20	63.0	60	25.2	100	2.9
21	62.1	61	24.4	101	2.7
22	61.1	62	23.5	102	2.5
23	60.1	63	22.7	103	2.3
24	59.1	64	21.8	104	2.1
25	58.2	65	21.0	105	1.9
26	57.2	66	20.2	106	1.7
27	56.2	67	19.4	107	1.5
28	55.3	68	18.6	108	1.4
29	54.3	69	17.8	109	1.2
30	53.3	70	17.0	110	1.1
31	52.4	71	16.3	111	1.0
32	51.4	72	15.5		
33	50.4	73	14.8		
34	49.4	74	14.1		
35	48.5	75	13.4		
36	47.5	76	12.7		
37	46.5	77	12.1		
38	45.6	78	11.4		
39	44.6	79	10.8		

Treas. Reg. Sec. 1.401(a)(9)-9

RMD Joint and Last Survivor Table – Life Expectancy

Ages	35	36	37	38	39	40	41	42	43	44	45	46
35	55.2	54.7	54.3	53.8	53.4	53.0	52.7	52.3	52.0	51.7	51.5	51.2
36	54.7	54.2	53.7	53.3	52.8	52.4	52.0	51.7	51.3	51.0	50.7	50.5
37	54.3	53.7	53.2	52.7	52.3	51.8	51.4	51.1	50.7	50.4	50.0	49.8
38	53.8	53.3	52.7	52.2	51.7	51.3	50.9	50.4	50.1	49.7	49.4	49.1
39	53.4	52.8	52.3	51.7	51.2	50.8	50.3	49.9	49.5	49.1	48.7	48.4
40	53.0	52.4	51.8	51.3	50.8	50.2	49.8	49.3	48.9	48.5	48.1	47.7
41	52.7	52.0	51.4	50.9	50.3	49.8	49.3	48.8	48.3	47.9	47.5	47.1
42	52.3	51.7	51.1	50.4	49.9	49.3	48.8	48.3	47.8	47.3	46.9	46.5
43	52.0	51.3	50.7	50.1	49.5	48.9	48.3	47.8	47.3	46.8	46.3	45.9
44	51.7	51.0	50.4	49.7	49.1	48.5	47.9	47.3	46.8	46.3	45.8	45.4
45	51.5	50.7	50.0	49.4	48.7	48.1	47.5	46.9	46.3	45.8	45.3	44.8
46	51.2	50.5	49.8	49.1	48.4	47.7	47.1	46.5	45.9	45.4	44.8	44.3
47	51.0	50.2	49.5	48.8	48.1	47.4	46.7	46.1	45.5	44.9	44.4	43.9
48	50.8	50.0	49.2	48.5	47.8	47.1	46.4	45.8	45.1	44.5	44.0	43.4
49	50.6	49.8	49.0	48.2	47.5	46.8	46.1	45.4	44.8	44.2	43.6	43.0
50	50.4	49.6	48.8	48.0	47.3	46.5	45.8	45.1	44.4	43.8	43.2	42.6
51	50.2	49.4	48.6	47.8	47.0	46.3	45.5	44.8	44.1	43.5	42.8	42.2
52	50.0	49.2	48.4	47.6	46.8	46.0	45.3	44.6	43.8	43.2	42.5	41.8
53	49.9	49.1	48.2	47.4	46.6	45.8	45.1	44.3	43.6	42.9	42.2	41.5
54	49.8	48.9	48.1	47.2	46.4	45.6	44.8	44.1	43.3	42.6	41.9	41.2
55	49.7	48.8	47.9	47.1	46.3	45.5	44.7	43.9	43.1	42.4	41.6	40.9
56	49.5	48.7	47.8	47.0	46.1	45.3	44.5	43.7	42.9	42.1	41.4	40.7
57	49.4	48.6	47.7	46.8	46.0	45.1	44.3	43.5	42.7	41.9	41.2	40.4
58	49.4	48.5	47.6	46.7	45.8	45.0	44.2	43.3	42.5	41.7	40.9	40.2
59	49.3	48.4	47.5	46.6	45.7	44.9	44.0	43.2	42.4	41.5	40.7	40.0
60	49.2	48.3	47.4	46.5	45.6	44.7	43.9	43.0	42.2	41.4	40.6	39.8
61	49.1	48.2	47.3	46.4	45.5	44.6	43.8	42.9	42.1	41.2	40.4	39.6
62	49.1	48.1	47.2	46.3	45.4	44.5	43.7	42.8	41.9	41.1	40.3	39.4
63	49.0	48.1	47.2	46.3	45.3	44.5	43.6	42.7	41.8	41.0	40.1	39.3
64	48.9	48.0	47.1	46.2	45.3	44.4	43.5	42.6	41.7	40.8	40.0	39.2
65	48.9	48.0	47.0	46.1	45.2	44.3	43.4	42.5	41.6	40.7	39.9	39.0
66	48.9	47.9	47.0	46.1	45.1	44.2	43.3	42.4	41.5	40.6	39.8	38.9
67	48.8	47.9	46.9	46.0	45.1	44.2	43.3	42.3	41.4	40.6	39.7	38.8
68	48.8	47.8	46.9	46.0	45.0	44.1	43.2	42.3	41.4	40.5	39.6	38.7
69	48.7	47.8	46.9	45.9	45.0	44.1	43.1	42.2	41.3	40.4	39.5	38.6

RMD Joint and Last Survivor Table – Life Expectancy

Ages	35	36	37	38	39	40	41	42	43	44	45	46
70	48.7	47.8	46.8	45.9	44.9	44.0	43.1	42.2	41.3	40.3	39.4	38.6
71	48.7	47.7	46.8	45.9	44.9	44.0	43.0	42.1	41.2	40.3	39.4	38.5
72	48.7	47.7	46.8	45.8	44.9	43.9	43.0	42.1	41.1	40.2	39.3	38.4
73	48.6	47.7	46.7	45.8	44.8	43.9	43.0	42.0	41.1	40.2	39.3	38.4
74	48.6	47.7	46.7	45.8	44.8	43.9	42.9	42.0	41.1	40.1	39.2	38.3
75	48.6	47.7	46.7	45.7	44.8	43.8	42.9	42.0	41.0	40.1	39.2	38.3
76	48.6	47.6	46.7	45.7	44.8	43.8	42.9	41.9	41.0	40.1	39.1	38.2
77	48.6	47.6	46.7	45.7	44.8	43.8	42.9	41.9	41.0	40.0	39.1	38.2
78	48.6	47.6	46.6	45.7	44.7	43.8	42.8	41.9	40.9	40.0	39.1	38.2
79	48.6	47.6	46.6	45.7	44.7	43.8	42.8	41.9	40.9	40.0	39.1	38.1
80	48.5	47.6	46.6	45.7	44.7	43.7	42.8	41.8	40.9	40.0	39.0	38.1
81	48.5	47.6	46.6	45.7	44.7	43.7	42.8	41.8	40.9	39.9	39.0	38.1
82	48.5	47.6	46.6	45.6	44.7	43.7	42.8	41.8	40.9	39.9	39.0	38.1
83	48.5	47.6	46.6	45.6	44.7	43.7	42.8	41.8	40.9	39.9	39.0	38.0
84	48.5	47.6	46.6	45.6	44.7	43.7	42.7	41.8	40.8	39.9	39.0	38.0
85	48.5	47.5	46.6	45.6	44.7	43.7	42.7	41.8	40.8	39.9	38.9	38.0
86	48.5	47.5	46.6	45.6	44.6	43.7	42.7	41.8	40.8	39.9	38.9	38.0
87	48.5	47.5	46.6	45.6	44.6	43.7	42.7	41.8	40.8	39.9	38.9	38.0
88	48.5	47.5	46.6	45.6	44.6	43.7	42.7	41.8	40.8	39.9	38.9	38.0
89	48.5	47.5	46.6	45.6	44.6	43.7	42.7	41.7	40.8	39.8	38.9	38.0
90	48.5	47.5	46.6	45.6	44.6	43.7	42.7	41.7	40.8	39.8	38.9	38.0

RMD Joint and Last Survivor Table – Life Expectancy

Ages	47	48	49	50	51	52	53	54	55	56	57	58
47	43.4	42.9	42.4	42.0	41.6	41.2	40.9	40.5	40.2	40.0	39.7	39.4
48	42.9	42.4	41.9	41.5	41.0	40.6	40.3	39.9	39.6	39.3	39.0	38.7
49	42.4	41.9	41.4	40.9	40.5	40.1	39.7	39.3	38.9	38.6	38.3	38.0
50	42.0	41.5	40.9	40.4	40.0	39.5	39.1	38.7	38.3	38.0	37.6	37.3
51	41.6	41.0	40.5	40.0	39.5	39.0	38.5	38.1	37.7	37.4	37.0	36.7
52	41.2	40.6	40.1	39.5	39.0	38.5	38.0	37.6	37.2	36.8	36.4	36.0
53	40.9	40.3	39.7	39.1	38.5	38.0	37.5	37.1	36.6	36.2	35.8	35.4
54	40.5	39.9	39.3	38.7	38.1	37.6	37.1	36.6	36.1	35.7	35.2	34.8
55	40.2	39.6	38.9	38.3	37.7	37.2	36.6	36.1	35.6	35.1	34.7	34.3
56	40.0	39.3	38.6	38.0	37.4	36.8	36.2	35.7	35.1	34.7	34.2	33.7
57	39.7	39.0	38.3	37.6	37.0	36.4	35.8	35.2	34.7	34.2	33.7	33.2
58	39.4	38.7	38.0	37.3	36.7	36.0	35.4	34.8	34.3	33.7	33.2	32.8
59	39.2	38.5	37.8	37.1	36.4	35.7	35.1	34.5	33.9	33.3	32.8	32.3
60	39.0	38.2	37.5	36.8	36.1	35.4	34.8	34.1	33.5	32.9	32.4	31.9
61	38.8	38.0	37.3	36.6	35.8	35.1	34.5	33.8	33.2	32.6	32.0	31.4

APPENDIX F: REQUIRED MINIMUM DISTRIBUTION (RMD) TABLES

RMD Joint and Last Survivor Table – Life Expectancy

Ages	47	48	49	50	51	52	53	54	55	56	57	58
62	38.6	37.8	37.1	36.3	35.6	34.9	34.2	33.5	32.9	32.2	31.6	31.1
63	38.5	37.7	36.9	36.1	35.4	34.6	33.9	33.2	32.6	31.9	31.3	30.7
64	38.3	37.5	36.7	35.9	35.2	34.4	33.7	33.0	32.3	31.6	31.0	30.4
65	38.2	37.4	36.6	35.8	35.0	34.2	33.5	32.7	32.0	31.4	30.7	30.0
66	38.1	37.2	36.4	35.6	34.8	34.0	33.3	32.5	31.8	31.1	30.4	29.8
67	38.0	37.1	36.3	35.5	34.7	33.9	33.1	32.3	31.6	30.9	30.2	29.5
68	37.9	37.0	36.2	35.3	34.5	33.7	32.9	32.1	31.4	30.7	29.9	29.2
69	37.8	36.9	36.0	35.2	34.4	33.6	32.8	32.0	31.2	30.5	29.7	29.0
70	37.7	36.8	35.9	35.1	34.3	33.4	32.6	31.8	31.1	30.3	29.5	28.8
71	37.6	36.7	35.9	35.0	34.2	33.3	32.5	31.7	30.9	30.1	29.4	28.6
72	37.5	36.6	35.8	34.9	34.1	33.2	32.4	31.6	30.8	30.0	29.2	28.4
73	37.5	36.6	35.7	34.8	34.0	33.1	32.3	31.5	30.6	29.8	29.1	28.3
74	37.4	36.5	35.6	34.8	33.9	33.0	32.2	31.4	30.5	29.7	28.9	28.1
75	37.4	36.5	35.6	34.7	33.8	33.0	32.1	31.3	30.4	29.6	28.8	28.0
76	37.3	36.4	35.5	34.6	33.8	32.9	32.0	31.2	30.3	29.5	28.7	27.9
77	37.3	36.4	35.5	34.6	33.7	32.8	32.0	31.1	30.3	29.4	28.6	27.8
78	37.2	36.3	35.4	34.5	33.6	32.8	31.9	31.0	30.2	29.3	28.5	27.7
79	37.2	36.3	35.4	34.5	33.6	32.7	31.8	31.0	30.1	29.3	28.4	27.6
80	37.2	36.3	35.4	34.5	33.6	32.7	31.8	30.9	30.1	29.2	28.4	27.5
81	37.2	36.2	35.3	34.4	33.5	32.6	31.8	30.9	30.0	29.2	28.3	27.5
82	37.1	36.2	35.3	34.4	33.5	32.6	31.7	30.8	30.0	29.1	28.3	27.4
83	37.1	36.2	35.3	34.4	33.5	32.6	31.7	30.8	29.9	29.1	28.2	27.4
84	37.1	36.2	35.3	34.3	33.4	32.5	31.7	30.8	29.9	29.0	28.2	27.3
85	37.1	36.2	35.2	34.3	33.4	32.5	31.6	30.7	29.9	29.0	28.1	27.3
86	37.1	36.1	35.2	34.3	33.4	32.5	31.6	30.7	29.8	29.0	28.1	27.2
87	37.0	36.1	35.2	34.3	33.4	32.5	31.6	30.7	29.8	28.9	28.1	27.2
88	37.0	36.1	35.2	34.3	33.4	32.5	31.6	30.7	29.8	28.9	28.0	27.2
89	37.0	36.1	35.2	34.3	33.3	32.4	31.5	30.7	29.8	28.9	28.0	27.2
90	37.0	36.1	35.2	34.2	33.3	32.4	31.5	30.6	29.8	28.9	28.0	27.1

RMD Joint and Last Survivor Table – Life Expectancy

Ages	59	60	61	62	63	64	65	66	67	68	69	70
59	31.8	31.3	30.9	30.5	30.1	29.8	29.4	29.1	28.8	28.6	28.3	28.1
60	31.3	30.9	30.4	30.0	29.6	29.2	28.8	28.5	28.2	27.9	27.6	27.4
61	30.9	30.4	29.9	29.5	29.0	28.6	28.3	27.9	27.6	27.3	27.0	26.7
62	30.5	30.0	29.5	29.0	28.5	28.1	27.7	27.3	27.0	26.7	26.4	26.1
63	30.1	29.6	29.0	28.5	28.1	27.6	27.2	26.8	26.4	26.1	25.7	25.4
64	29.8	29.2	28.6	28.1	27.6	27.1	26.7	26.3	25.9	25.5	25.2	24.8
65	29.4	28.8	28.3	27.7	27.2	26.7	26.2	25.8	25.4	25.0	24.6	24.3
66	29.1	28.5	27.9	27.3	26.8	26.3	25.8	25.3	24.9	24.5	24.1	23.7
67	28.8	28.2	27.6	27.0	26.4	25.9	25.4	24.9	24.4	24.0	23.6	23.2
68	28.6	27.9	27.3	26.7	26.1	25.5	25.0	24.5	24.0	23.5	23.1	22.7
69	28.3	27.6	27.0	26.4	25.7	25.2	24.6	24.1	23.6	23.1	22.6	22.2
70	28.1	27.4	26.7	26.1	25.4	24.8	24.3	23.7	23.2	22.7	22.2	21.8
71	27.9	27.2	26.5	25.8	25.2	24.5	23.9	23.4	22.8	22.3	21.8	21.3
72	27.7	27.0	26.3	25.6	24.9	24.3	23.7	23.1	22.5	22.0	21.4	20.9
73	27.5	26.8	26.1	25.4	24.7	24.0	23.4	22.8	22.2	21.6	21.1	20.6
74	27.4	26.6	25.9	25.2	24.5	23.8	23.1	22.5	21.9	21.3	20.8	20.2
75	27.2	26.5	25.7	25.0	24.3	23.6	22.9	22.3	21.6	21.0	20.5	19.9
76	27.1	26.3	25.6	24.8	24.1	23.4	22.7	22.0	21.4	20.8	20.2	19.6
77	27.0	26.2	25.4	24.7	23.9	23.2	22.5	21.8	21.2	20.6	19.9	19.4
78	26.9	26.1	25.3	24.6	23.8	23.1	22.4	21.7	21.0	20.3	19.7	19.1
79	26.8	26.0	25.2	24.4	23.7	22.9	22.2	21.5	20.8	20.1	19.5	18.9
80	26.7	25.9	25.1	24.3	23.6	22.8	22.1	21.3	20.6	20.0	19.3	18.7
81	26.6	25.8	25.0	24.2	23.4	22.7	21.9	21.2	20.5	19.8	19.1	18.5
82	26.6	25.8	24.9	24.1	23.4	22.6	21.8	21.1	20.4	19.7	19.0	18.3
83	26.5	25.7	24.9	24.1	23.3	22.5	21.7	21.0	20.2	19.5	18.8	18.2
84	26.5	25.6	24.8	24.0	23.2	22.4	21.6	20.9	20.1	19.4	18.7	18.0
85	26.4	25.6	24.8	23.9	23.1	22.3	21.6	20.8	20.1	19.3	18.6	17.9
86	26.4	25.5	24.7	23.9	23.1	22.3	21.5	20.7	20.0	19.2	18.5	17.8
87	26.4	25.5	24.7	23.8	23.0	22.2	21.4	20.7	19.9	19.2	18.4	17.7
88	26.3	25.5	24.6	23.8	23.0	22.2	21.4	20.6	19.8	19.1	18.3	17.6
89	26.3	25.4	24.6	23.8	22.9	22.1	21.3	20.5	19.8	19.0	18.3	17.6
90	26.3	25.4	24.6	23.7	22.9	22.1	21.3	20.5	19.7	19.0	18.2	17.5

RMD Joint and Last Survivor Table – Life Expectancy

Ages	71	72	73	74	75	76	77	78	79	80	81	82
71	20.9	20.5	20.1	19.7	19.4	19.1	18.8	18.5	18.3	18.1	17.9	17.7
72	20.5	20.0	19.6	19.3	18.9	18.6	18.3	18.0	17.7	17.5	17.3	17.1
73	20.1	19.6	19.2	18.8	18.4	18.1	17.8	17.5	17.2	16.9	16.7	16.5
74	19.7	19.3	18.8	18.4	18.0	17.6	17.3	17.0	16.7	16.4	16.2	15.9
75	19.4	18.9	18.4	18.0	17.6	17.2	16.8	16.5	16.2	15.9	15.6	15.4
76	19.1	18.6	18.1	17.6	17.2	16.8	16.4	16.0	15.7	15.4	15.1	14.9
77	18.8	18.3	17.8	17.3	16.8	16.4	16.0	15.6	15.3	15.0	14.7	14.4
78	18.5	18.0	17.5	17.0	16.5	16.0	15.6	15.2	14.9	14.5	14.2	13.9
79	18.3	17.7	17.2	16.7	16.2	15.7	15.3	14.9	14.5	14.1	13.8	13.5
80	18.1	17.5	16.9	16.4	15.9	15.4	15.0	14.5	14.1	13.8	13.4	13.1
81	17.9	17.3	16.7	16.2	15.6	15.1	14.7	14.2	13.8	13.4	13.1	12.7
82	17.7	17.1	16.5	15.9	15.4	14.9	14.4	13.9	13.5	13.1	12.7	12.4
83	17.5	16.9	16.3	15.7	15.2	14.7	14.2	13.7	13.2	12.8	12.4	12.1
84	17.4	16.7	16.1	15.5	15.0	14.4	13.9	13.4	13.0	12.6	12.2	11.8
85	17.3	16.6	16.0	15.4	14.8	14.3	13.7	13.2	12.8	12.3	11.9	11.5
86	17.1	16.5	15.8	15.2	14.6	14.1	13.5	13.0	12.5	12.1	11.7	11.3
87	17.0	16.4	15.7	15.1	14.5	13.9	13.4	12.9	12.4	11.9	11.4	11.0
88	16.9	16.3	15.6	15.0	14.4	13.8	13.2	12.7	12.2	11.7	11.3	10.8
89	16.9	16.2	15.5	14.9	14.3	13.7	13.1	12.6	12.0	11.5	11.1	10.6
90	16.8	16.1	15.4	14.8	14.2	13.6	13.0	12.4	11.9	11.4	10.9	10.5

RMD Joint and Last Survivor Table – Life Expectancy

Ages	83	84	85	86	87	88	89	90
83	11.7	11.4	11.1	10.9	10.6	10.4	10.2	10.1
84	11.4	11.1	10.8	10.5	10.3	10.1	9.9	9.7
85	11.1	10.8	10.5	10.2	9.9	9.7	9.5	9.3
86	10.9	10.5	10.2	9.9	9.6	9.4	9.2	9.0
87	10.6	10.3	9.9	9.6	9.4	9.1	8.9	8.6
88	10.4	10.1	9.7	9.4	9.1	8.8	8.6	8.3
89	10.2	9.9	9.5	9.2	8.9	8.6	8.3	8.1
90	10.1	9.7	9.3	9.0	8.6	8.3	8.1	7.8

Treas. Reg. Sec. 1.401(a)(9)-9

RMD MDIB Joint and Survivor Annuity Table
(maximum percentage for survivor)

Excess of Participant's Age over Beneficiary's Age	Applicable Percentage	Excess of Participant's Age over Beneficiary's Age	Applicable Percentage	Excess of Participant's Age over Beneficiary's Age	Applicable Percentage
10 or less	100	22	70	34	57
11	96	23	68	35	56
12	93	24	67	36	56
13	90	25	66	37	55
14	87	26	64	38	55
15	84	27	63	39	54
16	82	28	62	40	54
17	79	29	61	41	53
18	77	30	60	42	53
19	75	31	59	43	53
20	73	32	59	44 and greater	52
21	72	33	58		

Treas. Reg. Sec. 1.401(a)(9)-9

2021 Required Minimum Distribution (RMD) Tables

Proposed late in 2019, these updates to the RMD life expectancy tables have been finalized and will take effect in 2021.

Proposed RMD Uniform Lifetime Table – Distribution Period

Age	Factor	Age	Factor	Age	Factor
70	29.1	90	12.1	110	3.5
71	28.2	91	11.4	111	3.4
72	27.3	92	10.8	112	3.2
73	26.4	93	10.1	113	3.1
74	25.5	94	9.5	114	3.0
75	24.6	95	8.9	115	2.9
76	23.7	96	8.3	116	2.8
77	22.8	97	7.8	117	2.7
78	21.9	98	7.3	118	2.5
79	21.0	99	6.8	119	2.3
80	20.2	100	6.4	120 +	2.0
81	19.3	101	5.9		
82	18.4	102	5.6		
83	17.6	103	5.2		
84	16.8	104	4.9		
85	16.0	105	4.6		
86	15.2	106	4.3		
87	14.4	107	4.1		
88	13.6	108	3.9		
89	12.9	109	3.7		

Federal Register Document No. 2020-24723 (Nov. 5, 2020).

Proposed RMD Single Life Table – Life Expectancy

Age	Factor	Age	Factor	Age	Factor
0	84.5	40	45.7	80	11.2
1	83.7	41	44.7	81	10.5
2	82.7	42	43.8	82	9.9
3	81.7	43	42.8	83	9.2
4	80.8	44	41.8	84	8.6
5	79.8	45	40.9	85	8.1
6	78.8	46	39.9	86	7.5
7	77.8	47	39.0	87	7.0
8	76.8	48	38.0	88	6.6
9	75.8	49	37.1	89	6.1
10	74.8	50	36.1	90	5.7
11	73.8	51	35.2	91	5.3
12	72.8	52	34.3	92	4.9
13	71.9	53	33.3	93	4.6
14	70.9	54	32.4	94	4.2
15	69.9	55	31.5	95	3.9
16	68.9	56	30.6	96	3.7
17	67.9	57	29.7	97	3.4
18	66.9	58	28.8	98	3.2
19	66.0	59	27.9	99	3.0
20	65.0	60	27.1	100	2.8
21	64.0	61	26.2	101	2.6
22	63.0	62	25.3	102	2.5
23	62.0	63	24.5	103	2.3
24	61.1	64	23.6	104	2.2
25	60.1	65	22.8	105	2.1
26	59.1	66	22.0	106	2.1
27	58.2	67	21.2	107	2.1
28	57.2	68	20.4	108	2.0
29	56.2	69	19.5	109	2.0
30	55.3	70	18.7	110	2.0
31	54.3	71	17.9	111	2.0
32	53.4	72	17.1	112	2.0
33	52.4	73	16.3	113	1.9
34	51.4	74	15.6	114	1.9
35	50.5	75	14.8	115	1.8
36	49.5	76	14.0	116	1.8
37	48.6	77	13.3	117	1.6
38	47.6	78	12.6	118	1.4
39	46.6	79	11.9	119	1.1
				120 +	1.0

Proposed RMD Joint and Last Survivor Table - Life Expectancy

Ages	35	36	37	38	39	40	41	42	43	44	45	46
35	57.0	56.6	56.1	55.7	55.3	54.9	54.5	54.2	53.9	53.6	53.4	53.1
36	56.6	56.0	55.6	55.1	54.7	54.3	53.9	53.6	53.2	52.9	52.6	52.4
37	56.1	55.6	55.1	54.6	54.1	53.7	53.3	52.9	52.6	52.2	51.9	51.7
38	55.7	55.1	54.6	54.1	53.6	53.1	52.7	52.3	51.9	51.6	51.3	50.9
39	55.3	54.7	54.1	53.6	53.1	52.6	52.1	51.7	51.3	50.9	50.6	50.3
40	54.9	54.3	53.7	53.1	52.6	52.1	51.6	51.2	50.7	50.3	50.0	49.6
41	54.5	53.9	53.3	52.7	52.1	51.6	51.1	50.6	50.2	49.7	49.3	49.0
42	54.2	53.6	52.9	52.3	51.7	51.2	50.6	50.1	49.6	49.2	48.7	48.3
43	53.9	53.2	52.6	51.9	51.3	50.7	50.2	49.6	49.1	48.6	48.2	47.8
44	53.6	52.9	52.2	51.6	50.9	50.3	49.7	49.2	48.6	48.1	47.7	47.2
45	53.4	52.6	51.9	51.3	50.6	50.0	49.3	48.7	48.2	47.7	47.1	46.7
46	53.1	52.4	51.7	50.9	50.3	49.6	49.0	48.3	47.8	47.2	46.7	46.2
47	52.9	52.1	51.4	50.7	50.0	49.3	48.6	48.0	47.4	46.8	46.2	45.7
48	52.7	51.9	51.2	50.4	49.7	49.0	48.3	47.6	47.0	46.4	45.8	45.2
49	52.5	51.7	50.9	50.2	49.4	48.7	48.0	47.3	46.6	46.0	45.4	44.8
50	52.3	51.5	50.7	49.9	49.2	48.4	47.7	47.0	46.3	45.7	45.0	44.4
51	52.2	51.4	50.5	49.7	49.0	48.2	47.5	46.7	46.0	45.3	44.7	44.0
52	52.0	51.2	50.4	49.6	48.8	48.0	47.2	46.5	45.7	45.0	44.4	43.7
53	51.9	51.0	50.2	49.4	48.6	47.8	47.0	46.2	45.5	44.8	44.1	43.4
54	51.8	50.9	50.1	49.2	48.4	47.6	46.8	46.0	45.3	44.5	43.8	43.1
55	51.7	50.8	49.9	49.1	48.2	47.4	46.6	45.8	45.0	44.3	43.5	42.8
56	51.6	50.7	49.8	48.9	48.1	47.3	46.4	45.6	44.8	44.1	43.3	42.5
57	51.5	50.6	49.7	48.8	48.0	47.1	46.3	45.5	44.7	43.9	43.1	42.3
58	51.4	50.5	49.6	48.7	47.8	47.0	46.1	45.3	44.5	43.7	42.9	42.1
59	51.3	50.4	49.5	48.6	47.7	46.9	46.0	45.2	44.3	43.5	42.7	41.9
60	51.2	50.3	49.4	48.5	47.6	46.8	45.9	45.0	44.2	43.4	42.5	41.7
61	51.1	50.2	49.3	48.4	47.5	46.7	45.8	44.9	44.1	43.2	42.4	41.6
62	51.1	50.2	49.3	48.4	47.5	46.6	45.7	44.8	43.9	43.1	42.2	41.4
63	51.0	50.1	49.2	48.3	47.4	46.5	45.6	44.7	43.8	43.0	42.1	41.3
64	51.0	50.0	49.1	48.2	47.3	46.4	45.5	44.6	43.7	42.9	42.0	41.1
65	50.9	50.0	49.1	48.2	47.2	46.3	45.4	44.5	43.6	42.8	41.9	41.0
66	50.9	50.0	49.0	48.1	47.2	46.3	45.4	44.5	43.6	42.7	41.8	40.9
67	50.8	49.9	49.0	48.0	47.1	46.2	45.3	44.4	43.5	42.6	41.7	40.8
68	50.8	49.9	48.9	48.0	47.1	46.2	45.2	44.3	43.4	42.5	41.6	40.7
69	50.8	49.8	48.9	48.0	47.0	46.1	45.2	44.3	43.3	42.4	41.5	40.6
70	50.7	49.8	48.9	47.9	47.0	46.1	45.1	44.2	43.3	42.4	41.5	40.6
71	50.7	49.8	48.8	47.9	47.0	46.0	45.1	44.2	43.2	42.3	41.4	40.5
72	50.7	49.7	48.8	47.9	46.9	46.0	45.0	44.1	43.2	42.3	41.3	40.4
73	50.7	49.7	48.8	47.8	46.9	45.9	45.0	44.1	43.1	42.2	41.3	40.4
74	50.6	49.7	48.8	47.8	46.9	45.9	45.0	44.0	43.1	42.2	41.2	40.3
75	50.6	49.7	48.7	47.8	46.8	45.9	44.9	44.0	43.1	42.1	41.2	40.3
76	50.6	49.7	48.7	47.8	46.8	45.9	44.9	44.0	43.0	42.1	41.2	40.2
77	50.6	49.6	48.7	47.7	46.8	45.8	44.9	43.9	43.0	42.1	41.1	40.2
78	50.6	49.6	48.7	47.7	46.8	45.8	44.9	43.9	43.0	42.0	41.1	40.2

Proposed RMD Joint and Last Survivor Table - Life Expectancy

Ages	35	36	37	38	39	40	41	42	43	44	45	46
79	50.6	49.6	48.7	47.7	46.8	45.8	44.9	43.9	43.0	42.0	41.1	40.1
80	50.6	49.6	48.7	47.7	46.7	45.8	44.8	43.9	42.9	42.0	41.1	40.1
81	50.6	49.6	48.6	47.7	46.7	45.8	44.8	43.9	42.9	42.0	41.0	40.1
82	50.5	49.6	48.6	47.7	46.7	45.8	44.8	43.9	42.9	42.0	41.0	40.1
83	50.5	49.6	48.6	47.7	46.7	45.8	44.8	43.8	42.9	41.9	41.0	40.0
84	50.5	49.6	48.6	47.7	46.7	45.7	44.8	43.8	42.9	41.9	41.0	40.0
85	50.5	49.6	48.6	47.7	46.7	45.7	44.8	43.8	42.9	41.9	41.0	40.0
86	50.5	49.6	48.6	47.6	46.7	45.7	44.8	43.8	42.9	41.9	41.0	40.0
87	50.5	49.6	48.6	47.6	46.7	45.7	44.8	43.8	42.9	41.9	40.9	40.0
88	50.5	49.6	48.6	47.6	46.7	45.7	44.8	43.8	42.8	41.9	40.9	40.0
89	50.5	49.6	48.6	47.6	46.7	45.7	44.8	43.8	42.8	41.9	40.9	40.0
90	50.5	49.5	48.6	47.6	46.7	45.7	44.8	43.8	42.8	41.9	40.9	40.0
91	50.5	49.5	48.6	47.6	46.7	45.7	44.7	43.8	42.8	41.9	40.9	40.0
92	50.5	49.5	48.6	47.6	46.7	45.7	44.7	43.8	42.8	41.9	40.9	40.0
93	50.5	49.5	48.6	47.6	46.7	45.7	44.7	43.8	42.8	41.9	40.9	40.0
94	50.5	49.5	48.6	47.6	46.7	45.7	44.7	43.8	42.8	41.9	40.9	40.0
95	50.5	49.5	48.6	47.6	46.7	45.7	44.7	43.8	42.8	41.9	40.9	40.0
96	50.5	49.5	48.6	47.6	46.7	45.7	44.7	43.8	42.8	41.9	40.9	39.9
97	50.5	49.5	48.6	47.6	46.7	45.7	44.7	43.8	42.8	41.9	40.9	39.9
98	50.5	49.5	48.6	47.6	46.7	45.7	44.7	43.8	42.8	41.9	40.9	39.9
99	50.5	49.5	48.6	47.6	46.7	45.7	44.7	43.8	42.8	41.9	40.9	39.9
100	50.5	49.5	48.6	47.6	46.7	45.7	44.7	43.8	42.8	41.9	40.9	39.9
101	50.5	49.5	48.6	47.6	46.7	45.7	44.7	43.8	42.8	41.9	40.9	39.9
102	50.5	49.5	48.6	47.6	46.7	45.7	44.7	43.8	42.8	41.9	40.9	39.9
103	50.5	49.5	48.6	47.6	46.7	45.7	44.7	43.8	42.8	41.9	40.9	39.9
104	50.5	49.5	48.6	47.6	46.7	45.7	44.7	43.8	42.8	41.9	40.9	39.9
105	50.5	49.5	48.6	47.6	46.7	45.7	44.7	43.8	42.8	41.9	40.9	39.9
106	50.5	49.5	48.6	47.6	46.7	45.7	44.7	43.8	42.8	41.9	40.9	39.9
107	50.5	49.5	48.6	47.6	46.7	45.7	44.7	43.8	42.8	41.9	40.9	39.9
108	50.5	49.5	48.6	47.6	46.7	45.7	44.7	43.8	42.8	41.9	40.9	39.9
109	50.5	49.5	48.6	47.6	46.6	45.7	44.7	43.8	42.8	41.9	40.9	39.9
110	50.5	49.5	48.6	47.6	46.6	45.7	44.7	43.8	42.8	41.9	40.9	39.9
111	50.5	49.5	48.6	47.6	46.6	45.7	44.7	43.8	42.8	41.9	40.9	39.9
112	50.5	49.5	48.6	47.6	46.6	45.7	44.7	43.8	42.8	41.9	40.9	39.9
113	50.5	49.5	48.6	47.6	46.6	45.7	44.7	43.8	42.8	41.9	40.9	39.9
114	50.5	49.5	48.6	47.6	46.6	45.7	44.7	43.8	42.8	41.9	40.9	39.9
115	50.5	49.5	48.6	47.6	46.6	45.7	44.7	43.8	42.8	41.9	40.9	39.9
116	50.5	49.5	48.6	47.6	46.6	45.7	44.7	43.8	42.8	41.8	40.9	39.9
117	50.5	49.5	48.6	47.6	46.6	45.7	44.7	43.8	42.8	41.8	40.9	39.9
118	50.5	49.5	48.6	47.6	46.6	45.7	44.7	43.8	42.8	41.8	40.9	39.9
119	50.5	49.5	48.6	47.6	46.6	45.7	44.7	43.8	42.8	41.8	40.9	39.9
120+	50.5	49.5	48.6	47.6	46.6	45.7	44.7	43.8	42.8	41.8	40.9	39.9

Proposed RMD Joint and Last Survivor Table - Life Expectancy

Ages	47	48	49	50	51	52	53	54	55	56	57	58
47	45.2	44.7	44.2	43.8	43.4	43.1	42.7	42.4	42.1	41.8	41.6	41.3
48	44.7	44.2	43.7	43.3	42.8	42.4	42.1	41.7	41.4	41.1	40.8	40.6
49	44.2	43.7	43.2	42.7	42.3	41.9	41.5	41.1	40.8	40.4	40.1	39.9
50	43.8	43.3	42.7	42.2	41.7	41.3	40.9	40.5	40.1	39.8	39.5	39.2
51	43.4	42.8	42.3	41.7	41.2	40.8	40.3	39.9	39.5	39.1	38.8	38.5
52	43.1	42.4	41.9	41.3	40.8	40.3	39.8	39.3	38.9	38.5	38.2	37.8
53	42.7	42.1	41.5	40.9	40.3	39.8	39.3	38.8	38.4	38.0	37.6	37.2
54	42.4	41.7	41.1	40.5	39.9	39.3	38.8	38.3	37.9	37.4	37.0	36.6
55	42.1	41.4	40.8	40.1	39.5	38.9	38.4	37.9	37.4	36.9	36.4	36.0
56	41.8	41.1	40.4	39.8	39.1	38.5	38.0	37.4	36.9	36.4	35.9	35.5
57	41.6	40.8	40.1	39.5	38.8	38.2	37.6	37.0	36.4	35.9	35.4	35.0
58	41.3	40.6	39.9	39.2	38.5	37.8	37.2	36.6	36.0	35.5	35.0	34.5
59	41.1	40.4	39.6	38.9	38.2	37.5	36.9	36.2	35.6	35.1	34.5	34.0
60	40.9	40.1	39.4	38.6	37.9	37.2	36.6	35.9	35.3	34.7	34.1	33.6
61	40.7	40.0	39.2	38.4	37.7	37.0	36.3	35.6	34.9	34.3	33.7	33.2
62	40.6	39.8	39.0	38.2	37.5	36.7	36.0	35.3	34.6	34.0	33.4	32.8
63	40.4	39.6	38.8	38.0	37.2	36.5	35.8	35.0	34.4	33.7	33.0	32.4
64	40.3	39.5	38.6	37.8	37.0	36.3	35.5	34.8	34.1	33.4	32.7	32.1
65	40.2	39.3	38.5	37.7	36.9	36.1	35.3	34.6	33.8	33.1	32.5	31.8
66	40.0	39.2	38.4	37.5	36.7	35.9	35.1	34.4	33.6	32.9	32.2	31.5
67	39.9	39.1	38.2	37.4	36.6	35.7	35.0	34.2	33.4	32.7	32.0	31.3
68	39.8	39.0	38.1	37.3	36.4	35.6	34.8	34.0	33.2	32.5	31.7	31.0
69	39.8	38.9	38.0	37.1	36.3	35.5	34.6	33.8	33.1	32.3	31.5	30.8
70	39.7	38.8	37.9	37.0	36.2	35.3	34.5	33.7	32.9	32.1	31.3	30.6
71	39.6	38.7	37.8	36.9	36.1	35.2	34.4	33.6	32.7	32.0	31.2	30.4
72	39.5	38.6	37.7	36.9	36.0	35.1	34.3	33.4	32.6	31.8	31.0	30.2
73	39.5	38.6	37.7	36.8	35.9	35.0	34.2	33.3	32.5	31.7	30.9	30.1
74	39.4	38.5	37.6	36.7	35.8	34.9	34.1	33.2	32.4	31.6	30.7	29.9
75	39.4	38.4	37.5	36.6	35.7	34.9	34.0	33.1	32.3	31.5	30.6	29.8
76	39.3	38.4	37.5	36.6	35.7	34.8	33.9	33.1	32.2	31.4	30.5	29.7
77	39.3	38.4	37.4	36.5	35.6	34.7	33.9	33.0	32.1	31.3	30.4	29.6
78	39.2	38.3	37.4	36.5	35.6	34.7	33.8	32.9	32.0	31.2	30.3	29.5
79	39.2	38.3	37.4	36.4	35.5	34.6	33.7	32.9	32.0	31.1	30.3	29.4
80	39.2	38.2	37.3	36.4	35.5	34.6	33.7	32.8	31.9	31.1	30.2	29.3
81	39.1	38.2	37.3	36.4	35.4	34.5	33.6	32.7	31.9	31.0	30.1	29.3
82	39.1	38.2	37.3	36.3	35.4	34.5	33.6	32.7	31.8	30.9	30.1	29.2
83	39.1	38.2	37.2	36.3	35.4	34.5	33.6	32.7	31.8	30.9	30.0	29.2
84	39.1	38.1	37.2	36.3	35.4	34.4	33.5	32.6	31.7	30.9	30.0	29.1

Proposed RMD Joint and Last Survivor Table - Life Expectancy

Ages	47	48	49	50	51	52	53	54	55	56	57	58
85	39.1	38.1	37.2	36.3	35.3	34.4	33.5	32.6	31.7	30.8	29.9	29.1
86	39.1	38.1	37.2	36.2	35.3	34.4	33.5	32.6	31.7	30.8	29.9	29.0
87	39.0	38.1	37.2	36.2	35.3	34.4	33.5	32.6	31.7	30.8	29.9	29.0
88	39.0	38.1	37.1	36.2	35.3	34.4	33.4	32.5	31.6	30.7	29.9	29.0
89	39.0	38.1	37.1	36.2	35.3	34.3	33.4	32.5	31.6	30.7	29.8	29.0
90	39.0	38.1	37.1	36.2	35.3	34.3	33.4	32.5	31.6	30.7	29.8	28.9
91	39.0	38.1	37.1	36.2	35.2	34.3	33.4	32.5	31.6	30.7	29.8	28.9
92	39.0	38.1	37.1	36.2	35.2	34.3	33.4	32.5	31.6	30.7	29.8	28.9
93	39.0	38.1	37.1	36.2	35.2	34.3	33.4	32.5	31.6	30.7	29.8	28.9
94	39.0	38.1	37.1	36.2	35.2	34.3	33.4	32.5	31.6	30.7	29.8	28.9
95	39.0	38.0	37.1	36.2	35.2	34.3	33.4	32.5	31.5	30.6	29.8	28.9
96	39.0	38.0	37.1	36.2	35.2	34.3	33.4	32.4	31.5	30.6	29.7	28.9
97	39.0	38.0	37.1	36.2	35.2	34.3	33.4	32.4	31.5	30.6	29.7	28.9
98	39.0	38.0	37.1	36.1	35.2	34.3	33.4	32.4	31.5	30.6	29.7	28.8
99	39.0	38.0	37.1	36.1	35.2	34.3	33.3	32.4	31.5	30.6	29.7	28.8
100	39.0	38.0	37.1	36.1	35.2	34.3	33.3	32.4	31.5	30.6	29.7	28.8
101	39.0	38.0	37.1	36.1	35.2	34.3	33.3	32.4	31.5	30.6	29.7	28.8
102	39.0	38.0	37.1	36.1	35.2	34.3	33.3	32.4	31.5	30.6	29.7	28.8
103	39.0	38.0	37.1	36.1	35.2	34.3	33.3	32.4	31.5	30.6	29.7	28.8
104	39.0	38.0	37.1	36.1	35.2	34.3	33.3	32.4	31.5	30.6	29.7	28.8
105	39.0	38.0	37.1	36.1	35.2	34.3	33.3	32.4	31.5	30.6	29.7	28.8
106	39.0	38.0	37.1	36.1	35.2	34.3	33.3	32.4	31.5	30.6	29.7	28.8
107	39.0	38.0	37.1	36.1	35.2	34.3	33.3	32.4	31.5	30.6	29.7	28.8
108	39.0	38.0	37.1	36.1	35.2	34.3	33.3	32.4	31.5	30.6	29.7	28.8
109	39.0	38.0	37.1	36.1	35.2	34.3	33.3	32.4	31.5	30.6	29.7	28.8
110	39.0	38.0	37.1	36.1	35.2	34.3	33.3	32.4	31.5	30.6	29.7	28.8
111	39.0	38.0	37.1	36.1	35.2	34.3	33.3	32.4	31.5	30.6	29.7	28.8
112	39.0	38.0	37.1	36.1	35.2	34.3	33.3	32.4	31.5	30.6	29.7	28.8
113	39.0	38.0	37.1	36.1	35.2	34.3	33.3	32.4	31.5	30.6	29.7	28.8
114	39.0	38.0	37.1	36.1	35.2	34.3	33.3	32.4	31.5	30.6	29.7	28.8
115	39.0	38.0	37.1	36.1	35.2	34.3	33.3	32.4	31.5	30.6	29.7	28.8
116	39.0	38.0	37.1	36.1	35.2	34.3	33.3	32.4	31.5	30.6	29.7	28.8
117	39.0	38.0	37.1	36.1	35.2	34.3	33.3	32.4	31.5	30.6	29.7	28.8
118	39.0	38.0	37.1	36.1	35.2	34.3	33.3	32.4	31.5	30.6	29.7	28.8
119	39.0	38.0	37.1	36.1	35.2	34.3	33.3	32.4	31.5	30.6	29.7	28.8
120+	39.0	38.0	37.1	36.1	35.2	34.3	33.3	32.4	31.5	30.6	29.7	28.8

Proposed RMD Joint and Last Survivor Table – Life Expectancy

Ages	59	60	61	62	63	64	65	66	67	68	69	70
59	33.5	33.1	32.6	32.2	31.8	31.5	31.2	30.9	30.6	30.3	30.1	29.9
60	33.1	32.6	32.1	31.7	31.3	30.9	30.5	30.2	29.9	29.6	29.4	29.1
61	32.6	32.1	31.6	31.2	30.7	30.3	30.0	29.6	29.3	29.0	28.7	28.5
62	32.2	31.7	31.2	30.7	30.2	29.8	29.4	29.0	28.7	28.4	28.1	27.8
63	31.8	31.3	30.7	30.2	29.8	29.3	28.9	28.5	28.1	27.8	27.4	27.1
64	31.5	30.9	30.3	29.8	29.3	28.8	28.4	28.0	27.6	27.2	26.8	26.5
65	31.2	30.5	30.0	29.4	28.9	28.4	27.9	27.4	27.0	26.6	26.3	25.9
66	30.9	30.2	29.6	29.0	28.5	28.0	27.4	27.0	26.5	26.1	25.7	25.4
67	30.6	29.9	29.3	28.7	28.1	27.6	27.0	26.5	26.1	25.6	25.2	24.8
68	30.3	29.6	29.0	28.4	27.8	27.2	26.6	26.1	25.6	25.1	24.7	24.3
69	30.1	29.4	28.7	28.1	27.4	26.8	26.3	25.7	25.2	24.7	24.2	23.8
70	29.9	29.1	28.5	27.8	27.1	26.5	25.9	25.4	24.8	24.3	23.8	23.3
71	29.7	28.9	28.2	27.5	26.9	26.2	25.6	25.0	24.4	23.9	23.4	22.9
72	29.5	28.7	28.0	27.3	26.6	26.0	25.3	24.7	24.1	23.5	23.0	22.5
73	29.3	28.6	27.8	27.1	26.4	25.7	25.0	24.4	23.8	23.2	22.6	22.1
74	29.2	28.4	27.6	26.9	26.2	25.5	24.8	24.1	23.5	22.9	22.3	21.7
75	29.0	28.2	27.5	26.7	26.0	25.3	24.6	23.9	23.2	22.6	22.0	21.4
76	28.9	28.1	27.3	26.6	25.8	25.1	24.4	23.7	23.0	22.4	21.7	21.1
77	28.8	28.0	27.2	26.4	25.7	24.9	24.2	23.5	22.8	22.1	21.5	20.8
78	28.7	27.9	27.1	26.3	25.5	24.8	24.0	23.3	22.6	21.9	21.2	20.6
79	28.6	27.8	27.0	26.2	25.4	24.6	23.9	23.2	22.4	21.7	21.0	20.4
80	28.5	27.7	26.9	26.1	25.3	24.5	23.8	23.0	22.3	21.6	20.9	20.2
81	28.4	27.6	26.8	26.0	25.2	24.4	23.6	22.9	22.1	21.4	20.7	20.0
82	28.4	27.5	26.7	25.9	25.1	24.3	23.5	22.8	22.0	21.3	20.5	19.8
83	28.3	27.5	26.7	25.8	25.0	24.2	23.4	22.7	21.9	21.2	20.4	19.7
84	28.3	27.4	26.6	25.8	25.0	24.2	23.4	22.6	21.8	21.0	20.3	19.6
85	28.2	27.4	26.5	25.7	24.9	24.1	23.3	22.5	21.7	21.0	20.2	19.4
86	28.2	27.3	26.5	25.7	24.8	24.0	23.2	22.4	21.7	20.9	20.1	19.3
87	28.2	27.3	26.5	25.6	24.8	24.0	23.2	22.4	21.6	20.8	20.0	19.3
88	28.1	27.3	26.4	25.6	24.8	23.9	23.1	22.3	21.5	20.7	20.0	19.2
89	28.1	27.2	26.4	25.5	24.7	23.9	23.1	22.3	21.5	20.7	19.9	19.1
90	28.1	27.2	26.4	25.5	24.7	23.9	23.0	22.2	21.4	20.6	19.9	19.1
91	28.1	27.2	26.3	25.5	24.7	23.8	23.0	22.2	21.4	20.6	19.8	19.0
92	28.0	27.2	26.3	25.5	24.6	23.8	23.0	22.2	21.4	20.6	19.8	19.0
93	28.0	27.2	26.3	25.5	24.6	23.8	23.0	22.2	21.3	20.5	19.7	18.9
94	28.0	27.1	26.3	25.4	24.6	23.8	22.9	22.1	21.3	20.5	19.7	18.9
95	28.0	27.1	26.3	25.4	24.6	23.8	22.9	22.1	21.3	20.5	19.7	18.9
96	28.0	27.1	26.3	25.4	24.6	23.7	22.9	22.1	21.3	20.5	19.7	18.9

Proposed RMD Joint and Last Survivor Table - Life Expectancy

Ages	59	60	61	62	63	64	65	66	67	68	69	70
97	28.0	27.1	26.3	25.4	24.6	23.7	22.9	22.1	21.3	20.5	19.7	18.9
98	28.0	27.1	26.2	25.4	24.6	23.7	22.9	22.1	21.3	20.4	19.6	18.8
99	28.0	27.1	26.2	25.4	24.5	23.7	22.9	22.1	21.2	20.4	19.6	18.8
100	28.0	27.1	26.2	25.4	24.5	23.7	22.9	22.1	21.2	20.4	19.6	18.8
101	28.0	27.1	26.2	25.4	24.5	23.7	22.9	22.0	21.2	20.4	19.6	18.8
102	28.0	27.1	26.2	25.4	24.5	23.7	22.9	22.0	21.2	20.4	19.6	18.8
103	27.9	27.1	26.2	25.4	24.5	23.7	22.9	22.0	21.2	20.4	19.6	18.8
104	27.9	27.1	26.2	25.4	24.5	23.7	22.9	22.0	21.2	20.4	19.6	18.8
105	27.9	27.1	26.2	25.4	24.5	23.7	22.9	22.0	21.2	20.4	19.6	18.8
106	27.9	27.1	26.2	25.4	24.5	23.7	22.9	22.0	21.2	20.4	19.6	18.8
107	27.9	27.1	26.2	25.4	24.5	23.7	22.8	22.0	21.2	20.4	19.6	18.8
108	27.9	27.1	26.2	25.4	24.5	23.7	22.8	22.0	21.2	20.4	19.6	18.8
109	27.9	27.1	26.2	25.4	24.5	23.7	22.8	22.0	21.2	20.4	19.6	18.8
110	27.9	27.1	26.2	25.4	24.5	23.7	22.8	22.0	21.2	20.4	19.6	18.8
111	27.9	27.1	26.2	25.4	24.5	23.7	22.8	22.0	21.2	20.4	19.6	18.8
112	27.9	27.1	26.2	25.4	24.5	23.7	22.8	22.0	21.2	20.4	19.6	18.8
113	27.9	27.1	26.2	25.4	24.5	23.7	22.8	22.0	21.2	20.4	19.6	18.8
114	27.9	27.1	26.2	25.4	24.5	23.7	22.8	22.0	21.2	20.4	19.6	18.8
115	27.9	27.1	26.2	25.4	24.5	23.7	22.8	22.0	21.2	20.4	19.6	18.8
116	27.9	27.1	26.2	25.3	24.5	23.7	22.8	22.0	21.2	20.4	19.6	18.8
117	27.9	27.1	26.2	25.3	24.5	23.7	22.8	22.0	21.2	20.4	19.6	18.7
118	27.9	27.1	26.2	25.3	24.5	23.7	22.8	22.0	21.2	20.4	19.6	18.7
119	27.9	27.1	26.2	25.3	24.5	23.6	22.8	22.0	21.2	20.4	19.5	18.7
120+	27.9	27.1	26.2	25.3	24.5	23.6	22.8	22.0	21.2	20.4	19.5	18.7

Proposed RMD Joint and Last Survivor Table – Life Expectancy

Ages	71	72	73	74	75	76	77	78	79	80	81	82
71	22.4	22.0	21.6	21.2	20.8	20.5	20.2	20.0	19.7	19.5	19.3	19.1
72	22.0	21.5	21.1	20.7	20.3	20.0	19.6	19.4	19.1	18.9	18.6	18.4
73	21.6	21.1	20.6	20.2	19.8	19.4	19.1	18.8	18.5	18.2	18.0	17.8
74	21.2	20.7	20.2	19.7	19.3	18.9	18.6	18.2	17.9	17.6	17.4	17.2
75	20.8	20.3	19.8	19.3	18.9	18.5	18.1	17.7	17.4	17.1	16.8	16.6
76	20.5	20.0	19.4	18.9	18.5	18.0	17.6	17.2	16.9	16.5	16.2	16.0
77	20.2	19.6	19.1	18.6	18.1	17.6	17.2	16.8	16.4	16.0	15.7	15.4
78	20.0	19.4	18.8	18.2	17.7	17.2	16.8	16.3	15.9	15.6	15.2	14.9
79	19.7	19.1	18.5	17.9	17.4	16.9	16.4	15.9	15.5	15.1	14.7	14.4
80	19.5	18.9	18.2	17.6	17.1	16.5	16.0	15.6	15.1	14.7	14.3	14.0
81	19.3	18.6	18.0	17.4	16.8	16.2	15.7	15.2	14.7	14.3	13.9	13.5
82	19.1	18.4	17.8	17.2	16.6	16.0	15.4	14.9	14.4	14.0	13.5	13.1
83	19.0	18.3	17.6	17.0	16.3	15.7	15.2	14.6	14.1	13.6	13.2	12.8
84	18.8	18.1	17.4	16.8	16.1	15.5	14.9	14.4	13.8	13.3	12.9	12.4
85	18.7	18.0	17.3	16.6	16.0	15.3	14.7	14.1	13.6	13.1	12.6	12.1
86	18.6	17.9	17.2	16.5	15.8	15.2	14.5	13.9	13.4	12.8	12.3	11.9
87	18.5	17.8	17.1	16.4	15.7	15.0	14.4	13.8	13.2	12.6	12.1	11.6
88	18.4	17.7	17.0	16.2	15.6	14.9	14.2	13.6	13.0	12.4	11.9	11.4
89	18.4	17.6	16.9	16.2	15.4	14.8	14.1	13.5	12.9	12.3	11.7	11.2
90	18.3	17.5	16.8	16.1	15.4	14.7	14.0	13.4	12.7	12.1	11.6	11.0
91	18.3	17.5	16.7	16.0	15.3	14.6	13.9	13.2	12.6	12.0	11.4	10.9
92	18.2	17.4	16.7	15.9	15.2	14.5	13.8	13.2	12.5	11.9	11.3	10.8
93	18.2	17.4	16.6	15.9	15.2	14.4	13.7	13.1	12.4	11.8	11.2	10.6
94	18.1	17.4	16.6	15.8	15.1	14.4	13.7	13.0	12.4	11.7	11.1	10.5
95	18.1	17.3	16.6	15.8	15.1	14.3	13.6	12.9	12.3	11.6	11.0	10.5
96	18.1	17.3	16.5	15.8	15.0	14.3	13.6	12.9	12.2	11.6	11.0	10.4
97	18.1	17.3	16.5	15.7	15.0	14.3	13.5	12.9	12.2	11.5	10.9	10.3
98	18.0	17.3	16.5	15.7	15.0	14.2	13.5	12.8	12.1	11.5	10.9	10.3
99	18.0	17.2	16.5	15.7	14.9	14.2	13.5	12.8	12.1	11.4	10.8	10.2
100	18.0	17.2	16.4	15.7	14.9	14.2	13.5	12.8	12.1	11.4	10.8	10.2
101	18.0	17.2	16.4	15.7	14.9	14.2	13.4	12.7	12.0	11.4	10.7	10.1
102	18.0	17.2	16.4	15.7	14.9	14.2	13.4	12.7	12.0	11.4	10.7	10.1
103	18.0	17.2	16.4	15.6	14.9	14.1	13.4	12.7	12.0	11.3	10.7	10.1
104	18.0	17.2	16.4	15.6	14.9	14.1	13.4	12.7	12.0	11.3	10.7	10.1
105	18.0	17.2	16.4	15.6	14.9	14.1	13.4	12.7	12.0	11.3	10.7	10.0
106	18.0	17.2	16.4	15.6	14.9	14.1	13.4	12.7	12.0	11.3	10.7	10.0
107	18.0	17.2	16.4	15.6	14.9	14.1	13.4	12.7	12.0	11.3	10.7	10.0
108	18.0	17.2	16.4	15.6	14.9	14.1	13.4	12.7	12.0	11.3	10.7	10.0
109	18.0	17.2	16.4	15.6	14.9	14.1	13.4	12.7	12.0	11.3	10.7	10.0
110	18.0	17.2	16.4	15.6	14.9	14.1	13.4	12.7	12.0	11.3	10.7	10.0
111	18.0	17.2	16.4	15.6	14.9	14.1	13.4	12.7	12.0	11.3	10.6	10.0
112	18.0	17.2	16.4	15.6	14.9	14.1	13.4	12.7	12.0	11.3	10.6	10.0
113	18.0	17.2	16.4	15.6	14.9	14.1	13.4	12.7	12.0	11.3	10.6	10.0
114	18.0	17.2	16.4	15.6	14.8	14.1	13.4	12.6	12.0	11.3	10.6	10.0
115	18.0	17.2	16.4	15.6	14.8	14.1	13.4	12.6	11.9	11.3	10.6	10.0
116	18.0	17.2	16.4	15.6	14.8	14.1	13.3	12.6	11.9	11.3	10.6	10.0
117	17.9	17.1	16.4	15.6	14.8	14.1	13.3	12.6	11.9	11.2	10.6	9.9
118	17.9	17.1	16.4	15.6	14.8	14.1	13.3	12.6	11.9	11.2	10.5	9.9
119	17.9	17.1	16.3	15.6	14.8	14.0	13.3	12.6	11.9	11.2	10.5	9.9
120+	17.9	17.1	16.3	15.6	14.8	14.0	13.3	12.6	11.9	11.2	10.5	9.9

Proposed RMD Joint and Last Survivor Table – Life Expectancy

Ages	83	84	85	86	87	88	89	90	91	92	93	94
83	12.4	12.0	11.7	11.4	11.2	10.9	10.7	10.5	10.4	10.2	10.1	10.0
84	12.0	11.7	11.3	11.0	10.7	10.5	10.3	10.1	9.9	9.7	9.6	9.5
85	11.7	11.3	11.0	10.7	10.4	10.1	9.9	9.6	9.5	9.3	9.1	9.0
86	11.4	11.0	10.7	10.3	10.0	9.7	9.5	9.2	9.0	8.9	8.7	8.6
87	11.2	10.7	10.4	10.0	9.7	9.4	9.1	8.9	8.7	8.5	8.3	8.1
88	10.9	10.5	10.1	9.7	9.4	9.1	8.8	8.5	8.3	8.1	7.9	7.7
89	10.7	10.3	9.9	9.5	9.1	8.8	8.5	8.2	8.0	7.8	7.6	7.4
90	10.5	10.1	9.6	9.2	8.9	8.5	8.2	7.9	7.7	7.5	7.3	7.1
91	10.4	9.9	9.5	9.0	8.7	8.3	8.0	7.7	7.4	7.2	7.0	6.8
92	10.2	9.7	9.3	8.9	8.5	8.1	7.8	7.5	7.2	6.9	6.7	6.5
93	10.1	9.6	9.1	8.7	8.3	7.9	7.6	7.3	7.0	6.7	6.5	6.3
94	10.0	9.5	9.0	8.6	8.1	7.7	7.4	7.1	6.8	6.5	6.3	6.0
95	9.9	9.4	8.9	8.4	8.0	7.6	7.2	6.9	6.6	6.3	6.1	5.8
96	9.8	9.3	8.8	8.3	7.9	7.5	7.1	6.8	6.5	6.2	5.9	5.7
97	9.7	9.2	8.7	8.2	7.8	7.4	7.0	6.6	6.3	6.0	5.8	5.5
98	9.7	9.1	8.6	8.1	7.7	7.3	6.9	6.5	6.2	5.9	5.6	5.4
99	9.6	9.1	8.6	8.1	7.6	7.2	6.8	6.4	6.1	5.8	5.5	5.3
100	9.6	9.0	8.5	8.0	7.6	7.1	6.7	6.4	6.0	5.7	5.4	5.1
101	9.5	9.0	8.5	8.0	7.5	7.1	6.7	6.3	5.9	5.6	5.3	5.1
102	9.5	8.9	8.4	7.9	7.4	7.0	6.6	6.2	5.9	5.6	5.3	5.0
103	9.5	8.9	8.4	7.9	7.4	7.0	6.6	6.2	5.8	5.5	5.2	4.9
104	9.5	8.9	8.4	7.9	7.4	6.9	6.5	6.1	5.8	5.5	5.1	4.9
105	9.5	8.9	8.3	7.8	7.4	6.9	6.5	6.1	5.8	5.4	5.1	4.8
106	9.4	8.9	8.3	7.8	7.4	6.9	6.5	6.1	5.7	5.4	5.1	4.8
107	9.4	8.9	8.3	7.8	7.3	6.9	6.5	6.1	5.7	5.4	5.1	4.8
108	9.4	8.9	8.3	7.8	7.3	6.9	6.5	6.1	5.7	5.4	5.1	4.8
109	9.4	8.9	8.3	7.8	7.3	6.9	6.5	6.1	5.7	5.4	5.1	4.8
110	9.4	8.9	8.3	7.8	7.3	6.9	6.5	6.1	5.7	5.4	5.1	4.8
111	9.4	8.8	8.3	7.8	7.3	6.9	6.4	6.1	5.7	5.4	5.0	4.8
112	9.4	8.8	8.3	7.8	7.3	6.9	6.4	6.0	5.7	5.3	5.0	4.7
113	9.4	8.8	8.3	7.8	7.3	6.8	6.4	6.0	5.7	5.3	5.0	4.7
114	9.4	8.8	8.3	7.8	7.3	6.8	6.4	6.0	5.6	5.3	5.0	4.7
115	9.4	8.8	8.3	7.7	7.3	6.8	6.4	6.0	5.6	5.3	5.0	4.7
116	9.4	8.8	8.2	7.7	7.2	6.8	6.3	5.9	5.6	5.2	4.9	4.6
117	9.3	8.7	8.2	7.7	7.2	6.7	6.3	5.9	5.5	5.2	4.8	4.5
118	9.3	8.7	8.2	7.6	7.1	6.7	6.2	5.8	5.4	5.1	4.8	4.4
119	9.3	8.7	8.1	7.6	7.1	6.6	6.2	5.7	5.4	5.0	4.7	4.3
120+	9.2	8.6	8.1	7.5	7.0	6.6	6.1	5.7	5.3	4.9	4.6	4.2

Proposed RMD Joint and Last Survivor Table – Life Expectancy

Ages	95	96	97	98	99	100	101	102	103	104	105	106
95	5.6	5.5	5.3	5.1	5.0	4.9	4.8	4.7	4.7	4.6	4.6	4.6
96	5.5	5.3	5.1	4.9	4.8	4.7	4.6	4.5	4.4	4.4	4.3	4.3
97	5.3	5.1	4.9	4.8	4.6	4.5	4.4	4.3	4.2	4.2	4.1	4.1
98	5.1	4.9	4.8	4.6	4.5	4.3	4.2	4.1	4.0	4.0	3.9	3.9
99	5.0	4.8	4.6	4.5	4.3	4.2	4.1	4.0	3.9	3.8	3.8	3.7
100	4.9	4.7	4.5	4.3	4.2	4.0	3.9	3.8	3.7	3.7	3.6	3.6
101	4.8	4.6	4.4	4.2	4.1	3.9	3.8	3.7	3.6	3.5	3.5	3.5
102	4.7	4.5	4.3	4.1	4.0	3.8	3.7	3.6	3.5	3.4	3.4	3.3
103	4.7	4.4	4.2	4.0	3.9	3.7	3.6	3.5	3.4	3.3	3.3	3.2
104	4.6	4.4	4.2	4.0	3.8	3.7	3.5	3.4	3.3	3.2	3.2	3.2
105	4.6	4.3	4.1	3.9	3.8	3.6	3.5	3.4	3.3	3.2	3.1	3.1
106	4.6	4.3	4.1	3.9	3.7	3.6	3.5	3.3	3.2	3.2	3.1	3.1
107	4.5	4.3	4.1	3.9	3.7	3.6	3.4	3.3	3.2	3.1	3.1	3.1
108	4.5	4.3	4.1	3.9	3.7	3.6	3.4	3.3	3.2	3.1	3.1	3.0
109	4.5	4.3	4.1	3.9	3.7	3.5	3.4	3.3	3.2	3.1	3.1	3.0
110	4.5	4.3	4.1	3.9	3.7	3.5	3.4	3.3	3.2	3.1	3.0	3.0
111	4.5	4.3	4.0	3.9	3.7	3.5	3.4	3.3	3.2	3.1	3.0	3.0
112	4.5	4.2	4.0	3.8	3.7	3.5	3.4	3.2	3.1	3.1	3.0	3.0
113	4.5	4.2	4.0	3.8	3.6	3.5	3.3	3.2	3.1	3.0	3.0	3.0
114	4.4	4.2	4.0	3.8	3.6	3.4	3.3	3.2	3.1	3.0	3.0	2.9
115	4.4	4.2	3.9	3.7	3.6	3.4	3.3	3.1	3.0	3.0	2.9	2.9
116	4.3	4.1	3.9	3.7	3.5	3.3	3.2	3.1	3.0	2.9	2.8	2.8
117	4.3	4.0	3.8	3.6	3.4	3.2	3.1	3.0	2.9	2.8	2.7	2.7
118	4.2	3.9	3.7	3.5	3.3	3.1	3.0	2.8	2.7	2.6	2.6	2.5
119	4.0	3.8	3.5	3.3	3.1	2.9	2.8	2.6	2.5	2.4	2.3	2.3
120+	3.9	3.7	3.4	3.2	3.0	2.8	2.6	2.5	2.3	2.2	2.1	2.1

Ages	107	108	109	110	111	112	113	114	115	116	117	118	119	120+
107	3.0	3.0	3.0	3.0	3.0	3.0	2.9	2.9	2.9	2.8	2.7	2.5	2.3	2.1
108	3.0	3.0	3.0	3.0	3.0	2.9	2.9	2.9	2.8	2.8	2.7	2.5	2.3	2.0
109	3.0	3.0	3.0	3.0	2.9	2.9	2.9	2.9	2.8	2.8	2.6	2.5	2.3	2.0
110	3.0	3.0	3.0	3.0	2.9	2.9	2.9	2.9	2.8	2.7	2.6	2.5	2.2	2.0
111	3.0	3.0	2.9	2.9	2.9	2.9	2.9	2.8	2.8	2.7	2.6	2.4	2.2	2.0
112	3.0	2.9	2.9	2.9	2.9	2.9	2.9	2.8	2.8	2.7	2.6	2.4	2.2	2.0
113	2.9	2.9	2.9	2.9	2.9	2.9	2.8	2.8	2.7	2.7	2.6	2.4	2.2	1.9
114	2.9	2.9	2.9	2.9	2.8	2.8	2.8	2.8	2.7	2.6	2.5	2.4	2.1	1.9
115	2.9	2.8	2.8	2.8	2.8	2.8	2.7	2.7	2.7	2.6	2.5	2.3	2.1	1.8
116	2.8	2.8	2.8	2.7	2.7	2.7	2.7	2.6	2.6	2.5	2.4	2.2	2.0	1.8
117	2.7	2.7	2.6	2.6	2.6	2.6	2.6	2.5	2.5	2.4	2.3	2.1	1.9	1.6
118	2.5	2.5	2.5	2.5	2.4	2.4	2.4	2.4	2.3	2.2	2.1	1.9	1.7	1.4
119	2.3	2.3	2.3	2.2	2.2	2.2	2.2	2.1	2.1	2.0	1.9	1.7	1.3	1.1
120+	2.1	2.0	2.0	2.0	2.0	2.0	1.9	1.9	1.8	1.8	1.6	1.4	1.1	1.0

APPENDIX G
One Year Term Rates

The following rates are used in computing the "cost" of pure life insurance protection that is taxable to the employee under: qualified pension and profit sharing plans (Q 4093) split-dollar plans (Q 4017); and tax-sheltered annuities (Q 4056).[1]

For these purposes, the rate at insured's attained age is generally applied to the excess of the amount payable at death over the cash value of the policy at the end of the year.

Table 2001 can generally be used starting in 2001. P.S. 58 rates and other rates derived from Table 38 could generally be used in years prior to 2002. However, split dollar arrangements entered into before January 28, 2002, in which the contractual arrangement between the employer and the employee provides that P.S. 58 rates will be used may continue to use P.S. 58 rates. In 2001, either Table 2001 or the P.S. 58/Table 38 derived rates could generally be used.

See Q 246 for Table I, Uniform Premiums for $1,000 of Group-Term Life Insurance Protection and application of the rates.

---

1. Notice 2002-8, 2002-4 IRB 398; Rev. Rul. 66-110, 1966-1 CB 12.

Table 2001

One Year Term Premiums for $1,000 of Life Insurance Protection -- One Life

Age	Premium	Age	Premium	Age	Premium
0	$0.70	34	$0.98	67	$15.20
1	0.41	35	0.99	68	16.92
2	0.27	36	1.01	69	18.70
3	0.19	37	1.04	70	20.62
4	0.13	38	1.06	71	22.72
5	0.13	39	1.07	72	25.07
6	0.14	40	1.10	73	27.57
7	0.15	41	1.13	74	30.18
8	0.16	42	1.20	75	33.05
9	0.16	43	1.29	76	36.33
10	0.16	44	1.40	77	40.17
11	0.19	45	1.53	78	44.33
12	0.24	46	1.67	79	49.23
13	0.28	47	1.83	80	54.56
14	0.33	48	1.98	81	60.51
15	0.38	49	2.13	82	66.74
16	0.52	50	2.30	83	73.07
17	0.57	51	2.52	84	80.35
18	0.59	52	2.81	85	88.76
19	0.61	53	3.20	86	99.16
20	0.62	54	3.65	87	110.40
21	0.62	55	4.15	88	121.85
22	0.64	56	4.68	89	133.40
23	0.66	57	5.20	90	144.30
24	0.68	58	5.66	91	155.80
25	0.71	59	6.06	92	168.75
26	0.73	60	6.51	93	186.44
27	0.76	61	7.11	94	206.70
28	0.80	62	7.96	95	228.35
29	0.83	63	9.08	96	250.01
30	0.87	64	10.41	97	265.09
31	0.90	65	11.90	98	270.11
32	0.93	66	13.51	99	281.05
33	0.96				

"P.S. No. 58" Rates

One Year Term Premiums for $1,000 of Life Insurance Protection – One Life

Age	Premium	Age	Premium	Age	Premium
0	$ 42.10*	35	$ 3.21	70	$ 48.06
1	4.49*	36	3.41	71	52.29
2	2.37*	37	3.63	72	56.89
3	1.72*	38	3.87	73	61.89
4	1.38*	39	4.14	74	67.33
5	1.21*	40	4.42	75	73.23
6	1.07*	41	4.73	76	79.63
7	.98*	42	5.07	77	86.57
8	.90*	43	5.44	78	94.09
9	.85*	44	5.85	79	102.23
10	.83*	45	6.30	80	111.04
11	.91*	46	6.78	81	120.57
12	1.00*	47	7.32	82	130.86*
13	1.08*	48	7.89	83	141.95*
14	1.17*	49	8.53	84	153.91*
15	1.27	50	9.22	85	166.77*
16	1.38	51	9.97	86	180.60*
17	1.48	52	10.79	87	195.43*
18	1.52	53	11.69	88	211.33*
19	1.56	54	12.67	89	228.31*
20	1.61	55	13.74	90	246.45*
21	1.67	56	14.91	91	265.75*
22	1.73	57	16.18	92	286.25*
23	1.79	58	17.56	93	307.98*
24	1.86	59	19.08	94	330.94*
25	1.93	60	20.73	95	355.11*
26	2.02	61	22.53	96	380.50*
27	2.11	62	24.50	97	407.03*
28	2.20	63	26.63	98	434.68*
29	2.31	64	28.98	99	463.35*
30	2.43	65	31.51	100	492.93*
31	2.57	66	34.28	101	523.30*
32	2.70	67	37.31	102	554.30*
33	2.86	68	40.59	103	585.75*
34	3.02	69	44.17	104	617.42*

*Rates are derived by the editor from U.S. Life Table 38, and are based on the underlying actuarial assumptions of the P.S. 58 rates (see following pages).

P.S. 58 Rates Calculations

(Net annual premium per $1,000 − 1 year term)

For various tax purposes, P.S. 58 rates can be used for the net annual premium per $1,000 of one year term life insurance where there is only one insured. P.S. 58 equivalent rates (e.g., joint and joint and survivor rates) can also be determined where there is more than one insured (sometimes referred to as Table 38 rates). The derivation of such rates is described below for one and two insureds.

In each instance, the present value of $1,000 is discounted one year at 2.5% to $975.60. $975.60 is then multiplied by the probability of death of the insured(s) during the year. In each of the formulas below, substitute the appropriate q_x from Table 38 for each insured (where two insureds are involved, the second insured is referred to as y rather than x).

required interest rate = i = 2.5%
$1 \div (1 + i) = 1 \div 1.025 = .97560$
$\$1,000 \times .97560 = \$975.60$

q_x − probability of dying in each year of age (from Table 38)

    (e.g., q_x for person age 25 is .00198)

Where two lives are involved q_x and q_y are used

    qx is probability at first person's age
    qy is probability at second person's age
    (e.g., qx for first person, age 35, is .00329 and qy for second person, age 45, is .00646)

ONE LIFE
P.S. 58 rate = $\$975.60 \times q_x$
    (e.g., rate for person age 50 = $\$975.60 \times .00945 = \$9.22$)

TWO LIFE (Joint and Survivor, Second to Die)
P.S. 58 equivalent rate = $\$975.60 \times q_x \times q_y$

    (e.g., rate for persons age 60 and 70
    = $\$975.60 \times .02125 \times .04926 = \$1.02$)
    after first death use one life rate
TWO LIFE (Joint, First to Die)
P.S. 58 equivalent rate = $\$975.60 \times [(q_x + q_y) - (q_x \times q_y)]$
    (e.g., rate for persons age 60 and 70
    = $\$975.60 \times [(.02125 + .04926) - (.02125 \times .04926)]$
    = $\$67.77$)

Table 38

Age x	q(x)	Age x	q(x)	Age x	q(x)
0	$ .04315	35	$ .00329	70	$ .04926
1	.00460	36	.00350	71	.05360
2	.00243	37	.00372	72	.05831
3	.00176	38	.00397	73	.06344
4	.00141	39	.00424	74	.06901
5	.00124	40	.00453	75	.07506
6	.00110	41	.00485	76	.08162
7	.00100	42	.00520	77	.08873
8	.00092	43	.00558	78	.09644
9	.00087	44	.00600	79	.10479
10	.00085	45	.00646	80	.11382
11	.00093	46	.00695	81	.12358
12	.00102	47	.00750	82	.13413
13	.00111	48	.00809	83	.14550
14	.00120	49	.00874	84	.15776
15	.00130	50	.00945	85	.17094
16	.00141	51	.01022	86	.18511
17	.00152	52	.01106	87	.20032
18	.00156	53	.01198	88	.21661
19	.00160	54	.01299	89	.23402
20	.00165	55	.01408	90	.25261
21	.00171	56	.01528	91	.27239
22	.00177	57	.01658	92	.29341
23	.00183	58	.01800	93	.31568
24	.00191	59	.01956	94	.33921
25	.00198	60	.02125	95	.36399
26	.00207	61	.02309	96	.39001
27	.00216	62	.02511	97	.41721
28	.00226	63	.02730	98	.44555
29	.00237	64	.02970	99	.47493
30	.00249	65	.03230	100	.50525
31	.00263	66	.03514	101	.53638
32	.00277	67	.03824	102	.56816
33	.00293	68	.04160	103	.60039
34	.00310	69	.04527	104	.63286
				105	1.00000

One Year Term Premiums for $1,000 of Joint and Survivor Life Insurance Protection* (Second-to-Die)

AGE	5	10	15	20	25	30	35	40	45	50
5	.00	.00	.00	.00	.00	.00	.00	.01	.01	.01
10	.00	.00	.00	.00	.00	.00	.00	.00	.01	.01
15	.00	.00	.00	.00	.00	.00	.00	.01	.01	.01
20	.00	.00	.00	.00	.00	.00	.01	.01	.01	.02
25	.00	.00	.00	.00	.00	.00	.01	.01	.01	.02
30	.00	.00	.00	.00	.00	.01	.01	.01	.02	.02
35	.00	.00	.00	.01	.01	.01	.01	.01	.02	.03
40	.01	.00	.01	.01	.01	.01	.01	.02	.03	.04
45	.01	.01	.01	.01	.01	.02	.02	.03	.04	.06
50	.01	.01	.01	.02	.02	.02	.03	.04	.06	.09
55	.02	.01	.02	.02	.03	.03	.05	.06	.09	.13
60	.03	.02	.03	.03	.04	.05	.07	.09	.13	.20
65	.04	.03	.04	.05	.06	.08	.10	.14	.20	.30
70	.06	.04	.06	.08	.10	.12	.16	.22	.31	.45
75	.09	.06	.10	.12	.14	.18	.24	.33	.47	.69
80	.14	.09	.14	.18	.22	.28	.37	.50	.72	1.05
85	.21	.14	.22	.28	.33	.42	.55	.76	1.08	1.58
90	.31	.21	.32	.41	.49	.61	.81	1.12	1.59	2.33
95	.44	.30	.46	.59	.70	.88	1.17	1.61	2.29	3.36
100	.61	.42	.64	.81	.98	1.23	1.62	2.23	3.18	4.66

AGE	55	60	65	70	75	80	85	90	95	100
5	.02	.03	.04	.06	.09	.14	.21	.31	.44	.61
10	.01	.02	.03	.04	.06	.09	.14	.21	.30	.42
15	.02	.03	.04	.06	.10	.14	.22	.32	.46	.64
20	.02	.03	.05	.08	.12	.18	.28	.41	.59	.81
25	.03	.04	.06	.10	.14	.22	.33	.49	.70	.98
30	.03	.05	.08	.12	.18	.28	.42	.61	.88	1.23
35	.05	.07	.10	.16	.24	.37	.55	.81	1.17	1.62
40	.06	.09	.14	.22	.33	.50	.76	1.12	1.61	2.23
45	.09	.13	.20	.31	.47	.72	1.08	1.59	2.29	3.18
50	.13	.20	.30	.45	.69	1.05	1.58	2.33	3.36	4.66
55	.19	.29	.44	.68	1.03	1.56	2.35	3.47	5.00	6.94
60	.29	.44	.67	1.02	1.56	2.36	3.54	5.24	7.55	10.47
65	.44	.67	1.02	1.55	2.37	3.59	5.39	7.96	11.47	15.92
70	.68	1.02	1.55	2.37	3.61	5.47	8.22	12.14	17.49	24.28
75	1.03	1.56	2.37	3.61	5.50	8.33	12.52	18.50	26.65	37.00
80	1.56	2.36	3.59	5.47	8.33	12.64	18.98	28.05	40.42	56.10
85	2.35	3.54	5.39	8.22	12.52	18.98	28.51	42.13	60.70	84.26
90	3.47	5.24	7.96	12.14	18.50	28.05	42.13	62.26	89.70	124.52
95	5.00	7.55	11.47	17.49	26.65	40.42	60.70	89.70	129.26	179.42
100	6.94	10.47	15.92	24.28	37.00	56.10	84.26	124.52	179.42	249.05

*Rates are derived from U.S. Life Table 38. They are based on the underlying actuarial assumptions of the P.S. 58 rates. The method for deriving the rates is also based upon an unofficial informational letter of Norman Greenberg, Chief, Actuarial Branch, Department of the Treasury. The letter indicates that after the first death, the single life regular P.S. 58 rates are to be used. Due to space limitations, the table is presented in 5-year age increments. For planning purposes, it is suggested that each actual age be rounded to the nearest corresponding age in the table, or do the calculation described earlier in this appendix.

TABLE OF CASES

(All references are to question numbers.)

TABLE OF CASES

TABLE OF IRC SECTIONS CITED

(All references are to question numbers.)

INDEX

(Federal Income Tax , Q 645 – Q 818; Federal Estate, Gift, GST Tax, Valuation, Q 819 – Q 948)

(Federal Income Tax , Q 645 – Q 818; Federal Estate, Gift, GST Tax, Valuation, Q 819 – Q 948)

(Federal Income Tax , Q 645 – Q 818; Federal Estate, Gift, GST Tax, Valuation, Q 819 – Q 948)

References to question numbers. Tax Facts on Insurance & Employee
Benefits, Vol. 1, Q 1 – Q 986; Vol. 2, Q 3501 – Q 4161

(Federal Income Tax , Q 645 – Q 818; Federal Estate, Gift, GST Tax, Valuation, Q 819 – Q 948)

(Federal Income Tax , Q 645 – Q 818; Federal Estate, Gift, GST Tax, Valuation, Q 819 – Q 948)

References to question numbers. Tax Facts on Insurance & Employee
Benefits, Vol. 1, Q 1 – Q 986; Vol. 2, Q 3501 – Q 4161

(Federal Income Tax , Q 645 – Q 818; Federal Estate, Gift, GST Tax, Valuation, Q 819 – Q 948)

(Federal Income Tax , Q 645 – Q 818; Federal Estate, Gift, GST Tax, Valuation, Q 819 – Q 948)

(Federal Income Tax , Q 645 – Q 818; Federal Estate, Gift, GST Tax, Valuation, Q 819 – Q 948)

(Federal Income Tax , Q 645 – Q 818; Federal Estate, Gift, GST Tax, Valuation, Q 819 – Q 948)

References to question numbers. Tax Facts on Insurance & Employee
Benefits, Vol. 1, Q 1 – Q 986; Vol. 2, Q 3501 – Q 4161

(Federal Income Tax , Q 645 – Q 818; Federal Estate, Gift, GST Tax, Valuation, Q 819 – Q 948)

INDEX

(Federal Income Tax , Q 645 – Q 818; Federal Estate, Gift, GST Tax, Valuation, Q 819 – Q 948)

INDEX

References to question numbers. Tax Facts on Insurance & Employee
Benefits, Vol. 1, Q 1 – Q 986; Vol. 2, Q 3501 – Q 4161

(Federal Income Tax , Q 645 – Q 818; Federal Estate, Gift, GST Tax, Valuation, Q 819 – Q 948)

(Federal Income Tax , Q 645 – Q 818; Federal Estate, Gift, GST Tax, Valuation, Q 819 – Q 948)

References to question numbers. Tax Facts on Insurance & Employee
Benefits, Vol. 1, Q 1 – Q 986; Vol. 2, Q 3501 – Q 4161

(Federal Income Tax , Q 645 – Q 818; Federal Estate, Gift, GST Tax, Valuation, Q 819 – Q 948)

INDEX

References to question numbers. Tax Facts on Insurance & Employee
Benefits, Vol. 1, Q 1 – Q 986; Vol. 2, Q 3501 – Q 4161

(Federal Income Tax , Q 645 – Q 818; Federal Estate, Gift, GST Tax, Valuation, Q 819 – Q 948)

References to question numbers. Tax Facts on Insurance & Employee
Benefits, Vol. 1, Q 1 – Q 986; Vol. 2, Q 3501 – Q 4161

(Federal Income Tax , Q 645 – Q 818; Federal Estate, Gift, GST Tax, Valuation, Q 819 – Q 948)

(**Federal Income Tax** , Q 645 – Q 818; **Federal Estate, Gift, GST Tax, Valuation**, Q 819 – Q 948)

(Federal Income Tax , Q 645 – Q 818; Federal Estate, Gift, GST Tax, Valuation, Q 819 – Q 948)

(Federal Income Tax , Q 645 – Q 818; Federal Estate, Gift, GST Tax, Valuation, Q 819 – Q 948)

2021 TAX FACTS ON INSURANCE & EMPLOYEE BENEFITS

References to question numbers. Tax Facts on Insurance & Employee
Benefits, Vol. 1, Q 1 – Q 986; Vol. 2, Q 3501 – Q 4161

INDEX

M

(Federal Income Tax , Q 645 – Q 818; Federal Estate, Gift, GST Tax, Valuation, Q 819 – Q 948)

References to question numbers. Tax Facts on Insurance & Employee
Benefits, Vol. 1, Q 1 – Q 986; Vol. 2, Q 3501 – Q 4161

(Federal Income Tax , Q 645 – Q 818; Federal Estate, Gift, GST Tax, Valuation, Q 819 – Q 948)

References to question numbers. Tax Facts on Insurance & Employee
Benefits, Vol. 1, Q 1 – Q 986; Vol. 2, Q 3501 – Q 4161

INDEX

(Federal Income Tax , Q 645 – Q 818; Federal Estate, Gift, GST Tax, Valuation, Q 819 – Q 948)

INDEX

References to question numbers. Tax Facts on Insurance & Employee
Benefits, Vol. 1, Q 1 – Q 986; Vol. 2, Q 3501 – Q 4161

(Federal Income Tax , Q 645 – Q 818; Federal Estate, Gift, GST Tax, Valuation, Q 819 – Q 948)

CPSIA information can be obtained at www.ICGtesting.com
Printed in the USA
BVOW03s2051100816

458443BV00004B/12/P